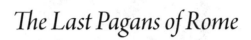

The Last Pagans of Rome

The Last Pagans of Rome

Alan Cameron

OXFORD
UNIVERSITY PRESS

2011

OXFORD
UNIVERSITY PRESS

Oxford University Press, Inc., publishes works that further
Oxford University's objective of excellence
in research, scholarship, and education.

Oxford   New York

Auckland   Cape Town   Dar es Salaam   Hong Kong   Karachi
Kuala Lumpur   Madrid   Melbourne   Mexico City   Nairobi
New Delhi   Shanghai   Taipei   Toronto

With offices in

Argentina   Austria   Brazil   Chile   Czech Republic   France   Greece
Guatemala   Hungary   Italy   Japan   Poland   Portugal   Singapore
South Korea   Switzerland   Thailand   Turkey   Ukraine   Vietnam

Published by Oxford University Press, Inc.
198 Madison Avenue, New York, New York 10016

www.oup.com

Oxford is a registered trademark of Oxford University Press

Library of Congress Cataloging-in-Publication Data

Cameron, Alan, 1938–
The last pagans of Rome / Alan Cameron.
p. cm.
Includes bibliographical references.
ISBN 978-0-19-974727-6
1. Christianity and other religions—Roman.   2. Church history—Primitive and early church, ca. 30–600.
3. Rome—History—Empire, 30 B.C.–476 A.D.   4. Christianity and other religions—Paganism—History—
Early church, ca. 30-600.   5. Paganism—Relations—Christianity.   6. Emperors—Rome.   I. Title.
BR170.C36 2011
261.2'20937—dc22   2010009147

Undertaken with the assistance of the Stanwood Cockey Lodge Foundation.

7 9 8

Printed in the United States of America
on acid-free paper

For old friends
TDB, GWB, WVH, PEK, JAN
and (once again)
for Carla

ACKNOWLEDGMENTS

The seeds that eventually grew into this volume were sown in articles I published as long ago as 1966 and 1977. It was in the 1980s that I first had the idea of turning my approach to the so-called pagan reaction into a book, and it was then that I began compiling the information on subscriptions that now fills chapters 12–14. It was also then that I came up with the title, which, as my ideas progressed, has turned out to be more ironic than I originally intended. It would (I suspect) have been a very different book if I had written it then. But I had not yet thought out all the issues to my own satisfaction, and other projects (mostly Greek) beckoned more insistently. Yet I never gave up on the last pagans, and at the turn of the millennium decided that the moment had come to pick up the threads again. The last decade or so has not only seen much important new work, but also the unexpected discovery of important new texts.

I have incorporated radically revised versions of three early articles, and substantially revised and updated the unpublished drafts of chapters 12–14. I more than once toyed with the idea of publishing the material on subscriptions separately, but in the end decided that, despite their bulk, they formed an essential part of the argument of *Last Pagans*, a perspective that would have been lost in a separate publication. All the rest has been written in the last few years. Chapters 17–18 were added at a late stage, provoked by the continuing emphasis in recent continental scholarship on the entirely lost (and surely trivial) history of Nicomachus Flavianus. At first I thought of publishing them separately, but given the ever increasing importance accorded this history in modern writing on the "pagan reaction," they too belong in this book.

My debt to the published work of Alföldi, Barnes, Bloch, Brown, Chastagnol and Paschoud (among many others) will be obvious. Many friends have sent me books and offprints, supplied information, commented on drafts or discussed problems with me over many years. I think particularly of Tim Barnes, Glen Bowersock, Christopher Jones, Franca Ela Consolino, Bob Kaster, Arnaldo Marcone, John North, Lellia Cracco Ruggini, Rita Lizzi Testa, Michele Salzman, Peter Schmidt, and Jim Zetzel. I am especially grateful to Michele for organizing a symposium on my views in May 2008 (and to Carmela Franklin for hosting it at the American Academy in Rome); and to Tim for generously taking the time to give the entire penultimate version of the manuscript a thorough critical reading, saving me from many errors.

I have also profited from criticisms and information of various sorts from Neil Adkin, Tom Banchich, Doug Boin, Philippe Bruggisser, Richard Burgess, J.-P. Callu, Giovanni Cecconi, Brian Croke, Michel Festy, Gavin Kelly, Dale Kinney, Hartmut Leppin, Neil McLynn, Silvio Panciera, Umberto Romano, Cristiana Sogno, John Weisweiler, and many others over the years. I wish I could recall the names of all those who asked questions after lectures that started a train of thought or led me to rethink an issue. Irene SanPietro helped with editorial work on a difficult manuscript, and David Ratzan performed the Herculean task of compiling the index. Hérica Valladares suggested the cover illustration. I am particularly grateful to the Andrew W. Mellon Foundation for awarding me an emeritus fellowship that covered many expenses, and to the Stanwood Cockey Lodge Fund of Columbia University for a generous subvention to defray the cost of publication. Finally, a special thank you to Stefan Vranka and the staff of Oxford Press USA for accepting so forbidding a manuscript in such difficult times, and for the promptest and most efficient operation I have encountered in forty years of publishing books.

CONTENTS

ILLUSTRATIONS

The Last Pagans of Rome

INTRODUCTION

The ruin of paganism, in the age of Theodosius, is perhaps the only example of the total extirpation of any ancient and popular superstition; and may therefore deserve to be considered, as a singular event in the history of the human mind

        —*Gibbon*, Decline and Fall of the Roman Empire, *Ch. xviii*

The last pagans of my title are the nobles of late fourth-century Rome. Although they spent their days moving between their grand Roman mansions and a variety of suburban villas, the oldest families owned estates all over Italy, North Africa, and many other parts of the empire, thus controlling the lives of hundreds of thousands. In the region of Hippo, according to Augustine, people said that if one particular noble converted, "no pagans would be left."[1] Sermons of the age constantly exhort landowners to destroy pagan shrines on their land (Conclusion). Prudentius singled out for special mention the first noble families to convert to the new faith (Ch. 5. 2). Biographies of the ascetic saints of the age always stress the rank and wealth repudiated by their heroes, from the younger Melania to Honoratus of Arles.[2] While insisting that it was of no importance, Jerome fantasized that his aristocratic groupies were descended from Camillus and the Scipios.[3]

We are reasonably sure that by ca. 450 there were few pagan nobles left. But there is very little reliable evidence about the earliest Christians in any given family, no statistics, and no conversion stories. Fortunately, my subject is not so much the conversion of the last pagans,[4] as how long they survived and what they did to defend the old cults. It is widely believed that pagans remained in a majority in the aristocracy till at least the 380s, and continued to remain a powerful force well into the fifth century (Ch. 5). On this basis the main focus of much modern scholarship has been on their supposedly stubborn resistance to Christianity. Rather surprisingly, they have been transformed from the arrogant, philistine land-grabbers most of them were into fearless champions of senatorial privilege, literature lovers, and aficionados of classical (especially Greek) culture as well as the traditional cults. The dismantling of this romantic myth is one of the main goals of this book.

---

1. *Ille nobilis, si Christianus esset, nemo remaneret paganus*, Aug. *Enarr. in Ps.* 54. 13.
2. *Vita Melaniae*, passim; Hilarius, *Vita Honorati* 4. 2.
3. Jerome, *Epp.* 54. 1, 4; 108. 1, 34.
4. Now treated in detail, from various angles, by Salzman 2002: see too Ch. 5. 2.

The idea that the aristocracy of Rome spearheaded a "pagan revival" at the end of the fourth century, culminating in a "last pagan stand" defeated at the battle of the river Frigidus, dies hard. The nature of the problem has changed in many ways following the reassessment of the cultural and religious life of late antiquity initiated by Peter Brown. But the thesis so eloquently expounded more than sixty years ago by Andrew Alföldi[5] and Herbert Bloch[6] lives on, if in modified form, in even the most recent histories of the late Roman West by scholars of repute.[7] More important perhaps, it is a fixture in countless more general books that allude in passing to the end of paganism. To cite only the most recent to come my way, the new English translation of Filippo Coarelli's archaeological guide to Rome dates the abandonment of the House of the Vestal Virgins to "the defeat of the last champions of paganism near Aquileia in 394." The context does not call for mention of these "champions." The battle of the Frigidus (Ch. 3) has simply become the canonical date for the definitive end of Roman paganism.

This view depends less on evidence than on a series of assumptions, many of which continue to be repeated as if established facts. There is only one narrative chapter (Ch. 2), describing the successive measures taken against paganism by Constantius II, Gratian, and Theodosius I. The other chapters reexamine these assumptions, sometimes (inescapably, given their often unquestioned hold in both popular and scholarly literature) in considerable detail. Readers may be surprised to discover how little evidence there is for this enduring myth—and how much that supports a very different story.

There has been much loose talk of pagan "revival," but it is not clear what form this revival is supposed to have taken. The term itself might suggest an increase in the number of pagans. But the 380s and 390s were undoubtedly a period when the pace of conversion to Christianity was accelerating (Ch. 5). "It is well known," claims one recent book, "that there was a resurgence of pagan activities and sympathy at Rome during the years 392–394."[8] What sort of activities? What kind of sympathy? A series of dedications by aristocrats from a single site of the Magna Mater in Rome is sometimes interpreted as a revival of "oriental" cults, which are held to have been what really drove the last pagans to take up arms in defense of the old ways. But the initiations they attest are more like a sort of upper-class freemasonry than cults with a genuine following (Ch. 4. 2). Sometimes "pagan revival" functions as a shorthand for the revival of secular literature in fourth-century Rome (Ch. 11). To be sure, Claudian and Ammianus were both pagans, but Claudian at any rate wrote for Christian patrons. Indeed, the late fourth- and early fifth-century West is rightly seen as the golden age of Christian literature, poetry no less than prose (Ambrose, Jerome, Augustine, Paulinus, Prudentius...).

---

5. Alföldi 1937, 1943, 1948, 1952, and many articles.
6. Bloch 1945; 1963; Bloch 1945 is the standard treatment (he lived till 2006: obituary by Jones 2008).
7. Potter 2004, 532; Demandt 2007, 166; Mitchell 2007, 88–89; van Dam 2007, 349; Coarelli 2007, 86. The most extreme recent example is Hedrick 2000.
8. Hunter 2007, 20.

Three aristocrats in particular have been identified as the core of a continuing pagan opposition: Vettius Agorius Praetextatus, Q. Aurelius Symmachus, and Nicomachus Flavianus,[9] all holders of priesthoods in the state cults. The most influential single source for this supposed opposition, often identified as the "circle of Symmachus," is Macrobius's *Saturnalia*, a dialogue in which none other than Praetextatus, Symmachus, and Flavian are the hosts at a symposium attended by a group of aristocrats and scholars who discuss at length such subjects as Vergil's knowledge of pagan cult (Ch. 16). It used to be taken for granted that Macrobius was himself a member of this pagan opposition. But the circle he depicts, like the "circle of Scipio" represented in Cicero's *De republica*, is an imaginary creation: the speeches he puts in the mouths of his interlocutors reflect his interests rather than theirs (Ch. 10. 5). Macrobius himself was almost certainly a Christian, and wrote a full half-century after his dramatic date (382). Several chapters are devoted to this important but much misunderstood work (Ch. 7, 10, 15, 16), which tells us more about the antiquarianism of Christian senators in the 430s than the beliefs of pagans in the 380s.[10]

It is the political aspect of the supposed pagan revival that has attracted most attention (Ch. 2, 3, 5). In 382, Gratian ordered the altar of Victory removed from the senate house, and withdrew the traditional public subsidies from the state cults. Symmachus led an embassy to court to protest. Two years later, now prefect of Rome, he wrote his celebrated formal appeal to Gratian's successor, Valentinian II, again asking for the restoration of altar and subsidies, again unsuccessfully. In 391 Theodosius I (it is claimed) decided that the time had come to go beyond these half measures and eliminate paganism. So he issued a comprehensive ban on all forms of non-Christian cult activity, which was rigorously enforced. This was the last straw for pagan aristocrats, who rallied behind the western usurper Eugenius (proclaimed on 22 August 392). In return for their support Eugenius (supposedly) restored both altar and subsidies, leading to a fully fledged revival of paganism at Rome, directed by his praetorian prefect Nicomachus Flavianus.[11] Very little of this story survives serious scrutiny.

Flavian's reputation as the pagan fanatic who "directed" this revival rests almost entirely on the interpretation of a single anonymous poem on the death of an unnamed pagan prefect devoted to exotic pagan cults. From the moment of its discovery in 1868, the prefect was identified as Flavian, and it was inferred that he had revived all the supposedly now forbidden cults mentioned in the poem. Even accepting the identification "revival" would be a stretch since the cults had been banned for barely three years. Nor does the poem say anything about the prefect *reviving* cults; he is simply ridiculed for believing in such nonsense.

---

9. Hereafter usually Flavian. Throughout this book, I assume that readers will consult *PLRE* for details of careers, even without explicit citations.
10. Study of the *Saturnalia* will in future be greatly facilitated by Kaster's new Loeb edition (3 volumes, 2010).
11. "Les Flaviens père et fils dirigent à Rome la réaction païenne," Chastagnol 1962, 242; cf. Piganiol 1975, 293; Matthews 1975, 241–42; Pietri 1976, 438–39, and so on.

More important, the clues in the poem simply do not fit Flavian. New evidence and new arguments prove beyond a shadow of a doubt that the prefect is Praetextatus, in which case the poem belongs in 384 rather than 394 (Ch. 8). This decade makes all the difference. For in 384 sacrifice had not yet been forbidden. Dated to 384 it simply provides evidence of permissible pagan practices, not a pagan "revival." At one stroke we lose not only virtually all the evidence there ever was for a pagan revival in the 390s but also for the belief that Flavian was its ringleader and inspiration.

The only other text that lends any support to the notion of Flavian as pagan paladin is a single paragraph in Rufinus's *Ecclesiastical History*, which describes him playing the role of *haruspex*, examining the entrails of a sheep before the battle of the Frigidus. This is regularly taken out of its context in Rufinus (where it simply balances Rufinus's picture of Theodosius no less improbably preparing for battle by praying to the saints) and treated as proof both of the pagan "revival" and Flavian's fanaticism. The exaggerated attention paid to the Frigidus in modern writings has had another unfortunate consequence (Ch. 3). The battle has been seen as a dramatic clash between paganism and Christianity, and the conclusion drawn that it was Theodosius's victory at the Frigidus that dealt Roman paganism its deathblow. The pagan revival was over almost as soon as it had begun.[12] This means that Roman paganism has been seen as a phenomenon that had to be suppressed by force. But there is no contemporary evidence that anyone saw the clash between Theodosius and Eugenius as a religious battle at all, and it is most unlikely that the Frigidus made any difference to the status of paganism at Rome. Since it was already in rapid decline by the 390s, it is not surprising that there is a very general correlation between Theodosius's victory and the decline of paganism (Ch. 2. 4). More generally, there is not a shred of evidence for the often-repeated assertion that the pagan nobility "rallied" to Eugenius's cause. The truth is that Flavian is the one and only pagan supporter of Eugenius we can actually name.

Flavian is also known to have written a history. Taking his fanaticism as axiomatic, a flood of recent publications has argued that this lost work "must have been" an attack on Christianity, a major source for later historians both Greek and Latin. But there is no reason to believe that it covered the empire at all rather than the Republic; or that it was a detailed political narrative rather than the barest of epitomes, like most fourth-century histories in Latin (Ch. 17–18). If it was so influential, why did not a single word survive?

The most widely held axiom of the "pagan opposition" model is that the aristocracy of Rome "displayed their pagan faith along with their attachment to classical taste" in the art they patronized and the literature they studied, driven by a consuming passion to preserve and propagate "pagan" culture. This is a venerable thesis, reformulated in a more subtle (but no more convincing) way by Robert Markus (taking both

---

12. "On sait que ce réveil païen fut de courte durée. Il est incontestable que la victoire de Théodose au Frigidus et le suicide de Nicomaque Flavien...ont frappé d'un coup mortel la vielle religion," Chastagnol 1960, 164.

pagan revival and pagan revolt for granted). According to Markus, the defeat of what he called "the pagan revolt" in 394[13]

> could easily have endangered the survival of the classical learning *with which it had been identified*. In the generation after Julian, and especially around the turn of the century, there is a perceptible hardening of attitude among Western Christians toward classical culture. *Classical education had become linked with pagan religion in a new way*. The link was forged in the heat of battle. The fiercely self-conscious vindication of their claims to sole rightful possession of classical culture struck a new note, introduced by the pagan reaction under Julian and renewed, intensified, in the 380s and 390s. What Christians had been ready to accept before 360, they were to question anxiously for the next forty or fifty years.

This emphasis is, I believe, mistaken. It is true enough that Julian was happy to exploit the double connotation (both cult and culture) of the term "Hellene," and his short-lived attempt to stop Christians teaching the classics implied a pagan monopoly on secular culture. But there was never any serious break in the devotion of Christian members of the Eastern elite to Greek grammatical, rhetorical, and even philosophical culture. Gregory Nazianzen at once repudiated Julian's attempt to appropriate Hellenism for pagans, and there is no sign of the sort of long-term anxiety about classical culture Markus suggested among cultivated Greek Christians of the fifth and sixth centuries.

Markus was certainly right to draw attention to a marked hostility to "pagan" (better secular) culture in Jerome, Paulinus of Nola, Augustine, and a few other western Christians (all of them highly cultivated men themselves). There was indeed a wave of asceticism that swept through the Christian aristocracy in the last decades of the fourth century. But it is a mistake to connect this hostility on the Christian side with the cultural activities of contemporary pagans. There is no evidence of any sort that pagans themselves felt called upon to defend their culture—or indeed that they saw it as "pagan" culture at all rather than the culture shared by all educated people. For while a few prominent Christian intellectuals attacked the classics (while ostentatiously quoting them in their own writings), lay Christian members of the elite continued to enjoy an education that consisted entirely of the classics. Symmachus, the only pagan aristocrat of the period whose writings allow us to form some impression of his culture, turns out to have been less well read than many of his Christian peers (Ch. 11, 14). There is no indication that he saw himself as a sponsor of a literary revival of any sort, much less a pagan revival. Least of all did he champion a revival of Greek culture (Ch. 15).

One of the most enduring (and improbable) assumptions, constantly repeated not only by historians but also in works on the history of scholarship and the

---

13. Markus 1974, 131 (my italics).

transmission of classical texts, is that pagan aristocrats of the period "devoted their ample leisure…to reading, copying and editing the texts of the classics."[14] The evidence—notes known as "subscriptions" in manuscripts of classical texts—is abundant, but should be interpreted in an entirely different and actually far more interesting and instructive sense. In order to establish this point I have assembled a complete dossier of subscriptions, Greek as well as Latin, in Christian as well as pagan texts, and reconsidered the copying and reading of texts in late antiquity (Ch. 12–14).

The traditional interpretation of these subscriptions has always formed the core of the widespread modern belief in a "classical revival" in late fourth-century Rome, sponsored by literature-loving pagan nobles. But it is difficult to know what could constitute anything so general as a "classical" revival. The most influential texts (Vergil, Terence, Cicero, Sallust) never fell out of favor and did not need to be revived. What did the late fourth century consider classical? If there was a revival of any period of Latin literature during these years, it is what we moderns would call the post-classical—Lucan, Statius, Juvenal (Ch. 11). The notion of a "classical revival" is particularly dear to art historians, who use it to explain any manifestations of "classicizing" style in the art of the age (Ch. 19).

The most learned, lively, brilliant, and colorful of my predecessors was Andrew Alföldi, whom I was privileged to know slightly in his old age.[15] In addition to an intimate knowledge of all the relevant texts, he was able to adduce as much again from the material culture of the age. I do not myself believe that more than a fraction of this material actually belongs to what Alföldi liked to think of as a fierce battle between the pagan aristocrats of Rome and the Christian state, but it certainly illustrates what I would prefer to call the secular culture of the age, a culture that imposed itself on cultivated Christians and so rightly belongs in this book. A number of chapters deal with the culture, both literary and artistic, of fourth- and early fifth-century Rome.

The first documented clash between the senate of Rome and the imperial court did not come till 357, when the altar of Victory was first removed from the senate house by Constantius II. Yet Alföldi had no doubt that the hostility of pagan senators to Christianity went all the way back to Constantine. Constantine's conversion, he insisted, "must have hit the Roman aristocracy amazingly hard," and from that moment they were engaged in a bitter struggle with one Christian court after another.[16] According to Krautheimer, "contemporary writings" suggest that Constantine's purpose in building his first large Roman church, S. Giovanni in Laterano, so far from the city centre was "to avoid or minimize friction with a strong pagan opposition headed by the senate and old families."[17] There are no such writings, just the

---

14. So even Markus 1974, 130, one of the most intelligent students of late antique culture.
15. See his delightfully patronizing dismissal of an early article of mine (Alföldi 1965/66, 83 n. 111), expressing his confidence that I would soon see that he was right.
16. Alföldi 1937, 1943, 1948, 1952, and many articles.
17. R. Krautheimer 1983, 2.

assumption that a Christian emperor "must have" wanted to replace the pagan temples of Rome with Christian churches.[18] But it is important to bear in mind Van Dam's recent warning that "before Constantine was a Christian emperor, he was a typical emperor."[19] The fact is that he exploited the monumental centre of Rome as a typical emperor.[20] There was no reason in principle for pagans to see Constantine's conversion as a threat. Rome had after all absorbed one new cult after another over the centuries. The most recent pre-Christian innovation in the religious sphere had been Aurelian's devotion to the cult of the Sun, which had led to the building of a splendid new temple, commemorative games, and the creation of a new college of *pontifices*, subsequently distinguished from the old ones as *pontifices Solis*.[21] Symmachus would surely have been satisfied with a compromise that added a college of *pontifices Christi*. He would not perhaps have wished to join this college himself, but would have been perfectly happy if his friend Praetextatus, notoriously curious about mystery cults, had done so.

An important new argument against the idea of a pagan opposition going back to the age of Constantine has recently been advanced by John Weisweiler. A small group of dedications on the bases of statues erected to fourth-century aristocrats in the Forum Romanum or Forum of Trajan (the two most important public spaces in late antique Rome) include a brief imperial letter authorizing the award of the statue and praising its recipient.[22] The earliest known example is a letter of Constantine granting the statue erected to L. Aradius Proculus while prefect of Rome in 337. Then we have the posthumous gold statue erected to Avianius Symmachus in 376, where the dedication refers to an "attached oration" (*adposita oratione*) inscribed on a now lost part of the base. The best known is the letter of Valentinian III that survives complete on the base of the statue erected to the elder Flavian in 431, on his rehabilitation (Ch. 6. 3). We also have fragments of two further imperial letters on the statue bases of two other fourth-century prefects of Rome, one of them perhaps [Ru]fius [Albinus], prefect of Rome in 389–91.

On the death of Praetextatus, Symmachus, in his capacity as city prefect, asked Valentinian II to grant permission for statues to the great man, explicitly requesting some words of praise from the emperor himself: "for praise is all the more illustrious if it comes from a celestial judgment" (*caelesti…iudicio:* the imperial letter on Avianius Symmachus's monument is characterized as a *perenne iudicium*).[23] In light of the texts

---

18. Too much attention has been paid to Zosimus's garbled story (ii. 29. 5, with Paschoud 2000, 234–40; and Fraschetti 1999, 76–134) that Constantine refused to ascend the Capitol to sacrifice and "incurred the hatred of the senate and people," whereupon he decided to found a new capital of his own. No one can agree which of his three Roman visits is meant (312, 315, or 326), and the motive for the foundation of Constantinople is absurd.

19. van Dam 2007, 11.

20. Curran 2000, 71.

21. Watson 1999, Ch. 11; unfortunately, nothing remains of the temple.

22. Weisweiler 2010. I am grateful to the author for showing me a copy of this important paper before publication.

23. *Rel.* 12. 4.

assembled here, there can be little doubt that Symmachus was asking for a brief imperial testimonial to include on Praetextatus's statue base.[24]

In the early empire it was only provincial grandees, people who in the ordinary way would never see an emperor, who solicited and prized letters from the emperor and had them inscribed on their monuments. But by the fourth century, when Roman aristocrats no longer enjoyed regular intercourse with the normally absent emperor, "closeness to imperial power became a more precious commodity," and a brief imperial testimonium inscribed on a statue base evidently added to the standing of even the most blue-blooded aristocrat. What is so intriguing about the surviving texts is that all those who can be identified are prominent pagans, people generally thought of as members of a pagan opposition. This must be coincidence; we can hardly doubt that similar letters adorned the statue bases of distinguished Christians. But it is nonetheless striking that members of the leading pagan families of the age all put so high a premium on the commendation of a now Christian emperor. And scarcely less striking that Christian emperors were so willing to flatter the vanity of pagan nobles.

All too often critics both ancient and modern have seen the Christianization of the Roman world in terms of conflict. Fifty years ago, a famous series of lectures was held at the Warburg Institute under the title *The Conflict between Paganism and Christianity in the Fourth Century.*[25] While late antique Christians certainly saw themselves as engaged in a battle with paganism, what is much less clear is whether pagans saw themselves fighting a battle against Christianity. The military metaphor implies that one side hopes to vanquish the other. Yet while militant Christians undoubtedly cherished hopes of stamping paganism out, and from the early fifth century on explicitly worked toward this end (Conclusion), there was no battle that pagans either could or perhaps even wanted to win. What sort of "victory" could they have hoped for? Many must have wished that Christianity had never entered the world, but by the 380s no one can have imagined that it would disappear. Most (certainly Symmachus, on the evidence of his speech on the altar of Victory) simply asked for coexistence, to be allowed to maintain the state cults. It is not even certain that all pagans felt it necessary to maintain blood sacrifice (Ch. 2. 4).

More than a century ago Samuel Dill justly remarked that "it would be a mistake to suppose that in general society the line between the two camps was sharply drawn."[26] Ignoring this warning, many scholars have assumed that pagans and Christians were constantly at each other's throats. One trivial illustration. Symmachus was annoyed when what he describes as "jealousy or ingratitude" robbed him of the normal honor of public statues after his proconsular year in Africa (373/74). His successor, Paulus Constantius, as it happens, is known to have been a Christian. So it is assumed that it

---

24. Presumably the emperor sometimes granted the request without including words of praise suitable for inscription.
25. Momigliano 1963.
26. Dill 1899, 12.

was because Symmachus was a pagan that Constantius blocked his statues.[27] But there is no evidence that Constantius was the guilty party, or, even if he was, that his obstructionism was due to the religious factor. It was not till much later that Symmachus emerged (briefly) as a pagan champion. The notion that any Christian would routinely do down any pagan (or vice versa) whenever he had a chance is entirely gratuitous. A subtle article by John Matthews has shown that, like many other aristocrats, Symmachus was engaged in feuds and quarrels throughout his life, on a variety of issues, social, economic, and purely personal.[28]

Pagan aristocrats play a large part in this book. Chapter 1 will justify the term "pagan." Here a few words on aristocrats. Both term and concept are modern, with no exact Latin equivalent. The closest is *nobilis*, variously defined (under the Republic, consuls and descendants of consuls; in the late empire, consuls or holders of the urban or praetorian prefecture). But such definitions do not capture the essence of aristocracy. As Chris Wickham has put it, an aristocrat is "a member of a (normally landed) political elite...who could wield some sort of power simply because of who he...was."[29] Sex. Petronius Probus and Q. Aurelius Symmachus, enormously wealthy landowners descended from generations of consuls, were undoubtedly aristocrats on this definition, destined to be VIPs from birth. But the historian Aurelius Victor, who rose from humble beginnings to become prefect of Rome, was not. Despite his illustrious office, Probus and Symmachus would not have recognized him as their social peer. A perfect ancient definition of aristocrat in this sense is offered by the first line of Probus's epitaph: *dives opum, clarusque genus, praecelsus honore* (wealthy, well born and distinguished in rank).[30] A new man like Victor could lay a (rather modest) claim to only the last of these titles.

In her comprehensive recent study, Michele Salzman employs the terms "senator" and "aristocrat" interchangeably, at one point explicitly stating that she uses the term "senatorial aristocracy...to refer to all holders of the senatorial rank of clarissimus."[31] While perfectly acceptable in itself, this usage blurs the distinction between run-of-the-mill senators and the old aristocracy, a distinction that is important for this book. By ca. 400 new policies initiated by Constantine and continued by his successors had enormously expanded the senate, until "there were something like 3000 jobs in each half of the empire leading more or less directly to senatorial status."[32] The many newer members were inevitably of more modest stock, less likely than scions of noble families to hew to the traditional cults.[33] More important, it was scions of the noble families who monopolized the many priesthoods in the traditional cults (Ch. 4). So

---

27. *Ep.* ix. 115; so Chastagnol 1962, 221; against, Matthews 1971, 122–23.
28. Matthews in Paschoud 1986, 163–75; see too Sogno 2006.
29. Gelzer 1969; Barnes 1974, 444–49; Badel 2005, 90–94; Wickham 2005, 153–257 at 153.
30. *CLE* 1347; Trout 2000.
31. Salzman 2002, 4, and passim.
32. Heather, in *CAH* 13(1998), 191; for a useful summary of the evidence, Chastagnol 1976, 51–69.
33. As recognized by Salzman 2002, 14.

even if Ambrose's famous claim that Christians enjoyed a majority in the senate in 384 is anywhere near the truth, that need not mean that a majority of the old families were now Christian. A new man like Aurelius Victor would never have been co-opted into one of the ancient priestly colleges simply because he was a pagan. It was from the ranks of the old aristocracy that we might expect to find reluctance to embrace Christianity, not the senate as a whole.

In consequence, this book employs the term "aristocrat" more narrowly and precisely than Salzman, to designate members of the old families, not any and all members of the senatorial order. From time to time I also employ the more general term "elite," normally to designate educated, comfortably off people who could not boast noble birth and did not aspire to (or at any rate win) positions in the imperial service. For example, on this definition Lactantius and Libanius, Ammianus, and the young Augustine, though not aristocrats or even senators, were members of the (or an) elite.

Roman paganism petered out with a whimper rather than a bang. But in minimizing the "pagan reaction," it should not be thought that my purpose is to belittle the last pagans, to dismiss them, in the vivid characterization of a recent critic, as "spinelessly self-regarding."[34] What this book attacks is less their failure to mount the defiant opposition of modern legend than the assumption that nobles like Praetextatus, Symmachus, and Flavian, in their capacity as priests of the state cults, must (or should) have seen it as their duty to do everything in their power to resist the encroachment of Christianity. But *pontifices* were not chosen by and did not represent the pagans of Rome in the way bishops were chosen by and represented the Christian community. There were in additions dozens of them, with no obvious leader, all landowners and officeholders first and priests second. Since most acquired their priesthoods in their teens or early twenties by virtue of birth (Ch. 4), it is unlikely that they saw themselves, or were seen by others, as the pagan champions they are depicted in modern works. It was not because he was an uncompromising pagan warrior that Symmachus was selected to head the embassy of 382 and write his famous speech of 384, but because he was known to be a moderate who enjoyed good relations with prominent Christians (Ch. 2. 1). Nor does his abundant correspondence suggest that he took any personal steps to further the pagan cause, by lobbying fellow aristocrats or court connections privately. Remarkably enough, his letters never so much as mention the withdrawal of cult subsidies or the altar of Victory (Ch. 2. 1). What the letters (and speeches) do show is that his main interests in life were networking, serving on embassies, and promoting the interests of his family (Sogno 2006). So shrewd a politician must have seen that by the 380s there was no battle pagans could hope to win.

---

34. So McLynn 2009, 572, citing Cameron 1999.

If the pagan aristocracy of Rome did not after all mount a defiant political and cultural rear-guard action, what did they do? For a while they continued to preside over the traditional cults, holding office, managing their estates, and occasionally reading a classical text in a cool seaside villa (Ch. 10. 6). When the government withdrew the funds necessary for public cults, they protested. When it became clear that protests were not going to achieve anything, it was only a matter of time before the remaining pagan nobles converted, less because of coercion and laws, than as the only way to continue holding office and preserve their ancestral role in Roman public life. Holding priesthoods in the state cults had brought them prestige—so long as those cults were the only game in town.[35] But even before the closing of the temples in 391, the writing was on the wall. It was now the church people were flocking to, and if the nobility was going to maintain its position, they too had to join the church, where their wealth and connections enabled them to maintain their traditional ascendancy, if in rather different ways (and continue to read the occasional classical text in the same villas).[36] Last-ditch resistance would have led to political suicide, and there were no pagan martyrs.

Paradoxically, perhaps in fact predictably, the Symmachi were to become one of the leading families in a now Christian Rome. Symmachus cos. 391 died a pagan, but his grandson, great-grandson, and great-great-grandson all became consuls (in 446, 485, and 522). It is frustrating that we know nothing about his son Memmius Symmachus beyond the age of eighteen in 402. He was brought up a pagan (p. 378), but there can be little doubt that he (or at latest his son, the future consul of 446) eventually abandoned the family paganism in order to further the family fortunes. A nephew, Aurelius Anicius Symmachus, who in all other respects followed the traditional career (proconsul of Africa and prefect of the city), evidently had one Anician parent and was already a Christian by 418–20.[37] Aurelius Memmius Symmachus cos. 485 was a pillar of the Christian establishment.

---

35. North 1992, 174–93.
36. See (e.g.) C. Pietri 1976; L. Pietri 2002, 253–63; Cooper and Hillner 2007.
37. Chastagnol, *Fastes* 281; C. Pietri 1976, 456–57.

1

PAGANS AND POLYTHEISTS

1

How did Latin *paganus* come to acquire its most famous meaning? The earliest documented meaning was apparently "rural," from *pagus,* a rural district. But to judge from surviving texts, the dominant meaning by the early empire was "civilian," as opposed to "military." Finally, soon after the middle of the fourth century, quite suddenly we find it as the standard Latin designation for non-Christians. It is less well known that by as early as the first century the word had passed into Greek (παγανός), where it still survives in the modern language—but only in the second of these three meanings.[1] How did the religious sense develop?[2] And why did it not develop in Greek?

Medieval writers assumed the rural derivation, on the ground that pagan practices tended to linger longest in the countryside.[3] So Baronius (1586), assuming that Christians dismissed nonbelievers contemptuously as country bumpkins. This seems to be the dominant view today.[4] Yet there are major objections. In the first place, this is not a perspective likely to have occurred to anyone as early as the fourth century, when, at any rate in the Latin-speaking western provinces, the primary and most conspicuous focus of paganism was still the city cults, presided over by the city elites, above all (as we shall see) in Rome itself.[5] Second, *paganus* is never used like *rusticus* or *agrestis* for "coarse" or "uncouth."[6] Notoriously, *rusticitas* stands for lack of polish and sophistication in Ovid,[7] but his one use of *paganus*, in a brief account of a rural festival, is entirely respectful.[8] Three examples in Apuleius all carry the sense "villagers" or "locals," again

---

1. *LSJ*, Lampe and Preisigke, s.v. παγανός, παγανικός, παγανεύω; H. Cuvigny and G. Wagner, *ZPE* 62 (1986), at 66–67 and P. Oxy. 3758, dated to 325; Grégoire and Orgels 1952, at 363–400.
2. Zeiller 1917; for more texts and a more systematic classification, Flury in *TLL* x. 1 (1982), 78–83 (add Aug. *Ep.* 11. 5. 2 Divjak and many examples in the new sermons published by F. Dolbeau); Mohrmann 1965, 277–89; Bickel 1954, 1–47; Demougeot 1956, 337–50; O'Donnell 1977, 163–69; Chuvin 2002, 7–15; Kahlos 2007, 22–26.
3. Le Goff 1980, 92–94.
4. "the term *pagani*, meaning inhabitants of the rural *pagi*, became synonymous with non-Christians," C. R. Whittaker, *CAH* xiii (1998), 308; Fowden 1993 and Athanassiadi/Frede 1999 below; Kahlos 2002, 6.
5. See (e.g.), Rives 1995; rural cults may have been more prominent in the East: Lane Fox 1987, 41–46.
6. So rightly Bickel 1954, 26–27; the closest example is Pliny, *NH* 28. 28.
7. Hollis 1977, 129–30.
8. *Pagus agat festum: pagum lustrate, coloni, / et date paganis annua liba focis,* Ov. *Fasti* i. 669–70; *annua pastorum convivia, lusus in urbe, / cum pagana madent fercula divitiis,* Propertius iv. 4. 75–76.

without a hint of condescension. When Sidonius describes his style as "not urban(e) elegance but rural simplicity" (*non urbanus lepos…sed pagana simplicitas*), he is claiming a virtue (albeit disingenuously), not a vice.[9] Finally, after a handful of references (again never pejorative) in technical literature like land surveyors and antiquarians such as Festus, by late antiquity this sense simply disappears from the everyday language.[10] More generally, it would be paradoxical if western Christians had called pagans by a name symbolizing lack of culture when eastern Christians called them by a name symbolizing culture itself ("hellene").

In support of the "civilian" derivation (which goes back to Alciati in 1582), Harnack drew attention to the widespread notion of Christians as soldiers of Christ, complemented by Christian reluctance to serve in the Roman army in the period before Constantine.[11] No Latin writer refers to Christians as *milites Christi* more often or emphatically than Tertullian. In his *De fuga in persecutione* of (probably) 208/9, successive chapters first compare Christians to soldiers and Christ to their general (*imperator*), and then distinguish bishops, priests, and deacons as officers (*duces*) from the "common soldiers" (*gregarius miles*), namely the laity.[12] If *paganus* had acquired its religious sense by 200, we should certainly have expected to find it somewhere in the fourteen hundred surviving pages of Tertullian. Yet in this sense he only uses *gentes, nationes*, and *ethnici* (note the title of his two-book *Ad nationes* = "Against [or addressed to] the pagans"). *Paganus* he uses just twice, both times clearly in the sense "civilian." At *De corona militis* 11 he claims that, in the eyes of the Lord, "a civilian who believes counts as a soldier, just as a soldier who believes counts as a civilian" (*apud hunc tam miles est paganus fidelis, quam paganus est miles fidelis*), which can only mean that Christ makes no distinction between soldier and civilian. How could he have written this if he had thought of *paganus* as implying "pagan"?[13]

Here too there are chronological objections. By the time the religious sense emerges in the mid-fourth century, Roman armies were beginning to be manned by Christians, and the Christian public, no longer a threatened minority, must have been ceasing to see itself as a militant movement. In any case, while in most of the thirty odd texts there is a clear contrast between civilian and soldier, there is never any suggestion of *hostility* between them. It makes no sense to see civilians as the *enemy* of these "soldiers of Christ." Soldiers are supposed to protect the civilian population. And if the religious sense is a natural extension of the civilian sense, why did it never develop in the Greek-speaking East, where *paganós* = civilian was firmly established?

On the "civilian" etymology, we should have expected *paganus* = pagan to develop earlier, on the "rustic" etymology, later. Of course, a new usage is likely to

---

9. Sidon. *Epp.* viii. 16. 3.
10. Naturally, we continue to find occasional examples in documents distinguishing between the inhabitants of *pagi* and *vici*: for example, *universi pagani seu vicani, AE* 1937, 121, l. 3 (dated to 18: xii: 335).
11. On both these points see Harnack 1981/1905.
12. *De fuga* 10–11; for the date, Barnes 1971, 47.
13. Not a rhetorical question, since some scholars have in fact argued precisely this: Grégoire and Orgels 1952, 388 ("*il est stupéfiant que…*"); Demougeot 1961, 354–65.

develop well before it is first recorded in datable surviving texts. But the distribution of *paganus* = pagan is peculiarly abundant and precisely dated: more than six hundred examples in at least fifteen different writers and texts datable between ca. 360 and 420 (476 in Augustine alone).[14] With only one exception (an inscription discussed in detail below), nothing earlier. We would surely have expected at least one or two earlier examples if this meaning had been known to such prolific Christian writers of the third or early fourth centuries as Tertullian, Cyprian, Arnobius, or Lactantius. Even after 360, some cultivated Christians never use it, at least in their writings. In his two detailed letters about the altar of Victory in 384, Ambrose uses *gentiles* nineteen times and *gentes* six times, never *paganus*, nor anywhere else in his abundant surviving writings. The so-called Ambrosiaster, writing in the 380s, uses *paganus* more than fifty times. Sulpicius Severus never uses *paganus*. Augustine (who nonetheless used the word freely) in two passage adds the qualification "those whom we have grown accustomed to call *gentiles* or, in the popular usage, *pagani*." We find the same formula in a law of 409 (*quos vulgo paganos appellant*).[15] Apparently, it was felt to be a popular, vulgar, or at any rate recent usage, not a term that educated people were willing to use without apology.[16]

All the other terms Latin-speaking Christians used for non-Christians were adapted from words Greek-speaking Jews had used for the goyim, the gentiles, from at least the second century B.C.: *gentes* and *nationes* from ἔθνη, *gentiles* (less often *ethnici*) from *ethnikoi*, *infideles* from *apistoi*.[17] All were words with distinctly hostile connotations. The more neutral "hellene" is a usage that goes back to the age of the Maccabees, when the hostile world of the gentiles was represented by the Seleucids.[18] Acts and the Letters of Paul frequently link "Jews and hellenes" as the addressees of early Christian preaching, where "hellenes" is by long-established convention generally rendered "Greeks," but nonetheless clearly denotes non-Christians rather than just Greek-speakers. Since the earliest converts were mostly Jews, this made sense to start with. But before long most Christians in the Greek-speaking provinces of the early empire were ethnically or at any rate linguistically Greeks, and "hellene" = non-Christian might have seemed paradoxical. Yet in the late antique East it emerged as the most widely used term of all.[19] This is because it came to encapsulate early Christian hostility to Greek culture, adumbrated in some passages of Paul but elaborately, not to say passionately, developed by the second-century Apologists.[20] Nonetheless, by the time

---

14. Figures from the Brepols online database; the next highest totals are in Ambrosiaster (54) and Filastrius (41).

15. Aug. *Ep.* 184bis. 3. 5 and in *Retract.* ii. 43. 1; *Cod. Theod.* xvi. 5. 46 (409), quoted below.

16. That is to say, Ambrose, Severus, and Jerome may have used it in conversation, but simply avoided it when writing.

17. See Bauer/Danker, *A Greek-English Lexicon of the New Testament* 3 ed. (2000), s.v. ἄπιστος 2, ἔθνος 2. a, ἐθνικός.

18. See the texts quoted in Bauer/Danker 2000, s.v. Ἕλλην 2. a and related words; Schürer 1979, 81–84.

19. Many examples cited by Jüthner 1923, 97–99, with n. 258 on 146–47; briefly, Bowersock 1990, 9–11; Sandwell 2007, 149; and (of course) Lampe s. vv. all the ἑλλην-words.

20. Ἕλλην = pagan is largely absent from the so-called Apostolic Fathers (E. J. Goodspeed, *Index Patristicus* [Leipzig 1907], s.v.), but becomes common in Aristides, Athenagoras and Tatian (see the useful index to Daniel Ruiz Bueno, *Padres Apologistas Griegos* [Madrid 1954], 935).

Christianity came to penetrate educated members of the elite, Greek was inescapably the language of Christian theology. Inevitably, the earlier outright hostility to classical culture became somewhat muted. Basil of Caesarea wrote an influential treatise on the profit Christian youths could draw from "hellenic literature,"[21] and the writings of the Christian Byzantines were to develop into perhaps the most learned and allusive literature ever produced. In consequence the word lost many of its pejorative associations, to the extent that more aggressive pagans, notably the Apostate Julian, defiantly and proudly embraced the equation hellene = pagan.[22] At the same time, unsurprisingly in an empire where many different languages were spoken, hellene-words continued to be used to identify Greek-speakers, particularly the verb *hellēnizo*, which was nonetheless just as regularly used of those who engaged in pagan practices. Obviously the context must always have been felt sufficient to distinguish these radically different senses, both of which persevered for another thousand years, till the end of the Byzantine world.[23]

As for Latin, while *ethnē* translated well enough (*gentes* and *nationes*),[24] for obvious reasons "hellene" did not. It made little sense to apply *Graecus* to a Latin-speaking western pagan who may not have even known Greek, and it is easy to see why *Graecus* = pagan failed to catch on in the West. We do in fact find a handful of examples in western writers familiar with Greek usage, evidently aware that they were using paradoxical terminology—in almost every case, instructively enough, glossed by *paganus*. In his commentary on Galatians 2. 3, where Paul calls his companion Titus a hellene (apparently in the ethnic sense),[25] Marius Victorinus notes "he was a Greek, that is to say pagan" (*Graecus erat, id est paganus*). A couple of pages later (ib. 4. 3) we find "among Greeks, that is to say among pagans" (*apud Graecos, id est apud paganos*). Even more explicit: "Greeks, whom they call hellenes or pagans."[26] Victorinus was writing ca. 360, the earliest firmly datable literary texts to use *paganus* = pagan, as well as the earliest known examples of *Graecus* = pagan. Further proof of the influence of Greek usage here is his coinage of the noun *paganismus* on the model of *hellenismos*.[27] By the early 380s we find *paganos, id est Graecos* in Filastrius of Brescia, together with a bizarre piece of Latinized Greek mythology that derives the word from "King Paganus, as the Greek poet Hesiod says" (*Pagano rege...ut ait Hesiodus Graecus poeta*)!28 Hesiod, of course,

---

21. Πρὸς τοὺς νέους ὅπως ἂν ἐξ ἑλληνικῶν ὠφέλοιντο λόγων, to give the work its full Greek title.

22. But by no means all pagans: Cameron 1993, 25–29; see too Bouffartigue 1991, 251–66.

23. See the Ἑλλην-words in E. Trapp, *Lexikon zur byzantinischen Gräzität* (Vienna 2001). Syriac had different words for "pagan" and "Greek," and so translators of late antique texts into Syriac "were able to make a clear verbal distinction between Greeks (and Greek culture) and paganism (and pagan cults)" (Bowersock 1990, 11).

24. For *gentes* in Latin, Löfstedt, *Late Latin* (1959), 74–75.

25. Evidently not realizing that ἕλλην here means that Titus was an ethnic Greek (rather than a Jew), Chrysostom (*Hom. in Gal.* 2. 3) explained what he took to be a reference to paganism in this passage as meaning that Titus "was born of Hellenic [i.e., pagan] parents."

26. *Graeci, quos Ἕλληνας vel paganos vocant, De homoousio recipiendo* 1. 13, p. 278 Henry/Hadot.

27. In his note on Galatians 4. 9.

28. Most of these texts are cited in full by Zeiller 1917, 79–80, 83–84; see too Chuvin 2002, 8–9.

had traced the (ethnic) hellenes back to King *Hellen*, son of Deucalion and Pyrrha.[29] Somewhat later, we still find the occasional example in Augustine (*Graecos, quos etiam paganos dicimus*).[30] Remarkably enough, the earliest datable writers to use *paganus* in this sense all treat it as the exact Latin equivalent of hellene = pagan.

This equivalence seems to have been generally recognized by translators. We find another example of *paganismus* in the Latin translation of Athanasius's *Life of St. Anthony* by Evagrius of Antioch, written between ca. 362 and 373,[31] where *ad paganismum* is a direct translation of *eis hellēnismon* in Athanasius. Then we have two examples in the old Latin translation of the twenty-fourth canon of the Council of Ancyra in 314, once again representing *hellēnismos* in the Greek original.[32] The same (probably fifth-century) translator also comes up with *paganizo* to represent *hellēnizo* in the sense "lapse into pagan ways."[33] Early in the fifth century Rufinus translated the title of Justin Martyr's lost *Pros Hellenas* as *Contra paganos*.[34] Even more instructive is Rufinus's translation of a quotation from Porphyry in Eusebius, claiming that the church father Origen was Ἕλλην ἐν Ἕλλησιν παιδευθεὶς λόγοις, a passage that is not easy to render both accurately and helpfully in any language. Lawlor and Oulton offer "a Greek educated in Greek learning," but this fails to explain why Eusebius goes on to accuse Porphyry of lying when he says (Lawlor and Oulton again) that Origen "came over from the Greeks" (*ex hellēnōn*). Obviously what Porphyry meant was that Origen "came over from the *pagans*," namely that he was born a pagan. This is clearly how Rufinus understood the passage, translating the first phrase *cum esset paganus et gentilibus, id est Graecorum studiis eruditus*, and the second *de superstitione gentili*.[35]

Down to the age of Constantine, such originally Jewish terms for enemies of the faith apparently sufficed. Earlier studies have paid insufficient attention to the fact that *paganus* is the one entirely new term to emerge. For those who favor the "rustic" etymology, *paganus* was depreciatory from the start, like all the others. According to Fowden, for example, it was because of its "derogatory" associations that Christians chose a term implying "rusticity." Athanassiadi and Frede gloss the word *peasant, rustic, unlearned*, and Kahlos even detects a "nuance of barbarism."[36] For O'Donnell it was "the whole point" of this usage to "address someone like Vettius Agorius Praetextatus as a 'hick' on the ground of a worship shared with men whose boots

29. Merkelbach and West, *Frag. Hesiodea* (1967), 4–5 (citing Filastrius 111 as *Cat.* F 3); most recently, Fowler 1999.
30. Aug. *De opere monach.* 13. 14 (*CSEL* 41. 555. 16); cf. id. *Quaest. Evang.* 1. 14.
31. *Vita Anton.* 78; for what is known about this work, Herzog and Schmidt 5 (1989), sect. 599. 3.
32. C. H. Turner, *Ecclesiae Occidentalis Monumenta Iuris Antiquissima* II. 1 (1907), 20b and 21a. The Greek original has not survived, but we have more or less complete versions in seven vernaculars: M. Geerard, *Clavis Patrum Graecorum* iv (Turnhout 1980), no. 8501.
33. Three times, Turner 1907, 20b and 22a, according to *TLL* x. 1. 78 the only occurrences of the word.
34. Rufin. *Hist. Eccl.* iv. 11. 11 and 18. 13; for the Greek title, Euseb. *Hist. Eccl.* iv. 18. 3–4.
35. Euseb. *Hist. Eccl.* vi. 19. 7 and 9; Rufinus's translation is to be found facing the Greek text in E. Schwartz's editio maior (1909; reprinted 1999).
36. Fowden 1993, 38; Athanassiadi and Frede 1999, 4; Kahlos 2002, 6.

squished with more than mud."[37] It is true that one or two Christian writers do exploit these associations. Orosius claims that pagans were so called "from the crossroads and villages of country places,"[38] and Prudentius at least once hints at the same idea (*stulte, pago dedite*).[39] But ancient writers loved to make etymological puns and jokes, most of them based on wildly speculative and often completely false etymologies.[40] Not only do these two or three texts (out of more than 600) not prove the "rural" etymology; they do not even prove that contemporaries believed it rather than simply exploited it to make an offensive point. Nor does it make much sense that the term selected as the direct Latin equivalent of hellene should imply rusticity and lack of learning. More important, we have seen that the term was felt to be vulgar or unfamiliar rather than insulting.

As for *paganus* = civilian, the fact that it appears so often in legal texts is enough to disprove the assumption sometimes made of a pejorative connotation here too. Nor is it easy to see any such connotations in Greek *paganós*. As we shall see again in the case of *paganus* = non-Christian, it is important not to confuse a particular context with the word itself. Naturally, it is pejorative when a Roman general in Tacitus tells his troops that they will be *pagani* if they do not win an upcoming battle (where Wellesley neatly renders *pagani* "you are finished as soldiers").[41] But in most of the thirty relevant texts we are clearly faced with a technical term. One particularly instructive case is a military register dated to A.D. 156 that lists a man who was promoted to centurion *ex pagano*. Obviously most centurions rose through the ranks, but this man was granted the post direct from civilian life, without any military service at all.[42]

What then are the connotations of *paganus* = non-Christian? Undoubtedly, many of the 600-odd fourth- and early fifth-century texts are very hostile. After all, most Christian writers who mention pagans do so not to praise them, but to criticize their blindness in not accepting the one true faith. Add to this the fact that late imperial laws were written in a ferocious, almost hysterical idiom,[43] and inevitably laws forbidding pagan practices share in the violent rhetoric of the genre. But there is no indication that those that specify *pagani* are any more violent than those that name *gentiles* or use some offensive periphrasis (examples below). On rather ill-defined grounds P. Borgomeo argued that *paganus* was a more negative term than *gentilis* for Augustine.[44] But I can find no unmistakable indication that the word was felt to be pejorative *in and of itself*. What needs accounting for is the appearance of a *new* term. There was no need for yet another pejorative term.

---

37. O'Donnell 1977, 168.

38. *ex locorum agrestium compitis et pagis*, Oros. *Adv. pag.* i, prol. 9.

39. Prud. *Peristephanon* x. 296; *Cathem.* xi. 85–88 (*sed cum fideli spiritu/concurrat ad praesepia/pagana gens et quadrupes/sapiatque quod brutum fuit*). Possibly too *Contra Symm.* i. 449, *sint haec barbaricis gentilia numina pagis*, though in context *barbaricis* clearly means "of barbarians," not "barbaric."

40. For a mass of material on this well-known phenomenon, see O'Hara 1996.

41. Tac. *Hist.* iii. 24, with Wellesley's commentary (Sydney 1972) and Penguin translation (1964).

42. Gilliam 1952, 75–78.

43. MacMullen 1986, 147–66.

44. Borgomeo 1972, 57–73.

On the contrary, by ca. 350, I suggest, Christians had become a sufficiently central and self-confident part of Roman society as a whole for a need to be felt for a *less* overtly polemical term to denote non-Christians. Even at the purely philological level, a collective plural like *ethnē/gentes* could not easily be applied to an individual. Latin *gentilis* could, but carried hostile connotations. Up to the age of Constantine, many Christians had looked on the entire Roman establishment as the enemy, and understandably employed sweeping, imprecise collective nouns like *ethnē/gentes* that implied a race apart, a race of persecutors.

But with the end of the persecutions and a Christian on the imperial throne, Christians must have begun to look on the non-Christians around them differently, no longer as automatic enemies but as misguided fellow citizens, fellow Romans in an increasingly dangerous world. Non-Christians were now individuals who lived next door or worked in the same office. Above all, they were converting in unprecedented numbers. The time had come for a less openly pejorative term to denote them. The well-established "hellene" was a word with enough positive associations to fill this role very satisfactorily in Greek, as well as being readily applicable to individuals (Is X a hellene?). In combination these must be the reasons it rapidly became the standard term in the eastern provinces. And we have seen that Marius Victorinus and Filastrius provide evidence of a short-lived attempt, in the period 360–80, to introduce "hellene" into Latin in the form of *graecus*, glossed *paganus*. In the event it was *paganus* that caught on, rapidly followed by a complex of derivatives clearly modeled on the *hellēn*-complex (*paganizo, paganismus*, etc.).

Christian preachers and polemicists might continue to denounce unbelievers in the old-fashioned way, but what sort of terms do we find in imperial legislation? It is perhaps more than coincidence that seventeen out of the first eighteen extracts in the chapter of the *Theodosian Code* entitled *De paganis, sacrificiis et templis* (xvi. 10),[45] running from 320/21 to 399, avoid using any specific term. *Paganus* appears in xvi. 10. 13, from 395, while all the rest are general prohibitions of the form "let no one…" or "we forbid anyone.…" But the final six extracts, running from 408 to 435, all use *paganus*. It is surely therefore significant that it is in a law of 409 that we find the apologetic formula *gentiles, quos vulgo paganos appellant* (xvi. 5. 46), implying that, in the eyes of those who drafted imperial laws at any rate, *paganus* = non-Christian was still felt to be a subliterary term. As late as a law of 416 we find the same gloss: those polluted *profano pagani ritus errore, hoc est gentiles* (xvi. 10. 21). Elsewhere in the Code *paganus* = pagan appears as early as a law of 370 (xvi. 2. 18), but in a law of 353 we find an unmistakable example of *paganus* = civilian, one in a series of laws about people winning honorary military rank and then trying to get out of their obligations as decurions or private citizens.[46] Apart from a single reference in the military writer Vegetius, writing in the 380s or 390s,[47] this is the latest surviving

---

45. This chapter title (of course) dates from 438, when the Code was published.
46. *Cod. Theod.* vii. 21. 2.
47. Without training in weapons, *nihil paganus distat a milite*, Veget. ii. 23. 14; for the date, Barnes, *Phoenix* 33 (1979), 254–57; further references in M. D. Reeve's OCT edition of 2004 (v–x).

example in a literary text of *paganus* = civilian. In most contexts the non-Christian sense obviously now became dominant, at least in Latin. In Greek *paganós*, however, the civilian sense remained dominant. There was no need for a new term for pagan in Greek, where "hellene" had for some time been standard usage.

It is instructive to compare certain similarities in the way *paganus* and "hellene" were used. While "hellene" was regularly applied quite neutrally to non-Christians, at the same time, although the word itself certainly had no pejorative etymology to color its use, a great many of the phrases and contexts in which it appears are grossly and unmistakably pejorative. It is an interesting exercise to compare the usage of the three mid fifth-century ecclesiastical historians, Socrates, Theodoret, and Sozomen. Not only did all three write within a decade of each other; they covered essentially the same period and same subject matter. Yet while Socrates and Sozomen both employ "the hellenes" freely in neutral contexts simply to identify non-Christian groups and activities,[48] there are few such neutral references in Theodoret. More often than not he uses pejorative periphrases: "those enslaved by impiety," "those devoted to the deceit of idols," "idolaters," "the impious," "unholy ones." When he does use "hellene" it is mostly in loaded formulas like "hellenic delusion" or "hellenic thorns."[49] We find the same with *paganus*. Laws forbidding pagan practices regularly use formulas like *pagana superstitio* or *profanus pagani ritus error.*[50] But this owes more to the stock minatory rhetoric of the imperial chancery than to etymology.

Just as with "hellene," some examples of *paganus* appear to be more or less neutral in tone. Perhaps the clearest illustration is the usage of Optatus of Milevis, in his treatise *Against the Donatists*, written ca. 384 (again among the earliest datable examples of the usage). For example, he glosses Paul's enigmatic "I planted, Apollos watered" at 1 Corinthians 3. 6 as follows: "I planted—that is, I made a catechumen of a pagan (*hoc est, de pagano catechumenon feci*)—Apollos watered—that is, he baptized the catechumen."[51] In another chapter he takes issue with the Donatist practice of counting converts previously baptized by Catholic bishops as no different from pagans and baptizing them again:[52]

> By some miracle you [the Donatists] have the audacity to say to each in turn "John Doe or Jane Doe, are you still a pagan" (*Gai Sei, Gaia Seia, adhuc paganus es aut pagana*)?"[53] A man who has already professed his conversion to God, you

---

48. See the indexes s.v. the Ἕλλην-words in Hansen 1995; and Bidez and Hansen 1960. Procopius writes of "the so-called Hellenes" (*BP* i. 20. 1; ib. 25. 10; *Anecd.* 11. 31; *Aed.* vi. 4. 12), but he "explains" Christian terms in the same way, as well as a number of other words not found in classical historians (Averil Cameron 1970, 151–53).

49. See the illustrations collected in the exemplary index to L. Parmentier's edition, *Theodoret Kirchengeschichte* (Leipzig 1911), 380 s.v. Ἕλληνες.

50. *Cod. Theod.* xvi. 10. 20; *Cod. Just.* i. 11. 8; *Cod. Theod.* xvi. 10. 21.

51. Opt. *Contra Don.* v. 7. 8 (ET M. Edwards, adapted).

52. Ib. iii. 11. 6–7, with Labrousse 1995, 98–100.

53. Opt. *Contra Don.* v. 7. 8 and 111. 11. 6–7.

call a pagan (*paganum vocas*)! A man who has already been baptized, not in our name or yours, but in the name of Christ, you call a pagan!…Anyone who has believed, has believed in the name of the Father, Son and Holy Spirit, and you call him a pagan after his profession of faith! If any Christian (God forbid) should falter, he can be called a sinner, but he cannot become a pagan again.

The two most intriguing details here are what looks like the official formula "John Doe or Jane Doe, are you still a pagan," and the assertion that even a bad Christian cannot become a pagan again once he has been baptized. There are also a number of neutral passages in various works of Augustine. For example, the following from one of the new sermons:[54]

But perhaps you are not going to come across pagans of this sort [namely those who get drunk after festivals]. Some pagans condemn those who abandon themselves to disgusting pleasures and bouts of drunkenness, and say: "Just as you have bad Christians, so we have bad pagans. Consider what good pagans are like." Then they name, for instance, wise men and philosophers.

Augustine styles Porphyry *nobilissimus philosophus paganorum*.[55] A law of 423 forbids "those persons who are truly Christians" to "lay violent hands on Jews and pagans (*paganis*) who are living quietly and attempting nothing disorderly or contrary to law."[56]

There can be little doubt that, in the absence of an existing term, *paganus* came to be treated as the Latin equivalent of "hellene." But *why*? Why *paganus*? In 1952 Mohrmann suggested a modified version of the "civilian" hypothesis: *paganus* meaning not just civilian in opposition to soldier, but anyone not belonging to a particular group, an outsider.[57] She cited an impressive number of illustrations, and the list can be extended. A wide range of such meanings is provided by the following entry in a bilingual glossary: ἰδιώτης (private citizen), ὁ μὴ ἄρχων (not in office), ἡ στρατευόμενος (not in the army): *privatus, paganus, plebeius*.[58] Every term is defined by what it is not rather than what it is. The most conspicuous feature of *paganus* is that, in all its meanings, it takes its precise color from an antonym. Originally rural as opposed to urban, then civilian as opposed to military, and finally pagan as opposed to Christian. We also find other such pairs. A passage of Cicero normally included under the first heading in fact implies a slightly different contrast: *pagani* as opposed to *montani*, an archaic formula apparently implying the entire population of Rome, both the original settlements on the Palatine and

54. S. Mayence 62. 97 = Dolbeau 1996, 373.
55. Aug. *Ep.* 234; *Civ. Dei* 22. 3.
56. *Cod. Theod.* xvi. 10. 24, issued at Constantinople on 8 June 423.
57. Mohrmann 1952, 118; for a more systematic treatment, *TLL* x. 1 (1982), 80. Courtney's note suggests "outsider" as a translation of *paganum* at Juvenal 16. 33.
58. *Corp. Gloss. Lat* II. 330. 48; the absence of the religious sense is probably to be explained by eastern rather than pre-Christian origin.

Esquiline hills and the surrounding farm land, the *pagi*.[59] A couple of legal texts distinguish the estates of the emperor, senators, and *pagani*, where *pagani* apparently denotes ordinary private citizens.[60] A recently published document from Oxyrhynchus uses Greek *paganós* a number of times interchangably with *demotai* "to describe those with no official positions."[61] In fact, we find Greek *paganós* in a variety of slightly differing contexts: private citizens as opposed to officials; lay clothes as opposed to monastic garb; everyday clothes as opposed to what one wears on festival days; a gladiator's personal as opposed to professional name; and even everyday chariot racing as opposed to the special events held on gala days.[62] By the tenth century there was even a verb παγανῶ = remove from office. The likelihood is that at least some of these meanings either go back to Latin *paganus* or would readily have been understood by Latin speakers from some (at least implied) antonym in the context. The soldier/civilian opposition is simply one example of a much wider and more general usage. It would not be surprising to find *pagani* in some newly found inscription relating to (say) membership of the Roman guilds (*collegia*), identifying those who were not members.

Here it is relevant to compare a formula employed by Greek-speaking Christians from as early as Paul: "those outside" (οἱ ἔξω, οἱ ἔξωθεν), meaning non-Christians. This too is a usage that goes back to pre-Christian times,[63] but became particularly common in Christian references to classical, that is to say non-Christian, culture: "external learning, wisdom, philosophy," often used neutrally or even as a compliment.[64] It is not easy to see how best to express the idea of "outsider" in Latin. The lack of a definite article excluded the elegantly unspecific "those outside" possible in Greek. The standard Christian way to refer to classical literature or learning in Latin was to use the word *saecularis*,[65] literally "learning of the world," but this was not an epithet that could be applied to a person. *Alienus, peregrinus* and *externus* were no doubt felt to be too hostile, implying as they did "foreign" or "non-Roman." For a combination of reasons now irretrievably lost, *paganus* was the word that caught on.

Particularly suggestive is the earliest datable nonliterary example of the religious sense, an epitaph from Catania in Sicily for a baby girl, erected by her father Zoïlus, *corrector* of the province.[66] Some critics have been reluctant to exploit an undated inscription, but it can at any rate be dated before 324, when the title of the governor of

---

59. Cicero, *De domo* 74, with R. G. Nisbet's commentary (1939), 137–38; *TLL* x. 1. 79, § 2. a; Tarpin 2002, 186–88.

60. Ulpian, *Dig.* xi. 4. 3: *divus Marcus … facultatem dedit ingrediendi tam Caesaris quam senatorum et paganorum praedia*; so too ib. xi. 4. 1. 2.

61. P. Oxy. 3758 (quotation from R. A. Coles on line 9, p. 164).

62. Grégoire and Orgels 1952; Oikonomidès 1972, 290; Dagron 2000, 127. For gladiators, J. Keil, *Akad. Wiss. Wien, Anzeiger* 79 (1942), 84–87; L. Robert, *Bull. Ép.* 1943, 336.

63. See LSJ, Bauer/Danker and Lampe s.v. ἔξω and ἔξωθεν. Iamblichus, *Vita Pythag.* 252, uses οἱ ἔξω of those outside the circle of Pythagoras.

64. ἡ ἔξω (θεν) παιδεία, ἡ θύραθεν (φιλο) σοφία; many examples cited in Cameron and Long 1993, 35–37.

65. *saeculares litterae, libri, codices, eruditio saeculi, saeculi disciplina*: *TLL* s.v. *littera* IIc2a and *litteratura*; on *saeculum* in the sense of what we would call the "secular" world, Löfstedt, *Syntactica* ii (Lund 1933), 470–72.

66. *CIL* x. 7122 = *ILCV* 1549; revised text by G. Manganaro in *AÉ* 1959, no. 23, with some useful notes.

Sicily was changed to *consularis*.[67] Since this makes it by a half-century the earliest-known example of the usage, we might hope to find some clue here about its origin. The girl, Julia Florentina, was *pagana nata*, lived for eighteen months and twenty-two days, and died *fidelis facta*, surviving her baptism by four hours. Ten days later she was buried in front of the church of the martyrs. A number of things about this touching dedication call for comment. First, in such a context there can be no question of any pejorative connotation. Second, even if Zoïlus's own conversion postdated Julia's birth, he cannot have considered a child (his own daughter) of less than two an active pagan. *Pagana* here must mean simply that she was not yet a full member of the church, more specifically that she was unbaptized.[68] Third, *pagana nata* is clearly and sharply contrasted with *fidelis facta*. That is to say, as in the many other cases just considered, *pagana* takes its precise color from an antonym in the context.

Following Mohrmann, then, I would suggest that the religious sense has nothing to do with either rustics or soldiers of Christ. At some time, around the end of the third or beginning of the fourth century, Christians began referring to those "outside" their community as *pagani*. It is unlikely that there was ever a conscious search for a new term. *Paganus* was simply the most natural term for any Latin-speaking community to apply to outsiders. To use a contemporary idiom, *paganus* represented "the other" in any group or community, in this case (of course) the other in a now Christian world. We have seen that cultivated folk thought it a vulgarism or neologism. But more and more people found it a convenient, at least potentially neutral way of referring to non-Christians, and eventually even the educated capitulated and it became standard. It was presumably at this stage that fancy by-forms and derivatives like *paganismus, paganitas, paganista*, and *paganizo* were coined.[69]

Take a recent case in English. Nobody really knows where gay = homosexual comes from. It is hard to believe that there can be any connection with old-fashioned phrases like "gay dog" or "gay Lothario," nor with the long-obsolete sense "prostitute" applied to women.[70] Scholars being scholars, one has even suggested a link with the use of "gai" in thirteenth- and fourteen-century Provençal poetry! According to Partridge, the sense has been "common" in the United States since ca. 1945.[71] The second edition of the *OED* offers citations from the 1950s, but it did not become widespread till the 1960s or 1970s.

The most intriguing thing about the word is not its ultimate derivation, but the fact that it caught on so rapidly, effectively eliminating all competition. And the reason it did so is surely that by the 1970s homosexuality had sufficiently entered the social

---

67. Chastagnol 1963, 371–72; Barnes 1982, 165.
68. So Mohrmann 1952, 114.
69. For *paganitas* (quite common) and *paganista* or *paganita* (very rare), see *TLL* x. 1. 78. 42–49, 50–77.
70. See the well-documented entry s.v. in *OED*; Burchfield, *The New Fowler's Modern English Usage* (1996), s.v.; Garner, *Oxford Dictionary of American Usage and Style* (2000) s. v.
71. Boswell 1980, 43 n. 6; Partridge, *Dictionary of Slang and Unconventional English*, 8th ed. (New York 1982), 450.

and cultural mainstream for a need to be felt for a neutral, nonspecific term, a term that neither depreciated homosexuals nor evoked uncomfortably explicit sexual associations (as "homosexual" itself does), a word that could be dropped casually in "polite" company. Words that fill a newly felt need sometimes catch on very quickly (computer-related terminology is an obvious recent illustration), and it is surely no coincidence that *paganus* caught on a generation after the Constantinian revolution.

2

Another point that may cause raised eyebrows in some quarters is my reluctance to use the currently fashionable "polytheist" in place of "pagan." There seems to be a growing sense that "pagan" is somehow objectionable. Among academics, it is Fowden who has most firmly articulated the objections, urging that "it is inappropriate to use a term derived from Christian apologetic to denote a religious culture whose study is struggling to emerge from Christian stereotypes."[72] True to his convictions, he used "polytheist" and "polytheism" throughout his valuable survey of late antique paganism in *Cambridge Ancient History* 13 (somewhat undermined by the index to the volume, where the entry for "polytheism" offers "see paganism"!). But it is relevant to point out straightaway that his negative reading of the word is colored by his mistaken appeal to the pejorative "rustic" etymology. It may be precisely because it was *not*, in itself, an overtly pejorative term that *paganus* caught on when and as rapidly as it did.

More surprisingly, there are signs that the word is not only felt to be unfair to late antique non-Christians but also offensive to present-day non-Christians. Several schools invited to participate in a conference on "paganism and Christianity" in London a few years ago refused to attend. Apparently, school authorities thought the term might cause offense to their many Hindu, Muslim, and Jewish students. Barnes has described a lecture he gave on late Roman paganism that called forth more discussion about his terminology than his thesis, and I myself have had the same experience. In an age of growing religious fundamentalism I certainly have no wish to cause offense, but this is surely a case of misplaced political correctness.

To be sure, there is a danger that pejorative language will foster or disguise biased thinking. We might well doubt the impartiality of a modern historian who used terms like "heathen," "infidel," or "idolater."[73] But whatever negative associations "pagan" may once have borne in Christian polemic are surely now confined to the rhetoric of American fundamentalist preachers. The Reverend Jerry Falwell infamously blamed indigenous "pagans and abortionists" rather than foreign terrorists for the 9/11 attacks

---

72. Fowden 1991, 119 n.*.

73. To judge from its *OED* entry, "heathen" regularly implies uncivilized and uncultivated. The very fact that it is now obsolete, at any rate in scholarly discourse, suggests that it has always been a more pejorative term than "pagan."

on New York. But such excesses aside, the current associations of "pagan" outside the Academy are overwhelmingly positive rather than negative. Anyone who searches the Internet for "pagan" will discover in a matter of minutes that it is now a key concept in New Age philosophy, Wicca, environmental awareness, and many other alternatives to the supposed tyranny of traditional organized religion.[74] Modern pagans (or "neo-pagans," as they sometimes call themselves) claim to practice an "earth-centred religion" that offers harmony with nature, ecological awareness, tolerance, and enhanced spirituality, and are delighted to derive their concerns from the original meaning of *paganus*, "country-dweller."[75] I would be the first to concede that this idealized late twentieth-century "paganism" has no genuine historical roots. Yet it is as much part of the baggage with which a twenty-first-century reader approaches the word as the Christian polemic of earlier centuries and Jerry Falwell. Add that the dominant modern academic representation of late Roman paganism has been as a romantic resistance movement, and it is verging on the absurd to suggest that any modern reader is likely to be led into a negative bias by the use of this word in a book on the last pagans.

It is true enough that early Christians used "paganism" as "a convenient shorthand for [a] vast spectrum of cults ranging from the international to the ethnic and local."[76] Athanassiadi and Frede write of "those who were grouped together as pagans by the Christian apologists, partly for reasons of convenience, partly for reasons of propaganda."[77] But this is more than just a question of convenience or propaganda—or (as Fowden put it) "the lazy cunning of Christian apologists."[78] There is a very real sense in which Christianity actually created paganism. The development has been described with exemplary clarity by North:[79]

> It is perhaps misleading even to say that there was such a religion as "paganism" at the beginning of our period....It might be less confusing to say that the pagans, before their competition with Christianity, had no religion at all in the sense in which that word is normally used today. They had no tradition of discourse about ritual or religious matters (apart from philosophical debate or antiquarian treatise), no organized system of beliefs to which they were asked to commit themselves, no authority-structure peculiar to the religious area, above all no commitment to a particular group of people or set of ideas other than their family and political context. If this is the right view of pagan life, it

---

74. As of 8 October 2008, Google offered more than 34 million hits for "pagan," excluding Wahhabi sites the great majority (as far as I persevered) favorable.
75. For a mass of current definitions of "pagan," see www.religioustolerance.org/paganism.htm; see too Hardman and Harvey (eds.), *Paganism Today* (San Francisco 1995) and Pearson, Roberts, and Samuel (eds.), *Nature Religion Today: Paganism in the Modern World* (Edinburgh 1998), both with extensive bibliographies. Half the contributors to both these volumes are academics.
76. Fowden 1993, 38.
77. Athanassiadi and Frede 1999, 4–5.
78. Fowden 1988, 173–82.
79. North 1992, 187–88.

follows that we should look on paganism quite simply as a religion invented in the course of the second to third centuries AD, in competition and interaction with Christians, Jews and others.

The lumping together of all non-Christian cults (Judaism excepted) under one label is not just an illustration of Christian intolerance. As far as the now Christian authorities were concerned, whether at the local, church, or governmental level, those who refused to acknowledge the one true god, whatever the differences between them, were for all practical purposes indistinguishable. Thus the objection that the term "pagan" "flattens out the diversity of religious experience" of non-Christians, and suggests the Christian perspective of a world divided into two distinct categories[80] is misplaced. Of course it does. We should not think of fourth-century non-Christians indignantly protesting that they were all being lumped together under an insulting sobriquet. No more bias is involved than when (say) European, Mexican, or Japanese nationals domiciled in the United States are nowadays all classified indifferently as "aliens." It would be absurd to object that the term does not do justice to their diversity. In the eyes of the U.S. government, whatever their ethnic or national origin, language or religion, they are indeed all aliens.

Fourth-century pagans naturally never referred to themselves as pagans, less because the term was insulting than because the category had no meaning for them. A pagan anxious to discover whether the person he was speaking to was a fellow pagan would get a more illuminating response by asking him whether he was a Christian! When the pagan Longinianus styles himself *homo paganus* in a letter to Augustine (*Ep.* 234), the tone of the letter suggests irony. He would certainly not have so styled himself writing to a fellow pagan.

No one planning to treat the non-Christian cults of late antiquity in and for themselves in all their variety and complexity will feel any need to use so unspecific a term as "pagan." She will simply write about the followers of Mithras, Isis, Marnas, and so on. And anyone studying (as Fowden brilliantly did) the role of monotheism in creating a universal state might justifiably find "polytheism" a more appropriate term for contrasting the role of religion in the pre- and post-Constantinian empire. But anyone planning to treat the attitude of the Christian establishment to non-Christian groups will find "pagan" a simpler and more accurate term. There seems little point in writing of the government issuing laws against polytheism when the laws themselves use terms like "gentiles," "*pagani*," and a variety of insulting periphrases. Indeed, those who employ the supposedly neutral "polytheism" in such a context[81] are in consequence (if unintentionally) making the Roman government appear less intolerant than it actually was.

Fowden also objected that the continued use of "pagan" and "paganism" by classical and Christian scholars is "one more sign of their isolation from other disciplines,

---

80. For example, Sandwell 2007, 10; so too Lee 2000, 10.
81. So Fowden in his chapter in *CAH* 13 (1998), 538–60.

particularly anthropology, where 'polytheism' is the norm." If "polytheism" is indeed the term most modern anthropologists employ (and that is far from clear),[82] this is not just because they perceive it as a modern, neutral alternative to "pagan." In themselves, monotheism and polytheism certainly can be value-free ways of classifying religions, but that is because they are also virtually content-free. As the online *Encyclopaedia Britannica* puts it, polytheism "characterizes virtually all religions other than Judaism, Christianity and Islam." Paganism has a much more restricted reference.

In modern academic writing "pagan" is both more and less than a synonym (pejorative or otherwise) for "polytheist." Whatever its connotations in the preaching of televangelists or Wicca Web sites, in current historical discourse, by long-established convention it is regularly employed as a shorthand for various facets of the non- or pre-Christian society of the Graeco-Roman world and its neighbours, excluding (for historical reasons) Judaism. For example, modern scholarly discussions of the age at which Roman girls married regularly distinguish between the evidence for Christian and "pagan" marriages.[83] It is also widely believed (whether rightly or wrongly is immaterial in this context) that women played a more prominent role in early Christian communities than their "pagan" counterparts.[84] In neither case does "pagan" have any reference, depreciatory or otherwise, to the religious beliefs of these people. It simply identifies social practices current in the non- or pre-Christian Roman world. In much the same way it is also now used in Jewish studies to identify non-Jewish cities or non-Jewish objects, imagery, practices, and art in the Jewish cities of Palestine.[85] It is also the standard term employed for their former religious practices in modern studies on the conversion of the Celts, Slavs, Vikings, and so on.[86] Purists might object to the usage, but it is widely accepted and not easy to think of a more succinct or convenient alternative. One might as well object to the collective use of "barbarian" to denote all and any peoples beyond the Roman frontiers, obviously depreciatory and making no distinction between long-established empires like Sassanid Persia and tribal groups like Goths and Huns. The reason no one does object is that barbarians have no modern constituency.[87]

Furthermore, for all its polysyllabic pretense to technicality, it would be naive to assume that "polytheism" itself is a term free of pejorative connotations. To start with, the relevant entries in Lampe's *Patristic Lexicon*[88] reveal it as a standard term of early Christian polemic, often linked with or glossed as idolatry and atheism. The Jewish

---

82. A survey of the Anthropological Index Online for the past thirty years showed far more hits for "paganism" than "polytheism."
83. Hopkins 1965, 319; Shaw 1987, 44 (glossing "pagan" as "early empire").
84. For a recent evaluation of this assumption, see Castelli 1998, 227–57.
85. S. Schwartz 2001, Ch. 4; Friedheim 2006.
86. For example, Jones and Pennick 1995, 132–37; Fletcher 1997, 6, and passim ("Celtic, Scandinavian and Slavonic paganisms").
87. I am speaking of general books; naturally, the experts (notably Goffart) object.
88. Svv. πολυθεΐα, πολύθεος and related terms (notably πολυθεομανία, madness of polytheism).

writer Philo refers in the most hostile of terms to polytheism as an evil that leads to atheism.[89] With the growth of the doctrine of the Trinity and veneration of saints, pagans soon began to turn the reproach back on Christians. Here is what John Chrysostom represents pagans saying already before the close of the fourth century: "Who is this Father? Who is this Son? Who is this Holy Ghost? How is it that you accuse *us* of polytheism when you have *three* gods?"[90] The Saracens said the same about the Crusaders, as have many others before and since, most conspicuously fundamentalist Muslims of modern Christians.

Even at the academic level, we can hardly claim to have altogether shaken off the condescending Eurocentric assumption that polytheism is a stage that mankind passes through on the way to monotheism. If it is true that polytheism has become the preferred term of modern anthropologists, that is because they have chosen to ignore all this baggage. But the fact that they intend it as no more than a mode of classification does not mean that all readers will accept it as such. To take an obvious example, Christians and Muslims tend to see Hinduism as a classic case of polytheism, but "all Hindus sometimes and some Hindus always insist that there is in reality only one God, of whom all the distinct gods and goddesses are but forms."[91] One man's taxonomy is another man's condescension.

No less important, polytheism inescapably implies a monotheist perspective. It would never have occurred to anyone in pre-Christian times to call himself a polytheist, and even as late as the fourth century, non-Christians in different parts of the empire would almost certainly have thought that classifying them according to whether they worshiped one or many gods blurred what they themselves would have considered far more significant differences. Cicero and Varro, for example, would have been surprised by the emphasis on the number of gods rather than the priestly colleges. Varro's *Antiquitates rerum divinarum* comprised sixteen books, the first thirteen devoted to priesthoods, shrines, festivals, and rituals, with only the last three coming to the gods.[92] A large part of the reason paganism yielded comparatively easily and rapidly (at least in the West) is precisely that pagans in different parts of the empire had so little in common.

Outside the academic context, current use of the term "polytheism" implies an aggressively monotheist perspective, whether Christian or Muslim. In this postmodern age, when poly- words (polyvalent, polysemous, and the like) have come to take on aggressively positive connotations, some attack monotheism as "imperialism in religion."[93] In the mouth of a Jerry Falwell or Osama bin Laden, polytheism is by no

---

89. *De confus. ling.* 42 (τῷ πολυθέῳ λεγομένῳ κακῷ); *De fuga* 114; *De praem.* 162; *De ebr.* 110; *De virt.* 214; *De decal.* 65; *De opif.* 171.

90. πῶς... ἡμῖν ἐκαλεῖ πολυθεῖαν; Jo. Chrys. *In Joann. Hom.* xvii. 4 (*PG* 49. 112).

91. Fuller 1992, 30.

92. For Varro's sixteen books, below p. 615n.231; cf. Cic. *De nat. deor.* iii. 5 and *De harusp. resp.* 18 for a similar emphasis.

93. Adler 1986, viii.

means just a term of taxonomy. Anyone who searches the Internet for "polytheist" or "polytheism" will discover a large number of Wahhabi denunciations of Jews, Christians, and even Shiite Muslims as polytheists. One Web site refers to Christians as "polytheist trinitarian pagans."[94] Whatever chances "polytheism" may once have had of becoming a scientific principle of classification have been overtaken by events. In the modern world, the sad truth is that very few terms in the religious lexicon are entirely neutral.

One much-debated issue in current research (Ch. 5) is the percentage of Christian officeholders at successive dates (350, 380, 420, and so on). Since the point of the exercise is to trace the rate of Christianization, for this limited purpose it is enough to classify all who cannot be shown to be Christians as pagans, whatever their actual beliefs (about which in most cases we have no information of any sort). From the point of view of our statistical inquiry all we need to know is, was he or wasn't he a Christian? If not, it doesn't soften the blow to classify him as polytheist rather than pagan. To take a somewhat different example, in standard usage "Visigothic paganism" and "Viking paganism" simply refer to whatever cults the Visigoths and Vikings practiced before they embraced Christianity.[95] It neither describes nor judges any actual beliefs they held before conversion; in itself it does not even entail the assumption that they were polytheists.

Paganism certainly *implies* polytheism, but not all pre-Christian cults were in fact polytheist. The truth is that from the earliest times down into late antiquity a great many pagans believed in the supremacy of one god or supreme power.[96] To be sure, most of them also assumed a plurality of subordinate gods, but is it helpful on this basis to classify them straightforwardly as polytheists? Fowden himself cites the well-known case of the grammarian Maximus of Madauros, writing to none other than his friend Augustine:[97]

> There is a Greek myth of uncertain authenticity that Mount Olympus is the dwelling-place of the gods. But we have the evidence of our eyes (*cernimus et probamus*) that the forum of our own town is occupied by a throng of benefi-cent deities (*salutarium numinum*). Yet who would be so foolish, so touched in the head, as to deny that there is one supreme god, without beginning, without natural offspring, like a great and powerful father? His powers, scattered throughout the material world, we call upon under various names, since (of course) none of us knows his true name. For "god" is a name common to all cults. Thus when we honour his separate parts by different forms of prayer, we seem to worship him entire.

---

94. www.answering-christianity.com; another site refers to Christians as "trinitos."
95. Thompson 1966, vii, 55–63; Jones and Pennick 1995, 132–37.
96. Athanassiadi and Frede 1999; see too Barnes 2001, 142–62; North 2005, 125–43.
97. *Ep.* 16. 1 (Sr. W. Parsons's translation, adapted); for the little that is known about Maximus, *PCBE* i. 733–34.

Despite the fact that Maximus closes his letter with the wish that the "gods preserve" Augustine (a routine formula, in this case presumably intended as a joke), it surely misplaces the emphasis to classify him as polytheist.[98] In modern terminology he was a "henotheist," someone who believes in one god, thought not to the exclusion of all others.[99] But this distinction would have been meaningless to fourth-century Christians, in whose eyes there was no difference between polytheists, henotheists, or indeed atheists. They were all pagans. Even monotheists would be pagans if their one god was not the one true god. For Christians, the key distinction was less between one god and many gods than between the one true god and false gods, whether one or many.[100]

Athanassiadi and Frede raise the surprising objection that it is "hardly appropriate" to characterize "highly articulate thinkers like Plotinus or Proclus" as pagans. The irrelevance of such an argument is sufficiently exposed by asking whether "polytheist" would be more appropriate, or even more descriptive. Neither term (of course) is a remotely *adequate* characterisation of the religious beliefs of *anyone*, whether a subtle philosopher like Proclus or an illiterate devotee of Mithras in the Roman army. But whatever else Proclus was, in the eyes of the Christian authorities he was indeed a pagan. In this case the irrelevance of the argument is further underlined by the fact that their fellow Greeks, Christians and pagans alike, would have called Plotinus and Proclus not pagans but *hellenes*, a characterisation both would proudly have accepted.

There are in fact more substantial and relevant objections to the term "pagan." The widespread use of formulas like "pagan reaction," "pagan propaganda," and even just "the pagans" in much earlier writing on the end of Graeco-Roman paganism has encouraged the mistaken idea that pagans *as a class* possessed unity of purpose and organization, at least in the face of the threat posed by Christianity. This is an assumption that has plagued a good deal of writing about late Roman paganism in particular. Since many of the last generation of Roman pagans came from the same social class, it has often been taken for granted that there was a "pagan party," led by a few prominent aristocrats. We shall see that this was not so. But it is an error that would not be lessened by using the term "polytheist" rather than "pagan."[101] Nor is the danger of seeing the decline of paganism too much in terms of Christian/pagan conflict in any way lessened by a change of terminology.

Much confusion has also been caused by loose use of phrases like "pagan literature" or "the pagan classics." To characterize the classics in this way has given rise to the misleading notion that pagans saw the classics as a buffer or even weapon against Christianity. We shall see that there is little reason to believe that pagans as a class were

---

98. Another famous example is Lucius's prayer to Isis under her many different guises in Bk xi of the *Metamorphoses*.

99. So Fowden 1993, 5, 40–41.

100. For the distinction between true and false religion, Jan Assmann, *The Price of Polytheism* (Stanford 2010).

101. Fowden, for example, refers to "the polytheist party in the senate" (*CAH* xiii [1998], 551).

any more devoted to the classics than cultivated Christians (Ch. 9–13). "Pagan" historiography (Ch. 14, 17–18) is a particularly dangerous notion, unmistakably implying writers with a consciously pagan agenda. There are one or two Greek anti-Christian histories (Eunapius, Zosimus), but no identifiable western, Latin example. Yet "polytheist" classics or historiography is no solution; rather terms with no specifically religious associations like "classical," "classicizing," or "secular." It is no less misleading to write of "pagan" art. While it may be a convenient and acceptable shorthand to distinguish (say) pagan from Christian sarcophagi, meaning those decorated with mythological scenes as opposed to those decorated with biblical scenes, to assume or argue that the former have a "pagan" message (see Ch. 19) implies a (so to speak) nondenominationally polytheist iconography that all non-Christians would recognize as such, whatever their individual beliefs. It also implies (indeed is often intended to imply) a consciously anti-Christian purpose. Obviously "polytheist" does not help here either. Once again, "classical," "secular," or just "mythological" is the simplest solution at a terminological level.

A random survey of a few recent studies of late antique society that employ "polytheist" instead of "pagan" turned up not a single case where the substitution of "pagan" could by any stretch of the imagination have been said to convey a negative bias of any sort. I like to think that in the following pages I use "pagan" less often and more carefully than most who have written on this subject. And where appropriate I occasionally use "polytheist." But in most cases "pagan" is the simplest, most familiar, and most appropriate term, and I make no further apology for using it.

2

FROM CONSTANTIUS TO THEODOSIUS

During his visit to Rome in 357, Constantius II ordered the altar of Victory removed from the senate house. Christian senators had understandably been distressed at having to watch while their pagan peers burned incense before senatorial meetings. Yet during that same visit Constantius walked around Rome admiring the ancient temples, and even filled vacancies in the pontifical colleges, evidently in his capacity as *pontifex maximus*.[1] The pious emperor may not have performed these duties enthusiastically, but no doubt saw them as a necessary quid pro quo. If he was going to grant a request from Christian senators, it was tactful to grant a parallel request from pagan senators. Though usually treated as a turning point in Christian intolerance, when viewed in context what this episode really illustrates is the policy of compromise even the most seemingly intolerant of Christian emperors pursued whenever possible.

Many Christians undoubtedly urged Constantius to go much further. Firmicus Maternus is one vivid and notably intemperate surviving illustration (Ch. 5. 1). But emperors were reluctant to offend the rich and powerful. Churchmen might put spiritual values first, but emperors faced more pressing priorities. The reason Constantius was in the West at all was a civil war, and while a few prominent Roman aristocrats had rallied to Magnentius (notably Proculus, prefect of Rome under Magnentius in 351–52), many others had left Rome to join Constantius (notably Adelphius, prefect of Rome from June to December 351). As it happens, Proculus was a pagan and Adelphius a Christian, but there is no evidence that allegiance during the war turned on religious sympathy. Even if it had, that was still an argument for conciliating powerful pagans as far as could be done without offending Christian opinion. It was no doubt explained to Constantius that Roman priesthoods were social prizes rather than religious vocations (Ch. 4), and that the pontiffs and augurs themselves never touched a knife or a sacrificial victim.

The altar of Victory was back in the senate house by 382, no doubt the result of an appeal to Julian on Constantius's death. Inevitably, Christian senators are bound to have renewed their demand for its removal on Julian's death. Some have argued that

---

1. Amm. xvi. 10. 4–12; Symm. *Rel.* 3. 7; Rüpke 2008, 58, implausibly claims that this "had nothing to do with the role of *pontifex maximus*, but must be seen in respect of the emperor's participation in senatorial appointments."

Julian's anti-Christian policies had a polarizing effect on Christian/pagan relations.[2] There may be some truth in this, but they certainly had no immediate or perceptible effect on imperial policy. The dates simply do not fit. Since the altar was clearly still there in 382, it follows that (passing over the short reign of Jovian) Valentinian I (363–75) must have turned down the appeal of the Christian party. This is put beyond doubt by the speech Ambrose put in the mouth of the (safely deceased) Valentinian I addressing his son Valentinian II, beginning: "You have misjudged me in thinking that I collaborated with the pagans. Nobody told me that there was an altar in that Roman senate house...."[3] This can hardly be true. Symmachus represents Valentinian looking down from heaven on (pagan) priests tearfully reproaching him "now that the custom which *he himself was glad to preserve* has been broken."[4] Valentinian famously did his best to be neutral in matters of religion,[5] and there can be little doubt that he decided to concede this point to powerful pagans.

It is natural to assume that Christian senators renewed their appeal to Gratian when he became senior western Augustus on the death of Valentinian in 375. But to start with he too must have refused, since it was not till 382 that he ordered the altar removed again. This refusal was presumably one element in the conciliatory policy toward the Roman aristocracy he pursued in the early years of his reign. In 382 he also took certain financial measures against the state cults, and most scholars have assumed that it was in connection with these two measures that he also repudiated the title of *pontifex maximus*. What we would like to know is *why* he embarked on what has traditionally been seen as a radical new policy toward paganism.[6]

The standard view is that in the first part of his reign Gratian was still under the influence of his old tutor Ausonius, held to explain the pro-senatorial policies of his early years. But after moving his court to Milan in 381 he fell under the influence of bishop Ambrose and abruptly turned against the pagan aristocrats he had previously been courting. Though often repeated as though undisputed fact, neither part of this hypothesis rests on any sort of evidence. The fact that Ausonius was on friendly terms with Symmachus does not prove that he was behind Gratian's early policy of courting the Roman senate. That policy was an inevitable reaction to the very hostile attitude to the aristocracy of Valentinian I's later years. Within months of Valentinian's death those responsible for this policy were either dismissed or executed.[7] Given the ever-present danger of usurpation, there had never been any point in treating so powerful a group so badly, and it is unlikely that the paganism of some of the most prominent senators was a factor in the new policy. Ausonius himself was undoubtedly a Christian,

2. Drake 2000, 436; Stark 2006, 196.
3. Ambrose, *Ep.* 72. 16 (= Maur. 17). References to Ambrose's letters are to Zelzer 1982.
4. *se culpatum putat more violato quem libenter ipse servavit, Rel.* 3. 20; cf. 3. 3.
5. *inter religionum diversitates medius stetit, nec quemquam inquietavit, neque ut hoc coleretur imperavit aut illud,* Amm. Marc. xxx. 9. 5. For more detail on Valentinian's religious policy, Lenski 2002, Ch. 5.
6. For this approach see Bowersock 1986, 298–307 at 303.
7. Matthews 1975, 64–69.

and the fact that, like many Christians of his generation, he was devoted to classical culture need not imply any sympathy for pagan cult. Nor was Ausonius's the only voice Gratian listened to. According to Zosimus, in the early days of his sole reign Gratian was under the influence of court eunuchs (p. 752). There is no evidence of any kind that Gratian was ever favorable to paganism as distinct from being attracted to secular culture.

On the other side, there is no real evidence for the all but universal assumption that Gratian ever fell under the influence of Ambrose. In autumn 378 he asked Ambrose for a statement of faith.[8] In the past this was interpreted as a request from a pious but (thanks to Ausonius) theologically untutored youth in search of spiritual guidance from a bishop known to be impeccably orthodox.[9] It was further assumed that Gratian at once succumbed to Ambrose's spell. But at this date Ambrose had not yet published any theological writings, and if it was instruction the emperor was looking for, there were many more senior and experienced bishops he knew better much closer to his court in Trier. Most of these bishops were Homoeans, naturally suspicious of the new Catholic bishop of Milan who had replaced the loyal Homoean Auxentius. It is much more likely that these Homoeans were suspicious of Ambrose and urged Gratian to demand a personal statement of faith. Ambrose's exact words are *fidem meam audire voluisti*, where the *meam* implies, not a theological treatise, but Ambrose's personal creed. Coming from an emperor, the *voluisti* is something closer to a command than a wish (indeed Ambrose later uses the term *mandaveras* of Gratian's request).[10] Ambrose rapidly fulfilled the request with *De fide* i–ii, to which he subsequently added three more books. Bk iii begins by claiming that "certain malicious minds, bent on sowing disputes, have provoked me to write at greater length." The natural implication is that Gratian had shown Bks i–ii to the bishops who had requested the statement for their approval. Not only did the emperor not fall under Ambrose's spell, Ambrose's polemical statement of faith was found wanting by his experts.[11] Furthermore, a year or so later Gratian agreed to "restore" a church in Milan to the Homoeans, apparently in response to a group of Milanese Homoeans and plainly without the courtesy of consulting Ambrose first.[12] It was presumably in response to this that Ambrose took the extraordinary step of refusing to meet with Gratian during his visits to Milan in 379 and 380.[13] It is hard to resist the inference that relations between Ambrose and Gratian were often strained.

As for the removal of the altar of Victory and the withdrawal of the subsidies, Ambrose himself explicitly disclaims any responsibility, and while (as we shall see) he

---

8. Nautin 1974, 229–44; McLynn 1994, 98–106; Barnes 1999, 165–74.
9. Conspicuously so the translation by H. de Romestin in the Nicene and post-Nicene Fathers series (1885).
10. For examples, Vidén 1984, 82, 88; Ambr. *De fide* i, pr.; iii. 1. 1.
11. See McLynn 1994, 112–18 for a full discussion.
12. McLynn 1994, 121–23.
13. So Barnes 1999, 171–73.

seriously misrepresents his past conduct on more than one occasion, there is no reason to question his veracity in this case. When recalling in 394 his role in dissuading Valentinian II from restoring the altar and subsidies in 384, Ambrose adds that he "was not responsible for their removal, but was responsible for preventing their restoration."[14] Why would he take pride in the one but repudiate any part in the other if he had been equally active in both?

The two celebrated letters to Valentinian II about the altar and subsidies have placed Ambrose so squarely in the center of the "debate" about the altar and subsidies that it is seldom appreciated that they were unsolicited by and almost certainly unwelcome to their recipient. It is instructive to note that when Ambrose came to write his funerary oration on Valentinian, he was tactful enough to suppress entirely his intervention. Instead we hear how[15]

> when all who were in attendance in the consistory, Christians and pagans alike, were saying that [subsidies and altar] should be restored, he alone, like Daniel, the spirit of God being stirred within him, denounced the faithlessness of the Christians, and opposed the pagans saying: "How can you think that I should restore what my pious brother [Gratian] has taken away?" For this would wrong both his religion and his brother, by whom he refused to be surpassed in piety.

This is certainly how Valentinian would have liked his Christian subjects to view his decision, but Ambrose's intervention made that impossible. If the young emperor had been intending to say no all along, he could not have claimed to be the lone voice of faith surrounded by waverers. If, on the other hand, he was thinking of the sort of compromise his father might have chosen (removing the altar but restoring the subsidies), that route too was made impossible by Ambrose.

More relevant in the present context, for all that Ambrose later claimed to have enjoyed close and affectionate relations with Valentinian, it is nonetheless clear from these two letters that he was not consulted about the senatorial embassy of 384. He heard about it through the grapevine, and wrote requesting a copy of Symmachus's petition. When he had read it he wrote a detailed refutation. The very fact that he was obliged to write is enough to prove that he was not consulted in advance and was not present either for the embassy or during the discussion of the petition. The second letter, certainly and possibly the first as well, was written after the decision had already been made, perhaps without any input from Ambrose at all. The notion that, because he lived in the same city as the emperor, Ambrose was a frequent visitor at court and so in a position to exert informal influence, is based on a misunderstanding of the nature of late Roman courts. Personal access to the emperor was strictly controlled by the *magister officiorum* (p. 202) and court eunuchs, a group with whom Ambrose had

---

14. *Ep. extra coll.* 10. 2 (= 57 Maur.), with *decerno* presumably used in the sense "vote in approval."
15. *De ob. Val.* 19 (trans. Liebeschuetz, adapted).

especially bad relations. If Ausonius exercised a strong influence over his former pupil, that was because he himself held office at court from 375–79, and was expected to offer advice. There is no evidence that Ambrose was a frequent (or welcome) visitor at the courts of either Gratian or Valentinian II.

On the basis of his speech about the altar of Victory, Symmachus has come to be regarded as an uncompromising champion of the pagan cause and a bitter opponent of Christianity. Symmachus himself would have been surprised by such a reputation. In the first place, it was surely for his oratorical ability and extensive experience as an envoy rather than for his religious commitment or expertise that he was chosen as senatorial spokesman. He begins by telling his imperial addressee that he is playing a double role: "as your prefect I am transacting public business and as an envoy I am presenting the message of my fellow-citizens." Both his father and father-in-law had served with distinction as senatorial ambassadors at court,[16] and Symmachus himself first did so at the court of Valentinian I at Trier in 369–70 when not yet thirty, as he was to again and again in later life.[17]

It is important to bear in mind that more than eloquence was required. An envoy who felt he had misjudged the tone of his formal speech might repair the damage at the emperor's table or in private lobbying at court. Until a brilliant paper by John Matthews, modern readers were content to mock the elegant emptiness of Symmachus's letters. Matthews showed that it was one of the prime functions of this "idiom" (as he rightly called it) "to function across the boundaries of religious difference (just as it also crossed the racial boundaries presented by the barbarian generals at court)."[18] Fellow pagans identified Symmachus as the man for the job precisely because, though a staunch pagan, he was known to be a moderate, with as many Christian connections at court as anyone in public life. It must have been obvious to even the most intransigeant pagans that tact rather than confrontation was called for if there was to be any chance of recovering the subsidies withdrawn by Gratian. The speech itself bears out this perspective. For all its eloquence (not to be equated with passion), this celebrated speech asks for no more than toleration of the state cults: "there must be more than one way to such a secret." It is clear that Symmachus was willing to settle for compromise and coexistence.

There is no reason to believe that he was involved in more than the first two of the (at least) six embassies that passed between senate and court on this issue. In 384 he took advantage of his position as prefect of Rome (the official intermediary between senate and emperor)[19] to renew the 382 appeal in the form of a *relatio*, one of the forty-

---

16. L. Aurelius Avianius Symmachus, *praefectus urbi Romae* (PVR) 364–65: *multis legationibus pro amplissimi ordinis desideriis apud divos principes functo* (*ILS* 1257); Memmius Vitrasius Orfitus PVR 353–56, 357–59: *legatus secundo* [= twice] *difficillimis temporibus petitu senatus et populi Roman* (*CIL* vi. 1739, 1740, 1741 [= *ILS* 1243], 1742).

17. On his many senatorial embassies, Matthews 1974, 75–77; Sogno 2006.

18. Matthews 1974; Salzman 2006, 352–67.

19. Chastagnol 1960, 66–68.

nine formal "reports" he sent to court in the course of his seven months in office. That year saw Praetextatus as praetorian prefect of Italy and Symmachus as prefect of Rome. Some have hypothesized the beginning of a pagan offensive, provoked by Gratian's measures. It is true that Praetextatus obtained an edict from court ordering the restoration of objects looted from temples, which Symmachus attempted to carry out, provoking accusations that he had arrested and tortured Christians (accusations that were conceded to be false by no less an authority than Pope Damasus).[20]

But they could not have taken these initiatives without their respective prefectures, to which they had been appointed by the emperor. Why did Valentinian II appoint two such prominent pagans to positions that allowed them to do this? More specifically, why did he authorize Praetextatus to restore looted objects to pagan temples?[21] The obvious explanation is that, well aware how upset a small number of powerful pagan nobles had been by Gratian's measures, he did his best to conciliate them in other ways, most strikingly in the exceptional honor accorded Praetextatus of designation to the ordinary consulship for 385. If he could not allow them public funds for the cults, he could at least allow them to protect the fabric of their temples. We have already seen that Constantius pursued a similar policy when he removed the altar in 357, and we shall soon see that in 389 Theodosius too felt obliged to conciliate the pagan nobility after turning down yet another embassy about the altar and subsidies.

The policy of clerics like Ambrose on such issues was very simple: no compromise. But for an emperor, bombarded with contradictory petitions and protests from all sides, compromise was the name of the game. It is a serious oversimplification to imagine that any fourth-century Christian emperor pursued a single, consistent policy toward pagans or paganism. Valentinian II must have known that many Christians would be distressed to see Praetextatus and Symmachus holding high office and restoring statues to temples. But the more political among them would recognize the trade-off for what it was. The restoration of a few statues was little enough compared with the loss of public subsidies for the cults. Nor were most aristocrats prepared to give up more than a few months of their precious *otium* to public office. Symmachus's prefecture, predictably enough, lasted barely seven months. When Praetextatus died later in 384 Symmachus was disheartened, and early in 385 resigned his prefecture, in effect abandoning his role as pagan activist. A decade later he was careful to keep his distance from the regime of the usurper Eugenius.

The third *relatio* has always been taken to represent Symmachus's own most deeply held convictions. But he was not speaking straightforwardly on his own behalf. While the formulation and the eloquence are his, it is likely that some details (especially the more philosophical arguments) were contributed by those who chose him as their representative. Nothing in his correspondence suggests that this was an issue he felt

---

20. Symm. *Rel.* 21, with Chastagnol 1960. 161–62; and Vera 1981, 153–60.
21. Since Valentinian himself was only thirteen in 384, the suggestion presumably came from advisers, unfortunately unidentifiable but unlikely to be pagans.

passionately about. As already remarked, his letters never mention embassies, sub-sidies, or even the altar of Victory. Precisely because they tell us so little about the supposed pagan reaction, it was once assumed that the published version of Symmachus's letters was carefully edited.[22] Certainly anything politically compro-mising would have been removed,[23] but his actions in 382 were common knowledge and his speech of 384 widely read and admired. Surviving letters to his older pagan friends and kinsmen refer so openly to pagan festivals and even to the meetings of the priestly colleges[24] that it is difficult to think of any reason why such lobbying should have been edited out.

Second, while the celebrated *relatio* is obviously the source of Symmachus's repu-tation as a pagan champion, it is less the speech than the detailed refutations by Ambrose and Prudentius that have given him this reputation. The speech itself is a remarkably moderate document, notable for its tact and reticence. Why did pagans decide to renew their plea only two years after Gratian rejected it in 384? Obviously because Gratian had been overthrown in a coup and killed. Many (and not only pagans) must have felt that this was a consequence of the new policy. Symmachus is careful to avoid even hinting at that possibility, but he does begin and end with Gratian, not indeed mentioning his death, but claiming instead that unscrupulous courtiers had failed to inform the young emperor about the embassy in 382, which was denied audience (p. 202). He then "reminds" Valentinian II that his father, Valentinian I, had not removed the altar. If Valentinian II had been disposed (as he might well have been) to grant the senatorial request, he could have accepted that Gratian was deceived by overzealous courtiers and reinstated his father's policy.

1: THE ALTAR OF VICTORY AND THE LOSS OF PUBLIC SUBSIDIES

If we may set aside the supposed influence of Ambrose, why did Gratian change his policy toward Roman paganism? Should we in fact be seeing a deliberate and rad-ical new policy here at all? It is the apparent combination of the removal of altar, with-drawal of subsidies, and repudiation of the title of *pontifex maximus* that has given rise to this assumption. According to Chastagnol, it was during a visit to Rome in 376 that Pope Damasus warned Gratian about the dangers of Roman paganism, and that Maecius Gracchus, prefect of Rome in 376–77, was already reflecting this new policy when he ostentatiously destroyed a Roman Mithraeum before accepting baptism.[25]

22. Against this assumption, McGeachy 1949, 222–29.

23. For example, all dealings with the usurper Maximus. Symmachus had been more careful with Eugenius, but even so he would have destroyed anything vulnerable to hostile interpretation.

24. E.g., *Epp.* i. 46, 47, 49, 51; ii. 34, 36, 53, 59; v. 85.

25. Chastagnol 1997, 40–41.

To take the last point first, there is no evidence that Gratian ever even visited Rome,[26] much less met Pope Damasus, and certainly no basis for assuming that Gracchus was following any sort of official policy. As for the altar of Victory, we have seen that its removal was an issue that had been raised again and again since 357. In all probability the initiative did not come from either Gratian himself or his immediate advisers. The natural assumption is that, when he moved his court to Milan in 380, Christian senators decided to renew their request to have the altar removed, just as pagan senators subsequently renewed their request to have it replaced when first Valentinian II and then Eugenius ascended the throne, approaching both a second time when they too moved their courts to Milan. Their spokesman may have been Anicius Auchenius Bassus, prefect of Rome in 382 and a Christian. Of course, we would like to know why Gratian eventually granted a request his father and perhaps he himself had earlier refused, but the answer may in part be no more than his general policy of courting the Roman senate, now increasingly Christian, and in part the increasing influence of powerful Roman Christians, now with easier access to a court in Milan.

Unsurprisingly, the altar of Victory affair has been endlessly discussed down the years. We have not only the plea for the restoration of altar and subsidies by Symmachus in his official capacity as prefect of Rome but also a point-by-point rebuttal by so well placed a contemporary as Ambrose, bishop of Milan. That is to say, we have a direct confrontation between the leading pagan and the leading Christian of the age. For many moderns, this is *the* conflict between paganism and Christianity. Yet no other ancient source so much as mentions it—not even Augustine, present in Rome at the time. Outside pagan senatorial circles the affair may not have been such a big deal as we tend to assume.

It is often described as a "debate," a debate that, if the two texts are considered in this light, Ambrose clearly wins. It is important to be clear at the outset that this is a misleading perspective. Ambrose makes a number of neat points at Symmachus's expense, but if Symmachus ever saw Ambrose's letters, he certainly never responded. Inevitably, therefore, Ambrose had the last word. There is no evidence that Symmachus himself even published his *relatio*, which has come down to us in two forms: in a much later, posthumous edition of his *relationes*; and disadvantageously sandwiched between Ambrose's two responses in Bk 10 of Ambrose's published correspondence.

Ambrose certainly scores some points. (1) Where Symmachus straightforwardly appeals to the importance of tradition, Ambrose points out that the Roman state had in fact continually modified its religious practices, adding new gods from conquered peoples. Seen in this perspective the eventual adoption of Christianity can be represented as in line with the best Roman traditions. But if this had been a real debate, Symmachus would undoubtedly have responded that, while Roman pagans had no objection to Christianity being *added* to the Roman cults, it was another matter entirely for a new cult to *replace* all the old cults. That was *not* the Roman way. (2) Why should

---

26. Barnes 1999, 168.

the state pay for the maintenance of pagan cults when it did not even maintain the Christian church? Once again, the argument is disingenuous. While not formally maintaining the church, Christian emperors had poured favors and money in its direction. (3) Ambrose claims that it was not the pagan gods but Rome's armies that had won all those wars down the centuries. Another good point, until we remember that elsewhere Ambrose himself insists that the Christian emperors of his own day won their battles, not by force of arms, but simply by their piety, in effect a Christian restatement of Symmachus's argument (Ch. 3). (4) Then there is the low number of Vestals. According to Ambrose, it was only with difficulty that they could recruit seven,[27] nor did they have to remain virgins for life. And even so they had to be paid! This is a particularly cheap jibe. Obviously this was not the total number of chaste pagan women.[28]

But before considering the arguments of the protagonists any further, it is essential to establish what exactly Gratian did in addition to having the altar removed. Since Symmachus claims that, despite removing the altar, Constantius "did not refuse funds (*inpensas*) for the Roman rituals,"[29] it has generally (and surely rightly) been inferred that Gratian *did*, in some way or other, "refuse" funds. After all, the very same sentence claims that Constantius "stripped away nothing from the privileges of the Vestal Virgins," and it is clear from Symmachus that Gratian did indeed strip away the privileges of the Vestals. The state cults were not financed directly from public funds, but (as in most parts of the Graeco-Roman world) from the income of estates willed to the temples over the course of the centuries.[30] The standard assumption, based on several passages of Ambrose, is that Gratian confiscated these temple estates, which had the status of public property.

But Lizzi has recently pointed out that Symmachus himself does not mention temple estates, concentrating instead on the privileges of the Vestals, especially their right to receive legacies.[31] Ambrose's letters, she argues, "were rhetorical pieces where the bishop selected what it seemed more convenient to say or not," while Symmachus's *relatio* "was an official document...with the sole purpose of obtaining the re-establishment of those pagan privileges Gratian's measures had suppressed." On this basis she privileges the evidence of Symmachus and suggests that only the Vestals were affected. Indeed, she goes on to argue that Gratian's measures, "far from proving that official paganism was dying, appear on the contrary as testimony to an attempt to check the economic effects which excessive devotion to the cult of Vesta was still producing in terms of legacies and donations of large landed estates." On this view, official Roman paganism was still thriving in 382. Not only did Gratian not remove its

---

27. In earlier times there were six (Wissowa 1912, 504 n. 5), but *Expositio Totius Mundi* 55, probably written soon after Constantius's Roman visit of 357 and well informed about Rome, also offers seven (see J. Rougé's edition [Paris 1966], 16). Ambrose is careful to use the ritual term *capere* of "taking" Vestals, and it would have weakened his point if he had got the number wrong.

28. Ambrose had already contrasted Christian and Vestal virgins in his earlier *De virginibus*; see Lizzi 1998.

29. *Romanis caerimoniis non negavit inpensas, Rel.* 3. 7.

30. Bodei Giglioni 1977, 33–76; Liebenam 1900, 68–73, 340–46.

31. Sym. *rel.* 3. 11, 13, 14, 15; Lizzi 2007, 251–62.

financial basis; he did no more than take steps to prevent the Vestals' resources actually increasing in the future.

But there are problems with this interpretation. The series of senatorial embassies to court (at least six between 382 and 394) strongly suggests that pagans found Gratian's measures very damaging indeed to the finances of the cults. And the distinction Lizzi draws between Ambrose's "rhetorical pieces" and Symmachus's "official document" is misleading. Symmachus was no less a rhetorician than Ambrose. He, too, carefully selected which topics to dwell on and which to skate over. It is unwise to base any argument on what Symmachus does *not* say. Concerned contemporaries on both sides knew exactly what the measures were, and who and what was affected. Neither Ambrose nor Symmachus had to address every detail.

Much has been written on the importance of the cult of Victory to the last pagans, but it was surely for rhetorical and psychological reasons that Symmachus devoted his best efforts to Victory, in the hope that Christians at court would be impressed by the link he drew between recent military defeats and the removal of her altar. In the aftermath of the catastrophic defeat of Adrianople, this was the argument most likely to hit home with Christians as well as pagans. As for the actual altar, Symmachus loyally represents it as the place where senators swore allegiance to the emperor, glossing over its far more obvious and significant role as a locus of pagan cult offerings, vividly evoked by Ambrose (two separate descriptions of Christian senators with eyes streaming from the smoke and choking on cinders).[32]

The withdrawal of the Vestals' privileges was less a frontal attack on paganism than an attempt to transfer their no-doubt extensive financial resources to the state. Symmachus contrives to make it seem petty and vindictive by claiming that their emoluments were now being used to pay dock workers,[33] protesting that even freedmen were allowed to receive legacies (*Rel.* 3. 14–15). Unlike all the other *publici sacerdotes*, Vestals were entirely supported by state funds. From the rhetorical point of view, it was surely because they were potential objects of sympathy that he devoted so much space to spinster ladies abruptly turfed out of their modest apartments.[34]

Nine out of the twenty sections of Symmachus's plea are concerned with financial issues, a point gleefully exploited by Ambrose, who refers at least a dozen times to what he represents as the pagan obsession with money. Sometimes in general terms ("we glory in [the] blood [of martyrs], they worry about cash"),[35] but no fewer than

32. Ambrose, *Ep.* 72. 9 (= Maur. 170 and 73. 31 [= Maur. 18].

33. Still a popular tactic in political rhetoric (taxes spent on nuclear weapons rather than school lunches...).

34. "If the privileges of his own college had also been removed, [Symmachus] would not have hesitated to say so clearly" (Lizzi 260). But the *pontifices*, secure in their estates, were not dependent on public support.

35. *nos sanguine gloriamur, illos dispendium movet* (*Ep.* 73. 11); *de dispendiis queruntur* (*Ep.* 72. 4); *virginitas quae pretio emitur* (73. 12).

eight times he represents the pagans as asking for "the cost of sacrifice,"[36] once even claiming that "their rituals cannot survive without money."[37] We cannot dismiss so consistent a refrain as "rhetoric." That the financial losses even Symmachus acknowledges included the confiscation of estates receives confirmation from a rescript of Honorius sent to Carthage in August 415, commanding that[38]

> in accordance with the constitution of the sainted Gratian... all land assigned by the false doctrine of the ancients to their sacred rituals shall be joined to the property of our privy purse. Thus, from the time when public expenditure on the worst superstition was forbidden, the revenues shall be exacted from the unlawful possessors thereof.... We decree that this regulation shall be observed not only throughout Africa, but throughout all regions situated in our world.

Lizzi insists that this law has nothing to do with the decree of Gratian as she reconstructs it from Symmachus. But it fits perfectly Ambrose's remark that "no one has deprived the temples of votive offerings (*donaria*) or the *haruspices* of legacies; *only estates were confiscated,* and this because they [the pagans] did not use in a manner worthy of religion what they defended by right of religion."[39] The first clause responds to Symmachus's complaint about the ban on legacies to Vestals, listing two options apparently not affected by Gratian's measures: votive offerings to temples and legacies to *haruspices.* Such precise claims would be counterproductive if not true. Here at least we must privilege the evidence of Ambrose. Clearly, estates that Christians saw as underwriting pagan cults were confiscated by Gratian. A law addressed to the proconsul of Africa in 408 reiterates an earlier ban that "withdrew revenues from the temples," this time assigning them to the army.[40] What can this be but the decree of Gratian to which Symmachus and Ambrose refer?

Were temple estates still available as late as 382? Ambrose claims that it was "now many years since the rights of the temples (*iura templorum*) were abolished all over the world,"[41] which might seem to imply that the rights of Roman temples had also long since been abolished. Yet the point of that "all over the world" might be that,

---

36. *ad usus quoque sacrificiorum profanorum praebere sumptum* (*Ep.* 72. 3); *sumptum sacrificiis profanis dari* (ib. 9); *de superstitionis impensis* (ib. 10); *sumptus sacrificiorum* (*Ep. extra coll.* 10. 2); *ad usus quoque sacrificiorum profanorum praebere sumptum* (*Ep.* 72. 3); *sumptum sacrificiis profanis dari* (ib. 9); *de superstitionis impensis* (ib. 10); *sumptus sacrificiorum* (*Ep. extra coll.* 10. 2 = Maur. 57).

37. *illi caerimonias suas sine quaestu manere posse non credunt* (*Ep.* 73. 11).

38. *omnia enim loca quae sacris error veterum deputavit, secundum divi Gratiani constituta nostrae rei iubemus sociari, it ut ex eo tempore quo inhibitus est publicus sumptus superstitioni deterrimae exhiberi, fructus ab incubatoribus exigantur* (*Cod. Theod.* xvi. 10. 20. 1).

39. *Nemo tamen donaria delubris... denegavit; sola sublata sunt praedia, quia non religiose utebantur his quae religionis iure defenderent,* Ambr. *Ep.* 73. 16.

40. *templorum detrahantur annonae, Cod. Theod.* xvi. 10. 19; the fuller version in *Sirm.* 12 (line 22) reveals that this is a reiteration of an earlier ban, addressed to the PPO of Italy but forwarded by him to the proconsul of Africa.

41. *certe ante plurimos annos templorum iura toto orbe sublata sunt,* Ambrose, *Ep.* 73. 19.

since these rights had been abolished everywhere else, it was now high time that Roman temple estates were abolished *as well*. That this is the preferable interpretation would seem to be borne out by a passage in his later speech (392) on the death of Valentinian II:

> Rome had sent envoys in order to recover the rights of the temples (*propter recuperanda templorum iura*), the unholy prerogatives (*privilegia*) of their priesthoods,[42] the performance of their sacred rites.... And when [Valentinian II] was confronted with the precedent of his father [Valentinian I], that during his reign no one had taken them (*ea*, = *templorum iura* etc) away, he replied: "you praise my father because he did not take them away. I have not taken them away either. Did then my father restore them, that you can demand that I must restore (*reddere*) them? Finally, even if my father had restored them, my brother [Gratian] took them away, and in this I would rather imitate my brother."

The same phrase, *iura templorum*, equated with the "unholy prerogatives of their priesthoods" and the "performance of their sacred rites." Later in the speech Ambrose describes how the day before his death Valentinian had again "refused the privileges of the temples" (*templorum privilegia denegavit*), repeating this formula on the following page.[43] The senatorial embassy had evidently pointed out to Valentinian that his father had *not* taken away the "rights of the temples," suggesting that he should follow his father's rather than his brother's example.[44] "Rights" and "privileges" of the temples are vague phrases, but surely imply temple estates rather than the privileges of the Vestals. If so, then these rights were evidently not withdrawn until after Valentinian I—and so by Gratian. There may also be another text. Zeno, bishop of Verona, attacks landowners who allegedly protect "smoking shrines" on their estates and are "struggling every day to hang on to their temple rights."[45] Landowners struggling to hang on to their "temple rights" look very much like Symmachus and his pagan peers in the 380s.[46]

Presumably till then the social standing and influence of the aristocratic priests of the state cults (Ch. 4) had secured exemption for the Roman temple estates. We may recall the case of the 364 law forbidding nocturnal sacrifices.[47] Praetextatus, then proconsul of Achaea, obtained an exemption for the Eleusinian Mysteries, presumably

---

42. *sacerdotiorum profana privilegia, De ob. Val.* 19; Liebeschuetz 2005, 373, translates *profana* "secular," but compare *sacrificiorum profanorum* and *sacrificiis profanis* (*Ep.* 72. 3 and 9).

43. *De ob. Val.* 52 and 55.

44. "What his father had omitted he completed, what his brother had decided he safeguarded," Ambrose, ib. 55.

45. *ius templorum ne quis eripiat cotidie litigatis, Tract.* i. 25. 89.

46. Zeno's exact dates are unknown; his death is usually placed ca. 379, but links with Ambrose's *De officiis* (Lizzi 1990, 162) from the mid-380s would support a date after 384 (cf. Lizzi 1989, 4 n. 8).

47. Nocturnal sacrifices had always been forbidden because of their presumed association with black magic. When accused of performing *nocturna sacra* two hundred years earlier, Apuleius did not dare to belittle the charge, and concentrated his defence on discrediting the evidence (bird feathers and soot) and the accuser (*Apol.* 57–60).

protesting that the emperors cannot have meant to include such age-old and (above all) respectable rites in their ban.[48] In a letter to his brother Celsinus Titianus, precisely datable shortly before his death in 380 while *vicarius* of Africa, Symmachus reports that a pontifical treasurer (*pontificalis arcarius*) called Rufus is visiting Africa to maintain the college's rights to its estates in Vaga, an ancient city 105 km west of Carthage (an episcopal seat for at least 150 years).[49] He urges Titianus to do all that is in his official power and personal zeal to help Rufus.[50] As late as 380 the Vaga estates were threatened but not yet lost to the college of pontiffs.[51] One of the laws cited above reveals that some African "temple revenues" had still not been reassigned as late as 408.

These revenues no doubt paid for a multitude of routine expenses connected with the state cults over and above the cost of sacrificial animals. But nothing upset Christians so much as the idea of animal sacrifice. Whether or not public celebrations of the state cults were still accompanied by sacrifice as late as the 380s (below), since few Christians were likely to watch them and know for sure, it was safe for Christian polemic to focus on this aspect. The hostile language of both Ambrose and the laws is enough to suggest why Symmachus avoided explicit mention of estates that he knew would be characterized as "paying for sacrifice." He alludes just once to the expense of what he refers to by the vague term *caerimoniae*. Better to focus on Victory and Vestals. His concentration on the Vestals can in fact be reconciled with the traditional interpretation. The writings of the land surveyors frequently mention estates owned by the Vestals,[52] and it may be that it was mainly the income from these estates that kept the state cults going.[53] The ban on legacies was presumably intended to bar rich pagans from circumventing the confiscations by leaving the Vestals new estates. But whether or not it was temple estates separate from the Vestals' estates that Gratian confiscated, curiously little attention has been paid in the past to the sheer number of attempts made to get them restored. It was enough to assume that the men involved were pagan fanatics. But even so that would not explain why the *financing* of the cults was apparently felt to be so crucial.

Why was the money so important? Some scholars have argued that it was simply the expense of the cults that most concerned Symmachus and his peers. Paschoud saw Symmachus himself as a miserly parvenu, unwilling to part with his own money.[54] According to McGeachy, "Control of the priesthoods meant control of landed estates" and "Roman paganism, deprived of government support, would no longer be a source

---

48. Zosimus iv. 3. 2–4. All senior officials had to come from one or the other of two families, the Eumolpidae and Kerukes: Kevin Clinton, *The Sacred Officials of the Eleusinian Mysteries* (1974).

49. *Ep.* 68, with Callu's note. On Vaga, Lepelley, *Les cités* ii. 228–30 (not citing this text).

50. *ut sequestratum paulisper officium regressus adripiat.*

51. These estates must have supported Roman rather than local temples, if a pontifical *arcarius* was involved.

52. Campbell 2000, 71, 83, 85, 131, 185; for commentary, 361–62; Wildfang 2006, 70–73.

53. It should be added that the Vestals played a role in at least ten annual public festivals: Wildfang 2001, 223–56.

54. Paschoud 1967, 79–83; Cameron 1999, 477–505, showing that the family goes back at least to the third century.

of income and prestige to the aristocracy."[55] But there were a great many priests, and it is unlikely that there was enough of a surplus to contribute substantially to the wealth of any individual priest. We happen to know the emoluments of Arval brethren: from the reign of Trajan right down to the 220s they received the princely *sportula* of 100 denarii each time they participated in the annual banquet.[56]

The altar of Victory has always been the center of attention for modern scholars, but pagans would hardly have been satisfied if Gratian or Valentinian II had given way on the sole issue of the altar but stood firm on cult subsidies. When giving a brief history of the issue in a letter to Eugenius, Ambrose summarizes the goal of Symmachus's *relatio* as "restoring (*reddi*) what was withdrawn from the temples," identified a couple of sentences later with "the expense of sacrifice," without even mentioning the altar.[57] A page or so later he characterizes the petitions to Eugenius himself in the same words: "the envoys asked you to restore [subsidies] to the temples" (*petierunt legati ut templis redderes*). This formula in effect excludes the altar, which pagans wanted restored to the senate house, not a temple. In his funerary speech on Valentinian II a year earlier Ambrose described the senatorial envoys as coming "to recover the rights of the temples and the unholy privileges of their priesthoods," again without even mentioning the altar of Victory. Clearly the subsidies were the real issue.

According to three separate passages of Zosimus, the key fact about the traditional pagan rituals of Rome was that they had to be performed publicly and at public expense. If true, this would explain all those embassies. First a passage (iv. 59. 3) that represents Theodosius coming to Rome after the Frigidus and telling Roman senators that

> the treasury was burdened by the expense of rites and sacrifices and that he wished to abolish them, not only because he did not approve of them, but also because the army needed more funds. Although the senators said that rites not performed *at public expense* were not performed properly, for this reason the rite of sacrifice ceased, and other rituals handed down from their forefathers were abandoned.

The second (v. 38) describes how Stilicho's wife, Serena, removed a necklace from a statue of Cybele and disrespected a Vestal,

> when Theodosius the elder came to Rome after the suppression of the tyrant Eugenius and instilled in everyone a contempt of the holy rites by refusing to finance religion with *public money*. The priests and priestesses were driven out and the temples deprived of all worship.

---

55. McGeachy 1942, 151 and 142; against, Baynes 1955, 361–66.
56. Nos. 64. I. 51 and II. 39; 68. II. 21; 69. 55; 94. III. 14; 99a. 16; 100b. 19; 102. 3 in Scheid 1998; Syme 1980, 112; and Scheid 1990b, 514–16, 529–30.
57. *templis quae sublata fuerant reddi.... sumptus sacrificiorum (Ep. extra coll.*10. 2).

There are problems with both texts, first because Theodosius did not go to Rome after the Frigidus;[58] and second because, while the detail about the end of sacrifice fits Theodosius's ban on sacrifice, the speech about the expense of sacrifice fits Gratian much better. The senators' response implies that this was the first time the question of the cost of the cults had come up, and here the contemporary evidence of Symmachus and Ambrose points unmistakably to Gratian's measures in 382. It looks as if Zosimus, who apparently knew nothing about Gratian's anti-pagan measures, mistakenly ascribed them to Theodosius (Ch. 17. 6). He would not be the first to make this error. Quodvultdeus of Carthage, writing between 445 and 451, claims that Symmachus's speech about the altar of Victory was addressed to Theodosius,[59] and we find a similar error in the manuscript tradition of the third *Relatio* itself, which give the addressee as Theodosius instead of Valentinian.[60] Zosimus's coverage of fourth-century western affairs is thin, but this is not (I suspect) the only reason he fails to mention the altar of Victory, since this is a silence he shares with all the ecclesiastical historians (even Rufinus, writing in Aquileia in 402) and all the chroniclers. In fact, it is worth pointing out that, if Ambrose had not taken it upon himself to intervene, we would only have known about Gratian's measures and the senatorial protests from Symmachus's speech. While causing great distress to the pagan senators of Rome, Gratian's measures seem to have made little impression anywhere else. It was Theodosius who went down in history as the emperor who proscribed paganism, and it is perhaps not surprising that Gratian's contribution was transferred to his more celebrated successor.

The third text is the story of the Etruscan *haruspices* in 408, who claimed to know a ritual that would drive Alaric away from Rome, but only "if it was performed at public expense, with the senate going up to the Capitol and performing the appropriate ceremonies both there and in the fora of the city" (Ch. 5. 3). The fact that all three Zosiman texts emphasize the need for public funding and public performance supports the conclusion that all derive from the same pagan source consulted by his source Olympiodorus during his Roman visit.[61] Despite the confusion about emperor and context, the detail about the need for public funding of the cults is intrinsically plausible. It fits the clear distinction drawn by the Antonine antiquary Pompeius Festus between "public rituals, which are performed on behalf of the people *at public expense*" and "private rituals, which are performed for individual men, families and households."[62]

---

58. Cameron 1968 at 248–65 argued in favor of this visit in 394, but I now believe that Ensslin 1953 was right to reject it; see too Döpp 1975, 73–83.

59. Quodvultdeus, *Livre des promesses* iii. 38. 41, R. Braun II (ed.) (Paris 1964), 568.

60. Ambrose (of course) knew that it was addressed to Valentinian (*rettulerat vir amplissimus Symmachus, cum esset praefectus urbis, ad Valentinianum, Ep.* 57. 2).

61. The story of Serena's impiety during Theodosius's visit in 394 is a back reference in Zosimus's account of her execution in 409; so both references to the visit probably derive from Olympiodorus, whose narrative began in 407.

62. Festus, *De verborum significatu*, 284. 18 Lindsay; Ulpian, *Dig.* 1.1.1.2.

That the state cults of Rome were indeed financed from public funds is a solidly documented fact.[63]

No other text says that they *had* to be paid for by the state or that they *had* to be performed publicly. But then neither issue had come up before. Until Gratian, everything to do with the state cults had been paid for out of public funds, and until Theodosius all rituals of the state cults had been performed publicly. It was not till Gratian and Theodosius that Roman pagans were faced, first with the withdrawal of public funds, and then with being forbidden to perform their rituals publicly. It was entirely natural that they should have protested that public funding and public performance were indispensable features of the traditional cults.

If it is the indispensability of public funding that lies behind Symmachus's *Relatio* and the series of pagan embassies to court, then it is unlikely that Gratian's confiscation of the relevant funds (whether temple or Vestal estates) was perceived by anyone except Roman pagans as a new policy, a concerted assault on Roman paganism. Emperors from Constantine on had been confiscating civic revenues all over the empire, temple estates among them, as part of a general policy of exercising tighter control over civic finances. Julian briefly restored estates confiscated by Constantius, but most of them were again confiscated by Valentinian and Valens.[64] If the Roman temple estates managed to escape confiscation, it was only a matter of time before a government in urgent need of money to pay troops finished the job. In 382, in the aftermath of Adrianople, raising troops was a priority, whereas in 394–95 Theodosius had more troops than he knew how to handle (p. 119). There was no reason why Gratian or his advisers should have anticipated the indignant senatorial reaction. Members of the priestly colleges were wealthy men who could easily have paid for the expenses of the festivals and the stipends of the Vestals and temple personnel out of their own pockets.

Why then were they reluctant to foot the bill themselves? As we shall see in more detail in chapter 4, there is an obvious sense in which the leaders of Roman paganism were the pontiffs and other *publici sacerdotes*. But however seriously they took their duties, these were not men who had devoted their lives to a religion they had in their maturity been elected to represent and defend. Take Symmachus himself, a loyal pagan who had done his duty in 382 and 384, yet a moderate, respected by Christians and pagans alike. If he had made good the loss of public money for financing the state cults, he would have been accused, to use Ambrose's phrase, of "paying for sacrifice." Not many pagans can have been willing to embrace so total an identification with the state cults.

---

63. Liebenam 1900; Marquardt 1884, 78–87; see too Rives 1995, 28–39; § 77 of the lex Irnitana gives regulations for expenditure on *sacra* (J. González [ed.] with M. H. Crawford, *JRS* 76 [1986], 173, 224). The financing of cult is also prominently detailed in the Caesarian Lex Coloniae Genetivae (M. H. Crawford, *Roman Statutes* [1996], no. 25).

64. Delmaire 1989, 641–45; Liebeschuetz 2001, Ch. 5, esp. 175–77; Goddard, in Ghilardi, Goddard, and Porena 2006, 282–88.

Private contributions had always been encouraged. In earlier times the rich and ambitious had paid for the building and repair of temples as well as baths, porticos, bridges, and aqueducts, in part at least because such expenditure reinforced their standing as public benefactors. We know of four cases of restoration of pagan temples in late fourth-century Rome. In 357/9, Symmachus's father-in-law, Orfitus, restored a temple of Apollo; in 367/8, Praetextatus restored the portico of the Dei Consentes in the Forum and demolished private buildings that had been erected too close to temples; in 374, Claudius Hermogenianus Caesarius repaired the portico of the temple of Bonus Eventus damaged by a flood; and between November 375 and August 378, Sempronius Faustus, prefect of the corn supply, restored the temple and portico of Isis at Portus, the latest datable official restoration of a pagan temple in the name of the emperors.[65] The first three are all known from other sources to have been pagans.

Praetextatus's dedication of the portico of the Dei Consentes characterizes the statues as *sacrosancta simulacra*, but it is going too far to interpret the (heavily restored) formula *cultu in f[ormam antiquam restituto]* as implying a restoration of *cult* rather than just ornamentation.[66] Philippus, PVR ca. 400, restored a nymphaeum *ad pristinum cultum*; Roman nymphaea were not cult sites.[67] It is also important to add that, since all these men were acting in their official capacity as prefects of the city, they were not spending their own money. The same applies to the case from Ostia; a *praefectus annonae* was likewise entitled to draw on public funds. The main role of Isis in the harbor of Rome was as patron of the corn supply, and so her temple was appropriately restored by the *praefectus annonae* at public expense (p. 695).

By the fourth century, many of Rome's centuries-old public buildings and monuments were inevitably in urgent need of restoration. In 366 Symmachus père restored the Aurelian bridge; in 377 Probianus restored the Basilica Julia; in 414 Albinus restored baths on the Aventine; ca. 443 Quadratianus restored the baths of Constantine.[68] In every case these were projects undertaken or supervised by prefects of Rome in office. At any given moment there must have been a long list of buildings in need of restoration, from which new prefects would presumably choose. It was probably only the more committed pagans who opted for temples. There must have been many who took care to choose less controversial projects such as bridges, baths, or aqueducts. One example is Volusianus Lampadius, a *pontifex Solis* and tauroboliate. During his two year tenure of office (365–66) he sponsored more restorations than any other prefect we know of: he erected or moved a number of statues;[69] restored a *castellum* for the Aqua Claudia;[70] and claimed to have restored no fewer than thirteen bridges between Rome

---

65. Ward-Perkins 1984, 88; Chastagnol 1969, 135–44. For a different perspective, Lizzi Testa 2001, 671–707.
66. *ILS* 4003; Bloch 1945, 203–9; Kahlos 1995, 41.
67. Known from three dedications: *CIL* vi. 1728 and 31912, with *CIL* vi. 8. 3 (2000), 4785; see p. 518.
68. For the sources and a few other examples, Ward-Perkins 1984, 42, 187.
69. Listed by Chastagnol, 1962, 168–69.
70. *CIL* vi.3866 = 31963 = *ILS* 5791.

and Ostia.[71] More generally, Ammianus mocks him for having his name inscribed on buildings as though he had built rather than just restored them.[72] But despite his obvious personal religiosity (p. 144), not a single temple.

The choices made by Orfitus and Praetextatus drew attention to their commitment to maintain the deteriorating fabric of Rome's temples, a commitment that was still acceptable to popular opinion in the 350s and 360s. Nor was it their own money they were spending. As for both Praetextatus and Claudius, it was not actual temples they restored, but their porticos, public areas outside the temples. Faustus also restored the portico of the temple of Isis at Portus. There is no record of any temples restored by either of the Symmachi,[73] and while the elder Flavian was never prefect of Rome, the younger Flavian was, and so far as we know he restored no temples either.

The fact that no known temple restoration can be dated later than the 370s has been linked to Gratian's measures: "In 382 a decree was issued banning the use of public funds on pagan temples."[74] That is to say, it is assumed that pagans were eager to restore temples, and had to be prevented by law. There is certainly no evidence for any such ban. The reassignment of temple revenues would have removed one possible source of funding, but there was nothing to stop a pagan using his own money if he wanted. Chastagnol combined the absence of dated temple restorations after 378 with his own identification of the Philippus who played a role in the erection of the church of S. Paolo fuori le mura in 390 as city prefect, and concluded that in 382 pagan temples lost their status as public monuments, which was transferred to Christian churches.[75] He took it for granted that Gratian embarked on a radical policy of eliminating paganism in 382. But it was only two years later, in 384, that Valentinian II authorized Praetextatus and Symmachus to restore looted statues to their temples.

It is in fact clear from the pronouncements of successive western governments down to the Ostrogoths that Roman temples continued to be considered public monuments, and were protected under dire penalties from spoliation.[76] An edict of Honorius in 399 reveals that zealots had been producing laws forbidding sacrifice as justification for destroying or despoiling them.[77] While no temple is known to have been restored later than 378, it was not the intention of either emperors or kings that such prominent monuments in the city center should be left to collapse. In 510/11 Theodoric complained that temples that he had "assigned for repair have instead been given over to demolition."[78] The fact that it has survived to the present day in such excellent shape suggests that the Pantheon was carefully maintained during the two centuries when it

---

71. *AE* 1975, n. 134 (more bridges than were previously known to exist).
72. Amm. Marc. 27. 3. 7.
73. For the temple of Flora see Ch. 8. 4.
74. Meiggs 1973, 593; so too Ward-Perkins 1984, 86; Kahlos 1995, 40.
75. Chastagnol 1966, 436–37; and 1969, 142–43; on the identification of this Philippus, p. 518.
76. See now Fauvinet-Ranson 2006, 116, 213–17, 234–36, 277–79.
77. *Cod. Theod.* 16. 10. 15; cf. *Nov. Maj.* 4. 1–2; Goddard 2006, 282–86.
78. Cassiod. *Variae* iii. 31. 4 (trans. Barnish); Fauvinet-Ranson 2006, 116.

was no longer an active temple and before it was turned into the church of S. Maria ad martyres in the early seventh century. An imperial rescript of 368 or 370 was "read in the Pantheon," presumably now used as some sort of assembly hall.[79] As late as 472/73 the city prefect Anicius Acilius Aginatius Faustus restored, not indeed a temple, but a statue of Minerva damaged by the collapse of a roof in a fire during a civil disturbance.[80]

The decline of temple restorations by prominent pagans is surely due less to legal prohibitions than to their increasing reluctance to be identified with sacrifice. There is very little evidence for private patronage of the state cults in the fourth century as a whole.[81] By the last decades of the century pagan senators may have felt that contributing to the repair of a pagan temple identified them too conspicuously with a now increasingly unpopular cause.

2: PONTIFEX MAXIMUS

That leaves Gratian's repudiation of "the ancient pagan title of *pontifex maximus*," allegedly "an uncompromising break with polytheism and the old gods of Rome."[82] But it is not easy to see why this should have been such a decisive signal to the pagans of Rome. It was almost four centuries since the office had been held by a Roman aristocrat, and during that period its imperial holders had vastly expanded its scope and powers.[83] To give a single illustration, from as early as Augustus emperors were regularly consulted and gave detailed rulings on the qualifications for and privileges of the Eleusinian priesthoods at Athens.[84] While first- and second-century emperors had at least spent much of their time in Rome and so fulfilled the primary obligations of the office toward the civic cults of Rome, by the 380s it had been well over a century since any emperor had resided in Rome. Constantine paid three brief visits (312, 315, and 326), Constantius II one (357), Theodosius one (389), and Gratian himself not even one. Constantius's visit was probably the last occasion on which an emperor had attended to pontifical business in person.

The date and context of Gratian's repudiation have been much debated over the years, but the most basic question of all has not been raised since the seventeenth century. Did it happen at all?[85] The only source is a digression on the *pontifex maximus* in a chapter of Zosimus shot through with absurdities and errors from start to finish (Ch. 17. 8). Sixteenth- and seventeenth-century scholars denounced it as a pagan

---

79. *Cod. Theod.* xiv. 3. 10 (*lecta in Pantheo*).
80. *simulacrum Minerbae, CIL* vi. 526 = *ILS* 3132; Fraschetti 1999, 157–70; Orlandi 2004, 475.
81. Ward-Perkins 1984, 87.
82. Chadwick 1976, 114. For a more sceptical assessment, Errington 1997, 33 n. 63; Leppin 2003, 246 n. 84.
83. Gordon in Beard and North 1990, 201–34; Millar 1977, 447–56. After 204 there is no record of any emperor taking part "in the periodic meetings of any college" (Rüpke 2008, 60).
84. Millar 1977, 449–50.
85. This section repeats material from the fuller treatment in Cameron 2007, 341–84.

slander, refusing to believe that any Christian emperor had ever consented to accept the office in the first place. But the evidence of inscriptions now makes it certain that they did. If the first few Christian emperors accepted the title, sooner or later (it might seem) one *must* have refused it, and, given the explicit testimony of Zosimus that it was Gratian, the apparently concerted measures of Gratian against the Roman cults seemed to provide the obvious context. It has also been taken for granted that all subsequent Christian emperors followed suit.

The first problem is Zosimus's claim that Gratian refused the pontifical robe when the pontiffs brought it to him at the beginning of his reign (367). For a Roman inscription of 370 shows Valentinian, Valens, and Gratian all bearing the title.[86] Nor can we interpret the beginning of his reign as the moment when he became senior western Augustus on Valentinian's death in 375 or even sole ruling Augustus on Valens's death in 378. For in his *Gratiarum actio* of 379 Ausonius compares Gratian to Vestal, *flamen* and *pontifex* in his chastity,[87] and even compares the "election" for his own consulate to the pontifical elections, "seeing that you [Gratian] who presided over them are *pontifex maximus* and a participator in the designs of God" (§ 42). On the grounds that Theodosius "never used or refused the title," Alföldi argued that it must have been dropped by January 379, the date of Theodosius's accession.[88] But this still runs up against Ausonius, who did not deliver his speech till the second half of 379, at court in Trier. Could Ausonius, himself a Christian, have been so gauche as to use this of all imagery if the emperor who had appointed him consul had so recently rejected the title on religious grounds?

The fact that Theodosius is never attested with the title proves nothing. Two dedications come into play (*ILS* 780 and 781), but it is not just *pontifex maximus* they lack, but the whole of the second half of the standard litany of imperial titles. In illustration here is Gratian's full style as given on the 370 inscription, as it happens the latest known inscription to offer the full style:[89]

> Fl. Gratianus pius felix maximus victor ac triumphator semper Augustus, *pontifex maximus*, Germanicus maximus, Alamannicus maximus, Francicus maximus, Gothicus maximus, *tribuniciae potestatis III, imperator II, consul primum, pater patriae, proconsul.*

The full style had become exceptionally rare by this date. There are in fact only three other examples known for the half-century after Constantine, one each for Constantius II, Julian, and Valentinian.[90] The great majority of fourth-century and all

86. *ILS* 771; *CIL* ii. 450*–452*, purporting to be milestones naming Valentinian, Valens, and Gratian as *pontifex maximus* in the neighbourhood of Emerita, are all forged on the basis of *ILS* 771.
87. § 66; cf. too *Augustus sanctitate, pontifex religione* (§ 35); Rüpke 2008, 63.
88. Alföldi 1937, 37.
89. *ILS* 771, with abbreviations expanded for the sake of clarity.
90. *ILS* 732 and 753; *CIL* ii. 4733 (known only from eighteenth-century copies) from Corduba for Valentinian (*cos. II* and so 368, though Hübner suggested *cos. III* for *cos. II p.p.*, which would give 373).

later dedications commemorating emperors offer (omitting victory titles) only *pius felix maximus victor ac triumphator semper Augustus* (or some minor variation). Since it is only in the full titulature that we ever find *pontifex maximus* (together with the entire sequence from *tribuniciae potestatis* to *proconsul*, italicized above), it is not significant that the two inscriptions naming Theodosius, both of which offer the now standard abbreviated titulature, do not include it. Since we have no edicts or letters of Theodosius I offering the full titulature, there is simply no way of knowing whether he used or refused the title of *pontifex maximus*.

There is in fact no reason to believe that the full style was ever formally abolished or even significantly modified. This is more than an argument from silence, nor is it a mere technicality. Though extremely rare, it nonetheless survived for at least another century and a half. There is one example each from the fifth and sixth centuries: an edict of Marcian and Valentinian III from 452; and a letter of Anastasius from 516. Remarkably enough, given the protracted discussion about Gratian's repudiation of the title, no one seems to have appreciated the significance of the fact that both documents include the title *pontifex*.

Here is the style accorded Valentinian III and Marcian in an imperial letter dated 7 February 452 (correcting a few obviously corrupt minor details):[91]

> Imperatores Caesares Flavius Valentinianus, *pontifex inclitus*, Germanicus *inclitus*, Alamannicus *inclitus*, <Francicus *inclitus*,> Sarmaticus *inclitus*, tribuniciae potestatis vicies septies, imperator vicies septies, <consul septies> et Flavius Marcianus, *pontifex inclitus*, Germanicus *inclitus*, Sarmaticus *inclitus*, Alamannicus *inclitus*, Francicus *inclitus*, tribuniciae potestatis ter, imperator iterum, consul.

And here is the style of Anastasius in a letter addressed to the senate of Rome in 516:[92]

> Imperator Caesar Flavius Anastasius, *pontifex inclitus*, Germanicus *inclitus*, Francicus *inclitus*, Sarmaticus *inclitus*, tribunici<ae potestatis XXV>, imper<ator> XXV, consul tertio, pius, felix, victor ac triumphator semper Augustus, pater patriae, proconsul.

These are official documents.[93] If we compare the titulature of these two letters with the 370 dedication of Valentinian I, Valens and Gratian, the only difference (apart

91. *ACO* 2. 3. 346. 38–347. 3; for details, Barnes, *Roman Emperors*, forthcoming, Ch. 2. To the best of my knowledge, the first scholar to mention these texts in this connection was P. Batiffol in *Bulletin de la societé nationale des antiquaires de France* 1926, 222–27, but they have been ignored in recent discussions.
92. *Coll. Avell.* no. 113, with Barnes, forthcoming.
93. Paschoud 2006, 69, dismisses these imperial letters as "des éléments ténus et très postérieurs," despite the fact that the first at any rate is a half-century earlier than Zosimus, and both are official documents!

from iteration numbers and victory titles) is the substitution of *inclitus* for *maximus* throughout. So systematic a change must be both intentional and official. From the late second century on emperors often added a *maximus* to their victory titles (*Parthicus maximus* and the like). This *maximus* too was regularly replaced by *inclitus* in the fifth century. In 312 Constantine assumed a *maximus* to indicate that he was senior Augustus, and most of his successors followed suit. By the fifth and sixth centuries this *maximus* as well was usually changed to *inclitus*.[94] Surprising though it might seem, *maximus* and *inclitus* apparently came to be felt as in some way equivalent imperial titles.

The inclusion of iteration numbers for the emperor's *tribunicia potestas* and the titles *pater patriae* and *proconsul* in the titulature of Valentinian III, Marcian, and Anastasius may fairly be seen as meaningless antiquarian survivals. But the case of *pontifex* cannot be dismissed so lightly. Proof that it is to be taken seriously, now explicitly reinterpreted in a Christian sense, is provided by a number of acclamations addressed to both Marcian and Theodosius II in the *Acta* of the Council of Chalcedon: "emperor and priest, you have restored the church, pious and orthodox, pious emperor, emperor and priest" (*pontifici imperatori, ecclesias tu correxisti; pio et orthodoxo, pio imperatori, pontifici imperatori*).[95]

If Gratian repudiated the title of *pontifex maximus*, how is it that we find Valentinian III, Marcian, and Anastasius not only continuing to style themselves *pontifex* in formal documents, but in effect the fifth-century equivalent of *pontifex maximus*? Ullmann, the only scholar to attempt an explanation, suggested that the title had been recently revived at this period, in connection with contemporary disputes about papal primacy.[96] Yet if Gratian had repudiated the title on the grounds that he was a Christian, how could a later Christian emperor have revived it? We are bound to wonder whether *any* emperor *ever* formally and finally repudiated the title. All we can say with certainty is that it does not appear in the abbreviated titulature in general use. Whatever Gratian did and whenever he did it, it is an inescapable fact that Marcian and Valentinian III are formally styled *pontifex* (if *inclitus* rather than *maximus*) in an official document of 452.

What then are we to make of Zosimus's digression? However distorted and fictionalized in its present form, it must conceal some initiative taken by Gratian concerning the imperial pontificate. Every emperor up to and including Gratian was styled *pontifex maximus*, later emperors *pontifex inclitus*. In 382 Gratian in effect disestablished the state cults of Rome, provoking controversy and protest. In the course of these protests he was (I suggest) reminded that he was in fact *ex officio* head of these cults. One response would have been to repudiate the title. Instead he surely disputed so restricted an interpretation of his religious authority. Pagan senators of Rome may well have continued to look on the imperial *pontifex maximus* as head of the state cults

---

94. Kienast 1996, 40–44, 26; Dessau's index to *ILS* iii. 1. 307–13; Rösch 1978, 159–71.
95. Theodosius: *ACO* II. 1. 1, p. 138. 28 Schwartz; II. 2. 1, p. 54. 7; II. 3. 1, p. 121. 6. Marcian: *ACO* II. 2. 2, p. 102. 21; II. 1. 2, p. 353. 29; II. 3. 2, p. 438. 35; II. 3. 2, p. 439. 17. The Greek versions offer ἱερεῖ or ἀρχιερεῖ.
96. "die Wiederaufname des Pontifex-Titels," Ullmann 1977, 27.

of Rome. But this was far too narrow a definition of the priestly powers of even Augustus, let alone Constantine. For centuries now the emperors had claimed authority over all forms of religious expression within Roman territory.

Since the term *pontifex*, taken by itself, was acceptable to Christians, the obvious solution was to modify the title by removing the *maximus*, and thereby signal the dissolution of its link with the state cults of Rome. An *alternative* limiting or defining epithet was then required, one that would distinguish the imperial *pontifex* from both pagan *pontifex* and Christian priest. For whatever reason, *inclitus* was the epithet chosen. And once the *maximus* in *pontifex maximus* became *inclitus*, there was a certain logic in changing every *maximus* in the imperial titulature to *inclitus*.[97]

Always an elevated, archaic word, at home in epic and the historians, it was (it seems) precisely in the 380s that *inclitus*[98] made its rather surprising entry into the imperial titulature.[99] The earliest inscriptional examples are dated to 400/401 and 418.[100] But in his *Relationes*, official requests and reports addressed to court in his capacity as prefect of Rome in the course of 384, just two years after Gratian's measures, Symmachus regularly styles Valentinian II and Theodosius *inclyti victores ac triumphatores semper Augusti* (or something very similar), no fewer than ten times.[101]

On the traditional assumption, Christian emperors continued to bear the title *pontifex maximus* as long as they did so as not to antagonize their pagan subjects, still in a majority in the early decades of the fourth century. Though not false, this is nonetheless a misleading perspective. According to Dio, writing of Augustus but from the perspective of the third century, in virtue of their tenure of the supreme pontificate the emperors "control all sacred and religious matters."[102] The emperor gradually came to monopolize the role of symbolic religious mediator for the whole empire. While Constantine and his Christian successors did not (of course) directly invoke their pontifical authority, it was in effect in this capacity that they legislated about church affairs, endowed churches and convoked councils to deliberate church doctrine.[103] To surrender the office might have been held to weaken the emperor's claim to play this role in church affairs, a claim welcomed by most Christians in the heady days of the first Christian emperor, if increasingly questioned when some of his successors fell into heresy.

---

97. Not that *maximus* altogether disappears from imperial titles in the fifth century, as can be seen from the lists of documents and inscriptions in Rösch 1978.

98. For the various spellings, O. Prinz, "Inclutus," *Glotta* 29 (1942), 138–47; for more information, Cameron 2007.

99. *TLL* s.v. *inclitus* 2; O'Brien 1930, 135; the indexes (under emperors' names) to O. Guenther's *Collectio Avellana* (1895) and R. Schieffer's *Index Prosographicus* to *ACO* i–iv (1982); Rösch 1978, 44–45, 86–87.

100. *CIL* viii. 969; *Coll. Avellana* no. 14. 3 (p. 59. 16 Guenther); cf. too *Coll. Avellana* no. 35 (*Victor Honorius inclytus triumphator semper Augustus*). Two other African dedications with similar formulas fall between 395 and 408, and 383 and 408, respectively (Cagnat/Merlin, *Inscriptions latines d'Afrique* [Paris 1923], 276, 314.

101. For a complete list, Vera 1977, 1035–36; for further details, Cameron 2007.

102. Dio 53. 17. 8.

103. Voelkl 1964; Ullmann 1976, 1–16; with Barnes 1981, 49–51. More generally, see too the chapter "The emperor and his church" in Frend 1972, 50–103.

So Gratian did not after all repudiate the office of *pontifex maximus*. He redefined his priestly authority in less specific terms. His action was therefore less pointedly or dramatically anti-pagan than hitherto supposed. Indeed, it is far from clear that we are justified in identifying a drastic new policy toward paganism at all in 382. The questions of the altar of Victory and the confiscation of temple estates had both come up again and again before 382. It was not inevitable that pagans would take such a hard line about the need for public funding, and Gratian may well have been surprised by the inflexibility of the senatorial reaction. The altar and subsidies undoubtedly became a flashpoint in pagan-Christian relations in late fourth-century Rome, but not because of a premeditated imperial decision to eliminate paganism. It is important to bear in mind that Gratian did not ban the cults.

3: THEODOSIUS AND THE CULTS OF ROME

Little is known about the religious policies of Magnus Maximus (after his fall his acta were naturally annulled). He was a devout Christian who went down in history as the first Christian emperor to put a heretic to death.[104] It is not expressly attested that pagan senators petitioned him to restore the altar and subsidies, but the fact that Ambrose represents the dead Gratian telling Valentinian II not to do "what even the enemy who raised arms against him had not done"[105] strongly suggests that Maximus too formally rebuffed a senatorial embassy.

In August 388 Theodosius invaded Italy and defeated Maximus. While posing as the savior of Valentinian II, in practice he quietly marginalized the youth who was in fact the senior member of the imperial college. Pacatus Drepanius's panegyric of July 389 before emperor and senate in Rome contrives to say almost nothing about Valentinian, while openly proclaiming that the future rulers of the Roman world will be the two (even younger) sons of Theodosius (*Pan. Theod.* 16. 5; 45. 3). During his visit to Rome, despite turning down another petition about the altar and subsidies late in 389, Theodosius took care to conciliate its governing class, pagans no less than Christians. His first appointment to the prefecture of Rome was the historian Aurelius Victor, followed by Rufius Albinus (Ch. 14. 2). In 389 the elder Flavian was appointed *quaestor sacri palatii*, and then the following year promoted to the praetorian prefecture of Italy, Africa, and Illyricum. Symmachus was designated to the extraordinary honor (for a civilian who had not held court office—and had supported Maximus) of ordinary consul for 391.

It is often asserted that Theodosius "fell under the spell" of these pagan grandees.[106] But not for long, because in February 391 he issued his celebrated law (discussed

---

104. Sulp. Severus, *Vita Mart.* 20; *Dial.* II. 6–7; Stancliffe 1983, 113, 129, 156; Birley 1983, 13–43.
105. Ambrose, *Ep.* 72. 16.
106. E.g., Bloch 1945, 222.

below) banning pagan sacrifice. Obsessed with the idea of pagan/Christian conflict, modern scholars tend to see Symmachus, Flavian, and Albinus first and foremost as pagan leaders and infer that all or most of their public actions were intended to further the pagan cause, and that any imperial gesture of favor to them was a concession to paganism. But this was only one aspect of their role in the social and political life of late antique Rome. What Theodosius saw was surely first and foremost immensely wealthy and influential landowners, men worth conciliating *despite* their paganism. Well aware that he had been compelled to oppose them on an issue they felt deeply about, he must have been apprehensive that, when he returned to the East, they might be tempted to throw their influence behind another usurper more willing than Maximus to give way on that issue. The obvious solution was to be as conciliatory as he could on other fronts—not unlike a Democratic president of the United States appointing one or two Republicans to key posts in his administration.

He pursued a similar policy in the East. On the death of his aggressively pious praetorian prefect Cynegius (384–88),[107] Theodosius turned to the pagan Tatianus (388–92), also appointing his son Proculus to the prefecture of Constantinople. In 391 Tatianus, like Cynegius, was accorded the honor of the consulate. The most natural explanation for these appointments is that, aware that Cynegius's excesses had caused ill will among the many remaining pagans, he decided to appoint a moderate, widely respected pagan in his place.

The *magister officiorum* Rufinus waged a campaign against Tatianus and Proculus, and eventually prevailed on Theodosius to depose them both and appoint him *praefectus praetorio*. Since Tatianus and Proculus were both pagans and Rufinus a fiercely committed Christian, few have been able to resist the temptation of seeing this as the cause of the hostility between the two factions. But that is not the way our most detailed source saw it, and since that source is the pagan Zosimus, we might have expected him to make the most of a Christian vendetta. There is probably no need to see any more here than the sort of struggle for power that goes on at every court. After all, it was the pious Theodosius who had appointed Tatianus and Proculus in the first place.

It is both implausible and unnecessary to see Theodosius going through a phase of being well disposed to pagans. The solution is simply that, in East and West alike, he did his best to work with traditional elites as far as he could, even when, like Tatianus, Symmachus, and Flavian, they were pagans. When he returned to the East he needed influential western supporters. His western designs were complex, not to say devious. In the short term it seems clear that he was planning to administer Italy, Illyricum, and Africa from Constantinople himself, and confine Valentinian II to the prefecture of Gaul, under the thumb of the (as he hoped) loyal Arbogast. In the long term he was evidently hoping to supersede this lone survivor of the previous dynasty with one of

---

107. For reservations about Cynegius's reputation as a destroyer of temples, see below p. 798.

his own sons when a suitable opportunity arose.[108] That opportunity was to arise sooner than he could have anticipated with the death of Valentinian in 392 and the usurpation of Eugenius. In 389–91, accompanied by the young Honorius, he spun out his western stay as long as he dared in the hope of creating a favorable climate for his more remote intentions. It was obvious that he could not count on the support of the independent Ambrose. Indeed, he could not *count* on anyone once he was back in the East.

Under the circumstances it is understandable that some of the pagan aristocrats he was courting should have misread his attentions and interpreted personal favors as favors transferable to the Roman cults. They were emboldened to repeat their petition. A senatorial embassy (a small one, according to Ambrose) tried to see Theodosius in Milan (apparently late in 389), unsuccessfully thanks to a personal (though evidently unwelcome) intervention by Ambrose (who admits that did not dare go near the emperor for several days afterwards).[109] Yet it is unlikely that either Symmachus or Flavian were among these petitioners. In 384 there had been a real possibility of Valentinian II returning to his father's policy of neutrality rather than reaffirming what had turned out to be the confrontational new policy of Gratian. It was a reasonable gamble that Valentinian would prefer to identify with his father than with the half-brother who had kept him under something close to house arrest (p. 646) But once he had reaffirmed Gratian's policy, it became impossible for any later Christian emperor to restore either altar or subsidies. Symmachus cannot have been willing to jeopardize his hard-won recovery from his earlier lapse of judgment in supporting Maximus.[110] And Flavian is not likely to have been prepared to jeopardize his now flourishing career at court.

That there were still some pagan senators who felt strongly about the issue is proved by the fact that, once Theodosius was back in the East, yet another embassy was sent to Valentinian in Gaul, shortly before his death on 15 May 392, the fifth in total and the second to Valentinian.[111] Why did they think it worth trying Valentinian again? By confining Valentinian to Gaul, Theodosius was evidently hoping to prevent him establishing the sort of rapport with Italian landowners he himself had done his best to establish during his nearly three years in Italy. A fragment from the lost history of Sulpicius Alexander describes Valentinian as "shut up in his palace at Vienne," where for the remainder of his short life he was to be a puppet of Arbogast.[112] The senators were presumably trying to drive a wedge between Valentinian and Theodosius, "offering [him] an opportunity to outbid his partner."[113] For while Theodosius

---

108. Presumably, he was planning to install Arcadius, already Augustus since 383, in Italy and Africa. Fortunately, for his future designs he was never faced with the complication of Valentinian II marrying and producing a son.

109. *senatus legatio... licet non totus senatus*, Ambr. *Ep.* 57. 4.

110. Just how hard won is explained in detail by Sogno 2006, 71–76.

111. (1) to Gratian (382); (2) to Valentinian II (384); (3) to Maximus; (4) to Theodosius (389).

112. Greg. Tur. *HF* ii. 9; Zos. iv. 53–54; McLynn 1994, 333–36.

113. McLynn 1994, 335.

continued to administer Italy, Africa, and Illyricum from Constantinople, Valentinian, technically senior Augustus, had administered Italy and Africa from Gratian's death till Maximus's invasion, and it was not clear that his writ no longer ran there. He may have been tempted by the senatorial invitation, but, no doubt under Arbogast's guidance, once again said no.

One other, less familiar text has a bearing on Valentinian II's attitude to pagan cults. While Roman state festivals were dependent on public funds, those provided by provincial priests were not.[114] The most important text for the imperial cult in the new post-Diocletianic Italian provinces is the Hispellum inscription, banning sacrifice at a new cult of Constantine (p. 141). Scarcely less interesting is the so-called *Feriale Campanum*, an inscribed calendar found in the amphitheatre of Capua.[115] It lists seven festivals "by command of the emperors" (*iussione domnorum*), dated to 22 November 387. By this date Maximus was master of Italy, but since 22 November is the anniversary of Valentinian II's proclamation, the document may have come from his court. Surprise has often been expressed that a Christian emperor should have authorized what have been called "provocatively non-Christian" festivals.[116] But though undeniably *pre*-Christian, they are above all local celebrations ("a lustration to the *iter Dianae* on 25 July"; "a procession to the *iter Averni* on 27 July," etc). What we should be asking is why *any* emperor would be asked to authorize festivals that had surely been celebrated in Campania every year for centuries. In the light of the Hispellum inscription, the obvious explanation is that the provincial priest, one Romanus junior, was anxious to make sure that the festivals for which he was responsible conformed to the law. Accordingly (I suggest), he formally submitted to court a short list of seven festivals from which all objectionable features had been carefully removed. Did these preapproved festivals survive the Theodosian ban on sacrifice? Probably—at least for a while. While churchmen no doubt railed against them as pagan abominations, emperors were reluctant to curtail the traditional pleasures of their subjects, so long as there were no offerings at altars or sacrifices.

4: THEODOSIUS'S ANTI-PAGAN LEGISLATION

It is commonly believed that, on Valentinian II's death, Arbogast and Eugenius soon succumbed to the continuing pressure from pagan senators in Rome and restored the altar of Victory and cult subsidies, the celebrated "last pagan revival." The notion that Eugenius's brief reign saw a pagan revival presupposes both that there is good evidence for such a revival, and that it was necessary because all forms

---

114. For what little is known about provincial priests in late antique Italy, see Cecconi 1994, 83–106.
115. A. Degrassi, *Inscr. Ital.* xiii. 2 (1963), 282–83 (with plate); Cecconi 101–5; Trout in Mathisen 1997, 162–78.
116. *iure mirandum est*, Degrassi l.c.; Trout 1997, 168.

of pagan worship had been finally and decisively forbidden by Theodosius. Both assumptions are highly dubious.

To take the second point first, it is a commonplace that the reign of Theodosius marked a turning point in the decline of paganism. This may be true, but it is far from certain that the explanation, hitherto taken for granted, is legislation. Theodosius's laws are assumed to be the result of (another) dramatic new policy shift, a long-meditated decision that the time had finally come to eliminate paganism: "the policy of tolerance until now observed in the West by Theodosius thus abruptly came to an end"; "The face Theodosius now presented [February 391] to the Western ruling classes was not the urbane ruler mixing easily with senate and people [as in 389], but the persecuting fanatic."[117] Theodosius's anti-pagan legislation has been assumed to differ from all earlier anti-pagan laws in two ways: first, in going further than earlier laws; and second, in being enforced and effective. Neither point has ever been explicitly argued or documented; rather they are simply assumed as an inevitable corollary (and explanation) of the further assumption that Eugenius's rebellion represented a reaction to the new anti-pagan policy. A classic circular argument.

This new policy is supposed to be enshrined in three successive laws, issued in February 391 (from Aquileia), June 392 (from Milan), and November 392 (from Constantinople).[118] The November 392 law is beyond question a comprehensive ban on pagan worship in every form, not only animal sacrifice, but offerings of incense, wine, and even garlands hung on trees, threatening offenders with confiscation of property. Whether it was systematically enforced is another matter, but given the brief interval between the three laws it is naturally tempting to take them together as a single initiative. The first was addressed to Rome, the second to Alexandria. According to Fowden, "The two cities thus singled out were potent symbols, both of catholic Christian dogma and, embarrassingly, of surviving polytheism. *But the constitutions were also intended for universal application.*"[119] In illustration he cites an extract from the third law, addressed to the praetorian prefect of the East, as if the three laws were interchangeable and the third could be used to interpret the first two.

But how do we know if a given law was "intended for universal application"? In their full form (never preserved in the extracts included in the Theodosian Code), laws addressed to praetorian prefects sometimes close with some such instruction as the following: "cause this regulation to come to the knowledge of all by means of letters issued to the governor of each province, so that edicts duly posted shall publish this regulation to the whole world."[120] Thus an extract of a law in the Code addressed to a single provincial governor might be the only surviving copy of a law circulated by higher authority to

---

117. Bloch 1945, 223–24; Williams and Friell 1994, 70; for similar views, Fowden in *CAH* xiii (1998), 553; Ando 2001, 384–85.

118. *Cod. Theod.* xvi. 10. 10–12, with commentary by Rougé, Delmaire, and Richard 2005, 438–47.

119. Fowden, *CAH* xiii (1998), 553.

120. *Const. Sirm.* 9; cf. 16; Matthews 2000, 186.

all governors. Since the November 392 law was addressed to Rufinus, praetorian prefect of the East, we would be justified in assuming that copies were sent to all provincial governors within his jurisdiction. But the West was emphatically not within his jurisdiction.

It is *possible* that a similar law was sent to the praetorian prefect of Italy, Africa, and Illyricum—at this time the pagan Nicomachus Flavianus. But no such law survives, and there is no evidence for any such assumption in the law of February 391 addressed to the prefect of Rome. This law has been variously described as "a death sentence against paganism," "the first edict to proscribe paganism," the "legal death" of paganism, a "comprehensive ban on pagan sacrifice," and "a trumpet blast to the pagans which…they heard and understood."[121] As already remarked, it is further assumed that it was in large measure the enforcement of this law that drove the last pagans of Rome to defend their way of life on the field of battle.

But if we look at the text of the law itself (or rather the excerpt preserved in the Theodosian Code), it is simply not the wide-ranging general prohibition of pagan cult so often assumed. Stock minatory rhetoric aside, its two provisions are (1) to ban sacrifice and (2) to ban access to temples. Unlike the law of November 392, it does *not* in fact ban all acts of pagan worship. Emperors had been forbidding sacrifice for three-quarters of a century. And though it is often implied that forbidding access to temples was an innovation,[122] this too appears as early as a law of 356.[123] Indeed, it goes back before even Constantine to the age of Diocletian. In the Theodosian context it has naturally been assumed that the ban was directed at pagans. But canon 56 of the Council of Elvira (ca. 300) forbids *Christian* officials to set foot in pagan temples. For centuries, participating in sacrificial ceremonies had been a standard part of the duties of Roman magistrates. Local bigwigs who happened to be Christians were also expected to attend. Naturally, this was a problem for Christian officials, and the Elvira canons lay down very strict bans on participating in any way in sacrifice. A Constantinian law of 323 forbids Christian clergy to be "compelled" to "celebrate" sacrifices, presumably meaning attend ceremonies at which sacrifices were performed rather than actually perform ritual acts themselves. Eusebius claims that Constantine forbade pagan governors to sacrifice.[124] The law may in fact have forbidden all governors to sacrifice, but even if it was restricted to pagans, the point was presumably to prevent situations where Christian dignitaries might be pressured to participate. By the close of the century, we might suspect that the opposite situation was more common: compliant Christian dignitaries willing to attend such ceremonies, to the disgust of their more rigorist peers.

Nor does the law purport to be binding on the population at large. Its one novel feature is its concern to ban public officials from participating in sacrifice or entering

---

121. Piganiol 1975, 285; Palanque 1933, 251; N. King 1960, 78; cf. Stein 1959, 209; Chuvin 1990, 65; Lee 2000, 123.

122. "Mais il y ajoute l'interdiction de fréquenter les temples…," Gaudemet 1972, 598.

123. *Cod. Theod.* xvi. 10. 4; on the date, Seeck 1919, 41–42.

124. *Cod. Theod.* xvi. 2. 5; Euseb. *VC* 2.44.

temples. Those found guilty of so doing will be liable to fines, ranging from four to fifteen pounds of gold. These are certainly stiff penalties, but why this particular emphasis? What was the overall purpose of the law? As recent research on the Theodosian Code has made abundantly clear, time and again if we look carefully at the text of a law addressed to a local official we find indications that it is the government's response to a specific request from that official to deal with a local situation.[125] That is to say, the surviving law is often, in effect, the original request sent to court by some local official, approved, reformulated, and returned to him as instructions.

In the case of the February 391 law, it looks as if Roman Christians had complained to court about public officials setting a bad example by attending pagan rituals and entering temples. It has (of course) been suggested that it is simply a copy of a more general law sent to the praetorian prefect of Italy,[126] but its provisions seem tailored specifically to the jurisdiction of the prefect of Rome, where the power of the land-owning aristocracy that traditionally monopolized both the prefecture of Rome and the Italian governorships must have made it particularly hard to enforce bans on sacrifice. Nothing in the text of this law as it has come down to us suggests that it is anything more than a response to a specific local situation rather than a dramatic new shift in Theodosius's policy toward paganism at large.

It is not likely that the surviving extract from the February 391 law simply happened to omit the more stringent and far-reaching provisions of the November 392 law sent to the prefect of the East. For the June 392 law, while briefer and differing in its verbal formulation, offers essentially the same provisions as the February 391 law, forbidding sacrifice and entering temples, and laying down fines for officials who enter temples. Moreover, its unique address to two different local officials, "Evagrius the Augustal prefect and Romanus, count of Egypt," strongly suggests that it was not a general law, but a rescript responding to a specific request, an assumption supported by the Alexandrian context.

The situation that provoked the request is well known.[127] Theophilus, bishop of Alexandria, had antagonized pagans by converting a disused temple into a church and exposing sacred objects to public ridicule; pagans responded by rioting. Rufinus, Socrates, and Sozomen all claim that an appeal was made to court, with Sozomen naming the officials who made the appeal as Evagrius the *praefectus augustalis* and Romanus the count of Egypt, both also named in a fifth-century Alexandrian chronicle and by the pagan Eunapius.[128] Theodosius is said to have responded with a rescript pardoning the rioters but ordering the destruction of the Serapeum. These are the same officials mentioned in the address to the 16 June law, though since it goes no

---

125. Harries and Wood 1993; Matthews 2000; Errington 2006.
126. Gaudemet 1972, 600.
127. For full documentation and bibliography, Thelamon 1981, 157–279; Baldini 1985, 97–152; Hahn 2008, 335–65.
128. Soz. *HE* vii. 15. 5; Eunapius gives Euetius (*VS* 472, vi. 11. 2), but no such prefect is known and Evagrius is the standard correction.

further than forbidding officials to enter temples, this cannot be the rescript the Christian writers describe. But since it is addressed, unusually, to the two officials involved in the eventual destruction of the Serapeum, it may reflect an earlier stage in a developing situation. But an imperial order to destroy a major functioning temple in a major city would be without parallel, and both pagan and Christian sources assign the primary responsibility to Theophilus. The final page of the Alexandrian chronicle carries on the left-hand side an illustration of Theophilus standing above Serapis holding a Bible, while on the right monks storm the Serapeum.[129] Theophilus may have claimed to be enforcing imperial orders, but surely exceeded them.

There is no basis for Fowden's suggestion that Rome and Alexandria were specially selected as hotbeds of paganism, ripe for a new Theodosian hard line. The truth is that the February 391 and June 392 laws do not go much beyond earlier laws banning sacrifice. It is the November 392 law, addressed to Rufinus as praetorian prefect of the East, that marks a new stage in anti-pagan legislation. Rather than Theodosius himself, it was surely Rufinus, a man of stern and conspicuous piety, who was the moving force behind this law, as he must have been for the very similar anti-pagan law issued on 7 August 395, seven months after Theodosius's death, and a series of laws against heretics, some before, some after Theodosius's death.[130] Whether even the November law was as inflexibly enforced as usually assumed is a question that need not trouble us for the moment. What matters in the present context is that there is no evidence that it was ever sent to Italy. This means that there is no solid evidence for any absolute Theodosian ban on pagan worship in the West before the rebellion of Eugenius.

The "dramatic new policy" interpretation is usually explained in terms of Theodosius falling under the influence of Ambrose, often spoken of as though documented fact.[131] But there is not a shred of evidence for Ambrose exerting any such influence on Theodosius. At this juncture it is improbable. Ambrose himself admits that his interference in Theodosius's dealings with the senatorial embassy of 389 was unwelcome. According to the manuscripts, the emperor "agreed to my request (*insinuationi meae assensionem detulit*), and so (*sic*) for several days I did not approach him, nor did he take it amiss (*nec moleste tulit*), because he knew that I was not doing it for my own advantage, but for his and that of my soul."[132] But if Theodosius agreed, why did Ambrose stay away? The Maurist editors inserted a *tandem*: "the emperor *eventually* agreed to my request." Liebeschuetz obtained much the same sense more neatly by emending *detulit* to *distulit*: "the emperor *delayed* his assent to my request." That is to say, on both versions Ambrose stayed away until Theodosius had reached a decision. Yet that still does not explain why Theodosius might have been expected to be angry. If Ambrose had not raised the issue himself, why should it ever have occurred to

---

129. For a reproduction with commentary, Hahn 2008, 364–65.
130. *Cod. Theod.* xvi. 10. 12–13 and xvi. 5. 23–26 (the last two dated 13 and 30 March 395).
131. The assumption is so widespread that it would be superfluous to cite authorities.
132. *Ep. extra coll.* 10. 4.

anyone that Theodosius was angry with him? That the emperor was indeed furious is
put beyond doubt by another letter of Ambrose to Theodosius himself about the
Thessalonica massacre written a month or two after this confrontation:[133]

> I saw that I alone of all your court had been stripped of the natural right of
> hearing, with the consequence that I had also been deprived of the power of
> speaking. *For you have frequently been offended because I obtained knowledge of a
> number of decisions taken in the consistory.* As a result, I no longer enjoy what is
> available to all, even though the lord Jesus says: "nothing is hidden that shall
> not be made manifest." I nevertheless showed as much respect as I could to
> your imperial will, for I made sure that you would have *no cause for anger* by
> acting in such a way that it was impossible for any report relating to imperial
> decisions to reach me.

Not only was Ambrose not the emperor's counsellor and confidant. Evidently,
Theodosius was so angry that, for a while at least, he gave strict orders that Ambrose
was not even to be told what was being discussed in the consistory. Apparently, he had
been hoping to deal with the embassy about the subsidies before Ambrose heard
about it. And yet this is the very moment when Theodosius is supposed to have fallen
under Ambrose's spell and decided on a tougher policy toward paganism.

On other grounds too the "dramatic new policy" assumption is far more problematic than usually recognized. It is important here to distinguish between what
Theodosius might have wished to do as a good Christian in an ideal world, and what
was practical politics for an emperor in a real world recovering from a bitter civil war.
He must have known that the altar and subsidies affair had upset a number of powerful aristocrats, and the most natural explanation of the favors he showered on such
grandees in 389/91 is that he was doing his best to conciliate them short of granting
the one thing they really wanted. Ambrose's heavy-handed interference may well have
upset these delicate overtures. The last thing the emperor wanted to do just before he
returned to the East was antagonize the still-powerful pagan lobby of Rome he had
been taking such pains to win over. And any such anxieties he entertained on this
score were fully justified. Within barely a year of his return another usurper was sitting
on the western throne, with the elder Flavian as his praetorian prefect.

The eve of his departure for the East would have been a singularly poor moment to
choose for a major anti-pagan initiative in the West. Once back in the East he would have
very limited power to enforce his new policy, above all because the chief officials he was
leaving in place behind him were all pagans. The February 391 law was addressed to the
prefect of Rome, Rufius Albinus.[134] This has often been claimed to be "ironic," but that is

---

133. *Ep. extra coll.* 11. 2 (= Maur. 52); McLynn 1994, 313–15; Liebeschuetz/Hill 2005, 263–64.
134. *Cod. Theod.* 16. 10. 10; MSS have PPO, but not only was Flavian PPO at this time; eleven other laws
    and four inscriptions attest him as PVR (Chastagnol 1962, 233–34).

hardly the word. Theodosius must have known that Albinus was a pagan, as was the man he himself had appointed to the prefecture of Italy, the elder Flavian. If he was planning a serious onslaught on pagan cults in the West, the worst possible way to launch it would have been to address the first law to a pagan and then return to the East. Even if he thought Albinus honorable enough to publish the law and punish any infractions that came to his notice, he must have realized that he could not count on the sort of energetic, single-minded enforcement he got from pious eastern ministers like Cynegius and Rufinus. Under the circumstances, we are bound to reconsider the assumption that the 391 law was either intended or (more important) perceived as a deathblow to paganism, rigorously enforced, provoking widespread resentment and resistance.

Its main provision was a ban on animal sacrifice. From the sons of Constantine (if not Constantine himself) on, edict after edict was issued forbidding sacrifice. The fact that such bans continued down into the sixth century has often been taken to prove that they were ineffective and that sacrifice continued regardless.[135] According to an influential article by Kenneth Harl, "The edicts of Theodosius abolished neither sacrifices nor pagans." Pagans certainly not, but sacrifice perhaps. According to Harl, animal sacrifice "had always been central to pagan worship, and…gained new emphasis in the fourth century as the Roman monarchy embraced the new faith and moved steadily against the cults." Others too have assumed that sacrifice continued to thrive down into the 380s.[136] This is a claim based, not on evidence, but on a priori assumption (so long as there were pagans, sacrifice must have continued).[137]

But an important article by Bradbury has shown that, in major eastern cities like Antioch at any rate, public sacrifice had virtually disappeared from civic festivals even before Julian, in part because of imperial legislation, but also because of changes in the public funding available for the purpose, such as it was now transferred to circus and theatre entertainments.[138] Notoriously, Julian sacrificed beasts by the hundred, but this was considered excessive even by admirers like Ammianus and Libanius.[139] "Do the people of Ilion still sacrifice?" wrote Julian himself to Pegasius, the future apostate bishop of Ilium. Eunapius describes how the prefect Anatolius "boldly" sacrificed at Athens in 359.[140] According to Libanius, writing about the festival of the Kalends: "the altars of the gods do not receive today everything they once did, *since the law forbids it,* but *before the ban* the beginning of this month [January] saw many fires, much blood, much smoke wafting up to the skies."[141] Theodosius, he claimed in a speech of 386, did

---

135. See especially Trombley I (1993), Ch. 1.
136. So recently N. Belayche, in Georgoudi, Koch Piettre, and Schmidt 2005, 343–70; Fowden, *CAH* xiii (1998), 551.
137. "pagans could not properly revere and commune with the divine without sacrifices," Harl 1990, 7–27 at 7.
138. Bradbury 1995, 331–56.
139. Amm. 22. 12. 6–7; Lib. *Or.* 12. 80; 18. 170.
140. Julian *Ep.* 79; Eunap. *VS* 10. 6. 8.
141. *Or.* ix. 18 (unfortunately undatable), with J. Martin's introduction in the Budé Libanius vol. 2 (1988), 187–91.

not "banish from the temples and altars either fire or incense or the offerings of other perfumes."[142] Put together, these texts clearly imply that by Libanius's day public sacrifice no longer took place, at any rate in Antioch. What could be more revealing than Julian's own account of how he arrived at the Antiochene suburb of Daphne expecting extravagant sacrifices, only to find not a single beast waiting for him.[143] Not one? If this is true, it would seem that the infrastructure for producing sacrificial animals no longer existed. In earlier times they were presumably selected and prepared months in advance for the appropriate festival occasions. Beasts that fitted the often very precise requirements could not be produced out of thin air on a few days' notice.

It might be argued that sacrifice lasted longer in the West, given the role of the aristocracy in the state cults. Yet in sharp contrast to the eastern texts just cited, there is not a single piece of direct evidence either way—surely a significant silence. In 386 Libanius claimed that sacrifice (*to thuein*) had not yet been forbidden in Rome and Alexandria.[144] But it is not clear that his language necessarily implies actual blood sacrifice. Just as *sacrificare* can be used for offerings of cakes, wine, or incense,[145] *thuein* too can be applied equally to bloody and bloodless sacrifices.[146] Nor can we be sure that he was either well informed or up to date, still less that he was referring to public celebrations of civic cult. The last documented and dated example of public sacrifice at Rome is Ammianus's reference to Tertullus "sacrificing in the temple of Castor and Pollux at Ostia" in his capacity as prefect of Rome in 359, presumably "the ludi of the Castors at Ostia" dated to 27 January by Polemius Silvius, an official celebration paid for out of public funds.[147] Symmachus refers to sacrifices being performed at Spoleto ca. 378, but adds that they were not made "in the public name."[148] It may be that Libanius had heard of the *taurobolia* celebrated in the Phrygianum (two in 377, one in 383, and the last known in 390), but that was in private. In Rome the authorities (the city prefect, usually a fellow aristocrat) may have been prepared to turn a blind eye to what their peers did in private.

But by the 380s the public sacrifices that had traditionally accompanied public festivals of the state cults would have outraged the now substantial Christian population of Rome. After all, in addition to the actual sacrifice there was the butchering and distribution of the meat for the massive banquets that followed. As early as St. Paul Christians had wrestled with the problem of avoiding sacrificial meat. Yet we hear nothing of protests about it in fourth-century Rome, nothing more than trite clichés

---

142. Lib. *Or.* xxx. 8, trans. A. F. Norman (slightly rearranged).
143. Jul. *Misop.* 361d–362b.
144. Lib. *Or.* xxx. 33 and 35.
145. Many examples in Scheid 2005, Ch. 1 (*sacrificium deae Diae ture vino fecerunt*); Scheid 1998, no. 69, 31; and so forth.
146. Bruit Zaidman and Schmitt Pantel 1992, 32–33; Bauer-Danker, *Greek-English Lex. of the New Test.*[3] s.v. θύω 1; Christians and pagans alike regularly use θύω and θυσία metaphorically (much material in Petropoulou 2008).
147. Amm. xix. 10. 5; Stern 1953, 84–85; Chastagnol 1960, 139; Meiggs 1973, 343–45.
148. *sacrificiis … saepe repetitis necdum publico nomine Spoletinum piatur ostentum, Ep.* 1. 49.

about showers of blood in Prudentius and the *Carmen contra paganos*. Writing in 393 Ambrose characterizes the confiscated subsidies as "funds for sacrifice" (*sumptus sacrificiorum*), but there is only one reference to sacrifice in his two letters responding to Symmachus during the famous "debate." Taken out of context, his remark that pagans "celebrate their sacrifices everywhere"[149] might seem proof enough, but in context his point is that, since pagans are able to sacrifice anywhere they want (in 384 it had not yet been banned), why do they need to sacrifice in the senate house where there are now lots of Christian senators? The offering he then describes is clearly the burning of incense, not animal sacrifice.[150]

In the complete absence of evidence nothing can be proved, but I suspect that, in the West as in the East, by the 380s (if not earlier) public rituals no longer routinely included animal sacrifice. As early as 333/5 we find Constantine laying down that celebrations of the imperial cult at Hispellum should not be "defiled by the deceits of any contagious superstition" (*ILS* 705).[151] He must have known that rituals of the imperial cult would not be Christian. He was not forbidding pagan rituals, just animal sacrifice, the one ritual Christians found absolutely unacceptable.[152] Here as early as the 330s we have at least one pagan festival in Italy where no blood was spilled. And since we find a Christian *flamen* of the imperial cult in North Africa datable between 364 and 366,[153] it looks as if sacrifice had been discontinued there too as early as the 360s.

Preaching in 404, Augustine contrasts his Christian congregation with their pagan parents; then (the 370s–380s) the temples were full of people offering incense, now the churches are full of people praising god.[154] Parents spattered with sacrificial blood would have made the point far more dramatically, but Augustine knew (I suggest) that his listeners' parents had long since given up sacrifice. Imperial bans of animal sacrifice were probably not so unsuccessful as often assumed. In major cities, at any rate, sacrifice may have been dropped from public festivals from as early as the 370s. As long as there was no public sacrifice, down to the 390s Christian governments were sensible enough not to be too concerned about what people thought, said, or did in private.

Laws forbidding sacrifice continue to be issued well down into the fifth century, and have always been assumed to prove that sacrifice continued. No doubt it did here and there, especially in remote areas. But it would be unwise to infer that every such law was provoked by a documented report of sacrifice, especially in cities. As we shall see in more detail in the Conclusion paganism lasted much longer for Christians than pagans. And for Christians, paganism always implied sacrifice.

---

149. *Ep.* 57. 2; *Ep.* 73. 31 (*sacrificia sua ubique concelebrant*).
150. Sacrifice could consist of offerings of incense, cakes, fruit, meal, wine: Beard, North, Price II (1998), Ch. 6. 4; Scheid 2005.
151. *ILS* 705. 46–47; Cecconi 87–96; Lee 2000, 92–93; van Dam 2007, 53–57, 115–17, 363–67.
152. Oddly disputed by van Dam 2007, 32–33.
153. See the texts analysed in Chastagnol 1978, 44–48.
154. *Sermo* Dolbeau 21. 16; Dolbeau 1996, 285.

As already remarked, things changed dramatically with the eastern law of 392, forbidding pagan cult in every form. But the western law of 391 simply repeated the ban on sacrifice (perhaps provoked by complaints about the *taurobolium* of 390 in the Phrygianum, not public but not entirely private either). As for the ban on entering temples, most rituals took place outside the temples themselves. The watching public would never enter a temple. Most pagans may have felt that they had made substantial concessions and were now conforming to the law.

That the 391 law was not construed as a dramatic shift in policy is in effect implied by the evidence of none other than Ambrose himself, who carefully enumerates three successive senatorial embassies petitioning for the restoration of state subsidies for the Roman cults *after* February 391: one to Valentinian II (May 392) and two to Eugenius (later in 392 and in 393/4). In the first case he writes of "the privileges of the temples" and of the others he twice uses the phrase *reddere templis*, "restore to the temples," presumably with *sumptus*, "expenses," understood (his biographer Paulinus twice uses the phrase *sumptus caerimoniarum* of these embassies). With this use of *reddere*, compare *De ob. Val.* 19: "everyone present, Christians no less than pagans, said that [these things] should be restored [*reddenda*]."[155] It seems clear that what Ambrose had in mind was the request Symmachus had made in 382 and 384.

Yet on the traditional interpretation, while Gratian had merely withdrawn public subsidies from the Roman cults, Theodosius altogether forbade them. If this is really how Roman pagans of the early 390s perceived Theodosius's legislation, if it was really this that drove them to open revolt, why is it that they continued again and again to petition for the restoration of the subsidies? Had not the issue of state subsidies been rendered irrelevant overnight by the absolute ban of 391, rigorously enforced? Surely what these embassies should have been asking for now is the lifting of Theodosius's ban. Yet there is no hint of this in Ambrose's account of the three successive senatorial embassies after 391. He writes as though they had the same goals as the pre-391 embassies.

It might seem self-evident that imperial laws, precisely dated original documents emanating directly from court, should form the bedrock of any attempt to trace the religious policies of Theodosius. Yet a fascinating article by Malcolm Errington has shown that contemporaries apparently did not take his legislation on religion quite as literally and seriously as most modern scholars.[156] The basis of this disconcerting claim is a close study of the treatment of Theodosius's attitude to pagans and heretics in the four ecclesiastical historians who cover the period: Rufinus, who wrote (in Latin) in 402/3; and Socrates, Theodoret, and Sozomen, who wrote (in Greek) one after another in the 440s.

It is important to be clear that this is not just an argument from silence. Errington rightly conceded that the failure of (say) Ambrose and Augustine[157] to single out

---

155. Ambr. *Ep.* 57. 5–6; Paulin. *Vita Ambr.* 26; Ambr. *De ob. Val.* 19: *et cum universi qui aderant Christiani pariter atque gentiles dicerent esse reddenda.*

156. Errington 1997, 398–443, to which I am much indebted; see too Errington 2006, Ch. 8.

157. At *CD* v. 26 Augustine refers to Theodosius's *iustissimis et misericordissimis legibus adversus impios*, but the context is the battle against Arianism.

Theodosius's legislative activity as a key part of his fight against paganism is not necessarily significant. It was enough for both their purposes to emphasize the emperor's personal piety and the success of his fight. But ecclesiastical historians are a different matter. Their goal was to trace the course of the (orthodox) church's victory over all rivals. Not only this. The three Greek historians all wrote after the publication of the Theodosian Code in 438; Sozomen was a lawyer and undoubtedly knew Latin, as also did Socrates. All four were working in the tradition of Eusebius's *Ecclesiastical History* (books 1–9 of Rufinus are actually an abridged translation of Eusebius). The most original feature of Eusebius's *Ecclesiastical History*, the reason it will always remain an indispensable foundation for the history of the church, is that it incorporates some 250 original documents, quoted in full, and another 100 summarized at length.[158] The three Greek writers likewise included a large number of original documents, letters of bishops, synods, and emperors, especially Constantine and Constantius II (Rufinus rather fewer, in keeping with the smaller compass of his work). Yet they virtually ignore the almost two hundred laws included in Bk 16 of the Theodosian Code.

According to Socrates (e.g.), Theodosius persecuted no heretics except Eunomius, whom he exiled. "Of the others, he interfered with none of them and forced nobody into communion with himself; but he allowed them all to assemble in their own places and entertain their own opinions on points of Christian faith." According to Rufinus too, writing of Theodosius's efforts to "drive out heretics" after his return to the East in 391, "he exercised such moderation in doing so that, rejecting all motives of revenge, he took measures to restore the churches to the Catholics only insofar as the true faith could make progress once the obstacle to its being preached had been removed."[159] The modern historian, familiar with the nineteen ferocious laws of Theodosius proclaiming that all "vicious doctrines hateful to god and man" are "forbidden by both divine and imperial laws and shall forever cease,"[160] can only register astonishment at such a verdict. Even if we allow that Socrates and Rufinus simply did not know about these laws (hardly conceivable in the case of Sozomen, given their recent publication in the code, his knowledge of Latin, and the fact that he was a lawyer), if they were treated as seriously at the time as they have been by modern critics, contemporaries must have been aware of their effect. Yet it seems clear that the other sources Socrates and Rufinus consulted, whether written or oral, cannot have conveyed the atmosphere of intolerance and persecution the laws suggest.

Here we may compare Sozomen's assessment of Theodosius's legislation against heretics:[161]

> By issuing legislation the emperor forbade the heterodox to meet in churches and teach about the faith and appoint bishops.... And he prescribed severe

---

158. For a useful brief account, Lawlor and Oulton 1928, 19–27.
159. Socr. *HE* v. 20. 4–5; Ruf. *HE* xi. 19.
160. *Cod. Theod.* xvi. 5; quotations from 5. 12 and 5. 5.
161. Soz. *HE* vii. 12. 12.

penalties in the laws. *But he did not impose them*, for he was anxious not to punish but to frighten his subjects, so that they would come to agree with him in religious matters. For this reason he also praised those who converted voluntarily.

None of the three explicitly applies the principle of frightening rather than punishing to anti-pagan legislation, but it is intrinsically probable that, like earlier Christian emperors, Theodosius did in fact follow the same policy in this area too. Bishops and evangelists might clamour for fierce laws and stringent penalties, but experienced administrators knew that this was not an effective way to change people's hearts and minds.

Here is Gregory of Nazianzus, in his *Invective against Julian*, probably early in 363:[162]

> Have the Christians ever inflicted on your people anything similar to what you have so often inflicted on us? *Have we taken away any of your freedom of speech* (parrhesia)? Have we incited any raging crowds against you, or magistrates willing to exceed their instructions? Whose lives have we put in danger? Rather, *whom have we deprived of holding office and other honors due to members of the elite*? In a word, to whom have we done anything like the many acts and threats you made against us?

And here is John Chrysostom, writing at Antioch in 378/9, addressing pagans:[163]

> No one has ever made war on them. Nor are Christians allowed to use force or violence to combat error. They must provide for the salvation of men by persuasion, speech and gentleness. *That is why no Christian emperor could ever issue decrees against you* such as the devil-worshippers issued against us.

He goes on to explain that the error of pagan superstition spontaneously collapsed on its own. Here is Gregory again, in his autobiography, writing perhaps in the early 380s:[164]

> I do not consider it good practice to coerce people instead of persuading them. Persuasion has more weight with me, and indeed with those very people I direct toward God. Whatever is done against one's will, under the threat of force, is like an arrow artificially tied back, or a river damned in on every side of its channel. Given the opportunity it rejects the restraining force. What is done willingly, on the other hand, is steadfast for all time. It is made fast by the

---

162. Or. iv. 98; J. Bernardi, *Gregoire de Nazianze, Discours 4–5* (Paris 1983), 244–46.
163. *In Babylam* 13: *PG* 50. 537 = M. A. Schatkin, C. Blanc, and B. Grillet, *Jean Chrysostome Discours sur Babylas* (Paris 1990), 106–8.
164. *Carm.* II. 1. 11. 1292–1304; A. Tuilier, G. Bady and J. Bernardi, *Saint Grégoire de Nazianze: Oeuvres poétiques* tome 1 (Paris 2004), 178 date the poem, improbably, as late as 388.

unbreakable bonds of love. The emperor [Theodosius], it seems to me, keeps this in mind, and to this extent keeps fear within bounds, winning over everybody gently, and setting up voluntary action as the unwritten law of persuasion.

A recent commentator was surprised by the tone of this passage, judging that it depreciated Theodosius's well-known efforts to promote the orthodox cause.[165] All three texts are no doubt to some extent disingenuous, and all three antedate the anti-pagan legislation of 391–92. But they postdate several surviving laws banning sacrifice in the strongest possible terms. It is hard to believe that Gregory and Chrysostom were making a claim they knew to be absolutely false. Surprising though it might seem, it looks as if they did not take all those ferocious denunciations so literally as most modern scholars. Or perhaps they recognized that the goal of the laws was first and foremost to stop sacrifice rather than win hearts and minds (that would come later). Gregory's emphasis on the importance of persuasion rather than force also appears in Prudentius, writing ca. 394 of conversions after the Frigidus (quoted on p. 121), claiming that none of the converts were intimidated by force: "all are convinced by reason alone and follow their own judgment, not a command." Augustine refers to the law closing the temples of Carthage in 399 as being *contra paganos*, and then adds "or rather *for* the pagans, if they had any sense" (*immo pro paganis, si sapiant*).[166]

As far as Roman paganism is concerned, particularly instructive is Socrates's claim that "the emperor Theodosius during his short stay in Italy conferred the greatest benefit on the city of Rome."[167] This was the period when, on the standard view, he proclaimed "paganism's death sentence." But what Socrates reports is his measures to eliminate two "infamous abuses": kidnapping visitors to work in bake-houses and serve as prostitutes; and condemning women caught in adultery to work in brothels. Not a word about laws banning paganism.

No less instructive are the summaries of Theodosius's laws and policies about paganism in Rufinus and Sozomen. First Rufinus, whose *Ecclesiastical History* appeared in 402–3, only twelve years after Theodosius's supposedly so crucial law of February 391. Yet all Rufinus says is the following: "the cult of idols, which on the initiative of Constantine and thereafter had begun to be neglected and destroyed, collapsed in Theodosius's reign."[168] Remarkably enough, he does not credit the emperor with any specific initiative to bring about this end. Sozomen's summary is a bit more detailed:[169]

---

165. See the note in Tuiler et al. (n. 164) 182.
166. Aug. *Sermo* 62. 18.
167. Soc. *HE* v. 18.
168. *idolorum cultus, qui Constantini institutione et deinceps neglegi et destrui coeptus fuerat, eodem* [= Theodosius] *imperante conlapsus est* (*HE* xi. 19); Errington 1997, 402.
169. Soz. *HE* vii. 20. 1–2; Errington 1997, 429–30.

For when the emperor saw that the habit of past times still attracted his subjects to their ancestral forms of worship and to the places they revered, at the beginning of his reign [379] he stopped them entering and at the end destroyed many of them. As a result of not having houses of prayer, in the course of time they accustomed themselves to attend the churches; for it was not without danger to offer pagan sacrifice even in secret, since a law was issued fixing the punishment of death and loss of property for those who dared to do this.

But it is surprisingly ill informed, especially from a lawyer. The first known Theodosian law to prohibit access to temples dates from 391, not 379, and no surviving law orders the destruction of temples.[170] Sozomen is probably generalizing here from Rufinus's account of the destruction of the Serapeum, supposedly authorized by an otherwise unknown imperial rescript. Punishment by loss of property is prescribed in the November 392 eastern law. The decisive factor in the eventual conversion of pagans, Sozomen concluded, was the closure of the temples. Augustine praises Theodosius for "commanding that the statues of the pagans should be everywhere overthrown,"[171] but no such law survives. On the contrary, a number of laws forbid the destruction or spoliation of temples. Not one of the ecclesiastical historians portrays Theodosius as the emperor who finally forbade paganism by law.

What now of the claim—hitherto taken for granted—that Theodosius's anti-pagan laws were rigorously enforced. This is a question that has received surprisingly little attention, apart from the simplistic assumption that pagan officials were unlikely to enforce anti-pagan laws. That may well have been so, but it is important to add that it was no part of the responsibility of *any* official to enforce the law in the way that modern states enforce the law.[172] The virtual absence of a regular police force to which infractions might be reported and who would then take action is one obvious problem. That was up to private individuals, who were expected to produce the necessary evidence and witnesses. If they failed to prove their case, such private would-be enforcers of the law were liable to be prosecuted, in turn, themselves. Bands of monks could attack shrines in rural areas with relative impunity, but those who presided over the cults of Rome were members of the landowning aristocracy (Ch. 4), and it cannot have been easy to find witnesses willing to impeach their own landlords in court.

It may be useful to underline why Gratian's more modest measures were effective in a way that no direct anti-pagan legislation could ever have been. Bans require not only the provision of penalties for infractions—and realistic penalties imposed for every infraction—but constant policing. The effectiveness of any ban depends on how energetically it is enforced and how easy it is to avoid detection. Gratian did not

---

170. Theodoret's claim that Theodosius "issued laws ordering the dissolution of the shrines of the idols" (*HE* v. 21. 1) is therefore also false.
171. *simulacra gentilium ubique evertenda praecepit*, Aug. *CD* v. 26. 48.
172. Briefly, J. Harries 1999, 93–96.

ban any activities. He simply ordered the confiscation of the revenues of certain estates that had till then financed the state cults and supported the Vestal Virgins. These were not measures that could be ignored. Once the revenues had been reassigned to other purposes, they were simply not available for their traditional ends. Whence those endless senatorial embassies trying to get them reinstated.

In what circumstances are laws most likely to be obeyed? Even rigorous enforcement is seldom in itself sufficient (and may be self-defeating) if the laws are unpopular and the practices they forbid commonplace. To take the most infamous example in modern times, the U.S. law forbidding the manufacture, sale, and consumption of alcohol was doomed to failure from the start. Laws forbidding adultery, homosexual practices, and abortion are hard to enforce and generally ineffective. Many people believe that the so-called "war on drugs" is likewise bound to fail because there are simply too many people willing and able to buy drugs. A more revealing modern analogy is the recent ban on smoking in public buildings and restaurants in the United States and many European countries.[173] The reason this ban has been as successful as it has is, first, because nonsmokers are now in an aggressive (not to say self-righteous) majority in these societies; and second, because it is limited to public places and makes no attempt to ban smoking itself. Drastic measures against paganism were bound to fail so long as pagans represented, at first a majority, and, until the late fourth century, a substantial minority of the population of the empire. On any hypothesis, the best that could be achieved was the prevention of public practices. If Theodosius's laws banning public cult celebrations were more successful than previous laws, this is mainly (I suggest) because there were fewer pagans by the 390s.

The idea that Theodosius's anti-pagan laws were fiercely enforced is an inference back from the baseless conviction that it was the resentment they fostered that led to a pagan reaction, the rebellion of Eugenius. There is no reason to doubt that the reign of Theodosius was a tipping point in the conversion of the Roman world, but not (or not primarily) because of his anti-pagan legislation. As far as the West at any rate is concerned, it may be that Rufinus's seemingly naive conclusion really does reflect what most early fifth-century lay Christians were content to believe: "in Theodosius's reign the cult of idols...collapsed." Prudentius said much the same, praising Theodosius for closing the temples (p. 348).

There is a particularly intriguing witness to this attitude in a sermon of Augustine delivered in Carthage in 401: "if the Roman gods have abandoned Rome, why do they still exist here?"[174] Nor is this just a personal reflection of Augustine. In the preceding paragraph he represents his congregation shouting "Like Rome, like Carthage." Given the date, the allusion must be to the recent closing of pagan temples and removal of cult statues in Carthage by the counts Gaudentius and Iovius. So a chronicle at this

---

173. I am here developing a remark by Wolf Liebeschuetz at a symposium in the Monastery of Bose in October 2008.

174. *si ergo, inquam, dii romani Romae defecerunt, hic quare remanserunt*, Sermo 24. 6 (*CCL* 41 [1961], 332).

point being maintained in Carthage (*templa gentilium demolita sunt Ioviano et Gaudentio comitibus*, under 399).[175] In view of the context (the closing of temples), Augustine cannot have been thinking of the Frigidus, fought far from Rome, but of the now closed temples of the city of Rome.

When Rufinus, Prudentius, and Augustine made such claims, they did not (of course) believe there were no pagans left in Rome. But with sacrifice gone and the temples closed, *public* paganism was dead. Rufinus's *idolorum cultus...conlapsus est* (xi. 19) refers not to the victory at the Frigidus (xi. 3 2–33) but to his much longer and more detailed account (xi. 22–30, almost a third of his final book) of the defeat of paganism in Alexandria, symbolized in the destruction of the Serapeum, a defeat that Rufinus clearly treats as a "paradigm"[176] for the final defeat of paganism in the Roman world.

No Christian wanted to believe that Christianity had to be established in the Roman world by force. Rather it was part of the divine plan. Had not God long ago engineered the birth of Christ to coincide with the arrival of the *pax Augusta* so that Christianity could more easily spread throughout the empire (the *praeparatio evangelica*)? The conversion of Constantine marked the beginning of the final stage, but the fact that Constantine himself, Constantius II, and Valens had all slipped into heresy left the final establishment of an orthodox Christian empire to Theodosius. Yet Theodosius did not achieve this by issuing laws or winning battles.[177] As we shall see in the next chapter, Rufinus's detailed account of the Frigidus ascribes victory to Theodosius's piety and prayers.

5: EUGENIUS AND THE STATE CULTS

We come at last to the "last pagan stand." All modern accounts of Eugenius's usurpation assume that he was pro-pagan from the start and, though himself a (lukewarm) Christian, eventually allowed his reign to take on the character of a pagan revolt.[178] According to Straub, the very beard he is shown with on his coins marks him as a philosopher and so tolerant of pagans, an argument still taken seriously in several recent studies.[179] But he had been a teacher of rhetoric, not philosophy, and Christ, the apostles, and the saints are all shown in the style of the philosopher with a beard.[180] So are Honorius, Theodosius II, and even Ambrose.

---

175. *Cons. Const.* s.a. 399; Burgess 1993, 203, 243. The Gallic Chronicle of 452 generalizes this entry to *toto orbe Romano antiquae superstitionis templa destructa* (*Chron. Min.* i. 650).

176. So Hahn 2008, 345.

177. While acknowledging the piety of both Valentinian I (xi. 10) and Gratian (xi. 13), Rufinus no doubt thought that both reigned too short a time to fulfil this role. More important, perhaps, was the passage of another two decades.

178. So most notably J. Straub's entry "Eugenius" in *RAC*; for a sensible corrective (though not going far enough), Szidat 1979; most extreme recent example, Hedrick 2000.

179. Straub, *RAC* 6. 860–61; Grierson and Mays 1992, 74; Leppin 2003, 206; Demandt 2007, 166.

180. Zanker 1995, 290.

Once we eliminate the *Carmen contra paganos* (*CCP*) from the debate, we are left with just four pieces of evidence: (1) his selection for the throne by the supposedly pagan Arbogast; (2) his appointment of Nicomachus Flavianus, supposedly a pagan fanatic, as his praetorian prefect; (3) Christian representations of the battle between Theodosius and Eugenius as a confrontation between paganism and Christianity; and (4) most important, his supposed restoration of the subsidies to the pagan cults. We shall see that the evidence for Arbogast's paganism is much weaker than hitherto assumed; in any case, there is a world of difference between simply being a pagan and leading a pagan revolt. As for Flavian, not only is there no solid evidence that he was a pagan fanatic (much more on this later); we must not forget that it was the pious Theodosius who first appointed him praetorian prefect. Eugenius merely invited him to continue in office, perhaps hoping that this would reassure Theodosius about his intentions. The question of Christian representations of the Frigidus will be dealt with at length in the following chapter.

That leaves the key assumption, hitherto taken as established and uncontroversial fact: that Eugenius restored the subsidies to the state cults. It is in fact far from clear that he did anything of the sort. The only evidence is a vague and ambiguous letter Ambrose wrote (or claims to have written) to Eugenius himself,[181] and a more explicit statement in Paulinus's *Life of Ambrose* based on this letter. The fact that Paulinus is more explicit than what is undoubtedly his source has not aroused the suspicion it should have. The letter itself contrives to *imply* that Eugenius restored the subsidies while carefully stopping short of actually saying so. But if Eugenius really did what Gratian, Maximus, Valentinian II, and Theodosius had all steadfastly refused to do, why the vagueness and ambiguity? Why not condemn his action directly and explicitly? In view of the importance of this letter for the hypothesis of a pagan revival, it deserves a much more careful and detailed examination than it has so far received.

The letter purports to be a belated response to (at least) two letters from Eugenius that Ambrose claims to have deliberately left unanswered. It professes to explain both why he did not reply to these earlier letters and why he left Milan before Eugenius moved his court there in spring 393. If Eugenius really did restore the subsidies, that *could* explain why Ambrose left Milan,[182] though given his record we might have expected him to remain and continue the battle against paganism. What it does *not* explain is why he refused to answer Eugenius's letters.

Ambrose claims that he refused because he "foresaw what would happen."[183] But how can this be? How can he have taken so provocative a step simply on the basis of a feeling that Eugenius would one day restore the subsidies? Some have argued that Eugenius was known to be well disposed to pagans before his accession. But he must have reassured the Christian community by refusing, as Ambrose himself concedes in

---

181. *Ep. extra coll.* 10 2–6; Zelzer 1982, 205–8.

182. "My reason for leaving Milan was my fear of the Lord," the letter begins.

183. *Ideo etiam in primordiis imperii tui scribenti non rescripsi, quia istud praevidebam futurum* (§ 11).

this very letter that he did, not one but two separate senatorial embassies petitioning for the restoration of the subsidies. Why should Ambrose have continued to fear the worst after so apparently convincing a demonstration?

The real explanation for his refusal to meet Eugenius is not in doubt. Like Symmachus, so long as Theodosius refused to recognize the new regime, Ambrose was anxious to keep his distance. Symmachus could do this by refusing office, remaining in Rome or one of his villas, and maintaining a low profile. But as bishop of an imperial capital, Ambrose was more exposed. If he remained in Milan he could hardly avoid meeting an emperor now resident in that city. Indeed, Ambrose and Symmachus shared a very particular reason for keeping their distance: both had been burned during the usurpation of Maximus. Like Eugenius, Maximus too had eventually invaded Italy and set up court in Milan, and Symmachus had been unwise enough to attend his consular inauguration there in January 388 and deliver a panegyric. Nothing is known of Ambrose's actions during this period (itself a significant silence), but since he did not flee the city and does not claim to have refused to meet Maximus, he must have met and offered so pious a Catholic the sacraments—and no doubt, like Symmachus, attended his consular inauguration. Theodosius evidently forgave Ambrose as he forgave Symmachus. But it would not have been prudent to risk making the same mistake twice.

Ambrose closes his letter by claiming that "for a long time I stifled and concealed my distress and determined to give no hint to anyone, but now I may no longer pretend, nor am I at liberty to be silent." But when anxious that Valentinian II and Theodosius might give way on the issue of the subsidies, he immediately threw the whole weight of his position and eloquence into the fray, threatening the young Valentinian and infuriating Theodosius. Why did he feel that he had to conceal his anxieties about Eugenius and keep them to himself, uncharacteristic behaviour for Ambrose in any circumstances? Why not write him the same sort of stern exhortation he had sent Valentinian?

The letter at once gives the impression that Ambrose is going to accuse Eugenius of restoring the subsidies by announcing a review of the various stages in the continuing saga of the senatorial embassies.[184] He then details five successive embassies to court: the one to Valentinian II known from Symmachus's *Relatio* of 384; another to Theodosius in Milan in late 389; a third to Valentinian II in Gaul in May 392; and then the two Eugenius refused. But he also alludes to what modern scholars have *inferred* to be a third occasion on which Eugenius finally restored the subsidies. Since this paragraph of the letter (§ 6) is central to the argument and more allusive and problematic than generally realized, it calls for detailed analysis. Having briefly described Valentinian's refusal, Ambrose continues as follows:

> But when your clemency [Eugenius] took over the helm of government, it was later discovered (*compertum est postea*) that these gifts were made (*donata illa*)

---

184. *ut ordinem rerum custodiam, strictim recensebo quae ad hoc spectant negotium*, § 1.

to men outstanding in public life, but practising pagans (*gentilis observantiae viris*). And it might perhaps be said (*fortasse dicatur*), august emperor, that you did not yourself restore [funds] to the temples (*templis reddideris*), but made gifts to men who had served you well (*bene meritis de te donaveris*).

A few lines later he repeats this claim in almost the same words with slightly more detail:

During your reign, envoys asked that you restore [funds] to the temples (*petierunt legati ut templis redderes*). You did not do it. Another embassy asked again. You refused. But later (*postea*) did you think it right to make gifts to those same envoys (*ipsis qui petierunt donandum putasti*)?

What are "these gifts" not further specified (*donata illa*) made to eminent pagans, and why were they only "discovered later"? Some have assumed that *donare* (repeated three times) is no more than a stylistic variation for *templis reddere*, an oblique way of saying that Eugenius yielded to a third senatorial embassy. Croke and Harries, for example, render *donandum* "that the request should be granted,"[185] thus unmistakably implying that Eugenius straightforwardly granted the petition of a third senatorial embassy. But both passages quoted above draw a clear distinction between *templis reddere* and *donare*. And "perhaps it might be said…that you did *not* yourself restore…*but* made gifts" implies that what Ambrose construed as *in effect* restoring the subsidies would have been characterized by Eugenius himself as nothing more than making personal gifts to individuals who happened to be pagans.

Nothing here licenses the idea of a third embassy. There were just two, both of which Eugenius refused. But it was "later" (*postea*, twice repeated) discovered (by whom?) that he had made personal gifts to members of one or both of these embassies. The personal nature of these gifts is further underlined in a later paragraph: "Who grudges your *giving* (*donavisti*) to others what you choose? We do not pry into your *generosity*, nor do we envy others their *gifts*."[186] But the remainder of the letter implies, without ever making a specific accusation, that personal gifts to prominent pagans were *equivalent* to restoring the subsidies. The closest he comes is at the end of § 7: "although they persisted, was it not your duty, emperor, out of reverence for the most high, true and living God, to oppose them no less persistently, and to deny what was harmful to the holy law?" (It should be noted in passing that this sentence, like several others in the letter, unmistakably addresses Eugenius as a Christian.) Even after the Frigidus, addressing Theodosius himself, all Ambrose says, vaguely enough, is that Eugenius "involved himself in sacrilege" (*se sacrilegio miscuisset*).[187]

---

185. Croke and Harries 1982, 56.
186. *Quis invidet quoniam quae voluisti aliis donavisti? non sumus scutatores vestrae liberalitatis, nec aliorum commodorum invidi,* § 8.
187. *Ep. extra coll.* 2. 2 (= Maur. 61).

With perhaps the sole exception of Neil McLynn,[188] modern scholars have simply accepted Ambrose's innuendo[189] as fact. According to Palanque, for example, at this point Eugenius "gave his support unreservedly to the pagan party."[190] The standard explanation of the "gifts" is that Eugenius realized that it was politically impossible for a Christian emperor to restore the subsidies directly, and so employed the subterfuge of channeling the necessary funds indirectly through personal gifts to individual pagan senators. Ambrose is supposed to be letting Eugenius know that he has seen through the subterfuge.[191] It will be noted that this interpretation of Ambrose's words *presupposes* what we are supposed to be proving, namely that Eugenius was well disposed to pagans. It also presupposes that these pagans were numerous and powerful enough to be worth conciliating at the price of so transparent a subterfuge. Yet the fact is that Flavian is the only pagan we can actually name who played any part in Eugenius's rebellion.

This is no doubt a *possible* interpretation of Ambrose's words taken by themselves. But it is not a likely interpretation in context. In the first place, we have seen that, according to pagans, the state cults only worked if publicly funded and (no less important) publicly celebrated. It was not so much lack of funds that was the problem as their source. "Laundering" funds through private hands was no solution, least of all to the question of public celebration. In the second place, on Ambrose's own evidence, Eugenius had already rebuffed two embassies, which hardly suggests that he was known to be well disposed to pagans and just looking for a way to restore the funds.

Many moderns have taken the further step of assuming that the gifts were at once put to use, and that Rome was soon awash in the blood of public sacrifice.[192] But if the recipients of Eugenius's gifts had actually used them to finance pagan cults, how could Ambrose have failed to say so, loud and clear? Nor could the subterfuge of "laundered" funds have remained a secret to be discovered "later." Above all, nothing in what Ambrose either says or hints at implies that Eugenius revoked Theodosius's ban on sacrifice. All he does is exhort Eugenius in the vaguest of terms to reflect on the power of God, who "sees the hearts of all men," warning him that people will pay attention less to what he does than to what he intends. If the worst Ambrose can say is that people will judge Eugenius by his *intentions* rather than his acts, it does not look as if the recipients of his gifts had actually done anything with them at the time of writing, let alone used them to finance the cults. How, after all, could people know his intentions? The claim that God "sees the hearts of all men" clearly implies that nothing mortal men could see had yet happened.

---

188. "perhaps the most audacious of all the misinterpretations the bishop perpetrated," McLynn 345.
189. Perhaps more accurately characterized as *suggestio falsi*.
190. Palanque 1933, 282 ("donne alors son appui sans réserves au parti païen").
191. So even the sceptical O'Donnell 1978, 137 and 139; Leppin 2003, 209.
192. "à la fin de 393...les fonctionnaires païens organisèrent ouvertement et pompeusement les cérémonies de l'ancien culte aux frais du fisc, et les temples furent à nouveau construits et réparés à la charge de l'État," Chastagnol 1960, 163; Matthews 1975, 241–43.

The elaborate biblical analogy from the age of the Maccabees that follows likewise fails to support the standard interpretation. On the occasion of quinquennial games at Tyre under Antiochus Epiphanes, Ambrose reports, the high priest Jason sent envoys from Jerusalem with 300 silver drachmas to spend on a sacrifice to Hercules. But the envoys, being men of god, used the money for triremes instead, with the result that "persecution gave way to the faith of our fathers and paganism yielded."[193] If the senatorial envoys had used Eugenius's gifts to finance sacrifices, why quote as a "similar case"[194] a story in which Jason's envoys *refused* to use the king's money for sacrifices? If anything, the biblical analogy implies that the senatorial envoys had *not*, or at any rate not yet, used their gifts to finance sacrifices. The best Ambrose can come up with is the claim that *if* they do, people will blame Eugenius.

According to many scholars, the letter either formally or implicitly excommunicates Eugenius, or at any rate threatens him with excommunication if he does not change his policy.[195] The truth is that it goes no further than the vaguest of exhortations (God "knows the innermost secrets of your heart"; Eugenius must "submit to God," §§ 7–8). As for the supposed threat of conditional excommunication, as McLynn shrewdly remarked, "perhaps the most significant thing about the letter is that it does not ask Eugenius to do anything, not even to revoke his gifts."[196] If he had really granted the pagan envoys what they asked, Ambrose would surely have demanded that he revoke the concessions at once. We have only to think of his earlier indignant tirades when Valentinian II was merely considering the same request.

There is in fact an obvious alternative explanation of Eugenius's "gifts": that he was trying to conciliate influential pagans whose petition he had felt obliged to refuse by offering them *something else* in consolation. We have seen that this is exactly what Theodosius did, offering Albinus the prefecture of Rome, Flavian two posts at court in succession, and Symmachus the consulship for 391. For Ambrose as for many ecclesiastics, it was imperative to rebuff any and all pagan overtures. But emperors, ever conscious of the insecurity of their rule and always reluctant to antagonize the rich and powerful, were anxious to soften the blow of refusal wherever possible. According to Eusebius, when settling disputes Constantine would make gifts from his own resources to the loser so that both parties might leave his court happy.[197] In all probability Eugenius's gifts to the envoys (no doubt estates) had nothing to do with the cults. Note that "it was later discovered" (a vague, impersonal passive) contrives to suggest that the gifts were somehow underhand or furtive. But of course if they were just personal gifts to individuals, there was no need for anyone except the donor and

---

193. *II Macc.* 4. 18–20; Ambr. *Ep. extra coll.* 10. 9 (= Maur. 57).
194. *huiusmodi quaestio temporibus superioribus.*
195. Piganiol 1972, 291; Lippold 1980, 48; O. Faller, *Sancti Ambrosii Opera* 7 (Vienna 1955), 114*; Homes Dudden 1935, 425; Palanque 1933, 281; Seeck 1913, 246.
196. McLynn 1994, 347 n. 185.
197. Euseb. *VC* iv. 4; cf. McLynn 1994, 343.

donee to know anything about them. Emperors had enormous resources, and at all periods made gifts of all sorts to all sorts of people.[198]

The main reason modern critics have been misled by Ambrose's innuendos is undoubtedly the fact that his biographer, the deacon Paulinus, was already misled within a decade and a half of Ambrose's death. Zelzer's wonderful edition includes useful summaries of Ambrose's letters to emperors. In this case she explains what she evidently recognized to be the obscurity of Ambrose's text by quoting at length from Paulinus.[199] There are certainly no ambiguities or obscurities in Paulinus's narrative. The only question is the source of this clarity and certainty. Since §§ 26 and 31 of Paulinus's *Life of Ambrose* are two of the only three texts that directly implicate Flavian in any sort of overtly pagan initiative, it becomes essential to assess its quality and (above all) its authority.

In general the *Life of Ambrose* has received a remarkably favorable press.[200] Palanque praised its sincerity, veracity, and critical sense. With Paulinus's sincerity and veracity I have no quarrel, but his critical sense and (above all) his accuracy are another matter. Even the sceptical O'Donnell characterized Paulinus as "a first-hand witness who also had Ambrose's own letters to draw upon." As far as the letters go, we may add that Paulinus drew on letters not included in the published collection of Ambrose's letters, most important, the letter to Eugenius (more later on these uncollected letters). But Paulinus did not enter Ambrose's service till after the Frigidus,[201] and though he certainly knew Ambrose's letters and also Rufinus's *Ecclesiastical History*, he read his texts very carelessly, drew unjustified inferences from them, and freely embroidered those inferences. Another factor is that, like many ecclesiastical writers, Paulinus saw heresy as more of a danger than paganism.[202]

The clearest illustration of his tendency to embroider is his account of the Thessalonica massacre. Notoriously, Theodosius ordered troops to punish the people of Thessalonica for killing one of his generals in a riot, and things got out of hand. The Christian community in Milan was shocked. Ambrose at once left the city to avoid awkward confrontations, and wrote a very skilful letter in his own hand suggesting that the emperor make public penance, since he did not dare to offer him the Eucharist in the present circumstances.[203] Theodosius agreed to the plan, and (as Ambrose reported five years later, no doubt with some exaggeration) "threw on the ground all the royal attire he was wearing, wept publicly in the church... and prayed for pardon with groans and tears." This brilliant solution, in McLynn's words, "turned

---

198. Millar 1977, 491–506, and the index entry "gifts from emperor" (642–43).
199. Zelzer 1982, lxxxvii–lxxxviii.
200. Briefly, Palanque 1933, 409–16; Homes Dudden 1935, 715; M. K. Kaniecka, *Vita Sancti Ambrosii* (1928); Mohrman and Bastiaensen 1975; Lamirande 1983; Moorhead 1999, 9–12; and McLynn 1994 are more critical.
201. O'Donnell 1978, 137–38; Paredi 1963, 208.
202. So Lamirande 1983, 106–8.
203. *Ep. extra coll.* 11 (= Maur. 51); McLynn 1994, 323–30.

the catastrophe into a public relations triumph."[204] But this was far too tame for Paulinus, who had Ambrose forbid Theodosius entry into his church and participation in the sacraments until he had done public penance.[205] At this,

> the emperor declared to him: "David committed adultery and also homicide." But at once the reply was given: "You who have followed him as he sinned, follow him as he corrected himself." When the most clement emperor heard this he so took it to heart that he did not scorn public penance.

The mere fact that a Roman emperor had publicly abased himself before a bishop was astonishing enough, and it is not surprising that some contemporaries, unaware of Ambrose's letter, assumed that Ambrose had publicly ordered Theodosius to do so. Paulinus's extravagant account of Ambrose humiliating a defiant emperor is pure fiction. All that happened in church was that bishop and emperor acted out the roles Ambrose had laid down in his letter.[206] But Paulinus did not simply invent his scene of confrontation. He misread and dramatized an obscurely phrased sentence in Ambrose's letter. "On the very night," Ambrose wrote, "in which I was preparing to go away, you *seemed* (*visus es*) to have come to the church, but it was not permitted to me to offer the sacraments."[207] Nor did he invent the biblical parallel of King David's sin and penance. Ambrose's letter had discussed David at some length, though as a model rather than a defiant warning.[208] Once again, Paulinus embellished his source.

Since this paragraph of the letter begins with the claim that Ambrose was "writing in my own hand for you alone to read" (*scribo manu mea quod solus legas*), what he must mean is that he had a dream or vision of Theodosius arriving at church, perhaps invented to dramatize his point: namely, that if Theodosius were to arrive in church before making some public atonement for the massacre, Ambrose would find it difficult to offer him the sacraments. It is important to note (and admire) the subtle way Ambrose makes this point. He does not say: "*if* you come to church, I *will* not offer you the sacraments." He conjures up a vision in which he was "not allowed" to do so, by some higher power unspecified.[209] Ambrose knew perfectly well that in real life he would never have dared publicly to refuse to offer Theodosius the sacraments.

But such subtlety was wasted on Paulinus. Writing as he was twenty years after an event he had not witnessed and that was already passing into legend, Paulinus had no doubt that the bishop he so admired was capable of defying an emperor, and he read

---

204. *De obitu Theod.* 34; McLynn 1994, 315–30 at 323; see too Moorhead 1999, 192–96.
205. *Vita Ambr.* 24.
206. For the details of the penance, McLynn 1994, 326–28.
207. *Ep. extra coll.* 11. 14.
208. Ambrose went on to treat David in a separate work, the *Apology of David*, much of which is an invitation to penitence: see Hadot and Cordier 1977, 33–43; briefly, Moorhead 1999, 194–96. He also evokes David in *De obitu Theodosii* 27 and 34: see Gerbenne 1999, 168–71.
209. At § 13 he goes a little further, saying *offerre non audeo sacrificium si volueris adsistere*, but this still falls well short of the threat we find in Paulinus.

this into Ambrose's words.[210] Thus was born the legend of Ambrose barring the door of his church to Theodosius, a legend that was to do more for his posthumous reputation than any of his actual achievements.[211]

Armed with this clear and specific illustration of the way Paulinus misread and embroidered Ambrose to the point of falsification, we may return to his account of Eugenius's supposed restoration of the subsidies:[212]

> But when Theodosius had left Italy and was at Constantinople, an embassy was sent to the emperor Valentinian [II], who was in Gaul, in the name of the Senate by Symmachus, then the prefect of the city, regarding the restoration of the altar of Victory and the subsidies for the cults.... Not long after (*non multo post*) Eugenius's accession, when Flavianus the prefect at that time and Count Arbogast petitioned for the altar of Victory and the expense of the state cults— something Valentinian of august memory, though still a youth, had refused— *forgetful of his faith he granted their petition.*

Where Ambrose details five earlier embassies about the subsidies, Paulinus has only two. Of course, he was not obliged to be exhaustive, but he was obliged to be accurate. Yet although he clearly had Ambrose's letter to Eugenius in front of him as he wrote (§ 27 quotes a dozen lines verbatim), he incorrectly dates Symmachus's *relatio* (384) after Theodosius's return to Constantinople (391) and assumes that it was addressed to Valentinian II in Gaul instead of Milan, confusing two embassies Ambrose had carefully distinguished. Paulinus's narrative gives an impression of accuracy and chronological precision that is entirely baseless.

Then, omitting the two embassies Eugenius refused, Paulinus represents him restoring the subsidies "not long after" he began to rule. Why "not long after"? Because he *inferred* that, when Ambrose said "when your clemency took over the helm of government," he meant *immediately* after he took over.[213] The inference was not unreasonable, but nonetheless mistaken (and implicitly contradicted by the interval required for the two embassies Eugenius refused). This is no trivial point. If Ambrose's letter had not survived, this passage would have been considered firm evidence that Eugenius restored the subsidies immediately after his accession. It was presumably this text that led Piganiol to claim, falsely, that, as Eugenius marched into Italy in spring 393, he "sent the Roman senate an order to replace the altar of Victory."[214] In fact, the second unsuccessful embassy surely postdates the establishment of his court at Milan in summer 393.

---

210. He was also no doubt influenced by Rufinus's claim that Theodosius did penance after being "reproved by the priests of Italy" (*cum a sacerdotibus Italiae argueretur, HE* xi. 18).
211. Dagron 2003, 105–6, 111–13, 295; Mannix 1925, 9–21; briefly, Moorhead 1999, 211–12.
212. *Vita Ambr.* 26.
213. Paulinus's *suscepit imperium* is a more prosaic adaptation of Ambrose's high-flown *imperii suscepit gubernacula* in this very passage.
214. Piganiol 1972, 291.

These inaccuracies illustrate just how sloppy (not to put it more strongly) Paulinus can be even when the correct information was clearly stated in his source, a single letter of Ambrose. What did he do when that source became allusive and evasive? Ambrose's letter is not at all the straightforward enumeration of facts it purports to be. While its *stated* purpose was to explain why Ambrose left Milan before Eugenius's arrival in spring 393, his *real* purpose was to make himself scarce, so as to escape being obliged to offer Eugenius the Eucharist and accept invitations to court, confrontations that might later prove embarrassing if Theodosius deposed Eugenius as he had Maximus. This was a tactic Ambrose had used on several occasions—twice with Gratian (in 379 and 380)[215] and once with Theodosius after the Thessalonica massacre. But it was hardly a motive he could own up to, least of all when writing to Eugenius himself.

If Eugenius had really restored the subsidies and Flavian had really revived sacrifice, Ambrose might have claimed to be in personal danger. As one staunch recent believer in a pagan revival put it, he "was forced to flee."[216] But if so, why is it that Theodosius too, immediately after the Frigidus, rebuked Ambrose for deserting his post (see p. ###)? Once again, Paulinus is more explicit than Ambrose. Immediately after stating that Eugenius restored the subsidies, he proceeds (§ 27): "when the bishop learned this, he left the city of Milan." That is to say, he states as fact that Ambrose left Milan because he had learned about the restoration of the subsidies. There can be no doubt that Ambrose's letter was Paulinus's source, yet he develops Ambrose's vague hints into a firm statement. As Chastagnol observed, Eugenius's restoration of the state subsidies "is clearly attested by Paulinus."[217] So it is. But with what justification?

More important still, this passage of Paulinus offers an apparently precise detail not known from any other source. Those who presented the senatorial petition are identified as "Flavian the prefect at the time and Count Arbogast" ("*petentibus Flaviano tunc praefecto et Arbogaste comite*"). Hitherto this has been treated as uncontroversial fact. What more likely than that a known pagan fanatic was a prime mover in getting the subsidies restored? But there are serious grounds for scepticism. Both the context and (more specifically) the use of the term *petentibus* imply that Paulinus is identifying Flavian and Arbogast as senatorial envoys ("*te imperante* petierunt legati *ut templis redderes*," as Ambrose himself put it). But neither Flavian nor Arbogast can have been members of an embassy to court. Both were ministers at court, and while they might have influenced Eugenius's response to the envoys behind the scenes, that is not what Paulinus, our only source, says. Arbogast had been Eugenius's generalissimo and Flavian his praetorian prefect since the beginning of the reign. If they were really the pagan power behind the nominally Christian throne, why did they wait so long before acting? We should also bear in mind that Arbogast did not stop Valentinian II turning down another embassy in Vienne shortly before his death. That makes three occasions

---

215. Barnes 1999, 172–74.
216. Hedrick 2000, 45.
217. Chastagnol 1969, 143, n. 3.

in succession when Arbogast was the power behind two different thrones and yet allowed senatorial embassies to be rejected. It is not easy to believe this man an ardent pagan. If so, why did he wait till the fourth attempt before acting?

Paulinus's identification of the envoys is surely no more than a guess. Having decided that he wanted names for the wicked pagans left unnamed by Ambrose, he turned to perhaps the only other written source he knew for these events, the *Ecclesiastical History* of Rufinus.[218] According to Rufinus, the pagans prepared for the confrontation with Theodosius by sacrificing *Flaviano tunc praefecto* (*HE* xi. 33). Paulinus incorporated the phrase unaltered, even down to the ablative absolute construction (*Flaviano tunc praefecto et Arbogaste comite*). The other name he got from the end of the same chapter of Rufinus, where Arbogast is said to have fought *deo adverso*, from which (I suggest) Paulinus *inferred* that he was a pagan (p. 110).

Here we should compare a later chapter in Paulinus (§ 31) that offers another otherwise unattested story about Flavian and Arbogast. Before leaving for the Frigidus, they supposedly vowed that, when they returned victorious, "they would turn the Basilica of Milan into a stable, and enlist the clergy in the army."[219] So long as Flavian was assumed a pagan fanatic, these words were regularly cited as yet another colorful illustration of his fanaticism. But every aspect of the story counsels caution. To start with, there is the recurrence of the same two names. Then there is the fact that at best this is that most dubious of all types of reported utterance, the unfulfilled intention. The threat about the clergy is sufficiently unrealistic to look more like a joke, and the threat about the stable is a commonplace. When consoling a friend on the death of his nephew, Jerome listed a number of recent disasters the young man will be spared, not least barbarian incursions resulting in the slaughter of priests, the demolition of churches and "horses stabled at the altars of Christ."[220] Ten minutes' Googling produced a host of reports of French and German invaders of Russia, Turkish invaders of Armenia and Cyprus, and even the British in New York in 1776 turning churches into stables.

More immediately relevant, a passage in the sixth-century chronicler Malalas suggests an altogether different perspective on the threat about the stable: Theodosius demolished three temples on the Acropolis in Constantinople, turning the temple of Helios into a courtyard that he donated to the Great Church; the temple of Artemis into a gaming hall; and "the temple of Aphrodite into a carriage-house for the praetorian prefect."[221] While Malalas is by no means a good source for fourth-century history, he is fairly reliable on public buildings and monuments.[222] He remarks that the gaming hall continued to be known as "the temple" in his own day, and that the next street was still known as "the deer," which is explained by an earlier passage describing the temple of

---

218. For Paulinus's knowledge of Rufinus's *HE*, see Pellegrino 1961, 16–19; Lamirande 1983, 25, 105; Mohrmann and Bastiansen 1975, 309, 314.
219. *V. Ambrosii* 31.
220. Jer. *Ep.* 60. 16. 3.
221. καρουχαρεῖον τοῦ ἐπάρχου τῶν πραιτωρίων, Mal. *Chron.* p. 267. 81 Thurn = p. 345 Bonn.
222. Moffat in Jeffreys 1990, 87–109.

Artemis as possessing (appropriately enough for the goddess of hunting) a statue of a deer.[223] According to a third passage of Malalas, in 324 Constantine had deprived these same three temples of their revenues.[224] In consequence, they must soon have ceased to be functioning cult centers, and by the 380s may well have been in effect disused.[225] The initiative to dismantle them probably came from his aggressively anti-pagan praetorian prefect Maternus Cynegius rather than Theodosius himself ("Like the Duke of Plaza Toro, Theodosius the Great led his regiment from the rear").[226] In this case a connection with Cynegius is strongly suggested by the fact that the temple of Aphrodite became the carriage-house of the praetorian prefect. These temple conversions in Constantinople cannot be later than Cynegius's death in 388, and such scandalous news is bound to have reached the West. When the two texts are brought together, the coincidence in detail is surely striking: a church/temple turned into a stable by/for a praetorian prefect.

If there is any basis to the threat reported by Paulinus, the pagan prefect of the 390s was just threatening to do to a Christian church what the Christian prefect of the 380s had actually done to a pagan temple. That threats were believed to have been made is borne out by Ambrose's remark about "faithless and sacrilegious men threatening the churches of the Lord with cruel persecution,"[227] though, once again, he leaves these pagans unnamed. The Malalan parallel lends some support to the threat about the stable and its attribution to Flavian. But it makes little sense to attribute it to Arbogast as well as Flavian. Paulinus apparently thought of Flavian and Arbogast as a pair, his wicked pagans. He uses the identical formula, simply reversing the order of the names: *Arbogastes tunc comes et Flavianus praefectus*. As so often elsewhere, Paulinus is just adding color and specificity to a general remark of Ambrose.

Was Arbogast even a pagan? So it has generally been assumed—on the evidence of Paulinus. But the only other text to say so is Orosius, who undoubtedly drew on Paulinus (p. 109). Two texts suggest that he was actually a Christian. According to John of Antioch, Arbogast was the son of Bauto, and Ambrose implies that Bauto was a Christian.[228] Paulinus himself records an anecdote that supports this assumption. According to an eyewitness, Arbogast once proudly told a Frankish prince at a banquet that Bishop Ambrose was a close personal friend with whom he often dined. "That explains your victories, Count," replied the Frank, "because you are dear to a man who says 'stand still' to the sun, and it stands still."[229] Whether or not he was a Christian, to have enjoyed so long and successful a career in the service of Gratian and Theodosius, Bauto must have had good relations with Christian courts. Outside these two very

---

223. Malalas p. 221. 74 Thurn = p. 292 Bonn.

224. ἐκέλευσεν ἀχρηματίστους τοῦ λοιποῦ διαμεῖναι, Mal. p. 248. 59 = p. 324. 5 = p. 176 Aus.

225. Mango 1985, 18, 33–34.

226. Brown 1971, 106. Matthews 1975, 140–42; Fowden 1978, 62–64.

227. *Expl. Psalm.* 36. 25, p. 91. 4–19 Petschenig; cf. Paschoud II. 2 (1979), 498.

228. Jo. Ant. F 280. 15–18 Roberto (187M); Ambr. *Ep. extra coll.* 10. 3 (57 Maur.); *PLRE* i. 159 (unnecessarily doubting the relationship).

229. Paul. *Vita Ambros.* 30; Ambros. *De obitu Val.* 26–27.

dubious passages of Paulinus, there is no basis for seeing him as a pagan, much less the ringleader of a pagan rebellion.

There are in fact good reasons for treating the entire context of this second anecdote as suspect. Flavian and Arbogast made their threat (Paulinus alleges) "because the church had spurned gifts from an emperor who had polluted himself with sacrilege (*qui se sacrilegio miscuerat*), and refused to grant him the privilege of praying with the church." Yet it is simply incredible, above all in Ambrose's absence, that the church of Milan would dare to spurn (*respuo*) gifts from an emperor residing in the city and refuse to allow him to attend services. Even Ambrose himself was never so bold. The "polluted himself with sacrilege" is taken verbatim (right down to the pluperfect tense) from the letter Ambrose wrote Theodosius immediately after hearing of the victory at the Frigidus (*qui se sacrilegio miscuisset*),[230] where the reference is clearly to the mysterious gifts he makes so much of in the letter to Eugenius. The "spurning" of these gifts is inferred from another passage in the letter to Eugenius, two questions Ambrose addresses Eugenius: "How will you offer gifts to Christ?" and "How will the priests of Christ distribute your gifts?"[231] But in Ambrose these are *rhetorical* questions. What he means is, having given presents to prominent pagans, how will you have the face to offer gifts to the church, and what will the church do faced with accepting such tainted gifts? These are in fact exactly the same rhetorical questions Ambrose had addressed to Valentinian II in 384, when he heard of Symmachus's embassy to court: "What will you answer the priest who says to you 'The Church does not want your gifts because you have adorned pagan temples with gifts; the altar of Christ spurns (*respuit*) your gifts.'" Once again, Ambrose did not have any specific gifts in mind. The questions are rhetorical because he knew that the church could not afford to "spurn" an emperor or his gifts. That is why he made himself scarce when he heard that Eugenius was planning to come to Milan. Paulinus turned these rhetorical questions into real gifts really spurned. Once again, these two letters of Ambrose were undoubtedly his source, but (as before) he goes far beyond what Ambrose himself had either said or implied.

Ambrose's letters were not only Paulinus's source but (together with Rufinus) his *only* source for this entire episode.[232] In 412/13 when he wrote his *Life*, he was living in North Africa (probably Carthage),[233] unable to consult potential informants in Milan. In the case of Theodosius's penance for the Thessalonica massacre the question of additional sources does not arise since the confrontation in church never happened. As for the restoration of the subsidies, what source could a humble deacon have had for the composition of a senatorial embassy that addressed the emperor in his consistory? Eugenius, Flavian, and Arbogast had all died as traitors, and no one involved in

---

230. *Ep. extra coll.* 2. 2 (= Maur. 61).
231. *Quomodo offeres dona tua Christo?* § 8; McLynn 1994, 351–52.
232. The few other sources Paulinus names are cited as witnesses to "miracles": V. Ambr. 14, 44, 46, 47, 50, 51, 52, 54 Kaniecka 1928, 11; Palanque 1933, 412.
233. *PCBE* ii. 2. 1655–58.

the senatorial embassies to Eugenius was likely to give interviews. Not even Ambrose himself is likely to have known who said what in Eugenius's consistory.

No statement by Paulinus based on an extant letter of Ambrose that goes beyond what Ambrose says merits credence. The only one we are concerned with here is his claim that Eugenius restored the subsidies. If Eugenius did *not* restore the subsidies, then Paulinus's identification of those who persuaded him to do what he did not do *cannot* be authentic. There may be some basis to the threats, though since Ambrose's own reference to those who threatened the church gives no names, once again suspicion is in order. It is especially suspicious that he twice offers the same pair of names as Rufinus. It looks as if Flavian and Arbogast were the only pagans Paulinus could name. In all probability both his stories about Flavian's aggressive pagan behavior are fabrications.

To return to Ambrose's letter to Eugenius, over and above the problems already raised, it simply cannot be what it appears to be, the actual letter Ambrose wrote Eugenius just before leaving Milan in spring 393. While purporting to explain to Eugenius why he was leaving, what the letter actually does is justify Ambrose's conduct under Eugenius to Theodosius. Nor would it be the first time Ambrose had fabricated such a self-justification. The clearest parallel is *Ep.* 30 to Valentinian II, purporting to describe his second embassy to Maximus at some date between 385 and 387. Yet instead of describing the second embassy, most of the letter is devoted to the first embassy in 383, and represents Ambrose addressing Maximus with a frankness, not to say impudence that is not only incredible in itself but would have completely torpedoed the peace he was supposed to be negotiating. What Ambrose actually did during this embassy was skilfully persuade Maximus not to invade Italy in 383 when it was at his mercy. He could not possibly have done this by taking the defiant approach so vividly described in the letter. What Valentinian must have wanted to hear at the time Ambrose is supposed to have been writing was the outcome of the *second* embassy, of which the letter says virtually nothing. There can be little doubt that, while some details may derive from a genuine letter written at the time, in its present form *Ep.* 30 was completely rewritten for publication after Maximus's death to present the bishop as a fearless and unrelenting opponent of the usurper.[234] The truth is that, while Valentinian II left for Thessalonica when Maximus seized Milan, Ambrose remained there and so must have worked out a modus vivendi with the new regime, a relationship about which both his own writings and Paulinus's biography observe a discreet (and understandable) silence.

Much the same is surely true of the letter to Eugenius. We have seen that Ambrose left Milan to avoid confrontations with emperors on at least three other occasions. On none of those occasions did he explain or justify his absence, evasively pleading illness or other engagements instead. On this occasion, burned by his blunder with Maximus,

---

234. So Liebeschuetz 2005, 349–57, whose arguments I accept and summarize.

he was presumably planning to stay away until the issue between Theodosius and Eugenius was decided. So why offer an explanation that would have made it impossible for him to return if Eugenius won, thus rendering the stratagem pointless? Above all, why so elaborate an explanation? If Eugenius had really restored the subsidies, whether directly or indirectly, he obviously knew what he had done and the merest hint would have sufficed. Why then the long review of earlier attempts to get the subsidies restored, fully a third of the letter?

This review suggests that the letter was written for a wider audience that might not be familiar with the history of the question. Here we have another parallel among Ambrose's imperial epistles, the long letter he sent Theodosius about the affair of the synagogue at Callinicum. The local bishop had led a band of monks to loot and burn the synagogue, and Theodosius angrily ordered him to rebuild it and the monks to be punished. Ambrose urged the emperor to cancel both rebuilding and punishment. Theodosius agreed to drop the rebuilding, but refused to pardon the monks. In the first eight sections, as Liebeschuetz points out,[235] Ambrose "provides information which the emperor had already discussed with his advisers, and even acted on. It is information which the emperor did not need, but which a wider readership would need." He suggests that this part of the letter "was from the first intended for the general public as well as the emperor." More probably it was added or rewritten for publication. In the version published in Ambrose's collected correspondence, an edition supervised by Ambrose himself,[236] the letter closes with the threat that, unless the emperor pardons the Christians who burned down the synagogue, Ambrose will raise the matter in church.[237] That this is a later addition is proved by the fact that a small group of letters omitted from the collected correspondence preserves a different version that lacks this final paragraph.

Ominously enough, the group omitted from the published correspondence also includes the letter to Eugenius. The most significant other letter in this group is a brief missive to Theodosius written immediately after the Frigidus, responding to the accusation that Ambrose had left Milan because he did not believe that Theodosius would defeat Eugenius. That is to say, it was not Eugenius who had demanded an explanation for Ambrose's absence from Milan, but Theodosius. Ambrose indignantly denies the accusation, claiming that he never had a moment's doubt "that divine support would be on the side of your Piety," and that the true reason for his departure was "avoiding the presence of one who was contaminated with sacrilege."[238] Suspiciously enough, the letter to Eugenius provides a detailed (if allusive) justification of this cryptic claim.

As for Ambrose's insistence that he had refused to respond to any of Eugenius's letters from the beginning of the reign, clearly he protests too much. As if aware that

235. Liebeschuetz 2005, 96.
236. Liebeschuetz 2005, 27.
237. *Ep.* 74. 33 (= Maur. 40) = *Ep. extra coll.* 1a, with Liebeschuetz 2005, 111 n. 2.
238. *Ep. extra coll.* 2. 1, with Liebeschuetz 2005, 216 n. 2.

so sweeping a claim was implausible (and easily refutable), he concedes that "when there was occasion to perform my duty on behalf of anxious individuals, I both wrote letters and made petitions."[239] But why would he take such pains to make so fine a distinction when writing to Eugenius himself? The truth is that he was really writing for the eyes of Theodosius, attempting to show that he had kept his dealings with the usurper's court to the absolute minimum consonant with his episcopal duties and his responsibilities to others.

As for the "sacrilege," this is the dubious claim that Eugenius gave money to pagans. But on Ambrose's own evidence, the gifts he makes so much of were not discovered till "later," later (presumably) than the two embassies he refused. So when would that be? The first of these embassies presumably approached Eugenius soon after his accession in 392, and the second a year later, after his arrival in Milan, when no hope remained of accommodation with Theodosius, and pagan aristocrats might have hoped that he would now be more willing to seek the support of Italian landowners.[240] If the gifts were later than this, that must have been *after* Ambrose had left Milan. So they cannot have been the reason he left. The letter cannot have been written at the time it purports to have been written.

In the immediate aftermath of Eugenius's defeat, accused of deserting his post by Theodosius, Ambrose was naturally anxious to justify his conduct under the usurper's regime. Not daring openly to accuse Eugenius of restoring the subsidies when contemporaries who were present would have known that he had not, he contented himself with vague innuendo. But when considering which of his letters to include in a collected edition after Theodosius's death, he decided to omit both accusation and defense. In imitation of the younger Pliny's letters, Ambrose's were published in ten books, those in Bks i–ix addressed to a variety of friends and colleagues on religious subjects, while Bk x consisted of letters addressed to emperors or concerning public affairs: the Altar of Victory debate, the Callinicum affair, the conflict with the empress Justina, the finding of the remains of the martyrs Gervasius and Protasius, and his oration on the death of Theodosius. That it is to say, Bk x collects in one place all the most spectacular episodes of Ambrose's public career.[241] The letter to Eugenius and the letter to Theodosius after the Frigidus clearly did not belong in this context. Both are evasive responses to an embarrassing accusation that may have served their immediate purpose of conciliating the victorious Theodosius, but added nothing to the list of Ambrose's triumphs. Much wiser to omit all mention of Eugenius from the published correspondence. But the letters Ambrose himself had prudently omitted were found among his papers and published by some admiring (but politically naive) disciple, perhaps (as Zelzer plausibly suggests) his deacon and future biographer Paulinus, who certainly knew and quotes from them.[242]

---

239. *Ep. extra coll.* 10. 12 (Liebeschuetz's translation).
240. So (e.g.) Matthews 1975, 240.
241. On Bk x, see the detailed discussion in Zelzer 1983, xix–lxxi.
242. See Zelzer 1982, lxxxiv–lxxvi.

6: PROIECTUS AND THE "TEMPLE OF HERCULES"

Three other texts have been adduced in support of the claim that Eugenius restored the subsidies. First, Zosimus's claim that Theodosius withdrew public funds from the pagan cults. According to Chastagnol, he did this because Eugenius had restored them.[243] But it is much more likely that Zosimus mistakenly ascribed Gratian's measures to Theodosius (p. 645). Second, Rufinus's elaborate description of Flavian performing public sacrifice before the Frigidus. For those who believed that Eugenius restored the subsidies, it was natural to see this text as proof that he also revoked Theodosius's ban on sacrifice. But as we shall see in the following chapter, Rufinus's description may well be pure fiction. Even granted that Flavian performed such a ritual, by itself that proves no more than that the Theodosian ban was not strictly enforced. Flavian was after all a praetorian prefect. Who was going to stop him?

The final text is the now famous fragmentary dedication of Numerius Proiectus that formed the starting point for Bloch's 1945 study. On the standard interpretation, Proiectus restored a temple of Hercules in Ostia in his capacity as prefect of the corn supply "under the emperors Theodosius, Arcadius and Eugenius."[244] The prefect of the corn supply was a subordinate of the prefect of Rome, at this time the younger Flavian. Everything seemed to fit. The dedication is securely dated to the reign of Eugenius, apparently attests the restoration of a pagan temple, and names an official who answered to one of the Nicomachi Flaviani. Here, it has always been assumed, is unmistakable epigraphic proof of the pagan revival. Chastagnol added a further argument, claiming that the temple must have been restored at public expense and so provided concrete proof that Eugenius restored the subsidies.

The date is secure, but none of the other assumptions. In the first place, we have seen that there is no basis for the argument about the use of public funds. More important, Douglas Boin has reexamined the question of the site hitherto identified as the temple of Hercules Invictus at Ostia, a large, central structure near the Forum,[245] and identified it instead as a temple of Vulcan, the principal god of the city. Of course, that does not in itself exclude the possibility that Proiectus restored a temple of Hercules somewhere else in the neighborhood. But there is no literary or epigraphic evidence for any sort of temple of Hercules at Ostia.

As for the Proiectus dedication, it is often carelessly stated that he restored a *temple* of Hercules. But all the surviving text says is that he restored the "*cella* of Hercules." Assuming that *cella* refers to the room inside a temple where the image of the god stood, Bloch claimed that "*cella Herculis* is equivalent to *templum Herculis*," and since

---

243. Zos. iv. 59. 2–3; Chastagnol 1960, 163; 1969, 143.
244. *AE* 1948, 127; for a photo, Bloch in Momigliano 1963, pl. #.
245. Briefly, Meiggs 1973, 347–50; see now Boin 2010.

then scholars have stated that Proiectus restored a temple as though this was a straight-forward, solidly documented fact.[246] It is true that, in literary texts, it is not uncommon for the part to be used for the whole (*carina* or *puppis* for *navis*), the figure known as synecdoche. But *cella* is *never* used for *templum*, not even in the poets.[247] In his *Fasti* (e.g.) Ovid frequently has occasion to mention temples. The word *templum* itself he uses fifty-two times, *aedes* sixteen times, *delubrum* eight times, *fanum* three times, and *sacellum* twice. The metrically so convenient *cella* not once. Bloch cited a single text from the *Acta* of the Arval Brethren, *ante cellam Iunonis reg(inae)*. Actually this is a regular formula in these *Acta*, but what Bloch failed to notice is that each time it is preceded by the words *in Capitolio*. Clearly the reference is to the temple of Jupiter Optimus Maximus on the Capitol, which had three *cellae*, one each for Jupiter, Juno, and Minerva (there are references throughout the *Acta* to offerings made *in Capitolio Iovi Iunoni Minervae*).[248] In this context the formula means exactly what it says: certain rituals of the Arvals were performed in front of the *cella* of Juno (not either of the other two *cellae*) at the temple of the Capitoline Triad.

The word *cella* is also used in a variety of quite different senses, usually of small rooms (a wine cellar, a poor man's hut, a prostitute's cubicle, a monk's cell) but also of large public areas. One much-discussed case is the supposedly unsurpassable *cella soliaris* in the Baths of Caracalla, where the epithet means equipped with *solia*, baths.[249] Four late antique inscriptions from African baths refer to the restoration or refurbishing of a *cella soliaris*. Other late antique inscriptions from baths refer to the restoration of a *cella natatoria*, a *cella balnearum*, *cella thermarum*, *cella unctuaria*, *cella frigidarii*, and *cella vestibula*.[250] Pliny describes the large and spacious *cella frigidaria* in the baths of his Laurentine villa; and also the *cella frigidaria* of his Tuscan villa, which contained a sizable pool.[251] Clearly *cella* was the standard term for a variety of rooms or halls in bath complexes, to judge from the frequency with which they were refurbished in late antiquity, often elaborately decorated and adorned.

Cella Herculis cannot refer to a temple of Hercules, nor would it be a natural way even to refer to the *cella* in a temple of Hercules. In all probability what Proiectus restored was a hall in one of the many bath complexes at Ostia,[252] perhaps, as Boin suggests, the baths at the Porta Marina gate, where in the 1770s Gavin Hamilton found four statue groups representing Labors of Hercules, now in the Vatican.[253] It would be natural for a hall in a bath complex decorated with the labors of Hercules to have been

246. E.g., Bloch 1945, 202, 234; Chastagnol 1960, 164; 1969, 143; Matthews 1975, 241; Szidat 1979, 499; Ward-Perkins 1984, 88; Hedrick 2000, 45; Leppin 2003, 209; and so on.
247. As can be seen at a glance from the entry in *TLL* iii (1906–12).
248. Scheid 1998, 99a20, and seven other places, with the note on p. 288, l. 20; Scheid 12c11, and passim.
249. *HA* Carac. 9. 4, with DeLaine 1987, 147–56.
250. All listed in Fagan 1999, 368–69; DeLaine 1987, 156.
251. Plin. *Epp.* ii. 17. 11; v. 6. 25.
252. Listed in Meiggs 1973, 404–20, 590; Fagan 1999, 402.
253. Palma 1978–80, 137–56.

known as *Cella Herculis*. Proiectus's restorations had nothing whatever to do with any pagan revival.

To pull the threads together, there is no serious evidence that Eugenius revoked or modified in any way the anti-pagan measures of either Gratian or Theodosius. As we shall see in the next chapter, Augustine and Prudentius make no distinction between the religious policies of Eugenius and the pious Maximus, and, with the exception of the self-exculpatory letter to Eugenius, no other text of Ambrose does either.

3

THE FRIGIDUS

1

In his continuation of Eusebius's *Ecclesiastical History*, written in 402/3, Rufinus of Aquileia gives a vivid account of the confrontation between Theodosius and Eugenius by the river Frigidus. The pagans (*pagani*) prepared for battle with endless sacrifices, Theodosius by fasting and prayers. Flavian prophesied victory for Eugenius by examining sheep entrails, and then took his own life because his prophecies proved false. Theodosius threw down his weapons in mid battle and called upon God for help, whereupon a miraculous wind arose, turning the enemy's weapons back upon themselves. Despite the brave efforts of Arbogast, God was against him (*adverso deo*), and "more glory accrued to the devout sovereign's victory from the failed expectations of the pagans than from the death of the usurper (*tyrannus*), the pagans whose empty hopes and false prophecies meant that the punishment of those among them who died was less grievous than the shame of those who survived."

Rufinus's account proved influential, among contemporaries and successors as well as modern historians. According to Hedrick, most of the Greek sources for Eugenius "*confirm* that the usurpation had some religious connotation."[1] But all the most widely cited Christian accounts of the battle (those of Augustine, Sozomen, and Theodoret) are derived from Rufinus.[2] This is not to say that Rufinus is their only source, or that they follow him slavishly. Augustine, for example, adds a quotation from Claudian. But even Augustine follows Rufinus more closely than he admits. For example, he claims to have his account of the miraculous wind from "soldiers who were present" (*milites...qui aderant*), a claim taken literally by many critics. Yet he borrowed this very phrase from Rufinus's "officers who were present" (*qui aderant duces*).[3] All three undoubtedly derive the basic outline of their accounts—a victory

---

1. Rufin. *HE* xi. 33, tr. Amidon; Hedrick 2000, 72 (my emphasis).
2. Theodoret's indirectly, through Sozomen or a Greek translation of Rufinus. The question of this Greek translation is linked to the question of the lost *Ecclesiastical History* of Gelasius of Caesarea (for a useful survey, see Amidon 1997, xiii–xvii). The standard view is that much of Rufinus's narrative down to the death of Valens was translated from Gelasius, but van Nuffelen 2002 has now made it probable that the history ascribed to Gelasius is a pseudonymous compilation of the mid fifth century. Fortunately, the controversy does not affect the chapters discussed here, which are indisputably original work by Rufinus.
3. Duval 1966; Courcelle 1969 (this important study will be drawn upon further below).

over paganism won by prayer—from Rufinus. Thus we should not be overly impressed by the fact that we have four different witnesses to this version. Augustine, Sozomen, and Theodoret add seemingly significant details, but (as we shall see) these are embellishments rather than genuine facts, based on theological considerations rather than independent factual sources.

Back in the days when people took it for established fact that the Frigidus represented the last pagan stand in the West, it was assumed that contemporaries saw it as a confrontation between paganism and Christianity. But there is far less authentic evidence than often assumed for treating Eugenius's brief reign as favorable to paganism (Ch. 2), and in chapter 8 we shall see that the most important single source for the traditional assumption, the *Carmen contra paganos* (*CCP*), has nothing whatever to do with his revolt. With that eliminated, Christian accounts of the battle have become the principal remaining source for the very existence of a "pagan revival."

Modern studies of the battle itself have been mainly concerned to trace the course of events.[4] Earlier accounts treated all sources equally as transmitters of details that could be combined into a composite picture: a battle that lasted for two days, with the first day going in Eugenius's favor and the second, thanks to the miraculous wind, turning the tables. Rufinus, Socrates, and Sozomen were faulted for offering a single day, but it is only Theodoret, the latest and (as we shall see) overall least trustworthy of all surviving sources,[5] who specifies two days. I am inclined to agree with Matthias Springer's recent contention that the sources are simply not of a nature or quality to permit such a reconstruction, and this chapter incidentally advances new considerations in favor of this position.

Most modern critics have taken Christian representations of the Frigidus more or less literally as historical narratives that describe the defeat of a dangerous pagan uprising, reflecting a perspective unique to the special circumstances of Eugenius's rebellion. There are problems with this assumption, nor is it enough to concede (as often done) that some of the writers may have exaggerated. The distortion that must be allowed for goes much deeper than simple exaggeration. The truth is that all these accounts are stylized in ways that call into question their claim to be considered historical narratives at all in the modern sense.

In the first place, impiety of one sort or another (dishonoring the gods, robbing temples, magic practices) had long been one of the stock accusations against tyrannical rulers or enemies of the state.[6] To give a single early illustration, Augustus boasted that he had replaced ornaments that his defeated rival M. Antonius "had taken into his private possession" in all the temples of Asia.[7] But such accusations came to assume a

---

4. The basic studies are Seeck and Veith 1913; Paschoud, *Zosime* 2. 2 (1979), 474–500; Springer in Bratož 1996, 45–93; and Paschoud 1997, 277–80. For a balanced recent account, Leppin 2003, 216–20.
5. Not counting later and derivative sources. For a version that attempts to rehabilitate Theodoret, Brasseur 1938.
6. For a collection of texts, Ziegler 1970, 1–25.
7. *Res Gestae Divi Augusti* 24.

sharper and more specific focus in the wars of Christian emperors. It was in the age of Constantine that the term *tyrannus* took on the specialized sense "usurper," often with the additional connotation of a persecutor of Christians.[8] Indeed, as time passed the connotations of impiety and persecution came increasingly to dominate, as illustrated by the fact that both Hilary of Poitiers and Lucifer of Cagliari explicitly style the pious but Arian Constantius II *tyrannus*,[9] despite the unimpeachable legality of his claim (as a legitimate son of Constantine) to the throne. And Athanasius comes close to doing so by describing him as inflicting more cruel punishments on the orthodox "than earlier tyrants and persecutors."[10]

Eusebius describes Maxentius "putting his trust in devices of magic rather than the goodwill of his subjects," while Constantine "relied on the help that comes from God," adding the illustration of Moses' victory over the chariots of Pharaoh and (most famously) Constantine's mysterious vision in the sky. Lactantius too, after describing Maxentius's recourse to the Sibylline books, tells the story of Constantine having the sign of the cross inscribed on his army's shields.[11] Eusebius also recurs again and again to Licinius's hostility to Christianity contrasted with Constantine's piety. The fact is that Eusebius was prepared to label any and all rivals of Constantine as persecutors.[12] As MacCormack put it, "In the Christian empire of the fourth century the enemy of religion and the enemy of the state were explicitly united as one."[13] Nor were even pagan writers unaffected by the trend: two probably pagan panegyrists of Constantine condemn Maxentius and his troops alike as "impious." Since the emperor's power was thought to come from God, it was impious for anyone to oppose the legitimate emperor of the day.[14]

It says much for the power of such propaganda that modern historians have been so reluctant to accept that Magnentius, defeated by Constantius II at Mursa in 351, was a Christian, preferring partisan literary sources to the contemporary coinage.[15] The most instructive illustration is the story that Constantius saw a vision of the cross in the sky before the battle. This is one of those rare cases where it is possible to trace the evolution of such a story.[16] Cyril, bishop of Jerusalem, wrote a (surviving) letter to Constantius, who was at the time in the West preparing for his campaign against Magnentius, telling him that people in the Holy Land had seen a cross in the sky on 7 May 351. There is no reason to doubt that some striking meteorological phenomenon

---

8. Barnes 1996, 55–65; Neri 1997, 71–86; see Barnes 58–60 for the connotation "persecutor."
9. Hilary, *In Constantium* 7. 5; ib. 11. 3 brands his regime a *tyrannis*; *nostri temporis tyrannus*, according to Lucifer, *De non parcendo* 23. 35 (p. 240, G. F. Diercks [ed.] 1978); cf. ib. 21. 44 (p. 236); ib. 31. 9 (p. 254); *Moriundum esse* 3. 26 (p. 270).
10. Athan. *Hist. Arian.* 40. 2.
11. Euseb. *HE* ix. 9. 3–5; *VC* i. 27–32, and i. 36. 1; Lact. *MP* 44.
12. *HE* x. 8–9; *VC* i. 57; ii. 18 and 26–27 (a letter of Constantine himself); iii. 1–3.
13. MacCormack 1981, 150.
14. *Pan. Lat.* xii (ix). 17. 2; *Pan. Lat.* iv (x). 6. 2 and 7. 1; Burdeau 1964, 39.
15. Ziegler 1970, 53–73; Bastien 1983, 268–72; Barnes 1993, 101–2; Rubin 1998, 124–41.
16. For more details, Chantraine 1993/94, 430–41; Bleckmann 1999, 58–68.

was so interpreted by Christians on that day, presumably over a very limited geographical area. Cyril interpreted it as a sign of divine favor, an indication that with God as his ally (*symmachon*) Constantius would carry the standard (*tropaion*) of the cross.[17] The military metaphors make it likely that Cyril had the coming campaign against Magnentius in mind. But according to Philostorgius, the cross was also visible during the battle of Mursa (28 September), inspiring Constantius and his army with invincible bravery, but terrifying Magnentius and his troops "inasmuch as they were utterly given over to the worship of demons."[18] Obviously, it is most unlikely that this rare meteorological phenomenon happened on both 7 May and 28 September in two widely separated locations, and there can be little doubt that the second occurrence is a doublet of the first. Philostorgius's final phrase cannot be taken seriously as evidence. Even if we allow that Magnentius himself might have had pagan leanings, it would be absurd to suppose that his entire army shared them.[19] If Constantius was fighting, as the Arian Philostorgius believed, under the banner of the cross, it was axiomatic that Magnentius must have been an enemy of the true faith. Naturally, there is no trace of this version in the orthodox ecclesiastical historians, for whom it was Constantius who was the heretic.[20] It is in effect an Arian counter-version of the vision of Constantine.

Magnus Maximus, a man of deep Christian piety and unimpeachable orthodoxy,[21] posed more of a problem. Having been initially recognized by Theodosius, he was not even technically a usurper.[22] But if he was defeated by another Christian emperor of unimpeachable orthodoxy, there had to be a reason. According to Orosius, though a lesser warrior, Theodosius excelled Maximus in faith alone. Ambrose implies that God allowed Theodosius to defeat Maximus because he was soft on Jews (a warning to Theodosius not to follow the same path).[23] According to the deacon Paulinus, Theodosius's penance for the Thessalonica massacre "prepared a favorable victory for him," evidently referring to the defeat of Eugenius. For the orthodox ecclesiastical historians, it was for his "treachery" in "murdering" Gratian that Theodosius took justified vengeance on Maximus.[24] The Arian Philostorgius says nothing about treachery and attacked the orthodox Gratian instead. He also depreciates Theodosius by explaining that he entrusted the campaign to his generals, as though he did not take the field against Maximus in person.[25]

---

17. Cyr. Jerus. *Ep. Const.* in *PG* xxxiii. 1165–76 at 1172. For later references, Socr. *HE* ii. 28. 22; Soz. *HE* iv. 5; *Const. Cpol.* s.a. 351 (*Chron. Min.* i. 238); *Chron. Pasch.* s.a. 354 (trans. Whitby and Whitby, Liverpool 1989, 31 with n. 94); Theoph. *Chron.* A.M. 5847 (pp. 69–70 Mango-Scott).

18. Philost. *HE* iii. 26, p. 52. 7 Bidez.

19. Rubin 1998, 133–41 implausibly argues that Magnentius was trying to placate a largely pagan army.

20. The only other text to associate the vision with the battle of Mursa is the *Chronicon Paschale*, at this point deriving from an Arian-influenced source (see Whitby and Whitby 1989, 31 n. 94).

21. The prime document on his orthodoxy is his letter *Contra Arianos* (*Coll. Avell.* 39), quoted by Rufinus, *HE* xi. 16.

22. Brandt 1999, 58–68; Vera 1975, 277–82; Barnes 1996, 64.

23. *sola fide maior*, Oros. vii. 35. 2; Ambrose, *Ep.* 40 (74). 22–26; Homes Dudden 2 (1935), 375.

24. Paulin. *Vita Ambros.* 24; Rufin. *HE* xi. 17; Soc. v. 11 and 13; Soz. vii. 13–14; Theod. v. 15; see too Paulinus, *Vita Ambr.* 19. On Gratian's posthumous rehabilitation, McLynn 1994, 155.

25. Philostorgius, *HE* x. 5 and 8.

A second motif relevant to accounts of the Frigidus campaign is that emperors who enjoyed the favor of God are regularly said to have defeated their enemies without fighting, without shedding blood, or by prayer alone. It is often said that the first examples of the motif occur in Ambrose, ranging from the *De fide* of 378 (victory comes *fide magis…quam virtute militum*) to his obituary on Theodosius in 395.[26] But there are earlier examples. Eusebius writes of Constantine continuing to win "his usual bloodless victories" into old age, and a dedication to Constantine by a governor of Thrace praises him for winning "bloodless victories from West to East."[27] Again, we find occasional examples in pagans. The Gallic rhetor Nazarius praises Constantine for defeating Maxentius in "a victory so happy and bloodless that you would not believe that they struggled in a dangerous war, but only that punishment was demanded from the impious"; and Themistius writes of Valens defeating the usurper Procopius "without spilling blood."[28]

The claim is made both in general terms and in accounts of actual imperial victories (where it is naturally often untrue, or at any rate a gross exaggeration). Paulinus of Nola's 26th poem, written under the threat of barbarian invasion,[29] illustrates the theme at length, citing a host of biblical illustrations (Joshua, Hezekiah, and Daniel): "arms have always needed faith, but faith has never needed arms." According to Paulinus, the sign of the unconquered cross affords surer protection than legions and walls.[30] Sermons 85 and 86 of Maximus of Turin, likewise written under the threat of invasions, make the same point, citing David, who slew Goliath "not with an iron spear but with a spiritual sword."[31] As the *exempla* cited suggest, the ultimate source of this conviction is the Old Testament: "The Lord said to Joshua, 'See, I have handed Jericho over to you'"; "The Lord gave victory to David wherever he went"; "the people of Judah prevailed, because they relied on the Lord," and many similar passages.[32] On the other hand, whenever Israel suffers a defeat, it is because its people turned to other gods: "The Israelites did what was evil in the sight of the Lord, and the Lord gave them into the hand of Midian." Ten verses later we discover that they had been "paying reverence to the gods of the Amorites."

To turn to specific late fourth-/early fifth-century examples, according to Rufinus, Chrysostom, Paulinus of Nola, Orosius, and Theodoret, Theodosius won a

---

26. Ambrose, *De fide* i. 3; *Ep.* 51. 6; *De obitu Theod.* 7 and 10; Zecchini 1984, 391–404; Heim in Duval 1974, 267–81; much material too (though lamentably ignorant of scholarship in English) in Heim 1992.
27. Eus. *VC* vi. 53; *SEG* 51 (2001), 695; Tantillo 1999, 73–95 at 81–83.
28. Naz. *Pan. Lat.* iv. 7. 1; Nazarius may have been a Christian: Nixon and Rodgers 1994, 334–42; Them. *Or.* vii. 9 (90a.4). The claim at *Or.* xvi. 19 (213A) that Theodosius defeated the Goths ἀναιμωτί is rather different, since the reference is to a negotiated surrender or treaty.
29. Probably written in 401, before the battle of Pollentia: Trout 1999, 118.
30. *Carm.* 26. 156–57, 103–10; Heim 1992, 293–301.
31. *Serm.* 85; B. Ramsey, *The Sermons of St. Maximus of Turin* (New York 1989), 205, 336, 345.
32. Joshua 6. 2; 8. 1; 10. 10; 11. 8; 2 Samuel 8. 6; 2 Chronicles 13. 18; 2 Chronicles 14. 12; and so on. This conception was in fact widespread in the ancient Near East: for a collection of texts and survey of the extensive modern literature, see Lori L. Rowlett, *Joshua and the Rhetoric of Violence* (Sheffield 1996), Ch. 4 and 5.

"bloodless" victory over Maximus. This is a half-truth at best. While his capture at Aquileia involved little fighting (perhaps the result of treachery), this was after two fierce and bloody earlier engagements, at Siscia and Poetovio, graphically described by a contemporary panegyrist.[33] Orosius goes on to claim that both Theodosius and Honorius won a series of victories both internal and external "spilling little or no blood" (vel nullo vel minimo sanguine).[34] According to Orosius again, Gildo the rebel count of Africa was defeated by his brother Mascezel by prayer, winning victory without war and vengeance without slaughter; and Honorius defeated the huge "pagan" army of Radagaisus in yet another bloodless victory.[35] According to Theodoret, Theodosius's troops did not receive any casualties after the miraculous wind at the Frigidus. According to Socrates (vii. 23), the defeat of the western usurper John in 423 was ascribed to the prayers of Theodosius II. Sulpicius Severus preserves the story that Constantius spent the battle of Mursa praying in a martyr-ion nearby.[36] The orthodox Severus is hostile to Constantius, accusing him of cow-ardice, but in all probability the original version simply ascribed victory to the emperor's prayers.[37] Valens's defeat at Adrianople was easy to explain: had he not been an Arian heretic?[38] And Julian (of course) had been a pagan. From one per-spective or another the pious (defined as orthodox) always win and the impious (whether pagan or heretic) always lose. More important, the converse is also true: those who win must be pious, and those who lose must be impious.

Finally, the very fact that what is at issue here is a detailed account of a battle should give us pause. After all, Rufinus was writing a history of the church. Obviously the outcome of certain battles was important to the church, but not battles in and of themselves. No battle is described so elaborately by any of the ecclesiastical historians as the Frigidus. No details are given of any of Constantine's victories. Battles were only of interest to ecclesiastical historians for the light they cast on the piety and orthodoxy of the victors.[39] It is worth taking a brief look at the only three battle descriptions we find (omitting the Arian Philostorgius's description of Constantius's victory at Mursa). First, Socrates's account of the struggle against the Arian Gaïnas in 400, where we have angels intervening and a sudden wind that destroyed Gaïnas's fleet. Second, Socrates's account (vii. 23) of how, thanks to the prayers of Theodosius II, an angel (disguised as a shepherd) led Aspar through the marshes surrounding Ravenna to

---

33. For the various versions of the capture, Nixon's notes in Nixon and Rodgers 1994, 510 n. 147. For Siscia and Poetovio, Pacatus, Pan. Theod. 34–36, with Nixon's notes.
34. Ruf. HE xi. 32; Chrys. PG 63. 491 (quoted below); Oros. vii. 35. 5–9; Theod. v. 15.
35. Oros. vii. 36. 2–5 and 37. 15.
36. Chron. ii. 38. 3; G. de Senneville-Grave, Sulpice Sévère: Chroniques (Paris 1999), 312, 448.
37. Nazarius describes Constantine's victory over Maxentius at the Milvian Bridge as "bloodless," Pan. Lat. iv (x). 7. 1. Like his daughter, Nazarius may have been a Christian (Nixon and Rodgers 1994, 334–42).
38. On the date of the conversion of the Visigoths (to Arianism), Thompson 1966, Ch. 4.
39. Or for the opposite; thus Sozomen (vii. 1–2) and Theodoret (iii. 20) devote quite a bit of space to the death of the Apostate Julian in battle.

defeat the usurper John in 425. Finally, there is Socrates's narrative of the Persian campaigns of Theodosius II, portrayed as religious wars provoked by persecution of the Christians in Persia. Once again, he emphasizes repeatedly that it was God who gave victory to the Romans, with the help of angelic intervention.[40] The one common feature all three share with the accounts of the Frigidus is that they attribute victory to the intervention of the God of the (orthodox) Christians.

Thus even without the miraculous wind, it was always likely that Theodosius's victory at the Frigidus would be represented, by the orthodox at any rate, as proof of his piety and the power of prayer. That was put beyond question by the mere fact of his victory. On the other side, the mere fact of his defeat proved Eugenius deficient in this area, and, pagan revival or no, the presence of the pagan Flavian at his right hand was the obvious place to look for an explanation. Without actually accusing Eugenius himself of paganism, Rufinus contrives to imply that, like Magnentius's troops in Philostorgius, his entire army consisted of pagans. Given the emphasis on Theodosius's "reliance on the aid that comes from true religion" (*verae religionis fretus auxilio*), the two references to the enemy as "the pagans" (*pagani*), the claim that when Theodosius began to force the Alpine passes "the demons were the first to flee," and not least the closing claim that Arbogast "strove in vain against God," incautious readers were likely to draw the conclusion that the Frigidus was a straightforward case of a Christian army fighting a pagan army. So Theodoret, for example, who represents the battle as a direct confrontation between Hercules and the cross. Sozomen did not go quite so far, but made the inference implicit but unstated in Rufinus that Eugenius was "by no means sincere in his profession of Christianity" (vii. 22. 4).

This is undoubtedly false. Eugenius himself was certainly a Christian, and so were most members of his court and many of his troops. As for the implication that Theodosius's entire army was Christian, that cannot be true either.[41] Much of the rank and file in the eastern army were barbarians, at this date predominantly Arians or pagans.[42] It may well be that, in general, soldiers were prepared to accept the religion of their commanders, but many of Theodosius's officers were still pagans. Until his sudden death shortly before the campaign, the man picked to command his cavalry was Richomer, a pagan. At least one of his federate commanders, Saul, was a pagan, and two others, Alaric and Gaïnas, were Arians. A number of senior eastern generals continued to be pagans or Arians well down into the fifth century.[43] It would be many years before the Romans would field an army that consisted entirely of orthodox Christians.

---

40. Soc. *HE* vi. 6 and vii. 18–20. Theodoret (v. 39) gives harrowing details of the sufferings of martyrs in Persia during this period, but nothing about the wars. Socrates' prolixity is no doubt in part explained by the influence of contemporary panegyrics and epic poems, three of which he cites by name: the *Gaïnea* of Eusebius Scholasticus and Ammonius (vi. 6. 35–37); and the empress Eudocia on the Persian wars (vii. 21. 7–8).

41. So Szidat 1979, 504–5; Leppin 2003, 216.

42. Tomlin 1998, 21–51; Lee 2007, 176–211.

43. Plinthas, Ardabur, Aspar, and the younger Ardabur (cos. 419, 427, 434, and 447) were all Arians, and Fravittas cos. 401, was a pagan.

2

Hitherto, historians have treated Rufinus's sentences about Flavian as straightforward reportage of hard facts that can be used to build up a detailed picture of his religious beliefs. According to Hedrick, for example, "Rufinus...*mentions* Flavian's *predilection* for sacrifice and the arts of prediction,"[44] as though he might have "mentioned" any number of other interests but just happened to pick these ones.

Let us take a closer look at all this apparently circumstantial detail in context and in the light of these literary and theological traditions. The account begins with the preparations of the two sides for the coming battle. Theodosius got ready by fasting and prayer and prostrating himself before the shrines of saints and martyrs. He also consulted John of Lycopolis, the same holy man he had consulted before marching against Maximus.[45] Rufinus then describes the pagan preparations:

> But the pagans, who are always giving fresh life to their errors with new ones (*qui errores suos novis semper erroribus animant*), renewed their sacrifices (*innovare sacrificia*) and stained Rome with the blood of their accursed victims, examining the entrails of cattle, and, from their foreknowledge based on these organs, announced that Eugenius was sure of victory. Flavian, who was prefect at the time, performed these rites according to his superstition and with enormous enthusiasm, and because of his assertions—for his reputation as a man of wisdom was very high—they were sure that Eugenius would prevail.

Taken out of context, with its references to "new errors" and "renewing sacrifices," this extract might well seem to support the widespread modern assumption that Flavian directed a general pagan revival. But read in context the picture is less clear-cut. Rufinus's point throughout is that the war was not won on the field of battle, but in the hearts of men. Just as Theodosius's preparations consisted of prayers and a prophecy by a Christian holy man (§§ 5–6), so too the pagans' preparations consisted of a prophecy, one based, in keeping with the nature of their beliefs, on the examination of a slaughtered animal's entrails. The first sentence might seem to imply indiscriminate sacrifice, but on closer examination its three elements—sacrifice, examination of entrails, and prophecy—describe, from a Christian viewpoint, the successive stages of a single practice: extispicy, the art of the *haruspex*. Of course, extispicy was not really prophecy, but a way of discovering whether a specific course of action under consideration, in this case the coming battle against Theodosius, had divine approval. Hyperbole aside, Rufinus is simply accusing Flavian of predicting Eugenius's victory

---

44. Hedrick 2000, 72 (obviously my italics).
45. More on John of Lycopolis below.

through extispicy. Rather than "revive the practice of sacrifice," *innovare sacrificia* should be translated "sacrifice again and again."[46]

Rufinus is not here describing anything so general as the revival of pagan sacrifice, nor is he even primarily interested in Flavian. His focus is on the folly of prophecy based on so futile a conception as animal sacrifice. He develops the point further by going on to describe Flavian killing himself in embarrassment at the failure of his prophecy. Rufinus is the only source to mention Flavian's suicide, which he seems to place *before* the battle, with the explanatory comment that he "judged that he deserved death because of his error rather than his crime." Modern scholars trying to reconstruct the sequence of events have understandably been puzzled. How can the prophecy have been falsified before the battle began? Assuming that the battle lasted for two days, some have inferred that Flavian killed himself after some minor engagement on the first day.[47] But why should he have abandoned hope before the final battle, and is the battle not supposed to have gone in Eugenius's favor on the first day? Paschoud's explanation is simply that Rufinus's account is muddled.[48] No, there is a much more revealing explanation.

We have only to follow Rufinus's own narrative, though it works on a theological rather than historical plane. After describing the prophecy, Rufinus continues as follows:

> But when Theodosius, confident in the assistance provided by true religion, began to force the Alpine passes, *the first to flee were the demons,* fearfully aware of how deceitfully they had received the many victims offered to them in vain (*primi... daemones in fugam versi*). Next were those who taught and professed those errors, especially Flavian, who was weighted with more shame than guilt.

In Rufinus's narrative Flavian's suicide follows, not the defeat of some contingent in Eugenius's army, but the flight of the demons to whom he had sacrificed in vain. Moderns naturally tend to gloss over references to demons in a historical narrative, but these demons play a key part in what Rufinus saw as the "true" sequence of events, a spiritual rather than merely narrative sequence. Flavian took his own life *not* (Rufinus claims) because Eugenius's troops were defeated in battle, but because he realized that his gods were deserting him. His account falls into two parts: first the falsification of the pagan prophecy of victory; then the (inevitable) pagan defeat in battle. Flavian, the pagan prophet, belonged in the first part. But these two parts are not consecutive on the chronological plane. Rufinus has no interest in specifying at which stage of the battle or hour of the day Flavian died. His entire account is more interpretation than

---

46. For *innovare* = *iterare*, see *TLL* vii. 1. 7 (1951), 1717.
47. E.g., Stein (1959), 217; King 1960, 88.
48. Paschoud 1979, 485.

narrative, on the Christian no less than the pagan side. Just as Theodosius wins by faith and prayers rather than fighting, so paganism loses by its intrinsic falsity rather than its inferior military prowess. In all probability no more was known about Flavian's death than the fact that he did not survive the Frigidus.

Let us turn now to the beginning of Sozomen's account of the rebellion:[49]

> A certain Eugenius, by no means sincere in his profession of Christianity, aspired to sovereignty and assumed the symbols of imperial power. He thought he would succeed in his enterprise because he was led on by the words of men who claimed to see the future by examining the livers of sacrificial victims and from the course of the stars. Men of the highest rank among the Romans were addicted to these things, notably Flavian, *then praetorian prefect*, a learned man active in politics. He was believed to be highly skilled in every form of prophecy. He persuaded Eugenius to take up arms, assuring him that he was destined for the throne, that he would be victorious in battle, and that the Christian religion would be abolished.

It should be clear that the entire passage is no more than an embellishment of Rufinus.[50] Over and above the general similarities between the two passages, both emphasize Flavian's prophetic expertise.[51] Sozomen even kept Rufinus's remark that Flavian was "prefect at the time" (*tunc praefecto* ~ ὁ τότε ὕπαρχος). Given his obvious debt to Rufinus, it is unlikely that his two additional details, Flavian's otherwise unattested astrological accomplishments and the predicted abolition of Christianity, derive from an independent source.[52] They are simply embellishments of Rufinus's general point about Flavian's prophetic expertise. Similarly, where Rufinus says only that "the pagans" thought Eugenius would defeat Theodosius because of these prophecies, Sozomen claims that he was led to seize the throne in the first place by Flavian's prophecies. This is demonstrably false. Eugenius did not seize the throne; he was chosen by Arbogast three months after the death of Valentinian II. The only area in which Sozomen offers genuine information not in Rufinus concerns the prophecies of John of Lycopolis, drawn from monastic sources (below).

The two remaining Rufinus-influenced accounts, those of Augustine and Theodoret, have attracted more attention than Rufinus himself. Both add details that, if based on genuine evidence, would have important implications for the idea of a pagan revival. These details are so attractive (not to say necessary) to true believers

49. Soz. *HE* vii. 22. 4–5.

50. See Hansen's preface in J. Bidez/G. C. Hansen, *Sozomenus Kirchengeschichte* (Berlin 1960), xlvii.

51. *magna enim erat eius in sapientia praerogativa* ~ ἐπιστήμη παντοδαπῆς μαντείας, where *praerogativa* is used in the general sense "distinction": *TLL* x. 2. 6. 797. 65–798. 38.

52. Rufinus seems to have been the only detailed source for the battle known to the ecclesiastical historians.

that few have questioned their credentials.[53] So (e.g.) Bloch, followed in many later studies:[54]

> Flavian emphasized the religious character of the coming battle. On the ledges which flanked the prospective battlefield he had set up statues of Jupiter with thunderbolts of pure gold. Standards with the picture of Hercules were carried before the army.

Hedrick recurs again and again to Flavian's "appeal to Jupiter at the battle of the Frigidus," and claims that Hercules "was singled out as a special patron of the pagan cause...at the Frigidus."[55] After pointing out that Jupiter and Hercules had been the protecting deities of Diocletian and Maximian, Bloch went on to follow Theodoret in characterizing the battle itself as a showdown between "Hercules and the Cross." On purely a priori grounds this is improbable in the highest degree. In the first place, while declaration of war in pagan times was preceded by consultation of the gods and sacrifice,[56] the Romans never went to war under the "standard" of Jupiter or any other god. That is a Christian perspective.[57] Second, the supposedly so significant *link* between Jupiter and Hercules is an entirely modern construction, based on Christian sources. Each deity is mentioned separately in one ancient text each: Augustine (Jupiter) and Theodoret (Hercules). No source says anything about "ledges which flanked the prospective battlefield."

Let us begin with Hercules. Theodoret does not actually specify standards: he simply refers to Hercules "leading" Eugenius's army.[58] Leppin has recently illustrated the technique of Socrates, Sozomen, and Theodoret by a comparison of their versions of, precisely, the battle of the Frigidus, concluding that "Theodoret's aspiration towards theological consistency has grave consequences for his reliability as a historical source. He has no qualms about stylizing or, to put it bluntly, of falsifying history."[59] To give a couple of illustrations, the night before the battle Theodosius is said to have dreamed that he saw two men in white raiment riding on white horses. After identifying themselves as John the Evangelist and Philip the Apostle, they told him they had been sent to fight on his side. A common soldier is said to have had the same dream.[60] Epiphanies of heroes and saints on white horses (in earlier Roman times

---

53. For Leppin 2003, 218, the stories are not necessarily false despite the lateness of the sources, and even the sceptical Courcelle (1969, 123) derived them from a common written source.
54. Bloch 1945, 235–36. So (e.g.) Thélamon 1981, 317, and already Palanque 1933, 285; more recently Ando 2001, 384; Potter 2004, 532.
55. Hedrick 2000, 70 and 51; cf. 45–46, 72, 229.
56. Beard, North, Price 1 (1998), 43–45.
57. As implicitly recognized by Potter 2004, 532: "For the first and only time would an army that identified its cause with that of the gods confront an army that had identified its salvation with the Christian God."
58. *HE* v. 23. 4, p. 324. 26 Parmentier.
59. Leppin in Marasco 2003, 231–33.
60. Theod. *HE* v. 24. 5–7; on (supposedly) shared dreams, Harris 2009, 42.

usually Castor and Pollux) are found in battle accounts of many nations and periods down into the modern era.[61] Theodoret's direct "source" here may have been the dream of Didymus the Blind in which, at the very moment Julian was killed, he saw figures on white horses proclaiming that Julian was dead. Didymus's vision is reported by both Sozomen and Palladius.[62]

Theodoret also claims, against all the evidence, that Theodosius's army was hopelessly outnumbered and, thanks to the miraculous wind, suffered not a single casualty. While it is impossible to exclude the possibility that he came across some independent witness to the battle, the real objection is that Theodoret was simply not interested in factual details. His account is well over twice as long as those of Socrates and Sozomen, with most of the additional material consisting of visions and invented speeches designed to underline the religious message. In fact, if we read Socrates, Sozomen, and Theodoret in sequence, it is obvious that each account expands the religious significance of the battle. The same applies to their accounts of the death of Julian and of Christians supposedly martyred under Julian, where Sozomen and Theodoret have a mass of unhistorical detail missing in Socrates.[63]

David Woods has recently interpreted these allusions to Jupiter and Hercules as "distorted references to the standards of just two units, the *Ioviani Seniores* and the *Herculiani Seniores*."[64] His argument is largely based on the *Passion of Saints Bonosus and Maximilianus*, two standard-bearers supposedly tortured and executed at Antioch under Julian for refusing to remove the sign of the cross from their standard.[65] Woods inferred that Constantine had pagan images removed from military standards that Julian then replaced, thus making military standards "a matter of controversy during the religious conflict of the fourth century." Notoriously, Constantine is said to have had the sign of the cross painted on the shields of his troops following a dream before the Battle of the Milvian Bridge, but even if this is accepted as fact, all it means is that a small cross was added to the main device that covered the whole shield (as shown on a well-known statuette of Constantine discussed by Alföldi).[66] There is certainly no reason to believe that all the hundreds of traditional devices of the various units were *replaced* by the cross, nor is there any evidence (e.g., in the more than 150 shield devices illustrated in the *Notitia Dignitatum*) that the addition of a cross became general practice.[67] When Jerome cites as an illustration of the rapid

61. Cracco Ruggini 1972, 265–72; Pritchett 1979, 11–46 (whose latest example is an appearance of St. James "careering on his milk-white steed" at the battle of Otumba in Mexico on 7 July 1520).

62. Pallad. *Hist Laus*. 4. 4; Sozom. *HE* vi. 2. 6–7. For Theodoret's debt to Palladius, Urbainczyk 2002, 49–50.

63. Leppin 1996, 112 n. 56 (it is not certain that Theodoret actually wrote after Sozomen); Penella 1993, 31–43.

64. Woods 1995, 61–68.

65. BHL 4721; I have used the reprint of T. Ruinart's edition by B. Galura (3 [Augsburg 1803], 363–72).

66. Lactantius, *De mort. persec.* 44. 5; Alföldi 1959, 179, with fig. 1; on Constantine's "dream," Harris 2005.

67. Inset crosses would no doubt have been invisible on the scale of these illustrations, but the fact remains that the original devices clearly continued to be considered primary.

decline of paganism that "soldiers' standards bear the sign of the Cross,"[68] he is either speaking metaphorically or making a sweeping generalization on the basis of the story about the Milvian Bridge.

Only one standard was transformed by the conversion of Constantine, the emperor's own, the so-called *labarum*, carried by an elite corps of guards renamed *praepositi labarum*.[69] The handful of depictions of shields with chi-rho devices on coins and other monuments seem to be restricted to imperial bodyguards. According to Eusebius, Constantine used the *labarum* "against every opposing and hostile force and commanded replicas of it to lead all his armies." If the emperor was leading his troops in person, then it could be said that his army was following the cross. In a heavily military context Firmicus Maternus exhorts Constantius II and Constans to "raise up the banner of faith";[70] and Cyril of Jerusalem represents Constantius II carrying the standard (*tropaion*) of the cross against Magnentius.[71] A consular diptych datable to 406 shows Honorius depicted as an infantryman holding the *labarum*, a banner on a pole bearing the legend *In nomine Christi vincas semper*. In Prudentius, Theodosius urges Roma to "acknowledge my standards, on which the figure of the cross leads the van, either gleaming in jewels or fashioned of solid gold on long shafts."[72] The evocation of gold and jewels underlines that he is referring to the emperor's personal standard, not the shields borne by the rank and file of his armies. There is no reason to believe that either the standards or the shield devices of the army as a whole were modified in any way. After all, the point of legionary standards, held aloft on long poles, was to distinguish the many different units of the army, so that commanders knew who was where, to serve as rallying points, and to convey signals and commands. The shield devices illustrated in the *Notitia* reveal an amazing variety of geometrical patterns and animal motifs.[73] Earlier scholars were sceptical about the authenticity of these illustrations, but some have now been confirmed by contemporary representations.[74]

Woods successfully identified a modest amount of "accurate and detailed information about the personalities and events of the reign of Julian" in the *Passion of Saints Bonosus and Maximilianus*, but the trial and torture scenes are pure fiction, as are the grounds alleged for their trial. According to Downey, the two men "refused to remove the Christian symbol, the *labarum*, from their standards."[75] But what the text actually says is that they refused to remove the cross from their *labarum*. The writer

---

68. *vexilla militum crucis insignia sunt*, Jer. *Ep.* 107. 2.

69. For earlier practice, Speidel 1994, 98; for the *praepositi labarum*, Frank 1969, 142–45 (the term is only found once, and should perhaps be corrected to *praepositi labari*; a contracted gen. plural is improbable in this context).

70. Woods 1997; Euseb. *VC* i. 31; Firm. Mat. *De err. prof. rel.* 20. 7 (*erigite vexillum fidei*).

71. Cyr. Jerus. *Ep. Const.* in *PG* xxxiii. 1172.

72. Prud. *Contra Symm.* i. 464–68; cf. ii. 713–14; Cameron 2007.

73. Dennis 1982, 51–59 at 56; Berger 1981, 43–57.

74. Speidel 1992, 414–18; Woods 1997; Berger 1981.

75. Woods 1995, 25–55 (at 55); Downey 1961, 392; Bowersock 1978, 107.

was ignorant enough to think that *labarum* was Latin for the standard of a palatine legion such as the Herculiani or Ioviani.[76] And there can be little doubt where he got this misconception. The only evidence for Julian removing the cross from military standards is Gregory Nazianzen's rather vague claim that he "attacked" the *labarum* that was carried in front of the Roman army,[77] meaning that he had the cross removed from his personal standard. The author of the *Passion* evidently thought Gregory was describing a general attack on Christian standards.

Hercules leading Eugenius's army is simply an imaginary counterpoise to the Constantinian *labarum* that, as Theodoret knew from Gregory and Eusebius, led the armies of Christian emperors. But while the aggressive pagan Julian had the cross removed from his personal standard, Eugenius was at least a nominal Christian. He must have gone to war with the *labarum* just like his Christian predecessors. Nor are there any grounds for invoking the Ioviani or Herculiani.[78] It is not even certain that the standard of the Herculiani bore an image of Hercules. Their shield device in the *Notitia* is that ubiquitous imperial symbol, the eagle. The confrontation between Hercules and the cross is simply part of Theodoret's theological stylization. It is not hard to think of reasons why he picked Hercules to represent paganism. In his *Cure for Hellenic Maladies* he had dwelt particularly on Hercules as the classic case of a mortal man deified by credulous posterity, a mortal, moreover, whose life on earth had been devoted to drunkenness and debauchery.[79]

If Theodoret's Hercules has nothing to do with the Herculiani, the statues of Jupiter certainly have nothing to do with the Ioviani. According to Augustine, after the battle,

> Theodosius threw down the statues of Jupiter *which had been consecrated against him* by I know not what rites (*Iovis simulacra quae adversus eum fuerant nescio quibus ritibus velut consecrata*) and set up in the Alps. The thunderbolts of these statues, which were made of gold, he laughingly and generously gave to his messengers, who...joked that they would like to be struck by such thunderbolts.

Some have argued that Augustine's "against him" (*adversus eum*) is to be taken quite literally: these were apotropaic statues put where Theodosius's men found them specifically to keep him from crossing the Alps.[80] The rites Augustine refers to so

---

76. As recognized by Woods 1995, 62. Actually the text as we have it itself does not mention either legion, but the title styles them soldiers *de numero Herculianorum seniorum* (an authentic detail).

77. τολμᾷ δὲ καὶ κατὰ τοῦ μεγάλου συνθήματος ὃ μετὰ τοῦ σταυροῦ πομπεύει καὶ ἄγει τὸν στρατὸν εἰς ὕψος αἰρόμενον, Greg. Naz. *Or.* 4. 66 (p. 174 Bernardi). Sozomen's claim (*HE* v. 17. 2–3) that Julian had images of Zeus, Ares, and Hermes painted on the standard is probably no more than embroidery of Gregory.

78. It might be added that there were also Ioviani and Herculiani in Theodosius's army, *iuniores* as opposed to *seniores* (*Not. Dign.* Or. v. 3–4).

79. Theod. *Graec. Aff. Cur.* iii. 26–29 and viii. 12–18; for the priority of the *Cure*, Canivet 2000, 28–31.

80. Turcan 2000, 162–63.

disdainfully are identified as theurgic, presumed (without evidence) to be one of Flavian's specialities.[81] It is true that there are one or two (distinctly dubious) cases of late antique apotropaic statues erected at boundaries to prevent invaders,[82] but there is a much simpler and better documented explanation for statues of Jupiter in the Alps. The natural place for shrines of Jupiter, the Roman sky god, was on the top of hills or mountains, and many such shrines are in fact found so sited.[83] No one setting up apotropaic statues at short notice for a very specific purpose would be likely to lug them up to the tops of mountains.

Furthermore, the apotropaic interpretation presupposes that the statues were known to have been recently consecrated (by Flavian, of course). But this is not what Augustine, our only source, actually says. It ignores (as does the translation cited above) a key word in the Latin: the *velut* before *consecrata*. The statues were "as it were" consecrated against Theodosius. That is to say they were *not* actually consecrated against him but *appeared* to have been, or might have been thought to have been. And if they were not set up for the purpose, then the accompanying rites Augustine mentions are likewise imaginary. Unlike Theodoret's Hercules-standards, these statues of Jupiter may actually have existed, but almost certainly they had nothing whatever to do with Eugenius or Flavian—or the fourth century. Even if Augustine got his information from someone who was present, what could this informant actually have told him? The most likely explanation is that, while travelling through the Alps, Theodosius's messengers came upon shrines of Jupiter on mountaintops where they had stood for centuries.

3

It is often stated that accounts of the battle fall into two distinct categories, the pagan version opposed to "the unanimity of Christian historiography in presenting the clash as an encounter between a pious Christian ruler and an impious pagan usurper."[84] This is a serious oversimplification. The reason we have as many as four accounts of this version is because the three later writers (Augustine, Sozomen, and Theodoret) all follow Rufinus. Yet this is by no means the only Christian version. There are in fact four other Christian accounts, none of which say anything about the defeat of paganism.

Modern accounts of the Frigidus have paid little attention to these versions. Much the earliest surviving eastern version is a sermon preached by John Chrysostom in the Church of the Holy Apostles in Constantinople, on the anniversary of Theodosius's

---

81. Duval in Bratož 1996, 95–107; Hedrick 2000, 45–46 ("profoundly significant").
82. For a sceptical discussion of the two best-known cases, Treadgold 2004, 715–17, 727.
83. As realised long ago by Mommsen 1870, 362; Wissowa 1912, 116 n. 5; Le Gall 1969.
84. Sivan 1994, 586.

death, probably 17 January 399. Since this text has not been used in earlier accounts of the battle, it is worth citing in full:[85]

> It was with these arms that he deposed tyrants, both the first [Maximus] and the second [Eugenius]. The first without effort or spilling blood, raising his trophy without losing even a fraction of his army. As for the second, although there was a battle, it was Theodosius alone who destroyed him [Eugenius]. When the two armies were drawn up facing each other, and clouds of spears were hurled, and his own troops were being turned back by the violent onslaught of the enemy, Theodosius leapt from his horse, threw his shield on the ground, and fell to his knees calling for help from heaven, transforming the site of the battle into a church, fighting with tears and prayers, not arrows and javelins and spears. At this a sudden wind arose, and the spears of the enemy were blown back on those who had thrown them. Seeing this, the enemy, who till then had been breathing fury and slaughter, changed tack, acclaiming Theodosius as their emperor. They bound the arms of their fellow-soldiers behind their backs and surrendered them. And the blessed Theodosius returned covered in glory, not from the victory alone but from the way he had won it. Unlike other emperors, his soldiers did not share the victory with him. On the contrary, it belonged to him alone, and to his faith. This is why we judge him blessed and say that he is not truly dead.

This is not just a passing reference. It is a detailed account of what is clearly represented as Theodosius's final and greatest achievement as a Christian emperor. Chrysostom treats the battle as an extreme example of the importance of prayer. It was not Theodosius's army that won the battle, but Theodosius himself, alone, by prayer. Obviously the tone is both panegyrical and theological. If Chrysostom had been familiar with the claim that, in addition to vanquishing Eugenius, Theodosius had also vanquished paganism, why not mention it in this of all contexts?

Next in date comes Philostorgius, perhaps the most significant of the alternative versions:[86]

> On arriving at the Alps, [Theodosius] seized them by treachery and, having met the usurper near the river called Frigidus, and having fought a fierce battle in which very many were killed on both sides, at length victory turned aside from the usurper and placed the crown on the lawful emperor.

---

85. *PG* 63. 491 (my translation); for a French translation, Paschoud 1997, 279. The equivalent of another 4 Migne columns remains unpublished in Cod. Athon. Stavron. 6, ff. 79ᵛ–84; Wenger 1956, 38–39; Aubineau 1989.

86. Phil. *HE* xi. 2, p. 133 Bidez.

The brevity is in part due to the fact that this is a summary by Photius. But brevity alone does not explain the absence of the miraculous wind, imperial prayers, or pagan/Christian confrontation. Nor can we credit Philostorgius with a distaste for the supernatural. We have seen that he ascribed Constantius's victory over Magnentius to a celestial vision of the cross. The explanation is simply that an Arian writer could not attribute either victory or miracles to the prayers of an anti-Arian emperor.[87] Philostorgius treated Theodosius's victory as a straightforward case of the triumph of the stronger over the weaker. He may have suppressed the triumphalist anti-pagan version for the same reason, though (since he did not know Rufinus) it is just as likely that he simply did not know it.[88] The fact that he (mistakenly) identified Eugenius as a pagan suggests that he knew something of it but did not choose to emphasize this aspect.[89] We may be sure that, if Theodosius had chanced to be an Arian, none of our orthodox sources would have said anything about the power of his prayers or the defeat of paganism.

As for Socrates, in most respects he follows Rufinus fairly closely (Theodosius prays, Bacurius fights bravely, and the miraculous wind turns the enemy's spears against themselves). But there is not a word about Flavian and the pagan preparations or the defeat of paganism. This is the more striking in that, like Sozomen, Socrates certainly knew Rufinus at firsthand (citing him by name no fewer than nine times). Indeed, he began by following Rufinus quite closely, but when revising the first draft of his work in the light of various writings of Athanasius he became increasingly distrustful, especially for chronology (ii. 1), and in his later books only cites him for events in which Rufinus was himself a participant (iii. 19. 8; iv. 24. 8; iv. 26. 25). In fact, even when following Rufinus he sometimes omits details he judged implausible.[90] If he had just stated the outcome of the battle and pressed on, the omission might have seemed less noteworthy. In fact, he gives a very full account, including such relatively minor details as the bravery of Bacurius. The only thing he omitted was the pagan/Christian dimension of the battle, so central to what we know to have been his main source. Intriguingly enough, while mentioning Bacurius's bravery, he even drops Rufinus's emphasis on its inspiration, Bacurius's Christianity. The very fact that he omitted what modern scholars have considered the most important aspect of the battle should make us wonder whether we were right to consider it so important. For whatever reason, the undoubtedly pious Socrates clearly did not.

No less remarkably, though clearly familiar with both the Rufinus and Augustine versions, Orosius too dropped the anti-pagan coloring of his sources. While he

---

87. Leppin 2001, 111–24 (121 for the Frigidus).
88. On Philostorgius's sources (which included Eunapius and Gelasius), see J. Bidez, *Philostorgius Kirchengeschichte*[2] (Berlin 1962), cxxxiv–cxl.
89. Ἕλληνα δὲ τὸ σέβας, p. 133. 11 Bidez.
90. Hansen 1995, xliii; Urbaincsyk 1997, 49–59.

identified Arbogast (probably mistakenly) as a pagan, there is no suggestion that Eugenius too was a pagan, and no mention of Flavian, Jupiter, or Hercules.[91] Around 560, Cassiodorus's protégé Epiphanius produced a variorum *Ecclesiastical History* that consists of excerpts from Socrates, Sozomen, and Theodoret translated into Latin. The chapter on the Frigidus (ix. 45) includes substantial extracts from all three, but, for whatever reason, omitted the bits of Sozomen and Theodoret that depicted the battle as a pagan/Christian confrontation.

Finally, we may turn to what is generally, though misleadingly, known as the "pagan" version, represented by Zosimus and John of Antioch.[92] Both reflect the account of what we know to have been Zosimus's main source for the period, Eunapius of Sardis, like Zosimus an aggressive pagan. Eunapius's history went down to the year 404 and cannot have been published later than ca. 420, when he would have been in his seventies.[93] What Zosimus and John actually offer is a rather confused account, featuring an unhistorical eclipse of the sun, in which Theodosius wins by attacking Eugenius's men at dawn while they were still sleeping after a late dinner. The classification "pagan" is predicated, perversely enough, on the assumption that Eunapius deliberately suppressed both the pagan revival and the miraculous victory won by Theodosius's prayers. According to Buck, for example, his account "was designed to save the honor of the pagan gods by ignoring the conflict of paganism and Christianity," which is why it "omitted completely not only the statues of Jupiter and Hercules, under whose protection the pagans fought, but also the Bora, the wind which gave the Christian army victory."[94]

But this is not nearly so satisfactory an explanation as usually supposed. In the first place, it presupposes as axiomatic not only a full-blown pagan revival but also the literal truth of Rufinus's account, complete with the embellishments of Augustine and Theodoret. Even so, why would an aggressively pagan historian ignore or suppress what he was bound to consider the false and absurd claim that Christianity defeated paganism at the Frigidus? The obvious pagan response to such a claim was to deny rather than suppress it. To suppress it would be tantamount to conceding that it was true; it would not conceal the fact that the Frigidus did in fact spell the effective end of Roman public paganism. Zosimus's very next chapter describes Theodosius exploiting his victory by going to Rome and urging its pagan elite to convert. But they refuse, thus implicitly rebutting the Christian claim. Theodosius then abolishes pagan rites, which Zosimus represents as leading to the decline and fall of the Western Empire (iv. 59). Elsewhere in his history Zosimus shows no embarrassment at reporting the various setbacks suffered by paganism from Constantine on, and he is particularly hostile to Theodosius.

---

91. Oros. *Hist. Adv. Pag.* vii. 35. 12.
92. "La version païenne," Paschoud, *Zosime* 2. 2 (1979), 475–78; so too M. Springer 1996, 50–52.
93. On Eunapius's dates, a controversial subject, see Liebeschuetz in Marasco 2003, 177–201.
94. Buck 1988, at 48–53.

It is often argued that Eunapius's eclipse is a pagan answer to the miraculous wind, on the grounds that it is introduced to explain Eugenius's defeat.[95] But how would an eclipse explain defeat in a way that was less embarrassing to pagans than a sudden storm? Both were likely to be seen as divine manifestations in favor of the eventual victor, and while sudden storms are common enough (especially in the neighborhood of the Frigidus in September),[96] eclipses are far rarer and so more likely to be seen as signs from heaven. In fact, it is not uncommon for sudden storms to be turned into eclipses in literary texts for dramatic effect.[97] A good parallel is provided by the second battle of Cremona in A.D. 69, where the bright moon that puts Vitellius's troops at a disadvantage in Tacitus's account is turned into an eclipse by Dio.[98] The seventh-century Christian chronicler John of Antioch offers essentially the same version (with a more detailed account of the unhistorical eclipse), which he too obviously got from Eunapius. But John had also read one of the Christian versions and added Theodosius's prayer to what he took from Eunapius, which in effect turned the eclipse into an omen favoring Theodosius, resulting in an account not so very different from the version we find in the ecclesiastical historians.[99]

Taken by itself, without reference to Rufinus, Augustine, or Theodoret, there is no trace of a pagan/Christian dimension in Zosimus's account of the battle. Like Zosimus (who describes Eugenius as "terrified" by Theodosius's advance), John blames the defeat on Eugenius's inexperience. Arbogast Eunapius praised as brave and incorruptible, Eugenius as learned and virtuous.[100] But not so much as a hint that either favored paganism. It seems that, like Philostorgius, Eunapius treated Theodosius's victory as just another triumph of the stronger over the weaker. There is no detectable pagan agenda. It is simply a *secular* version, what we would expect to find in a secular history.

In light of the silence of Chrysostom, Philostorgius, and Socrates, the true explanation of Zosimus's failure to mention the pagan/Christian dimension of the battle may be nothing more than ignorance. It has long been realized that Eunapius was poorly informed about western events, to the extent that he apparently knew nothing about the saga of the altar of Victory or Gratian's withdrawal of subsidies from the pagan cults—very surprising omissions in a pagan historian, only really explicable in terms of ignorance (p. 47). Moreover, depending on just when and where he composed the final installment of his history, Eunapius may actually have written before the wind miracle entered the Greek historical tradition (next section).

---

95. So Paschoud, *Zosime* 2. 2 (1979), 477.

96. Kovač in Bratož 1996, 109–18.

97. Out of 250 references to eclipses in ancient literature, more than 200 are false: see Demandt 1970, discussing the Frigidus on 22 and 52.

98. For Cremona, Tac. Hist. iii. 23; Dio 65. 11; Demandt 1970, 22.

99. Joh. Ant. F 280. 37–69 R = 152.M; it is true that John places Theodosius's prayer after the eclipse, but that does not affect its potential status as a manifestation of divine will.

100. Zos. iv. 53–54; Eun. F 58. 1–2.

4

According to Hedrick, even those willing to minimize the role of religion in the actual Frigidus campaign "must concede that in the aftermath influential Christian authors such as Ambrose and Augustine conceived of the usurpation as a pagan revolt."[101] There is in fact no evidence whatever for any such *contemporary* conception, least of all in Ambrose. It does not appear until Rufinus, who was followed, with important qualifications, by Augustine. Writing as he was in 402/3, Rufinus may look like a virtually contemporary source for 394, but he had been far away in the Holy Land at the time, and a very different perspective had developed in the course of those eight intervening years. As for Augustine, it is instructive to note that, despite sticking closely to Rufinus's narrative throughout his account of the Christian emperors of the fourth century,[102] he entirely dropped the vivid description of the "pagan" preparations for the Frigidus. Since he added the story about the statues of Jupiter, he evidently believed that Eugenius had pagan supporters, but Eugenius himself he brackets with Maximus as just another usurper (p. 122). There is no suggestion of a pagan revolt.

It has not, I think, been sufficiently appreciated that Ambrose, the only exactly contemporary western source with firsthand access in Milan to participants in the battle itself, says nothing about either a pagan revolt or a confrontation between paganism and Christianity. It is worth examining the references in Ambrose in chronological order, without preconceptions.[103] In the three earliest, even the miraculous wind is conspicuous by its absence.

First there is a letter to Theodosius himself written immediately after Ambrose received news of the victory, in September 394:[104]

> Thanks be to the Lord our God who has responded to your faith and piety. He has refashioned an ancient type of holiness, letting us see in our time what we marvel at as we read the Scriptures, namely the mighty presence of divine help in battles, so that mountain heights have not slowed up the course of your coming, nor did enemy arms prove any obstacle.

After explicitly evoking divine help in battles on a biblical scale, the best Ambrose can come up with is a speedy transit of the Alps and facility at coping with enemy arms! There is no suggestion here of anything so dramatic as a miraculous wind that

---

101. Hedrick 2000, 85; at xiv he claims that they "represented the revolt in *exclusively* religious terms" (my italics).
102. On which see especially Duval 1966 and Courcelle 1969.
103. Paschoud's useful list of sources for the Frigidus (*Zosime* 2. 2 [1979], 488–500) does not in fact include all relevant texts of Ambrose.
104. *Ep.* 61. 3 (*Ep. extra coll.* 2. 3, p. 179 Zelzer).

turned those enemy arms against themselves during the actual battle.[105] Second is a follow-up letter to Theodosius, no later than (say) November 394:[106]

> It is said that your victory was granted in the manner of the ancients, with ancient portents (*vetustis miraculis*) like those of the blessed Moses, the blessed Joshua son of Nun, of Samuel, and of David. It was granted not by man's foresight but by the outpouring of heavenly grace.

Once again Ambrose attributes the victory to divine help, citing the usual Old Testament precedents. But Ambrose saw the hand of God in all victories won by orthodox emperors. Zelzer identified the *vetusta miracula* as the miraculous wind, but the Old Testament normally just assigns God the credit in very general terms ("The Lord gave victory to David" or the like).[107] There is no basis for seeing specific acts of divine *intervention* behind such remarks. More important, there is nothing here about paganism—and again no wind.

Next comes § 7 of Ambrose's funerary oration on Theodosius (*De obitu Theodosii*), delivered on 25 February 395:

> You will recall, I am sure, what triumphs the faith (*fides*) of Theodosius acquired for you. When, because of difficulties in the terrain and the hindrance of camp followers, the army line came down to battle a little too slowly and because of your delay in offering battle the enemy seemed to insult you, the *princeps* leaped down from his horse and, advancing alone before the line, said: "Where is the God of Theodosius?"

This may be the ultimate source for the detail of Theodosius leaping off his horse in Chrysostom.[108] But in Chrysostom, as in Rufinus and his followers, Theodosius's dramatic battlefield prayer is immediately followed by the miraculous wind.[109] In Ambrose, however, all that happens is that he "aroused all" with his words (*quo dicto excitavit omnes*). In the most obvious context imaginable, the wind is not even mentioned. Yet Ambrose nonetheless compares Theodosius's victory to Old Testament victories throughout.

---

105. *hoc loco ad miracula insolita alludit, quibus deus victoriam de Eugenio relatam illustravit*, notes Zelzer ad loc., citing Augustine. But Ambrose himself goes on to illustrate very minor phenomena.

106. *Ep.* 62. 4 (*Ep. extra coll.* 3. 4, p. 181 Zelzer).

107. The closest parallels to the miraculous wind would be the collapse of the walls of Jericho or the hailstorm that fell on the Amorites when they were already in flight, the day the sun stood still (Joshua 6. 20; 10. 11–14).

108. So MacCormack 1981, 336 n. 249. It is unlikely that Chrysostom could read Latin, but it is natural to suppose that copies of Ambrose's funeral oration accompanied Theodosius's body on its return to Constantinople, and that its more striking details became known among Greek-speakers.

109. *post illam imperatoris precem... ventus ita vehemens exortus est...*, *HE* xi. 33 (p. 1039. 5 Mommsen); "at this a sudden storm arose..." (Chrysostom).

For Ambrose's one and only reference to a miraculous wind we have to wait another month, until his sermon on Psalm 36. 15 delivered between 19 and 24 March 395:[110]

> For spears often rebound on those who have thrown them. This happened in the recent war, when faithless and sacrilegious men attacked a man trusting in the Lord, and tried to snatch his throne away from him, making dire threats of persecuting the churches of the Lord, so that suddenly a wind arose which tore their shields from the hands of the faithless and turned all their spears and missiles back on the army of the sinner.

The miraculous wind is the high point of most surviving accounts of the Frigidus. Sudden storms during the first week of September are indeed common in this area.[111] But they are normally accompanied by torrential rain (not mentioned in any of these texts),[112] which might have been expected to inconvenience both sides equally. A storm consisting solely of a wind that affected only one side is neither probable in itself nor in keeping with local conditions. And a storm that literally blew spears back on those who had thrown them is sheer fantasy.

In the context of his sermon it was not Ambrose's purpose to describe the battle, but to illustrate the verse he was explaining: the sinner whose malice hurts only himself. Like the good preacher he was, he cast around for a vivid illustration, and found it in a sudden storm that hit the field of the Frigidus. Like the trained rhetorician he was, he naturally felt free to exaggerate to underline his point, producing what, in a sermon, was a perfectly acceptable hyperbole.[113] Yet why does he fail to mention the wind in those three earlier passages where he had ascribed Theodosius's victory to divine assistance?

The answer is there in the text if we just read the following sentence. There is no suggestion in Ambrose that the storm came in answer to the emperor's prayers—or even during the battle. It took place *before* the battle. "*The enemy had not yet arrived,* and already they could not withstand the onslaught of a wind. They were being laid low by their own javelins and, worse still, these wounds affected their minds more than their bodies" (*adhuc hostis deerat, et iam illi ventorum proelia ferre non poterant, suisque spiculis sternebantur et, quod peius est, non erant corporum graviora vulnera illa quam mentium*). Ambrose's point is that Eugenius's troops were already demoralized by this sudden storm *before* the battle. Another half-dozen lines continue the motif of men wounded by their own weapons, but it soon becomes clear that these are now metaphorical weapons. Like any skilful preacher, Ambrose has returned to his text:

---

110. Palanque 1933, 552–53; Homes Dudden 1935, 689–90.
111. Gerbenne 1999, 173–75; Kovač in Bratož 1996, 109–18.
112. As Paschoud 1997, 278, remarks, the darkness that accompanied or preceded the downpour might explain the eclipse version.
113. A *decens veri superiectio*, in Quintilian's terminology: *Inst.* 8. 6. 67; Lausberg 1998, § 909, p. 410.

those who act from malice destroy themselves. The degree of reality that lies behind this moral lesson is unclear (if the enemy had not arrived yet, why were Eugenius's men throwing their spears?), but let us concede that the troops were indeed disconcerted by a sudden storm. Ambrose himself, our earliest, best-placed, and most authoritative source is perfectly clear that it did *not* happen *during* the battle. We are surely bound to accept this chronology. What possible motive could he have had to move it from during to before the battle? Here is our explanation for his earlier silence. Since the only storm Ambrose knew came before the battle, naturally it never occurred to him that it was the answer to Theodosius's prayers during the battle, much less the turning point of the battle. The only thing about it that caught his interest was the moral of wickedness defeating itself.

Verbal parallels strongly suggest that it was from Ambrose (*iacula in ipsos qui ea iecerint refunduntur... tela... retorqueret*) that Rufinus got his formulation of the wind-miracle (*tela hostium in eos qui iecerant retorqueret*).[114] Since he had returned from Palestine and was living in Aquileia when he wrote the *HE*, it is reasonable to assume that he was familiar with the writings of Ambrose, no doubt conveniently available to him in the library of his patron Bishop Chromatius of Aquileia, a friend of Ambrose. It is tempting to conclude that it was Rufinus who transformed a minor prebattle curiosity into a major battlefield miracle. Yet Rufinus was not in fact the first person to take this step.

Surprisingly, ironically enough, that was the new court poet Claudian, according to Augustine a staunch pagan. Yet despite its superficial classicizing veneer, his panegyric on Honorius's third consulate, recited at Milan early in January 396, closely follows the official line: an emperor beloved by God for whom a miraculous wind turned the enemy's spears against themselves:[115]

> Te propter gelidis Aquilo de monte procellis
> obruit adversas acies revolutaque tela
> vertit in auctores et turbine reppulit hastas.
> o nimium dilecte deo, cui fundit ab antris
> Aeolus armates hiemes, cui militat aether
> et coniurati veniunt ad classica venti.

For your [Honorius's] sake the north wind overwhelmed the enemy line with its icy mountain storms, hurled their weapons back on the throwers and drove back their spears with its blast. You are indeed beloved of god, you for whom Aeolus pours armed tempests from his cave, you for whom the elements do battle, and the winds come together at the sound of your war-trumpets.

---

114. For fuller discussion, Courcelle 1969, passim; see too Perrelli 1995, 261–62.
115. *III Cons. Hon.* 94–95. The fact that the emperor Claudian is addressing is Honorius, to whose auspices (as consul) he credits his father's victory, is irrelevant to the point at issue.

The same paradox expressed in much the same terms and words as Ambrose. Yet while the shared conceit of spears being blown back on those who threw them[116] leaves little doubt that Claudian knew Ambrose (if only indirectly), he was surely also influenced by another, much older text: Silius's account of the battle of Cannae. Expanding on a brief statement in Livy, Silius represents Juno ordering Aeolus to release a wind (the Vulturnus) that blew sand in the face of the Romans, blinding them, causing their spears to fall uselessly behind them, and blowing their swords aside when they were about to strike the foe. Claudian undoubtedly knew Silius,[117] and it makes a neat reversal to turn the wind responsible for Rome's most infamous defeat into the wind that gave Theodosius his greatest victory. Silius's two conceits are slightly different from Claudian's, but one major motif Claudian surely took from Silius was the sudden wind that turned the tide of battle. As for Ambrose, Claudian may have been in Milan as early as March 395 to hear him preach in person. Paradox and hyperbole were the essence of panegyric, and no one could have faulted a verse panegyrist for making the most of Ambrose's storm. It may be more than coincidence that Claudian's earlier reference to the Frigidus (*Panegyric on Olybrius and Probinus* 103–13) has nothing about the miraculous wind. For it was recited at Rome in January 395, before Ambrose's sermon. Claudian does not say in so many words that this wind came in answer to the emperor's prayers, but he nonetheless clearly implies that it came during the battle at his bidding (Silius's wind came at a goddess's bidding). Since his first appearance at Rome in January 395 Claudian had become the new poetic sensation. His poems were widely read (Augustine cites this very passage in his account of the Frigidus), and no doubt found readers in Constantinople.[118]

This might explain Chrysostom. The detail of Theodosius leaping down from his horse to pray is only otherwise known from Ambrose's *De obitu*. It does not appear in Rufinus and so is also missing from all his derivatives. Chrysostom also has the miraculous wind in much the same form as Rufinus three years before Rufinus wrote.[119] While it is conceivable that Chrysostom got to know the highlights of *De obitu*, it is hard to believe that he had any knowledge of the sermon on Psalm 36. If Claudian's *III Cons. Hon.* was read in Constantinople, it is likely to have found Greek imitators, which Chrysostom is likely to have read or heard. He may have got both details from the same work, a panegyric by some bilingual visitor from the West that combined both Ambrosian details in the same work, with the miraculous wind filtered through Claudian.

If Rufinus read Ambrose through the filter of Claudian, that would explain why (like modern scholars) he ignored or overlooked "the enemy had not yet arrived." By

116. So far as I have been able to discover, a conceit unknown to classical poetry or rhetoric.
117. Ware 2004, 168–69; Livy 22. 46. 9; Silius, *Punica* ix. 491–524. Silius is clearly influenced here by Vergil's account of Juno ordering Aeolus to loose the winds against Aeneas's fleet in *Aeneid* i. 81–90, but there is no sign that Claudian had Vergil in mind. Polybius has nothing about a wind, and most scholars regard it as "an invention of Roman propaganda" (Walbank's note); Dewar 1994.
118. For the evidence, Cameron 1970, 242–46; Whitby 1985, 507–16.
119. τὰ μὲν βέλη τῶν ἐναντίων κατὰ τῶν ἀφιέντων ἐφέρετο, *PG* 63. 491.

transferring Ambrose's wind from its original metaphorical and spiritual context into what purports to be a historical narrative, he turned it into a miracle. What started out as a trope in a sermon gave the miracle of the wind its place in the evolving saga of the Frigidus.

Back to the pagans. This wind arose, Ambrose explained in his sermon, "in the recent war, when faithless and sacrilegious men (*infideles et sacrilegi*) attacked a man trusting in the Lord," and goes on to describe them "shooting poisoned arrows of perfidy against the people of Christ from the quiver of their hearts." It might seem obvious that these people must be pagans. But any unsuccessful challenger of a victorious Christian emperor was likely to be so characterized. In such a context, Maxentius, Licinius, Magnentius, and Magnus Maximus would be *infideles et sacrilegi* no less than Eugenius. Moreover, it is one thing for a partisan of the victor to blacken the name of defeated rebels by implying that they were unbelievers, and quite another to claim this as solid evidence that the revolt itself was inspired by paganism.

If the Frigidus had really been perceived by contemporaries as the final defeat of paganism, we should expect to find clear evidence in *De obitu Theodosii*, a public eulogy of the emperor pronounced in Milan barely four months after the battle.[120] Some scholars have indeed so read it.[121] Yet there are only two unmistakable references to paganism in the entire speech. First a curiously oblique passage in *De obitu* 4 in which "supplanting the perfidy of tyrants" is linked to the stamping out of worship of idols. It might seem tempting to see an allusion to the suppression of a pagan revolt here,[122] but closer analysis reveals the reference to be much more general. In the first place the plural *tyranni*, obviously including Maximus as well as Eugenius, prohibits exclusive focus on the Frigidus. In the second, the entire paragraph is shot through with allusions to the biblical story of Jacob. Honorius performs the burial rites for his father after forty days just as Joseph performed the burial rites for his father Jacob after forty days. Theodosius is said to have "supplanted" (*supplantavit*) the perfidy of tyrants because Jacob "supplanted" his brother Esau (Genesis 25. 25; 27. 36),[123] and to have "hidden the idols of the gentiles" (*abscondit simulacra gentium*).[124] "For," Ambrose explains, "his faith has hidden (*abscondit*) all worship of idols and stamped out all their rituals."

This is not at all the straightforward statement of contemporary fact it appears to be. Why that curious *abscondit*, usually translated "put away" (implying "abolish") but properly "hid" or "buried"? Once again this is a biblical allusion, to Jacob's wife Rachel stealing the gods of her father, Laban, and then "hiding" them by sitting on them and

---

120. The *De obitu* was delivered on 25 February 395.
121. "Ambrose chooses to stylise it into a battle against paganism," Errington 1997, 399.
122. So, for example, the recent discussion, by Gerbenne 1999, 161–76 at 172.
123. *celebrat...quadragesimam patris Jacob, supplantatoris illius, et nos celebramus Theodosii quadragesimam, qui imitatus Jacob supplantavit perfidiam tyrannorum, De obitu Theodosii* 3–4; cf. 54–55.
124. Errington 1997, 399, improbably claims that these *simulacra* are the pagan idols set up before the battle.

claiming that she was having her period (Genesis 31. 34–35). Ambrose is in fact drawing here on his own sermons on Jacob delivered in 386,[125] where he had interpreted Rachel's "hiding" (*abscondit*) of these "idols of the gentiles" as proving that they were unclean. A few chapters later (Genesis 35. 4) Jacob "buries the foreign gods" of the Hivites beneath a terebinth tree. In his *De Jacob* Ambrose had interpreted this "burying" (*abscondo* again) of the "idols of the gentiles" (*simulacra gentium*) as proof that the "faith of the church has destroyed every practice of paganism" (*fides enim ecclesiae omnem observantiam gentilitatis abolevit*).[126] Taken by itself, the claim in *De obitu* 4 that "the faith of Theodosius has hidden all worship of idols and stamped out all their rituals" might well seem to imply an impressive recent defeat of paganism. But when we discover that Ambrose himself made exactly the same claim in almost exactly the same words eight years before the Frigidus, right down to the (in the context of *De obitu* puzzling) self-quotation about "*hiding* idols," its contemporary relevance and factual basis is inevitably much diminished.

The second reference to paganism in *De obitu* comes in § 38:

> Whoever during life fittingly celebrates the Pasch of the Lord shall be in perpetual light. Who celebrated it more gloriously than he who removed sacrilegious errors, closed temples, destroyed idols? For in this was King Josiah preferred to his ancestors.

Once again, the entire passage is modeled on an Old Testament text, this time 2 Kings 23,[127] where Josiah king of Judah destroys the altars and idols of false gods and commands all the people to celebrate the Pasch of the Lord (where Pasch = Passover). Naturally, it is significant that Theodosius is compared to the one Old Testament king who attempted to stamp out the paganism of his day, but nothing in the context suggests that this achievement was due to the recent victory at the Frigidus. Rather it is represented as a timeless consequence of Theodosius's piety. In an earlier section Ambrose had compared Honorius to King Josiah, and, more than two years before the Frigidus, Valentinian II as well.[128]

The victory itself is mentioned only three times in *De obitu*, in each case as an illustration of the emperor's piety rather than for its own importance or even to illustrate his prowess as a commander. When he leaps off his horse to pray (§ 7) we are merely told that he "aroused all," with no reference even to the enemy, let alone paganism. The second passage is § 34: although he had won a glorious victory, because of the slaughter of the enemy Theodosius abstained from the sacraments until he recognized the grace of God toward him in the arrival of his children

---

125. Homes Dudden 1935, 683; Moorhead 1999, 135.
126. *De Jacob* ii. 5. 25 and ii. 7. 33 (C. Schenkl [ed.], CSEL xxxii. 2, 1897, pp. 46–23, and 51. 13).
127. Or the parallel narrative in 2 Chronicles 34–35.
128. *De obitu Theodosii* 15 (*prae ceteris regibus Israel Domini pascha celebravit et ceremoniarum abolevit errores*); *De obitu Valentiniani* 57 (*ita domini pascha celebravit ut omnes retro principes superaret*).

(Honorius and Placidia).[129] This is cited as one of many illustrations of Theodosius's willingness to do penance.

The third passage is § 10. After describing how Elisha, surrounded by Syrians, prayed to God to blind them, Ambrose argues that perfidy is a form of blindness (*ubi perfidia, ibi caecitas*). "Deservedly, then," he continues, "was the army of unbelievers (*exercitus infidelium*) blind."[130] What he is accusing this "army of unbelievers" of is *perfidia*, a term that in Ambrose denotes any repudiation or perversion of *fides*,[131] in this context almost certainly disloyalty, as in § 2 (*ultorem perfidiae* after a reference to *exercitus fidem*) and 6 (*perfidiam tyrannorum*). Again and again, Ambrose appeals to the loyalty the army owed to its two new emperors, especially the ten-year-old Honorius (§§ 2, 6, 8), and one out of many passages in Claudian reveals why. This is from a speech of Theodosius addressing Arcadius in a dream, describing the immediate aftermath of his own death:[132]

> cum divus abirem
> res incompositas (fateor) tumidasque reliqui.
> stringebat vetitos etiamnum exercitus enses
> Alpinis odiis, alternaque iurgia victi
> victoresque dabant. vix haec amentia nostris
> excubiis, nedum puero rectore quiesset.
> heu quantum timui vobis, quid libera tanti
> militis auderet moles, cum patre remoto
> ferveret iam laeta novis. dissensus acerbus
> et gravior consensus erat.

When I was raised to heaven I left disorder and chaos behind, I admit. The army was still drawing their forbidden swords in that bitter Alpine conflict [the Frigidus]; conquerors and conquered alike gave rise to conflict in turn. This madness could scarcely have been calmed by my vigilance, much less by the rule of a boy. How I feared for you what the uncontrolled might of so many soldiers might dare, when, with your father gone, there came a feverish desire for change. Discord was dangerous enough, but unanimity more dangerous still.

The loyalty of the two now uncomfortably combined armies to their child emperor was a more urgent consideration in February 395 than the fate of paganism. As in the sermon on Psalm 36, *infidelis* is not precise enough, in the absence of any other pointer

---

129. *filiorum … adventu*: for the inclusion of Placidia, Paulin. *V. Ambr.* 32, with Oost 1968, 60 n. 63.
130. Mannix thought that *caecus* here alluded to the effects of the miraculous wind, but while a sandstorm might blind, this was simply a wind, and there is no other reference to the miraculous wind in *De obitu*.
131. Madec 1974, 232, citing many examples in n. 274.
132. *De bello Gildonico* 292–300 (Loeb translation, adapted). For the other passages, notably *In Rufinum* ii. 105–19, Cameron, 1970, 162–65, 171–72.

in the context, to prove a reference to paganism rather than the impiety predicated of any and all opponents of a legitimate Christian emperor. As many critics have noticed, here as elsewhere in the speech Ambrose regularly plays on the two meanings of *fides*, (religious) faith and (political) loyalty.[133]

The two passages in *De obitu* that proclaim the end of paganism (§§ 4 and 38) are overshadowed by four other themes allotted far more space and emphasis: Theodosius's clemency, humility, and penitence; and above all his Christian faith and the loyalty owed to the sons who have inherited both his throne and his faith. First clemency. *De obitu* is full of references to Theodosius's clemency (§§ 12, 13, 14, 25, 26, 33, 39). The only other emperor identified among Constantine's Christian heirs is Gratian, and the fact that Ambrose twice links Theodosius with Gratian in heaven (§§ 39 and 52) has led some to conclude that his purpose was to link their campaigns against paganism. Tempting though this might seem, there is nothing in the context of either passage to suggest such a purpose. On the contrary, both passages stress the clemency of the two emperors ("in this world they took delight in pardoning many" § 52). It was Ambrose who had taken the lead in urging the emperor to pardon rebels and their kin. Augustine too emphasizes Theodosius's clemency after the battle, as does Paulinus the deacon.[134] So too, despite those "pagan" trimmings that misled earlier critics, did Claudian, combining piety and clemency in a single sentence.[135] The emperor himself affected regret about Flavian's suicide, claiming that he would have spared him.[136] If pagan resentment played any part in Eugenius's usurpation (which is doubtful), given the extreme youth of the new western emperor Honorius and the uncertain loyalty of the army, the immediate aftermath of Eugenius's defeat would have been the worst possible moment to embark on the campaign of forced conversions some have postulated.

Yet according to Hedrick, immediately after the Frigidus "Theodosius insisted that the surviving pagan elite convert." He cites two texts, neither of which comes close to supporting so extreme a claim, one each from Augustine and Prudentius. First Augustine:[137]

> The sons of his enemies (*inimicorum suorum*), whose fathers had been slain not so much by his command as by the violence of war, took refuge in a church even though they were not yet Christians. Wishing to take advantage of this situation to make Christians of them (*Christianos hac occasione fieri voluit*), and loving them with Christian charity, he did not deprive them of their property, but indeed increased their honors.

---

133. See particularly Steidle 1978, 103.
134. McLynn 1994, 354; Aug. *CD* v. 26; Paulin. *Vita Ambr.* 31.
135. *non insultare iacenti / malebat; mitis precibus, pietatis abundans, / poenae parcus erat* (*IV Cons.* 112–14).
136. *ILS* 2948, line 16; Hedrick 2000, 3.
137. Hedrick 2000, xv, 56, 71; Aug. *CD* 5. 26.

Taken by themselves, the words *Christianos...fieri voluit might* imply forced conversion.[138] But the combination of the context and the limiting formula *hac occasione*
support a milder translation, such as that of Dyson (quoted above), or David Knowles
(Penguin): "Theodosius wished them to become Christians, since the occasion thus
offered." There is a world of difference between bringing pressure to bear on sons of
ringleaders (presumably no more than a handful of senior officials) who had actually
taken refuge in Christian churches, and ordering the conversion of all remaining
pagans. Augustine gives no names, but the younger Flavian did not lose his property
and was soon reappointed to high office. It is going too far to claim that Theodosius
pardoned him *on condition* that he convert to Christianity.[139]

The second text is a fanciful account by Prudentius of mass conversions of Roman
senators following an exhortation by Theodosius, again immediately after the Frigidus.
To start with, the exhortation is fiction, since we know that Theodosius did not in fact
go to Rome or address the senate. And even if it be conceded that the eloquent speech
Prudentius supplies reflects an imperial letter or speech to a senatorial embassy in
Milan, the conversions that supposedly followed were, he emphasizes, entirely
voluntary. He describes a formal motion in the senate to ban the worship of idols:[140]

> A large number cross over to the side where our noble emperor's motion calls,
> *as free in mind as in foot.* No room is there for resentment; *no one is intimidated
> by brute force;* it is clear to see that such is their will; *all are convinced by reason
> alone and follow their own judgment, not a command.* And our good leader,
> requiting earthly services with equal rewards, gives to the worshippers of idols
> a share of the highest dignities, allows them to vie with the repute of their fam-
> ilies, and forbids not to men who are still in the coils of paganism a career in
> the highest worldly ranks when they have deserved them.

While implying that few pagans were left, Prudentius was obviously very concerned
to underline that no one was forced to convert. Symmachus himself, as Prudentius's
poem illustrates, continued to remain in high public esteem despite his unrepentant
paganism.

Theodosius's penitence is a favorite Ambrosian theme. It receives renewed
emphasis in *De obitu* (§§ 13, 27–28, and especially 34). The themes of his faith and
piety run right through the speech, with victory on the field of battle just one of its
rewards. In a remarkable digression toward the end of the speech Theodosius's faith is
set in a historical context going back to Constantine. Rather surprisingly, the primary
credit is assigned to his mother the Augusta Helena, who not only (so Ambrose

---

138. For *volo* used (especially of emperors) in the sense "order," see Vidén 1984, 82.
139. Chastagnol 1962, 242; Sogno 2006, 80. There is no direct evidence that Flavian was one of those who
    took refuge in a church.
140. *Contra Symm.* i. 608–15.

claims) discovered the True Cross, but also the nails that had pinned Christ to it.[141] These nails she had fashioned into a diadem and a bit for her son's bridle, the diadem as a symbol of empire, the bit as a curb that lifts the eyes of emperors heavenward to seek Christ rather than downward to the corruption of the world.[142] Constantine used both and "passed on his faith to the emperors who succeeded him."[143]

The relevance of this lengthy digression (§§ 40–51, a sixth of the entire speech) has been much debated.[144] It is the most elaborate of four different treatments of essentially the same theme: the transmission of faith. The first of the other three is Theodosius himself leaving his sons the "legacy of his piety" (*pietatis suae reliquit heredes*, § 2). The second the heritage of faith among the patriarchs Abraham, Isaac, and Jacob, with Honorius playing the role of Joseph to Theodosius's Jacob (§§ 3, 4, 9). And the third is a reverse illustration: the four separate passages in which Theodosius is praised for deposing usurpers (*tyranni*) in the plural, §§ 4, 53, 56, and most explicitly 39, where as a pendant to Theodosius embracing Gratian in heaven in the assembly of the saints, Ambrose describes Maximus and Eugenius in hell together, "teaching by a miserable example the wickedness of taking up arms against their emperors."[145] The fourfold repetition makes it clear that, though writing in the immediate aftermath of the Frigidus, Ambrose drew no significant distinction between the crimes of Maximus and Eugenius. More remarkably still, § 39 represents Theodosius embracing Gratian, "who no longer grieves for his wounds, for he has found an avenger," thus (by implication) saying more about the defeat of Maximus than Eugenius.

Maximus and Eugenius are often linked as the two successive usurpers deposed by Theodosius in other contemporary texts, such as Claudian and, more important, Prudentius (*gemini bis victor caede tyranni*). The relevance of Prudentius to the Frigidus has often been overlooked. The bulk of the first book of the *Contra Symmachum* seems to have been written shortly after the Frigidus, before Theodosius's death in January 395 (Ch. 9. 4). Like Zosimus, though from the opposite perspective, it implies that Rome was sunk in paganism till Theodosius, fresh from his victory at the Frigidus, urged the senate to convert.[146] In the opening lines Prudentius claims to have believed that Theodosius had already eliminated the disease, but then the plague broke out anew (*renovata lues*, i. 5). It is tempting to identify this "renewal of the plague" with Flavian's "pagan revival" under Eugenius, but nothing in the rest of Prudentius's narra-

---

141. Ambrose is the earliest surviving source for this celebrated but unhistorical story. Borgehammar 1991, 60–66, and Drijvers 1992, 108–13, both argue that Ambrose got it from the lost *Ecclesiastical History* of Gelasius. But if Gelasius wrote no earlier than the mid-fifth century (n. 3), we should perhaps return to the old view that the legend developed in the West (Borgehammar 1991, 8 n. 6), which would explain why Chrysostom had apparently not heard of it as late as the 390s (Drijvers 95) and why the Greek ecclesiastical historians all seem to be dependent on Rufinus.

142. For the various traditions about these nails, Borgehammar 1991, 48–49, 62–63.

143. *fidem transmisit ad posteros reges*, § 47.

144. Duval 1977, 274–86; Steidle 1978; Bonamente 1979; Consolino 1984 and 1994.

145. Note too § 56, where Italy is "freed a second time from tyrants" (in the plural).

146. Prud. *Contra Symm.* i. 410; i. 408–631.

tive supports so precise an identification. Indeed, after elaborately developing the metaphor of Theodosius's "cure" for twenty lines, at 22–27 he briefly touches on the unsatisfactory "medicine" applied by the "tyrants." They did no more than see what suited the needs of the moment, with no thought for the future. They deserved poorly of both the people and the senate by *allowing* them to plunge headlong into hell together with Jupiter and all the rest of the gods:

> heu, male de populo meriti, male patribus ipsis
> blanditi, quos praecipites in Tartara mergi
> cum Iove siverunt multa et cum plebe deorum.

He then returns to the more successful measures of Theodosius. There is no suggestion that either of the "tyrants" had actively fostered paganism. They are mentioned as inferior predecessors, yardsticks for measuring the achievement of Theodosius himself. The fact that Prudentius does not distinguish Maximus from Eugenius in this of all contexts hardly suggests that he saw Eugenius as sponsoring a pagan revival. For Maximus was a devout Christian. The implication is simply that *neither* took their responsibilities as Christian emperors seriously and "allowed" (*siverunt*) Rome to wallow in paganism. In the eyes of serious Christians, this had been true of most earlier Christian emperors. In this context, the implication is that paganism revived on Eugenius's watch simply because he failed to enforce Theodosius's anti-pagan laws.

For those content to accept Rufinus's account as a faithful narrative of a pagan/Christian confrontation that was decided at the Frigidus, it was natural to look for corroborating evidence in Ambrose and Prudentius. But the moment we set Rufinus on one side and look at the relevant passages of Ambrose and Prudentius by themselves, without preconceptions, even collectively they provide nothing approaching the proverbial smoking gun.[147] Nothing more than vague innuendos about pagan troops, which look even less impressive when we bear in mind that there were at least as many pagan troops in Theodosius's army. Not one clear statement linking Eugenius to paganism. If the victory at the Frigidus had really been perceived by contemporaries as a victory over paganism, we should expect to find much more explicit and emphatic evidence in the abundant writings of so well placed a contemporary as Ambrose. As for Prudentius, not a word about the actual, very recent battle that had determined Eugenius's fate.

Nowhere, perhaps, is the silence more eloquent than in those two letters Ambrose wrote to Theodosius immediately after the Frigidus. To be sure the reference in the first to Eugenius's "sacrilege" alludes, however obliquely, to favors allegedly conferred on pagans. But this has nothing to do with the Frigidus. Ambrose is replying to a letter from Theodosius reproaching him for deserting his post in Milan six months earlier.

---

147. Ambrose's letter to Eugenius has been discussed in detail in chapter 2.

He denies the accusation, claiming that he was just "avoiding the presence of one who had polluted himself with sacrilege."[148] The "sacrilege" to which he refers is those mysterious "gifts" discussed in chapter 2. That is to say, the only allusion to paganism in these two letters is Ambrose's specious retrospective justification of his own behavior six months *before* the Frigidus. There is not a hint of a recent pagan threat hanging over the heads of all good Christians now triumphantly averted.

Ambrose's silence might help to explain Chrysostom's silence, if we assume that it was (ultimately) from Ambrose that Chrysostom got the details of Theodosius leaping off his horse to pray and the spears blown back on the men who threw them. It is also worth emphasising that, when writing about the Frigidus, Chrysostom too began, like Ambrose, by linking Eugenius with Maximus. Even Augustine treated Maximus and Eugenius together in a chapter titled "On the faith and piety of Theodosius Augustus," introducing Eugenius as just "another *tyrannus* unlawfully substituted in the place of that emperor."[149] Emphasis on the importance of piety and prayer in dealing with usurpers is by no means an innovation of Christian accounts of the Frigidus. It goes all the way back to Constantine.

No less tellingly, Ambrose's silence is also reflected in Paulinus's *Life of Ambrose*. Paulinus seems to have first entered Ambrose's service after the Frigidus. He returned to Milan with Ambrose in mid- to late September 394, arriving, as he remarks with the precision of someone who was there, one day before Theodosius.[150] If Rufinus's account had really reflected the perception of contemporaries, we should have expected everyone still to be talking about the defeat of paganism. Yet Paulinus does not even mention the battle. He dismisses the entire saga of Eugenius's defeat in an ablative absolute (*extincto Eugenio*, § 31).

5

None of the sources closest to the event treats the Frigidus as the final confrontation between paganism and Christianity in the West. This perspective first appears in Rufinus.[151] If it was Claudian who first put the miraculous wind during rather than before the battle, it was surely Rufinus who invented the motif of pagan/Christian confrontation, though "invented" is perhaps too strong a term, with inappropriate implications of deceit. He was not so much inventing as adding color and specificity to the impiety that contemporary Christians must inevitably have predicated of Eugenius in the light of his defeat by the pious Theodosius. While Ambrose did not explicitly make the point himself, if asked he too would surely have agreed that God

---

148. *non enim ego ecclesiam Mediolanensium dereliqueram domini mihi iudicio commissam, sed eius vitabam praesentiam qui se sacrilegio miscuisset, Ep.* 61. 2 (*Ep. extra coll.* 2. 2, p. 178. 10–13 Zelzer).
149. *CD* v. 26; as Marrou 1951, 247–49, showed, the chapter titles go back to Augustine himself.
150. *Vita Ambros.* 32.
151. A point missed even by the subtle and sceptical McLynn 1994, 353.

granted Theodosius victory because Eugenius was soft on paganism. And if, as suggested in chapter 2, the letter Ambrose claims to have written to Eugenius before the Frigidus was in fact written (or at least rewritten) after, then the fact that he accuses the usurper of nothing more than making undefined "gifts" to prominent pagans would become even stronger evidence against the notion of a final clash between paganism and Christianity.

On top of this, as Courcelle pointed out, Rufinus's chapter on the Frigidus is very much a literary set piece.[152] Classical historians had long treated battles as opportunities for rhetorical display.[153] In general, as already remarked, ecclesiastical historians had no interest in battles as such. But Theodosius died only four months after the Frigidus, and since, like most historians of recent events, Rufinus prudently decided not to continue his narrative into the reign of living emperors, inevitably the defeat of Eugenius was the last event in his book. It is not surprising that he was tempted to make the Frigidus a fitting climax to the reign of a great Christian emperor.

Where Ambrose has Theodosius simply get off his horse to pray, Rufinus makes him climb up on a rock so that he could see and be seen by both armies. Courcelle cites a passage from Livy where Hannibal climbs onto a high point "whence he could be seen far and wide."[154] Zecchini preferred to explain Rufinus's divergence from Ambrose here by a different source, the panegyric *super victoria* [singular] *tyrannorum* that Gennadius ascribes to Paulinus of Nola.[155] But Sivan was surely right to identify this lost work as celebrating Theodosius's victory over Maximus and his co-emperor Victor in 388/9.[156] In any case, even if it postdated the Frigidus, since according to Gennadius Paulinus had represented Theodosius winning "by faith and prayer rather than arms" (*fide et oratione plus quam armis*) and since Paulinus himself explained his purpose as proclaiming Theodosius "not so much an emperor as a servant of Christ," it is unlikely that he gave a description of the battle.[157] Not that Rufinus was interested in factual details anyway. In real life, of course, Theodosius would not have done anything so foolish as expose himself to enemy fire simply in order to pray (Hannibal climbed on a rock so that he could address his troops more effectively *before* the battle). A more likely influence here is Exodus 17. 9–12, where Moses climbs to the top of a hill and raises his hand in prayer so that Joshua might defeat the Amalekites.

---

152. "un tableau de bataille très littéraire, d'allure épique," Courcelle 1969, 117.

153. For an old but wide-ranging overview, Peter 1897,2. 307–13.

154. *stans in edita rupe, unde et conspicere et conspici ab utroque posset exercitu* (Rufinus) ~ *Hannibal in promuntorio quodam, unde longe ac late prospectus esset* (Livy 21. 35. 8).

155. Genn. *Vir. ill.* 49; Zecchini 1987, 47–48.

156. Most scholars have dated the work to 394/5 (for detailed bibliography, Guttila 1990, 139–54; Mratschek 2002, 221–27), but see Sivan 1994, 577–94. For firmly dated inscriptions commemorating the defeat of Maximus and Victor as joint *tyranni*, see *ILS* 789 and 821.

157. Paul. Nol. *Ep.* 28. 6. Paulinus would have been writing far away in his villa in Spain, with no access to independent firsthand information about the course of the battle (and a year before the miraculous wind had entered the story). Since Ambrose's *De obitu Theodosii* likewise represents Theodosius as "not so much an emperor as a servant of Christ," it may well have been influenced by Paulinus.

The most important example (of course) is the transference of Ambrose's pre-battle storm to the battle itself. Whether or not Rufinus was influenced by Claudian, verbal parallels show that he drew on Ambrose's sermon on Psalm 36. Seen from a modern perspective and judged by modern standards, he was creating a miracle where none existed in his source. But in all probability Rufinus saw Ambrose's prebattle storm as a miracle too, and thought of himself as simply dramatizing his narrative by giving it a more central placing. There is also a lesser but still significant example. According to Ambrose, the actual words of Theodosius's prayer were "where is the God of Theodosius?" Rufinus gives him a speech with epic tones (*huc veni, porrige dexteram tuis*), and introduces a biblical quotation (Psalm 113. 10): "why should the nations say 'where is their God'?" (*quare dicunt gentes, ubi est Deus eorum*),[158] thereby making explicit a conflict between the Christian God and pagan gods that is at most implicit in Ambrose.

Nor is it only Flavian who plays a typological rather than strictly historical role in Rufinus's re-creation of the Frigidus. He is full of praise for the bravery of Bacurius, a former Georgian chieftain whom he had got to know personally while they were in Palestine, a man "outstanding in his faith and piety." In an earlier book he gives a detailed account of the conversion of Georgia to Christianity apparently provided for him by Bacurius.[159] It is no coincidence that the only four participants in the battle he names (apart from Theodosius and Eugenius) fall into two neatly contrasted pairs: two prophets, Flavian and John of Lycopolis, the false versus the true; and two warriors, Bacurius and Arbogast, the noble Christian barbarian versus the misguided pagan barbarian.

6

So what do all these Frigidus texts really tell us about Flavian and the pagan revival? Very little—perhaps nothing at all. We may eliminate Sozomen at once as entirely derivative, adding nothing but embellishment to Rufinus's praise of Flavian's prophetic expertise. As for Rufinus, the fact that he singled out Flavian as the pagan face of Eugenius's administration proves little. After all, Flavian *was* the most conspicuous (perhaps the only) pagan in Eugenius's administration. In all probability the only pagan Rufinus could name. The claim that Flavian was well known for his skill in divination has hitherto been thought to find confirmation in an independent pagan source, Macrobius's claim that he was an authority on augural law.[160] On this basis Rufinus has been held to provide genuine information about Flavian's interests and expertise, characteristic interests for a pagan ringleader. But at least three reservations

---

158. Psalm 78. 10; cf. Psalm 113. 10; Joel 2. 17; Micah 2. 10.
159. *HE* x. 10–11; Thélamon 1981, 93–95; Paschoud, *Zosime* 2. 2 (1979), 464; Zecchini 1987, 35–37; Braund 1994, 246–52.
160. *Sat.* i. 24. 17; so (e.g.) Leppin 2003, 209.

are in order. In the first place, as we shall see in chapter 7, Macrobius was almost certainly a Christian. In the second, augury (looking for and interpreting signs from heaven) is different from extispicy (inspecting the entrails of sacrificial animals). Augurs had nothing to do with inspecting entrails; that was the job of the *haruspex*. Augury and extispicy were two entirely different ways of ascertaining the favor of the gods.

Third, it was not the purpose of either Rufinus or Macrobius to record biographical facts about Flavian. For Rufinus, Flavian simply represented false prophecy as opposed to the true prophecy of John of Lycopolis. As for Macrobius, his purpose was to illustrate the knowledge of augural law displayed by *Vergil*, not Flavian. Once it is recognized that Macrobius was a Christian, the explanation of his selection of Flavian for this particular role is obvious: Rufinus's praise of his "wisdom" (*sapientia*) in this area. Macrobius turns out not to be an independent witness after all.

Much has often been made of a Greek oracle, supposedly circulated by pagans, according to which Christianity would last for 365 years and then disappear. We know about this curious prophecy from a long discussion in Augustine's *City of God*.[161] It is alleged to be a promise obtained by St. Peter from demons after sacrificing a one-year-old boy (i.e., a child who had lived 365 days).[162] If, with Augustine, we count from the traditional date for the Crucifixion (A.D. 29), that takes us to 394, the year of the Frigidus. It is naturally tempting to link the oracle to Eugenius's rebellion and (more specifically) to its supposed prophet, the elder Flavian. Few modern writers have been able to resist the temptation.[163] But not only does Augustine, our only source, *not* mention Flavian, he does not mention Eugenius either. Indeed, his own interpretation of the oracle *excludes* both Flavian and Eugenius. Remarkably enough, when adding 365 to 29, he *miscounted*, arriving at 398. Is this, as Dyson assumes, just a slip? If so, it is a slip that Augustine at once exploited by pointing out that the following year (399) saw the closure of pagan temples in Carthage. Thus for Augustine the fateful year marked the end of paganism rather than Christianity.[164] The closure of pagan temples in Carthage was no doubt a landmark for those who lived in North Africa, but if Augustine had known a pagan interpretation of the oracle as predicting Eugenius's victory, would he not have used it in his account of the Frigidus? Would not Rufinus too have used it in his account, which lays such emphasis on the failure of pagan predictions of victory?

Most critics have assumed that the oracle was either an anti-Christian fabrication from the start, or at any rate interpreted in an anti-Christian sense by pagans. This

---

161. *CD* 18. 53–54; Hubaux 1948, 343–54; O'Meara 1959, 67–72; Chadwick 1984, 125–26.
162. On the motif of divination by child sacrifice, Chadwick 1984, 125 n. 2.
163. Seeck 1913, 248; Geffcken 1920, 161; Klein 1971, 54 n. 81; Wytzes 1977, 171–72; Thélamon 1981, 313; Amidon 1997, 112; *PCBE* ii. 1. 827; Hedrick 2000, 44–45; Honoré 1989, 9; Adamik 1995, 189; Romano 1998, 23.
164. If Augustine had deliberately fudged his calculation to this end, why not make the coincidence exact by arriving at 399 rather than 398.

assumption has been thought to find support in the further assumption (in itself plausible) that the oracle comes from the *Philosophy from Oracles* of Porphyry, an author assumed (less plausibly) to be well known to the last pagans of Rome.[165] But the only interpretations we know of are Christian. Since Augustine begins his calculations by remarking on the vanity of trying to establish the date of the coming of Antichrist and the Final Judgement (citing three failed attempts), this oracle was surely another such *Christian* attempt. Filastrius of Brescia, writing between 385 and 391, records just such a Christian calculation, based on Isaiah's claim (61. 2) that he was sent "to proclaim the year of the Lord's favor" (*annum dei acceptabilem*), interpreted as 365 years till the Second Coming.[166] Filastrius rejects this prediction on the grounds that it was already "more than 400 years" since the coming of the Lord. The fact is that there are no grounds for believing that the oracle was even known to pagans, much less exploited in connection with the confrontation between Eugenius and Theodosius—still less (in the absence of any evidence of any kind) by Flavian.

To return to Rufinus, having described Theodosius's preparations in some detail, he needed something to balance them on the pagan side, something that would correspond to Christian expectations of pagan divination. Rufinus was an educated man, whose writings reveal him surprisingly well informed about some aspects of augury and extispicy, presumably from his knowledge of the classics rather than observation.[167] Naturally, extispicy suited his purpose better than augury. Christians found watching the movements of birds silly enough, but solemnly examining the entrails of dead animals was disgusting as well as silly. Since Rufinus's description corresponds so perfectly with the worst Christian expectations of a pagan diviner, we are bound to wonder whether he simply made it up—or at any rate added color and detail out of his imagination. There is a parallel of sorts in Augustine. To underline the importance of the defeat of the pagan barbarian Radagaisus in 406 (Ch. 5. 3), Augustine claimed that "he used to sacrifice to Jupiter every day," to the delight of Roman pagans.[168] The truth is that nothing whatever was known about this shadowy barbarian. He certainly did not sacrifice to the very Roman god Jupiter, nor can Augustine have had any information about how often he did so. He simply invented these details to dramatize the danger Radagaisus posed.

Rufinus implies that Flavian conducted the extispicy in person, but Flavian was a *pontifex*, not a *haruspex*. He also implies that the ritual was performed publicly (whence the embellishments of Hercules-standards and statues of Jupiter in Theodoret and Augustine). Flavian may have consulted *haruspices*, but he cannot possibly have done so publicly on behalf of Eugenius and his entire administration and army.

---

165. O'Meara 1959, 67–72; Chadwick 1984, 125–26; Ch. 15.
166. Fil. *Heres.* 106, p. 65 Marx; *PCBE* ii. 1 (1999), 818.
167. Linderski 1981, 213–15.
168. Aug. *CD* v. 23; *Sermo* 105. 13.

Nor is it only Flavian's preparations that have been written up. Let us take a closer look at Rufinus's account of Theodosius's preparations:

> He made ready for war by arming himself not so much with weapons as with fasts and prayers; guarded not so much by the night watch as by nightly vigils in prayer, he would go round all the places of prayer with the priests and people, lie prostrate in sackcloth before the reliquaries of the martyrs and apostles, and implore assistance through the faithful intercession of the saints.

Did Theodosius do *all* these things? Did he really lie prostrate in sackcloth? Rufinus has undoubtedly added color and detail here too. Theodoret added apostles on white horses, and Sozomen too expanded Rufinus's dossier. After setting out from Constantinople, Theodosius stopped at a church of John the Baptist and prayed for the Baptist's help. Months later, at the very moment (Sozomen claims) that the battle was being fought, a demoniac abused the Baptist, and cried out "You are defeating me and laying snares against my army"[169]—presumably addressing the devil.[170] The emperor may well have prayed at this church, but the rest is later embellishment. Above all, Rufinus's *emphasis* must be the very opposite of the truth. While Theodosius's piety is beyond question, on any realistic assessment, as an experienced and conscientious but not very successful general, he is bound to have devoted as much time and effort as he possibly could to conventional military preparations. It is revealing here to contrast the detailed account by Pacatus of his preparations for the campaign against Maximus: although (he claims) marching not so much to fight as to punish an unworthy enemy, "yet you carried out the war with such careful planning and so many calculations that you seemed to be preparing to meet some Perseus or Pyrrhus or even Hannibal himself." According to Philostorgius, Theodosius spent the entire winter before he set out for the West preparing for the campaign against Eugenius.[171] It was from the theologians rather than military sources that Rufinus got his emphasis on prayer as the best preparation for battle.

As for the prophecies of John of Lycopolis,[172] they too have been adjusted to fit Rufinus's context and purpose. Here we are fortunate to have what must have been Rufinus's source, the (now anonymous) *Historia Monachorum* (*HM*), an account in Greek of a pilgrimage to Lower Egypt by seven monks in the winter of 394–95, which Rufinus himself translated into Latin a year or so after finishing his *Historia Ecclesiastica*. The *HM* begins its life of John of Lycopolis by claiming that he foretold to the emperor Theodosius everything that happened in the world by the will of God, including "the revolt of tyrants and their prompt defeat, and the destruction of the barbarians who

---

169. Soz. vii. 24. 2 and 8.
170. So O'Donnell 1978, 139.
171. Pacat. *Pan. Theod.* 32, with Nixon in Nixon and Rodgers 1994, 495–98; Phil. *HE* xi. 2.
172. Thélamon 1981, 341–43.

attacked him."[173] Obviously we cannot be sure exactly what John said, but this text is as close as we could ever hope for. The seven pilgrims visited John himself in Lycopolis, and while they were there he produced one final prophecy (dying soon after): that the news of the Frigidus had just reached Alexandria on that very day, and that Theodosius would shortly die a natural death.[174]

The neutral "prompt" defeat of the *HM* did not suit Rufinus for either "tyrant." So he made John prophesy a "bloodless" defeat for Maximus, in keeping with the now common Christian belief that pious emperors won by prayer alone. "Prompt" was even less appropriate for the Frigidus, so he made John foretell a victory "with great bloodshed on both sides." The temptation to make prophecies and predictions more accurate by retroactively adjusting them against the historical record is almost irresistible. Sozomen goes one step further by making John prophesy to Theodosius himself that he would defeat Eugenius and then die (vii. 22. 8). Theodoret follows Rufinus in making John prophesy a bloodless victory over Maximus and one "with much slaughter" over Eugenius (v. 24. 2).[175]

Since Rufinus has either improved or invented virtually every detail in his picture of Theodosius's preparations for battle, we need not take his "pagan" preparations as literally as most modern critics have. The description of Flavian's sacrifice is an integral part of the preparations of the two sides for battle *in Rufinus's chapter*. Moderns have read more into it than even Rufinus intended by taking it out of this context and inserting it into an entirely different context, the modern hypothesis of a revival of paganism at Rome. In its original context it is an exercise in what the rhetoricians call *enargeia* (a "vividly detailed depiction... through the enumeration of (real or invented) observable details")[176] designed to balance the equally fanciful description of the very different preparations of Theodosius. Just like Augustine's picture of Radagaisus's daily sacrifices to Jupiter, it was never meant to be treated as a straightforward record of literal fact. It was perhaps because he appreciated this that Socrates dropped the section when adapting Rufinus's account. It may be more than coincidence that, on the very next page of his book, Socrates expressly repudiates the techniques ancient historians used to play up or down the events they were describing.[177]

One final point. How important was the Frigidus in the grand scheme of things? On the standard modern view, it was a watershed of European history; Eugenius's defeat crushed the pagan reaction and sealed the fate of paganism in the West. But not even Rufinus makes so extravagant a claim. Would things have turned out so very dif-

---

173. τήν τε τῶν τυράννων αὐτῷ ἐπανάστασιν καὶ τὴν ταχεῖαν πάλιν αὐτῶν ἀναίρεσιν, *HM* i. 1, p. 9 Festugière.
174. *HM* i. 64, p. 35 Festugière.
175. It seems hard to doubt that Theodoret drew directly on Rufinus here, presumably in a Greek translation, though the version printed below the Latin text in Mommsen's edition (p. 1036) omits this detail.
176. Lausberg 1998, § 810, p. 359.
177. Socr. *HE* vi. 1. 3 (the Frigidus closes Bk v, except for a brief epilogue).

ferently if Eugenius had won? It is unlikely that he would have been ambitious enough to try to conquer the eastern provinces,[178] so in all probability the same division between East and West would have ensued, with Arcadius ruling in the East.[179] We have seen that Eugenius did not restore the subsidies, but even if he had won and restored both subsidies and sacrifice, there is little reason to believe that this would have halted the steady and surely now irreversible spread of Christianity, or that paganism could ever have recovered its hold on the populace at large—or indeed survived much longer than it did. Roman paganism was not extinguished on the field of battle or even by imperial laws. It died a natural death, and was already mortally ill before Theodosius embarked on his final campaign.

---

178. So, briefly, Demandt in Bratož 1996, 31–43 at 40–41. There is little reason to believe that Arbogast could have succeeded where Stilicho failed.

179. If Theodosius had survived his victory by a decade or so, that just might have forestalled by a generation the surely inevitable split between East and West.

4

PRIESTS AND INITIATES

Much of our evidence for the religious affiliations of pagan aristocrats comes from inscribed dedications—more indeed than most people probably realize. In simpler times it was taken for granted that inscriptions provided a peculiarly uncomplicated sort of evidence, bare facts not mediated by human art or bias. We have now come to realize that few facts are bare. We need to know what sort of monuments these dedications were inscribed on, where they were erected, by whom, and with what purpose. After all, if it is their honorands' private religious beliefs they are supposed to be attesting, why was it considered appropriate to record this sort of information on public dedications? And which dedications were in fact public?

1: ROMAN PRIESTHOODS

Let us begin with the largest category, priesthoods of the Roman state cults. Much has been made of the priesthoods held by the last few generations of Roman aristocrats. Since the traditional priesthoods were monopolized by men of noble birth, in modern studies this has often been interpreted as proving that aristocrats were the champions of the traditional cults. The evidence is not quite so straightforward. Herbert Bloch wrote of these men having a "policy" of "advertis[ing] . . . their various religious activities and achievements" on dedications and epitaphs.[1] Many other critics have tacitly followed this approach, taking it for granted that anyone epigraphically attested as a *pontifex* was a devout pagan. Implying as it does that they were deliberately and defiantly proclaiming their paganism, this is a misleading perspective.

In the first place, by the late fourth century the great majority of these dedications were inscribed on private monuments, erected in cult settings or private houses (§ 4). Without these dedications, in most cases we would not know that these men were pagans at all. More important, listing priesthoods on dedications and epitaphs was by no means an innovation of the fourth century. Already in the first they were regularly included in cursus inscriptions, normally placed conspicuously out of chronological sequence at the beginning or end of a man's career together with his

---

1. Bloch 1945, 211.

highest honors (the consulship or proconsulship of Asia or Africa).[2] The cursus of the younger Pliny lists his consulate and augurate out of sequence before a detailed list of posts held:[3]

> consul, *augur*, curator alvei Tiberis et riparum et cloacarum urbis, praefectus aerari Saturni...

Priesthoods were regarded as political rewards rather than religious responsibilities. There can be no question that Pliny valued his augurate at least as highly as his consulate.[4] In theory the colleges co-opted new members themselves, but in practice they supplied nominations to the emperor, who, on top of being *pontifex maximus*, was a member of every college.[5] Not surprisingly, he was careful to keep so important a source of political patronage under his personal control. Our sources often speak as if priesthoods were straightforwardly within the emperor's gift.[6] The locus classicus is a passage of Seneca on the sort of honors the dissatisfied ambitious man hopes for from the emperor:

> He has given me the praetorship, but I had hoped for the consulship; he has given me the twelve *fasces*, but not made me *consul ordinarius*; he bade the year be dated by my name, but failed me with regard to a priesthood; I was co-opted into a priestly college, but why only one?

The future emperor Galba received the *ornamenta triumphalia* and three priesthoods, one major and two minor, as a reward for victories in Africa and Germany.[7]

Priesthoods were ranked as major and minor, with the four *amplissima collegia* (*pontifices, augures, quindecimviri sacris faciundis,* and *septemviri epulonum*) the most sought after. In 274 Aurelian established the new college of *pontifices Solis*, at once counted among the major priesthoods.[8] After 274 the original pontiffs styled themselves *pontifices maiores*,[9] though from around the middle of the fourth century we occasionally find the style *pontifices Vestae*, first known from four parallel dedications commemorating the second city prefecture (357–59) of Symmachus's father-in-law

---

2. Lewis 1955, 10; Sherwin-White 1966, 272.
3. *CIL* v. 5262 (= *ILS* 2927), 5263 and 5667. Elisions (...) indicate the omission of one or more administrative posts. In citing cursuses in this chapter, I (a) expand abbreviations and supplement reasonably certain missing letters without indication; (b) italicize priesthoods; and (c) separate posts with a comma. There would be no point in translating such lists, but for ease of comprehension I give all posts and titles in the nominative case.
4. Pliny, *Epp.* ii. 1. 8; iv. 8; x. 13.
5. See the section "Cooptatus in omnia collegia" in Rüpke 2005, 1603–5.
6. Lewis 1955, 16–17; Millar 1977, 355–58.
7. Seneca, *De ira* iii. 31. 2; Suet. *Galb.* 8. 1; F. Millar 1977, 297–99.
8. Christol 1986, 65, 167–68.
9. The style *pontifex maior* is in fact occasionally found earlier, to distinguish from the *pontifices minores*: Panciera 2006, 995.

Memmius Orfitus.[10] Praetextatus is twice styled *pontifex Vestae*, but true conservatives like Symmachus and Flavian preferred the more traditional *pontifex maior*.

By the late empire, and especially after the conversion of Constantine, the approval of the mostly absent emperor must have become more and more a formality and the membership of the colleges more and more exclusive and self-perpetuating. Already in the first century something like a third of all holders of major priesthoods were allowed to inherit them from fathers, grandfathers, or other kinsmen. And the well-born were not only permitted but also encouraged to hold several. Accumulation of one major and one or more minor priesthoods was always common, but the first man known to have held two major priesthoods is P. Cluvius Maximus Paullinus, cos. ca. 143. After that, only two more before the reign of Aurelian: C. Fulvius Plautianus, cos. II. 203, and Octavius Appius Suetrius Sabinus, cos. 214 and 240.[11] By the fourth century accumulation of even the major priesthoods became common.

Almost all the minor priesthoods are last attested in the third century. In the case of the Arvals, the argument from silence is particularly strong. Up till 241 the acta inscribed in the grove of Dea Dia are now complete enough to supply the names of almost the entire brotherhood over a period of 250 years. Then a gap of more than sixty years before a single name dated to 304, inscribed on the back of the acta for 134–35 (itself an ominous sign of the dilapidation of the sanctuary).[12] The presumption is that this was an attempt to revive a defunct order under the tetrarchs when, in Victor's words, "the oldest cults were accorded the utmost respect." But this "desperate attempt" was short-lived; none of the fourth-century pagan priests discussed in this chapter were Arvals.[13]

Just one Salius palatinus stands on record, C. Vettius Cossinius Rufinus cos. 316. A dedication by two otherwise unknown and undatable pontiffs of Vesta records the refurbishing of the *mansiones* of the Salii.[14] The fact that they claim to have made their repairs *pecunia sua* has often been taken to imply a date after 382 (and so to reflect the "pagan revival"), but, given the lack of any Salii later than Rufinus, as with the Arvals a short-lived tetrarchic revival is more likely. Three men are described as *duodecimvir urbis Romae*, a college created in connection with the temple of Venus and Roma dedicated by Hadrian in 135, generally known as *templum urbis* in late antiquity:[15] T. Fl. Postumius Titianus cos. II 301; M. Aurelius Consius Quartus in a dedication from the early 340s; and Caelius Hilarianus in a dedication dated 13 May 377.[16]

---

10. Chastagnol 1962, 139–40.

11. For sources and bibliography, Rüpke 2005, nos. 1275, 1773, and 2557.

12. Scheid 1990b, 139; Scheid 1992, 219–23. The last sign of use at the baths in the Arval grove is a purse of coins dated to 334/5, from which Scheid and Broise 1987, 275–77, inferred that the sanctuary was closed by Constans's law of 341 (*Cod. Theod.* 16. 10. 1). But no other Roman cult seems to have been affected by this law, and the fact that tablets of the Acta were reused in the adjacent basilica of Saints Faustinus and Viatrix built by Pope Damasus (Scheid and Broise 1980, 242–48) suggest that it had been abandoned.

13. *veterrimae religiones castissime curatae, Caes.* 39. 45; "tentative désespérée" Scheid 1990a, 738–40.

14. *ILS* 4944 (misinterpreted by Curran 2000, 207 n. 266).

15. Wissowa 1912, 340; Chastagnol 1987, 277 n. 37.

16. *ILS* 1249; *CIL* vi. 1419b; *ILS* 4148; also -*anus* in *ILS* 1198.

Did the minor priesthoods disappear, or simply lose prestige? The fact that another dedication for Cossinius Rufinus of the same date omits his Saliate suggests the possibility that other minor priesthoods might have survived into the fourth century but (like the suffect consulate) were no longer considered worth listing.[17] Postumius Titianus's duodecimvirate is usually assumed to have been acquired late in life, since it is not listed among his priesthoods in an early cursus.[18] But it may be that the fourth-century nobility no longer bothered to list minor priesthoods. Consius Quartus and Caelius Hilarianus were rather minor figures.

The fact that accumulation of major priesthoods begins about the time minor priesthoods disappear suggests a general decrease in the number of priesthoods. While it is natural to connect this decrease with the spread of Christianity, that need not imply that the state cults as a whole were already in general decline. In order to maintain the exclusivity of the colleges, there had to be fewer places than candidates. In the high empire there were perhaps as many as forty *pontifices* and augurs and at least twenty *XVviri*; the *septemviri epulonum* may have remained at ten, and the number of *pontifices Solis* is unknown. That makes perhaps as many as eighty places in the major priesthoods alone, not to mention several hundred minor priesthoods.[19]

In the first and second centuries there may have been enough priesthoods to go around much of the Roman elite on an even division. Whence the practice of cumulation, to ensure that there was competition. It was an essential feature of the system that a man like the younger Pliny, a wealthy and deserving public servant but on the fringes of the aristocracy, should be kept waiting till his forties. By the mid-fourth century, when perhaps no more than half the aristocracy remained pagan, it may be that any noble who wanted could obtain a major priesthood, which would explain the decline in the minor priesthoods.

For centuries, most aristocrats listed their priesthoods along with all their other *honores* on cursus inscriptions as a matter of course, with no thought of "advertising…their religious activities," and there is no reason to suppose that the situation had changed by at any rate the age of Constantine. The prestige value of Roman priesthoods is clearly enough illustrated by their inclusion in the cursus. But more specific details are illustrated by their location within the cursus. Revealingly enough, some cursuses list priesthoods at the point in the honorand's career they were awarded. For example, Julius Celsus suff. cos. 92 evidently became a *quindecimvir* between his governorship of Cilicia and a consular post; and Terentius Gentianus suff. cos. 116 a *pontifex* between his consulship and governorship of Macedonia. More revealing still, the two priesthoods of Valerius Festus suff. cos. 71

---

17. *ILS* 1217; *CIL* vi. 32040; quoted in Chastagnol 1962, 63–64. Even in earlier times, membership of the Salii was not always mentioned (Christol 1986, 65 n. 7).

18. Chastagnol 1962, 44; *PLRE* i. 919; PIR[2] P. 899 (p. 380).

19. For a convenient brief list of all the priesthoods with the best modern estimate of their numbers, Rüpke 2007, 223–28; see now the annual lists in Rüpke 2005 (ET 2008).

appear at differerent points in his cursus, presumably because he won them on different occasions.[20]

This practice underlines the equivalence of priesthoods to public offices. It remained standard right down to the end of paganism. For example, Q. Flavius Maesius Egnatius Lollianus Mavortius, cos. 355: quaestor, praetor, *augur*, consularis alvei Tiberis…; Turcius Apronianus Asterius, PVR[21] 362–64: suffect consul, quaestor, praetor, *quindecimvir*, corrector Tusciae et Umbriae…; Memmius Vitrasius Orfitus, PVR 353–55 and 357–58: quaestor, praetor, suffect consul, *pontifex Solis, quindecimvir, pontifex maior*, consularis Siciliae…;[22] Symmachus cos. 391: quaestor, praetor, *pontifex maior*, corrector Lucaniae et Brittiorum…; and the elder Flavian: quaestor, praetor, *pontifex maior*, consularis Siciliae….[23]

There is also a smaller group where the priesthoods appear together at the very beginning of the honorand's career: Furius Placidus, cos. 343: *pontifex maior, augur, quindecimvir*, corrector Venetiarum…; Vulcacius Rufinus: *pontifex maior*, consularis Numidiae…(347);[24] Clodius Octavianus: *pontifex maior*, consularis Pannoniarum…(363);[25] L. Aur. Avianius Symmachus PVR 364/5: *quindecimvir, pontifex maior*, praefectus annonae….[26] The *PLRE* entries for this second group state that the priesthoods need not have been held as early as this. But why not? It is true that priesthoods are sometimes listed out of sequence at the beginning of a cursus, but only when they are placed together with the honorand's highest posts. Thus the younger Pliny (*consul, augur*…). And such was the cachet of multiple priesthoods that, even when won at different times, they were sometimes grouped together out of sequence, in order of rank, at the beginning of the cursus.[27] Thus the infamous Fabricius Veiento, with three consulships and four priesthoods under the Flavians. His one surviving dedication reduces his *honores* to just *cos. III* followed by his priesthoods spelled out in full.[28] But in every case in the second group of fourth-century dedications the highest post appears in its proper position in the sequence, at the opposite end of the cursus from the priesthoods.

In both groups distinguished here priesthoods precede the honorand's first significant post, normally a provincial governorship. The only difference between them is that in the first group the offices that precede the priesthoods are one or more of the trio quaestorship, praetorship, and suffect consulship. By the mid-fourth century the quaestorship was held by aristocrats as early as the mid-teens; the praetorship in

20. *ILS* 8971, 1046, 989, with Syme *RP* vi. 423; see too *RP* iv. 404. For another case of priesthoods at two different points in a cursus, Q. Pomponius Munatianus Clodianus in the late third century: *AE* 1974, 129, with Christol 1986, 224–38.

21. For the sake of brevity I use the convenient ancient abbreviations PVR = *praefectus urbis Romae* and PPO = *praefectus praetorio*.

22. *ILS* 1223, 1224a; 1229 (early career); 1243.

23. *ILS* 2946 and 2947.

24. *ILS* 1237; *PLRE* i. 782–83.

25. *ILS* 1253; *PLRE* i. 637.

26. *ILS* 1257; *PLRE* i. 865–66.

27. Many examples collected by Syme vi. 423–24.

28. *PIR* P. 654 (Silvanus); *ILS* 1010; *PIR* F. 91 (Veiento).

or before the early twenties; and the suffect consulship (now often spurned by the nobility) in the early twenties.[29] The praetorship still involved some real duties, but its main function, accompanied by extravagant games, was to mark a young noble's entry into public life.[30] The one feature common to all members of the second group is that they do not list either quaestorship or praetorship, in all probability because they were taken for granted in an aristocratic career. The slightly abbreviated cursus given Praetextatus on his monument in the Forum Romanum omits the quaestorship and praetorship recorded in his two surviving full cursuses.[31]

Whether or not the men in this second group actually held either quaestorship or praetorship, their priesthoods are probably listed in chronological sequence at the beginning of the cursus. Two of a group of eight late third-century dedications by urban praetors to Hercules at the Ara Maxima show praetors who are already *quindecimviri sacris faciundis*.[32] From the age of Augustus on it had been common for members of the nobility to win their priesthoods as early as this (Augustus himself acquired his first pontificate at the age of fifteen),[33] and there is no reason to doubt that all these fourth-century nobles acquired their priesthoods in the traditional way by their early twenties, before holding their earliest provincial command.

In the early empire new men had to wait rather longer, till just before or after the consulship (which then meant mid- to late thirties).[34] Here too the old pattern continued. The long career of a rather minor figure of the age of Constantine, C. Iulius Rufinianus Ablabius Tatianus, is an instructive case:[35]

> Rufiniani oratoris filius, fisci patronus rationum summarum, adlectus inter consulares iudicio divi Constantini, legatus provinciae Asiae, corrector Tusciae et Umbriae, consularis Aemiliae et Liguriae, *pontifex Vestae matris et in collegio pontificum promagister, sacerdos Herculis*, consularis Campaniae.

The long sequence of junior posts, culminating in the governorship of Campania, the most prestigious of the Italian governorships, makes it clear that Tatianus was a man of undistinguished origins who worked hard to achieve his modest success. It was not till near the end of his career that he was rewarded with two priesthoods, the second a mysterious title unattested before the fourth century, but apparently carrying some prestige, since Praetextatus was a *curialis Herculis*.[36]

---

29. Chastagnol 1958, 221–53 = 1987, 83–115.
30. On the age of praetors, Chastagnol 1958, 238; and 1992, 243–47. *Cod. Theod.* vi. 4. 1 envisages quaestors younger than sixteen years old.
31. *CIL* vi. 1779a, with addenda in vi. 8. 3 (2000), p. 4758; so too the dedication by his child (*ILS* 1258), p. 158.
32. 314a and 318 at *CIL* vi. 312–19 (cf. *ILS* 3402–9); for the date of 315 see Chastagnol 1962, 32; Iun. Priscillianus Maximus (in the 290s) is another praetor with two priesthoods (*PLRE* i. 589).
33. Howe 1904, 9–11; Lewis 1955, 25–26; Syme vi. 421–22.
34. For a summary of the evidence, Scheid 1990b, 160–70.
35. *CIL* X. 1125; *PLRE* i. 875–76.
36. *ILS* 1259, abbreviated to a bare *curiali* on *CIL* vi. 1778. There is also an apparently fourth-century *pon[tifex] Herculis* on *CIL* vi. 30893 (with Mommsen' note).

Next, two more distinguished careers. First the case of Rufius Caeionius Volusianus cos. 311 and 314. As one of five illustrations of characteristic senatorial careers in the age of Constantine, Chastagnol presented Volusianus's cursus as follows:[37]

Suffect consul, *pontifex Solis, augur*, corrector Italiae (282–9), proconsul Africae, [*praefectus praetorio* (PPO), *praefectus urbi Romae* (PVR), consul ord. II (311)] comes, PVR II (313–5), consul III (314).

That would be a characteristic *aristocratic* career. But the placing of the two priest-hoods[38] in second and third place is pure speculation. They do not appear in the only full cursus we have for Volusianus, dating from (or soon after) 314, which omits the posts bracketed above, since they were held under Maxentius. Two fragmentary inscriptional lists imply that the priesthoods were late acquisitions,[39] which would be surprising in an aristocrat. The explanation is provided by the horoscope of a Roman senator Barnes has identified as Ceionius Rufius Albinus cos. 335, Volusianus's son.[40] According to the horoscope, this man's father won two ordinary consulates before being driven into exile by his enemies. Only Volusianus and Albinus fit the data of the horoscope.[41] The one detail it supplies relevant to the present context is that Volusianus's origin was undistinguished.[42] Not surprisingly for a successful man, he made a brilliant marriage[43] and founded one of the great houses of the fourth century. Yet he was not himself of noble birth. It may be that it was not till after his consulship in 314, while he was prefect of Rome, that he was finally invited to join the exclusive fraternity of the *XVviri sacris faciundis*.

Second, Fabius Titianus, who after three provincial governorships and a post at court became consul in 337, PVR in 339–41, PPO (of Gaul) in 341–49, and finally PVR again in 350–51 under Magnentius.[44] No dedication earlier than 350 records a priest-hood, but a votive inscription of that year offers the following cursus: "*XVvir sacris faciundis,* consul ordinarius, iterum praefectus urbi." His names do not suggest any aristocratic connection, and the obvious explanation is that, for all his long and distin-guished career, Titianus too was not of noble birth. But in every age the nobility has always been happy to marry their daughters to powerful new men, and the elder

---

37. Chastagnol 1982, 171.
38. By an uncharacteristic error Chastagnol in addition named the wrong priesthoods.
39. Barnes 1982, 121.
40. Firm. Mat. *Mathesis* ii. 29. 10–20; Barnes 1975, 40–49.
41. However, it is remarkable that, while supplying a detailed career for Albinus, the one detail Maternus omits is the highest, his consulship. I suggest that a couple of words have fallen out of the text (by homoeoteleuton): *in administrationem Campaniae primum destinatus est, deinde Achaiae proconsula-tum, post vero ad Asiae proconsulatum et <ordinarium consulatum et> praefecturam urbi Romae* (p. 81. 17–19 Kroll-Skutsch).
42. *paternum genus ostendit ignobile,* p. 82. 7 Kroll-Skutsch.
43. Probably a Nummia Albina, descended from a long line of consuls; Barnes 1975, 44–45.
44. For the details, Chastagnol 1962, 107–11; *PLRE* i. 919–20.

Symmachus chose one of Titianus's daughters (Symmachus had a brother called Celsinus Titianus)[45] and he was finally admitted to the magic circle of the priestly fraternities. As though to the manner born, in his 350 dedication he adopts the traditional abbreviated cursus of the truly great: consulship, two urban prefectures—and the coping stone, his new priesthood.

It is not without justification that membership of the priestly colleges in the early empire has been treated "as an aspect not of Roman religion but of the history of the senatorial élite."[46] And in the fourth century, as before, it is clear that the qualifications for a priesthood remained either noble birth or (a distant second) a distinguished career. When making his point that, despite removing the altar of Victory from the senate house, in other respects Constantius II treated Roman paganism with great respect during his 357 visit, Symmachus describes how he "filled up the priesthoods with *nobles*" (*replevit nobilibus sacerdotia*).[47] Grandees like Rufius Volusianus and Fabius Titianus had to wait till perhaps their fifties to be admitted. In earlier centuries the emperor would have rewarded promising newcomers earlier than this, but when the decision was left entirely to existing members of the colleges, they were likely to be less welcoming.

The fact that they continued to structure their dedications in the same way does not in itself prove that the honorands themselves continued to look on their priesthoods as social prizes. Indeed, there must always have been some pontiffs who took the religious aspects of their posts seriously. In the Republic and early empire it was taken for granted that those who presided over the cults of the city should be chosen from among the elite. But the growing pressure of Christianity, with its very different priests, elected at a mature age to lead communities of Christians, may eventually have prompted more religiously inclined pagans to see their pontifical duties in a new light.

It is natural to wonder whether Praetextatus was one such. Macrobius presents him as a religious expert, and one of the poems inscribed on his funerary monument describes him dismissing his worldly *honores* as "fleeting and trifling" compared to his various initiations:

> quid nunc honores aut potestates loquar
> hominumque votis adpetita gaudia,
> quae tu caduca ac parva semper autumans
> divum sacerdos infulis celsus clues?

The cursus on his monument *distinguishes* between his priestly and political honors. After a list of priesthoods and initiations, the transition to public offices is marked, uniquely on the surviving evidence, by the formula *in re publica vero*:

---

45. Chastagnol 1962, 218; *PLRE* i. 1146, stemma 27.
46. Gordon in Beard and North 1990, 221. Significantly enough, the subtitle of Lewis 1955 was *A Study of the Nobility*.
47. *Rel.* 3. 7.

D(is) M(anibus). Vettius Agorius Praetextatus, augur, pontifex Vestae, pontifex Solis, quindecemvir, curialis Herculis, sacratus Libero et Eleusiniis, hierophanta, neocorus, tauroboliatus, pater patrum. *In re publica vero*: quaestor candidatus, pr(a)etor urbanus, corrector Tusciae et Umbriae, consularis Lusitaniae, proconsule Achaiae, praefectus urbi, legatus a senatu missus VII, praefectus praetorio II Italiae et Illyrici, consul ordinarius designatus.

It is worth emphasizing that there is no hint of this perspective in the cursuses of Praetextatus's supposed fellow pagan champions, Symmachus and the elder Flavian. In both cases their one priesthood (*pontifex maior*) is listed in its chronological place between an early praetorship and their first provincial governorship. It is also worth emphasizing that, in an age when so many pagan grandees held two, three, or even (like Praetextatus) four Roman priesthoods, both Symmachus and Flavian held only one each.

It is tempting to attach a similar significance to the four priesthoods that prominently open the cursus of L. Aradius Valerius Proculus cos. 340, whose distinguished career ran from about 315 to 351:[48]

> *Augur, pontifex maior, quindecimvir sacris faciundis, pontifex Flavialis,* praetor tutelaris, legatus propraetore provinciae Numidiae, peraequator census provinciae Callaeciae, praeses provinciae Byzacenae, consularis Europae et Thraciae, consularis Siciliae, comes ordinis secundi, comes ordinis primi, proconsul prov. Africae…perfunctus officio praefecturae praetorio, comes iterum ordinis primi intra palatium, praefectus urbi, consul ordinarius.

On this basis Proculus has been described as a "devout" or "zealous" pagan, a "païen engagé," a "grand seigneur païen." But it is entirely possible that he simply acquired all these priesthoods before a late praetorship.

In a cursus from the 380s it might have been legitimate to suspect a defiantly pagan emphasis. But in 340 Christianity posed no imminent threat to Roman paganism. The priesthoods are simply details in the litany of Proculus's *honores*. Much has been made of the fact that he restored the portico of a temple of Cybele and Attis in Carthage while proconsul of Africa.[49] But porticoes were public amenities. Dedications throughout the century reveal proconsuls of Africa sponsoring the restoration of public buildings in Carthage, most of them at public expense.[50] The state monitored major building projects, and it is unlikely that Proculus had a free hand. The probability is that he chose from a list of buildings needing renovation provided by local

---

48. Barnes 1982, 119–20.
49. *CIL* viii. 1694; Matthews 1973, 185. Chastagnol 1962, 100, carelessly writes *altar*; the inscription is incomplete, but enough survives to make clear that he restored a portico: Lepelley, *Cités* ii. 14.
50. Lepelley, *Cités* ii. 13–53.

authorities. That he chose a temple rather than (say) baths may reflect his personal inclination, but it does not make him a zealot.

In addition to being an *augur, pontifex maior,* and *quindecimvir,* Proculus appears on three of these dedications with the short-lived but instructive title *pontifex Flavialis.* Shortly before the end of his reign Constantine allowed the Umbrian town of Hispellum to erect a temple to the imperial house, the *gens Flavia,* on the condition that it was not to be polluted by sacrifice.[51] A dedication found at Hispellum reveals a local official of equestrian rank as *pontifex gentis Flaviae.* He is described as the *editor* of gladiatorial games and theatrical shows, evidently those mentioned in Constantine's letter to Hispellum.[52] Presumably, this man did most of the actual work with Proculus as honorary colleague (perhaps on the strength of property he owned in the area) to elevate the status of the cult. Proculus cannot have become *pontifex Flavialis* before the establishment of the cult, about 333.

While the *pontificatus Flavialis* was technically a "pagan" cult, it was a cult sanctioned by and actually named after Constantine. Its award was a mark of imperial favor. Though an aristocrat of old Rome, Proculus enjoyed high favor with Constantine. His cursus lists three conferments of the title of *comes,* the third time *intra palatium,* implying that he served at court in Constantinople. The base of his statue in the Forum of Trajan preserves a flattering letter from Constantine himself (p. 9). A pagan who publicly reproduced such a letter from the first Christian emperor can hardly be described as exercising "independence...in the face of the Constantinian dynasty."[53] He was still sufficiently influential at court to obtain the (for an aristocrat) rare distinction of an ordinary consulate from Constans in 340. The fact that the usurper Magnentius called the grand old man out of retirement to be prefect of Rome in 351 is not to be seen as an attempt to curry favor with pagans, but rather as part of his well-documented attempt to win recognition from Constantius II, by appointing a tried and trusted Constantinian supporter.

A closer look at Proculus's cursus as a whole (we have four copies, three from the family house on the Caelian Hill)[54] reveals perhaps the longest and most boastful cursus of the age, no fewer than twelve offices or titles, including a number of minor items one would hardly expect to see solemnly spelled out in the career of such a grandee.[55] In context, the *pontificatus Flavialis* makes it clear that Proculus's cursus begins as it does for reasons of prestige rather than pagan pride. He may have been a pious pagan, who took his priestly duties seriously. But it is a misunderstanding of the nature and function of Roman state priesthoods to proclaim such men pagan champions, let alone leaders of a pagan party.

---

51. *ne aedis nostro numini dedicata cuiusquam contagiose superstitionis fraudibus polluatur, ILS* 705, line 46.
52. C. Matrinius Aurelius Antoninus (*ILS* 6623); *PLRE* i. 75; and Lepelley in Christol 1992, 355–58.
53. Salzman 2002, 76.
54. Quoted in full by Chastagnol 1962, 96–100; cf. *PLRE* i. 747–48.
55. For example, *peraequator census provinciae Callaeciae,* an official charged with revising the census, generally regarded as "onerous...[and] a disagreeable imposition" (Jones, *LRE* ii. 537, iii. 156 n. 35).

2: "ORIENTAL" INITIATIONS

The other main category of dedications is those attesting priesthoods and initiations in what have traditionally been called "oriental" cults. The distinction goes back more than a century to the work of Franz Cumont, summarized in his classic *Oriental Religions in Roman Paganism* (1911).[56] The basic thesis is that during the early empire it was the ecstatic cults of the Orient that met the spiritual needs left unfulfilled by the empty ritual of the state cults. The very term "oriental," with its implication of direct contact with exotic eastern cults, is misleading. Some of these cults (notably Isis, Magna Mater, and Mithras) had long been domesticated (the latter perhaps even invented) in Rome. Cumont also virtually ignored the still-popular mysteries of Dionysus, which ultimately derived from archaic Greece.[57] Yet while the inadequacy of the term "oriental" is now universally recognized, in the absence of a succinct and satisfactory alternative, I propose to go on using it, without scare quotes, as a convenient shorthand.

It was not long before this thesis was applied to the "pagan revival" of the fourth century, by Robinson, who concluded that "the main strength of the pagan revival was supplied primarily by the oriental religions."[58] There is no doubt some truth in this view. The actual religious experiences these dedications commemorate were no doubt more emotional than anything the state cults could offer. But there are many problems with the stronger formulation developed in Bloch's famous article of 1945, namely that it was the oriental cults that energized the last generation of pagans to resist the encroachment of Christianity on the state cults.

The main evidence for these oriental initiations and priesthoods is a series of dedications that record exotic-sounding initiations and priesthoods for a handful of members of the fourth-century Roman nobility.[59] These dedications may be divided into two main groups. First, seven found at the site of a Mithraeum in the Campus Martius in Rome, all concerned with a single family.[60] Second, a couple of dozen dedications mostly from a shrine of Magna Mater and Attis on the Vatican hill known as the Phrygianum.[61] Some still survive; some have not been seen since they were dug up in 1609 during the construction of St. Peter's. According to Matthews these dedications reveal cults that "convey an atmosphere of personal and emotional intensity" that has "little to do with the state cults."[62] This may be true of the actual

---

56. Latest French edition 1929, reprinted in 2006 with an introduction by C. Bonnet and F. van Haeperen.

57. Nilsson 1957.

58. Robinson 1915, 87–101 at 89.

59. All these inscriptions have been republished by M. J. Vermaseren, *Corpus Inscriptionum et Monumentorum Religionis Mithriacae* 1 (The Hague 1956) [= *CIMRM*] and *Corpus Cultus Cybelae Attidisque* 3 (Leiden 1977) [= *CCCA*]. It has to be said that both text and notes offered in these two works are shockingly inaccurate.

60. *ILS* 4267a–e, 4268, and 4269; Vermaseren, *CIMRM* 1 (1956), 171–73, nos. 399–406; Griffith 1998.

61. Platner-Ashby 1929, 325–26; Vermaseren in *CCCA* 3 (1977), 47–49.

62. Matthews 1973, 177, 179.

initiations commemorated by these dedications. But is it true of the dedications themselves? Are they really as "private" as Matthews (after many others) assumed? They are private in that they were inscribed in or around temples rather than on monuments erected in the public spaces of Rome. But they were not completely inaccessible to the general public.

Let us begin with the Campus Martius group. Five report the promotion of unnamed persons to various grades on eleven occasions in 357, 358, 359, 362, and 367 by Nonius Victor Olympius, described as *pater patrum*, and his two sons Aurelius Victor Olympius and Aurelius Victor Augentius, both described as *pater*. In 376 Aurelius Victor Augentius, now *pater patrum*, promoted his son Aemilianus Corfo Olympius (described as a boy, *puero*), to the rank of *hierocorax*. Finally, in (probably) 382/3 Tamesius Augentius Olympius refers to grand "temples of Apollo" (i.e., Mithras) built by his grandfather Victor (presumably Nonius Victor Olympius) and an even grander cave built by himself.[63] Since grandfather was promoting his sons in the 350s and 360, Olympius's dedication can hardly be dated earlier than the 380s, in which case his claim that his own cave "requires no public funds" (*sumptusque tuos nec, Roma, requirit*) may well allude to Gratian's withdrawal of public funds for the public cults.

The social and geographical context is clear. We have three generations of the same family dominating one particular Mithraeum, from the 350s to the 380s. No adult family member held a lesser post than *pater*, and none of the seven dedications name any of the other members of the congregation. While we need not doubt the spiritual importance of the cult to the Olympii, family control was apparently their first priority. Such family cult organizations are no new phenomenon among the Roman elite. The best-documented case is a dedication of A.D. 165/70 from Torre Nova by more than four hundred members of a Bacchic thiasos in honor of their priestess, Pompeia Agrippinilla, wife of M. Gavius Squilla Gallicanus cos. 150, and a descendant of Pompey's historian and friend Theophanes of Mytilene.[64] The initiates (*mystai*) are listed in twenty different categories with four of the most senior the husband, daughter, brother, and sister of Agrippinilla. It is natural to assume that all or most of the others are family retainers or dependents (given that three hundred of them bear Greek names, presumably slaves and freedmen). It would be interesting to know how many members there were in the Mithraeum of the Olympii. I would guess at most a hundred or two rather than thousands.

Here we have clear evidence of a Mithraic community located somewhere on the property of the Olympii. The fact that the people the Olympii promote to the lesser Mithraic grades are never named strongly implies that they were not fellow members of the elite, presumably, like the Torre Nova thiasos, members of their household and

---

63. *antra, ILS* 4269. 5, which I take to be a poetic plural *metri causa*.

64. *PIR²* G. 114 and *P.* 667; for the family tree, *PIR²* P. 625 stemma (p. 274). For the dedication, A. Vogliano and F. Cumont, *AJA* 37 (1933), 215–70, with pll. xxvii–xxvix; *IGUR* i. 160; Bruhl 1953, 275–76; Nilsson 1952, 524–41. For its date (165/70) and the people named, Alföldy 1979, 521–31 and 543–44; Scheid 1986, 275–90. The monument is now on public view in the Metropolitan Museum of Art in New York.

retainers. The very fact that it was a family affair makes it unlikely that the Olympii had any thoughts of proselytizing beyond the family circle, that is to say their immediate dependents.[65] Another consequence of the support of such a community by wealthy private individuals (initiations were not cheap), is that, once the family died off or lost interest, the cult itself was likely to disintegrate (dependents may not all have shared their high priest's enthusiasm). While the Mithraeum of the Olympii seems to have survived Gratian's anti-pagan measures of 382, there is no evidence that it outlived Tamesius Augentius Olympius.

During his city prefecture of 376/7 Furius Maecius Gracchus destroyed a Mithraeum and received baptism.[66] It would be interesting to know which Mithraeum. Not, I suggest, an active one run on the family grounds by a powerful clan like the Olympii. By 376 Mithraism was in terminal decline, and there were doubtless a number of more or less abandoned Mithraea in or around Rome, easy targets for a Christian convert eager to prove his mettle.

Next the Phrygianum. Not quite the family business run by the Olympii, but the dedications do reveal strong family connections nonetheless. Prominent among this group are C. Caeonius Rufius Volusianus *signo* Lampadius, city prefect in 365, his son Ceionius Rufius Volusianus, one daughter, Sabina, and another, Rufia Volusiana, with her husband, Petronius Apollodorus. Also two further Caeonii: Alfenius Caeionius Iulianus Kamenius and Rufius Caeionius Sabinus.[67] Like the priests of the state cults, all members of the nobility, with just one exception: Sextilius Agesilaus Aedesius. As his detailed cursus informs us, this man started out as a lawyer in Africa, then obtained a legal post at court and served in a number of rather minor palatine ministries before finally becoming *vicarius* of the Spains. But for a chance remark of Ammianus we might well have wondered what so modest a figure was doing in these circles. Ammianus happens to remark that Aedesius was a "very close friend" of Volusianus Lampadius (15. 5. 4). It must have been this personal relationship that gave him his entrée into such grand company.

Some of the Phrygianum dedications list only initiations and priesthoods. For example,[68] Petronius Apollodorus (dated to 370):

pontifex maior, XVvir sacris faciundis, pater sacrorum dei invicti Mithrae;

Ulpius Egnatius Faventinus (376):

augur pub(licus) p(opuli) r(omani) Q(uiritium), pater et hieroceryx D(ei) S(olis) I(nvicti) Mithrae, archibucolus Dei Liberi, hierofanta Hecatae, sacerdos Isidos;

---

65. As Nilsson 1952, 541, remarked of Agrippinilla, "elle ne fit pas de propaganda parmi le peuple, mais créa un collège composé de sa famille."
66. Jer. *Ep.* 107. 2; Chastagnol 1962, 200.
67. See McLynn 1996, 327; Duthoy 1969, 102–3.
68. *CIL* vi. 509 and 511; *ILS* 4148, 4149, 4151.

Rufius Caeonius Sabinus (377):

> pontifex maior, hierophanta deae Hecatae, augur publicus populi Romani Quiritium, pater sacrorum invicti Mithrae, tauroboliatus;

Caelius Hilarianus (377):

> duodecimvir urbis Romae, pontifex Solis, hieroceryx invicti Mithrae, sacerdos dei Liberi, sacerdos deae Hecatae;

Q. Clodius Flavianus (383):

> pontifex maior, XVvir sacris faciundis. septemvir epulonum, pontifex dei Solis;

and L. Ragonius Venustus (390):

> augur publicus populi Romani Quiritium, pontifex Vestalis maior.

In view of the fact that the Phrygianum was a shrine to Magna Mater and Attis and most of these dedications were inscribed on altars dedicated to Magna Mater and Attis, it might seem entirely reasonable to infer that they proclaim private religious allegiances in a private location. But there are two complicating factors. First, although most of the dedications commemorate altars to Magna Mater and Attis following the *taurobolium*, all the priesthoods listed concern *other* cults, both Roman and oriental. Why list all their other priesthoods when commemorating the one initiation performed on this site? Second, at least two give detailed regular cursuses.

One we have already considered, the full account of his modest career given by Sextilius Aedesius in 376 (*ILS* 4152); first administrative posts, followed by priesthoods and initiations. Then there is Clodius Hermogenianus Caesarius PVR 374:

> Clodius Hermogenianus Caesarius, v. c., proconsul Africae, praefectus urbis Romae, XVvir sacris faciundis, taurobolio criobolioque perfecto...aram dicavit.

But the best illustrations are Ceionius Rufius Volusianus junior (390)[69] and Alfenius Ceionius Julianus Kamenius (374). First Volusianus, who lists just one office, presumably his only major administrative post, but boastfully takes up more than half his dedication by naming both father and mother complete with titles:

---

69. I distinguish this man from his homonymous father (C. Ceionius Rufius Volusianus signo Lampadius) as Volusianus junior, although the suffix is not in fact found in surviving ancient texts.

ex vicario Asiae et Ceioni Rufi Volusiani v. c. et inlustris ex prefecto pretorio et ex prefecto urbi et Caecinae Lollianae clarissimae et inlustris feminae deae Isidos sacerdotis filius.

Evidently a man anxious anxious to make up for the shortcomings of his own career by underlining the nobility of his birth, on both sides. As for Kamenius, his Phrygianum dedication (19 July 374) lists only priesthoods, as follows:[70]

> v. c., septemvir epulonum, pater et hieroceryx sacrorum summi invicti Mithrae, hierophanta Hecatae, archibucolus dei Liberi, aram taurobolio criobolioque percepto dicavit.

But we are fortunate enough to have three other versions of Kamenius's cursus. First, two from monuments erected in the family house soon after he laid down the office of *consularis Numidiae*, at a date unknown before 381, augmented by two Roman priest-hoods.[71] And finally, his epitaph (dated 4 September 385, when he was forty-two), virtually identical except for the addition of one further post, the vicariate of Africa.[72]

> v.c., quaestor, praetor triumphalis, *septemvir epulonum*, magister numinum, pater sacrorum summi invicti Mithrae, hierophanta Hecatae, archibucolus dei Liberi, *XVvir sacris faciundis*, tauroboliatus deae Matris, *pontifex maior*, consul-aris Numidiae, vicarius Africae.

The omission of the quaestorship and praetorship from the Phrygianum cursus has several parallels (p. 137). The explanation of the additional post is not in doubt. Kamenius's vicariate (securely placed in 381) postdates his Numidian governorship. This is surely also the explanation for his two additional Roman priesthoods. That would also explain why they are separated from his first Roman priesthood, which, like so many young men of noble birth, he acquired immediately after his praetorship. He *might* have grouped all his Roman priesthoods together, like Praetextatus. But since he did not choose this option, the obvious alternative arrangement was simple chronological sequence. That would explain why the two additional Roman priest-hoods are separated from each other. Kamenius's priesthoods, like his administrative offices, are arranged in strict chronological order of their acquisition, all of them won before his first provincial governorship in Numidia.

   More important, if we had only Kamenius's Phrygianum dedication, we might rea-sonably have concluded that its litany of titles reflected private religious allegiances,

---

70. *AE* 1953, 238 = *CIMRM* i. 515 Vermaseren; Duthoy no. 34; for his career, *PLRE* i. 474–75.
71. *CIL* vi. 1675 (= 26 Duthoy = 516 Vermaseren) and 31940. 31940 offers *mag(istro) num(inum?)* for the *mag(istro)* of 1675.
72. *ILS* 1264.

allegiances he had no wish to reveal beyond the walls of the Phrygianum. But the three other dedications all include the same litany of titles, in their entirety. How private can these cults have been? The actual *taurobolia* commemorated in the Phrygianum dedications were no doubt performed in secret, but the Phrygianum itself and all those altars the *tauroboliati* provided were hardly private. They are simply one aspect of the ostentatious expenditure expected of public figures like priests, commemorated in the usual way by dedications making clear in detail just what important people they were. This is why the dedications include *every* honor they had won.

Furthermore, the final version on Kamenius's funerary monument (found in what must have been a family villa at Antium) begins with a ten-line poem proclaiming how he has equaled the achievements and virtues of his father, grandfathers, and forefathers, an ornament to his family and the senate, cut off too soon, deeply lamented by his wife and children. Not a word about his priesthoods or the gods. This is a clear case where titles like *pater sacrorum summi invicti Mithrae* and *archibucolus dei Liberi* seem to have been treated straightforwardly as *honores* to be listed at the appropriate points in his cursus, along with his Roman priesthoods and administrative posts.

What then of the five men whose Phrygianum dedications list only priesthoods? The obvious explanation is that these were the only titles these men had earned at the date of the dedications. Not one of them is known from any other source. Certainly none are known to have reached high office. Some may still have been in their early twenties. Our clearest control here is the cursus of Kamenius: all eight of his priesthoods are listed between his praetorship and first provincial governorship. At the time of his own Phrygianum dedication in 374, at age thirty-one, Kamenius himself had not yet won his first governorship.

It is unfortunate that we do not have the Phrygianum dedication of Volusianus Lampadius himself, apparently the doyen of this last generation of initiates. But we do have a very similar dedication found on the Aventine, presumably from another temple: *Ruf. Volusianus v. c., pater, ierophanta, profeta Isidis, pontifex dei Solis vot(um) solvi* (*ILS* 4413). The fact that it begins with his senatorial rank and ends with a single state priesthood suggests that this is an early cursus, before he had won his first governorship. Oddly enough, despite having eleven dedications of one sort or another we do not have a single full cursus. But the abbreviated dedication to a cult statuette of Attis found at Ostia takes care to mention his multiple prefectures (*Volusianus v.c. ex praefectis tauroboliatus donum dedit*).[73] Volusianus was obviously a religious enthusiast. It must be significant that the Phrygianum was filled with dedications by his family and friends.

All in all, this little group of dedications does not at all give the impression of a private (much less secret) religious fraternity. The eyes of modern scholars eagerly searching for evidence of personal religion tend to gloss over all the worldly details they supply. Vermaseren's Corpus of Mithraic dedications on occasion actually omits

---

73. *AE* 1945, 55; Meiggs 1973, 401; photo, Bloch 1963, pl. 10.

such information as irrelevant and distracting.[74] I suspect that most contemporaries would have read these dedications first and foremost as cursus inscriptions of Very Important Persons.

Given the solid epigraphic evidence for aristocratic interest in Mithras and Magna Mater, there is what might seem a surprising gap in the epigraphic evidence for Isis. For Alföldi, Isis worship was Christianity's most dangerous rival in late fourth-century Rome.[75] It was on this basis that he identified a series of medallions struck in Rome with reverses of Isis, Anubis, the Nile, and the Sphinx as "pagan propaganda" produced by the aristocracy (Ch. 19. 1). But most of the evidence cited is trite clichés of anti-pagan polemic. Isiac priests with shaven heads are ridiculed in all four verse invectives studied in chapters 8 and 9, and to cite one of the few texts missed by Alföldi, in a context where he obviously just means "pagans," Ambrose evokes those who "shave their heads and eyebrows when attending the mysteries of Isis" (*Ep.* 27 [58]. 3). Two of the invectives cite Vergil's "barking Anubis" (*latrator Anubis*), and in a famous passage of the *Confessions* (8. 2. 3) Augustine describes the nobility as devoted to "monstrous gods of every kind and Anubis the barking dog."[76] Ambrosiaster ridicules a man wearing a dog's head dashing in all directions "looking for the body parts of Osiris the adulterer."[77] Were such figures really to be seen on the streets of Rome every day? The truth is that Christian polemic tends to dwell on the gods of Egypt (a) because shaved heads and eyebrows, tambourines, and dog-headed gods were so much easier to mock than dignified aristocratic pontiffs; and (b) because this mockery goes back to the classical poets themselves. Anubis is already barking in Propertius (iii. 11. 42) and Ovid (*Met.* ix. 690) as well as Vergil. Such polemics tell us more about the classical culture of the writers than contemporary pagan practice.[78] The fact is that only one of the Phrygianum dedications names a priest of Isis, that of Faventinus, dated to 376, where *sacerdos Isidos* is only one of his five priestly titles. Then there is Volusianus Lampadius, with *profeta Isidos* as one of four priestly titles in an early dedication (no later than the 350s). Isis does not appear among the ten priestly titles of Praetextatus.[79] Symmachus never mentions Isis, Osiris, or Anubis. Nothing suggests that Isis remained a serious competitor as late as the 380s.

It is likely enough that the enthusiasm these nobles shared for all these exotic cults was in some sense a reaction against the rising tide of Christianity. But the traditional claim that such cults were part of a *battle* against Christianity, with these men as its leaders, is not convincing. It would be hard to conceive of a more exclusive, elite form

---

74. For example, see his note on *CIMRM* 520 (Aedesius).

75. Alföldi 1937, 40, 43–44.

76. In fact, Augustine goes on to develop the quotation, describing these gods as "monsters who once bore arms against Neptune and Venus and against Minerva, gods that Rome once conquered and then implored for aid." His point is that in Vergil the Romans defeat the Egyptian gods at Actium, but now they hold sway over Rome.

77. *Quaest. vet. et nov. test.* 114. 11 (p. 131 M.-P. Bussières [ed.], SC 512, Paris 2007).

78. See O'Donnell's sensible note on the passage (3 [1992], 18–19).

79. His wife, Paulina, is described as *Isiaca* on *ILS* 1260, but not on 1259, Praetextatus' funerary monument.

of religious expression than these initiations. They can hardly have deluded themselves into supposing that this was the way to rally rank-and-file pagans against Christianity, much less cause defections.

The one thing all Phrygianum dedicants share is the *taurobolium*, the sacrifice of a bull for the benefit of one person (§ 4). Most of them were also Mithraists, every one either a *pater* or *pater patrum*. The Olympii no doubt presided over a genuine community of Mithraists, even if only members of their own household. But it is hard to believe that these other nobles all just happened to have reached the highest grade in a number of different Mithraic congregations. Furthermore, in every case these Mithraic titles are just one in a sequence of top grades in other cults. For example, Aedesius, Faventinus, Kamenius, Sabinus, Sabina, Praetextatus, and Paulina were all hierophants of Hecate as well as *tauroboliati* and (the males among them) Mithraic *patres*. Three of them, Aedesius, Kamenius, and Faventinus, were also *archibucoli* of Liber, a Dionysiac title widely attested in Asia Minor in earlier centuries.[80]

It is natural to assume that all this religious activity was part of the conservatism of the last pagans. Certainly this was why they did their best to preserve the state priesthoods. Yet is it really true that they made "a final effort to *preserve* all the oriental cults."[81] The priestly titles we find in the Phrygianum inscriptions do not at all suggest the cults of Cybele, Mithras, or Isis as they were celebrated in early imperial Rome.

Take Mithraism. Throughout the early empire Mithraism had always been a cult of the military, and was in decline by the beginning of the fourth century. Alison Griffiths has argued that the prestige of Mithraism rose after the tetrarchs restored a shrine of Mithras at Carnuntum in 308, describing the god as the *fautor* of their *imperium* (*ILS* 659).[82] This is not convincing. Carnuntum had been the site of a legionary camp from the early second century, and the Mithraists there were overwhelmingly soldiers. The fact that Mithraism found favor with soldier emperors is not likely to have influenced the aristocracy of Rome. This unexpected flowering of Mithraism in late fourth-century Rome is an innovation rather than either a survival or a revival.

The *archibucoli* are also a puzzle. *Bucoli* derive from some early Dionysiac festival in which the god was worshipped in the form of a bull, tended by "herdsmen," who performed a ritual dance.[83] We may well doubt whether our aristocrats still performed the traditional dance. It is in keeping with their other titles that none of them is anything less than an *archibuculus*. What sort of organization does that imply? The Torre Nova thiasos numbered eleven *bucoli*, eight *bucoli sacri*, and three *archibucoli*. But all bore Greek names, implying (as we have seen) that they were slaves or freedmen: the *archibucoli* ranked no higher than eighth in the hierarchy of

---

80. The evidence is collected by W. Quandt, *De Baccho ab Alexandri aetate in Asia Minore culto*, diss. (Halle 1912), 251–54; Kern, *RE* 3. 1 (1987), 1013–17; Cumont, *AJA* 37 (1933), 247–49; Nilsson 1957, 48, 52–56, 58–60.

81. For example, Vermaseren 1977, 180 (my italics).

82. Clauss 2000; Griffiths 2000.

83. Lucian, *De Saltatione* 79.

the thiasos, whereas Aedesius, Kamenius, and Faventinus were clearly at the top of their hierarchy.

There are indications that these aristocratic hierophants were not quite at home in the sacred Greek terminology that obviously gave them so much pleasure. Faventinus and Hilarianus both style themselves *hieroceryx*, sacred herald, of Mithras,[84] an official often found in temples and at festivals all over the Greek world, but not otherwise attested in the abundant Mithraic dossier (why would a group that met in caves need heralds?). It is tempting to conjecture that this reflects a misreading of the term *hierocorax* (*corax* or raven was one of the standard Mithraic grades). The dedication of Aemilianus Corfo Olympius mentions *hierocoracica*, the tokens or symbols of the *corax*.[85]

According to Turcan, these grand titles "presuppose at least the temporary survival of a whole organization of cultic societies." Certainly, they might seem to *imply* such an organization. But Burkert has raised serious questions about the size and nature of mystery cult followings.[86] Whether or not we are prepared to agree with his claim that, even in earlier times, *no* mystery cult can be called a religion, the cults of this little band of late fourth-century aristocrats seem to amount to little more than initiations by exclusive groups. The *taurobolium* was normally undergone once in a lifetime—or at most twice (two dedications mention a second performance after twenty years).[87] Nine of our little band are described as hierophants of Hecate, and the reference in the dedication of Lampadius's daughter Sabina to the "nights of dread Hecate" implies the traditional nocturnal initiation.[88] Praetextatus was initiated into the mysteries at Eleusis, and Paulina into the mysteries of Hecate on Aegina and Dionysus at Lerna, presumably during Praetextatus's proconsulate of Achaea in 364, when he managed to get Eleusis exempted from a recent law forbidding nocturnal sacrifice.[89] These too must have been once-in-a-lifetime experiences. The *archibucoli* of Bacchus presumably also presided over a mystery cult. But this little group of dedications is the only evidence there is for celebration of the mysteries of Hecate and the "herdsmen of Bacchus" in Rome.

In the ordinary way each *pater* (e.g.) *should* imply a separate Mithraeum and congregation, but the office has surely been reconceived on the lines of the state priesthoods. Just as there could be up to twenty *pontifices* of equal rank, so there could be as many *patres* or *archibucoli* as there were suitable candidates among the elite. There was no need for a congregation; if a ritual required an audience, retainers on their estates sufficed. If this was a battle against Christianity, it was fought by an army in which everyone was a general.

---

84. *ILS* 4153 and 4148.
85. For an illustration of these tokens, Clauss 2000, 133.
86. Turcan 1996, 326; Burkert 1987, Ch. 2.
87. *ILS* 4153 (Faventinus) in 376; ib. 4154 (Volusianus junior) in 390.
88. *CIL* vi. 30966; Duthoy 22, no. 31; *CCCA* 3 (1977), no. 238.
89. Zos. iv. 3. 2–4. For Paulina' titles, *ILS* 1259–61.

It has often been suspected that in their late fourth-century form some of these cults, notably the *taurobolium*, were influenced by Christianity. There may be something in this. Aedesius's claim that he had been *in aeternum renatus* (*ILS* 4152) is suggestive. But this need not imply that Cybele would save everyone who turned to her, the lowly as well as the rich and powerful. Even if many or all the unknown members participated in initiations, this can hardly be seen as a proselytizing cult, trying to compete with Christianity.

In this context Praetextatus's famous quip that he would become a Christian if he was made pope takes on a new meaning. Nobles like Praetextatus and Kamenius would not have been happy to find themselves rank-and-file catechumens, gathering in groups with women and children to be instructed by some lowborn presbyter. They took it for granted that they were born to be top dogs in any religion they joined. In 404 Augustine complains that the pagan elite of Carthage "refuse to be humble so that they can become Christians."[90] This attitude goes far to explain the failure of late Roman paganism to offer any effective resistance. The answer of these nobles to the crisis of Roman paganism was to experiment with more and more cults themselves rather than offer guidance or leadership to their humbler fellow pagans, much less devise some way of uniting all pagans in a common cause.

Where did all these initiation cults come from? The earliest documentation both for the initiations themselves and for their cumulation in one person is a Phrygianum dedication dated to 15 April 313, commemorating a *taurobolium* by an otherwise unknown C. Magius Donatus Severianus *v. c.*, who proclaims himself *pater sacrorum invicti Mithrae, hierophantes Liberi patris et Hecatarum*. Three slightly earlier dedications commemorate *taurobolia* by L. Cornelius Scipio Orfitus, an *augur*, in 295; Iulius Italicus, *XVvir sacris faciundis*, in 305, and an Antoninus, *pontifex* and *XVvir sacris faciundis*, in 350. Another dated to 319 commemorates a *taurobolium* by a woman called Serapias, *sacrata [deum] Matris et Proserpinae*, with Fl. Antonius Eustochius, *sacerdos Phryx maximus*, officiating and in the presence of unidentified members of the college of *XVviri sacris faciundis*.[91] All three men were evidently nobles, to judge from their Roman priesthoods, but Serapias (an Egyptian name) is styled merely *honesta femina*, implying equestrian rank (319).[92] Only in Severianus (313) do we find all four of the cults practiced by our little band of late fourth-century diehards: Mithras, Bacchus, Hecate, and Magna Mater. And Severianus, though a senator, was not (to judge from his names) of noble birth. Even the earliest in the series are men who held Roman as well as oriental priesthoods.

With the single exception of Antoninus (350), there is a gap of more than fifty years between Severianus and what we might call the Volusianus Lampadius group. This gap may be due to more than chance. It is not just that only one Phrygianum dedication has survived from this period. There is no evidence from any other source

---

90. *Sermon* 198. 59 (Dolbeau 26).

91. *ILS* 4145 and 4143 (cf. 4144); *CIL* vi. 498; *ILS* 4146.

92. For this connotation of *honestus*, Garnsey 1970, 239.

either. It may be significant that Firmicus Maternus's rant against pagan cults, published in the 340s, mentions neither Hecate nor (in a chapter mocking worship of
Bacchus in the form of a bull)[93] his aristocratic "herdsmen." By contrast, the *Carmen
contra paganos* of 384 ridicules its prefect (Praetextatus, as we shall see) as *Bacchique
comes Triviaeque sacerdos*, surely an allusion precisely to the combination of these two
initiations.[94] If there had been a continuous sequence of *taurobolia* from 295 to 390, we
should expect to have more evidence between 320 and 370. Most of the inscribed
altars were found in 1609, but more recent excavations have not changed the picture:
one in 1949 turned up Kamenius's altar, dated to 374; and another in 1959 an anonymous altar dated to 13 August 376, the same date as two of the 1609 altars.[95] In all probability the gap is real, and the 370–90 series reflects a revival of these cults by a single
group, the circle of Volusianus Lampadius.

Attempts have sometimes been made to link the Roman revival of Mithraism
among the Roman aristocracy with the attempted pagan revival of Julian.[96] But other
objections aside, the dates simply do not fit. The earliest initiations at the mithraeum
of the Olympii are dated to 357, well before anyone in Rome can possibly have known
either that Julian was a pagan or, more important, that he would become Augustus.
The *taurobolia* of the Volusianus group are a little later, mostly in the 370s. That is to
say, earlier than Gratian's measures against the state cults. Three fall later than this
(two dated to 383, one to 390), but none later than the banning of sacrifice in 391. They
are thus not easy to connect in any straightforward way with any of the hypothesized
"pagan reactions," whether under Julian, Gratian, or Theodosius.

If there was anything so organized as a "pagan party" in late fourth-century Rome,
the Phrygianum group must have been prominent members. It is thus the more
striking that Symmachus, whose public life ran from 365 (his first governorship) to
402, never mentions a single one of them in his extensive correspondence, addressed
to or mentioning several hundred members of the late Roman elite.[97] That he should
not mention *any* of them must be more than coincidence. We are bound to infer that
they were at any rate not among his inner circle of friends, nor even acquaintances he
considered worth cultivating.

Some of them may have been friends of Praetextatus, an initiate in some of the same
mysteries. Yet I have the impression that Praetextatus was not a member of this group.
In the first place, he was an important figure in his own right, not (like most of the
group) a child or dependent of Volusianus. Second, though a *pater patrum, tauroboliatus*,
and hierophant (presumably of Hecate) like most of them, he also boasted other titles

---

93. *De errore profanarum religionum* § 21. Even if the *mulierem quidem triformi vultu* of § 5. 1 is Hecate,
    Maternus himself did not so identify her.
94. *CCP* 71 (Trivia = Hecate); see p. 284.
95. Vermaseren, *CCCA* 3 (1977), nos. 245a, 241b, 233, 242; McLynn 1996, 326 n. 53.
96. For example, Hackethal 1968, 244–45.
97. Even if Sabinus is identified with the Sabinus mentioned (but not written to) a couple of times in
    letters of Symmachus (*PLRE* i. 793), that does not imply a relationship.

none of them had: *curialis Herculis* and *neocorus*, as well as being an initiate in the Eleusianian mysteries. His wife, Fabia Paulina, was *tauroboliata*, an Eleusinian initiate, a hierophant of Hecate, and an initiate of Dionysus, but she emphasizes that she was initiated into the original mysteries of Hecate on Aegina and of Dionysus at Lerna.[98] There is perhaps a hint here that Praetextatus and Paulina had experienced the real thing rather than the ersatz mysteries now being celebrated in Rome.

If there was no unified pagan party in late fourth-century Rome, this helps to explain why there was no concerted pagan reaction.

3: ROMAN AND ORIENTAL

What then of Bloch's thesis that it was oriental rather than state cults that inspired political resistance to Christianity? If there were a clear correlation between the holding of oriental priesthoods and politically active pagans, it would be a hypothesis worth testing. But there is no such correlation. Quite the opposite. As Bloch's own well-known table of priesthoods held by members of the fourth-century aristocracy clearly shows, virtually all male members of the Phrygianum group held Roman as well as oriental priesthoods, sometimes several. Of those whose noble birth rendered them eligible, only one lacks a Roman priesthood: Rufius Volusianus junior. And in this case the explanation is surely to be found in the date of the dedication, 390 (more below).[99] It is hardly surprising that Aedesius, a retired bureaucrat of modest attainments, was not judged worthy of the honor. The otherwise unknown Leontius mentioned in one of the two Greek inscriptions in the Phrygianum was a visitor from the East. But the otherwise unknown Crescens named in the same dedication was *XVvir* and *pontifex Solis*.[100] There is one fragmentary inscription that, according to Matthews, "does not look as if it went on to mention public priesthoods."[101] But this overlooks the possibility that the Anonymus was a young man who acquired his Roman priesthood(s) *after* his Mithraic title. There is a distinct possibility that *every* eligible member of the Phrygianum group before the 380s held at least one Roman priesthood.

There is no solid basis for the once-popular notion that there were two streams in late Roman paganism, the "traditionalists" (like Symmachus), who confined themselves to the Roman state cults, and the "orientalists" (like Praetextatus) who turned to the exotic rituals of the East. Avianius Symmachus wrote a series of verse portraits of some of the great men of his time: to Valerius Proculus cos. 340 he ascribed *simplex caelicolum cultus*.[102] What is the force of *simplex*? It is hardly a formula anyone would

---

98. For Paulina' titles, *ILS* 1259–61.
99. ILS 4154 = Duthoy 25; so Matthews 1973, 182.
100. *CIL* vi. 30780 = Duthoy 30 = Vermaseren 237; Matthews 1973, 182.
101. *AE* 1953, 237 = Vermaseren 240; Matthews, 1975, 182.
102. Quoted in Symm. *Ep.* i. 2. 4.

apply to Praetextatus or the members of the Phrygianum group. Proculus held three traditional priesthoods (*augur, pontifex maior, quindecimvir sacris faciundis*).[103] It is natural to infer that Avianius was alluding to the fanciful, nontraditional titles paraded by some of his pagan peers, but that need not imply active disapproval. In any case, since virtually all the orientalists we can identify also held at least one traditional priesthood, there is no way of discovering on this evidence which cults they valued most. Symmachus may not have shared Praetextatus's enthusiasm for mysteries, but there is no reason to believe that this was a matter of serious disagreement between them. On the other hand, Praetextatus certainly shared Symmachus's concern for the traditional cults (several of Symmachus's letters to him actually discuss pontifical matters).

Note the way Rufius Caeonius Sabinus and L. Ragonius Venustus lovingly spin out their augurates into the pompous title *augur publicus populi Romani Quiritium* (and Venustus his pontificate into *pontifex Vestalis maior*). Note too that one of the two epigrams that adorn Sabinus's altar gives a brief "poetical" description of each of his five priesthoods:[104]

> antiqua generose domo, cui regia Vestae
> pontifici felix sacrato militat igne,
> idem augur, triplicis cultor venerande Dianae
> Persidicique Mithrae antistes Babilonie templi
> taurobolique simul magni dux mistice sacri.

Noble scion of an ancient house, for whom as pontiff the house of Vesta stands firm, happy in her sacred fire; you are augur as well; venerable worshipper of Diana of the triple form [= Hecate]; Babylonian priest of the Persian temple of Mithras; at the same time mystical leader of the great bull-slaying rite.

Nothing here suggests that Sabinus differentiated in any way between his two Roman and three oriental priesthoods. No less important, line 1 implies that all five (and not just the first two) are linked to his noble birth.

There is also a more specific problem with the assumption that orientalists were more politically active. Only three of the orientalist group seem to have been people of any consequence or influence: Volusianus Lampadius, Praetextatus, and Kamenius. Lampadius won his first prefecture in 354 and his second in 365. His son Volusianus junior underwent his second *taurobolium* after twenty years in 390, by when he must have been at least forty, and so born no later than 350—and perhaps much earlier. Lampadius was presumably born no later than ca. 315, in which case he may have been dead by the 380s. Praetextatus died in October or November

---

103. His title *praetor Flavialis* was an innovation, but in no sense exotic or "oriental"; indeed it was a priesthood of the imperial cult.

104. *CIL* vi. 511; the best text is *CLE* 1529.

384, Kamenius in September 385. Praetextatus and Kamenius were alive to support Symmachus in 384,[105] but all three were probably dead *before* the so-called last pagan stand.

Who then were the supposedly orientalist senators who supposedly urged Eugenius to make concessions to paganism in 392–94? The elder Flavian, so most scholars have always believed. Flavian has always been held to be an arch-orientalist. But on what basis? The only grounds ever adduced are the identification of the unnamed prefect of the *Carmen contra paganos* as Flavian. This assumption is fundamental not only to Bloch's study but to every modern account of the rebellion of Eugenius. We shall see in chapter 8 that it is mistaken: the prefect cannot be Flavian, nor can the poem be as late as 394. Of course, while the lapse of the identification removes what used to be considered the positive evidence that he was an orientalist, it does not in itself prove that he was not. But there is another objection.

Flavian's one surviving cursus mentions a single, Roman priesthood. This cursus has to be studied in tandem with Symmachus's cursus, because they are a pair, dedications to statues of Symmachus and Flavian erected side by side in the palace of the Symmachi on the Caelian hill by Memmius Symmachus, son of the one and grandson-in-law of the other:[106]

Eusebii, Q. Aur. Symmacho, v. c.	Virio Nicomacho Flaviano, v. c.
quaest(ori), praet(ori), pontifici	quaest(ori), praet(ori), pontifici maiori,
maiori, correctori Lucaniae et	consulari Siciliae, uicario Africae,
Brittiorum, comitis ordini tertii,	quaestori intra palatium,
procons(uli) Africae, praef(ecto)	praef(ecto) praet(orio) iterum,
urb(is), cons(uli) ordinario,	cons(uli) ord(inario),
oratori disertissmo,	historico disertissimo,
Q. Fab(ius) Memm(ius) Symmachus, v. c.,	Q. Fab(ius) Memmius Symmachus, v. c.,
patri optimo	prosocero optimo

The two dedications were carefully composed to balance each other, with the last three lines in each case identifying the dedicatee's claim to literary distinction and relationship to the dedicator. Each mentions just one priestly title, *pontifex maior*. If Flavian was the enthusiast for oriental cults he is traditionally assumed to be, why no oriental titles? Here is Bloch's explanation:[107]

> the addition of any other sacred office possibly held by Flavian would have upset the balance of the two inscriptions.... If Flavian, e.g., was a *tauroboliatus* or a priest of Isis, Symmachus's son was under no obligation to mention these

---

105. Not that there is any direct evidence of such support.
106. *CIL* vi. 1699 and 1782 = *ILS* 2946–47.
107. Bloch 1945, 210.

things. They were Flavian's private affair which he could and undoubtedly did divulge in inscriptions set up by himself. Yet none has survived.

The argument is weak at best. The addition of Symmachus's signum in the genitive has already left the balance less than perfect,[108] and the various offices are differently abbreviated in the two dedications. More important, there is simply no basis for Bloch's claim that oriental priesthoods were a man's "private affair," not to be mentioned "in an inscription set up in his honor by someone else." On the contrary, we have seen that their holders seem to have treated them as public *honores* no less than their Roman priesthoods.

Matthews (who was in no doubt that Flavian was the prefect of the CCP and so an ardent orientalist) agreed with Bloch's arguments, but went on to object that "they apply to precisely the same degree to Symmachus as they do to Flavian."[109] Accordingly he was willing to entertain the possibility that Symmachus too was an enthusiast of oriental cults. He rightly emphasized that the silence of the third *relatio* is no real objection. The *relatio* is wholly concerned with the state cults, and it would have been irrelevant to bring in Isis and Mithras (and counterproductive, since the oriental cults were so much easier for Christians to make fun of).

Yet the arguments of both scholars are nonetheless misguided. Both *presuppose* the identification of Flavian as the prefect of the CCP. On that assumption, Flavian *was* an orientalist and so, for whatever reason, Memmius Symmachus *must* have deliberately omitted all his oriental priesthoods and initiations. For Matthews, if he omitted Flavian's initiations, why not Symmachus's too? But with the lapse of the identification, all such possibilities lapse. The reason Memmius Symmachus does not list oriental priesthoods for either Symmachus or Flavian is the obvious one. They did not have any.

The distinction between public and private priesthoods is mistaken. There is no case of a man known to have held both state priesthoods and mystery initiations who omitted only the latter on a dedication. All surviving dedications (whether public or private) either include all a man's cult titles, or none—itself an indication of their equivalence. We are surely bound to conclude that both Symmachus and Flavian held *only* Roman priesthoods, one each. It should be remembered that, while Macrobius appropriately cast Praetextatus as an expert on oriental cults, Flavian's contribution (unfortunately lost) was to have been on the very Roman topic of augural science.

The distinction we should be drawing is between public and private *dedications*. Bloch's table listed sixteen dedications with priesthoods and initiations from the last third of the fourth century. All but one come from either a cult site or a private house (e.g., all four dedications that attest Orfitus's three Roman priesthoods). If we look at Bloch's table from this perspective, his claim that pagan nobles were "advertising" their religious activities loses its force. Indeed, Niquet made the opposite claim, that

---

108. Flavian too had a signum, revealed by a dedication from Lepcis Magna (*Inscr. Rom. Trip.* 475).
109. Matthews 1973, 188.

in the decades after Constantine they deliberately dropped their priestly titles from public dedications, with only one exception to the "rule," the posthumous statue of Avianius Symmachus in the Forum Romanum (377).[110]

It is true that Symmachus's statue is the latest surviving public monument to list pagan priesthoods. But it is also the only such Roman monument from the entire fourth century, which makes it hard to see it as an exception, or to link any such "rule" to Constantine. It is also true that we have numerous dedications by fourth-century pagan city prefects to statues they erected or buildings they restored that do not include priesthoods. But dedications *by* officials in office seldom give a complete cursus and so seldom include priesthoods, normally naming just their current office. Thus Volusianus Lampadius, vainest of all late Roman grandees, is named in eleven dedications, only two of which, both from cult sites, list his priesthoods. Of the nine monuments he restored as city prefect (365–66),[111] four describe him as just *praefectus urbi*, the other five add that he was a former praetorian prefect. It is only dedications in honor *of* officials that give a complete cursus, routinely including priesthoods along with all their other titles.

The first undoubted case of the deliberate omission of a priesthood from a full cursus[112] is the posthumous dedication rehabilitating the elder Flavian in 431, an omission some have invested with enormous significance (Ch. 5.5). But the fact that there is only one such public cursus *with* a priesthood in fourth-century Rome makes it hard to know whether omission or inclusion is more significant. Avianius must have been in his early sixties when he died in 377. Some peers who, like him, had picked up their priesthoods in the 330s may not have been so willing to "advertise" them in the changing climate of the 370s. We should also bear in mind that the dedication to Avianius's monument was probably drafted by his son, Q. Aurelius Symmachus, a notable champion of the traditional priesthoods. There is almost certainly one case of omission well before 431, the posthumous statue of Praetextatus erected in the Forum Romanum in 385. All we have is a fragment, but enough survives to make it virtually certain that priesthoods (which come before public posts on Praetextatus's other dedications) were not included:[113]

> [Vettio Agorio Praet]extato
> [v(iro) c(larissimo), correctori Tusciae et U]mbriae
> [consulari Lusitaniae, proc]onsuli Achaiae,
> [praef(ecto) urb(i), praef(ecto) Ill]yrici et Italiae....

---

110. Niquet 2000, 178.

111. All except *AE* 1975 n. 134 cited in full by Chastagnol 1962, 164–69.

112. While including his two priesthoods, Avianius' cursus in fact omits his minor offices.

113. *CIL* vi. 1779a, with the addenda at *CIL* vi. 8. 3 (2000), p. 4759; and Niquet 2000, 238. It has been suggested that the priesthoods were listed on one side of the base, but such a division of titles would be without parallel. In addition, we have another (private) dedication that indisputably omits all Praetextatus' priesthoods (below).

Niquet assumed that what she saw as a change of policy between the dedications of Symmachus in 376 and Praetextatus in 385 reflected Theodosius's decision to eliminate paganism. This is improbable. Christian emperors were concerned to stop pagan practices. It was not against the law to be a pagan, and few were likely to have been bothered if individual pagans chose to include all those silly titles in their cursus. The initiative probably came from the family of Praetextatus.

In the high empire the man in the Roman street knew, when comparing two otherwise parallel cursuses, that priesthoods implied noble birth and imperial favor. But by the second half of the fourth century priesthoods must have come to be viewed quite differently, by both Christians and pagans. The Christian man in the street was likely to see a *pontifex* as something like a pagan bishop and a *quindecimvir sacris faciundis* as someone personally stained with the blood of sacrifice. Aristocrats would not have continued to spend fortunes on games (Symmachus 2,000 pounds of gold on the praetorian games of his son) unless popular favor was still important to them. When they held (as most of them did sooner or later) the prefecture of Rome, they were faced with the delicate responsibility of provisioning the city. There were constant famines and riots. The elder Symmachus was not the only noble to have his fine Trastevere mansion burned down by a rampaging mob. In an increasingly Christian Rome it was unwise for nobles to run further risks by "advertising" their paganism to everyone who passed their dedications in the public spaces of Rome on a daily basis. The reason members of the Roman elite had in the past routinely listed priesthoods along with the rest of their *honores* was the prestige they brought. Even before the 380s it was becoming clear that they were now becoming liabilities. It was not prudent to flaunt them.

The monuments of Praetextatus are an instructive case study.[114] The dedication to the funerary altar he shares with his wife, Paulina, is probably the best known and most discussed epigraphic text of the fourth-century West. Famously, it lists all ten of his priesthoods and initiations, as does the dedication to a statue erected in his honor more than two years after his death. The three poems inscribed on the funerary monument underline the evident pride he took in these cult titles. Even so it would be a mistake to see Praetextatus defiantly proclaiming them to the world. Both dedications come from private locations.[115] We also have one further dedication to the memory of Praetextatus, this time by a son or daughter. Praetextatus is styled the *parens* of the (unnamed) dedicator, presumably another dedication from a private house, where the identity of this child of the great man would have been obvious. Yet here the priesthoods are omitted. Given the private context, the natural assumption is that this child was either a Christian or a moderate pagan who did not want visitors to assume that (s)he shared father's obsessive religiosity. It may have been this same child, especially if a male with his career ahead of him, who chose to drop the priesthoods from the public monument in the Forum Romanum.

---

114. For the various Praetextatus monuments, see Niquet 2000, 237–52.
115. For full bibliography, see the addenda to both dedications in *CIL* vi. 8. 3 (2000), pp. 4757–60.

An earlier case of a son apparently unhappy about a father's priesthoods is Placidus Severus, *vicarius* of Rome in 364–65. The augurate of his father, Q. Flavius Maesius Egnatius Lollianus *signo* Mavortius, city prefect in 342 and consul in 355, is commemorated in four Campanian dedications of 337, all evidently following the same script, since all give it in the full form *augur publicus populi Romani Quiritium*. Years later Severus honored Lollianus with a dedication in the family house on the Aventine that offers every detail of his cursus in full *except* for the augurate, but praised him as *pater religiosus*.[116] *Religiosus* need imply no more than "behaving with scrupulous integrity" (*OLD* 8), but we should bear in mind that Lollianus was the dedicatee of an astrological work by Firmicus Maternus that repeatedly uses the adjective with reference to cult observance.[117] It looks as if Severus respected but did not share his father's brand of piety. These are cases to be borne in mind by those who take it for granted, without evidence, that the younger Flavian pursued his father's paganism throughout his own long life.

4: THE TAUROBOLIUM

The taurobolium is by far the most notorious ritual celebrated by the last pagans of Rome, thanks to a vivid account by Prudentius. In view of the importance of this description for modern interpretations of the role of oriental cults in the "pagan revival," it must be quoted in full:[118]

> In order to be made holy (*consecrandus*), the high priest (*summus sacerdos*) goes down into a trench dug deep in the ground wearing an extravagant headband (*infulatus*), his temples bound with fillets (*vittis*) for the occasion and his hair clasped with a golden crown, while his silken robe is held up with the Gabine girdle (*cinctu Gabino*). Above him they lay planks to make a stage, leaving the timber-structure open, with spaces between; and then they cut and bore through the floor, perforating the wood in many places with a sharp-pointed tool so that it had a great number of little openings. Hither is led a great bull with a grim, shaggy brow, wreathed with garlands of flowers about his shoulders and encircling his horns, while the victim's brow glitters with gold, the sheen of the plates tinging his rough hair. When the beast for sacrifice has been stationed here, they cut his breast open with a consecrated hunting spear (*sacrato venabulo*) and the great wound disgorges a stream of hot blood, pouring on the plank-bridge below a steaming river which spreads billowing out. Then through the many ways afforded by the thousand chinks it passes in a shower, dripping a

---

116. *ILS* 1223, 1224a, b, c; 1225 + 1232 = *CIL* vi. 37112; *CIL* vi. 8. 3 (2000), p. 4819.

117. *religiosus sane erit et cultor deorum* (ii. 11. 12); *erunt religiosi in deorum cultu* (ii. 50. 8); *erunt sane religiosi iusti cultores deorum* (ii. 128. 13); see the index verb. in the Kroll/Skutsch/Ziegler edition, 2 (1913), 515.

118. *Per.* x. 1011–50 (Thompson' Loeb translation, slightly adapted).

foul rain, and the priest in the pit below catches it, holding his filthy head to meet every drop and getting his robe and his whole body covered with corruption. Laying his head back he even puts his cheeks in the way, placing his ears under it, exposing lips and nostrils, bathing his very eyes in the stream, not even keeping his mouth from it but wetting his tongue, until the whole of him drinks in the dark gore. After the blood is all spent and the *flamines* have drawn the stiff carcase away from the planking, the *pontifex* comes forth from his place, a grisly sight, and displays his wet head, his matted beard, his dank fillets and soaking garments. Defiled as he is with such pollution, all unclean with the foul blood of the victim just slain, they all stand apart and give him salutation and do him reverence because the paltry blood of a dead ox has washed him while he was ensconced in a loathsome hole in the ground. (1011–50)

Will you have me speak also of that hecatomb of yours [i.e., you pagans], when a hundred beasts at a time fall by the knife and the gore from all the separate slaughters swells into a flood, so that the *augures* almost have to swim to make their way through the sea of blood. (1051–55)

In an earlier chapter, I argued against using loaded terms like "fanatic," but anyone who quite literally bathes in the fresh blood of a bull and then proudly displays himself or herself dripping with that blood to the applause of the assembled company really does look like a fanatic. The contrast between this and simply presiding over the state cults is indeed extreme.

One critic calls Prudentius's account our "most reliable and detailed description"; another "a clear exposition." According to yet another,[119]

> There are no doubt a few exaggerations due to Christian zeal in his version of the rite, but we have no reason to believe that the more important points are incorrect or invented. *Moreover the other texts obviously refer to a similar ceremony.*

On the contrary, the entire passage is pure fiction from start to finish.[120] In the first place, since it was so obviously Prudentius's purpose to expose the *taurobolium* as both disgusting and ridiculous, we should expect it to be at best a caricature of the truth. Cumont took it for granted that Prudentius wrote as an eyewitness.[121] Yet not only is it inconceivable that a Christian was allowed to watch such a ritual; as McLynn points out, the very fact that Prudentius himself describes the initiand emerging from the pit to cheers "from afar" (*eminus*) in effect concedes that the ritual itself was conducted in private.

---

119. Vermaseren 1977, 102 (with a garish illustration on 104); Rutter 1968, 239; Duthoy 1969, 104.
120. So McLynn 1996, 312–30, one of those articles I wish I had written myself.
121. Cumont 1929, 63 ("témoins oculaire").

According to Rutter, the *CCP* "confirms Prudentius's account." Only if we assume its truth. Otherwise it merely describes the initiand changing into rags and being "polluted by the blood of the bull" (57–62). Anyone standing close to a sacrifice was liable to be splashed by a bull having its throat cut. And even this conflicts with Prudentius, who has a "high priest" (*summus sacerdos*) dressed, not in rags, but in his best silk toga tied with a Gabine knot wearing a headband (*infula*) decorated with fillets (*vittae*). Prudentius envisages his initiand as a Roman priest dressed in the costume he has read about in the Latin poets. But those who underwent the *taurobolium* did not do so in their capacity as public priests, but as private individuals. Prudentius apparently has no conception of the difference between the public activities of Roman *pontifices* and private initiation rituals. Note too that the victim is stabbed in the breast with a hunting spear, instead of having its throat cut by a knife, and that the initiate, described as a *pontifex*, is surrounded by *flamines* (1042–43), thus mixing up state priesthoods and exotic initiation rites. In rituals of the state cults, it would have been servile *victimarii* who both performed the actual sacrifice and dragged away the carcase, certainly not *flamines*.

It should also be noted that the account of the *taurobolium* is immediately followed by a denunciation of hecatombs. Prudentius was apparently unaware that hecatombs are a feature of Greek, not Roman cults. Prudentius was a Spaniard who may have paid a single visit to Rome.[122] In all probability he had no firsthand knowledge of Roman paganism. The man who could describe a panting, foaming fanatic spouting Sibylline Oracles (*Apoth.* 439–40; cf. *CS* ii. 893) obviously knew nothing about the real guardians of the Sibylline Oracles, the sober *quindecimviri sacris faciundis*. Goddard has inferred that the *quindecimviri* were still active till 408, when Stilicho had the Sibylline books burnt.[123] But as we shall see in chapter 6, it was Christian Sibyllines Stilicho burned, not the books of the *quindecimviri*.

What appear to be descriptions of contemporary pagan ritual in Prudentius are either clichés of anti-pagan polemic (bald Isiac priests shaking tambourines),[124] or details recollected from his reading of the classics. The martryr Lawrence "foresees" the day when a Christian emperor will close and bar the temples of Rome (*Peristephanon* ii. 473–84): from that day the people will begin to desert the temples and rush to the churches, men who had once been *luperci* or *flamines* will kiss the shrines of martyrs. Since Prudentius is so obviously thinking of Theodosius's legislation of 391, it is tempting to infer that he is referring to actual holders of these ancient priesthoods at that time. In *Peristephanon* x. 161–65 he vividly describes naked *luperci* running through the streets of Rome, as he does again in *CS* ii. 862–63. But the last two named *luperci* on record are C. Iulius Camilius Galerius Asper cos. 212, and L. Crepereius Rogatus, of the late third or possibly early fourth century.[125] Lactantius too ridicules those *qui nudi, uncti,*

---

122. His Roman visit has been much discussed: for a summary of the arguments, Shanzer 1989, 461 n. 1.
123. Goddard 2007, 280.
124. Firm. Mat. *De errore prof. rel.* 2; *Carmen ad Senatorem* 21–27; Prudentius, *Contra Symmachum* i. 631.
125. *PIR²* I. 232; *PLRE* i. 767; Wiseman, *JRS* 85 (1995), 16; for a list of all known *luperci*, Rüpke 2005, 599.

coronati…luto obliti currunt (*Div. Inst.* i. 21. 25), but there is no evidence that he ever visited Rome or saw the festival. Since the *uncti* echoes Cicero's description of Mark Antony as *lupercus* (*Phil.* 13. 31), like Prudentius, he is surely drawing on literature, not life.[126]

As for the fifteen *flamines*,[127] we know of only two later than the first century, Terentius Gentianus cos. 211, a *flamen Dialis*; and Iulius Silvanus Melanio, an equestrian holder of one of the minor flaminates in the third century.[128] But at *Apoth.* 460–88 Prudentius describes a *haruspex* wearing fillets (*vittatus*) examining the entrails of a cow sacrificed to Hecate (!) by the axes of the *pontifices* under Julian, attended by a *flamen* wearing bay leaves on his head.[129] Prudentius had no idea who the *flamines* were or what they did (or used to do). He did not even know the best-attested thing about them, that they wore a special spiked cap (*galerus* or *apex*).[130] Donatus included much material on *flamines* in his Vergil commentary, almost all of which Servius, writing in the 420s, omitted, probably because he considered it too obscure or unfamiliar for his pupils (Ch. 16. 6). These three texts of Prudentius are wholly insufficient to prove that the *flamines* still existed in the late fourth century.

Prudentius's classical reading is on prominent show in his two references to the taking of auspices. First *CS* i. 237–40: "offerings are made to Janus…with auspices and sacred feasts, which the wretches still keep in its long-established honor, and carry on the festal rejoicing of the Kalends," a passage treated by F. Heim as a precisely dated reference to the official taking of auspices.[131] Then there is *Perist.* x. 146–47, evoking consuls feeding chickens with meal (*farre pullos pascitis*). Several scholars have been incautious enough to see a contemporary allusion here to the taking of auspices, but the giveaway is his mention of *consuls*. Evidently, Prudentius is thinking of consuls taking the auspices before setting out on campaign half a millennium earlier in the pages of Livy (where the formula *pullos pascere* recurs often).[132] We find the same cliché of consuls feeding chickens in Minucius Felix and Salvian.[133] It is hardly necessary to add that by the 390s most consuls were Christians, with the imperial family heavily represented.[134] More telling is the remark of the pagan Servius, writing ca. 420, that

---

126. On the Lupercalia, below §§ 6.
127. Vangaard 1988, 24–29. I am not counting *flamines* of the imperial cult, which, though derived from the original *flamines*, are a different phenomenon: Weinstock 1971, 305–8; Fishwick i. 1 (1993), 164–8.
128. Vanggaard 1988, 70–73; for a list of all known *flamines*, Rüpke 2005, 588–90. Egger 1962, 79–80, followed by Rüpke/Glock 2005, 823, no. 941, takes *Iovis antistes* in *ILS* 3404 = *CLE* 869 (a praetor called Perpetuus) as identifying a *flamen Dialis*, and then identifies the man as Betitius Perpetuus, *corrector Siciliae* in 312/24. Possible, but both elements in the reconstruction are speculative, and this would be a century later than the last known *flamen*.
129. Pure fiction, based on Lactantius' account of a Christian disrupting the divination of a *haruspex* under Diocletian (*De mort. pers.* 10).
130. Discussed in detail by Vangaard 1988, 40–45.
131. Heim 1988, 41–53 at 43 (a paper often cited, but wholly uncritical).
132. Livy 6. 41. 8; 10. 40. 4; 22. 42. 8.
133. Minucius Felix 25. 12; 26. 3; Salvian vi. 12–13 (read as a contemporary reference by Goddard 2007, 281).
134. Exceptionally, both consuls of 391 (Symmachus and Tatianus) were pagans.

"our ancestors *used to* do everything according to auspices."[135] As for his frothing Sibylline priests, Prudentius's source here is beyond question Vergil, writing of the Sibyl herself, not her priests.[136]

Like many Christians, knowing nothing about contemporary paganism, Prudentius simply assumed that what he had read about pagans doing in Livy or Vergil they still did in his own day. We find this even in Macrobius, who repeatedly makes his interlocutors refer in the present tense to long-obsolete pagan practices as though they were still current in the 380s. Since Christians were (understandably) reluctant to watch pagan rituals, it is hardly surprising that their ideas about what pagans actually did derived from the classical texts the more cultivated among them knew so well.

To return to the *taurobolium*, the fairly abundant epigraphic evidence suggests an entirely different sort of ritual. Nothing more than the sacrifice of a bull, after which either its blood or its testicles (*vires*) were put in a ritual vessel known as *cernus*. On the basis of Prudentius's account alone a dramatic transformation in the nature of the ritual has been hypothesized.[137] But if the taurobolium was no more than the sacrifice of a bull, then the only difference from traditional sacrifice would be that it was performed in the interest of an individual rather than the state.

The Phrygianum dedications suggest not so much a vigorous pagan revival as a small group of individual pagans unwilling to embrace Christianity and desperately experimenting, searching for an alternative route to what Symmachus had called "so great a secret" (*tam grande secretum*). All the top people seem to have been top people in all the cults. Even if we assume that there were many other initiates beside our aristocrats, such cults were exclusive bodies. They did not proselytize for recruits. Even if *all* the cults nominally presided over by Praetextatus, Kamenius, and their peers had had thousands of adherents, what was their stake in the expensive initiations of their high priests? What sort of allegiance could such priests expect from the adherents of their cults? How much attention could men with estates and careers to manage devote to so many different cults? What happened to the rank and file once the high priest died?

5: THE DECLINE OF THE PRIESTLY COLLEGES

Symmachus's correspondence implies that the priestly colleges were still flourishing as late as the 380s. But his letters reveal that absenteeism from both festivals and pontifical meetings was common, with both Praetextatus and Flavian frequent offenders. For example, in *Ep*. ii. 34 Symmachus expresses surprise that Flavian will not be returning to Rome in time for the festival of the Magna Mater

---

135. Serv. on *Aen*. iv. 340; on Servius' imperfects, see p. 168.
136. With *bacchantis* in *CS* ii. 893, cf. *bacchatur* in *Aen*. vi. 78; with *anhelus* in *Apoth*. 439, cf. *Aen*. vi. 48.
137. Duthoy 1969, 121.

on 27 March. In *Ep.* ii. 59 he says he is returning to Rome for the festival of Vesta (9 June), and hopes that Flavian will be there to participate in the designation of his son Memmius as quaestor. Apparently, he did not feel able to count on him being in Rome anyway for the festival of Vesta. *Ep.* ii. 53 replies to a reminder (which he insists was unnecessary) from Flavian about some festival involving a fast (perhaps that of Ceres on 4 October). To judge from the sequel, Flavian had playfully asked Symmachus to take his place. Evidently, yet another festival he missed. *Ep.* ii. 36 to Flavian deplores the decision of the Vestals to erect a statue to the memory of Praetextatus. Apparently, Symmachus had been unable to carry a vote at the college of pontiffs, in part (it seems) because Flavian had once again been absent.

In *Ep.* i. 51 Symmachus tells Praetextatus he has decided to return to Rome earlier than he had originally intended because of troubles there (probably a food shortage). On top of this there are his pontifical duties, it being the month for which he was responsible (*officium stati mensis*). In earlier times, he goes on, it was common to delegate such duties to a colleague, but Symmachus felt he could not do this "when so many are neglecting their priestly duties" (*in tanta sacerdotum neglegentia*). It is here that he makes his much-quoted remark that "it is now a way of currying favor for Romans to desert the altars" (*nunc aris deesse Romanos genus est ambiendi*). What has not been sufficiently appreciated is that this is *not* a comment on the small numbers of pagans left because of the inroads of Christianity. It is a complaint about the small number of *pontiffs* who took the trouble to show up, whether at meetings of the college or at the festivals. It is clear from the letter's close that Praetextatus was away from Rome, and although this could be because it was not his month, nonetheless Symmachus strikes a reproachful note.

Ep. i. 47 reproaches Praetextatus for vacationing at Baiae while Symmachus performs his pontifical duties in Rome, and while the tone is playful ("there is much to be discussed in our college; who allowed you a holiday from your public responsibilities?"), Symmachus devotes four sentences to the point. *Ep.* i. 49 tells Praetextatus about attempts to expiate publicly some portent at Spoletum, promising to inform him of the decision of a special meeting of the college of pontiffs. Once again, Praetextatus was clearly absent. *Ep.* i. 46 reports a decision of the colleges concerning the public performance of cult acts, and an imperial edict apparently related to cult statues. Unfortunately, Symmachus gives no details, evidently assuming that Praetextatus was familiar with the issues involved, even though, yet again, he was evidently not present at the meeting. Symmachus was a member of only one college, the pontiffs. When we reflect how many other colleges Praetextatus belonged to, it does not seem likely that he can have devoted much time to the affairs of any one of them.

Were the priestly colleges really still a going concern? Perhaps in 380, but hardly by the late 390s. According to Christophe Goddard, "The last pagan priest we know of, Rufius Antonius Agrypnius Volusianus…was a Roman pontiff who died after his conversion in Constantinople in 437."[138] Did the college really still exist nearly forty years after Symmachus's death? Actually, there is no evidence whatever that Volusianus was a pontiff. Indeed, we shall see in the next chapter that there is no good evidence that he was even a pagan.

Reference is often made in this connection to Orosius's story that Tertullus, consul in 410, made a speech in the senate that opened as follows: "I shall speak to you, conscript fathers, as consul and pontifex, of which offices I hold the one and hope for the other."[139] This speech has always been held to prove him a militant pagan.[140] But if the reference were to the college of pontiffs, the two wishes would be curiously incommensurate. The consulate was the supreme honor available to a private citizen (even rarer now that so many went to emperors and their sons), while membership of the priestly colleges (even assuming they still existed) was a distinction shared with scores of others, a distinction that came to nobles like Tertullus unsolicited in their teens.[141]

It is hard not to connect this text with a strikingly similar passage in Paulinus of Nola, urging Augustine's young protégé Licentius in 396 to renounce his worldly ambitions and follow Augustine's footsteps: "If you heed and follow Augustine... then indeed you will be fashioned consul and priest (*formatus consul et pontifex*), not in the phantom of a dream, but in reality." And then, "For Licentius will be truly a pontifex and truly a consul (*vere enim pontifex et vere consul*), if you hug the footsteps of Augustine... tread the ways of God in close attendance on your master, so that you may learn... to *deserve* the priesthood (*sacerdotium*)."[142] To be both consul and *pontifex* had been the summit of a Roman noble's ambitions since the days of the Republic.[143] Paulinus's first *consul et pontifex* symbolizes the traditional worldly success Licentius is currently pursuing, while the *vere pontifex et vere consul* represents a spiritual version of this success, leading after a long apprenticeship to a priesthood he deserves, which must be a Christian priesthood. If Tertullus's speech is correctly reported, his *patres conscripti* confirms that he too was building on the traditional formula; like Paulinus, the priesthood he hopes for must also be Christian, hardly less than a bishopric, perhaps (if it is comparable to the consulate) the papacy itself.

The latest Roman *pontifex* known is Symmachus himself, who died in 402. No *pontifex*, *augur*, or *quindecimvir* is known to have lived later than 402. All those we can positively identify (Albinus, Flavian, Kamenius) were more or less exact contemporaries of Symmachus, that is to say men who lived till the 380s, 390s, or early 400s, but acquired their priesthoods in the 360s. Nothing further is known about Q. Clodius

---

138. Goddard in Ghilardi 2006, 294.
139. "Loquar vobis, patres conscripti, consul et pontifex, quorum alterum teneo, alterum spero," Oros. vii. 42. 8; Paschoud, *Zosime* 3. 2 (1989), 46; *PLRE* ii. 1059.
140. Most recently, Salzman 2002, 65.
141. Assuming that Tertullus was one of the Insteii Tertulli: *PLRE* i. 883–84; ii. 1060. The way to win such a priesthood was to be nominated by a member of one of the colleges, not to make a speech in the senate.
142. Paul. Nol. *Ep.* 8. 1.
143. E.g., Cic. *De harusp. resp.* 12; *De prov. cons.* 21; Val. Max. 4. 2. 1; Oros. ii. 5. 10 (from Livy).

Flavianus and L. Ragonius Venustus, holders of various Roman priesthoods, beyond their Phrygianum altars dated to 383 and 390, respectively. Both might have been a year or two younger than Symmachus—but not significantly younger. Bloch identified the Postumianus mentioned in the opening chapters of Macrobius's *Saturnalia* with a Postumianus who is attested on an undated Roman dedication as *pontifex Solis*, *quindecimvir*, and Mithraic *pater patrum*. But this dedication might be as much as a century earlier than Macrobius's interlocutor, who could not have been younger than Symmachus in any case.[144]

More telling is the altar dedicated by Ceionius Rufius Volusianus in 390. Here we have a pagan noble, at least forty years old,[145] son of Volusianus Lampadius, without a single Roman priesthood. And this in the Phrygianum, surrounded by altars commemorating the Roman priesthoods of his fellow nobles. In the ordinary way he should have picked up at least one by his early twenties. If he performed a *taurobolium* he was obviously a pagan. So why no Roman priesthoods? Then there is the younger Flavian. He was no doubt brought up a pagan, but there is no actual evidence that he ever held a priesthood.

Goddard claimed that the great Roman families remained pagan down to the late fifth century. But it is important to distinguish between the possibility that a few (perhaps more than a few) nobles continued in the privacy of their homes to drop a few grains of incense on a domestic altar, and the continued existence of the priestly colleges. According to Liebeschuetz, when Gratian renounced the title of *pontifex maximus*, this meant that "there would be no one to fill vacancies in the priestly colleges, which would therefore die out."[146] But for a half-century before even the conversion of Constantine, emperors had spent so little time in Rome that by 382 there must have been several generations of priests co-opted into the colleges without imperial approval. The reason Constantius II approved appointments in person in 357 must in part be because he was directly asked during his Roman visit, but more important because he was at the time very anxious to conciliate the aristocracy of the West before returning to the East. It is not likely that (say) Valentinian I, notoriously unsympathetic to the Roman nobility, was approached. Nor is it likely that either Gratian or Theodosius directly abolished the priestly colleges. What would have been the point in so provocative an act? The colleges had no power in themselves. They simply provided an opportunity for *publici sacerdotes* to meet and discuss issues affecting their various colleges. But once pagan rituals had been banned, there was nothing left to discuss.

At a practical level, the continued functioning of the colleges must have depended on mustering a quorum, that is to say a quorum for each of the four major colleges. And while there are bound to have been a few pontiffs and augurs unknown to us who lived beyond 402, were there really enough to fill four separate sets of meetings? Those

---

144. Macrob. *Sat.* i. 1–2; *CIL* vi. 2151; *PLRE* i. 719; Matthews 1967, 497–98.
145. He performed a second *taurobolium* after twenty years: *ILS* 4154 = Vermaseren *CCCA* 244.
146. Liebeschuetz/Hill 2005, 61.

who consult the lists of priests in Rüpke's recent *Fasti Sacerdotum* (2005/2008) might be inclined to answer in the affirmative. But the format of annual lists is problematic for this purpose. While it was reasonable to include (e.g.) Q. Aurelius Symmachus as *pontifex Vestae* every year from 361 to 402, to record the names of those who held three or four major priesthoods under each of those priesthoods every year for thirty or forty years gives a misleading impression of the total number of priests and the vitality of the colleges. Rüpke's lists also tend to prolong lives (and so tenures) further than the evidence warrants (e.g., Ulpius Egnatius Faventinus, listed as *augur* from 361 to 390, when he is not known to have lived later than 376).[147]

Even so, Rüpke was able to list only one name later than 402, Fl. Macrobius Longinianus, praetorian prefect in 406–8. But this depends on the unwarranted identification of the prefect Longinianus with a pagan Longinianus who corresponded with Augustine, and the assumption that the *sacerdotia* Augustine's correspondent mentions are Roman priesthoods (Ch. 5. 3).

The fact is that, on the evidence we have, Symmachus († 402) is the latest known pontifex, Praetextatus († 384) the latest known *augur*, Kamenius († 385) the latest known *quindecimvir*, Coelia Concordia (385) the latest known Vestal, and Q. Clodius Flavianus (if he outlived Kamenius) the latest known *septemvir epulonum*. In a letter of 400 Jerome evokes Caecina Albinus the *pontifex*, listening fondly as his Christian granddaughter chants Alleluia.[148] Albinus was a contemporary of Symmachus, who cannot have lived much later than this. There is no indication that any pagan noble born later than ca. 360 (the generation of the younger Flavian) ever held any of the old priesthoods. The colleges were not abolished; they simply faded away as their older members died off, in the first decade of the fifth century.

Moderns tend to assume that nobles with many priesthoods were more dedicated pagans. In fact, the accumulation of more than two major priesthoods in a single person should probably be seen as an early sign of the decline of the priesthoods. Nobles who expected to hold public office on top of all the other responsibilities attendant on wealth and influence cannot have done justice to the duties of three or even four separate priesthoods.[149] It may be that someone like Symmachus, who restricted himself to a single priesthood and took the trouble to attend as many meetings as he could, was actually serving the state cults better than those who ostentatiously filled their cursuses with a multitude of priesthoods they had no time for.

Books ii–vii of Symmachus's letters were published posthumously by his son. But Symmachus himself revised and published Bk i, and was presumably planning to

---

147. In the German edition the improbably named M. Philonius Philomusus Eugenianus is listed every year from 381 to 400, on the basis of a modern forgery: CIL vi. 736 = 30823 ("monumentum quin novicium sit nullo modo dubitandum," Huelsen). Removed from the lists of the English translation (2008).

148. Jerome, *Ep.* 107. 1.

149. Three men are known to have held four priesthoods: Praetextatus, Kamenius, and Q. Clodius Flavianus.

publish the rest when death intervened. He had surely completed the selection and arrangement of at any rate Bk ii, letters to the elder Flavian, a delicate task young Memmius would hardly have undertaken without his father's guidance (Ch. 10). If so, Bk i probably appeared in the late rather than early 390s, when the *sacerdotum neglegentia* complained about in 383 (*Ep.* i. 51) was more advanced. It would be naive to suppose that at this date so prominent a pagan did not give careful thought to the inclusion of letters referring to the priestly colleges, letters he had written before the disestablishment of the cults. It is not mere chance (I suggest) that the letters he selected give the impression that up till then the college of pontiffs at any rate was flourishing, and that Symmachus himself was the only member of the college who took his duties seriously.

6: CONCLUSION

There is little evidence that official Roman paganism survived the fourth century. By this I do not mean that Roman paganism itself died out (in a variety of ways and forms it never entirely died). Nor do I mean that no individual pagans were left. But there can (I would argue) be no serious doubt that the formal apparatus of the state cults as administered by the various priestly colleges was gone. There is one highly significant piece of evidence that has never so far been exploited by historians. The grammarian Servius frequently and systematically refers to *pontifices, flamines,* and countless details of sacrifice and other cult practices in his Vergil commentary, published in (at latest) the 420s, *in the imperfect tense* (Ch. 16. 3). This, that, or the other was what the priests *used to* do or say (*sacrificabant, rogabant, immolabant, dicebant, faciebant,* etc.). This is the way all the late antique commentators refer to details of the state cults, but none of the others can be dated so early and so precisely. It is not just a single ritual that Servius is referring to, but everything to do with the priests and rituals of the state cults of Rome.

It might be argued that Servius, a pagan himself, most of whose pupils would now be Christian, was taking care to distance himself from the old rituals. But how would writing of these rituals as if they were all extinct when some of them were still performed achieve this? For reasons discussed in detail in chapter 16, Vergil's knowledge of pontifical and augural law had been a central preoccupation of his commentators since the first century. As the last known western pagan commentator working in a now Christian world, Servius might have been expected to take one of two lines with this material: either (in the interests of self-preservation) to minimize or drop it altogether; or (assuming the pagan reaction model), whether openly or indirectly to defend this approach against Christian criticism. He did neither. The only difference between his notes on such topics and those of his main source, the commentary of Aelius Donatus (dating from ca. 350, before any serious Christian inroads against the cults), is that where Donatus had used present tenses, Servius systematically substituted imperfects.

The natural inference is that as early as the 420s the apparatus of the state cults as a whole no long functioned. Above all, the regular use of imperfects with respect to the activity of pontiffs and augurs implies that the priestly colleges no longer existed.

It is often assumed that a few at least of the traditional festivals long continued to be celebrated. That some festivals continued in some form is likely enough, though there is less evidence than often supposed, nor is that evidence very revealing. The Calendar of 354 offers a very full list of the festivals and games (*ludi*) still celebrated in mid fourth-century Rome.[150] That (of course) was long before Gratian and Theodosius. In all probability most continued in some form down to the 380s, though (as we have seen) it is likely that the more objectionably pagan features (most obviously animal sacrifice) were eliminated. Rutilius arrived at Faleria when the Heuresis of Osiris was being celebrated in November 417, but, though himself a pagan, all he reports is villagers relaxing and enjoying themselves (*De red.* i. 373–76).

From almost a century after the Calendar of 354 we have the Calendar of Polemius Silvius (449), which lists the Carmentalia, Parentatio tumulorum, Lupercalia, Quirinalia, Terminalia, Quinquatria, Natalis urbis Romae, and Lavatio. But it would be rash to infer that all were still celebrated, much less in anything approaching their original form, with offerings at altars. As Mommsen pointed out, Silvius clearly based his list on a copy of the Calendar of 354, omitting (as Silvius himself remarks in his preface) all the obviously pagan names (e.g., Isidis navigium, Iunonalia, Neptunalia, Saturnalia, Volcanalia), and keeping those whose pagan origin was less obvious.[151] He evidently did not know that the Lavatio (27 March) commemorated the washing of the statue of the Magna Mater, since he identified it as the Resurrection of Christ![152] In the case of other festivals he included he emphasized history rather than cult (*Carmentalia, de nominis matris Evandri*). If this was his method,[153] there is no reason to believe that he had any actual evidence for the continued performance of any of the pagan festivals he included.

The long series of illustrated calendars may cast a little more light here. As Stern pointed out, in a well-preserved late second- or early third-century mosaic pavement from el-Djem in Tunisia, no fewer than nine months are illustrated by scenes of pagan festivals. The Codex Calendar of 354 has reduced the number of pagan festivals illustrated to four; while an early fifth-century mosaic from Carthage has only one.[154] And that one is the consular games of the first week of January, which, like many other *ludi*, certainly continued. The long series of consular diptychs show consuls, all now Christian, spending fortunes year after year on their (now entirely de-paganized) consular games in both Rome and Constantinople, right down to the Basilius who celebrated the last consulate of all, at Rome, in 541.[155]

---

150. Salzman 1990.
151. In *Chronica Minora* 1 (Berlin 1892), 513–14; Stern 1953, 32–35.
152. *Lavationem veteres nominabant; Resurrectio,* in A. Degrassi (ed.), *Inscr. Ital.* 13. 2 (Rome 1963), 266.
153. For some reservations, see Salzman 1990, 242–43.
154. Stern 1981, 431–75.
155. Cameron and Schauer 1982; Cameron 2007, 195.

It has often been assumed that the Lupercalia (15 February), attacked in a well-known pamphlet by Pope Gelasius, was maintained by a core of stubborn pagans able to resist the power of the church for a full century after Theodosius. Yet it is hard to believe that the charade nostalgically watched by Christians in the 490s retained any genuinely pagan elements. To start with, the senator who defended the festival, and to whom Gelasius's letter is addressed, was undoubtedly a Christian, since Gelasius begins by excommunicating him.[156] Perhaps the most striking thing about the letter is Gelasius's failure to use what might have seemed the most obvious argument of all against the continued performance of the festival: the fact that it was now more than a century since all pagan festivals had been banned by law. How could he have failed to make this point if the Lupercalia of the 490s had been in any sense an authentic pagan ritual? Indeed, Gelasius mocks the inauthenticity of the festival as it was now performed, pointing out (explicitly citing as his source the "second decade" of Livy) that in olden times it was the nobility who ran through the streets of the city nude and Roman matrons whom they whipped with strips of goatskin.[157] Now it was the dregs of the population (*viles trivialesque personas*), by which he probably meant *actors*.[158] Nor does he mention pontiffs or *luperci*. Apart from the addressee, he mentions only "backers" (*patroni*), again undoubtedly Christians. It seems clear that the college of *luperci* no longer existed in 495. A scholiast on Juvenal writing a half-century before Pope Gelasius, in Rome, wrote (using the imperfect tense we have seen to be so telling in Servius) that "sterile women *used to* offer themselves to the Luperci for purification."[159] Clearly, this no longer happened. The celebration that took place in the streets of Rome in the 490s was not in any sense a genuine pagan survival but a completely de-paganized re-creation of one of the most picturesque festivals of ancient Rome. Nothing in Gelasius's letter suggests (as often assumed) that his attack was successful. Indeed, he concedes that earlier popes had tried to get it stopped without success, which suggests that the civil authorities did not share his own anxiety.

Modern historians tend to take it for granted that holders of the state priesthoods must have been the principal champions of the pagan cause. But while (as already remarked) some Christians may have identified *pontifices* as the pagan equivalent of bishops, their role in Roman paganism was actually very different. The college of pontiffs determined the date of festivals, administered burial law, and (in earlier times) advised the senate on religious matters.[160] They played a role in a

---

156. *Cum Christianum videri velit et profiteatur et dicat*... (*Coll. Avellana* [1895–98], no. 100. 3 = G. Pomarès, *Gelase I: Lettre contre les Lupercales* [Paris 1959], 164). For a new interpretation of this puzzling text, to which I am indebted, McLynn 2008, 161–81, together with North's contribution to the same volume (pp. 144–60).

157. Evidently, Gelasius did not want his opposition to the Lupercalia to be put down to ignorance. Elsewhere in the letter he quotes entire lines of Lucan and Juvenal (§§ 14 and 20).

158. *Apud illos enim nobiles ipsi currebant et matronae...vos...deduxistis...ad viles trivialesque personas, abiectos et infimos, Coll. Avell.* 100. 16 = Pomarès 1959, 174; Cameron 2004, 512–13.

159. *steriles mulieres februantibus Lupercis se efferebant et ferula verberabantur* (Schol. Vet. on Juv. ii. 142); on the date of the Juvenal scholia, Cameron 2010.

160. For what pontiffs actually did, Beard and North 1990, 19–48; Porte 1989, 131–44; van Haeperen 2002.

handful of festivals, but were not, *as pontiffs*, significant public figures (after all, there were twenty of them at full strength, not to mention the scores of augurs, *quindecimviri* and *septemviri*).[161] They did not represent, and certainly never addressed publicly, any sort of congregation. It is typical (and significant) that at the beginning of his *Relatio* Symmachus identifies himself as prefect of Rome and voice of the senate, not *pontifex*.

There is no reason to suppose that pontiffs were more pious than other pagans, or in any but a purely titular sense pagan leaders. In view of their wealth and social importance *as aristocrats* they were certainly the most authoritative representatives of Roman paganism, and so the obvious spokesmen to protest at the Christian abrogation of state subsidies for the cults in 382. On the other hand, they were not necessarily the most committed champions available. Indeed, the very fact that they were so prominent, both socially and politically, may have meant that most were unwilling to commit their prestige too decisively to a losing cause. *Pontifices* did not in any sense represent a pagan community in the sense that Christian clergy represented the Christian community. With a few pagan counterparts to bishops like Athanasius or Ambrose to rally the troops, the fate of Roman paganism just might have been different. But pagan priests known to have been appointed in their teens and twenties on the basis of birth and connections could hardly command either the authority needed for the task or the respect of their Christian counterparts. More important, it does not seem to have occurred to them to make the attempt. Men like Kamenius, Praetextatus, Flavian, and Symmachus were first and foremost aristocrats and landowners, not priests. The very fact that their descendants continued to hold high office in a Christian world is enough to show that it was their families and estates, not the cults, that they saw as their primary responsibilities.

It is instructive to contrast the fate of the priesthoods of the imperial cult. In Roman North Africa, such was the range of responsibilities and privileges these priests enjoyed[162] (notably the games they provided and paid for) that they survived the loss of their specifically religious functions. Already by the late fourth century we find Christian *flamines* of the provincial cult.[163] In Rome, on the other hand, not only did the repeated senatorial protests irrevocably identify pontiffs with paganism. For all their social prestige, Roman priests did not, in their capacity as priests, provide games or even pay for the publicly funded festivals they superintended. Their games they gave in a different capacity, as quaestors, praetors, or consuls, and this they continued to do down into the sixth century. Lacking as they did the flexibility to modify the cults so that they could continue without the subsidies, with disestablishment the *publici sacerdotes* lost their religious duties and functions. Since their social position did not depend on the priesthoods (as that of provincial priests did), it is not surprising

---

161. For Roman priests in the public life of Rome, Rüpke in Eck 2005, 283–93.
162. For a convenient list, Rives 1995, 88.
163. Chastagnol and Duval 1974, 87–118; Lepelley 1979, 362–79.

that those with the most to lose were willing to limit their protests and quietly let them go.

Nonetheless, in default of any evidence that "oriental" cults were the driving force Bloch and many others have assumed, we are left with the undoubted fact that some at least of the last pagans made repeated attempts to get state funding of the traditional Roman cults restored. Perhaps after all it was the state cults that provided the last resistance, such as it was, to Christianity.

Addendum to p. 162: Lizzi Testa, "*Augures et pontifices*: Public Sacral Law in Late Antique Rome," in A. Cain and N. Lenski (eds.), *The Power of Religion in Late Antiquity* (Ashgate 2009), 251–78 at p. 267 argues that Prud. *Perist*. iv. 527–28 records the conversion of a real Vestal. But her very name, Claudia, shows that he was thinking of the famous Claudia Quinta of myth (Ovid, *Fasti* iv. 305–44).

5

PAGAN CONVERTS

Ever since Gibbon enumerated the "secondary" causes for the spread of Christianity (the primary cause, naturally, being "the convincing evidence of the doctrine itself"), historians have sought to trace, date, and account for the Christianization of the Roman world. It is clear that the conversion of Constantine was a turning point, though there is less agreement about the extent of pre-Constantinian Christianity. Thanks to the support of a succession of Christian emperors and an aggressive church, by the beginning of the fifth century paganism was in rapid decline. What this book seeks to discover is how rapid (and how defiant) this decline was.

Until recently, it was taken for granted that the fourth-century Roman world was divided straightforwardly between pagans and Christians. The question was how to determine the relative proportions and the date and rate of conversion from one to the other. But not only are we faced with all the usual problems of the ancient historian about lack and quality of evidence. Even more problematic is the assumption that these are the sort of questions we could answer if only we had more evidence. It should be recognized straightaway that they are questions only a Christian would have asked at the time:

> The image of a society neatly divided into "Christian" and "pagan" is the creation of late fourth-century Christians, and has been too readily taken at its face value by modern historians. Unlike Christianity, with its growing worldwide cohesiveness, "paganism" was a varied group of cults and observances.... It existed only in the minds, and, increasingly, the speech-habits, of Christians.

As Henry Chadwick charmingly put it, "Pagans did not know they were pagans until the Christians told them they were."[1] Even then, no pagan would have thought of himself as a pagan except in relation to Christians.

It is also a problem that we have so few conversion stories—for the aristocracy, none. Fascinating as Augustine's incomparable account of his own conversion is, such confessions are always misleading in one way or another. More important in the present context, Augustine had never really been a pagan. We have the outline of a conversion for one minor member of the nobility, a certain Firmicus Maternus, *vir*

---

1. Markus 1990, 28; Chadwick 1985, 9.

clarissimus, inferred from his two surviving works: the *Mathesis*, an astrological work undoubtedly written by a pagan, and *De errore profanarum religionum*, the most intemperate surviving work of Christian polemic. What we do not have, unfortunately, is a narrative, any account of how and why Maternus turned from paganism to such an aggressive form of Christianity.[2]

If we had only his *Mathesis*, he would have been confidently classified as a pagan. The ferocious polemic of the *De errore* might seem to imply a powerful conversion experience between the two works that produced an evangelical fervor.[3] But there is another possibility, persuasively argued by Caseau.[4] Given the suspicion inevitably aroused by opportune conversions among ambitious members of the elite, such converts were under some pressure to prove their conversions genuine. Take Arnobius's *Adversus Nationes*. Though often described as Christian apologetic, according to Jerome Arnobius wrote the book to convince a bishop, sceptical because in his pagan days he had attacked Christianity, that he was a genuine convert.[5] While this need not detract from the sincerity of Arnobius's conversion (no one was likely to pretend to be a Christian in the age of Diocletian), it does call the sincerity of his polemic into question. Constans issued a law banning sacrifice in 341, and since *De errore* (343/50) repeatedly apostrophizes Constantius and Constans (fourteen times, in fact), urging them to ban sacrifice by law and overthrow pagan temples, it has often been assumed that Firmicus was a fanatic urging them to go even further.[6] Indeed, a law of Constans addressed to Taurus as praetorian prefect and dated to 346, banning sacrifice and ordering temples closed, has been claimed to be "a response to Firmicus or to the mood which he represented."[7] But Taurus did not hold this office till 355, and the date of the law is generally now corrected to 356,[8] in which case the link to Firmicus vanishes. Again, without questioning the sincerity of his conversion, we may nonetheless question his motive in writing. We should bear in mind that his *Mathesis* (337) opens with a flattering dedication to a prominent pagan, Lollianus Mavortius, whose distinguished career Firmicus obsequiously traces from office to office, apostrophizing him no fewer than thirty times in the course of his book, just as he repeatedly apostrophizes Constantius and Constans in *De errore*.[9] While no doubt delighted to observe the conversion of a former pagan man of letters and protégé of pagan aristocrats, sceptical Christians might need to be convinced that he really had rejected his pagan past.

More speculatively, there is the case of M. Aurelius Consius Quartus. A Roman dedication of the 340s gives him the correctorship of Flaminia-Picenum, by when he was already *pontifex maior, promagister iterum*, and *duodecimvir*. A flattering public

---

2. The missing first two folios of the unique manuscript may have contained some biographical material.
3. So Festugière 1944, 9.
4. Caseau 2007, 39–63, with earlier bibliography.
5. Jer. *Chron.* s.a. 326–27; Simmons 1995, 6–9.
6. *Cod. Theod.* xvi. 10. 2 and 3; Firm. *De err.* 16. 4; 20. 7; 29. 1.
7. Forbes 1970, 17.
8. *PLRE* i. 879–80; Delmaire et al. 2005, 432.
9. See Barnes 1975, 40.

dedication from Hippo a decade or so later lists four more governorships, culminating in the proconsulate of Africa—but no priesthoods.[10] Did he convert (as many pagans must have) between the late 330s and early 360s, or is there some more mundane explanation for the omission of his priesthoods at Hippo?

One case (discussed in more detail later) that we know to have been based on mature reflection rather than self-advancement, is Augustine's account of the conversion of the celebrated pagan professor Marius Victorinus.[11] After studying Christian writings for some years in private, Victorinus told his friend the Christian priest Simplicianus that he was "now a Christian." "I shall not believe that or count you among the Christians," Simplicianus replied, "until I see you in the church of Christ." "Do then walls make a Christian?" Victorinus famously responded. They had this conversation many times, until one day he finally said to Simplicianus, "Let's go to church; I want to become a Christian" (*volo Christianus fieri*). Not the least interesting detail in this story is the implication that, but for Simplicianus's insistence, Victorinus might have continued to believe that his personal acceptance of Christian teaching was enough to make him a Christian, without the need to confess his faith publicly in church. That public confession in front of a crowd of their social inferiors must have been particularly hard for Roman aristocrats.

For those brought up in the world of civic cults and private initiations, it cannot have been easy to comprehend the exclusive, absolute commitment Christianity demanded. During much of the fourth century, there must have been many who took a genuine interest in Christianity and presented or considered themselves as Christians but, while rejecting sacrifice to what they were willing to accept were false gods, still followed (say) pagan burial customs, continued to watch a favorite festival, or occasionally consulted a *haruspex*. Rigorists would have dismissed such folk as no better than outright pagans. Depending on which side the evidence in such cases comes from, the modern historian, grateful for *any* evidence, would render a firm verdict one way or the other—a verdict that might have been contested at the time. Take Bacurius, an Iberian chieftain who rose to the rank of *magister militum* in Theodosius's army at the Frigidus. Rufinus was in no doubt that he was a sincere Christian, but Libanius seems to have thought of him as a pagan (*PLRE* i. 144). Both men actually knew him, and, by itself, the opinion of either would have been considered decisive by any modern scholar. But what do we do with both?

Sandwell has recently studied religious identity in late fourth-century Antioch, where we have extensive evidence on both the pagan and Christian side in the voluminous writings of Libanius and John Chrysostom.[12] For Chrysostom (she concludes), pagan and Christian were "fixed and clear-cut identities." You were either one or the

---

10. *ILS* 1249; *AE* 1955, 150; Chastagnol 1987, 202–3.
11. Aug. *Conf.* viii. 2. 3–4. The story continues for several pages, and it is important to try to distinguish the factual account the elderly Simplicianus gave the young Augustine from the imaginative color added by Augustine (Victorinus's fear of his "devil-worshipping" aristocratic patrons and so on).
12. Sandwell 2007.

other. Members of his congregation were constantly warned that they could not be considered Christians if they engaged in any activities that Chrysostom judged irredeemably pagan (attending pagan festivals, consulting soothsayers, even wearing amulets, not to mention sacrificing). Libanius, on the other hand, "allowed people a more flexible approach to religious interaction in which they could play down their religious allegiance in certain circumstances in order to ease relations with others and then emphasize it again when it was useful or necessary to do so."

The classic illustration is Domitius Modestus, who professed Christianity under Constantius, came out as a pagan under Julian, and returned to (Arian) Christianity again under Valens. When Libanius wrote to him shortly after his promotion by Julian he simply remarked on his open acknowledgment of the gods he had long admired in private. The sophist Hecebolius made the same double switch, and though Libanius does mention (without actually naming him) that his Christianity helped him become Julian's tutor, he does not mention his two subsequent switches.[13]

In 1923 R. Guignebert posited a category he called "semi-Christians." There were no doubt many who, while no longer fully pagans, were not yet fully Christians either, but "semi-Christian" is not a term contemporaries would have chosen. Chrysostom applies it only to Judaizing Christians, never pagans.[14] And when Faustus the Manichee called Christians semi-Christians, Augustine responded that "something that is 'semi' is imperfect in some respect, but still not false in any respect," adding that all Christians were striving to make their faith more perfect.[15] Manichaeans, he said, were *pseudo*-Christians. More recently, Kahlos has conjured up a group she calls *incerti*.[16] No doubt there were many Christians unsure just what they believed. But there must also have been many who were in no doubt what they believed, but were nonetheless found wanting by more rigorist peers, whether because they were thought to believe false doctrine, or simply because they still went to the circus (Ch. 21). To this day there are sects that see "true" Christians as a select society of saints in a corrupt world, while others believe that one day the whole world will bow before Christ.

Rather than a simple division between pagans and Christians, I would posit as many as five overlapping categories. In characterizing them it is important to avoid the tendentious labels that have so bedeviled past scholarship: fanatics, zealots, extremists, diehards, devout on the one side; time-servers, conformists, opportunists, trimmers, lukewarm, indifferent, or weak-kneed on the other.[17] I prefer the neutral terms "committed" and (occasionally) "rigorist." On the two extremes of my fivefold grouping I would place committed Christians (Ambrose and Augustine) and committed pagans (Praetextatus and Symmachus); then, on the one side center-Christians, on the other center-pagans. Center-Christians would include both time-servers and

---

13. Lib. *Ep.* 804. 5; *Or.* xviii. 12; *PLRE* i. 605–8; Libanius had a grudge against Hecebolius (Kinzig 1993).
14. Χριστιανὸς ἐξ ἡμισείας, Chrys. *Adv. Jud.* i. 4 (*PG* 48. 844); Brottier 2004, 439.
15. Aug. *Contra Faust.* i. 3 and ii. 2, the only occurrences of the word in Latin.
16. Guignebert 1923, 65–102; Kahlos 2007.
17. The delightfully tendentious "weak-kneed" comes from Dill 1899, 20.

sincere believers who were nonetheless not interested in or well informed about details of theology, and saw no reason to reject secular culture (Ausonius). Center-pagans would be people brought up as pagans but with no deep investment in the cults themselves (people like Servius).

In between would be the (for a time) perhaps rather large group of those who for one reason or another resisted straightforward classification (people like Bacurius). I would not suppose that there was ever more than a relatively small proportion of the entire population in either of the "committed" groups. The major shift, as I see it, would be from the center-pagan to the center-Christian category. From about 340 to (say) 430 I would guess that some three-quarters of the one passed into the other.

2

In attempting to trace this shift our biggest problem is the complete lack of both numbers and dates. There are two ways of creating numbers and dates (of a sort). The first is to investigate how late we find pagans appointed to the highest offices of state. Here the starting point must be a massive volume by von Haehling (1978), assembling every scrap of information about the religion of every holder of the six highest offices of state between 324 and 455.[18] His book concludes with a series of tables, listing pagan and Christian officeholders under each emperor, both as absolute numbers and as a percentage of all officials known.

Von Haehling assumed that within this period a substantial proportion of all holders of these offices is known (86 percent was his estimate), and that the religion of approximately half of this total could be determined with some probability. On his calculations, 20 percent of Constantine's appointments were Christians; 22 percent of Constantius II's (337–61); 31 percent of Valentinian I's (364–75); and 50 percent of Gratian's (375–83). On this basis he concluded that the reign of Gratian marked a turning point. But if Gratian's reign had really been a watershed, we should expect this shift to be reflected in the longer and much better documented reigns of Theodosius I (379–95) and Honorius (395–423). Yet on von Haehling's figures only 27 percent and 34 percent, respectively, of their appointees were Christians.

There are also other problems with these figures. Many rest on single sources subject to all the usual uncertainties. More important, they represent offices held rather than officeholders. Remarkably enough, von Haehling counted men who held two of the offices he treated twice, and some three times. The 787 offices held included in his survey represent only 584 different officeholders. In addition, he almost certainly underestimated the number of holders of these offices who are simply unknown. To return to his figures for the reign of Gratian (which was, after all, very short), while

---

18. Praetorian prefects, prefects of Rome and Constantinople, proconsuls, prefects of Egypt, and *magistri militum*.

Christians clearly predominate, Christians and pagans combined represent less than two-thirds (61 percent) of the total number of known officials, not to mention the unknown.

It was certainly an error to count posts rather than people, but the error does not falsify von Haehling's results quite as fundamentally as it might seem. The fact that (say) a Christian emperor filled two or three different vacancies in his administration with the same pagan does after all mean that on two or three occasions when he might have appointed a Christian he appointed a pagan. Barnes's main criticism is that von Haehling undercounted Christian appointees under Constantine and Constantius; mine that he overcounted pagans under Honorius (§ 3) and Valentinian III (§ 4).[19]

Take the sixteen pagans and ten Christians von Haehling lists for Constantine. Four of the pagans have been counted twice and one four times. In addition, Barnes transferred two pagans to the other camp, giving nine Christians and six pagans. Following the same method for the reign of Constantius II, instead of twenty-one pagans and eighteen Christians, he ended up with twenty-two Christians and only ten pagans. These are dramatically different proportions, and Barnes drew a very firm conclusion: "The claim that a majority of the holders of high administrative offices under the Christian emperors continued to be pagan until the reign of Gratian is quite simply false." The Christianization of the Roman elite, he argues, took place faster and reached a critical point earlier than generally believed.

As we shall see, this is probably true. But it is doubtful whether it can be proved by a handful of cases based on such uncertain evidence. Take two of Constantine's longest-serving ministers: Junius Bassus, praetorian prefect for fourteen years (318–31) and consul in 331; and Domitius Zenophilus, holder of three proconsulates and consul in 333.[20] Barnes includes Bassus among "consuls *attested* as Christians," on the basis of a speculative identification of an anonymous Christian consul represented on a fragmentary Roman sarcophagus. Other identifications are just as likely, especially if the portrait represents a suffect consul.[21] A dedication Zenophilus made to Aesculapius and Hygieia might seem to prove him a pagan. Barnes less plausibly suggests a nominal Christian falling into old ways because (as the dedication implies) he was ill at the time.[22]

Acilius Severus, PVR 325–26 and cos. 323, is also included in the "attested as Christians" column on the strength of the assumption that this is the Severus to whom Lactantius dedicated two (lost) books of letters. But the single name Severus is hardly enough to warrant a firm identification, and Lactantius's first six books of letters, including those dedicated to Severus, seem to have been devoted to classical themes:

---

19. Barnes 1994a and 1995a.
20. Novak 1979, 308–10.
21. Schumacher 1958, 100–120, not considering the possibility of a suffect consul; as we shall see later (p. 731), suffects wore the full consular regalia on their inauguration; though bearded, the man's face looks young.
22. Barnes 1994a, VII, 5.

philology, metrics, geography, and philosophy.[23] Jerome gave a copy to Pope Damasus, who found them long-winded and tedious.[24] Why would Lactantius be concerned to dedicate works of this nature to a Christian? It is *possible* that one or all of these three were (or became) Christians (Bassus's son died a Christian). But there is no real evidence, just the assumption that Constantine's most trusted ministers "must have been" Christians. If they were not, the entire assumption is called in question.

Barnes laid much weight on a passage in the second book of Prudentius's *Contra Symmachum* that lists converts to Christianity among the aristocracy of Rome. The two books of the poem were published together soon after the battle of Pollentia in 402, but the context of this passage is the immediate aftermath of the Frigidus at Rome, and there are grounds for believing that the core of Bk i was originally written soon after the Frigidus, as a panegyric on Theodosius (Ch. 9. 4). Theodosius delivers a lengthy harangue (i. 415–505), whereupon "the fathers leap for joy" (*exultare patres videas*), throw off their pontifical robes,

> iamque ruit, paucis Tarpeia in rupe relictis,
> ad sincera virum penetralia Nazareorum
> atque ad apostolicos Evandria curia fontes,
> Amniadum suboles et pignera clara Proborum.

and now, leaving just a few on the Tarpeian rock [meaning the Capitol, site of the temple of Jupiter Capitolinus], the senate of Evander rushes to the pure sanctuaries of the Nazarenes and the baptismal waters of the Apostles, descendants of the Amnii, and the famed sons of the Probi.

Then follows a list of Christian converts among the Roman aristocracy—evidently thought of as the traditional bastion of paganism. Four can be identified with certainty, the rest are family names that admit of more than one possible identification. The most detailed and penetrating analysis is an article by Barnes and Westall, whose main flaw lies in their assumption that Prudentius was as well informed about the late Roman aristocracy as they.[25] However diligent his inquiries, it would not have been easy to obtain reliable information about the earliest noble converts. Their Christian grandchildren in the very different world of the 390s had every reason to exaggerate. All Prudentius needed was a few prominent Christian family names.

We may begin with line 552: the *pignera clara Proborum* must refer to Anicius Olybrius and Anicius Probinus, the brother consuls of 395. In his panegyric on the

---

23. For the fragments, S. Brandt, *Lactantii Opera* 2. 1 (Vienna 1893), 155–58; A. Wlosok, in Herzog and Schmidt 5 § 570. 11. To judge from F. 3 and 4, the two books dedicated to Demetrianus contained Christian material, but then he is also the dedicatee of *De opificio Dei*.

24. *quo fit, ut et legenti fastidium generet longitudo, et, si qua brevia sunt, scolasticis magis sint apta quam nobis de metris et regionum situ et philosophis disputantis*, Damasus ap. Jer. *Ep.* 35. 2. 1.

25. Barnes and Westall 1991, 50–61. For his modest career as a bureaucrat, Palmer 1989, 24–31.

pair Claudian styles them *pignora cara Probi*.[26] They were the sons of Sex. Petronius Probus cos. 371, though since their mother Anicia Proba was the dowager head of the family after her husband's death ca. 390, *Proborum* should perhaps be translated (with Barnes and Westall) "Proba and Probus."

> fertur enim ante alios generosus Anicius urbis
> inlustrasse caput: sic se Roma inclyta iactat.
> quin et Olybriaci generisque et nominis heres
> adiectus fastis, palmata insignis abolla,
> martyris ante fores Bruti submittere fasces
> ambit, et Ausoniam Christo inclinare securem.

For it is said that a noble Anician before all others shed lustre on the city's head (so glorious Rome herself boasts). And the inheritor of the blood and name of Olybrius, though he was entered on the consular fasti and enjoyed the splendour of the palm-figured robe, was eager to lower Brutus's rods before a martyr's doors and humble the Ausonian axe to Christ.

The *enim* implies that what follows explains the preceding line, and Olybrius and Probinus were indeed Anicians. Lines 554–57 identify Hermogenianus Olybrius cos. 379, father of Anicia Proba. But the unnamed Anician first convert (*generosus Anicius*) is not so easy to pin down.

No fewer than three Anicii stood high in the favor of Constantine: (1) Amnius Anicius Julianus, PVR 326–29 and cos. 322; (2) Sex. Anicius Paulinus, PVR 331–33 and cos. 325; and (3) Amnius Manius Caesonius Nicomachus Anicius Paulinus, PVR 334–35 and cos. 334.[27] Barnes labels all three "consuls attested as Christians," but there is no direct evidence about a single one of the three. Number 2 is styled *benignus* and *sanctus* on a fragmentary dedication, which has been thought to "imply a Christian."[28] Yet while both epithets are often applied to Christians, neither is used to *designate* an ordinary lay Christian. In fact, both appear just as often in pagan inscriptions, especially epigraphic poetry.[29] Particularly striking is the epitaph of the pagan hierophant Alfenius Ceionius Iulianus Kamenius († 385), which refers to his *sanctum parentem* and addresses him as *sancte Kameni* (CLE 654. 1 and 4). The fact that the dedication

---

26. *Pan. Ol. et Prob.* 143; it is generally assumed that Prudentius was echoing Claudian here, but the reverse is equally possible.
27. No. 3 is the son of no. 1 and nephew of no. 2. For brevity I use the contemporary acronyms: PPO = *praefectus praetorio*, and PVR = *praefectus urbi Romae*.
28. Chastagnol 1960, 53 n. 3; Novak 1979, 291; von Haehling 1978, 366, no. 5.
29. M. L. Fele, C. Cocco, E. Rossi, and A. Flore, *Concordantiae in Carmina Latina Epigraphica* (Hildesheim 1988), 1036–40; there is no entry for *benignus* in the index of Christian vocabulary in E. Diehl, *Inscriptiones Latinae Christianae Veteres* 1–33 (Berlin 1925). According to Fronto, Marcus Aurelius was *tam sanctus uxori, tam fratri bonus ac benignus* (*ad M. Caes.* v. 48); note too *v(irgini) v(estali) sanctae benignissimae*, CIL vi. 2131.

to a statue of no. 3 in the Forum of Trajan does not include any pagan priesthoods might *suggest* that he was a Christian, but falls short of proving it, and another dedication by the tanners' guild is inscribed on a reused Dionysiac altar, with Dionysiac imagery on three of its four sides. One further detail: a name probably to be restored as [*Am*]*n. Anicius P*[*aulinus*] is included on what appears to be a list of pagan priests of Rome datable to either ca. 300 or ca. 320.[30] One of the other names, the poet (and PVR in 329 and 333) Publilius Optatianus Porphyrius, undoubtedly became a Christian, so Paulinus too might subsequently have converted. Nonetheless, this document can hardly be said to support the assumption.

Barnes and Westall want to go further back even than the age of Constantine. Accepting Champlin's argument (suggestive, though not compelling) that Ovinius Gallicanus cos. 317 was a Christian, and assuming that Prudentius knew this, they argued that "Prudentius' stress on *ante alios* should point to a date significantly earlier than the 320s," and suggest Anicius Faustus cos. 298. But this presupposes improbably detailed knowledge of Anician family history. More important, it would imply that the Anicii were not opportunists, but genuine converts from an age when Christians were still persecuted. Prudentius's vague *fertur* may reflect nothing more than an Anician family boast, not easy to refute in the Theodosian age.

Finally, i. 558–60:

> non Paulinorum, non Bassorum dubitavit
> prompta fides dare se Christo, stirpemque superbam
> gentis patriciae venturo attollere saeclo. 560

The ready faith of the Paulini and Bassi did not hesitate to surrender to Christ and to lift up the proud stock of a patrician clan to meet the age that is to come.

It used to be taken for granted that *Paulinorum* alludes to the Gallic noble Paulinus of Nola, but Barnes and Westall claim that the context, "blue-blooded aristocrats of the Roman metropolis," is against this, preferring Anicius Paulinus PVR in 380.[31] But once again that overestimates Prudentius's knowledge and sense of relevance. At the very moment he was writing these lines the renunciation of rank and wealth by Paulinus of Nola "captured the contemporary imagination." To quote a single illustration, from Ambrose: "what will the senators say when they hear: a man from that family, that lineage."[32] Paulinus of Nola was the first name that would occur to anyone listing prominent Christian converts in the mid-390s. It is unlikely that Prudentius would have left him out just because he was a member of the Gallic rather than Roman

---

30. Groag, 1926/7, 102–9; T. Barnes 1975, 173–86.
31. Barnes and Westall 1991, 54; so too Chastagnol 1962, 207.
32. Ambrose, *Ep.* 6. 27. 8; Trout 1999, 2–3.

aristocracy—if indeed he knew.[33] If so, there is no evidence that Anicius Paulinus PVR 380 was a Christian.

While emphasizing early noble converts, the context in which Prudentius inserts his list is mass conversions after the fall of Eugenius. After his victory at the Frigidus Theodosius turns his gaze on Rome, a city "beset with black clouds," and bids her put off her gloomy garb; her head is befouled with vapors, and smoke pours over her face. He sees murky shades, dark spirits, and black idols flitting about her. That is to say, Rome is still sunk in paganism. The emperor's lengthy harangue (i. 415–505) bids her "put aside her childish festivals, her absurd ceremonies, her shrines that are unworthy of so great an empire" (*deponas iam festa velim puerilia, ritus / ridiculos tantoque indigna sacraria regno*, 499–500). Then comes the passage just quoted about Evander's senate throwing off their pontifical robes and rushing to be baptized. Whoever the first noble Christian, taken as a whole the passage implies that the nobility of Rome was largely pagan right down to the Frigidus. So the very text cited for early conversions offers an exceptionally (indeed improbably) late date for widespread conversions. Of course, Prudentius is exaggerating so that he can credit Theodosius with inspiring mass conversions, and his own list of converts provides one or two conspicuous earlier examples. But if his picture is so distorted, how do we decide which parts to take literally and which not?

There are also more general problems with this approach. As early as the 330s Eusebius was complaining about those who "adopted the false facade of the Christian name" and "crept into the church with fraudulent purpose through fear of the emperor's threats."[34] Men seeking office had a stronger motive than most to profess Christianity. Christians were contemptuous of those who (as they saw it) pretended to be Christians in order to advance their careers. But those who did so may not have seen themselves as pretending, or indeed doing anything in the least dishonest or dishonorable. They were simply honoring their emperor's chosen god, just as their grandfathers had honored Aurelian's choice of Sol.

Nor should we take it for granted that Christian emperors appointed Christians rather than pagans whenever possible. Ammianus, the most detailed narrative source we have for the period, never implies that any emperor (even Julian)[35] selected officials for their religion. It is true that, in keeping with the tone of a secular history, he plays down the role of religion in late antique life. But we might have expected so opinionated a writer to at least hint if some official he particularly despised (Petronius Probus, e.g.), got his job because he was a Christian (p. 223). In fact, Probus held most of his offices under Valentinian I, notoriously the most impartial of the Christian emperors in religious affairs.

---

33. The *Gracchi* who pulled down images of the gods in lines 61–65 refer to Furius Maecius Graccus, PVR in 376/7, who destroyed a Mithraeum and was baptized during his prefecture (Chastagnol 1962, 198–200).

34. Euseb. *Vita Con.* iv. 54. 2; iii. 66. 1; MacMullen 1984, 56.

35. Julian certainly preferred pagans (82 percent on von Haehling's figures), yet Ammianus does not mention the fact.

Theodosius I deliberately appointed a number of influential pagans during his Italian stay of 388–91 (Ch. 2. 3). Constantine too needed the cooperation of the immensely rich and powerful nobility of Rome, especially when he was in the East or campaigning on some distant frontier. He could hardly have avoided appointing one or two Anicii to high office, whether or not they were Christians. In the case of Aradius Proculus, PVR in 337, he contributed a eulogy for the base of a gold statue in his honor (p. 9). Two holders of pagan priesthoods were among Constantius's most trusted ministers: Vulcacius Rufinus, with three praetorian prefectures and a consulship, and Symmachus's father-in-law, Memmius Vitrasius Orfitus (who may actually have married a niece of Constantius).[36]

More important, there is little reason to believe that any emperor's ministers represent a cross section of society as a whole, least of all the society of fourth-century Rome. Here we are fortunate enough to have a genuine and more abundant set of statistics, deriving from a source that has yet to be fully exploited by historians, the more than twelve thousand[37] sculptured sarcophagi found in and around Rome, dating from the early second to the early fifth century. Few are dated exactly, but most can be assigned a date to within a couple of decades on stylistic grounds. On the latest available figures there are 788 pagan and 71 Christian sarcophagi dating from 270–300; 317 pagan and 463 Christian from 300–330; and only 12 pagan but 325 Christian from 330–400.[38] Christian are already outnumbering pagan sarcophagi before the death of Constantine.

These figures need a few words of explanation. First, in this context "pagan" means no more than decorated with the traditional themes familiar from the second and third centuries (mythological, Dionysiac, hunting, seasons, etc.).[39] So while "pagan" sarcophagi might continue to be commissioned by traditionalist Christians, no pagan is likely to have ordered the scenes from the Bible that decorate so many Christian sarcophagi. Second, the fashion for elaborately carved stone sarcophagi rapidly declined in the course of the fourth century, barely surviving into the fifth.[40] That explains the startling lack of proportion between the 463 Christian sarcophagi between 300–330 compared with only 325 for the entire rest of the century, when there must obviously have been many more Christians.

Marble (sometimes imported) was expensive, and those carved in high relief required months of expert labor.[41] Purchasers of sarcophagi must have been well to do, though to judge from the names engraved on the few surviving lids, as in the early

---

36. Cameron 1996, 295–301.
37. I owe this figure, which includes a large number of fragments as well as the magnificent complete specimens illustrated in every book on Roman and early Christian art, to Björn Christian Ewald.
38. Dresken-Weiland 2003, 64–65. Such precise figures must be taken with a grain of salt, but are approximately correct.
39. For a pie chart illustrating the popularity of different themes at different times, Ewald, *JRA* 16 (2003), 564.
40. Brandenburg 2002.
41. For information on prices for sarcophagi, Dresken-Weiland 2003, 76–80.

empire, mostly below the level of the nobility (Junius Bassus PVR 359 is the only identifiable aristocrat).[42] If we add to those 463 the 77 from 270–300, 540 Christian sarcophagi between 270 and 330 reveal Christianity firmly entrenched among the propertied classes of Rome under the tetrarchs, and rapidly increasing its hold after the conversion of Constantine.

Salzman, rightly assigning less weight to imperial pressure, argues that her own statistics, based on a wider pool of evidence than just officeholders, support the implication of "statements of contemporaries" that the shift of balance from pagans to Christians occurred in the 380s and 390s. But these are invariably the statements of *Christian* contemporaries. Such statements tend to fit into one or the other of two categories according to the point the writer is making: *either* paganism is now on the run, *or* the temptations of paganism are all around us. The same writer may even take both approaches in the same poem or sermon. We have just seen that Prudentius's *Contra Symmachum* implies that the aristocracy remained sunk in paganism till the Frigidus, when they converted en masse. Both claims are grotesque distortions. In his account of the conversion of Marius Victorinus, Augustine claims of the period around 350 that "almost all the Roman nobility was enthusiastic for the cult of Osiris and monstrous gods of every kind,"[43] often cited as a statement of fact. But Augustine's purpose was to highlight the shock he imagined that the conversion of a fashionable professor must have caused. Rufinus's claim that paganism "collapsed" under Theodosius, though an impression shared by many contemporaries, refers to the closing of the temples (Ch. 2. 4) rather than the winning of minds. When emphasizing in 405/6 that Christianity had spread all over the world, Augustine claimed that there were now "very few" pagans left.[44] Later remarks in his many writings give a much less confident impression.

There is more to be said about Symmachus's claim that he was charged to present his appeal about the altar of Victory by "the senate." Over the years there has been a futile debate about whether or not there was a Christian or pagan "majority" in the senate in 384.[45] Futile, because in all ages politicians claim to represent the majority, if only (when outvoted) a "silent" majority; futile too because the votes of any assembly turn on such factors as when the meeting is held, how much notice is given, and (above all) on how exactly the motion is framed. Even if there had been a majority of Christians present, many are bound to have been center-Christians, unwilling to vote yes if confronted with (say) the motion: "In view of the current barbarian threat, should this house turn its back on a tradition that has brought Rome a thousand years of victory and prosperity"? According to Ambrose, some Christians in Valentinian II's consistory urged him to grant the senatorial request. The question of "majority" is a distraction. There were undoubtedly many Christian senators by 382, not necessarily either holders of high office or members of the noblest families.

---

42. Dresken-Weiland 2003, 30–41; Borg forthcoming.
43. *Conf.* 8. 2. 3; for the rest of this instructive passage, see Ch. 5. 2.
44. *paucissimi, Contra Cresc.* iii. 63. 70.
45. Sheridan 1966, at 188–93; Matthews 1975, 206–7; Fowden, *CAH* 13 (1998), 551.

The closing of the temples in the first half of the 390s marked the end of public paganism, but that tells us nothing about hearts and minds. The numbers and dates are simply not there to fix a tipping point.[46] Though it would be impossible to prove, occasional flashpoints like the altar of Victory conflict may actually have slowed down the steady drift of middle-of-the-road pagans into middle-of-the-road Christianity, making it harder for pagans on the brink of conversion to accept a faith that apparently repudiated Victory. Whatever the proportion of Christian and pagan officials under Constantine and Constantius, the evidence of the sarcophagi strongly supports the more general Barnes thesis that this drift was well under way before the death of Constantine.

Salzman rightly emphasizes the importance of such intangible factors as Christianity's gradual acquisition of the "status and respectability" that were so essential to aristocrats.[47] Here we are fortunate to have the evidence of two precisely dated high-quality Christian artefacts, and another not quite so firmly dated: the Calendar of 354, the Junius Bassus sarcophagus of 359, and the Esquiline treasure. The original of the calendar has not come down to us, but it is clear from the later copies that it was a sumptuously illustrated book of lists, by the leading calligrapher of the age, Pope Damasus's friend Furius Dionysius Filocalus. It contained not only all the traditional festivals but also an Easter cycle and list of the bishops of Rome. Its dedicatee was called Valentinus, possibly a brother (or uncle) of Q. Aurelius Symmachus.[48]

The Bassus sarcophagus is justly celebrated as a masterpiece of classicizing high relief sculpture. There are also dozens of other high-quality Christian sarcophagi lacking exact dates but judged even earlier, to cite only one, the so-called Two Brothers Sarcophagus, generally placed between 330 and 350.[49] On rather imprecise art historical grounds, Shelton dated the Esquiline treasure between 330 and 370. The weak point in her argument is distinguishing the Christian bride Proiecta of the Esquiline casket from the Christian bride Proiecta, whose death in December 383 not yet seventeen years old is commemorated by Pope Damasus.[50] Most have identified the two, in which case the casket would date from ca. 380, but two Proiectas and an earlier date cannot be excluded. The high-end art market of Rome was clearly targeting rich Christians of noble birth as early as the 350s.

Then there are Jerome's attacks on the Christian society of Rome during his stay of 382–85. Scores of passages lambaste the Roman clergy for their greed, venality, hypocrisy, gluttony, and corruption, nor does he spare the Christian nobility on whom they

---

46. The point at which "momentum for change becomes unstoppable," Malcolm Gladwell (*The Tipping Point*, 2000).

47. In addition to Salzman's discussion, see, more generally on the importance of status, Lendon 1997, 36–47.

48. Salzman 1990; Valentinus 7 and 12 in *PLRE* i; and 2 in *PLRE* ii.

49. Deichman et al. 1967, no. 45; magnificently illustrated in Grabar 1968, 243–45; for illustrations of other Constantinian Christian sarcophagi, Grabar 239–68.

50. For the arguments on both sides, Cameron 1985, 135–45, and Shelton 1985, 147–55.

preyed.[51] Many texts could be cited, but one must suffice. Jerome warns that the virgin should shun widows:

> To see them in their capacious litters, with red cloaks and plump bodies, a row of eunuchs walking in front of them, you would fancy them not to have lost their husbands but to be seeking them. Their houses are filled with flatterers and guests. The very clergy, who ought to inspire them with respect by their teaching and authority, kisses these ladies on the forehead, and, putting forth their hands (so that, if you knew no better, you might suppose them in the act of blessing) take wages for their visits.

Jerome's vivid sketches are (of course) exaggerations, not to say caricatures, inspired as much by literature as real life. But they clearly imply an established, surely second-generation Christian elite, not a few recent converts.

This earlier generation is documented by a pamphlet (cited as *Gesta*)[52] written in 368/9 by a supporter of Pope Damasus's rival, the anti-pope Ursinus, claiming that "ladies of quality (*matronae*) so loved Damasus that he was known as the ladies' ear-tickler (*matronarum auriscalpius*)." It is important to be clear that this is more than a personal attack on Damasus's morals. Ammianus's account of the struggle in which 137 of Ursinus's followers were killed is immediately followed by a description of unnamed celebrities who are "enriched by gifts from ladies of quality (*oblationibus matronarum*)...ride in carriages, dress splendidly, and outdo kings in the lavishness of their table."[53] While no doubt exaggerating, Ammianus is drawing here on a pro-Ursinian pamphlet like the *Gesta*. He knew that the fighting took place in the Basilica Sicinini (named in a document of 367), knew exactly how many died, and not only, like the *Gesta*, specifies *matronae* as Damasus's patrons but uses the Christian term *oblatio*.[54]

Furthermore, in July 370 an edict was addressed specifically to Damasus forbidding clerics to visit the homes of widows and wards (*viduarum ac pupillarum*) or to accept anything either by gift or testament from "women to whom they have attached themselves privately under the pretext of religion."[55] "Ear tickling" was apparently a vivid metaphor for coaxing money and favors out of rich women, a practice for which Damasus evidently became notorious. In fact, it helps to explain Jerome's famous anecdote about Praetextatus telling Damasus that he would convert at once if he could be bishop of Rome, a joke implying that, in the eyes of a leading pagan noble of the 360s, the bishop of Rome was a man of wealth and power, a priest with the social status of a pontifex or augur.

---

51. Wiesen 1964, passim.
52. From its (misleading) title *Quae gesta sunt inter Liberium et Felicem episcopos* (*Collectio Avellana*, O. Guenther [ed.] [1895] no. 1. 10); Pietri 1976, 408–23.
53. xxvii. 3. 11–15 (Hamilton 1993, adapted).
54. Pietri 1976, 410 ("archives préfectorales"); *Coll. Avell.* 6 (160 dead); *TLL* s.v. *oblatio*, 9. 2. 73–78.
55. *Cod. Theod.* 16. 2. 20, according to the subscription, "read in the churches of Rome."

But the ear tickling of Roman *matronae* did not begin with Damasus. According to Theodoret, citing a contemporary Roman source, again probably related to the *Gesta*, during his Roman visit of 357 Constantius II was pressured into restoring the exiled Liberius to the see of Rome by the *wives* of important officials.[56] Mothers, wives, daughters, and sisters have traditionally been seen as an important factor in the conversion of the nobility, an assumption recently questioned by Salzman.[57] However this may be, Christianity was undoubtedly making substantial inroads into aristocratic (especially female) society as early as the 350s and 360s.

It has traditionally been assumed that paganism remained dominant well into the fifth century. This is little more than speculation, based not on evidence but assumptions, assumptions that will be reassessed in the course of this book. Least of all did paganism retain any sort of intellectual hegemony in elite Roman society at the end of the century. By the early 380s fashionable Christian ladies were studying the Bible with Jerome. In the early 390s Pope Siricius and Ambrose were worried by the success of Jovinian's anti-ascetic teaching among cultivated Christians (p. 212), and a year or two later the teachings of another "heretic," Pelagius, were further dividing the Christian elite of Rome.[58] These were the hot issues of the age.

3

To return to officeholders, how long after the death of Theodosius do we find western pagans holding the highest offices of state? According to von Haehling, there were eleven pagan prefects of Rome after 395, and Chastagnol added one more. Earlier in the fourth century, pagans, many of them aristocrats, certainly dominated the prefecture of Rome. But did this tendency really continue throughout the first quarter of the fifth century? Even if it did, a dozen pagan prefects after 395 would not in itself prove that paganism remained a powerful force among the Roman elite. In fact, we shall see that there were less than half this number. Here is the list:

395–97: Florentinus
398: Felix
399–400: Nicomachus Flavianus junior
401: Protadius
401/2: Fl. Macrobius Longinianus
402: Caecina Decius Albinus
403/7: Postumius Lampadius
408–9: Gabinius Barbarus Pompeianus

---

56. Theod. *HE* ii. 17. 1–4; on his source (cited ib. 15. 10), A. Martin et al., *Theod. HE* 1 (2006), 87–89; Maier 1995.
57. Salzman 2002, Ch. 5.
58. See Brown's papers on "The Patrons of Pelagius" (1972, 183–226); and Maier 1995.

409: Priscus Attalus
409–10: Marcianus
414: Rutilius Claudius Namatianus
417–18: Rufius Antonius Agrypnius Volusianus

Von Haehling and Chastagnol also list five pagan praetorian prefects, a number we can effectively reduce to one, since Lampadius, Longinianus, Volusianus, and the younger Flavian also appear on the list of city prefects:[59]

406–8: Fl. Macrobius Longinianus
409–10: Lampadius
428–29: Volusianus
430: Macrobius Ambrosius Theodosius
431: Nicomachus Flavianus junior

There is in fact no good evidence that more than four of these city prefects and perhaps not even one of the praetorian prefects were really pagans. Setting aside the younger Flavian for more detailed treatment in § 4, let us begin with the first three city prefects: Felix and the brothers Florentinus and Protadius, both Gauls.

Von Haehling's argument about Felix rests entirely on a letter Symmachus wrote to a certain Hadrianus in 397/8 (*Ep.* vii. 58), reporting that he had sent copies of two of his speeches to Felix and Minervius (a third brother of Florentinus and Protadius), whom he describes as "distinguished men, endowed with the priesthood of virtue and letters" (*inlustres viros virtutum ac litterarum praeditos sacerdotio*). Von Haehling inferred from *sacerdotio* that both men were pagans, and if Minervius was a pagan, so too (he assumed) were both his brothers.[60] But it should be obvious that the word is being used metaphorically here, with a sort of chiasmus: *virtutum* is being applied to Minervius, at the time holding the financial post of *comes rerum privatarum*, and *litterarum* to Felix, then *quaestor sacri palatii* and so charged with drafting imperial laws.[61] Cassiodorus often uses *sacerdotium* metaphorically,[62] and we shall encounter several similar metaphors (*adytum, cultus, mysteria, penetral, sacraria*) in chapter 16. 6.

That does not prove Felix a Christian, but he can hardly have been a committed pagan. After holding office under Eugenius, not only was he immediately promoted to *quaestor sacri palatii* by Honorius, in 396 Symmachus thanked him profusely for putting in a good word with the new regime for both himself and the younger Flavian.[63] As for Florentinus, Minervius, and Protadius, Protadius was the recipient of some of Symmachus's most flowery and affectionate letters, and on that basis dubbed by

59. On the younger Flavianus's three urban prefectures, Ch. 14. 2.
60. Von Haehling 1978, 389; see Callu's note ad loc.
61. For their careers, see *PLRE* i. 459; 603; Delmaire 1989, 149–52.
62. Service under a pious emperor and the proper discharge of public office are both "a kind of priesthood," *quoddam sacerdotium* (Cass. *Variae* i. 12. 4 and vi. 3. 9; cf. vi. 19. 5).
63. Symm. *Ep.* v. 47, with Callu's notes and Seeck, *Symmachus* cliv–clv.

Chastagnol "a fervent defender of paganism." Chastagnol also claimed Florentinus as a pagan for being the dedicatee of Claudian's *De raptu Proserpinae*.[64] But like Felix, all three brothers were appointed to high office immediately after the Frigidus. Florentinus became *quaestor* at the beginning of 395 and prefect of Rome by summer 395. Minervius was appointed to some unidentified post at court in 395 and in quick succession to the *comitiva* of the *res privata* and *sacrae largitiones* in 397–99. Protadius arrived at court in Milan in 395, evidently hoping to ride the family bandwagon, but was not immediately successful and returned to Gaul. Yet by 400 or 401 he too was PVR, presumably having held some lesser post in the interim.[65]

Once again, von Haehling was misled by a Symmachan metaphor. One typical letter to Protadius (iv. 26) closes with the sentence: "even if I am not your equal in elegance of style, I shall strive to match you *constantia religionis*." For von Haehling, *constantia religionis* proved Protadius "unwaveringly loyal to the old religion."[66] But *religio* is Symmachus's favorite word (more than fifty examples) for the duties of friendship, or for friendship itself.[67] It is hard to believe that all three brothers could have met with such remarkable success in the immediate aftermath of the Frigidus if they had been committed pagans. The obvious assumption is that, like so many cultivated Gauls (Ausonius, Pacatus Drepanius, Paulinus of Nola),[68] they were at any rate center-Christians.

Next Longinianus (401–2), a correspondent of Symmachus, who received *Epp.* vii. 93–101, a man in high office at court from ca. 399 and so to be identified as Fl. Macrobius Longinianus, *comes sacrarum largitionum* in 399–400, PVR in 401–2, and PPO in 406–8. The only possible grounds for seeing him as a pagan is to identify him as the Longinianus with whom Augustine corresponded at some date unknown after 395, a philosopher who had at one time held pagan priesthoods of some sort (p. 167). But there is nothing beyond the single name and approximate date in favor of identifying the two Longiniani. Nothing in the nine letters of Symmachus suggests that his man was a pagan, still less a philosopher. And nothing in Augustine's letter suggests that his Longinianus was a person of high rank: while the heading of his letter to Volusianus runs *domino illustri et merito insigni et praestantissimo filio* (*Ep.* 137), his letters to Longinianus are headed just *Longiniano* (*Ep.* 233, 235). In the text of the letter, Volusianus is styled *excellentia tua* (§ 20), while Longinianus is just *benevolentia tua* (*Ep.* 235. 1).[69]

Furthermore, the prefect Longinianus built a baptistery in the church of St. Anastasia at the foot of the Palatine, known from a dedication that describes the church as a "house of faith."[70] Since the dedication praises his distinction and loyalty

---

64. Chastagnol 1962, 248, 253.
65. *PLRE* i. 363; 603; and 751; Chastagnol 1962, 253–55.
66. Symm. *Ep.* iv. 26; "an der alten Religion unbeirrbar," p. 400.
67. As shown by Wistrand 1972, 229–31. More examples could be added from Lomanto 1983.
68. That is to say (of course) Paulinus before his conversion to the ascetic life.
69. For *excellentia tua*, "used chiefly for laymen of high official standing," O'Brien 1930, 45.
70. *ILCV* 92 (known from a medieval copy); for St. Anastasia, Pietri 1976, 461–64, 490.

but does not actually say that he was a Christian, it has been inferred that he was a pagan.[71] It no doubt occasionally happened that a pagan prefect was obliged ex officio to superintend the building of a church, since the first five lines eloquently describe the power of baptism to wash away sins, it seems perverse to suppose that Longinianus was not himself a Christian.

In 405/6 a horde of Goths led by a chieftain called Radagaisus invaded Italy. According to Augustine and Orosius, Roman pagans were encouraged by the news that Radagaisus was a pagan into clamouring for the restoration of sacrifice (Ch. 3. 6). But this barbarian will hardly have shared the sophisticated, tolerant Roman paganism of Roman aristocrats, who must have been as well aware as their Christian peers that Radagaisus was not likely to treat pagan nobles any differently from Christian bishops or holy nuns. Fears aroused by the invasion were soon dispelled, because the Goths were completely defeated by Stilicho at Fiesole. Christians made much of the victory, the first time a Christian army had decisively defeated the Goths.[72] These vague assertions (by people who were not in Rome at the time) are often taken to illustrate the continuing influence of paganism in Rome,[73] but they are surely no more than Christian propaganda.

Lampadius, Pompeianus, Attalus, and Marcianus have been woven into a continuing story of pagan reaction late in the first decade of the fifth century.[74] First Pompeianus. According to Zosimus, during Alaric's siege of Rome in 408,[75]

> Pompeianus, the prefect of the city, came upon some Etruscans visiting Rome, who said that they had freed a city called Narnia from danger; prayers to the gods and ancestral observances had caused violent thunder and lightning, which had driven off the barbarian besiegers. After talking with these men Pompeianus turned to how the priests could help. *Taking into consideration the prevailing religion* and anxious to proceed with caution, he laid the whole plan before Innocent, the bishop of the city. Innocent considered the city's safety more important than his own convictions and allowed them to perform what they knew in private. But the priests declared that the only way their rites would benefit the city was if the traditional ceremonies were performed at public expense, with the senate processing up to the Capitol and performing the necessary rites there and in the public spaces of the city. No one dared to participate in the ancestral worship, so they dismissed the Etruscans, and turned to flattering [Alaric] as best they could.

---

71. Mastandrea 1978, 523–40; Rüpke 2 (2005), 992–93 (no. 1697); von Haehling 1978, 311–13 sensibly registers him as a Christian.
72. Full discussion in Cameron 2007, 191–202.
73. For example, Pietri 1976, 442.
74. Heinzberger 1976, 144–221; Matthews 1975, 290, 296; Pietri 1976, 443–45; Demandt/Brummer 1977, 496–501.
75. Zos. v. 41. 1–3, with Paschoud's notes on pp. 275–80.

We have another account of this intriguing episode in Sozomen (both reflecting the well-informed contemporary pagan history of Olympiodorus):[76]

> After the siege had lasted for some time, and fearful ravages had been made in the city by famine and pestilence ... those among the senators who still adhered to pagan superstition thought it necessary to offer sacrifices on the Capitol and in other temples. Certain Etruscans, who were summoned by the prefect of the city, promised to drive off the barbarians with thunder and lightning. They boasted of having performed a similar exploit at the Tuscan city of Narnia, which Alaric had passed by on his way to Rome, after failing to capture it.

Nothing in Zosimus's account, taken by itself, suggests that Pompeianus was a pagan. While the formula "taking into consideration the prevailing religion" reveals the historian as a pagan, it tells us nothing about the prefect.[77] For the first time in eight hundred years barbarians were besieging Rome, and here were some people who claimed to know a ritual that would drive them away. In such a crisis many Christians would have been tempted. Sozomen no doubt *assumed* that Pompeianus was a pagan, but the only source to say that he was is a chapter in the Greek *Life of Saint Melania*, describing how the noble Melania and her husband, Pinianus, liquidated all their property:[78]

> And when they left Rome, the prefect of the city, who was a very ardent pagan (*hellenikotatos*), decided along with the entire Senate to have their property confiscated to the public treasury.... By God's providence, it happened that the people rebelled against him because of a bread shortage. Consequently he was dragged off and killed in the middle of the city.

This is surely no more than an inference by the biographer, whether from the story of the Etruscans (which he does not mention but surely knew from Sozomen)[79] or based on his own conviction that only a pagan would attempt to confiscate the property of the saintly Melania and Pinianus. But the disposition of their estates was a cause célèbre at the time, and there is no reason to believe that paganism played any part.[80] Their (no doubt mainly Christian) kin were trying to block what they saw as the irreponsible liquidation of family property, and the main goal of the senate was finding the money to meet Alaric's demand of five thousand pounds of gold and thirty thousand of silver to lift his siege.

---

76. Soz. *HE* ix. 6. 3–4; Matthews 1970; Gillett 1993; Treadgold 2004.

77. For various interpretations of this formula, Paschoud, *Zosime* 3. 1 (1986), 276.

78. *Vita Melaniae* 19, p. 166 Gorce.

79. It is suggestive that, like Sozomen, the biographer does not name the prefect. The *Life of Melania* was written in the early 450s, shortly after the appearance of Sozomen's history.

80. For further objections to the more elaborate speculations of Demandt/Brummer 1977, see Deichman et al. 1967, 104–8.

As for the biographer's claim that Pompeianus was a "hellene," Byzantines regularly apply the term loosely to Christians with unpopular or theologically dubious views. For example, Cyrus of Panopolis, poet, prefect, and consul in 441, who ended his days as a bishop and patron of Daniel the Stylite; Orestes, prefect of Egypt in 415, baptized by the patriarch of Constantinople;[81] and the jurist Tribonian, often cited as illustrating the "tenacity" of paganism in the age of Justinian.[82] Some scholars even believe that the emperor Anthemius was planning a "final" pagan revival in the West as late as the 470s,[83] on the strength of a statement by the neoplatonist Damascius that he was *hellenophrōn*.[84] Others describe him as a devout Christian,[85] and Latin sources suggest no more than a misunderstanding by Greek-speakers of the fact that Anthemius was unpopular in the West because he was a *Greek*, that is to say, a Greek-speaking easterner, denigrated as *Graecus imperator* and *Graeculus*.[86]

Another aristocrat thought to attest to the "persistence" of paganism in early fifth-century Rome is Apronianus, husband of Avita and niece of the elder Melania.[87] In his birthday poem for St. Felix in January 407, Paulinus of Nola asks what new thing the year has brought him, and names[88]

> Apronianus, the glory of the family of Turcii, a boy in years but old in the sensations of the flesh,[89] a noble in the ancient stock of Rome, but more famous in his title as Christian. The fame of his ancient and of his recent birth are intermingled; he is a longstanding member of Rome's senate, but new to Christ.

That is to say, Paulinus appears to consider Apronianus a recent convert in 407. The Turcii had been a prominent pagan family (Apronianus's grandfather, Secundus Asterius, and great-uncle, Apronianus Asterius, had both held pagan priesthoods), which (according to Moine) made his conversion a "scandal" for the pagan party and a great coup for Christians.[90] But was there still a pagan party around to be scandalized as late as 407? Palladius describes how Melania returned to Rome in 400 and "catechized and made a Christian of Apronianus, a hellene," whom she also prevailed upon

---

81. For many illustrations, Rochow 1991, 133–56; Cameron 1982, 217–89 at 268; and 1993, 157, 246–48, 327.

82. The claim that Tribonian was a hellene derives from a Suda entry that is mainly based on Procopius—except for this one detail: Tony Honoré, *Tribonian* (London 1978), 64–67.

83. Vassili 1938; Courcelle 1969, 261–62; Pietri 1981, 420–22; Shanzer 1986, 25–26; O'Flynn 1991, 127; Orlandi 2004, 509.

84. Athanassiadi 1999, 198, F 77A (actually an indignant summary by Photius). As for Photius's further charge that Anthemius had a "secret plan to restore the abomination of idolatry," if it was secret, how did anyone know about it? The fact that Messius Phoebus Severus, PVR and western consul in 470, studied philosophy in Alexandria (Damascius) does not prove him a pagan, still less a patron of other pagans.

85. ἄνδρα Χριστιανικώτατον, according to Theophanes, *Chron.* 5957.

86. Sidonius, *Ep.* i. vii. 5; Ennodius, *Vita Epifanii* 50.

87. So Salzman 2002, 81.

88. Paul. Nol. *Carm.* 21. 210–15.

89. *aetate puerum, sensibus carnis senem*, presumably an allusion to the fact that he had sired two children.

90. Moine 1980, 28.

to live in continence with his wife.[91] But Apronianus appears as the patron of Rufinus and dedicatee of several of his translations from Origen, Basil, and Gregory Nazianzen as early as 398–99. In the preface to the Origen translation Avita is described as Apronianus's "sister in Christ."[92] Melania's return to Rome from the East is securely dated to 400, by when Apronianus must already have been a Christian. Palladius's use of the technical term "catechized" suggests that he was a catechumen. What Melania did was convince him to accept baptism and embrace the ascetic lifestyle. In the ascetic circles of Paulinus, Palladius, and Melania, "hellene" need imply no more than that he had till then refused baptism and continence. We are not obliged to believe that Apronianus was ever an out-and-out practicing pagan. Another uncle had married Proiecta and is named in the Christian inscription to the casket in the Esquiline treasure (*Secunde et Proiecta vivatis in Christo*), implying that one member at least of the couple was a Christian ca. 380 (if not earlier).[93]

To return to Pompeianus, it is instructive to compare the role assigned the senate in the two versions. According to Sozomen, the first stage in the affair was pagan senators eager to sacrifice on the Capitol, while in Zosimus the Etruscans say that their ritual only worked if senators participated in a procession to the Capitol. It is only the Christian version that describes a senatorial initiative. In Zosimus, the Etruscans just happened to be in Rome, and Pompeianus knew nothing about their rites before meeting them. Moderns, convinced that there was still a powerful pagan element in the senate, privilege Sozomen, but the more detailed and less tendentious account of the pagan Zosimus is surely to be preferred. Why would a pagan have played down the pagan context of the episode? On the other hand, it is obvious why the Christian Sozomen would have played up the failure of what he saw as a dangerous pagan plot.

We may be sceptical about the claim that the pope agreed to the ritual provided it was performed in secret,[94] but the priests' response that it only worked if performed publicly and at public expense rings true (p. 46). And so does Pompeianus's consultation of the pope. As prefect of Rome, he had the authority to allow the ceremony. But a public performance could not have escaped the notice of the Christian community, and if not authorized by the church would have been likely to provoke riots. It might be added that, while processing to the Capitol was a traditional ritual, a rite that produced thunder and lightning and drove barbarians away was not.[95] This episode does not belong in a narrative of pagans trying to revive their traditional cults.

Next Postumius Lampadius, city prefect at some time between 403 and 407 and then praetorian prefect in 409, often identified with a supposedly pagan Lampadius who corresponded with Augustine.[96] But nothing in Augustine's letter suggests that his

---

91. Ἀπρονιανόν, Ἕλληνα ὄντα, κατήχησε καὶ χριστιανὸν ἐποίησε, Pallad. *Hist. Laus.* 54. 4.
92. Murphy 1945, 111; Moine 1980, 32.
93. On the Esquiline treasure, Cameron and Shelton 1985, 135–55.
94. A detail understandably omitted by Sozomen.
95. Not even Briquel 1997 could find any but a legendary parallel for conjuring lightning.
96. *Ep.* 246; so Chastagnol 1962, 260; von Haehling 1978, 316.

Lampadius was either a pagan or a person of high rank. Where Augustine addresses Volusianus as *excellentia tua* (p. 189), Lampadius is merely *caritas tua*, a formula of general use, not implying a person of high status.[97] In any case, no one who read the letter carefully could be in much doubt that Augustine's Lampadius was a Christian, a believer in astrology who had consulted Augustine about fate. In his reply Augustine offers an explanation that he hopes will safeguard Lampadius's faith (*fidei tuae*), and then deplores the way Lampadius excuses his sin and so turns away "from the remedy of confession" (*medicamento confessionis*).[98] The fact that Augustine had recently seen this man (evidently in Africa) is also strongly against the identification with a prefect of Rome.

On 3 November 409 Priscus Attalus, at the time prefect of Rome, was proclaimed emperor by Alaric and "a clique of romantic pagan senators."[99] But it is only a Greek ecclesiastical historian, Philostorgius, who calls Attalus a hellene. He said the same about an earlier usurper, Eugenius, on that occasion certainly in error.[100] Some have indeed proclaimed a mini pagan revival of 409–10, following on the affair of the Etruscan priests in 408: the one-time pagan Attalus appointed Lampadius praetorian prefect, Marcianus city prefect, and Tertullus consul, all three allegedly pagans.[101] It is assumed that this is the apostate Marcianus mentioned in the *Carmen contra paganos* (*CCP*), dated to 394. But we shall see in chapter 8 that the *CCP* dates from 384. Given the twenty-five-year interval, this identification is improbable. It is possible that the city prefect of 409 is a Marcianus who held office under Eugenius,[102] but that falls far short of proving him a pagan. We have just seen that Tertullus was a Christian. Whether or not Attalus was ever a pagan, since he immediately accepted baptism on his elevation it is clear that he was willing to put career before religion, in which case appointing pagans to his administration would have undermined the effect of his own baptism.

According to Sozomen, Attalus's fall upset both pagans and Arians, the former because they had *conjectured* from his interests and his early education that he would openly declare his paganism and restore the traditional temples, festivals, and sacrifices;[103] the latter because he had been baptized by Sigesarius, bishop of the Goths, an Arian, and would restore them to the position they had enjoyed under Constantius and Valens.[104] It should be emphasized that this is not a factual report of what either pagans or Arians believed. It is a claim by an orthodox Christian depreciating an unsuccessful usurper. The fact that he is said to have been baptized rather than converted suggests that he was not only not a pagan but already a catechumen.

---

97. O'Brien 1930, 52–53.
98. *Ep.* 246. 1.
99. Brown 1972, 190.
100. *HE* xii. 3, p. 142. 2 Bidez (Ἕλλην δὲ τὴν δόξαν); xi. 2, p. 133. 11 for Eugenius.
101. Matthews 1975, 295–96; Paschoud, *Zosime* 3. 2 (1986), 44.
102. *PLRE* i. 555, Marcianus 14 (accepting the 394 date for *CCP*).
103. τεκμηράμενοι τῆς Ἀττάλου προαιρέσεως καὶ τῆς προτέρας ἀγωγῆς εἰς τὸ προφανὲς ἑλληνίσειν αὐτὸν ἡγοῦντο καὶ τοὺς πατρίους ἀποδιδόναι ναοὺς καὶ ἑορτὰς καὶ θυσίας, Soz. *HE* ix. 9. 1.
104. *PCBE* ii. 2. 2066; Thompson 1966, 163.

There is no serious evidence that a single one of this quartet was a pagan at all, much less a committed pagan. This is not to say that all city and praetorian prefects after 395 were Christians, much less pious, committed Christians. Caecina Decius Albinus is one of the interlocutors in the *Saturnalia*, and so (in Macrobius's judgment anyway) a pagan in 382. But he was appointed governor of Campania in 397/8, and either *quaestor sacri palatii* or *magister officiorum* (possibly both in succession) at the court of Honorius in 398/9 before becoming prefect of Rome in 402.[105] There is no evidence that he actually held office under Eugenius, but clearly his paganism did not stand in the way of his advancement. It will no doubt be suggested that he was one of the nobles Prudentius represents as converting after the Frigidus. But it is unlikely that Macrobius would have chosen so conspicuous a convert for his band of pagans. More generally, the rapid and brilliant post-Frigidus career of so prominent a pagan aristocrat lends little support to the notion that Eugenius was supported by pagan aristocrats as a class. The same applies to Messala, praetorian prefect in 399–400, if he too was a pagan (p. 394).

There is no solid evidence that any of the perhaps four pagan city prefects were committed, active pagans, not even Rutilius Namatianus, whom we shall see to have been something less than the unregenerate pagan of so many modern studies (Ch. 6. 2). More generally, it is important to bear in mind here Peter Brown's perceptive remark that Christian emperors[106]

> put very little direct pressure on individual pagans.... Rather, from time to time, the emperors took measures to render pagan worship incapable of being performed in public.... These governmental actions were sporadic. It was Christian opinion which invested them with an aura of inevitability.

It is a mistake to see the occasional pagan prefect in the first decade or two of the fifth century as proof that paganism remained strong and anti-pagan legislation ineffective. No individual pagan could have used the nine or ten months of his prefecture to do much more for the pagan cause than restore a few statues. Indeed, pagans who accepted high office from Christian emperors were more likely to be seen as collaborators than champions of the cause. Heresy was the real worry for both church and court. As far as paganism was concerned, it was enough that there was no more sacrifice and the temples were closed. The stragglers would soon come over.

4

Many historians have proclaimed a second (or third) "pagan reaction" in the 430s. The evidence alleged is threefold: 1) the "rehabilitation" of the elder Flavian in 431, the

---

105. *PLRE* i. 35–36; Chastagnol 1962, 258–59.
106. P. Brown, 2003, 74.

year of his son's praetorian prefecture; 2) a sequence of three supposedly pagan praetorian prefects of Italy (Volusianus, Macrobius, and the younger Flavian);[107] and 3)
the publication of Macrobius's two "pagan" books in or around the year of his
prefecture. If all three really were committed pagans, holding office in sequence, we
might indeed feel obliged to examine the possibility of a pagan revival of some sort
under the weak Valentinian III. Furthermore, if pagans were able to exercise this sort
of influence as late as the 430s, we might feel obliged to take similar evidence alleged
from the earlier decades of the century more seriously.

Let us begin with the three prefects. First, Volusianus, prefect in 428–29, son of
Rufius Albinus, prefect of Rome in 389. Thanks to his inclusion among Macrobius's
interlocutors, Rufius Albinus is generally considered a paladin of the pagan cause. In
real life he married a Christian wife who gave birth to a Christian daughter.[108] So
Volusianus had a Christian mother and sister, and was uncle to none other than that
formidable Christian ascetic the younger Melania. Some aristocrats (the Turcii and
Symmachi) chose to spend most of their time taking care of private affairs, content to
hold the bare minimum of public posts consonant with their dignity (an Italian
governorship, proconsulate of Africa, and prefecture of Rome). Others pursued posts
at court as well as the traditional senatorial career, notably the Nicomachi. It is possible that such men secretly dreamed of the restoration of sacrifice, but those with
ambitions at court could not afford subversive agendas. Their priority was evidently
holding office and perpetuating the family name, wealth, and power. Two such were
Volusianus and the younger Flavian. Such ambitions required compromise.

While resident in Carthage in 411/12, Volusianus conducted an urbane but respectful
correspondence with Augustine on a series of problems he had with Christianity. He
seems to have moved in circles where such issues were discussed by a mixed group of
pagans and Christians (among them aristocratic exiles from the sack of Rome),
including Augustine's Christian friend Marcellinus (future dedicatee of the *City of
God*), who urged Augustine to take Volusianus seriously and forwarded additional
problems Volusianus had raised privately with him.[109] It is usually taken for granted that
Volusianus was a pagan at the time, but several hints in these letters suggest that he was
actually a catechumen, notably the fact that one of the points on which he sought
Augustine's guidance (and which Augustine dealt with at length in his reply) was the
belief widespread among men of status that baptism was incompatible with the
demands of a public career.[110] Particularly striking is the question "who can solve the
uncertainties in which I am entangled?" (whether or not the anonymous speaker
Volusianus is quoting was himself), and Marcellinus's remark that Volusianus "is being
drawn away from firm belief in the true god" (*a veri dei stabilitate…revocatur*).[111]

---

107. Von Haehling 1978, 606–8; Grünewald 1992, 485.
108. The mother of Albina 2 (mother of the younger Melania) and Rufius Volusianus: *PLRE* i. 33 and 38.
109. Aug. *Epp*. 132, 135, 136, 137, 138; Moreau 1974, 6–181 at 123–28; *PCBE* 1. 686–87.
110. *Ep*. 138. 9–15, quoting and responding to Volusianus's words in *Ep*. 136.
111. *Ep*. 135. 1 and 136. 1.

It has further been assumed that he remained a pagan until a deathbed "conversion" at Constantinople a quarter century later in 437, described in the *Life of Melania*.[112] It is true that the biographer begins by describing him as "still a hellene," but we have seen how slippery a term this is. When Melania found him sick and, in her anxiety to get him to accept baptism, threatened to tell the emperor, he replied as follows, according to the biographer, supposedly an eyewitness:[113]

> I exhort your holiness not to take from me the gift of self-determination with which God has honored us from the beginning. For I am completely ready and long to wash away the stain of my many errors. But if I should do this by the command of the emperors, I would gain it as if I had come to it through force and would lose the reward of my free decision.

If this bears any relationship to what Volusianus actually said, it is the response of a catechumen rather than a pagan. Even if it is pure fiction, it is not a speech any Christian biographer was likely to invent for a man he believed to be an out-and-out pagan dramatically converted on his deathbed. A week or so later Melania, seriously ill herself, is expressly warned that he might die a catechumen,[114] though in the event further inquiry revealed that he had been baptized in time. If he remained a catechumen for many years,[115] Volusianus was no doubt a poor Christian, the despair of his pious niece. But there is no evidence that he was ever a committed pagan, much less as late as his prefecture of 428–29. As Peter Brown wrote in 1967, Volusianus was born into "a post-pagan world," a man who at best knew the pagan cults from books, not the streets and temples.[116]

Next, the younger Flavian, prefect in 431–32. For Grünewald as for many others, converted or not, both Flavian and his son Nicomachus Dexter remained pagans at heart,[117] their true sentiments sufficiently revealed by their "edition" of Livy—in fact (as we shall see) no more than a proofreading of a copy made for a friend in 400, with no bearing at all on fifth-century paganism (Ch. 14). As for Dexter, he cannot have been more than four or five when sacrifice was forbidden. There are no sufficient grounds for assuming regardless that, deep down, he shared his long-dead grandfather's paganism. With a record three tenures of the city prefecture, for a late fourth-century Westerner an altogether exceptional proconsulate of Asia and a praetorian

---

112. *V. Mel.* 50; Chastagnol 1956, 253. So emphatically Fraschetti 1999, ix–x.

113. *Vie de Mélanie* 50–55; Deichman et al. 1967, 62–68, with commentary on 129–33. Quotation from § 53 = p. 65 Clark.

114. κινδυνεύει τελευτῆσαι κατηχούμενος, § 54 fin.

115. One of the great pastoral problems of the age was the large number of permanent catechumens who put off their baptism until a serious illness or some other emergency threatened (van der Meer 1961, 148).

116. P. Brown 1967, 298; see too p. 797.

117. Both Chastagnol and von Haehling classify him as a Christian, but only a "nominal" Christian.

prefecture in his seventies, it seems clear that holding public office was especially important to the younger Flavian.

As for Macrobius, he has almost always been assumed an out-and-out pagan. But as we shall see in chapters 7 and 16, once we look beyond the subject matter of his two books, there is nothing in the presentation to make him a pagan at all. Whatever their personal feelings, all three prefects were probably at least nominal Christians. Certainly center-Christians rather than committed Christians. Macrobius undoubtedly kept a soft spot in his heart for the old ways. But only the younger Flavian was old enough to have seen pagan sacrifice in the temples rather than just read about it in books. And it must be significant that Macrobius discreetly refrained from including him along with his father among his all-pagan interlocutors.

By 430 it was more than twenty years since pagans had been banned from holding imperial office,[118] and while the law was not strictly enforced, officials who made no secret of their hostility to Christianity were certain to provoke protest and risk the embarrassment of dismissal. After two such disgraces Flavian was not likely to court a third. In addition to the débâcle of 394, he had been dismissed for flogging a town councillor during his proconsulate of Asia in 383, and reduced to ignominious flight to escape further retribution.[119] Symmachus had to bail him out, but such an arrogant violation of long-standing custom recently reinforced by law would have terminated the career of anyone less well connected.[120] It was Symmachus again whose patient diplomacy restored him to imperial favor after 394. How did Symmachus achieve this? By withdrawing from pagan activism after the failure of his petition in 384 and prudently taking no part in Eugenius's rebellion. The lesson of his prudence cannot have been lost on his son-in-law. But for Symmachus's survival of the coup with influence intact, the younger Flavian might never have been restored to favor, office, and power.

5

The hypothesis of a pagan reaction in the 430s presupposes a pagan reaction in 392–94; it also presupposes that the elder Flavian was its "ringleader." The moment these two claims are cast in doubt, most of the basis for seeing his "rehabilitation" in 431 as another pagan reaction disappears. A recent book by Hedrick characterizes Flavian as the "chief ideologue" of the 392–94 reaction, and makes much of his *abolitio memoriae*:[121]

---

118. Zos. v. 46. 3; *Cod. Theod.* 16. 5. 42 (408).
119. Libanius, *Or.* 28. 5; Symm. *Ep.* iii. 69. 2; *PLRE* i. 345; Matthews, in *Xenia* 23 (1989), 18.
120. *Cod. Theod.* xii. 1. 85 of 381 imposed a penalty of twenty pounds of gold plus fifty for the offender's staff and *perpetua infamia*, which among other legal disabilities entailed disbarment from public office. The flogging of curials was also deeply shocking to public opinion: P. Brown 1992, 52–55.
121. Hedrick 2000, xiv–xv, and passim.

In the years immediately following 394, he came to be regarded by some Christians as an irreconcilable and militant foe of Christianity...the moving spirit behind the "last pagan resistance to Christianity": in short, in retrospect he came to exemplify the despised old order in its death throes. For a long time after his condemnation he was unnamed in any source....Suddenly, in the 430s, he appears as a prominent character in two texts: Macrobius's *Saturnalia* and the inscription of rehabilitation.

This is indeed a widely held view. But it is absolutely baseless. By comparing the smashing of the statues of Piso and Sejanus, Hedrick contrives to imply that Flavian suffered *abolitio memoriae* in the fullest and most insulting sense, a complete erasure of memory that makes its allegedly sudden revocation in 431 seem to demand an explanation in the context of that time. But the sanctions imposed on the disgraced were seldom systematically imposed or permanent,[122] and the key factor in Flavian's case is that his offense was taking the wrong side in a civil war. Reconciliation is always the wisest course in the aftermath of civil wars, and imperial policy toward those who had served Eugenius was conciliatory from the beginning. There is constant reference to Theodosius's *clementia* in the earliest sources (Ch. 3. 4). And a law of 21 April 395 allowed the validity of virtually all transactions from the period of the "tyrant," laying down that "the names of the calamitous consuls only shall be abolished,"[123] meaning Eugenius himself and Flavian, western consuls in 393 and 394. That was inevitable (Theodosius had appointed his own consuls in their place). We may assume that at this point Flavian's name was stricken from the bases to his statues in the public spaces of Rome. Even so, *abolitio* was not carried out systematically, since his only other surviving dedication, the base to a statue commemorating his vicariate of Africa by the city of Lepcis Magna in 377, stands undamaged in the forum of Lepcis to this day.[124]

Less than a month later, on 18 May 395, a full amnesty was proclaimed. Honorius announced that "if any man was in the imperial service in the time of the tyrant or was given any administrative post or filled any place of honorary rank...he shall not sustain the brand of infamy (*notam infamiae*) or be polluted by any title of disgrace."[125] This certainly included the younger Flavian (soon restored to office), and that it also included his father is proved not least by the letter Symmachus wrote to the younger Flavian later the same year[126] telling him that his reputation with the people was

---

122. We now have the benefit of several important modern studies: Flower 2006 and Varner 2000 and 2004.

123. *Cod. Theod.* 15. 14. 9.

124. J. M. Reynolds and J. B. Ward-Perkins, *Inscr. of Roman Tripolitania* (Rome 1952) no. 475. Coincidentally, a dedication commemorating the African proconsulate of Cn. Calpurnius Piso was left undamaged in the forum of Lepcis (Flower 2006, 136).

125. *Cod. Theod.* 15. 14. 11; this amnesty did not (of course) mean that they could count offices held under the usurper.

126. For the date, Seeck 1883, clxii; Marcone 1983, 59.

restored and referring unmistakably to his "father's restoration" (*paterna reparatio*).[127]
Seeck thought that *reparatio* referred to the rehabilitation documented by the dedication of 431.[128] But if this took place as early as 395, what happened in 431? Full rehabilitation so soon is unlikely. But the *reparatio* Symmachus describes involved Flavian's
"memory" (*memoria*) and his son's "safety" (*salus*). It must have been a measure of
substance, and since it is firmly datable to 395, the obvious explanation is that, like his
son, the elder Flavian too benefitted from the general lifting of the "brand of infamy."

This did not mean that his name could be restored to his public monuments. That
would have been a positive honor, requiring specific imperial authorization. The reinscribing of his monuments had to wait until 431. But the amnesty of May 395 did
remove the *infamia*. This would explain why, shortly after Symmachus's death in
402, his son Memmius Symmachus felt able to include in his father's published
correspondence an entire book containing almost a hundred letters to Flavian.
Evidently, this young man, a twenty-year-old with his career before him, felt no appre-
hension that such a publication might damage his prospects.

There are many objections to the notion of Flavian as pagan "ideologue." But not
the least is the fact that a number of the letters Memmius included show the two
friends openly discussing pagan cults and festivals. Nor is there anything polemical or
defiant about these allusions. What is so intriguing about them is precisely that they
are so casual (Ch. 4. 5). Even granting the lifting of the *nota infamiae*, we might have
expected Memmius to play safe by deleting these letters at any rate. That he did not is
perhaps the clearest single proof that Flavian's paganism was *not* the source of his *infamia*. That was simply and solely the consequence of being a usurper's chief minister—
above all being unwise enough to accept a consulate from him.

Memmius also erected a statue to Flavian, his grandfather-in-law, in the family
house on the Caelian Hill, which went so far as to include that consulship in the dedication—and his priesthood. This was a private house, but the house of a Roman aristocrat in a fashionable part of town was hardly altogether private space. He would
never have dared to do either of these things if the *abolitio* of April 395 had still been in
effect. So if Flavian's *infamia* ended in May 395, then at one stroke the "rehabilitation"
of 431 loses most of the significance it holds in the mythology of pagan revival. Flavian
did not lurk in a limbo of disgrace for thirty-seven years, to the festering resentment of
a still-powerful pagan community, but for a little over eight months. All that happened
in 431 was the reinscription of his public monument.

The dedication to this monument is inscribed on a statue base discovered in the
Forum of Trajan in 1849.[129] The inscribed surface is so uneven that it may be the

127. Symm. *Ep.* vi. 1; Sogno 2006, 82.
128. Seeck, *RE* 6. 2 (1909), 2511. Matthews 1975, 247 n. 1, enigmatically remarks that Flavianus's "reputation
    was 'protected' under the succeeding regime."
129. *CIL* vi. 1782 = *ILS* 2948; German translation in Grünewald 1992, 465–66; French in Chastagnol 1976,
    107–9; English in Hedrick 2000, 2–3. There are several mistakes in the inscription (Hedrick 2000,
    252–58), and I have no confidence that I understand every word of the rambling, not to say incoherent
    chancellery rhetoric.

original defaced base, scraped and reinscribed with a new dedication.[130] It is natural to infer that it was the embarrassment of this defaced monument in so prominent a place that rankled, and prompted the younger Flavian to decide that the time had finally come to eliminate all trace of the family disgrace. It was not just a new cursus that was required to make the monument whole, but the accompanying imperial eulogy that marked out the truly great (p. 9). For obvious reasons it would have been premature to ask for the restoration of so prestigious a distinction in 395 when the family was relieved enough to have escaped *infamia*. But a generation later, when Eugenius's rebellion was fading into ancient history and Flavian's son and grandson were now praetorian and city prefects,[131] the time had finally come.

Let us begin with the dedication before turning to the imperial letter:

> To Nicomachus Flavianus, consularis of Sicily, vicar of Africa, quaestor at the court of the blessed Theodosius, twice praetorian prefect of Italy, Illyricum and Africa, because of his worth and prestige in the senate and as a public official (*virtutis auctoritatisque senatoriae et iudiciariae ergo*), a statue *restored* (*reddita*) in honor of his son, Nicomachus Flavianus, consularis of Campania, proconsul of Asia, frequently[132] prefect of the city and currently praetorian prefect of Italy, Illyricum and Africa.

It should be clear that the real honorand is the younger Flavian. The elder's rehabilitation is merely hinted at in the single word *reddita*. The imperial letter begins by referring obliquely to the "interruption" in his honors (*interpolatum...honorem*); then "let us recall to the monuments of his worth and his titles" (*in monumenta virtutum suarum titulosque revocemus*) a man whom Theodosius

> desired to survive for us and be spared for you—many of you remember his words before you—so that you may realise that whatever Flavian suffered from underhanded insinuations (*caeca insimulatione*) was far from [his own] wishes. It was the kindness (*benevolentia*) the emperor showered upon him and even his *Annals* (which he wanted his quaestor and prefect to dedicate to him) that excited the jealousy of scoundrels (*livorem improborum*).

Flavian is not being pardoned for past transgressions. There were none. Nothing but malicious lies spread by scoundrels. We are reminded of Symmachus's claim (*Rel.* 3. 1) that his embassy to the court of Gratian was denied an audience by scoundrels

---

130. See the description in Hedrick 2000, 249–50 (with new text and full bibliography). Hedrick himself hints at but stops short of making this inference.

131. City prefects in office often oversaw the repair of buildings and erection of statues (Chastagnol 1960, 45–46, 51–52). But the fact that Nicomachus Dexter describes himself as former prefect suggests that the work was tactfully done at family rather than public expense.

132. *saepius*; on the explanation for this curiously evasive formula, Ch. 14. 2.

(*improbi* again). This accusation too is usually dismissed out of hand, but there was surely something to it. Emperors seldom reversed themselves, and if Gratian had seen the ambassadors he would no doubt have refused their request anyway. But as Sogno has pointed out,[133] to refuse even to see them was insulting. Those who find a radical new approach to paganism here may not be troubled by the insult, but it would be very surprising in Gratian, who had hitherto gone out of his way to conciliate the senate. When faced with refusing the same request, both Valentinian II and Theodosius did their best to soften the blow (Ch. 2). Some have assumed that Symmachus's scoundrels are Ambrose and Pope Damasus, but that too would have been improbably insulting. More important, Ambrose simply did not have the power. Symmachus does not say that these scoundrels poisoned the emperor's mind against the embassy, but very precisely that they denied it an audience. Only one official had the power to grant or refuse petitioners an audience, and that was the *magister officiorum*.[134] It so happens that the man who held this office at Gratian's court in 383 was a certain Macedonius, accused of misconduct on Gratian's death and due to be tried by none other than Symmachus in 384.[135] Deflecting blame for the failure of the embassy from Gratian to Macedonius was a neat way of preparing the ground for a fresh attempt with Gratian's successor.

When faced with hostility or failure, Symmachus's technique was to deflect attention from the real source of that hostility or failure, and blame the jealousy of personal enemies.[136] To turn back to the imperial letter, the Nicomachi undoubtedly had enemies. In a letter of uncertain date we find Symmachus complaining to the *magister militum* Ricomer that subordinates of his have been intriguing against both Flaviani without his knowledge.[137] A letter to Rufinus claims that he was so devoted to Flavian as to "upset the *improbi*."[138] The letter that informs Flavian junior about the removal of his *infamia* refers to "the notorious, unceasing envy (*livor*) of our colleagues" that has incited the plebs against him.[139] Sogno plausibly infers that enemies of the Nicomachi took advantage of Flavian junior's vulnerability in the months after the Frigidus. Typically, Symmachus blames the family troubles on personal jealousy. Just so the imperial letter of 431 focuses on the malice of personal enemies.

The *suggestio falsi* is breathtaking. Flavian is now the innocent victim of slanderous attacks; Theodosius was saddened by the death of a man he had elevated to the highest offices of state. His request for the dedication of the *Annales* is represented as the culmination of imperial favors lavished on this outstanding public servant. The point

---

133. Sogno 2006, 48.
134. Boak and Dunlap 1924, 92.
135. Vera 1981, 27; *PLRE* i. 526; Symm. *Rel*. 36.
136. As illustrated by Matthews 1986, 163–75.
137. *Ep*. iii. 69; dated by Callu to 382, but (like iii. 58 and 66) perhaps written to Ricomer at court in Milan in 389–91. For the present purpose it makes little difference.
138. *ad improborum dolorem, Ep*. iii. 86. 2.
139. *collegarum vero notissimus pervicax livor, Ep*. vi. i; Sogno 2006, 81–82.

was not to proclaim Flavian's continuing fame as a historian (Ch. 17. 1), but to suggest that he was held in high esteem by the emperor against whom he had in fact rebelled. There is no more than one glancing hint of Eugenius's revolt: Theodosius's wish that Flavian should "survive for us and be spared for you."

Much has been made of the fact that Flavian's cursus omits his priesthood, but by 431 it was a half-century since anyone had included priestly titles on any public dedication (not even the family of Praetextatus). Perversely enough, it has been thought "significant" that the imperial letter makes no reference to Flavian's paganism, as though this was the real purpose of the rehabilitation.[140] But (of course) this presupposes that Eugenius's usurpation was perceived as a pagan rebellion. Above all, it is difficult to see how studiously *not* mentioning Flavian's paganism was supposed to evoke his paganism.

Thirty-seven years after the Frigidus, the "pagan ringleader" of modern textbooks may have appeared to contemporaries much as he does in Macrobius's *Saturnalia*, a great man of a bygone age, whose one mistake was to have joined the wrong side in a civil war. A pagan, to be sure, but then so were the ancestors of many good Christians of the 430s. Fifth-century Christian aristocrats felt no embarrassment about their pagan forbears. According to Cassiodorus it was "in imitation of his kinsmen" that Aur. Memmius Symmachus cos. 485 wrote his *History of Rome* (one of the historians implied by the plural must have been the elder Flavian).[141] Symmachus (according to Cassiodorus), "a modern imitator of ancient Cato, transcended the virtues of the men of old by his holy religion."[142] That is to say, his Christianity is an extra layer on top of the qualities he has inherited from his pagan ancestors. Despite their paganism, those ancestors are not rejected.

The writings of Symmachus not only continued to be read and admired. His literary fame actually increased in the fifth and sixth centuries. His eloquence receives glowing tributes from Christian writers on all sides: Ambrose, Prudentius, Prosper, Sidonius, Cassiodorus, Ennodius.[143] The Bobbio palimpsest that preserves all we have of his speeches was written in Italy ca. 500,[144] and it must have been in response to this growing fame that books 8–10 of his letters and the *Relationes* were first published several decades after his death in 402 (Ch. 10. 3). They must have been preserved in the family archives, evidently by some now Christian descendant.[145] One particularly revealing illustration missing from Polara's survey of those who read or quoted Symmachus is Caesarius, bishop of Arles from 502–42. In his entire voluminous oeuvre, Caesarius cites only three secular authors: Vergil (the same passage three times), Juvenal, and

---

140. Hedrick 2000, passim; Grünewald 1992, 474.
141. *parentesque suos imitatus, Origo gen. Cass.* 10 (= *Anecdoton Holderi*), L. Viscido (ed.) (Naples 1992), 38.
142. *antiqui Catonis fuit novellus imitator, sed virtutes veterum sanctissima religione transcendit*, ibid.
143. Polara 1972, 3–16; for Ennodius, see the list of echoes in F. Vogel's edition (1885, 332).
144. *CLA* i. 29 and iii p. 20.
145. Perhaps in the 430s rather than a century later (so Marcone 1988).

Symmachus.[146] That is to say, Symmachus's well-documented reputation as defender par excellence of the old gods in no way detracted from his influence as a stylist.

A certain Vettius Agorius Basilius, not certainly identifiable but clearly a late fifth- or early sixth-century descendant of Vettius Agorius Praetextatus, preserved the only surviving copy of the scurrilous poem on his famous ancestor (Ch. 8). Late antique men knew not to take invectives too seriously. Anyone of any importance was liable to make enemies. Like the younger Flavian, Basilius too no doubt put the abuse down to *caeca insimulatio* and *livor improborum*. It was part of the price of fame.

Because of his association with the "pagan revival" of 392/4, it has always seemed obvious that the rehabilitation of the elder Flavian in 431 must imply another pagan "revival" of some sort, or at any rate some sort of concession to the pagan aristocracy of Rome.[147] But did any such body still exist? What sort of concessions could realistically have been sought in the 430s? The restoration of sacrifice was out of the question, and the priestly colleges long defunct. Short of participation in the old cults, most other aspects of the traditional aristocratic lifestyle had now been embraced by their Christian descendants. Any attempt to restore the old cults would have outraged not only the Roman church but the now overwhelmingly Christian population of Rome. As we shall see in the chapters that follow, one of the most striking and important aspects of the Christianization of the Roman aristocracy is that "the secular traditions of the senatorial class, traditions which one might have assumed bound up with the fate of their pagan beliefs, came to be continued by a Christian aristocracy."[148]

Flavian's rehabilitation has usually been treated as an event of considerable importance, requiring an explanation in terms of the wider political and religious situation of the 430s. The nominal ruler of the West was the child emperor Valentinian III (425–55), at this point in his inglorious reign under the competing influence of his mother, Galla Placidia, and his all-powerful master of soldiers Aetius. On Stein's view, the rehabilitation was an early illustration of the policy of the then newly dominant Aetius to conciliate the aristocracy of Rome. For Oost, this was the policy rather of Galla Placidia.[149] Yet it is hard to see why the aristocracy at large, even the few remaining pagans among them, would be pleased by such a gesture. As we have just seen, like any aristocratic family, the Nicomachi were engaged in constant rivalry with their peers, and not just Christians. A letter of Symmachus expresses anxiety that the pagan Euangelus will bad-mouth the younger Flavian at court in 397.[150] Their fall from power in 394 must have delighted those rivals, pagans no less than Christians.

146. M.-J. Délage, *Césaire d'Arles: Sermons* 1 (Paris 1971), 95. The Symmachus citations seem to have been taken from Sidonius (*Ep.* viii. 10, cited by name, *Symmachianum illud*). In one sermon (217. 3) Caesarius cites it as *illa sapientis viri sententia*; in a second (236. 4) as *illam sententiam saecularem quidem sed valde utilem*.

147. Solari 1936, 357–60; Grünewald 1992, 486, with earlier references.

148. Brown 1961, 4.

149. Stein 1959, 340; Twyman 1970, 480–503; Oost 1968, 231 (for whom the letter was written by Placidia herself!).

150. That is to say, the "real" Euangelus, not the Macrobian interlocutor (Ch. 7. 9).

A less grandiose explanation will suffice. The inscription does indeed have an agenda beyond the rehabilitation of a man dead thirty-seven years: to promote the Nicomachi, past, present and future. Even after the lifting of *infamia* in 395, that defaced monument in the Forum of Trajan was an embarrassment for the entire family. The initiative for imperial rescripts came from members of the consistory, in particular from the praetorian prefect.[151] The younger Flavian took advantage of the opportunity presented by his own prefecture to make a personal request a weak emperor was unlikely to deny his chief minister: the imperial eulogy. It was not Aetius or Galla Placidia who drafted the imperial letter, but Flavian himself—as put beyond doubt by the use of his father-in-law's trick of blaming setbacks on the jealousy of rivals. The family could now hold up their heads and see their great ancestor's name and titles where they belonged in the public places of Rome together with his peers, complete with the all-important "eternal commendation" of an emperor.

The new inscription ends as it began with the younger Flavian:

> The honor of the younger Flavianus, which, thanks to his father's upbringing, has often been praised by us and our predecessors, seems only half complete compared to *the summit of the praetorian prefecture which his providence and industry enhances every day*, unless he finally recovers the integrity of his whole house and family.

Particularly significant is the final sentence, which holds up his "descendants" (in the context evidently including Nicomachus Dexter, who superintended the erection of the statue) for the same admiration as Flavian himself. Dexter no doubt had sons and/ or nephews with expectations of rank and privilege.

---

151. "The *suggestio* ... was usually put forward formally by a praetorian or city prefect," Harries 1988, 164.

6

PAGAN WRITERS

How late do we find pagan writers revealing their paganism in their writings? Once upon a time this seemed an easy question. Mythological poets like Claudian and Nonnus were unhestitatingly identified as pagans, defiant pagans. Nowadays we make more allowance for the influence of the literary tradition on Christian writers in secular genres. There are a number of Latin writers of the late fourth and early fifth centuries whose religious beliefs have been repeatedly debated over the years: Ausonius, Claudian, Rutilius Namatianus, Macrobius, Martianus Capella, Pacatus Drepanius, to name the most prominent.

It is often claimed of writers who fall into this category that such and such a passage "could not have been written by a Christian." At best, this means that a well-informed and observant Christian is not likely to have written thus. But a poorly informed or not very pious Christian might have. And even a well-informed and observant Christian might have if he was writing in a classicizing genre, for example an epithalmium or a panegyric, whether in prose or (especially) verse. If all we had from the pen of Sidonius Apollinaris was his imperial panegyrics, and we knew nothing about his life beyond these poems, it might well have been argued that he was a pagan. It might have seemed surprising to find a pagan celebrating (as Sidonius did) Christian emperors of the 450s and 460s, but the Egyptian pagan Pamprepius briefly enjoyed high favor at court in Constantinople in the late 470s.[1] The survival of Sidonius's correspondence puts it beyond doubt that he had always been a Christian, who eventually entered the church and ended his days as a bishop. As late as 468 (his panegyric on Anthemius), audiences at western courts clearly still enjoyed classicizing poetry full of the old mythology.

All too often, having inferred, usually on the basis of just one or two passages, that one of these writers is a pagan, some critics at once take the further steps of assuming that he must therefore have been hostile to Christianity, assign him to "pagan circles," and then look for signs of covert polemic. The polemic is always covert, never open, because (we are assured) pagans did not dare to speak their mind openly. Alföldi, Straub, and Chastagnol are the classic exponents. More recently, here is Shanzer, writing on Martianus Capella: "Too often a discreet silence on the part of a pagan author is taken for lack of conviction, rather than a refusal to recognize Christianity and an unwillingness to get involved in the possible legal consequences of professed

---

1. Cameron in Bagnall 2007.

paganism." Her claim that the "esoteric material in Martianus' work would have been prosecutable" is improbable in itself and further undermined by the lack of any known prosecution for any pagan work. Her emphasis on Martianus's knowledge of Iamblichus and the Chaldaean oracles proves nothing. Both were known to the Christian Synesius. Praetextatus's speech on solar theology in Macrobius's *Saturnalia* (she even less probably suggests) is "a rationalizing, monotheistic, pagan answer" to Christian attacks on the incredible multiplicity of pagan deities.[2]

Such an approach presupposes that any and all pagans should be expected to be actively hostile to Christianity simply by virtue of their paganism. The grammarian Servius is often assumed to have been engaged in an implicit battle against the rising tide of Christianity (Ch. 16). Many scholars have operated on this assumption without stating it so bluntly. But it is by no means obviously true of even the most prominent western pagans: Symmachus, for example. There is simply no evidence that Christians in authority actually punished the expression of pagan sentiments.[3] Obviously, there must have been some limits. But so far as we know courteous disagreement was never forbidden. A full treatment would fill another book. What follows is no more than a few disconnected sketches on a handful of individual writers.

1: RUTILIUS NAMATIANUS

Many (too many) studies have been devoted to the religious beliefs of Rutilius. One or two outliers have allowed the possibility that he was a Christian; the great majority have concluded that he was a pagan, with many insisting that he was an ardent pagan who hated Christians. The key passages are his denunciations of monks and Jews, traditionally read as indirect attacks on Christianity, and above all his attack on Stilicho for burning the Sibylline books.[4] Since his voyage can be securely dated to autumn 417 and his famous little poem not long after, it would be important if a prominent pagan could be shown to express such views openly this late. Claudio Bondi's 2003 film *de Reditu (il ritorno)* represents Rutilius returning to Gaul in order to raise an army to overthrow the Christian government of Ravenna (excerpts available on YouTube). He would (I suspect) have been very disappointed if he had tried to rally the now largely Christian aristocracy of Roman Gaul for any such attempt.

My purpose is more limited than these studies. I do not believe that such propositions can be proved. Take the case of Claudian. Augustine calls him "alien from the name of Christ," but we do not know whether he had positive information or was just guessing from his poems. Orosius calls him a "most stubborn pagan," but otherwise simply copied the passage he quotes from Augustine. The "pagan" imagery of which

---

2. Shanzer 1986, 136, 27; Cameron and Long 1993, 32–33; see Ch. 7. 13.
3. Chastagnol 1991, 40–42; against, Cameron 1965, 240–48; Syme, *Roman Papers* 3 (1984), 899–909.
4. Corsaro 1981, 55–93; Wolff, Lancel, and Soler 2007, xiii–xvii.

critics once used to make so much is now recognized to be purely literary.[5] While there is no way of discovering his personal beliefs, there is one thing we do know for certain: all his poems were written for Christian patrons and publicly performed in front of an overwhelmingly Christian audience at court in Milan and (later) Ravenna. Claudian was more than a court panegyrist. He was at the center of a literary circle at court. His minor poems include several addressed to high imperial officials, some certainly and all probably Christians. In addition, he enjoyed a close personal relationship with the pious empress Serena, to whom he addressed several poems, one thanking her for finding him a wife.[6] Clearly his poetry appealed to at any rate my "center-Christian" group. If he was a pagan, he cannot have been considered a militant pagan by those who knew him best. And if Claudian's "pagan" poems were so popular with Christians, then the argument that other works of "pagan" character must have been written by and for pagans loses much of its force.

Interpretation of Rutilius's *De reditu suo* has been transformed since 1970, when Mirella Ferrari unexpectedly found thirty-nine fragmentary lines from Bk ii, till then lost except for the first sixty-eight lines.[7] The most important gain is the discovery that the poem as a whole cannot after all be interpreted straightforwardly in terms of Rutilius's supposed paganism. We now know that the invective against Stilicho at the beginning of Bk ii was followed (and balanced) by a eulogy of the patrician Constantius, a devout Christian. Whatever we decide about the attack on Stilicho for burning the Sibylline books (ii. 51–56), the main thrust of the attack is clearly Rutilius's conviction that Stilicho betrayed Rome to the Goths, an accusation by no means confined to pagans. In a paper on Stilicho's supposed treachery written before Ferrari's discovery, Cracco Ruggini suggested that Rutilius's attack on Stilicho was "probably a polemic against the policies of Constantius."[8] A reasonable suggestion on the evidence then available, consistent with the assumption that his resentment against Stilicho was largely inspired by the latter's supposedly anti-pagan policies. But we can now see, on the contrary, that the condemnation of Stilicho's treachery prepares the ground for praise of Constantius for repairing the damage and finally bringing the Goths to their knees. This newly discovered praise of Constantius also undermines the old assumption that *De reditu* is a private poem, intended for an audience of the poet's pagan friends, which in turn further lessens the likelihood that it is any sense a pagan manifesto.

In the most famous passage of his poem, Rutilius eloquently describes how Rome has always risen with renewed and increased strength from her defeats, whether the Gauls, the Samnites, Pyrrhus, or Hannibal. More than a century ago Dufourcq

---

5. For more details and older views, see my *Claudian* (1970).

6. Cameron 1970, 393–402; *cm* 50 must be read as an attack on Jacobus's excessive devotion to the cult of saints, not as an attack on the cult itself: Vanderspoel 1986; Consolino 2004; D. Woods, *CQ* 41 (1991), 571–74.

7. Ferrari 1973, 1–41; for the most recent text and discussions of these lines, Wolff, Lancel, and Soler 2007, xlvii–lv.

8. Cracco Ruggini 1968, 447 n. 64.

suggested that this was a discreet pagan reply to Augustine's thesis (in *CD* i–iii) that these same early defeats proved that the pagan gods did not exist. Courcelle tried to strengthen the argument, arguing that Rutilius knew *CD* iv–v as well.[9]

There is in fact one further scrap of evidence. In the course of a bitter invective against the Jews (i. 395–98), Rutilius makes the point that, ironically enough, it was Titus's conquest of Judaea that dispersed the Jews throughout the world:

> latius excisae pestis contagia serpunt,
> > victoresque suos natio victa premit.

> Once the pest was destroyed its contagion spread far and wide;
> > the conquered nation overwhelmed its own conquerors.

Commentators have long noticed the close similarity in both thought and language between the last line and fragment 42 of Seneca's *De Superstitione*, also an invective on the Jews: "the customs of this detestable race have become so prevalent that they have been adopted in every part of the world; the conquered have imposed their laws on their conquerors" (*victi victoribus leges dederunt*). That captive Greece had captured Rome was a commonplace, but Seneca is Rutilius's only known predecessor in applying the same epigram to the Jewish Diaspora. There can be little doubt that he is echoing Seneca's words.

But where did he read them? Seneca's prose writings were not fashionable in the pagan circles of the later empire. His style was severely criticized by Fronto and Gellius, and he is seldom quoted by the grammarians. Nor did he share to the same degree in the revival of interest in Silver Age writers at the end of the fourth century.[10] On the other hand, he was widely read and admired by Christians. As early as the second century close parallels to New Testament ideas and phrases were noted in his writings, and to Tertullian he was *Seneca saepe noster*. By the fourth century it was even believed that he had known St. Paul, and a correspondence between them (in bad Latin) was duly produced to prove it.

Jerome went so far as to include Seneca in his catalogue of Christian writers. Of all his works, *De Superstitione* was the one most likely to be read by Christians rather than pagans. For the attack it contains on the Roman state religion was, according to Augustine, "fuller and sharper" than even Varro's (*CD* iv. 10)—obviously a Christian perspective, but nonetheless a judgement borne out by the extant fragments. It is hardly surprising that of the fifteen that survive only one is quoted by a grammarian, one by Tertullian—and the remaining thirteen by Augustine in the *City of God*.[11] In all

---

9. Dufourcq 1905, 488–92; Courcelle 1964, 104–7.
10. Macrob. *Sat.* pr. and i. 2. 7 quote from Sen. *Epp.* 84 and 47 more or less verbatim, probably at second hand.
11. O'Daly 1999, 109, 250–51.

probability Rutilius derived his knowledge of this passage from the same source as us, *CD* vi. 11, a chapter titled "What Seneca thought about the Jews." If Rutilius had read *CD* i–v, why not vi too? Books i–iii appeared in 412, iv–v in 414/15, and vi–xi in 416. Since Rutilius was writing in October 417, it is not difficult to picture him skimming the early chapters of the latest installment.

Yet this would not make it a pagan reply. Rutilius does not turn the passage against Augustine. He simply borrows it for his own anti-Jewish polemic. No Christian reader would have taken any exception to these sentiments. As for his emphasis on Rome's recovery from past disasters, that can be sufficiently explained in terms of a different aspect of the date. For five years after their sack of Rome in 410, the Goths had continued under Athaulf and Wallia to cause trouble to the Romans, until, early in 416, the patrician Constantius starved them into surrender in east Spain. Thereafter they fought as allies of Rome against the other barbarians in Spain.

Since we now know that Bk ii went on to praise Constantius's settlement of the Gothic problem, there can be no doubt that i. 141–44 allude precisely to the Gothic defeat of 416.

> ergo age, sacrilegae tandem cadat hostia gentis:
>   submittant trepidi perfida colla Getae.
> ditia pacatae dent vectigalia terrae:
>   impleat augustos barbara praeda sinus.

Come then, let a sacrilegious race fall at last in sacrifice; let the trembling Goths bend their treacherous necks in surrender. Let the pacified lands pay rich tribute and barbarian booty fill [Rome's] majestic lap.

It may well be that Rutilius was unimpressed by Augustine's inference from Rome's pre-Christian defeats. But there is no need to interpret his own emphasis on Rome's resilience in terms of anti-Christian polemic. It is sufficiently explained by the defeat of the Goths, the most recent and (as it must have seemed to everybody at the time, Christians no less than pagans) spectacular illustration of his theme. After only six years, Rome had risen above its worst disaster in almost a millenium and defeated the enemy who inflicted it. Courcelle aptly quotes the parallel of Orosius, writing in the following year (418), who from his very different standpoint took a similarly optimistic view of the future of the empire under the new Romano-Gothic alliance. Most commentators explain *sacrilegae...gentis* as the sacrilege of attacking Rome, which might well be what Rutilius had in mind. But many contemporaries were likely to think of the Goths' Arianism. If Rutilius really read as far as Bk vi of the *City of God* without attacking its thesis, that does not suggest an aggressive pagan.

To return to the attack on the Jews, the context is highly circumstantial: Rutilius's indignation at a Jewish innkeeper who overcharged him. In addition, he begins by denouncing circumcision, emphatically rejected by Christians, before rehearsing a series of traditional anti-Jewish motifs of Roman satire.[12] According to Lana, "It is obvious that Rutilius could not speak freely in his poem."[13] On the contrary. He seems to give free rein to his strongest feelings in these invectives. And now we know that Bk ii went on to praise the administration of Constantius, it is difficult to see why he should have felt unable to speak freely. There was no reason why any contemporary, Christian or pagan, should see this for anything but what it was: an open attack on Jews, not a covert attack on Christians.

The same applies to the two attacks on monks. It is important to bear in mind how very different from simple conversion to Christianity or even organized monasticism is the extreme form of asceticism—withdrawal to an uninhabited island—that Rutilius attacks in both passages (i. 439–52 and 515–26). It is not surprising that he reacted with horror to these island hermits. He was meant to. The most alarming account of the phenomenon comes (predictably enough) from the pen of Jerome, who describes how, in 374, his boyhood friend Bonosus, a young man of culture, wealth, and rank, gave them all up to live in sackcloth on a desolate, dangerous, and terrifying island, forever surrounded by the din of waves crashing against bare rocks. This overwrought picture was clearly intended to inspire horror as much as admiration. Nor is the reason far to seek. The first generation of western hermits had been overwhelmed by reading the *Life of Antony*. They were trying to re-create the world of the Desert Fathers with all its most extreme privations in Italy and Gaul. In the absence of real deserts, the abundance of uninhabited islands was the natural alternative—as Jerome himself reveals by describing a pious young man as "burning daily to make his way to the monasteries of Egypt…or at least to live a lonely life in the Dalmatian islands."[14] This is why he insists that there was not a blade of grass or a leaf of shade on Bonosus's island.

The earliest known example is St. Martin, who lived for a year or two ca. 358 on the island of Gallinaria with a single companion.[15] The generally hostile reaction of urban elites was not unconnected with the fact that deportation to an uninhabited island (*relegatio*) had long been a standard form of imprisonment for members of the Roman elite. Ammianus records two cases of relegation to the Dalmatian island of Boae in 361 and 368,[16] and some Priscillianist heretics were sentenced to exile on the remote Scilly Isles.[17] It has been suspected that Martin's was a case of imprisonment rather than

---

12. Schenkl 1911, 392–410. According to Gager 1985, 56, "Circumcision came to be seen as a synonym for Judaism itself." At i. 389 Rutilius applies the much-discussed phrase *radix stultitiae* to Judaism, and many have been tempted to identify *stultitia* as Christianity (see now the note in Wolf, Lancel, and Soler 2007). But the nine following lines are exclusively devoted to Judaism, and given Christianity's emphatic rejection of Judaism, this would be an improbably antiquarian way for a pagan to attack Christianity as late as the fifth century.

13. Lana 1961, 167.

14. *Jer. Ep.* 3. 4–5; *Ep.* 60. 10 (396); cf. *Ep.* 118. 5 (406).

15. *V. Mart.* 6. 5, with Fontaine 1968, 599–602.

16. Amm. Marc. 22. 3. 6 and 28. 1. 23.

17. Sulp. Sev. *Chron.* 2. 51. 4.

voluntary withdrawal,[18] and it is surely no coincidence that both Jerome (*carcerem*) and Rutilius (*ergastula*) introduce prison terms, albeit metaphorically, into their descriptions.

Some of these islands resembled the Egyptian desert less than others. The Lérins Islands, for example, off the French Riviera, a fifteen-minute boat ride from modern Cannes. The Lérins community were not wild-eyed hermits, but Gallic aristocrats, men of culture and natural authority, many of whom wrote books and engaged energetically in the ecclesiastical politics of the region.[19] One of them gives the game away with a lyrical description of the place as a *locus amoenus*.[20] But Hilarius, in his biography of the founder, St. Honoratus, did his best to maintain the forbidding desert stereotype: when Honoratus arrived the islands had been abandoned[21] (he claimed) because of poisonous snakes, which miraculously withdrew the moment the saint landed![22]

The Lérins settlements date from ca. 400/410. By ca. 386 Ambrose knew of a number of island hermits; in letters of 399 and 406 Jerome refers to such hermits being supported by his friends Fabiola and Julianus.[23] Around 398 Augustine wrote to the abbot of the community on Capraria (the subject of Rutilius's first invective), and (according to Orosius) their prayers helped Mascezel's expedition against Gildo in that year.[24] Island hermits were clearly a newly fashionable phenomenon of Rutilius's day (he must have been born 370/380).

The context of the second attack on the monks (i. 517–26) is as circumstantial as the attack on the Jews. As his ship passed by the uninhabited island of Gorgo, Rutilius was reminded of a fellow countryman, a young man of good family with an excellent marriage, who had thrown it all away to live in squalor and solitude there. Why should this invective have made anyone think of ordinary urban Christians, most of them just as appalled by these island hermits as pagans.[25] Twenty years before Rutilius wrote, a monk called Jovinian, though a celibate himself, attacked what he saw as the exaltation of celibacy over the married state as a "dogma against nature." His views were eventually condemned, but for a while they drew much popular support in the Christian community of Rome.[26] Other Christians, most notoriously but not only Jerome, accused Roman monks of gluttony and hypocrisy.[27] Monasticism, especially in its most extreme form, threatened the traditional way of life of the Roman aristocracy.[28]

---

18. Fontaine 1968, 600.
19. Courcelle 1968, 379–409; Mathisen 1989, 83–85 (culture); 85–140 (politics).
20. *aquis scatens, herbis virens, floribus renitens, visibus odoribusque iucunda…*, Eucherius, *De laude eremi* 42.
21. Though certainly settled in earlier times: Strabo 4. 1. 10; Valentin (next note) 108 n. 1.
22. Hilarius, *Vita Honorati* 15 = *Vie de Saint Honorat*, M.-D. Valentin (ed.) (Paris 1977), 106–10.
23. Ambr. *Hexaemeron* iii. 5. 23; Jer. *Ep.* 77. 6 (399) and 118. 5 (406).
24. Aug. *Ep.* 48; Oros. vii. 36. 5.
25. For a list of "Inseleremiten," Lorenz 1966, 11.
26. Duval 2003; Hunter 2007.
27. Wiesen 1964, 86–90; *Consultationes Zacchaei et Apollonii* iii. 3. 1–2, with Hunter 2007, 59.
28. Fontaine 1979; Gordini 1983; Hunter 2007.

By no means all Christians agreed that (as Rutilius put it) "the divine is nurtured in filth."[29] Many Christian members of the elite had reservations enough about sons and daughters giving away their money and adopting the ascetic lifestyle in cities or on family estates (Paulinus of Nola and the younger Melania a decade or so earlier). But the danger of desert islands (on top of their prison associations) was something altogether different. There is no reason most contemporaries should not have taken both invectives at face value as attacks on island hermits rather than Christians in general. Indeed, many conservative Christians would have warmly endorsed such hostility to this alarming development.

The fourth of the poet's invectives accuses Stilicho of betraying Rome to the Goths and burning the Sibylline books (ii. 41–60). The latter accusation has always been identified as the clearest single proof of Rutilius's paganism and requires more extended discussion. It has often been taken for granted that Stilicho's treatment of the Sibylline books was a deliberately anti-pagan act, sometimes connected with his spoliation of the gates of the Capitol recorded by Zosimus.[30] But Stilicho's motive in stripping the Capitol gates was surely his need for gold to pay the four thousand pounds of gold demanded by Alaric in 405,[31] not hostility to paganism. He normally did his best to conciliate the pagan aristocracy, so far as he could without making any concessions on the religious front.[32]

The Sibylline books had long been a marginal (if picturesque) element in the complex of rituals that made up Roman paganism, consulted at irregular intervals in times of danger or disaster. And from the reign of Augustus on, only emperors were authorized to order consultation, which they did very rarely, and only when it suited their own ends.[33] There is no good evidence that they were consulted at all between the late first and mid-third centuries. It is hard to see why they should have been "associated in the post-Constantine period with militant paganism."[34] Certainly there is nothing to link them with the generation of Symmachus or the banning of sacrifice, as often assumed on the basis of one or two references in the *Historia Augusta*. Symmachus himself never mentions them, nor did the pagan Eutropius find room for a single reference in his potted account of one thousand years of Roman history. Servius too shows little interest. Donatus devoted a long note to sacrifices performed by the *quindecimviri sacris faciundis*, the priests responsible for consulting the books. But Servius, writing in the 420s, dropped it. He knew that during the empire they were housed in the temple of Apollo, but by his characteristic use of the imperfect (*servabantur*, "used to be kept") he treats them as a thing of the past (Ch. 16).

---

29. *illuvie caelestia pasci*, i. 523.
30. v. 38. 5; Mazzarino 1938, 249–50; Paschoud, *Zosime* 3. 1 (1986), 266. It is true that the Sibylline books were originally kept on the Capitol, but Augustus had long ago moved them to the temple of Palatine Apollo.
31. Zos. v. 29. 9; Paschoud iii. 1 (1986), 220, 267.
32. Cameron 1970, 230–41; Marcone in Paschoud 1986, 145–62.
33. Parke 1988, 210.
34. Bird 1994, 146.

The *HA* reports an obviously fictitious debate in which one senator reproaches his colleagues for delaying to consult the books under Aurelian; the author then cites an (obviously forged) letter from Aurelian with the same complaint, expressing astonishment at their hesitation "as though they were deliberating in a Christian church rather than a temple of all the gods" (*Aur.* 20. 5). Certainly a hit at Christianity, but also at the senate, nor is it obvious that this debate is "propaganda" for the Sibylline books. The writer was apparently unaware that the books were not consulted about military problems and that only the emperor could order consultation.[35] The last known occasions when they were consulted do not suggest any pagan bias. Maxentius supposedly consulted them before the Battle of the Milvian Bridge in 312, and was told (with suspiciously Delphic ambiguity) that enemies of Rome would perish;[36] Julian ordered them consulted about his Persian expedition in 361, and then disregarded the warning not to leave his frontiers that year.[37] If anything, both stories are hostile to pagan emperors.

To link interest in the Sibylline books with the "pagan revival" of the 390s is to overlook a couple of intriguing texts that point to much earlier interest. According to Aurelius Victor (361) and the so-called *Epitome de Caesaribus* (395), when consulted about the threat from the Goths in 269/70, the Sibylline books decreed that the "foremost man in the senate" should consecrate himself to victory. When Pomponius Bassus offered himself, the emperor Claudius II claimed the honor instead, and routed the Goths by sacrificing his own life, "reviving the tradition of the Decii."[38] Claudius may have consulted the books, but the only fact here is his death soon after defeating the Goths (according to Eutropius and the *HA* from the plague). This is certainly a fiction, but from the age of Constantine at latest, and it is difficult to discern any specifically pagan purpose.

Even in the *HA*, references to the Sibyllines are not always to the "official" books kept in the temple of Palatine Apollo. The clearest illustration is the claim that they foretold the accession of Hadrian.[39] This could not have been the result of a formal consultation, restricted to times of crisis, when the *quindecimviri* would identify a passage in the Sibyllines that seemed relevant and make a recommendation. For example, the Lives of Gallienus (5. 5) and the Gordians (26. 2) record consultations after earthquakes, in both cases recommending the performance of specific rituals. Whether true or not, these are at any rate plausible scenarios. But a formal consultation about the identity of a future emperor (by definition under his predecessor) is inconceivable.

Yet it is not pure invention. There can be little doubt that what the writer had in mind here is a passage in the twelfth in the surviving corpus of "unofficial" Sibylline

---

35. Paschoud 2002, 357–69, has pointed out that, for a pagan, the writer is curiously ill informed about pagan cults, though I am not attracted by the idea that he was a renegade Christian.

36. Reported by both Lactantius, *De mort. pers.* 44. 8 and Zosimus, ii. 16. 1 (rather surprisingly accepted as fact by Paschoud, *Zosime* 1² [Paris 2000], 220).

37. Amm. Marc. 23. 1. 7.

38. Victor 34. 2–5; *Epit.* 34. 3.

39. *HA Hadr.* 2. 8.

Oracles that does indeed offer an unmistakable (if obviously post eventum) prophecy of the reign of Hadrian: "he will have the name of a sea beginning with the first letter of the alphabet [Adriatic], in four syllables...and dedicate temples in all cities, inspecting the world on his own feet."[40] The claim that the emperor Tacitus was likewise "promised by the Sibylline books" (*HA Tac.* 16. 6) reflects a similar conception, whether or not the writer was simply inventing.

This is a fact of the highest significance. By late antiquity, appeal to Sibylline Oracles need have no connection with the Sibylline books of Roman cult—indeed seldom does. "Unofficial" collections of Sibylline Oracles had been circulating for centuries, many of those that survive Jewish or Christian. Augustine's scholarly friend Flaccianus, proconsul of Africa in 393, showed him a Greek Sibylline with a Christian acrostic describing the Last Judgment. A century earlier Lactantius quoted a number of Sibylline prophecies of Christ. It is generally accepted that the twelfth and thirteenth oracles were circulating together by the mid-third century,[41] and it seems clear that the author of the *HA* consulted Greek sources (p. 779).

To return to Rutilius, which Sibylline books did Stilicho burn, and why? As Demougeot saw a half-century ago, his motive must have been to eliminate a *current* Sibylline prophecy unfavorable to himself or his policies.[42] A quarter-century after the disestablishment of the cults, there could be no question of a formal consultation of the books formerly kept in the temple of Palatine Apollo—even supposing they survived the fire of 363.[43] Five years earlier Prudentius had included the Sibyl in a list of pagan oracles now silent, drawing an absurdly unhistorical picture of raving Sibylline priests and priestesses (p. 161). Evidently, he knew nothing about the unsensational activities of the surely now defunct college of *quindecimviri*.

The oracle in question must have been one of the multitude of unofficial Sibyllines, many of which do indeed contain prophecies of the fall of Rome, prophecies naturally very disturbing to any Roman government faced with a hostile barbarian army in Italy. According to the Christian Palladius, Alaric's capture of Rome was "long ago foretold in prophecy," by which he must have meant the Sibylline prophecy that Rome would become a ruin (Ῥώμη ῥύμη), already known to Lactantius.[44] In its earliest redaction, the so-called Tiburtine Sibyl "foretells" a mighty warrior called Constantine who will humble the Hellenes (= pagans) and found Constantinople (330), but then goes on to warn her not to boast, because she will not rule for sixty years. In its extant form this text is in prose, but there are telltale traces of the original hexameters.[45] It was evidently

---

40. *Sib. Or.* xii. 163–75; another possible link is the claim at *HA Marcus* 24. 4 that the famous rain miracle came in answer to his prayers. The only other text to make this claim is (again) *Sib. Or.* 12, at line 200.
41. Aug. *CD* 18. 23 = *Or. Sib.* viii. 217–50; Ogilvie 1978, 28–33; Potter 1990, 154–57.
42. Demougeot 1952, 83–92.
43. As Amm. Marc. 23. 3. 3 claims.
44. Pall. *Hist. Laus.* 54. 7; Sib. Or. viii. 165; iii. 363; Lact. *Div. Inst.* vii. 25. 7. The Metaphrastic text of Palladius actually cites the Sibyl at this point p. 148. 9 Butler).
45. Alexander 1967, 14, lines 94–95. For more details, Cameron 2001, 45–52.

composed between 378 (there is an oblique allusion to the death of Valens on the field of Adrianople) and 390, the date prophecied for the fall of Constantinople.

The end of the fourth century was an age in which prophecies of doom circulated thick and fast. We have already touched on the pagan oracle in Greek hexameters described by Augustine that predicted the end of Christianity 365 years after the resurrection (Ch. 3. 6). Then there is the sermon Augustine preached on the fall of Rome in 410, which gives a detailed account of a prophecy that Constantinople would be destroyed by fire from heaven "a few years ago" under Arcadius (395–408). When the appointed day came, a fiery cloud hung over the city. Other sources link celestial manifestations with an earthquake datable to 395 or 396.[46]

Extravagant comparisons are so routine in late antique poetry that no one has paid much attention to the comparison with Nero that follows in Rutilius's poem: "Stilicho's victim [Rome] was immortal, Nero's mortal; Stilicho destroyed the mother of the world, Nero his own." But if we attend to the context, no Roman emperor is evoked more often in the surviving "unofficial" Sibyllines than Nero.[47] Even in his lifetime, a purported Sibylline verse claimed that a matricide would be the last of the descendants of Aeneas.[48] Oracles referring to Nero were often reinterpreted as prophecies of later public enemies,[49] and Rutilius's rather strained comparison suggests that such a prophecy was reinterpreted for Stilicho.

In a poem recited at Rome in 402, a few years before Stilicho's action, Claudian gives a long list of omens and portents that caused people to worry as Alaric advanced into Italy: birds, thunderbolts, an eclipse of the moon, and "the linen [book] that guards the destiny of Rome with its fateful song."[50] While undoubtedly using language that evokes the "official" Sibylline books of Roman tradition, once again he cannot possibly be referring to an actual consultation of those books. It is inconceivable that Honorius ordered a consultation, and that the passage produced was a prophecy of doom. It must again be one of the "unofficial" Sibyllines, which Claudian links to Roman destiny because they are so full of references to the fate of Rome. Caesar's crossing of the Rubicon was followed, according to Lucan, by a long series of terrible portents: new stars, comets, thunderbolts, eclipses (lunar and solar), Alpine snow suddenly vanishing, talking animals, monstrous births, and "dire prophecies from the Sibyl of Cumae passed from mouth to mouth." Here too commentators assume a reference to the official Sibyllines.[51] At this date it is not impossible that the senate ordered a consultation, but the *quindecimviri* would never have come up with a prophecy of doom. This must be an early reference to an unofficial Sibylline prophecy.

---

46. O'Reilly 1955, § 7, 68–70. For the other sources and full analysis, Cameron 2001, 47–50.

47. See the index to J. Geffcken's edition (p. 240, s.v. Römische Kaiser).

48. ἔσχατος Αἰνεαδῶν μητροκτόνος ἡγεμονεύσει, quoted in Dio 62. 18. 3; so too *Sib. Or.* v. 363.

49. Potter 1990, 300–302.

50. *quid carmine poscat / fatidico custos Romani carbasus aevi, Get.* 231–32.

51. *diraque per populum Cumanae carmina vatis / volgantur,* Lucan i. 564–65, with R. J. Getty's note (Cambridge 1955).

A few lines later Claudian dismisses all the prophetic manifestations he has just described as "womanish wailings." He would never have treated an official consultation of the Sibylline books on the emperor's orders so contemptuously. On the contrary, we are meant to see all these portents and oracles as uninformed and (above all) misguided defeatism—misguided because in 402 this wave of defeatism was triumphantly routed by Stilicho's (as it seemed at the time) decisive victory over Alaric at Pollentia. But it reappeared when Alaric reappeared stronger than ever outside the walls of Rome in 408. It was around this time that Jerome published his commentary on the book of Daniel, interpreting Daniel 8. 11 as predicting the fall of Rome. A number of Christian writers at this period saw Alaric and his Goths as harbingers of Antichrist.[52] Stilicho presumably seized and destroyed all such defeatist prophetic texts he could lay his hands on. He was following good precedent. No less a person than Augustus, in his capacity as *pontifex maximus*, burned thousands of lines of Sibylline Oracles deemed "unsuitable," retaining for future consultation only what he had personally authorized (among other things presumably weeding out all prophecies of doom).[53] If the Sibyllines Stilicho burned included what remained of the books rescued from the temple of Apollo, that would explain why pagans were angry. But given the fact that so many unofficial Sibyllines were thought to have prophesied the birth of Christ, many Christians must also have been disturbed.

I am happy to agree that Rutilius was probably, though perhaps not (as his latest editors claim) "incontestably" a pagan.[54] In addition to all the usual arguments and assumptions, they insist that the Rome Rutilius celebrates in his famous eulogy (i. 47 164) is a pagan Rome, that he completely ignores the numerous Christian basilicas that adorned the city by 417. But this is entirely to misunderstand the passage. The Rome of Rutilius's eulogy is not the brick and marble fifth-century city but Roma the symbol and personification of an empire. Roma is apostrophized as the goddess who made a single fatherland for nations far apart (63), made a city of what was once a world (66), the goddess every corner of her dominion celebrates (79). In the diction of poetry, *dea Roma* means no more than the personification with helmet, shield, and one bare breast that are her attributes in art and literature, Christian no less than pagan, down into the sixth century. Rutilius's white-haired Roma rejuvenated by the defeat of the Goths derives from Claudian, but then so does Prudentius's Roma, rejuvenated by her conversion to Christianity.[55] Above all, Rutilius's Roma is the Rome that recovered with renewed strength from even its worst defeats, by Gauls, Samnites, Pyrrhus, Hannibal, and now Goths. To have introduced Christian churches would have destroyed the unity and purpose of the passage. Not even the most pious Christian could have claimed that Christianity helped Rome defeat Brennus and

---

52. Courcelle 1964, 22, 33, 43–44; Demougeot 1952; nothing new in Doignon 1990, 120–46.
53. Suet. *Aug.* 31. 1.
54. "incontestablement païen," Wolff, Lancel, and Soler 2007, xiii.
55. Claud. *de bello Gild.* 21–25, 208–12; Rutil. 115–54; Prud. *CS* ii. 655–767; Cameron 1970, 274–76, 364–69. Rutilius gives Roma a turreted helmet, perhaps thinking of Lucan i. 188.

Hannibal. No educated fifth-century Christian would have found anything objectionable in Rutilius's stirring eulogy of Rome.

The fact that Rutilius attacks island hermits twice may suggest that he found the phenomenon more disturbing than his Christian peers. He may have felt that Christianity was more prone to such antisocial extremes than the old cults. He may have offended clerics and rigorists. But if we place his four invectives in a contemporary social and religious context, they are unlikely to have struck most lay Christian contemporaries as offensive. He surely did not intend his poem as a pagan manifesto, nor would most Christians have so read it.

2: MARIUS VICTORINUS

If asked to name a fourth-century pagan champion, many readers of Augustine's *Confessions* would think of the celebrated pagan rhetor and philosopher Marius Victorinus: "until he was of advanced years he was a worshipper of idols and took part in sacrilegious rites. . . . Old Victorinus had defended these cults for many years with a voice terrifying to opponents." A couple of pages later we are told that "special pleasure was felt at the conversion of Victorinus's heart, in which the devil had an impregnable fortress, and of Victorinus's tongue, which he had used as a mighty, sharp weapon to destroy many."[56] On this evidence it is tempting to count Victorinus as an active member of the "pagan opposition." But as Markus has seen,[57]

> The process of thought which had brought the neo-Platonist thinker and Latin rhetor to find in Christianity an expression of the true philosophy is transformed in Augustine's account into a dramatic renunciation of a militant pagan past, and a painful break with the circle of his aristocratic friends. . . . The image of conversion in terms of crossing from one of the front lines on a battlefield to the other belongs to the 390s rather than to the 350s.

It is also a purely Christian perspective. Victorinus himself, who became a prominent Christian theologian and polemicist, like St. Paul before him and Augustine after, in retrospect no doubt exaggerated the militancy of his pagan past. Since he could not have held one of the traditional priesthoods, reserved for the nobility, as far as the state cults are concerned it is unlikely that he ever actually "took part in sacrilegious rites" except as a spectator. There is no reason to believe that his religious trajectory either began with hostility to Christianity or involved the rejection of an active pagan past. All we know for certain is that he was a longtime student of Neoplatonism who at some point began to study Christian writings, and was eventually won over.

---

56. *Conf.* 8. 2. 3 and 8. 4, with J. J. O'Donnell's commentary, vol. 3, 1992, 19.
57. Markus 1974, 7; cf. Markus 1990, 29.

If Victorinus's pagan writings had perished, scholars might reasonably have assumed, on the basis of Augustine's characterization, that they "must" have been aggressively anti-Christian. In fact, among his lost works we know of translations of Aristotle's *Categories* and *De interpretatione*, the former in eight books complete with a commentary; and a work *De syllogismis hypotheticis*.[58] The subject matter cannot readily have lent itself to religious polemic. Among his surviving works we have part of an *Ars grammatica*, and a detailed commentary on Cicero's *De inventione*. No one would expect to find polemic here either, but one passage positively leaps out at us. When commenting on *De inv.* i. 29. 44, Victorinus distinguishes between two sorts of arguments, those that merely make probable and those that prove irrefutably (*aut probabiliter ostendens aut necessarie demonstrans*). Things proved irrefutably are those that "cannot happen or be proved otherwise," and the illustration Cicero himself gives is: "if she has born a child, she has slept with a man" (*si peperit, cum viro concubuit*). Victorinus qualifies this claim, arguing that irrefutable arguments scarcely apply to human relations, where probability is the most we can hope for:[59]

> If the probable depends on what *seems* true, the irrefutable must depend on what *is* true. But in human affairs the truth is hidden (*verum latet*) and everything is subject to conjecture. So there can be no irrefutable arguments. In human affairs things can only be irrefutable to the extent that human opinion (*opinio humana*) allows them this power. Moreover, according to the opinion of the Christians (*Christianorum opinio*), the argument "if she has born a child, she has slept with a man" is *not* irrefutable, nor the argument "if he has been born, he will die." For among them it is certain (*manifestum*) that someone *was* born without the intervention of a man and did *not* die (*sine viro natum et non mortuum*).

It is clear that Victorinus wrote these words while still a pagan, and tempting to see them as polemic against the twin notions of virgin birth and resurrection.[60] But as a careful analysis by Pierre Hadot has made clear, this would be a mistake.[61] To start with, while Victorinus may not at the time of writing have accepted the Christian position, it is to misunderstand his argument as a whole to see even scepticism here, much less polemic. His point, which he goes on to discuss at considerable length, is that very few propositions relating to human affairs are susceptible of irrefutable proof. He cites several more examples: the existence of an underworld, the existence of gods, whether the world had a beginning or not (235. 28). These are "opinions" (*opiniones, dogmata*), the sort of thing we can never make more than probable. Nor does everyone find the same things probable. Romans find one thing just, barbarians another (234. 39). In this

---

58. Schanz iv. 1. 155–56.
59. C. Halm, *Rhetores latini minores* (Leipzig 1863), 232. 35–44.
60. So de Labriolle 1934, 360–61.
61. P. Hadot 1960, 12–17; see too Courcelle 1963, 69–74; and Hadot 1971, 47–54.

context Christian belief in the virgin birth simply functions as a neat qualification of the seemingly irrefutable argument about the birth of a child necessarily implying sexual intercourse. And Victorinus picks on this particular argument, not because it gave him the opportunity to attack Christianity, but because it happened to be the example Cicero offers in the passage under discussion. Thus he is able to show that an example long considered irrefutable would no longer be so considered by everyone.

The antithesis he draws between truth and opinion is a Platonic doctrine heavily emphasized by the Neoplatonists. The specific claim that in human affairs "the truth is hidden" derives from Porphyry, as shown by a passage of Macrobius, *latet, inquit* [*Porphyrius*], *omne verum*,[62] where the quotation continues with a description of the soul trying to discern truth through a veil of darkness. In a later passage Macrobius uses the verb *opinor* in the same way of what men find probable. It is clear from the examples both cite that (presumably following Porphyry) they saw religion as the clearest example of an area where men's most firmly held "opinions" were liable to differ sharply. In context, the truth of Christian "opinion" was simply irrelevant to Victorinus's point. While Christians would have been happy to agree that the virgin birth constituted an exception to Cicero's argument, they would have been less happy to see it cited as a case of the inevitable relativism of religious belief.

Victorinus's conversion may not have been the dramatic event a superficial reading of Augustine might imply. The day he made his public profession in church may well have caused a sensation, but he had been quietly studying Christian writings for a long time by then, as he admitted privately to Augustine's informant, a Milanese priest called Simplicianus who had been close to Victorinus in Rome forty years before (Ch. 5. 1). It is natural to infer that the passage in the *De inventione* commentary is an early indication of this interest in Christian writings.

Of course, it is possible that he let slip polemical asides in class, like the fifth-century Egyptian grammarian Horapollon.[63] But the surviving "pagan" writings of Victorinus do not at all give the impression of a pagan controversialist. On the contrary, they suggest that his conversion was a slow process based on private study, not a sudden rejection of a militant pagan past. And once converted, he turned his attention to the fight against heresy, not paganism.

3: AMMIANUS MARCELLINUS

There has never been any question that Ammianus was a pagan. Unusually for a pagan, he refers quite openly to Christians and Christianity, sometimes favorably, more often not. He is usually seen as a moderate, tolerant pagan. Barnes has recently

---

62. *Comm. Somn. Scip.* i. 3. 18; Hadot and Courcelle, ll. cc.
63. Zach. Schol., *Vita Severi* (Patr. Orient. ii. 1. 6) 1903, 15–23.

argued against this view. He makes a number of good points, but he has not convinced me that Ammianus indulges in covert as well as open polemic.[64] This section does no more than touch on two topics.

First, the claim that Ammianus "sets out to marginalize Christianity by deliberately understating the role that Christians and Christianity played in the political history of the fourth century," in particular by "leav[ing] out completely the ecclesiastical affairs that occupied a large amount of Constantius' time during the years for which his account is extant."[65] This is (I believe) a misunderstanding of the nature (and limitations) of Ammianus's history. As Averil Cameron and I pointed out long ago, his apparent avoidance of Christian terms as if unfamiliar (*Christiani ritus presbyter, ut ipsi appellant*, to give a typical illustration) is no more than a classicizing affectation.[66] We find exactly parallel apologetic formulas in the work of Christian secular historians, most conspicuously Procopius. For the very same unclassical reference acquired by "presbyter" compare the late fifth-century Malchus: "the priest, whom the Christians call presbyter"; and Procopius: "he donned the garb of the priest whom they are accustomed to call presbyter".[67] According to Barnes, our argument

> is valid in general, but it has been given a misleading application. In contrast to Ammianus, Procopius makes his Christianity clear in several passages. But when Ammianus twice glosses the word *synodus* with the phrase *ut appellant*, he implies that one of the commonest forms of political assembly in the fourth century was an exotic rarity.

But the fact that Procopius elsewhere "makes his Christianity clear" is irrelevant. The key point is that both were writing history in the grand style, restricted to events traditionally considered important (war and politics) and written in the style and vocabulary of the classical historians.

It was the *genre* that marginalized Christianity. Procopius too deliberately omitted almost all ecclesiastical affairs from his narrative,[68] despite the fact that religious divisions were even more important under Justinian than Constantius II. Well aware how incomplete a picture of the politics of the age his *Wars* gave, Procopius says a bit more about ecclesiastical affairs in his less classicising *Secret History*, and more than once makes an (unfulfilled) promise of a separate ecclesiastical history. It is instructive to consider his curiously detached, almost Herodotean characterizations of this projected supplement to the *Wars*: "a conflict (*stasis*) had arisen among the inhabitants

---

64. Barnes 1998, esp. Ch. 8, with *JRS* 99 (2009), 294.
65. Barnes 1998, 81–82.
66. Note too *coetus…eiusdem legis cultorum, synodus ut appellant*, Amm. xxxi. 12. 8; xv. 7. 7; xxi. 16. 18; and often elsewhere: Cameron and Cameron 1964, 316–28.
67. Malchus F 20 line 139 Blockley (having just apologized a few lines earlier for the term *magistriani*, ib. line 122); Proc. *Wars* i. 25. 31.
68. Averil Cameron 1985, 36, 131.

concerning those matters over which the Christians fight among themselves, as will be told in my work on the subject"; "the measures that were taken with regard to the Christians will be described in my subsequent narrative."[69]

One or two scholars have questioned Procopius's Christianity, and Kelly has recently claimed that "the Christian persuasion of some of the Byzantine historians whom [Cameron and Cameron] cite is not necessarily clear-cut."[70] That some were less than fully committed Christians is possible. That they were all out-and-out pagans, as late as the sixth century so hostile to Christianity that they could not bring themselves to refer to presbyters without apology, is beyond belief. That this is not the explanation in the case of Procopius is put beyond doubt by the fact that he apologizes in exactly the same way for using "Hellene" in the unclassical sense "pagan" ("the so-called Hellenes," *SH* xi. 31)! Whatever their religious convictions, avoiding Christian terms and marginalizing Christian affairs was dictated by considerations of style and genre. Barnes objects that Ammianus is inconsistent in his terminology, no less often using Christian terms without apology. Yet Procopius too is inconsistent in exactly the same way.[71] Since such terms must in fact have been perfectly familiar to everyone even by Ammianus's day, even purists must have thought it overly pedantic to apologize every single time.

As the case of Procopius makes clear, two centuries after Ammianus ecclesiastical affairs were still not felt to belong in a traditional narrative history, not to mention the fact that providing even an outline of the ecclesiastical politics of the age would have required an entirely different sort of research and expertise—and a different narrative structure. Nor did Ammianus entirely exclude ecclesiastical politics. He let one striking incident in by the back door. One of his regular sections was events at Rome, pegged to successive prefects of Rome. By this route he included the exile of Pope Liberius under the prefecture of Leontius (356), something of a stretch, because all Leontius did was have Liberius spirited out of Rome in the middle of the night and taken to court at Milan. But it allowed Ammianus to explain that Liberius was exiled because he refused to endorse Constantius's exile of Athanasius with the "higher authority" of the bishop of Rome. Even without a context, this is a revealing glimpse of Constantius's obsession with controlling the church. Nothing covert here. The accusation he reports that Athanasius practiced divination and magic is confirmed by the ecclesiastical historians.[72]

Second, inferences from individual passages. The most detailed portrait of any non-imperial individual in Ammianus is his devastating attack on Petronius Probus (xxvii. 11. 1–3). According to Barnes, "In the chorus of praise for Probus, there are only two

---

69. *Wars* viii. 25. 13; *Secret History* xi. 33; cf. xxvi. 18; i. 14.
70. Kaldellis 2004; G. Kelly 2008, 68 n. 114. For Procopius, see rather Averil Cameron 1985, Ch. 7; briefly Treadgold 2007, 177; for Malchus, Treadgold 2007, 103.
71. Averil Cameron 1970, 151–53, for a list of Christian terms in Procopius, in § 6 those used with apology, in § 10 those without. For a collection of such formulas in Malchus, Blockley 1981, 77.
72. Amm. xv. 7. 6–10; Rufin. *HE* x. 16; Socr. *HE* i. 27. 18; Soz. *HE* iv. 9. 10.

dissenting voices," Jerome and Ammianus, and he takes it for granted that the reason for Ammianus's attack was Probus's Christianity. But the very fact that the Christian Jerome accuses Probus of "destroying the provinces he governed" in his greed (s. a. 372) at once undermines this claim. As for that "chorus of praise," it is precisely that, dedications in honor of Probus by his own clients and a panegyric on his sons by Claudian. We should hardly expect to find criticism here. The truth is that all we know about Probus's Christianity is that he was baptized on his deathbed. There is no evidence that he was an active member of the Christian community in his lifetime. In any case, Ammianus mentions innumerable other Christians in his narrative favorably enough.

There is no reason to believe that Christianity was the source of Ammianus's hostility to Probus in particular or the Anicii in general. If Ammianus had a personal axe to grind (which is entirely probable), it would be enough that Probus was one of those who had refused or withdrawn his patronage. It is going too far to infer from these passages that he "makes it clear that he regarded Christians as corrupt in every way."[73]

His account of Olybrius's city prefecture is another fascinating illustration of Ammianus's technique:

> He never deviated from a humane policy, and took great pains to ensure that no word or act of his should be accounted harsh. He punished slander severely, pruned the profits of the treasury wherever he could, drew a sharp distinction between right and wrong, and all in all was an admirable judge and very mild towards those he governed. Nevertheless, these good qualities were overshadowed by a defect, which did little harm to the community but was discreditable in a high official. His private life verged on the luxurious and was almost entirely devoted to the stage and to women, though his liaisons were not criminal or incestuous. (28. 4. 2)

A seemingly glowing testimonial—with a sting in the tail. Once again, Barnes detects an explanation in terms of Olybrius's Christianity. But this would be a strangely oblique way of attacking a man for his religion. Then there is Ammianus's account of the capture of the Mesopotamian city of Bezabde by the Persians (20.7.9 [B. 87]):

> The bishop incurred suspicion, which in my opinion was ill-founded but obtained wide currency, that he had had a secret meeting with Sapor, in which he had pointed out which parts of the walls were weak on the inside and therefore best to attack. What seemed to lend plausibility to this suspicion was that after his visit the enemy deliberately directed his engines against the danger spots where the walls were crumbling, as if he were exultantly taking advantage of information about conditions inside the town.

---

73. Barnes 1998, 117–18, 180.

Barnes is undoubtedly right to see Matthews's claim that Ammianus "defends the bishop…against unjust suspicions" as misguided. If Ammianus had really thought the allegation of treachery a baseless slander, he would either not have mentioned it at all or else justified his own opinion. As it is, he supplies evidence in support of the accusation. Barnes more plausibly argues that, like Tacitus, Ammianus is using rumor "to suggest disreputable conduct or a dishonest motive while taking no authorial responsibility for the dubious information thus conveyed."[74] But he surely goes too far in drawing the wider conclusion that "in Ammianus's opinion, Christians were intrinsically unpatriotic."

Compare the rather similar passage where Ammianus describes the city prefecture of the elder Symmachus, "a man of the most exemplary learning and discretion" and a pillar of the pagan establishment:

> Through his efforts [Rome]…can boast of a splendid and solid bridge which he restored and dedicated, to the great joy of the citizens, who nevertheless some years later demonstrated their ingratitude in the plainest way. They set fire to his beautiful house across the Tiber, enraged by a story, invented without a shred of evidence by some worthless ruffian, that Symmachus had said he would rather use his wine to quench lime-kilns than sell it at the reduced price that the people were hoping for. (27. 3. 4)

Once again, Ammianus claims not to believe the accusation, but if he had really thought it a baseless slander, why repeat it at all, especially since the fire happened "some years later"? He must have realized that the anecdote was more memorable than his account of the bridge. Note too that this chapter of Ammianus goes straight on to the prefecture of Volusianus Lampadius, a long and uniformly hostile account. Volusianus was so vain that he took it amiss if even his spitting was not praised, again with a devastating final touch, that he was occasionally (*non numquam*) strict and honest. Volusianus was the head of a clan of tauroboliates (Ch. 6. 2). Yet according to Barnes, "That does not exclude the possibility that the prefect had been a Christian under Constantine, when it would have helped his career."[75] Not only is this the rankest speculation. While Christians were scathing about the falsity and insincerity of those who professed Christianity for advancement, there is little evidence that it bothered pagans much. Ammianus criticizes Domitius Modestus as a flatterer of Valens, but, like Libanius, never alludes to his switches from Christian to pagan and back again according to the religion of the emperors he was serving.[76] Remember too his portrait of the arrogant and uncouth Memmius Vitrasius Orfitus, the younger Symmachus's father-in-law.

---

74. Barnes 1998, 87–88.
75. Barnes 1998, 116.
76. Amm. xxix. 1. 10–11; *PLRE* i. 605–8; see p. 326.

The fact that he openly mocked three of the most prominent Roman pagans of the second half of the fourth century should make us hesitate before postulating covert mockery of prominent Christians. Why resist the more commonsense conclusion: that Ammianus found Orfitus's arrogance and lack of culture, Volusianus's vanity, Symmachus's contempt of the masses, Probus's greed and ambition, and Olybrius's womanizing equally offensive.

Barnes and Kelly are right to argue that Ammianus was more hostile to Christianity than generally supposed. It is obviously significant that his praise of the modest life-style of "certain provincial bishops" immediately follows his account of a battle between Damasus and Ursinus for the papacy that, "it is agreed (*constat*)," left 137 dead bodies in a church.[77] But this is not quite the "ironic juxtaposition" Kelly suggests. Once again, Ammianus is openly drawing on a Christian text, the Ursinus dossier (p. 186), to show Christians in an unfavorable light. This openness is surely more instructive about Christian tolerance of dissent than all that supposed covert polemic.

4: JULIUS OBSEQUENS

It has been suggested that Julius Obsequens's little collection of prodigies was, if not a pagan counterpart to Orosius or Augustine, at any rate some sort of pagan interpretation of Roman history.[78] It is a peculiarly difficult work to interpret: no surviving manuscript, nothing known about the writer, the beginning lost.[79] The most prudent course would be to set it aside as undatable (perhaps as early as the second century). But suppose (with Schmidt) we date it to the early fifth century, where does that get us? Rossbach rightly pointed out that many chapters of Obsequens seem to link prodigies to successful or unsuccessful events at Rome. For example: "showers of stones on the Aventine were expiated by a nine-day observance; there was a successful campaign in Spain" (§ 2). Obsequens, he concluded, was a good pagan who believed in the importance of expiating prodigies in the traditional way.[80]

Whether or not this is what Obsequens thought (and it would be a strange thought for a late fourth-century pagan, writing four centuries after the state had abandoned public expiation of prodigies), this was certainly not genuine Republican practice. Prodigies were not any strange happening, but a very restricted range of happenings, mainly damage done to temples and statues by storms, unusual births (whether animal or human), and unusual precipitation (hail, blood, or milk). Furthermore, these happenings had to be officially recognized as *prodigia* by the senate (*suscepta*),

---

77. Amm. xxvii. 3. 11–15; G. Kelly 2008, 4.

78. Schmidt 1968.

79. The title (*ab anno urbis conditae quinquentesimo quinto*) gives the starting date as 259 B.C., but the surviving text begins at 190. If the information is authentic, the title must have been taken from an explicit rather than incipit in the now-lost manuscript used for the Aldine edition (1508).

80. Rossbach 1897, 3–4; his edition (1910), xxxiv; Peter 1897, 347; P. Schmidt 1968, 224.

and then they were dealt with (*procurata*) by one of several forms of expiation.[81] Expiation was supposed to ward off whatever evil the prodigy portended and that was the end of it. There is no evidence that subsequent military successes were ascribed to successful expiation, or military failures to failure to expiate. In any case, even in Obsequens the link is often unclear. For example, in 92 B.C. an immense number of prodigies are elaborately expiated—and a barbarian tribe devastates Macedonia (§ 53; cf. 63). If Obsequens's purpose was to stress the importance of expiating prodigies for winning the favor of the gods, why include examples that conspicuously contradicted his thesis? Five out of the first twenty chapters consist of nothing but a list of prodigies without any reported outcome (§§ 1, 5, 7, 14, 15), and in four of these there is no mention of expiation. It is true that expiation of *prodigia suscepta* could be taken for granted,[82] but if it was Obsequens's purpose to stress the importance of expiation, he could hardly afford to omit this step in the process.

Furthermore, Obsequens does not restrict himself to prodigies proper. His later chapters include a number of omens and even dreams of private citizens. This shift from public prodigy to private omen mirrors a genuine contemporary shift of interest reflected in the biographies of Suetonius and the *HA*. Dreams and omens prove nothing about the due performance of traditional pagan rites. Whatever its date, it is difficult to discern any clear religious purpose in Obsequens's book. His interest in prodigies and omens may have been simply antiquarian. It is particularly unfortunate that the beginning of the work is missing, since it might well have included an explanatory preface that would have answered at least some of our questions.

In order to counter the pagan claim that it was the abolition of sacrifice that had led to recent disasters, Augustine devoted Bk iii of his *City of God* to disasters suffered by Rome before the birth of Christ. But he did not include prodigies among those disasters. Indeed, he made fun of them: "I say nothing of manifestations which were more remarkable than harmful; talking oxen, unborn infants shouting words while still in the womb, flying serpents, women turning into men, hens into cocks and so on."[83] To Augustine's immense catalogue of pre-Christian disasters there was in fact a simple pagan answer: Rome had survived them all with ever-increasing strength. But since it was now four centuries since the senate had paid any attention to the traditional prodigies, much less formally expiated them, it is difficult to see why late fourth-century pagans would have been impressed by Obsequens's list. Talking oxen and flying serpents would surely have been an embarrassment.

Yet according to Hedrick, "Even in Honorius' time prodigies continued to be observed, interpreted, and expiated."[84] If by this he means that traditional practice continued unchanged down to the 390s, this is undoubtedly false. Traditional

---

81. MacBain 1982; see John North, *JRS* 76 (1986), 254–57, and in North and Beard 1990, 54–55.
82. For a convenient list of prodigies together with the form of expiation, MacBain 1982, 82–105.
83. *CD* iii. 31. Sex-change *prodigia* are in fact very rare (not in Obsequens, though cf. Livy 24. 10. 10; Macbain 1982, 127 n. 238); the hens changed into cocks example is presumably a joke.
84. Hedrick 2000, 56, cf. 69.

practice was abandoned as early as the age of Augustus. When Symmachus tells his son-in-law in 401 that the city is disturbed by "signs" (*ostenta*), the most serious of which was the suffect consul being thrown out of his ceremonial carriage on the way to his inauguration (*Ep.* vi. 40. 1), this is no more than the sort of "bad omen" identified by superstitious people at all periods of human history. Ammianus often mentions omens and portents, particularly during his account of Julian's Persian expedition. In another context, when reporting the birth of a two-headed child (xix. 12. 20), he remarks that "portents of this kind often occur, pointing to various outcomes; *but as they are no longer expiated by public rites* as they were in the old days (*ut apud veteres publice*), they pass by unheard of and unknown." This is just the sort of prodigy we find recorded by Livy and Obsequens, yet despite using the verb *expiare*, it is clear that Ammianus does not have traditional Republican practice in mind. In the old days, once the prodigy had been expiated, it was as though it had never happened. It was not, like Ammianus's string of omens and portents, regarded as an omen of future disaster.

A letter to Praetextatus about a portent at Spoletum (*Ep.* i. 49) refers to a whole series of sacrifices performed by various authorities (nineteen in fact, eight to Jupiter and eleven to Fortuna Publica), all of them (he laments) in vain (*nequiquam*). What is going on? It seems that pagans in Spoletum had been expecting these sacrifices to bring about some perceptible improvement in the situation. But there was no empirical way of judging whether or not expiatory sacrifices had "worked." If the proper forms had been followed, it was simply assumed that the expiation had warded off whatever evil the prodigy had portended.[85] Symmachus goes on to say that, despite all the sacrifices, "the portent of Spoletum has not yet been *publicly* expiated" (*necdum publico nomine…piatur*). There is no need to say more here about the importance of public observance.[86] It seems that the nineteen expiatory sacrifices Symmachus lists had been made by individual pagans privately. The authorities had presumably not allowed a public sacrifice in the traditional style. It is tantalizing that we do not know either the date of this letter[87] or the nature of the portent.

5: LATINIUS PACATUS DREPANIUS

I close with a case that has been put on an entirely new basis by an unexpected discovery: Latinius Pacatus Drepanius, a younger friend of Ausonius, who describes him as an outstanding poet. Hitherto he has only been known as the author of the last in date of the twelve so-called Panegyrici Latini, delivered before Theodosius in Rome

---

85. Unless the sacrifice itself was judged a failure, but it is hard to believe that nineteen successive victims could have been found defective.
86. When Symmachus asks his brother, then vicar of Africa, to help maintain pontifical ownership of some temple estates in Vaga, he refers to "public benefit" (*publica utilitas, Ep.* i. 68).
87. Seeck's 378 (p. lxxxix) is no more than a guess.

sometime between June and August 389.[88] It has been plausibly conjectured that it was Drepanius himself who compiled the corpus of the Panegyrici Latini, all of which, like Drepanius, have strong Gallic connections.[89] Imperial panegyric is a highly conventional form, to start with apparently unaffected by the conversion of Constantine, who is the subject of no fewer than five of the speeches. They are characterized by "a neutral monotheism which would be acceptable to Christians and pagans alike."[90] Nonetheless, a number of passages have led most scholars to conclude that Pacatus Drepanius was a pagan.[91] For example, phrases like "the god who is your consort" (6. 4), "divine beings (*divina*) enjoy perpetual motion" (10. 1, referring to Theodosius), and "that god who shares in (*particeps*) your majesty" (18. 4).[92] Among those who came out of Emona in procession to greet Theodosius, § 37 describes *flamines* venerable in their purple robes and *pontifices* wearing *apices*, the conical hat worn by various pagan priests. But no mention of Christian clergy. Section 4. 5 has been generally thought to go further than most divine comparisons:

> Let the land of Crete, famous as the cradle of the child Jupiter, and Delos, where the divine twins learned to crawl, and Thebes, illustrious as the nursemaid of Hercules, yield to this land. We do not know whether to credit the stories we have heard, *but Spain has given us a god we can actually see"* (*deum... quem videmus*).

Would even the most liberal Christian have followed classicizing conventions that far? In this case the answer is yes.

Thanks to a brilliant recent discovery by Turcan-Verkerk, we now know that Drepanius (as he should be called) was not only a Christian, but the author of devotional poetry. We can now read one of his poems, an openly Christian piece titled *On the Paschal Candle* (*De cereo paschali*).[93] The poem has long been known, but was attributed in error to a ninth-century poet, Florus of Lyons.[94] The only manuscript (*Paris BNF lat.* 7558) contains a series of works by Gallic writers, with *De cereo paschali*, ascribed to Drepanius, immediately preceded by poems by Claudius Marius Victor, Ausonius and Paulinus of Nola, and followed by Florus. The context is thus solidly the poetry of late antique Gaul. With the aid of online databases Turcan-Verkerk was able to list countless parallels with both the panegyric on Theodosius and the poems of Ausonius and Paulinus. To take a single example, the reference to perpetual motion at *Pan.* 10. 1 reappears in *De cereo* (line 1–2) as well as in a couple of

---

88. Delmaire 1989, 126; Nixon and Rodgers 1994, 443.
89. Nixon and Rodgers 1994, 6; Rees 2002, 23.
90. Liebeschuetz 1979, 300.
91. E. Galletier, iii. 50–51; Von Haehling 1978, 432–33; Delmaire 1989, 127.
92. Nixon and Rodgers 453 n. 25.
93. Turcan-Verkerk 2003; C. E. V. Nixon, *Gnomon* 78 (2006), 126–30.
94. On whom see (briefly) Raby 1953, 196–99.

passages of Ausonius.[95] There can be no question that the poem should be restored to the fourth-century Pacatus Drepanius, the only writer of any period who bore this unusual name.

More than any other speech in the corpus of the Panegyrici, Drepanius's "borrows ideas and phraseology from all or almost all the other speeches in the collection," and most of the passages just cited are modeled on phrases in the others.[96] His poetry too is written in the traditional style in close imitation of classical models. Indeed, he shows a wide familiarity with classical poets, not only Vergil and Ovid, but Lucretius, Manilius, and Statius. The poem begins with the nonspecific apostrophe *Alme deus rerum,* and the long invocation that follows could as easily be from a monotheistic pagan hymn until line 18, where we are told that the assembled worshippers celebrate "one deity under three names." Lines 19–23 offer a mild polemic against the noise, incense, and blood involved in the nocturnal celebration of the Eleusinian and Dionysiac mysteries, but if the two references to the Trinity (line 18 and by implication lines 26–27), the apostrophe *Christe* at line 45, and line 30 (*intacto pregnans utero dedit innuba mater*), were removed, it would be impossible to say with certainty that the poem celebrated a Christian rather than pagan vigil. Interestingly enough, Drepanius, a contemporary of the austere Paulinus, is more consistently classicizing than even Ausonius. The eighty-five-line prayer included in Ausonius's "Daily Round," though written in his usual classicizing hexameters, is full of overtly Christian ideas like original sin, explicitly rejects blood sacrifice, and evokes Elias, Enoch, and David. Drepanius's classical culture stands out in sharper relief in that there is not a single allusion to the Bible, here again unlike his contemporary and fellow disciple of Ausonius, Paulinus of Nola, who not infrequently quotes Scripture in his poems.[97]

With Drepanius's description of *pontifices* and *flamines* quoted above, we may compare a speech that for some reason Drepanius did not include in the corpus of the Panegyrici, the *Gratiarum Actio* of his teacher Ausonius, undoubtedly a Christian, comparing Gratian's chastity to that of Vestals, *flamines,* and *pontifices.*[98] This passage of Ausonius is more intriguing than has (I think) been appreciated. Being virgins, Vestals were naturally supposed to be chaste, but there was no such requirement or expectation for *flamines* and *pontifices.* Perversely enough, to treat them as exemplars of chastity, as though all Roman priests were holy men, seems to be a Christian perspective. Drepanius's reference to *flamines* and *pontifices* probably recalls some description of a civic procession in an earlier panegyric where *flamines* and *pontifices* were singled out for their social prominence.

---

95. Turcan-Verkerk 2003, 72, note.
96. Nixon and Rodgers 1994, 6; cf. *Pan.* 2. 10. 5; 9. 2. 4–5; 7. 17. 3; 2. 2. 5. Given (a) the very large number of panegyrics that must have been composed year by year on every emperor and (b) what Rees 2002 (188) nicely calls the "innate transience of the genre," it is surely significant that Pacatus shows such familiarity with precisely these speeches.
97. Green 1971, 54–60.
98. Auson. *Grat. act.* 14.

This is a discovery with important ramifications. It is not just the puzzle of Pacatus Drepanius that has finally been solved. The solution raises the bar for similar puzzles in the future. If the pious Christian his poem reveals him to have been can refer to "the god who is your consort," describe the dress of *flamines* and *pontifices* as venerable, and call a Christian emperor to his face "a god we can see," it makes it harder to know at what point we can say with confidence that this or that classicizing formula could not have been written by a Christian.

7

MACROBIUS AND THE "PAGAN" CULTURE OF HIS AGE

1

Macrobius's *Saturnalia* is a key text for any evaluation of the intellectual interests of the elite of late fourth- and early fifth-century Rome. Some of the most distinguished "nobles and other learned men" of the age gather to devote the holiday from which the dialogue takes its name to literary conversation. In the first category we have Vettius Agorius Praetextatus, Q. Aurelius Symmachus, (Virius) Nicomachus Flavianus, (Publilius Caeionius) Caecina Albinus, (Ceionius) Rufius Albinus, Euangelus, and a young man called Avienus. In the second, the philosopher Eustathius, the rhetorician Eusebius, the doctor Dysarius, the Egyptian Cynic Horus, and Servius, who had recently set up school as a grammarian. A nice mix of amateurs and professionals, age and inexperience, Romans and foreigners, allowing different perspectives in the discussions that follow.[1]

The principal interlocutors are cultivated men, enthusiasts of the old learning, anxious to keep alive the old traditions. The function of those who are represented as challenging their elders and betters (Avienus, Dysarius, and Euangelus) is to force them to formulate (for the reader's benefit) views they would otherwise have taken for granted in such company. And all are pagans, Praetextatus, Symmachus, and Flavianus the most prominent pagans of the age. The dramatic date (as we shall see) is 382, the eve of the withdrawal of state subsidies from the traditional cults. And there is much discussion of pagan sacrifice and priestly practice. It is not surprising that modern readers have assumed the *Saturnalia* to be a showcase for pagan culture, according to some nothing less than a work of pagan propaganda. Indeed, study of the *Saturnalia* has overlapped with study of what has become known as the "pagan revival" of the late fourth century. Those gathered in Macrobius's pages have been identified as the circle of Symmachus—or (as some prefer) the circle of Praetextatus. It was long taken for granted that Macrobius was himself a member of this circle. But was he even a contemporary? When did he live? And what was the purpose of his work?

The writer's full name and rank—Macrobius Ambrosius Theodosius, *vir clarissimus et inlustris*—are attested in the titles and explicits to most books of both *Saturnalia*

---

1. With twelve guests, Macrobius is obviously ignoring Varro's upper limit of nine (Gellius 13. 11); there are twenty-one named guests at Athenaeus's banquet, not to mention various unnamed extras: Baldwin 1976, 38–39.

and the *Commentary on the Dream of Scipio*. There are a number of close and often extended parallels between the two works, and in every case there is either more detail or the subject matter arises more naturally in the context of the passage in the *Commentary*.[2] The natural conclusion is that *Commentary* was written before *Saturnalia*. Both are dedicated to his son Eustathius, and the prefaces to both proclaim their principal aim to be his education (implying that *Saturnalia* followed *Commentary* at no great interval). The preface to the *Commentary* refers to their joint readings of the *Republics* of Plato and Cicero, suggesting a boy in his teens rather than a small child. That fits well enough with the writer's illustrious rank (mentioned in the titles to both works), unlikely to be conferred on a man before his forties.

Three Macrobii held office at the turn of the fourth and fifth centuries: a vicar of the Spains in 399–400, a proconsul of Africa in 410, and a *praepositus sacri cubiculi* in 422. At one time all three were identified and assumed to be the writer, with the *Saturnalia* dated ca. 395 and the *Commentary on the Dream of Scipio* a decade or so earlier.[3] The *praepositus* can be ruled out at once. A *praepositus* must have been a eunuch. Yet the writer undoubtedly had a son, born of his own flesh (Pr. 1). The vicar of 399–400 and the proconsul of 410 *could* be the same man.[4] Barnes has recently argued that, as in the early empire, proconsuls of Africa continued to be appointed for a year at a time, with the year of office beginning and ending first in April and then from 407 in October.[5] On this basis only one year between 391/2 and 414/5 gives problems: precisely 409/10, where we find Macrobius attested on 25 June 410, and Palladius on 16 August and 25 September. If so, then either Macrobius was replaced before his term expired, or the date of the law is wrong. If the date is wrong, all is uncertain. If he died or was removed from office, that augurs ill for the promotion needed to provide the necessary rank of *vir inlustris*.

L. Jan's suggestion that the writer was born in North Africa is sufficient explanation of the "other sky" under which he was born.[6] We may compare Claudian's characterization of Africa as "another sky."[7] It is often inferred from his apology for lacking "the native elegance of the Roman tongue" that Latin was not his native language.[8] More probably this is no more than one of those mock modest apologies for "rusticity" so popular among late antique writers.[9] Against the earlier explanation that he was a Greek, some have pointed to his occasional mistranslations from Greek[10]

---

2. This is a revised and pruned list of the examples collected by Wissowa 1880, 12: *Comm.* 1. 6. 27 ~ *Sat.* vii. 5. 21; *Comm.* 1. 12. 1 ~ *Sat.* i. 17. 63; *Comm.* 1. 20. 1 ~ *Sat.* i. 17. 3; *Comm.* 1. 9. 2 ~ *Sat.* i. 6. 6; *Comm.* 1. 17. 14 ~ *Sat.* i. 18. 15; *Comm.* 1. 6. 60 ~ *Sat.* vii. 5. 20; *Comm.* 1. 6. 81 ~ *Sat.* vii. 9. 3.

3. Following the standard article, Georgii 1912.

4. *PLRE* ii. 698; Chastagnol 1959, 191–203.

5. Barnes in Phoenix 37 (1983), 259–60.

6. *Macrobii opera* 1 (1848), 6; there are two African bishops called Macrobius (*PCBE* i. 662–63).

7. *alterius convexa poli, Gild.* 2.

8. pr. 12; Flamant 1977, 124.

9. Curtius 1953, 83–84, 411–12. For example, Corippus, Johannis 37, *rustica Romanis dum certat Musa Camenis*.

10. Wissowa 1880, 15; Flamant 1977, 93–94.

contrasted with his obvious familiarity with Latin literature. There is a more powerful objection. In all three of his books Macrobius writes as a Latin speaker. Examples in the *Saturnalia* might be disallowed on the grounds that the speakers are mostly Romans—for example, "what the Greeks call *idein*, we call *videre* by adding the letter V" (i. 15. 16) in the mouth of Praetextatus. But there are innumerable examples in the two other works: for example, *Comm.* 1. 5. 9, "a surface (*planities*), which the Greeks call *epiphaneia*"; and from his *De verborum graeci et latini differentiis vel societatibus*: "we Romans say *curro, percurro*, they say *trecho, diatrecho*."[11]

2

There is a different and decisive reason for rejecting all known Macrobii. To contemporaries the writer was not known as Macrobius at all, but as Theodosius. As seen as early as 1614 by Jacques Sirmond and restated in 1938 by Santo Mazzarino,[12] there is solid and unambiguous evidence from within a century of the writer's death. Flamant objected that the use of proper names in late antiquity was "fanciful," and that while the possibility that he was known as Theodosius cannot be excluded, "it seems more reasonable to respect tradition" (meaning medieval tradition).[13] We may begin with some differences between late antique and medieval practice.

Although the old distinction between praenomen, nomen, and cognomen had long since disappeared by ca. 400, there were nonetheless well-established principles in late Roman nomenclature. Elite western males normally bore three or more names that commemorated various family connections; and in contexts that called for only one name, it was almost always the last and always the same name.[14]

The few exceptions known are the result of an understandable desire to avoid confusion between homonyms in the same family. To take two interlocutors of the *Saturnalia* as examples, Caecina Decius Albinus, son of Publilius Caeonius Caecina Albinus, was known as Decius rather than Albinus to distinguish him at a glance from his father. Flamant misleads when he writes of the father that the other interlocutors "arbitrarily" call him Caecina one moment and Albinus the next.[15] He was misled by the informality of the urbane literary dialogue of the *Saturnalia*—and the need to distinguish him in that specific context from another homonym, the interlocutor Rufius

---

11. *GLK* v. 599. 22 = p. 13. 5 de Paolis.
12. Mazzarino 1938, a brilliant paper published at the age of twenty-two; so too Sundwall 1915, 139, no. 467.
13. Flamant 1977, 93.
14. For a more systematic analysis, Cameron 1985, 164–82; the argument about the last name was first made (as Bruce Barker-Benfield pointed out to me) by Sirmond, in the preface *De propriis nominibus* to his first edition of Sidonius (Paris 1614), notae p. 7, citing the cases of Cassiodorus, Palladius, and Macrobius.
15. Flamant 1977, 91–95, closely followed by Armisen-Marchetti 2003, ix.

Albinus. This, not caprice, is the explanation for the subtle variation in (e.g.) iii. 14. 1–2: *subiecit Rufius Albinus, antiquitatis non minus quam Caecina peritus: miror te, inquit, Albine...et Caecina...et Rufius....*In the pages of Macrobius, Vettius (Agorius) Praetextatus is normally Praetextatus but occasionally Vettius; Q. Aurelius Symmachus normally Symmachus, but occasionally Aurelius or Q. Aurelius (never Quintus alone). But in official contexts (e.g., the addresses of imperial laws) both Rufius and Caecina are always styled Albinus, just as Decius Albinus is always Decius; so too invariably Flavianus, Praetextatus, Symmachus. On no hypothesis could Macrobius Ambrosius Theodosius have been called, in one-name contexts, both Macrobius and Theodosius.[16]

It has been objected that "Theodosius" could not be the principal name because it does not reappear in the family while "Macrobius" does. But this is to misunderstand the nature and function of family names in late antique Rome. It is true that the family name is sometimes found last and used as the diacritical: for example the Symmachi. But there are other families where the family name is seldom if ever the diacritical. For example the Nicomachi: (Virius) Nicomachus Flavianus's son was Nicomachus Flavianus, his grandson (Appius) Nicomachus Dexter. Not least there is the greatest of all late Roman houses, the Anicii. Out of the forty men and women in *PLRE* i–ii called Anicius/-a, only three have it as their diacritical, no fewer than twenty-nine as their first name. The Macrobii were one of those families where the family name regularly came first. We now have evidence for three successive generations (below): Macrobius first, followed by a different diacritical in each generation (Theodosius, Eustathius, Eudoxius).

To turn to medieval practice, men were often known by only one name followed by a title, ethnic or sobriquet: Ermoldus Nigellus, Paulus Diaconus, Sedulius Scottus, Walafrid Strabo. When faced with a sequence of three or four names, medieval copyists were liable to assume that their bearer was likewise called by the first of his names. It is no coincidence that it was during the Middle Ages that so many polyonymous late antique writers—Palladius Rutilius Taurus Aemilianus, Venantius Honorius Clementianus Fortunatus, Rutilius Claudius Namatianus, Martianus Minneius Felix Capella, all known to contemporaries by their last names—came to be called by their first names.

The habit of singling out Macrobius's first name rests, not on genuine ancient tradition, but on the application of medieval practice to ancient nomenclature. Of the hundred earliest manuscripts of the *Commentary*,[17] seventy-five carry a title, incipit or explicit (sometimes all three) offering the writer's name. Twenty-seven offer Macrobius Ambrosius Theodosius (fifteen complete with rank);[18] twenty Macrobius Ambrosius (eleven with rank); twenty-three Macrobius alone.[19] Macrobius Ambrosius and

---

16. As airily suggested, without discussion or documentation, by Armisen-Marchetti 2003, xiv. I was unable to find a single example when doing the research for Cameron 1985.

17. Information from Munk Olsen 1982. Macrobius was not among the authors he studied directly, but he did list those MSS of the *Commentary* that include Cicero's *Somnium*, less than half the total but the earlier half. According to Barker-Benfield in Reynolds 1983, 224, there are 113 MSS of the *Sat.* and 230 of the *Comm.*

18. Including such misreadings of *v.c. et inl.* as *viri consularis* or *viri eloquentissimi.*

19. In this sample, no other combination appears more than once.

Macrobius are not so much alternative traditions as simply abbreviations; for we sometimes find Macrobius Ambrosius or Macrobius alone *combined* with Macrobius Ambrosius Theodosius in the same manuscript.[20] That is to say, even in cases where the exemplar offered all three names complete with rank, the copyist would often only copy it in full once and elsewhere use Macrobius alone.

Now for the late antique evidence. First two men from the same social class sharing the same intellectual interests: Boethius[21] and Cassiodorus both offer Macrobius Theodosius.[22] So do the excerpts from a work on the Greek and Latin verb.[23] And all known representatives of La Penna's family V and Willis's IIb[24] of the *Saturnalia* offer *Macrobii Theodosii v. c. et illustris*. That the explicits to Bks iii and vii in these manuscripts preserve authentic information is confirmed by the traces they preserve of the likely original division of the work into three days rather than seven books.[25]

These witnesses all omit the same element in the full nomenclature, the Ambrosius. Outside the most formal contexts a man with three or more names never used them all; the standard practice (as in the early empire)[26] was to use two, normally the same two. For example, (Publius Caeionius) Caecina Albinus, (Virius) Nicomachus Flavianus. So too Macrobius (Ambrosius) Theodosius. Boethius and Cassiodorus could be expected to know this.

Even earlier and more authoritative is the subscription and explicit to Bk i of the *Commentary* in a very early copy of the work:[27]

> Aurelius Memmius Symmachus v.c. emendabam vel distinguebam meum Ravennae cum Macrobio Plotino Eudoxio v.c.
> Macrobii Ambrosii Theodosii v.c. et inlustris de Somnio Scipionis liber primus explicit, incipit secundus.
>
> I, the honorable Aurelius Memmius Symmachus, corrected and punctuated this my copy at Ravenna with the honorable Macrobius Plotinus Eudoxius.
> End of Bk. i of the honorable and illustrious Macrobius Ambrosius Theodosius's commentary on the *Dream of Scipio*: beginning of Bk. ii.

Such subscriptions were normally set out with considerable formality in the blank spaces between books by the subscriber himself. Whenever they can be checked, the names and titles they offer are invariably correct (Ch. 12–14). It is true that explicits cannot

---

20. Olsen nos. 121.7; 163; 237. 5; 260.5; 343; 393; 428; 530.
21. *In Isagog. Porph.* 1, S. Brandt (ed.) (*CSEL* 48) 1906, 31. 21.
22. *Expos. Psalm.*, M. Adriaen (ed.) (*CC* 1) 1958, 30. 20; 116. 125.
23. Neap. Lat. 2; see now de Paolis 1990, 5, 174, 178–89, with p. xv n. 17.
24. Marshall in Reynolds 1983, 234–35; de Paolis 1986/7, 134–35; Carton, *TAPA* 96 (1965), 30.
25. *Macrobii Theodosii v.c. et illustris conviviorum tertii diei* (explicit to Bk vii); Jan i (1848), xxxi–xxxii; Marinone 1967, 39–41.
26. Schulze 1904, 488–89; Instinsky 1969, 12, 4–6 (for the circle of the younger Pliny).
27. Barker-Benfield in Reynolds 1983, 224; for a recent discussion of the manuscript evidence, Armisen-Marchetti 2003, lxxii–lxxxviii; for the text of the subscription, Armisen-Marchetti 134.

normally claim the same authority as a subscription by two readers working within a half-century of the writer's death, but this is a special case. The three earliest manuscripts that carry the subscription, all three important witnesses not directly related,[28] offer it immediately before the explicit in exactly this form. The obvious inference is that this is the explicit that closed Bk i in the copy produced by Symmachus and Eudoxius.

In the explicit, the writer is described (as in many incipits and explicits to the *Saturnalia* as well) as *v(ir) c(larissimus) et inlustris*, the correct style for the five highest offices of state. In the subscription, both Symmachus and Eudoxius are merely *v(ir) c(larissimus)*, indicating no more than nominal membership of the senate. No more is known of Eudoxius, but Symmachus (the father-in-law of Boethius) enjoyed a long and distinguished career, prefect of Rome, consul in 485, and patrician. In the dedication of Boethius's *De Trinitate* both Boethius and Symmachus are given their full names in correct sequence and full current titles of rank (*v. c. et inl. excons. ord. (atque) patricius*). As we shall see in chapters 12–14, aristocratic subscribers all but invariably included all the titles they were entitled to. The probability is that the task of correcting the *Commentary* was completed before Symmachus had won his first illustrious office, the prefecture of Rome, held a year or two before his consulate in 485.

The most telling single piece of evidence is the dedication to Macrobius's *De verborum graeci et latini differentiis et societatibus* (which otherwise survives only in excerpts): *Theodosius Symmacho suo*. The name Symmachus is always the final, diacritical element in the family nomenclature, and the dedicator is clearly using his diacritical too. Then there is the dedication to the *Fables* of Avianus (or, as we shall see, Avienus). The "excellent Theodosius" (*Theodosi optime*) whom Avianus addresses is surely (as generally accepted) Macrobius.[29] (1) He is represented as equally at home in literature both prose and verse: "Who could speak in your company on either oratory or poetry" (*nam quis tecum de oratione, quis de poemate loqueretur?*). According to Murgia, this "seems to imply that Theodosius is an orator and a poet."[30] But that would surely require *in* rather than *de* with both nouns (or the bare ablative), nor is *quis tecum…de poemate loqueretur* a natural way to praise a man for his poetry. Avianus goes on to claim that his dedicatee "in both forms of literature outstrips Athenians in Greek learning and Romans in Latin" (*cum in utroque litterarum genere et Atticos Graeca eruditione superes et Latinitate Romanos*), where the reference to learning surely implies that he is a critic or scholar. It would be difficult to think of any writer of the age who might be more aptly so characterized than Macrobius, author of learned works on both Vergil and Cicero. (2) He is praised for his *graeca eruditio*, and while it is easy to depreciate Macrobius's learning, he had clearly read a fair number of Greek books at firsthand in a world where the ability to read Greek fluently was becoming rare

---

28. For details, see Armisen-Marchetti 2003, lxxvii–lxxxvii.
29. Allowed even by Küppers 1977, 48f., who disputed everything else I wrote about the fabulist in Cameron 1967a.
30. Murgia 2003, 68.

(Ch. 15). (3) He is also praised for surpassing Athenians in his Greek scholarship and Romans in his Latin. This is a curiously precise compliment, implying that Theodosius himself was neither Greek nor Roman (otherwise he would have been praised for surpassing *other* Athenians and *other* Romans). We may recall that he was born "beneath another sky."

So despite the preference of the Middle Ages for Macrobius, the late antique evidence unequivocally supports Theodosius. To get around it, Flamant offers a remarkably perverse reading of the subscription, deriving from an assumption that colors his entire book, that Macrobius was a card-carrying member of a pagan underground permanently at war with the Christian authorities. According to Flamant, it is "striking to note" that the copy referred to was "private." This he infers from *emendabam...meum*. He further claims that the writer did not dare to publish openly so pagan a book; since the copy in question belonged to Symmachus, not even Eudoxius had a copy of his own:[31]

> Publication of the *Saturnalia* and *Commentary* amounts to no more than the circulation of the original copy among a few close friends. The silence that surrounds both books down to Boethius (who will learn of them by the same route) confirms this hypothesis.

But there is nothing unusual about this *meum*. It is the standard way a subscriber refers to his own copy: for example, "temptavi emendare...*meum*" in Sabinus's subscription to Persius or "relegi *meum*" in a manuscript of Boethius (for many more examples, p. 435). As we shall see, the physical copies in which these subscribers actually wrote were private, but the works they contained had been published in the ordinary way. It is true that Symmachus does not identify the copy against which he corrected his own. But the fact that he did the job together with a descendant (probably grandson) of the writer creates a presumption that Eudoxius was able to supply a family copy—if not the writer's autograph, at any rate a copy corrected against it. Yet Flamant, carried away by his two *idées fixes* of secret publication and Macrobius as principal name, concluded instead that the writer's names were already out of sequence in Symmachus's copy. All that remained was to suggest that Boethius and Cassiodorus got their information from this same "corrupt" edition, and the way was clear to prefer the medieval evidence and reinstate "tradition."

But what likelihood is there that medieval copyists had access to an authentic tradition unknown to Boethius, Cassiodorus, and the writer's grandson? It is among the Theodosii of the *Code* we should be looking, not the Macrobii. As it happens, Theodosius is a much less common name among the western governing class than might have been suspected. The Christian prosopography of North Africa shows only one.[32] Of the

---

31. Flamant 1977, 137.
32. Aug. *Ep.* 222. 3; *PCBE* i. 1109.

twenty-one Theodosii from the fourth and fifth centuries listed in *PLRE* i–ii, only one (excluding members of the imperial family) held the rank of *vir inlustris*, the praetorian prefect of Italy in 430.[33]

This identification, which would imply a date after 430 for his literary activity, is now generally accepted by historians, though some dissent was expressed in other quarters.[34] Since the point is central to a true understanding of both Macrobius and the last pagans of Rome, a fresh study is in order, taking objections and improvements into account, incorporating a key piece of new evidence, and (more important in the context of this book) adding a new interpretation of the supposedly "pagan" culture of the *Saturnalia*.

Both *Saturnalia* and *Commentary* are dedicated to a son called Eustathius.[35] A bronze tablet of unknown provenance (*ILS* 813) attests a certain Plotinus Eustathius as prefect of Rome under some regrettably unnamed emperors and the patrician Ricimer, that is to say between the outside limits of 451 and 472. Eustathius was the name of Macrobius's son; and at *Comm.* i. 8. 5 he proclaims Plotinus "chief with Plato among the teachers of philosophy." What name more appropriate for a neoplatonist to give his son—a name only otherwise found among the aristocracy in his only other identifiable descendant, Macrobius Plotinus Eudoxius.

The suggestion that Plotinus Eustathius was Macrobius's son, advanced in 1966, has now been put on a quite different footing by Silvio Panciera's publication of a new inscription from Rome revealing that this man's full name was *Macrobius* Plotinus Eustathius.[36] Eustathius was only a child when he received his father's two dedications. If that was ca. 430, as here suggested, then by ca. 460 he could have been in his forties, the right sort of age to be urban prefect. Furthermore, by ca. 480, he could have had a son of his own in at least his twenties, a contemporary of Aurelius Memmius Symmachus, the future consul of 485, with whom he revised the text of the *Commentary*. The following stemma surely compels assent—and excludes a date substantially earlier than ca. 430 for Macrobius's literary activity:

Macrobius Ambrosius Theodosius, praetorian prefect 430

|

Macrobius Plotinus Eustathius, city prefect 461/65

|

Macrobius Plotinus Eudoxius, friend of Symmachus cos. 485

---

33. The only other possibility is the Theodosius *primicerius notariorum* in office in 426—in all probability the same man at an earlier stage of his career: § 16 end.

34. Cameron 1966, 25–38; for later discussions, Paolis 1986–87, 113–32; Armisen-Marchetti 2003, viii–xiv.

35. Rather than Eustachius: Marinone 1967, 63; De Paolis 1986/7, 150.

36. F.l. Macrobius Pl[otinus E]ustathius, v(ir) [c(larissimus)…]…[ex ab]strusis lo[cis…]aen…, Panciera *Tituli* 4 (1982), 658–60, with Tav. XXIV. 1 = 2006, 1101–2.

The new inscription, though very fragmentary, reveals that Eustathius was one of a number of magistrates (often urban prefects) of the late fourth and fifth centuries who spent from their own pockets to restore and transfer to more appropriate settings neglected statues. The usual formula in such dedications is that the official rescued the statue from some hidden, out of the way, deserted, obscure, dirty or squalid spot (*abditi, avii, infrequentes et inculti, obscuri, sordentes, squalentes loci*). Here the phrase is [*ex ab*]*strusis l*[*ocis*]; the statue had been hidden away somewhere. It has often been assumed that the reference is to statues removed from disused or ransacked pagan temples. But the earliest examples date from the end of the third century, and the prefects involved seem to be indifferently pagan or Christian.[37] More probably these dedications simply represent a continuing policy of urban renewal. The antiquarian in Macrobius would have been proud of a son who spent his time and money salvaging and refurbishing precious relics of the Roman past.

3

In the first chapter of the *Saturnalia* Macrobius (it would be pedantic to start calling him Theodosius again at this late hour) concedes that he has included among his interlocutors "one or two" (*unus aut alter*) whose "mature years fell later than the age of Praetextatus." He cites (after Athenaeus) the venerable precedent of Plato, who made Parmenides and Socrates dispute *de rebus arduis* although "the latter as a boy could hardly have met the former in his old age...with Plato to support me I do not need to count up on my fingers the ages of the interlocutors."

Does this mean that Macrobius represented one or two characters older than they actually were at the dramatic date of the *Saturnalia*? So I assumed in 1966. So too Marinone, who placed Servius's date of birth nearer 380 than 370, assuming that, though represented in the dialogue as a young man, in reality he just was a boy at the time.[38] The only interlocutors who come into question are Avienus, Servius, and Decius Albinus. All the others were undoubtedly old enough to debate *de rebus arduis* with Praetextatus, and some comment is made about the youth of precisely these three. But why warn about the anachronism and then show them young in addition? Perhaps, as Bruggisser has argued,[39] the anachronism lies less in the age assigned them at the dramatic date than in what they are given to say so young: they are represented as speaking with an erudition and authority beyond their true age at the time.

---

37. Ward-Perkins 1984, 43–44; Curran 1994, 46–58, arguing for "the beautification of the late antique city." It has been argued that (e.g.) *sordentes* implies the pollution of pagan temples, but the verb is in fact regularly applied to dilapidated buildings in need of repair (*ILS* 5510, 5702, 5733). For a list of inscriptions, Panciera 2006, 1102.

38. Marinone 1970, 188, going further than his edition (1967, 33, "intorno al 370"); so too Holtz 1981, 225.

39. Bruggisser 1984, 162–73.

The clearest illustration would be Servius. Though represented as having only recently begun to teach (*inter grammaticos doctorem recens professus*) and full of becoming modesty,[40] Servius is nonetheless spoken of as "by far the greatest professor of all," excelling "the teachers of old by his learning."[41] Vergil is a major theme of the *Saturnalia*, and Servius was the leading Vergilian authority of his generation. Just as Eusebius is presented as the outstanding Greek rhetorician, Dysarius the outstanding doctor, and Symmachus the outstanding orator, so in the interest of the discussion Servius is anachronistically accorded the authority of his more mature years.[42] What we know about Decius's career bears out this interpretation. He was *consularis* of Numidia some time between 388 and 392, governor of Campania in 397–98, and city prefect in 402. His father (himself an interlocutor) is said to have been a contemporary of Symmachus (*Sat*. i. 2. 15), who was born ca. 340. Chastagnol conjectures that Decius was born ca. 365, in which case he would indeed have been too young for scholarly debate in 382.

Of Servius's works other than the Vergil commentary, a treatise on metre is dedicated to a young noble called Albinus, described as "glory of the *praetextati*,"[43] that is to say a youth of less than sixteen years, younger than Servius himself. Chastagnol and Flamant identified him with the interlocutor Rufius Albinus, but a man who was prefect of Rome in 389 could not have been less than sixteen at the earliest possible date for Servius to have written anything. As for Caecina's son, Decius Albinus, championed by Zwierlein,[44] if born ca. 365, he must have been an older contemporary of Servius. It is obviously most unlikely that Servius wrote such a work before he was himself sixteen. Decius Albinus can also be eliminated on other grounds: as we have seen, he was known as Decius, not Albinus.

Servius's dedication goes on to give another clue: the young Albinus is said to be "spurred on by the *daily* example of his father and grandfather (*cotidie urgearis exemplo*), to whom literature owes the greatest reverence." That is to say, his father and grandfather were both still alive. Surely Decius's son, Caecina Decius Aginatius Albinus, whose first recorded post is a precocious urban prefecture in 414, when he was *vitae flore puer sed gravitate senex*.[45] The two living literary forbears would then be Decius and his father, Caecina, both prominent enough in the world of letters to be interlocutors in the *Saturnalia*. Caecina, still alive ca. 400 (Jerome, *Ep*. 107. 1), was Symmachus's contemporary, and Aginatus Albinus cannot have been born later than ca. 390 to be prefect in 414—nor much earlier, given the dates of his father and grandfather. His sixteenth birthday would have fallen ca. 405. If so, Servius's *de centum metris* would have been written between 400 and 405.

---

40. i. 2. 15; 4. 4; ii. 2. 12, 13; vii. 11. 1, 3, 10.
41. i. 2. 15; 1. 24. 20; vi. 6. 1; vi. 7. 3, 4; vii. 11. 2.
42. i. 2. 7; i. 7. 1; v. 1. 7.
43. *GLK* iv. 456.
44. Zwierlein 1983, 36–38.
45. Rutilius, *De reditu* i. 470: Barnes, *Phoenix* 37 (1983), 264.

Confirmation of the aristocratic connections implied by this dedication and his participation in Macrobius's gathering is provided by the preface to Servius's *De metris Horati*, which he claims to have written "while enjoying leisure in Campania."[46] Evidently, he had access to one of those Campanian estates where the rich liked to spend their time when it was too hot in Rome. No doubt it belonged to the (otherwise unidentifiable) *d(ominus) n(oster)* Fortunatianus to whom the book is dedicated.[47]

If Servius had just begun to teach as a *grammaticus* in 382, he cannot have been born later than ca. 360. Such a date is supported by a letter of Symmachus addressed *Servio* that Seeck dated on other grounds to 396.[48] Nothing in the letter identifies its recipient as a grammaticus, but given the extreme rarity of the name[49] and the care Macrobius seems to have taken over such details, it may be that Servius really was known (however slightly) to Symmachus, in which case he may have achieved a certain measure of renown by 396.

The identity of Avienus is more problematic. Socially speaking, the interlocutors fall into two groups: in Macrobius's own words, "aristocrats and other learned men" (i. 1. 1). In the first group, Praetextatus, Symmachus, Flavianus, the Albini, and Euangelus.[50] In the second, men of more humble birth who qualify by their various professional specialties: Dysarius, Eusebius, Eustathius, Horus, and Servius. Avienus has no specialty. Despite the fact that, like the professionals, he is introduced by only one name, he is surely (as Küppers argued) an aristocrat.[51] When we first meet him he is waiting at Praetextatus's house with Rufius Albinus when the other guests arrive. Because Eustathius refers to "your Apuleius" when addressing Avienus, Barnes claimed him for an African.[52] But in the mouth of a Greek, here as elsewhere in Macrobius, the possessive simply identifies a Latin speaker.[53]

The key text is i. 6. 26, where, while explaining how aristocratic *cognomina* were passed down from generation to generation in the great families, Praetextatus turns to Avienus: "So too your own Messala, who derives his name from the *cognomen* won by Valerius Maximus when he captured the famous city of Messana in Sicily." The distant ancestor is M.' Valerius Maximus Messala cos. 263. B.C. But who is "your Messala"? Both Davies and Marinone translate "your friend Messala," but two other combinations suggest a closer relationship. Gennadius Avienus cos. 450 is said by Sidonius to have belonged to a family known as the Corvini,[54] and one of his grandsons bears the

---

46. *cum in Campania otiarer, GL* iv. 468. 6; Kaster 1988, 359.
47. The *d. n.* would seem to rule out identification with the rhetorician C. Chirius Fortunatianus (Schanz-Hosius IV. 1. 184–85) suggested in *PLRE.*
48. *Ep.* viii. 60, with Seeck cxcix; cf. lxii and lxv.
49. Only one other example in *PLRE* i–iii, one in *PCBR* i (both Africa in 384) and not one in *ILS* or *ILCV.*
50. Despite his uncouth manners, Evangelis is at any rate a landowner, with an estate at Tibur (vii. 16. 15).
51. Küppers 1977, 40–47. Decius and Postumianus (below), both aristocrats, are likewise given only one name.
52. vii. 3. 24; Barnes 1982, 79.
53. As noted by Jan; cf. (again from Eustathius) *Homerus vester Mantuanus* (i. 16. 43) and *hic vester*, again of Vergil (v. 2. 17); and from another Greek, Eusebius, *in Cicerone vestro* (v. 1. 4).
54. *Ep.* i. 9. 4; *PLRE* ii. 193–94. This connection was already made by De Rossi, *ICVR* i p. 328; Küppers 1967.

name Messala.[55] The Corvini must (it seems) have claimed descent from M. Valerius Messala Corvinus cos. 31.[56] It seems natural to infer that Macrobius's Avienus belonged to the same family.

K. Smolak argued that the interlocutor Avienus was one of the many sons of the geographical and astronomical poet Rufius Festus Avienus.[57] But unlike so many fourth-century aristocrats, who boasted of descent from the nobility of the Republic, the poet made much more modest claims about his ancestry, publicly tracing his descent from the Neronian philosopher Musonius Rufus and the second-century Rufii Festi, all equestrians from his native Volsinii.[58] No son of the poet could have switched the family story so dramatically as to claim descent from the Republican Valerii.

The interlocutor Avienus should be identified with the fabulist Avianus, whose name should in fact be spelled Avienus.[59] Most manuscripts of the *Fables* give the author's name as Avianus, but three of the earliest give Avienus. Avienus is also found in Eugenius of Toledo, a well-informed ninth century grammatical work, and four medieval library catalogues from France and Germany.[60] For Küppers, Avienus arose from confusion with Rufius Festus Avienus. The exact converse is more likely. Not only were the latter's geographical and astronomical poems scarcely read in the Middle Ages,[61] an inscription from Bulla Regia has revealed that his correct name was Postumius Rufius Festus *qui et* Avien*i*us. That is to say, the final element is Avien*i*us, not Avienus; and a *signum* or nickname, not a *nomen* (in formal contexts he was known as Festus).[62]

There is also the consideration that the *Fables* are dedicated to a Theodosius who must be Macrobius. Under the circumstances it would be understandable and appropriate for Macrobius to have returned the compliment by casting their author as one of his interlocutors. It was after hearing that he was going to receive a dedication from Varro that Cicero decided to make Varro an interlocutor in his *Academica*.[63] Moreover, at the end of a section (vii. 8. 8.) lifted from Alexander of Aphrodisias's *Problemata physica* (i. 52) on why heavier food is sometimes easier to digest than lighter food, Macrobius adds a less relevant illustration "of his own" (as Jan notes in his commentary): the reed bows before the wind that tears an oak tree out of the ground. The story of the oak and the reed happens to be one of Avianus's *Fables* (no. 16). In the circumstances it is natural to conclude that Macrobius took his picturesque illustration from his friend the fabulist.[64]

---

55. Fl. Ennodius Messala 2 cos. 506 in *PLRE* ii. 759–60.
56. *Ep.* i. 9. 4; *PLRE* ii. 193–94; for the posterity of Messala Corvinus, Syme 1986, 227–43, with stemma IX.
57. In Herzog and Schmidt 5 § 557.
58. The Rufii Festi of Volsinii are in fact very solidly documented: Matthews 1967.
59. Cameron 1967a; against, Küppers 1977, 10–64; in favor, Schmidt 2009, 68–76.
60. *GLK* Supp. 174. 15; 183. 30; 185. 23; for the other references, Cameron 1967a, 390–92; Gaide 1980, 8–9.
61. Smolak in Herzog and Schmidt 5 § 557. 6 C.
62. For more detail, Cameron 1995, 252–62.
63. Cic. *Att.* xiii. 12. 3.
64. Schmidt 2009, 72–74, citing further parallels between them, argues that Avianus drew on Macrobius.

4

How closely can we pin down the dramatic date of the dialogue? The *terminus ante quem* is 384, when Praetextatus died. In 1966 I argued for 384 itself, a potent year in the decline of the pagan cause. I now believe that Macrobius had a slightly earlier date in mind, the *Saturnalia* (17–22 December) of 382. There can be little doubt that he was thoroughly familiar with the conventions of the literary symposium and dialogue. Much of the relevant material has been collected by Martin and Flamant, though their interpretations are not always subtle or sympathetic. For example, two of the stock figures (going back before even Plato to Homer) are the uninvited guest and (a later development) the Cynic.[65] Of the two, only the Cynic has an established function, to provoke the other interlocutors by his contrariness. But Macrobius makes his uninvited guest play the role of the Cynic, while his Cynic is a perfect gentleman. Flamant suggests that Macrobius misunderstood the conventions. We shall soon see that he was influenced by a more practical consideration.

That Macrobius knew Cicero's *De Republica* well is proved by his commentary on the *Somnium Scipionis*. In addition, he deliberately evokes a number of other Ciceronian dialogues:

> If men such as Cotta, Laelius and Scipio will be discussing the weightiest matters in the writers of old for as long as Roman literature endures, men of similar stature and no less merit, Praetextatus, Flavianus, Albinus, Symmachus and Eustathius, may be permitted to speak in the same way. (i. 1. 4)

Cotta was featured in *De Oratore* and *De Natura Deorum*; Laelius and Scipio in *De Senectute* and *De Republica*. A notable convention of the genre, ultimately deriving from Plato's *Phaedo*,[66] was to set the scene of a dialogue shortly before the death of the principal interlocutor. The dramatic date of *De Senectute* is 150 B.C., a year before the death of the elderly statesman Cato; the dramatic date of *De Oratore* is 91, only ten days before the death of the great orator Crassus (*De Oratore* iii. 6); *De Republica* is set in 129, shortly before the death of Scipio Aemilianus. Tacitus's *Dialogus* is probably another case.[67] *De Amicitia* offers an interesting if self-explanatory variation on the pattern: Laelius leads a discussion on friendship shortly after the death of his lifelong friend Scipio. And in a sort of parody of the convention, Trimalchio closes his dinner party with a drunken preview of his own funeral.[68]

Macrobius was certainly familiar with the convention, since he twice alludes to Scipio's impending death in his *Commentary* (vii. 9; viii. 2). Another dialogue he surely

---

65. Martin 1931, 64–79; Flamant 1977, 197–98.
66. Most doubt whether Macrobius had read the *Phaedo* (see Flamant 1977, 587), but it depends what is meant by "read." It is unlikely that he was completely ignorant of the *Phaedo*.
67. For more details, Cameron 1967a, 258–61; Bartsch 1994, 104–5.
68. Petronius, *Sat.* 78.

knew at firsthand—one very much after his own heart—is the *Deipnosophists*.[69] Athenaeus too explicitly states that his principal interlocutor Ulpian died a few days after the feast.[70] Praetextatus was both host and principal interlocutor. On any hypothesis the *Saturnalia* is set not long before his death. The question is, how long? The examples of the *Phaedo* and *Deipnosophists, De Oratore* and *De Republica* might suggest an interval of only days. But *De Senectute* was set a year before Cato's death. While it was appropriate for an old man to describe the blessings of old age, he could hardly be convincing on his deathbed. That moment was better suited (as in the *Phaedo*) to a discourse on the immortality of the soul.

Praetextatus was still alive on 9 September 384. But he was dead by 1 January 385, when he was to have entered on the consulship for that year. The festival of the *Saturnalia*, concerning which Praetextatus himself is made to give a long disquisition in Bk i, began on 17 December. The conversations Macrobius describes purport to have taken place on the eve of the festival and its first three days—that is to say, 16–19 December.

Only during a holiday could busy Roman aristocrats have managed to devote three consecutive days to uninterrupted discussion. In 1966 I assumed that Macrobius chose the nearest holiday to the day on which Praetextatus died, just as Cicero chose the holidays closest to the deaths of Scipio and Crassus. Yet the situation cannot be so simple. It was not till the second week of January that Decius Albinus (who had been unable to attend) is represented as calling on Postumianus to hear his account of the conversations he had missed. Postumianus was so busy with his law practice that Decius had waited till the holidays "which fill much of January" (*Sat.* i. 2. 1), evidently meaning the Agonalia and Carmentalia, falling on 9, 11, and 15 January. This itself (it should be underlined) is a piece of calculated antiquarianism. For by Macrobius's day the traditional Roman system of *dies fasti* and *nefasti* was no more, following a law of 389.

When Postumianus begins his tale he says nothing about Praetextatus having died since 19 December. We cannot disregard dates that Macrobius himself spells out so precisely. The dramatic date of the dialogue cannot after all have been December 384. Perhaps then (as Ronald Syme suggested to me in 1966) the *Saturnalia* of 383, "the eve of a crisis." This would explain some surprising silences. Unlike Cicero, Macrobius says nothing about the political situation at his dramatic date. It is understandable that he should have chosen not to speak openly about Gratian's attack on the state cults. But this is not his only silence. During much of 384 Symmachus was city and Praetextatus praetorian prefect and consul designate. The pressure of Postumianus's legal work is twice mentioned, but not a word on the holidays providing a welcome relief from the burdens of office for Symmachus and Praetextatus. And yet, while

69. *Athenaei enim convivium ante oculos fuisse Macrobio docet universa Saturnaliorum forma, docet ratio et dispositio dialogi similis, docet argumentorum in tanta varietate tanta similitudo* (Kaibel, 1 [1887], xxxi–xxxii). Courcelle 1948, 10–11, argued for a common source, but see Martin 1931, 286, and below, p. 584.

70. xv. 686C; Athenaeus's host is a certain (P. Livius) Larensis; on him and the more serious problem of the identification of Ulpian, Baldwin 1976, 21–42.

Symmachus, as city prefect, would naturally have been resident in Rome, the praetorian prefect should have been at court in Milan. Nor is there a word on Praetextatus's impending consulship. In December 384, Praetextatus would surely (if alive) have been overseeing the preparations for his consular inauguration, at this date normally held at court when the emperor was in residence. Furthermore, if Praetextatus is the prefect of the *Poem against the Pagans* (Ch. 8), he was seriously ill for three months before his death. Macrobius must have known this much about the lives of his most important protagonists, and why suppress such circumstantial details?[71]

Praetextatus did not become praetorian prefect until spring 384, and so might well have been in Rome for the *Saturnalia* of 383. But rather than just settle for 383, perhaps we should take a closer look at the role the festival itself plays in Macrobius's book. The parallel with the holidays in Cicero's dialogues is inexact. The Ludi Romani are only mentioned by name once in *De Oratore*.[72] The *Saturnalia* are mentioned by name fifty times in Macrobius, not to mention many indirect allusions; nearly thirty pages are devoted to the origin of the festival. Cicero's Ludi Romani do no more than identify a holiday ten days before Crassus's death. It is hard to believe that Macrobius devoted so much attention to the *Saturnalia* simply to fix a date—especially since he does *not* in fact fix it. Whether or not he foreshadowed Praetextatus's death in one of the now missing later parts of the dialogue, he certainly does not do so in the part actually devoted to the *Saturnalia*.

We must direct our attention to other aspects of the dramatic situation. Cicero set both *De Republica* and *De Oratore* during moments of political crisis, the divisive consequences of the tribunates of Tiberius Gracchus and Livius Drusus, respectively. The year 384 saw not only the death of Praetextatus, but the defeat of Symmachus's plea for the restoration of the altar of Victory and state subsidies to the pagan cults. Perhaps it is not so much the death of Praetextatus that hangs over Macrobius's *Saturnalia*, as the death of Roman paganism. In the eyes of contemporaries, they may have seemed closely linked. However little Praetextatus could have done if he had lived, his death at such a moment was a major blow to his fellow pagans. Symmachus resigned his prefecture and opted out of the battle.

Modern scholars tend to pick the year 394 as the last crisis of western paganism. But Gratian's withdrawal of state subsidies to the cults was arguably the blow from which they never recovered. Pagans made at least six successive attempts to get the ban rescinded (Ch. 2). Cicero set his heroes squarely in the thick of the political troubles of his dramatic dates. Scipio was the leader of the anti-Gracchan faction in 129; Crassus delivered the most brilliant speech of his life attacking the consul Philippus on the eve of the Social war.[73] Macrobius chose not to do this. Instead he showed his

---

71. There are lacunae in ii, iii, and iv, but the beginning of the work was the obvious place for such allusions.

72. i. 14; alluded to at i. 57; ii. 13; iii. 1–2.

73. *De Republica* i. 19; vi. 12; *De Oratore* i. 24; iii.1f.; Astin 1967, 238–41; E. Rawson, *JRS* 62 (1972), 33–45.

protagonists in relaxed discussion of the old state cults as though they were still thriving and unthreatened. The last moment that was possible was the eve of Gratian's disestablishment of the cults, the end of 382. The *Saturnalia* of 382 (it might be argued) was the last major public holiday before the first of the successive strokes of doom that overwhelmed Roman paganism.

But let us recall those words quoted above from the opening of the *Saturnalia*, where "men like Praetextatus and Flavianus" are compared to "men like Cotta, Laelius and Scipio." When Cicero wrote *De Republica*, *De Oratore*, and *De Natura Deorum*, all his interlocutors were long since dead. In fact, although in some dialogues Cicero cast himself and his friends as interlocutors, he had originally intended *neminem includere in dialogos eorum qui viverent* (*Att.* xiii. 19. 3). And he never mixes the living with the dead. In choosing contemporary interlocutors there was always the risk of giving offence to those left out: witness his rewriting of the *Academica* to substitute Varro for Brutus when he heard that Varro had been dropping hints to Atticus that he would like to be represented—and his hesitation at the last moment whether or not to write Brutus back in again.[74]

It is here that Döpp raised his principal objection to the original formulation of my thesis, making the surprising claim that Cicero *did* mix the living and the dead—and precisely in *De Natura Deorum*. In fact, *De Natura Deorum* is the only member of a third category of dialogue in which the only surviving interlocutor is Cicero himself. Its dramatic date is 77 or 76 and it purports to be a discussion in which (like Tacitus in his *Dialogus*) Cicero took part as a young man. Cicero (like Tacitus) himself contributes nothing to the dialogue, less even than Decius Albinus to the *Saturnalia*. The other interlocutors, as in *De Republica*, *De Amicitia*, and *De Senectute*, are all men of an earlier generation, long dead when Cicero wrote.

Macrobius chose Praetextatus and his circle for the same reason. Like Cicero, he was evoking great names of the *past*. And surely when he wrote they were *all* dead. Flavianus died in 394, Symmachus in 402. Caecina Albinus was still alive in the period 400/405; Euangelus in 397; Postumianus in 395 when, since his grandfather was alive in 314, he must have been fairly old.[75] Eusebius represents himself and Dysarius as "knocking at the door" of old age at the dramatic date (vii. 10. 1). Decius was a much younger man, but there is no direct evidence that he lived beyond 402. Horus, a boxer before he turned to philosophy, was an Olympic victor in 364, when presumably in his twenties or thirties.[76] Rufius Albinus was alive when Rutilius wrote in 417, but nothing suggests that anyone except Servius and Avienus lived any later.

Were Servius and Avienus still alive? Avienus was apparently the younger, since his youth is mentioned more often and more emphatically than Servius's. In fact, it is this very feature of his characterization that suggests that he too was dead when Macrobius

---

74. See Plasberg's preface to his Teubner edition (1922), iiif.
75. Chastagnol 1987, 254–56.
76. See his entry in *PLRE* i. 445.

wrote. It is youthful ignorance that prompts most of Avienus's interventions. Early on it leads him to make a fool of himself. At *Sat.* i. 4. 2–3 he expresses surprise at some archaism used by Caecina Albinus. Caecina replies with nothing but a tolerant smile, and Symmachus asks Servius to explain. When Servius has finished, Avienus indignantly objects to this cult of archaism: "You might as well be talking with Evander's grandmother." This time no less a person than Praetextatus delivers a crushing rebuke: "Hush, pray...let us not insolently abuse the reverence we owe to antiquity, mother of the arts."[77]

Within the structure of the dialogue this ignorance is (of course) a dramatic device, allowing Avienus to ask more basic questions than his wiser fellow guests. More interestingly, as Kaster acutely pointed out, Avienus is "the one participant whose character undergoes a development during the course of the dialogue." He does not learn his lesson all at once. The very next time he opens his mouth it is to "interrupt, as was his way" (i. 6. 3). But by later books he is applying himself to his betters with the utmost deference (v. 1. 2; vi. 7. 1–4; vii. 2. 1), winning high praise for his readiness to learn (vii. 3. 23). Avienus is nothing less than a "link between the age of Praetextatus and Macrobius's own"—the proof that Macrobius's generation can still learn from the past.[78] This is his main function in the dialogue.

Schmidt has suggested that Avienus was actually a younger contemporary of Macrobius, who published his *Fables* after the *Saturnalia*. But it is doubtful whether the real Avienus would have been flattered to be included, not for the reputation of his mature years, but as an example of youthful ignorance reproached and redeemed. He was surely dead when Macrobius wrote—an older contemporary recently dead. It was perhaps the reflection that Avienus's lifetime formed a bridge between his own and Praetextatus's generation that gave Macrobius the idea of using him in this way.

5

From Thilo to Döpp, it has been taken for granted that Servius's *Aeneid* commentary was not published when Macrobius wrote.[79] Yet this can scarcely be reconciled with the dates so far established: Servius born no later than ca. 360 and *Saturnalia* published no earlier than 430. Nor can the problem be eased by supposing that the commentary was a work of Servius's old age. For cross-references establish that the *Aeneid* was actually the first of his Vergil commentaries, followed by the *Bucolics* and finally the *Georgics*.

---

77. *nec insolenter parentis artium antiquitatis reverentiam verberemus,* i. 5. 4.
78. Kaster 1980, 42–48, developed in more detail by Schmidt 2009, 64–68.
79. Döpp 1978, 630, followed by Brugnoli, *EV* iv (1988), 806, refers Servius's allusion (on *Aen.* vii. 604) to Gothic ferocity to Alaric. But this would have been as appropriate in 440 as 380—or at any time in between.

The case for the priority of Servius boils down to one argument:[80] if Servius's commentary had been available to Macrobius, surely he would have used it when compiling the series of Vergilian interpretations he put into Servius's mouth at *Saturnalia* vi. 6–9. As it is, Servius is made to repeat page after page copied from Gellius. The argument is less compelling than might appear. Indeed, a much stronger case can be made for its converse. For the truth of the matter is that, despite their common concern with Vergil and approximate contemporaneity, *neither* shows any knowledge of the other.

If the *Aeneid* commentary were later than the *Saturnalia*, then, if he was born by 360, that would entail that most of Servius's works were written after the age of seventy. We may surely exclude the possibility that both published simultaneously and so independently. Even if neither actually quotes from the other, Macrobius explicitly presents Servius as the great Vergil authority of his age. Although careful to preserve his dramatic fiction by introducing a modest young man who has only recently begun to teach in 382 (*Sat.* i. 2. 15), he goes on to praise him in terms that barely maintain the fiction; already by i. 24. 8 he is said "to excel the teachers of old." At vi. 6. 1 Caecina refers to the "ready store of annotation" (*adnotationis*) he has built up from "explaining" (*enarrando*) Vergil to the youth of Rome every day. The words *adnotatio* and *enarrare* (the latter used again of explanations put in Servius's mouth at vi. 7. 2)[81] suggest line-by-line commentary rather than after-dinner conversation. Why after all would Macrobius import Servius into Praetextatus's circle *as a Vergil commentator* at the cost of anachronism if he were not known as a Vergil commentator at the time of writing? It might be urged as a last resort that at the time of writing Servius was known to be working on his commentary but had not yet published. Yet every Latin *grammaticus* spent most of his time commenting on Vergil. Alone in his generation Servius *published* a commentary on the whole of Vergil, a commentary that soon eclipsed all competition, even Donatus.

Those who believe that the *Saturnalia* appeared first have to explain why Servius did not quote or even mention Macrobius. He would after all have had every reason. Does he not himself appear as one of Macrobius's pundits? What about the seventy-odd Vergilian interpretations put in his own mouth, almost none of them (as we shall see) reflecting his published view of the passages in question? According to Marinone, the Vergilian interpretations in the *Saturnalia* are not Macrobius's *personal* views but material transcribed from his sources, monographs on Vergilian topics or treatises like Gellius. So there were no genuinely "Macrobian" interpretations to quote or refute. But in what way are Macrobius's interpretations *more* derivative than those of Servius, who likewise for the most part copied them from earlier sources—often the very same sources as Macrobius (Ch. 16)?

But if Servius had published first, there are a number of reasons why Macrobius might have chosen *not* to quote him. First and most obvious, it would have violated

80. Marinone 1970, 181–211.
81. The *vox propria* of the grammarian's activity (*TLL* v. 2. 550 β).

his dramatic fiction to quote from a book not published till a generation after his dramatic date. Second, it would have been inartistic, not to say tedious, to quote at length from a recent work that he could expect to be in the hands of all serious readers. Third, Servius posed Macrobius a problem he did not have with his other interlocutors. None of the others had published a voluminous work on the very subject assigned him in the dialogue; Macrobius had a free hand with them. Given the importance of the *grammaticus* in everyone's initiation into Vergil, it was natural that he should want one among his interlocutors, a professional to balance the learned amateurs. Servius was the best known in the neighborhood of his dramatic date, yet Macrobius cannot have wished to be circumscribed by the published views of the real Servius. There had always been a certain tension between men of letters and professional grammarians, clearly documented in several passages of the *Saturnalia* itself. It would be surprising if a man who elsewhere speaks so slightingly of grammarians (p. 590) had given his unqualified approval to even the most famous of the breed. Indeed, Kaster has identified some specific respects in which the views of the Macrobian Servius differ markedly from those of the real Servius.

In his first utterance, Macrobius's Servius appears as a champion of archaic usage against the "modernist" attack of the ignorant young Avienus. Avienus takes exception to the forms *noctu futura* and *die crastini*. Servius in reply cites a number of examples of *noctu*, but for the other expression only an analogy, *die quinti* from Coelius Antipater, to which Praetextatus adds the praetorian formula *die noni*.[82] As Kaster saw, this is not just something the real Servius happens not to mention. It is something he would *never* have said. Servius is above all things a prescriptive grammarian, constantly drawing attention to the "rules" Vergil violates and warning his students what the poet "should have said" (*debuit dicere*)—meaning (of course) what they should be saying.[83] Servius of all people would never have advised a student to extend an anomalous usage by analogy. In a note on *Aen.* i. 4 he starts straight off by warning his pupils that there are lots of peculiar usages in Vergil "and we do not invent others on their basis" (*nec ad eorum exemplum alia formamus*). This recurring Servian use of the present (*formamus, ponimus, dicimus*) has a strongly prescriptive force, in effect *formare, ponere, dicere debemus*.[84]

For Marinone (as for most other critics) it seemed incredible that Macrobius should draw on Gellius if he had Servius himself at hand.[85] But what if it was not the *views* of the

---

82. Both taken from Gellius x. 24. Gellius himself cited no example of *die crastini*. It was presumably the lemma (*"die pristini," "diecrastini" et "diequarti" et "diequinti," qui elegantius locuti sint, dixisse, non ut ea nunc volgo dicuntur*) that suggested both word and treatment to Macrobius. The lemmata derive from Gellius himself (Holford-Strevens 2003, 30) and in any case are already present in the fourth-century Vatican palimpsest (P. K. Marshall, in his OCT, 1 [1968], v–vi).

83. Kaster 1988, 171–81.

84. So Kaster 1988, 181, citing examples where *dicimus* "plainly serves the purpose for which *debuit dicere* is used elsewhere." But as J. N. Adams pointed out (*CR* 41 [1991], 100–101), there are also many cases where it does not.

85. Marinone 1970, 203.

real Servius he wanted, but the authority of an idealized Servius as one more mouth-piece *for his own views*? In vi. 7–9 Servius is represented discussing a series of problem-atic passages in Vergil, in every case reproducing material from Gellius (ii. 6; v. 8; 16. 6; 18. 5). The Gellian material is skilfully divided up between Avienus and Servius so that the inexperienced Avienus puts texts and problems before the master for his solutions.

Significantly enough, however, it is again almost all material that the real Servius not only did not but *would* not have used. Marinone found it significant that in vi. 6 the Macrobian Servius briefly characterizes no fewer than fifty-seven passages, only nine of which are provided with any remotely similar comment by the real Servius. But so gross a discrepancy can hardly be put down to simple ignorance of the real Servius. Given the fact that Macrobius drew on Servius's own principal source, namely Donatus, we should expect greater overlap than this on as many as fifty-seven passages picked at random. We need to pay more attention to the context. For some thirty pages the two Albini have been illustrating Vergil's debt to earlier poets, when Caecina suggests that Servius should quote "some of the poet's own inventions, not borrowed from the ancients or, if so, adapted in a bold, original but tasteful manner."[86]

Excellent idea, cries the modern reader, who has had quite enough of Vergil's bor-rowings. But anyone familiar with the real Servius will recognize that this is not one of his specialties: *nove dictum*, "novel phrase," is not a positive term in Servius's critical lexicon. For Servius, what is *nove dictum* offends against some rule: on *sacris litatis* at iii. 221: *"diis litatis" debuit dicere... ergo nove dixit; nove... cum proprie...*, "novel, because properly..." (ix. 48). More succinctly, *satis nove et adfectate*, "novel and affected" (*Aen.* iii. 221), *nove et satis licenter*, "novel and against the rules" (viii. 268). The half-dozen examples of *nove* in the DS scholia do not carry the same degree of disapproval.[87] There is an amusing definition of the limits within which *novitas* is tolerated in Servius's commentary on Donatus's *Ars*: if deliberate and "supported by appropriate prece-dent," it passes muster as a "figure" (*figura*); if inadvertent, it is a "fault" (*vitium*).[88] Macrobius's "original but tasteful" (*nove quidem sed decenter*) the real Servius would have dismissed as an oxymoron.

Like the five preceding chapters of the book, vi. 6 too is excerpted from some prob-ably first-century polemical treatise, this time rebutting the charge of plagiarism by quoting original Vergilian turns of phrase. There is no basis for associating any of this material with the real Servius. In most of the fifty-seven passages the Macrobian Servius cites for their originality, the real Servius has no note at all. Where he does, it is not enthusiastic.[89] For example, where the Macrobian Servius holds up *vir gregis* = he-goat (*Buc.* vii. 7) for our admiration, the real Servius disapprovingly notes "inappropriate:

---

86. *ab ipso figurata, non a veteribus accepta, vel ausu poetico nove quidem sed decenter usurpata*, vi. 1. 1.
87. On the DS scholia, essentially Donatus, see Ch. 16, passim.
88. *quicquid scientes facimus novitatis cupidi, quod tamen idoneorum auctorum firmatur exemplis, figura dici-tur. quicquid autem ignorantes ponimus, vitium putatur* (*GL* iv. 447. 8–10); Kaster 1988, 174.
89. For a classified list of examples, Uhl 1998, 463–75.

only applies to human beings." On iii. 339 he objects that Vergil's use of *superare* for *vivere* is "novel and without a parallel" (*sane nove, et caret exemplo*). Where the Macrobian Servius admires *tepidaque recentem / caede locum* (*Aen.* ix. 455–56), literally "a place fresh with warm blood," for its novelty, Servius raps out the label *hypallage* and credits "many critics" with the banalization *tepidumque recenti* ("a place warm with fresh blood"). The Macrobian Servius draws attention to the extended humanization of the bees in *Geo.* iv, notably the *Quirites* of 201. "Boldy said," comments Donatus with apparent approval (preserved in DS); no comment in Servius.

In at least three cases the Macrobian Servius uses Gellian material that is also found, slightly abbreviated, in Servius Danielis (DS). That is to say, it is Donatan material that the real Servius deliberately omitted (p. 574). In each case problematic or puzzling phrases are explained with reference to parallels from archaic writers, Cato, Ennius, and Accius.[90] It can hardly have been ignorance alone that led Macrobius to credit his fictitious Servius so systematically with views so different from those of the real Servius. He could, after all, so easily have assigned him an area of Vergilian scholarship in which the real Servius excelled.

It is thus particularly striking that it is in this of all contexts that Macrobius puts in Servius's mouth the often quoted lament: "this is what comes of our neglect of the classics; since our generation has deserted Ennius and all the old books, we are ignorant of much that would be clear to us if we were more used to reading the old authors" (vi. 9. 9). Servius is not the only character to whom this sentiment is assigned: Rufius Albinus claims that by imitating them Vergil has kept alive the old poets "whom we are beginning to mock as well as neglect."[91] But vi. 9. 9 is much the most emphatic statement, and it is Servius again who is represented as apprehensive that people now find Ennius contemptible "amid the more polished elegance of our own age" (i. 4. 17).

There can be no doubt that by the early fifth century archaic Latin writers were again in eclipse. While complete texts of the early writers were no longer current, passages imitated by Vergil were kept alive in commentaries up to and including that of Donatus. But by the end of the fourth century there came about a change of taste that was to be decisive for the ultimate fate of early Roman poetry. During the course of the century almost the entire range of early imperial literature came back into vogue. Not surprisingly, it was some while before this change of taste penetrated the conservative world of the *grammaticus*, but it had finally done so by Servius's day (Ch. 11).

Laments about the neglect of old writers began in the age of Nero, with Valerius Probus, whose successful attempt to revive their study played an important part in the second-century archaizing movement.[92] Earlier critics assumed that, when

---

90. On *vexasse* (*Buc.* vi. 76), *equitem* (*Geo.* iii. 116) and *squalentem auro* (*Aen* x. 314) in vi. 7. 4–17 and vi. 9. 8–12 (from Gellius ii.6 and 18. 5).

91. vi. 1. 5; cf. vi. 3. 9.

92. Suet. *De gramm.* 24; Jocelyn 1967, 61–62.

plagiarizing his texts from works of this period, Macrobius simply included the comments along with the texts. This goes too far. The references to neglect of old writers come in the symposiastic frame, to which he devotes considerable care, not in the lists of quotations. Avienus's sneering description of the incompetent grammarian who gave a poor answer to his question (vi. 9. 1–3) is closely modeled on Gellius's description of an incompetent grammarian who gave him the same answer to the same question (*NA* 16. 6). But the skilful way Macrobius adapted his source to his own context makes clear that he was consciously making the sentiment his own.

In the circumstances, for Macrobius to make Servius lament the neglect of Republican writers is surely more pointed than it seems at first sight. Such a sentiment could have been assigned to any of his antiquarians, yet he selected the one whose abundant published work reveals him the least appropriate mouthpiece. It is precisely the Republican quotations in Donatus that the real Servius systematically omitted in favor of "modern" poets (Ch. 11 and 16). By contrast, such parallels as there are between Macrobius and the Servian corpus are overwhelmingly with the richer DS material Servius omitted. That is to say, the real Servius represents the modernizing tastes that Macrobius, through his fictitious Servius, so deprecates.

This systematic misrepresentation of the real Servius must be deliberate. Donatus would have suited his purpose better, but he was long dead by Macrobius's dramatic date.[93] Servius was by no means simply an abridged Donatus; he had a better sense of meter and prosody and sometimes shows better judgment in choosing between interpretations—and in cutting out some of the foolishness that was coming to dominate Vergilian studies (Ch. 16). But he was not nearly so interested in Macrobius's two primary areas of interest: early Republican writers and the details of Roman priestly practice. One final point. The degree of misrepresentation of the real Servius strongly suggests that when Macrobius wrote he too was safely dead.

6

Not surprisingly, a number of Macrobius's interlocutors are either mentioned in Symmachus's letters or received letters from him. It is not the least of the objections to the traditional assumption that Macrobius was himself a contemporary and intimate of Praetextatus and Symmachus[94] that there are no Macrobii (or Theodosii) anywhere in Symmachus's correspondence. If the *Saturnalia* had been published during Symmachus's lifetime, it is even harder to explain his failure to mention it. For almost

---

93. Jerome dated Donatus's floruit to 354 (*Chron.* s. a.); Holtz 1981, 18–19, placed his birth ca. 310, and wondered whether he was still alive when his pupil Jerome left Rome in 385. The evidence of Macrobius suggests not.

94. "The author of the *Saturnalia* belonged to this circle not only on account of his literary and religious interests, but also socially" (Bloch 1945, 206).

two-thirds of his nine hundred surviving letters belong to the period between 395 and his death in 402—precisely the period in which the composition of the *Saturnalia* used to be set. Yet Macrobius was certainly the friend of *a* Symmachus (witness the dedication of the *De differentiis*, "Theodosius Symmacho *suo*"). With Q. Aurelius Symmachus himself ruled out, evidently a Symmachus of a later generation.

If the *Saturnalia* did not appear till after the publication of Symmachus's letters (between 402 and 408), naturally this was where Macrobius turned for information about Symmachus and his friends.[95] For example, two of the stock characters required for a literary symposium were a doctor and a Cynic.[96] Where did Macrobius find his doctor, Dysarius, and the Egyptian philosopher/pugilist Horus, whom he describes as a Cynic? Dysarius happens to be the only doctor mentioned in Symmachus's *Letters*, an *amicissimus vir* described as the outstanding doctor of the age in very similar terms to Macrobius's characterization.[97] As for Horus, in the ordinary way one would scarcely have expected to encounter a man with so suspect a social background at Symmachan soirées. But Symmachus does refer to a philosopher called Horus as a "long-time dear friend," praises his erudition, and adds that he "counts it among the chief gifts of fortune to enjoy the company of people of quality"[98]—a wish that Macrobius fulfilled for him. Since Symmachus does not say that Horus was either Egyptian, a Cynic, or a former boxer, Macrobius must have had some other source for these details. Libanius mentions a student of rhetoric called Horus who was an Egyptian and an Olympic victor.[99] But Macrobius may just have invented the detail about his being a Cynic to fulfil the requirements of the genre.

More important, where did he find his uninvited guest, the boorish Euangelus? On the usual view, Euangelus is an invented character, so named because he is meant to be seen as a Christian. Since his principal role in the dialogue is to disparage Vergil and deny him the erudition praised by the other interlocutors, it might indeed seem tempting to conclude, with virtually all modern critics, that Macrobius expected readers to understand Euangelus as representing Christian hostility to classical culture. As we shall see in chapter 16. 8, this is a major misunderstanding of the *Saturnalia* as a whole. Euangelus is unmistakably represented as a pagan, and his aggressive, antagonistic behavior is simply a structural device designed to create some appearance of

---

95. This note gives a selection from a list of parallels kindly sent me by James Willis suggesting that Macrobius had read Symmachus's letters: *viros edecumatae honestatis* (Sym. 3. 49; 3. 51) ~ *edecumatos...sodales* (Mac. i. 5. 17; ii. 1. 8); *multiiugis paginis* (Sym. 1. 13) ~ *multiiugis libris* (Mac. ii. 1. 8); *laetitia...ostentatrix sui* (Sym. 1. 37. 1) ~ *sui ostentatrix continentia* (Mac. vii. 4. 3); *clam te esse non patior* (Sym. 4. 70. 1; 1. 16. 1; 1. 44. 1) ~ *clam te esse non pateris* (Mac. vi. 7. 3); add *insubidas* (i. 4. 1) ~ *insubide* (vii. 14. 3).

96. *Sat.* i. 7. 2–3; J. Martin, *Symposion* (1931), 79–92; 69–79.

97. *qui inter professores medendi summatem iure obtinet locum* (Symm.) ~ *qui tunc praestare videbatur ceteris medendi artem professis* (Macr. i. 7. 2); *ep.* iii. 37; also mentioned in *ep.* ix. 44, both letters of reference (which is why they specify his profession).

98. *Ep.* ii. 39; *PLRE* i. 445.

99. *Ep.* 1278; the other texts are all collected in *PLRE* i. 445.

controversy among Macrobius's interlocutors, on the analogy of Cicero's dialogues, in which the principal speakers all advance different points of view. Macrobius faced more of a problem since his principal interlocutors are all represented as more or less uncritical admirers of the past. His two main devices to provoke disagreement are Avienus's ignorance and Euangelus's contrariness.

Nor is Euangelus pure invention, because a man of that name is mentioned in a letter of Symmachus dated to 397. Nor can there be much doubt why Macrobius chose this man for the role of agent provocateur in his dialogue. Symmachus's letter describes how his impetuosity (*incautus animus*) made him willing to take risks, a man who was "no friend" of his son-in-law, the younger Flavian (*Ep*. vi. 7. 2). Flavian (he adds) will be distressed to hear that Euangelus, his "enemy" (*aemulus*), is leaving for court on the same errand as Flavian (Honorius's consular celebrations in Milan).[100] Flavian's fears that Euangelus will do him harm at court have usually been taken to imply that he was a Christian.[101] Yet we must resist the temptation to see everything in terms of Christian-pagan conflict. As Ammianus's *History* so memorably reveals, the Roman upper classes lived in a world of rivalry and feuds, and Flavian's arrogance won him enemies from an early date. It is unlikely that this bad blood between Flavian and Euangelus was widely known, but in the published correspondence he stood out for all to see as just the sort of man whose "unwelcome arrival" would "bring a frown to most of the guests" (*Sat*. i. 7. 1).

Macrobius uses the imperfect tense of all three: Euangelus *erat*; Horus *habebatur*; Dysarius *tunc…videbatur*; the *tunc* is a giveaway in itself, betraying a writer of a later age. We saw earlier that Macrobius transposed the roles of Cynic and uninvited guest in his dialogue, and we can now see why. Not a misunderstanding of the conventions after all. Horus the Cynic was a dear friend of Symmachus while Euangelus was a troublemaker and a personal enemy of the younger Flavian. It was more in keeping with the known personalities of the interlocutors to assign Euangelus the role of devil's advocate.

On the chronology here proposed (soon after 430), the *Saturnalia* was written some fifty years after its dramatic date. Flamant thought that the personality of Praetextatus stood out too vividly for so long an interval, comparing Cicero's portraits of Crassus and Antony. On the contrary, one of the strongest arguments in favor of a late date is precisely the absence of personal details or touches of intimacy: Praetextatus "with his usual gravity…with the unruffled kindliness he showed to all alike…for all his unfailing forbearance, serenity and strength of character" (i. 5. 4; i. 7. 2, 5). This sublime figure is not a real person, but an idealized Roman senator and sage. The very parallels Flamant cites undermine his point. For Cicero's *De Oratore* was composed thirty-six years after its dramatic date (91/55); *De Republica* seventy-five years after (129/54–51).

---

100. For *aemulus* in Symmachus, see Matthews 1986, 163–75.
101. Marcone 1983, 72; Callu, *Symmaque: Lettres* 3 (1995), 151; and most earlier critics.

7

Georgii's dating of the *Saturnalia* to 395 was problematic in itself, quite apart from the many pointers to a much later date. On the one hand, to present such champions of the pagan cause as Praetextatus, Symmachus, and Flavian discussing pagan festivals in private conclave only a year after the débâcle of the Frigidus might seem to identify its author as a militant pagan—except for what they are actually given to say. In particular, it is hardly conceivable that anyone writing in the vicinity of 395 would assign the elder Flavian a speech on, of all subjects, augural law (i. 24. 17). According to Rufinus, he had employed haruspicy to prophesy victory for Eugenius (Ch. 3)—a prophecy famously and embarrassingly falsified.

In 395 the younger Flavian was living in retirement and disgrace, obliged to convert and repay his father's salary as praetorian prefect. Believers in a continuing pagan reaction have always been reluctant to accept that his conversion was genuine. For Hartke and Chastagnol and more recently Grünewald,[102] he paid only lip service to Christianity, all the while secretly pursuing his destiny as leader of the pagan cause. What he actually did during his period of disgrace was bide his time and use his connections (notably his father-in-law, Symmachus) to ingratiate himself with the new Christian regime in Milan.

Those who have claimed the *Saturnalia* as a work of pagan propaganda can have read only extracts. One believer in the early date went so far as to call it a pagan "machine de guerre,"[103] Yet if the book has a pagan agenda, why is its paganism so relentlessly antiquarian? The first subject discussed by this notorious band of pagans is the genitive plural of the word *Saturnalia*. Why no reference to the state of those same festivals in the fourth century? Why (above all) no hint of Christianity? The traditional explanation is contemptuous silence, most eloquently expressed more than a century ago by Gaston Boissier:[104]

> At the very moment he shows them meeting to celebrate one of their most ancient and respected festivals, the emperor was preparing to ban sacrifices and close the temples. A few years later, when Macrobius was writing his book, the religion he glorifies was proscribed, persecuted, close to destruction. And yet not a word in his book betrays this sad state of affairs. Not one reference to the dangers paganism was running and to which it would succumb. The author, a loyal pagan (dévot), must have been profoundly grieved, but he reveals nothing of this grief. It is natural that he should feel a furious hatred towards the religion that was suppressing his own and would supplant it; yet the name

---

102. Hartke 1940, 164; Chastagnol 1962, 242; Grünewald 1992, 481.
103. Türk 1963, 327–49.
104. Boissier 1 (1891), 208–12 (my translation); so too (e.g.) Flamant 1977, 687.

of Christianity is not so much as mentioned. We may be sure that he was thinking of it all the time, to curse and revile it; yet he never speaks of it.

It was in the pages following this passage that Boissier enunciated his famous doctrine of a general pagan "conspiracy of silence" about Christianity. He had been amazed to find no mention of Christianity in the pagan grammarians, orators, poets, and historians of the age.

The silence is deafening enough, but is *conspiracy* the right word or *contempt* the right explanation? Occasionally, no doubt, but to assume it everywhere is not only to create a widespread pagan resistance without any direct evidence[105] but to misunderstand a fundamental feature of the secular culture of the age. The traditions of such long-established literary genres as classicising poetry, ceremonial oratory, and historical writing effectively barred mention of so alien a subject as Christianity. Indeed, for many, Christians and pagans alike, these restrictions were a positive advantage. More will be said on the subject in later chapters: for the moment it will suffice to refer to Liebeschuetz's discussion of the "neutral monotheism" of fourth-century panegyric as providing "a wide area of common ground between Christians and pagans."[106] We should not be misled by the polemical writings of an aggressive Christian minority. For the majority on both sides who wished to avoid confrontation, the "conspiracy of silence" was actually a welcome solution.

Most of all does the hypothesis of contemptuous silence conflict with the relaxed, nostalgic tone of the conversation Macrobius puts in the mouths of his band of pagans. Once we recognize that the *Saturnalia* was written a half-century later, an entirely different and far simpler explanation offers. The most striking single feature of the mise-en-scène of the book is the way the interlocutors constantly speak about pagan sacrificial practice in the present tense. A few illustrations will give some idea of the tone of this part of the discussion: "it is impossible to make an acceptable offering to the gods by prayer alone, but he who prays to the gods must also lay hold of the altar with his hands" (iii. 2. 7); "it is well known that, when sacrifice is to be made to the gods above, purification is effected by ablution of the body, but aspersion alone is deemed enough when an acceptable offering is to be made to the gods of the lower world" (iii. 1. 5);[107] "it is also a duty of the pontiffs to make known the names which properly belong to sacred places" (iii. 4. 1); "the celebration of a religious festival consists of the offering of sacrifices to the gods or the marking of the day by a ritual banquet or the holding of public games in honour of the gods" (i. 16. 4); "while the victim is being slain no legal business may be done, but in the interval between the

---

105. "the contemporary Christian menace...can only be inferred," Levine 1966, 210; many similar judgements could be cited.
106. Liebeschuetz 1979, 285–302.
107. Servius on *Aen.* iv. 635 gives an abbreviated version of this note in the imperfect tense (*aspergebantur...abluebantur*).

slaying of the victim and the placing of the offering on the altar such business may be done, although it is again forbidden when the offering is being burned."[108]

Hitherto even those who have minimized the paganism of the *Saturnalia* (and that includes my own 1966 discussion) have taken it for granted that such passages (which could be multiplied almost indefinitely) are at any rate a natural reflection of the author's paganism. Yet it should be noted that there is no suggestion that these rituals are true or necessary, still less that they are neglected, endangered, or banned. Within the world of the *Saturnalia* they are simply taken for granted. The point at issue is not sacrifice itself, but some picturesque attendant detail: when aspersion rather than ablution is sufficient; which are the intervals during sacrifice when legal business may be transacted. These are scarcely central issues of late fourth-century paganism.

A recent study assumes that holding the altar while praying was still important to fourth-century pagans.[109] But Macrobius only raises the point because he is explaining why *Vergil* makes his heroes do so at *Aen.* iv. 219 and vi. 124, and the only evidence he cites is a fragment of Varro on the *origin* of the gesture. There is no suggestion that this was current practice. Compare *Sat.* iii. 12. 3: "it is agreed (*constat*) that those who now (*nunc*) sacrifice at the Ara Maxima are crowned with laurel." According to another recent study, "The attentive observation of this ritual detail suggests that Macrobius' diners speak as contemporary witnesses of the cult's activity, an impression confirmed by the usage of the present tense."[110] But on top of misinterpreting the present tense, this fails to take account of *constat*, Macrobius's stock formula for an interpretation agreed on by earlier commentators (p. 611). His source is not autopsy, but the scholarly tradition. Indeed, he goes on to cite Bk ii of Varro's *Antiquitates*. The reference of that "now" is not 382, but the period after rather than before the foundation of Rome. It is Varro's now, not Macrobius's. As we shall see in chapter 16, Macrobius found both details at second- or thirdhand in Vergil commentaries.

In fact, almost all these passages on sacrificial and pontifical practice come in discussions of Vergil. Any reader of Vergil must be struck by the large number of passages that refer to or describe cult acts, notably sacrifice.[111] Since Vergil's aim was mainly aetiological, the rituals he describes were often archaic by his own day; many must have been obsolete and all but forgotten by even the most learned pagans by the fourth century. Explaining such references for modern readers was (and remains) a scholarly task requiring considerable expertise in archaic Roman religion. Since so much of the *Saturnalia* is devoted to elucidating other aspects of Vergil's art, why resist the obvious explanation here?

Macrobius could simply have written an expository treatise on Vergil's debt to archaic Roman religion. Instead, he chose to cast his material in the form of a dialogue.

---

108. i. 16. 3; cf. i. 15. 22 on the days when *nefas est sacra celebrari*; i. 16. 2f., *festi dis dicati; festis insunt sacrificia epulae ludi feriae*; and iii. 4. 1, *pontificalis observatio est.*
109. Saggioro 2002, 252–53.
110. McDonough 2004, 657.
111. For a convenient list of such texts, Bailey 1935, 42–59.

At a purely stylistic level, this saved him the labor of translating the innumerable present tenses of his sources into cumbersome imperfects.[112] More important, the dialogue form enabled someone writing for a (by the 430s) almost entirely Christian readership to distance himself from potentially dangerous subject matter while at the same time producing something closer to a work of literature than a philological treatise. A key element in the mise-en-scène of a literary dialogue was the choice of interlocutors. In Macrobius's case the choice was especially delicate. If his interlocutors were to discuss such matters with the right degree of expertise, seriousness and respect, obviously they could not be Christians.

Since it was a well-established convention to set literary dialogues in the past,[113] the obvious solution was to set the scene far enough back to have all pagan interlocutors. Inevitably, that meant *before* Gratian's disestablishment of the cults. In a mis-en-scène constructed with any serious regard for the political realities of its dramatic date, pagans who took the apparatus of the state cults seriously could not have been represented ignoring the restrictions imposed in 382, much less the subsequent outright proscription of sacrifice in 391. What Macrobius wanted was a context in which pagans could be shown talking about the old cults as if they were still a going concern. He wanted to show Praetextatus, Symmachus, and Flavian discussing pontifical trivia and picturesque details rather than the threat of Christianity and the future of paganism. December 382 was the last moment when those present tenses he needed were possible.[114] Not too long before then, or he would lose the advantage of interlocutors who were still well-known names—and had living descendants he could compliment through praise of their ancestors.

Certainly Macrobius excluded the Christian threat that hung over the real pagan world of 382, but not out of resentment or fear. Fifty years after the event, his purpose in presenting his interlocutors as pagans could be seen as literary rather than religious. He chose the eve of the crisis of Roman paganism as his dramatic date, not because he was interested in the crisis of paganism, but because he was interested in *pre*-crisis paganism. His theme was more the paganism of Vergil than the paganism of Symmachus and Praetextatus.

Nothing in the manner of his exposition suggests that he was a believer, still less that his aim was to promote belief. The core of his material is solidly antiquarian. Once a new topic is under way, all pretence of urbane after-dinner conversation is gone: without pausing for breath, the interlocutor of the moment produces an unbroken stream of citations from obscure monographs many centuries old. Both the quotations

---

112. More on these present tenses in Ch. 16.

113. Most of the forty-three Christian dialogues analyzed by P. L. Schmidt, by contrast (in Furhrmann 1977, 103–80), are set in the present, naturally enough since most are concerned with contemporary theological issues.

114. It is not known whether Gratian's measures fell as late in the year as December 382, and Macrobius himself may not have known the exact date. The Theodosian compilers were apparently unable to find a copy to include in their Code of 438.

and often enough the controversies that lie behind them are second- or thirdhand. But at the beginning and end of these antiquarian extracts Macrobius did his best to create the illusion of a real dialogue among real pagans. Whence the "pagan sentiments" put into the mouths of his interlocutors: they are part of the mise-en-scène.

At i. 24. 22, the slave "whose duty it is to burn incense before the Penates and maintain the storeroom" (*cui cura vel adolendi Penates vel struendi penum*, based on *Aen.* i. 703, *cura penum struere et flammis adolere Penatis*) in Praetextatus's house informs his master that his fellow slaves have finished their annual feast. At one level the writer's purpose is certainly to show us that Praetextatus is a good pagan. Not however to promote paganism, but simply to provide background and prepare us for the subject matter of the dialogue. So too i. 17, where Avienus asks Praetextatus about what we now call solar syncretism: "I have asked myself earnestly and often how it is that we worship the sun sometimes as Apollo, sometimes as Liber, and at other times under a number of other different styles." Since Avienus is the youngest of the interlocutors and the closest to Macrobius's own generation, it is certainly instructive that he is so unmistakably represented as a pagan. But we must be careful not to misplace the emphasis. Avienus is not being held up for admiration or imitation as a follower of the old ways. On the other hand, this is not just the sort of casual pagan reference we might expect to find in a pagan writer. It is purely dramatic, another skilfully devised element in the mise-en-scène. Given the decision to have an all-pagan group, what more natural than that a new topic should be introduced by one pagan asking another "Why do we worship" in such and such a way? There are in fact many other such passages. At the end of the first's day's discussions Flavian announces that "*his* Penates" (*Penates mei*) will be honored to host the company next day (i. 24. 25). Praetextatus describes how "in our sacred rites we call on Janus... (*in sacris quoque invocamus*) as Janus Geminus, Janus Pater" and a variety of other names (i. 9. 15). The Egyptian Horus tells Avienus that in the worship of Saturn "*your* rite (*ritus vester*) differs from that of the Egyptians" (i. 7. 14), where the "your" identifies Roman pagans.

8

While it was necessary for the subject matter of Macrobius's dialogue that his interlocutors should be pagans, he uses them for antiquarian rather than specifically pagan ends. Even when they discuss religious questions, their exchanges and polemic alike are concerned with the establishment of colorful facts by appeal to old books, not the religious questions themselves. They are presented (as fifty years after their death they could be) as scholars first and pagans second, modern versions of the Ciceronian ideal of *viri clarissimi et sapientissimi* (*De Rep.* i. 13).

We have an instructive parallel to this attitude in the reinscription of the monument in honor of the elder Flavian in the Forum of Trajan in 431 (Ch. 5. 4), ignoring his paganism and treating him as a great man of an earlier generation victimized by personal enemies. If Macrobius is indeed Theodosius, prefect of Italy in 430, then it is unlikely that he had published either *Commentary* or *Saturnalia* by 430, since before then he did not hold the illustrissimate securely attested by the titles to both works. The composition of the *Saturnalia* is thus to be placed precisely in the period following the rehabilitation of an idealized Flavian. We need not suppose that Macrobius wrote at the instigation of the younger Flavian. There is no trace of apologia for the elder Flavian, nor is he singled out in any way from the other interlocutors.[115] But it is natural to suppose some sort of connection between these two more or less contemporary enterprises. At the very least, the reinscription of the monument will have eased any doubts he had and illustrated in a concrete way the purification that the passage of the years could bring. In fact, Macrobius took it one step further. In his pages Flavian appears as more than a famous man of letters; his devotion to the old cults, glossed over in the imperial letter, is made explicit, as it could be now that the cults themselves were safely gone.

It is also suggestive—and surely more than coincidental—that so many of the contemporaries and colleagues of the prefect of 430 should have had forbears who appear in the *Saturnalia*. The praetorian prefect of Italy in 431 was the younger Flavian, and the prefect of Rome a year or so before 431 his nephew the elder Flavian's grandson, Nicomachus Dexter. In 429 the praetorian prefect was Rufius Albinus's son Rufius Volusianus. It is surely Volusianus who explains the inclusion of Rufius Albinus. As for Macrobius, it will be recalled that he dedicated a book *Symmacho suo*. Which Symmachus? Memmius Symmachus, the son of Q. Aurelius Symmachus, is not attested in any office after his praetorship in 401, and it has often been assumed that he died young. But we have so little documentation for the early fifth century that the discovery of an inscription attesting him as prefect of Rome in the 420s would come as no surprise. He had a son, Q. Aurelius Symmachus cos. 446,[116] evidently the father in turn of Aurelius Memmius Symmachus cos. 485. We have already found Symmachus cos. 485 in the company of Macrobius's grandson, and on balance I am inclined to identify Macrobius's friend as Memmius Symmachus.

The work opens with a certain Postumianus repeating to Decius Albinus an account of the discussions at the *Saturnalia* he had heard from Eusebius (*Sat.* i. 2. 1–14). Second-order narrators are a conspicuous feature of Platonic dialogues, but why these particular names? In 382 Decius Albinus was too young for the actual dialogue, but why introduce him at all? The explanation is surely a compliment to another of Macrobius's contemporaries, Decius's son Caecina Decius Aginatius Albinus, prefect of Rome in 414 and 426, prefect of Italy in 443–49, and consul in 444.[117] The compliment also embraced Decius's father, the interlocutor Caecina

115. At least in what survives; it must be borne in mind that Flavian's major contribution in Bk iii is lost.

116. The entry in *PLRE* ii. 1042–43 gives his name as just Symmachus, overlooking the version given in the consular date to *Nov. Val.* 21. 1; presumably the Q. Aur. *Symmchi v. c.* on the Flavian amphitheatre seat *CIL* vi. 32162, less plausibly identified with the consul of 485 in *PLRE* ii. 1044 (Cameron 1982, 144).

117. *PLRE* ii. 50–53; Chastagnol, *Fastes* 273–74. A long career, sometimes divided between two men.

Albinus. According to Macrobius, Caecina and Symmachus were contemporaries and close friends. But though Decius received seven letters (vii. 35–41, datable to 396–98), there is no letter to Caecina, nor (like Rufius Albinus) is he mentioned in letters to others (Ch. 10. 5).

As for Postumianus, there is the eloquently named Rufius Praetextatus Postumianus, consul in 448 and prefect of Rome twice before that date. The implied connection with both Praetextatus and Postumianus is very suggestive.[118] And if Avienus, the youngest of the interlocutors, was the grandfather or great-uncle of Gennadius Avienus cos. 450, one of the two most powerful men of his day,[119] Macrobius surely knew the (for us) missing generation between them. We have seen already how Macrobius chose some of his minor interlocutors: we can now see why he chose the aristocrats he did—and why the Symmachi, Flaviani, and Albini are so prominently represented. The interlocutors of the *Saturnalia* reflect less the original circle of Praetextatus in the pagan 380s than their descendants, the circle of Macrobius himself in the Christian 430s.

But there is one omission that, once noted, demands an explanation: the younger Flavian. Born ca. 358 and so about twenty-four in 382, he was perfectly old enough to be shown taking part in a learned discussion held that year. Why then is he not among the interlocutors of the *Saturnalia*? The Caeonii Albini, father and son, are both represented, though Decius Albinus was not even as old as the younger Flavian in 382. Given the fact that he was still alive and prominent as late as 431, it must have crossed Macrobius's mind to include him, if only along with Decius in the proem as one of the younger characters who missed the actual gathering.

There are two possibile explanations, not mutually exclusive. First, on the evidence so far analyzed, Macrobius followed the traditional custom of excluding the living from the company of his interlocutors. If he published the *Saturnalia* in the early 430s, it may be that he excluded Flavian quite simply because at the time of writing he was still alive. If so, then he is not likely to have published the book long after 431, when Flavian was already in his mid seventies.

Perhaps more important, by the 430s Flavian had professed Christianity for nearly forty years. For Macrobius to present him discussing the old cults in the vividness of dramatic dialogue (in the present tense) with such notorious pagans as Symmachus, Praetextatus, and his own father would have been an unwelcome reminder that he too had once been an active member of that band. At the very moment he was so conspicuously promoting himself on the basis of his father's rehabilitation, he could not afford any suggestion that the family paganism was still alive. Important as the concept of cultural continuity is in the *Saturnalia*, in this area at least, by making sure that all his

---

118. Mentioned in letters of Symmachus in 395–96: *PLRE* i. 719; Matthews 1967, 499–502 for Postumianus.
119. See his entry in *PLRE* ii. 193–94.

interlocutors were safely dead, Macrobius preserved a discreet distance between his own day and the age of Praetextatus.[120]

9

It used to be taken for granted that the *Saturnalia* painted a firsthand picture of the interests and ideals of the circle of Symmachus. But if Macrobius wrote in the 430s, this view must be abandoned. Nor is it just that Macrobius saw the age of Praetextatus through the rose-colored spectacles of one who had heard of it only from old men. Kaster has warned against emphasizing what he calls "the purely elegiac aspect of the dialogue," as if the age of Praetextatus was a golden age irretrievably past. He suggests a rather different emphasis: "*not long ago* there were great men *just as* in the time long past. Macrobius's moralizing recreation...is meant to provide a metaphor and model for his own day."[121] The age of Praetextatus as it is portrayed in the pages of the *Saturnalia* is Macrobius's own construction and has a contemporary purpose.

Nor should we suppose that Macrobius thought the culture and wisdom of the age of Praetextatus beyond his own contemporaries. Just as Cicero cannot really have considered Crassus and Antonius better or more learned orators than himself, so we should not make the mistake of supposing that Macrobius looked on himself as no more than epigone and amanuensis. It is after all his words we are reading, not those of Praetextatus and Symmachus. When he laments contemporary neglect of the great writers, he does not include himself. Far from it. The *Saturnalia* was intended to remedy the situation; it was a polemical work. Macrobius was in effect trying to spearhead a revival of antiquarian scholarship.

This is why he was willing to use the principle of analogy to extend an archaic usage into the present. It is simply one aspect of his "ideal of cultural continuity."[122] Just as the generation of Praetextatus and Symmachus were "men of similar stature and no less merit" than Scipio and Laelius; just as Avienus, the youngest member of the company, learns from his older contemporaries in the course of the dialogue; so likewise Macrobius's generation can learn from the material he has collected. Both *Commentary* and *Saturnalia* are dedicated to his son, and the prefaces make clear his pedagogical purpose. But it is not the limited education of the schools he has in mind. As he says of the *Saturnalia*: "much knowledge, much instruction, examples drawn from many ages, but informed by a single spirit" (pr. 10).

The new date also has repercussions on the wider story of the Greek renaissance of the following century. In the still-standard work of Pierre Courcelle, "Beginning

---

120. Schmidt 2009 identifies Avienus as Gennadius Avienus cos. 450. But it is surely incredible that Macrobius would so emphatically draw attention to the paganism of a living, younger contemporary.
121. Kaster 1980, 260.
122. Kaster 1988, 174.

with the first third of the fifth century, all trace of literary culture disappeared in Italy.…No literary work…reveals any trace of Hellenism.…There was nothing to foretell the splendid outburst of Greek literature induced by the reign of Theodoric at the beginning of the sixth century."[123] He was working on the assumption that Macrobius wrote in the fourth century. But with Macrobius's three books situated where they belong in the 430s, and Martianus Capella's *De nuptiis Philologiae et Mercurii* redated to the same general period,[124] the discontinuity is much less sharp. Macrobius can be seen rather as the harbinger of the Boethian revival. His *Commentary* was studied by Symmachus the future consul of 485 with the aid of the writer's grandson, and soon after by Boethius and Cassiodorus. With Macrobius and Servius put in their proper place, there is little to suggest that the real circle of Symmachus proper boasted any serious Greek scholars (Ch. 15). There may be an added significance in the dramatic date of the *Saturnalia*; it was the death of Praetextatus, who, if not a scholar, at any rate dabbled in the study of Aristotle, rather than the death of Symmachus that marked the end of an era.

The most distinguished writer of the age *not* on Praetextatus's guest list is the future historian Ammianus Marcellinus. In Bk 22. 7 Ammianus mentions that Praetextatus happened to be in Constantinople when Julian arrived there at the end of 361 and was appointed proconsul of Achaea. He then tells a series of anecdotes about Julian's behavior at Constantinople, most of them unattested elsewhere. When he goes on to add that "Praetextatus was present on all these occasions," we are surely justified in inferring that Praetextatus was his informant. Why else should he have thought to say this and how else could he have known?[125]

It was presumably in Rome that he met Praetextatus, in the early 380s. Given the social gulf between them, it would be going too far to infer a friendship, but more than a chance encounter is implied. One would like to believe that Praetextatus recognized some of the remarkable qualities of this Greek ex-soldier who had set himself the daunting task of continuing Tacitus down to his own times. They had a number of interests in common.[126] But even if Macrobius had known of the connection, Ammianus was not really the sort of interlocutor he wanted. He was neither a gentleman nor a scholar, nor was it genuine associates of Praetextatus he wanted, but people with links to the elite of his own day. Though a great admirer of the Roman past, Ammianus's specialty was the history of the very recent past. While embodying some of the noblest Roman traditions, he was not a suitable spokesman for the antiquarian topics that interested Macrobius.

There may also be more specific reasons. It has not escaped notice that Ammianus paints a strikingly different picture of the pursuits of the Roman aristocracy at the end

---

123. Courcelle 1969, 147–48.
124. Cameron 1986, 320–28.
125. *aderat his omnibus Praetextatus*, 22. 7. 6; Matthews 1989, 23.
126. Matthews, *Ammianus* 124–25, 428–35; J. Szidat, *Mus. Helv.* 39 (1982), 132–45.

of the fourth century:[127] degenerate, haughty, avaricious drones, interested only in racing, dicing, and eating, men who locked up their libraries like the family vault, *detestantes ut venena doctrinas*. Ammianus may well have meant to exempt Praetextatus, whom he elsewhere praises highly, from his polemic. But he did not mention Symmachus at all, nor did he credit Praetextatus (or any other aristocrat) with any serious intellectual interests.[128]

Where Ammianus criticizes them for their cruel, unfeeling treatment of slaves (28. 4. 16), Macrobius puts an eloquently high-minded plea for a more humane attitude (taken from Seneca, *Ep.* 47) into the mouth of Praetextatus (i. 11. 1–50). Yet it is Ammianus, not Macrobius, who more accurately reflects the attitude of at any rate Symmachus, which, as his own letters reveal, "ranges from callous cruelty to a sort of vexation at having to bother with such fellows."[129] Despite the fame his history must have brought him, and despite the fact that Macrobius shared some of Ammianus's literary prejudices (against Juvenal, e.g.), clearly the author of this polemic would not have fitted comfortably into Macrobius's mutual admiration society. We can perhaps go further. It is surely more than coincidence that Macrobius praised his little band for precisely the virtues that according to Ammianus the aristocracy of Rome so conspicuously lacked.

Ammianus attacks their lavish and ostentatious banquets (28. 4. 13; xiv. 6. 16). Macrobius dwells time and again on the frugal, unpretentious character of the meals his heroes eat: why, they did not even know the meaning of some of the extravagant menus they had read about in the books of the ancients (iii. 13. 2; 14. 1; 17. 12)! Macrobius denies that any actor had ever darkened the portals of Praetextatus and his friends (ii. 1. 7; iii. 14. 3). According to Ammianus aristocratic houses echoed continually with the sound of singing and music, and *pro philosopho cantor, et in locum oratoris doctor artium ludicrarum accitur* (14. 6. 18). Ammianus complains that in their exclusiveness they despised anyone born outside the *pomerium*: they would expel an *honestus advena* (Ammianus himself) from the city in time of food shortage—but allow foreign dancing girls to stay. Macrobius took care to include among Praetextatus's guests three Greeks and even an Egyptian. And no one would see a dancing girl in any of their houses (ii. 1. 5–7).

It might seem improbable that these very specific assertions and denials were based on genuine information about the lifestyle of Praetextatus and his friends. But Macrobius may (e.g.) have come across the letter in which Symmachus claims that, even at the seaside, he "led a consular life" (*vitam agimus consularem*): "no singing in the boats, *no extravagance at table*, no visits to the baths and no splashing when the young folk swim."[130] It would not be surprising if he had sought to qualify Ammianus's slashing

---

127. There is much denunciation of the upper classes of late fourth-century Rome in Jerome too, though women and the clergy were his main butts: Wiesen 1964.

128. xxvii. 9. 8–10 and xxii. 7. 6; his praise of Symmachus's father is somewhat undermined by the anecdote about the burning of his Trastevere mansion (xxvii. 3. 3).

129. McGeachy 1942, 92.

130. *nullus in navibus canor, nulla in conviviis helluatio, nec frequentatio balnearum nec ulli iuvenum procaces natatus* (*Ep.* viii. 23 to Marcianus in 396: Seeck 1883, cxcii).

denunciation of the whole senatorial order, some of whom he was portraying as Scipio and Laelius reincarnate. If so, this would add one more qualification to the pagan interpretation of the *Saturnalia*. For Ammianus was a pagan. It was not just Christian attacks on his heroes that concerned Macrobius; in this area he was defending the character and morals rather than religion of the class to which he himself belonged.

10

So was Macrobius himself a pagan? Surely not—at any rate not a committed pagan. One of the most widely discussed passages in the entire *Saturnalia* is the long discourse on solar theology put in Praetextatus's mouth in Bk i (17–23), arguing that almost all the gods of the Graeco-Roman pantheon (and a few others as well) represent one aspect or another of the sun. It is widely agreed, to quote from a recent account by Liebeschuetz, that, in its approach to monotheism, Praetextatus's speech[131]

> is one of the principal sources for the last stage of Roman paganism, more precisely for the interpretation of their traditional religion by the last generation of pagan senators... Praetextatus does not simply proclaim that all the polytheistic gods are fundamentally aspects of one supreme deity, he also argues that the supreme god, of whom all the others are aspects, is the sun.

Three unargued assumptions common to more or less all modern writing on Macrobius underlie this approach. First, that the *Saturnalia* as a whole reflects the religious views of "the last generation of pagan senators." Second, and more specifically, that this speech reflects, by and large if not in detail, the real views of the real Praetextatus. And third, that Macrobius himself shared these views. Liebeschuetz did not explain how he reconciled these assumptions with the late date for Macrobius (which he accepted). But if Macrobius was writing fifty years after Praetextatus's death, all three become problematic.

Of course, *if* Macrobius was a committed pagan, it is possible that, though writing in the 430s, he made a serious effort to reconstruct the religious beliefs of Symmachus and Praetextatus in the early 380s. But we have just seen that the interlocutors he chose do *not* in fact represent an authentic literary circle of that period. Macrobius chose his interlocutors for their connections to his own circle in the 430s, all or most of whom must have been Christians. More important, the *Saturnalia* is *not* a work of history, and it is a fundamental error (to be sure often made) to treat it as such. It is a literary dialogue—in its frame if not its subject matter in effect a work of fiction. Macrobius did not originate any of his material. With the sole exception of the

---

131. Liebeschuetz 1999, 186; so too O'Donnell 1970, 66–67.

dialogue frame, he adapted or in some cases simply copied it from a variety of earlier sources, as put beyond doubt by the few cases where they can be identified.

As we shall see in more detail in later chapters, like Cicero's dialogues (which he had clearly studied), it is a vehicle for material that interested Macrobius. He made no sustained attempt to represent the actual views of the individual interlocutors into whose mouths he puts the material he had collected. To be sure, in the interests of verisimilitude he did his best to match up speeches and interlocutors in a very general way. Thus Servius speaks about details of language in Vergil; Symmachus the orator and Eusebius the rhetorician about rhetoric in Vergil; Dysarius the doctor on medicine, and so on. The reason Macrobius assigned Praetextatus his material on solar syncretism is simply that oriental religions were well known (not least from his funerary monument) to be his specialty. It does not follow that they were Macrobius's specialty. It is simply another illustration of the pains to which he went to match his material to the interests and expertise of his interlocutors.

No less relevant is the overwhelmingly antiquarian rather than religious *treatment* of cult material in the *Saturnalia* (analysed in detail in Ch. 16). Shanzer objected that "the antiquarian label is not sufficient to explain Macrobius's work," appealing, like Liebeschuetz, to Praetextatus's speech, which (she claimed) is "thrown into relief compared to the rest of the *Saturnalia*" and "can be taken as a fair indication" of the writer's own pagan beliefs.[132] That "thrown into relief" is something of a giveaway. Is it really justifiable to treat a brief passage conceded to be atypical as the key to the entire work? Quite apart from the several hundred other pages of the book, virtually ignored in this approach, the context makes clear how we are meant to read Praetextatus's speech.

How are the other interlocutors represented as greeting it? On the Liebeschuetz-Shanzer view, we should expect one of them to praise the great man for summing up so clearly what they all believed but could never have put so well themselves. Quite the contrary (i. 24. 1):

> As Praetextatus ended his discourse, the company for a while regarded him in wide-eyed wonder and amazement. Then one of the guests began to praise his *memory*, another his *learning*, and all his *knowledge* of the observances of religion; for he alone, they declared, knew the secrets of the nature of godhead, he alone had the intelligence to apprehend the divine and the ability to expound it.

Two details stand out here. First, the other interlocutors treat Praetextatus's exposition first and foremost as a display of *erudition*, just like all the other antiquarian material elsewhere in the *Saturnalia*. Second, they react as though it was all *new* to them. Liebeschuetz was honest enough to be puzzled by the second detail. If

---

132. Shanzer 1986, 135–36; Flamant 1977, 654 ("Macrobe ne pouvait mieux signifier qu'il en fait son porte-parole").

Praetextatus's speech represents "the interpretation of their traditional religion by the last generation of pagan senators," what was it that they found new? Not (he assumes) "the idea that the sun was the supreme deity, nor the identification of quite a number of specific deities with the sun or with powers of the sun, nor indeed the underlying theory that all the gods of polytheism represented aspects of the one supreme god."[133] What then? Given the pains Macrobius took with the frame of his dialogue, on the Liebeschuetz-Shanzer view this is a question that deserves a serious answer.

When discussing the sources of Praetextatus's speech, Liebeschuetz remarks that "there is no need to suppose that Macrobius had to 'follow' any single principal source. He surely was a very well-read man.... So the outline of the speech can well be Macrobius's own." Reasonable as this might seem, it is to treat Praetextatus's speech as a special case. Macrobius himself never lays claim to *any* originality, and where we are in a position to check, he did indeed follow single sources closely for long stretches. Notoriously, he follows Gellius so closely that in many places the Macrobian text has the authority of a manuscript of Gellius. Much the same is true of Plutarch's *Table-talk*, which Macrobius often follows so closely that at one time his few slight differences were thought to imply that he drew on a fuller text than the one that has come down to us.[134] In the case of Praetextatus's speech it has long been agreed that Macrobius's ultimate source must have been Porphyry, though an important study by Mastandrea has produced strong arguments in favor of a Latin intermediary, the pagan theologian Cornelius Labeo.[135] In all probability i. 17–23 is nothing but a series of excerpts from Labeo.[136] In a very general sense, of course, a writer usually excerpts an earlier text because he approves of what it says. Yet we cannot make so straightforward an assumption about a work like the *Saturnalia*. Most of its subject matter simply cannot be categorized in this way. The entire book is a mass of miscellaneous antiquarian material assembled from a wide variety of sources, much of it lists of passages from earlier writers imitated by Vergil.

While Macrobius obviously found Labeo's material interesting enough to rescue from oblivion, I cannot see any indication that it was more important to him than the rest of his antiquarian material—still less that it represented a deeply personal religious credo. The reputation of the *interlocutor* as a religious expert makes it natural to wonder how far this section reflects the real beliefs of *Praetextatus*. According to Bloch (e.g.), "The views put forward...agree so closely with everything we know about Praetextatus that Macrobius must either have used a lost treatise by Praetextatus himself or gathered his information from people who had an excellent knowledge of Praetextatus and his ideas."[137] But if the section really derives from an actual work by a

---

133. Liebeschuetz 1999, 196.
134. P. K. Marshall in his OCT of Gellius, 1 (1968), xix; Hubert 1938, 307–17.
135. Flamant 1977, 652–79; Mastandrea 1979, 169–80.
136. Macrobius himself frankly admitted that much of his book was "faithfully set out in the actual words of the old writers" (*ipsis antiquorum fideliter verbis*, pr. 4).
137. Bloch 1945, 207–8.

man who, among other religious offices, held the super-grade of *pater patrum* in the cult of Mithras, then it is hard to explain a startling omission from the otherwise exhaustive list of deities identified as manifestations of the Sun: Mithras!

For Shanzer, Macrobius must have been aware that what he was transcribing was "in effect, a defense and rationalisation" of polytheism.[138] But by definition there can be no one form of polytheism. There is no reason, for example, to believe that a traditionalist like Symmachus would have conceded such centrality to solar syncretism. *If* we had independent evidence that Macrobius was a committed pagan, it might be legitimate to look for apologetic or polemic beneath the antiquarian surface. But in default of such evidence, the transcription of such a passage cannot in itself prove the transcriber a committed pagan. Many Christians pillaged the erudition of both Porphyry and Labeo without themselves accepting its implications. To cite only one example, an antiquary of the mid-sixth century, John the Lydian excerpted several of the very same passages of Labeo as Macrobius.[139]

Even in the case of Cicero's dialogues or Tacitus's *Dialogus*, it is a misunderstanding of the nature of the form to claim (as earlier critics so often used to) that this or that character or speech reflects the author's own views. It is the beauty and the challenge of the form at its best that the writer puts something of himself into every speech, leaving it to the reader to draw his own conclusions. In the case of antiquarian treatises in dialogue form (the *Deipnosophists*, to quote an obvious example), it makes no sense even to ask the question; the antiquarian likes it all. If asked to identify personal sentiments in Macrobius, it is precisely the antiquarian declarations I would point to, notably the much-quoted profession of faith put in the mouth of Rufius Albinus: *vetustas quidem nobis semper, si sapimus, adoranda est* (iii. 14. 2). This is not only a recurring Macrobian motif; it is also explicitly formulated in the author's preface.

The omission of Mithras from the list of solar identifications is a puzzle on any hypothesis—above all on the hypothesis that Macrobius was a pagan. For Flamant, it was simply a consequence of the fact that Porphyry, his source at this point, was not interested in Mithras.[140] Quite untrue, as it happens. A series of references in two surviving works (*On abstinence* and *On the Cave of the Nymphs*) suggest on the contrary that Porphyry took a keen interest in Mithraism.[141] Mithras appears in a parallel list of solar identifications in Martianus Capella, which clearly derives from the same tradition as Macrobius.[142] Turcan took a different line, arguing that Christians disapproved more

---

138. Shanzer 1986, 136; "it seems impossible that Macrobius…would not be aware of its implications" (ib.).
139. See the verbal parallels between *Sat.* i. 9, 12–14, 17–21, and a number of passages in Labeo (whom John cites by name four times) set out by Mastandrea 1970, 21–47, 56–65, 170–72.
140. Flamant 1977, 673.
141. Discussed in detail by Turcan 1975, 24f. and 62f.; see too Clauss 2000, 42, 51, 68, 76, 82, 135–36, 144.
142. i. 13, with Shanzer 1986, 133–37; and ii. 190–93 (at 191), with Lenaz 1975, 56–59. Macrobius's list: Apollo, Dionysus, Hades, Mars, Mercury, Asclepius, Salus, Hercules, Sarapis, Adonis, Attis, Osiris, Horus, all twelve signs of the Zodiac, Nemesis, Pan, Saturn, Jupiter, and Adad; Martianus's list: Apollo, Dionysus, Serapis, Osiris, Mithras, Dis, Horus, Typhon, Attis, Hammon, Adonis.

strongly of Mithraism than of other pagan cults. On this view, Macrobius deliberately dropped the reference to Mithras in his source to protect himself. Yet the evidence suggests on the contrary that Christians found the rituals of Isis, Magna Mater, and Attis, all three quite openly included in Macrobius's list, even more repugnant. To quote only the most relevant example, all three are prominently featured in an anonymous Christian invective on Praetextatus that refers to Mithras only indirectly.[143]

A far simpler explanation suggests itself once we reconsider the assumption that Macrobius was a pagan. Mithraism was long since dead by the 430s. Macrobius had surely never seen a functioning Mithraic cave, nor, for all its popularity in the second and third centuries, was Mithraism prominently mentioned in the sort of books he read. While surely familiar with the list of initiations on Praetextatus's funerary monument, Macrobius may not have realized that the abbreviation *PP* stood for *pater patrum*, the highest grade in the Mithraic hierarchy.[144] To a Christian of the 430s whose knowledge of paganism was largely derived (as Macrobius's was) from the poets and antiquarians, Mithras was not a name with the recognition factor of Dionysus, Osiris, or Adonis. The earliest reference to Mithras in Latin literature comes as late as Statius,[145] and for preference Macrobius read nothing later than Vergil. Even Claudian mentions Mithras only once in passing, compared with elaborate descriptions of Attis and Cybele.[146] The answer is surely that, like the late antique commentator on Statius's *Thebaid*, an approximate contemporary,[147] Macrobius knew very little about Mithraism.

It is often alleged that the *Commentary* too is the work of a pagan. According to its latest editor, it "goes against all the evidence" to consider Macrobius even a "lukewarm" Christian.[148] Yet the only evidence cited is (once again) Praetextatus's speech on solar syncretism and neoplatonic doctrines like the three hypostases and the descent of the soul that are alleged to be incompatible with Christian teaching. The *Commentary* is certainly a work that derives from the pagan philosophical tradition without the slightest hint of Christianity. But then the same is true of Boethius's *Consolation of Philosophy*. In Chadwick's words, the *Consolation* "is a work written by a Platonist who is also a Christian, but is not a Christian work."[149] Yet there is little or nothing in the *Consolation* inconsistent with Christianity either. By and large this is also true of the *Commentary*: for example, II. 10. 5–16 is about as close as a Platonist

---

143. Turcan 1984, 224–26. *sub terra quaerere solem* at CCP 47 looks like a reference to Mithras, though given the many other solar identifications (e.g., line 109, *Attin…praedicere solem*), other interpretations are possible.

144. On other fourth-century Mithraic dedications, we find the even more cryptic abbreviation *PSIM*, for *pater sacrorum invicti Mithrae* (ILS 4148, 4153).

145. *Theb.* i. 716–20; Turcan 1992, 203–4.

146. *Stil.* i. 63; *Rapt.* i. 202–13; *Eutr.* i. 277–80; and ii. 279–303; *Gild.* 117–20.

147. See his garbled note on the famous description of Mithras at *Theb.* i. 716–20; Cumont 1899, 29; Bidez and Cumont 1938, 225–38.

148. Armisen-Marchetti 2003, xviii–xix.

149. Chadwick 1981, 249.

could come to reconciling the philosophical doctrine of the eternity of the universe with Christian teaching of a creation.[150] At II. 5. 22–26 Macrobius playfully mocks those opposed to the idea of a spherical earth inhabited on the other side. It is true that some Christians rejected the Antipodes (notably Lactantius and Augustine), but many pagans did so just as vehemently (notably Lucretius and Plutarch), and it is altogether implausible to infer (with Flamant) that Macrobius's (very mild) polemic was directed against Christians.[151]

A recent study of the mystical Neoplatonic notes on the descent of the soul incorporated in Servius's commentary on *Aeneid* vi (also a major theme of the *Commentary*) takes it for granted that they are part of the "battle of dying paganism against the triumphant doctrines of Christianity."[152] According to another recent critic, "Macrobius borrowed heavily from Iamblichus and Porphyry, and in so doing declared an allegiance to Hellenic philosophy and religion."[153] His debt to Iamblichus is much less certain than that to Porphyry, and that to Porphyry often indirect.[154] We should also bear in mind that Porphyry wrote with great learning on a wide variety of subjects, most of them in no way "pagan." More specifically, Porphyry's *De regressu animae* with its "doctrine of detachment from the flesh and of a return to God had a profound impact on Christian minds."[155] The fact that both *Commentary* and *De Nuptiis* were admired and imitated within a couple of generations by Fulgentius and Boethius[156] makes it hard to believe that cultivated lay Christians saw them as works with a significant pagan content or purpose. As with the *Saturnalia*, some passages in the *Commentary* might have pagan implications if we knew on other grounds that the author was a committed pagan. But they are secondary to the aim and character of the work as a whole. The *Commentary* is a philosophical and scientific complement to the literary and religious antiquarianism of the *Saturnalia*.[157]

My own feeling is that Macrobius could not have written about the minutiae of pagan sacrifice in the distanced, casual way he does at the time he does if he had been a committed pagan himself. Three chapters that have been generally overlooked may have a bearing on the question of the audience at which the *Saturnalia* was aimed.

---

150. The brevity of the historical record "seems to argue against the eternity of nature"; he concludes that the world was made by God but before time. It seems to me a mistake of emphasis to conclude (with Flamant 1977, 628–36) that this is "l'une des thèses majeures que l''hellénisme' n'a cessé d'opposer aux chrétiens." The fact is that a philosophical Christian could have accepted the argument.

151. Flamant 1977, 469–74.

152. Setaioli 1995, 629–49 at p. 631.

153. Ando 2001, 371, citing Courcelle 1969, 46.

154. See Mastandrea 1979 for Cornelius Labeo as a Latin intermediary.

155. Courcelle 1969, 417.

156. For Boethius's use of the *Comm.*, Courcelle 1967, 116–24; for Martianus and Boethius, O'Daly 1991, 19–22; and Fulgentius, Stahl, Johnson, and Burge 1971, 56–57. For Flamant 1977, 698, it was only "the chance of a family legacy" that put the *Commentary* into Boethius's hands.

157. Flamant 1977, 680–86, draws a similar parallelism between the two works—but then adds his own tendentious conclusion that this is a Roman civilisation "qu'il entend opposer au Christianisme envahissant" (686).

First, ii. 4. 11, where, alone among secular writers,[158] Macrobius alludes to the story of the Massacre of the Innocents—in the course of a chapter on the jokes of Augustus. On hearing of "the two-year-old children Herod the king of the Jews had killed," Augustus quipped that he would rather be Herod's pig than his son. This can hardly be the original form of the joke. Augustus cannot have known the gospel of Matthew (ii. 16), nor does Matthew say that Herod's own son was included. It must be a Christian adaptation of an original joke alluding to Herod's well-attested execution of three of his adult sons.[159] But Macrobius writes as though he could expect his readers to take the story for granted. If this falls short of proof that he was a Christian, it makes it hard to believe that he was writing for pagans.

Second, at i. 16. 6 Macrobius briefly categorizes the various sorts of Roman holidays: fixed (*stativae*), movable (*conceptivae*), extraordinary (*imperativae*), and market days (*nundinae*). The last sort, he says, "are the concern of the rustics and country folk (*paganorum itemque rusticorum*), who assemble to attend to their private affairs and market their wares." *Itemque rusticorum* serves to define *paganorum*,[160] and the reason Macrobius takes care so to define it is obvious enough. For any Roman antiquarian who had done his homework, *paganus* meant "countryman." But among Christians, of course, the standard meaning of the word was now "pagan" (Ch. 1). In view of the concentration of his book on pagan festivals, Macrobius did not want his readers, by the 430s overwhelmingly Christians, to misinterpret *paganorum* and *Paganalia* in the present context. Again, he would not have needed to take such a precaution if he had been writing for pagans.

Finally, it is suggestive that Macrobius puts in Euangelus's mouth the claim that "he too"—meaning as well as Praetextatus—had attended lectures on pontifical law (iii. 10. 2). This is one of those details in the skillfully constructed "pagan" mise-en-scène of the work already discussed. But no one can have given classes on pontifical law as late as the fourth century. The once-extensive learned literature had entirely perished by then, represented by a handful of brief fragments preserved by early imperial antiquarians and Vergil commentators (p. 607). This is surely the perspective of a Christian, accustomed to catechetical classes for young Christians and taking it for granted (mistakenly) that pagans too routinely received instruction in the elements of their religion (p. 797). It is hard to believe that any pagan as interested in

---

158. And so in earlier times exploited by fundamentalists, notably the Reverend Jean Masson, *The Slaughter of the Children of Bethlehem as an Historical Fact in St. Matthew's Gospel vindicated: and the suspected Christianity of Macrobius who also mentions the same Fact disprov'd* (London 1728), appended to the second edition of Edward Chandler, *A Vindication of the Defence of Christianity* (1728), a response to doubts raised by Anthony Collins, *A Discourse of the Grounds and Reasons of the Christian Religion* (1724).

159. On which see Schürer et al. (eds.), 1 (1973), 293–94. The pig alludes (of course) to Jewish dietary laws.

160. For connective *itemque*, Kröner, *TLL* 7. 2. 538. 6; no example in Symmachus's letters but several in his *Relationes* (16. 1; 19. 1; 20. 2; 36. 2; 38. 2); perhaps a bureaucratic formula. J. C. Zeune (1774) suggested *id est*.

pontifical law as Macrobius professes to be could have made such a blunder. In a later chapter we shall see that, for all the importance he appears to assign to it, he actually knew next to nothing about pontifical law.

On purely historical grounds it is unlikely that a committed pagan would be appointed prefect of Italy as late as 430 (Ch. 5. 3). Nor is it likely that a man bearing the name Theodosius, unknown to elite western society before the Theodosian dynasty, a man born in the reign of and evidently named after Theodosius I (379–95), had pagan parents.

Not that it makes much difference for a proper understanding of the *Saturnalia*. On the one hand, an antiquarian devoted to Cicero, Vergil, and Neoplatonism, who happened also to be a Christian, could have written two such books without feeling that it compromised his faith. On the other, if a pagan, he was not writing with a specifically pagan agenda. Rigorists would certainly have deplored the obvious enthusiasm of the *Saturnalia* for the details of pagan cult, but few cultivated lay Christians would consider this sort of sentimental, literary paganism any real threat to the faith. If challenged, Macrobius could always have replied that, by setting his dialogue on the eve of Gratian's disestablishment of the cults, he was in fact pointedly confining his pagan interlocutors within their historical moment. Now that the actual sacrifices were gone for good, it was safe to romanticize one of the more picturesque elements in the classical texts (above all Vergil) that everyone still read.

8

THE POEM AGAINST THE PAGANS

1

The so-called *Carmen contra paganos* (*CCP* for short) is an anonymous invective in 122 classicizing hexameters on the death of an unnamed pagan prefect. The sole surviving copy consists of three leaves in a late fifth- or early sixth-century hand attached to a contemporary codex of Prudentius (Par. lat. 8084). Some interpretations have been prepared to allow a considerable interval (as much as forty years) between the death of the prefect and the writing of the poem.[1] It seems to me, as it seemed to its first commentators in the 1870s, more natural to assume that such a trivial piece of doggerel was written very soon after its subject's death, within days rather than even weeks, let alone years.

The mention of a pagan Symmachus in line 114 establishes a late fourth-century date. More controversially, it was early inferred that lines 28–33 allude to a military uprising.[2] Morel, De Rossi, and Mommsen at once identified this hypothesized uprising with Eugenius's rebellion of 392–94, and the prefect with the elder Flavian, who took his own life when Theodosius won the day at the Frigidus (5 September 394).

Since the subject of the poem was both prefect and consul, as Flavian was in 394, the poem was assigned to this year and interpreted as an attack on Flavian written shortly after his death. The tirade against pagan cults it contains was read as a reflection of the pagan revival he supposedly directed. Schenkl went so far as to claim that, since there was no reference in the poem to the death of Eugenius, it must have been written in the brief interval between the suicide of Flavian and the execution of Eugenius.[3]

For almost a century this identification was thought so secure that the poem was regularly cited under the title *Carmen adversus Flavianum*. Yet there is no unmistakable reference to any specific date or event, much less to Flavian himself, and a number of other names have also been proposed. The only one to win the support of anyone but its proposer is Praetextatus, who died a month or two before reaching the consulship for which he had been designated late in 384. As early as 1867 Morel listed four names, and Mazzarino later added one more:

---

1. Grünewald 1992, 462–87.
2. Romano 1998 and Bartalucci 1998 give useful surveys of the various interpretations, and there are also bibliographies in Markschies 1994 and Adamik 1995.
3. Schenkl 1879, 73 (quoted with approval by Schanz-Hosius IV. 1² [1914], 222).

L. Aur. Avianius Symmachus (père), PVR 364, died cos. des. 376; Q. Aur. Symmachus (fils), PVR 384, cos. 391, died 402; Vettius Agorius Praetextatus, PVR 367, PPO 384, died cos. des. 384; Virius Nicomachus Flavianus, PPO and cos. 394, died 394; Gabinius Barbarus Pompeianus, PVR 408–9, died 409.

The successful candidate must fulfil a number of conditions. He must have been (1) consul (*te consule*, 112); (2) prefect (*praefectus*, 25); he must have (3) died a protracted death (*tracta morte*, 27), if we are to press line 121, of dropsy; (4) been a pagan (passim); and (5) had an heir called Symmachus who restored a temple of Flora (112–14). More generally (6), the circumstances of his life as well as death must make sense of the poem as a whole.

But we should not expect all these conditions to be met in the most obvious or straightforward way. The poem is, after all, an invective, full of hyperbole and heavy-handed irony. As with most invectives, some of its accusations are bound to be unfair, some paradoxical, some sheer invention. Most commentators have taken it for granted that *Symmachus heres* in 113 must be a legal heir, but why make so much of so literal a connection? Musso devoted five pages to the universal respect in which Praetextatus was held, arguing that such a paragon could not possibly be the murderous fanatic of the *CCP*.[4] But invectives always caricature their subjects. Claudian's *In Rufinum* and *In Eutropium* are malicious travesties, grossly unfair to Rufinus and Eutropius. Another problem is the by now highly conventional nature of anti-pagan Christian invective. We must beware of twisting a personal or contemporary reference out of invective commonplaces.

What has always seemed to me the only satisfactory solution (namely Praetextatus) was first briefly stated by Ellis in 1868 and more authoritatively argued by Cracco Ruggini in 1979, for many of the right reasons.[5] Yet Cracco Ruggini made two important tactical errors, and consequently failed to carry general conviction. First, she confined herself to arguments in favor of Praetextatus, taking it for granted that the case for Flavian would then automatically lapse. Second, she did not ground her identification in a systematic analysis of the poem as a whole. In consequence, she accepted some long-standing misinterpretations of individual passages that have continued to be cited in support of Flavian (§§ 4–5). The real objection to Flavian (whose case has been vigorously restated a number of times since her monograph)[6] is not just that he does not satisfy all the requirements. More important, the structure, tenor, and themes of the poem as a whole simply do not fit what we know of Flavian and his part in the rebellion of Eugenius.

---

4. Musso 1979, 215–19.
5. Ellis 1868, 80; Cracco Ruggini 1979; and 1988.
6. Most fully by Musso 1979; see too Grünewald 1992; Markschies 1994; Adamik 1995; Romano 1998; taken for granted by Thrams 1992, 199–200; most recently (but with no new arguments) by Coşkun 2004.

The *CCP* is virtually the only evidence there is for a pagan revival—if (and only if) its prefect is Flavian. So it is not surprising that those committed to a pagan revival are reluctant to consider alternative identifications. It has seldom been recognized that the arguments in favor of the two Symmachi are technically stronger than those for Flavian. The reason that, despite their "qualifications," neither has received a fraction of the attention devoted to Flavian is revealing. Neither provides any support for the notion of a pagan reaction under Eugenius.[7]

2

Those who have read Eugenius's rebellion into the poem have done so by taking a word here and a line there out of context and virtually ignoring the rest of the poem, a procedure sometimes justified by dismissing it as so irretrievably incompetent as to defy ordinary interpretation. Undeniably the poet had a shaky command of prosody and syntax, his transitions are abrupt, and he had an unaccountable predilection for the imperfect subjunctive. But a few false quantities do not inescapably entail imbecility of mind and incapacity to string two coherent thoughts together. If we are going to convict anyone of ignorance and incompetence, it should be the scribe. In many cases his errors have reduced the text to gibberish. He was presumably a Latin speaker, but it seems clear that he was unfamiliar with the diction of classicizing poetry, or even the names of pagan deities: for example, *Panasque* (70) appears as *poenasque*; *Megales* (65) as *magalis*; *Ceres* (96) as *caeris*; *Cybellae* (106) as *cirillae*.

A rehabilitation would be out of place. It is undeniably a poor piece of work—but not so bad that any meaning a critic wants can be twisted out of it. Much (especially the second half) runs smoothly enough, and has considerable rhetorical power. More important, the poem as a whole has a clear and intelligible structure, and no interpretation that does violence to or ignores this structure deserves to be taken seriously.

Lines 1–22 are an introduction on the criminal absurdities of the pagan gods: Jupiter's incest with Juno, his amorous disguises as bull, swan, and shower of gold; naked Venus weeping for the death of the pretty mortal Adonis; gods who quarrel among themselves.[8] Another commonplace is the futility of prayer if even the gods themselves are governed by fate (*regitur fato si Iuppiter ipse*, 17–18).[9] Perhaps the most significant aspect of this preface is its very triteness. Almost every phrase can be paralleled from almost any other Christian invective against the pagan gods. As far as the preface goes, the subject of the invective to follow might be no more than an identikit

---

7. With characteristic brilliance and ingenuity Mazzarino 1974, 398–461, argued at length for the elder Symmachus, but not even the most loyal of his disciples seems to have followed him.
8. For material on these commonplaces, Perelli 1988, 241–54.
9. This last motif is discussed in detail by Lenaz 1980.

pagan seen through Christian eyes rather than the infamous rebel of 394. The point is underlined by the ironic acrostic DI PII, "pious gods," offered by lines 1–5.[10]

Sections 2–3 of this chapter are (I believe) the first serious attempt to analyze the poem as a whole and trace a consistent meaning and purpose from start to finish.[11] While they draw attention to details that support or refute the various identifications as they arise, full analysis of the more controversial passages is postponed till §§ 4–5. A complete text and translation are provided in an appendix, and ideally the reader should (re)read the entire poem from start to finish before proceeding any further— and then again afterward.

The poem proper begins with line 23. Referring to his catalogue of immoral Olympians, the poet asks whether these are suitable leaders (*ducibus*) from whom "to hope for health," *sperare salutem*, a phrase carefully repeated in the final line of the poem (for its meaning and importance, underlined by the ring composition, see later). This brings us to lines 25–38, the key part of the poem for the Flavian hypothesis. Unfortunately, these are the most obscure and difficult lines in the poem, partly because of one or two desperate corruptions, but mainly because no one has ever tried to make coherent sense either of the passage as a whole or of its relationship to the rest of the poem. On the standard interpretation, the lines evoke the proclamation of a state of emergency in Rome, involving a protracted purification of the city and the arming of the people. I say "evoke," not "describe," because this interpretation rests on four words taken out of context, one of them an emendation: *lustravit* (29), *seditio* (31—the emendation), *iustitium* (32), and *saga* (33). If we reject the emendation and interpret the three other words as contemporary readers would have understood them, the whole passage takes on an entirely different meaning: it describes the extravagant mourning the prefect's death inspired in Rome (§ 4). What did he do to deserve this? asks the poet (25 and 46), and lines 38–45 answer this question.

Much of the rest of the poem is a list of the various pagan deities and rituals that he is said to have observed, but interspersed among them are a few other misdeeds: offering food tainted by the smoke of incense at his banquets (41–42), providing gladiatorial games (43–45), and destroying old buildings (38–40). Lines 78–86 accuse him of seducing Christians away from the faith, which would suit Flavian well enough. But offering tainted food and destroying old buildings would be something of an anticlimax in the indictment of a man who had rebelled against his emperor.

Thanks to the poor quality of our copy, there are a number of details that may never be fully understood. But there is one passage where text, meaning, and emphasis alike are crystal clear, lines 87–97, a series of rhetorical questions asking what good this or that god has done the prefect:

---

10. First pointed out by Perelli 1988, 253–54.
11. The skimpy section on "struttura" in Bartalucci 1998, 42–43, does no more than offer a summary of the poem, finding so little coherence that he toys with the idea that it is no more than a sequence of "epigrams."

> Quid *tibi* diva Paphi custos, quid pronuba Iuno,
> Saturnusque senex potuit praestare sacrato?...
> quid, miserande, Ceres, subrepta Proserpina matri,
> quid *tibi* Vulcanus claudus, pede debilis uno?

> What could the divine guardian of Paphos [Venus], or Juno goddess of marriage or old Saturn do for you, a consecrated man?...What about mother Ceres, you wretch, what Proserpina stolen away from her mother? What lame Vulcan, with his one weak foot?

The implied answer (of course) is no good at all. In a poem about Flavian we might have expected the poet to ask what good all these gods did the *city*. Instead, he focuses entirely on the personal needs of the prefect rather than the harm he did the city (not to mention the empire). And the remainder of the poem continues and develops this perspective. Line 110 tells of his attempt to win public office (*procerum...honores*) through "magic arts," and the concluding section (114–22) describes in detail how his wife heaped the altars of all the gods with offerings but, while attempting to "move Acheron," instead sent him headlong down to the depths of hell. In the context, "moving Acheron" must mean influencing Death, that is to say, persuading Death to spare him;[12] she makes these offerings *in the hope of saving his life.*

In context, the point of the rhetorical questions in 87–97 must be that the prefect has been vainly trying one god after another in the hope of saving his own life. This also explains the emphasis on his long-drawn-out death (25–27):[13]

> dicite: praefectus vester quid profuit urbi,
> quem Iovis ad solium raptum iactatis abisse,
> cum poenas scelerum tracta vix morte rependat?

> Tell me, what has your prefect done to help the city, the man you boast was snatched I a away to the throne of Jupiter, whose agonizing death scarcely atones for his crimes?

What is a *tracta mors*? What but a slow, painful death, put beyond serious doubt by the *tandem* in 29 (*metas tandem pervenit ad aevi*): "*at last* he came to the end of his life."[14] Against Praetextatus it has always been urged that, according to Symmachus, he died a natural death. Yet while Symmachus's words (*fata rapuerunt, functus est lege naturae,*

---

12. In the Vergilian model (*flectere si nequeo superos, Acheronta movebo,* Aen. vii. 312), of course, the verb has a "more cataclysmic implication" (Horsfall 2000, 218).

13. With Matthews, I accept Froehner's brilliant *iactatis abisse* for *tractatus babisset* in the manuscript. Morel's *trabeatus* is superficially attractive, but how did the prefect come to die in his consular robes before he became consul?

14. For an anthology of interpretations, Adamik 1995, 220; his own, no more than "the death he suffered," is very weak, especially in an invective.

naturae lege resolutus) might reasonably be held to exclude murder, suicide, and accident, they do not exclude a slow death by painful disease. No more does Jerome's claim that he participated in a public procession a few days before his death.[15] People with painful terminal conditions are not necessarily bedridden. On the other hand, it is not easy to square a long-drawn-out death with Flavian's suicide.[16] The natural assumption is that he cut his wrists or fell on his sword.

This emphasis on the prefect's death explains in turn why the phrase *sperare salutem* frames the core of poem:

> Convenit his ducibus, proceres, *sperare salutem* (23) . . .
> desine post hydropem talem deflere maritum,
> de Iove qui Latio voluit *sperare salutem.* (121–22)

"Is it appropriate, senators, to hope for *salus* from these leaders" (namely the pagan gods)? The general view, based on the apostrophe "senators" (*proceres*), is that *salus* in 23 = *salus reipublicae*, and that this line alludes to some danger hanging over Rome.[17] But the passage goes on to evoke the prefect's death in considerable detail, not this hypothesized danger to Rome. And the phrase is repeated in the final line of the poem (122), where again emphasis falls exclusively on the prefect's death. The key to the whole poem lies in realizing that *salutem* here refers to the prefect's *health*.[18]

Many critics have translated line 122 "hope for salvation from Jupiter *for* Latium," where Latium is assumed to stand for Rome.[19] This is not impossible, but De Rossi was surely right to take *Latio* with *Iove*, and identify a reference to Jupiter Latiaris.[20] For Christians Jupiter Latiaris meant only one thing: human sacrifice, supposedly still performed as late as the age of Constantine.[21] The practice is mentioned with horror by numerous fourth-century Christian writers, the most relevant being two other anti-pagan verse invectives of the same period.[22] This gives a neat final point: the prefect has been praying for *salus*—his own, of course—to a god who demanded human sacrifice!

To be sure, *salus* can be used of the public weal, but only in contexts where the reference is clear. Symmachus uses the word more than seventy-five times in his

---

15. *Rel.* 10. 2; 12. 1; Jer. *Ep.* 23. 3; Musso 1979, 237.
16. Lenaz 1978, 565, compares *durante tractu et lentitudine mortis* in Tacitus's account of the long, drawn-out death of Seneca (*Ann.* 15. 64. 3), but that was obviously a special case.
17. So even Cracco Ruggini 1979, 89.
18. So Bartalucci 1998, 168 on 122, but without perceiving its importance for the poem as a whole.
19. Manganaro 1961, 45; Romano 1998, 52.
20. Sometimes known as Jupiter *Latii* (*CIL* xi. 6310); De Rossi 1868, 63; so too Lenaz 1978, 556–57; Cracco Ruggini 1979, 115. Perhaps we should write *Latii* here.
21. Tertull. *Apol.* 9. 5; *Scorp.* 7. 6; Minuc. Fel. *Oct.* 30. 4; Firm. Mat. *De err.* 26. 2. For more examples and brief discussion, Rose, *Mnem.* 55 (1927), 273–79; Rives, *JRS* 85 (1995), 75. According to both Lactantius (*Div. Inst.* i. 21. 3) and Porphyry (*De abstin.* ii. 56. 9, ἔτι γε νῦν τίς ἀγνοεῖ), apparently here influenced by Christian propaganda, it still happened as late as 300. It is generally assumed that Christians misinterpreted the execution of criminals in the games held for the Feriae Latinae.
22. Prud. *Contra Symm.* i. 396; Paul. Nol. *Carm.* xxxii. 109–12. So already Ellis 1868, 79.

correspondence,[23] eight times with a political reference, but only in the formulas *salus civium, salus publica*, or *salus reipublicae*. Some twenty times of greetings offered or received, and well over thirty times of the physical health of individuals, whether himself, his family, or his friends. On the reading of earlier critics, a variety of words and phrases (*lustravit, iustitium, saga, urbi…inferre ruinam*) seemed to provide the context necessary for a politico-military reading of *salutem* in 23 and 122. I hope to show that, in context, these words do not in fact carry any of these associations, either individually or collectively. In which case the natural assumption, in a poem about the death of a man clearly stated to have died a slow and painful death, is that in both 23 and 122 *salus* means *health*.

The final proof is the reference to dropsy in 121. Is this dropsy a medical or a moral condition? Remarkably enough, some scholars have been willing to combine dropsy and suicide,[24] though most Flavian-fanciers have assumed a metaphor.[25] But this is not a solution that can be simply assumed. Whether used literally or metaphorically, a word must make appropriate sense in its immediate context. Dropsy (now known as edema) is properly an abnormal accumulation of fluid in the body caused by heart, liver, or kidney failure, now seen as a symptom rather than a disease. Like so many diseases, it was often used in antiquity as a metaphor for a moral failing,[26] the standard analogy (since sufferers were supposed always to be thirsty)[27] being avarice. First found in Aristotle and common in Hellenistic diatribe, it was no doubt best known to a fourth century Latin poet from Horace and Ovid.[28]

There are also one or two fifth-century texts where the metaphorical sense appears to be pride, but in all these cases the context leaves no room for doubt. For example, in Claudianus Mamertus, "he swelled with the dropsy of pride and wasted away with the fever of envy." It is sometimes thought that Prudentius's hymn on St Lawrence provides an example:[29]

> hunc, qui superbit serico, / quem currus inflatum vehit,
> hydrops aquosus lucido / tendit veneno intrinsecus.

this man, who vaunts himself in his silk and is puffed up with pride as he rides in his chariot, a watery dropsy of the soul within distends with transparent poison.

But since 237–38 so clearly portray this man as arrogant, it would be very feeble if the moral vice his disease concealed turned out to be arrogance. Kudlien has shown

23. Neatly set out by Lomanto, *Concordance* (1983), 831–33.
24. "Vielleicht war er schon krank in den Krieg gezogen," Schenkl 1879, 72–73.
25. Most emphatically Musso 1979, 238–40.
26. Bramble 1974, 35–38; Kudlien 1962, 104–15.
27. So notable a feature that (as Heinrich von Staden pointed out to me) diabetes, another condition characterized by constant thirst, was also sometimes known as ὕδρωψ: Urso 2000, 59–60.
28. Horace, *Odes* ii. 2. 13 (with Nisbet and Hubbard's notes); Ovid, *Fasti* i. 213–17; Kudlien 1962, 107–8.
29. Claud. Mam. *De statu animae* iii. 8 (*hydrope superbiae tumuit*); Prud. *Per.* ii. 237–40.

that the series of medical metaphors that runs right through lines 229–64 draw on the standard Graeco-Roman moral repertory.[30] We should therefore expect this imposing figure to turn out to be a miser.

Elsewhere in the *CCP* it is the folly, cruelty, and wickedness of the prefect the poet attacks. When he is styled *inflatus* at line 58, the reference is to his wealth rather than his arrogance, the bloated millionaire who put on rags for the taurobolium (*quis tibi, taurobolus, vestem mutare süasit, / inflatus dives subito mendicus ut esses*). The poet might have added arrogance or even greed to his other vices earlier in the poem. But to introduce either notion so abruptly so near its conclusion would give it a distracting emphasis. More specifically, the *post* in the final apostrophe—"desine *post hydropem talem* deflere maritum"—clearly implies that, however interpreted, this condition somehow explains why the prefect's wife should abandon her attempt *Acheronta movere*. How could arrogance or greed come to play such a role?

Dropsy fits both context and *post*. "After the dropsy" means "after/once he had developed dropsy." Though not named till line 121, the prefect's illness has been presupposed throughout the poem, and its nature was presumably known to informed contemporaries (dropsy was a conspicuous condition). Advanced dropsy was considered terminal (Hadrian, Theodosius I, and Honorius all died of it), and (so the poet implies) the prefect and his wife should have accepted the inevitable. He was after all an old man (*sexaginta...annis*, 67). Instead, he devoted his last three months (28–29) to begging false gods to prolong his life. There is also (I suggest) another layer of meaning in the repeated *sperare salutem* (23 and 122). While the prefect himself and his wife were praying to their gods for the restoration of his *health*, the Christian reader cannot help thinking of the Christian connotation of the word, *salvation*. If it was salvation the prefect wanted, obviously he was praying to the wrong gods.

Another detail that supports this reading of the poem is the claim in line 62 that the poet hopes to live for twenty years after the *taurobolium* (*vivere...viginti...in annos*). This is explained by two dedications in the Phrygianum, dated to 376 and 390, recording the repetition of the *taurobolium* after twenty years.[31] Apparently some initiates thought of the ritual as being valid for a specified period only, after which it needed to be renewed. Whether or not they actually believed that it gave protection in this world as well as the next, the poet is obviously implying that the prefect underwent this absurd and messy rite in the hope of extending his life.

So the point of the poem as a whole is that the prefect was a sick man desperate to prolong his life. Lines 110–12 give him a motive; he is hoping to win *procerum honores*:

> artibus heu magicis *procerum dum quaeris honores,*
> sic miserande iaces, parvo donate sepulchro.
> sola tamen gaudet meretrix te consule Flora.

---

30. Kudlien 1962, 112.
31. *ILS* 4153 (Ulpius Egnatius Faventinus) of 376; ib. 4154 (Ceionius Rufius Volusianus) of 390.

Alas, while seeking the honours of the nobility by your magic arts, you are brought low, wretch, rewarded with a tiny tomb. The only one to rejoice in your consulship is Flora the whore.

What are these *honores* he seeks? Evidently the sort of posts sought by members of the elite (*proceres*), worldly honors. But which ones? By the time of his death the elder Flavian had won both the highest offices to which a private citizen could aspire, the praetorian prefecture and the consulate. But in the last months of 384 Praetextatus was still on the brink of the culminating honor of his career. He was consul designate, and had only to live till 1 January, a simple enough goal that he failed to reach, evidently because of a terminal illness. The prefect of the poem was likewise seeking some high office, which he failed to attain (*dum quaeris honores / sic miserande iaces*) because of the dropsy, despite his own and his wife's supplication to a veritable pantheon of pagan gods and goddesses. The "magic arts" with which he sought this office are not some new development, but simply all the pagan rites listed in the preceding fifty lines. That the office he failed to win was indeed the consulate is proved by the ironic *te consule* in the following line.[32]

3

Even before we turn to the real meaning of the various passages alleged to refer to the events of 392–94 (§ 4–5), it should be clear that the subject of the *CCP* cannot possibly be Flavian.

(1) Obviously our prefect did not commit suicide. This is proved not only by the reference to dropsy but by the thrust of the poem as a whole: a dying man praying to his gods to *prolong* his life. An invective on the fallen Flavian was bound to handle its subject's death very differently. Many contemporaries will have respected him for choosing suicide over surrender. As Bloch put it, "Flavian chose the death of Cato Uticensis and followed even in this last act the ancient tradition of Rome."[33] Theodosius himself is said to have regretted his death. We may doubt whether he shed real tears, but he may have regretted the suicide.[34] Christians understood only too well the value of martyrdom. Any posthumous invective on Flavian was bound to focus on his life and treason rather than his death.[35] And a Christian invective was likely to condemn his suicide (Augustine devoted much of the first book of his *City of God* to arguing that suicide is never permissible, even for Christian virgins raped by

---

32. As already seen by Mazzarino 1974, 409, though arguing for the elder Symmachus.
33. Bloch 1945, 240; Stein 1959, 217; Matthews 1973, 180; the title of Romano 1998 is *L'ultimo pagano*.
34. Notoriously, Stalin did his best to suppress the news of Hitler's suicide in the Soviet Union (H. Trevor-Roper, *The Last Days of Hitler*⁷ (London 1995), xlvii–liv).
35. Interestingly enough, John of Antioch depreciated the suicide of Arbogast as revealing his barbarian nature.

barbarians, explicitly condemning Lucretia, the outstanding pagan example of preferring suicide to dishonor).[36]

(2) The CCP nowhere even hints at treason. To be sure, the word *prodidit* appears in line 38—but in connection with wine![37] There is vague talk about hating peace, loving war and seducing Christians away from the true faith, but not a word about rebellion against the emperor. While Christians, like many modern historians, later exaggerated the religious dimension of Theodosius's victory, it is impossible to believe that a poem on Flavian's death could have completely ignored its political dimension. How could the poet have written 122 lines of invective on Flavian without even mentioning the most important indictment of all?

(3) The Flavian hypothesis presupposes that the long list of gods and goddesses represents the cults Flavian revived. Bloch (e.g.) wrote of his *"revival* of the whole pageantry of the ancient cults."[38] Yet while the core of the poem (lines 46–120) consists of little more than a catalogue of pagan rituals, there is no hint that *any* of them had been revived. On the contrary, the implication is that they were still thriving, implying a date *before* Theodosius's law of 391.[39] The prefect is simply (and repeatedly) mocked for putting his trust in these false gods. In Christian eyes it was far worse to restore false gods once dethroned than simply to believe in them in the first place.[40] The latter could be put down to mere ignorance; the former argued deliberate perversity. If the prefect had just revived all these cults, how could the poet have failed to say so?

(4) Lenaz thought that the lack of reference to "the miracle of the Frigidus" was a fatal flaw in the case for Flavian,[41] but we have seen that this "miracle" was unknown to contemporaries. On the other hand, the role of prayer and piety in the victory was certainly a contemporary theme, and it would be incredible to find no reference of any kind to Theodosius's victory in a Christian invective on Flavian written in the immediate aftermath of the Frigidus.

Committed Flavian-fanciers have brushed these deafening silences aside as unimportant, on the grounds that the poet was only interested in Flavian and Rome. Since Flavian killed himself halfway though the battle, "what would have been the point in speaking about it in an invective whose only purpose was to attack and make fun of his fallen adversary?"[42] This simply will not do. We may agree that a post-Frigidus invective on Flavian was not obliged to *describe* the battle. But since the poet's main concern was his subject's death, and Flavian undoubtedly killed himself during or after and because of the battle, how could he have failed even to mention the cause and context of his death?

---

36. Trout 1994, 53–70.
37. A "locus desperatus" (Bartalucci ad loc.); *prodidit* must be corrupt.
38. Bloch 1945, 230–31; for a particularly emphatic statement, Matthews 1975, 242.
39. So Consolino in Consolino 1995, 319.
40. So the *Carmen ad quendam senatorem* (Ch. 9. 1), lines 41–45, 72–73.
41. Lenaz 1978, 567–70, citing all the relevant texts on the Bora.
42. Romano 1998, 17; cf. Adamik 1995, 190 n. 29.

There is one further preliminary caveat, one that applies equally to all candidates. What most strikes the reader of the *CCP*, claims Romano, is its actuality; it is no scholastic exercise.[43] But this is not an easy distinction to draw. It is not just the prologue that is full of commonplaces of the genre. The *CCP* is one of many anti-pagan invectives. To name only works from the second half of the fourth century, we have (in prose) Firmicus Maternus, Ambrosiaster, and Maximinus the Arian; and (in verse) the anonymous *Carmen ad quendam senatorem* and *Carmen ad Antonium*, Prudentius's hymn to the martyr Romanus (*Per.* x), subtitled *Contra gentiles*, and, most elaborate of all, the two books of his *Contra Symmachum*.[44] All these works raise much the same objections in much the same language, heavily indebted to the Apologists of the second and third centuries.[45]

It has often been assumed that the cults listed straightforwardly reflect those actually observed by the prefect. But there are some thirty-five names on the list, many of them hardly serious figures in late Roman civic cult: Bellona, Neptune, Pan, Vulcan, Fauns, and nymphs. It is unlikely that Flavian was known to be a devotee of Neptune or Pan or the Fauns.[46] Most of these names are here simply because they are bêtes noires of Christian Apologetic. Saturnus because Christians liked to wax indignant about a god who ate his own children;[47] Attis because of the perversion of a god who castrated himself; Vulcan because of the absurdity of a lame god (*claudus, pede debilis uno* echoes *claudus deus et debilis* in Minucius Felix 22. 5); Pans and satyrs because of their lecherous propensities; nymphs because Christians mocked the notion of making gods of creatures who "lived at the bottom of a pool like frogs";[48] Venus and the vote of Paris (96) because of the frivolity of a goddess entering a beauty contest; Janus *bifrons* (93), not because Flavian celebrated the Compitalia in January 394,[49] but because Christians liked to make fun of a god who could walk backward. The bald priest of Isis shaking tambourines (98–99) appears again and again in Christian invectives (p. 148). Many names come from the poets rather than cult: *latrator Anubis* and *pronuba Iuno* (the latter absurdly inappropriate for a sexagenarian male) from Vergil; Pan, Fauns, and satyrs from Nemesianus.[50]

One scholar, failing to appreciate that *vidimus* in 103 is simply a stock first-person narrative device to convey vividness,[51] inferred that 103–7 are an eyewitness description

---

43. Romano 1998, 21.
44. For a brief survey, Cracco Ruggini 1979b, 119–44. For the four poems, next chapter; for Maximinus, Gryson 1980, 66–79; for Ambrosiaster (Ps-Aug. *Quaest. vet. et nov. test.* no. 14), Bussières 2007.
45. Vermander 1982, 3–128.
46. Cicero has a character in *De nat. deor.* (iii. 15) make fun of Fauns.
47. See Clarke 1974, 283 n. 296.
48. Prud. *Peri Steph.* x. 241–25.
49. So Phillips 1988, 383–84 (writing of the poet's "vivid eyewitness tone"); see rather Minuc. Fel. 22. 5 again.
50. Nemesianus: *lasciva cohors* (66) and *Faunosque deos... Satyrosque Panasque* (69–70) ~ *Faunique senes Satyrique procaces... lasciva cohors* (Nem. *Buc.* iii. 25, 46); *iuga ferre leones* (103) ~ *iuga... ferre leones* (Nem. *Buc.* iv. 54); Ihm, *Rhein. Mus.* 52 (1897), 211.
51. More than thirty examples of *vidimus* and *vidi* in Vergil alone. *Vidi egomet* in Horace, *Serm.* i. 8. 23 is a parody of this device, as noted in Ps-Acro's note ad loc.

of Flavian driving a wagon drawn by a team of lions, "brandishing the silver reins in his hands." On this basis he went so far as to date Flavian's presence in Rome by the dates of the festivals he allegedly celebrated "on their correct days of the Roman calendar," between 21 March and 3 May![52] Here it is the lions (actually from Nemesianus) that are the giveaway. Who can take seriously the idea of a praetorian prefect driving lions though the streets of Rome with silver reins?

Bartalucci has recently pushed the argument from conventional motifs to its extreme, denying the *CCP* all actuality: not an attack on a specific pagan prefect after all, but simply what it has often been called, a *Carmen contra paganos*. Perhaps (he suggests) an attack on a composite figure, combining details from the lives of several different late fourth-century pagans.[53] There is an element of truth here. The greater part of the poem is indeed an attack on paganism, paganism (in the words of Fontaine) "incarnate in one of its most distinguished Roman representatives."[54] But it is also more than that; there are several highly specific details. If this is a picture of Pagan Everyman, why is it that three of the most specific of these details (the consulate, the dropsy, and demolishing ancient buildings in Rome) have nothing whatever to do with paganism? While it is theoretically possible that each of these details identifies a different pagan, why do so with details irrelevant to their paganism? Above all, the unremitting focus of the poem on its subject's *death* makes it inevitable that its first readers would identify him as whichever prominent pagan had recently died after a long illness.

It seems to me impossible to resist the conclusion that the *CCP* attacks one and only one pagan, a recently deceased prefect designated for the consulship—whether or not he lived to give his name to the year. Furthermore, despite the conventional nature of much of the anti-pagan invective, even here there are some very specific details.

For example, it is clear from the extended context in which he places his account of the *taurobolium* (57–77) that the poet knew that it formed part of the cult of Magna Mater. The idea of repeating the *taurobolium* after twenty years seems to be a recent development within the cult, unknown to earlier Christian invective. As we shall see later, it must have also been from public dedications that the poet derived his knowledge of the term *sacratus*. Another detail redolent of contemporary practice is *Triviaeque sacerdos* in line 71,[55] assuming that Trivia = Hecate. No fewer than nine members of the late Roman elite are described as hierophant or *sacerdos* of Hecate, and six out of the nine (including Praetextatus) are also described as *sacerdos, sacratus* or *archibuculus Liberi*,[56] initiate of Liber/Bacchus/Dionysus. This perhaps allows us to press the combination *Bacchique comes Triviaeque sacerdos* in line 71.

52. Matthews 1975, 242; cf. Matthews 1970, 478; Bloch 1945, 230–31.
53. Bartalucci 1998, 34–35, reviving an idea thrown out casually by Ellis 1868, 80.
54. Fontaine 1981, 219.
55. A tag from Vergil (*Aen.* vi. 35 and x. 537), but not necessarily lacking contemporary reference.
56. See columns 10 and 11 in the table of priesthoods in Bloch 1945; Collins-Clinton 1977, 36 n. 94.

While we need not take the prefect's alleged devotion to Fauns and satyrs too seriously, we are bound to accept that he was an initiate of "oriental" cults. Of our front-runners, only Praetextatus qualifies on this count. Not only is there no independent evidence that Flavian took any interest in such initiations; whatever his personal preferences, on any hypothesis the main gravamen of the Christian indictment against Flavian was his (alleged) role in the restoration of state funding to the traditional cults. Rufinus appropriately enough confined himself to Flavian's participation in the traditional craft of haruspicy, which played him and the pagan cause so fatally false. Yet our poet is clearly more interested in the colorful absurdities of Attis, Anubis, Cybele, and Isis.

4

A number of passages call for more detailed discussion. First lines 28–29, the immediate sequel to the description of the prefect's death:

> mensibus iste tribus totam qui concitus urbem
> lustravit, metas tandem pervenit ad aevi.

The man who feverishly traversed the whole city for three months finally reached the limits of his life.

What is the prefect doing here? On the Flavian interpretation, *lustravit* is held to refer to a purification ceremony (*lustratio*) held as part of the "pagan revival."[57] Cracco Ruggini thought that Praetextatus conducted a *lustratio* in connection with the famine of 384. Musso argued that only a consul (and so Flavian) could perform a *lustratio*. It was (she claims) the atmosphere of religious fanaticism at Rome before the conflict with Theodosius that led to the revival of this ancient ritual of purification, last heard of in A.D. 271.[58]

But nothing we know of *lustrationes* suggests that they lasted longer than twenty-four hours. It is inconceivable that even the "fanatical" Flavian devoted three months to this one ritual. Did he have nothing else to do? And what was he doing in Rome in the first place? As chief minister of an emperor facing war against a formidable opponent, his place was at court in Milan.[59] Praetextatus was also praetorian prefect in the year he died, but he is not attested in office after 9 September, and may well have spent his last few months at home in Rome, where he died.

---

57. For an anthology of variations on this view, Adamik 1995, 220; Bartalucci 1998, 110.
58. Musso 1979, 220–25, collects much information about these rituals.
59. Matthews 1970, 478, argues that Flavian came to Rome "in the early months of 394," but without evidence.

Furthermore, while *lustrare* is certainly the verb for performing a ritual *lustratio*, it also bears a variety of other meanings, especially in the poets. Without some pointer to ritual in the context, it normally means "encircle," "traverse," or "survey." Even in its ritual sense, the idea of movement is central, since a *lustratio* consisted of a *procession around* the place or object to be purified.[60] When commenting on *Buc.* 5. 75, *lustrabimus agros*, both Macrobius and Servius gloss the verb as *circumire*.[61] In Ovid's *Fasti*, a poem largely concerned with Roman festivals, the ritual sense is naturally common. In a passage of Silius, after a reference to altars in the preceding line we naturally identify a ritual element in the phrase *lustratis moenibus*. But without such a pointer, *moenia lustrat* in two passages of Ovid's exile poetry simply means "circles the walls," of enemy attackers besieging a city.[62] A particularly clear example is *Aen.* ix. 57–58, "huc turbidus atque huc / lustrat equo muros," where Turnus is circling the Trojan camp looking for a way in.

The verb appears again at *CCP* 72 of Bacchic dances, *lustrare choros et molles sumere thyrsos*, where it is usually translated "lead the dances," an otherwise unattested sense of the word.[63] It has long been noticed that this line is copied verbatim from *Aen.* vii. 390–91, *molles tibi sumere thyrsos, / te lustrare choro*, addressing Bacchus, where *lustrare choro* means "circle in the dance" or "dance around," as at *Aen.* x. 224, "agnoscunt longe regem *lustrantque choreis*," "circle [the king] with dancing rings."[64] What has not been noticed in this context is that two late antique and many Carolingian manuscripts read *lustrare choros* at *Aen.* vii. 391.[65] Modern editors rightly reject *choros*, but this was surely the reading in our poet's text of Vergil. If so, he will naturally have thought *lustrare choros* Vergilian Latin for dancing a Bacchic dance. Neither Vergilian model nor present context provides any basis for seeing ritual connotations here.[66]

What compels us, with no pointer in the context, to assume a ritual meaning in 29? There is in fact a negative pointer, the three months, obviously absurd for a ritual *lustratio*. And how would the ritual sense fit the other half of the sentence in which it stands: "the man who feverishly 'purified' the city for three months finally died." If the point of this purification was to protect the city, why is it linked to the death of an individual? Flavian-fanciers simply ignore the context, but if we read the two clauses together in sequence, it is obvious that there must be a connection between the three months and the fact that the prefect "eventually" (*tandem*) died. *Tandem* must in effect mean after three months.

---

60. See the entry *lustro* in *OLD, TLL,* and *EV* iii (1987), 287–90 (S. Fasce and A. Palma); "frequent in non-ritual contexts, in the sense 'move around,'" Horsfall's note on *Aen.* vii. 391; briefly, Ward Fowler 1919, 96–98.

61. Macr. *Sat.* iii. 5. 7 (*lustrare significat circumire*); Serv. on *Buc.* v. 75 (*lustrare hic circuire*).

62. Silius, *Punica* xii. 752; Ovid, *Tristia* iv. 1. 78; *Ex Ponto* i. 2. 19.

63. So Croke and Harries 1982; "guidare i cori," Manganaro 1961 and Romano 1998.

64. Harrison 1991, 133.

65. M² and R; see Geymonat's text and Horsfall's note on vii. 391.

66. Bartalucci 1998, 140, insists that *lustrare* must bear a religious sense here too, but he produces no supporting evidence, and it makes no sense to link an ancient Roman purification rite with Bacchic dancing.

Urbem lustravit means no more (I suggest) than "traversed the city." This might seem utterly banal. Yet throughout the second half of the poem the prefect is accused of supplicating all the gods in Rome to prolong his life. This must have involved visiting all their temples. Line 91 mentions a trip to the temple of Serapis, and the following line asks what promises Mercury made him "on his rounds" (*eunti*). The poet implies that a sixty-year-old with a terminal condition should have accepted the inevitable instead of rushing from temple to temple in a vain search for *salus*. I would translate 28–29 as follows: "the man who feverishly crisscrossed the entire city for three months eventually came to the end of the road." Ambrosiaster makes a similar point about the undignified behavior of the devotee of Isis "dashing in all directions looking for the body parts of Osiris the adulterer."[67]

In the case of a sufferer from dropsy there might be an additional allusion here. Why is the prefect's movement described as "rapid" or "agitated" (*concitus*)? According to Mazzarino, because he is driven by religious passion;[68] according to Perelli, because he is represented as a man out of control, like the typical tyrant figure in an invective.[69] Neither seems entirely satisfactory in what purports to be a description of his literal movement around the city. There is another possibility. It was widely believed that exercise (walking and even running) was good for dropsy.[70] Perhaps the poet is making malicious fun of the fact that the dropsical prefect had been spotted *jogging*!

We have already seen that *sperare salutem* in 23 and 122 does not, as previously thought, refer to some danger threatening Rome, but simply to the prefect's health. It is this nonexistent "danger to Rome" that has been widely held to explain lines 32–33, the most important single passage for the Flavian interpretation:

> quis tibi iustitium indixit,[71] pulcherrima Roma,
> ad saga confugerent populus quae non habet olim.

> Who declared this *iustitium* for you, most beautiful Rome? Are the people to don the *saga* they have not worn for so long?

A *iustitium* is a suspension of the law courts and public business, in early Republican times often proclaimed during a military crisis and followed by conscription of troops.[72] The *sagum* was the military cloak.[73] On the strength of the formula *tumultum*

---

67. *per omnia se circumfert loca…, Quaest. vet. et nov. test.* 114. 11 (p. 131 Bussières 2007).
68. Mazzarino 1974, 456 n. 146, also comparing *raptum* (26), *subito* (44 and 58), and *praecipitem* (120).
69. See Bartalucci 1998, 44, 110.
70. *multum ambulandum, currendum aliquid est*, Celsus, *De medicina* iii. 21; *curres hydropicus*, Hor. *Epi.* i. 2. 34; see particularly Caelius Aurelianus, *Tardae passiones* (*Corp. Med. Lat.* vi. 1. 2, G. Bendz and I. Pape [eds.], 1993) iii. 137, 141–42, 145–46.
71. *incussit* Cod., but the *vox propria* for proclaiming a *iustitium* is *indicere* (Oakley on Livy vii. 6. 12).
72. More than a dozen examples: for the *dilectus*, Brunt, *Italian Manpower* (Oxford 1971), 629. The only comprehensive treatment (still useful but hardly definitive) remains Nissen 1877; Oakley 1998, 126–27.
73. Wilson 1938, 104–10.

decerni, iustitium edici, saga sumi…dilectum haberi used by Cicero against the pro-consul Mark Antony in 43 B.C.,[74] De Rossi and Mommsen argued that these two lines reflect a crisis that led to the declaration of a state of emergency and the arming of the urban plebs. Flavian-fanciers have always identified this emergency as the outbreak of war between Eugenius and Theodosius.[75]

This is utterly incredible. In the first place, it had been over five hundred years since the last proclamation of a *iustitium* for a military emergency.[76] This sort of *iustitium* was a Republican institution (proclaimed by the consuls or senate) that naturally lapsed under the empire.[77] Whether or not Flavian restored the state cults, he certainly did not restore the Republic. Nor will it do to postulate the use of an obsolete formula for current procedure. Eugenius fought Theodosius with the regular military resources at his disposal. There is not the remotest possibility of a mobilization of the civilian population of Rome. Yet the reference to the "people" who had not worn *saga* for so long unmistakably identifies the population of Rome, with the *olim* serving to underline the Juvenalian emphasis on the present impotence of a once-proud warrior people.[78] The poet must be referring to something that happened in Rome.

By identifying the prefect as Pompeianus, lynched during Alaric's first siege of Rome in 409, Manganaro was at least able to explain the emphasis on Rome (Zosimus actually mentions the inhabitants arming themselves).[79] Unfortunately, this identification fails on every other count. Matthews weakly argued that "there is nothing to exclude the possibility" that Flavian proclaimed another *iustitium* in 394.[80] But the situation in 394 was entirely different. No siege of Rome, and no likelihood of one. Assuming that, even on their different identifications of the prefect, they still had to find an emergency that would explain the *iustitium*, Mazzarino and Cracco Ruggini picked riots over wine and grain shortages in 375 and 384, respectively.[81] But grain and wine riots were regular occurrences in fourth-century Rome, and we know enough about both years to be certain that no such extreme measures were either necessary or taken.[82]

How would contemporaries have understood the proclamation of a *iustitium*? For more than five hundred years the phrase *iustitium indicere* had meant only one thing in ordinary usage: to proclaim a period of public *mourning*.[83] It is important to be clear

---

74. Cicero, *Phil.* 5. 31; again at 6. 2.
75. For a recent statement, Adamik 1995, 221.
76. Perhaps 111 B.C., in connection with the Jugurthine War (Cic. *Pro Plancio* 33); Cicero used the traditional formula against Antony (*Phil.* 5. 32), but it is unlikely that he really expected to mobilize the Roman plebs.
77. Nissen 1877, 150.
78. nam[*populus*] *qui dabat olim / imperium fasces legiones omnia, nunc se / continet atque duas tantum res anxius optat, / panem et circenses*, Juv. x. 78–81. *habet olim* obviously recalls Juvenal's *dabat olim*.
79. Manganaro 1960, 210–24; Zos. v. 40. 1.
80. Matthews 1970, 473.
81. Mazzarino 1974, 422–24; Cracco Ruggini 1979, 86–89.
82. Ruggini 1995, 157–52, 724; Kohns 1961, 146–48, 168–82.
83. As firmly stated long ago by Nissen 1877, 148–52; see too Vollmer 339 n. 4; Wesch-Klein 1993, 91–101; on imperial funerals see too Fraschetti 1990, 42–120.

that this is not a figurative, later extension of a "true" *iustitium*.[84] The word itself signifies no more than a suspension of the law courts (*ius sistere*), though it normally involved a suspension of business in general and leisure and religious activities as well. Shops, baths, taverns, and temples were closed; auctions, weddings, circus, and theatre games were canceled.[85] The original purpose was to ensure that everyone of military age was free to assemble for immediate mobilization. But closing the courts and shops was also a standard preliminary for public mourning, not only as a mark of respect but to enable and encourage everyone to attend the funeral.[86]

The earliest on record for an individual was proclaimed on the death of Sulla, the first true public funeral at Rome.[87] But the connotations of public grief were no innovation of the late Republic. When news of the defeat at the Caudine Forks reached Rome (320 B.C.), people adopted every form of mourning; the shops around the forum were closed and "a *iustitium* began spontaneously before it was even proclaimed."[88] Tacitus describes a similar spontaneous *iustitium* on the death of Germanicus.[89] What this must mean is that the people *anticipated* the senatorial decree by closing shops and discontinuing their regular business and leisure activities the moment they heard the news.

From Augustus on *iustitia* were normally (but not exclusively) proclaimed on the death of members of the imperial family. They are explicitly attested for C. and L. Caesar, Augustus, Germanicus, Drusus, Drusilla, Hadrian, Pius, Severus, Constantine, and Jovian.[90] By the late second century we also find them in the world of fiction. In Apuleius's *Golden Ass*, when Psyche's fate is announced "a *iustitium* was at once proclaimed"; and Ausonius describes Priam mourning Hector *iustitio publico*.[91]

That *iustitium* in *CCP* 32 likewise describes public mourning is put beyond doubt by the reference to *saga* in the following line. The Ciceronian formula links the donning of *saga* with the proclamation of a *iustitium* and the conscription of troops—but not in the way most scholars have assumed. It is not the newly conscripted troops who put on the *sagum*, but the civilians who remained in Rome. The first known example of this curious practice is attested by the Livian *Epitome* for 91 B.C. After the first Roman reverse in the Social War, "the people put on the *sagum*" (*saga*

---

84. As implied by Cracco Ruggini 1979, 86 ("un vero *iustitium*"), with 85 n. 252.
85. The word was rendered in Greek as ἀνοχαὶ δικῶν, ἀπραξία, or ἀργία: see Mason 1974, s. vv.
86. This is spelled out in so many words in *CIL* x. 3903, an Augustan dedication from Capua: [*ne*]…*possit esse inped*[*itus populus ne fun*]*us…frequentet*; for commentary, Vollmer 1893, 346–49. The fullest list of activities suspended is to be found in the Pisa decree on the death of C. Caesar (*ILS* 140 = EJ² no. 69).
87. Granius Licinianus, p. 33. 3 Flemisch; Weinstock 1971, 348–49.
88. Livy ix. 7. 8, with Oakley's commentary (Oxford 2005), 111.
89. *audita mors adeo incendit ut ante edictum magistratuum, ante senatus consultum sumpto iustitio desererentur fora*, Tac. *Ann*. ii. 82. 3.
90. Tac. *Ann*. i. 16. 2; *Ann*. i. 50 1; *Ann*. ii. 82; Suet. *Tib*. 52. 1; *Galba* 10; *Fasti Ostienses* (A.D.19): *VI idus Dec(embres) iustitium ob excessum G*[*er*]*manici*; *Fasti Cuprenses* (A.D.4): *Romae iustit*[*ium indictum est* (C. Caesar); *SHA Marc*. 7. 10; Victor, *Caes*. 20. 6; *SHA Marcus* 7. 10; Euseb. *Vita Const*. iv. 69; Symm. *Or*. i. 8.
91. Apul. *Met*. 4. 33; Auson. *Per. Hom*. 24.

populus sumpsit); after a victory over the Samnites the following year "*saga* were laid aside *at Rome*" (*Romae saga posita sunt*). A more detailed version of the second passage is preserved by Orosius: when news of the Roman victory reached Rome, "the senators laid aside their *saga*, that is to say the dress of mourning (*vestem maeroris*) which they had put on at the outbreak of the Social War," and returned to their togas.[92] Velleius too writes that the vicissitudes of the Social War were so bitter that the people "put on *saga* and long remained in that dress." Lucan provides a fictitious account of yet another spontaneous *iustitium* of this kind. After a series of portents,[93]

> ferale per urbem
> iustitium; latuit plebeio tectus amictu
> omnis honos.

> the law courts closed and gloom descended on the city;
> all people of rank were disguised in common dress.

This "common dress" put on by "people of rank" was the cheap, woollen *sagum*.[94] Scipio Aemilianus is said to have worn a black *sagum* during the Numantine campaign "in mourning for the disgrace of his army," and Horace describes Antony donning a *lugubre sagum* after his defeat at Actium.[95] A number of passages in Cicero's *Philippics* refer to senators putting on the *sagum* when Roman armies were in danger during the Mutina crisis and exchanging it for the toga when the danger passed.[96] Cicero's words are borne out by Livy's account of the crisis.[97] In all these cases the *sagum* is less a military uniform than any dark cloak suitable for mourning.

It is this well-documented practice of putting on mourning dress during a public crisis that links the earlier state of emergency sense of *iustitium* to the later public mourning sense. The funerals of Augustus, the prospective heirs who predeceased him, and his many successors were treated as public disasters, following the pattern of the funerals of Sulla and Caesar the dictator.[98]

92. Liv. *Epit.* 72–73; Oros. v. 18. 15; even if *hoc est vestem maeroris* is Orosius's gloss on his Livian source (so Nissen 1877, 128 n. 4), it does no more than reflect the obvious implication of the passage.
93. Vell. Pat. ii. 16. 4; Lucan ii. 17–19, with E. Fantham's note (Cambridge 1992), 83.
94. The *sagum* is "merely a rectangle of heavy cloth" woven from rough wool, N. Goldman, in Sebesta and Bonfante 1994, 232.
95. Plut. *Apophth. Scip. Min.* 16 = *Mor.* 201C; cf. Polyaenus 8. 16. 2. Hor. *Epod.* 9. 28, with Porphyrio's note.
96. *Phil.* 6. 9; 8. 6; 8. 31; 12. 16; 13. 23; 14. 1, 2, and 3. It is usually assumed that *saga sumere* is different from *vestem mutare*, a formula found several times in Cicero (*Pro Sest.* 26 and 54; *Pro Planc.* 29 and 87; *In Pis.* 17; also Livy vi. 16. 4 and *Epit.* 105; Tac. *Ann.* ii. 29. 1; EJ² 69. 22), also referring to the donning of mourning dress. They are distinguished by J. Heskel in Sebesta and Bonfante 1994, 142–43. But three passages of Dio that mention the senate "changing clothes" (37. 43. 3; 40. 50. 1; 41. 3. 1–4) look as if they refer to *iustitia*. For other references to mourning dress for the senate, Talbert 1984, 218–19; *RE* s.v. "Trauerkleidung" and "Luctus."
97. Liv. *Epit.* 118; so too Dio 46. 31. 2.
98. Weinstock 1971, 348–55.

In both the literature and the epigraphy of the empire, *iustitium* is common both as a technical term for the proclamation of an official period of mourning and more generally (especially in late antiquity) for any sad event that causes or merits widespread grief.[99] In the state of emergency sense I have found no example later than Livy.[100] According to Juvenal, if a great man's house is burned down,[101]

> horrida mater,
> pullati proceres, differt vadimonia praetor.

> nobles appear in mourning, their ladies with hair dishevelled,
> the praetor adjourns his hearing.

Mazzarino surprisingly misunderstood this passage, assuming that a *iustitium* in the state of emergency sense was proclaimed because of the fire. This made it a perfect parallel for his own thesis that *CCP* 32 alludes to a state of emergency proclaimed on the burning of the house of Symmachus père in 375. But this ignores the context. Juvenal is contrasting the different reactions people have to the sufferings of rich and poor. No one lifts a finger to help the poor man if his house burns down, but if it happens to a millionaire, people behave *as if* it is a public disaster.[102] The praetor closes the courts, women put on mourning, and senators the cheap, dark clothing worn by the common people.[103] What we have here is a classic (if imaginary) case of a public mourning *iustitium*. In the present context its main interest lies in the implication that, as late as the early second century, *iustitia* were not an exclusively imperial prerogative, but might be proclaimed at a local level by a praetor.

There is in fact an implicit allusion to the practice of donning *saga* for a funeral in another fourth-century Christian text: the elegiac poem on the lid of the sarcophagus of Junius Bassus, who died in office as prefect of Rome on 25 August 359. According to the sixth couplet,[104]

> fle]vit turba omnis matres puerique senesque,
> fle]vit et abiectis tunc pius ordo togis.

---

99. E.g., Mamertinus, *Grat. Act. Iul.* 9. 3; Pacatus, *Pan. Theod.* 24. 2; Sidonius, *Ep.* ii. 8. 1; Ennodius, *Vita Epif.* 122; Cassiodorus, *Var.* ii. 3.2.

100. According to Suet. *Galb.* 10. 2, Galba declared a *iustitium* as governor of Hither Spain in 68, in order to enroll additional troops.

101. Juv. iii. 212–13 (Niall Rudd's translation, Oxford 1992); the scholia gloss *pullati* as *cum nigris vestibus lugentes* (p. 44 Wessner). *differe vadimonia* is found of a *iustitium* in at least two inscriptions relating to public funerals, dating to A.D.56 and 70, respectively (*vadimoniis exsequiarum eius causa dilatis, AE* 1972, 174; and *vadimon[iis honoris cau]sa dilatis, CIL* vi. 31293, with *PIR²* F.352, p. 168).

102. Mazzarino 1974, 422–24; see rather S. M. Braund's commentary (Cambridge 1996), 210–11.

103. *pullatus* is regularly used of both the cheap attire of the *plebs* (Quint. vi. 4. 6; ii. 12. 19; Pliny, *Ep.* vii. 17. 9) and of mourning clothes worn by members of the elite: e.g., Ammian. xxix. 2. 13; [*pullis*] *amictos togis, Tab. Siar.* fr. b, col. I, 3 (M. Crawford [ed.], *Roman Statutes* [1996], p. 516).

104. *AE* 1953, 239; *CIL* vi. 8. 3 (2000), 41341 (with photos and up-to-date bibliography); for revised text and discussion, Cameron 2002, 288–92.

> All the people wept, mothers, children and old men;
> the pious senate wept also, *discarding their togas.*

In the light of the texts cited here, there can be little doubt why the senators discarded their togas: they put on *saga* instead. We find the same link between *iustitium* and senatorial mourning dress in the so-called *Consolatio ad Liviam,* a lament on the death of the elder Drusus: "the courts are silent...no purple [stripe] is seen in all the Forum."[105]

The fact is that *iustitium* in *CCP* 32 is not at all the quaint archaism everyone has assumed. The word is actually rather common in the classicizing poets of late antiquity, with examples in Prudentius, Dracontius, Corippus, and Avitus, in every case unmistakably implying public mourning.[106] Prudentius refers to a *iustitium* in Egypt when the chariots and horses of Pharaoh were swept away in the Red Sea (*Cath.* v. 73–80). Two passages in Dracontius (writing in the 490s) are especially relevant.[107] First,

> maxima iustitium victoria grande paravit,

> A mighty victory produced tremendous grief.

This is the victory won by Manlius Torquatus the younger, and the grief is the result of his execution by Torquatus the elder for disobedience while winning it. Interestingly enough, although *iustitium* here is clearly nontechnical, a few lines later Dracontius (anachronistically) suggests that, if the younger Torquatus had been killed by the enemy, a formal *iustitium* would have been declared in his honor:

> res publica tota doleret,
> pullati proceres, *vadimonia nulla fuissent.*

> the whole state would be grieving, senators would be in mourning,
> and the courts would be closed.

The obvious debt to Juvenal (*pullati proceres* and *vadimonia*) makes it clear that Dracontius (correctly) understood Juvenal's *differt vadimonia praetor* as a public mourning *iustitium.*

Second,

> his dictis gemit aula ducis sub luctibus atris;
> *moenia iustitio foedant* et plangitur urbe,

---

105. *Consol. Liv.* 185–86; for other links between this poem and the Bassus poem, Cameron 2002, 289–90. See too already Livy ix. 7. 8 (*iustitium...lati clavi, anuli aurei positi*), with Oakley's note.

106. Prud. *Cath.* v. 80 (*arcis iustitium triste tyrannicae*, "a sad day of mourning for the tyrant's city"); Cor. *Ioh.* 3. 360 (*iustitium meruit*); Alc. Avit. *Carm.* v. 301 (*iustitium iustum cogit maerere merentes*).

107. Drac. *Laud. Dei.* 3. 383, 386–87; *Rom.* 8. 597–98.

At these words the king's court groaned in dark grief;
  they deface the walls with mourning and there is weeping in the city.

Here *foedant* is being used in the sense "spoil the appearance of," "make ugly";[108] in the context, evidently by hanging dark banners of mourning on the city walls. Once again we may compare the *Consolatio ad Liviam*: "the city groans, and puts on one countenance of woe" (line 181). These texts explain *pulcherrima Roma* in CCP 32. To be sure *pulcherrima* is a standing epithet of Roma,[109] but why at precisely this point in the poem? Surely because *iustitium* and *saga* would conjure up for contemporary readers the picture of a city draped in the drab paraphernalia of mourning. The manifestations of public grief have cast a pall of ugliness over the beauty of Rome. The Christian poet is shocked at such a display of grief for a pagan, and neatly exploits the archaic military associations of *iustitium* and *saga* to make a Juvenalian jibe.

As so often in the *CCP*, it is essential to pay attention to context and emphasis. On the state of emergency interpretation, it must have been the prefect himself who proclaimed the emergency. But that does not explain the incredulous *quis*: "*who* proclaimed the *iustitium*?" Why ask who if it was obvious who, none other than the subject of the poem? The implication of the question is that the *iustitium* was unauthorized or undeserved. This makes perfect sense if it was an honor accorded the prefect by someone else, an honor the poet considered inappropriate for a pagan.

But appropriate or not, a *iustitium* for a private citizen was not impossible. Private citizens were still occasionally granted public funerals complete with *iustitia*. Ammianus describes indignantly how ca. 372 Valens forced high dignitaries, two former consuls included, to walk before the coffin of his favorite astrologer in mourning clothes (*pullati*, perhaps recalling Juvenal).[110] And the fact that family retainers were not allowed to carry the coffin of Junius Bassus (*nec licuit famulis domini gestare feretrum*) and senators "discarded their togas" to participate in the procession suggests that he too enjoyed a public funeral.

Little is known about non-imperial public funerals, beyond the obvious fact that they were paid for out of public funds.[111] But it seems clear that members of the elite at large rather than just members of the family carried the coffin, and some distinguished senator was chosen to deliver the eulogy. A famous example is Tacitus's eulogy of Verginius Rufus in A.D. 97.[112] Nine are attested between Augustus and Trajan, at least two of which (those for L. Volusius Saturninus and T. Flavius Sabinus in 56 and 70, respectively) included formal *iustitia*. And we are surely bound to take at face value the fact that Ammianus uses the word of the astrologer's funeral. In the context it can

---

108. See OLD s.v. 2a and b; TLL s.v.

109. Notably Verg. *Geo.* ii. 534 (*pulcherrima Roma*); for many more examples, Gernentz 1918, 57.

110. Amm. 29. 2. 15.

111. Vollmer 1893, 321–64, remains basic; Wesch-Klein's *Funus publicum* (1993) is more up to date; briefly, Talbert 1984, 370–71.

112. Wesch-Klein 1993, 83–90; Plin. *Ep.* ii. 1. 1 and 6.

hardly be construed metaphorically as grief, since Ammianus makes it clear that no one else shared Valens's grief. Like the *CCP* poet, he carefully uses the official term to underline the contrast between the scale of the honor and the unworthiness of its subject. In the case of non-imperial funerals the *iustitium* was probably limited to the city where the man died and the day of the funeral itself.[113] In *CCP* 32 the *tibi* clearly limits the prefect's *iustitium* to the city of Rome.

Flavian died in disgrace and defeat, and cannot possibly have received a public funeral. Indeed, one of the best-documented facts about the rather vague process modern scholars have called *damnatio memoriae* is the banning of mourning.[114] On this ground alone he can be excluded from consideration. But it is a well-documented fact that Praetextatus's death was greeted with extravagant demonstrations of grief (§ 8 below). Whether, like Junius Bassus twenty-five years earlier, he was granted a public funeral there is no way of knowing. But when Symmachus describes how "the people refused the usual pleasures of the theatre," this could be identified as one item in a spontaneous *iustitium*. From C. Caesar in A.D. 4 to Constantine in 337, cancellation of circus and theatre entertainments was a regular provision of *iustitia*, here anticipated by the people.[115] In any case, as city prefect at the time and so the chief judicial authority in Rome, Symmachus himself (like Juvenal's praetor) had the authority to close the courts on the day of the funeral.

The prefect's death leads us to line 111:

sic, miserande, iaces parvo donate sepulcro.

The small tomb mentioned here has often been held an argument against Praetextatus, in view of his grandiose surviving funerary monument. But commemorative monuments are not at all the same thing as tombs. The poet is simply making the common point that *any* tomb is a small place for great ambitions to come to rest.[116] The classic illustration is Alexander the Great, most memorably put by Juvenal, one of the few classics our poet really knew: while a single world was not enough for his ambition, a coffin suffices for his body (*unus Pellaeo iuveni non sufficit orbis...sarcophago contentus erit*). In the no less sharp formulation of his fifth-century scholiast, "quem vivum mundus non ceperat, mortuus *exiguo loco* contentus est." The world was full of grandiose monuments to Alexander, but his actual body, in Statius's words, "Babylon confines in a narrow tomb" (*angusto Babylon premit sepulchro*).[117] Dracontius

---

113. In the ordinary way a *iustitium* lasted until the funeral was over: Vidman 1971, 209–12. Imperial *iustitia* covered a wider area and longer period: for Constantine, see Euseb. *V. Const*. iv. 69; on the evidence of Tacitus the one for Germanicus seems to have lasted for months (Woodman and Martin 1996, 104–5).

114. Flower 2006, 76, 84, 172.

115. *recusavit populus sollemnes theatri voluptates, Rel*. 10. 2; *ILS* 140 = EJ² 69. 30; Euseb. *V. Const*. iv. 69.

116. So Cracco Ruggini 1979, 108 n. 323; Shanzer 1986, 240.

117. Juv. x. 168–73, with *Schol*. p. 173 Wessner; Stat. *Silvae* ii. 7. 93–95.

writes of the souls of heroes disdaining the confines of a *vile sepulchrum*, where the context makes clear that it is the confinement, not the cheapness of the tomb, that is at issue. Jerome's letter to Marcella makes essentially the same point about Praetextatus: "a few days ago the highest dignitaries of the city walked before him…now he is desolate and naked."[118]

The rhetorical questions in the two lines that immediately precede the *iustitium* (30–31) are especially puzzling:

> quae fuit haec rabies animi? quae insania mentis? 30
> †sediovt† vestram posset turbare quietem

What madness of soul was this, what insanity of mind? What…might disturb your peace?

Baehrens ingeniously conjectured *seditio ut* for the gibberish[119] at the beginning of 31, enthusiastically adopted by most Flavian-fanciers as an explicit reference to Eugenius's rebellion.[120] If the emendation fitted neatly into the syntax and restored good sense, it might be worth considering. But it does neither. What would be the sense in: "what was this madness, what was this folly, in order that sedition might disturb your rest." Whose folly, and whose rest? The poet uses *vester* four times elsewhere, twice in the prologue, where it obviously refers to the pagans addressed in line 1: *Iuppiter hic vester* (9) and *sacratis vestris* (24).[121] But in 25 (*praefectus vester quid profuit urbi?*) and 46 (*sacratus vester urbi quid praestitit?*) the emphasis on the city implies "you Romans." In 31 likewise it is natural to refer *vestram* to the *Roma* apostrophied in the following line: "what madness, what folly…would disturb your rest, beautiful Roma." The madness is usually assumed to be the prefect's, but the poet does not begin to describe his behavior till line 34, and, however criminal and foolish, why would it disturb anyone's rest?

All previous interpretations have been predicated on interpreting *iustitium* in 32 as a state of emergency. Once we assign the word the only meaning it can bear in contemporary Latin, everything falls into place, and for the first time the entire passage makes sense as a whole. The poet is addressing the people of Rome on the subject of a prefect who has recently died. It is the noisy excesses of their foolish grief that are disturbing Rome's peace and quiet. In 25 and again in 46 he asks them what good the

---

118. Drac. *Rom.* ix. 28; Jer. *Ep.* 23. 3.

119. Adamik reads SED OVT or OVI; at my request, Jean-Pierre Callu and Marie-Pierre Laffitte, conservateur général of the BNF, have confirmed that the manuscript offers SED OVT with what looks like an erased I between the D and O. Callu also points out that initial SED might have been retrojected from line 34, in which case the original reading might have begun quite differently.

120. So most recently Adamik 1995.

121. Cracco Ruggini 1979, 89, interprets *quies* as more or less a technical term of civic law and order, citing *necessaria quaedam Romanae quieti* at Cassiodorus, *Var.* ix. 19. 2. But obviously the *Romanae* there makes all the difference. There is no call to read so much into so commonplace a word without any pointer in the context.

prefect has done the city? No one seems to have wondered what the point of this emphatically repeated question is. The poet affects to be astonished at the sight of the city in mourning (*iustitium, saga*), and asks incredulously what the prefect has done for the city to deserve this outpouring of grief.

Another passage held to point to Flavian is 112–14:

> sola tamen gaudet meretrix te consule Flora,
> ludorum turpis genetrix Venerisque magistra,
> composuit templum nuper cui Symmachus heres.

Flora alone rejoices in your consulship, Flora the whore, shameful mother of games and teacher of Venus, for whom your heir Symmachus recently built a temple.

A number of critics have found *Symmachus heres* a major objection to Praetextatus, principally (it seems) because they assume a *legal* relationship. For Cracco Ruggini, the heir is Q. Aur. Symmachus, son and heir of his father Avianius Symmachus, city prefect in 384–85. Musso used the same explanation to argue for Memmius Symmachus, son and heir of Q. Aur. Symmachus.[122] But while it is not impossible that *Symmachus heres* might mean "the younger Symmachus," the context surely leads us to expect this person to be the prefect's heir.[123] For Matthews, the heir was the younger Flavian who, having married Symmachus's daughter, "is accurately described as *Symmachus heres*." Hardly. Symmachus's heir would be his own son, Memmius Symmachus.

For Cracco Ruggini, Symmachus completed the renovation of a temple of Flora begun before his death by Praetextatus. Musso objected that no such renovations could have been undertaken at state expense after 382, arguing that Memmius restored the temple as part of his quaestorian games in 393, as part of Flavian's "pagan restoration."[124] But his quaestorian games did not fall during Flavian's consular year (394), nor is there any other evidence for temple restoration forming part of any games— nor is it likely, given the expense of the games themselves. Furthermore, Q. Aur. Symmachus took care to keep his distance from Eugenius's regime.

According to Matthews, these lines offer "a specific point of information, as firm and precise as any in the poem."[125] Specific, but not firm and hardly "information." We must not overlook the strange but emphatic qualification: Flora *alone* rejoices in his consulate. What is the point of that *sola*? If the prefect was really consul, how can he possibly have had only one admirer, and that a goddess? What of his wife and

---

122. Both refer to *Olybriaci generisque et nominis heres* in Prud. *Contra Symm.* i. 554. But it is one thing to praise an aristocrat in terms of his descent from long-dead ancestors, and quite another to use *heres* to distinguish the younger of two homonyms while the elder (in Memmius's case) is still alive.

123. The one strength of Mazzarino's identification is Symmachus père as prefect and Symmachus fils as heir.

124. Cracco Ruggini 1979, 111; Musso 1979, 191–203; Roda 1973, 81.

125. Matthews 1970, 470; as he rightly argues, it must therefore exclude Pompeianus.

family? And why did Flora rejoice because of a temple built by someone *other* than the prefect himself? Even within the hyperbolic terms of an invective there must be some basis for this puzzling complex of remarkably precise claims.

It has often been held a fatal hole in the case for Praetextatus that he was never consul. Yet he was consul designate when he died. If he had just lived till 1 January 385 the year would ever after have been known by his name, a fact mockingly and repeatedly underlined by at least one contemporary. In a letter written perhaps only days after the event, Jerome contrasts Praetextatus's death with the recent death of his friend Lea. Like the poet, he refers to Praetextatus obliquely by title; while Lea is in heaven, the "consul designate" is in hell. He goes on to draw a vivid picture of Lea "in the bosom of Abraham looking on the rich man in his purple, the consul *not yet in his triumphal robe*, but already cursed, begging for a drop of water from the tip of her finger."[126] Finally, when telling his famous anecdote about Praetextatus and Damasus thirteen years later, Jerome again refers to him as "the wretch who died consul designate."[127] There was good reason for connecting Praetextatus's death with his failure to become consul. It was common knowledge that he was ill and died just before reaching the consulate to which he had been designated. Our poet is surely making the same point.

We saw in an earlier chapter how Praetextatus got permission from court to allow Symmachus, in his capacity as city prefect, to recover objects looted from pagan temples (Ch. 2. 1). Little was done before Praetextatus died, but it may be that the one temple that managed to recover its plundered statues was Flora's. The advantage of this hypothesis over Cracco Ruggini's is that it is an independently documented collaboration between Praetextatus and Symmachus in a matter concerning the restoration of pagan temples. Both their names will have been included in the dedication commemorating their work, in which Praetextatus will naturally and properly have been styled *consul designatus*—perhaps even just *consul*.

Once a man had been designated consul he was regularly so styled in official documents,[128] normally but not invariably with the limiting participle *designatus*. The cursus inscription to a statue of Symmachus's father erected by the senate after his death while still consul designate in 376 describes him simply as *consul*.[129] In a letter sending his apologies for not attending the upcoming inauguration of Syagrius, Symmachus addresses the consul designate straightforwardly as *consul amplissime*.[130] When asking the emperors to erect statues to Praetextatus a month or so later he styles him "the

---

126. *Ep.* 23. 2 and 3; the bosom of Abraham, the rich man in purple, the finger and the water come from Luke 16. 19–24, which Jerome is paraphrasing.

127. *miserabilis Praetextatus, qui designatus consul est mortuus, c. Ioh. Hier.* 8.

128. For examples and discussion, Cameron in *CLRE* 18–20.

129. *Symmacho v.c. praefecto urbi consuli pro praefectis praetorio…*(*ILS* 1257); Symmachus's speech of thanks to the senate for supporting his father's nomination (*Or.* iv) was delivered earlier that year, but much of it implies that he was already consul.

130. *Epp.* i. 101; none of his other letters to consuls designate specify that they are still designate: for example, to Ausonius (*Epp.* i. 19, 20, 21); Neoterius cos. 389 (*Epp.* v. 38); Theodorus cos. 398 (*Epp.* v. 5–6, 10–11).

man you justly appointed consul."[131] Since he did not live to give his name to the year, the inscription commemorating this refurbished temple of Flora may indeed have been the only epigraphic monument to Praetextatus's consulate. That would explain perfectly how "only Flora the whore found any satisfaction in your consulate."

That leaves one detail. How could Symmachus be Praetextatus's heir? Whether or not there was really a pagan party, contemporaries, like posterity (Macrobius, e.g.), certainly looked on Praetextatus and Symmachus as the two most distinguished pagans of the age. And in the year 384 they held the two highest civilian offices in the West together. If ever there was a moment when paganism seemed poised to seize back the initiative, it was 384. Then Praetextatus died. As the author of a plea for the restoration of the altar of Victory that very year and the official charged by Praetextatus himself to restore looted statues to temples, Symmachus must have seemed his obvious successor as leader of the pagan cause. The word *heres* is not infrequently used of a wider sort of succession.[132] Symmachus calls his father "legitimate heir of the literature of old," and Jerome his friend Paula "the heir of Paul whose name she bears," obviously meaning spiritual heir, since the rest of the sentence is devoted to her biological genealogy.[133]

In the event Symmachus proved a broken reed. Within barely a month of Praetextatus's death he resigned his office and retired to his estates in Campania. If this is the sort of succession the poet had in mind, then he was writing before February 385, by when Symmachus had left office and failed to take up his legacy.[134] The *heres* need not imply that the restoration of the temple postdated the prefect's death, only that Symmachus became his heir on his death.

5

Two passages (51–56 and 78–86) represent the prefect in an aggressive, not to say murderous light. First 51–56:

> fundere qui incautis studuit concepta venena,
> mille nocendi vias, totidem cum quaereret artes;
> perdere quos voluit, percussit, luridus anguis,
> contra deum verum frustra bellare paratus,
> qui tacitus semper lugeret tempora pacis   55
> ne<c> proprium interius posset vulgare dolorem

---

131. *quem iure consulem feceratis, Rel.* 12. 5; four surviving cursus inscriptions describe him as *consul desig-natus* (*CIL* vi. 1777–80; *ILS* 1258–59), all quoted by Chastagnol 1962, 172–73.
132. *TLL* s.v. *heres* I. B *sensu laxiore* (col. 2654) and *sensu translato* (2655).
133. Symm. *Ep.* i. 3. 2; Jer. *Ep.* 108. 1.
134. Chastagnol 1962, 226.

eager to spray the poisons he had devised on the unwary, seeking a thousand ways of doing harm and as many contrivances. Those he wanted to ruin he struck down like a ghastly snake, ready as he was to fight the true God in vain. He would always lament in silence times of peace, unable to proclaim his own deep grief.

Critics have solemnly debated this "time of peace" the prefect lamented, variously identifying one period or another of good relations between pagans and Christians.[135] But does anything in this entire passage refer to the real world at all? Is the poet seriously accusing the prefect of indiscriminate murder by *poisoning*? If so, then he can hardly be thinking of the Frigidus. The solution lies in another direction entirely.

This "lurid serpent" who laments times of peace, fights against the true god, and pours poison down the throats of the unwary is no mortal man but—the *devil*. The devil regularly appears in Christian Latin texts (especially poetry) in the guise of a serpent, often simply as *serpens* or one of its more poetical equivalents (*anguis, coluber, draco*). There are countless examples in poets of the turn of the century like Damasus, Paulinus of Nola, Prudentius, and Claudius Marius Victor.[136] A variety of epithets underline different aspects of his evil presence: *antiquus, callidus, cruentus, improbus, perfidus, profanus, tortuosus*—and even (as in *CCP*) the graphic *luridus* (sallow, ghastly, lurid). According to Evagrius's Latin translation of the *Life of Antony* (§ 40), when tempted by the devil in the form of an old monk, the saint recognized *luridam faciem serpentis*. In many of these passages there is explicit reference to the serpent's *venenum*. According to Prudentius, for example, the serpent sprays all earthly things with his poison.[137] The closest single parallel is perhaps Paulinus 19. 72–73 (written in 405), describing how

> *lividus* incassum *serpens* fremit ore cruento,
> *lugens* humanam ieiuna fauce salutem.

> The spiteful serpent vainly hisses with its bloodstained mouth,
> and with hungry jaws laments the salvation of mankind.

Here, just as in *CCP* 54–56, the serpent laments (*lugeret ~ lugens*) human happiness.

Mille nocendi vias in l. 52 is borrowed from the *mille nocendi artes* known to the Fury Allecto in *Aen.* vii. 338. Not surprisingly, a great many Christian writers applied

---

135. For the various suggestions, Bartalucci 1998, 128–29.
136. Paul. Nol. 27. 573, 31. 83 and 107 (*serpens*); 31. 184 (*anguis*); 19. 158 and 28. 248 (*draco*); 19. 161 (*coluber*); Prud. *Per.* 6. 23, *Cath.* 3. 126, *Symm.* i pr. 38 (*coluber*); *Cath.* 3. 111 (*draco*); *Apoth.* 406, *Cath.* 9. 91, 6. 141 (*serpens*).
137. Prud. *Per.* 14. 113–15: *draco...terrena...omnia / spargit venenis*; at *Ditt.* i. 1 Eve is stained by *venenum* from the serpent's mouth; Damasus 1. 21, *serpentis dira venena*; Victor, *Alethia* 395, *serpens dira veneno*; ib. 410–22, the *serpens* with his *venenum*; Paulinus 16. 52–57, the devil *rabidis inflavit colla venenis* and pours his venom into the hearts of the wicked; 5. 31–34, God is begged to ward off the *venenum* with which the *serpens* destroyed Eve; 15. 156–58, God wards off the *venena* of the *serpens antiquus*.

this tag to the devil, the earliest known being Martin of Tours and Paulinus of Nola.[138] Contemporary Christian readers would at once have identified *luridus anguis* as the devil. The prefect is being identified as one of the forms the devil took in Rome of the 380s. That is certainly a damning assessment, but at the same time it removes the "time of peace" and the accusation of poisoning from the human realm. It is the souls, not the bodies of the unwary, that are being poisoned.

The second passage is 78–86, describing how the prefect tried to seduce Christians away from the true faith, on the Flavian identification one of the most important passages for the hypothesis of an aggressive pagan reaction:

> Christicolas multos voluit sic perdere demens,
> qui vellent sine lege mori, donaret honores
> oblitosque sui caperet quos daemonis arte, 80
> muneribus cupiens quorundam frangere mentes
> aut alios facerĕ prava mercede profanos
> mittereque inferias miseros sub Tartara secum.
> solvere qui [....] voluit pia foedera, leges,
> Leucadium fecit fundos curaret Afrorum, 85
> perdere Marcianum †sibi† proconsul ut esset.

In his madness he wanted to destroy many Christians. He would give rewards to those willing to die outside the <Christian> law, men whom, forgetful of themselves, he would ensnare through demonic artifice, seeking to weaken the minds of some by gifts and turn others away from God for a paltry reward, sending the wretches down with him to hell as an offering to the dead. Being eager to break the sacred laws and pious commandments, he persuaded Leucadius, in charge of the estates of Africa, to corrupt Marcianus so that he might be his proconsul.

The last two lines are firmly anchored in the real world, and, taken out of context, the first might be thought to imply actual warfare. But the emphasis falls on those "*willing* (*qui vellent*) to die outside the law": not people dying in battle, but people prepared to die outside the faith, that is to say, abandon Christianity and risk going to hell *when* they die. The sweeping "destroy" (*perdere*) of line 78 is at once qualified by "ensnare" and "weaken," with bribes and gifts, not warfare; and the objects of these attacks are "some," "others," Leucadius and Marcianus. It is frustrating that Leucadius and Marcianus are otherwise unknown, but the context suggests no more than apostasy in return for the bribe of some office (Conclusion). As before, all this warfare is spiritual, and its victims are a few individuals, not whole armies. We might compare Augustine's description of the tongue of the rhetorician M. Victorinus in his pagan days as "the

---

138. For numerous examples, cited in full, Courcelle 1984, 542–49.

great, sharp weapon with which he had destroyed many."[139] The fact that the prefect does these things *daemonis arte* (80) picks up the demoniac inspiration of 51–56 (*mille nocendi…artes*, 52). None of this fits Flavian's role in the rebellion of 392–94.

6

Let us take a closer look at the claim that the prefect was "snatched up to the throne of Jove" (line 26). With Froehner's *iactatis* for *tractatus*, this becomes a pagan boast that the Christian poet is mocking. While perfectly acceptable for Flavian, it fits Praetextatus much better if we take into account Jerome's claim, in a letter written only days after his death (*Ep.* 23. 3), that Praetextatus "is a prisoner in the foulest darkness, not (as his wretched wife falsely claims) in the royal abode of the Milky Way." Jerome repeats the point in another contemporary letter (*Ep.* 39. 3), reproaching Paula for not believing that her daughter Blesilla is in heaven when "the devil's handmaid" (namely Paulina) fantasizes that her unbelieving husband is in heaven (*infidelem maritum fingit in caelum*).

The fact that Jerome makes essentially the same point twice suggests that Paulina really did make such a claim—which he expected Paula to recognize. Why "devil's handmaid" (*ancilla*)? Perhaps because Paulina refers to herself as "handmaid to the gods" (*famula divis*) in her only known work, the long and moving poem on Praetextatus inscribed (together with two on her by Praetextatus) on his surviving funerary monument.[140] Where did she say that Praetextatus was in heaven? The natural assumption is in the same poem. Yet there are problems with this hypothesis. In the first place, the poem itself contains no such explicit claim. Second, Jerome must have written long before the completion and erection of the monument. Third, the standard modern treatment of these poems, by Polara, argues that they were inscribed years later and written by someone else in the names of the couple.[141]

It is certainly odd to find husband and wife addressing each other on their joint funerary monument. On general stylistic grounds Polara argued that all three are by the same hand, in which case the writer could not have been Praetextatus, since the poem ascribed to Paulina mentions his death. And while Paulina could have written this poem, it is perhaps unlikely that she wrote the other two, both of which praise her to the skies.

But it is not hard to overcome these difficulties. In the first place, while the poems are undoubtedly similar, Paulina's has two metrical irregularities absent from the two poems ascribed to Praetextatus.[142] The metrical practice of the other two (admittedly

---

139. *quo telo grandi et acuto multos peremerat, Conf.* 8. 4. 9.

140. *CIL* vi. 1779 = *ILS* 1259; some brief notes in F. Buecheler, *CLE* (*Anth. Lat.* ii. 1, 1882), 111.

141. Polara 1967, 40–65; for some second thoughts, Polara in Consolino 2000, 107–26.

142. The second-foot spondee *exemplum de me* in 34 (where Buecheler outrageously "corrects" to *exempla*) and fourth-foot anapaest *famulam divis dicas* in 24.

only eighteen lines) is stricter. Second, Paulina's contribution is a highly idiosyncratic and deeply personal piece, not at all the sort of poem one expects to find on a funerary monument. She refuses to speak of Praetextatus's public career, on the ground that he considered such honors transient and trivial, and devotes more than a third of the poem to their shared religious life, in particular to the fact that he initiated her into all his mysteries. Third, there is the extreme disproportion in length between the three poems: Paulina forty-one lines, Praetextatus six and twelve lines, each the sole inscription on one side of the monument. It might seem natural that the poem on Praetextatus, obviously the more important person, should be the longest of the three, yet it is in fact more about Paulina than Praetextatus. With only minor modifications much of it could in fact have been transferred to the much shorter poems on Paulina. Anyone commissioned to provide one poem for each of the three sides of the monument would surely have produced three more conventional poems of much the same length.

Except for a four-line appendix to Paulina's poem, all three are couched in the present tense throughout as if both were alive. While this can be explained naturally enough as a dramatic device, another possibility is that the three poems were actually written during the lifetime of the couple. This would better explain the rather abrupt final four lines in which Paulina briefly laments Praetextatus's death and expresses her conviction that they will soon be together again:

> his nunc ademptis maesta coniunx maceror.
> felix, maritum si superstitem mihi
> divi dedissent, sed tamen felix, tua
> quia sum fuique postque mortem mox ero. (38–41)

Now, robbed of these things, I, your grief-stricken wife, am wasting away. Happy would I have been had the gods granted that my husband outlive me. Yet I am still happy because I am yours, was yours, and soon shall be yours after death.

The transition is unsatisfactory. In context, the "things" she has lost (*his nunc ademptis,* 38) must be the various honors (*insignia,* 37) she has won through Praetextatus and which have made her the envy of her peers. Yet Praetextatus's death did not really take any of these things away. What she lost was Praetextatus himself.[143] The awkward transition suggests that lines 38–41 are a later supplement to an otherwise complete poem written by Paulina herself while Praetextatus was still alive. In comparison with the leisurely treatment of their shared initiations, the expression of her grief is curiously perfunctory. I suggest that the three poems were not originally composed for inscription on a funerary monument. They are, after all, remarkably long and personal for such a purpose and location. As an alternative occasion I suggest the fortieth

---

143. *te nunc adempto* would have made a more satisfactory transition, picking up ten earlier examples of *tu* and *te.*

wedding anniversary commemorated on the front on the monument (*coniuncti simul vixerunt ann(os) xl*).

Fully half of Paulina's poem is devoted to the fact that Praetextatus had encouraged her to share all his mystery initiations. Her proud claim that through Praetextatus "though unknown, I am known by all" (*ignota noscor omnibus*), implies a notoriety (confirmed by the two letters of Jerome) that may not have met with the universal approval she claims. Paulina is one of only two women named in Symmachus's extensive correspondence (the other being the Vestal Virgin Primigenia found guilty of unchastity).[144] We may contrast his praise of his own (unnamed) daughter's more traditional skill at working wool! We have already seen that Paulina disagreed with Symmachus about the proper commemoration of her husband (p. 725). On any hypothesis the monument was inscribed in two stages. The eccentric spacing on the front shows that room was left beneath Praetextatus's cursus for the subsequent addition of Paulina's, as often happens (then as now) on joint monuments for husband and wife. Paulina (I suggest) had an existing poem of her own inscribed on the rear with a brief appendix to make it funerary. Praetextatus's poems on Paulina were added later together with her cursus after she died.

A partial parallel is provided by the tombstone of a poet who must have died at about the same time: Rufius Festus *signo* Avienius. His son Placidus added to his own funerary epigram a poem by Festus "about himself to the goddess Nortia."[145] In it the poet looks back contentedly on his life, honors, marriage, children, ancestors, and local religious traditions, evidently in old age. Whether or not he wrote it with this aim in mind, Festus's poem (perhaps an excerpt from a longer work) makes a highly appropriate epitaph. Toward the end of their lives Praetextatus and Paulina may likewise have written (and if not formally published, at any rate circulated among their friends) a cycle of poems about their life together.

If the poems were available before the completion of the monument, that would explain how Jerome came to know them so soon. Symmachus too seems to have known Paulina's poem as early as Jerome. In the very letter in which he requests the emperor to erect statues to Praetextatus's memory, Symmachus remarks that he makes the request "not because he would wish for any such earthly reward, for he spurned all physical pleasures as merely transitory" (*gaudia corporis...ut caduca calcavit, Rel.* 12. 2). According to Paulina,

> quid nunc honores aut potestates loquar,
> hominumque votis adpetita *gaudia*,
> quae tu *caduca* ac parva semper autumans
> divum sacerdos infulis celsus clues. (18–21)

144. Symm. *Ep.* i. 48 (Paulina); ix. 147–48 (Primigenia).
145. *R. Festus v.c. de se ad deam Nortiam,* ILS 2944, with Cameron 1995, 252–53.

> Why should I mention your high offices, and the joys men seek in their prayers,
> which you have always considered transient and trivial, well known as you are
> in your priestly headbands as a priest of the gods.

Since the letter clearly predates the statue, it has hitherto been taken for granted
that the poem imitates Symmachus. This is not impossible. Yet the idea is more pow-
erfully developed in the poem, where there is a radical contrast between worldly and
spiritual rewards, whereas in Symmachus no more is implied than that Praetextatus
thought statues ostentatious. Nor is this a mere *praeteritio*; remarkably enough, in
thirty-nine lines the poem mentions none of Praetextatus's worldy honors.[146] The
probability that Symmachus echoes the poem would be increased if Jerome, likewise
writing before the erection of the statue, did so too.

According to Jerome, Paulina claimed that her dead husband was now *in lacteo caeli
palatio*. There is no such precise claim in the poem. Nothing closer than lines 8–9, where
Paulina praises Praetextatus for his study of the writings (Greek and Latin) of "the wise,
to whom the gate of heaven lies open."[147] According to one widespread view, usually classified as Pythagorean, it was to the moon that human souls went after death, and the
moon itself is sometimes identified as the "gate" of heaven.[148] For others it was the Milky
Way, and the tropical signs of Cancer and Capricorn were held to be the "gates" through
which souls had to pass on their way to and then back from heaven.[149] It is unlikely that
Jerome was simply embellishing Paulina's words on the basis of his own knowledge, since
this line refers, not to Praetextatus's own posthumous location, but to his study while alive
of philosophers who wrote on the subject. Furthermore, Jerome's own contrast between
the palace in the sky envisaged by Paulina and the foul darkness of hell where Praetextatus
has really gone suggests that he is quoting her actual words. The phrase *in lacteo caeli palatio* calls forth two observations. First, "milky palace of the sky," with its transferred epithet,
is the elevated diction of poetry, meaning "palace in the Milky Way." Second, we have only
to invert the first two words and we have the greater part of an iambic senarius: *caelī lāctĕō
pălātĭō*. I suggest that Jerome's quotation is an actual fragment from another poem by
Paulina, not included on the Praetextatus monument.[150]

Let us return to the *CCP* and the pagan boast that the prefect "was snatched up to
the throne of Jove." Although the boaster is not here identified as the prefect's wife, the

---

146. It is true that they are listed in full in the cursus inscription on the front, but even so on most monuments where there is a poem as well as a cursus inscription, the main purpose of the poem is to evoke
the offices held in more poetical style: e.g., *ILS* 1241–42 for Proculus PVR 337 (Chastagnol 1962, 98);
AE 1953, 239 for Bassus PVR 359 (Chastagnol 150); *ILAlg* I. 1285 for Olybrius PVR 368–70 (Chastagnol
181); *ILS* 1269 for Probus cos. 406; and indeed *AE* 1928, 48 for Praetextatus himself during his proconsulate of Achaea (Chastagnol 175).

147. *soforum, porta quis caeli patet*, line 9; and cf. l. 40–41, *tua / quia sum fuique postque mortem mox ero.*

148. Cumont 1942, 177–252 (178 and 201 n. 1 for the "gate" motif).

149. Mac. *Comm. Somn. Scip.* i. 12. 2; Cumont 1929, 301–2, n. 28. Symmachus represents the soul of
Valentinian I looking down *ex arce siderea* in *Rel.* 3. 20.

150. Or at any rate not on the surviving monument; there may have been others.

other half of Jerome's contrast does appear at the end of the poem (116–22), where it is the incessant prayers and vows of the prefect's wife that have "sent the wretch headlong to hell" (*praecipitem inferias miserum sub Tartara misit*). Indeed, a little earlier in *Ep*. 23. 2 it is precisely *in Tartaro* that Jerome places Praetextatus. Just like Jerome, the Christian poet makes fun of the contrast between the hoped for and actual destination of his pagan victim's soul after death.[151] More significant still, both link this change of direction to his wife's prayers. This certainly fits Praetextatus better than any other candidate.

7

To sum up, there are decisive objections to Flavian, and every argument produced in his favor fits Praetextatus better. There are in addition seven details that point specifically to Praetextatus, none perhaps individually compelling but cumulatively (I would submit) irresistible:

(1) The poet makes much play with the word *sacratus* (lines 6, 34, 46, 76, 88, and 95), always ironic. The two most obvious cases are lines 34 ("sed fuit in terris nullus sacratior illo") and 46 ("sacratus vester urbi quid praestitit, oro"). It is not a standard term of pagan cult.[152] But it does occur repeatedly in the celebrated monuments listing the initiations of Praetextatus and his wife:

> d. m. Vettius Agorius Praetextatus augur, p[o]ntifex Vestae, pontifex Sol[is], quin-decimvir, curialis Herc[u]lis, *sacratus* Libero et Eleus[ni]s, hierophanta, neocorus, tauroboliatus, pater patrum…et Aconia Paulina c.f., *sacrata* Cereri et Eleusiniis, *sacrata* apud Eginam Hecatae, tauroboliata, hierophantria. (ILS 1259)

On another inscription Paulina is styled *sacrata* no fewer than three times:

> *sacratae* apud Eleusinam deo Iaccho Cereri et Corae, *sacratae* apud Laernam deo Libero et Cereri et Corae, *sacratae* apud Aeginam deabus. (ILS 1260)

It was evidently standard (though never common) imperial Latin for an initiate (in a literary text first attested in Apuleius).[153] Inscriptions attest *sacrati* of Mithras, and Arnobius and Augustine both use it of initiates.[154] Since the word could also mean "cursed," it is easy to see why a Christian would be amused by its repeated application to Praetextatus and his wife and prompted to exploit the double meaning. Jerome

---

151. The jibes of Jerome and the *CCP* poet might explain why Paulina chose not to have the Milky Way poem inscribed on the monument.
152. Adamik 1995, 217 (on line 6) claims that *sacratus* in the *CCP* = *pontifex*, which cannot be true.
153. *Metam*. xi. 23, 24, and 27, with Gwyn Griffiths 1975, 308.
154. Clauss 1992, 21; Arnob. *Adv. pag.* v. 19; Augustine, *Ep.* 17. 4; *City of God* ii. 26.

reacted in the same way. In his letter to Marcella he suggests that, just as the beggar Lazarus in heaven looked on the rich man in the torments of hell, so the pious Lea looks upon the dead Praetextatus as *non palmatum consulem, sed sacratum* (*Ep.* 23. 3), which I take to mean "not now a consul in his triumphal robes but a man cursed."[155] Prudentius makes the martyr Romanus address his pagan persecutor as "sacrate," where it seems natural to find the same double meaning.[156] As we shall see, it may be more than coincidence that Jerome and the *CCP* poet both make the same pun.

(2) The poet claims to be addressing those who worship the Sibyl's cave, the lofty Capitol of Jupiter, the Lares of Priam, the shrine of Vesta, the goddess who married her brother (Juno), the cruel boy (Cupid), and then (line 6) those "whom only the purple *toga praetexta* consecrates" (*purpureā quos sola facit praetexta sacratos*). Most critics see line 6 as simply a roundabout way of identifying *pontifices*, entitled to wear the *toga praetexta* on festal occasions.[157] But most aristocratic Roman pagans were pontiffs. And how are pontiffs made *sacrati*? And why by the purple toga *alone*?[158] Many other elite Romans besides pontiffs were entitled to wear the *praetexta*, and there were other pontifical insignia. When the poet goes to such pains to make a claim that is both untrue and irrelevant we at least expect it to be witty. There is only one explanation that supplies the required point: his subject is an initiate (*sacratus*) called—Praetextatus![159] Our poet was not the only contemporary to play on Praetextatus's name in this way. Macrobius does so too.[160]

(3) In his letter on the death of Lea, paraphrasing a passage in Luke, Jerome draws a vivid picture of Praetextatus in hell begging Lea, who is in heaven, for a drop of water from the tip of her finger.[161] There need be no particular reason for Jerome's choice of this particular passage of Scripture. Anyone suffering in the fires of hell would naturally be thirsty. But sufferers from dropsy were believed to be permanently thirsty. If Praetextatus suffered from dropsy, then (as Cracco Ruggini saw) Jerome would be making a clever and malicious joke.[162]

(4) The prominence accorded to the prefect's wife at the end of the poem not only fits the prominent role accorded to Paulina on Praetextatus's monument, but, more significant, Jerome's letters on Praetextatus's death. Writing to both Marcella and Paula he gloatingly refers to Paulina's pathetic belief that her husband was in heaven

---

155. "non encore promu, mais déjà sacré," Labourt, where "sacré" preserves the ambiguity of the Latin.
156. *Per.* x. 226 (not so taken in the Loeb).
157. Wytzes 1977, 160; Adamik 1995, 217.
158. This *sola*, like the *sola* in l. 112, is one of many illustrations of the importance of paying due attention to the poet's *emphasis*, so central a feature of an invective.
159. This too was seen by Ellis 1879, 80; cf. Ruggini 1979, 78.
160. Macr. *Sat.* i. 6. 3, 25–26. Even if we date Firm. Mat. *De err.* as late as 346, it is out of the question that the *praetextatus* in 18. 6 could also be Praetextatus (so Cracco Ruggini 1998, 507, maintaining her impossible view that Praetextatus, sixty years old in 384, participated in the foundation of Constantinople in 330!).
161. Jer. *Ep.* 23. 3 ~ Luke 16. 19–24.
162. Cracco Ruggini 1979, 83; and 1998, 506 n. 27.

when he was actually in hell.[163] The objection that Flavian too may have had a loyal pagan wife misses the point. Paulina was something of a public figure and pagan activist in her own right, as the poems on her husband's funerary monument so eloquently proclaim. Jerome represents Christ reproaching Paula for lacking the conviction (albeit misguided) of a "pagan woman" (*ethnica*) that her loved one was now in heaven, in the following sentence further characterizing this woman as "the devil's handmaid." Obviously, he expected Paula to identify this unnamed woman.

(5) As Bloch engagingly observed, the deities supposedly worshipped by the prefect are "nearly identical with those worshipped by Praetextatus and his wife."[164] So convinced was he of the traditional identification that it did not occur to him that this was because the prefect *was* Praetextatus!

(6) On f. 45 of the manuscript that carries the *CCP* stands the signature †[VE]TTIVS AGORIVS BASILIVS, not in the hand of the original text scribe, but in a hand that added a number of marginal metrical notes.[165] The natural presumption is that this is the name of an early owner. It has hitherto been supposed that this Vettius Agorius Basilius is to be identified as the Vettius Agorius Basilius Mavortius cos. 527 who "revised" the *Epodes* of Horace.[166] That cannot be. These three names are all that were ever written, and it is inconceivable that, when signing his name in full with some formality, the consul omitted his diacritical name. William Jefferson Clinton does not sign himself William Jefferson. The owner of the manuscript must be some other member of the family. But whoever he was and whatever his date (no earlier than the late fifth century), he was clearly a descendant of *Vettius Agorius* Praetextatus.

Of course it may be that Basilius did not know the identity of the prefect (the poem has no title in his copy). It is also possible that the leaves that carry it (which are written in a different hand and glued onto the rest of the manuscript) were added later than Basilius's day. But the obvious inference is that he knew that it was a poem on his famous pagan ancestor and attached it to the most appropriate book in his library. Mazzarino surprisingly used the same argument *against* identifying the prefect as Praetextatus, on the grounds that no one would want a scurrilous invective on his great-grandfather.[167] I must confess I should be delighted to come across anything of the sort on an ancestor of mine.[168] It is surely a stronger argument for the identification than against.

(7) The last piece in the puzzle (at any rate the last we are likely to find) was published by Dolbeau in 1978. Among various items of early Christian poetry recorded in a library catalogue describing the lost holdings of the Benedictine abbey of Lobbes in

---

163. *Ep.* 23. 3 and 39. 3.
164. Bloch 1945, 230.
165. *CLA* v (1950), 571 *a*; for more information, Winstedt 1904, 112–15.
166. Cameron 1998, 28–39.
167. Mazzarino 1938, 260–61.
168. Compare the eagerness of present-day Australians to claim descent from authentic British convicts.

the eleventh and twelfth centuries, there appears the title *Damasi episcopi versus de Praetextato praefecto urbis*.[169] What are the credentials of this title?

Flavian-fanciers have dismissed it as no more than a baseless medieval guess.[170] It is true that brief texts tended to be copied into manuscripts containing longer works and in consequence often picked up the ascriptions of such works in error. Of the two other anonymous Christian verse invectives we have from this period, one acquired the title *Ad Antonium* from the opening line of the poem, and was ascribed to Paulinus of Nola, probably an accidental consequence of being copied along with the poems of Paulinus. The *Carmen ad senatorem* was less appropriately copied in manuscripts of and ascribed to Cyprian. It is important to be clear that the Lobbes title is quite different in character, involving as it does three separate elements, all (whether correct or not) well grounded and plausible: subject (Praetextatus), title (prefect), and author (Bishop Damasus). Prefect was an obvious guess since the word appears in the poem, but not so the names Praetextatus and Damasus. The only ancient sources where a medieval reader was likely to come across Praetextatus are Macrobius and Jerome—neither of whom identifies him as prefect.[171] And Damasus is only otherwise known for writing on saints and martyrs. A medieval reader reduced to guesswork would surely have guessed Symmachus (named in the poem) as subject and Prudentius (author of a *Contra Symmachum*) as poet. The only surviving copy was indeed attached to a manuscript of Prudentius. Such an accumulation of plausible and internally coherent information must go back to late antiquity.

Damasus took inordinate pride in his poetry, and worked his name and a poeticized version of his title into some twenty of his epigrams, not counting those where it is given in an accompanying prose dedication. If he wrote the *CCP*, he might be expected to have published it openly under his own name. On the other hand, since it is not a work to bring much credit to its author (especially if he was pope), it may at first have circulated anonymously. In the eighteenth century it might have carried some such title as *On a notorious public figure recently deceased, by a member of the clergy*. But one or two friends must have been in the know, nor can it have been easy to conceal the authorship of a poet-pope whose style must have become notorious. Signed copies of his epigrams were magnificently engraved on martyr-tombs all over Rome by his friend the calligrapher Filocalus. The identity of the subject will naturally have been obvious to all, and in the small world of the Christian elite of Rome in 384 the identity of the author cannot long have remained a secret.

In a later article Dolbeau added the important further discovery that the early eleventh-century poet Heriger of Lobbes echoes a couple of passages from the *CCP* in

---

169. Dolbeau 1978, 30, no. 238.

170. So Grünewald 1992, 475 n. 49, with no explanation or justification; likewise Adamik 1995, 194 n. 46 (misunderstanding the argument of Shanzer he cites in support) and Romano 1998, 19.

171. The latter point is made by Cracco Ruggini 1998, 502.

a poem of his own.[172] Passing over less certain cases, it will be enough to cite the following double echo:

> non hic Iunonis nuptae cum fratre sororis…
> nec Phebi numquam verum cortina locuta, (Heriger, *Vita Usmari* i. 348, 358)
> incestosque deos, nuptam cum fratre sororem…
> quis numquam verum Phoebi cortina locuta est. (*CCP* 4, 7)

The phrase *Phoebi cortina* comes from *Aen.* vi. 347, but not the framing *verum…locuta*. We also now know that Heriger shows knowledge of a number of other poets listed in the Lobbes catalogue.[173]

The final proof is the identification (albeit mistaken) of the subject's office as city prefect. The original title presumably offered just *Praetextato praefecto*, and someone added *urbis* on the basis of the strongly Roman emphasis of the *CCP* to which so many modern critics have drawn attention. Whatever we make of the ascription to Damasus, there can no longer be any doubt that the *versus…de Praetextato praefecto urbis* preserved in the library at Lobbes in the eleventh century were indeed the *CCP*. If the library had survived, no one would ever have had any doubt about the identity of the prefect.

<h1 style="text-align:center">8</h1>

If the prefect of the *CCP* is Praetextatus, half the title offered by the Lobbes ascription is correct. That is enough to disprove the notion that it is simply a medieval guess. It also creates a presumption that the other half is correct. Is it really possible that Pope Damasus wrote the *CCP*? There are in fact three separate questions here. Could Damasus have written so *bad* a poem? Could he have written so *unpleasant* a poem? Was he alive at the time it was written?

First, chronology. One fixed point is Damasus's death on 11 December 384. The other is that Praetextatus must have been dead before the end of the year—or he would have become consul on 1 January 385. Some have put Damasus's death first, mainly on the basis of the dramatic date of Macrobius's *Saturnalia*, assuming that Praetextatus is portrayed alive during the Saturnalia (17–22 December) of 384.[174] But I hope to have shown that the dramatic date is not 384, but 382 or at latest 383 (Ch. 7. 4). Since Jerome's letter contrasting the deaths of Blesilla and Praetextatus does not mention the death of Damasus, it has been generally assumed that Damasus was still alive at the time, and accordingly that he died

---

172. Dolbeau 1981, 38–43.
173. Babcock 1986, at 209–21.
174. Shanzer 1986, 241–42; Cracco Ruggini 1979, 115 ("negli ultimi giorni di dicembre del 384").

after Praetextatus.[175] The argument is not compelling, but that does not prove the assumption incorrect.

If an ingenious but fragile series of combinations by Domenico Vera holds, Praetextatus was alive on 2 but dead by 10 December.[176] Obviously, that would leave very little time for the CCP. But if any one of the links in this chain fails, the date fails, and one is particularly weak: the claim that, since Symmachus does not identify Bauto as consul designate in *Rel.* 47 (datable by the gladiatorial games it mentions no earlier than 2 December), Praetextatus must still have been alive at the time. But he does not *identify* Bauto at all. The unnamed *dux* he mentions might be one of at least two other western *magistri militum*. Obviously, Symmachus cannot be expected to specify the future honors of a man he does not name.[177]

Since they so often held it themselves and never appointed more than the traditional two per year, the ordinary consulate was not only the highest honor the emperors could bestow on private citizens, but exceptionally rare.[178] The consular inauguration was a very grand affair with an entire week's games involving months of preparation and enormous expense. It would have detracted considerably from the honor to ask anyone to fill in for someone else at ten days' notice. For his games, Bauto was no doubt able to take over some of the arrangements long since set in motion by Praetextatus, but the personalized ivory diptychs consuls distributed could not simply be transferred from one man to another, and we happen to know that Bauto's were ready in time. We also know that Augustine, newly appointed rhetor of Milan, was ready with a panegyric for Bauto on 1 January.[179] The latest law addressed to Praetextatus as praetorian prefect is dated 4 September 384, and once we leave Macrobius out of account, there are no grounds for placing his death later than November or even October.[180]

Not that we need to allow more than a couple of days for the composition of 122 lines of doggerel. On the basis of *nuper* in 113, it has sometimes been argued that the temple of Flora was renovated after the prefect's death, implying an interval between his death and the writing of the poem.[181] But the poet uses temporal adverbs very freely to fill out his lines (*subito* four, *semper* six times), and even though he only uses *nuper* once, it would be rash to press its chronological implications. It is enough that it implies the later end of the three months' duration of the prefect's illness. Once it is recognized

---

175. *Ep.* 39; so Cavallera 1922, 23–24. For, Chastagnol 1962, 224; against, Shanzer 1986, 241 n. 50; Rebenich 1992, 164 n. 137.

176. Vera 1981, 341–42; and in *Koinonia* 7 (1983), 133–42; Shanzer 1986, 241–42.

177. Bauto is the standard guess (Seeck, Stein, Piganiol, Vera), on the assumption that the consulate must be a reward for a recent victory, but Arbogastes and Rumoridus cannot be excluded (Demandt, "Magister militum" in *RE* Supp. xii [1970], 607–12). There is also another possibility: as Seeck suggested, the substitute consul could have been Arcadius, not Bauto at all (*CLRE* 19).

178. For imperial monopolization of the consulate, Cameron in *CLRE* 5–6.

179. Symm. *Ep.* iv. 15; Aug. *Contra litt. Petiliani* iii. 25. 30; Courcelle 1950, 80–82.

180. Vera also argues that the *sollemnes theatri voluptates* the people refused on the news of his death (Symm. *Rel.* 10) were those of 12–14 December, but obviously there are earlier possibilities.

181. Chastagnol 1969, 143 n. 4 ("assez longtemps après"). I leave out of count Grünewald's gap of forty years.

that *iustitium* refers to the mourning inspired by news of his death, it should be clear that the poet was writing no more than a day or two after. The symptoms of dropsy were so conspicuous that it must have been common knowledge that Praetextatus was seriously ill. Modern newspapers regularly have draft obituaries of the sick and elderly ready, and Damasus may well have sketched out his invective in anticipation.

The philological issue calls for a more minute inquiry. According to Romano, nothing in the style or prosody of the *CCP* suggests Damasus, and Cracco Ruggini agrees that it is simply not good enough for Damasus.[182] Paschoud goes so far as to praise Damasus for "his perfect mastery of classical meter and diction."[183] Recent years have seen a more positive assessment of Damasus's verse, universally condemned by earlier critics for its poverty of thought, metrical errors, and repetitious style.[184] But rehabilitation should not be pressed too far. While individual epigrams have a certain rugged dignity, when read in sequence they reveal a very limited vocabulary of classicizing formulas endlessly recycled with minimal variation. This is exactly the style of the *CCP*.

First a few examples from Damasus: the formula *servat/servas qui altaria Christi* closes 16. 5; 32. 2; and 48. 4; *tulerat/portant qui ex hoste tropaeum* closes 15. 4 and 16. 4; *rapuit/raperet...regia caeli* closes 11. 11; 16. 3; 25. 2; and 47. 3; *feritate tyranni* 18. 6; 40. 6; and 43. 2; *iussa tyranni* 8. 3; 21. 1; and 35. 1; *mira fides rerum* opens 1. 11; 8. 5; and 46. 6. Finally, the entire line *tempore quo gladius secuit pia viscera matris* (of the persecutions, where *mater* = the church) is repeated five times in exactly the same form (17. 1; 31. 1; 35. 5; 43. 1; and 46. 3).

We find a very similar repetition of formulas in *CCP*:[185] *latrator Anubis* closes both 95 and 100; *Megalensibus actis* closes 77 and 107.[186] For similar rather than identical phrases: *artibus heu magicis* (110) ~ *carminibus magicis* (119); *comitem Bacchi* (49) ~ *Egeriae nymphae comites* (70) ~ *nympharum Bacchique comes* (71). With the last formula, compare Damasus 16. 4 (*comites Xysti*) and 25. 3 (*crucis invictae comites*). For repetition extending over a whole line, note the following:

mittereque inferias miseros sub Tartara secum	83
praecipitem inferias miserum sub Tartara misit	120

Where we may also compare Damasus 2. 7:

inferni rapiant *miserum* ne *Tartara* taetri.

---

182. Romano 1998, 19; Cracco Ruggini 1998, 515; so most other critics (Fraschetti 1999, 71).

183. Paschoud 2006, 358.

184. Fontaine 1986, 115–45, with a bibliography of recent studies.

185. Not counting effective repetition like the *quid prodest*? rhetorical questions.

186. Baehrens and Shackleton Bailey both assumed that the second *latrator Anubis* was repeated in error, ousting the original text. This is certainly possible, but what of *Megalensibus actis* and the other repetitions?

The next two lines repeat two different formulas, identically articulated:

> Sarapidos cultor, Etruscis semper amicus   50
> Saturni cultor, Bellonae semper amicus.   68

where we may also compare *Christi perfectus amicus* in Damasus 50. 6. I have already mentioned the repetitious use of temporal adverbs as metrical stopgaps in *CCP*. Damasus does this too. *CCP* has *subito* four times and *semper* six times; Damasus *subito* five times, *semper* three times, *tunc* six times, *nunc* four times, and *hinc* six times.

Next, metrical practice. Every critic has deplored the number of "false" quantities in *CCP*. Value judgments aside, the only relevant factor in the present context is that there are proportionately almost exactly as many in Damasus (*CCP* 17 in 122 lines; Damasus 40 in 320 complete lines). But over and above the simple "errors" we often find in late antique poets (*CCP* 45, *profānare*; Dam. 2. 3, *fābulas*; 44. 3, *decōrans*), we also find one or two shared idiosyncracies. (A) Both allow *qu* to lengthen short vowels: e.g., *purpureā quos* in *CCP* 6; *votāque* in *CCP* 116. This is almost a mannerism in Damasus: *telāque cruenta* (8. 7); *regnāque piorum* (20. 5; 25. 5; 39. 8; 43. 5). There are occasional examples in other late antique poets (many emended away by modern editors), but proportionately fewer.[187] (B) *CCP* twice shortens final *a* in adverbs: *contră* (54) and *sexagintă* (67). Damasus too does this. Not only *posteă* (28. 8) and *octogintă* (67. 13), but *sexagintă* twice (10. 3; 43. 2).[188]

Classicizing poets should not be judged by prosody alone. It may be instructive to compare the practice of Gregory Nazianzen, a learned man, famous orator, and prolific poet, whose verse is notable for literally hundreds of "false" quantities. It is hard to believe that so keen a reader of the fastidious Callimachus (whom he often quotes)[189] was not aware of the correct quantities. Whatever his motives, his practice shows that an otherwise cultivated and technically competent poet might simply not bother about the traditional quantities—especially those at variance with contemporary pronunciation. Like Gregory's, the hexameters in both Damasus and *CCP* are in other respects monotonous in their correctness. In Damasus 296 out of 320 lines have a strong caesura in the third foot (92.5 percent); in *CCP* 113 out of 122 lines (92.6 percent). In both works all but one of the remaining lines have a trochaic break in the third followed by a strong break in the fourth foot. Every hexameter line in both works ends with a two- or three-syllable word. The proportions are virtually identical.

---

187. L. Mueller, *De re metrica poetarum latinorum* (St. Petersburg 1894), 382–83, 443; Paul. Petr. vi. 93, *fractāque* (*fert atque* Petschenig); vi. 442, *plenāque* (*plena atque* Petschenig).

188. Less impressive because commoner is the fact that both lengthen naturally short syllables when they bear the metrical stress. Damasus: *sequerîs Hyacinthe* (46. 3); *populūs ubinam* (35. 5); *CCP*: 13, 44, 46, 50, 73, 82.

189. Cameron 1995a, 334–36.

Then there is the question of elisions. Like most late antique poets, both in general use elision sparingly, mostly of short syllables. But both also share one striking mannerism. Damasus has no fewer than twelve heavy elisions after relative words, concentrated in two positions: seven in the fourth foot (*qu(i) altaria servant*), four in the first (*qu(i) intemerată fide*), and one in the second foot (*vulnera qu(ae) intulerat*).[190] There are four exactly parallel heavy elisions after relative words in the 122 lines of *CCP* (once again, almost exactly the same proportion): *qu(ae) insania mentis*, 30; *qu(i) Hierium*, 47; *fundere qu(i) incautis*, 51; *omnia qu(ae) in templis*, 114.

There are in addition several close verbal parallels between *CCP* and Damasus:[191] (1) "haec Damasus *cumulat supplex altaria donis*" (Dam. 33. 3) ~ "ipsa mola ac manibus coniunx *altaria supplex / dum cumulat donis*" (*CCP* 116–17). Obviously, *Aen.* xi. 50 (*cumulatque altaria donis*) lies behind both passages, but they also share one detail not in Vergil, the *supplex*. (2) Both share the unusual phrase *concepta venena* (Dam. 46. 7 ~ *CCP* 51), emended because of its oddity by some editors. (3) In the very next line of the *CCP*, "carnificumque *vias* pariter tunc *mille nocendi*" (Dam. 27. 2) ~ *mille nocendi vias* (*CCP* 52). Once again, a Vergilian phrase (*mille nocendi artes, Aen.* vii. 337) lies behind both. Courcelle devoted a separate article to countless echoes of this one phrase in later poets.[192] The original Vergilian *artes* is found in every passage he lists save for these two.[193] In the light of these parallels, a few others, less striking in themselves, deserve mention. (4) *dextra laevaque* in *CCP* 105 and Damasus 57.6; (5) *quaereret inventum* in *CCP* 101 (of the corpse of Osiris) and *quaeritur inventus* in Damasus 21. 11 (of the corpse of the martyr Eutychius); (6) *pia foedera* in *CCP* 84 and Damasus 1. 5; (7) the *vester* that appears so often (five times) in *CCP* is also common in Damasus (four times in five lines in *Ep.* 28).

No less striking are the similarities in the texts they know. Both Damasus and the author of *CCP* are steeped in Vergil, and positively stuff their lines with Vergilian tags.[194] But neither could really be described as a learned poet.[195] Vergil is the only classic either seems to know well, underlined by the crudity with which they reproduce whole phrases almost or entirely unaltered. Between fifty and sixty specific passages are echoed in the 122 lines of *CCP*. Damasus knew Juvencus's *Evangelia* and *CCP* Juvenal, but we would hardly expect to find Juvencan echoes in *CCP* or Juvenalian echoes in epigrams on martyrs. But both do betray knowledge of the biblical Cento of Faltonia Betitia Proba.[196] With *ex hoste tropaea . . . / tulerat* at Proba 5–6 compare *tulerat*

190. Dam. 7. 2, 5; 15. 4; 16. 4, 5, 6; 21. 8; 32. 2; 34. 2; 40. 5; 48. 4; 59. 3.

191. First noted by Ihm 1899, 208–12.

192. Courcelle 1947, 219–27; more examples in Courcelle 1984, 539–48.

193. Not counting a Christian epitaph obviously based on the Damasan epigram: Courcelle 1984, 541. On dubious "genetic" grounds, Shanzer 1986, 246, argues that *CCP* imitated Damasus.

194. On Damasus and Vergil, Ferrua's edition; on *CCP* and Vergil, Ihm 1899, 209–10; Adamik 1995, 213–14. Their sheer number can be best appreciated in Romano 1988's apparatus of imitations.

195. It is an exaggeration, with Cracco Ruggini 1998, 515, to credit the author of *CCP* with "an excellent knowledge of classical authors"; so too Mazzarino 1974, 448.

196. Ihm 1895, 195; so too Shanzer 1986, 245, arguing that Proba drew on Damasus.

quae ex hoste tropaea at Damasus 15. 4. Then there is *pia foedera* at Proba 1, Damasus 1. 5, and *CCP* 84; and *penetralia cordis* at Proba 11 and Damasus 50. 5. Finally, note *iurgantesque deos* in Proba (17) and *CCP* 22, in both places evoking the quarrelling Olympians of epic poetry (p. 328).

It is not in itself surprising that two Christian poets should know so recent a work as Proba's Cento, though it is nonetheless striking that both should recall phrases from its twenty-eight-line preface. Much more remarkable is the fact that both knew Petronius's *Satiricon*. In chapter 11 we shall be considering the late fourth-century revival of interest in early imperial literature. Petronius benefited less from this revival than any other major first-century writer. There is no unmistakable allusion in any surviving writer before Damasus—and the *CCP*.[197] A poem in *Satiricon* 128. 6 begins with the following line, *nocte soporifera veluti cum somnia ludunt*, unmistakably echoed in Damasus 21. 9, *nocte soporifera turbant insomnia mentem*. *CCP* 71, *nympharum Bacchique comes*, is no less clear an echo of the beginning of another Petronian poem a few pages later, *nympharum Bacchique comes* (*Satiricon* 133. 3).[198] The only other writers of the age to show any knowledge of Petronius (and that minimal) are Prudentius and Jerome.[199] The fact that both Damasus and *CCP* imitate poems in the same part of so long and little known a work as the *Satiricon* stands out the more in light of their apparent ignorance of much better known poets like Ovid, Lucan, and Statius.

The material assembled thus far shows that the style, metrical practice, and texts drawn on by Damasus match exactly the style, metrical practice, and texts drawn on by the author of the *CCP*. There is a remote possibility that another poet shared all these features,[200] though the fact that he would have to be an exact contemporary only increases the improbability. But there is a final detail that clinches the matter.

More than a century ago Ihm drew attention to a truly remarkable idiosyncrasy of Damasus: complete avoidance of copulative *et* (*et* = and).[201] But no one has noticed that there is no example of copulative *et* in *CCP* either. Both are relatively short texts (320: 122 lines), but even so it cannot have been easy to avoid using the commonest single word in the Latin language. We are bound to conclude that in both cases the avoidance is deliberate. Both overwhelmingly preferred enclitic *que*, but where *-que* was impossible, both Damasus and *CCP* preferred the more elevated *ac* to the mundane *et*.[202] To be precise, in the 320 lines considered genuine Damasus by Ferrua, there

197. K. Müller, *Petronius*[4] (Stuttgart 1995), xxx. Macrobius knew that Petronius Arbiter wrote erotic fiction (*Comm.* i. 2. 8) and Marius Mercator quotes Petronius and Martial as models of obscenity (*PL* 48. 126–27, 133), but no sign that either had actually read any.

198. Note too *carminibus magicis* at the beginning of *CCP* 119 and Petron. 135. 12. 13. And with *totam…urbem / lustravit* in 28–29, Ted Champlin reminds me of *lustravi oculis totam urbem* in Petron. 11. 1.

199. Prud. *Contr Symm.* ii. 179 ~ Petr. F 48. 7; Jer. *Ep.* 130. 19 = Petr. F 24; Müller 1995, xxx. I am not counting grammarians, whose knowledge is likely to be derivative.

200. Prudentius (e.g.) has four examples of short syllables lengthened by -qu (*CS* i. 630; *Apoth.* 320; *Cath.* x. 5; *Per.* iii. 80).

201. Ihm 1895, 195–96; see too Ferrua's index verborum (p. 273).

202. For the "elevation" of *ac*, D. O. Ross Jr., *Style and Tradition in Catullus* (Cambridge, Mass. 1969), 27–33.

is no example of *et* = and, one of *ac* (1. 16), two of *atque*, forty-five of enclitic *-que*, and two of *et* = *etiam*. In the 122 lines of the *CCP*, there is no example of *et* = and, one (perhaps two) of *ac* (72, 116),[203] none of *atque*, twenty-six of *-que*, and two of *et* = *etiam* (15 and 59).[204] The proportions are startlingly similar.

Why would anyone do this? Latin poets had always preferred *-que* (long since vanished from the living language)[205] to *et*, largely because of its metrical convenience in a language less rich than Greek in short syllables. But no other poet, whether classical or contemporary, comes even close to banning *et*. Vergil, the ultimate yardstick in Latin poetic diction, preferred *-que* to *et* by the modest proportion of 4,168: 3,159. In Claudian (round numbers) the proportion is 2,300: 1,250; in Sidonius (poems), 540: 430. If we turn to the three surviving anti-pagan verse invectives, the texts closest in time and genre to the *CCP*, in Prudentius's *Contra Symmachum* the proportion is 316: 334; in the *Carmen ad senatorem* 18: 10; in the *Carmen ad Antonium* 49: 40. That is to say, all save Prudentius, who slightly prefers *et*, slightly prefer *-que*. It is difficult to comprehend why anyone should choose to go so far beyond the practice of all other Latin poets, but coincidence may safely be excluded. Avoidance of *et* can only be seen as a deliberate hyper-poeticism.[206] As in the case of Nonnus, virtuosity is sometimes an end in itself.[207] It passes belief that two different, exactly contemporary poets went to so bizarre an extreme independently.[208]

Even without their shared avoidance of *et*, the sheer number and variety of similarities between Damasus and *CCP* (verbal, metrical, prosodical, stylistic) are impressive, the more so when we take into account the small compass of the two texts and (not least) their very different nature and genre.[209] It is never possible to ascribe an

---

203. At 116–17 the MS offers *ipsa molat manibus coniunx altaria supplex / dum cumulat donis. molat* ("grinds") makes no sense in the context, and in the light of *Aen.* iv. 517 (*ipsa mola manibusque piis altaria iuxta*) Dobbelstein's *mola et* looks tempting. Yet both text and meaning of *Aen.* iv. 517 are uncertain (F and Serv. read *molam*; see Pease, Austin, and Geymonat ad loc.), and in the light of the poet's avoidance of *et*, we should probably accept Ellis's *mola ac* (Ellis 1868, 79).

204. *et quisquam supplex veneratur templa tyranni* (15), imitated from *Aen.* i. 48 (*et quisquam...*), where "*et* marks a querulous or indignant note" (R. G. Austin ad loc.). For *et* = *etiam*, see *TLL* v. 2. 906.74. Note that Bartalucci, evidently unaware of the implications of the Damasan parallel, interprets *et* in 59 = *etiam*.

205. Löfstedt 1911, 87; Leumann, Hofmann, Szantyr, *Lat. Grammatik* 2 (Munich 1965), 473–76.

206. Two other similarities. First, both like puns on proper names: for *CCP* see p. 306 on *praetexta* (6); for Damasus, Cameron 1985a, 138. Second, both indulge in occasional hyper-archaism. Damasus twice has *mage* for *magis* (16. 9; 19. 7), found once in Vergil but nowhere else later than the Augustan age (Harrison on *Aen.* x. 481).

207. Though the self-imposed metrical rules with which Nonnus bound himself (see R. Keydell's edition [1959], 35*–42*) were accompanied by meticulous observance of the traditional quantities.

208. We may also exclude the possibility that one imitated the other. Why would anyone want to, and who would have noticed? No modern scholar has.

209. The only idiosyncracy of *CCP* that cannot be paralleled in Damasus is the eccentric imperfect subjunctives. But it is usually the tense as much as the mood that is problematic, and most are surely either corrupt or governed by conjunctions in omitted lines. Baehrens and Shackleton Bailey posited a lacuna between 10 and 11, and I would posit another between 40 and 41, where the transition is intolerably abrupt, quite apart from the unexplained *ornaret, daret* and *poneret* in 41–43. Adamik's explanation in terms of vulgar usage (1995, 202–3) is unconvincing in a heavily classicizing poem.

anonymous work to a known writer with absolute certainty. But that is not the issue here. Though transmitted anonymously in Par. lat. 8084, in the manuscript Heriger read at Lobbes in the eleventh century, *CCP* was ascribed to Damasus. The only question now is whether there is any justification for disregarding this ascription. I submit that the shared avoidance of *et* provides all the confirmation that could be required. *CCP* and the epigrams of Damasus were written by one and the same author, namely Damasus.

This discovery naturally raises new questions about the character of Pope Damasus. In 384 he was almost eighty, and relied heavily on his new secretary Jerome, to whom he delegated the task of responding to his official correspondence.[210] "I was the spokes man of Damasus of blessed memory," Jerome boasted fifteen years later, looking back on his time in Rome.[211] If Damasus wrote the *CCP*, Jerome surely had a hand in it. More than one critic has drawn attention to Jerome's venomous fascination with the circumstances of Praetextatus's death. There are in fact four specific points of agreement between Jerome and the *CCP*:[212] (1) both emphasize the fact that their pagan subject went to hell, not heaven; (2) both emphasize the futile role played by his wife; (3) both make play with the longed-for consulate he did not live to enjoy; and (4) both exploit the term *sacratus* ironically.

That Jerome shared in the actual writing of *CCP* seems unlikely. We have two brief specimens of his hexameter verse, two epitaphs for his friend Paula, written in 403.[213] Given their brevity and unfamiliarity, it may be worth transcribing them here. The first (A) from the tomb itself (*titulus sepulchri*), the second (B) on the entrance to the cave in which it stood (*in foribus speluncae*):

> A: Scipio quam genuit, Pauli fudere parentes,
> Gracchorum suboles, Agamemnonis inclita proles,
> hoc iacet in tumulo, Paulam dixere priores.
> Eustochiae genetrix, Romani prima senatus,
> pauperiem Christi et Bethlemitica rura secuta est.
>
> B: Respicis angustum praecisa rupe sepulchrum?
> hospitium Paulae est, caelestia regna tenentis.
> fratrem, cognatos, Romam patriamque relinquens,
> divitias, subolem, Bethlemiticŏ conditur antro.
> hic praesepe tuum, Christe, atque hic mystica Māgi
> munera portantes hominique rĕgique deoque.

Though fluent enough, these lines consist (like the *CCP* and Damasus) of a string of clichés loosely strung together. Traina and Consolino will not allow "a learned man

---

210. Rebenich 1992, 144–45; on the relations between Jerome and Damasus, see too Kelly 1975, 82–87.

211. *Ep.* 45. 3. 1.

212. Vera 1983, 137–39; Cracco Ruggini 1998, 503–7.

213. *Ep.* 108. 33. 2; Consolino 1988, 226–42.

like Jerome" to shorten the final syllable of *Bethlemiticŏ* or the first of *rĕgique*, the form in which all manuscripts present B 4 and 7. But Jerome's undoubtedly wide familiarity with Roman poetry would not in itself have enabled him to write correct classicizing verse without considerable practice.[214] We should also bear in mind that this is a critic who judged Damasus *elegans in componendis versibus.*[215] Both print Traina's conjecture *Bethlemiti* (found in one ninth-century MS). This could be right, but Jerome does use the same adjectival form in the last line of A. As for B 6, it is easy enough to write *homini*, but the threefold -*que* in *hominique regique deoque* is rhetorically effective, and it may be that this is a case where the rhetorician triumphed over the metrician in Jerome. He was perhaps misremembering Juvencus i. 250, *regique hominique deoque*, which he quoted in one of his commentaries.[216]

Despite a taste for satire, it is not likely that Jerome undertook anything so ambitious as a full-dress verse invective himself. But he surely discussed the project with Damasus, and may have given him a few ideas. The verses are indisputably Damasus's, but the inspiration may in part be Jerome. This would explain why we find Damasus sinking to the level of scurrility we expect from the pen of Jerome on the rampage. On other evidence there is little indication that Damasus was on notably bad terms with Praetextatus, nor did he intervene personally in the altar of Victory affair earlier that year.[217] He even wrote a letter to court rebutting the accusation that Symmachus had been persecuting Christians to further Praetextatus's project of restoring pagan statues to their temples. But a dignitary of the church who finds it appropriate to preserve a judicious neutrality in his official capacity may nonetheless yield to unworthy instincts in private, especially if egged on by Jerome.[218]

9

But why? Research on the *CCP* has been overwhelmingly concerned with the riddle of its subject, paying curiously little attention to its motivation, presumed self-evident. According to one critic, it was intended to denounce the "crimes" committed by Praetextatus during his prefecture.[219] But no one really believed he was a criminal. It was not criminal acts, however defined, that worried even Jerome and

---

214. I speak from experience, having learned with much labor (and taught others) to compose Latin and Greek verses. On the same basis I have to reject Dolbeau's suggestion (1981, 42 n. 21) that the poor quality of the *CCP* might be due to lack of revision due to Damasus's sudden death. Metrical blunders are not the sort of thing ancient poets wrote in their rough drafts and removed during revision.

215. Jer. *De vir. ill.* 103.

216. *Comm. Matth.* i. 2. 11.

217. Pietri 1976, 429–31.

218. We need not take too seriously Romano's objection that the poem shows too little Christian charity to be the work of a pope. As Dolbeau shrewdly remarks, "Le fait de choisir Jérôme comme familier n'est pas la marque d'un caractère paisible" (1981, 43 n. 23).

219. Puglisi 1981, 235.

Damasus, but Praetextatus's moral and intellectual standing in the Roman community. It was this, if anything, that led to apostacies among the Christian elite. If Praetextatus had been converted on his deathbed, all would have been forgiven. His only crime was being a widely respected pagan, and the greater part of the *CCP* is appropriately concerned with the falsity of his beliefs. We have seen that the poet repeatedly refers to the prefect's death, and (unlike all the other candidates) we know a good deal about the circumstances of Praetextatus's death.

The evidence of Symmachus and Jerome combines to document an outburst of public grief. Symmachus wrote four letters to court on the subject, full of phrases like *summo patriae gemitu, dolor omnium,* and *populi Romani inusitatum dolorem.* This is from the first:

> When first the painful rumour about him spread abroad in Rome, the peo-
> ple refused the usual pleasures of the theatre; with loud shouts (*multa
> adclamatione*) it testified to his glorious memory and was angry at the malice
> of fortune.

Sceptics might be inclined to discount the "loud shouts" of the people, but in a later letter to court Symmachus enclosed copies of these acclamations, attesting "the strong feelings the citizens expressed about his admirable qualities and his honesty on the day he died." Even Jerome admitted that "the entire city was in shock."[220] But he imme-diately added that the man was now in hell. This is exactly the attitude and aim of the *CCP*, to prick the bubble of sentiment aroused by the great man's death.

It is one of the more amiable human weaknesses to celebrate the good rather than bad qualities of controversial figures on their deaths. Praetextatus was a man whose many virtues were universally admired, and not by pagans alone.[221] Even without a formal *iustitium*, the funeral of a Roman aristocrat was a grand affair, an elaborate pro-cession with music, mourners, and grandiloquent eulogies. More generally and more worrying still, it was a moment for affectionate recollections and anecdotes. Jerome and the author of the *CCP* were surely trying to counteract what must have struck them as a dangerously inappropriate outpouring of emotion for an altogether unworthy subject. Their goal was to remind the faithful that this charismatic and popular pagan was now burning in the fires of hell.

The poem's concentration on the prefect's death and insistence that he had *not* gone to heaven (26, 83, 110) only really make sense if it was written within days of his death. Some Christians may have found it harder than others to answer Symmachus's

---

220. Symm. *Rel.* 10. 2; 11; 12. 2; 24. 3; Jer. *Ep.* 23. 3.
221. Much of the eulogy in Ammianus (*praeclarae indolis gravitatisque priscae senator*, xxii. 7. 6) and Symmachus is fairly general, but Symmachus also gives a concrete illustration: "if any benefit ever passed to him under the terms of a will, he immediately passed it back to the nearest kin of the tes-tator" (*Rel.* 12. 3). For an anthology of texts, Musso 1979, 215–21.

question whether there was really only one way to so great a secret. Many of the more tolerant and broad-minded among them were surely wondering whether it was really necessary to believe that so great a man was condemned to everlasting hellfire. Jerome and the author of the *CCP* were clearly anxious to answer that question in the affirmative.

When making his formal request to court for statues to be erected in Praetextatus's memory, Symmachus refers more than once to envy and malice. The emphasis seems too pointed to imply no more than the envy that attends any great man.[222] It was perhaps Christian invectives like Jerome's and the *CCP* he had in mind.

---

222. *hoc uno punit invidiam* [sc. Praetextatus] *quod tantum ei mors ad gloriam contulit, ut huic quoque fortunae livor debeat invidere,* Rel. 12. 1; Vera 1981, 103.

9

OTHER CHRISTIAN VERSE INVECTIVES

1

The *Carmen contra paganos* (*CCP*) is by no means a unique document of its age. Three other anti-pagan poems in hexameter verse date from the same time and place, give or take a decade: the so-called *Carmen ad quendam senatorem* (*CAS*) mistakenly ascribed to Cyprian; the *Carmen ad Antonium* (*CAA*) preserved among the poems of Paulinus of Nola, though certainly not by him;[1] and, most elaborate of all, the two books of Prudentius's *Contra Symmachum* (*CS*).

The author of *CAS* states his reason for writing in verse:

> quia carmina semper amasti
> carmine respondens properavi scribere versus.

Since you are so fond of poetry, I am hastening to answer you with a poem.

He knows that the senator will appreciate a poem, and so he states his case in the form of a poem, in the hope that it will be more likely to convince. So too Paulinus of Nola writes to the young Licentius, a would-be poet, that "I will lead you to the Lord, the inventor of every kind of harmony, by the metres of poetry."[2]

If as many as four such invectives have survived—each by a different route—the probability is that many more once existed. *CAS* and *CCP* are highly rhetorical and, if not learned poetry, at any rate anxious to show off their knowledge of the various cults they depreciate. It is also striking (and, as we shall see, characteristic) that it is the Christians who adapted this new vogue to a very practical and contemporary end. Though none of them betray any unmistakable verbal reminiscences, it seems natural to link this sudden vogue for hexameter invective with the fourth-century rediscovery of Juvenal (Ch. 11). The Lucillus mentioned by Rutilius (*De reditu* i. 598) is said to have written satires worthy of Turnus and Juvenal. It is no doubt significant that the only two surviving quotations of Turnus are found in the Scholia to Juvenal and Servius.[3] Probinus cos. 395 also wrote satirical epigrams.

---

1. "Both the thought and metre are foreign to Paulinus," R. Green 1971, 130–31; Morelli 1912, 481–98.
2. *Ep.* 8. 3, trans. Walsh.
3. Courtney 1993, 362–63.

We have just seen that the ironic jibe at *CCP* 33 about the people donning a *sagum* recalls Juvenal's jibe on the present taste for bread and circuses of the *populus...qui dabat olim / imperium fasces legiones* (10. 74–79). And *perituras fundere voces* at *CCP* 19 echoes Juv. i. 18, *periturae parcere chartae* (see too Bartalucci's note). *CAS* 12–13 on the effeminate priests of the Magna Mater and 26–27 on Isis also have a Juvenalian ring. Note the following on effeminate Isis-worshippers:

> leniter incedunt mollita voce loquentes,
> lassatosque tenent extenso *pollice* lumbos.

These men "walk lightly, speaking with effeminate voice, their loins exhausted with extended thumb," that is to say if (with F and H, the ninth- and tenth-century manuscripts that carry the poem) we read *pollice*. It might seem tempting to recall Juvenal's description of the effeminate men who "scratch their heads with a single finger,"[4] but the rationale behind this custom attributed (no doubt falsely) to effeminate men is reluctance to disturb carefully arranged hair. Nor does *extenso pollice* make good sense; *extendere* should mean "stretch" or "distend," not "extend" ("with finger extended," Croke and Harries), and *pollex* means thumb, not finger. We should print the correction *podice* suggested by an early hand in F, "with rectum stretched." This would explain perfectly why their "loins" are exhausted.[5] And then we might more appropriately compare Juvenal ii. 12, *podice levi*, "with smooth rectum." More generally, according to CAA 93, the devotee of Magna Mater *femineos vitat coitus patiturque viriles*.

According to Bloch, the *CAS* provides "additional testimony for the spirit of defection which spread among the Christian members of the Roman aristocracy at this time.... The poem fits admirably the revival under Flavianus and, like the [*CCP*], it was presumably written soon after the revival's end."[6] Obviously, the new date for the *CCP* will affect this interpretation of the other poems. Thanks to the discovery that *CCP* avoids *et*, we are now able to state with absolute certainty that *CAA* and *CAS* were at any rate not written by the author of *CCP*, though there are a few links between them. For example, there is some similarity between *CAS* 25–27,

> si quis ab Isiaco consul procedat in urbem,
> risus urbis erit: quis te non rideat autem
> qui fueris consul nunc Isidis esse ministrum,

If any consul enters the city from [?a temple of] Isis, he will be a laughingstock for the city. Who will not mock a man who used to be a consul, and is now a servant of Isis?

---

4. Juv. ix. 133 (with Courtney's note); cf. Calvus F 18 (cited by the Juv. scholia ad loc.).
5. For *lumbi* as a somewhat vaguely conceived "seat of sexual desire," Adams 1982, 48.
6. Bloch 1945, 232.

and *CCP* 98–99:

> quis te plangentem non risit, calvus ad aras
> sistriferam Fariam supplex cum forte rogares?

Who did not laugh at you as you mourned, whenever you came to the altars
with shaven head as a suppliant, to beseech rattle-bearing Faria [Isis]

Prudentius too dismisses the rites of Isis, laughable with their bald priests (*ridendãque
suis sollemnia calvis*, 630),[7] as does Paulinus of Nola (*Carm.* XIX. 111–16, 129–31). There
is also an interesting parallel between the accounts of the annual finding of Osiris in
CCP and *CAA*. First *CCP* 100–101:

> cumque Osirim miserum lugens <   > Isis
> quaereret, inventum rursum quem perdere posset.

when mourning wretched Osiris, [as Isis] sought the one she would lose again
when found?

Then *CAA* 119–20:

> nescio quid certe quaerunt gaudentque repertum
> rursus et amittunt quod rursus quaerere possint.

Yes, they look for something and rejoice when they have found it,
and lose it again so that they can hunt for it again

Ovid wrote of *numquamque satis quaesitus Osiris* (*Met.* 9. 693), a passage quoted
(though mistakenly attributed to Lucan) by Lactantius with the ironic comment *semper enim perdunt, semper inveniunt*.[8] According to Firmicus Maternus, "You find
nothing but a statue you hid yourself, to search for and grieve for again."[9] According to
Martianus Capella, Isis loved Osiris so much that "she was never satisfied with finding
him (*numquam eum contenta sit invenire*). Shanzer suggests "a jab at Christian polemic"
(Shanzer 1986, 63), but if anything he is saying the same thing as the Christians.[10] The
joke that they deliberately lose the statue of Osiris so that they can look for it again
seems to be original with these two poets.[11] But in neither case is the similarity close

---

7. Did Prudentius perhaps pick up the unusual lengthening before *qu* from Damasus/*CCP*, for whom it
   was a positive affectation?
8. *Div. Inst.* 1. 21. 21; cf. too Tertull. *Adv Marc.* 1. 13. 5.
9. *De errore prof. rel.* ii. 9.
10. i. 4, p. 3. 12 Willis; Shanzer 1986, 63.
11. It is not to be found, for example, in so rich an inventory of such abuse as Firm. Mat. 2. 9, *simula-
    crum…quod iterum aut quaeras aut lugeas*.

enough to prove direct influence, let alone in which direction. And if there were many other such poems, both themes might turn out to have been commonplaces of the genre.

There are two much closer parallels between *CAS* and *CAA*. First *CAS* 45,

> cur *linquenda* tenes aut cur *retinenda relinquis*?

> why do you cling to what you should renounce, why do you renounce what you should cling to?

and *CAA* 149–50:

> qui *linquenda* colunt contraque *colenda relinquunt*.

> they worship what they should renounce and renounce what they should worship.

Or *CAA* 8:

> dicentes quae sunt fugienda, sequenda, colenda.

Then *CAS* 85,

> non erit in culpa *quem paenitet ante* fuisse,

and *CAA* 238–39,

> *quem paenitet antea* lapsum[12]
> non facit in numero turbae peccantis haberi.

Both passages come at or near the end of their respective poems, urging that repentance will bring forgiveness of past sins.

If the *CCP* had celebrated the death of the elder Flavian and the failure of the "pagan revival," then it might have been worth considering whether the other poems fitted the same context. *CCP* accuses its prefect of seducing Christians from the faith, and *CAS* addresses a once-Christian senator who has abandoned his faith, but there is no suggestion that this senator was the victim of such a Svengali. The one thing *CAS* and *CAA* do share with *CCP*, albeit in different ways, is the lack of any political dimension. None of the three contains any hint of treachery or rebellion.

---

12. It would be easy to repair the metre with *paenitet ante <re>lapsum*, but that might be correcting the poet.

The author of *CAA* claims to have "examined all the sects…and found nothing superior to belief in Christ" (1–3). For long he too was uncertain, tossed by many a storm until the church received him in its harbor of safety and set him in a calm anchorage after his stormy wanderings (153–55). That is to say, he was once a pagan (incidentally, the strongest proof that the author was not Paulinus of Nola). When he comes to his assessment of the various sects and cults, his tone becomes more shrill, but the irenic, conciliatory tone in which he begins hardly suggests a period of polarization such as the aftermath of the fall of Eugenius. When he asks with mock incredulity why the followers of Isis "do not hide their rites instead of parading them through the public places" (117–18), the context makes clear that it is not the illegality of the rites to which he is alluding, but their absurdity, of which the Isiacs should be ashamed. Ambrosiaster's *Contra paganos*, written in the mid-380s, makes much of the shame pagans should feel for the disgrace of their rites (p. 796). The implication is that the rites were not yet illegal: the poet was writing before 391.

CAA opens by apostrophizing a man called Antonius:

> Discussi (fateor) sectas, Antonius, omnes

Many critics have argued that Antonius is the name of the poet, but it is more natural for a writer to begin by identifying his dedicatee rather than himself.[13] Chastagnol, assuming that the poem was addressed to a pagan to urge him to convert, identified Antonius with Rufius Antonius Agrypnius Volusianus, uncle of the younger Melania, famously baptized on his deathbed in Constantinople in 437.[14] But nothing in the poem suggests that the addressee is a pagan, and there is certainly no exhortation to convert. The natural assumption is that Antonius is a fellow Christian, possibly Claudius Antonius cos. 382 (p. 372).

Chastagnol was prepared to date the poem as late as the 430s, assuming (of course) that paganism remained strong in Rome well into the fifth century. But Marinella Corsano has recently noticed that two entire lines are pirated verbatim in a (barely) metrical Roman epitaph dated precisely to 4 October 389.[15] Lines 5–6 of the epitaph run as follows:

> tunc poterit mors ipsa mori cum tempore toto
> vita perennis erit, veniam d[a]bit omnibus unam.

Then death itself will be able to die when life will last for all time, and will offer one forgiveness for all.

The source is clearly *CAA* 233–34,

---

13. See the many parallels cited in the useful recent commentary by Palla and Corsano 2002, 24–28, 94.
14. Chastagnol 1987, 246–47.
15. *ICUR* n.s. V (1971), 13355; Corsano 2000, 39–43.

> tunc poterit mors ipsa mori, cum tempore toto
> vita perennis erit.

The second half of line 6 comes from ten lines earlier in *CAA, veniam dabit omnibus unam* (222). The fact that the borrowed material comes from two different parts of the poem is enough to exclude the possibility of a common source. *CAA* cannot have been written later than the late 380s, well before the Frigidus.

The author of *CAS* likewise writes as though Isiac processions were still to be seen on the streets of Rome, which would rule out Mazzarino's date of 404/5.[16] Sordi has recently suggested accepting the ascription of the poem to Cyprian and so dating it a century and more earlier, ca. 250, arguing that the words *improba secta* placed in the mouth of the apostate at line 63 refer to Christianity, and must therefore have been written before Constantine.[17] But at any date a pagan could be represented depreciating Christianity, and 250 would be improbably early to find a Christian senator, even if he did later renounce his faith.

Rosen more plausibly argued that the senator had become a Christian under Constantius II (337–61) and then lapsed under Julian (361–63).[18] But I am less happy with his assumption that the poet's silence about the traditional Roman cults implies that they were still flourishing, which depends in turn on his (surely mistaken) assumption that the Roman senate remained almost entirely pagan till the 390s.[19] Actually his thesis depends, as formulated, on yet another assumption, common to all modern work on the poem, that this apostate must be a Roman senator and that the poet was writing in Rome. But nothing in the poem itself points to Rome, and the *senatorem* in the title is clearly a guess, as proved by the qualifying *quendam*. An eastern city is equally possible. Earlier in the fourth century Latin was still widely spoken and even written in the East.

Some critics have doubted whether the apostate is a real person at all.[20] There are certainly grounds for scepticism about some details. He is reproached for chanting vile hymns, *respondente tibi volgo et lacerante senatu* (29–30), which should mean that the people applauded and the senate condemned his behavior. Does this mean that the senate was now Christian (Mazzarino), or just that, though still mainly pagans, they disapproved of his shameful behavior (Rosen)? It is not easy to identify a period when the Roman plebs might have been more pro-pagan than the senate. And while it is plausible enough in itself that a convert might abandon his faith after a "few years" (line 44), did he really return to the worship of Magna Mater and Isis, allowing the poet to claim that he shaved his head and shook tamborines, wearing the soft slippers of the Galli and hobnobbing with effeminates and sodomites? Did he really carry

---

16. Mazzarino 1974, 395.
17. Sordi 2008, 149–54.
18. Rosen 1993, 393–408.
19. Rosen 1993, 393; against this last assumption, see Ch. 6. 1.
20. Consolino in Consolino 1995, 317; against, Rosen 1993, 402.

complaisance so far[21] as to embrace precisely those cults Christian controversialists took most pleasure in ridiculing? The poet also makes much of the spectacle of a consul as a minion of Isis (26–27)? Very few Roman senators won consulates in the second half of the fourth century,[22] and not one who could be identified as an apostate Christian. Yet if the poet just wanted to create an identikit apostate, why make so much of so atypical a feature?

Once we consider the possibility that the poet was writing in Antioch or Constantinople rather than Rome, an eminently qualified candidate at once presents himself: Domitius Modestus, an eastern official who had been Count of the East under Constantius (358–62), prefect of Constantinople under Julian (362–63), and again under Valens (369–70), who elevated him to a long tenure of the praetorian prefecture of the East (370–77) and finally the consulate (372).[23] Though in the eyes of his close friend Libanius a pagan, Modestus professed Christianity under Constantius II, but came out openly as a pagan under Julian. Under Valens he professed Christianity again, and became an aggressive enforcer of Valens's pro-Arian policies.[24] Successive emperors were evidently less concerned about his personal beliefs than his loyalty and efficiency. But those who took their religion seriously were understandably scandalized that such an unscrupulous opportunist continued to prosper. His consulate may have been the last straw. While it is unlikely that he openly engaged in any pagan activities after his baptism (as an Arian) under Valens, Rufinus at any rate continued to think of him as a pagan.[25]

An eastern identification would also help to explain another puzzling detail. The poet claims that the apostate's motive was to ingratiate himself with the plebs, and that if their indignation had so moved him, he would have become a Jew (49–50). That a Christian senator of Rome might become a Jew to win popular favor is a surprising and improbable notion. But in some eastern cities Judaism retained its attraction for Christians. While it is unlikely that there were many formal apostasies, in Antioch at any rate many Christians continued to observe some aspects of Jewish law and even attend some Jewish festivals, much to Chrysostom's distress.[26] For most of Modestus's tenure of the praetorian prefecture, Valens's court was based in Antioch. As for *lacerante senatu*, the council of Antioch is likely to have been largely Christian by the 370s.[27]

Domitius Modestus, one of the most prominent and powerful easterners of his age, a man notorious for his switches from pagan to Christian and back again, and a consul to boot, fits the bill to perfection. If so, *CAS* would date from the early 370s, probably not long after Modestus's consulate in 372. All three invectives would then

---

21. To paraphrase Housman on the identity of Ovid's Ibis (*Classical Papers* iii [1972], 1040).
22. Nine between 350 and 400; the suffect consulship was no longer important (Ch. 19. 7).
23. For his career, *PLRE* i. 605–8, with Dagron 1974, 246–47.
24. Dagron 1974, 242–44, 292; Sandwell 2007, 6–8, 258–59; van Dam 2002, 106–35.
25. Ruf. *HE* xi. 5.
26. Wilken 1983; Brottier 2004.
27. Liebeschuetz 1972, 225.

date from well before the Frigidus. Ultimately, the most interesting and important thing about this nexus of anti-pagan poems is their classicizing form and diction rather than any facts they may or may not convey about individual pagans or pagan revivals.

2

Several attempts have been made over the years to establish links between *CCP* and the most important and prolific Latin poet of the turn of the century, Claudian.[28] Since it is hard to imagine Claudian imitating such doggerel, his priority (it might seem) could be taken for granted; and since his major works can all be dated to within a matter of months, a firm terminus ante quem could be established. Manganaro used supposed echoes of Claudian to support his identification of the prefect as Pompeianus, prefect of Rome in 408. None of the parallels so far produced are compelling. The closest is *CCP* 111, *sic, miserande, iaces, parvo donate sepulchro*, which seems to combine two phrases of Claudian: *hic miserande iaces* from *In Eutr.* ii. 460, and *parvo procede sepulchro* from *In Eutr.* i. 458. But neither phrase is particularly striking, and the context in both passages of Claudian is somewhat different. In any case, now we know that *CCP* was written by Damasus, the argument that Claudian must be source rather than borrower loses much of its force. Whatever its literary shortcomings, even Claudian may have glanced at a scurrilous poem by so celebrated a contemporary figure as Pope Damasus.

I would turn the argument upside down. It is the *lack* of parallels between Claudian and these poetasters that I find striking. If any of these Christian pamphleteers had been writing after the recent appearance of the two most brilliant invectives in Latin since Juvenal, we should expect to find unmistakable traces in their work. For example, all three poems mock the effeminate behavior of the castrated priests of Attis (*CCP* 72–77, 109; *CAS* 9–20; *CAA* 88–93). Book i of Claudian's *In Eutropium* contains the most savagely detailed and brilliantly witty inventory of castration and effeminacy motifs ever compiled.[29] We might reasonably expect to find some echo in one at least of these poems if they had been written in or after 399.

3: FALTONIA BETITIA PROBA

There is one other, slightly earlier, Christian poet who needs to be discussed in this context, Faltonia Betitia Proba, whose only surviving work is a Christian Vergil *Cento*.[30] Shanzer has drawn attention to a verbal parallel between the *Cento* and the

---

28. Perelli 1988, 209–25; Shanzer (n. 25 below) 245–46; Consolino in Consolino 1995, 320.
29. Long 1996.
30. Clark and Hatch 1981; Herzog in Herzog and Schmidt 5 § 562.

CCP. Since the *Cento* was written perhaps ca. 370, this would provide a useful (if unsurprising) terminus post quem. Yet this was not Shanzer's argument. Instead she identified the author as Betitia Proba's granddaughter Anicia Faltonia Proba, wife of Petronius Probus, arguing that the *Cento* imitated the *CCP* instead of vice versa.[31] Since the *Cento* was clearly known to Jerome by 394,[32] that would effectively exclude any candidate later than Praetextatus.[33]

This would be useful corroboration of the preceding chapter—if it were true. Since the date and identity of the first Christian poet in the Roman aristocracy—a woman at that—is a matter of some importance in itself over and above its relevance to the date of the *CCP*, a reexamination of the evidence is in order.[34] Shanzer's argument falls into two parts: the identification, and the priority of the *CCP*. It will be best to begin with the second, since a date after 384 would effectively exclude the elder Proba.

The lines in question come from Proba's preface, not yet Vergilian cento but (however derivative) original composition by Proba herself (lines 13–17):

> non nunc ambrosium cura est mihi quaerere nectar,
> nec libet Aonio de vertice ducere Musas;
> non mihi saxa loqui vanus persuadeat error
> laurigerosque sequi tripodas et inania vota
> *iurgantesque deos procerum* victosque penates. (13–17)

No longer do I care to seek ambrosial nectar, nor does it please me to lead down the Muses from the Aonian peak; let no vain error persuade me that rocks talk, or to pursue laurelled tripods, and heroes' empty vows and quarrelling gods and conquered Penates.

Next the *CCP* (lines 20–24):

> nuda Venus deflet, gaudet Mavortius heros,
> Iuppiter in medium nescit finire querellas
> *iurgantesque deos* stimulat Bellona flagello.
> convenit his ducibus, *proceres*, sperare salutem?
> sacratis vestris liceat componere lites?

Naked Venus weeps while Mars rejoices, and Jupiter has no idea how to stop their complaints; Bellona eggs on the quarrelling gods with her whip. Senators,

---

31. Shanzer 1986; 1994, 75–96. The second article is a response to Matthews 1992, 277–304, which effectively rebutted all her original arguments except for the alleged borrowing from the *CCP*.
32. *Ep.* 53. 7; Schanzer 1986, 239 n. 36.
33. Not completely, of course; if the *CCP* were written shortly after Flavianus's death (September 394), there is just time for Proba to have read it before writing a poem that Jerome had read by 396.
34. Matthews 1992, 277–304; R. Green 1995, 551–63; and 1997, 548–59. I have added a few arguments of my own.

is it possible to hope for salvation with leaders like this? Can your consecrated ones solve these disputes.

According to Shanzer,

> The occurrence of the three elements, *iurgantes, deos,* and *proceres,* two of which are not particularly common, so close to one another in related contexts cannot be accidental. This is a clear indication of a genetic relationship between the two poems. I have been unable to find a third possible source of the words, so will work on the assumption that one must be dependent on the other.

She makes much of the *procerum* in Proba, echoing (she assumes) the vocative *proceres* in the following line of *CCP; procerum* she construes as a direct reference to the *CCP*, "those wrangling gods of the senators" (237). This is her proof of the priority of the *CCP*. But the word is used quite differently in the two passages. The author of the *CCP* is addressing living senators of fourth-century Rome, while Proba is simply listing traditional literary devices of the pagan poets that she, a devout Christian, will not use in her poem.

Comparison with *Pegaseium nectar* in Persius[35] is enough to show that the *nectar* of line 13 is water from Hippocrene. There is no need to cite parallels for the most widespread of all dramatizations of poetic inspiration: the Muses tripping down Helicon. Next come talking rocks and laurel-bearing tripods. There are no independent talking rocks in Greek mythology. The rocks belong with the tripods, jointly evoking the Delphic oracle. The Pythia was regularly depicted seated on a tripod or descending into a Delphic cave.[36] *Parnasia rupes* in Vergil (*Buc.* 6. 29) springs to mind, and Lucan has a possessed Delphic priestess scattering tripods inside her cave (5. 169–73). Martianus Capella refers to the "talkative grottoes of the sacred cave."[37] Paulinus of Nola similarly rejects both Muses and Apollo, represented by a cave (x. 19f.). In another poem Paulinus inserts Helicon into the same twin rejection of Apollo and the Muses, in terms very reminiscent of Proba's *Aonia de vertice ducere Musas*:

> non ego Castalidas, vatum phantasmata, Musas
> nec surdum *Aonia* Phoebum *de rupe* ciebo. (xv. 30–31)

What now of the last three items on Proba's list?

> et   inania vota
> iurgantesque deos procerum victosque penates.

---

35. *Prol.* 14; cf. Honestus, *AP* ix. 230, ἐκορέσθης/ Πηγασίδος κρήνης νεκταρέων λιβάδων.
36. See the sources quoted in J. Fontenrose, *The Delphic Oracle* (Berkeley 1978), 200f.
37. *sacrati specus loquacia antra* (11, p. 16 W); cf. πέτρα Δελφῶν in Aeneas of Gaza, *Epp.* 17. 12.

To construe the central phrase as "those wrangling gods of the senators" does violence
to its context, the traditional sources of poetic inspiration. Poets are seldom senators
and senators seldom poets. To identify *procerum* as a reference to fourth-century senators isolates *vota* and *penates*. *victosque penates* is a taunt from Juno's speech at *Aen.* i.
68, repeated by Turnus at viii. 11. Christian polemicists were naturally delighted to
exploit a central pagan text admitting that Rome was founded under the auspices of
defeated gods.[38] But how does the phrase fit *here*, and what are the "empty vows" of the
preceding line? Whose vows?

I suggest that, just as the rocks and tripods of 15–16 collectively designate Apollo,
so the vows, quarrels, and conquered gods likewise collectively depend on the genitive
procerum. Who then are these *proceres*? They are simply the human heroes of the
Aeneid. Rather than derive *procerum* from some hypothetical contemporary source,
why not the one certain source of a Vergilian cento, Vergil himself? *proceres* is after all
the standard Vergilian term for the heroes of his poem, whether Greek (*Danaum proceres*, vi. 489; *Myrmidonum proceres*, xi. 403), Trojan (*o proceres*, iii. 103; *alii proceres*,
i. 740; *agnovere deum proceres*, ix. 659; viii. 587), or others (*delectos populi ad proceres*,
iii. 58; *lecti proceres*, x. 213; *in medio procerum*, xii. 213).

The opening lines of Proba's preface describe a poem she had written at some earlier
date; however, we identify its subject apparently a traditional classicizing epic or panegyric. In putting into Vergilian verse the stories of the Old and New Testaments, she was
writing a Christian epic. Perhaps the single most striking feature of the structure of the
Aeneid (as of most classical epics) is its divine framework. The humans do little that has
not been approved of or suggested by the gods, who are constantly quarrelling among
themselves. Not surprisingly, Christians found these quarrels of the gods scandalous.[39]
The one thing Proba could not possibly do in a Christian epic was make the action depend
on the whims and quarrels of Jupiter, Juno, and company. This is the point she is making
in lines 16–17. The heroes of the *Aeneid* (its *proceres*) are constantly offering up *vota* to the
gods (some thirty times, in fact), gods who are continually quarrelling, gods who, by
Vergil's own admission, have been defeated. Proba promises that her epic will have none
of this nonsense. The *non nunc* with which this section of her preface begins suggests that
her earlier poem (like Claudian's panegyrics and historical epics) *did* invoke the Muses
and employ the traditional divine machinery. This need not mean that she wrote them as
a pagan; merely that she followed the same conventions as Claudian. We find all the traditional divine framework in the Christian Sidonius more than a century later.

On this interpretation, both *iurgantesque deos* and *procerum* are integral parts of
Proba's context. *procerum* is not, after all, proof that *iurgantesque deos* is a "precise

---

38. As Augustine acidly put it, "itane istis *penatibus victis* Romam, ne vinceretur, prudentes commendare
debuerunt," *Civ. Dei* i. 3; cf. *Sermo* 81. 9, with Hagendahl 1967, 324, 390, 417–18; Shanzer 1986, 237 n. 24.

39. Tert. *ad nat.* i. 10. 38; *Apol.* 14. 2; Min. Fel. *Oct.* 24. 2; Aug. *CD* 4. 30; already Cicero, *de nat. deor.* i. 42
(*eorum bella proelia pugnas…discidias discordias…querellas*), with A. S. Pease's comm. on *Aen.* iv (1955,
284–85).

quotation" from the *CCP*.[40] On the other hand, *proceres* had long outgrown its poetic origins to become a standard elevated term for senator; an imperial law dated 3 May 361 lays down as a quorum for the passing of a senatus consultum *decem e procerum numero* who had previously held the consulate.[41] The *CCP* twice apostrophizes its *proceres* (23 and 106). So if it were the later of the two poems, there would be no need to derive its use of the word from Proba, where it is used in a completely different sense.

Neither idea nor execution is distinctive. The motif of quarrelling gods was common in Christian polemic, and anyone wishing to make the point in the formulaic language of hexameter verse was likely to hit on *iurgantesque* or *rixantesque deos* (*superos* or *divos* would have made it hard to work in the connective, required by the syntax in both poems). It may be that the later of the two writers remembered the phrase from the earlier, but since this is the only verbal coincidence between them, there are no internal grounds for determining priority.

As for the identification of the poet, Shanzer approached the issue confident that she had proved the *Cento* later than 384. Without that proof there are no serious grounds for calling into question the remarkably solid and unanimous evidence in favor of the elder Proba.

Three early manuscripts of the *Cento* and two other sources offer the following items of information about the poet (I have numbered each item separately). Both incipit and excipit in Vat. Reg. lat. 1666 (s. XI) identify her as (1) *Flatoniae Vetitiae Probae cl(arissimae) feminae*, that is to say *Faltoniae Betitiae Probae*. This is in fact the only evidence for the full name of the elder Proba. According to the lost Mutinensis (s. X) used by Montfaucon, she was (2) *Proba uxor Adelphi*, (3) *mater Olibrii et Alicpii*, and (4) wrote on the war of Constantine [in fact, Constantius II] *adversus Magnentium*. Another manuscript, Pal. lat. 1753 (s. IX/X), calls her (5) *Aniciorum mater* and (6) *uxor Adelphii expraefecto urbis*. Finally, (7) Isidore of Seville identifies Proba as *uxor Adelphii proconsulis*,[42] and (8) the recently published catalogue of the Benedictine abbey of Lobbes (s. XI/XII) styles her *Valeriae Probae Aniciae*.[43]

According to Shanzer, only items 5 and 8 deserve credence, all the rest being muddled medieval guesswork. Hagith Sivan was also sceptical of the medieval evidence.[44] But to dismiss 1–4 and 6–7 as muddled guesswork is to ignore not only their basic accuracy (assuming identification with the elder Proba) but also their internal coherence. *uxor Adelphii* (2, 6), *expraefecto urbis* (6), and *mater Olibrii et Aliepii* (3) are precise details corroborated for the elder Proba by contemporary sources. Her husband, Clodius Celsinus *signo* Adelphius, was prefect of Rome in 351, and a certain Faltonius Probus Alypius held the same office in 391. The names of the latter make him a highly plausible

---

40. Shanzer 1986, 237.
41. *Cod. Theod.* 6. 4. 12; cf. Symm. *Or.* 4. 6, *nunc idem principes nostri quod proceres volunt.*
42. *De vir. ill.* 22. 18.
43. Dolbeau 1978, 30, no. 238; and 1981, 39–40.
44. Sivan 1993, 141. All relevant texts are cited in *PLRE* and Chastagnol 1962.

son for Faltonia Betitia Proba, and by a lucky chance an inscription identifies his older brother: Q. Clodius Hermogenianus Olybrius, cos. 379, who derives his Clodius from his father. The securely documented brothers Alypius and Olybrius are clearly the brothers Aliepius and Olibrius of the Mutinensis. In her preface Proba claims previously to have written a poem on a civil war. The war between Constantius and Magnentius (351–53) mentioned in the Mutinensis (4) overlaps with Adelphius's city prefecture.

To be sure there are one or two confusions, but none of them points to an original identification with the younger Proba. For example, the marginal note in Pal. 1753 identifying the husband mentioned in line 689 as *Alipyum virum suum* is a mistake and no doubt a guess, but is better explained as a confusion with Betitia Proba's son Alypius than Anicia Proba's husband, Petronius Probus. *Constantini* for *Constantii* in the Mutinensis is insignificant in itself and still points to Betitia rather than Anicia Proba. Magnentius clearly points to Betitia rather than Anicia Proba. As for Isidore, Shanzer's scepticism about his sources is misguided;[45] the fact that he correctly identified Betitia Proba's husband as Adelfius lends no support to the case for Anicia Proba. Whether or not the proconsulate (7) is an error, this is the one otherwise undocumented post Adelphius is likely to have held.[46] For the proconsulate of Africa in the fourth century was practically monopolized by the Roman aristocracy (a fact unlikely to have been known to Isidore). If it is a confusion, it is not a confusion that points to Petronius Probus.[47]

Aniciorum mater in Pal. 1753 (5) Shanzer identifies as a "major confusion" pointing to the younger Proba. The younger Proba was indeed mother to (at least) five children who bore the name Anicius, and accordingly celebrated as the doyenne of the Anicii in letters of Augustine and Jerome and Claudian's panegyric of her consular sons Olybrius and Probinus. It is thus the most likely of the eight details to be a guess. It is also the least specific of the details, offering no actual names. Anyone familiar with Claudian's poem might (understandably) have confused Proba the mother of Olybrius and Probinus with Proba the mother of Olybrius and Alypius and simply given the family name. This same MS goes on to state in the explicit (6) that Proba was *uxor Adelphii expraefecto urbis*, correctly naming the husband of the elder Proba. If Proba wrote on the war against Magnentius, by then Adelphius would certainly have been ex-prefect. Furthermore, the text of Proba in this MS immediately follows two other early mid-fourth-century works: the *Ars grammatica* of Marius Victorinus, and the *De metris* of Aelius Festus Aphthonius, giving the latter the equestrian rank of *vir perfectissimus*, a title that did not survive the fourth century. As Matthews put it, "The ascriptions of authorship in Pal. lat. 1753, far from being suspect or confused, seem quite unusually accurate."[48] As for the *Valeriae Probae Aniciae* of the Lobbes catalogue (8),

---

45. For more detail, Matthews 1992, 285.
46. Accepted (e.g.) by Chastagnol 1962, 133–34.
47. Probus did hold the proconsulate of Africa, but was best known for his four tenures of the praetorian prefecture.
48. For more details, see I. Mariotto, *Marii Victorini Ars grammatica* (Florence 1967), 35–36; Matthews 1992, 285–88; Schmidt in Herzog and Schmidt 5 § 525. 1.

the younger Proba was not called Valeria[49] and Anicia was not the last of her names.[50] This garbled entry is far from solid support for the younger Proba.[51]

In a second paper Shanzer attempted to explain what she describes as "the confusion between grandmother and granddaughter" by postulating a biographical notice that mentioned both, supposedly misinterpreted by some medieval copyist. But not one of the errors in the Proba tradition can in fact be explained by such a confusion. All arise from confusion *between* details in the domestic biography of the elder Proba. On any hypothesis the author of this notice had access to detailed and accurate information about the family of Betitia Proba—but apparently knew not a single name from the immediate family of the younger Proba. More than confusion or guesswork is involved when we have so many accurate details about Betitia Proba's kin but not one identifying the more distinguished mother, husband, and three consular sons of Anicia Proba.

Third, why even mention a maternal grandmother from a minor aristocratic family like Betitia Proba in the biography of a grand dame like Anicia Proba? Betitia's only claim to fame (which Shanzer denies) rests on her identification as the poet. The ancestors we would expect to find mentioned in a notice on Anicia Proba are Tyrrania Anicia Iuliana, the mother from whom she derived her Anician blood; her grandfather Adelphius; her father, Olybrius; and above all her infamous husband, Petronius Probus. Of these four names, the only two to appear are Adelphius and Olybrius, and they are quite specifically identified as the husband and son, respectively, of the elder, not the grandfather and father of the younger Proba.[52] This alone is surely conclusive proof that the primary subject of this biographical notice was the older, not the younger Proba.

Given its obvious importance as the only other dating handle, Shanzer's treatment of Proba's account of her civil war poem is curiously unsystematic. In both articles she raises a couple of literal-minded objections to the notion of a historical epic and casually floats (without substantiating) the possibility of a mythical subject. But there is only one civil war in Greek myth, that of Polyneices against his brother Eteocles (though he was the only one of the Seven who was a Theban), and at least three details in Proba's description do not fit it. First, "cities so often bereft of countless citizens" (*innumeris totiens viduatas civibus urbes*, line 7); the Seven sacked neither Thebes nor any other city, and they themselves were the principal casualties. Second, shields "polluted with the slaughter of fathers"; none of the Seven killed their fathers. Third, Shanzer objects that there was never a peace treaty to be violated between Constantius

---

49. Perhaps (as Dolbeau suggested) a mistaken expansion of *Val*(*tonio*), in which case evidence for the earlier Proba.

50. Anicius/-ia, though common enough in this prolific family, is normally found in first, never last place.

51. *Aniciae* could have been added by someone with the better-known Proba in mind, but if Claudian was the source of this interpolation, the error must have been earlier than the Lobbes catalogue; for Babcock 1986, 203–21, has shown that, though a MS of Claudian was available in X/XI Lobbes and read with some care by (among others) Heriger of Lobbes (†1007), its selection did not include the panegyric on the Anicii.

52. And Olybrius is paired with his brother Alypius, who has even less right to appear in Anicia Proba's immediate family tree than her grandmother.

and Magnentius (*temerasse duces pia foedera pacis*, line 1). But quite apart from the obvious explanation that *pia foedera pacis* is simply a poetic phrase for *pacem*, there were no such treaties in the Theban saga either.

Shanzer further argues that *regum crudelia bella* is not consistent with Constantius's war against Magnentius, a legitimate emperor suppressing a usurper. But it is important to bear in mind that these lines do not come from the actual poem written "long ago," which was no doubt careful to style Magnentius *tyrannus*. Five years after the actual victory Constantius was tactless enough to celebrate a belated triumph during his visit to Rome in 357 (which had supported Magnentius). A famous passage of Ammianus (written in the late 380s) reflects Roman disapproval of this triumph celebrated by Romans over Romans:[53]

> As if the temple of Janus had been closed and all his enemies overthrown, [Constantius] was eager to visit Rome after the death of Magnentius and celebrate, without title, a triumph over Roman blood. For he did not vanquish any nation that made war on him in person...but wanted to display an inordinately long procession, banners stiff with goldwork and the splendour of his retinue to a populace living in perfect peace and neither expecting nor desiring to see this or anything like it.

A few years later (404) we find even stronger condemnation of civil war triumphs in Claudian.[54] Writing her *Cento* a decade or more after the event under a new dynasty, it would not be surprising if Proba took a more cynical view of the war, as simply a struggle for power between two dynasts.

There is a second retrospective passage (now in the form of cento) at 45–47:

> namque—fatebor enim—levium spectacula rerum
> semper equos atque arma virum pugnasque canebam
> et studio incassum volui exercere laborem.

> For—yes, I shall admit it—I used to sing of trivial spectacles, always horses, arms of men, and battles, and was anxious eagerly to toil at a pointless task.

According to Shanzer the terrible losses of the civil war between Constantius and Magnentius could not have been described as *levium spectacula rerum* (from *Geo.* iv. 3). But these lines refer to more than the specific poem described in 1–7. They follow Proba's rejection of classicizing literary devices and, as the imperfect *canebam*[55]

---

53. 16. 10. 1–2; similar views in 21. 16. 15.
54. *VI Cons. Hon.* 393–406; Vera 1980, 89–132. McCormick 1986, 81, goes too far in treating Ammianus's disapproval as nothing but personal hostility to Constantius.
55. *canebat* in *Aen.* ix. 777, one of the not infrequent "cheats" in Proba's cento (conveniently indicated by italics in Schenkl's apparatus of imitations).

shows, evoke in general terms everything she "used to write" before devoting her gifts to Christ (no doubt a few panegyrics and other *pièces d'occasion* as well as the epic). Very different is the tone of 1–7, closing with the words *satis est meminisse malorum* (line 8). It would be odd to recall mythical disasters with such reluctance. These "evils" so sombrely described—death, slaughter of kin, and depopulation of cities—surely imply a real civil war in the recent past, not a mythical war in the remote past.

A real civil war would not in itself exclude Anicia Proba. But the one other biographical detail that can (perhaps) be inferred from the *Cento* is that the poet's husband was still alive when she wrote (*o dulcis coniunx*, line 693). Anicia Proba's husband Probus died some time between 388 and 390.[56] By 388 (or even 390) she cannot "long ago" (*iamdudum*, line 1) have written a poem on the only civil war of her lifetime up to that point, that against Magnus Maximus in 388. The war against Magnentius would have been the obvious conjecture even if it had not been explicitly named by the ascription in the Mutinensis. Shanzer calls the text of the ascription unsure, and suggests keeping *Constantini* and reading *Maxentii* for *Magnentii*. But for obvious reasons scribes were peculiarly liable to write *Constantini* for *Constantii*,[57] and the war against Maxentius fell long before the lifetime of Betitia, while her husband was prefect of Rome under Magnentius. The war of 353 is thus the only civil war available for *either* Proba.[58]

Tim Barnes has cautiously advanced a new argument in favor of the later Proba.[59] An inscription on a column that apparently once formed part of Adelphius's tomb makes it clear that his wife predeceased him.[60] Now when recording how an official called Dorus brought a charge of treason against the *magister equitum* Arbitio in 356, Ammianus refers to an earlier book where he had described the same Dorus laying a similar charge against "Adelfius the urban prefect." That is to say, Adelfius was accused of treason (*altiora coeptantem*, Ammianus's standard formula) during his prefecture, held under Magnentius. Since Dorus evidently survived and prospered, Barnes assumes that Adelfius was prosecuted and convicted, in which case "it would seem reasonable to infer that [he] was probably sentenced to death rather than merely to exile." If so, then he would have been dead before the final battle between Constantius and Magnentius, and if his wife predeceased him, she could not have celebrated that battle.

But there are obviously other possible outcomes. It seems incredible that a Roman aristocrat with no power base should be accused of aiming at the purple. Adelphius was prefect from 7 June–18 December 351. Magnentius was decisively defeated on 28 September 351 by Constantius at Mursa, and Constantius offered amnesty to any

---

56. *PLRE* i. 739; Matthews 1975, 230 n. 5; 1989, 480 n. 27; Shanzer 1986, 244.

57. For example, three out of the first five occurrences of Constantius/–ia in Ammianus xiv (1. 1; 7. 4; 7. 12).

58. For A. Olivetti's theory that the remarkably detailed and often fanciful account of Constantius's campaign against Magnentius in Zosimus ii. 45–53 derives from Proba's poem, see Paschoud's notes. Even if Zosimus (or perhaps rather Eunapius) did draw on a poetic source, it would surely have been in Greek.

59. Barnes 2006, 249–56.

60. *Clodius Adelfius…uxori incomparabili et sibi fecit* (*ILCV* 1850); Barnes 252–53 shows with many parallels that the sequence *uxori et sibi* always implies a living husband and dead wife.

supporters of the usurper willing to change allegiance.[61] The charge against Adelphius was surely "treasonable" correspondence with Constantius, and if he had any sense he anticipated trial by leaving Rome and making for the court of Constantius, probably with many other nobles deserting the sinking ship.[62] If so, both he and his wife might have lived another decade or two, allowing her time to write a poem on the Magnentian War and her later *Cento*.[63]

There is not one really solid argument in favor of Anicia Proba, and two arguments against that neither Barnes nor Shanzer mention. First an argument from silence. If the younger Proba had been a well-known poet, we should certainly have expected Claudian to mention it in his panegyric on her two sons. Literary culture was highly prized in the Roman upper classes, and a tactful panegyrist would always discover it in his subject if there was the slightest basis in fact. Only once did Claudian have a chance to develop the theme in any detail, in his panegyric on Mallius Theodorus, the only authentic man of letters among the subjects of his panegyrics. But the importance of the theme is sufficiently indicated by the fact that in no fewer than three cases he praised his subjects for *studying* literature, for simply reading the classics: Honorius, his young bride, Maria, and Stilicho's wife, Serena.[64] In a genre with such well-established conventions, listeners would draw the obvious inference from the absence of this topic; the panegyrist was then obliged to lay the emphasis elsewhere instead. For example, we justifiably infer from Claudian's concentration on Stilicho's military and administrative virtues that he was not a literary man.

The invitation to celebrate the consulships of two members of the greatest family in Rome, Anicius Olybrius and Anicius Probinus, was Claudian's big chance, his first major poem in the West. Both the new consuls dabbled in poetry. A recently discovered anthology has presented us with a translation of a Greek epigram by Probinus (*Ep. Bob.* 65), and a poetic epistle Claudian sent to Olybrius praises his "*prona facultas*" in verse (*cm* 40. 3–4). His principal patron was naturally Anicia Proba herself, the dowager head of the family. If she had really been a published poet, author of a classicizing epic as well as the *Cento*, it would have been positively insulting to pass over the fact in complete silence while praising her youthful sons' poetic trifles. Yet in his panegyric he simply praises the brothers for their poetic attainments (*Pieriis pollent studiis, Pan. Prob. et Olybr.* 150), without a word on the example or teaching of their mother. In sharp contrast, Claudian devotes several lines to describing how Serena taught her daughter Maria, Honorius's bride, to read the poets of Greece and Rome (*Nupt.* 230–37). Even in a trifling quatrain on Serena's washbasin, Claudian takes care to call her *docta* (*cm* 45. 3). If Anicia Proba had been a famous poet, how could so consummate a courtier have failed to remark that her sons were worthy pupils of such a mother. He did not do so because they were not.

---

61. Julian, *Or.* i. 38A–B; Zosimus ii. 53. 2.
62. For other nobles who rallied to Constantius, Chastagnol 1960, 420–22.
63. Barnes 249 points out that he was born no later than ca. 303.
64. *IV Cons. Hon.* 396–400; *Nupt.* 233–37; *c.m.* 30. 146–59.

Second, in a letter to Paulinus of Nola written in 394, Jerome mocks Vergilian centos, calling them "puerilities," and while he does not name names, he cites a line from Proba's *Cento* (403 = *Aen.* i. 664 and ii. 650) and refers contemptuously to a "garrulous old woman" (*garrula anus*). No one has ever doubted that he had Proba in mind.[65] According to Sivan and Barnes, he writes of her as if she was still alive.[66] Arguably so, but would a toady like Jerome have poured such scorn on the richest, noblest, and most powerful woman in Rome? This is not a rhetorical question. In a letter written in 414, to the Anician heiress and nun Demetrias, Jerome included an extravagant eulogy of her grandmother, none other than Anicia Proba, "the most illustrious woman in the Roman world" (*Ep.* 130. 7). If Anicia Proba was the poetess, it does not look as if Jerome knew it.

The importance of restoring the first Christian poet of Rome to her rightful date and context lies in establishing that Claudian was not after all the first poet to reintroduce classicizing epics on contemporary wars into Latin literature. It has sometimes been inferred from her preface that Proba was born a pagan, but if this had been so she would hardly have confined herself to repudiating pagan literary motifs. I would infer rather than she was born a Christian, in which case it is instructive to find a Christian writing traditional epico-panegyrical poetry. We have also identified some commonplaces of anti-pagan polemic. But as far as the *CCP* is concerned we are no further forward. The author of the *Cento* cannot have been born later than ca. 320. So if there is any connection between the two poems, it must be the author of the *CCP* who imitates the *Cento*.

4 · PRUDENTIUS AND SYMMACHUS

Finally, the one anti-pagan poem we know to have been written not long after the fall of Eugenius, the two-book work of Prudentius misleadingly known for short as *Contra Symmachum* (*CS*). The poem is not in fact an invective against Symmachus, who is treated throughout with remarkable courtesy. The full title is *Contra orationem Symmachi*, and Bk ii is indeed a detailed and systematic refutation (in 1,132 lines) of Symmachus's most famous speech, his plea for the restoration of the altar of Victory in 384. The two books appear to have been published together after Stilicho's defeat of the Visigoths at Pollentia in 402 (explicitly mentioned at ii. 718–20), and it has generally been assumed that they were also written together in or soon after 402. We shall see that there are in fact strong grounds for believing that at any rate the narrative core of Bk i dates from late 394, as first suggested in 1883 by Émile Faguet and developed with slightly different arguments by Harries (1984) and Shanzer (1989).[67]

---

65. For a useful account of Jerome's criticisms see Springer 1993, 96–105.

66. Sivan 1993, 142; T. Barnes 2006, 256.

67. Faguet 1883, 24–27; Harries 1984, 69–84; Shanzer 1989, 442–62. Against the suggestion that *CS* i was originally written in 391 (Callu 1981, 235–39), see Shanzer 1989, 451–53.

Why is the date of Bk i important? Let us begin with its prologue:[68]

> credebam vitiis aegram gentilibus orbem
> iam satis antiqui pepulisse pericula morbi,
> nec quidquam restare mali, postquam medicina
> principis immodicos sedarat in arce dolores.
> sed quoniam renovata lues turbare salutem   5
> temptat Romulidum, patris imploranda medella est,
> ne sinat antiquo Roman squalere veterno
> neve togas procerum fumoque et sanguine tingui.
> inclitus ergo parens patriae, moderator et orbis,
> nil egit prohibendo vagas ne pristinus error   10
> crederet esse deum nigrante sub aëre formas.

I used to think that Rome, once sick with her pagan errors, had by now entirely rid herself of the dangers of her old disease and that no evil remained now that the emperor's healing measures had assuaged the grievous pain in the city. But since the plague has broken out anew and seeks to throw in confusion the well-being of the race of Romulus, we must beg for a remedy from our father, that he not let Rome sink again into her old filthy torpor, nor allow the senators' togas to be stained with smoke and blood.

The *princeps* referred to in lines 4 and 9 must be Theodosius I, and the *medicina* of line 3 must be his anti-pagan laws of 391–92 (note particularly *prohibendo* in line 10). But what is the "new plague" (*renovata lues*) mentioned in line 5? In the belief that these lines were written in 402 and refer to the current state of Roman paganism, some critics have assumed that the "new plague" was a resurgence of paganism in that year.[69] Since it would be surprising if Prudentius had done no more than produce another refutation of Symmachus nearly twenty years after the event, it is undeniably tempting to suppose that his purpose was to counter a new attempt by Symmachus to restore the altar. Since at least a half-dozen attempts were made, there is no objection in principle to yet another. If this were so, Symmachus might after all be reclaimed as a pagan extremist.

Yet there are overwhelming objections. In the first place, nothing else we know about Symmachus suggests that he took any active part in promoting the pagan cause after his resignation from the prefecture of Rome in January 385. There is certainly no sign that he played any part in the revolt of Eugenius. This is why he still enjoyed an influence at court he was able to exploit to restore the fortunes of the younger Flavian. Second, by 402, when all forms of sacrifice had been banned for a decade, it was inconceivable that Honorius would grant a request turned down by three Christian

---

68. For the moment I am setting on one side the balancing prefaces in Ascelpiads to the two books.
69. Poinsotte 1982, 34; Demougeot 1951, 287; Pietri 1976, 441–43.

predecessors, one of them his own father. Third, nothing in the poem itself supports this view—nor outside it either. It is true that the senate prevailed upon Symmachus to go to Milan as a senatorial legate in the winter of 402, but this was surely in connection with the economic hardships caused by Alaric's invasion.[70] It is also true that, on the evidence of both Claudian and Symmachus, Stilicho seems to have been anxious to conciliate the Roman aristocracy, but there is no evidence that he was willing to make any concessions to paganism.[71]

Of course, Symmachus *might* have taken the opportunity of his presence at court to renew his plea, but it could hardly have been the *same* plea. The ban on sacrifice in 391, repeatedly renewed thereafter, had entirely changed the terms of the debate. While Symmachus's speech of 384 had not lost its power as a plea for tolerance, by 402 it was irretrievably out of date in practical terms. Any pagan appeal composed in 402 would have had to face up to the ban on sacrifice. Restoring the altar of Victory and the subsidies of the Vestals would be pointless by themselves. The altar could not have been used. No Roman senator with any sense of the political realities of the day could have entertained the hope that the ban on sacrifice would be lifted as late as 402.

But the arguments Prudentius refutes in such detail over the course of the 1,132 lines of Bk ii are those Symmachus had presented in 384. Of course, if Symmachus had reformulated his case in 402, it is natural that he should have repeated *some* of the same arguments, yet it is *precisely* the arguments of 384 Prudentius refutes. Yet how could Symmachus have been so unwise as to repeat in 402 the argument that Gratian's measures of 382 had caused the bad harvest of 383. For there was an excellent harvest in 384, as Ambrose gleefully pointed out at the time. To be sure there had been problems with the corn supply of Rome on several occasions between 384 and 402,[72] but these problems had many causes other than famine, in the period after 394 often political, given the cold war between East and West, the revolt of Gildo, and the depredations of Alaric in first Illyricum and later Italy itself. Furthermore, there must have been several years in which there were perfectly satisfactory harvests. By 402 the argument that the abandonment of sacrifice endangered the harvest had repeatedly been proved invalid. A reflective pagan might have reformulated the connection between true belief and worldly success from the pagan side as Augustine was to do from the Christian side. But the Symmachus Prudentius refutes did not do so. He simply repeats the long-exploded argument of 384.

This does not mean that *CS* had no contemporary significance, just that its significance has nothing to do with a new attempt to restore the altar of Victory. In his own terms Ambrose had already long since supplied what most Christians found a satisfactory answer to most of Symmachus's arguments. Yet there was one argument that

70. Sogno 2006, 84–85.
71. Cameron 1970, 199, 227, 230–42; Matthews 1975, 265–70.
72. Kohns 1961, 182–214; Ruggini 1995, 152–76.

was not so easily answered, the argument, significantly enough, with which *CS* ii begins: "who is such a friend of the barbarians that he does not need the altar of Victory?" During the millennium that Rome had worshipped Victory, she had been uniformly successful. The occasional defeat had always been soon redeemed. When Symmachus wrote these words in 384, it had been six years since the Roman defeat at Adrianople. The Romans had not managed to redeem this devastating defeat in the interval. Not only had Theodosius not defeated the Goths in battle, many were alarmed at what seemed his dangerously conciliatory policy toward the Goths. The situation did not change after 384. Indeed, it had deteriorated alarmingly. In 395 Alaric had raised the standard of revolt inside Roman territory, and despite two campaigns, Stilicho too had failed to defeat the Goths. Many, and not only pagans, must have been wondering whether Symmachus had been right after all. The Marcellinus to whom Augustine dedicated his *City of God* was but one among many Christians disturbed by the succession of disasters under recent Christian emperors. Would it really be such a terrible thing to restore that altar? Then in 402, finally, Stilicho defeated Alaric at Pollentia. It is surely no coincidence that Prudentius lays such stress on the fact that it was *dux agminis imperiique / Christipotens…iuvenis* and his *parens Stilicho* who won that victory, after worship at Christ's altar (ii. 709–12).

The actuality of the events behind Prudentius's poem lay not in a renewal of Symmachus's appeal, but in the battle that answered the most potent question raised by his original appeal. Despite refusing to convert, Symmachus himself had not suffered disgrace or eclipse. The extensive correspondence from the last decade of his life makes it clear that he remained influential and widely respected, by Christians no less than pagans, a respect that is reflected in Prudentius's poem.[73] Unlike Praetextatus in *CCP*, Symmachus himself is treated with studied courtesy in *CS*. His *relatio* was still circulating and still finding admiring readers. It was a short piece, elegant and eloquent, without rancor or polemic—but no less dangerous for that. Claudian had written an epic on Pollentia (*De bello Getico*) and others too had probably produced panegyrics. Instead of focussing on the battle, Prudentius stressed the fact that a Christian emperor had finally and (as it seemed at the time) decisively defeated those apparently invincible Goths.

That Victory was indeed in the forefront of people's minds after Pollentia is underlined by a striking (though often misunderstood) passage of Claudian, in his *Panegyric on the Sixth Consulate of Honorius*, recited in Rome in January 404 on the occasion of Honorius's triumphal entry.[74] Honorius has entered the senate house, and

---

73. Symmachus seems to have died in 402, but Prudentius's respectful tone suggests he was still alive at the time of writing. The date is based on evidence in the letters of 402 that Symmachus was weak and ill, and no surviving letter can be dated to a later year. Obviously, we cannot rule out the possibility that he had some disabling illness, and remained among the living for another year or two. But his political life at any rate ended in 402.

74. On this passage, see Dewar 1996, 392–97.

> adfuit ipsa suis ales Victoria templis,
> Romanae tutela togae, quae divite pinna
> patricii reverenda fovet sacraria coetus
> castrorumque eadem comes indefessa tuorum
> nunc tandem fruitur iunctis,[75] atque omne futurum
> te Romae seseque tibi promittit in aevum. (597–602)

Winged Victory herself, protectress of the Roman peace, was present in her temple, she who with golden wing shelters the awesome sanctuary where the fathers assemble, she who is also the unwearied companion of your [Honorius's] wars; now *at last* she takes her joy in your union, and for all eternity she promises that you will belong to Rome and she to you.

For the senate house as a temple and for the statue's golden[76] wings we have an exact parallel in Prudentius himself (*aurea quamvis / marmoreo in templo rutilas Victoria pinnas / explicet, CS* ii. 27–29). Beyond question Claudian is referring to an actual statue of Victoria in the senate house, and when, after describing her as the unwearied companion of Honorius's wars, he claims that she is "finally" (*tandem*) united with him, he too must be referring to Pollentia. In an earlier poem, Bk iii of his panegyric on Stilicho, recited in Rome in 400, Claudian represents Stilicho too visiting the senate house:

> quae vero procerum voces, quam certa fuere
> gaudia, cum totis exsurgens ardua pennis
> ipsa duci sacras Victoria panderet aedes...
> adsis perpetuum Latio votisque senatus
> adnue, diva, tui. Stilicho tua saepius ornet
> limina teque simul rediens in castra reducat. (*Stil.* iii. 202–14)

What were the acclamations of the senators, how unfeigned their rejoicing when Victory, soaring aloft with outspread wings, herself threw open her holy temple to her general.... Be ever present to Latium, and grant, goddess, the prayers of the senate. May Stilicho often adorn your doors and bear you back with him to his armies.

Once again, behind the poetic language Claudian is associating the statue of Victory in the senate house with Stilicho's actual military successes (at this point in fact rather meager). Claudian's great nineteenth-century editor Theodor Birt thought that the later passage was alluding to a restoration of the altar of Victory by Stilicho, otherwise unattested. Many have assumed that Constantius and (after him) Gratian had the

---

75. *iunctis* is difficult and the variant *votis* no better (see Dewar's note).
76. For *dives* = golden, see Dewar on 598, esp. Verg. *Aen.* vi. 195 (the golden bough).

statue as well as the altar removed, and some complain that "altar and statue are not clearly distinguished in the texts."[77] But Ambrose cites Symmachus's demand that "*old altars must be returned to their statues*, ornaments to their shrines,"[78] which clearly implies that the statue never left the senate house.

In the 1880s Rodolfo Lanciani demolished a foundation wall on the Caelian Hill that turned out to be filled with bits of statues deliberately broken up to be used as rubble, one of which he identified as a Victory, recomposed from 151 fragments. Lanciani claimed that it came from the Symmachan house on the Caelian, and had been smashed by a Christian mob after the failure of the "pagan revolt" in 394. [79] This dramatic hypothesis has not weathered well: not to mention serious doubts about the very existence of a "pagan revolt," the wall in question is almost certainly too early; there is no evidence that the statue was found in the house of the Symmachi; and the statue itself has recently been reidentified as Isis![80] No less serious an objection, it was not Victory herself that upset Christian senators in 359 and 382, but her altar, upon which pagans dropped grains of incense before senate meetings.[81] The texts that preserve the celebrated "debate" only refer to an altar; Ambrose indeed uses the word no fewer than eighteen times. Lacking as she did mythical adventures, family, and love life, Victoria had always been more of a personification than a full-fledged goddess, and was to be the only "pagan" deity to survive the end of paganism on the coinage (including Theodosius's) and official art of the Christian empire, down into the seventh century.[82] While most Christian senators will have been outraged by a smoking altar, there cannot have been many willing to face up to the symbolism of removing the personification of Victory from the senate house. There is no reason to believe (and certainly no evidence) that the statue was ever removed. So when Claudian evokes Victoria welcoming Honorius to the senate house, he is by no means taking the pagan side in the continuing debate. Birt was understandably impressed by the fact that in his Stilicho panegyric Claudian directly echoed a Symmachan phrase: *amica trophaeis* (*Stil.* iii. 205) ~ *amicum triumphis* (*rel.* iii. 3). "Who is such a friend of the barbarians that he does not need the *altar* of Victory" was Symmachus's question. Pollentia proved that Christians could still achieve Victory *without* that altar.

Symmachus's question must have become increasingly disturbing over the years since Adrianople. Pollentia finally allowed a complete Christian response, and that is what *CS* ii provides. But what is the explanation of Bk i? In recent years it has come to

77. Pohlsander 1969, at 594; Grierson and Mays 1992, 82.

78. *Sed vetera, inquit*[Symmachus], *reddenda sunt altaria simulacris, ornamenta delubris*, Ambrose, *Ep.* 73. 10. This sentence does not actually appear in *Rel.* 3; perhaps from some document relating to Symmachus's attempt to restore statues to temples during his prefecture.

79. R. Lanciani, *Ruins and Excavations of Ancient Rome* (London 1897), 346–48; and in *Wanderings through Ancient Roman Churches* (Boston 1924), 73–74.

80. Coates-Stephens 2001, 228–31; for the Isis identification, Bertoletti, Cima, and Talamo 2006, 48–50 (otherwise repeating most of the inaccuracies in Lanciani's vivid narrative).

81. Herodian v. 5. 7; Ambr. *Ep.* 17. 9; 18. 31.

82. See (e.g.) A. R. Bellinger and M. A. Berlincourt, *Victory as a Coin Type* (New York 1992); J. W. E. Pearce, *RIC* 9 (1953), 316; J. P. C. Kent, *RIC* 10 (1994), 481–83; Grierson and Mays 1992, 81–82.

be recognized that the *Contra Symmachum* is a curiously complex work. Matching prefaces in Asclepiads about Saints Paul and Peter, respectively, give a specious unity to two books that have very little else in common. Only Bk ii lives up to the title borne by the poem as a whole. Bk i does not even mention Symmachus (and then without naming him) until line 622. The core of the book (i. 42–407) is a rambling general attack on paganism. The first half of this section (42–296) argues that most pagan gods were originally just kings deified by a credulous posterity; the second half (297–407) that other gods were originally natural forces like water and fire (Neptune and Vulcan). This is thoroughly conventional stuff, with no specific focus or contemporary reference. Given its length and entirely general character, it does not make a particularly appropriate introduction to the saga of the altar of Victory. The section on the deification of natural forces provided an opportunity to introduce and belittle Victoria, a personification, but Prudentius did not take it. For this he waited till Bk ii, where he makes rather puerile fun of the idea of a winged maiden directing the weapons of panting soldiers (27–67). Apart from the epilogue there is literally nothing in the first 621 lines of Bk i that sets the scene for a refutation of Symmachus.

There are also other important differences. The only emperor mentioned in Bk i is Theodosius. He is not actually named, but since the events related in the relevant sections (1–41 and 408–624) undoubtedly refer to the brief period of Theodosius's sole rule between the Frigidus (6 September 394) and his death (17 January 395), he must be the emperor in question. Furthermore, the very fact that he is not named strongly suggests that he was alive when Prudentius wrote.[83] In addition, as Harries remarked, Bk i "celebrates a wide range of Theodosian achievements, but his fathering of Arcadius and Honorius, reigning emperors in 402, is not among them."[84] Book ii, on the other hand, as befits a poem written in 402, is addressed to Arcadius and Honorius, with no reference to Theodosius. The exactly contemporary poems of Claudian frequently introduce Theodosius together with his two sons, but in Claudian there is never the slightest doubt that Arcadius and Honorius are the reigning emperors, and that Theodosius, now dead, is being evoked in flashbacks or speaking to them in dreams.[85] Yet nothing in Bk i suggests that Prudentius was writing about the past.[86] Perhaps the clearest indication is i. 37–39:

> parete magistro
> sceptra gubernanti. monet ut deterrimus error
> utque superstitio veterum procul absit avorum.

---

83. Especially in apostrophes by orators and poets, reigning emperors are almost never identified by name, simply styled βασιλεύς or *princeps*, with or without epithets. In the case of the numerous (inevitably brief) Greek epigrams of the imperial age, this often makes identification very difficult.

84. Harries 1984, 75.

85. Notably *IV Cons. Hon.* 212–418, a speech of advice on kingship, closing *haec genitor praecepta dabat* (l. 419); and *De bello Gild.* 225–320 (a dream), where at the close Theodosius is actually referred to as *divus* (320).

86. So rightly Shanzer 1989, 445, 447–50.

Obey a teacher who wields the sceptre. He gives warning that the wicked error and superstition of our forefathers be put away.

Taken by itself, the *monet* might be considered a historic present, but it is not easy to believe that anyone writing under Honorius would tell his readers to obey Theodosius "who wields the sceptre" (present participle), without any reference to those who had succeeded to his power on his death. Whatever his achievements, a dead emperor no longer "wields the sceptre." As Faguet saw, the natural inference is not just that Theodosius was alive when Prudentius wrote these words, but present in the West.[87] No less important, there is no reference in Bk ii to the transmission of power from Theodosius to his sons, and no explanation of the chronological gap between 394 and 402.

Let us take a closer look at the two "Theodosian" passages, i. 1–41 (quoted in part above) and 408–624. For 41 lines Theodosius is praised for dispelling the "error and superstition of our ancestors," and then comes a bizarre rhetorical question: "Is Saturnus thought to have ruled our Latin forefathers better?"—better, apparently, than Theodosius rules Rome today. This is a forced and clumsy transition to that long general attack on paganism (i. 42–407), with no contemporary reference, cut short by a no less clumsy transition back to Theodosius: "such are the rites, drawn from the early days of our ancestors, that entangled and defiled the centre of imperial power when an emperor who had twice defeated tyrants [Theodosius in 394] turned his eyes in triumph on her noble battlements" (408–11).

The first part of the second Theodosian passage, the third major section of Bk i (415–505), is a speech put in the mouth of Theodosius urging the senators to cast aside their paganism, allegedly followed by mass conversions. A brief section (already discussed in chapter 5. 2) lists a number of aristocratic converts by name (i. 551–65). While claiming that some of the most blue-blooded families in Rome had long since converted, the passage as a whole implies that the entire aristocracy was still wallowing in paganism until Theodosius's exhortation. The explanation of the inconsistency must be the competing claims of different patrons. On the one hand the emperor, whom Prudentius is anxious to credit with the conversion of the aristocracy as a whole; on the other, powerful Roman families who would be insulted to be included among the unconverted. As already remarked, this makes it difficult to use as evidence. But it does have a bearing on the notion that it was a new senatorial embassy about the altar of victory that prompted Prudentius to write. In Bk ii he credits Arcadius and Honorius with the defeat of paganism:

> hac me labe ream modo *tempora vestra* piarunt;
> vivo pie *vobis auctoribus*, impia pridem
> arte Iovis, fateor.

---

87. "haec verba Theodosium non mortuum, non in Oriente longinquo gubernantem, sed praesentem significant," Faguet 1883, 25.

It is only your times that have cleansed me from this guilty stain; under your guidance I lead a pious life, impious (I confess) in earlier times, through the deception of Jupiter.

But in Bk i Theodosius is the "only man" (*vir solus*) who prohibited "ancient error" (*pristinus error*), and his exhortation leads senate and people alike to reject paganism and Rome to devote herself to Christ (506–615).

What is the explanation of these inconsistencies between the two books? Harries suggested serial composition, as in the case of Claudian's multi-book poems. The two books of the *In Rufinum* and *In Eutropium* are separated by a year or more, and the incomplete *De bello Gildonico* is obviously the first book of what must have been planned as a multi-book work. In addition, *In Eutropium* ii and *De bello Gildonico* are preceded by brief hexameter prologues that clearly reflect a later situation that the rest of the poem, evidently last-minute additions to bring the poems up to date at the last moment.[88] That is to say, the later books and prologues *continue* the story. But while Bk ii of CS reflects a later date than Bk i, there is no *continuity* between the books. More specifically, Bk i contains absolutely nothing on Symmachus's celebrated speech, the ostensible subject of both books. I am more attracted by Shanzer's theory that Bk i was "patched together…largely from pre-existing material," perhaps two different poems, "a standard invective against pagan gods combined with a panegyrical treatment of Theodosius's anti-pagan legislation."[89] This is convincing as far as it goes. It accounts for most of the inconsistencies, but it still does not *explain* the two-book work as we have it.

According to Shanzer, a "painstaking and perfectionist poet does not rustle up old drafts and glue fragments together in a manner suggestive of a feverish journalist unless he has an urgent reason." For Shanzer the reason was a fresh attempt to have the altar restored. Yet the cobbling together of earlier drafts into Bk i contributes nothing to the contemporary relevance of the poem as a whole. Indeed, it actually obscures the purpose of Bk ii. If all we had was Bk ii, minus its first four lines (another clumsy transition), it would have been obvious from the start that Prudentius's purpose was (finally) to answer Symmachus's question about barbarians. But the emphasis on Theodosius in Bk i leaves the reader's mind confused as she approaches Bk ii.

If Prudentius had decided to reuse existing material at the planning stage of his poem, he was craftsman enough to harmonize old and new better. Most obviously, he would surely have eliminated the stark chronological disconnect between the two books. It would not have taken much actual rewriting; a modified framework would have sufficed. For example, begin Bk i with an apostrophe to Arcadius and Honorius; then a flashback to Theodosius: we all thought the aristocracy had finally abandoned paganism in 394, but it lingered on, thanks to the usurpers. Now with Pollentia

---

88. Cameron 1970, 76–79, 115, 134–38; Cameron 2000, 142.
89. Shanzer 1989, 457–62.

Honorius has added a coping stone to the achievement of his father. Virtually the whole two books as we have them could have been accommodated in such a framework with no more than two or three brief new link passages.

Shanzer herself saw the preexisting material she posited as unpublished drafts. Perhaps so. But there is no need to make this assumption. Most writers incorporate bits from a variety of drafts in larger projects, but they normally revise, rearrange, or adapt such material (presumably in any case unfinished and so needing more work) more or less drastically to harmonize with their current conception. At ca. 250 and 350 lines each, the two poems she identified are quite long enough to have been published separately, especially since the panegyric on Theodosius would have been an early work by an as yet little-known writer.[90] But they would have been much shorter than all his other hexameter poems: *Apotheosis* (1,084 lines); *Hamartigenia* (966); *Psychomachia* (915); *CS* ii (1,132). My own suggestion is that it was when sorting and arranging his various poems for republication in the collected edition securely documented by the *praefatio* in 405 that Prudentius decided to gather his three anti-pagan hexameter works together into a single two-book poem. This would explain why he did so little rewriting. The surviving two-book work might have been more appropriately titled "A reply to Symmachus and other anti-pagan hexameter poems."

In fact, Prudentius did little more than split his panegyric on Theodosius into two parts (1–41 and 408–621), to sandwich his invective against the pagan gods 42–407) and add an epilogue apostrophising Symmachus (622–57), introduced by yet another awkward transition—awkward, because Symmachus has not been so much as mentioned in the 621 preceding lines of Bk i. Nor is he actually named even here:

> *ipse* magistratum *tibi* consulis, ipse tribunal
> contulit auratumque togae donavit amictum,
> cuius religio tibi displicet, o pereuntum
> adsertor divum.

It was he [Theodosius] who conferred on you [Symmachus] the office of consul and the judgment seat, and gave you the gold-wrought toga to wear, he whose religion does not win your approval, you upholder of dying gods.

It is clear from the context that *ipse* is Theodosius, but first-time readers, ancient no less than modern, must initially have been surprised by the *tibi*. Not only has Symmachus never so far been mentioned by name, there has been no mention of the altar of Victory either, the supposed subject of the poem as a whole. While there can be no doubt that the *tibi* does address Symmachus, nothing has prepared the reader

---

90. In addition, in their original form, both postulated poems are likely to have had prologues and epilogues that did not fit the new context. As Shanzer rightly points out, the postulated panegyric would have resembled a lost panegyric on Theodosius by Paulinus of Nola, which is said to have praised him "for winning by faith and eloquence rather than force of arms" (see p. 125).

for his abrupt, anonymous introduction at this point. And while the praise of Symmachus's eloquence prepares us for the refutation of his speech in Bk ii, it still does not supply the much-needed *narrative* connection between the two books. Nothing in the epilogue points later than Theodosius and 394, so there is still no explanation for Bk ii opening with an apostrophe to Arcadius and Honorius in 402. Prudentius's bridge from Theodosius to Symmachus is once again forced: the claim at i. 616–21 that Theodosius continued to reward deserving pagans with high office. But this refers to 394, so the "for example, Symmachus" that follows is historically unjustified. Symmachus was consul in 391, and held no offices of any kind after that.

Prudentius was no bungler. There are no such inconsistencies and awkward transitions in his other long hexameter poems, nor (I suspect) would we have found them in the *CS* if the two books had been written one after another in a continuous process of composition. But once he had decided to combine his two earlier anti-pagan invectives into a "first" book *Contra Symmachum*, he devoted little effort to the necessary links and transitions, relying on the balancing Asclepiad prefaces to tie the two books together.

An influential article by F. Solmsen has long been held to have proved that a brief passage at the end of Theodosius's speech in Bk i (501–5) alludes to a law of 399 forbidding the destruction of pagan works of art.[91] Since the material incorporated in Bk i evidently received some revision for the two-book edition, it is not impossible in itself that Prudentius added a few lines "to reflect a change of imperial policy towards statues in pagan temples."[92]

But if read in context, the passage has no connection with this law. Theodosius is ordering the Romans to put aside their childish festivals and absurd ceremonies, and

> marmora tabenti respergine tincta lavate,
> o proceres: liceat statuas consistere puras,
> artificum magnorum opera; haec pulcherrima nostrae
> ornamenta fuant patriae, nec decolor usus
> in vitium versae monumenta coinquinet artis

wash marble that is spattered with putrid blood, senators. Your statues are the work of great artists; let them stand clean. Let them be the fairest ornaments of our nation, and let no debased usage pollute monuments of art and make them serve an evil purpose.

The law of 399 was intended to stop fanatics and vandals destroying pagan works of art. That is not Prudentius's point at all. Theodosius is protesting at the fact that so

---

91. *Cod. Theod.* xvi. 10. 15 (issued at Ravenna); Solmsen 1965, 310–13; Shanzer 1989, 451–52; Barnes and Westall 1991, 60–61. Palmer 1989, 260, thought the allusion was to a less specific (eastern) law of 382, *Cod. Theod.* 16. 10. 8.

92. Barnes and Westall 1991, 60.

many beautiful Roman monuments, perhaps temples as much as statues, are *dirty*, spattered with the blood of sacrifice. He wants them *washed*, and when he says he wants statues to stand *puras*, he means literally as well as figuratively and morally clean. There is no question in Prudentius of the destruction of pagan monuments. The point at issue is the end of sacrifice. All visitors to Rome were struck by the splendor of its monuments and statues:[93] but all this splendor was polluted (according to Prudentius) by the blood and smoke of sacrifice.[94]

This interpretation is confirmed by a closely parallel passage in *Peristephanon* ii, a long account of the martyrdom of St. Lawrence. While he is being tortured, Lawrence has a vision of the future conversion of Rome:

> video futurum principem
> quandoque, qui servus Dei
> taetris sacrorum sordibus
> servire Romam non sinat,
>   qui templa claudat vectibus,
> valvas eburnas obstruat,
> nefasta damnet limina,
> obdens aenos pessulos.
>   tunc pura ab omni sanguine
> tandem nitebunt marmora,
> stabunt et aera innoxia,
> quae nunc habentur idola.

I foresee one day an emperor who will be the servant of God and will not allow Rome to be slave to vile, abominable rites. He will close and bar her temples, block their ivory doors, shut their unholy entrances, making them fast with brazen bolts. *Then at last her marbles will shine bright, cleansed from all blood, and bronze statues that are now considered idols will stand free from guilt.* (*Per.* ii. 473–84)

It has long been realized that the princeps who will one day do all this must be identified as Theodosius. It should also be clear that Theodosius must still have been alive when Prudentius wrote these lines. If writing under Honorius, he could not have been so tactless as to assign Theodosius sole credit for the end of paganism. His emphasis on the physical closing of temples reflects one of the provisions of Theodosius's anti-pagan law of 391. What has not been appreciated is that here too praise of Theodosius for ending paganism is immediately followed by the claim that, in consequence, statues

---

93. Gernentz 1918, 56–61; above, p. 217.
94. As already argued in chapter 2. 4, this passage should not be considered evidence that blood sacrifice was still being publicly performed as late as this.

(evidently statues in pagan temples) will be cleansed of blood. There are verbal as well as thematic parallels between the two passages (*puras* ~ *pura*; *consistere* ~ *stare*); in *CS* Theodosius is begged not to allow (*sinat*) Rome to sink into its ancient squalor, in *Per.* ii he does not allow (*sinat*) Rome to be a slave to pagan rites. The probability is that the two poems were written at about the same time. An earlier passage in Theodosius's speech in *CS* mocks (as many Christians did) the idea of worshipping man-made, perishable objects such as statues (i. 435–41), but that does not mean that Prudentius wished to see them destroyed. There is no contradiction with the later passage.

Nothing in either *CS* i. 501–5 or *Per.* ii. 481–84 suggests that the statues he mentions stood in any danger of destruction. He does not say (as the law of 399 does)[95] that they *should* be preserved as works of art. He states as fact that, when sacrifice ends they *will* "stand free of guilt" (*stabunt...innoxia*); in *CS*, it is the senators he begs to *allow* them to stand clean as works of art. According to Solmsen, "Read in the context of the entire oration [the *CS* passage] is a surprising and rather weak conclusion... an anticlimax." Only if Prudentius was introducing a reference to recent imperial legislation—but not if their transformation into pure works of art was an automatic consequence of the end of sacrifice. Before accepting Solmsen's judgement we should bear in mind that the second passage quoted is the conclusion of St. Lawrence's speech just as the first is the conclusion of Theodosius's speech. Prudentius clearly saw this point as a climax in both poems.

There is no reason to believe either reference to statues a later insertion. There is nothing in *CS* i that need be later than 394.[96] More important, the parallels between the two passages support the conclusion that the major part of *CS* i was written during the lifetime of Theodosius. The reason I have examined the genesis of this intriguing poem at such length is that, if my explanation is accepted, we would have not one antipagan hexameter invective by Prudentius, but three: one dating from immediately after the Frigidus; a second of entirely general character, undatable; and a third inspired by Pollentia in 402.

5

There were, of course, other Christian poets writing in classicizing meters and genres, in both Greek and Latin.[97] One of the stranger developments in Christian

---

95. *volumus publicorum operum ornamenta servari*, Cod. *Theod.* xvi. 10. 15.

96. Barnes and Westall 1991, 51, 55–58, argue that i. 551, *Amniadum suboles et pignera clara Proborum*, an allusion to the two Anician consuls of 395, is an interpolation (by an early reader, not Prudentius). I would agree that the line does not really fit between i. 550 and 552, but would prefer to accept it as written by Prudentius (the future consuls of 395 would have been known by late 394) and transfer it between 560 and 561.

97. Some of this concluding section is borrowed from Cameron 2004, 327–54, where I also treat similar developments in Greek poetry.

Latin literature is the biblical paraphrase in classicizing hexameters: Sedulius, Arator, Cyprianus Gallus, Claudius Marius Victorius, Avitus.[98] Whatever bishops and clerics might say, cultivated lay Christians evidently continued to find the uneducated style of the Bible unappealing, and needed the incentive of classicizing meter and diction to sweeten the pill. Sedulius's preface to his *Carmen Paschale* is particularly revealing:

> There are many for whom the attraction of studying secular literature lies in the charms of poetry and the pleasures of verse. These men pay little attention to anything they read in prose because they take little pleasure in it. But anything they see sweetened with the blandishment of verse, they greet with such eagerness of heart *that they commit it to memory* and store it away by constant repetition.

Whether or not anyone memorized Sedulius's poem in its entirety, brief passages and striking phrases may well have stuck in the memory of people trained since childhood to memorize poetry. Interestingly enough, he subsequently rewrote the poem in prose. As was only to be expected, by classical standards the poetic version is more consistently successful. An epigram of Claudian's purports to be a reply to a friend who had asked him for something in prose. Sorry, he says: "the Muses say no to prose; I speak only poetry" (*verba negant communia Musae; carmina sola loquor, cm* 3). No doubt a joke, but probably in essence true enough nonetheless. It is unlikely that Claudian could have produced classicizing prose as pure as his classicizing verse.

There can be little doubt that poetry was more attractive than prose to most late antique men of culture.[99] Why otherwise did Paulinus of Nola, a man with serious reservations about the value of secular culture, write so many classicizing poems in so many different genres? It is sometimes suggested that Christian poets like Paulinus, Prudentius, and Gregory of Nazianzus (all three wrote classicizing poems in many genres) had a polemical purpose, to provide a Christian alternative to classical pagan poetry. There is no doubt some truth in this, but such an assumption perhaps overlooks the sheer pleasure men of letters took in the process of versification.[100]

Damasus has already appeared in these pages as the author of *CCP*. But he also belongs in the wider context of this epilogue. Damasus's greatest achievement was what has been called the Invention of Christian Rome. During the eighteen years of his papacy (366–84) he discovered and adorned the tombs of scores of martyrs in and (especially) around Rome, and inscribed these tombs with often-substantial elogia in his own classicizing hexameters, magnificently carved by Furius Dionysius Filocalus,

---

98. Roberts 1985; Green 2006.
99. Not to all, however, and notably not to Augustine: see Mestra 2007, 11–28.
100. Openly admitted by Gregory, who wrote almost 18,000 lines of classicizing verse: Cameron 2004, 333.

the greatest calligrapher of the age.[101] After Damasus, Rome could lay claim to a glorious Christian past that in its own way was as extensive and tangible as its pagan past. These verses, if neither genuinely learned nor subtle, were steeped in Vergilian echoes. While it would go too far to suggest that they made conversion more socially acceptable to pagan nobles, they did at any rate give Rome's Christian past a distinctively Roman, classical color.

The best-known and most prolific Christian poets at the turn of the fourth century are (of course) Paulinus of Nola and Prudentius. Both knew the classical poets intimately, and wrote for cultivated readers able to appreciate their skill and learning. One of Paulinus's earliest poems (generally dated ca. 390, long before the first Latin works of Claudian) is a eulogy of John the Baptist, *Laus Sancti Iohannis* (*Carmen 6*). As Roger Green remarks, it is better classified as a panegyric than a biography. Like so much of Paulinus's poetry, the very vehemence with which he rejects the trappings of pagan poetry underlines his familiarity with it.[102] This is particularly obvious in his one *epithalamium*, in which he explicitly rejects Juno, Cupid, and Venus, thereby revealing his (and his prospective readers') knowledge of their prominence in traditional secular *epithalamia*.[103] The bulk of Paulinus's poems were *natalicia*, commemorating St. Felix every year from 395 to 407 on his feast day, 14 January. Here it is less the occasional debt to secular birthday poetry that impresses,[104] than simply the fact that he chose to honor his local martyr with a hexameter poem. In retrospect, his annual poems on St. Felix may remind us of Claudian's regular performances at the court of Honorius during those very same years (395–408). As time passed Paulinus no doubt heard of and read Claudian's work, but he cannot yet have done so when he recited his first *natalicium* in January 395. The *natalicia* are in some ways the least classicizing of Paulinus's poems, unsurprisingly, given their subject matter, the life and miracles of a Christian saint. But he must nevertheless have been writing for an audience that appreciated and was accustomed to public recitation of praise poetry in classicizing hexameters.

If Betitia Proba was writing such poems as early as the 350s, Claudian surely had other predecessors, whose work was of such modest quality and ephemeral interest that it failed to survive. There can be little doubt that Claudian is the key figure in the development of encomiastic poetry in the Latin West. It is proof enough that his poems are the first of their kind to survive and were so widely imitated by his successors. But the fact that he had predecessors helps to explain that very success. In subject matter and genre no less than in style, he was writing for an audience able to appreciate what he had to offer. But what is so interesting and indeed important about Proba as a predecessor, as one who paved the way for Claudian, is that she was a Christian.

---

101. For a clear account of his activity, Curran 2000, 142–55; Trout 2003, 517–36.
102. R. P. H. Green 1971, 21–22; Walsh 1975, 17; Trout 1999, 85–86.
103. *Carmen* 25; Green 1971, 35–37; Roberts 1989, 337–38; Trout 1999, 215–17.
104. So Walsh 1975, 7; Green 1971, 29.

The brilliance of Claudian's invectives is likewise liable to blind us to the fact that here too he had predecessors: the Christian hexameter invectives studied in this chapter. Why this form? Obviously, because their authors, hoping that pagans as well as Christians would read them, thought they would reach a wider and more appreciative audience in classicizing verse (*quia carmina semper amasti, / carmine respondens properavi scribere versus, CAS* 3–5). *CCP, CAA,* and *CAS* date from one to three decades before the earliest poems of Claudian. Like Claudian's invectives, they too show the influence of Juvenal, especially the *CCP*. Once again, Claudian is following, not initiating a trend. And it is a trend whose earliest surviving late antique representatives were Christians.

10

THE REAL CIRCLE OF SYMMACHUS

1

"It was through their devotion to classical culture that the senatorial aristocracy made their most vital contribution to the life of the Later Roman Empire." So J. A. McGeachy in his sober and careful study of Symmachus (1942), a verdict that was already traditional and has not been seriously challenged since: aristocrats were men of letters who delighted to spend their leisure in study, correcting and annotating manuscripts, listening to philosophers, writing poetry or history. Naturally, most of these aristocratic litterateurs were pagans; their paganism and their enthusiasm for classical culture lent each other mutual support.[1]

This is surely a most surprising claim. A cultural movement spearheaded by the aristocracy of Rome? The very idea of any substantial part of aristocratic society in any age devoting its leisure to scholarship will astonish anyone familiar with the private life of the animal down the millennia.[2] Above all, aristocrats cut off (as Symmachus and his peers were) from their hereditary role as masters of the universe.[3] European aristocrats in the early twentieth century divided their time between hunting and shooting on their estates and the cafés, casinos, and spas of Biarritz, Cannes, and Monte Carlo. In a wide-ranging study of early medieval aristocracies, Wickham has recently remarked that "this emphasis on a literary lifestyle is unusual among aristocracies."[4] Is it really credible that late Roman aristocrats turned to a life of literature and scholarship?

Lommatzsch, who practically invented the idea, was more aware of the paradox than those who have embellished it since.[5] At no time during the long centuries of the Republic and early empire did the aristocracy of Rome either take much interest or achieve any distinction in literature or scholarship. All the household names come from outside this charmed circle: Ennius and Terence, Cicero and Catullus, Vergil and

---

1. McGeachy 1942, 153; for an emphatic statement, Chastagnol 1992, 336.
2. "Historians have not in the main been much impressed by standards of aristocratic learning. It may be that members of a hereditary elite are less likely than ambitious newcomers to gravitate to the forefront of intellectual enquiry," Jonathan Powis, *Aristocracy* (Oxford 1984), 45.
3. Fourth-century aristocrats exercised considerable power in virtue of their extensive estates, and some continued to hold a restricted range of offices, but they no longer had any *hereditary* entitlement to the highest offices of state.
4. Wickham 2005, 153–258 at 158.
5. Lommatzsch 1904, 185.

Horace, Lucan and Seneca, Pliny and Tacitus. In most ages aristocrats have at best played the role of patrons of the arts. The most that might plausibly be claimed is that literature-loving pagan aristocrats, even if they wrote little or nothing themselves, nonetheless actively patronized those who did, exploiting the religious connotations and presuppositions of the venerable literary heritage that clearly meant so much to educated folk in late antiquity. The reason it is specifically pagan *aristocrats* who have been credited with this devotion to the classics is (of course) because it was pagan aristocrats who monopolized the priesthoods of the old pagan cults (Ch. 5).

In the case of the aristocracy of late fourth-century Rome the paradox is further heightened by the fact that Ammianus Marcellinus, the most important pagan Latin writer of the age, included two remarkable invectives on the Roman aristocracy,[6] on top of arrogance, vanity, ostentation, superstition, gluttony, and cruelty accusing them (not least) of devotion to trivial pursuits like dicing, chariot racing, and dancing girls rather than the liberal arts. Critics have often played down these passages, largely on the grounds that it "must have been" precisely for aristocrats that Ammianus wrote— and, since he was a pagan, for pagan aristocrats. But quite apart from the fact that there is little in his history to which most Christians could take exception, the notion that aristocrats (pagan or Christian) were the only or natural audience for his work implies an implausibly simplistic social structure for so large and central a city.

There must have been hundreds of potential readers and patrons among the elite of Rome outside the few score genuinely aristocratic families. We have only to list some of those he names as likely sources for this or that detail: Aurelius Victor (PVR 389), Hypatius (cos. 351, PPO 382–83), Syagrius (PPO 380–82, cos. 381), and Constantius II's grand chamberlain Eutherius.[7] All lived at Rome during some of the period Ammianus was living and writing there. All important men, but none of them members of the aristocracy. In fact, the only aristocrat among his likely sources is Praetextatus, and Praetextatus died in 384, the best part of a decade before Ammianus finished his history. In the fourth century as in earlier centuries, the most cultivated men came from outside the ranks of the aristocracy: Ausonius, Ammianus, Claudian, Augustine, Jerome.

Ammianus (it is said) judged the many from bad experiences of a few; his criticisms are commonplaces. To be sure they are commonplaces—and not just commonplaces that can be paralleled from Greek and Latin texts. They match well enough the criticisms of aristocratic leisure activities in many other ages. But the fact that Ammianus's two invectives are full of commonplaces does not (as often inferred) mean that they are simply "rhetoric" and can be ignored. Commonplaces tend to be used precisely when they fit. They may exaggerate a situation or paint it in heightened or overly conventional colors, but they are rarely applied to situations they do not fit at all. If anything, Ammianus says surprisingly little about the aristocratic passion for hunting, so vividly documented in the art of the age (particularly mosaic floors found

6. *nobiles* (14. 6. 21 and 24); *nobilitas* (28. 4. 6).
7. Matthews 1988, 15, 100–101, 377.

on the grounds of aristocratic estates).[8] The explanation may be ignorance due to lack of invitations to attend such hunting parties. Matthews has shown that many of the accusations in these two digressions are born out by details recorded elsewhere in Ammianus's narrative.[9]

It is instructive to note that in at least two passages Ammianus's reproach turns on a deficiency of patronage rather than personal accomplishment on the part of these nobles. "Men of learning and sobriety (*eruditos et sobrios*) are shunned as bringers of bad luck who have nothing to contribute"; "the few houses that once had the reputation of being centres of serious culture (*studiorum seriis cultibus*) are now given over to the trivial pursuits of passive idleness, and echo with the sound of singing, flutes and lyres. It is the singer they invite instead of the philosopher, theatre impresarios instead of orators."[10] In the context, when he goes on to make his famous claim that "their libraries are like tombs, permananently closed," the implication is not just that the owners themselves did not read, but that they did not allow anyone else to read.

Then as now it was hard for serious students to find all the books they needed, and those with well-stocked libraries were expected to allow the less fortunate free access to their treasures. Here is Plutarch's account of the famous library of L. Lucullus cos. 74 B.C.:

> He assembled a large number of books (carefully copied), and the manner in which they were used was more honorable to him than their acquisition. For his libraries were open to all, and the colonnades which surrounded them and the reading-rooms (*scholasteria*) were accessible to Greeks without any restriction. They went there as if to an abode of the Muses, and spent whole days there in company with one another, gladly dropping their other pursuits. Lucullus himself often spent time with scholars (*philologoi*) in the colonnades.

Though a cultivated man with literary interests, Lucullus was not himself a scholar, philosopher, or poet. But he knew how to play the role of patron of letters. Cicero confirms the essential accuracy of this picture. He describes how, one day when he was at his Tusculan villa and found that he needed certain books he knew to be in the library of Lucullus's Tusculanum, he went there to borrow them, as he often did. To his surprise he found Cato there, sitting in the library, surrounded by Stoic texts. "What are you looking for here, you who have so many books of your own?" asked Cato, a neat segue into the discussion of Stoicism that forms Bk 3–4 of *De finibus*.[11] While the mise-en-scènes of Ciceronian dialogues are not to be taken literally (§ 5), there is no reason to doubt that Lucullus's library really was a place where men of letters in search of rare (especially Greek) books might meet.

---

8. Briefly, Anderson 1985, Ch. 7.
9. Matthews 1989, 414–21; den Hengst in den Boeft et al. 2007, 159–79.
10. 14. 6. 15 and 18.
11. Plut. *Lucull.* 42 (ἤ τε χρῆσις ἦν φιλοτιμοτέρα τῆς κτήσεως) ; Cic. *De fin.* iii. 7 and 10.

Ammianus's complaint is revealingly echoed by Caesarius of Arles a century later, in the preface to a collection of his sermons. After begging readers not only to read and reread the book themselves but to lend it to others to read and copy, he ruefully adds that there are all too many even among the clergy "who like to own beautifully copied and bound books, and keep them locked up in their libraries (*ita armariis clausos tenent*) so that they neither read them themselves *nor let others read them*."[12]

According to Heather, "A totally different vision of the senatorial life parodied by Ammianus emerges from the *Saturnalia* of Macrobius, where a series of experts…is portrayed as gathering to engage in serious discussions of literature, religion and antiquarian lore."[13] But it is essential to bear in mind that Macrobius's "vision" is *imaginary*, his interlocutors amateurs, not experts, and the learning he puts in their mouths copied from learned texts of long ago (§ 5). To be sure his vision remains significant as an *ideal* of senatorial *otium*, but an ideal no longer realized. Indeed, we have already seen that Macrobius may actually be responding to Ammianus's criticism (Ch. 7. 12).

Of course, Ammianus does not mean that these people were actually illiterate. All members of the Roman elite knew Vergil, Terence, Cicero, and Sallust from school. Some (like Symmachus) would deepen and extend this knowledge of the classics in adult years. Others would never open another book. A few may really have devoted their lives to nothing but idleness and luxury. Others will just have been too busy with the duties of office or the responsibilities of running their estates. It is difficult to see why people like this should have identified the texts Christians and pagans alike read in school with worship of the old gods.

Take Memmius Vitrasius Orfitus, Symmachus's father-in-law, damned in a celebrated phrase of Ammianus as "less instructed in the liberal arts than befitted a member of the nobility."[14] But not a mere boor or idler, for the very same sentence praises his judicious administration and legal skill. We all know intelligent, industrious, and successful people who simply do not read for pleasure. As it happens, Orfitus was a prominent and active pagan, not only *pontifex Vestae, pontifex Solis*, and *quindecimvir sacris faciundis*, but restorer of a temple of Apollo during his second urban prefecture.[15] But given his lack of literary interests, it is hard to believe that he saw any connection between cults and culture.

The fact that pagan deities and practices are prominently featured in some (not all) classical writings has led many scholars to assume that fourth-century pagans could not fail to be conscious of the link between "pagan" literature and pagan belief. But while it was natural for Christian readers of the classics to be struck by the mention of pagan gods, this was not why pagans themselves read such texts. Much of the divine apparatus of ancient poetry bore little relation to living cult practice, and many of the divine immoralities endlessly pilloried by Christian polemicists were embarrassing to

---

12. *Serm.* 2 Morin = M.-J. Délage, *Césaire d'Arles: Sermons au peuple* 1 (Paris 1971), 278–80.
13. Heather, *CAH* 13 (1998), 193.
14. *splendore liberalium artium minus quam nobilem decuerat institutus* (14. 6. 1).
15. *PLRE* i. 651 (where *praefuit ipse sacris* in Symm. *Ep.* i. 1. 3 is mistakenly referred to Orfitus).

serious-minded pagans, who did their best to rationalize them away. Pagans referred to the classics as "the old writers" (*veteres*). The modern term "pagan classics" corresponds to Christian labels such as books, authors, literature "of the gentiles."[16] But even Christians often used less polemical terms: "secular" books, authors, or literature,[17] that is to say, like the contemporary Greek Christian formula "external" or "foreign" wisdom,[18] literature "of the world" rather than literature of faith. While a few extremists condemned all classical literature, for most Christians it was quite literally the culture of the world. The Christian community never developed or even contemplated an alternative Christian educational system, whether at the primary or secondary level, and the reason is obvious. The traditional grammatical and rhetorical education was felt to fill the secular needs of society well enough. Changing the educational system would have meant changing the definition of culture, in effect the definition of the elite.[19] The traditional system had the irreplacable practical advantage of having established standards that were accepted in every corner of the Roman world. What we misleadingly call "pagan" culture fulfilled an overwhelmingly social function.

It was one thing for a Christian to deprecate preoccupation with form rather than content in a speech or the prominence of pagan gods in poetry. But to be *ignorant* of Cicero or Vergil was something else altogether, especially for a lay Christian with a secular career in mind. Even those, like Jerome and Augustine, who most warmly commended the simple style of Scripture, could not resist the temptation to show of their classical culture when writing to members of the elite (§ 4), whether pagan or Christian. Nor was this just a matter of personal vanity. Even bishops who spoke to their congregations in a simple style needed the traditional rhetorical style for their dealings with secular authorities, whether at the municipal or imperial level. Anyone who wants to be taken seriously by those in authority has to some extent to play the game according to the rules. The ability of a public figure like Augustine to get things done rested in no small measure on his reputation as a man of culture and learning.[20] At a purely practical level there was simply no alternative preparation for public life.

It is not as if more than a handful of the classics (notably Livy and Vergil) carried any substantial religious freight.[21] Many carried very little (Caesar, Quintilian, Martial). The classic dearest to Symmachus's heart was undoubtedly Cicero. Not only the writer he most often named, quoted, and imitated (his highest accolade is *Tullianum*, "Ciceronian"), but the source of much information and many anecdotes.[22] Yet the specifically pagan content in most of Cicero's speeches is low,[23] and from an early date

---

16. *gentilium libri, gentiles litterae, auctores gentiles, gentilium codices*: TLL s.v. *gentilis* IV A–B1a.

17. *saeculares litterae, libri, codices, eruditio saeculi, saeculi disciplina*: TLL s.v. *littera* IIc2a and *litteratura*.

18. ἡ ἔξω(θεν) or θύραθεν παιδεία or σοφία and similar phrases: for a selection, Cameron and Long 1993, 35–36.

19. Brent Shaw, *BMCR* 7 (1996), 519.

20. Marrou 1938, 96–104.

21. Varro was another matter, but he had never been a school author and most of his many works were effectively lost by the late fourth century, read by Augustine but not Symmachus (Ch. 16. 12).

22. Kroll 1891, 9–11, 61–76.

23. The exceptions are the *Catilinarians, De domo*, and *De haruspicum responsis*; Goar 1972, Ch. 2.

Christians pounced on *De divinatione* and *De natura deorum* as an armory of weapons against paganism. In their different ways Sallust and Juvenal too could be read as denouncing the vices of pagan Rome. This was certainly how Augustine read Sallust.[24]

It might have been different if there had been a danger of the classics losing their place in the curriculum. But there was never the remotest chance of this. If anything, the Christian state increased its commitment to maintaining grammarians and rhetoricians to produce men with the rhetorical training required in the ever-expanding imperial service. The very idea of a contrast between the cultural attainments of bureaucrats and aristocrats would have surprised contemporaries. In the schools at least the future of the classics was assured; luxury texts of Vergil, Cicero, and Livy proliferated in the Christian world of the fifth and sixth centuries.

What then is the evidence on which this paradoxical modern consensus is built? Is this aristocratic cultural reaction as securely documented as generally supposed? Did pagan aristocrats really use the classics as weapons in a battle against the new religion? What could this mean? How could they do it? Pagans certainly had no monopoly on classical and classicising literature. But the fact that some pagans were literature lovers does not mean that all literature lovers were pagans. More generally, is it helpful to study either the late Roman aristocracy or late Latin literature in terms of Christian versus pagan?

According to Niquet, public and private dedications alike show that "culture and learning" formed a central element in senatorial class consciousness, proving that Ammianus's criticisms were "unfair to most senators."[25] But the great majority of the dedications she assembled praise no more than the honorand's *eloquentia*, regularly listed as one in a series of what Neri has called a senator's "public virtues."[26] L. Turcius Secundus is "*eloquentia* iustitia integritate auctoritate praestans" (*ILS* 1230); Anicius Auchenius Bassus "aeque *diserto* ac nobili, provisione efficacia vigore *eloquentia* moderatione praestanti" (*ILS* 1262); and the elder Symmachus is praised for "auctoritas, prudentia adque *eloquentia*" that is "pro dignitate tanti ordinis" (*ILS* 1257), "in keeping with the dignity of the senate." In this context the inclusion of *eloquentia* was not meant to imply that, over and above all the practical virtues required of a senator, the honorand was also a man of letters and learning. *Eloquentia* was one of the practical virtues, a necessary qualification for any man of affairs, something "in keeping with the dignity of the senate." In the preamble to his panegyric on Theodosius, delivered in Rome in 389, Pacatus Drepanius claims to be nervous about speaking in front of the Roman senate "because of its inborn and hereditary gift of eloquence."[27] Rutilius Namatianus praises Messala, a praetorian prefect, for showing "what kind of dwelling-place eloquence demands; each man will be as eloquent as his desire to be

24. O'Daly 1999, 82–84, 97–98, 240–46.
25. "Bildung und Gelehrsamkeit mit dem senatorischen Standbewusstsein untrennbar verbunden bleiben," Niquet 2000, 167–72 at 167.
26. Neri 1981, 175–201.
27. Pac. Drep. *Pan. Lat.* ii (12). 1. 3; Neri 1981, 199.

good."[28] Mere flattery in both cases, no doubt, but flattery based on a long-standing ideal of senatorial eloquence, an ideal still reflected in the dedications under discussion. Oratory was no longer so central a qualification for public life as in Cicero's day, when even men of action like Crassus the triumvir and Pompey were expected to perform in court, but senators were still expected to be able to deliver a competent speech. A few (the Symmachi, father and son, and Symmachus's father-in-law, Orfitus) were called upon to serve on embassies to court, where their eloquence served a very practical purpose.

As Marrou underlined long ago, there was a world of difference between calling a man *eloquens* (a standing epithet in any senatorial cursus) and *doctus* or *eruditus*.[29] The funerary monument of Vettius Agorius Praetextatus and the dedications that praise Petronius Probus as "most eloquent *and erudite* (*eruditissimo*) in all matters"[30] are not typical of their age and class. It is also misleading to include in this dossier the private funerary monument of Rufius Festus Avienius, several of whose learned poems survive. And while the fact that the poets Claudian and Merobaudes were rewarded with senatorial rank and a statue in the Forum of Trajan shows that poets were still honored, it tells us nothing about the cultural attainments of rank-and-file senators. Ammianus's blanket condemnation is no doubt exaggerated and unfair. But the bulk of Niquet's dedications do not disprove his complaints; they simply illustrate a traditional ideal that he felt that many of them no longer lived up to. He would no doubt have conceded that Orfitus was *eloquens*; it was *doctrina* that he lacked. It is worth adding that, since Orfitus was dead by 370 and Ammianus did not come to Rome till the 380s, his celebrated put-down cannot be a personal judgment. He must have heard it from Orfitus's peers.

As for the often-repeated claim that culture and learning are seldom mentioned in Christian funerary inscriptions, pagan funerary inscriptions do not often mention them either. If we confine our inquiry to dedications honoring fourth-century Roman aristocrats, praise of eloquence and learning is by no means confined to pagans. Two of the most prominent nobles cited above were Christians: Petronius Probus and Anicius Bassus. Pacatus too was a Christian.

An impressive looking dossier of cultural activities claimed for pagan aristocrats of the late fourth century can be found in all the standard modern accounts. But (oratory aside) very little rises to the level of either literature or scholarship. Some of these people, the historian Aurelius Victor (e.g.), were not aristocrats at all, but men of humble origins who rose to the ranks of the elite by their own efforts, precisely because of their literary culture. As for the claim that pagan aristocrats "edited" classical texts, there is not a single certain example. As we shall see in chapters 12–14, the vast majority

---

28. *De reditu* 275–76, a poetical version of Cato's *vir bonus dicendi peritus*.

29. Marrou 1938, 105–24.

30. *litterarum et eloquentiae lumini* (ILS 1265); *disertissimo atque omnibus rebus eruditissimo patrono* (ILS 1266).

document the work of Christians. The fact that Lollianus cos. 355 was the dedicatee of a book on astrology does not prove that he was an expert himself, much less a man of general culture. Boethius mentions a certain Albinus who "is said to have written" on geometry and dialectic,[31] frequently identified with Macrobius's interlocutor Caecina Albinus, without the slightest justification. There is no reason to believe that Boethius's Albinus was either a senator or even wrote in the fourth century, but if so he is more likely to have been Caeionius Rufius Albinus cos. 335, described as *philosophus* on a Roman dedication.[32]

Just about the only fourth-century pagan of aristocratic birth who produced any substantial literary corpus was the poet Rufius Festus Avienius, a generation before the crisis of Roman paganism. The only pagan aristocrat with any pretensions to scholarship (grossly exaggerated by moderns, as we shall see in later chapters) is Praetextatus. Neither a scholar nor an original writer, Symmachus himself barely earns the modest characterization of man of letters: while admired for his *eloquentia*, nothing in his surviving writings suggests that he laid any serious claim to *doctrina* (Ch. 11). All that the subscriptions really prove is that, well down into the sixth century, members of the now Christian Roman elite (by no means just the aristocracy) took pleasure in owning and reading luxury texts of the classics. That is important enough in itself. If there had been no market for the expensive, sturdy codexes in which the classics began to be copied in the two centuries before the onset of the dark ages, fewer might have survived.

2

Within the ranks of the aristocracy many scholars have identified an inner core of literary pagans, the so-called "Circle of Symmachus," actively nurturing the classics and sponsoring pagan writers in the hope of recalling waverers to the fold. It is (I suspect) the chance congruence of two factors, one ancient and one modern, that has saddled Symmachus with this unlikely role: Macrobius's *Saturnalia*, where he appears as one of the three hosts to a fictitious literary gathering; and Otto Seeck's wonderful edition of Symmachus's *Letters* (1883), with its massive introduction identifying every correspondent and his family. As a consequence, Symmachus has always been seen as the central figure in late fourth-century Roman society.

That is to say, Symmachus has been treated as the Pliny of his age. This is a natural comparison to make, but at the same time it calls forth a number of qualifications and reservations. In the first place, while Pliny may not have had a literary circle in the Macrobian sense, he corresponded with some fifty people who were either writers of some sort themselves or with whom he discussed literary topics.[33] Nor can there be

---

31. Boethius, Περὶ ἑρμ . i. 4 Meiser; Chadwick 1981, 84.
32. *ILS* 1222, reedited as *CIL* vi. 8. 3 (2000), no. 41318 (p. 5051).
33. Guillemin 1929, 23; White 1975, 299.

any question that his letters cast a flood of light on the literary world of his age, or that Pliny himself was a keen and active patron of letters. But while Symmachus's correspondence reveals a man (incidentally a pagan) who set a high value on literary culture, fewer than twenty of his more than 130 correspondents could be described as literary in any way, and his occasional remarks on the work of these friends consists of little but elegant flattery. Apart from citing a few poems by his father and himself,[34] the only specific works by contemporaries he mentions are Ausonius's *Mosella* (i. 14), a declamation by the rhetor Palladius (i. 15), a translation by his friend Naucellius (iii. 11), a history being written by an anonymous senator (ix. 110), and the Greek poet Andronicus (viii. 22).

Pliny too praises the work of his friends, but the big difference is that they were constantly sending each other copies of their works and soliciting criticism. Nor was this just a way of fishing for praise. It seems clear that genuine criticisms were communicated and embodied in these draft compositions.[35] Several letters show Symmachus sending friends copies of *published* speeches,[36] notably his *Pro Trygetio*, a political speech presumably distributed more for its contents than to solicit literary criticism.[37] But I have not found any case of Symmachus circulating speeches for suggested improvements. The well-known letter about Ausonius's *Mosella* is not a response to a draft. Indeed, it is a complaint that Ausonius had not sent him a copy at all. There is no indication that the translation Naucellius sent him was an unpublished work he was expected to criticize, and the copy of Naucellius's poems he returns he returned because it had been bound up wrongly (p. 478). There are no comments and no sign that any were expected. Of course, this does not prove that Symmachus and his friends did *not* circulate their drafts like Pliny and his friends. But there is no evidence that they did. Nor is there any evidence in Symmachus's letters of the salons for the reading of new works that Pliny considered such an important tool for the nurturing of literary talent. Nor can a single writer of the age be identified as the beneficiary of his patronage. These differences between Pliny and Symmachus are the more striking in that the evidence on which they are based is, formally speaking, virtually identical: nine books of private correspondence.

Unlike Pliny's circle, the circle of Symmachus as it appears in much modern scholarly writing is not, paradoxically enough, based on the solid and abundant evidence of his correspondence. The list of members is more a matter of definition than evidence. Since it is assumed to be an association of pagan literary men, all pagan literary men of the right time and place are assumed to belong. Those for whom there is no evidence are said to hover on its "fringes." On no better evidence than a palaeographical dating to the neighborhood of 400, a luxury artefact like the illustrated Vatican Virgil that

---

34. *Ep.* i. 1, i. 2, i. 8; brief notes on these poems in Courtney 1993, 447–53.
35. Guillemin 1929, 42–59; Cova 1966.
36. *Ep.* iv. 29. 1; iv. 45. 1; v. 9. 1; vii. 58. 1; Callu vol. 2, 111 n. 1.
37. *Ep.* i. 44. 3; i. 52; i. 78. 1; 1. 105; v. 43; Sogno 2006, 23–25.

happens to contain representations of sacrifice is assigned to the "circle of Symmachus" (Ch. 19. 3), as though this were the only possible source for such patronage.

At one time Ammianus, Claudian, and Rutilius Namatianus were all confidently assumed to be Symmachan protégés. It was during the last decade of Symmachus's life, the period from which most of his letters have survived, that Claudian won instant fame as the most brilliant and prolific Latin poet of the age and Ammianus published the most elaborate and important history of Rome in Latin since Tacitus. It was in Rome itself that Claudian made his debut and Ammianus worked, wrote, and gave recitations. Another Egyptian poet, the obscure Andronicus of Hermupolis, wrote to Symmachus with a copy of some poems. Symmachus replied with extravagant praise (comparing them to Homer!), and promised to publicize them in Rome (not that he seems to have done so). But he neither wrote to nor even mentioned either Claudian or Ammianus. Nor (unlike Pliny again) does he ever mention attending recitations or literary performances of any sort. For example, though frequently referring to the consular celebrations held both at court in Milan and once in Rome during the last two decades of his life, not once does he mention the customary panegyric (several of them by Claudian).

The old view that a letter of Symmachus to an unnamed historian (*Ep.* ix. 110) was addressed to Ammianus is now discredited.[38] It is true that he twice mentions Symmachus's father, Avianius Symmachus, with approval, the second time praising him as a man of "exemplary learning and conduct." But then there is that unflattering anecdote he repeated (p. 224), and the barb about Orfitus's culture would not have pleased his son-in-law. Symmachus himself served as proconsul of Africa during the elder Theodosius's campaign against the African rebel Firmus, winning his commendation for some service or other.[39] If he had so wished, somewhere in his long account of Theodosius's campaign Ammianus could easily have slipped in "ably assisted by the proconsul Symmachus, later consul," as he does with other important contacts (e.g., Neoterius, "later consul," xxvi. 5. 14). There was also another opening. The first emperor to remove the altar of Victory from the senate house (as we know from Symmachus himself) was Constantius II, during his Roman visit of 359, so memorably described by Ammianus.[40] A brief reference forward to Symmachus's greatest claim to fame would not have been out of place. Indeed, it must have been hard for a pagan writing ca. 390 in Rome to resist the temptation. But Ammianus did.

As for Rutilius, there is nothing beyond their common paganism to associate him with Symmachus. Not only is he not mentioned by either Symmachus or Macrobius, his famous little poem *De reditu suo* was not written till 417/8. Pagan literary circles no doubt still existed. Rutilius's poem lists a number of high-placed friends, some (by no means all) literary men (Lucillus, Messala, Protadius), some pagans (Lucillus, Messala, and perhaps Rufius Volusianus), but some Christians (Protadius).

---

38. Cameron 1964, 15–28.
39. Symm. *Ep.* x. 1. 2 (addressed to Theodosius).
40. Symm. *Rel.* iii. 5; Amm. xvi. 10, with the additional fragments discovered by Cappelletto 1983; Cameron 1989.

Much has been made of Symmachus's remark that *iter ad capessendos magistratus saepe litteris promovetur*,[41] as if it implied some special appreciation of literature. Yet his point is that men of letters are deservedly promoted to high offices of state. There are many other such letters recommending rhetoricians and a handful of philosophers for administrative posts of one sort or another.[42] All they show is that Symmachus shared the general view that magistrates should be cultivated men. He also supported a certain number of unknowns for teaching positions. This is certainly to his credit. They might be fairly called his protégés, but there is no indication that he took a personal interest in anything these people actually wrote (if they did) rather than their qualifications for office. They are all praised in the same clichés. As for the quality of his judgement, it is interesting that he took the trouble to preserve his letters about such otherwise unknown "philosophers" as Barachus and Serapammon—and threw away the one commending a brilliant young African who was to prove one of the most influential thinkers of the millennium. It has been suggested that Symmachus deliberately selected Augustine for the chair of rhetoric at Milan in the hope that this ardent young Manichee (as he then was) would stir things up in the Catholic circles of the western capital. That is a nice thought. But it is going too far to claim that he "gravitate[d] around the pagan circle of Symmachus," even "for a short moment."[43] Augustine's own remark that he "canvassed" (*ambivit*) Manichaean friends to support his application does not suggest any previous relationship with Symmachus, nor does the fact that he got the job on the basis of an audition (*dictione proposita*).[44]

A grammatical work by Servius quotes from a Symmachan speech, but the one letter to Servius appears in a book not originally intended for publication and does not touch on literary themes.[45] No writings of Servius are dedicated to Symmachus, while two of his books name other patrons (Albinus and Fortunatianus).

Then there is Arusianus Messius, who compiled a collection of phrases from Vergil, Sallust, Terence, and Cicero that includes another quotation from a speech by Symmachus. On the strength of this we are asked to believe that, though not mentioned in the letters, Messius "seems to have been close to Symmachus." He may indeed have been trying to curry favor with a potential patron, but that does not mean he shared Symmachus's religious views (as it happens, the first person to quote from Messius's book was St. Ambrose). And there is worse to come. Messius's book is dedicated, not to Symmachus, but to Anicius Olybrius and Anicius Probinus, two members of the leading Christian family in Rome. Rather than abandon Messius's supposed closeness to Symmachus, we are now told that even the Christian Anicii "were interested in the literary efforts of the pagan circles."[46] To such extremes was a good scholar driven simply

---

41. *Ep.* i. 20. 1 (to Ausonius); cf. *scis enim bonas artes honore nutriri*, i. 79 (to Ausonius's son Hesperius).
42. McGeachy 1942, 158–61.
43. P. Brown 1967, 67.
44. *Conf.* v. 23, with O'Donnell's commentary (2. 320–21); see too now Ebbeler and Sogno 2007, 230–42.
45. *Ep.* viii. 60; see further below.
46. Bloch 1963, 212.

because he took it as axiomatic that secular literary activity would be sponsored by pagan "literary circles." The truth is that Symmachus's name does not appear in a single literary dedication of the age. Of course, given his reputation as a man of letters, it is likely that many a budding writer sought his patronage, but no surviving letter responds to any such request. Some writers of the age surely looked on themselves as Symmachan protégés, but none that we can identify. The large number of letters commending aspirants for office makes it clear that Symmachus wished to be remembered as an influential patron, but there is little to suggest that he saw himself specifically as a patron of letters.

Claudian too began his career under the auspices of Christian aristocrats—the same patrons indeed as Messius. In 395 he recited a panegyric on the joint consulate of Olybrius and Probinus. Why did he pick the Anicii rather than the Symmachi? Perhaps sheer opportunism, correctly identifying them as a wealthy and powerful family in high favor with the ruling house. But it may be that he also saw them as a more appreciative audience for his work (again correctly, since Symmachus reveals no awareness of having ever heard of Claudian). Of all the many people to whom Claudian dedicated poems or with whom he corresponded on literary topics, not one is known to have been a pagan and most were certainly Christian. If there *was* a pagan party at Rome, they must have counted him irretrievably committed to the Christian camp.

Olybrius and Probinus were two of the five children of S. Petronius Probus, the most powerful aristocrat of his generation, holder of four praetorian prefectures and consul in 371.[47] Most of the eighteen surviving dedications in his honor dwell on the many offices he held and the splendor of his ancestry. But others, as we have seen, praise him in addition as a "luminary of letters" and "most erudite in all matters."[48] It is easy to dismiss such compliments by interested parties to important men. Yet much of the evidence cited for the cultural interests of pagan aristocrats is of the same nature. Flavian's history, of which so much has been made in recent years, is known exclusively from dedications by members of his own family; and most of the evidence for portraying Praetextatus as a scholar derives from claims made by his widow on his funerary monument![49] Epigraphic praise of the cultural attainments of Probus are more detailed than for any aristocrat of the age except Praetextatus (Symmachus and Flavian included), and there is no obvious reason to take them any less seriously.

Ausonius confirms Probus's reputation as an orator, and the compliment that he "combined Ulysses's hail and Nestor's honeyed flow with the voice of Cicero," trite though it is, nonetheless implies that he could speak in Greek as well as Latin, an accomplishment certainly not matched by Symmachus.[50] Symmachus's selection of the young Augustine for preferment is paralleled by Probus's selection of the future

---

47. In addition to the entry in *PLRE* i. 736–40, see Novak 1980, 473–93; Cameron 1985, 164–82.
48. *litterarum et eloquentiae lumini* (*ILS* 1265); *disertissimo atque omnibus rebus eruditissimo patrono* (*ILS* 1266).
49. For reservations on the evidence of Macrobius's *Saturnalia*, below §§ 5.
50. *Ep.* 9 (12). 13–15.

bishop Ambrose to serve on his *consilium*, likewise on the basis of his rhetorical skill. It should also be noted that one of Symmachus's six letters to Probus contains a literary allusion that he later repeats in letters to two of his literary friends.[51]

McGeachy made much of Symmachus's concern for the education of his son, but Probus was no less concerned for the education of his sons. To this end he asked Ausonius for copies of the *Fables* of Titianus and the *Chronica* of Cornelius Nepos. Ausonius equipped his gift with a long poetic dedication to Probus that (as Robin Nisbet has seen) opens with an echo of Catullus's famous apostrophe to his native Sirmio (*perge, o libelle, Sirmium, / et dic ero meo ac tuo / ave atque salve* ~ Catullus 31. 12, *salve venusta Sirmio, atque ero gaude*). Ausonius obviously expected Probus, like Catullus born in Verona and at the time of writing resident in Sirmium, to spot the echo and appreciate the play on Sirmio/Sirmium.[52] Catullus's modern fame is liable to blind us to the fact that he was not a late antique classic (unknown, it seems, to both Symmachus and Servius).

That Probus's sons grew up with an interest in poetry and oratory is claimed by Claudian in his panegyric on their consulate and now confirmed by the presence of at least one classicizing epigram by Anicius Probinus in the *Epigrammata Bobiensia*.[53] What may be the epitaph for his third son, Anicius Probus cos. 406, proclaims him too a poet.[54] The boys' maternal great-grandmother was the renowned poetess Faltonia Betitia Proba, author of a surviving Christian cento and one or more classicizing epics or panegyrics (Ch. 9. 3).

It has often been thought that Petronius Probus himself was a poet. A poem transmitted between Cornelius Nepos's *Lives of Foreign Generals* and his other works in the three best manuscripts has been read as implying that Probus dedicated a book of poems by himself, his father (Petronius Probinus cos. 341), and grandfather (Petronius Probianus cos. 322) to Theodosius I.[55] No one who has made this claim apparently took the trouble to read the poem. The *auctor* who identifies himself as Probus is neither poet nor aristocrat, but a *calligrapher*.[56] And the emperor to whom he presented this manuscript was not Theodosius I, but that well-known amateur calligrapher Theodosius II. But a man does not need to be a poet himself to be a patron of letters. The Probus to whom the poet Rufius Festus Avienius dedicated his *Ora maritima* was surely Petronius Probus.[57] If so, it is significant that, like Claudian, Avienius, though

51. Paulinus, *Vita Ambrosii* 5; Symm. *Ep.* i. 58 (to Probus), v. 68 (to Olybrius and Probinus), and vii. 15 (to Attalus): the story of Atilius Serranus summoned from the plough to the consulate (see Callu's note).

52. McGeachy 1942, 155–59; Auson. xxvii. 9. b. 1–3, p. 202 Green; Nisbet 1995, 83.

53. Nos. 65 and perhaps also 55, 56, and 70: Speyer 1959, 113–20.

54. *carmine doctiloquus*, CLE 1408. 2 = ILCV 64. 2. The poem only gives the one name Probus, but calls its honorand *spes generis clari, magnorum gloria patrum…clarior in patria nobilitate Probus* (lines 1 and 6).

55. See the entries for all three men in *PLRE* i; Chastagnol 1962, 83; Novak 1980, 490; Shanzer 1986, 247; Bruggisser 1993, 26; Sivan 1993, 151; Nisbet 1995, 83; Lançon 1995, 199.

56. *AL* 783; for a better text (interpreted as here, following Jahn), Marshall 1977, 1–2.

57. Cameron 2002a; Cameron 1995, 258 (more sceptical).

never mentioned by Symmachus, was a pagan. For all we know Probus's attitude to Christianity and classical culture may have been much like that of Ausonius, with whom he was evidently on close terms. We should not be surprised to find the leading Christian aristocrat of the generation before the Frigidus patronizing pagan men of letters and encouraging his sons to do the same.

3

There is another way of approaching the "circle" of Symmachus, remarkably enough never systematically tried. The only pagan aristocrat from whose pen we have an oeuvre substantial and varied enough to test the hypothesis of a pagan literary circle and cultural reaction is Symmachus himself. We can take a closer look at the people Symmachus actually wrote to and the surviving letters he sent them.

First a few necessary preliminaries on the editing and publication of his correspondence.[58] It used to be thought, on the basis of explicits to Bks ii and iv claiming that they were "published after [Symmachus's] death by Q. Fabius Memmius Symmachus his son," that all ten books were put together by Memmius.[59] But marked structural and chronological differences between Bks i, ii–vii, and viii–x suggest rather publication in three separate stages. In Bks i–vii letters are grouped by correspondents, while in Bks viii–ix letters to the same addressees are not grouped together, there are several thematic groups with different addressees, a great many anonymous letters, overall less important addressees, and an altogether disproportionate number on the subject of Memmius's praetorian games in 401.

Earlier discussions took refuge in the assumption that Memmius simply lost interest in his task, and that viii–x represent the unclassifiable "odds and ends" of Symmachus's files.[60] But that does not really explain even the anonymous letters,[61] much less the thematic groupings or the inclusion in viii–ix of additional letters to correspondents previously grouped in i–vii.[62] These last were presumably deliberately omitted when the original selection was made.[63] Roda was surely right to argue that it was only ii–vii that Memmius published. Books viii–x were a separate, later instalment

---

58. What follows is mainly based on Callu 1 (1972), 18–22; Vera 1977, 1003–36; and 1981, lxxxix–xcv, 438–42; Roda 1979; 1981a; and 1981b, 58–79; Marcone 2008, 63–72; Sogno 2006, 60–62.

59. For a brief statement of this position, Matthews 1974, 66–68.

60. *pro certo habeo, iuvenem editorem longi operis taedio captum schedulas, quae supererant, ita uti in patris scriniis compositae vel potius incompositae iacebant, librariis describendas tradidisse,* Seeck 1883, xxvi; for a less hostile statement, Matthews 1974, 67–68.

61. The occasional anonymous letters in ii–vii are presumably to be put down to scribal omissions.

62. For example, ix. 88, anonymous but probably to Ausonius; 112, anonymous but probably to Petronius Probus; and ix. 43, 124, and 126, probably to Rusticus Julianus, Florentinus, and Anicius Probinus: Roda 1981a, 280; and 1981b.

63. It is easy to see why Symmachus himself might have chosen to omit ix. 88, a very deferential letter initiating his correspondence with Ausonius. The letters included in i (13–43) present the two men as equals.

compiled from what remained in the family archives in response to Symmachus's growing fame as an epistolographic model.[64]

The explicits naming Memmius are both preserved in the only Carolingian manuscript of the Letters (Par. lat. 8623). A similar heading survives for Bk x in a lost MS quoted in Juretus's edition of 1580: *continens epistolas familiares ad imperatores, sententias senatorias et opuscula, editus post eius mortem a Q. Flavio [sic] Memmio Symmacho v.c.* As Roda saw, there are significant differences between this and the undoubtedly ancient explicits to Bks ii and iv, which do not characterize the contents of individual books. The same lost MS also described Bk ix as *continens commendatitias*. Since most of the other books contain commendatory letters, this detail can hardly be authentic. All that survives of Bk x is two early letters, one to the elder Theodosius (375) and one to Gratian (376). Theodosius was not an emperor but since Gratian was, Bk x may have been devoted to correspondence with the imperial family (perhaps in chronological sequence), presumably to match the Plinian total of nine books private and one official correspondence.[65] But that does not mean that we have to accept the detail about Memmius, surely added on the basis of the two undoubtedly authentic explicits. It is a pity we cannot be sure how much else in the heading is authentic, because *epistolas familiares ad imperatores* would imply that the *relationes*, official letters to emperors, were not included.

It was once thought that Symmachus himself published the *relationes* soon after leaving office early in 385, but the lack of any principle of arrangement (whether emperors addressed, date, or subject matter) and the fact that so many of the headings are incorrect are insuperable objections to this assumption.[66] The heading to the most famous of all (3), on the altar of Victory, is not only incorrect (naming Theodosius, not Valentinian II as principal addressee), but typically conflicts with numerous indications in the text of the letter itself. The editor who devised these headings was apparently unaware that, even when intended for one particular emperor, such documents were properly addressed to the entire imperial college. Vera rightly insisted that such gross ignorance of official usage could not be ascribed to Symmachus himself. The solution must be that the *Relationes* were published from copies kept in Symmachus's files, where the headings and imperial apostrophes were left blank or indicated by acronyms such as *DDDNNN* (*domini nostri*, three in number), to be filled in by the secretary who produced the final version.[67]

Much of the material in Bks viii–ix is of considerable historical value, but it is easy to see why Symmachus himself might have considered it too slight and repetitious

---

64. Book ix consists almost entirely of commendatory letters, giving it virtually textbook status.
65. Sidonius too eventually published nine books, explicitly citing the Plinian precedent in ix. 1. 1. Individual books seem to have been published separately, or in small groups: see Stevens 1933, 171–73; and J. Harries 1994, 7–10.
66. Vera 1977, 1003–36; and 1981, lxxxix–xcv; Sogno 2006, 33–34; Callu 2009, xxxix–lix.
67. For example, the fact that in *Rel.* 12 we find the apostrophe *domini imperatores Valentiniane Theodosi et Arcadi inclyti victores ac triumphatores semper Augusti* shows how the acronym *DDDNNN*, often found elsewhere, was meant to be expanded.

(and the *Relationes* too technical) for publication.[68] Nor is it likely that Memmius would have wanted to include all those letters on his own praetorian games. If this analysis of Bks viii–ix is accepted, there is an important consequence for the study of Symmachus's circle: any addressee known only from viii–ix was passed over when the original selection was made.

The inclusion of letters to the future pretender Priscus Attalus (vii. 15–25) proves (as Seeck saw long ago) that ii–vii appeared before Attalus's first proclamation in 409. Nor is it likely that letters to Stilicho (iv. 1–14) would have been included after his execution in 408. The probability is that ii–vii were published not long after Symmachus's death in 402.

As for Bk i, Kroll pointed out long ago that the great majority of Symmachus's archaisms occur in Bk i of his *Letters*.[69] A more systematic investigation by Haverling (like Wölfflin before her) disputed some of Kroll's examples while still concluding that there were many more of them (both lexical and syntactic) in Bk i. Haverling also identified more poeticisms and neologisms in i than ii–ix.[70] Then Callu observed that no letter in Bk i can be dated later than the late 380s, whereas all the other books contain letters going down to shortly before Symmachus's death.[71] Books ii–vii all contain a certain number of letters to younger contemporaries, whereas no one included in Bk i lived later than ca. 390.[72] It is natural to connect stylistic elaboration with contents and conclude that Bk i was revised and published by Symmachus himself in the (perhaps late) 390s.

Bruggisser argued that the stylistic elaboration of Bk i was original, simply a consequence of the fact that he was addressing men of considerable prestige and culture.[73] There may be something in this: Symmachus certainly adjusted style to correspondent (more on this below). But it cannot be the whole explanation. If Ausonius and Praetextatus were in a class by themselves, many correspondents in later books were at least as cultivated and distinguished as the rest of the correspondents addressed in Bk i. Some letters in ii–vii are very elaborate indeed (notably those to Protadius, iv. 17–34), while we find archaisms even in letters to the less important correspondents of Bk i.

Few would doubt that Symmachus did something to prepare his letters for publication. Pliny and Sidonius carefully revised theirs,[74] and it would be surprising if Symmachus had been content to leave his just as he originally wrote them two or

---

68. While composing the *Relationes* (with the exception of *Rel.* 3), we may picture Symmachus complaining, with the younger Pliny, *scribo plurimas sed inlitteratissimas litteras* (*Ep.* i. 10. 9).
69. Kroll 1891, 31–41; cf. E. Wölfflin, *ALL* 7 (1892), 616–17.
70. Haverling 1988, 136–37; 254–55.
71. Callu 1972, 18 (noted already by Peter 1901, 146); cf. too Bruggisser 1993, 27. What follows is an amplified and fortified version of Callu's argument.
72. Petronius Probus must have died about then: Matthews 1975, 230; all the others probably earlier.
73. Bruggisser 1993, 25–30.
74. *retractatis exemplaribus enucleatisque*, Sidon. *Ep.* i. 1. 1; for Pliny's revisions, Sherwin-White 1966, 11–20.

three decades earlier. There was nothing he prized more than *verborum vetustas*,[75] and it would be natural enough for him to have added a few archaisms during revision.[76]

If Bk i was published together with ii–vii, why do ii–vii all contain a preponderance of recent letters while i contains nothing later than 385? Bruggisser argued that Bk i was intended to evoke a specific phase of Symmachus's career, the reign of Gratian, allegedly a golden age for the senate of Rome. But however impressed Symmachus may have been by the pro-senatorial measures of Gratian's opening months, he must soon have been undeceived. From 377 on Gratian stopped appointing aristocrats to the prefecture of Rome,[77] and then in 382 came the measures that led to the disestablishment of Roman paganism. It is hard to believe that any pagan could have looked *back* on the reign of Gratian as a golden age for the senate of Rome.

As for the inclusion of officials of that period like Hesperius, Antonius, and Syagrius (i. 75–107), to most readers of Memmius's posthumous edition they would no longer have been names to conjure with. Nor do the actual letters they received lend any support to Bruggisser's thesis. Books i–ii of the correspondence of both Pliny and Sidonius contain earlier letters than the later books.[78] In both cases the natural inference is that these books were published before the later books. In the case of Symmachus there is no steady chronological progression from first to last book. While letters in Bk iii run from ca. 370 to 390, and in iv from ca. 398 to 402, the basic principle of arrangement is grouping by recipient.[79]

Symmachus's letters were widely admired (he claimed that people stole them in transit).[80] Having already published at least one collection of his speeches,[81] it would not be surprising if he had decided to publish a selection of his correspondence as well. It would have been tactful to select correspondents who were not only men of prestige but also safely dead, as the eight included in Bk i all were by (say) 390.[82] As for Bruggisser's further thesis that Bk i had a cultural goal, the "validation and restoration of antiquity,"[83] this makes better sense if we attribute such a design to Symmachus himself rather than the still teenage Memmius.[84]

---

75. Bruggisser 1993, 317–18; and below, p. ##.
76. It was no doubt during revision that Sidonius added some of the many direct quotations from Pliny and Symmachus as well as the classics ("It is not easy to believe that a casual correspondence ... would contain so many quotations from two prose authors," Stevens 1933, 60–63, 171–74).
77. Piganiol 1975, 226; Bruggisser 1993, 200–233; Chastagnol 1960, 437–38.
78. Pliny, Sherwin-White 1966, 27–31; Sidonius, Harries 1994, 7.
79. Sogno 2006, 61–62.
80. ii. 48; McGeachy 1942, 121, mistranslates and misinterprets ii. 12 in the same sense, but Symmachus's point is just that people who have promised to deliver his letters quickly then dawdle on the way (so Callu's translation, but his note on ii. 48 cites ii. 12 as a parallel).
81. Seeck 1883, v–x; McGeachy 1942, 17–22; Pabst 1989.
82. Or at any rate, like Ausonius far off in Bordeaux, permanently out of touch with Symmachus after 379.
83. Bruggisser 1993, 434 (and passim).
84. Not that such themes are restricted to Bk i; the letters to Naucellius in iii. 10–16 are another conspicuous illustration. There is much of value in Brugisser's detailed analyses, but his generalisations suffer from concentrating on barely a third of Bk i to the exclusion of the remaining eight books.

It has often been assumed that Memmius was responsible for both selection and arrangement.[85] But the *editus* of the subscription means "published," not "edited," and if Symmachus published Bk i himself, it was no doubt (like the first books of Pliny and Sidonius)[86] a trial balloon. Its obvious success must have encouraged him to continue. The fact that Bk i differs so sharply from the other books in the matter of archaisms suggests that Symmachus had not yet begun stylistic revision of the remainder. But there is reason to believe that he had at least made a preliminary selection and arrangement of material before death intervened. The fact that Bk i opens with letters to his father and Bk vii with letters to his son suggests a plan devised by Symmachus himself, a plan that foresaw just seven books.[87] Inside this ring structure Bks ii and vi both have single addressees, the Nicomachi Flaviani father and son (vi jointly to the younger Flavian and his wife, Symmachus's daughter). Memmius surely did no more than prepare the manuscript for publication.[88]

How much editing was required? A century ago Seeck argued that all letters to or concerning the usurpers Maximus and Eugenius were deleted, and Peter that the correspondence as a whole was censored to make it more palatable to Christian readers.[89] If Peter were right, its present form might give a misleading impression of Symmachus's dealings with pagans and attitude to paganism.

It is certainly not the case that all letters addressed to pagans or of pagan content were weeded out. As we shall see in what follows, too many of both sorts remain. While there are no letters to Maximus, Eugenius, or Arbogast, there is an entire book (ii) of letters to the elder Flavian. Croke tried to minimize the degree of political editing as well. While accepting the deletion of letters to Maximus, he argued that Symmachus did not have close enough relations with either Eugenius or Arbogast to warrant censoring his letters to them.[90] But his argument that Symmachus's letters "never say anything at all of political affairs" and so would not have "contained any information which could be considered treasonable" goes too far.[91]

It is not just a question of "information." Having narrowly escaped retribution for his involvement in the usurpation of Maximus, and being the oldest friend of the elder Flavian, Eugenius's praetorian prefect, Symmachus had to tread more carefully than most. It was easy to refuse office in the new regime, but given his central role in the social and diplomatic life of the western elite, it is likely that he was bombarded with invitations from court that were not so easy to refuse without offense—not least from

---

85. "Symmachus' letters were carefully culled and edited by Memmius," Salzman 2006, 360.
86. For Pliny's books, Sherwin-White 1966, 20–41; for Sidonius, Stevens 1933, 171–73; and Harries 1994, 7–10. Since both lived to see all nine books published, they may have made further revisions when republishing the separate books as a corpus.
87. Sogno 2006, 62.
88. So already Peter 1901, 148. Memmius was still very young at the time.
89. Peter 2 (1897), 34, a view widely quoted but not repeated in his 1901 study of Symmachus's letters.
90. McGeachy 1949, 222–29; Croke 1976, 533–49.
91. As does the argument that Symmachus would have had no cause to "seek out the friendship" of a Frankish general like Arbogast. Symmachus *always* sought out relations with the power brokers of the day.

his friend Flavian. However hard he tried to distance himself from the regime, there must have been a paper trail vulnerable to hostile interpretation.

But Croke was right to point out that 402 would be late in the day to delete letters that might compromise him with Eugenius. Symmachus himself surely went through his files the day after the news of the Frigidus. Libanius reports examining his files after the Theodorus conspiracy of 371, and the complete gap in his correspondence between 365 and 388 (the usurpations of Procopius and Maximus) can hardly be accidental.[92] Symmachus was not so paranoid as this, but he will surely have taken care to remove anything likely to compromise himself or his family. The whole of his correspondence with the younger Flavian before 394 is missing,[93] and while we can hardly doubt that he deleted all letters to the elder Flavian touching directly on the Eugenian regime, he left some letters from that period. The emperor referred to (though not named) in ii. 81 must be Eugenius, and at least two letters refer openly to the celebration of Flavian's canceled consulate (ii. 83 and 84).[94] The task of distinguishing between what could safely be left and what had to go was not one that could be left to his inexperienced teenage son.

But neither father nor son (it seems) considered it necessary to edit out all pagan references. As we shall see in the remainder of this chapter, there is a hint of the paganism of almost every pagan Symmachus corresponded with somewhere in the letters to him. There are especially frequent references (more than twenty) to the elder Flavian's paganism. It is remarkable enough that Memmius saw no risk in publishing so soon after the event so detailed a record of his father's relationship with a man publicly branded as a traitor. But it is even more remarkable that, despite Christian emphasis on the role of paganism in the victory at the Frigidus, he saw no need to edit out references to pagan priesthoods and festivals (ii. 34, 36, 53, 59). By the time of Symmachus's death less than a decade later, these were no longer (apparently) things that had to be hushed up and only whispered to fellow pagans.

If Bk i was published in Symmachus's lifetime, we are entitled to assume that he gave considerable thought to its contents and arrangement. The correspondents included are Avianius Symmachus (his father), Ausonius, Praetextatus, Petronius Probus, Celsinus Titianus (his brother), Hesperius (Ausonius's son), Antonius, and Syagrius. Only three are known pagans (his father, brother, and Praetextatus), and the letters to all three allude freely to pagan festivals and priestly duties. But at least four of the other five were definitely or probably Christians.

In addition to eleven letters from Symmachus to his father (hereafter Avianius), there is also a long letter from Avianius announcing his intention of producing a new version of Varro's *Hebdomades*, an illustrated biographical dictionary of famous Romans. To this end he included seven brief hexameter poems on prominent Roman figures of his own and the preceding generation (one of them, as it happens,

---

92. *Or.* i. 163, 175–77; *Or* xxxii. 27; Norman 1992, 28–34.
93. Marcone, *Comm. iv* (1983), 53.
94. iv. 17 to Protadius thanks him for his sympathy, perhaps concerning Flavian's death.

perhaps a Christian).[95] Symmachus exclaims in reply that these poems are better than Varro's. In another letter he praises Avianius as "the sole authentic representative of Ciceronian eloquence in our own age," and for drawing on "whatever is charming in the poets, authoritative in the orators, reliable in the historians and learned in the grammarians" (compliments that naturally lose much of their weight in a letter from a son to his father). Avianius features prominently in the modern catalogue of aristocratic literary pagans. But not to mention the execrable quality of the verses,[96] the fact remains that this is all that was ever completed of this ambitious project. Though celebrated in his day for his oratory, so far as we know Avianius never published a line in his life.

Nonetheless, there can be little doubt that Symmachus intended his father, conspicuously featured at the beginning of the book, to cut an exemplary figure: devout pagan and distinguished man of letters. But what of the rest of the book? The next block consists of thirty letters addressed to Ausonius. This is the evidence on which Ausonius has been proclaimed a key member of Symmachus's circle. Literary allusions and compliments fly thick and fast. But the correspondence is effectively limited to the period when Ausonius was a power at Gratian's court,[97] and, having never in his life set foot in Rome, he can hardly be counted as a member of Roman literary circles. Above all he was a Christian. By all means the sort of liberal Christian with whom Symmachus could feel at home. But if it had been Symmachus's purpose to proclaim the centrality of the pagan element in pagan culture, it would have undermined the whole concept to concede that a Christian could master it just as well. The fact that Symmachus assigned Ausonius so prominent a place in his book and underlined his own deep admiration for the older man's learning and poetry suggests on the contrary a very different purpose: to remind the more aggressive Christians of the 390s that classical culture was *not* an exclusively pagan preserve; that it was something distinguished Christians valued and even emulated.

In third place comes Praetextatus, another exemplar of pagan piety and old-fashioned learning. But after him we have Petronius Probus, the most prominent Christian aristocrat of the day, father of the Christian consuls of 395.[98] Then Celsinus Titianus, a pagan of no great distinction, included out of family piety as a beloved brother now deceased. Lastly, three praetorian prefects of the 370s and 380s, Hesperius (Ausonius's son), Antonius, and Syagrius, the first two at least surely Christians. Claudius Antonius, cos. 382, was a kinsman by marriage of the emperor Theodosius. An allusion that is rather difficult to interpret may imply that he wrote classicizing tragedies,[99] but as a marriage connection of Theodosius he is likely to have been a Christian. Having been

---

95. Petronius Probianus: Chastagnol 1962, 83.
96. See the brief notes in Courtney 1993, 447–53.
97. Bowersock in Paschoud 1986.
98. Letters to Olybrius and Probinus are collected in Bk v.
99. Symm. *Ep.* i. 89. 1 (with Callu's note); *PLRE* i. 77; Martindale, *Historia* 16 (1967), 256.

compromised once by his support of a usurper, it is not surprising that Symmachus should wish to claim an imperial kinsman as one of his closest friends.

The keynote of the book is thus compromise and conciliation. Pagan readers would be pleased that Symmachus made no secret of the devotion to the old gods he shared with Praetextatus, but Christians would be reassured to see how many prominent Christians he corresponded with. We find much the same recipe in the second instalment (Bks ii–vii), unlike i published after the Frigidus: a handful of pagans, some but by no means all men of letters, but a preponderance of Christians.

Bk ii contains only letters to the elder Flavian. Book iii, twelve correspondents, two of them literary pagans: the poet and antiquary Naucellius and the medical writer Siburius. An orator called Eutropius has been mistakenly identified as the historian because one of the letters to him has been thought to allude to the *Breviarium*.[100] After a hyperbolic reference to Gratian's recent military successes, Symmachus remarks that his language is more in the style of a panegyric than a letter, and then adds: "but I leave this to be written up by you above all, given your literary skill" (*sed haec stilo exequenda tibi ante alios, cui pollet Minerva, concedimus*). This is supposed to allude to *Brev.* 10. 18. 3: Eutropius will stop with the death of Jovian "because what follows must be told in more elevated style; I am not so much passing it over as reserving it for more elaborate treatment" (*nam reliqua stilo maiore dicenda sunt, quae nunc non tam praetermittimus quam ad maiorem scribendi diligentiam reservamus*). According to Vanderspoel, Symmachus is urging the historian to keep his promise and write a history of current events in the grand style. But this is to misunderstand a stock formula. "More elaborate treatment" means, not an expanded continuation of his history, but panegyric, the only style appropriate for current events.[101] Symmachus is making exactly the opposite point: that his correspondent is better qualified than he in the art of panegyric. This alone is enough to prove that he is *not* the author of the *Breviarium*, written in the plainest of styles, eschewing all artifice.

Two of the three letters to Siburius (iii. 44–45) have a strong literary flavor, but only a glancing hint of his paganism. As for Naucellius (iii. 10–16), four of Symmachus's seven letters to him are heavy with classical allusions (iii. 11, 12, 13, 15), but only a couple of hints of paganism. He translated a Greek historical work (iii. 11. 3), and a dozen or so of his poems (to which Symmachus alludes in the same letter) were first published fifty years ago in a little anthology known as *Epigrammata Bobiensia*.

These poems survive in a single Renaissance manuscript, copied from the same now lost Bobbio codex of the early eighth century that carried Rutilius Namatianus and (probably) Julius Valerius's Latin translation of the *Alexander Romance*.[102] On the

---

100. *Ep.* iii. 47 (end of 378); Seeck 1883, cxxxii; Matthews 1975, 8–9; more recently Vanderspoel 2001, 284–85.

101. Cameron 1995, 467.

102. Ferrari 1973, 23–25; Reeve in Reynolds 1983, 339–40; Fo 1992, 133–34; M. Rosellini, *Iulii Valerii Res Gestae Alexandri Macedonis* (Stuttgart 1993), vi–viii.

(in itself reasonable) assumption that this sequence reflects an early fifth-century collection, Ferrari argued that the "dominant and characteristic note" of the collection is paganism, and that it was assembled in a "pagan milieu," connected to the "circle" of the Symmachi, soon after 417, the date of Rutilius's poem. But we have already seen that Rutilius's paganism should not be overstated, and the paganism of the *Alexander Romance* is non-existent (p. 555).

As for the *Epigrammata Bobiensia*, more than forty of its seventy poems are direct translations from the Greek, mostly Hellenistic or early imperial ecphrastic epigrams. Number 37 consists of seventy hexameters in the person of the Flavian poetess Sulpicia lamenting the woes of Rome under Domitian; 39–40 are by the Augustan poet Domitius Marsus, celebrating Atia the mother of Augustus. Of the dozen or so poems by Naucellius,[103] 1–9 celebrate his home in Spoleto, his warm springs, his baths, and himself. Two (48 and 57) were written for his friend Nonius Atticus cos. 397 (also a friend of Symmachus).[104] It is a "pagan" anthology only in the sense that its contents are classicizing. The only other iden-tifiable contributor beside Naucellius was a Christian, Anicius Probinus cos. 395 (author of 65 and perhaps also 55, 56, and 70).[105] One of these poems (70) is a lampoon on someone called Romulus addressed to someone called Bassus. In context, Bassus is probably Anicius Auchenius Bassus cos. 408 (a kinsman of Anicius Probinus) and Romulus, Pisidius Romulus, prefect of Rome in (probably) 406, both Christians.[106] Bassus wrote a funerary poem on the death of Augustine's mother Monnica.[107]

Munari identified Naucellius himself as the author of all unascribed poems and the compiler of the collection, but there are metrical objections, and it is unlikely that a poet would include the work of others in a book of his own poems. Number 57, addressed to Nonius Atticus and hoping for immortality for his verses, seems to be the opening poem in a book dedicated to Atticus. Yet it cannot fulfil this function where it stands.[108] It follows that the Bobbio anthology contains excerpts from an earlier collection published by Naucellius together with material from elsewhere. The translations from Greek epi-grams are clearly inspired by Ausonius, who spent all his life in Gaul (Ch. 15. 9). Since Rutilius too was a Gaul, and his poem describes his return to Gaul, we are hardly entitled to assume that the original of the Bobbio anthology reflects Roman literary interests, still less a "pagan milieu." Clearly it was put together by a man with classical interests, but in the mid-fifth century that is not enough to prove him a pagan. Since the earliest pos-sible date is twenty years after Symmachus's death, it is entirely gratuitous to infer a con-nection with either Symmachus himself or even his mythical circle. Naucellius's book was dedicated to Nonius Atticus, not Symmachus. And whether or not Naucellius was

---

103. Some anonymous in the MS, and ascribed to him by conjecture.
104. Often (Seeck, *PLRE*) styled Nonius Atticus Maximus, but the Maximus must be stricken: Cameron 1985, 109.
105. Speyer 1959, 113–20.
106. So already Munari 1955, 21–22.
107. *AL* i. 670; *PLRE* ii. 220; *PCBE* ii. 1. 271.
108. Speyer 1959, 74–84.

still a pagan when Symmachus knew him, he long outlived his younger contemporary and died a Christian, buried in the basilica of S. Paolo fuori le mura in the 420s.[109]

Book iii closes with three Theodosian generals (one known from another source to have been a pagan) and the infamous Christian prefect Rufinus (subject of an invective by Claudian) assassinated in 395.[110] Book iv has eight addressees, every one (in all probability) a Christian. First comes Stilicho, Honorius's chief minister and general from 395–408, followed by two to the general Bauto.[111] Although himself a Christian, Bauto had sided with Symmachus in the affair of the altar of Victory. Yet one of Symmachus's letters to Bauto reveals that they had a serious falling out the following year—a particularly instructive warning not to reduce all signs of conflict to the conflict between paganism and Christianity. If the altar of Victory issue had been (as usually supposed) the paramount issue in Symmachus's world, we might have expected him to cultivate an influential Christian ally at court at all costs. But something else intervened, and Bauto insulted Symmachus by waiting a year before sending him the mementos of his consulate in January 385. The fact that there are only two letters to Bauto strongly suggests they had never been close.

The chief point of interest in Bk iv is the letters addressed to Protadius (iv. 17–34), perhaps the most carefully wrought and allusive block in the entire correspondence. "You breathe the flowers of Helicon," enthuses Symmachus, claiming that he did not "rear Amyclaeans or Molossans" (meaning hunting dogs) when a youth and will not do so now that his "white beard is falling beneath the razor" (alluding to several passages of Vergil).[112] *Ep.* iv. 24 has a citation of Sallust; iv. 28 elaborate metaphors of writing; iv. 33 poetic references to oracles; iv. 34. 2 quotations from Plautus and Juvenal; iv. 29 sends Protadius some of Symmachus's speeches through one of his brothers; iv. 18 and 32 refer in detail to Protadius's studies in Gallic history.[113] Symmachus evidently took great pains composing these letters, and Protadius reciprocated. The second in the series begins with a refusal to believe Protadius's claim that he has been hunting, since "your letters breathe the thyme of elegance."[114] That is to say, so elaborate and allusive is their style that Symmachus affects to believe that Protadius has been at his books rather than hunting.[115]

Another little group that shows the same signs are the letters to the future short-lived emperor of 409–10, Priscus Attalus (vii. 15–25): for example, 18 and 20 are

---

109. His metrical epitaph (*ICUR* n.s. ii. 5017), identified by Champlin 1982, was carved by the same hand as another (ib. 4886) dated to 427. There is no Christian symbol or formula in what survives, but the more than a thousand other epitaphs found in the cemetery of S. Paolo are (naturally) all Christian (ib. 4775–5786).

110. The fact that he was nonetheless included suggests that, like Tatianus and Proculus, Rufinus was posthumously rehabilitated, perhaps after the fall of the eunuch chamberlain Eutropius.

111. For the probability that Bauto was a Christian, see p. 85.

112. iv. 18. 1 (Vergil, *Geo.* iii. 345, 406; *Buc.* i. 29).

113. Studied in detail below, pp. 523–26.

114. *Falso apud me venandi studio gloriaris, cum thymum facundiae spirent litterae tuae, Ep.* iv. 18.

115. A compliment he had previously used in a letter to Praetextatus (*Ep.* i. 53).

miniature ecphraseis and 19–20 are full of mythical allusions. When Symmachus evokes Attalus's "recent studies in both Latin and Greek," again this is an inference from allusions in Attalus's latest letter.[116] Late antique men of letters who took them-selves seriously engaged in a sort of contest of allusions, each trying to impress or outdo the other.[117] Symmachus goes so far as to imply that the elegance achieved by both Protadius and Attalus was based on research rather than the inspiration of the moment—and this was intended as a compliment. It is therefore the more significant that, though Attalus may still have been a pagan (p. 194), Protadius was a Christian.

We saw in an earlier chapter that some critics mistakenly assumed on the basis of their literary interests that the Gauls Protadius and his brothers Florentinus and Minervius were pagans. Though from Trier rather than Bordeaux, they were surely liberal Christians in the Ausonian mould. But it is important not to misunderstand this notion. There were no doubt many who converted to improve their prospects at a Christian court. But at the same time there have always been sincere Christians able to keep belief and culture apart[118]—a compartmentalization that may have been easier in the age of Ausonius than the age of Jerome, but was still possible and surely not uncommon. We are not entitled simply to assume that Protadius and his brothers were timeservers, but even if they were that does not make them crypto-pagans, active mem-bers of a supposed cultural resistance. It is unlikely in the highest degree that they were open pagans. The man for whom Symmachus fashioned his most carefully wrought allusions to the "pagan" classics in Bks ii–vii was almost certainly a Christian.

Next Longinianus, who received *Epp.* vii. 93–101, a man in high office at court from ca. 399 and so to be identified as Fl. Macrobius Longinianus, *comes sacrarum largitio-num in* 399–400, PVR in 401–2, and PPO in 406–8. We saw in chapter 6 that there is no basis for identifying him with a pagan Longinianus known to Augustine. It may be added that there is no hint of intimacy in these letters—and no literary allusions either. They are Symmachus's standard business letters. No fewer than four are devoted to the rehabilitation of Flavian, and none antedate Longinianus's emergence as a power at court. Not only is there not a shred of evidence that he was a pagan, he was neither a close friend nor a literary friend, but one of the many rising men in the new regime Symmachus carefully cultivated to further the career of his son-in-law.

According to McGeachy's statistics, 54 of Symmachus's 134 correspondents "were pagan or probably pagan; 33 were Christian or probably Christian."[119] He adds that 443 letters "were addressed to known and probable pagans" and only 259 to Christians, resulting in a total of 63 percent to pagans. This statistic is very misleading, in that it counts all 172 of those addressed to the two Flaviani on the pagan side, despite the younger Flavian's probable conversion (of which more below). If we subtract his 81 letters from the pagan total, that leaves a ratio of 362:259. If we transfer them to the

116. *Lectitasse autem te in multo otio utriusque linguae auctores, ipse index fuisti*, vii. 18. 3.
117. A nice fictional example is Julian's contest with Priscus in Gore Vidal's *Julian*.
118. The obvious example that comes to mind is English Victorians: see particularly Jenkyns 1980.
119. McGeachy 1949, 226–27.

Christian total, that gives 362:340. And the fact that an entire book of 91 letters is addressed to the elder Flavian skews any statistic based on the sheer number of letters. If we go further and eliminate the many otherwise unknown names in Bks viii–ix, and restrict ourselves to the books prepared for publication by Symmachus himself and Memmius, we end up with an altogether different balance: 56 correspondents, of whom fewer than 20 were known pagans.

Of course, some of those whose religion is unknown may have been pagans. But a large proportion of the surviving letters date from the last decade of Symmachus's life, and their addressees must for the most part have been younger men, disproportionately more likely to be Christians. Especially so the dozens of officials he pestered with requests concerning Memmius's praetorian games in 401.

When Symmachus was born ca. 340, there may have been few Christians in the circles in which he moved. Most of his elders, if not his peers, will have been pagans. By the time he died in his early sixties in 402, that world had passed; all his elders and many of his peers were dead. Whether or not all post-Frigidus officeholders were Christians, in the absence of evidence to the contrary it will have been prudent to assume that they were. It is unlikely that many were open or committed pagans.

On the traditional view, Symmachus was a last-ditch champion of the old order. But recent research on the vocabulary and technique of his correspondence has revealed a rather different figure, a skilful politician, a master of reconciliation and compromise.[120] Where earlier scholars vied with one another in condemning the verbosity and triviality of his letters, we have now come to see how perfectly his uncontroversial polite sonorities papered over cracks in the social fabric.

For the Alföldi school, Symmachus's politeness to Christians was a mask covering deep inner resentment and hostility. But whatever his real feelings (which of course we cannot know), this is surely to misplace the emphasis. It is significant enough that he wrote such letters—and in such quantities. Whether or not he had to grit his teeth to do it, the fact remains that Symmachus transferred his diplomatic skills to Christian correspondents without so much as a ripple in the even tenor of his rhetoric. To use a modern analogy, a conservative elderly male lawyer or professor might not feel at his ease dealing with (say) black, female, or gay junior colleagues. But if he nonetheless does it, skillfully, elegantly, and (to outward appearances) enthusiastically, he is setting an example for younger peers to follow. By publishing his correspondence in the form and at the time he did, whatever his personal feelings, Symmachus was setting an example of cooperation rather than resistance.

He does not modify his manner in any obvious way when writing to Christians. Yet there is in fact a discreet clue to when he is writing to pagans. In a number of letters he evokes a plurality of gods, sometimes clearly implying that his correspondent is a fellow pagan, sometimes in routine phrases like *deos oro* or *deorum favor*.[121] We might

---

120. Above all Matthews 1974, reprinted in Matthews 1985.
121. Lomanto 196–97, 203.

expect a polytheist to use the plural in such phrases as casually as a monotheist might use the singular. Von Haehling refused to allow a "neutral expression like *deorum favor*" any probative value when assessing the evidence for the paganism of Messala, PPO in 399–400.[122] This was because he did not investigate the distribution of such phrases. Formulaic though Symmachus's letters are, he nonetheless employs the formulas with sensitivity and skill. In this case, of the twenty-one correspondents addressed in these fifty-five letters, ten were certainly and another six or seven probably pagans. No fewer than sixteen occur in letters to the elder Flavian, four in letters to his father and his brother Titianus, four more in letters to Praetextatus, two to Naucellius, and one to his son Memmius (vii. 1), surely brought up a pagan. The other known or likely pagans are Attalus (vii. 21), Marinianus (iii. 24), Messala (vii. 92), Siburius (iii. 44), and Hiero-phantes (v. 2), the last possibly a description rather than a proper name. In at least five further cases (Almachius, Censorinus, Magnillus, Priscillianus, Romanus), though nothing else is known about the men, the form of the polytheistic reference suggests that the addressee shared the writer's paganism.[123] There is nothing to suggest that another three (Lucillus, Valerianus, and an anonymous) were Christians.[124]

But six recipients are known or likely Christians. Ausonius[125] is no surprise, given his penchant for using the imagery of pagan priesthoods in his own writings. But Petronius Probus is perhaps unexpected.[126] We have already seen that Probus was a more cultivated man than he is often given credit for, but the relevant factor here may be chronological. The letters to both Ausonius and Probus date from the 370s or even earlier,[127] long before the anti-pagan legislation of 382. Symmachus may not have felt it necessary to take account of Christian susceptibilities before then. Writing to the sternly Christian Rufinus in 390, Symmachus closes with the words (in Callu's trans-lation): "mes voeux s'addressent *aux Dieux*." This overtranslates the original, a much vaguer formula: *voto divina convenio*.[128]

The other recipients—at least on the text printed by Seeck and Callu—are Florentinus (iv. 51), Marcianus (viii. 23), Manlius Theodorus (v. 13), and Faltonius Probus Alypius (vii. 68). Since the first three at least are men of letters, that would fit traditional assumptions well enough. But there is a complication. In the case of

---

122. Von Haehling 1978, 308; so too Rivolta Tiberga 1992, 91–92, 115.
123. Almachius: *si dii iuverint voluntatem*; Censorinus: *si bene destinata dii iuverint*, viii. 27. 3; Priscillianus: *deorum te benignitas muneretur*, viii. 5; Romanus: *salutis praesides deos comprecor*, viii. 70. For Magnillus, where the text is uncertain, see further below.
124. viii. 21; viii. 69; ix. 83.
125. *ita me deis probabilem praestem*, i. 14. 5; *dii te pro tanta gratia munerentur*, i. 21.
126. *Dii modo optata fortunent, salutem reipublicae in solido locent*, i. 57.
127. Ausonius's *Mosella* may date from 368: Sivan 1990, 383–94. i. 57 was written at a time of political uncertainty while Probus was holding high office. Since his four prefectures date from 364, 366, 368–75, and 383–84 (Cameron 1985, 178–82), and in later years Symmachus and Probus were barely on speaking terms, the letter might date from as early as the 360s; i. 58 dates from 366 (181 n. 82). There is no good reason (with Callu) to date it as late as 383.
128. *Ep.* iii. 90.

Florentinus and Theodorus (as in two examples in letters to Magnillus), the manuscripts are divided between singular and plural.[129] In all four cases the same manuscripts divide the same way. According to Seeck (tacitly followed by Callu), "A Christian interpolator occasionally changed *deos* to the singular."[130] On this basis he emended two examples of the singular to plural without manuscript support, both in the same letter to Avianius Symmachus. First the formula *deo volente* (i. 3. 5), which he "corrected" to *diis volentibus*. It is true that the only witnesses we have here are the same florilegia (ΦVR) that offer the singular in the other four cases. But there are at least fifteen further passages where we find the singular without a plural variant. And a great many (more than fifty, in fact) where we find the plural with no singular variant. Even polytheists occasionally appeal to a single god. For example, alongside countless examples of *deos precor, deorum munere* and the like we find a handful of similar expressions in the singular in the letters of Pliny.[131] A certain and conspicuous example in Symmachus himself is *Rel.* iii. 5, "everywhere is full of god (*omnia quidem deo plena*) and nowhere is safe for perjurors," where the text is guaranteed by the Vergilian echo, *Iovis omnia plena.*[132] There is no variant and no cause for doubt in another example Seeck missed, in a letter to the elder Flavian.[133]

The second passage Seeck emended is more serious: where all manuscripts offer *deum magna pars veneratur,* he "corrected" to *deos magna pars veneratur* (i. 3. 4). In this form the passage is regularly cited, with no indication that *deos* is an emendation, in illustration of Symmachus's delight at finding so many pagans at Beneventum on his visit there ca. 375! Perhaps so. But in a city with a long Christian tradition laying claim to several Diocletianic martyrs,[134] Symmachus's praise of the public-spirited Beneventans for spending from their own pockets to rebuild their city after an earthquake need not be limited to pagans. Nor does the context lend any support to such a reading of the passage. Symmachus goes on to say that the hospitality offered him by the Beneventans was generous to the point of becoming burdensome, and he left sooner than he had intended so as not to distract them from their rebuilding. This was disingenuous. He must in fact have been apprehensive that, if he accepted too much hospitality, he would risk being put under an obligation to contribute to the earthquake fund himself. It should be added that, even if we read *deos* and assume that he had pagans in mind, the fact remains that Symmachus beat a hasty retreat instead of staying to offer encouragement or discuss matters of common interest. In the mouth of a pagan, *deum veneratur* could hardly be construed as a reference to Christianity, but neither would it be so aggressively pagan a

129. Langlois 1974, 94–95. Florentinus (iv. 54): *diis quippe auctoribus* (P); *deo … auctore* (VRM). Theodorus (v. 13): *praefata ope deorum* (PΠ); *p. o. dei* (VRMF). Magnillus: *promptum deorum favorem,* PΠ; *p. dei f.,* ΓΦVM (v. 20). *si diis votum iuverint,* P; *si deus votum iuverit,* VM (v. 17).

130. See the note in his apparatus to i. 3. 4 (p. 4 line 30).

131. *adfuit tamen deus voto* (*Ep.* i. 12. 8); *promissis deus adnuat* (i. 22. 11); *si deus adnuisset* (vii. 24. 3).

132. *Buc.* iii. 60; see Vera 1981, 34–35.

133. *adiutu dei,* ii. 26; the variants here (*adiutu diei* and *ad nutum dies*) merely confirm the singular.

134. Delehaye 1933, 300.

reference as *deos veneratur*. It might be no more than an unpolemical comment on the piety of the Beneventans, anxious to repair their damaged temples, whether pagan or Christian (the quake will not have discriminated). In view of Symmachus's reputation as a defender of the old gods, it is at least as likely that some medieval reader occasionally "corrected" singulars to plurals rather than vice versa. No firm decision is possible. But under the circumstances the letters to Florentinus and Theodorus cannot be counted among the examples of polytheistic references in letters to Christians. If the singulars are correct they would prove the opposite.

That leaves only Marcianus and Alypius. Alypius was the scion of a noble Christian clan, but there is no evidence that he was a Christian himself, and we know of at least one cousin who was an outright pagan, Clodius Hermogenianus Caesarius PVR 374.[135] A letter to Flavian raises the possibility that Alypius was another black sheep. Symmachus tells Flavian, at the time with Eugenius's court in 393, that Alypius has long been eager to visit court, recommending him to invite Alypius to his consular celebration, with allusive talk of benefits he will receive and protection he can offer from the "cloud of a previous enmity" that hangs over Alypius. Callu suggests that, being a member of an "antipagan clan," Alypius hoped that the personal support of Symmachus and Flavian would protect him from being a victim of Eugenius's regime.[136] But there is no evidence that the Anicii were actively hostile to pagans, much less that Eugenius persecuted Christians. On the usual scenario, Flavian himself is the pagan ringleader. The "enmity" was surely one of those personal feuds to which the aristocracy was so prone. But if Alypius really appealed to Symmachus to intercede with Flavian on his behalf during Eugenius's regime, he was evidently not afraid to compromise himself with Christians. The *deos* in vii. 68 is perhaps enough to suggest that he was actually a pagan.

Symmachus's usage turns out to be far from casual. Every notable pagan he corresponded with received a letter with a polytheistic reference,[137] but perhaps not a single committed Christian, at any rate in the last decade or so of his life. One name we might have expected to find on the list of polytheistic references is the younger Flavian, on the popular view a dedicated crypto-pagan even after his conversion. In fact, there is not a single reference to gods in the plural—only one rather vague allusion to things that are "in the hands of the heavenly powers."[138] It is time to take a closer look at these letters.[139]

---

135. Clearly related to Clodius Hermogenianus Olybrius PVR 368–70 and cos. 369: Chastagnol 1962, 192–93.
136. Callu i. 207 n. 3.
137. In view of the doubts raised above about the identification of the correspondent Eutropius with the author of the *Breviarium*, it is perhaps more than chance that there are no polytheistic references in the letters to Eutropius.
138. *nunc in caelestium manu est*, vi. 75.
139. All eighty-one letters are in fact addressed jointly to Flavian and his wife (Symmachus's daughter) under the heading *Nicomachis filiis*, and some part of many of them is clearly addressed to his daughter. But there can be little doubt that the greater part of the correspondence concerns his son-in-law rather than his daughter.

Interestingly enough, the correspondence with the younger Flavian (Bk vi) was more radically censored than the letters to his father (Bk ii), no doubt because by the time Bk ii appeared the principals were both safely dead. But the younger Flavian was still a young man, like his father a man driven by ambition. He could not afford to be compromised. We have already seen that no letter in Bk vi falls earlier than autumn 394. Not only everything from the Eugenian period but everything since his marriage to Symmachus's daughter in 388 was deleted. It was surely directly after the Frigidus when not just Flavian's future but his very life hung in the balance that Symmachus himself, in both their interests, destroyed the entire correspondence. Memmius (and Flavian) no doubt ran a cautious eye over the post-Frigidus letters as well before publication. Conceivably it was at this stage that polytheistic references were eliminated. But given his anxiety to restore his son-in-law's fortunes, Symmachus must have composed these letters with great care, and more probably he refrained from using them in the first place. The contrast with the free use of such formulas in the letters to the elder Flavian suggests that Symmachus employed them consciously and deliberately.

There is a complementary statistic pointing in the same direction. A small number of letters (fifteen, to be precise) contain formulas evoking a single god (*deo iuvante* or the like). Notably so the two form invitations to Memmius's praetorian games in 401, most of which must at that date have been sent to Christians.[140] No fewer than three are addressed to the younger Flavian.[141] No one else received more than one. Naturally, this does prove him a sincere Christian. But given the precision of Symmachus's usage, the combination of three monotheistic formulas and the lack of polytheistic formulas in as many as eighty-one letters can hardly be put down to coincidence.

Those who think of Symmachus as a last-ditch pagan stalwart take it for granted that he expected his son and son-in-law to carry on the torch. Things can hardly have been so black and white at the end of his life. In 384 Symmachus himself had done what he could in a fight where there had been at best a possibility of compromise. Since then it had become all too clear that victory was out of the question and toleration the most that could be hoped for. By the time Memmius held his first public office, the praetorship of 401, it must have been clear to so shrewd a political observer as Symmachus that the Symmachi and Nicomachi could not expect to maintain their position in the Christian world of the fifth century if they persisted in their paganism. Having already held both city prefecture and consulate, Symmachus himself entertained no further hopes of public office and did not need to compromise. But the younger Flavian was still on the threshold of his career, and Symmachus was solicitous enough of his prospects to avoid any implication that he was a practicing pagan. In the four years after the Frigidus Symmachus devoted all his energy and diplomatic skill to the rehabilitation of his now formally Christian son-in-law, and lived to see his efforts rewarded with

---

140. *praefato divinitatis favore, Ep.* viii. 71; *divinitatis honore praemisso,* viii. 72.
141. *deo iuvante,* vi. 65. 2; *praefata dei venia,* vi. 19. 1, 68. 1.

Flavian's city prefecture of 399. It must have occurred to him that if Memmius was to enjoy a career like his own he too would one day have to make the same compromise.

Why did Symmachus pay such meticulous attention to what might have seemed entirely routine formulas? At one level it is just one aspect of his obsessive courtesy, the care he took to tailor every letter to its addressee, gracefully alluding to his interests and achievements and avoiding anything that might be construed as inappropriate or disagreeable. But there is perhaps another factor at work as well. A number of Libanius's letters allude in one way or another to the paganism of some of his correspondents. Such letters tend to cluster around the reign of Julian, and it has usually been assumed that they document a "pagan party" in Antioch that was reinvigorated by the accession of a pagan emperor. But an important new book by Sandwell has produced an intriguing reassessment of these letters. While retroactively painting a picture of the reign of Constantius as an age of persecution for pagans, the truth is that Libanius himself had enjoyed great personal success during these years, building up a large network of connections among powerful Christians.[142] While there can be no question that he remained a pagan all his life, Julian's more enthusiastic followers (and to start with perhaps Julian himself) seem to have suspected him of being a sycophant who had put career and connections before cult.[143] The reason he refers to their shared devotion to the old gods when writing to certain correspondents at this period (Sandwell argues) is that he was trying to reassure them that he was indeed still one of them, not one of the many timeservers who had switched allegiance to suit the times. Such references supply more than biographical facts about the correspondents; they have a contemporary agenda.

Moderns have grown so accustomed to thinking of Symmachus as the public face of Roman paganism that they tend to overlook the fact that by as early as 385 he had quietly withdrawn from the struggle. While not perhaps as vulnerable as Libanius to the accusation of sycophancy, he did spend much of the last fifteen years of his life cultivating his connections rather than defending the cults, connections inevitably now mainly Christian. Publishing his correspondence thus posed a problem. On the one hand, in the interests of his son and son-in-law, he wanted to make it clear to the now Christian establishment that the Symmachi were not all the intransigeant pagans the altar of Victory affair might suggest. Whence the inclusion of letters to so many prominent Christians. On the other hand, he did not want his fellow pagans to think that he had abandoned the cause he once defended so eloquently. It is this (I suggest) that explains the systematic and surely deliberate use of polytheistic formulas and one or two other striking features. Since he included so many letters to Christians, the mere presence of letters to prominent pagans would prove little in itself. Whence not just the skilfully placed formulas, but the detailed references to cult celebrations and meetings of the pontifical college (pp. 163–8), not to mention the inclusion of an

---

142. Sandwell 2007, esp. 218–20.
143. For accusations of flattery, Sandwell 2007, 222–24.

entire book of letters to the elder Flavian. Symmachus took care to leave posterity in no doubt that he was a loyal Roman pagan to the last.

4

It has always been taken for granted that both the elder and younger Flavian were key members of this hypothesized pagan cultural resistance. The elder wrote a history that (though lost without trace) has been proclaimed a key document in the anti-Christian movement (Ch. 17–18), and has also been credited with a Latin translation of the Life of the pagan miracle-worker Apollonius of Tyana (Ch. 15. 5). The younger Flavian has won even wider fame as an "editor" of Livy, and both father and son have been claimed at one time or another as authors of the so-called *Historia Augusta* (Ch. 17. 1). These claims will all be considered in due course. For the moment, let us see what light Symmachus's letters cast on their cultural attainments in general.

We have seen that it is not hard to identify Symmachus's literary correspondents. While none of his letters fall below a certain standard level of elegance and orotundity, those to men of letters are regularly distinguished by often-elaborate classical allusions or flattering references to the correspondent's style—sometimes both. The chapter "on letters" in Julius Victor's *Ars rhetorica* specifically recommends adjusting style to correspondent.[144]

Symmachus was by no means alone in this sort of variation. Well-read Christians like Augustine and Jerome did it too. Hagendahl has shown in revealing detail that the number and source of quotations in Jerome's letters vary according to "not only the contents of the letter but also the social position of the addressee and his degree of education."[145] The clearest example is the remarkable range of (often extended) classical quotations in just two of his letters to Paulinus of Nola: over and above numerous passages of Cicero and Vergil, we find Quintilian, Pliny the Younger, Philostratus, Publilius Syrus, Plautus, Horace, Persius, and Lucan.[146] Here we have a classic example of one highly educated man showing off to another. There would (of course) have been no point in such a display if he had been writing to someone who would not appreciate or even disapprove of it. In this case both parties were Christians.

The same is true of Augustine. *Epp.* 16–17 to Maximus of Madauros and 91 to Nectarius of Calama are full of classical quotations. These men were pagans, but two others who received similar letters, Marcianus (*Ep.* 258) and Darius (*Ep.* 231),

---

144. *epistola, si superiori scribas, ne iocularis sit … si inferiori, ne superba; neque docto incuriose, neque indocto diligenter*, R. Giomini and M. S. Celentano (eds.) (Leipzig 1980), 105. 36 (*indiligenter*, Halm, *Rhet. Lat. Minores* [1863] 448. 17, mistakenly).

145. Hagendahl 1958, 191–209; 246–60 (quotation from 208). According to Pease 1919, 161, Jerome was "greatly influenced by the character, and still more the culture, of those to whom he wrote, and to the sophisticated he allowed himself a freedom from which he abstained when addressing the more easily scandalized simplicity of the monks at Bethlehem."

146. *Ep.* 53; 58: Hagendahl 1958, 185–91.

were undoubtedly Christians, Darius a third-generation Christian.[147] It should also be noted that the two pagans were by no means aristocrats. Both were Africans, Maximus a small-town schoolteacher and Nectarius a small-town alderman.[148] Darius was at any rate a man of high rank, styled *vir illustris* by Augustine,[149] but nothing suggests that Marcianus was.[150] Augustine himself was a product of small-town Africa.

I myself would turn the traditional hypothesis on its head and argue that knowledge of the classics was taken far more seriously by people of modest origins, well aware that literary culture was their one avenue to positions of profit and power. Two examples we can document are Augustine and Aurelius Victor, both Africans. Born to a modest family in Thagaste, Augustine was lucky enough to catch the eye of a local grandee who paid for his education. Having won himself a chair in a capital city by his rhetorical proficiency, he might have hoped before long to win a provincial governorship and a post at court. Victor proudly boasts that, though born on a small farm to a father of no education, he had achieved his success though education (*rure ortus tenui atque indocto patre, Caes.* 20. 5). We should not (of course) imagine that Victor's father was an illiterate peasant; rather a small landowner, no doubt literate, but without the polish given by a rhetorical education at Carthage or Rome.

People like Augustine and Victor owed their careers entirely to the culture they worked so hard to acquire. It is scarcely likely that aristocrats would have set the same store on attainments that the lesser orders could acquire by hard work. An aristocrat's career did not *depend* on his culture. Some (like Symmachus) might pride themselves on it, but an Orfitus (e.g.) could count on high office whether or not he could lace his letters and conversation with apposite quotations. What shocked Ammianus was the fact that a good many Roman aristocrats did not come up to cultural standards he took for granted among educated people of his own station in life.

We find the same sort of intellectual snobbery in the young Augustine's disillusionment when he finally met Faustus the Manichee. It is worth taking a closer look at this assessment by a young man who, though not yet a Christian, had never really been a pagan:[151]

> I soon discovered that he was ignorant of the liberal arts except for literature, and even here his knowledge was conventional. He had read some speeches of Cicero, a very few books by Seneca, some of the poets, and such volumes of his

---

147. *PCBE* i. 264–65, 691–92; *PLRE* ii. 347–48 (Darius).

148. *PCBE* i. 733–34 (Maximus 3) and 776–79.

149. *Ep.* 231 dates from 429, and given the unusual name, possibly Darius the praetorian prefect of the East in 436–37 (*PLRE* ii. 347–48).

150. Hardly the Marcianus of *CCP* or (if they are different) Symmachus's correspondent of that name: *PCBE* i. 692.

151. *Conf.* v. 11 (Chadwick, much adapted). As O'Donnell ad loc. remarks, "The list of *auctores* need not be taken as literally accurate."

own sect as were written in decent Latin.[152] Since he practised speaking every day, this was the basis of his eloquence, made more agreeable and attractive by his self-control and a certain natural grace.

Not the way Christian controversialists usually characterize heresiarchs. It is a balanced and (above all) professional assessment, conceding that Faustus was a fluent and witty speaker, but (to adapt Ammianus's phrase) "less instructed in the liberal arts than was fitting." It would be interesting to know on what grounds Augustine felt able to limit the classical texts Faustus knew to Cicero and "a few books by Seneca." When he arrived in Milan he at once went to see whether another celebrated speaker deserved his reputation. Ambrose turned out to be "less witty and entertaining" than Faustus, but "more learned" (*eruditior*).[153] Elsewhere people were beginning to seek illumination from illiterate holy men,[154] but Augustine, like Ammianus, was of the generation and social class for whom it was a man's literary culture that made the all-important first impression.

To be sure, Augustine's letters to Volusianus, the one Roman aristocrat he corresponded with,[155] are sprinkled with quotations from Cicero, Sallust, Vergil, and Lucan.[156] But Volusianus's letter to Augustine had made it clear that he was a man of culture,[157] and Augustine treated many Christians of his acquaintance to just as full and varied a diet. For example, he wrote Marcellinus (the dedicatee of the *City of God*) a letter complementing the one to Volusianus, quoting Cicero, Sallust, Varro, Terence, and Juvenal.

Naturally enough, Symmachus drew the same sort of distinctions among his correspondents. The following received two or more "literary" letters: Antonius (i. 89, 91, 93), Ausonius, Avianius, Naucellius, Olybrius, Praetextatus, Probinus, Protadius, Siburius, Syagrius (i. 92, 95, 96). As many again received only one: Andronicus (viii. 22), Eutropius (iii. 47), Hesperius (i. 78), Lucillus (viii. 21), Marcianus (viii. 23), Probus (i. 58), Theodorus (v. 9), Valerianus (viii. 69), and three anonymous (ix. 72, 84, and 110), of whom the first and third might be the same man.[158] Then there is the question of Symmachus's use of Greek words.[159] Leaving out of count words such as *holosericus, archiater, apophoreta,* and *diptychum* that are found in Latin script in other late antique Latin writers, there are four words that manuscripts transmit in Greek characters, and two more that were probably

---

152. I take it the point is that he could not read Manichaean texts in Greek, obviously a serious shortcoming in a purported authority on Manichaean teachings.
153. *Conf.* v. 23.
154. Brown 1971 = 1982.
155. As we have already seen (p. ##), there is no evidence that Volusianus was ever a pagan.
156. *Ep.* 137; the references are listed in Hagendahl 1967, 745.
157. Moreau 1974, 125.
158. One letter to Florentinus (iv. 52) describes Symmachus's pleasure in receiving letters from all three brothers in quick succession, and the "varied charm" of each.
159. Haverling 1988, 132–35.

originally written in Greek.[160] It is suggestive that all six letters are addressed to "literary" correspondents:[161] Avianius (i. 1. 2); Ausonius (i. 14. 2); Eutropius (iii. 47); Siburius (iii. 44. 1); the anonymous historian (ix. 110); and Marcianus (viii. 23. 1).[162]

Of the first group, four were probably pagans, five Christians; of the second, perhaps as many as five or even six pagans. But seven of this second group (four or five pagans) are represented in Bks viii–ix only, letters not included in the original selection. The presumption is that they were either less close friends or less important people. Either way, no support here for the notion that pagan men of letters belonged to Symmachus's inner circle.

Two specific illustrations. A letter that has always played a central role in any account of the pagan cultural resistance is ix. 13 of 401 to Valerianus on the supposed "editing" of Livy (Ch. 14). If the Valerianus of viii. 69 (388/89) is the same man, he was probably a pagan. But given the distribution of the letters between different books this cannot be regarded as certain (nor the further identification as Valerianus PVR in 381).[163] Even on the most favorable hypothesis this was a man Symmachus wrote to twice in thirteen years and whose letters were not grouped together in the early books with his more important correspondents. Then there is the letter to the poet Andronicus (viii. 22), clearly a response to an unsolicited bid for patronage.

Though his own culture is a good deal less wide than often supposed, Symmachus may well have been better read than most of his peers in the Roman elite. Being in addition possessed of considerable sensitivity and tact, just as he avoided polytheistic phrases when writing to Christians and only used Greek words when writing to those who knew Greek, so he took care not to be too literary when writing to generals, bureaucrats, and less cultivated fellow aristocrats. There was no point in embarrassing such people with allusions they might not recognise and could not replicate. But when writing to people who shared his literary interests, he pulled out all the stops. No modern reader equipped with the rudiments of the same classical education as Symmachus can fail to detect the difference between his run-of-the-mill letters and his literary letters.

Which sort did he write to the two Flaviani? The elder Flavian was Symmachus's oldest friend, recipient of an entire book of his correspondence, ninety-one letters ranging in date from 364 to the very eve of his death in 394. They show every sign of intimacy, and even after a certain amount of editing, make no secret of his devotion to the old gods. Yet not one of them mentions a literary topic, contains a literary allusion,

---

160. Whether or not he wrote *amusoteros* in Latin characters at *Ep.* 1. 14. 2, he clearly intended the Greek comparative ἀμουσότερος. And since there is no other attestation of *emmetrus* as a Latin word (*TLL* v. 510), we should probably write ἔμμετρα *verba* at *Ep.* i. 1. 2. I reject Seeck's introduction of λόγος by emendation at 1. 15. 2 (see p. 537).

161. The occasional use of Greek words was another recommendation of Julius Victor: *Graece aliquid addere litteris suave est, si id neque intempestive neque crebro facias*, Halm 448. 29.

162. This Marcianus cannot be certainly identified (*PLRE* i. 556–57), but viii. 23 is full of archaisms (see Callu's note on p. 190 of his Budé edition).

163. All three identified by Chastagnol 1962, 208; Callu on viii. 69 is more cautious.

or praises his erudition. The lack of a literary dimension in so large a sample cannot be put down to chance. The eighty-one letters to the younger Flavian likewise contain no literary allusions of any sort.[164]

This is more than an argument from silence. Whether out of courtesy or self-promotion, Symmachus took considerable pains to give the impression that he shared the outlook and interests of his correspondents. We have already seen how significantly placed the polytheistic references and Greek words are. Let us take another example from the letters to Praetextatus. *Ep.* i. 48, after making the trite point that man is born to suffer adversity, then recommends "leaving it to the disputations of philosophers"; i. 47, as well as discussing pontifical responsibilities, likewise implies that its addressee is not only a philhellene but also something of a philosopher. We know from Boethius as well as his widow that Praetextatus was indeed something of a philosopher.[165]

No fewer than three letters commend philosophers to Flavian (among them the Horus we have already met as one of Macrobius's interlocutors), once with the explanation that "you profess a knowledge of such things."[166] Another letter (ii, 46) reminds Flavian that Socrates always made the best of his setbacks (it was this sage principle that helped Symmachus to bear the bitter disappointment of his Saxon gladiators committing suicide before Memmius's praetorian games!).[167] A passage of Macrobius represents him as remembering something from a Greek philosopher (in fact Aristotle).[168] Such hints imply that Flavian affected some philosophical expertise. In the light of these hints it is tempting to identify as Nicomachus Flavianus the otherwise unknown Flavianus to whom John of Salisbury ascribes a work titled *De vestigiis sive de dogmate philosophorum*, full of trivial and unhistorical anecdotes about philosophers—much like the one Symmachus quotes to Flavian.[169]

The fact that, on the evidence of a much-discussed passage of Sidonius, Flavian took an interest in Philostratus's *Life of Apollonius of Tyana* harmonizes well with these philosophical interests. On the other hand, if (as often mistakenly inferred from this passage) he had *translated* Philostratus into Latin, we might have expected Symmachus to mention the fact. He is full of praise for Naucellius's translations from the Greek.[170] As we shall see (Ch. 15), Flavian simply subscribed his personal copy of Philostratus.

So while as many as four letters imply an interest in philosophy, not one in almost a hundred suggests that he was a serious connoisseur of literature—still less that he took any interest in history. Take Symmachus's letters to Theodorus, a philosopher

164. As briefly remarked by Marcone in Paschoud 1986, 117.

165. Bruggisser 1993, 391–94; see too Ch. 15, p. 542.

166. ii. 29 (Maximus); ii. 39 (Horus); ii. 61 (Serapammon).

167. *Ep.* ii. 29 (Maximus); ii. 39 (Horus); ii. 61 (Serapammon); ii. 46.

168. *Sat.* vii. 6. 15.

169. So Schaarschmidt 1862, 103–7; C. C. J. Webb's edition, vol. 1 (Oxford 1909), xlvi.

170. He does not mention Praetextatus's translation of Themistius's Aristotle paraphrases, but then Praetextatus was an older man he knew less well and most of the twelve letters to him date from the last years of his life. The translation may have been an early work.

and old friend. Yet only one letter even approaches the standard Symmachan literary epistle: v. 9, asking for Theodorus's opinion on one of Symmachus's speeches. But (unlike the letters to Praetextatus) no classical allusions. It may be more than coincidence that there are no quotations from the poets in Augustine's correspondence with the pagan philosopher Longinianus.

On the traditional view, historiography (in the form of supposed replies to Augustine's *City of God*) and philosophy have been held to be central components of a monolithic "pagan" culture uniformly dear to the hearts of all serious pagans. Philosophy in particular, in the form of Neoplatonism, has been widely held to provide the intellectual underpinning of late Roman paganism. The evidence is just not there (Ch. 15). On the one hand, when writing to philosophical friends Symmachus explicitly disavows philosophical expertise; on the other, he does not treat them (with the exception of the more versatile Praetextatus) to the classical allusions he reserves for his literary friends. Philosophical friends did not in general share his literary interests, nor he their philosophical interests.[171]

The culture that defined a well-educated late antique gentleman consisted essentially of knowledge of Cicero and the classical poets and a training in rhetoric. History was never studied as a subject in its own right; and philosophy was an advanced subject, studied by a tiny minority. Symmachus's knowledge of both was limited to anecdotes, mainly drawn from Cicero or rhetorical handbooks rather than firsthand acquaintance with historical or philosophical texts.

Thus even if he *had* known its author, the *Breviarium* of Eutropius, for all its utility, was not likely to impress him *as literature*. He may have referred to it for information, but it will not have been a work he read and reread in the way he read and reread his Vergil, Cicero, and Sallust. It had no stylistic pretensions, much of the history it covered was recent, and the fact that Eutropius himself was a pagan would not have been enough to give it the cachet of a classic.[172] The same applies to the *Caesares* of Aurelius Victor, and even the more ambitious *Res gestae* of Ammianus.

The letters to Praetextatus make a very different impression. It is not just his widow's poem on the funerary monument that proclaims his knowledge of Greek and Roman literature (prose and verse) as well as philosophy. Symmachus's letters contrive allusions to Homer and Hesiod and to both Greek and (ancient) Roman history on top of the philosophical allusions and references to pagan festivals and priesthoods—virtually everything that interested Praetextatus in just a dozen letters. Nothing could illustrate more clearly the care Symmachus took to tailor letters to addressees. By the same token nothing could underline more clearly the significance of the lack of literary references in the far more numerous letters to the elder Flavian.

---

171. Against the idea that Symmachus was familiar with Porphyry, Ch. 15.
172. In iii. 50 Symmachus claims that *veterum scripta* (i.e., the classics) have taken the place of conversation with Eutropius in his absence. But there is no implication that Eutropius himself was a devotee of the classics.

Symmachus himself never uses any such formula as "pagan culture" or "pagan classics." Like the grammarians of the age, he speaks only of "the old writers" (*veteres*). When he praises the style of his friends, it is almost always for catching the archaic qualities of these archetypes. His father, for example, is the "true heir of the ancients" (*iustus heres veterum litterarum*), by which (in the context) he means his "Ciceronian" style.[173] Naucellius "imitates the ancients" (*veteres aemularis*), himself an "exemplar of antiquity" (*vetustatis exemplar*).[174] Praetextatus too he praises for the "antiquity of his diction" (*verborum vetustas*). In all these cases the context makes clear that the compliment identifies, not the pagan content or character or even what we would call the style of their writing,[175] but simply their use of archaic diction. Particularly instructive is a letter playfully taxing the pagan Siburius for pushing archaism too far, suggesting ironically a return to the songs of the Salii, the tables of the Decemvirs, and (like Cato) beginning speeches by invoking Jupiter and the rest of the gods.[176] Thus the only passage where Symmachus directly links style to pagan worship is a joke, an excess of archaism rejected (he warns) even by Cicero.[177]

All such allusions come in letters to Symmachus's "literary" friends.[178] But in ninety-one letters there is no such praise of Flavian's style, evocation of the antiquity of his diction, or any suggestion that he spends his leisure reading the ancients. The one letter that praises his eloquence (*facundiae tuae copiis*, ii. 8) is no exception, since the reference is to his duties as *quaestor sacri palatii*, in which capacity he was expected to cast imperial laws into the chancery style of the age. Just so when Claudian praises Theodorus's eloquence, he is referring to the style of the edicts he issued as *magister memoriae*.[179] The one Symmachan letter that hails him as a connoisseur of style again refers to contemporary style (one of Symmachus's own speeches)[180] We have seen that Augustine, a rhetor himself, drew a distinction between mere eloquence and erudition. Faustus was a more entertaining speaker than Ambrose, but his inferior in erudition. Flavian and Theodorus (and Orfitus too) may have excelled in the mandarin prose of the day, whether orally or in writing. But that did not make them men of learning as the term was generally understood.

There has been much debate whether Flavian's *Annales* covered the Republic or empire (Ch. 17–18). I would suggest that Symmachus's failure even to mention his oldest friend's historical work supports the latter alternative. Whether or not he wrote an anti-Christian history or translated the *Life of Apollonius*, such ventures cannot

---

173. *unus aetate nostra monetam Latiaris eloquii Tulliana incude finxisti*, i. 3. 2.

174. iii. 15. 1; iii. 11. 2; *spectator tibi veteris monetae solus supersum*, iii. 12. 2.

175. On Symmachus's conception of style, p. 738.

176. iii. 44. 1, with which Callu compares Servius *Aen.* xi. 301.

177. One letter to Memmius touches on style (vii. 9), praising the rhetorical flourishes in his last letter, but suggesting that such figures are more at home in speeches. Letters (he advises) should be more informal—that is to say (of course) should take pains to give the impression of informality.

178. The addressee of ix. 123 is unknown, but clearly "literary."

179. *oracula regis / eloquio crevere tuo*, Pan. *Theod.* 36, 333; *PLRE* i. 901.

180. v. 9. 2. Theodorus also compiled a little manual on metre (Keil, *GL* vi. 485–600).

after all be seen as characteristic manifestations of a monolithic "pagan" culture actively sponsored by Symmachus and his circle.

On the best evidence we have (the best we could have, for that matter), personal letters from his oldest friend, the man hailed as the ringleader of the pagan reaction turns out (it seems) not to have shared Symmachus's enthusiasm for the classics. As we saw earlier (§ 1), this does not mean that he was illiterate. He had read all the basic texts at school and could doubtless recognize a familiar quotation from Vergil or Sallust. And we know that he could write the florid prose of the age as expertly as any of his peers.[181] Like Theodorus, he was an educated man with serious tastes who devoted the intervals of leisure in a busy public career[182] to philosophy rather than literature.

But unlike Symmachus (or, on occasion, Augustine or Jerome), he did not write his letters in his library, pausing to check the details of a half-remembered anecdote in Cicero or Valerius Maximus.[183] This is why Symmachus did not write Flavian the same sort of allusive literary letters he sent Ausonius and Protadius. When Symmachus himself so clearly acknowledged that even Christians of his acquaintance knew the classics better than Nicomachus Flavianus, the "last of the pagans," knowledge of the classics can hardly be equated with paganism.

5

To a greater extent than its aficionados perhaps realize, the notion of a pagan cultural offensive is based on a misreading of the nature and purpose of Macrobius's *Saturnalia*. It is largely the *Saturnalia* that has given rise to the modern assumption that it was classical culture that fueled the paganism of the last pagans. Yet it was not Macrobius's purpose to *re-create* the pagan society of the 380s, but simply to devise a suitable set of interlocutors as mouthpieces for material he himself had collected on topics he himself found interesting. Nothing in the surviving text suggests that Macrobius thought of his interlocutors as the only literary figures of the age, much less that he identified cult and culture.

His principal model was Cicero's literary dialogues, a revealing parallel. For they have often been misread in the same way, with the same result. For a long time it was taken for granted that Cicero was trying to re-create a historical "Circle of Scipio." But it was not for their actual political wisdom that he selected Scipio and Laelius as his interlocutors, but for the time in which they lived, the last days of a republic uncorrupted by the Gracchi. He was simply using appropriate names from the past as more authoritative spokesmen for his own views. We need only change "philhellenes" into

---

181. We may have some specimens in the constitutions that survive from his tenure as *quaestor palatii*: Honoré 1989.
182. It is worth emphasizing that both men devoted much more time to office than Symmachus.
183. See the examples quoted in Kroll 1891, 17–21.

"pagans" and every word of Astin's sceptical assessment of the circle of Scipio can be transferred to the circle of Symmachus.[184] Astin warned of the danger of exaggerating

> the uniqueness of these cultural and intellectual interests; and from that there
> seems to have developed a tendency to think of the "circle" as a kind of club to
> which all Roman *literati* or philhellenes would naturally belong. A further
> development is then to identify this supposedly highly distinctive cultural
> group as a distinctive political group whose outlook and policies were
> conditioned by these cultural interests.

While doing his best to get the historical details of his mise-en-scène as accurate as possible,[185] the views expressed are Cicero's or, in the philosophical dialogues, Cicero's adaptation of his Greek sources. He made no attempt to reproduce the actual views of Cato, Scipio, Crassus, or whoever on the subjects in question (in most cases he probably did not even know them).[186] For example, his portrait of the orator Crassus is detailed, rounded, and perhaps more generally true to life than any other of his interlocutors.[187] But there is no reason to believe that Crassus shared Cicero's interest and expertise in rhetorical theory, and the detailed technical precepts put in his mouth undoubtedly represent a combination of Greek theory and Ciceronian experience—as is put beyond doubt by their broad agreement with the discussion in the *Orator*, where Cicero is speaking in his own person. More generally, the claim in the preface to *De oratore* ii that Crassus and Antonius were better educated than most people believed is surely a dramatic fiction to lend verisimilitude to the improbably learned speeches Cicero assigns them, and illustrate his own conviction that only a man of broad culture could be a successful orator.[188]

An even clearer example is L. Lucullus, cast as spokesman for the Academy in the first edition of the *Academica*. Book ii of the first edition begins with a detailed introduction claiming to reveal the little-known fact that Lucullus was actually something of a philosopher in his spare time (ii. 1–4). This was not only untrue but absurd, as Cicero himself at once admitted. It is pure dramatic fiction, designed to invest the discourse of Lucullus that follows with some semblance of verisimilitude. Cicero had second thoughts at once, ruefully admitting to Atticus that Lucullus "could never have dreamed of such abstrusities."[189] He produced a second edition

---

184. Astin 1967, 294–306; Zetzel 1972.
185. No fewer than six letters to Atticus bear on research Cicero did on the interlocutors of a dialogue he never in fact wrote: Badian 1969, 54–65; Sumner 1973, 155–76. More generally, Rawson 1991.
186. In the words of its latest commentator, "There is no reason to believe that anything said in [*De republica*] is an accurate reflection of anything ever said by any of the participants" (Zetzel 1995, 12). On the setting and form of Cicero's dialogues, ib. 3–13.
187. Jones 1939, 318–20.
188. His detailed descriptions of both men participating in discussions with philosophers and rhetoricians in Greek in Athens is surely exaggerated, if not entirely fictitious: Rawson 1985, 6.
189. *Att.* xiii. 19. 5 (= 326 S–B). It is true that Plutarch represents Lucullus as something of a philosopher (*Lucull.* 42), but, as the context shows, this was an inference from Cicero's *Academica*, evidently the first edition.

transferring the role to Varro. It may be, as he claimed defensively in a letter to Varro himself, that Varro would approve the views now put in his mouth. But at this point Varro had not yet seen the speech itself, originally composed for Lucullus and (as Cicero admits) amounting to little more than a Latin version of Antiochus of Ascalon. "I dare say you will be surprised," Cicero adds, "at our holding a conversation that never actually took place, *but you know the convention of dialogues*."[190]

No contemporary familiar with these conventions would have made the error of identifying Macrobius's much-quoted chapters on solar theology (*Sat.* i. 17–23) as Praetextatus's own views. Given his well-known interest in oriental cults, Praetextatus was simply the most appropriate spokesman for such material, just as Crassus was the most appropriate spokesman for Cicero's views on oratorical theory. But the fact that Praetextatus enjoyed exotic initiations need not mean that he was an expert on exotic religious texts. Only one of Macrobius's interlocutors published works that survive to provide a check on what is said about him and put in his mouth: Servius. The results are instructive. Although the Macrobian Servius is given the *sort* of things the real Servius wrote about to say, not a word of it derives from his real writings. Indeed, in many ways it actually contradicts what the real Servius said (Ch. 7. 5).

As we shall see (§ 6), the cultivation of philosophical *otium* by members of the elite continued down to the end of the fourth century. Augustine's Cassiacum dialogues, however improved and embellished in their literary presentation, undoubtedly reproduce the content of real discussions among real people at a real time and place.[191] But the *Saturnalia* is a purely imaginary re-creation of the conventions of the genre.[192] The obnoxious Euangelus was a real member of the Roman elite ca. 380, but everything said about him in the *Saturnalia* is dramatic fiction. He is cast as the stock character of the uninvited guest, and his boorish provocation of the other interlocutors is simply a dramatic device (Ch. 16. 7). Dysarius the doctor and Horus the Cynic are likewise entirely fictional characters as they appear in the pages of Macrobius. Only their names and professions are real, taken from letters of Symmachus.

While taking some care (as Cicero did) to avoid outright anachronism, Macrobius was neither obliged nor expected to give an accurate account of the interrelationships, the cultural attainments, or even the interests of his interlocutors. His only concern was to pick speakers who lived at more or less the right time and place and were not obviously unsuited to the subject matter he intended to put in their mouths. Even after the determination of the true date of the *Saturnalia*, it has still been generally assumed that Macrobius preserves independent biographical information, just as reliable as that inferred from Symmachus's correspondence. But the very fact that he apologizes for "one or two" anachronisms (i. 1. 5) reveals at once that his interlocutors were not even

---

190. *Fam.* ix. 8 (= 254 S–B).
191. As convincingly established by Madec 1986.
192. To take a different sort of example, Chastagnol 1992, 336, oddly identified the room where the guests gather in *Sat.* i. 6. 1 as Praetextatus's actual library. Praetextatus may well have had a fine library, but the room described by Macrobius is simply an element in the mise-en-scène.

all contemporaries. It is therefore suggestive that only two of the twelve are actually attested by the correspondence as genuine friends of Symmachus. In one or two cases Macrobius may have had other evidence (e.g., the claim that Horus was a former boxer, which he is perhaps unlikely to have invented). But that is not really the point. Whatever the interrelationships of their historical counterparts, given the fiction of a dinner party as context, naturally the interlocutors have to be represented as friends.

One detail central to the cultural resistance hypothesis that, remarkably enough, has never been questioned is the *erudition* ascribed to all the interlocutors. But it is to confuse literary genres (dialogue for history) to suppose that this is intended as a realistic portrait. If the subject matter of the dialogue is antiquarian, naturally the interlocutors have to be learned. For example, when Macrobius describes Rufius and Caecina Albinus as "by far the most learned of our contemporaries" (vi. 1. 1), his immediate purpose is simply to prepare us for the long sequence of obscure quotations from Republican poets he is about to put in their mouths. There is no warrant for inferring that in real life the Albini were authorities on the Republican poets, texts that had long since disappeared by the fifth century. Macrobius himself knew no more of them than the series of often-unintelligible excerpts he had copied at second- or thirdhand from various antiquarian monographs.[193] Both Albini were no doubt well-educated men by the standards of their age and class (from his letter to Augustine, we know that Rufius's son Volusianus quoted Vergil elegantly and appropriately). But it is to misunderstand not only the conventions of the genre but the social context to identify them as scholars. They are meant to be *gentlemen*, cultivated amateurs.

At his first mention of Caecina Albinus, Macrobius claims that he and Symmachus were "closest of friends by reason of their age, their habits and their pursuits." This has often been accepted as solid fact. Yet on what must be regarded as the definitive evidence of the correspondence, it is the elder Flavian who was Symmachus's oldest and closest friend. We have already seen that it was in Symmachus's correspondence that Macrobius found some of his minor interlocutors (Dysarius, Euangelus, and Horus). But it was *not* here that he found the Albini. There is not a single letter to either of them. In the entire correspondence there is just one letter headed *Albino* (viii. 25). It was not included in the books published by Symmachus himself or his son, and the respectful formality of the phrase *reverentia tua* makes it unlikely that this man was either a contemporary or a close friend.[194] Callu was astonished to find (as he thought) only this trace "of the ties between the two traditionalist senators." But not only is this to privilege Macrobius's later fiction over firsthand contemporary evidence, it also presupposes what we are trying to prove, namely that paganism was the basis for friendship in the circle of Symmachus, and that all pagan literary men were friends.[195]

---

193. See the detailed analysis of the sources of *Sat.* vi. 1–5 by Jocelyn 1964/5. Hollis 2007, 8, unwisely assumes that Macrobius consulted original texts.

194. *Reverentia tua* is a formal address to a person of high standing: O'Brien 1930, 7–8.

195. Callu 1995, 191. There is no evidence outside Macrobius that either of the Albini was a man of letters.

Here we may compare the case of Messala and Lucillus.[196] Both were poets, both friends of Rutilius Namatianus as well as Symmachus, and polytheistic references in Symmachus's letters to them imply that both were pagans (vii. 92; viii. 21). Messala was also a brother of the interlocutor Avienus (p. 241). According to one modern commentator, he was a member of the "pagan circle of Symmachus."[197] Twelve letters from Symmachus (vii. 81–92) make him an acquaintance at least, but paganism and poetry notwithstanding, the allusion to his literary fame is formal (vii. 91), there are no literary allusions in the other letters, and no hint of intimacy. As for Lucillus, there is just one letter in Bk viii thanking him for the gift of some writings. On the traditional view, having paganism and literature in common should have been enough for such men to make common cause. It is hardly surprising to discover that in the real world friendship depends on more personal factors.

It might be suggested that Macrobius had another source now lost to us for linking the Albini to Symmachus. But he must have realized that Symmachus's correspondence was the decisive authority on such a matter. Since most of the hundreds of people Symmachus wrote to were acquaintances rather than friends, it is not likely that he *never* wrote to two of his closest friends. The explanation is as simple as it is revealing. Macrobius did not care. It was no part of his purpose to identify Symmachus's real friends or reconstruct a genuine pagan literary circle of the 380s. All he needed was a group of more or less cultivated pagans who flourished in the 380s. As we saw in chapter 7, Macrobius's choice of interlocutors reflects his own circle rather than the circle of Symmachus and Praetextatus. He chose the Albini to honor their fifth-century descendants.

More than mere prosopographical details are involved. We have already seen that not all Symmachus's pagan literary acquaintances were intimates while some of his closest literary friends were Christians. We now discover that two key members of Macrobius's supposed pagan scholarly brotherhood—the Albini—turn out to have been neither scholars nor intimates. Servius was a scholar but not an intimate, a crucial generation younger. For if he was too young to know Praetextatus, he was too young to know sacrifice as an adult. In their different ways all these factors undermine the idea of a late fourth-century scholarship-inspired pagan reaction.

The modern idea that Symmachus, Praetextatus, and the elder Flavian were the literary doyens of late Roman society (and so in the forefront of this hypothesized pagan offensive) derives from their portrayal as the three hosts in Macrobius's fiction. How do the real Praetextatus and Flavian compare with their counterparts in the

---

196. From the reference to hunting (viii. 21), clearly a landowner, and so not (as Roda supposed) the painter of ii. 2 and ix. 50. From the reference to writings, especially in view of the rare name, surely the satirist Lucillus who was the father of Rutilius's friend Decius and CSL some time (*olim*) before 417 (*De red.* i. 599–614); see Callu's note; C. H. Keene's edition), 35.
197. Castorina 1967, 223.

pages of Macrobius? Eight letters in Bks i–ii reveal Symmachus talking about pontiffs, portents, and festivals with Praetextatus (i. 46, 47, 49, 51) and Flavian (ii. 34, 36, 53, 59). It was surely these very letters that gave Macrobius the idea of casting his material in the form of a dialogue with precisely these three as hosts. Another letter accuses Praetextatus of spending his leisure "rummaging in old books" (i. 53), which might have suggested that he was an antiquarian. But read in context, this is simply an elaborate compliment on the elegance of Praetextatus's style. The combination of archaic diction and novel ideas in his letter *suggests* (Symmachus playfully claims) that Praetextatus has been at his books instead of hunting.

It is only Praetextatus that Symmachus himself so characterizes. He says nothing of the sort about Flavian. The principal contributions of the Macrobian Praetextatus and Flavian were on pontifical and augural law in Vergil (Flavian's unfortunately lost). Flavian was a pontifex and Praetextatus augur and quindecimvir as well, so both may have had a smattering of sacral law. But they cannot have been *experts* on a subject on which the learned literature had long since disappeared (Ch. 16. 10). The speeches Macrobius puts in their mouths represent his research, not theirs.

In chapter 15 we shall see that the same objection undermines another far-reaching assumption: that the "circle" of Symmachus saw a revival of Greek culture. But there is one respect above all in which Macrobius's mise-en-scène is unrealistic and implausible: the way his pagan interlocutors ignore the Christian threat to their way of life. This silence has not (of course) passed unnoticed, and various attempts have been made to explain it away. One view is the blindness of the last pagans, living in a fool's paradise, unable to comprehend the danger in which they stood. Forty years after the banning of sacrifice this passes belief. The most popular is fear of Christian reprisals.[198] Yet while fifth-century pagans were forbidden to visit their temples, perform sacrifice, or hold public office, they were not forbidden to speak about the old cults. If that were so, the *Saturnalia* would never have been written at all. How could it rally pagans to devote hundreds of pages to the cults as though they were still flourishing, with no hint of the danger that hung over them?

Once again, the true explanation is much simpler and more revealing. Macrobius had no interest in *late antique* paganism. *That* is why he gives no sense of the crisis that threatened it at the very moment of his dramatic date. It was *Vergilian* paganism that interested him. All he wanted was a group of pagans to talk about picturesque details of a timeless Roman paganism that, in his ignorance of genuine late antique paganism, he imagined to have remained unchanged from Vergil to Praetextatus. As we have already seen (Ch. 7), it was precisely to avoid dealing with the "pagan reaction" of the decade 383–94 that he picked a date before Gratian's anti-pagan measures of 382.

---

198. Cicero claimed that it was to avoid causing offense that he chose interlocutors from the past (*Q. fr.* 3. 5. 2).

6

A final objection to assigning a political or religious dimension to Symmachus's love of the classics is that his letters set it in a quite different and entirely traditional context. As Kroll noted more than a century ago, Symmachus regularly implies that the best place to commune with *veterum scripta* was a villa in the country. Again and again his letters describe the joys of studious leisure on a cool suburban estate, whether for himself or his literary friends.[199] The diversion of choice for many rich Romans vacationing on their estates was hunting. But Symmachus, like Pliny before him, disclaimed both interest and expertise, and affects to believe that his closer friends likewise devoted their country trips to reading rather than hunting.[200]

Symmachus and his friends were following a social pattern that goes back through Pliny to the age of the Republic. Cicero and his peers regularly kept their libraries in their various villas, where they did their serious reading and writing. We have already glanced at the library in Lucullus's Tusculan villa, and Cicero is known to have had libraries in at least four of his villas. When at his Cumanum he would use the rich library in Sulla's villa, then owned by his friend Faustus Sulla.[201] A number of Pliny's letters quite straightforwardly identify country retreats with the leisure to read and write.[202] The fact that so many busts and statues of famous writers and philosophers have been found in excavations at villa sites likewise suggests that this is where their owners liked to do their reading.[203] But there was an important shift of emphasis between the age of Cicero and the age of Symmachus. For Cicero, learned leisure was a poor alternative to a life in politics.[204] For Symmachus as for many members of the late Roman elite, "an affectation was studiously maintained that the burdens of responsibility entailed by the possession of public office were an unwelcome intrusion upon a senator's leisure."[205]

Symmachus consistently represents the study of literature as a private, leisure activity of gentlemen, prosecuted on their estates in the intervals of a busy life, relaxation from the cares of public office or private business. "While you leave Rome for court," he writes to Eutropius, "I am settling down to read in my suburban retreat."

---

199. Kroll 1891; *me in secessu anteurbano adserui lectioni…vicem sermonis tui veterum scripta funguntur…interventus familiaris negotii rupti otium meum*, iii. 50 (to Eutropius); *tibi et rusticari et erudiri plurimum licet*, iv. 32 (to Protadius); [*agri quies*] *et aeris praestat salubritatem et pabulum lectionis*, v. 78 (to Hesperius); iv. 44 (to Minervius); viii. 21 (to Lucillus); vii. 18. 3 (to Attalus). On the material evidence for all these villas, see Sfameni 2006.

200. i. 53 and i. 47. 2 picture Praetextatus reading rather than hunting on his estates; iv. 18. 1–2 repeats the claim for Protadius; cf. Pliny, *Ep.* i. 6 (to Tacitus).

201. Rawson 1985, 40–42; Grimal 1969, 361; Fedeli in Cavallo 1988, 34–38; Casson 2001, 69–73.

202. *Epp.* i. 3; i. ix; ix. 36; Grimal 1969, 421–22; Hoffer 1999, 29–44 ("Villas: Factories of Literature"); Méthy 2007, 373–78.

203. Neudecker 1988, 64–74; Zanker 1995, 203–13; Stirling 2005; Marzano 2007, 96–101.

204. André 1966, 279–334.

205. Matthews 1975, 9; McGeachy 1942, 44–45. Not that senators actually avoided public office: Roda 1985, 95–108.

Unfortunately, some personal business came up, and he had to put his books aside and return to town.[206] Two Livy subscriptions and another in manuscripts of Augustine's *De trinitate* bear witness to work done on country estates. We have already touched on the *Epigrammata Bobiensia*, prominently featuring work by the nonagenarian Naucellius. Those who had expected exciting new light on the pagan revival were to be sadly disappointed. The most interesting thing about these poems, as Peter Brown shrewdly remarked, is precisely "that they have nothing new to contribute; they mirror exactly this quiet world, dominated in its literary expression by the traditional forms of the good life."[207] It is summed up in poem 5:

> hic studia et Musis otia amica colo...
> vivere sic placidamque iuvat proferre senectam,
> docta revolventem scripta virum veterum.

> Here I pursue my studies and my leisure devoted to the Muses... Thus I delight to live and extend my calm old age, re-reading the learned books of the writers of old.

No hint of a pagan agenda. Naucellius just sat in the shade somewhere on his estate at Spoleto quietly reading and rereading the "learned books of the old writers." In the preface to a monograph on the meters of Horace, the grammarian Servius claims that it was "when I was at my leisure in Campania"[208] that he turned to Horace. That is to say, aping the ways of his betters, he represents what is clearly a piece of scholarly research as the casual product of a few days' leisure in the country.[209]

This notion of gentlemanly studious leisure was by no means restricted to pagans. The best-documented Christian example has already been cited: Augustine and his followers in the immediate aftermath of his conversion at Cassiacum.[210] So too Paulinus of Nola in the early days of his withdrawal from public life: "after I finally seemed to win rest from calumnies and wanderings, unbusied by public affairs and far from the din of the marketplace, I enjoyed the leisure of country life, surrounded by pleasant peace."[211] Another letter of Paulinus describes how his friend Aper, "spending little time in cities, grew to love the intimate remoteness of the silent countryside, not putting leisure before business or withdrawing from what is useful to the church, but avoiding the bustle of the churches which almost rival the crowds of the forum" (*Ep.* 38. 10). Symmachus's Christian friend Mallius Theodorus withdrew from a

---

206. Symm. *Ep.* iii. 50.
207. P. Brown 1961, 1–2.
208. *cum in Campania otiarer, GL* iv. 468. 6.
209. As acutely noted by Kaster 1988, 66.
210. P. Brown 1967, 115–16; *Christianae vitae otium*, in Augustine's own phrase, *Retract.* i. 1. 1.
211. *Ep.* 5. 4, trans. Walsh; Fontaine 1972, 571–602.

distinguished public career to "dedicate his leisure to the Muses" (*otia Musis*), in the words of his panegyrist Claudian. The preface to Rufinus's translation of Origen's commentary on *Numbers* reveals him in the company of his aristocratic patrons on one of Melania's estates in Sicily, translating Origen while Alaric burned Rhegium on the other side of the straits.[212]

By the close of the century the rising tide of asceticism rendered the notion of Christian withdrawal to the peaceful comfort and abundance of an aristocratic estate problematic.[213] There is no mention of leisure or villas in the biography of an early fifth-century aristocratic "drop-out" like the younger Melania. But in 386 Augustine's Cassiacum dialogues frequently allude to discussions taking place in the luxurious warmth of baths, and we hear of fine baths on one of the African estates of the elder Melania, decorated with a poem inscribed by the celebrated society calligrapher Furius Dionysius Filocalus.[214] As we have already seen, while "at leisure" (*otiosi*) during the course of their philosophical discussions, Augustine's little Christian band devoted many entire days and a part of every day to reviewing the *Aeneid*—a remarkable real-life parallel to Macrobius's fictional symposium.

A number of consequences may be drawn. First, the centrality of the country retreat in this conception of literary *otium* spectacularly underlines the elite nature of the culture it fostered. It is precisely the fact that it was above all a social marker that explains why the traditional culture was so enthusiastically embraced by Christian members and would-be members of that same elite. For the same reason it is unlikely even to have occurred to pagans to use the culture they shared as a weapon in the battle against their Christian peers—much less to proselytize their inferiors.[215] It was the only culture there was. The idea that love of the classics formed a bond between pagans in particular rather than members of the elite in general is neither probable in itself nor borne out by the available evidence. It follows that the notion of aristocrats (of all people) "propagating" this culture scarcely makes sense. It was only a fraction of his peers to whom Symmachus wrote his "literary" letters—and some of them were Christians.

---

212. Claudian, *Pan. Theod.* 61–66; Wilson 1990, 218.
213. See especially Trout 1988, 132–46.
214. Aug. *C. Acad.* iii. 1. 1; *De beata vita* i. 6; iii. 17; *De ord.* i. 8. 25; ii. 6. 19; AL 120 R with Cameron 1992, 140–44.
215. As pointed out in Ch. 13, texts without word division and punctuation were in any case inaccessible to any but those trained from childhood to use them.

11

THE "PAGAN" LITERARY REVIVAL

1

There is no question that the fourth century saw a revival of Latin literature. It could hardly be otherwise. After the nadir of the third century there was only one way to go. But in much of the modern literature it has been widely characterized as a pagan revival and associated with the aristocracy of late fourth-century Rome, reacting to the threat of Christianity. This is perhaps the single most serious obstacle to a true understanding of this important development.

Early in the second century the direction of Latin letters began to change sharply, to move away from the rhetoric and point and polish of the so-called "Silver Age" toward archaism. The term "Silver Age" is modern, and many no longer consider it a helpful label, attributing as it does a greater homogeneity to the literature of the first century A.D. than it actually possessed. But we are not here concerned to do justice to the variety of first-century literature, but rather to trace the fortune of a few of its most conspicuous representatives, mainly poets, who share an artificiality, a striving for effect, a taste for erotic learning, bravura descriptions, and impassioned speeches that does set them apart.

There had always been a strain of archaism in Latin literature.[1] It is enough to mention Sallust, Vergil, and Tacitus. Old and even obsolete words were thought to convey the appropriate degree of dignity for a history of Rome's past or an epic poem. But what had formerly been no more than one prominent element in the style of his-toriography and epic became the all-pervading goal of writers in every genre in the age of Fronto and Aulus Gellius. Some have thought that the second-century archaizing movement could be explained solely in terms of an internal development within Latin literature, as the gradual victory of this archaizing tendency over all others.

This explanation is surely inadequate. An affectation for linguistic archaisms is one thing, the utter rejection of the literature of the preceding century quite another. And yet this is just what some Latin writers of the second century did. It cannot be a coin-cidence that Greek literature was undergoing a similar change of direction at this time: the movement we know as the Second Sophistic. The archaizing movement is best explained as a combination of both these factors. On the one hand, Latin writers of

---

1. Marache 1952; Lebek 1970; Holford-Strevens 2003.

the late first and early second centuries felt dissatisfied with the increasing stridency and artificiality of Silver Latin poetry. On the other, they could not but be impressed by the glittering revival of Greek letters. And the key to the Greek revival had been a rejection of the present and a return to the great old writers of a golden age. If Latin writers could just do the same, perhaps Latin literature would be restored to sanity.[2]

But however disquieting the excesses of Silver Latin rhetoric, it was not possible to renew Latin literature simply by turning back the clock. The Greek classical authors to whom the Second Sophistic looked back—Demosthenes, Plato, Thucydides—were among the greatest writers of all time. The same was not true of the revered models of Fronto and Gellius: Ennius, Cato, Accius, Lucilius, Sisenna. Rightly or wrongly, the Romans had always looked back on the age of Ennius and Cato as a *moral* golden age; but as literature, the writings of the second century B.C. were not classics by any definition. For all their merits, these were writers fumbling for a style, a vocabulary, above all for an identity, as they sought to come to terms with the all but overwhelming influence of a recently discovered Greek literature.

Imitation of these early Roman writers could not form the basis of a vital Latin literature. What Latin writing we have from the second century A.D. seems predominantly concerned with linguistic archaism, with reproducing quaint and frequently obsolete words and forms attested in second-century writers rather than current usage—the latter seldom mentioned without a shudder.[3] Words, not ideas, were the business of the Antonine man of letters. The only notable work to survive from this age, significantly enough, is the *Golden Ass* of Apuleius, from the linguistic point of view an unmistakable child of the archaizing movement, but in its subject matter and treatment a version of a Greek novel. Indeed, we actually possess a version of its Greek original.

The political crisis of the late third century doubtless had its effect. Patronage of the arts would inevitably be affected by wars and inflation. But it is not so clear that such things stop writers from writing. War had always been the prime theme and inspiration of ancient historical writing, and the third century saw the production of a large number of histories in Greek: the massive chronicle of all Roman history compiled by Dio Cassius; Herodian and Dexippus. It may be true that the Greek provinces suffered less during the third-century invasions. Yet unlike Rome, Athens was actually besieged by the Herulian Goths—and none other than the historian Dexippus led the Athenian defense.[4] Even in the West, the second and third centuries produced some remarkable and important Christian writers: Minucius Felix, Tertullian, Cyprian.

It is particularly striking that one of the most influential intellectual movements of Late Antiquity flourished in Rome in the darkest days of the third-century crisis: the philosophical revival we call Neoplatonism. But Plotinus and the most influential of

---

2. Russell 1990, 13.
3. Marache 1952; 1957.
4. Millar 1969, 12–29.

his disciples (Porphyry and Iamblichus) were Greeks. The truth is that it was only secular Latin literature that suffered this catastrophic decline in the third century. There can be little doubt that the decline owed less to the public misfortunes of the empire than to the false trail laid by the archaizing movement. This trail led nowhere, and nowhere is where secular Latin literature went.

For the better part of two centuries the post-Augustan poets were spurned or left unread. Not one is named or quoted in Gellius's *Noctes Atticae*. But by the end of the fourth century the writers of the Silver Age were again in favor, and the archaic writers again in eclipse. This is one of the most important strands in the story of the fourth-century revival of letters. The almost complete lack of secular literature in the late second and early third centuries makes it difficult to trace the story of the decline of the archaizing movement and the rediscovery of the post-Augustans. Archaizing was never expressly repudiated, but in practice came less and less to influence actual usage.

The revival of interest in Silver Age literature is not in itself surprising. Even at the height of the archaizing movement, Roman elite education had remained basically rhetorical in nature. The increasing formality of Roman public life called for an ever-increasing variety of speeches. By the end of the third century, as the corpus of the Panegyrici Latini reveals, Latin oratory was clearly flourishing. It was inevitable that anyone with a rhetorical training who chanced to pick up a text of Seneca, Lucan, Statius, or Juvenal would find it appealing.

Archaizers certainly continued into the fourth century, though among teachers and scholars rather than poets and orators, most conspicuously Nonius Marcellus in early fourth-century North Africa, with his dictionary of Republican Latin, and Fl. Sosipater Charisius, author of an influential *Ars grammatica*, both probably in the first half of the fourth century.[5] Something like half of Charisius's examples come from Vergil, almost all the others from Republican texts, many from Ennius, Naevius, Lucilius, Pacuvius, and other archaic writers. Charisius's work is the more significant in view of its obvious didactic and practical goals. In § 2. 13 (pp. 253–89 Barwick) Charisius gives a long list of adverbs with supporting illustrations, many archaic and obsolete. To take two at random, *necessum* is cited from the elder Cato and Afranius; and the phrase *obviam esse* from Sallust, Sisenna, Cato, and Plautus. No explanation of the list is offered; no hint (e.g.) of the key difference that *necessum* was now wholly obsolete while *obviam esse* remained current usage. So remote an authority as Augustus is said to have reproached Tiberius for using *perviam* instead of *obiter*, while the "divine Hadrian" is cited for the suspicion that *obiter* is "not Latin, though it is said to occur in Laberius." We find the same range of examples (Vergil and Republican writers) in the *Ars grammatica* of Diomedes, perhaps from the third quarter of the fourth century.

---

5. Schmidt in Herzog and Schmidt? 5 § 523. 2, with Kaster 1988, 253, 394 (rightly rejecting Usener's correction of Chrestus in Jerome, *Chron*. s. a. to Charisius).

2

When and where did people start reading again the books that had been gathering dust through most of the second and third centuries? The main objections to the modern preoccupation with the role supposedly played by the pagan aristocracy of late fourth-century Rome are that the revival (a) began long before then, (b) in many different parts of the Roman world, and (c) had nothing to do with paganism or (d) Roman aristocrats. Indeed, some of the first signs of a rekindled interest in post-Augustan writers come from cultivated Christian writers. Aristocrats after all are usually at best patrons rather than initiators of literary movements.

Already under Constantine, Lactantius quotes several times from Ovid (both *Fasti* and *Metamorphoses*), Persius once, and two lines each from Juvenal and Lucan by name. It is true that the passage he cites as Lucan is in fact Ovid, though he does cite a couple of lines of Lucan anonymously in the following paragraph.[6] In a sceptical analysis of Lactantius's knowledge of Latin poetry, Ogilvie was inclined to suspect that he found Juvenal and Lucan in a commonplace book. He was right to be sceptical about Lactantius's quotations of Ennius, Lucilius, Naevius, and Plautus, most of which he may well have got from Cicero or other intermediaries.[7] But the passages of Ovid and Lucan he transposes both concern Osiris, and what sort of intermediary would quote passages about pagan gods from authors few people were reading? The answer is surely that he confused quotations jotted down in his own commonplace book. I see no reason to doubt that Lactantius read (at least some) Lucan and Juvenal for himself—though only in part because they were coming back into fashion. More important, he was searching for ammunition to attack paganism.

Just so at about the same time Eusebius was conducting an even more ambitious search through hundreds of neglected and unfashionable Greek texts, both Classical and Hellenistic, while preparing his *Evangelical Preparation* and *Demonstration*.[8] A century earlier Tertullian had read Pliny the Younger and Tacitus as well as Juvenal for the same reason.[9] This is why Lactantius turned to Cicero's *De natura deorum*, Lucretius, Euhemerus (in Ennius's translation), and prophetic works like the Sibylline Oracles and Hermetica.[10]

Still under Constantine, we find the Spanish presbyter Iuvencus imitating Ovid, Lucan, Statius, and even Silius and Valerius Flaccus in his *Evangelia*, dated by Jerome to 329–30. Iuvencus is untypical in a different way: as an epic poet, he had a particular

---

6. *Div. Inst.* i. 21. 20–21; Ovid, *Met.* 9. 693; Luc. 9. 158–59.
7. Ogilvie 1978, 7–19.
8. Carriker 2003; Kofsky 2000.
9. Barnes 1971, 201–4.
10. Ogilvie 1978, Ch. 3 and 5, passim.

motive to familiarize himself with the Latin epic tradition.[11] His principal poetic source and model was unquestionably Vergil, imitated on every page. Nonetheless, it is clear that texts from the entire range of post-Augustan poetry were available where and when both Lactantius and Iuvencus wrote.

Lactantius was presumably educated in his native Africa. It is suggestive that another writer to show early knowledge of the post-Augustans was also an African, Nemesianus, writing in the 280s. Like Iuvencus, Nemesianus too turned overwhelmingly to Vergil. Indeed, he seems to have set himself explicitly in the Vergilian succession, with a set of *Eclogues*, a didactic poem (*Cynegetica*), and the promise of an epic on the deeds of the short-lived emperors Carinus and Numerian.[12] While affecting the odd archaism (*ollis* and *mage*, *Cyn*. 264 and 317), Nemesianus was clearly familiar with Statius, both *Silvae* and *Thebaid*. He has to be seen as a harbinger of the fourth-century renaissance. The author of the perhaps early fourth-century *Pervigilium Veneris* also knew Statius.[13]

As for Iuvencus, even without Jerome's reference to his "most distinguished birth," his many names and praenomen (C. Vettius Aquilinus Iuvencus) would have suggested an old family and so the best education money could buy.[14] It is natural to assume that he was related to Vettius Aquilinus cos. 286. In general the elite culture of the Roman world, both Greek and Latin, seems to have been remarkably homogeneous. But just as Valerius Probus was encouraged to find archaic authors still popular in mid first-century Berytus,[15] so it may be that the post-Augustans continued to be read in some of the more remote outposts of empire after they had fallen out of fashion in Rome. We might expect to find Tacitus and Pliny holding their own against the archaizing tide in Gaul, and Seneca and Lucan in Spain. Paradoxically, however, it may have been the Christians who first started shaking the dust off such texts.

According to A. Wlosok, in turning to Cicero and Vergil, respectively, Lactantius and Nemesianus represent a new Classicism. This seems an odd perspective, given that most archaizers respected Cicero and Vergil. Lactantius was a great admirer of Seneca as well as Cicero.[16] I should prefer to emphasize the tilting of the balance away from archaism. A half-century earlier, for example, in addition to Cicero, Minucius Felix admired both Fronto and Fronto's bête noire Seneca.

Other indications can be seen in early fourth-century Gaul. Gaul had suffered badly from the unrest of the third century, and Constantius I devoted much effort to restoring

---

11. For example, Iuv. iv. 215 *nutrimina pinguia flammae* ~ Ov. *Met*. 15. 352 *alimentaque pinguia flammae*; Iuv. ii. 179 ~ *Met*. 7. 90; Iuv. i. 175 = *Theb*. 10. 209 (*caeli secreta*); Iuv. i. 213 = *Theb*. 1. 351 (*tenebrosa volumina*); Iuv. iii. 230 ~ *Theb*. 7. 810; Iuv. iii. 390 ~ *Ach*. 1. 198; Iuv. iv. 611 = *Theb*. 10. 580 (*sententia vulgi*); i. 8 = Luc. 1. 129 = ii. 105 (*vergentibus annis*); Iuv. i. 682 = Sil. 15. 235 (*per prona*); Iuv. i. 499 = Val. Flacc. 1. 673 (*consurgere in iras*); Iuv. ii. 66 = Val. Flacc. 2. 488 (*dona salutis*). Many parallels are cited in J. Huemer's edition of 1891; but see the reservations in Green 2006, 10–13.

12. *Cyn*. 58–81; K. Smolak in Herzog and Schmidt 5 § 555.

13. On the PV, see Cameron 1984.

14. *nobilissimi generis Hispanus*, *De vir. ill*. 84; for a brief account, Herzog in Herzog and Schmidt 5 § 561; for much more detail, see now Green 2006, 1–134.

15. Suet. *Gramm*. 24. 2, with Kaster's note.

16. Ogilvie 1978, 73–77.

schools and education there. The state thus contributed to the revival of culture in the last decade of the third century. Our knowledge of Constantius's rebuilding of the schools of Gaul derives from the earliest of the so-called Panegyrici Latini, a corpus of eleven Gallic panegyrics dating from 289 to 389.[17] Not even the earliest of these panegyrists were real archaizers. Their models were Cicero and the younger Pliny. That is to say, they saw themselves in the logical and historical tradition of Roman oratory as it developed from the late Republic into the early empire. The corpus as we have it was probably assembled by the Gaul Pacatus Drepanius, whose panegyric on Theodosius, the latest in time (389), stands in second place, immediately after Pliny's on Trajan. Even the earliest members of the corpus, nos. 10 (2) and 11 (3) by Mamertinus on Maximian in 289 and 291, show Pliny's influence.[18] It is not surprising that local patriotism kept study of Pliny's oratory alive regardless of literary fashions elsewhere.

The schools of Gaul enjoyed a high reputation throughout the fourth century; Roman aristocrats would send their sons to Gallic rather than Roman professors. Symmachus himself had studied with a Gallic rhetor, and he made his own son do the same.[19] The best-known representative of the culture of mid fourth-century Gaul is Ausonius (as we have seen in Ch. 10. 3).

Ausonius has often been classified as an honorary or one-time member of the "circle" of Symmachus. This is doubly misleading. In the first place, Ausonius (born ca. 310) was a full generation older than Symmachus (born ca. 340), and he certainly derived his culture from the schools of Gaul, not from contact with Symmachus. In the second place, Ausonius was a Christian. He does not parade his Christianity in his writings, to be sure, but that does not justify the sneers of those moderns who have dismissed him as a lukewarm or nominal Christian, and in effect treated his works as evidence of pagan tastes. This is an unhelpful perspective, less because (trivially) it is unfair to Ausonius as a person, than because (more important) it deflects attention from the well-documented phenomenon, of which Ausonius is no more than the most conspicuous example, of enthusiasm for classical culture among Christians, especially Gallic Christians. After all, Ausonius's favorite and best-known pupil, Paulinus of Nola, a deeply committed and active Christian, was (if with a less easy conscience) scarcely less well read in at any rate the Latin classics than his teacher. Paulinus's friend Sulpicius Severus was also a man of wide classical culture.[20]

A Renaissance catalogue of Ausonius's works discovered in 1971 mentions the titles of four hitherto unknown: (1) a poetical history of usurpers (*De imperatoribus res novas molitis*) from Decius and Diocletian, "according to Eusebius of Nantes"; (2) a chronicle from the beginning of the world to his own day; (3) a book on the names of Hebrew and Athenian months; and (4) a book on the traditions of the Hebrews and interpretations

---

17. For an up-to-date summary account, Schmidt in Herzog and Schmidt 5 § 185–98; Rees 2002.
18. Klotz 1911, 535.
19. Symm. *Ep.* ix. 88. 3; vi. 34; Haarhof 1920; Étienne 1962, 235–64.
20. Green 1971, Ch. 2–3; Stancliffe 1983, 55–70.

of Hebrew names.[21] Eusebius of Nantes (*Nanneticus*) looks like the man cited by Evagrius for a history of the emperors from Octavian to Carus (283), one of whose two fragments describes a siege of Tours (not far from Nantes) in the 250s.[22] This would explain the odd phrase *res novas molitis*. In the ordinary way a history of usurpers might seem very strange,[23] but it would be natural enough for Ausonius to have celebrated the series of usurpers who created the so-called Gallic Empire of 260–74, presumably treated in some detail by Eusebius. The world chronicle points to Christian influence, more particularly to the Chronicle of the other Eusebius (of Caesarea), who also wrote an influential work *On the Place-names in Holy Scripture*, perhaps a source for the book on Hebrew traditions and names. If these new titles reflect authentic lost works of Ausonius, they would add a new dimenson to Ausonius's Christian culture.

To return to his "pagan" (better secular) culture, Ausonius knew all the usual school authors (Vergil by heart, as his erotic Vergil cento shows, composed in just one day—without a concordance). He also knew all the Silver Age poets: he quotes easily and often from Seneca, Lucan, Statius, Juvenal,[24] and, like his colleagues the Gallic panegyrists, he was also familiar with the younger Pliny. Little or nothing survives from Ausonius's youth, but it would be implausible to suppose that he first read all these writers in later life. The two panegyrics on Maximian (10 and 11) of 289 and 291 are both heavily influenced by Cicero and Vergil;[25] number 11 contains an unmistakable quotation from Ovid's *Heroides*;[26] number 10 (321) contains at least one unmistakable echo of Lucan;[27] and number 6 (310) seems to have known Tacitus.[28] Ausonius too seems to echo one or two Tacitean epigrams.[29]

The implication is clear: by the middle of the fourth century Gaul had already experienced a full-scale revival of early Imperial Latin literature.

3

Over the past few decades much careful research has been devoted to tracking down classical allusions in the works of late antique writers (especially Jerome and Augustine), picking up a line of research generally left in abeyance since the nineteenth

---

21. See Reeve 1977, 112–20; and Green 1981, 226–36.

22. *FHG* V. 21–23 = *FGrH* 101; the identity of this Eusebius has been much discussed: Sivan 1992; Burgess 1993.

23. Naturally one thinks of the *HA*, though its usurpers are interspersed with its legitimate emperors.

24. See the testimonia in the editions of Schenkl, Peiper, and Prete; Green 1991; Green 1977.

25. Klotz 1911, 536–39, 547–48, 550, 555, 564. Klotz's suggested Ennian reminiscences (539) are hardly persuasive.

26. Klotz 1911, 531–40. *ubi silvae fuere, iam seges est,* Pan. Lat. xi (3). 15. 3 ~ *iam seges est ubi Troia fuit,* Ovid. *Her.* i. 53; on the dates, Nixon and Rodgers 1994, 42–43, 76–79.

27. *Pan.* x (4) 29. 5, *sonat ictibus umbo* ~ Luc. 6. 192; Bonaria 1958, 497–99; ib. 30. 1 ~ Luc. 2. 209–19; Vinchesi 1979, 5; Ovid, Klotz 539.

28. *Pan.* vi. (7). 9. 2; Baldwin 1980, 175–80; Nixon and Rodgers 1994, 231 n. 40 (212–14 for the date).

29. *Caes.* (xxiii) 12, 54–55, 85, with Green 1991, 558, 560, 563, 565.

century. But individual writers have usually been treated in isolation, or at most com-pared with one other writer for specific likes or dislikes. The results of these separate investigations have yet to be systematically combined into one picture. Still less has any attempt been made to compare the reading habits of Christians and pagans. Those who have seen pagans exploiting pagan literature as a weapon in the struggle against Christianity seem not to have noticed that educated Christians were reading all the same books.

The theory and practice of literary imitation have been much studied in recent years.[30] This chapter is not concerned with such questions; its sole purpose is to dis-cover which classical writers were *known* to fourth- and early fifth-century writers and members of the elite. To this end I have not attempted to distinguish unconscious echoes from deliberate imitations or even direct quotations (for more on these distinc-tions, Ch. 20. 6). Of course, while it is obvious that quotations or allusions prove knowledge (of a sort), it is not so obvious that their absence proves ignorance. Even the best-read writers are not obliged to quote or allude to everything they have read. Yet the argument from silence is stronger than it might seem. The literary culture that was so indispensable to the late Roman elite was based on deep knowledge of a limited range of texts rather than a more general knowledge of a wider range (see p. 487). And it was evidently considered desirable to advertise this knowledge, sometimes in what might be considered a rather crude way. Symmachus, Jerome, and Augustine positively stuff their letters to more learned correspondents with learned quotations, while not bothering when writing to those who would not recognize such displays (Ch. 10. 4).

Members of the elite undoubtedly took pains to advertise their culture by quoting or alluding, whether to figures from Greek or Roman mythology, history, or philos-ophy, or verbal allusions to classical texts. Jerome seems to have kept a special notebook for quotations and allusions suitable to the several score often very elaborate prefaces with which he adorned his works (Ch. 20. 6). All educated people were expected to recognize and respond to quotations from Cicero, Sallust, Terence, and (above all) Vergil, the more cultivated to a wider range of texts as well. Direct quotation is unprob-lematic, but (as we shall see) it is not uncommon to find quotations taken at secondhand from some intermediary who is not mentioned. Such quotations are not therefore evi-dence for firsthand familiarity with the author quoted. Nor is it just the uneducated who do this; one of the worst offenders is the most learned man of his day, Jerome.

We may begin with the decline of the archaizing movement. Terence (the main school-author after Vergil) is perhaps the only Republican poet Jerome, Ambrose, and Augustine really knew at firsthand.[31] It is sometimes supposed that Ausonius still read the archaic poets. But his quotations of Ennius are limited to one of his donnish tours

---

30. Most recent work has been devoted to the poets: e.g., Hinds 1998; for a prose writer, see now Kelly 2008, 161–321.
31. Jerome: Hagendahl 1958, 270–74; Adkin 1994, 187–95; Hagendahl 1967, 378; Courcelle 1972, 223–31.

de force, a piece titled *Grammaticomastix* in which every line ends in a monosyllable, four of them quoted from Ennius. Here are two (3 and 17):

> Ennius ut memorat, repleat te "laetificum gau"...
> unde Rudinus ait "divum domus altisonum cael."

The first may in fact be a fabricated hyper-ennianism. Skutsch was willing to accept the other three as genuine,[32] but even so Ausonius is more likely to have found them ready collected in some grammatical work than while reading a complete text of Ennius. Another poem he claims to have written in "the style of Lucilius" (if, with most editors, we correct the manuscript reading *Luciano* into *Luciliano*), but it has to be said that there is nothing remotely "Lucilian" about the poem.[33] Yet Ausonius seems to have a firsthand knowledge of Plautus.[34]

Ammianus too may have known Plautus at firsthand.[35] For Augustine, Ennius, Naevius, Pacuvius, Caecilius, and even Plautus are "mere names known from Cicero and Varro"; Jerome's quotations of Naevius and Ennius likewise come from Cicero, and a couple of references to Plautus imply a low opinion. Ambrose has a couple of proverbial expressions from Plautus—including one he attributes to Plato because he found it already so misquoted in Apuleius![36] It is true that a late fourth-century contorniate features the tragedian Accius, whence Alföldi and Green inferred that he was still being read in the fourth century.[37] Contorniates for Terence, Sallust, Horace, and Apuleius certainly celebrate current favorites, but what of those for Euripides and Theophrastus? There is no real evidence that Accius was still being read rather than just known from one or two familiar quotations. He is only quoted once in the whole of Servius.[38] Many contorniate types reflect much earlier motifs in many different media (Ch. 19. 1). The Accius type no doubt originated in the archaizing period.

More than a century ago Birt tried to prove that Claudian had read Ennius and Lucilius. But the parallels he cited are not close, and in all probability Claudian read them in the form of quotations in the same sources as us. When investigating Claudian's literary debts in 1970 I was already sceptical, as was Skutsch in his edition of Ennius (1985).[39] Against this wider context, it now seems even less likely. Paulinus of Nola quotes well-known lines of Ennius twice and Plautus perhaps once.[40]

---

32. Skutsch 1985, 18–19, 726–29.
33. *De herediolo* pr. (Green 1991, 282); a friend who claimed to write satirical poetry is compared to Lucilius (*Ep.* 11 to Tetradius; Green, 625).
34. See Schenkl's edition (1883), 267–68; Green 1991, 597, 620, 644.
35. Kelly 2008, 172, 193–96, 208–9.
36. Hagendahl 1967, 691; 1958, 103, 165, 168, 203, 274; Courcelle 1972, 224–25.
37. Alföldi and Alföldi 1990, 51, 103–4; Taf. 33. 5–8; Green 1971, 50.
38. With another twelve quotations in the DS additions (on which, see Ch. 16, passim).
39. Cameron 1970, 315; Skutsch 1985, 19–20.
40. Green 1971, 50.

A century ago Kroll made a thorough study of Symmachus's knowledge of earlier writers, discovering to his surprise that Symmachus too knew very little of the archaic writers beyond Plautus (whom he echoes quite often, from several different plays) and Terence.[41] Despite affecting a considerable number of *verbal* archaisms (*ain tandem, fors fuat, aliquantisper, obnixe, optato, praeut, obgannire*), Symmachus's direct knowledge of archaic *literature* seems minimal. His three quotations from Ennius and one from Naevius were all quoted by Cicero before him, the line of Naevius three times. Moreover, most of these archaisms occur in Bk i of his *Letters*. If this is the one book he published himself (Ch. 10. 3), it is natural to infer that it was during the process of revision that he introduced most of these archaisms, drawing on a grammatical work rather than the casual fruits of his reading. For very few are actual quotations from archaic writers. The implication is that Symmachus cultivated an ideal of archaism that he could only realize with the aid of textbooks.

What of Macrobius? While urging his readers not to neglect Republican texts, it is unclear how well he really knew them himself. It might seem paradoxical to say this of a writer who quotes Ennius alone more than fifty times. Yet the many hundreds of archaic quotations that fill the pages of the *Saturnalia* are seldom, perhaps never, the result of his own reading of original texts (Ch. 7 and 16). They are mostly copied in the form of preexisting lists from earlier monographs, the general nature if not the specific identity of the source being recognizable by such telltale traces as alphabetical sequence of titles or anti-Vergilian polemic where it is out of place in Macrobius's own context. For all his pleas in favor of the old writers, there is no indication that Macrobius himself ever read or even consulted (say) an original text of Ennius's *Annales*, a play of Accius, a speech of Cato, or even, more remarkably, given his professed enthusiasm for the minutiae of pagan cult practice, a text of Varro (Ch. 16. 12).

For the middle of the fourth century, we have fairly precise evidence for Rome. The greatest scholar of the age, Jerome, recorded in his *Chronicle* that in the year 353 his own teacher Donatus and the rhetor Marius Victorinus were flourishing at Rome. Donatus undoubtedly played a part in the Latin revival, though his precise role is hard to pin down. He wrote three enormously influential works: an *Ars grammatica*, and massive commentaries on Vergil and Terence. Most later grammarians wrote commentaries on Donatus's *Ars*, and all later writers on Vergil and Terence pillaged his two commentaries. The surviving Vergil commentary of Servius derives almost all its erudition from Donatus. Donatus's commentary is lost, but can to some extent be reconstructed from the additional notes preserved in the fuller, Daniel version of Servius, known as DS (Ch. 16). But there are two important respects in which Servius's commentary differs from Donatus's.

First, Servius omitted many of the older and more obscure quotations he found in Donatus; second, he added a considerable number of new quotations, mainly from the post-Augustans, but also from Horace. It was not just to make room for the

---

41. Kroll 1891, 26–29.

new quotations that the old ones were dropped. To give some specific illustrations, Servius never quotes Naevius, whereas there are nine quotations in the DS scholia (essentially Donatus) together with another five in Donatus's Terence commentary.[42] At least twenty-five other Republican authors quoted in the DS scholia are never quoted at all by Servius, or quoted in abbreviated form, often dropping the title or book number supplied by Donatus. Some writers he quotes occasionally he seems to have had no real firsthand knowledge of. For example, he cites Catullus six times, but in every case the citation is so misleading as to suggest that he never actually had a text of Catullus in his hands.[43] Of the twelve DS quotations from Nigidius Figulus, Servius has only one.[44]

To some extent the explanation is no doubt, as Lloyd put it, that Servius "seems obviously a school edition while DS appears to be the remnant of a more comprehensive work...designed for the use of scholars."[45] Certainly Servius has a mass of elementary grammatical notes conspicuous by their absence from the more or less contemporary scholia on Juvenal and Statius, who were not school texts.[46] It is easy to see why a grammarian might have felt that citations of Republican historians and discursive notes on pontifical minutiae were not suited to his more elementary purposes. But Servius did more than just drop certain topics and illustrations.

The point is neatly illustrated by Lloyd's comparison of the Plautus quotations in Servius and the additional DS scholia. Not only do DS have seventy-three more than Servius; the Servius quotations are in general much shorter, and only eleven out of forty-seven identify the play quoted from, whereas forty-five of the seventy-three additional DS quotations identify the play. More striking still, out of the twenty-nine Servius quotations from surviving plays, fifteen are so free that the passages are sometimes difficult to identify. By contrast, of the sixty-one DS quotations from surviving plays, only seven are at all free, though nowhere near as free as the Servius quotations. As Lloyd saw, it is most unlikely that scribal competence or incompetence could be responsible for so systematic a variation, especially since Servius's Terence quotations, by contrast, are both more frequent and more extensive than DS (137 as against 85) and in general surprisingly accurate. It is hard to resist the conclusion that Servius had a much closer firsthand knowledge of Terence than of Plautus. Though aware that Plautus was important enough to be quoted nearly fifty times, he reduced the length of the quotations he found in Donatus, dropped the play titles, and did not bother to check the actual text of his quotations against a text of Plautus. The greater accuracy of his Terence quotations suggests that he did check them against a text. We find the

---

42. Rowell 1957, 113–19; W. Strzelecki, *Cn. Naevii...* (Leipzig 1964), xii–xvii; Jocelyn 1965, 143.
43. Lloyd 1961, 291–341 (the basic study); Goold 1970, 136–38.
44. Lloyd 1961, 299–302, 307, pointing out that Sisenna is quoted by Nonius more often than all other Republican historians combined, presumably for his extreme archaizing.
45. Lloyd 1961, 323; Goold 1970, 135.
46. It may be that Donatus's commentary had less of this elementary material; the DS addenda are no help here, since there was always enough in Servius.

same difference in the treatment of Ennius. All the longer quotations and all the quotations ascribed to specific books occur in DS.[47]

The difference between DS and Servius is striking throughout the entire range of Republican quotations, prose and verse. Of the sixteen Republican historians quoted in DS, Servius quotes from only two, Cato and Sisenna.[48] Obviously, Servius's omissions are eloquent proof of the second and final rejection of archaic literature. But does their inclusion in Donatus prove that they were still being read up till ca. 350? Almost certainly not—at any rate not in complete texts, as opposed to brief quotations in the commentators. It is not likely that so drastic and widespread a shift in taste should all have come about in the half-century between Donatus and Servius.

Many of the omitted quotations are not intrinsically difficult or advanced, nor are the many quotations from imperial poets that Servius added intrinsically easy. Naevius and Ennius are now subjects for graduate seminars while undergraduates read Lucan and Juvenal, but this is because Lucan and Juvenal have survived complete while Naevius and Ennius exist in barely intelligible fragments. For second-century students they were just texts like any others, quoted for a detail of information or Latinity.[49] We find exactly the same double process in the later Horace scholia. Pseudo-Acro dropped almost all the citations of Republican writers he found in Porphyrio and substituted references to Juvenal, Lucan, and (above all) Vergil. Porphyrio never quotes Juvenal or Statius, and Lucan only twice.[50] On balance, it is hard to doubt that the omission of Republican and addition of imperial quotations represents a genuine and important change of taste.

For the period ca. 390 we have the evidence of Ammianus that Juvenal was felt to be a popular but decadent taste. In a famous passage he poured scorn on idle aristocrats who "hated learning like poison" and devoted their leisure to the scandalous biographies of Marius Maximus—and Juvenal (xxviii. 4. 14). Juvenal is the only imperial Latin poet Macrobius himself quotes, once only, and it may be significant that the quotation is put in the mouth of the boorish Euangelus just when he is about to commit the unforgivable crime of accusing Vergil of ignorance (*Sat.* iii. 10. 2).

Just as most of Servius's quotations come from Donatus, so most of Donatus's come from his predecessors. One case we can pin down is his note on *Buc.* vii. 33, which cites Varro and the *Megalenses* of the Republican dramatist Atta to illustrate the word *sinum*. The apparently pre-Donatan *Scholia Veronensia* cite both passages as coming from the commentary of the early third-century Asper.[51] Archaizers like Fronto and Gellius may have relished Atta, but scarcely Donatus and his contemporaries. We may infer with some confidence that the greater part of the archaic

---

47. Lloyd 1961, 314–22. Skutsch 1985, 40–41.
48. Lloyd 1961, 299–302.
49. Beginning Latin students today pay more attention to history and culture and less to grammar and syntax than their equivalents a century ago, but that does not in itself make the classes either more or less advanced.
50. For the authors cited by Porphyrio, Diederich 1999, 317–34.
51. Asper (p. 574) also quoted passages from Cicero and Plautus not included in DS; Donatus was no doubt selective, as any commentator coming late in a tradition has to be.

illustrative matter we now read in DS and Servius was originally collected and incorporated into the exegetical tradition in the age of Asper. Thereafter, it simply maintained its place in successive Vergilian commentaries until Servius took the final step of expelling all but the most basic items. The clearest illustration is provided by the now well-documented culture of Donatus's most famous pupil. As we have already seen, Jerome had virtually no active knowledge of archaic Roman poetry.

Horace was little read after the mid-second century, mentioned only once by Gellius and twice by Macrobius. Servius quotes him 251 times, compared with only 20 citation in the DS scholia.[52] The few DS citations probably reflect the exegetical tradition Donatus was reproducing rather than his personal taste, since his student Jerome cites Horace 65 times.[53] In Servius we find the full range of Silver Latin poets: not only Persius (34 quotations) and Lucan (119), but Statius (63), Juvenal (74), and occasionally Martial (4). There can be no serious doubt that the greater part of these quotations from the Silver Age poets was added by Servius himself. There are no such quotations in the DS additions in Servius, nor in Donatus's *Ars*, nor in the abridged and interpolated version we have of his Terence commentary. We may compare the probably sixth-century *Scholia Bembina* on Terence, substantially based on Donatus's commentary on Terence, and Cledonius's commentary on one of Donatus's *Artes*; both contain numerous quotations from Lucan, Statius, and Juvenal, which they certainly did not find in Donatus (whose *Ars* at least is extant in its original form). Another nice illustration of the change of emphasis in Servius is the way he closes his *Life* of Vergil, in other respects virtually identical to Donatus's, by comparing the beginning of the *Aeneid* (*arma virumque*) with the opening lines of the epics of Lucan (*Bella per Emathios*) and Statius (*Fraternas acies*); and for the title *Aeneis* he quotes the form *Theseis* from Juvenal i. 2.

The difference can be clearly appreciated in a comparison of successive treatments of the same point. In his *Ars* (*GL* IV. 378), Donatus discusses and illustrates the two genitive plurals of *domus*: *domorum* and *domuum*. In his Vergil commentary (*Aen.* ii. 445), Servius included Juvenal 3. 72 (*viscera magnarum domuum*), as do the later grammarians Pompeius (*GL* V. 192), Cledonius (*GL* V. 47), and Priscian (*GL* II. 309), whereas the pre-Servian Diomedes (*GL* I. 307), like Donatus, does not.[54] In the well-known section on literary genres in Bk III of Diomedes's *Ars grammatica*, the chapter on satire cites only Lucilius, Horace, and Persius (*GL* I. 485). It has been much debated whether or not Diomedes took this section from Suetonius,[55] but it is remarkable that he did not see fit to add Juvenal, whatever his source offered. Similarly, the chapter on elegy cites only Propertius, Tibullus, and Gallus, not Ovid.

---

52. Lo Monaco 1995, 1203–24; Geymonat 1998, 30–39.
53. Hagendahl 1958, 281–83.
54. The fact that the extant commentary on Donatus's *Ars* that passes under the name of Servius does not quote it proves nothing either way, since by common consent it is a substantially abridged version of the original Servian commentary: *GL* IV. 434; Holz 1981, 227–29.
55. Schmidt in Herzog and Schmidt 5 § 524.

In his *Apologia* against Rufinus Jerome lists the commentaries on classical authors, which he imagines Rufinus read as a boy (they had at some point been schoolfellows): Asper on Vergil and Sallust, Vulcatius on Cicero's speeches and Victorinus on his dialogues, Donatus on Terence and Vergil, and others unspecified on Plautus, Lucretius, Horace, Persius, and Lucan. The list is full enough to suggest that it is virtually complete. The implication is that they had read Persius and Lucan at school but not Juvenal and Statius. Persius and Lucan are indeed the only post-Augustan poets Jerome seems to have known at all well. Persius he quotes more than twenty times, Lucan seven times;[56] Senecan tragedies twice;[57] and Statius not at all.

Lucan is the only post-Augustan quoted in the extant Donatus Terence commentary (on *Eun.* 348). That Lucan was perhaps the only post-Augustan poet Donatus knew is suggested by Servius's note on *Aen.* xii. 365, *ac velut Edoni Boreae...*:

> It should be noted that Donatus was mistaken to write *Edonii* here, with short *dŏ*, following Lucan i. 675, *Edonis Ogygio decurrit plena Lyaeo*. For it is certain that Lucan shortened the syllable.... Statius, following both Vergil and the rules, has *tristius Edonas hiemes Hebrumque nivalem* (*Theb.* v. 78), not *Edonias*.

The situation is a good deal more complex than this slipshod note reveals. To start with, Servius has egregiously misquoted the line of Statius (in fact *dulcius Edonas hiemes Arctonque prementem*), and all surviving MSS of Statius read *Edonias* rather than *Edonas*. But for Claudian's imitation in *Cons. Stil.* i. 123 (*Edonas hiemes*), the true reading might have remained in doubt. We may also wonder whether Donatus really proposed emending Vergil on the basis of Lucan.[58] Nonetheless, Servius's note makes little sense unless Donatus's note had quoted Lucan but not Statius. We have already seen that the fifth-century Pseudo-Acro Horace scholia add hundreds of references to Juvenal missing from the earlier Porphyrio scholia, in the case of the *Odes* at least far less relevant than the many citations of Republican writers they drop.

It is not surprising that Persius and Lucan, who both wrote early enough to win the commendation of Quintilian, should have been acknowledged by the grammarians before Juvenal and Statius. But we need not suppose that Juvenal and Statius were actually "rediscovered" later. Seneca's tragedies seem to have been the last of the major Silver Age poems to come back into favor. Apart from one or two uncertain echoes in Ausonius,[59] and a fair number in Claudian and Prudentius, Jerome twice echoes the *Troades* and Augustine quotes a line each from *Phaedra* and *Troades*.[60] The unwary

---

56. Hagendahl 1958, 284; Hagendahl argued that he only read Lucan in old age, on the grounds that four quotations come in works written between 408 and 414 and a fifth in 394/5. But since then a further echo has been spotted in a letter dating from ca 374 (*Ep.* 1. 3 ~ Luc. 1. 24–26); R. Godel, *MH* 21 (1964), 68.

57. *V. Malchi* 9 ~ *Tro.* 510–11; *Adv. Iov.* 2. 6 ~ *Tro.* 371–72; Schmidt 1972, 47–48.

58. The second hand in the Medicean (s. V) offers *Edonios*.

59. See Green's edition (1991), 252, 365, 372, 375.

60. Hagendahl 1967, 476–77; Schmidt 1978, 43–58; Zwierlein 1984, 46–57; for Prudentius, Palmer 1989, 188–93.

have been misled by a quotation from the *Oedipus* in a Renaissance manuscript into thinking that Servius (or Donatus) quoted Seneca at least once.[61] But the manuscript in question contains Servius enhanced with additions by learned Renaissance readers, often texts not otherwise cited by Servius.[62] The fact that Servius did not after all draw on Seneca in his Vergil commentary proves little in itself. Not being in hexameters, Senecan tragedy did not provide such suitable illustrative material as Lucan and Statius. But a number of the metrical illustrations in Servius's *Centimeter* reveal considerable familiarity with Senecan tragedy.[63] The later grammarians likewise quote Seneca only occasionally.[64] As Schmidt has suggested, these highly rhetorical works were surely read in the school of the rhetor rather than the grammarian.[65] A long passage from the *Thyestes* is quoted in the probably fifth-century scholia on Statius,[66] not (as we shall see) a work in the grammatical tradition.

It was perhaps Persius's very difficulty as much as his moral and literary qualities that won him a place in the classroom, since he was equipped with a commentary before Juvenal ever put pen to paper. Charisius, writing after Donatus but before Servius, quotes Persius four times—but not the other three. The one surviving Charisius manuscript seems to quote *Lucan(us)* once for the form *dii* instead of *die* or *diei* (i. 126K = 161. 8 Barwick). But since Lucan is nowhere else quoted in Charisius and in any case does not use this form, Wessner was surely right to suppose a mistaken expansion of *Luc*(ilius) or *Luc*(retius). The *HA* quotes Persius by name[67]—not that many will be disposed to believe that the emperor Alexander Severus really whispered *in sanctis quid facit aurum* (*Pers.* ii. 69) when refusing to make gold offerings in temples. Lucan is quoted as early as the end of the third century by Sacerdos and the metrical writer Aphthonius, and then again by Diomedes,[68] who wrote between Charisius and Servius; none of the three quote Statius or Juvenal. The Christian poet Faltonia Betitia Proba seems to have known Lucan well.[69]

A recent survey by Neil Adkin allows only four definite Juvenalian reminiscences in Jerome, none in early works.[70] If a writer with Jerome's taste for satire and invective had read Juvenal properly at an early age, we should certainly have expected to find more frequent and obvious traces than this. By contrast, he was intimately acquainted

---

61. *Oed.* 1057, DS on *Aen.* xii. 395; Zwierlein 1983, 36.
62. Paris. lat. 7965, with Thilo, i (1881), xci–xciii ("Itali e libris a Servio neglectis exempla petiverunt"); I am grateful to Charles Murgia for pointing this out to me.
63. Zwierlein 1983, 36. No direct quotations, because the metrical illustrations in this work (*GLK* iv. 456–67) are all invented: Schanz iv. 1 (1914), 176.
64. Ps. Probus, *GLK* iii. 224. 22; 246. 19; Priscian, *GLK* ii. 253. 7–9. Diomede's two metrical citations (*GLK* i. 511. 23; 517. 30) derive from an earlier source.
65. Schmidt 1978, 46; cf. Quint. 10. 1. 129, *multae in eo claraeque sententiae*; Ennodius recalls reading Seneca *adulescentiae meae…temporibus, Pro Syn.* 38, p. 54. 15 Vogel.
66. *Schol. Stat. Theb.* iv. 530, p. 230 Jahnke.
67. *Alex. Sev.* 44.9.
68. Vincesi 1979, 3–4.
69. Green 1997, 554, 556.
70. Adkin 1994, 69–72.

with the satires of Horace and Persius. There is a very obvious contrast here with the invectives of Claudian, studded with Juvenalian echoes, imitations, and devices.[71] We may conclude with some confidence that Jerome did not read Juvenal at school and never really made good the omission in later years.

Augustine's knowledge of the post-Augustans reveals the same bias. His favorite was Lucan, whom he quotes more than twenty times, though apparently not before ca. 400. Next comes Persius, quoted ten times from 387 on. Juvenal is represented by one extract of eight lines quoted (presumably direct from a text) in a letter "unusually rich in classical elements" (*Epp.* 138. 16), and two allusions in the *City of God* (i. 2; ii. 23), all late works (411/12 and 413). Statius he does not quote at all, but one line each from Seneca's *Phaedra* and *Troades*.[72] The only post-Augustan poet Ambrose seems to know is Lucan, one clear allusion to the very beginning of the *Pharsalia*.[73]

Sulpicius Severus provides an interesting minor contrast. His main debt, not surprisingly given his historical interests, is to the historians, not only Sallust but also Tacitus, whom he knew well.[74] Among the poets, in addition to Terence and Vergil, he quotes Ovid, Statius, and perhaps Juvenal.[75] The Statius quotation is particularly telling. St. Martin liked to eat fish at Easter, but one Easter none was available. Martin bade his deacon go down to the river and try his net. At the first cast he caught a huge pike, which he brought back to the monastery rejoicing, like Hercules "when he brought home to applauding Argos the captive boar."[76] This is no secondhand quotation. The man who could produce a line that so brilliantly evoked both the pride of the deacon and the amazement of his fellow monks clearly knew his Statius intimately—and at firsthand. Yet even so, aware that (given his subject matter) some readers might disapprove of such showiness, Sulpicius at once apologized, identifying his quotation offhandedly as "some poet or other" and adding in parenthesis "a learned quotation since I am talking to learned men."[77] When describing in his *Chronicle* how the waters of the flood subsided he neatly quotes a phrase from the flood in Ovid's *Metamorphoses*.[78] It may be significant that he was educated in Bordeaux, where the examples of Ausonius and Paulinus of Nola suggest that the poets of the Silver Age were studied more thoroughly than elsewhere.

For Symmachus we may return to Kroll's findings: a fair number of verbal echoes of Ovid; one or two of Lucan; more surprisingly, a couple of Silius; and more than twenty parallels with Statius, from both *Silvae* and *Thebaid*.[79] No more than a half-dozen strike me as actual reminiscences, but the others certainly bear witness to a general familiarity with the idiom. There is one apparent echo of Juvenal, perhaps not

---

71. Long 1996, 321–35.
72. Hagendahl 1967, 476–77; O'Donnell 1980, 159.
73. *Ep.* vi. 14 ~ Luc. i. 1–3; Sister Charles, *Greece and Rome* 15 (1968), 191.
74. For Sallust, Fontaine 1975, 355–92; for Tacitus, van Andel 1976, 40–48.
75. van Andel 1976, 25; Stancliffe 1983, 60–61, 84.
76. *Dial.* iii. 10. 4, quoting *Theb.* viii. 751.
77. *nimirum ut dixit poeta nescio quis—utimur enim versu scholastico quia inter scholasticos fabulamur.*
78. *Chron.* i. 3. 4 ~ *Met.* i. 346; *longae pacis malo* in *Chron.* i. 24. 4 may recall *longae pacis mala* in Juv. vi. 292.
79. For knowledge of Silius, see p. 512.

to be pressed (p. 537). Of prose writers, apart from many echoes of Cicero and Sallust, the two chief school texts, the one book he certainly owned, read, and constantly turned to, revealingly enough his major source for Republican history, was the *Facta et dicta memorabilia* of Valerius Maximus.[80] More surprisingly, in view of the celebrated Symmachan "edition" (Ch. 14), very few signs that he had read Livy; certainly no preoccupation. It might be added that Christians turned to Valerius Maximus just as enthusiastically as pagans when in search of the appropriate historical example or anecdote. It will be enough to refer to Lactantius and Sulpicius Severus.[81]

Symmachus's literary culture turns out to be thoroughly conventional, neither reactionary nor progressive. While cultivating verbal archaisms, he had no real knowledge of the Republican poets; some knowledge of the post-Augustans, but by no means one of those (in Ammianus's phrase) "who devote all their attention to reading Juvenal and Marius Maximus." Like Ammianus himself, Symmachus may have read some Juvenal, but he no doubt agreed that he was a vulgar taste of the trendy. As for Macrobius, though hardly the authentic archaizer he pretends to be, he was enough of a conservative to resist the vogue for the post-Augustans. As we saw, he puts his one quotation from Juvenal in the mouth of the boorish Evangelus (*Sat.* iii. 10. 2), and shows no knowledge of any other post-Augustan poet. In the pages of Macrobius, Servius is represented as afraid that people now find Ennius contemptible "amid the more polished elegance of our own age" (i. 4. 17). This "more polished elegance" is the style of Pliny and Statius, Lucan and Juvenal. That is to say, Macrobius, unreconstructed archaizer that he was, disapproved of the revival of Silver Age literature.

At one time it seemed obvious that Symmachus's nine books of private and one of public correspondence were modeled on the correspondence of Pliny,[82] but after listing every parallel he could, Kroll rightly concluded that even collectively there was no proof of any real familiarity. There is another way of reaching the same conclusion. Nothing could be less like the richly descriptive and anecdotal letters of Pliny than the brief notes of Symmachus, seldom consisting of more than a salutation or commendation, skilfully tailored to the addressee.[83] If only Symmachus had given us Plinian portraits of Praetextatus or Flavian or Petronius Probus—or even Ambrose. Furthermore, Symmachus's letters were not originally published in the form in which we now have them (Ch. 10. 3). Symmachus himself probably published Bk i, Bks ii–vii were published after his death by his son Memmius, and Bks viii–x and the *Relationes* several decades later. Book x is in any case a somewhat uncertain quantity. All that survives is two letters, to the elder Theodosius and Gratian, and a heading of doubtful authenticity (p. 367). If Symmachus himself and Memmius published only Bks i–vii between them, there is nothing to suggest that either knew of Pliny's ten-book correspondence.

---

80. Kroll 1892, 82–88; 55–58 for the post-Augustan poets.
81. Klotz 1942, 29–32; Ogilvie 1978, 43–46; for Severus, Stancliffe 1983, 60–61.
82. So I argued myself in Cameron 1965, 295–96.
83. Callu 1 (1972), 22–25; Marcone 1988, 144–46.

The earliest example of a correspondence published on the Plinian model, revealingly enough, is that of a Christian bishop, Ambrose, as revealed in the Vienna Corpus edition of Ambrose's Letters begun by Otto Faller and completed by Michaela Zelzer. It seems clear that Ambrose himself selected and arranged his letters for publication shortly before his death, probably ca. 395.[84] The first nine books are hardly private letters, being mainly concerned with biblical exegesis, but they are addressed to private citizens, while Bk 10 consists of letters addressed to emperors and concerning public affairs. Not only letters, but documents such as his oration on the death of Theodosius. There is little evidence that Ambrose really knew Pliny's letters, but he must have been familiar with the layout of the ten-book collection.

Nearly a century later Sidonius too published his letters in nine books, and there are many close verbal echoes of Pliny scattered throughout. Indeed, so detailed are many of these reminiscences that some at least must surely have been either introduced or at any rate made more pointed during the editorial process, which we know Sidonius himself supervised.[85] To return to the fourth century, Ausonius must have known Pliny, because he quotes Pliny as precedent for his own erotic verse, evidently alluding to *Ep.* 4. 14. 4.[86] Jerome undoubtedly derives some anecdotes from Pliny.[87] Tempting as it might seem to suppose that Symmachus saw himself as the Pliny of his age, the truth is that Pliny was more to the taste of Jerome and Ambrose.

Tacitus found few readers in late antiquity. The claim in his *HA* biography that the emperor Tacitus (275–76) had ten new copies of his famous "ancestor" made every year and placed in libraries (*Tac.* 10. 3), though often taken seriously as the first sign of a Tacitean revival, is no more than a silly joke (p. 755). Pagans and Christians alike found the period of the empire less appealing than the Republic, whether for its virtues and victories (pagans) or its disasters (Christians). Kroll found a half-dozen fairly convincing echoes of both *Histories* and *Annals* in Symmachus. And Aurelius Victor seems to have known the early books of the *Annals* well.[88] That the *HA* preferred Suetonius was only to be expected, though it is a little surprising to find outright polemic against Tacitus, explicitly disavowed as a model.[89] No doubt such passages are not to be taken seriously, but even so there is clearly no sense, in a source often held to be the incarnation of pagan senatorial

84. See the prefaces to their edition in *CSEL* 82. 1 (1968); 2 (1990); 3 (1982); 4 (1996); in addition, Zelzer 1977, 351–62; Savon 1995, 3–17; and Barnes 2001, 357–61.
85. Stevens 1933, 61–64; Harries 1994, 7–10.
86. Auson. *Nupt. Cent.* p. 139. 4 Green.
87. Cameron 1965, 289–98; Jones, *Phoenix* 21 (1967), 301; Hagendahl 1974, 226–27; Trisoglio 1973, 343–83.
88. Kroll 1891, 95–97; Bird 1984, 95.
89. *Prob.* ii. 7; *Aurel.* ii. 2, in both passages bracketed with Livy, Sallust, and Trogus: Syme 1991, 358–71; 451–58.

traditions, that Tacitus was regarded as a significant representative of classical (much less specifically pagan) values. From Tertullian to Orosius and Sulpicius Severus, it was Christians who read Tacitus for his subject matter, Nero's persecutions in the *Annals*, and the Jewish war in the *Histories*. Sulpicius Severus in particular was strongly influenced by Tacitus's style as well.[90] No trace of the historical works in Augustine, whose historical interests lay in the Republic, but he does quote the final sentence of the *Dialogus* in an early work.[91] A passage of Jerome features prominently in every modern discussion of the scope of Tacitus's major works, his remark that "Cornelius Tacitus wrote the lives of the emperors in thirty books from Augustus to the death of Domitian."[92]

4

It is instructive to turn from Servius's commentary on Vergil to the scholia on Juvenal and Statius. Servius's goal was twofold: to introduce his students to the greatest, most perfect, and (above all) most learned of all poets; and to teach them to write good Latin. It was not easy to do both at the same time, not least because Vergil's Latin is often eccentric and irregular. Inevitably, literary criticism receives pretty short shrift. The Juvenal and Statius scholia are very different, in two main respects. First, they contain almost none of the elementary grammatical notes that dominate Servius's commentary; clearly Juvenal and Statius were not school authors. Both commentators evidently felt that they could take basic philological competence for granted. Second, neither commentary is learned in the way Servius is. This is partly because the interpreter of Juvenal and Statius was not faced with the problem of doing justice to several centuries of monographs and commentaries by predecessors. And partly because of the form that exegetical tradition had taken, with its emphasis on Vergil's learning, in its turn a defensive reaction to the earlier polemic against his supposed "thefts" and "mistakes" (Ch. 16).

Unencumbered by either predecessors or a learned exegetical tradition, commentators on the post-Augustans could simply provide what they thought would help the average reader. These two offer in fact much the same as their modern counterparts: the Juvenal scholia attempt to identify names and explain *realien*; the Statius scholia quote literary models (especially Vergil and Lucan) and comment on plot and myth.

---

90. See van Andel 1976, 40–48; Barnes 1977, 341–45.

91. Aug. *Contra Acad.* iii. 3. 6 (p. 38. 76 Green) ~ Tac. *Dial.* 42. 3. Many other literary dialogues close with similar formulas, but only Tacitus uses exactly the same words as Augustine (A. Gudeman, *Tacitus Dialogus*[2] [1914], 510).

92. *In Zach.* 14. 1–2.

Juvenal is an interesting test case. We shall see in the following chapter that there is no evidence for or probability in the widespread assumption that Juvenal was "rediscovered" by Servius and "edited" by his pupil Niceus. Servius did not do anything so dramatic as "rediscover" Juvenal—or Lucan or Statius. The revival of interest in Juvenal was in full swing by the time he set up school ca. 380. What he does deserve the credit for is being realistic enough to face up to the change of taste and illustrate Vergil by authors people were actually reading instead of a series of fragments transferred from one commentary to another over the centuries. The modern scholar naturally regrets the substitution of surviving authors who imitated Vergil for quotations from his sources that are otherwise lost.[93] But one of the factors that contributed to Servius's success was surely that his commentary more faithfully reflected the living culture of late antiquity.

The changes in literary taste that characterized the fourth-century West did not all occur at one time or in one place. In Gaul, it seems, people were reading virtually the whole corpus of Silver Latin poetry by the middle of the century. In Rome they had hardly started by then, though the teaching of Donatus and his colleague Victorinus (whose specialty was Cicero) had at any rate shifted the balance away from archaic and toward classical writers. It was left to Servius, at the beginning of the fifth century, to complete the process in both directions by adding the new and eliminating much of the old.

This revival of the whole range of early imperial Latin poetry is a central feature of western elite culture at this time. Among other things, it helps to explain the enormous and instant success of Claudian. More so than any other representative of the late fourth-century poetic revival, Claudian could replicate the whole range of early imperial poetry. He catches to perfection every trick of style, point, and word order that are so characteristic of Lucan and Statius, and his savage invectives have more than a touch of Juvenal's spirit as well as his language and manner.

It is not enough, with modern literary histories, to emphasize Claudian's remarkable talent. It is just as important that he came at exactly the right moment. A century earlier literary circles would not have been ready for a new Statius or a new Juvenal. In 395 they were. Educated westerners in 395 were able to appreciate Claudian as connoisseurs. Many a passage depends for its very comprehension on the reader appreciating the neat adaptation of a phrase of Lucan, Statius, or Juvenal. The fact that his immediate audience was the Christian court at Milan rather than some paganizing salon in Rome merely underlines the power and universality of the Silver Age revival. Symmachus attended Stilicho's consular inauguration at Milan in January 400, and it is hard to believe he was not present for the recitation of Claudian's panegyric. His surprising failure even to mention Claudian suggests that he did not find these modern re-creations of the classics much to his taste.

---

93. For Servius's contemporaries this material was still available in Asper and Donatus.

The fame of Claudian leads us to another intriguing aspect of late antique literature: the overtaking of prose by poetry. Poetry began to colonize areas formerly thought the province of prose. One minor illustration is the use of classicizing verse for public dedications. The tomb of the great Christian plutocrat S. Petronius Probus was adorned with two classicizing elegiac poems totalling forty-eight lines—incidentally a nice illustration of the fact that this development was a universal taste, not limited to pagans. An even more (literally) conspicuous illustration is the many epigrams Pope Damasus wrote for inscription on tombs of martyrs throughout Rome. Their literary quality is low, but they are at any rate full of Vergilian echoes (Damasus's sole venture into hexameter invective has already been discussed in Ch. 8).

5

This change in taste was real and important. If by some chance the empire had not survived the third-century crisis, if something like the Dark Ages we know had descended around A.D. 250, then we might well have had many works of Cato, Ennius, and other archaic writers now lost, but few or no works of Lucan, Statius, Juvenal, and other Silver Age writers that we now possess. Imagine Renaissance drama without the tragedies of Seneca, or modern historiography of the Roman Empire without the younger Pliny or Tacitus. But the empire did survive its political crisis, and Cato and Ennius were decisively ousted by Lucan and Juvenal, Pliny and Tacitus.

Despite the fact that the fourth century saw the triumph of Christianity and the rapid decline of paganism, there is no real evidence in either literature or art that classical was identified with pagan, or that any specific classical texts, whether archaic or post-Augustan, were valued or exploited by pagans for their religious content. Many have succumbed to the temptation to read religious goals into Macrobius's championing of archaic literature, but not only is it far from certain that he was a pagan, it was the undoubtedly pagan Servius who played a key role in the final dethronement of archaic writers from the school curriculum. It may be (as suggested earlier) that Macrobius was indirectly attacking Servius, but if so, this polemic clearly had nothing to do with Christianity. As for the eclipse of archaic by post-Augustan writers, that too had nothing to do with the success of Christianity or the failure of paganism. The earliest fourth-century readers of the Silver Age poets were all Christians (Lactantius, Iuvencus, Ausonius).

Not the least interesting aspect of the Silver Age revival is that it ran alongside of and in no way counter to the growth of a specifically Christian literature in the fourth century. Much of Juvenal attacks the vices of pagan Rome, and Statius's *Thebaid* was considerably less pagan than the *Aeneid*. Lucan repudiated the traditional Olympian framework for his epic, and (as C. S. Lewis famously pointed out) the deities who people Statius's poems are abstract personifications rather than the old Olympians.

The tendency was carried much further in Claudian.[94] The potent medieval figure of Natura came directly from Statius and Claudian.[95] It is hard to imagine Prudentius's *Psychomachia* without Statius's *Thebaid*. Ultimately, the fourth-century revival was important because it was the literary tastes of the fourth (rather than the second) century that were passed on to the Christian Middle Ages and so to the modern world.

---

94. *The Allegory of Love* (Oxford 1936), 75–76.
95. Economou 1972, 42–50.

CORRECTORS AND CRITICS I

1: INTRODUCTION

The "editing" of classical texts has long been identified as one of the principal ways the pagan aristocracy of Rome tried to maintain and promote the old order.[1] Actually "editing" is altogether too grand a word for the very modest activity involved. At the end of certain works (or individual sections or books within those works) some manuscripts preserve subscriptions, notes stating that some person with impressive sounding titles has "emended," "reviewed," or "checked" the text at such and such a time and place. Some of these subscribers are familiar names, and it is clear that many were members of the elite of their day. For Christian texts we have a handful of originals, some signed, most unsigned. For classical texts we have only two indisputably original sets (in the Puteanus of Livy's third decade and the Fronto palimpsest, both fifth-century); and one late antique copy (the Medicean Vergil). Most, inevitably, are medieval or even renaissance copies.

There is as yet no comprehensive inventory of these subscriptions, and this very lack has played no small part in modern misinterpretations.[2] For example, the fact that Otto Jahn (quite understandably) restricted his famous collection of 1851 to classical texts has given rise to a widespread assumption that subscriptions are only (or mainly) found in classical texts, and manifest a new concern to preserve such texts. There are in fact a great many exactly parallel subscriptions in Christian texts, far more indeed than those collected by Reifferscheid as a supplement to Jahn in 1873. More late antique subscriptions survive in the various works of Augustine (some original) than any classical text.

There are also a great many anonymous subscriptions, deliberately omitted by both Jahn and Zetzel (1981), who limited themselves to those that included proper names. Both omitted (e.g.) the only original secular subscriptions that can be directly tied to interventions in the text by the subscriber's handwriting (those in the fifth-century Puteanus of Livy).[3] There are also a number of similar subscriptions in Greek

---

1. I make no attempt to list even a selection of the modern works in which this is stated as established fact.
2. Jahn 1851; Reifferscheid 1873; Büchner in Hunger 1961; Zetzel 1981, 211–31; 1980, 38–59; Petitmengin 1983, 365–74; Pecere 1986; 1990 (both illustrated): unpublished typescript by R. W. Hunt. The material in Hedrick 2000, chapter 6 draws on an earlier version of my research but with his own interpretation. I have done my best to integrate Greek with Latin, Christian with pagan, manuscript evidence with literary texts, and (above all) to trace a social and historical development.
3. There are several different hands in the Fronto palimpsest, and the subscription in the Medicean Vergil is a copy.

texts, both secular and Christian. These too have never been systematically collected. Though laying no claim to completeness, this and the two following chapters cite more than twice the number of subscriptions included in any published list (interpreting the term to include any note preserved in a manuscript relating to the production or circulation of late antique texts). The additional material suggests a rather different interpretation of their function, more modest but in its own way no less important.

Extravagant claims have been and continue to be made for these subscriptions. I single out five assumptions in particular, every one mistaken: that most of the subscribers were (1) pagans and (2) Roman aristocrats; (3) that the subscribers chose texts that both reflected and were intended to spread their pagan sympathies; (4) that they were consciously preserving precious pagan texts in danger of being lost; and finally (5) that they were performing some sort of serious editorial activity. Thus the standard account by Bloch:[4]

> And yet, while their fight for the ancient religion ended in failure, they gained on another front a victory which has made their names immortal: they rescued the works of the great Latin authors out of the darkness into which they had fallen during the anarchy of the third century, copied and emended them in the fashion inherited from the great scholars of Alexandria and so prepared editions which were improved texts, and which were to form the starting point for the mediaeval tradition of these authors. Without the assiduous activity of these men, much of Latin literature that has come down to us would have been irretrievably lost.... This is the historical achievement of the pagan revival at the end of the fourth century.

So too, more quaintly, W. M. Lindsay:[5] "The younger scions of aristocratic houses, as soon as they had completed their studies at the University, tried their "prentice hands" on new editions of these dethroned kings of literature." In its outlines (the classics as a bulwark against the rising tide of Christianity, illustrated by Macrobius's *Saturnalia*), the idea goes back to Jahn.[6]

The classics were certainly the staple of late antique culture. But quite apart from the simplistic assumption that classical culture was more enthusiastically pursued by pagans than Christians, the Bloch interpretation rests on three further fallacies, worth stating briefly before we consider individual subscriptions in detail. First, the very

---

4. Bloch 1945, 240–41; for the first four points, Pecere 1986 and Cavallo 1977, 93–96; for the fifth, Dain 1975, 119–21. The account in Reynolds and Wilson³ 1991, 39–43, plays down their earlier emphasis on "pagan revival," though continues to employ the question-begging term "recension." For an extreme recent example, Lançon 1995, 197–99.

5. Lindsay 1903, 1; likewise Wattenbach 1896, 324.

6. "Ein Hauptbollwerk...war die Litteratur, in welcher die Kraft der heidnischen Auffassung und Cultur wurzelte...," Jahn 1851, 365; but no trace in the earlier study of Lersch 1845, 229–74.

idea of identifying love of literature with textual scholarship. It is only a minority in any age that has ever seen any virtue in "improving the text" of the classics—and they have usually been depreciated as tasteless pedants by the lovers of literature. Pope's ridicule of Bentley springs to mind. We have already seen that it is a radical misunderstanding of Macrobius's *Saturnalia* to suppose that his aristocratic interlocutors are meant to be scholars rather than cultivated amateurs. It was a gentleman (Euangelus) who put down the one professional scholar in the company (Servius) with a contemptuous "professor" (*grammatice*).[7] There is not the slightest sign that Symmachus (e.g.) was interested in scholarship rather than literature.

Second, while it is true enough that the fourth century saw a revival of interest in a number of authors neglected or rejected in the second and third centuries, this revival began in the age of the Tetrarchs and was largely complete by the middle of the century (Ch. 11). Yet the earliest datable late antique subscriptions (Apuleius and Livy) fall in 395 and 401, and the great majority much later. On chronological grounds alone there is no basis for linking the supposed "revision" the subscriptions document with the rediscovery of forgotten texts. And while the idea that texts became corrupt during a long period of neglect might seem attractive, the reverse is actually more likely. If fourth- and fifth-century readers were having copies made from second-century exemplars that had been gathering dust in family libraries, the quality of their text is likely to have been higher without the chain of gradually deteriorating copies that might otherwise have intervened.[8] It should be emphasized that the numerous late antique commentators on such texts never refer to recent editions or editors.

Third, subscriptions in manuscripts are simply the wrong place to look for scholarship. The sort of late antique books that survived the Dark Ages to be read and copied in the Carolingian Age were not scholarly editions, but large-format (often square or almost square)[9] sturdily bound, often illustrated volumes carefully copied in beautiful, legible script on high-quality parchment—expensive books, coffee-table books, not the sort of texts that have ever been known for their scholarly credentials. The reason they survived the centuries that did not read them is that they were durable objects of beauty, preserved for their appearance and value rather than content.[10] A very few such books have survived to the present day, and the fact that most subscriptions name members of the elite is enough to show that the lost books they attest were of the same nature. Scholarly readers who collated manuscripts certainly still existed (most of them Christian, as we shall see), but we should not expect to find any trace of their work in the luxury books of the age.

---

7. Macr. *Sat.* ii. 2. 12.
8. Corruptions generated by an unfamiliar script are another matter (p. 500).
9. For a sample list of the measurements of surviving examples, Cavallo, 1997, 206–9.
10. In addition, the original text could be (and often was) washed off and the parchment reused for a new book.

2: GREEK SUBSCRIPTIONS

Not counting the middle Byzantine Lucian subscriptions discussed later, nor the thousands of original scribal colophons in Byzantine manuscripts, late antique subscriptions in Greek fall into three main groups:[11] those to scholia on classical texts, those to texts of the Greek Bible, and those to mathematical texts. First those to scholia.[12] At the end of most books in the tenth-century Venetus A of the Iliad, for example: "in the margins, Aristonicus's *Critical Signs*, Didymus's *On the Aristarchan Recension*, extracts from Herodian's *Iliac Prosody* and Nicanor's *On Homeric punctuation*." That is to say, these four books were the source of the marginal scholia in this manuscript. At the end of Aristophanes's *Clouds* in the eleventh-century Venetus (and a few later manuscripts): "colometry from Heliodorus; marginal notes from Phaeinus and Symmachus and some others."[13] In the tenth-century Laurentianus of Apollonius of Rhodes: "scholia from Lucillus of Tarrha, Sophocleios and Theon"; at the end of the *Orestes* in two Euripides manuscripts "<copied> from various exemplars; scholia from the commentary of Dionysius in its entirety and various extracts"; another at the end of the *Medea* adds "extracts from Didymus."[14]

Like most of their Latin counterparts, these subscriptions are not original. It is unlikely that all these works by the first- and second-century scholars they name survived intact into the tenth or eleventh century to be directly consulted by Byzantine copyists. There can be little doubt that in most if not all cases these subscriptions were copied from late antique exemplars. Clearly those responsible for the late antique exemplars were themselves scholars who had taken care to identify the sources they at least had directly consulted when compiling the scholia with which they enriched their texts.

As for biblical texts, a series of sixth- or seventh-century subscriptions in biblical manuscripts, both Greek and Syriac, quote an earlier series of subscriptions to various books of the Septuagint prepared ca. 300 by Pamphilus of Caesarea and his disciples Antoninus and Eusebius the church historian. Most specify that the text was copied from the Hexapla or Tetrapla of Origen and "corrected" by Pamphilus and his collaborators.[15] Origen's two great works, which included (at least) four different versions of the Greek Bible, were never published, but kept for consultation in Pamphilus's library in Caesarea, where Jerome consulted them a century later. Just like the Latin subscribers, Pamphilus and his collaborators worked in pairs, one collating while the other corrected. To cite just one example, from II Ezra in the Codex Sinaiticus: "copied from and corrected against the Hexapla of Origen; Antoninus collated, I Pamphilus corrected."[16]

---

11. Vogel and Gardthausen 1909; with Cutler 1981, 328–34.
12. For a brief account, Cavallo 1992, 98–104.
13. K. J. Dover, *Aristophanes Clouds* (Oxford 1968), cxi–cxii; and *Frogs* (Oxford 1993), 95–96.
14. Zuntz 1965, 272–74.
15. For full details, Mercati 1941, 1–48; Devréesse 1954, 123–24; Jenkins 1991, 261–77.
16. μετελήμφθη καὶ διωρθώθη πρὸς τὰ Ἑξαπλᾶ Ὠριγένους· Ἀντωνῖνος ἀντέβαλεν, Πάμφιλος διόρθωσα.

For the New Testament, another batch of sixth- and seventh-century subscriptions (in Greek, Syriac, and Armenian) to various books refer to a copy "in the library of Caesarea in the hand of Pamphilus."[17] No subscription is mentioned this time, but how else was Pamphilus's hand identified after two centuries?

Lastly, author subscriptions to mathematical works. First, a note appended to the heading of Bk 3 of Theon's commentary on Ptolemy's *Almagest*: "commentary (*hypomnema*) of Theon of Alexandria on Bk 3 of Ptolemy's *Mathematical Syntaxis*, edition revised (*ekdoseōs paranagnōstheisēs*) by my daughter Hypatia the philosopher." Exactly parallel are three explicits to commentaries by the sixth-century Eutocius on Archimedes: "commentary by Eutocius of Ascalon on Bk 1 of Archimedes *On the Sphere and Cylinder*, edition revised by Isidore of Miletus the engineer, my teacher."[18] Though deriving from the author, these notes are found in only one manuscript and were apparently not thought of as forming an integral part of the title. Earlier editors and critics assumed that the reference was to the (subsequent) revision of these commentaries by Hypatia and Isidore, respectively. In fact, a distinction is being drawn between the commentary, the unaided work of the author, and the text he was explaining, which had been revised for him by a collaborator. This is put beyond doubt by the subscriptions to Bks 1 and 2 of Theon: "commentary of Theon . . . with his own edition." There are similar notes to all four books of Eutocius's commentary on Apollonius of Perga's *Conic Sections* ("in his own edition," *tēs kat'auton ekdoseōs*). But Hypatia and Isidore are not being acknowledged for simply proofreading the text for errors. Revision of mathematical texts involved correcting or simplifying or even adding to the author's proofs and modernizing his terminology.[19]

Nonetheless, the purpose of the subscriptions was still basically the same as in the other two groups: to state the authority of the text being offered the reader. The same applies to the very few other late antique Greek subscriptions we know of. The ninth-century chronicler Syncellus claims to have consulted a "very accurate, well accented and punctuated" copy of the Bible from Caesarea in Cappadocia that carried a similar subscription by St. Basil. Basil's subscription had evidently specified the source against which his copy had been made and collated, unfortunately not repeated by Syncellus.[20] This too was surely more than just Basil's personal text. It is natural to assume that (like Victor of Capua's New Testament, discussed below) it was intended to serve as a master copy for members of his flock who wanted an accurate Bible.[21]

The only other late antique Greek subscriptions known to me derive, like those of Pamphilus and his colleagues, from Caesarea in Palestine. First one to an eleventh-century Vienna manuscript of Philo: "Bishop Euzoïus had new copies made in

---

17. Zuntz 1945, 15–16; Devréesse 1954, 159–68.

18. The other two are identical in the relevant respects; for all details, see Cameron 1990, 103–27.

19. Heath 1926, 46–63.

20. Βασίλειος . . . ἀντιβαλὼν διωρθώσατο, Syncellus p. 382 Dind. = 240. 12 Moss.

21. It may have incorporated the chapter divisions Basil planned to introduce: Vaganay and Amphoux 1991, 112.

codexes,"[22] strikingly borne out by the near-contemporary evidence of Jerome: Euzoïus (bishop of Caesarea from ca. 367–79) "with much labor attempted to restore (*instaurare*) the dilapidated library of Origen and Pamphilus on parchment (*membranis*)."[23] Jerome's *instaurare* clearly reflects the imprecise ἀνενεώσατο used in place of the standard "copied," "collated," or "corrected." It seems that Euzoïus sponsored (whence the middle *aneneōsato*, "had new copies made") the recopying not just of Philo, but of other texts he found in damaged or illegible papyrus rolls. This may explain the imprecise and impersonal character of the subscription. In the Vienna manuscript its four words are written at right angles to each other in the form of a cross.[24]

In all probability this device was affixed to all works recopied under Euzoïus's initiative. It must have been while working in the library that Jerome came across the subscription, no doubt in a number of different books, to judge from his claim that Euzoïus attempted to restore the entire library. Given the ambitious nature of the project, no more than replacement of the damaged rolls can have been envisaged; nor, given his own episcopal responsibilities, can Euzoïus have done much of the actual work himself. The fact that Pamphilus's subscriptions were reproduced and his hand identified as late as the seventh century suggests that his copies were already parchment codexes.

Caesarea seems to be the only place where the process of replacing papyrus rolls that must have been taking place all over the Graeco-Roman world can be documented and even to some extent dated.[25] A speech of Themistius from January 357 refers to a team of copyists established by Constantius II to make new copies of texts "crumbling through long neglect,"[26] and a rescript of 372 recommends the appointment of skilled Greek and Latin scribes to copy and repair manuscripts.[27] Both texts refer to the library of Constantinople, apparently founded by Constantius.[28] Neither mentions rolls, but the new copies must have been codexes.

Particularly noteworthy is the subscription "copied from and collated against an exemplar from among Origen's own books" between Bks i and ii of Origen's *Against Celsus* in a thirteenth-century manuscript.[29] For the identical subscription has now turned up in the same place on a seventh-century papyrus.[30] More than a century ago P. Koetschau suggested that the original of this subscription derived from an edition by

22. Εὐζόϊος ἐπίσκοπος ἐν σωματίοις ἀνενεώσατο, Cod. Vind. theol. gr. 29, with Runia 1993.
23. Jer. *De vir. ill.* 113; according to *Ep.* 34. 1 (if not interpolated) Euzoius's predecessor Acacius began the recopying. Euzoius's σωματίοις does not in itself imply parchment codexes, but Jerome had handled the actual books.
24. See the photos in Runia 1996, 480–81, figs. 1–2.
25. On the importance of Caesarea in the history of the Christian book, Grafton and Williams 2006.
26. Themistius, *Or.* iv. 59d–60c, of 1 January 357 (reading μικρᾶς in l. 5); Cavallo 1986, 90.
27. *Cod. Theod.* xiv. 9. 2. Olymp. fr. 32 M = 1. 31 B may refer to the repair of old papyrus rolls: Lewis 1974, 65n.
28. Paschoud, *Zosime* 2. 1 (1979), 99; Vanderspoel 1995, 99 n. 132.
29. Koetschau 1889, 33–38, 66–67; Borret 1967, 23–24.
30. μετεβλήθη καὶ ἀντεβλήθη ἐξ ἀντιγράφων [ου pap.] τῶν αὐτοῦ Ὠριγένους βιβλίων, Borret 1967, 34–42.

Eusebius or Pamphilus.[31] "Edition" is hardly the right word if the copy in question was made from Origen's personal copy, but it may have been one of the many books of Origen Pamphilus is said to have copied in his own hand.[32] On the other hand, it might equally have been some other reader who consulted Origen's papers in Caesarea.

Whoever it was, his purpose was evidently to claim a uniquely authoritative text. We may compare two in a series of original marginalia in the so-called Palatine Anthology of 930/40, based on the slightly earlier Anthology of Constantine Cephalas (ca. 900):[33] "collated up to this point against the copy of the Lord Michael," and "thus far the epigrams of the late Lord Michael, which he copied in his own hand from the book of Cephalas."[34] The writer had collated his copy against a text that had itself been copied directly from Cephalas's autograph. Obviously, his purpose in supplying these details was to underline the authority of his copy.

There is an interesting parallel of a sort from a much earlier date among the Herculaneum papyri. The subscription to a copy of Bk 28 of Epicurus's *On Nature* notes "<from> old <copies>," and then (after a few missing words), "written [or copied] under <the archonship of> the Nikias <who held office> after Antiphanes."[35] The care taken to distinguish Nikias archon in 296/5 B.C. from two later archons of the same name (282/1 and 266/5), not to mention the fact that the word *archon* is omitted, put it beyond reasonable doubt that the exemplar of the Herculaneum copy was made and dated in Athens itself—and later than at any rate 282/1. In short, a copy dating from the lifetime of Epicurus himself.[36]

The only Latin subscription to cite authoritative sources in this way is also the only one that antedates the late fourth century. It attests a revision (*emendavi*) of Cicero *De lege agraria* ii by the second-century Statilius Maximus "according to Tiro, Laecanianus, Domitius and three other old <scholars>."[37] Statilius was a professional scholar, author of a work *On rare words in Cicero*, cited twenty times by the fourth-century grammarian Charisius.[38] His revision purports to be based on the texts of six earlier scholars, and his subscription also correctly dates the speech in question (to 63 B.C.) and assigns it a number (XXIV), apparently from some scholar's chronological list of Cicero's speeches.[39] He may actually have cited individual readings by the earlier scholars he names, in

---

31. Koetschau 1889, 66–67; accepted by Borret 1967, 43.
32. Jerome, *De vir. ill.* 75.
33. Palatinus graecus 23 + Parisinus suppl. graecus 384; Cameron 1993, 99–159 (here 111).
34. ἕως ὧδε ἀντεβλήθη (on *AP* vii. 428); ἕως ὧδε τὰ τοῦ κυροῦ Μιχαὴλ (on *AP* vii. 432).
35. [ἐκ] τῶν ἀρχαίων … ἐγ[γ]άφη ἐπὶ Νικίου τοῦ μ[ε]τὰ Ἀν[τι]φάτην, Cavallo 1983, 59. I am grateful to Steve Tracy for up-to-date information on Athenian archons.
36. Perhaps the date Epicurus (†270) wrote the book in question, though none of the dozen or so other rolls containing books of *On Nature* carry dates or subscriptions.
37. *Statilius Maximus rursum emendavi ad Tironem et Laecanianum et Dom(itium) et alios veteres III*: Zetzel 1973, 225–43; Pecere 1982, 73 123; Martin 1984, 145–54.
38. *De singularibus apud Ciceronem* (Charisius 252. 16 Barwick); the fragments are cited and discussed in detail by Zetzel 1974, 107–23 (with some reservations by Timpanaro 1986, 197–209).
39. The number should perhaps be XXVIII in the complete dated sequence: Zetzel 1973, 229.

the manner of a small number of Greek papyri with marginal variants ascribed by name to critics such as Theon, Apion, Aristonicus, and Nicanor.[40] For example, scholia in the first-century Louvre Alcman papyrus refer to readings by Aristophanes, Pamphilus, and Aristarchus; a marginal note in a slightly earlier Alcman papyrus records that the poem was "written in the margin (*paragegraphetai*) in exemplars of Bk 5 as well; in that book it is bracketed (*periegegrapto*) in Aristonicus's exemplar, but not in Ptolemaeus's."[41] If Grenfell and Hunt were right to identify a marginal abbreviation in a second-century Homer papyrus as *hai archaiai*, that would nicely parallel Statilius's collective *veteres* designating the three unnamed early critics.[42] Galen repeatedly refers to readings in "old copies" unspecified, and the Epicurus subscription from Herculaneum refers to "old <copies>."[43] For the combination of named and unnamed authorities we may compare the subscription already cited to Aristophanes's *Clouds*: "colometry from Heliodorus; marginal notes from Phaeinus and Symmachus and some others." "Others" (*alloi, alii*) to refer to alternative views or readings is standard in commentaries and marginal notes from the Hellenistic period on.

The later secular subscriptions in Latin manuscripts are more concerned with stating the credentials of the subscriber than his text. It will be enough for the moment to cite just two characteristic examples, those to Livy 7 and Horace's *Epodes*: *Emendavi Nicomachus Flavianus v. c. ter praef(ectus) urbis apud Hennam*; and *Vettius Agorius Basilius Mavortius v. c. et inl(ustris), ex-com(es) dom(esticorum), ex-consul ordinarius legi et ut potui emendavi conferente mihi magistro Felice oratore urbis Romae*. We learn in detail what very important persons Flavian and Mavortius were, but nothing about the source of either their text or their corrections. There is an obvious contrast with most of the Greek subscriptions just listed, which identify the source copied or collated but do not name the subscriber at all.

Clearly Statilius was making much wider claims than Flavian and Mavortius. Not like them a gentleman certifying that his private copy had been duly corrected (with or without the aid of a professor), but a scholar who had sought out the six earliest copies of *De lege agraria* he could find, no doubt with a view to determining whether they supported the sort of rare (usually archaic) forms he was interested in. As the years passed there was an obvious danger that forms used by Cicero would be replaced by forms familiar to later copyists (to quote one of the examples Statilius himself discussed in his monograph, the adverb *rare* rather than *raro*, not attested in surviving

---

40. All earlier work is superseded by McNamee 2007.

41. *PMG* 1, Schol. A (p. 6 Page), with Turner 1987, 44; *PMG* 3 (p. 12 Page). Against a coronis in a first- or second-century papyrus of Simonides someone noted in the margin "not in the exemplar" (οὐκ ἦ(ν) ἐν τ(ῷ) ἀντιγ(ράφῳ), *PMG* 519, F 1 col. ii. 4–5, presumably another exemplar of his own, not the exemplar our papyrus was copied from.

42. P. Oxy. 445 iii; but McNamee 2007, 38, deciphers it as Ἀρ(ιστάρ)χ(ου), citing several similar abbreviations.

43. παλαιὰ ἀντίγραφα, Galen XVI. 474 and 751 Kühn and other passages quoted in H. Kühlewein, *Hippocrates* 1 (1894), xlvii. Eustathius also regularly uses the term οἱ παλαιοί, no doubt reflecting earlier practice: van der Valk 1963, 8 n. 31, 186–87, 603.

Ciceronian manuscripts). Whatever the authority of Statilius's witnesses or the quality of his judgment,[44] here was a scholar who collected variants and had criteria for distinguishing between them.

Not so his successors. We shall see that, for all their grandiose trimmings, the *emendatio* the late antique Latin subscriptions document seldom represents anything more than the routine correction to which any properly produced ancient book was subjected.[45]

3: SUBSCRIPTIONS BY OWNERS AND OTHER PRIVATE SUBSCRIPTIONS

Bloch sketched a picture of pagan aristocrats emending texts "in the fashion inherited from the great scholars of Alexandria." That was an extravagant notion, long abandoned by editors, though often still repeated by historians. Students of the text of Horace (e.g.) no longer talk about a "Mavortian recension."[46] Mavortius did no more than check his own text against its exemplar—and even this he did with the help of a professor. But even seemingly innocuous phrases like "improving the text" rest on the anachronistic assumption of a stable vulgate that individual ancient readers could improve by collation of manuscripts—and also imply an edition prepared for publication. Indeed, this view has been reasserted in two influential recent manuals that describe subscribers as producing "editions" that were "increasingly more correct and reliable," and go on to claim that "engagement in this first humanism was regarded as a fundamental duty of the intellectual and politician."[47]

The most extreme illustration of this approach is Hedrick's far-fetched reading of the letter of Valentinian III rehabilitating the elder Flavian, which begins as follows:

> to preserve against the pitfalls of mankind's lot the honor of men eminent and renowned in public life when it has been interrupted for a while (*interpolatum aliquatenus*), and to recall the memory of the departed to eternal fame, is a sort of correction of his fate (*emendatio quaedam eius sortis videtur*).

According to Hedrick, there is a metaphor "running through the letter" that "suggests an equivalence between the rehabilitation of Flavian and the correction (*emendatio*)

---

44. Whether or not any of his manuscripts were outright fakes (Zetzel 1973, 238–43; Jocelyn, *Gnomon* 60 [1988], 200), it is unlikely that they were as old as he thought; but provided he cited variants, his preference for archaisms need not have falsified the text.

45. According to Hedrick 197, "For Cameron, the practice of correcting manuscripts is ultimately to be regarded as culturally insignificant." On the contrary, I would maintain that chapters 12–14 reach more wide-ranging conclusions about the culture of copying texts and reading in late antiquity than the traditional view embraced by Hedrick.

46. To give the merest sample of the literature on this pseudo-subject, Pasquali 1952, 377; Brink 1971, 30–31; Cavarzere 1992, 47–49.

47. Conte 1994, 632, repeated in Graf 1997, 273.

of texts." This is alleged to allude to the supposed Nicomachan correction of the text of Livy (Ch. 14), and more generally to "elite interest in the correction of texts."[48] This approach presupposes (of course) that the corrections implied by these subscriptions represent something more scholarly than simple checking against exemplar, something that (Hedrick claims, without a scrap of evidence) brought the correctors respect and admiration. At the verbal level, his reading of the imperial letter rests on just two words, the juxtaposition of *interpolatum* and *emendatio*. But neither ancient nor even humanist critics ever used *interpolare* in the textual sense it has acquired in modern times[49] (not that this meaning, deliberate insertion of alien material, would make any metaphorical sense applied to *honorem*).[50] Here it undoubtedly bears the well-attested sense "interrupted"; his *honor* was withdrawn for thirty-seven years, and is now restored.[51] As for *emendatio*, "emendation" in the textual sense is but one specialized sense of a word that is far more often used in a variety of more general senses, here obviously "restoration."[52] Flavian's friend Symmachus, for example, uses *emendo* or *emendatio* twenty times, only twice of correcting a text,[53] the other eighteen times in a variety of other senses. Of these eighteen, not one offers even the possibility of an indirect allusion to correcting texts.[54]

The activity of the Latin subscriber is usually summed up in the word *emendavi*. But while English "emend" conjures up critical editions sparkling with the conjectures of a Bentley, Housman, or Shackleton Bailey, Latin *emendare* refers to the removal of *menda*, "faults," of many different sorts. Even in a literary context, the commonest sense is "polish," whether of an author's stylistic improvements to his own work, or revisions suggested by readers he has consulted before publication.[55] When applied to correcting manuscripts it *could* be used of a serious scholarly revision based on philo-logical research, but is far more often applied to the routine process of checking copy against exemplar. On the basis of a reference to collation in the Mavortius subscription, it has been widely assumed that subscribers collated manuscripts. The truth is that only two secular subscriptions mention more than one exemplar: those to Martianus

---

48. Hedrick 2000, 171–213.
49. *TLL* s.v.; Rizzo 1973, 287.
50. Hedrick's translation of *aliquatenus interpolatum* as "corrupted to some degree by interpolations" is nonsense at both the literal and metaphorical level. Later, more fancifully and even less plausibly, he claims that "the errors of the past are conceived as interpolations—matter that is not integral or original to the truth" (212).
51. *TLL* vii. 1. 15. 2244 B, *interruptio, temporaliter*.
52. For the various senses, see the entries *emendatio, emendo* and related terms in *TLL*.
53. Symm. *Ep.* i. 2. 1 and ix. 13. 1; for the list, Lomanto's Concordance, p. 239.
54. Hedrick cites Symm. *Rel.* 3. 6 as "an analogous use of this metaphor": *corrigit enim sequentem lapsus prioris et de reprehensione antecedentis exempli nascitur emendatio*. But this depends on his translation of *lapsus* as "slip" (= copying error), where in the context a far stronger word is required: "for a mistake on the part of a predecessor [Constantius's removal of the altar of Victory] is a lesson to the successor [Valentinian I], and censure of past error leads to its being corrected [the altar being replaced]" (Liebeschuetz and Hill 2005). No contemporary, whether Christian or pagan, could possibly have thought of replacing the altar of Victory as correcting a copying error.
55. As in the chapter on *emendatio* in Quintilian (x. 4); Delvigo 1990, 71–110; Rizzo 1973, 249–75, and passim.

Capella and the first decade of Livy. We shall see that in the overwhelming majority of cases, the corrector was simply collating his personal copy against the exemplar from which it had just been made. No research, no learning, no literary taste even was required. Just a careful comparison of copy and exemplar.

There is no evidence of any kind or date for Hedrick's assumption that subscribers "circulated their corrected manuscripts" and received "credit for the corrections." No surviving secular subscription implies a text destined for circulation (much less publication) rather than private use. Those who see scholarship behind every subscription seem not to have realized how many are purely personal notes of entirely private significance. It is time to consider individual cases.

First, three that seem to be nothing more than owners' signatures (the first two originals): *Ennodiorum*, written in rustic capitals on a blank page in a sixth-century Verona manuscript of Jerome's letters, implying ownership by some member of the great Gallic family of the Ennodii;[56] *Vettius Agorius Basilius*, in the sixth-century Puteanus of Prudentius (p. 307); and *Iuliani v.c.*, in the Puteanus of Statius.[57] We also find a couple of owner subscriptions on second-century papyri.[58] A much more elaborate form of owner's signature is to be found at the end of Bk ix in most manuscripts of Aulus Gellius: two elegiac couplets in which someone called C. Aurelius Romulus expresses his gratitude to "the noble Eustochius" for giving him a copy of Gellius; he wishes Eustochius long life for giving so dear a friend "such great things to teach."[59] Apparently, Romulus was a teacher with a rich friend. Another minor category comprises two notes that advertise the shop (*statio*) where the books in question were produced. While these make no direct mention of correcting, the names of the proprietors (Gaudiosus and Viliaric) were presumably enough to guarantee a properly corrected text (p. 438).

A larger category consists of notes incorporating apostrophes, heterogeneous, but best understood if grouped together. First the series of Gennadius subscriptions to successive books of Martial.[60] All fourteen books close with claims by a certain Torquatus Gennadius to have made corrections (*emendavi*). In addition, Bks 1, 7, 13, and 14 apostrophize *Quirine*, Bks 3 and 5 *Constantine*; Bks 2, 7, 8, 10, and 13 all say *lege* or *lege feliciter*; and 1, 3, 4, 7, 10, 12, 13, and 14 *floreas*. Assuming that Gennadius was a professor of rhetoric, Marrou thought he had corrected manuscripts for two pupils or collaborators.[61] Perhaps so, though I would emphasize the dedication rather than the correction. The verbs and vocatives are all paralleled on the dedication page of the

56. Verona XVII (15) (*CLA* iv. 489a) fol. 208ᵛ, a reference I owe to Marie Taylor Davis.
57. Zetzel 1981, 25.
58. ἐκ βιβλιοθή(κης) Πραξί(ου) Ἡρακλείδης ἀ (? πέγραψε), on the mime papyrus P. Lond. Lit. 97; and the genitive Σωσύου after the title of a grammatical work by Apollodorus on P. Mil. Vogl. i. 19 (Turner less plausibly saw a reference to the Roman "publishers" the Sosii).
59. *Cecropias noctes, doctorum exempla virorum, / donat habere mihi nobilis Eustochius. / Vivat et aeternum laetus bona tempora ducat, / qui sic dilecto tanta docenda dedit.* See P. K. Marshall, *Gellius* 1 (1968), viii.
60. For the texts, Lindsay's edition (1902), and Lindsay 1903, 3–4; Zetzel 1981, 211–13.
61. Marrou 1932, 105 = 1976, 68.

so-called Calendar of 354 (where there is no mention of correction): *Valentine floreas in deo, Valentine lege feliciter, Valentine vivas floreas, Valentine vivas gaudeas.*[62] Compare too *Romaniane vivat, Romaniane vivat* at the end of Bk i of the *Ad Herennium* in a Würzburg manuscript.[63] The third person in what is surely an apostrophe to a dedicatee is puzzling, perhaps to be corrected to *vivas*. Given the extreme rareness of the name, it is worth mentioning Marx's suggestion that the dedicatee might be Romanianus the friend and benefactor of Augustine.[64] Marx did not notice that Romanianus once asked to borrow Augustine's copy of Cicero's *De oratore.*[65] Augustine himself never cites the *Ad Herennium*, but he might nonetheless have owned a copy, and, of course, someone else might have given Romanianus his copy.

Romanianus ended his days as a Christian.[66] And the calendar was a work commissioned by or for a certain Valentinus, likewise a Christian (to judge from the Easter table and lists of popes and martyrs included), and executed by the calligrapher Filocalus, a friend of Pope Damasus, who signed his name on the same page (*Furius Dionysius Filocalus titulavit*). The Martial was surely likewise a calligraphic copy, prepared for Quirinus and Constantinus (perhaps brothers) and corrected by Gennadius, whether he was the donor or simply (like Victorianus in the Livy subscriptions) hired to correct the text. The most puzzling of the series is the subscription to Bk xiv, *cum tuis Gennadi vatibus Quirine floreas.* This can hardly be sound as it stands, but whatever we make of *vatibus*, the *cum tuis* is guaranteed by two other dedications. First a subscription to the *Breviarium* of Festus missed by Jahn and recently rediscovered by Michael Reeve: *lege Censorine cum liberis tuis propitio domino Christo semper;*[67] and an original subscription in a fifth-century manuscript of Priscillian: *lege Felix Amantia cum tuis in Christo Iesu domino nostro.*[68] The *cum tuis* presumably means "together with your family." The fact that Festus's *Breviarium* was a pagan work is obviously outweighed by the wish that Censorinus might read the book with the blessing of Christ (it is therefore unlikely that this is Symmachus's pagan friend Censorinus).

All these books were gifts, gifts presented to a family rather than an individual (*lege X cum tuis*). A nice contemporary parallel (except that we have no subscribed manuscript) is the copy of Titianus's *Fables* and the *Chronica* of Nepos that Ausonius sent Petronius Probus for the education of his children (*ad institutionem tuorum*).[69] There are several more dedicatory apostrophes in Christian texts: *lege Ianuariane feliciter in Christo* (*Letters* of Cyprian) and *tene in Christo felix Domitiana* (*Homilies* of Origen).[70]

---

62. See the reproduction of Barb. lat. 2154 f. 1 in Salzman 1990, fig. 1, facing p. 26.
63. Würzburg Mp. misc. f. 3 (s. IX); Zetzel 1981, 227.
64. Not listed in *PLRE* i–iii, and the only example in *PCBE* (i. 994–97) is Augustine's patron; see too Lepelley 1981, 178–82; F. Marx, *Incerti auctoris ad C. Herennium libri iv* (Leipzig 1894), 1–4, followed by Taylor 1993, 243–50.
65. Aug. *Ep.* 15. 1. Jerome knew the work (Marx 1894, 6–8).
66. At any rate a catechumen: *PCBE* i. 995–97.
67. In Bamb. E. III. 22 of Festus: Leitschuh 1895, 33; Reeve, *Gnomon* 69 (1997), 510.
68. Würzburg M. p. th. q. 3 (*CLA* ix. 1431; s. V); Bischoff 1990, 185.
69. Auson. *Ep.* XXVII. 9, p. 201 Green.
70. Cod. lat. Monac. f. 2ʳ (s. IX); St. Gallen 87, p. 125 (s. IX); both cited by Bischoff 1990, 185.

We may add two similar notes preserved in several manuscripts of Jerome's *Life of St. Hilarion*. After the title: *in sanctis orationibus tuis memento mei decus ac dignitas virginum nonna Asella*; and at the end of the prologue: *opto ut in Christo permaneas et memor in orationibus tuis sis mei, virgo sacratissima*, words of greeting Jerome himself wrote in the copy he gave his old friend Asella (p. 770). It was not uncommon for writers to add such personal messages in their own hand, normally introduced in copies by the formula "and in another hand" (*et alia manu*). Unless the writer kept a copy of such details in his files (as Augustine's secretaries apparently did)[71] or the recipient's copy chanced to become the ancestor of surviving manuscripts, they would be lost. Here is one of many examples from Augustine, appended to a letter to Pelagius: "and in another hand: remember us and be pleasing to the Lord in safety, dearest and most missed of brothers."[72] A subscription of almost twenty lines attests a gift of sorts: the presentation of a copy of Arator's verse paraphrase of Acts to Pope Vigilius in 544, together with a vivid account of its public recitation for days on end with constant interruptions for applause and encores.[73]

It was apparently subscriptions that included apostrophes that led Hedrick to his claim that subscribers circulated their work. But the majority of such subscriptions do not even mention correction. It is just a detail that Gennadius corrected as well as dedicated his Martial. Symmachus presented Ausonius with an uncorrected copy of Pliny, and there is no reference to correction in the Festus, Calendar, Priscillian, Cyprian, Origen or Arator subscriptions. Ausonius too says nothing about correcting Nepos or Titianus, though he does apologize for the slowness of his copyists. In all these cases the correction may simply have been taken for granted, most likely because, like the copying, it was done by a professional of low status not considered worth mentioning.

One of the most fulsome and self-promoting of extant subscriptions advertises the work of a copyist (*scripsi...manu mea*), Flavius Theodorus son of Dionysius, *vir devotus memorialis sacri scrinii epistolarum et adiutor vir magnifici quaestoris sacri palatii*. Confirmatory detail is supplied by a subscription in a Boethius manuscript: *contra codicem Renati v.s. correxi, qui confectus ab eo est Theodoro antiquario qui nunc palatinus est*.[74] The subscriber corrected his copy against a manuscript written by "Theodorus the copyist (*antiquarius*) who is now a civil servant." Theodorus evidently copied the Boethius while still a full-time professional copyist and the Priscian after acquiring his (very modest) position in the civil service. This may explain why it took him so long to complete his copy of Priscian: the

---

71. As shown by Dekkers 1952, 130.

72. *Ep.* 146; *Ep.* 205 to Consentius: (*et alia manu*) *Deo vivas, dilectissime fili*; *Ep.* 131 to Proba: (*et alia manu*) *Deus verus et verax veraciter consoletur cor tuum, et protegat salutem tuam, domina insignis et merito illustris ac praestantissima filia*; *Ep.* 176 to Pope Innocent: (*et alia manu*) *memor nostri, in Dei gratia augearis, domine beatissime meritoque venerabilis, et in Christo honorande sancte pater*; *Ep.* 201, Honorius to Augustine: (*et alia manu*) *Divinitas te per multos annos servet incolumem*; *Ep.* 95, to Paulinus and Therasia: (*et alia manu*) *memores nostri, felices vivite, magna gaudia et solatia nostra sancti Dei*.

73. The only reliable edition of this subscription (if that is what it should be called) is by Chatillon 1963, 71–78; for an English translation (of a less satisfactory text), Llewellyn 1970, 75–76.

74. Zetzel 1981, 220–21 for all the subscriptions relating to Theodorus.

subscription to Bk 1 dates from 1 October 526, to Bk 17 from 30 May 527. Priscian's panegyric on the emperor Anastasius may date from around 512, but his other works can be
assigned no more precise date than the early decades of the sixth century.[75] Thus Theodorus
may have been making his personal copy of a newly published work. And the fact that versions of his subscription in five different parts of the work survive in so many later manuscripts suggests that this was an authoritative copy (perhaps the authorized copy) from
which others were made. None of these subscriptions mention correction, but this may
simply have been taken for granted. In combination, the Boethius and Priscian subscriptions imply that Theodorus's handiwork was well known. In the case of a literary text we
might have identified him as a calligrapher, the sort of person who produced beautiful but
inaccurate copies like the Romanus of Vergil. But no one would want a calligraphic copy of
a grammatical textbook extending to more than a thousand pages. Theodorus's name was
presumably thought to guarantee accuracy as much as penmanship.

The subscriptions in manuscripts of Solinus likewise proclaim the work of a copyist, though this time the emperor Theodosius II (*studio et diligentia domni Theodosii
invictissimi principis* and variants). Hedrick repeatedly appeals to Theodosius as the
most compelling illustration of the social importance of "correcting" manuscripts
("the emperor himself…").[76] This is a serious misunderstanding of the evidence.
Theodosius did not (of course) spend his days correcting manuscripts. He was a *calligrapher*. This was his nickname in the Byzantine tradition. He is said to have claimed
that, when at the circus, he never lifted his eyes from his calligraphy to the actual
races.[77] The emperor may have done beautiful work and it was only to be expected that
his subscriptions would be preserved in later copies, but this eccentric hobby did not
for a moment purport to be scholarship. Indeed, since it is unlikely that anyone dared
to correct the imperial hand, it may have accompanied an unusually poor text. A calligrapher called Probus copied a text of Cornelius Nepos for Theodosius, equipping it
with a long poetic dedication to the emperor, and it is probably the same man who
copied two other texts (the Cento of Proba and the Map of Agrippa) for the imperial
calligrapher, again with long prefatory poems.[78] Neither mentions correcting his text.

More valuable from a palaeographical point of view is the dated and localized
original subscription by the humble Ursicinus, *lector* in the church of Verona and
copyist of a manuscript of Sulpicius Severus dated to 1 August 517. Evidently with his
own professional needs in mind, Ursicinus used a combination of spacing and
punctuation to facilitate reading aloud at sight.[79] Last, the two earliest-known original

---

75. For what is known of the chronology of Priscian, Kaster 1988, 346–47.
76. Zetzel 1981, 215; Hedrick 2000, 197, 198, 203, 206, 223.
77. Geo. Mon. *Chron.* p. 604. 8 de Boor (ὁ καὶ καλλιγράφος); Mich. Glykas, in *PG* 158. 489D; Aldhelm,
   p. 203 Ehwald; *ILS* 802; Jahn 1851, 342–43; Momigliano 1977, 152; Lippold, *RE* Suppbd 13 (1972), 130.
78. Quoted and studied in Cameron 2002, 121–30.
79. *Perscribtus codix hec* [with *Verona* written above the *hec*]…*sub die Kal. Aug. Agapito v.c. c. ind. decimae
   per Ursicinum lectorem ecclesiae Veronensis*; *CLA* iv (1957), 494; Parkes 1993, 16 and 166–67, with pl. 4.
   For another subscription by a copyist, Eutalius the *antiquarius*, p. 495.

subscriptions (both in third- or fourth-century palimpsests) are by copyists. First, an incipit to a fragment of Seneca's otherwise lost *Life of His Father*: *Incipit eiusdem Annaei Senecae de vita patris feliciter scribente Meniciano die et lo(co) s(upra) s(criptis)*,[80] implying a more detailed, dated subscription to another work of Seneca earlier in the same manuscript. Second, the briefest of all signed subscriptions, in the Gellius palimpsest: on the otherwise blank front page of a quinion, something like *Cott.a..scribsit*.[81]

Most of the subscriptions gathered in this section do not even mention correction, much less collation. As for those that do, we may divide the corrected texts behind them into different categories. In § 4 we shall be reviewing a batch of copies corrected by students and professors. These were undoubtedly all personal copies, and presumably new copies. Many other subscribers also make it clear that it was their own copies they were correcting. For example, "temptavi emendare/legi emendans *meum*" in the Sabinus subscriptions to Persius; "relegi *meum*" and "relegi *meum* contra codicem Renati" in a manuscript of the logical tracts of Boethius;[82] "emendabam vel distinguebam *meum*" in Symmachus's subscription to Macrobius; Rusticus the deacon three times uses the phrase *in meo* of manuscripts he owned.[83] Then there is "legi et distincxi codicem" (Asterius in the Medicean Vergil); "Donatus presbyter...proprium [= "my own"] codicem...legi" (Rufinus);[84] "Donatus...proprium codicem...legi" again, this time an original subscription in a Monte Cassino manuscript of Ambrosiaster dated to 569.[85] Finally, another original is Victor of Capua's *legi meum* at the end of James in the Fulda New Testament (546).[86] The constant repetition of *meum* and *proprium codicem* makes it clear that in every case the manuscript subscribed was a personal copy, not a text prepared for circulation, much less publication. It will be observed that there is no difference between the formulas used for pagan and Christian texts.

Particularly instructive are subscriptions by well-known writers to copies of their own works (none unfortunately original): *Severinus Boethius vir clarissimus inlustris ex consule ordinario patricius legi opusculum meum* (Bk ii of his *De arithmetica*);[87] and *recognovi Hieronimus Bethleem meum tractatum* (Jerome, *Adversus Helvidium*).[88] One of Ennodius's declamations is followed in the oldest manuscript (s. IX) by the words

---

80. *CLA* i. 69: Lowe 2 (1972), 514.

81. Vat. Pal. lat. 24, f. 173ᵛ/172, as hesitantly read by E. A. Lowe (*CLA* i. 74). Editors (and J. Fohlen, *Scrittura e civiltà* 3 [1979], 215) offer a confident COTTA SCRIBSIT, but the traces of the second word seemed very uncertain to Shane Butler and myself in May 1998, even under ultraviolet light.

82. For the evidence, Jahn 1851 and Zetzel 1981.

83. *ACO* II. iii. 1 (1935), p. 227. 15; 243. 19; 342. 7; for Rusticus, see further below.

84. Metensis 225 (s. X); on the basis of the subscription (dated to 561), Koetschau (*Origenes Werke* 5 [Leipzig 1913], lix–lxii) reconstructed a "Codex Lucullanus" as the archetype of all extant MSS of Rufinus's translation of Origen Περὶ ἀρχῶν, copied in the same *castellum Lucullanum* as his Ambrosiaster MS (next note).

85. Casin. 150, p. 248 (*CLA* iii. 374a); many corrections in the same hand as the subscription.

86. E. von Dobschütz, *Zeitschr. f. d. neut. Wiss.* 10 (1909), 91.

87. Stangl 1882, 10.

88. *regonnovi* MS (Verona XV: *CLA* iv. 486).

Ennodius emendavi meum deo meo iuvante; and one of his letters by a *legi* in all manuscripts.[89] There are also three other less specific author subscriptions to letters of Jerome: *cursim contulimus Bethlem* and *emendavi in Bethlehem* (both *Ep.* 49, in different manuscripts) and *recog(novi) Betheem* (*Ep.* 54).[90] Boethius employed a more recherché formula at the end of Bk iv of his commentary on Cicero's *Topica*: *conditor operis emendavi*, "I the author corrected," with *conditor operis emendavi II* (= a second time) at the end of Bk v.[91]

In almost all these cases there can be no question of the corrector collating more than one exemplar. In most, the authors were probably certifying an official exemplar from which others might make or check further copies, like the one indisputable surviving example, a subscription in the Bamberg MS of Cassiodorus's *Institutions*: "original copy, against whose text all other copies are to be corrected" (*codex archetypus ad cuius exemplaria sunt reliqui corrigendi*). Lorenzo Valla added in his own hand an exactly parallel subscription to a copy of his Latin translation of Thucydides: "checked…so that this codex may be the original of my translation against which other copies can be corrected" (*recognovi…ut esset hic codex me(a)e translationis archetypus, unde cetera possent exemplaria emendari*).[92] There are many other examples in the writings of the humanists, often (as in this case) the official copy, but sometimes just the author's autograph.[93] At Bk i. 4. 4 Cassiodorus refers to a codex of the Psalter "to which you may turn if you run into errors," later described as *archetypus*.[94] Hardly less interesting is the note "to be copied from this point" (*abhinc scribendum*) that survives in an eighth-century manuscript of Augustine's *Questions on the Heptateuch*, apparently descended from the copy marked up by Eugippius for his collection of excerpts from Augustine compiled between 492 and 496. The passage that follows is among Eugippius's excerpts.[95]

But being authors rather than editors, Jerome and Boethius might also have taken the opportunity of making a few final changes in style or substance as well as just eliminating transcriptional errors. The same surely applies to the author-subscription of a little treatise on the date of Easter (*De ratione Paschae et mensis*) by the obscure chronographer Hilarianus. After mentioning people who had tried to get hold of his

---

89. *Dictio* 21, p. 265. 18 Vogel (*meam* B, but the other examples strongly suggest that Ennodius wrote *meum*); *Ep.* 5. 16, p. 193. 6 Vogel (theoretically a later corrector, but in view of the other example surely Ennodius himself). On the publication of Ennodius's works, see Vogel pp. xxix–xxx.

90. See Hilberg's apparatus to *Ep.* 49 and 54, *CSEL* 54. 387; 485.

91. So Stangl 1882, 9, citing all the manuscripts.

92. Rizzo 1973, 312; Grafton 1997, 11.

93. Rizzo 1973, 308–17.

94. *ad quem recurratis si vos mendositas fortassis offenderit*; cf. i. 15. 12 (pp. 22. 3 and 49. 7 R. A. B. Mynors [ed.], Oxford 1937). According to Mynors (p. x), the Bamberg subscription "seems likely to date from a time when the work was already in wide circulation," but I would prefer to ascribe it to Cassiodorus himself.

95. Acutely identified long ago by the Benedictine editors: Gorman 1980, 103. The longest-surviving subscription (more than twenty lines), attesting correction (*ut potui emendavi*) by a notary of the church of Naples called Peter in 581, is found in a ninth-century Paris MS of Eugippius's excerpts (Par. B.N. late 11642, f. 224; Gorman, ib. 102).

book before it was finished, he announces that it is now *emendatum* and adds a dated colophon: *Quintus Iulius Hilarianus explicuit, emendavit die III nonarum Martiarum Caesario et Attico consulibus* (5 March 397).[96] On so controversial a subject it must have been anxiety about his argument rather than copying errors that caused Hilarianus to keep his readers waiting.

4: SUBSCRIPTIONS IN MANUSCRIPTS COPIED FOR FRIENDS

Another context in which we encounter the correction of manuscripts is in the fulfilment of commissions for friends. Here the prime example is the copy of Livy Symmachus had made for his friend Valerianus, with apologies for the delay caused by the need for "careful correction" (Ch. 14). But he also wrote to Ausonius apologizing for sending a copy of Pliny's *Natural History* uncorrected.[97] Sidonius in person made a copy of his Greek text of Philostratus's *Life of Apollonius* for one friend, sent another some Varro, and the *Chronicle* of Eusebius ("as requested"), and, like Symmachus, apologized to yet another for the inadequate correction of a copy of part of the Old Testament.[98] We have already seen that subscriptions incorporating apostrophes (the Gennadius Martial) may derive from presentation copies. It makes no sense to suppose that such copies were subjected to anything more than the minimum correction necessary to secure a readable text.

The presentation of books to friends was just one aspect of the circulation of books in the Roman world. It has often been claimed that Christians copied their books privately while pagans relied on the book trade.[99] Both sides of this antithesis have been exaggerated. On the one hand, the more elegant of the surviving early Christian books must have been copied professionally. On the other, there is little evidence that even in the first and second centuries serious pagan readers were able to obtain more than a fraction of their needs by walking into a bookshop.

At all times most people of whom we have any knowledge (that is to say, members of the elite) seem to have acquired new books through presentation from the writer.[100] Anyone who wanted his own books to circulate would send copies to friends and urge them to have further copies made for distribution. So prolific a writer as Galen claimed that he wrote only for friends and pupils, not to see his books circulate and be read by future generations; when he discovered they were circulating without his permission, he became more cautious about his friends.[101] Whatever we make of Galen's professed

---

96. Turin I.b. vi. 28 fol. 81[b] of s. VI–VII (*CLA* iv. 438); on Hilarianus's treatise, see now Lana 1995, 73–89.

97. *en tibi libellos, quorum mihi praesentanea copia fuit, Ep.* i. 24; evidently he did not have a complete Pliny.

98. Sidon. *Ep.* viii. 3. 1; viii. 6. 18; v. 15. 1.

99. Cavallo 1977, 119; Pecere 1986, 27.

100. Starr 1987, 213–23; Norman 1960, 122–26.

101. *De ordine librorum*, XIX. 49–50 K = 80 Mueller, with van Groningen 1963, 1–17; Hanson 1998, 22–53.

lack of literary ambition, we are surely bound to accept that he did not distribute his books through professional booksellers.

There is surprisingly little direct evidence for the book trade in late antiquity. It certainly existed. Sidonius compares the library in a friend's house to the "shelves of a scholar or the tiers of the Athenaeum or the piled cabinets of the booksellers."[102] That certainly implies that he had seen bookshops with well-stocked shelves. We know of two such "shops" (*stationes*) by name, that of Gaudiosus in Rome[103] and Viliaric (a Goth described as a master *antiquarius*) in Ravenna. Viliaric, who was active in the first half of the sixth century, is also known from a subscription to a Ravenna charter of 551 in Gothic.[104] Both produced deluxe volumes, Gaudiosus Bibles, Viliaric a famous Orosius. At the other end of the scale, Augustine had works copied at the "shop of Maiorinus" (*officina Maiorini*) in Thagaste.[105]

A hyperbolic passage of Sulpicius Severus describes how his *Life of Martin* was introduced to Roman society by Paulinus of Nola, to the delight of the *librarii* "because there was nothing they could sell at a greater profit, more quickly or for a higher price."[106] But by late antiquity both *librarius* and *bibliopola* are terms applied to both booksellers and copyists,[107] suggesting that there may often have been no clear-cut distinction. Especially in the larger cities, many professional copyists must have worked for both booksellers and private patrons. Viliaric was less a businessman than a master craftsman, who no doubt fulfilled the commissions of his most important customers in person. There will have been a steady request for Bibles and secular staples like Vergil and Sallust, but the sudden demand for a new bestseller like the *Life of Martin* was surely satisfied by privately employed or freelance copyists as well as by bookshops. It is unlikely that bookshops could begin to supply the specialized needs of a scholar like Jerome. One of his letters gives a friend a list of theological books he wanted copied, all of them (he implies) available in the library of their mutual friend Rufinus of Aquileia.[108] Protadius asked Symmachus for copies of Livy, Caesar's *Bellum Gallicum*, and Pliny's *Bella Germaniae*.[109]

None of these were books likely to be kept in stock by fourth-century booksellers, who could not even have produced copies to order without access to an exemplar.

102. *Ep.* ii. 9. 4; for the Athenaeum, p. 537n. 57.
103. Known from the subscription *de statione Gaudiosi librarii ad vincula S. Petri civitate Romana*, in Angers Bibl. Mun. 24 (s. IX), f. 125ᵛ: D. De Bruyne, *Rev. Bénéd.* 30 (1913), 343–45 (*Gaudii libri*, cod.).
104. *Confectus codex in statione magistri Viliaric antiquarii*, subscription to Orosius Bk v in Laur. 65. 1, fol. 144ᵛ (*CLA* iii. 298); "Wiljarith bokareis," pap. 34 in Tjäder 1982, 95–96, and in *Studia Gotica*, U. E. Hagberg [ed.] (Stockholm 1970), 144–64 (with photo of the subscription on p. 148).
105. Aug. *Ep.* 15. 1; *PCBE* i. 667 s.v. Maiorinus 2.
106. Sulp. Sev. *Dial.* i. 23; Marrou 1949, 212–14.
107. See the entries for both words in *TLL*; Sidonius's *mercennarius bibliopola* at *Ep.* ii. 8. 2 doubles as copyist, and note *scribam tuum sive bibliopolam* at *Ep.* ix. 7. 1.
108. *quaeso ut tibi Reticii…commentarios ad describendum largiatur* [Rufinus], and *quaeso ut eos libros… librarii manu in charta scribi iubeas* (*Ep.* 5. 2).
109. Symm. *Ep.* iv. 18. 5; iv. 36. 2.

Very instructive in this connection is a private letter from Oxyrhynchus dating from ca. A.D. 170. In a postscript the sender asks his addressee to have some books copied for him:[110]

> Make and send me copies of books 6 and 7 of the *Characters in Comedy* (Κωμῳδούμενοι) of Hypsicrates. For Harpocration says that they are among Polion's books. But it is likely that others, too, have got them. He also has prose epitomes of Thersagoras' work on the myths of tragedy.

Another hand (perhaps the addressee's) adds the information that "according to Harpocration, Demetrius the bookseller has got them," presumably meaning Hypsicrates and Thersagoras. There is no way of knowing whether Demetrius the bookseller simply happened to have the books in stock or Polion lent his copies to Demetrius to be copied. Booksellers must often have filled private commissions.

It might be argued that, when Sidonius describes how someone arrived in town with a bag of books by a famous writer and all the local book lovers made copies, this is a picture of provincial life in an age of decline. But take Symmachus's complaint that Ausonius did not send him a copy of his *Mosella*: "although you distribute your books generously (excepting only me, of course), I shall still enjoy your work— thanks to the kindness of others" (*Ep.* i. 14. 5). Symmachus is not complaining because he did not get a complimentary copy and had to buy one. The author's "distribution" was the only way the poem circulated at all. The "kindness of others" means that Symmachus had a copy made by someone who was on Ausonius's mailing list. And this in fourth-century Rome, not fifth-century Gaul. Augustine seems to have been surprised that, despite a passion for books, his friend Alypius refused to take advantage of the privilege when he could have had them copied for his own use at the special rates to which his position in the imperial service entitled him.[111] Once again, fourth-century Rome.

According to Cavallo, the normal method of publication for Christian books was for the writer to deposit a certified copy with a friend who was authorized to allow copies to be made.[112] This view is largely based on Marrou's interpretation of a letter of Augustine to a certain Firmus in Carthage. Augustine had sent Firmus a copy of his *City of God*, asking him to allow "those brothers in Carthage who do not yet have a copy to transcribe it." But the recent publication of another letter to Firmus has revealed this to be a misapprehension.[113] Firmus was a young friend Augustine was hoping to convert, and the invitation to encourage others to make copies was simply

---

110. P. Oxy. 2192; Turner and Parsons, *GMAW*[2] no. 68.
111. *Conf.* vi. 10. 16; the exact reference of the phrase *pretiis praetorianis* cannot be determined.
112. Cavallo 1977, 119.
113. Marrou 1949, 208–24. But see now *Ep.* 2* Divjak, with Eno 1989, 17–30; van Oort 1993, 417–23.

a standard request such as Ausonius or for that matter Pliny the Younger might have made. Christian writers may have been more anxious for their books to circulate because of the urgency of their message, but the practice itself was nothing new, much less an innovation of Christian communities.

At all periods people lent books for copying,[114] though owners will normally have been unwilling to part with rare or fragile texts (Symmachus's complete Livy, e.g.) or despatch them any distance. Particularly informative is a letter from the Athenian philosopher Longinus complaining to Porphyry about the quality of his copy of Plotinus, and asking Porphyry to send him accurate copies of two works in particular, which he would collate and then return. Longinus was surprised that Plotinus's pupil Amelius had not corrected the copyists' mistakes, remarking that Amelius must have had more urgent duties than "this sort of attention."[115] The same letter warns Porphyry not to expect anything from Longinus; copyists were in such short supply that Longinus's were having to spend all their time making his copy of Plotinus. Evidently, Amelius had sent a complete Plotinus to Athens for Longinus to have copied and then return. To be able to criticize it, Longinus must have collated the work of his own copyists against Amelius's copy, which he assumed that Amelius had previously collated against Plotinus's master copy.

Libanius and his fellow sophists at Antioch all maintained private copyists, as did prolific ecclesiastics like Augustine and Jerome.[116] Symmachus occasionally mentions the *librarii* who wrote or kept copies of his and his correspondents' letters.[117] But having a privately made copy of a literary text corrected adequately may have been more of a problem. A wealthy Spaniard called Lucinius sent six copyists to Bethlehem to copy the principal writings of Jerome. Jerome warned the man that, although he had frequently urged the scribes "to collate carefully and check" (*ut conferrent diligentius et emendarent*), he could not guarantee the accuracy of their work. It seems that Lucinius had not made provisions for a qualified person to oversee the correction of his copies. Longinus was interested enough in Plotinus's work to do the job himself. An aristocrat at leisure on his estates may sometimes have been willing (as Sidonius was on one occasion),[118] but Jerome (like Symmachus) made it clear that he was too busy.

---

114. For Cicero, Starr 1987, 217; Rawson 1985, 43–44; for Augustine, Keenan 1935, 79–81; for a seventh-century example, Braulio *Ep.* 25–26 (*PL* 80. 674–75).

115. Porph. *Vita Plotini* 19–20. For προσεδρεία = attention or assiduity, LSJ s.v. 2; Lampe, s.v. 5; Armstrong's "supervision" implies προεδρεία, which is never found in this sense. According to Porphyry, Amelius's copy was in fact remarkably accurate, and the problem was Longinus's inability to understand Plotinus.

116. Norman 1960, 122; de Ghellinck 1946, 215–26.

117. *Epp.* i. 24. 1; ii. 35. 1; v. 85. 2; v. 86. 1. Cicero had a number of literary slaves and freedmen in addition to his beloved Tiro, though little is known about exact functions and duties: Treggiari 1969, 148–49, 253–64.

118. Jer. *Ep.* 71. 5; 75. 4; Sidon. *Ep.* v. 15. 1.

5: SUBSCRIPTIONS IN NEWLY COPIED TEXTS

The feature common to all subscriptions collected in the two preceding section is that they involve newly made copies. Many others imply the same. Dracontius first copied and then corrected (*descripsi et emendavi*) his Pseudo-Quintilian (below). It was a new copy of Julius Paris that Rusticius Helpidius Domnulus emended (*emendavi descriptum Rabennae*). Renatus corrected a manuscript of Boethius "made" (*confectus*) by Theodorus, the copyist mentioned in subscriptions to Priscian quoted above. In his subscription to Macrobius's *Commentary*, Aurelius Memmius Symmachus claims to have punctuated as well as corrected his personal copy (*emendabam vel distinguebam meum*). Asterius too did both to his Vergil text (*legi et distincxi codicem*, and again in the accompanying poem, *distincxi emendans*). While *emendatio* can cover many different things (from the scholarship of Valerius Probus[119] to school exercises), *emendatio* and *distinctio* combined clearly imply a virgin text, unpunctuated and uncorrected, fresh from the copyist. So a high proportion of the surviving subscriptions attest the correction of newly copied texts.[120]

This suggests an explanation both simpler and more basic than scholars engaged in philological endeavor or collation of manuscripts. The systematic correction of newly copied texts had been standard practice from the Ptolemaic age, as we know from innumerable literary papyri corrected in different hands or different inks.[121] "These routine operations [as Kenney put it] should not be magnified into genuinely philological procedures."[122] The procedure itself was fairly mechanical. The corrector normally worked with an assistant reading the text of the exemplar out to him, while he simply corrected any divergencies in his own copy.

This is so obviously the best way to check any text against its exemplar[123] that it remained in use down to and indeed long after the invention of printing. According to the Frisian scholar Viglius Zuichemus, writing in 1534, unless printing houses "have a learned corrector of delicate taste, however elegant their types...yet they lose praise unless the corrector's care is apparent." Working under the corrector, he adds, is the reader; proofs must be collated against the exemplar, "and if it is to be done properly it requires two men's work."[124] The different skills required are nicely spelled out in Jerome Hornschuch's *Orthotypographia* (1608): the corrector "must get used to anticipating the reader by at least one word. For by doing this he will see what needs to be

---

119. Suet. *De gramm.* 24. 2, with Kaster's commentary (1995), 260–63.

120. So already Jahn 1851, 367–68; note too such authorities as Pasquali 1952, 366; and Bischoff 1990, 43.

121. Turner 1968, 93; 1987, 15–16; McNamee 1981, a wider study than the title implies.

122. E. J. Kenney, *Cambridge History of Classical Literature* 2 (Cambridge 1982), 18.

123. There are many examples of laws, treaties, and the like being read out publicly so that there should be no dispute about their contents. For example, the law that texts of the three Attic tragedians should be read out from an authorized text for actors to check the correctness of their own copies: for many examples, Cameron 1990.

124. Gerritsen 1991, 144–63.

corrected and make a note of it in the margin a little before the reader catches him up. It is then up to the reader if he sees that the corrector is being held up by a number of mistakes to read more slowly, or to stop for a minute."[125] A vivid letter of Petrarch describes how he corrected a new copy of his own *Bucolicum carmen* while the exemplar was read aloud to him by a slow reader whose poor delivery helped him to catch errors he might have missed with a more experienced reader.[126]

Only the Martianus subscription actually specifies that the assistant read the text out (*contra legente Deuterio*), but Sidonius uses exactly this formula of a professional hired to correct the work of his copyist.[127] Cassiodorus too describes correcting his Bible "with friends reading in front of me" (DI i. 8). According to the Horace subscription, Mavortius corrected his text "with Master Felix collating for me" (*conferente mihi magistro Felice*). Since Mavortius had the copy and Felix the exemplar, strictly speaking neither could have been collating by himself. In the context, "collate" must be shorthand for Felix's role in the joint process, namely reading aloud from the exemplar. We find exactly the same usage in three of the Septuagint subscriptions: "Eusebius corrected with Pamphilus collating," and (twice) "Antoninus collated, Pamphilus corrected." The reader was the junior partner in the process (in Renaissance printing houses readers were normally apprentice correctors),[128] but when the two were social and intellectual equals, like Pamphilus, Eusebius, and Antoninus, they may well have alternated roles. This may be why six of the other Septuagint subscriptions offer the undifferentiated pairs "Pamphilus and Eusebius corrected."[129]

Several other Latin subscriptions offer another variation. Aurelius Memmius Symmachus corrected his Macrobius "with (*cum*) Macrobius Plotinus Eudoxius"; Domitius Dracontius corrected Pseudo-Quintilian "with (*cum*) his brother Hierius"; and a series of eight subscriptions shows an unnamed person correcting the works of Cassian with the help of three different assistants (*cum Simplicio, cum Gaudentio, cum Maximo*).[130] In the tenth century, Alexander of Nicaea corrected his copy of Lucian "with" (*meta*) three different assistants (p. 472). The Asterius subscription in the Medicean Vergil is corrupt in the form in which we have it, but on both the likely reconstructions Asterius is acknowledging the help of his "brother" Macharius, a man of much lower status than himself.[131] Since it is always the first named who claims to have done the actual correcting, the "with" must imply that the other read out the

---

125. Quotation translated by Grafton 1998, a characteristically learned and illuminating study.

126. *Fam.* 22. 2. 8; Rizzo 1973, 246. On "collation à deux" see too Petitmengin and Flusin 1984.

127. *nec semper illo **contra legente** qui promiserat operam suam* (*Ep.* v. 15. 1).

128. Devréesse 1954, 123–24, nos. 3, 4, 8; Grafton 1998, 63.

129. Devréesse 1954, 123–24, nos. 5, 9, 10b, 11 (διωρθώσαντο), 6, 7 (διωρθώσαμεν).

130. *emendavi in monasterio Silvaniano cum Simplicio*, at the end of *Inst.* i, ii, iii; *contuli cum Gaudentio in monasterio Silvaniano*, at the end of *Coll.* ii, iii, v, viii); all in Balliol 275 (s XIV in.), fol. 4ᵛ, 8, 10ᵛ, 58ᵛ, 63ᵛ, 73, 90: R. A. B. Mynors, *Catalogue of the Manuscripts of Balliol College Oxford* (Oxford 1963), 291. Mynors compares Manchester, John Rylands Library, lat. 49, s. XV: *contuli cum Maximo properante in monasterio* (end of *Inst.* xii). I owe this reference, unknown to editors of both works, to Bruce Barker-Benfield.

131. For the various possibilities, Cameron 1998, 33–35.

exemplar. We find the same formula in humanist subscriptions: Lorenzo Valla checked the manuscript of his translation of Thucydides "with the very Giovanni who copied it so excellently."[132] Salutati collated his own copy of Seneca's tragedies against a borrowed manuscript "with the aid of friends...so that my copy might as far as possible borrow the correctness of yours." This and many other humanist examples make it clear that such formulas imply the systematic correction of a new copy against a single exemplar.[133] The fact that Sidonius's reader sometimes failed to turn up so that the copyist had to correct on his own puts it beyond doubt that his function was simply to proofread a newly copied text.

That is to say, the corrector was not "improving" the text on the basis of scholarly expertise or further collation, but simply checking that copy conformed to exemplar, correcting scribal errors, and supplying missing words. A scholarly owner might subsequently add further corrections or collations of his own, but these will not have formed part of the original systematic correction. It was this that was signaled by the subscription *emendavi*. A number of surviving late antique manuscripts carry corrections in two or three different late antique hands, and the natural assumption is that they represent the work of successive owners.[134]

It was not a task that required erudition or even a feel for language and style, just alertness and diligence. A reader with such a feel would be alerted to corruption by what he felt to be bad Latin, bad sense, or bad meter, but the systematic correction of a new text was surely directed at the repairing of obvious errors and omissions as rapidly as possible rather than a careful reading of the text. Naturally it was best done at once, when the exemplar was still available. Otherwise it might never be done, and an uncorrected text was not only unreliable in itself but liable to spawn ever-more corrupt copies in turn. Strabo criticized commercial booksellers for "using bad copyists and not collating."[135] It was the combination that was fatal. Careful collation of a bad scribe's copy against his exemplar could repair the damage. A similar commentary on the quality of commercial editions is implied by a friend's request that Pliny himself should "correct and certify" a purchased copy of his speeches.[136] Martial did the same (vii. 11), and characteristically wrote the friend a poem about it: "You make me correct (*emendare*) my books with my own hand and pen, Pudens; what excess of love and approval that you want my trifles in autograph!"

Despite its elementary nature, this routine procedure was in its own way every bit as important as the philological or manuscript researches of the occasional scholar,

---

132. *idem ego Laurentius...recognovi, cum ipso Ioanne, qui eum tam egregie scripsit*, Rizzo 1973, 312.

133. *cum meis contuli ut de libro tuo mei correctionem, quantum foret possibile, mutuarer*, Epistolario 1, F. Novati (ed.) (1891), 124; Rizzo 1973, 246–48.

134. For the Vergil manuscripts, M. Geymonat's edition (1973, xix–xx); so too the Sinaiticus of the Greek Bible.

135. Strabo 13. 1. 54. Renaissance publishers were sometimes criticized for bad correctors: Grafton, 1998, 64, 66.

136. *petis ut libellos meos...recognoscendos emendandosque curem*, Pliny, *Ep.* iv. 26. 1.

which seldom affected copies used by the general reading public.[137] And not just for the classics. Augustine warns those who wish to study Scripture that "they must first focus on the task of correcting their manuscripts," using "reliable texts...with careful attention to the need for correcting errors (*emendatio*)." In one of the new letters he answers a query about a passage of Scripture by telling his correspondent that his text is in error and needs to be corrected (*emendetur ergo mendositas codicis*).[138] We shall see in § 6 how meticulously Victor of Capua corrected his New Testament.

It was in the very nature of the transmission of texts before the invention of printing that there could never be a stable vulgate. The quality of text in any given book always depended on three factors: the quality of its exemplar, the accuracy with which it was copied, and the care with which it was corrected. Copy and correction went hand in hand: when attempting to replace copies of books destroyed in a library fire at Rome, Domitian sent correctors as well as copyists to Alexandria.[139] A poor copy of a scholar's text, left uncorrected, might actually be less accurate than a carefully revised copy of a regular trade text. The dilemma is perfectly caught by Jerome: "there is no point in correcting a book unless the corrections are preserved by careful copyists."[140]

Those who are tempted to follow Bloch feel that the *emendatio* so elaborately evoked in late antique subscriptions "must have" consisted in something more than "mere proofreading." It is natural to compare this sort of *emendatio* to modern proofreading, and the operations themselves are certainly similar.[141] But there are two basic and far-reaching differences. First, printer's proofs are normally checked directly against the writer's autograph, and however badly the job is done (authors are often very poor proofreaders of their own writings) there is little likelihood of serious degradation of the text (publishers have always employed professional proofreaders as well). Second, once a book has been printed its text is fixed. This is not to say that new errors do not creep into later editions (Joyce's *Ulysses* is a notorious battleground),[142] but the text of most modern books remains essentially unchanged from edition to edition.

Not so ancient books. Every single manuscript copy ever made had to be checked afresh, every single word. Those who argue that *emendatio* must be more than "mere" checking of copy against exemplar have failed to appreciate how absolutely vital this procedure has been in the accurate transmission of hand-written texts down the centuries. It is impossible to copy a text of any length by hand without making mistakes, and it is especially difficult to avoid the most serious (and common) mistake of all, omission of whole phrases or lines. With a combination of erudition, ingenuity, and

137. McNamee 1981, 247–55.
138. *De doctr. Christ.* ii. 52; iii. 1. 1; *Ep.* *5. 3. 2 Divjak.
139. *missisque Alexandream qui describerent emendarentque*, Suet. *Domit.* 20.
140. Jer. *Vulg. Ezra pr.* (*PL* 28. 1403B).
141. Gilbert Highet once called textual criticism a "glorified form of proofreading"; Shackleton Bailey 1982, 106.
142. But this is less the result of progressive degradation than editorial emendation of hard to decipher author copy: Bruce Arnold, *The Scandal of Ulysses* (London 1991); John Kidd, *New York Review of Books*, 30 June 1988, 1–8; and 25 September 1997, 54–56.

taste miscopied words can often be correctly (or at least plausibly) restored, but the omission of a whole phrase or line can never be repaired by conjecture and is bound to produce further and deeper error. The clearest single proof that a manuscript has been checked against another copy is precisely the insertion of missing words or lines attested by other manuscripts (or unlikely to have been invented). The work of the modern proofreader is done once the book has been published. The work of the ancient *emendator* was never done. It only takes one bad copy that no one corrected to ruin all later copies that derive from it.

6: PAGAN SUBSCRIBERS?

Only three sets of subscriptions lend even prima facie support to Bloch's emphasis on the paganism of the subscribers: those to Livy 1–9, Apuleius, and Pseudo-Quintilian. The case of Livy is treated in detail in chapter 14. Here it is enough to point out that those who read the Livy subscriptions this way produce no evidence that Livy had a religious rather than romantic significance for late Roman readers, and (more seriously) ignore the fact that the Nicomachi were both Christian converts by this date.

Second, a series of eleven subscriptions in the Laurentianus of Apuleius's *Apology* and *Golden Ass* by a certain Sallustius.[143] The most detailed is found at the end of Bk 9 of the *Golden Ass*, which Sallustius "emended" at Rome in 395 and again at Constantinople in 397. Seeck identified the corrector with the Sallustius who was prefect of Rome (PVR) in 383, according to Bloch, a "family close to Symmachus and mentioned by him precisely in those years."[144] Having been formally accused of magic practices, Apuleius (it is argued) is a writer pagans would admire and Christians disapprove of.

This is pretty tenuous stuff. In the first place, there is simply no evidence that the *Metamorphoses* was more widely or appreciatively read by pagans than Christians. One of its few identifiable late antique readers was Augustine, who (interpreting the work autobiographically) refers in a surprisingly matter of fact (if sceptical) manner to Apuleius purportedly retaining his human faculties after being transformed into an ass. As for the claims some pagans made for his magical powers, Augustine more than once shrewdly objected that Apuleius himself disclaimed any such powers in his *Apology*—which was included (with two subscriptions) in Sallustius's copy.[145] It has been asserted that "the last book must have appealed to the worshippers of Isis,"[146]

---

143. Zetzel 1981, 213–14.
144. Bloch 1963, 214; cf. Reynolds and Wilson 1991, 40; Pecere 1986, 30–34, 217–18; Callu iii. 160. A subscription after § 65 of the *Apology* calls him C. Crispus Sallustius, where the "Crispus" assimilates him to the historian.
145. *sicut Apuleius in libris quos asini aurei titulo inscripsit sibi ipsi accidisse, ut accepto veneno humano animo permanente asinus fieret, aut indicavit aut finxit*, CD xviii. 18; *Ep.* 137. 13; 138. 18; CD viii. 19.
146. Bloch 1963, 214.

but it is by no means self-evident that serious pagans found Bk 11 sufficient recompense for the absurdities and immoralities of Bks 1–10—especially if, as Apuleius surely intended, they read Bk 11 as poking fun at the greed of Isiac priests.[147] Apuleius was best known in late antiquity as a philosopher. Augustine treats him with considerable respect, citing his *De deo Socratis* forty-three times (to be sure in disagreement, but praising his erudition in both Latin and Greek and styling him *Platonicus nobilis*). Macrobius too clearly knew Apuleius primarily as a philosopher, which explains why he was so shocked at his writing a "narrative full of imaginary adventures of lovers."[148] Even less enthusiastic is a letter ascribed to the emperor Severus in the *Historia Augusta* that pokes fun at the pretensions to literary culture of the usurper Clodius Albinus, when all he did was busy himself with "old wives' songs, the Milesian tales from Carthage of his friend Apuleius and other literary nonsense."[149] The *HA* is widely held to reflect pagan senatorial views. Finally, the year 395 would have been as inappropriate a moment for pagan propaganda as could well be imagined.

In any case, the identification simply cannot stand. In the first place, the single name and lack of titles (not even a *v. c.*) lend no support to the idea that Sallustius was a senior member of the elite at all. Second, the subscriber goes on to add a remarkably precise piece of information: *in foro Martis controversiam declamans oratori Endelechio*, where the last four words may be paraphrased "studying rhetoric with Endelechius."[150] Sallustius was just a student, still in his teens in 395. He could not possibly have been PVR in 383, and though the PVR had a younger son whose wedding Symmachus attended in 398, there is no reason to believe this son was even called Sallustius. With the lapse of the identification, there is not the slightest reason to believe the subscriber a pagan. Sallustius is a common enough name.

Worse still, Endelechius *can* be identified. He was a teacher of rhetoric, author of a poem *De mortibus boum*, a friend of Paulinus of Nola—and a Christian.[151] Naturally, we cannot allow a Christian to help young Sallustius disseminate so subversive an author, and it has been suggested, quite gratuitously and improbably, that it was only *after* helping Sallustius that Endelechius was converted! The fact that he was a professor of rhetoric proves nothing. At least one other professor of rhetoric in Rome itself at this very moment was a Christian; Magnus, a correspondent of Jerome honored with a statue from the senate.[152]

Third, the one possible pagan reference. After the eighteenth of the so-called *Major Declamations* ascribed to Quintilian, several manuscripts offer a subscription by someone called Domitius Dracontius, who claims to have "copied and corrected" his manuscript

147. So, briefly, Cameron 2010, 1070–77.
148. Hagendahl 1967, 17–28, 680–86. Macr. Comm. i. 2. 8: *argumenta fictis casibus amatorum referta, quibus vel multum se Arbiter* [sc. Petronius] *exercuit vel Apuleium non numquam lusisse miramur.*
149. *SHA V. Clod. Alb.* 12. 12.
150. Marrou 1932 = 1976.
151. *PLRE* ii. 975; Schanz-Hosius iv. 2 (1920), 361.
152. *PLRE* i. 535.

"from the copy of my brother Hierius, for myself, for my own purposes, *and for all the gods.*" In a parallel subscription (preserved in only two manuscripts) to the tenth declamation he further characterizes Hierius as "incomparable †arrico† of the city of Rome," locating their activity "in the school of the Forum of Trajan."[153] If we accept Lommatzsch's *oratore* for the corrupt word, it is tempting to identify this man with Hierius "orator of the city of Rome" to whom the young Augustine dedicated his first work, *De pulchro et apto,* ca. 380.[154] This would then be the earliest approximately datable subscription, and it would not be surprising if both men had been pagans. Augustine's Hierius was a Syrian, famous for his eloquence in Greek as well as Latin, and also for his philosophical expertise.[155] But there are other possibilities. With Rohde's *grammatico* or Dessauer's (less probable) *vicario,* Augustine's Hierius would not fit.[156]

A much later date would then become possible,[157] less hospitable to the pagan reference. In any case, *mihi et usibus meis et dis omnibus* is an odd collocation, and few have been happy with its implication that the gods read declamations. Haase suggested *dis<cipulis> omnibus,* Rohde *d<oct>is omnibus,* both appropriate for a teacher and a rhetoric textbook—neither compelling, but both more believable than the transmitted gods. Of course, attempts have been made to link Dracontius and Hierius to the "circle" of Symmachus and the "pagan revival." But over and above the fact that neither is mentioned in Symmachus's extensive correspondence,[158] what sort of pagan "propaganda" could they possibly have been producing? In content as in style, these pieces are virtually indistinguishable from the stock declamations preserved by the elder Seneca in the first century and composed by Bishop Ennodius in the sixth: model declamations in imaginary cases involving parricide, pirates, poisoning, torture, tyrants, and cannibalism. Sometimes we have speeches both for and against, as in the case of the call girl accused of poisoning a client (14–15) and the father who tortured a son accused of incest with his mother (18–19). Whether pagan or Christian, all members of the elite studied rhetoric, and the sensational themes were well calculated to kindle the enthusiasm of teenagers. To judge by six quotations from four different declamations, Pseudo-Quintilian made a strong impression on one Christian student, the young Jerome.[159] Though far from edifying, the themes are more comical than corrupting, and their specifically pagan content is close to zero. Two deal with astrology

---

153. L. Håkanson, *Decl. Quintiliano falso ascriptae* (Stuttgart 1982), xi, 371, 219; id. *ANRW* ii. 32. 4 (1986), 2282.

154. So A. Mazzarino 1975–76, 463; Schneider 2000a and b.

155. *Conf.* iv. 14. 21, with J. J. O'Donnell's commentary (1992, 246–51).

156. Proc. Gaza *Ep.* 145; *PLRE* ii. 559. For *vicario,* S. Mazzarino 1942, 384.

157. A Latin *grammaticus* called Hierius taught at Gaza ca. 500 (*PLRE* ii. 559), but he does not fit the Forum of Trajan.

158. So A. Mazzarino 1976; and Schneider 2000; Domitius Dracontius would have been known as Dracontius rather than Domitius, and so is unlikely to be the Domitius of Symm. *Ep.* ii. 76.

159. From 3, 10, 12, and 13, twice expressly naming naming Quintilian: Hagendahl 1958, 296–97. Lactantius quotes three times from the *Minor Declamations* with approval, as illustrating Christian ethics: Winterbottom 1984, 291, 395.

and magic (4 and 10), but hardly in a way that recommends their use. One of the two equipped with a subscription (10) is a wife's suit against a husband who had put a spell on her son's tomb to prevent his ghost appearing in her dreams. As it happens, this is one of the four that stuck in young Jerome's mind. Christian students continued to compose the same sort of declamations, using the same textbooks.[160] Ennodius's *Dictio* 21 is actually a reply to Pseudo-Quintilian 5.[161]

The few who still concern themselves with these declamations persist in seeing Dracontius as in some significant sense editing or revising the collection.[162] But the terms he uses are unusually informative and precise: what he did was make a copy of his own from Hierius's exemplar (*descripsi... de codice fratris Hieri*), and then check it for accuracy with Hierius's assistance (*legi et emendavi...cum fratre Hierio*). As we know from many other examples of the formula *emendavi cum X*, this means that one read the new text aloud while the other checked it against the exemplar. Not in any sense a "recension," since at best Dracontius's manuscript can have been no more than a faithful copy of a single exemplar. No editing, no pagan conspiracy; just a professional man obtaining the tools of his trade.

The series of fifteen subscriptions to successive books of Martial may be the work of another teacher of rhetoric. The most detailed appears after the dedicatory epigrams in Bk xiii: *emendavi ego Torquatus Gennadius in foro Divi Augusti Martis consulatu Vincentii et Fravitae vv. cc.* [namely 401].[163] Again the Forum Martis, as in the Sallustius subscription, the academic center of late antique Rome.[164] Taken by itself, it might seem that Gennadius, like Sallustius, was a student of rhetoric. But a Torquatus Gennadius is known to have been prefect of Egypt in 396 and proconsul of Achaea a year or two later, the subject of a poem by Claudian, who refers to both his posts and also calls him "second glory of the Roman forum." Presumably second after Cicero,[165] but surely identifying him as a rhetor rather than advocate. Once more, the date of his two offices (396–98) is strongly against the idea that he was a staunch pagan.

At least one other set are clearly the work of a student, the two subscriptions to Juvenal:[166] *legi ego Niceus apud M. Serbium Romae et emendavi* and *legi ego Niceus Romae apud Serbium magistrum et emendavi*. Given the rarity of the name Servius, the term *magistrum*, and the fact that the Vergil commentator Servius is known to have taught in Rome, there can be little doubt that Nicaeus was a student in Servius's school in the early years of the fifth century—that is to say, born after the ban on sacrifice.

---

160. Riché 1995, 39–40. The "pagan" character of Ennodius's *Dictiones* is actually more marked: 16 and 22 talk about Vestal Virgins and appeal several times to gods in the plural.
161. For a comparison of the two works, Håkanson, *ANRW* II. 32. 4 (1986), 2285–90.
162. Håkanson in Reynolds 1983, 335 ("a recension"); Sussman 1987, ix ("scrupulously prepared for publication"); Kragelund 1991, 274 ("occup[ied] himself seriously with the recension").
163. *Fragvitii* MSS; for the series, Zetzel 1981, 211–13.
164. Marrou 1932 = 1976, passim.
165. *PLRE* ii. 1124; Cameron 1970, 394, 402.
166. In *Leid.* 82 fol. 45ʳ (s. X) in the margin by *Sat.* 7. 4 in the hand of the scholiast: and in *Laur.* 34. 42 fol. 20ᵛ (s. XI) following *Sat.* 5.

Although he does not say so in so many words, it is likely that Servius helped him correct his manuscript. Like at least three other subscriptions of the period, it bears witness to nothing more than a schoolboy correcting his own text.

Though by his own admission thirty years old when he revised his Persius, Sabinus's claim to have done it "without a teacher" (*sine magistro*) is eloquent of the traditional context for such undertakings. In a later chapter we shall see that Nicomachus Dexter, known from his subscription to Bks 3–5 of Livy, must have been a schoolboy at the time, and the same may have been true of others. The one time of life all elite Romans corrected texts of the classics was in the school of the grammaticus or rhetor, no doubt in fine calligraphic copies presented to them by rich parents. The reason some of these schoolboys' texts became the ancestors of medieval manuscripts is simply that sturdy calligraphic codexes were likely to survive the centuries and end up as exemplars in some monastic or royal scriptorium.

Many of the other surviving subscriptions are found in manuscripts of textbooks, technical works, handbooks, and encyclopedias: Julius Paris's epitome of Valerius Maximus and Pomponius Mela's *De chorographia*,[167] Pliny's *Natural History*, Solinus, Vegetius, Priscian, and some Latin scholia on Galen.[168] None of these works could possibly be seen as part of a pagan program. They are simply books to which any educated person, whether pagan or Christian, might turn for information. As for the poets represented, whether classical (Terence, Vergil, Horace) or post-Augustan (Lucan, Persius, Juvenal, Martial), we saw in the last chapter that all were read by Christians and pagans alike.[169] The post-Augustans did indeed benefit from a revival in the course of the fourth century, but (as we have seen) this was an empire-wide movement, not limited to Rome, aristocrats, or pagans.

Least of all is there any basis for the claim that it is to the "editions" these subscriptions are supposed to bear witness to that we owe the very survival of classical literature, a "silent protest" against the triumph of Christianity? It is indeed occasionally the case that, directly or indirectly, all surviving manuscripts of certain authors derive from copies signed by a late antique subscriber.[170] When this happens, it is certainly better that the ultimate source of our text should have been a corrected copy rather than an uncorrected copy. But we have no way of knowing whether the corrector did a good job, and in several cases (as we shall see) we can be fairly sure he did not.

Caution is necessary, because subscriptions were sometimes added by collation to manuscripts deriving from different sources.[171] Yet there can be little doubt that (e.g.) all extant manuscripts of Apuleius's *Apology*, *Golden Ass*, and *Florida* derive from

---

167. Paris and Mela are both subscribed by the same man, Rusticius Helpidius Domnulus (Zetzel 1981, 216).

168. For the relevant subscriptions, briefly Zetzel 1981.

169. Zetzel 1981, 211–27; Reynolds 1983, 505 (index s.v. "subscriptions").

170. A point often overemphasized (notably by Lommatzsch 1904, 182).

171. For the Juvenal and Lucan subscriptions, A. E. Housman, *Lucanus* (Cambridge 1926), xiii–xviii; for Persius, Clausen 1963, 252–56; Zetzel 1981, 229.

Sallustius's copy. But for Sallustius, these works might not have survived, and if he had not corrected his copy, our text would be in a worse state than it is. At the other end of the literary spectrum, all extant manuscripts of Julius Paris, Pomponius Mela, and Vibius Sequester derive from the copy "emended" by Rusticius Helpidius Domnulus.[172] By grouping these three handbooks together in a single codex, Domnulus may be said to have performed a modest editorial function. Brief texts like this almost certainly stood a better chance of survival as a corpus. The Pseudo-Quintilianic *Minor Declamations* survive in a Carolingian MS that is also our best MS of the declamations of Calpurnius Flaccus, Antonius Julianus, and the excerpted tradition of Seneca the Elder, no doubt copied from the MS of some late antique professor of rhetoric.[173] But such editing as this involved had nothing to do with his writing the formula *emendavi* at the close of each book. That simply described the checking of copy against exemplar.

Sallustius's copy of Apuleius was not in any sense a "recension." Nor does the fact that he records having corrected his manuscript twice transform his efforts into a philological enterprise. Just as modern writers normally read proofs more than once, so a careful ancient corrector would often check his copy more than once. Statilius Maximus claims to have corrected Cicero's *De lege agraria* "again" (*rursum emendavi*).[174] Boethius jotted down the words "corrected twice" (*emendavi II*, where *II = bis*) in an author-subscription to Bk 5 of his commentary on Cicero's *Topica*.[175] And the subscription "corrected once" (*semel*) in a contemporary hand in a sixth-century manuscript of Augustine's commentary on the psalms implies something less than the corrector's usual standard.[176] Then there are two almost identical subscriptions by the presbyter Donatus, dated to 561 and 569, respectively, in copies of Ambrosiaster (a sixth-century original) and Rufinus (a tenth-century copy): *infirmus (et debilis) legi legi legi*.[177] While we cannot exclude sheer exuberance, it is more natural to suppose that Donatus added the second and third *legi* after a second and third reading of his copy.[178] One humanist scholar claimed to have checked his copy of Cicero *De oratore* seven times![179]

The closest parallel is provided by the Fulda New Testament, corrected twice in his own hand by Victor, bishop of Capua. To his first subscription (*legi*) dated 19 April 546, he subsequently added a second dated 12 April 547 (*iterato legi*).[180] Since we are

---

172. Vibius Sequester's *De fluminibus*, which follows Paris and Mela in Vat. lat. 4929, the archetype of all three works (Billanovich 1955 and 1993), probably stood in Domnulus's book, though it carries no subscription.

173. So Winterbottom 1984, xx; Sussman 1994, 19–20. Winterbottom himself suggested Domitius Dracontius, but there is no reason to believe that Dracontius played any sort of editorial role in the *Major Declamations*.

174. Although Statilius claims to have used six manuscripts, the *rursum* means that he checked his own copy twice.

175. Stangl 1882, 9; for the Cicero subscription, § 6 below.

176. *emendabi semel deo gratias*, Par. lat. 9533 (s. VI: *CLA* v. 587).

177. Casin. 150, p. 248 (*CLA* iii. 374a); Metensis 225 (the long version).

178. So Lindsay, *Pal. Latina* 2 (1923), 10.

179. G. Lamola in May 1428: Rizzo 1973, 176; for a medieval example of seven times, ib. 244.

180. For the text, von Dobschütz 1909, 90–91, with P. Corssen, 1909, 175–77; *CLA* viii. 1196.

fortunate enough to have Victor's actual copy, we are in a position to identify his corrections. They are very thorough, covering orthography and syllable division as well as scribal errors. But except for the Pauline epistles, he used just one exemplar, evidently the one from which he had had his copy made.[181] The quality of both text and script is high, its orthography no doubt an improvement on its source; the Pauline epistles are enriched with readings from a second source; and Victor further enhanced the usefulness of the book by adding a gospel harmony. He undoubtedly intended it to serve as a model for further copies. But for all its virtues, the Codex Fuldensis can scarcely be styled a "recension" of the Latin New Testament.

It may be that Sallustius had an opportunity to collate another exemplar in Constantinople. But he makes no such claim himself, and ten out of his eleven subscriptions mention only Rome. It was apparently just Bk 9 that, for whatever reason, he checked a second time two years later in Constantinople. There is no reason to believe that he was doing anything more than completing the correction of his own copy. He was not preserving an endangered text, nor (on the evidence of Augustine) was he reviving a forgotten text.

7: LATE ANTIQUE EDITIONS

In the course of his attack on a widespread assumption that surviving manuscripts of the classics derive from medieval archetypes, Pasquali argued that errors common to the entire manuscript tradition could be explained equally well by the ancient editions from which they all ultimately descended.[182] But as far as the Latin classics are concerned, there is no real evidence that late antique editions in the Alexandrian sense existed.[183] Not even in the case of Vergil. In the course of his massive commentary on Vergil, Servius cites hundreds of variants, but in a thoroughly unsystematic way. It is clear that he had no interest in constructing a text of his own. While he occasionally names earlier scholars who supported one reading or another, there was apparently no standard edition to which he could (or did) appeal.[184] We have three almost complete fifth- or sixth-century codexes and substantial fragments of four more. All but one carry corrections in one or more contemporary hands, and one (the Medicean) a subscription as well. But no clear relationship can be established between any of them. Certainly no authoritative recent edition lies behind them.[185] Statilius Maximus

---

181. Fischer 1963, 545–57.

182. Pasquali 1952, 21. The question of medieval archetypes remains controversial: Timpanaro 1981, 75, 136–38; Reynolds and Wilson 1991, 214–15.

183. Tarrant 1995, 101. On the other hand, a number of classic Greek mathematical works were equipped with texts as well as commentaries in the fourth to sixth centuries: Cameron 1990, 103–27.

184. Zetzel 1981, passim, and see further below.

185. Geymonat in Horsfall 1995, 304; against, Courtney 1981, 24, arguing for a common source, though not an "edition"; against Courtney, Timpanaro 1986, 181–82; Courtney again, 2002–3, 189–94.

seems to have made a serious recension of at least one of Cicero's speeches in the second century, which was the ultimate source of our surviving text of that speech. But we cannot assume that he edited the entire corpus, and even if he did, it is not likely that every one of the late antique copies that survived the Dark Ages to generate our surviving manuscripts reflects his edition.[186]

In this context, it may be worth discussing in detail two post-Augustan poets widely supposed to descend from late fourth-century editions by pagan scholars: Juvenal and Seneca's tragedies. First Juvenal. It has often been assumed that the credit for the "rediscovery" of Juvenal traced in the last chapter should be assigned to Servius and the circle of Symmachus.[187] The evidence alleged is as follows: (1) Ammianus attests a vogue for Juvenal among the elite of late fourth-century Rome; (2) the two subscriptions just quoted attest a certain Nicaeus correcting a text of Juvenal in the school of Servius at Rome; (3) Servius introduced citations of Juvenal to the grammatical tradition; (4) Macrobius portrays Servius as an intimate of Symmachus; and (5) Mommsen assigned the Juvenal scholia to the same milieu, the work of "a well-trained pagan scholar living in Rome" around the turn of the century.[188] Indeed, the fact (6) that the end of *Satire* xvi and the so-called O-fragment (thirty-four additional lines in vi offered by one otherwise unremarkable eleventh-century manuscript) are not only missing in all other manuscripts but also unknown to the scholia, has been explained by the dramatic rediscovery in Rome of a lone surviving manuscript of Juvenal, already defective by the age of Servius.[189] According to the most recent commentator, following the standard work by Knoche, "at some time between 352 and 399 the Satires were edited and published with a commentary."[190]

On the face of it, an impressive series of clues pointing to late fourth-century pagan circles in Rome. But there are overwhelming objections. In the first place, there is the sheer improbability of one grammarian in Rome successfully initiating a change of taste documented over the entire Roman world. Second, Servius lived fully a half-century too late to play any such role in the first place. Not to mention Tertullian and Lactantius in third- and early fourth-century Africa, there is Ausonius in mid fourth-century Gaul, who knew Juvenal well. Because he was a friend of Symmachus and lived to ca. 395, Ausonius has often been thought to fit the "Servian" hypothesis, and bracketed with Juvenalian readers of a later generation. But he was born ca. 310, and never visited Rome. Even if he discovered Juvenal later than his school days, there are echoes in his *Mosella* of ca. 371. Ausonius's pupil Paulinus of Nola, born ca. 355 and educated

186. On the thorny question of the various collections and combinations in which Cicero's speeches have survived, see the long entry by various writers in Reynolds 1983, 55–98.
187. Most elaborately by Knoche 1940, 34–52.
188. Highet 1954, 185–86; Wessner 1931, xl.
189. So (e.g.) Griffiths 1963, 107; Courtney 1967, 39–40, improbably supposing that the O-fragment disappeared even before the text was copied into a codex, with a copyist carelessly skipping over one column in a roll.
190. S. M. Braund, *Juvenal Satires: Book* 1 (Cambridge 1996), 38; Knoche 1940, 37. For the two termini, see below.

in Bordeaux, also knew Juvenal, as did Sulpicius Severus, born ca. 360 and likewise educated at Bordeaux.[191] Then there is Prudentius, born in 348; there is no reason to doubt that he picked up his enthusiasm for Juvenal at school in his native Spain.[192]

It is simply not true that Juvenal was "suddenly" rediscovered,[193] and certainly not in Rome. The anonymous Christian invective on Praetextatus, certainly influenced by Juvenal, dates from 384. Despite the role sometimes assigned him in this narrative, there is no evidence that Symmachus had more than a nodding acquaintance with Juvenal (p. 537). Symmachus was born ca. 340, Servius ca. 360. The obvious explanation is that the Roman vogue for Juvenal began in the 360s, after Symmachus's school days but in time for Servius's. If Juvenal was all the rage by the 380s, that is much too early for Servius, still in his twenties, to have been responsible. He too must have read Juvenal in school, wherever that may have been.

As for the scholia, they are much later than Mommsen supposed, up to a century later than Knoche's fourth-century edition.[194] There are indeed clear pointers in the scholia to the city of Rome: references to the Baths of Diocletian, praetorian games, and even to a measure of the city prefect of 352–53. And unlike many such compilations there are also signs of a single author (cross-references and references to views of other commentators).[195] Moreover, the fact that they preserve the only quotation of Marius Maximus outside the *Historia Augusta* nicely illustrates Ammianus's scornful linking of Juvenal and Marius Maximus. But the past tenses in his references to Roman cult practices show that the scholiast wrote *after* the ban on sacrifice (391), and the fact that he drew on Orosius (417) proves him a Christian. As for the loss of the O-fragment (only significant if it is authentic, which is far from certain)[196] and the end of *Satire* xvi, the commentary has not come down to us complete as a continuous work. What we possess has been reconstituted from excerpts entered in the margins of texts of Juvenal.[197] Naturally, we should not expect to find scholia on passages missing from the surviving manuscripts![198]

There is no evidence here that the O-fragment (if authentic) was lost by 400. And no justification for assuming that the text used several decades earlier by Ausonius and his pupils in Gaul derived from this same supposedly defective Roman exemplar. As for Nicaeus, we have already seen that he was probably just a student of Servius checking his personal copy in class. Nothing in his formulaic *legi et emendavi* warrants connecting him with a new edition of Juvenal (much less the scholia). For Knoche, this edition he postulated was a critical text. In general support of the notion, he appealed to the other

---

191. Green 1971, 49; Sulp. Sev. *Chron.* i. 24. 4, with van Andel 1976, 23.

192. Palmer 1989, 22–23, and (for Juvenal) 180–84.

193. "ganz plötzlich," Knoche 1940, 34.

194. Cameron 2010.

195. E.g., *ut superius dixi* on vi. 117, referring to the note on i. 71; Wessner 1931, xxxvi–xli.

196. Against, see now Willis 1989, 441–68; see too Tarrant in Reynolds 1983, 203 n. 22.

197. The "continuous" commentary we find (e.g.) in the Excerpta Sangallensia (s. IX) is no exception, since there are many indications that they too were patched together from marginal scholia to a text of Juvenal (Wessner. xii–xiii).

198. The one manuscript that preserves the O-fragment has no scholia.

critical editions of classical texts supposedly being prepared at this time by Symmachus and his protégés in the furtherance of their supposed cultural revival. More specifically, he believed that fortune had given him a page of this very edition in the form of the Antinoë Juvenal papyrus of ca. 500. The proof (he thought) lay in its two (very obvious) corrections, occasional punctuation and (above all) critical symbols. But there are no variants, and however impressive the critical symbols look, they seem to mean no more than "not sure what this means."[199] The ignorance and lack of understanding the scholia reveal are enough to prove that the papyrus was no scholar's copy.

Even if Knoche's edition had existed, the claim that all manuscripts later than ca. 400 "derive their basic text" from it would be arbitrary.[200] Texts of Juvenal were being copied all over the empire between ca. 350 and 550. The very fact that the *Satires* were so popular makes it all the more likely that they circulated among the smart set in the form of uncorrected, ever more corrupt luxury copies. We have seen that the seven surviving Vergil manuscripts of the age do not derive from a single source.

The second case is the tragedies of Seneca. Otto Zwierlein postulated a late fourth-century "edition" by some pagan scholar, once again appealing to the many other supposedly similar editions of the age.[201] The manuscripts of Seneca's tragedies notoriously divide into two families, known as E and A. The A-manuscripts are not only character-ized by interpolations and lacunae, but present the plays in a different sequence and even with different titles, not to mention including the Pseudo-Senecan *Octavia*. They also lack the metrical notes included in E. But shared errors nonetheless point to a common archetype, and the lack of shared minuscule errors suggests that this arche-type was late antique rather than medieval.[202]

Zwierlein thought he could date the first representative of the E-tradition between 380 and 394. The first of these termini comes from his date for Servius's *Centimeter*, apparently the source of the metrical notes in E; the second from an imitation in Claudian that seems to presuppose an error peculiar to the E-tradition. Unfortunately, the true date of Servius's book is 400/405 (p. 240), thus eliminating the interval between Zwierlein's two termini. Not that one banal corruption (*melius* for *medius*)[203] is enough to identify the progenitor of the E-tradition. Even if we concede that the ancestor of E was known to Claudian, nothing points to an "edition" rather than a personal copy. The few leaves we have of a fifth-century copy of the tragedies show affinities with both the E- and A-traditions, as (it seems) does the single page from a fourth-century codex recently found in Egypt.[204] It is no doubt true enough that the metrical notes in E are late

199. Roberts 1935, 199–209; on the diple obelismene at vii. 92, see Courtney's commentary (London 1980), 374.
200. Courtney 1967, 40.
201. So too Taylor 1993, 250, writing on the MS tradition of the *Ad Herennium*: "In order to combat the generally poor standard of manuscript tradition, a circle of men, acting upon the initiative of Symmachus (345–405), began to work on the correction of texts."
202. Zwierlein 1983, 24–39; Tarrant in Reynolds 1983, 378–81.
203. *mediusque* [*melius* E] *collo sedit Herculeo polus, HF* 72; Zwierlein 1983, 31–33.
204. Zwierlein 1983, 47–50; Markus and Schwendner 1997, 76.

antique rather than medieval, added by a reader capable of analyzing Seneca's lyric metres. But that allows us to descend at least as late as Boethius in the sixth century.

In a later study Zwierlein suggested as a specific motive for his postulated "edition" Seneca's enthusiasm for the Hercules saga (the sequence in E begins and ends with plays on Hercules), assuming that Hercules had a religious significance for the last generation of pagan men of letters.[205] But as he appears in the comparisons in Claudian's panegyrics Hercules is no more than a panegyrical commonplace. Whether or not Hercules was still an active object of cult, he is only mentioned once in passing by Symmachus as the mythical founder of the site of one of his villas.[206] Nor do either Symmachus or any of his pagan peers show any knowledge of Seneca's tragedies. Only four late fourth-century writers quote them, and three were committed Christians: Jerome, Augustine, Prudentius (p. 412). As for the fourth, whether or not Claudian was a pagan (which is far from certain), he wrote almost exclusively for Christian patrons.

Many classical texts descend from a single late antique copy. In Leighton Reynolds's image, the classical tradition follows the "lines of the hourglass, which funnels down to a narrow middle and then bellies out again." But the narrow middle is not the years 380–430, a period of intense literary activity and lavish book production, but the so-called Dark Ages, the seventh and eighth centuries, when "the flow of classical learning... was universally reduced to a trickle."[207]

The reason it is so often late antique copies that formed the basis for the medieval tradition of classical texts is not because fourth century pagans had performed a salvage operation.

The key factor was the copying of texts from fragile and bulky papyrus rolls onto the more capacious and (above all) more durable medium of the parchment codex. Seen in the long perspective, this was one of the great bottlenecks in the history of the transmission of texts. No book that was not transcribed from roll to codex was likely to survive the Dark Ages. But this process should not be compared with that other great bottleneck, the transliteration of Greek texts from uncial to minuscule in the ninth century. Byzantine scholars were self-consciously rediscovering texts unread for centuries and written in a script that even the educated found hard to read.[208] Contemporaries cannot have viewed transcription from roll to codex in such a light. There was no such radical change in script, and while the fourth century saw something of a literary revival, there are no grounds for linking it with the codex or the codex with either pagans or aristocrats.[209] To take only one example, we have more or less significant parts of nineteen late antique codexes of Vergil to just one roll,[210] and since

205. Zwierlein, 1984, 5–12.
206. Symm. *Ep.* i. 1. 5, with Courtney 1993, 448.
207. Reynolds 1983, xiii, vividly illustrating the point on p. xvi.
208. Lemerle 1986, 136, actually compared "the 'invention' of literary minuscule with the 'invention' of printing."
209. As often implied, for example by Fuhrmann 1994, 51–52.
210. M. Geymonat's edition (1973), xix–xxiii (only Π1 is a roll).

more than half are assigned to the fifth century or later, most of them must have been owned by Christians. It was Bishop Euzoïus who sponsored the transference of Pamphilus's library from roll to codex in the 360s.

The most attractive feature of the parchment codex for some aristocratic book lovers may have been the fact that it lent itself much better than the roll to decoration and illustration.[211] As many surviving books of the age reveal, there was a vogue among the wealthy for deluxe editions, of the Bible and patristic works as well as the classics. It was because they were legible and well preserved that Carolingian scholars selected such books as exemplars—though given a choice they may also have been impressed by the apparent authority of the Roman grandees occasionally named in subscriptions.

---

211. Bischoff 1990, 187.

13

CORRECTORS AND CRITICS II

8: SUBSCRIPTIONS AND CORRECTIONS

Ultimately, the purity of the surviving texts of the classics depended more on individual owners carefully checking copy against exemplar than on the odd scholar trying to "improve the text" by collating manuscripts. It is in any case far from clear that even the more scholarly readers of late antiquity had any clear concept of "improving the text" by collation. The prime example here is the Fronto palimpsest, with its margins full of variants added by the secondhand (C = Corrector). In a great many cases C explicitly designates them as variants rather than conjectures by the lemma $i(n)$ $a(lio)$ or $i(n)$ $a(liis)$, "in another copy," "in other copies" (he seems to have drawn on at least three different copies, though not necessarily directly; most of his variants surely came from the margins of only one or two actual texts). In addition, he made many hundreds of corrections directly into the text, by erasure, expuncture, or interlinear insertion. Obviously, what we would like to know is on what basis he sometimes directly altered his text and sometimes just quoted variants in the margins.

To the scholar familiar with the modern apparatus criticus, it might seem obvious to identify the marginal variants as rejected alternatives. But a careful study by Zetzel has shown that the situation is more complex.[1] Sometimes the variant is so obviously superior that it is hard to believe C could not see it; sometimes so obviously inferior that it is hard to see why he bothered to record it at all. The most plausible solution, one that would impose some degree of consistency on his choices, would be to identify the corrections made in the text as the result of collation against the original exemplar, and the marginal variants as the (later) product of collation against other manuscripts. This solution would incidentally underline the overriding importance of that routine first correction.

Divergences from the exemplar were automatically (and in most cases no doubt rightly) considered errors and corrected, while variants found elsewhere were simply recorded. It was the corrector's obvious duty to reproduce his exemplar exactly, especially if that exemplar had been (to all appearances) authoritatively corrected. Any reading that differed from it could confidently be expunged and replaced, whereas

---

1. Zetzel 1980, 49–55; the standard text is now M. P. J. van den Hout's Teubner (1988).

variants found in other manuscripts, however interesting, were of unknown authority.[2] As Zetzel rightly underlines, C never gives any indication of the value he attached to his variants. The next copyist could have produced a better text of Fronto simply by adopting some of these variants, but C gives no indication that this is what he was expected to do, and certainly no guidance as to which readings he should prefer.

It might be suggested that the Fronto palimpsest was a scholar's working copy, on which he recorded his collations with the intention of exploiting them later in a separate "edition." But the variants are jumbled up together with innumerable trivial jottings: "remarkable passage about love," (4), "praise of Cicero" (57), "acts of masculine bravery by Sempronia" (100). There are a handful grammatical notes,[3] but taken as a whole the marginalia can hardly be called a commentary, certainly not one designed for general circulation. The same applies to the trivial bilingual marginalia in two contemporary and two somewhat later hands in the Antinoë Juvenal, a single leaf from a parchment codex of ca. 500.[4]

The Fronto palimpsest is in fact clearly an owner's personal copy. Many of the marginalia were simply designed to remind him of passages he had found interesting for one reason or another. The variants he collected because variants were one of the inescapable features of an unstable vulgate. It was not that late antique readers thought them all equally true.[5] On occasion (like some modern editors) they may have wondered whether some variants went back to the author himself. But they must have been well aware that many were just plain wrong. Yet how were they to decide? It was a dilemma. Serious readers knew the importance of an accurate text—but they also knew that no two copies were identical. A passage of Strabo suggests that conscientious readers routinely collated other copies just to check the text of passages that interested them.[6] The only responsible course for a reader who (like most readers in every age) did not consider himself a textual critic was to ensure that his copy reproduced an authoritative exemplar as faithfully as possible—and to record variants for information.

Untypically, Galen frequently expressed opinions about variants in his commentaries on Hippocrates, opinions that seem to have influenced the text of surviving manuscripts, which is in substantial agreement with the readings he recommended. But then Galen was a critic as well as an expert in the subject matter of Hippocrates.[7]

It is striking how little interest even a professional scholar like Servius shows in deciding between the hundreds of variants he quotes. Zetzel assumes that Servius found most of these variants already cited by other scholars rather than by collating manuscripts himself.[8] No doubt so, but I should prefer to draw a distinction between systematic and occasional collation. I do not see Servius collating a manuscript

---

2. Intelligent ancient readers must have been as aware as modern editors that attractive solutions to problematic passages might as easily be conjectures as transmitted truth.
3. Zetzel 1980, 55.
4. Roberts 1935, 199–209.
5. Zetzel 1980, 56 n. 50; cf. Reeve, CP 80 (1985), 90.
6. Strabo 17. 1. 5 (790), with T. W. Allen PBSR 5 (1910), 77.
7. J. Ilberg in H. Kühlewein, Hippocratis opera 1 (1894), xxxv–lxiv; Pasquali 1952, 327–30; Hanson 1998, 22–53.
8. Zetzel 1981, 92–98.

systematically, in the manner of an ancient corrector or a modern editor. But he surely checked any texts that lay at hand when considering specific passages. To give an obvious example, when he was teaching, pupils will surely have asked him about variants in their own texts, which in the case of those from old families may on occasion have been books (or copies of books) of considerable antiquity. But the key fact is that Servius was a commentator rather than a critic. Collecting variants and correcting the text are not at all the same thing.

The Fronto subscriber's favorite term is *emendavi*, though he also uses *legi* and *recognovi*, with no discernible difference of meaning. Do these terms cover all his work on Fronto, including marginal variants and notes on the subject matter? Or just his corrections of the text? I would suggest that these three terms specifically denote only the corrections. In the case of subscriptions preserved in medieval copies, we normally have only the long ones at the end of books that give all those imposing biographical details. But original subscribed books often have a succession of shorter ones inside books, sometimes the single word *contuli*. Later copyists usually omit such details, and modern editors often follow suit. But a fair number survive, both in late antique originals and (less often) in copies. One manuscript of the new letters of Augustine offers *contuli* in twelve out of thirty letters,[9] and in one manuscript family a *contuli* is preserved after every letter but one in the first six books of the letters of Ambrose.[10] A sixth-century manuscript of the *City of God* preserves nine originals, including the even more explicit *exemplar contuli* after Bk x, unmistakably implying collation of copy against exemplar.[11] There are a number of other examples in other works of Augustine.[12] In Viliaric's sixth-century Orosius there is a *contuli* at the end of Bks 1 and 4 in the hand that made the earliest corrections.

The Fronto palimpsest itself provides a striking example. At the end of *Ad M. Caesarem* iv comes the first and longest subscription, which may once have given the corrector's name, though all that can now be read with certainty is *haec…legi emendavi*. Then *legi emendavi qui supra* (nine times), *legi emendavi* (twice), and (once each) *emendavi, legi*, and *recognovi*, all at the end of books or sections.[13] Given the many gaps in this lacunose palimpsest, there were presumably many others on pages now lost or illegible.

What was the purpose of repeating these notes at such short intervals? Certainly not to identify the subscriber, since most are anonymous. And surely not to indicate that the subscriber had made all his different sorts of corrections and marginalia on each successive section (if, like C, he was filling his margins he did not need any such reminder). No, he was indicating how far he had *corrected*. Since it

---

9. See 7–16 and 18–19 Divjak; Petitmengin 1983, 365–74, for a few examples after other letters of Augustine.

10. BFLG in the *CSEL* edition (82. 1–3) by O. Faller and M. Zelzer, best preserved in Berol. lat. fol. 908 of s. IX.

11. Par. lat. 12214 (*CLA* v. 635); Petitmengin 1983, 374.

12. Reifferscheid 1873, 3–4.

13. Van den Hout (ed.) 1988², xxxvi–xxxvii.

might not be necessary to enter corrections on any given page, and since, if neatly entered over erasures, they might be hard to spot, it was essential for a corrector to indicate just how far he had got in his last session. "Collate" is, after all, the meaning of *contuli*, as of its Greek equivalent for such interim notations, ἕως ὧδε (ἀντεβλήθη).[14] Although we seldom find these interim formulas in medieval copies of classical texts, it is significant that the more detailed subscriptions usually appear at the end of successive books within a work (Apuleius, Caesar, Livy, Martial, Pseudo-Quintilian).

9: DIFFERENT TERMS (*EMENDAVI, LEGI, RECOGNOVI, CONTULI, RECENSUI*)

Like many other subscribers, C seems to have used *legi, emendavi,* and *recognovi* more or less interchangeably. In his double subscription to *Metamorphoses* ix, after writing *legi et emendavi* in 395, Sallustius added *rursus recognovi* in 397, where the *rursus* implies that he is using the verbs interchangeably. Properly and originally, *legi* and *recognovi* were formulas appended by clerks to documents or court proceedings they had verified and by administrators to petitions or orders they had approved.[15] Here at least we have a number of originals, a variety of documents on both papyrus and stone with a *legi* or *recognovi* at the bottom. To cite one specific category, we have hundreds of certificates of honorable discharge from the army, which conclude with a formula stating that they are certified copies (*descriptum et recognitum*) of the original in Rome.[16] In the earliest nonofficial *legi* subscription I know (*Iader subscripsi; Polianus legi*), at the end of a letter of Cyprian, the purpose must again have been authentication rather than collation; several other passages in Cyprian's correspondence mention letters suspected of forgery or subscribed by brethren who had not read what they were signing.[17]

But when appended to copies of literary texts, *legi* and *recognovi* came to take on the same meaning as *emendavi* or *contuli*. Though the four terms seem to be used interchangeably, the fact that *legi* is so often combined with *emendavi*, usually in the formula *legi (et) emendavi* (so Sabinus, Niceus, Sallustius, Mavortius), suggests that (at any rate in earlier subscriptions) *legi* alone might imply less than *emendavi*. In the Fronto palimpsest we find *legi emendavi* a dozen times, *legi* alone just once. Thus when a sixth-century subscriber to Bk 8 of Caesar's *Gallic War* makes the limited claim *legi*

---

14. Devréesse 1954, 86; Cameron 1993, 116.

15. Often (especially *legi*) in Latin even on petitions written in Greek; both are represented in Greek by the same word, ἀνέγνων. A. Wilhelm, *Hermes* 55 (1920), 6–9, 29; B. Kübler, *RE* IV A. 1 (1931), 499–501; Petitmengin 1983, 372–73.

16. M. M. Roxan, *Roman Military Diplomas* (London 1978; London 1985).

17. *Ep.* 79 (p. 839. 4 Hartel); cf. *Ep.* 9. 2. 1; 49. 1. 4; 55. 5. 1, with G. W. Clarke, *The Letters of St. Cyprian of Carthage* 1 (1984), 224–26; 2 (1984), 117–18; 3 (1986), 169; 4 (1989), 225–26.

tantum,[18] he may have meant that he had "just read" his copy, that is to say, checked it as far as he could without collating it against another exemplar.

An example of *recognosco* in this sense has yet to be recognized in one of the new letters of Augustine. Some readers of Augustine's *De gestis Pelagii* were disputing his views, and accused the owner of the copy they were using, a certain Justus, of tampering with the text. Justus was so perturbed that he travelled to Hippo to check it: "collating (*conferens*) his copy with mine, *me quoque percognoscente* he discovered it to be perfectly sound."[19] The words left in Latin should mean, as indeed they are translated by Robert Eno, "which I was thoroughly acquainted with myself." But this makes no sense. Of course an author is "thoroughly acquainted" with his own books. But however well Augustine knew this one, even so he could not possibly be sure *without checking* that there were no unfortunate transcriptional errors in Justus's copy (if only something so mundane as an omitted negative) that wrought havoc with his theology. What he wrote was surely *me quoque recognoscente*: "with me checking it as well." Augustine himself helped to check Justus's copy against his own, one reading aloud while the other collated in the usual way.

C used all these terms in alternation to designate (I suggest) that all-important first correction against the exemplar. *emendare* and *recognoscere* was what Pliny's friend asked him to do to a copy of his speeches, in this case unquestionably meaning no more than correct copying errors.[20] Both interchangability and meaning are strikingly borne out by three of the Jerome author-subscriptions: *cursim contulimus Bethlem, emendavi in Bethlehem,* and *recog(novi) Betheem* (another passage adds *relegere* to the list of synonyms).[21] Note too *legi et distincxi* followed by *distincxi emendans* in his poem in Asterius's elaborate Vergil subscription; *legi ... emendans* in Sabinus on Persius; *relegi* in Renatus on Boethius. The word *relegere* is several times found in this sense in Augustine: note particularly *Augustinus haec dictavi et relectis subscripsi,* "I Augustine dictated this, checked it and affixed my subscription."[22] Rufinus uses *relegi* of checking the work of his monks while they are still copying[23] (here it should be noted in passing that, since he was checking the work of several scribes as they worked, his checking cannot have gone further than looking for obvious divergences or omissions from the exemplar). All these terms simply certify that the copies in question had been checked.

---

18. Julius Celsus Constantinus, Zetzel 1981, 222. The subscriptions are confined to the *Bellum Gallicum.* Editors of Caesar have always interpreted this formula "only the *Bellum Gallicum,*" i.e., not the *Bellum Civile,* etc., as well. But, as should be clear from the innumerable examples cited in this chapter, *legi/emendavi* formulas were placed at the *end* of blocks of text, and invariably referred to them. In a two-word formula like *legi tantum,* the adverb must qualify the verb, not an unexpressed object. If he had wanted to say "thus far," the standard formula was *hucusque.*

19. *Ep.* 4*, p. 27 Divjak; Eno 1989, 42 (with a useful introduction to the subject matter, 38–40).

20. *petis ut libellos meos ... recognoscendos emendandosque curem,* Pliny, *Ep.* iv. 26. 1. Since Pliny was after all the author, he might also have made occasional stylistic changes as well.

21. Petitmengin 1983, 373 n. 52; *Ep.* 71. 5.

22. *Ep.* 241; *Ep.* 238; 239.

23. *Apol. Hieron.* ii. 11 (quoted below).

It is worth lingering on Augustine, *Ep.* 1*A to Firmus, which begins by stating that he has sent Firmus all twenty-two books of the *City of God, etiam mihi relectos.* Ever since this letter was published there has been a debate about whether Augustine revised the *City of God,* and whether occasional variants in the text derive from a second edition.[24] According to O'Daly, it is an argument in favor of this hypothesis "that he considered his rereading worthy of mention." But while a complete revision of so long a work that had taken him so many years to write cannot be excluded, it would have been a massive undertaking. In the present context the natural assumption is that Augustine simply checked the copy he had had made for Firmus against his own master copy, presumably with the assistance of "my son, your brother Cyprianus" who, he adds, had recommended the revision. After each book he checked Firmus would have read some such subscription as *Augustinus ipse emendavi, conferente mihi Cypriano filio.* Given the author's personal involvement, Firmus's copy was no doubt more accurate than most, but nothing more.

The formula *contuli* has so far only been found in Christian texts.[25] Since *conferre* was the *vox propria* for comparing one manuscript with another (= Greek ἀντιβάλλειν), it seems unlikely that the distribution is significant. The explanation surely lies in the fact that *conferre* describes the process of collation rather than the correction it made possible. Jerome was always insisting on the need for copyists "to collate and check" (*ut conferrent diligentius et emendarent*).[26] The term *contuli* appears most often as an interim formula (after individual letters of Ambrose and Augustine). Two manuscripts of Rufinus's translation of nine speeches of Gregory Nazianzen offer the instructive subscription "thus far I collated against the copy of the Blessed Melania in Rome" (*usque huc contuli de codice sanctae Melaniae Romae*).[27] Since both manuscripts offer the subscription at the end of the seventh speech, we may infer that this was its original location. The form of his note (*usque huc* = Greek ἕως ὧδε) shows that the corrector was indicating the point up to which he had collated his copy against the text in the library of, or perhaps actually in the hand of, one of the two Melanias (the elder was Rufinus's principal patron, but the younger is said to have been a skilful and prolific calligrapher).[28] He was perhaps unable to complete his task. In the Bembinus of Terence (ca. 400) there is no subscription, but a number of corrections individually signed with the name Ioviales, three times with a *hucusque.*[29] To cite a probably much later example, Politian records a note he found in the margin of a *vetustissimus codex* of Cato's *De agricultura: huc usque de duobus emendavi, hinc de uno exemplario tantum.*[30] Whether the original subscriptions *contuli/emendavi utcumque* found after a couple of

---

24. O'Daly 1999, 38.
25. "un verbo quasi esclusivo della *subscriptio* cristiana," Pecere 1986, 25.
26. *Ep.* 71. 5; Arns 1953, 68–72.
27. O (*Roma*) and A (*Romae*), late IX and X s.: A. Engelbrecht, *Tyrannii Rufini Orationum Gregorii Nazianzeni novem interpretatio* (CSEL 46, 1910), xxxii–xxxiii, lx.
28. *V. Melan.* 23; 26.
29. For a list, R. Kauer, *Wien. Stud.* 20 (1898), 256–60; on the various correctors, Prete 1970, 25–48.
30. M. D. Reeve in Reynolds 1983, 41.

letters of Jerome and Augustine's *De paenitentia* mean "checked thus far" or "checked as best I could" (= *ut potui*) is unclear.[31] In any case, though the formula *contuli* happens not to occur in any surviving secular subscription, Mavortius used the verb in his Horace subscription (*emendavi conferente mihi magistro Felice*). It seems that *recognovi* or *emendavi* was preferred to signal the completed task. For example, in a Basilican manuscript of Hilary's *De trinitate* dated to 509–10, we find *contuli* at the end of books and quires throughout, but *emendavi* at the end of the final book.[32]

One other term is found in only one subscription: *recensui*, in the unfortunately undatable Calliopius Terence subscription. We have a number of medieval copies of what must have been a fine late antique illustrated Terence. In a recent study David Wright has dated their postulated late antique model to ca. 400, and then further identified it with the copy "edited" by Calliopius.[33] But the art-historical date is insecure and there are grounds for dating Calliopius later than the illustrated copy.[34] The single name and lack of titles suggests a much later date.

In at least eight passages Augustine uses *recenseo* of reviewing or checking passages to make sure what they said. For example, "if anyone doubts this, let him review that passage and pay attention to the context."[35] The most interesting is an anecdote about a former pupil called Eulogius who was now a rhetor himself. One evening he was reviewing the reading from Cicero he was going to give his class the following day (*recensens lectionem quam postridie fuerat [discipulis] traditurus*) when he came on a passage he simply could not understand.[36] If he had another copy at hand, he no doubt collated it in case the source of his difficulty was a corruption in the text, but his primary goal here was comprehension rather than correction. In the event, he fell asleep and Augustine explained the passage to him in a dream!

But we also find the word used of checking one manuscript against another. Jerome explained in a letter to Paula that he has been collating (*confero*) the edition of Aquila against the Hebrew text, with "the Prophets, Solomon, the Psalms and Kings already meticulously checked" (*examussim recensetis*).[37] In his polemic against Jerome, Rufinus cites some books that (he claims) Jerome thought he had revised so as to make them perfectly clear (*ad liquidum recensuisse*).[38]

Most illuminating of all are a couple of passages in Augustine's *Contra Academicos*. Augustine describes how he, his son Adeodatus, and Trygetius and Licentius, two of his pupils, spent almost a whole day "in reviewing Bk i of Vergil" (*in recensione primi*

---

31. Reifferscheid 1873, 3 (*utcumque* itself could bear either meaning).
32. *CLA* 1 (1934), 1a; Lindsay, *Pal. Latina* 2 (1923), 10.
33. Wright 1996, 41–56.
34. Grant 1986, 42, 96. The verb *recensui* lends no support to Wright's surprising suggestion (50) that Calliopius was "an entrepreneurial publisher identifying himself and advertising his product."
35. *Ep.* 148. 8; cf. 96. 9 (*recense sane epistolam meam*); 104. 5; 149. 5; 162. 3; 175. 1; 274. 1.
36. *De cura pro mortuis gerenda* xi. 13 (*CSEL* 41, 1900, 642), presumably the Ciceronian commentator Favonius Eulogius.
37. *Ep.* 32. 1; for the unusual form of the past participle, see the examples cited in *TLL* s.v.
38. *Apol.* i. 28.

libri Vergilii). A few days later they broke off their philosophical discussions to devote "about seven days" to "reviewing" (*recenseremus*) and also "discussing" (*tractaremus*) Bks ii–iv. In another dialogue composed at the same time he further describes how they "listened" (*audivi*) to a half-book of Vergil before dinner every day.[39] It seems clear that each of these three terms designates a different activity: *audire*, listening without interruption while someone simply read the text aloud; *tractare*, more discursive treatment of problem passages; *recensere*, word by word review of the text. One day apparently sufficed for the *recensio* of *Aen*. i, but nearly seven were spent on ii–iv, implying three to four hundred lines a day. That is about how long it would take one person to read his text aloud carefully while the others checked it against their copies. It is tempting to infer that Augustine is describing the process to which some of the surviving subscriptions bear witness. Not scholarship, but a scholarly review of the text by advanced students under the supervision of an experienced teacher. The finished product might have been signed (e.g.): *emendavi (recensui, recognovi) ego Licentius adiuvante Augustino magistro, ex oratore urbis Mediolanii*. None of the participants in this seminar were pagans. Though not yet baptized, most were at least catechumens.

A scholarly reader who took the trouble to revise his copy carefully was also likely to add notes of various sorts, both at the time and at intervals over the years. If the Bobbio Fronto had survived in its prepalimpsested form, it might have been possible to distinguish different layers of annotation in different inks, as Zuntz did for the Laurentianus of Euripides, showing that Triclinius annotated the manuscript on at least three different occasions.[40] We should not suppose that all the marginalia in the Bobbio Fronto were added in the course of just one reading and classified as different aspects of *emendatio*. Since readers often jotted down notes or references or collated individual passages when in doubt, the fact that a manuscript carried variants and marginal notes proved nothing about its credentials as a whole. What responsible prospective readers or purchasers wanted to know about a book they came across was whether it had been systematically corrected. That is what *legi/emendavi/recognovi* certified.

The point in their various ranges of meaning at which all these terms intersect is clearly "check," "certify as accurate." One new context in which *recognovi* was to become a standard formula is in the certification of the proceedings of church councils and public disputations. The earliest well-documented example is the conference between Catholics and Donatists at Carthage in 411. Groups of shorthand-writers (*notarii, exceptores*), two at a time on each side, would take everything down verbatim, the various versions would be carefully compared (*collatio*) and if necessary corrected (*emendatio*), and then the participants would sign with the formula *recognovi*.[41]

---

39. *Contra Acad*. i. 15; ii. 10; *De ordine* i. 8. 26.
40. Zuntz 1965.
41. Tengström 1962, 17–22; S. Lancel, *Gesta Conlationis Carthaginiensis* (Turnholt 1974), x–xiii; *Gesta* I. 7. 3; 9. 4; 12. 9; 22. 8; 24. 4; 26. 6; Teitler 1985, Ch. 2.

By the end of the fourth century, almost everyone concerned with the writing, copying, and checking of books would have had dealings with the law, bureaucracy, and church. One form of authentication naturally influenced another. *Legi* and *recognovi* came to be used interchangeably with *emendavi* because, when affixed to a poem or history, *emendavi* meant the same as *legi* or *recognovi* affixed to a legal or bureaucratic document or record of a public debate. All three were formulas for certifying an accurate copy.

Such checking was to remain one of the key stages in the routine of book production until (and after) the invention of printing. Humanists used the same terms as their late antique predecessors, normally *emendavi* or *recognovi*.[42] Both medieval and humanistic texts make it clear that correction was done at once, before the newly copied text was even bound. In a definition of what counted as a book in the eyes of the law, the jurist Ulpian excluded blank papyrus and unfinished books but included books that had been "fully written out" (*perscripti*) but not "hammered or ornamented," together with books "not yet glued together or corrected" (*emendati*). It looks as if correction was perceived as the final stage in the production of a book.[43]

There is late antique evidence pointing in the same direction. For example, in the Hilary manuscript of 509–10 just mentioned, we find *contuli* written (perhaps in the hand of Fulgentius of Ruspe) on the last page of successive quires by the quire numbers.[44] In the light of Rufinus's account of how he regularly checked quires (*quaterniones...relegi*) of Ciceronian dialogues copied by his monks on Mount Olivet *while they were writing*,[45] the implication is that the corrector checked quires individually before they were bound together. Rufinus was playing the role of the corrector or diorthotes in the professional copying house of earlier times. This is why Sidonius complained about his corrector's occasional failure to turn up. Copyist and corrector needed to work together to produce a book on schedule. In two other sixth-century Latin manuscripts we again find *contuli* written in the bottom corner of the last page of each quire by the quire number.[46] These manuscripts were no doubt produced in monastic scriptoria, but it is not likely that monks working in different places uniformly adopted new and different practices. Common sense suggests that this had been standard practice since the adoption of the codex.

---

42. Rizzo 1973, 243–44; for *recognovi* in Politian, Rizzo 279; but in humanist usage *emendatio* soon came to take on its modern sense of "conjecture" (Rizzo 1973, 267).

43. *Digest* xxxii. 52. 5. According to Roberts and Skeat 1987, 31 n. 4, *emendati* may refer to "the repair of minor blemishes in the material," but it is hard to believe that anyone disputing (say) whether a given volume was included in a legacy would raise so weak an argument; lack of final correction would surely be stronger.

44. *CLA* i. 1a, with *Suppl.* (1971), pl. VI and p. viii; Wilmart 1938, 293–305; Courcelle 1964, 197 with pl. 34a.

45. *in meis cellulis manentes, in monte Oliveti, quamplurimos ei* [for Jerome] *Ciceronis dialogos descripserunt, quorum ego et quaterniones, cum scriberent, frequenter in manibus tenui et relegi*, Rufinus, *Apol. Hieron.* ii. 11.

46. *CLA* iii. 304 (Ambros. Cim. 1) and v. 658 (Par. lat. 13367).

On f.45^r of the Puteanus of Prudentius stands the signature [+Ve]*ttius Agorius Basilius*. Though at the end of a book (Prudentius's *Cathemerinon*), this is an owner's signature rather than a subscription (p. 431). But if (as Winstedt argued) this is the contemporary hand that corrected the manuscript throughout, adding a number of omitted lines (evidently from the exemplar), then these corrections were surely made before binding. For the original threefold (re)numbering of the quires shows that the manuscript was written in three separate parts (f. 1–44 = quires i–vi; f. 45–123 = quires i–x; and f. 124–55 = quires i–iiii), and the signature appears on the first page of the second part.[47] The presumption is that Basilius wrote his name on the front page of the second part before the three parts were bound together, to ensure that the binder was not misled by the numbering of the quires.

10: DELUXE COPIES

By no means all corrected manuscripts were subscribed. For example, six out of the seven capital Vergils were corrected by contemporary hands, presumably against exemplars, to judge from the supplementation of missing words and lines. But only the Medicean was subscribed (and there are strong reasons for believing that the Asterius subscription and poem were added by a later copyist from another manuscript).[48] But subscribed or no, the Vergil manuscripts vividly illustrate how crucial correction was. The text of at least three of them was so carelessly copied that, without the ministrations of their correctors, they would have been practically unreadable. The beautiful uncial palimpsest text of Cicero's *De re publica*, perhaps from the lifetime of Symmachus, is likewise full of errors throughout, most of them removed by a competent corrector using the same exemplar as the copyist. Elaborate colophons at the end of Bks i and ii occupy an entire column, leaving plenty of space for the corrector to sign his name and as many titles as he wished. But he did not.[49] For an aristocrat who wanted a calligraphic Cicero or an illustrated Vergil, the basic need was not scholarly research, but careful correction. The two grandest and most luxuriously produced Vergils, the Romanus and Augusteus, have the worst text. Both are so large that "each bifolio required a whole sheepskin."[50] But the corrector of the Romanus caught only half of the grosser errors, and no one bothered to correct the Augusteus at all.

The Livy manuscripts provide another illustration. We have more or less substantial fragments of six late antique copies, all from the fourth or fifth century. No fewer

---

47. Winstedt, *CR* 17 (1903), 207; 18 (1904), 112; Cunningham 1958, 34.

48. See M. Geymonat's edition (1973), xix–xx, listing s. V–VI correctors for all save the Augusteus; Cameron 1998.

49. Strelitz 1874; K. Ziegler, *Cicero: De re publica*^{7} (Leipzig 1969), xxiii–xxxi, 80; for the colophons, van Buren 1907, 189.

50. Wright 1992, 27: Romanus 35 x 33. 5 cm; Augusteus 42 x 35 cm.

than three were left uncorrected: the Veronensis of the first decade; the Vatican fragments of the fourth (R);[51] and perhaps the Vindobonensis of the fifth.[52] The text of what remains of the fifth decade is so bad[53] that we can hardly lay all the responsibility on its scribe. And despite the efforts of its anonymous corrector, the same applies to the Puteanus of the third decade. Anonymus was able to straighten out simple mistakes, but not to repair the many more serious errors and omissions. In fact, his misguided interventions often made things worse; later copyists naturally tend to follow the corrected rather than the original text of the Puteanus.[54] Either Anonymus did not have an exemplar at all, or he had the same already corrupt (or illegible) exemplar from which the Puteanus had just been made. Both Vindobonensis and Puteanus were luxury books, copied in expert uncial hands. The scribes may have been ignorant or careless, but much of the blame surely rests with already corrupt, no doubt uncorrected, exemplars. The Puteanus subscriptions were written at Avellino, near Naples, presumably on some aristocratic estate.[55] This manuscript may therefore be the closest we are likely to come to an original classical text corrected and subscribed by a member of the fifth-century Roman elite. It is not a reassuring document.

But luxury Christian books were no different. Jerome repeatedly warns rich Christians that it is "correctness and accurate punctuation" (*ad fidem placeat emendata et erudita distinctio*) they should be looking for in copies of the Scriptures, not gilding and "Babylonian parchment." Again, "let those who wish have their old books or purple parchment picked out with gold and silver ... as long as they leave me ... books that are correct rather than beautiful" (*non tam pulchros codices quam emendatos*).[56] It is this last passage in which the word *uncial* first occurs, not in its technical modern sense of a type of script, but satirically, "inch-high letters."[57] A perfect example is provided by the early fifth-century Veronensis of Augustine's *City of God*, "conspicuous for the excellence of its calligraphy rather than of its text,"[58] perhaps from the same

---

51. *Multa quidem textus menda praebet ... neque aderat corrector*, McDonald, OCT 5 (1965), xl. On the other hand a *corrector aequalis* (F²) *emendavit* the Bamberg fragments (F): McDonald 1965, x. For the Veronensis, Ch. 14.

52. *CLA* x. 1472; P. Jal, *Tite-Live XXXI: livres xli–xlii* (Paris 1971), lxxxiii–lxxxviii. Though listing corrections in detail, C. Wessely has nothing on the man responsible in his one hundred-page preface to *Codex Vindobonensis latinus 15 photypice editus* (Leyden 1907). John Briscoe tells me that some corrections may be in a second hand (letter dated 12–viii–98), though he sees no reason to believe them drawn from a different exemplar.

53. Just how bad can be appreciated by anyone who studies a few pages of apparatus in Jal's Budé (1971–79) or J. Briscoe's Teubner of 1986.

54. *ingenio suo fretus lectiones sanas nunc instaurat, emendationes pravas nunc introducit*, P. G. Walsh in his Teubner of Bks 26–27 (1989²); cf. T. A. Dorey, in his Teubner of Bks 21–22 (1971), vii. It might have been thought that the copies would *always* follow the corrected text, but they are in fact remarkably inconsistent: F. W. Shipley, *AJA* 7 (1903), 193–97.

55. *recognobi Abellini*, at the end of Bks 21, 24, and 25.

56. *Ep.* 107. 12; *Vulg. Job pr.* (*PL* 28. 1083A); for other such passages, Arns 1954, 26.

57. So P. Meyvaert, *JTS* 34 (1983), 185–88.

58. E. A. Lowe in *CLA* 4 (1947), 491.

scriptorium as the no less splendid but even more careless Puteanus of Livy.[59] Viliaric's beautiful Orosius (ca. 550) is also a careless piece of work, but in this case most of the worst errors (notably the many omissions) were caught by a contemporary corrector, evidently collating against Viliaric's exemplar.[60]

The one calligrapher we can identify by name in late fourth-century Rome— Furius Dionysius Filocalus—seems to have worked exclusively for Christian patrons, in both parchment and stone. The Calendar of 354 we cannot judge, since all we have are Renaissance copies, nor his inscriptions on the baths of the elder Melania, known from an eighth-century copy. But many of the martyr-epigrams he inscribed for Pope Damasus have survived in their original magnificence.[61]

Asterius's poem is more informative than the subscription it accompanies. In it he begs the next reader to check again (the *legi relegi* of the documents) and forgive him if he overlooked any errors due to preoccupation with his consular games (to the cost of which he then passes):

> quisque *legas relegas* felix, parcasque benignus
> si qua minus vacuus praeteriit animus.

Whoever reads this, reread it fruitfully, and kindly forgive me if my busy mind has skipped over anything.

Though not the actual copy he checked, the Medicean illustrates his words well enough. The activity of the first corrector (M², formerly identified as the hand of Asterius) is limited to inserting omitted words and lines, correcting the more obvious errors—and occasional punctuation.

Asterius appears in a rather different light in another subscription, as the posthumous "editor" of the *Carmen paschale* of Sedulius. He claims to have found the poem "scattered" among the poet's papers, put it together, and published it "with every elegance."[62] Since he was working from the author's own papers, the editorial achievement for which he was so anxious to claim credit presumably consisted of little more than checking his own copy against the writer's autograph. In view of his emphasis on the elegance of the volume, the copy he corrected had presumably been made by a professional calligrapher.

---

59. *CLA* 4, 12; Reynolds 1983, 210–11; Conway and Johnson, OCT 4 (1934), xxx–xxxi; Lowe, *CLA* 5 (1950), 562.
60. See C. Zangemeister's edition (1882), vii–ix.
61. Ferrua 1942, 21–35; Salzman 1990, 202–4; Cameron 1992, 140–44.
62. *hoc opus Sedulius inter cartulas dispersum reliquit, quod recollectum, adunatum atque ad omnem elegantiam divulgatum est a Turcio Rufio Asterio v. c. exconsule ordinario atque patricio;* preserved in several MSS, earliest the s. VII Taur. E. IV 44: J. Huemer's edition (1885), vii. The date of Sedulius is uncertain: *PCBE* ii. 1344–45 ("entre 425 et 450"); Green 2006, 142–43. The Turin MS also carries a couple of subscriptions attesting collation by a certain Abundantius: *ego Abundantius hunc librum contuli* (p. 112) and the same (with *istum* for *hunc*) on p. 90.

11: THE ROLE OF RELIGION

According to D. E. Martin, late antique subscriptions reflect "a striking new departure from the traditional methods and philosophy of book editing."[63] But the *method* is exactly the same. It is only the naming of the subscriber that seems to be new. Why is it that we find people of rank proofreading manuscripts with such apparent pride? The standard explanation is pagan concern about the "preservation" of the classics. As McGeachy put it, "Mistakes in the texts of the classics weakened one of the strongest supports of paganism—its literature."[64] Yet (as we have seen) most identifiable subscribers are either known to be Christians or must be presumed Christians from their date. The force of this objection has been disposed of too glibly as "the eventual acceptance and preservation of pagan literature by the Christians, who took up the task when the pagan resistance faded."[65] That is to say, from the surviving Christian evidence we postulate a prior pagan initiative that Christians perpetuated without any apparent awareness of its original anti-Christian purpose. In chapter 19 we shall encounter much the same flawed assumption that fifth-century classicizing Christian art depends on a prior pagan initiative.

Surprisingly enough, the answer may after all lie ultimately in religion. I suggest, however, that this new preoccupation with the accuracy of the written word has Christian rather than pagan roots. Starting with the sacred writings themselves, Christian scholars soon extended their concern to the writings of the doctors of the church. In an age when true faith turned on the omission or inclusion of an iota, it was vital to have the most accurate texts possible. We have already noted the importance attached to obtaining certified copies of public disputations on Christian controversies. An early illustration of the Christian concern for authentication is the subscription found in one manuscript of the late second-century *Martyrdom of Polycarp*, tracing the sequence of copies between the writer and a disciple of Polycarp. Even if some elements in the pedigree raise doubts, its significance as an authenticating device remains unaffected.[66] Earlier studies have misplaced the emphasis. According to Pecere, Christianity brought about a "radical shift in the relationship between *scribere* and *emendare*" and a "redefinition of the system of book production and diffusion."[67] But this is both too vague and too extreme. Certainly Jerome had a religious motive for wanting accurate texts, but he made it absolutely clear that the only way to get them

---

63. Martin 1984, 149.
64. McGeachy 1942, 170; the most vigorous statement of this view is Lommatzsch 1904.
65. Martin 1984, 149; for a similar formulation, Lommatzsch 1904, 188.
66. H. Musurillo, *Acts of the Christian Martyrs* (Oxford 1972), 21; Barnes, *JTS* 19 (1968), 510–14. Such pedigrees are not completely new. According to Galen, Ptolemy Philadelphus had books that arrived in Alexandria classified by their place of origin, which may explain the Homeric texts classified by city names (Massaliote, Chian. etc.): Allen 1924, 291–94; for an even earlier colophon on the provenance of the Greek Book of Esther, see E. J. Bickerman, *Journ. Bibl. Lit.* 63 (1944), 339–62.
67. Pecere 1986, 25; on alleged new features in the diffusion of Christian books, see above.

was the old-fashioned way, collation and correction.[68] Toward the end of the second century Irenaeus of Lyons closed a book with the following oath, explicitly quoted and endorsed by Eusebius, Jerome, and (on two occasions) Rufinus:[69]

> I adjure you who transcribe this book, by our Lord Jesus Christ and by his glo-
> rious advent when he comes to judge both the quick and the dead, to collate what
> you have transcribed and to correct it carefully against the copy from which you
> have transcribed it; and likewise to transcribe this oath and insert it in your copy.

An impressive testimony to the concerns of generations of Christian scholars. But before we get carried away with grand notions of revolutionary Christian attitudes,[70] there are a couple of commonsense reservations to be born in mind. First, Jerome's own constant complaints about the idleness and inaccuracy of copyists, not to mention the multitude of execrable surviving copies of Christian books, make it all too clear that, oaths notwithstanding, in real life Christian scribes were no more accurate than their pagan predecessors. Second, there is nothing here (except for the formulation of the oath) to which any pagan could take exception. Indeed, many pagans in earlier centuries must have wished they could make their copyists swear such an oath.

On the evidence we have, it was Pamphilus and his collaborators who initiated or at any rate formalized the change we are investigating. Pagans had been carefully correcting their books for a half-millennium before the triumph of the church, but formal subscriptions in early imperial Greek literary papyri are extremely rare and invariably anonymous, an impersonal passive, the bare abbreviation di(*orthōthē*) ("corrected") added at the end of a book by the colophon.[71] It might be objected that most papyri are fragmentary and that we have relatively few colophons. But the majority of those we do have are not followed by subscriptions of any sort.[72] In fact, there are only two certain examples, papyri of *Iliad* 2 and 17, respectively.[73] To the best of my knowledge there is not a single such subscription attached to the scores of colophons we have on Herculaneum papyri.[74] And the same is true of the colophons preserved for the first two speeches in the recently published fourth-century Isocrates codex.[75] A marginal note "I Ammonius the grammarian, son of Ammonius, made

---

68. Many texts on the faults and errors of copyists and the importance of correction in Arns 1953, 68–72.
69. Eusebius, *HE* v. 20. 2; Jerome, *de vir. ill.* 35; Rufinus, in his translation of both Eusebius and Origen *De principiis*, pr. 3 = Jerome, *Ep.* 80. 3 (adding punctuation: see below).
70. Christianity was (of course) a book-centered religion in the way no pagan cult ever was, but I am here concerned with the purely material aspects of Christian books.
71. McNamee 1981, 25.
72. Except for stichometric notes about the number of lines copied: Turner, *GMAW*² (1987), nos. 14, 17, 18, 61.
73. P. Bodl. Ms. Gr. a. 1 (P); P. Ross. Georg. i. 4, both δι (ορθώθη); for a classified list of all annotated papyri of Homer, McNamee 1992, 15–51.
74. Or so I infer from the silence on the subject by Cavallo 1983.
75. Worp and Rijksbaron 1997, 87, 115; for the corrector, 24.

notes" in a second-century Homer commentary is no exception. This does not mean that Ammonius corrected the commentary,[76] but that he used it to mark up a text of Homer, that is to say, placed sigla in the margins to refer readers to the relevant notes in the commentary.[77]

The explanation is simple enough. In the early centuries books were always both copied and corrected by people of low status, slaves or freedmen specially trained for the purpose.[78] It was enough that they did their job; it was neither necessary nor appropriate that they should prove it by signing their (obscure and unimportant) names. Genuine scholarly editors would naturally have signed their work, but not by adding a bare "corrected" (*diorthōsa*) at the end of successive books. The only subscription we have to a scholarly edition (Statilius Maximus's *De lege agraria*) makes much more elaborate claims (Ch. 12. 2). The fact that so many papyri were corrected but not subscribed suggests that correction was simply taken for granted in professionally produced books. Given the complete absence of signed subscriptions in a half-millennium of literary papyri, it is surely more than coincidence that the first known Greek subscriptions to name subscribers are Christian, those by Pamphilus and his collaborators to the Septuagint. A man of Pamphilus's wealth and standing would never have devoted so much time and effort to proofreading texts of the classics. The classics could be left to lowly professionals, but the consequences of a mistake in Scripture were too serious for this.

It is important to be clear that Pamphilus and Eusebius were not really scholarly editors. They made no claim to have sought out or collated manuscripts of either the Old or New Testament.[79] While taking immense pains to produce the most accurate text they could, for the Septuagint they just copied Origen's text from the fifth column of his *Hexapla*. Jerome, with no thought of depreciating their efforts, describes them as publishing the labors of Origen.[80] And the only claim made for Pamphilus's New Testament text is that it was copied in his own hand (plausibly enough, given that he is said to have copied much of Origen in his own hand). Yet given their intimate familiarity both with the biblical text and its scholarly exegesis, their contribution was obviously not limited to a routine diorthosis. In his biography of his patron, Eusebius records that Pamphilus had many copies of the Scriptures made so that he could present them to anyone willing to read.[81] And many years later it was to Eusebius that Constantine addressed his famous request for fifty copies of the Scriptures, legible

---

76. ἐσημειωσάμην; Zuntz 1951, 193 n. 1.
77. P. Oxy. 221; McNamee 2007, 286, no. 1205; for scholiastic (or perhaps pedagogic) σημείωσαι, McNamee 1998, 274, 281, 286–87.
78. As rightly emphasized by Cavallo 1997, 212–13.
79. Against Zuntz 1945, 103–4, contrast K. Aland and B. Aland 1989, 66.
80. *codices…quos ab Origene elaboratos Eusebius et Pamphilus vulgaverunt*, *Prol. Paralip* (PL 28. 1393).
81. *scripturas quoque sanctas non ad legendum tantum, sed et habendum tribuebat promptissime* [i.e., he gave as well as lent copies]: *nec solum viris sed et feminis quas vidisset lectioni* [= ἀνάγνωσις] of reading Scripture: Lampe, *Patr. Lex.* s.v. A] *deditas. unde et multos codices praeparabat, ut cum necessitas poposcisset volentibus largiretur* (Jerome, *Apol. Ruf.* i. 9, quoting Eusebius); Zuntz 1945, 103–4.

and portable codexes written by experienced professional calligraphers.[82] He must have taken pains to see that these copies reproduced the text so laboriously corrected by himself, Pamphilus and Antoninus in the dark days of the persecutions. The truth is that Pamphilus and Eusebius acted less as scholars than as unusually conscientious publishers, except that they were more concerned to distribute than sell the accurate copies of Scripture they produced.

The Pamphilan colophons parallel the later Latin subscriptions in ways that have not been sufficiently appreciated. Most other surviving Greek subscriptions state the credentials of the text copied, but never name those who simply did the correcting. For example, the scholarly reader responsible for the late antique exemplar of the Venetus A of the Iliad gave names and titles for the works he excerpted for his scholia. But he did not name himself (nor does he claim to have either copied or corrected his text).[83] And the same is true of the subscription to Origen's *Against Celsus*: "copied from and collated against an exemplar from among Origen's own books," where the use of the impersonal passive need not imply that the subscriber himself did the actual copying and collating. Koetschau assumed that the subscriber's name was later omitted,[84] but why assume that it was ever there? We now know that it was already missing six hundred years earlier in the Toura papyrus.

Those who assign a pagan significance to the late fourth- and early fifth-century secular subscriptions were evidently unaware how closely they mirror the Pamphilan subscriptions in form. For example, the curiously precise custom of recording the name of the man who read out the exemplar as well as the man who actually corrected the copy. Compare, for example, the Horace subscription (*Mavortius...emendavi conferente mihi magistro Felice*) with the Septuagint subscription to II Esdra, "Antoninus collated, Pamphilus corrected," where (as we have seen) collated must mean collated *aloud*. Note too the *ut potui* in Mavortius's *legi et ut potui emendavi*, where such humility comes oddly from a Roman consul assisted by a professor of rhetoric. Here again we may compare Eusebius (on III Kings), "I Eusebius corrected as accurately as I could."[85] The earliest secular example of the formula is *prout potui* in the Persius subscription of 402; it was especially common in subscriptions to Christian Latin writings.[86]

An even closer parallel is provided by a series of original Byzantine subscriptions in the Vaticanus of Lucian by Alexander of Nicaea, writing around 930.[87] The one to Bk ii of the *True History* is typical: "I, Alexander, bishop of Nicaea in Bithynia, corrected <this

---

82. Euseb. *Vita Const*. iv. 36.
83. To take a later example, the compiler of the Palatine Anthology (930/40) names the sources he drew on for his own collection, copied substantial portions of text in his own hand, and in addition corrected and added ascriptions and scholia to the work of the various scribes he employed. But he never names himself (Cameron 1993, Ch. 5–6).
84. μετεβλήθη καὶ ἀντεβλήθη, Koetschau 1889, 66–67.
85. Ἀντωνῖνος ἀντέβαλεν, Πάμφιλος διόρθωσα; Εὐσέβιος διώρθωσα ὡς ἀκριβῶς ἐδυνάμην.
86. Reifferscheid 1873, 4, quotes several examples from manuscripts of Augustine; cf. too Lindsay, *Paleographia latina* 2 (1923), 11; Petitmengin 1983, 370. Bede claims to have corrected a Latin translation of the Life of St. Anastasius *prout potui*: *HE* v. 24, with Franklin and Meyvaert 1982, 373.
87. For the date, R. Browning, *Byzantion* 24 (1954), 426.

book> with the aid of my brother Jacob, metropolitan of Larissa."[88] First, the titles of both men recorded in full in an owner's private copy. Second the "with": compare Domitius Dracontius correcting his Pseudo-Quintilian "with (*cum*) his brother Hierius" and Aurelius Memmius Symmachus corrected his Macrobius "with (*cum*) Macrobius Plotinus Eudoxius." Alexander corrected his Lucian with three different assistants (his brother, a nephew, and a deacon).[89] Third, a remarkable structural parallel, the position of the emphatic "I": *diorthōsa egō Alexandros, emendavi ego Torquatus Gennadius* (Martial, six times), *emendavi ego Dracontius* (Ps-Quintilian), and *legi ego Niceus* (Juvenal).[90]

Since it is out of the question that Alexander followed western practice, we are bound to conclude that he was following the same Greek models as the late antique Latin subscribers. Zuntz indeed assumed that the Pamphilus subscriptions were modelled on earlier subscriptions to texts of the Greek classics. Where Pamphilus and Eusebius had taken Origen as their authority, according to Zuntz there "must have been" early copies of Homer with subscriptions like "taken from and collated against the text of Zenodotus."[91] But quite apart from the lack of evidence, this is highly unlikely in itself. In the first place, the various editors of Homer constantly differed from one another. Nobody would have followed one rather than another throughout. In the second, all of them were generally thought to have gone much too far.[92] Only a handful of their readings are found in the hundreds of Homer papyri.[93] Last, and most important, it is by no means certain that any of these critics (least of all Zenodotus) produced complete new texts consisting entirely of their own preferred readings. Rather, they revised and annotated existing texts.[94]

On the evidence we have, the subscriptions of Pamphilus and his disciples are the first of their kind, gentlemen playing the role of correctors without being professional scholars. Their names were guarantees of quality. It was not long before other prominent Christians followed their example. The fact that St. Basil used the same formula in the subscription to his carefully revised Bible (*antibalōn diōrthōsōato*) suggests that he was familiar with the Caesarea Bibles. The only subscribed late antique Bible to survive comes from the sixth-century West, Victor of Capua's meticulously corrected volume. It may have been Euzoïus, Eusebius's second successor as bishop of Caesarea, who

---

88. διώρθωσα ἐγὼ Ἀλέξανδρος ἐπίσκοπος Νικαίας τῆς κατὰ Βιθυνίαν μετὰ τοῦ οἰκείου ἀδελφοῦ Ἰακώβου τοῦ μητροπολίτου Λαρίσσης.

89. For the list, H. Rabe, *Scholia in Lucianum* (Leipzig 1906), 287.

90. Compare too *scripsi ego* in one of the Priscian subscriptions.

91. Zuntz 1951, 192.

92. Indeed, they were often subjected to ridicule (Düring 1941, 6–11).

93. If there are a few more in the medieval manuscripts, that is not because they derive from authoritative early copies, but because Byzantine readers took them from the scholia: according to T. W. Allen, of more than 874 known Aristarchan readings, only 80 appear in all of our nearly 200 medieval manuscripts, and 132 in none; of 413 Zenodotan readings, only 6 appear in all manuscripts, and 240 in none; fewer still in the papyri (*Homeri Ilias* 1 (Oxford 1931), 199); R. Janko, *The Iliad: A Commentary* 4 (Cambridge 1992), 22.

94. Montanari 1998, 1–20; M. L. West, *Homerus: Ilias* 1 (Stuttgart 1998), vi–viii. It might be added that Zenodotus is not mentioned in any of the scholar's texts listed by McNamee 2007, 39.

extended the same attention to nonbiblical writings—unless the subscription to Origen's *Contra Celsum* derives from Pamphilus (§ 2). The close parallelism between the Latin subscriptions and the subscriptions of Alexander of Nicaea suggests that the practice had spread to copies of the classics before the end of the fourth century. As it happens a number of Latin subscriptions come from the East, including the earliest known (Sallustius finished correcting his Apuleius at Constantinople in 397). An otherwise unknown Paul corrected his Lucan there at a date unknown.[95]

This is not a case where we can postulate a long-established pattern drawn upon by Christians and pagans alike. As we have seen, there are grounds for identifying precisely the common features as innovations by Pamphilus and his disciples in Caesarea. It is also important to add that the differences between the secular Latin subscriptions and those in the Septuagint manuscripts are as striking as the similarities.[96] Where Pamphilus and his colleagues identified themselves by a single name,[97] the Latin subscribers (like Alexander of Nicaea) normally give full names and titles. And where Pamphilus and his colleagues took care to indicate the scholarly credentials of their text, the Latin subscribers were mostly just correcting their own copies, normally against an unidentified exemplar, sometimes with the aid of a friend, sometimes entirely on their own.

It might seem tempting to hypothesize that pagans deliberately adopted these new Christian forms because they were trying to accord the classics the status of secular Scripture, "unmarred by error."[98] That would be a neat way of maintaining the hypothesis of a pagan reaction despite the prior Christian initiative. But this would presuppose that these hypothetical militant pagans, while despising Christianity and its literature, admired and emulated the scrupulosity of Christian book production. Yet there is nothing new about the procedure of collation and correction itself; it is only the detailed description of the procedure that appears to be new. In any case, the Latin subscribers reproduced only the form of these Christian subscriptions.

It is obviously more likely that those who first adapted these forms to private ends were Christians rather than pagans—not that many are likely to have recalled the Christian origin of the forms by the end of the fourth century. Anxious to identify a distinctively Christian attitude to the book, Pecere has argued that correction and subscription "acquired a juridical importance in the Christian book."[99] Certainly, Christians became increasingly concerned about questions of authenticity, but there is no need to see such concerns behind every subscription in a Christian book. A simple *contuli* at the end of a letter of Augustine or Ambrose meant no more than that it had been checked for accuracy. We have already seen that authenticating

---

95. Zetzel 1981, 223.
96. Zuntz 1951, 196, noted only the similarities in a brief comparison.
97. The title "confessor" (ὁμολογητής) given Antoninus in one subscription cannot have been original.
98. Martin 1984, 148.
99. Pecere 1986, 27.

subscriptions were a routine feature of legal and bureaucratic life. We should not presume a religious motive in books that belonged to bureaucrats who happened also to be Christians. Nor does it make much sense to distinguish between secular and Christian subscriptions when the secular books in question were subscribed by Christians.

By the end of the fourth century a much more far-reaching change had taken place in the world of the ancient book: the victory of the codex over the roll, the traditional medium for classical literature.[100] The advantages of the codex are obvious enough (more durable, more capacious, more handy for reference), yet there seems little doubt that Christians adopted it before the rest of the population, whether because they recognized these advantages or (as is perhaps more likely) because they originally wrote and then continued to copy their works in the parchment notebooks (*membranae*) generally used for subliterary purposes (especially business and the law)[101] rather than the rolls sanctified by art and tradition for literature proper. From as early as the second century most Christians seem to have read their Scriptures in codex form.[102] By ca. 400 most readers of the classics must have been Christians.

Another factor in the victory of the codex will have been its adoption by the law and the bureaucracy. The first two legal codes, significantly titled *Codex Gregorianus* and *Codex Hermogenianus*, appeared at the beginning of the fourth century. And by about the same date the codex also became the standard medium for storing bureaucratic information (the earliest documentary codex, listing military clothing requisitions, dates from 324–27).[103] Grammarians and rhetoricians must also have found the codex more useful for textbooks (we have seen how prominently students and teachers and professors of rhetoric are represented among the subscriptions). It is clear from the very numerous references in both Jerome and Augustine that *codex* was now standard Latin for "book."[104] By 400 it is unlikely that anyone remembered Christian priority.

In short, by the end of the fourth century most of the people likely to commission copies of the classics would either be or know Christians and have regular dealings with the law and bureaucracy, in both private and public contexts. The same scribes must often have been called upon to copy classical, Christian, legal, and technical texts indifferently. It is not surprising that all the various innovations in book production should eventually have come together, to be employed indifferently (and unself-consciously) by Christians and pagans alike.

---

100. Roberts and Skeat 1987; Harris 1991, 71–85.
101. On which see Roberts and Skeat 1987, 15–23.
102. Roberts and Skeat 1987, 38–66; Harris 1991, 73–77; Bagnall 2009.
103. Sheridan 1998; P. Beatty Panop. (T. C. Skeat [ed.] 1964) is a documentary codex dating from 339–45, made up from a reused documentary roll dating from 296–300.
104. Arns 1953, 122–28; Petitmengin, "Codex" in *Augustinus-Lexikon* 1 (1986–94), 1022–37 (*liber* 3,059 times, *codex* 636 times).

12: WHO WERE THE SUBSCRIBERS?

Who are the people who identify themselves so grandly in the surviving subscriptions to classical texts? Not only is there not a single pagan aristocrat among them, not one can be plausibly identified as pagan at all. And the truth is that, of those who can be dated before ca. 450, only Nicomachus Flavianus and his son Dexter can be claimed as aristocrats.

Fl. Iulius Tryfonianus Sabinus, the corrector of Persius, for all his impressive-sounding names, was simply a guards officer. Like a better-known *protector domesticus* with literary tastes (Ammianus Marcellinus), he was no doubt of respectable provincial stock, but scarcely well-connected if he could manage nothing better than a four-year posting to Spain and southern Gaul. Torquatus Gennadius, Domitius Dracontius, Hierius, and Felix were all professors (it was no doubt the connections he acquired as a successful rhetorician that won Gennadius his provincial governorships). It has been asserted that grammarians and rhetors "stood in a close relationship with the aristocracy."[105] But I know of no evidence pointing to a closer relationship with the aristocracy of Rome than with any other members of the elite.

Rusticius Helpidius Domnulus, whose subscriptions to Pomponius Mela and Iulius Paris date from around 450, was a bureaucrat in the imperial service at Ravenna, just the sort of person we might expect to find taking an interest in geographical and rhetorical works. He was also a pious Christian.[106] Also certainly Christian was the unnamed landowner who corrected "as best he could" a copy of Augustine's *De Trinitate* "on my Acherusian estate in the territory of Cumae in the province of Campania" in 556, perhaps the villa of Servilius Vatia memorably evoked in a letter of Seneca.[107]

At the end of all eight books of Caesar's *Gallic War* in one of the two manuscript families, we find the subscription *Iulius Celsus Constantinus v. c. legi*. In the case of Bk ii this subscription is immediately followed by another: *Flavius Licerius Firminus Lupicinus legi*.[108] Lupicinus is generally identified as a nephew of the Gallic aristocrat Ennodius, bishop of Pavia early in the sixth century,[109] but for no good reason Constantinus has often been dated up to two centuries earlier. Editors of Caesar continue to credit these

---

105. Cavallo 1977, 93.
106. *PLRE* ii. 374; Harries 1994, 122–24. Much less plausibly, S. Cavallin identified the subscriber as Helpidius, *comes sacri consistorii* in the East, present at the Council of Ephesus in 449 (*Sacris eruditi* 7 [1955], 49–66). But the subscriber's diacritical name was Domnulus, the same as the western quaestor.
107. *in provincia Campania in territorio Cumano in possessione nostra Acherusia*, in at least five MSS of s. XI to XIV: Aug. *De Trin.* 2, W. J. Mountain and F. Glorie (eds.) (1968), 535. Clearly a private estate, and so not the monastery of Eugippius (Mountain, i. lxxiii); cf. M. M. Gorman, *Rev. Bén.* 93 (1983), 28–29. For Vatia's villa, Sen. *Ep.* 55 (*Acherusio lacu*, § 6), with D'Arms 1970, 224–25.
108. For the evidence, W. Hering's Teubner edition (1987), xvi–xvii; Zetzel 1981, 222; Brown (n. 118) 112–23.
109. *PLRE* ii. 694, 315–16.

men with a "recension," the ancestor of one of the two manuscript families.[110] But the most natural explanation, given the many examples of two men working on a text together, is that Lupicinus was simply helping Constantinus correct one and the same text. The only difference is that (like the Livy subscribers, chapter 14) they signed their names separately. It is in fact common to find two separate *legi* subscriptions on original documents of the age, one from the official who approved the order or petition in question, the other from the clerk (or even scribe) who checked the text before passing it on to the official.[111]

The correctors of Caesar must both, at this date, have been Christians—and to judge from their names and connections, surely gentlemen rather than scholars, Lupicinus a Gaul of noble birth. Caesar's commentaries had never been numbered among the literary classics, and their specifically pagan content is very low.[112] It was not religion, nor even devotion to the classics, that inspired these men, but local patriotism. A century earlier another Gaul, Protadius, obtained a copy of Caesar's *Gallic War* from his friend Symmachus with the object of studying the history of his native Gaul.[113] In a list of works he studied ca. 520 with another Gallic aristocrat called Parthenius, the poet Arator names only one secular text: Caesar's commentaries.[114] Unsurprisingly enough, all the earliest manuscripts of the *Gallic War* and all the earliest references in medieval literature and entries in medieval library catalogues come from France.[115] It is striking how all these readers identified with the Roman conquerors of Gaul rather than the conquered Gauls. The Gallic panegyrists likewise praised the Aedui for collaborating with Caesar.[116]

If the name of Q. Aurelius Symmachus, as often claimed, could be included in the band of subscribers,[117] that might lend some support to the pagan salvage hypothesis, given Symmachus's known love of literature and support of the pagan cause. Unfortunately, he cannot. As we shall see in the following chapter, Symmachus himself played no direct part in the celebrated so-called "Symmachan" recension of Livy. All he did was offer to have a copy made for a friend and get a professional to do the correcting, with some assistance from his son-in-law. When sending Ausonius a copy of Pliny's *Natural History* he apologized for the carelessness of the copyist, adding that he "wanted to be appreciated for the speed of his own gift rather than the correctness of another's work" (*Ep.* i. 24). Thanks to this conceit we learn that, even if he had

---

110. O. Seel (1977³), xxvi; W. Hering (1987), v–vi (at any rate disputing the second point).
111. P. Oxy. 1106 (where the scribe added *legi scribus* at the bottom); P. Lond. 1663; P. Masp. 67130. 6; 67321. 11, 12; 67320. 6, 7; 67280. 5, 6 (all s. VI).
112. As early as Orosius we even find the commentaries ascribed to Suetonius (vi. 7. 2), an error no doubt assisted by Caesar's third-person narrative (which eschews all the auspices and portents that fill Livy's pages).
113. *Ep.* iv. 18. 5; cf. iv. 36. 2; Wightman 1975, 93–107.
114. *PLRE* ii. 126; 833.
115. V. Brown 1979, 106–7, 114–15.
116. *Pan. Lat.* 5. 2. 4; 9. 4. 1; 6. 22. 4: Woolf 1998, 3–4, 21–22.
117. Reynolds 1983, 207.

waited to have the books corrected, Symmachus had no intention of doing the work himself. The impersonal passive in his apology for the continuing delay in the correction of Valerianus's promised copy of Livy (*etiam nunc diligentia emendationis moratur, Ep.* ix. 13) implies the same.

One passage has indeed been cited as evidence that "Symmachus and his circle gave careful attention to the matter of securing correct copies of their own works," a letter to his nonagenarian literary friend Naucellius:[118]

> I have given the copy of your poems to a servant to return to you, and because the sequence of pieces was disturbed, I have sent my copy as well, so that you may correct both, and add others you are still composing.

But it makes all the difference that these are new poems direct from the author, not classics with a long manuscript tradition carrying with it the potential for a corrupt text requiring emendation. It looks as if Naucellius's amanuensis made a copying or binding error, and Symmachus simply restored what he took to be the correct sequence. Since the error was presumably mechanical (perhaps a bifolio folded the wrong way), it cannot have taken much skill to straighten it out. Furthermore, despite his *descripsimus*, we cannot even be sure that Symmachus actually made the second copy himself (below). The "correction" mentioned is the poet's own stylistic improvements, nothing to do with collation of manuscripts. Symmachus was celebrated among his contemporaries for his oratory and also for the elegance of his letters. He was proud of his literary culture. But nothing suggests that he had any philological expertise or interests. Even in the pages of Macrobius, oratory and rhetoric are his only specialties.

The only man among the pagan aristocrats assembled by Macrobius with any pretensions to scholarship is Vettius Agorius Praetextatus. As early as Jahn's pioneer study Praetextatus was included along with the subscribers, on the basis of five lines from the remarkable poem his wife Paulina had inscribed on his funerary monument:[119]

> tu namque quicquid lingua utraque est proditum   25
> cura soforum porta quis caeli patet,
> vel quae periti condidere carmina
> vel quae solutis versibus sunt edita
> meliora reddis quam legendo sumpseras.

> Whatever is written in either language, by the efforts of the wise, to whom the gate of heaven lies open, the poems the learned have composed, or what is written in prose, you improved what you found in your reading.

---

118. McGeachy 1942, 171.
119. "In the last verse, the allusion to the standard subscription formula *legi et emendavi* is unmistakable," Jahn 1851, 341; cf. Wytzes 1977, 140; *ILS* 1250, lines 25–29.

Paulina gives three illustrations of the sort of books Praetextatus read, in both Greek and Latin: philosophy (26), poetry (27), and prose (28). Whatever he read, she claims, he "improved" (*meliora reddis*, 29). According to Hedrick, Paulina "compares the transformation of texts through correction with the transformation of individuals through initiation into mystery cults."[120] Not only is there no hint of so fanciful a link in the poem, it does not even specifically mention the correction of texts. We have seen that the *emendatio* attested by the subscriptions consisted of checking text against exemplar. This process could not have "improved" any text; the most that it could achieve was to make the copy nearly as good as the exemplar (nearly, since it is axiomatic that any copy will introduce at least one mistake not present in its exemplar). Paulina cannot be alluding to the drudgery of systematic correction. There was nothing either scholarly or praiseworthy about checking a newly made copy against its exemplar. Whenever possible, scholars and gentlemen alike normally employed people to do both copying and correcting for them, not least because professionals were trained for the task and did it better (modern publishers likewise rely on professionals rather than authors for correcting proofs).[121] Accurate proofreading has nothing to do with scholarship or even literary taste, and scholars are often surprisingly poor proofreaders. Proofreading requires a particular combination of qualities, persistence and alertness rather than imagination or erudition.[122]

If Paulina had been talking about a Bentley or Housman, we might picture conjectures jotted down in the margins of his texts. But the modern analogy is misleading. In the first place, Bentley and Housman did not waste their time correcting printers' errors, but concentrated on problem passages they knew from the editions they were using to be more than mere misprints. If Praetextatus annotated his texts, the texts he annotated will already have been professionally corrected, texts that (like the editions used by Bentley and Housman) reflected the vulgate of his day, so that he could concentrate on questions of interpretation. The corrections to which Paulina alludes are surely meant to draw attention to Praetextatus's taste and erudition rather than (trivially) his ability to spot scribal errors.

Second, though ancient readers and critics must often in practice have corrected defective texts by conjecture, they seldom laid claim to any credit for doing so. There are a fair number of variants in the Vergilian text, both in the direct tradition (the extant manuscripts) and the indirect, mostly preserved in Gellius and the Vergilian

---

120. Hedrick 2000, 208.

121. The text of modern printed books is nonetheless sometimes surprisingly poor: for many examples, James Thorpe, *Principles of Textual Criticism* (1972)—a point to be pondered by editors of classical texts, who often seem to operate on the assumption that a perfect author's autograph is in principle recoverable. But take the case of Plotinus, who formed his letters poorly, divided his syllables incorrectly, paid no attention to spelling, and could not bear to reread anything he had written (Porph. *V. Plot.* 8). No doubt an extreme case, but a number of classical texts were left unfinished, and so lack the author's final *emendatio*.

122. Professional proofreaders sometimes collate *backward* against their exemplar to avoid being influenced by what they expect to see rather than what they actually see.

commentators. Many of these variants have been denounced (less often praised) as conjectures by scholars like Hyginus or Probus. But the texts in question never say more than (e.g.) *legit Probus*, and methodical studies by Timpanaro have found no reason to regard the majority as anything more than (in origin) transcriptional errors, subsequently defended by one critic or another.[123] A certain Dioscorides published an edition of Hippocrates under Hadrian, which Galen depreciated for its misguided alterations of the text. But since he apparently found these alterations in the form of marginal variants introduced by the lemma "perhaps,"[124] it cannot have been clear which were Dioscorides's own emendations and which simply readings from other manuscripts. Even in the case of Byzantine scholars like Planudes and Triclinius, who undoubtedly emended classical texts extensively, in any given case it is difficult to be certain precisely because they never identify emendations as such.[125] The closest I know of to a claim of authorship is the "I think" with which the contemporary corrector of the tenth-century Medicean of Aeschylus introduces his corrections.[126]

There is (of course) a sense in which subscribers who claim to have corrected their texts *solus* (Lucan), *sine exemplario* (Vegetius), *sine antigrapho, sine magistro* (Persius),[127] or with a *legi tantum* (Caesar), must have resorted to conjecture. But it is obvious from the way they formulate these claims that they regarded this as a *pis aller*. So far from boasting about their conjectures, they are in effect warning future readers that their text lacks external authority. In special circumstances an author might actually licence conjectural correction in advance. On the grounds that his copyists were "just beginners," Caesarius of Arles asks readers of his sermons to "correct appropriately" (*sicut expedit emendate*) any omissions or additions they detect, and have a more elegant and accurate copy made.[128]

Finally, unlike a Bentley or Housman, the Praetextatus we known from Macrobius was no textual critic to jot down conjectures in his margins. He was a cultivated gentleman, a man of letters and student of religion. While he might have collated other exemplars for the occasional problem passage, the notes in his margins surely explained subject matter and cited parallels. Notes like this would certainly have increased the utility of Praetextatus's books, thus "making them better." In any case, the emphasis falls less on the merit of individual improvements than on the variety of the texts he improved. It is the breadth and catholicity of Praetextatus's scholarship that Paulina, hardly an impartial witness, is praising.[129]

---

123. Pasquali 1952, 347; Timpanaro 1986; and Florence 2001.
124. ἴσως, Hanson 1998, 45 n. 80.
125. Zuntz 1965, 193–201; *The Greek Anthology: From Meleager to Planudes*, Cameron 1993, 353–55; Wilson 1983, 232–40.
126. οἶμαι, Wilamowitz, *Aeschyli Tragoediae* (Berlin 1914), xi–xii; West 1990, 323.
127. For the full text of these subscriptions, Zetzel 1981.
128. *Serm.* 2 Morin = *Sermons au peuple* i. 284 Délage.
129. The fact, it was said of H. J. Rose, that "the detective stories in the local library had their printers' errors corrected in his hand is some evidence of his omnivorous reading" (obituary in *The Times* [London], 8 February 1961).

13: PUNCTUATION AND ANNOTATION

We have already seen how different Statilius Maximus's "revision" of Cicero's *De lege agraria* was from the work documented by the late antique subscriptions (§ 2). He does not say *legi, relegi*, or *recognovi*, and for a good reason: he was not performing the routine activity these terms designate, but marking the completion of a genuinely philological enterprise.[130] His subscription is not typical of second-century subscriptions in literary manuscripts,[131] nor is it a precursor of the series that seems to begin in the late fourth century.

Apart from the Fronto palimpsest, only one late antique secular subscription implies anything more than routine correction: that of Securus Melior Felix, who claims to have revised his manuscript of Martianus Capella with the aid of "very faulty copies" (*ex mendosissimis exemplaribus*) unspecified. It should be noted straightaway that Felix was a professor of some distinction (*rhetor urbis Romae*, with the honorary rank of *vir spectabilis comes consistorianus*),[132] a much more likely person to collate manuscripts than an aristocrat, bureaucrat, or schoolboy, and better equipped than them to diagnose and emend corruptions. But the fact that he acknowledges a single assistant like all the other joint subscribers does not suggest a project of an entirely different order from theirs. And the location of the subscription in most of the manuscripts that carry it suggests that Felix only corrected Bk i (out of nine) in any case.[133] It is also puzzling that he found every copy he consulted corrupt, working as he was less than a half-century after Martianus wrote.[134] My own interpretation of the evidence is that, having concluded, presumably on grounds of sense, that the text of his own copy was bad, Felix decided to collate sample passages of Bk I in as many manuscripts as he could lay his hands on. The result confirmed the text of his own copy, which Felix construed as proof that they were all corrupt. One possible explanation is that all the copies he consulted derived from the same corrupt exemplar; another is that he was a poor judge of Martianus's often bizarre style. Either way, Felix is not so much boasting of his editorial achievement as warning the next reader of the limited resources at his disposal.

We may compare the probably sixth-century subscription to a small corpus of letters of Augustine in a ninth-century Paris manuscript: *legi Facistus iuxta mendosum*

---

130. Martin 1984, 151–55, rightly noting the influence of legal subscriptions, wrongly postulates legal influence on the Statilius subscription—which uses the traditional literary term *emendavi*. Statilius no more betrays an "attitude of slavish adherence to his 'authoritative texts'" (Martin 1984, 153) than any other subscriber, Greek or Roman.

131. It might seem tempting to infer from Gellius 18. 5. 11 that Gellius knew of a text of Ennius with a subscription (so Hedrick 2000, 172), but the words *quem fere constabat Lampadionis manu emendatum* imply on the contrary that "quel manoscritto non doveva avere una *subscriptio*" (Timpanaro 1986, 39).

132. For Felix's career, Cameron, *CP* 81 (1986), 320–23.

133. For a list of the relevant manuscripts, Préaux 1975, 102–4.

134. The consular date in Felix's subscription should be identified as 494 rather than 532 (Cameron 1986, 320–24).

exemplar.[135] Facistus (if that was really his name) is evidently apologizing for the poor quality of the only exemplar available to him.[136] Once again, we find exact parallels in early Byzantine manuscripts. A carefully corrected early ninth-century codex of mythographical and geographical texts carries three separate notations in a contemporary hand "corrected against a poor exemplar."[137] There appear to have been well-established conventions for subscriptions attesting correction. I have already suggested that, at any rate in a new copy, *emendavi* (*relegi, recognovi, contuli*) without further specification was understood to imply collation of (new) copy against exemplar.[138] Any other circumstances were normally specified, whether the assistance of a professional scholar (who could be assumed to have used an authoritative exemplar of his own), a defective exemplar, or no exemplar at all, as in the subscriptions to Lucan, Persius, and Vegetius. In the now lost subscription at the end of his copy of Livy's third decade, the corrector of the very corrupt Puteanus may not only have recorded his full name and titles, but owned up to the fact that he was "doing his best with the aid of very faulty copies" (*prout potui ex mendosissimis exemplaribus*).

Martianus's *De nuptiis Philologiae et Mercurii* was not a classic, but a fifth-century work of considerable scholarly pretensions. The same is true of Macrobius's commentary on the *Somnium Scipionis*, subscribed by Aurelius Memmius Symmachus cos. 485. Symmachus too, unlike his more notorious pagan great-grandfather, was a man of wide learning, a philosopher, and historian, mentioned with respect in the dedications of a number of scholarly works by Priscian and Boethius.[139] Thus the fact that two such difficult texts appear on the list of subscriptions proves nothing about the scholarly interests or expertise of the late Roman elite as a whole.

These are also the subscribed texts we might have expected to appeal least to Christians. We have already found cause to doubt the once popular view that either book was a work of pagan inspiration by a professed pagan, and the subscriptions allow us to add that within a few decades copies of both were being corrected by Christian scholars. The Martianus subscription explicitly invokes the aid of Christ (*Christo adiuvante*), and Aurelius Memmius Symmachus was a pillar of the Christian establishment of Rome. We have already seen that the "pagan" history of Festus also carries an explicitly Christian subscription. If anything, most subscriptions illustrate Christian acceptance of secular literature rather than pagan resistance to Christianity.

By far the most impressive (and best-documented) enterprise attested by a series of subscriptions is the Latin version compiled by Rusticus the deacon of the Acta of the Council of Chalcedon (451). The subscription that most fully characterizes his work stands at the end of the first session, dated 18 March 565. In it he gives name, title, and

---

135. *Ep.* 78 (Paris Nouv. acq. 1443, f. 156); Gorman 1983, 8, 30. *legi* alone = *emendavi* seems not to be found in subscriptions before the sixth century: Asterius (494); Victor (546/7): Donatus (561, 569).

136. The name is usually corrected to Faustus (Gorman 1983, 8), but why would so common a name be corrupted?

137. διώρθωται οὐ πρὸς σπουδαῖον ἀντίγραφον, Heid. Pal. gr. 398: Diller 1952, 6.

138. So already long ago Reifferscheid 1873, 6.

139. Schanz-Hosius IV. 2 (1920), 84; *PLRE* ii. 1046.

date in full like the secular subscribers, *Rusticus per gratiam Dei diaconus sanctae ecclesiae Romanae*. Like them he uses *emendare* for the completion of his task (*finivimus emendantes*) before giving more precise detail with the three verbs *contuli, annotavi, distincxi*.[140] We do not have the original, but the ninth-century Parisinus latinus 11611 preserves his edition in something like its original form and layout, complete with Rusticus's marginal notes and subscriptions,[141] allowing us to determine the significance of each term.[142]

Legi/emendavi/recognovi cover the whole process of checking a copy against its exemplar. All imply or include *contuli*, which by itself refers only to collation. *Contuli* he uses repeatedly, always very precisely in the sense "collate," often indicating which copies he collated. For example, "I could not find this session in the codex in the Akoimetae, but I collated another Greek codex" (*hanc actionem in Acu(manitano) codice non inveni sed alterum Graecum contuli*); "I got this reading by collating a Latin codex" (*hanc lectionem ex codice Latino contulimus*). In passing it should be noted that, when citing variants, Rusticus regularly uses a formula we also find in the Bobbio palimpsest and the Nicomachean Livy: *ia*, standing for *i(n) a(lio codice)*. His basic source was a manuscript kept at the Akoimetae monastery where he did most of his work (*Rusticus ex Latinis et Grecis exempl(aribus) maxime Acoemit(ani) monast(erii) emendavi*). This manuscript was in Greek but also contained Latin versions, as revealed by notes like *et ista in codice Acum(itano) iacet*.[143] For one session he depended entirely on the *Acumitanus* "because there was no other Greek codex."

One of the other Greek manuscripts he collated he identified as "a new parchment codex of the patrician Julia recently copied from an old papyrus codex which she herself told me used to belong to the brothers Proculus and Albinus the scholastici"—a remarkable example of concern for the pedigree of a manuscript source.[144] Another example is a subscription preserved in the eighth-century Echternach Gospels, dated to 558 and recording collation by some unidentified person against a codex reputed to have belonged to Jerome from the library of the presbyter Eugippius.[145] Not to mention

---

140. *distincti*, MSS; I have expanded and corrected abbreviations throughout.

141. All the details are printed in E. Schwartz's edition and fully discussed in his prefaces (*Acta Conciliorum Oecumenicorum* I. iv. 2 [1922], viii–xvi; and II. iii. 3 [1937], xii–xxiii); and Schwartz 1925.

142. In Ambros. G. 108 inf. (s. IX) we find three subscriptions by a doctor called Simplicius to some Latin scholia on Galen. In slightly different words all say *ex voce Agnello yatrosophista audivi, legi, contuli . . . et scripsi feliciter* (Zetzel 1981, 226). *Ex voce audivi* represents the Greek formula ἀπὸ φωνῆς, often found in MSS of Neoplatonist lecture notes to indicate that they were taken down from the dictation of the professor named (Richard 1950, 191–222). *Legi, contuli et scripsi* describe, respectively (in reverse order), how Simplicius made a fair copy of Agnellus's lectures, collated the copy against his dictation, and certified the correctness of the copy.

143. *ACO* II. iii. 1 p. 230 line 4.

144. *hanc actionem in Acu(mitano) codice non inveni sed alter(um) grecum contuli (ACO* II. 3. 3 p. 3. 2) . . . *quam inveni in codice patr(iciae) Iuliae membranaceo novo transcriptam ex codice vetusto chartaceo quem dixit ipsa fuisse de Proculi et Albini germanorum scholastic(orum)* (ib. p. 5. 18). Schwartz mistakenly identified Julia as the great Anicia Juliana (*PLRE* ii. 635–36), but there are chronological objections (see *CP* 81 [1986], 100–101).

145. *proemendavi ut potui secundum codicem de bibliotheca Eugipi praespiteri quem ferunt fuisse sci Hieronimi ind. vi post con. Bassilii v.c. anno septimo decimo*: Par. lat. 9389 f. 222v, with T. J. Brown in T. D. Kendrick et al., *Evangeliorum quattuor codex Lindisfarnensis* 2 (Lausanne 1960), 50–56.

the unique authority of Jerome for the text of the Gospels, Eugippius too, abbot of the Lucullanum monastery, source of a number of subscribed Christian texts,[146] was a name worth appealing to. With the sole exception of Statilius Maximus, no secular Latin subscription cites such a pedigree.

In Rusticus's usage *distincxi* means, not "punctuate," but "equip with critical signs," by which he means symbols (sometimes surviving in the Parisinus) to draw attention to the relevant marginal note. For example, this is how he identifies passages missing in some of his witnesses: "from this sign to that sign missing in my (copy) and in the *Acumitanus*, though I found it in another Greek (copy) just as it stands in the Latin (version)."[147] This use of *distinguere* is clearly attested in a number of passages of Jerome, notably a letter to Pammachius in which he describes the divergences from the Hebrew Bible in the Septuagint, "passages marked in church copies with obeli and asterisks" (*quae in exemplaribus ecclesiae obelis asteriscisque distincta sunt*). This is a "church" usage, and in the preface to his translation of the Pentateuch he traces it to Origen's *Hexapla*.[148] It is ironic to note that it was Christians rather than pagans who employed methods (in Bloch's phrase) "inherited from the great scholars of Alexandria."[149]

But Arns was surely mistaken to read this sense into Rufinus's addition to Irenaeus's oath, where the reference must be to punctuation: "let him correct [his copy] to the letter and punctuate it [*distinguat*] and let him reject an uncorrected and unpunctuated [*non distinctum*] text, in case difficulties in sense arising from lack of punctuation [*si distinctus codex non sit*] give rise to even greater obscurities for readers."[150] Obeli and asterisks are excellent ways of drawing attention to notes on details of text or interpretation, but the one thing they do *not* do is make any passage easier to read. It is careful punctuation that does that, especially in a difficult writer like Origen. We must accept that, even in subscriptions, *distinctio* can bear two distinct meanings. *Distinctio* as Rusticus used it was reserved for texts where there were substantially differing versions to be reported, not just a few variants, as in a text of Vergil or Livy. In a manuscript of the classics it would most naturally refer to punctuation.[151]

146. For a list, Riché 1992, 133–34; see too Gorman 1983, 7–30.
147. *a signo hoc usque ad signum istud in meo et in Acumit(ano) non est, in alio tamen Gr(aeco) sic inveni ut hic in Latino iacet, ACO* I. iii. 1, p. 243, lines 19–24. The other examples are all similar: Schwartz, I. iii. 3, p. xv.
148. *Ep.* 57. 11; cf. 134. 2; *Vulg. praef.* (*PL* xxii. 577); Arns 1953, 72 n. 4.
149. The point should not be exaggerated. Brock 1970, 215–18, has shown that, while Origen employed "Alexandrian" symbols to indicate passages missing or added in the various versions of the Greek Bible, the goal of the manuscript researches that led to his *Hexapla* was not to reconstruct the original text of the Septuagint, but to compare the versions used by contemporary Jews for purposes of debate and controversy. No less exaggerated is the insistence of Zuntz 1953 that Christian scholars employed "Alexandrian" methods in establishing the New Testament text. But however many manuscripts they consulted, the way Christian readers dealt with variants must have been quite different: no considerations of "propriety," no linguistic arguments—and no conjectures. Even Bentley planned to confine himself to manuscript readings in his projected edition of the New Testament.
150. Rufinus, Περὶ ἀρχῶν, pr. = Jerome, *Ep.* 80. 3; Arns 1953, 72.
151. In sixty-five-odd examples of *distinguere* and *distinctio* in the commentaries of Donatus and Servius, the reference is always to punctuation (Mountford and Schultz's index [1930], 55 s.v. *distinctio*).

Distinctio = punctuation is mentioned in only two secular subscriptions (Asterius's Vergil and Symmachus's Macrobius), not surprisingly, given that all surviving late antique literary texts, in whatever script, Christian or pagan, are written without word division or punctuation. Such punctuation as we find in surviving late antique books has generally been added by a later hand, often (it seems) later than the corrector.[152] When Sidonius praises Lupus, bishop of Troyes for both correcting and punctuating any book that passed through his hands,[153] the linking of the two activities implies newly copied books left unpunctuated by the original scribe. Fronto sent a friend a copy of Cicero he himself had corrected and punctuated (*emendatos et distinctos*).[154] Augustine begins his discussion of ambiguities in Scripture by warning people to check punctuation, quoting a number of illustrations. It is clear that even copies of Scripture were seldom punctuated.[155] The very fact that punctuation was a subject taught by the grammaticus proves that students were likely to be faced with unpunctuated texts—though punctuation is actually too narrow a term. At an early stage, students were shown how to prepare a text for reading (*praelectio*).[156] Since this meant reading aloud, instruction covered word division and (for verse) marking ambiguous quantities as well as dividing up clauses, sentences, and paragraphs—in short anything that contributed to correct and effective oral delivery. As Ausonius put it, "Punctuation [or perhaps "phrasing"] enhances meaning, and pauses give force to flat passages" (*distinctio sensum / auget et ignavis dant intervalla vigorem*).[157]

It was not only in the schoolroom that ancient readers read aloud. It is well known that people normally read aloud even to themselves. But this was more than just a custom to which there were occasional exceptions, like Ambrose, as described in a famous passage of Augustine's *Confessions.* It was an almost inevitable consequence of reading unpunctuated texts with no word division. To quote the conclusion of a technical discussion of the point by Paul Saenger, "the aural retention of inherently ambiguous fragments often was essential until a full sentence was decoded."[158] Nowadays we naturally think of silent reading as a much faster process, but it is unlikely that Ambrose (e.g.) could have read significantly faster just because he was not verbalizing his text if he had been reading an unpunctuated text with no word division. The text Augustine was so surprised to see him read silently was no doubt something he knew well, like the Bible.

This also explains an often-overlooked technical detail in the process of copying: the importance attached to meticulous syllabification. Trained scribes followed established rules when dividing words between lines: for example, *con-suleret*, not

---

152. G. B. Townend, *CQ* 19 (1969), 332–33; E. O. Wingo, *Latin Punctuation* (Mouton 1972), 23 n. 11, 25–27.
153. Sidon. *Ep.* ix. 11. 6.
154. Fronto, *Ad amicos* ii. 2, p. 187. 11 van den Hout².
155. When he advises checking in case *male distinxerimus* (iii. 2. 2), this need not refer to an incorrectly punctuated text. The word is often best translated "phrase" or "articulate" (so Parkes 1993, passim).
156. Parkes 1993, 10–12.
157. Auson. *Liber protr.* 49–50; Parkes 1993, 9.
158. Aug. *Conf.* vi. 3. 3, with O'Donnell's commentary (ii. 345); Saenger 1997, 8.

co-nsuleret or *cons-uleret*. The scribe of the early fifth-century Verona Livy followed the rules with scarcely a single exception throughout his long task.[159] In texts copied without word division or punctuation, readers had at least to be able to count on the correct syllabification of individual words or they were lost without a compass.

Gellius describes how he once showed up a boastful fellow who claimed to be an expert on Varro's *Menippean Satires* by asking him about a particular passage. The fellow slyly asked Gellius to read it out to him, but Gellius refused, on the grounds that, since he did not understand the passage, his reading would be "confused and poorly phrased" (*indistincta...et confusa*). He handed over an "old copy of proven correctness, clearly written,"[160] and the supposed expert made a fool of himself by mispronouncing the words and "mutilating the thoughts" (*sententias intercidebat*). It is clear from the nature of Gellius's accusation that the text must have been unpunctuated. Whether or not the story is true,[161] we are bound to accept its presupposition, that a carefully corrected text of some antiquity might nonetheless be unpunctuated.

To quote from the standard modern account of the subject,[162]

> It seems likely that punctuation was thought to be necessary only when a copy was to be employed for reading aloud...and that punctuation was regarded as unnecessary in copies for private reading, where it might interfere with the study of, or meditation on the text.

This assumption is borne out by the many surviving ancient texts that are either entirely unpunctuated, or equipped with no more than occasional pointing to prevent obvious misunderstandings. It would be absurd to suppose that these texts were never read at all down the centuries. The explanation must be that experienced ancient readers were capable of deciphering unpunctuated texts.

This tells us something important about both readers and texts. As the Gellius anecdote makes clear, not even a scholar could be expected to sight-read an entirely unfamiliar text. Trimalchio kisses a clever slave-boy because he could say his ten times table and read a book at sight (*librum ab oculo legit*). The expression also occurs in a glossary, which describes how the student first read out his *lectio* (presumably a text he had prepared), and "then an unknown text at sight rapidly" (*deinde ab oculo citatim ignotum*).[163] It was mainly *familiar* texts that members of the elite read in those luxury editions in undivided capital or uncial script. We saw in an earlier chapter that, despite his ancient reputation, Symmachus (e.g.) was not by modern standards a well-read

---

159. Lowe and Rand 1922, 8–9; Mommsen 1909, 107–9.
160. *Gellius, NA* 13. 31; *librum veterem fidei spectatae*, presumaby meaning corrected (a corrected copy could easily be identified by the presence of corrections, normally in a different hand or different ink).
161. Many such anecdotes in which Gellius represents himself putting down boastful ignoramuses are at any rate improved or dramatized versions of real incidents: Holford–Strevens 2003, Ch. 4.
162. Parkes 1993, 68.
163. Petron. *Sat.* 75. 4; *CGL* iii. 381. 63; Heraeus 1899, 34.

man. But contemporaries might not have thought this a fair assessment. Rather than reading a wide range of different texts, cultivated members of the elite seem to have read and reread the same old favorites, mostly texts they had first read long ago in school. They knew a few texts very well. Rereading a familiar text like Vergil in an unpunctuated text posed few problems.

This also helps to set in context another phenomenon touched on in an earlier chapter: reading as an elite, leisure activity, often reserved for a trip to the country. When Symmachus's elderly friend Naucellius describes himself as *docta revolventem scripta virum veterum* at leisure on his estate, the emphasis falls on the prefix, "rereading the learned books of the ancients."[164] Nowadays people value the ability to read fast, in order to assess, select, and retrieve information from many different sources.[165] It may be instructive to list a few of the features modern readers take for granted: a clearly printed and systematically punctuated text, systematic use of capital letters, frequent paragraphing, quotations marked off by quotation marks or (for longer blocks of text) indentation in smaller type, occasional use of brackets and parentheses or of italics or bold type for emphasizing individual words. It is hard to imagine skimming for information (as modern researchers do all the time) a pile of books lacking all these features. Insofar as it was necessary at all in late antiquity, gentlemen must have relied on secretaries and (when in office) career bureaucrats to do this sort of thing for them. We would probably be astonished if we were granted the opportunity of watching just how *slowly* even men of letters read literary texts—if they actually read themselves at all. Like the elder Pliny and no doubt many other members of the elite (especially those of advanced years), they may have preferred to be read to. Naucellius (e g) was still "reading" in his mid nineties.[166]

As for the two subscriptions that mention punctuation, it is no coincidence that in both cases the subscriber was working with an assistant. There can be little doubt that Macharius read aloud to Asterius from his own text of Vergil, taking care to pause where appropriate, while Asterius corrected and punctuated his text accordingly. The case of Symmachus's copy of Macrobius is rather different. This was neither a classic, nor a book to be savored for its style or diction. It was a work of learning, not easy for even a scholar to sight-read. In the closing words of the preface to his edition of Plotinus, Porphyry claims that, after arranging the various works and equipping them with headings and summaries, all that remained was to "put in the punctuation and correct any verbal errors." Remember too how strongly Rufinus emphasized the need for punctuation in his translations from Origen. Difficult nonliterary prose texts like Plotinus, Origen, and Macrobius must have been virtually unintelligible in the unpunctuated texts favored by members of the elite. Anxious to secure the best text he could, Symmachus checked his copy against a copy in the possession of the author's

164. *Ep. Bob.* 5. 8.
165. See Saenger 1997, 11.
166. For other examples, Cameron 1995, 45; for Naucellius, *PLRE* i. 618.

grandson. Whether or not the author's autograph, this was likely to be a corrected text with enough punctuation to eliminate ambiguities.

One last reflection on this issue. Nothing here supports the assumption that subscriptions document a concerted effort by pagans to promote the reading and proper appreciation of Rome's literary heritage. Quite the contrary. What they really illustrate is the care that fifth- and sixth-century Christians devoted to the text of their beloved classics. On a realistic assessment, unpunctuated luxury texts without word division, especially when (like the Romanus and Augusteus) inadequately corrected, must have been very hard for any but the most experienced readers to make any sense of at all.[167] These were copies custom made for private reading by members of the elite at leisure. In fact, like expensive editions of classics in tooled leather bindings advertised in glossy magazines today, they were books designed for show rather than reading. We may recall Jerome's contempt for Bibles copied in gold and silver on purple parchment.

Once again, it was Christians who took steps to make books more accessible to a wider range of readers—in the first instance, of course, Christian books. While it was a pity to misunderstand Vergil, misunderstanding Scripture could imperil one's immortal soul. Augustine devotes several pages of his *De doctrina Christiana* to stressing the importance of careful and correct punctuation (iii. 1–9). Over and above the usual principles, he prescribes in addition "the rule of faith." No punctuation yielding a text that conflicts with Christian teaching can be right. Jerome came up with a more practical solution, beginning each sentence with an indented capital letter, each clause on a new line, *per cola et commata* as he put it.[168] Ursicinus, significantly a "reader" (*lector*) in the church of Verona in 517, combined both methods in a carefully punctuated copy of Sulpicius Severus, obviously designed for easy reading.[169] From the sixth century on we begin to find systematic punctuation. But it was to be many centuries before word division was generally adopted.[170]

Two other terms require discussion: *describere* (found in two secular subscriptions) and *adnotare*. The latter is only found in Sabinus's subscription on Persius: "I tried to correct my copy without an exemplar and annotated it" (*temptavi emendare sine antigrapho meum et adnotavi*); and "I annotated my copy, correcting it as far as I could without a teacher" (*prout potui sine magistro emendans adnotavi*).[171] In a much-discussed passage of Suetonius, the second-century scholar Valerius Probus is said to have gathered together many copies of "old books" and taken care *emendare ac distinguere et adnotare*. These *notae* are generally thought to have been symbols placed in

---

167. While it can be argued that incorrect punctuation more or less compels misinterpretation, it can hardly be maintained that the "neutrality" of an unpunctuated text is much help to any but experienced readers.

168. Parkes 1993, 15–19; see particularly his pl. 1, an early fifth-century Vulgate possibly annotated in Jerome's own hand.

169. Parkes 1993, pl. 4, pp. 166–67.

170. The process is traced at length in Saenger 1997.

171. W. V. Clausen, *Persi saturae* (Oxford 1956), xxiii; for more details on the subscriptions, Clausen 1963.

the margin to draw attention to passages considered noteworthy for one reason or another.[172] There are what may be Proban signs in the margins of the Medicean Vergil, marking beginnings and ends of speeches, similes, and so forth.[173] The corrected and punctuated books of Cicero that Fronto sent his friend Volumnius Quadratus were also *adnotatos*. Textual notes, according to van den Hout, but the passages of Pliny to which he appeals suggest notes on style.[174] Parkes identifies Sabinus's *notae* as critical symbols of some sort.[175] But this is a guards officer on duty in Spain who on his own admission had neither an exemplar nor a teacher to guide him. What sort of critical work can he possibly have done?

Parkes does not seem to have known the Rusticus subscriptions with their triple claim *contuli, annotavi, distincxi*. Here at least *annotavi* cannot refer to critical symbols, already covered by *distincxi*. Since we have Rusticus's edition in essentially its original form, there can be no doubt that he is simply referring to what amounts to a skeleton commentary on the Chalcedon Acta. On almost every page (clearly set out in a separate register in Schwartz's edition) there are concise but informative marginal notes, mostly on textual points, but also occasional notes on subject matter, by no means restricted to theology. For example, when Cyril of Alexandria dates a letter "in the month of Mechir," Rusticus explains: "Mechir is what the Egyptians call February, beginning for them on our January 26." Against a reference to Uranius of Emesa he notes that it was while Uranius was bishop that the head of John the Baptist was found there "and placed where it belonged." The discovery of John's head at Emesa is described in detail by Marcellinus in his *Chronicle* s. a. 453, but without any reference to its subsequent location.[176] The critical notes quote variants and systematically indicate passages missing or added in one or other of his versions or copies. Unlike the Fronto scholiast, he seldom quotes trivial variants or obvious errors.

Jerome uses *adnotare* in the same way to refer to brief marginal notes. For example, "I rapidly dictated a translation, briefly noting on the side of the page (*ex latere in pagina breviter adnotans*) the contents of each chapter." Elsewhere he complains about a foolish copyist who interpolated his marginal notes into the body of the text (*miror quomodo e latere adnotationem nostram nescioquis temerarius scribendam in corpore putaverit*)![177] The Fronto scholiast never makes the claim *adnotavi*, presumably because his notes were random, the sort of heterogeneous marginalia anyone might jot down

---

172. *De gramm.* 24. 2, with R. A. Kaster, *Suetonius: De grammaticis* (Oxford 1995), 261–63; Jocelyn 1984; 1985.
173. O. Ribbeck, *Prolegomena critica ad P. Vergili Maronis opera maiora* (Leipzig 1866), 158–63.
174. Plin. *Ep.* iii. 13. 5; v. 12. 2; van den Hout, *A Commentary on the Letters of M. Cornelius Fronto* (Leiden 1999), 437. On any hypothesis, it is not clear why Fronto warns Quadratus that these notes are for his eyes only (*adnotatos a me leges ipse; in volgus enim eos exire quare nolim, scribam diligentius*, p. 187. 11 van den Hout² = i. 309 Haines).
175. "Sabinus...inserted *notae* before a few verses," Parkes 1993, 13.
176. B. Croke's otherwise comprehensive note (1995, 91–92) omits this text.
177. *Ep.* 57. 2; 106. 46; Arns 1953, 71–72. Servius uses *adnotavit* of a Vergilian explanation by Probus (*Aen.* xii. 605).

in his own copy. Rusticus's notes, by contrast, were a systematic and homogeneous commentary, both critical and exegetical, clearly deserving separate description.

Not only does Sabinus concede that he had neither exemplar nor teacher to help him, he did no more than "attempt" to correct the text. The burden of his contribution (I suggest) lay in his notes, a systematic attempt to elucidate Persius (whence the formula *adnotavi*). His book will have looked something like the Veronensis of Vergil, an indifferent text enriched with marginal scholia. But just as the Scholia Veronensia are excerpted from a learned Vergil commentary (probably the second-century Asper), so Sabinus's Persius scholia will have been excerpted from a commentary. We know from Jerome that there was a school commentary on Persius as early as the mid-fourth century (*Adv. Rufinum* i. 16), and the surviving so-called *Commentum Cornuti* clearly preserves some late antique lore. Sabinus may have done a competent job, but his marginal notes are bound to have represented a reduction rather than an expansion of his source. Whatever its merits (and we must bear in mind that he was a guards officer), hardly a work of scholarship. Unfortunately, neither of the two manuscripts that carry the subscription preserves a word of the scholia Sabinus so laboriously collected.[178]

Descripsi too should be regarded as exceptional. Members of the elite would occasionally write to family members or close friends in their own hands, but virtually everything else they dictated.[179] Symmachus dictated letters to even so old a friend as the elder Flavianus (*Ep.* ii. 31; 35). A remarkable passage of Augustine reveals that he did not write even the marginalia in his own books in his own hand: a secretary read the text aloud to him and then jotted down Augustine's comments. Two centuries earlier Fronto felt obliged to apologize when arthritis forced him to use a scribe to correct a friend's manuscript.[180] But of the thousand-odd books Augustine left behind in his personal library, his biographer, cataloguer, and confidant of forty years Possidius identified only one slim autograph of sixteen pages.[181]

We should not be misled by the fact that a few learned Byzantines of a later age (mostly monks) copied entire manuscripts. Although we have many works of Planudes and thousands of pages of Eustathius's rambling Homer commentaries in autograph, the scholia in Arethas's books are often in the hand of his copyists,[182] and Byzantines of status mentioned the fact if, exceptionally, they deigned to copy a few pages

---

178. See now W. V. Clausen and J. E. G. Zetzel, *Commentum Cornuti in Persium* (Munich 2004); and Zetzel 2005.

179. McDonnell 1996, 474–77; McGeachy 1942, 119.

180. *corrigam, sed librari manu, nam mihi manus dextra iam vexatur doloribus non mediocribus, Ad amicos* ii. 3 (to Volumnius Quadratus), p. 187. 15 van den Hout².

181. *Retract.* ii. 58; *quaternio una quam propria manu sanctus episcopus Augustinus initiavit*, Possidius, *Indiculus* 10³. 15, A. Wilmart (ed.), *Miscellanea Agostiniana* 2 (Rome 1931), 179; more generally Dekkers 1952.

182. Lemerle 1971, 214f.; note particularly the longer scholia in Moscow Greek 231, signed Ἀρέθα but in the hand of the scribe Stylianos (L. G. Westerink, *Byzantion* 42 [1972], 196–244). Modern attempts to determine whether this or that MS is or is not annotated in Arethas's own hand have paid too little attention to this fact.

themselves.[183] Late antique gentlemen might practice calligraphy as a hobby (Filocalus was a personal friend of Pope Damasus,[184] and Theodosius II an emperor). But only in the most pressing of circumstances would they play the humble role of copyist. The way Jerome refers to a text he had once copied in his own hand as a young man makes clear that this was exceptional;[185] and it was during a long period of imprisonment that a severely depressed Sidonius distracted himself by making a copy of Philostratus's *Life of Apollonius*.[186] In late antiquity, as in the age of Cicero, texts were normally copied by professionals of low status. It is true that, according to her biographer, that most blue-blooded of saints the younger Melania made calligraphic copies of the Bible to support her followers. But this is clearly represented, like her cheap clothes and fasting, as one of the many ways she deliberately abased herself.[187]

Only Domitius Dracontius among the subscribers implies that he corrected a copy he had made himself, and this is not the only possible interpretation of his words. McDonnell has plausibly suggested that, in a number of passages of Cicero that describe members of the elite of his day copying (*describere*) lengthy texts, the verb is being used in a causative sense, "have copied," just as nowadays we might say "I Xeroxed your article," when it was a secretary or student who actually toiled over the copying machine.[188] One example must suffice. After remarking in a letter to Atticus that he has received "the books" from Vibius, apparently a geographical poem by Alexander of Ephesus, Cicero adds: "a tasteless versifier and yet an ignoramus; but he's some use. *I am having them copied and sent back*" (*poeta ineptus, et tamen scit nihil; sed est non inutilis. describo et remitto*).[189] No one will believe that Cicero copied a multi-book work by a Greek poet he himself judged an ignoramus in his own hand.

A particularly clear illustration is provided by Jerome's claim that he never "had his dinner plates engraved with idols" (*idola caelata descripsi*). Since only silversmiths could have done the actual work, here at least *descripsi* must be causative. So too when Damasus writes *legi atque descripsi* of letters he had received from Jerome. Popes have better things to do than make copies of their mail. Nor is it likely that Symmachus himself copied Naucellius's poems, as his *descripsimus* might seem to imply; nor that the venerable Lupus, bishop of Troyes for a half-century, copied Sidonius's letters in person (the reference to punctuation and errors suggests that he simply corrected the work of professionals).[190] It may be that Dracontius likewise did no more than

---

183. αὐτοχειρί or ἰδιοχείρως: for examples, Cameron 1993, 130–31.

184. *Damasi papae cultor adque amator*, as he styles himself on commissions for the pope (18, 18A, and 27 Ferrua).

185. *mea manu ipse*, *Ep*. 5. 2.

186. *Ep*. viii. 3; Stevens 1933, 162–63; Ch. 15. 2.

187. *V. Melaniae* 23 and 26; obviously it is also relevant that it was the Bible she copied.

188. McDonell 1996, 484–85.

189. Cic. Att. ii. 20. 6 and ii. 22. 7 = 40 and 42 Shackleton Bailey, with his notes and translation (slightly adapted).

190. Jer. *Ep*. 27. 2; 35. 1; Symm. *Ep*. iii. 11. 4; Sidon. *Ep*. ix. 11. 6.

have his text copied before he corrected it. This is surely the implication of the passive participle in Domnulus's phrase *emendavi descriptum*.

14: CONCLUSION

Reynolds and Wilson write of the "sudden *re*appearance of subscriptions in secular texts during the last years of the fourth century" as implying an "apparent intensification of interest" in the correcting of such texts, arguing that the survival of so many "is some indication of the extent of the activity."[191] But the hundreds of corrected literary papyri from Hellenistic and early imperial times *without* signed subscriptions suggest that it was not till the fourth century that they first appeared. Subscriptions in Latin manuscripts earlier than this were surely likewise normally unsigned. With the exception of Statilius Maximus's edition of Cicero, the only Latin subscriptions that can be dated earlier than the fourth century document the work of professional calligraphers, not correctors (the Seneca and Gellius palimpsests). What mattered was not *who* corrected the manuscript, but simply the fact that the job had been done, and that could be discovered from a bare *di(orthōthē)* or *emendavi*.[192]

Most surviving subscriptions have come down to us at several removes through a process of copying and recopying from late antique originals. No informed ancient copyist would have made the faux pas of importing such notes from his exemplar into his copy. For to do so would imply that the copy he had just made had already been corrected! It was only later scribes who made this error, misled by the impressive litany of names and offices in the more elaborate subscriptions into supposing that they added authority to the text.[193]

The first subscriptions to name subscribers date from ca. 300, and the authenticating appendix to the *Martyrdom of Polycarp* may date from about the same time. We have seen that there are grounds for believing that the innovation was Christian. Yet though new in form, late antique subscriptions do not in fact represent a new development in the transmission of texts. It is not the collating that was new, but the elaborate identification of the collator and often his collaborator as well. It is not surprising that medieval copyists did not bother to reproduce anonymous subscriptions. The *contuli* preserved after almost every letter of Ambrose in one manuscript family is entirely missing in all the rest. Eight books in the Puteanus of Livy carry anonymous contemporary subscriptions (*recognovi, recognovi Avellini*), none of which are reproduced in a single one of its medieval descendants.[194] It would

---

191. Reynolds and Wilson 1991, 41 (my emphasis).
192. Scholarly readers would always look out for *emendata exemplaria* (Jerome, *In Is.* 16 = PL 24. 570).
193. The firsthand in the s. X Metensis of Rufinus quite properly marked the subscription of Donatus for deletion (n. 27 above, with Koetschau 1913, lx).
194. The subscriber's corrections are of poor quality, but that can hardly be why his subscriptions were omitted.

have been different if the subscriber had revealed himself to be a polyonomous Roman dignitary.

Luxury texts like the capital Vergil manuscripts (all but one unsubscribed) must have been commissioned by people of rank like those named in subscriptions. There is no basis I can find for supposing that subscribed manuscripts imply a different level of corrections from unsubscribed. The corrections in the Medicean Vergil are no different in kind from those in the other capital Vergil manuscripts. And some unsubscribed manuscripts (the Cicero palimpsest) were subjected to a far more careful and scholarly scrutiny than some subscribed ones (the Puteanus of Livy). There may have been a subscription at the now missing end of the Cicero manuscript, but there are no interim formulas as in the Fronto palimpsest. And while it is likely that all surviving secular subscriptions were originally written in codexes rather than rolls,[195] there is no reason to believe that they reflect the *first* transcription of the work in question from roll to codex. The only documented example we have of systematic transference from roll to codex is the Christian library of Pamphilus in Caesarea, sponsored by Bishop Euzoïus in the 360s.

The boastful practice of recording name and rank was new to the late fourth century—and even so the exception rather than the rule. Tempting though it might seem to invest the more imposing secular subscriptions with some special editorial significance, on closer scrutiny very little of the information they so proudly supply (name, rank, place, date) has any bearing on the quality or source of their corrections. The subscriptions in biblical manuscripts, on the other hand, like those in Rusticus's edition of the Acta of Chalcedon and indeed Statilius Maximus's Cicero subscription, state clearly just what sort of corrections and collations the subscribers claimed to have made, and on what authority. With just two partial exceptions (those to Persius and Martianus Capella), not even the most loquacious of the secular subscribers claim to have done any more than correct a personal copy, normally against its exemplar, though sometimes against the copy of a professor. Some admitted that they did not even have an exemplar. The mind boggles at what sort of "corrections" a guards officer with neither exemplar nor scholar to help him may have made in an exceptionally difficult text like Persius. And in the pages of the Puteanus of Livy we can actually see what happened when a corrector without an exemplar tried to emend a deeply corrupt text.

It has always been assumed that it was a new development for people of rank to perform an office earlier performed by professional correctors. But that does not elevate the office or imply "that this humble task took on greater importance than it once had." In their eagerness to see textual, social, and even religious significance in the subscriptions, moderns have paid insufficient attention to their most obvious feature: the few surviving original subscriptions are owner signatures in their very own books (Vettius Agorius Basilius's personal copy of Prudentius, Donatus presbyter's Rufinus; Ursicinus lector's Sulpicius Severus, Victor of Capua's New Testament). The majority

---

195. With the possible exception of the Statilius Cicero subscription, given its early date.

are medieval copies, copies (often at several removes) of books signed and annotated by fifth- and sixth-century dignitaries. For reasons too obvious to need stating, we have no such signed or annotated copies from earlier centuries, nor even copies of such copies. Gellius and Fronto claim to have seen manuscripts of Cicero and Vergil annotated by Tiro and other Republican critics, but even if they are not (as some may be) outright forgeries, they do not survive.[196] It was not till the arrival of the codex that we encounter books durable enough to survive till the Carolingian renaissance, some even to the present day.

Subscriptions written in personal copies by owners amount to a combination of the traditional correction certificate (*emendavi*) with a bookplate, identifying the owner of the book by his full name and titles. It was in part this pompous style that inspired the modern conviction that correcting manuscripts was a preoccupation of the highest dignitaries of state. But notoriously there was an explosion in rank and titulature at every level in the early Byzantine world. Many of the most impressive looking titles in subscriptions actually describe very modest offices (Theodorus the clerk who copied Priscian). By the fifth century, almost anyone educated and wealthy enough to own deluxe copies of the classics would be entitled to append some imposing formula to his name. Symmachus repeatedly protests at the growing "modern" custom of adding titles of rank to the headings of private correspondence, apologizing elaborately when a copyist of his own did it to one of his letters to the elder Flavian.[197] Incredibly, even when correcting a copy of one of his own books, Boethius added all his titles in full. Euzoïus, Rusticus the deacon, and Victor of Capua spelled out their ecclesiastical offices in the same way. In their pomposity at least, the subscriptions we have been studying are simply one aspect of the increasing bureaucratization of late Roman life.

According to Hedrick,[198]

> The fact that the wealthiest and most influential men in the empire ... occupied themselves with the correction of manuscripts is already a strong indication that the practice has some social significance. Men like these were able, after all, to delegate such tasks to their dependents.

But were they? Rather than an active new enthusiasm of the elite, correcting their own manuscripts was surely an unwanted consequence of the scarcity of qualified correctors, a scarcity felt even by wealthy litterateurs like Symmachus. What better illustration than the sheer number of uncorrected late antique manuscripts?

Why should there have been such a scarcity? Actually there may not have been a scarcity at all in absolute terms. It was the demand that had increased exponentially. With the ever-growing requirements of church and bureaucracy, there were almost

---

196. Zeztel 1973, 230–43.
197. *Ep.* ii. 35. 1; iii. 44. 1; iv. 30. 2 (*redeamus quin ergo ad infucatos nominum titulos*); 42. 2.
198. Hedrick 2000, 203, 198.

certainly far more copyists (many doubling as stenographers)[199] than in earlier centuries.[200] But the great majority will only have been capable of reading and writing the standard business script of the age. As we learn from Diocletian's Price Edict, those who could produce *scriptura optima* were paid more than twice as much per hundred lines.[201] An eastern rescript of 372 recommends the appointment of four Greek and three Latin *antiquarii* "skilled in writing" to produce and repair manuscripts for the library of Constantinople.[202] Clearly they wanted specialists, able to decipher near-illegible, centuries-old script, and capable of replacing worn or damaged pages in matching script. Much of the work required may have involved transference from roll to codex, but by 372 there may also have been many venerable codexes in need of repair.

There is reason to believe that the new term *antiquarius* designated copyists who specialized in the capital scripts reserved for luxury editions.[203] Viliaric's magnificent Orosius was the work of a *magister antiquarius*, and a fifth-century Hilary in Verona written in a "delicate and graceful uncial of the oldest type" is subscribed in tiny Rustic capitals with the colophon *scribit antiquarius Eutalius*.[204] Deluxe texts were not only written in a finer script, they were sometimes copied on purple parchment in gold or silver characters. If the subscribed copies of the classics discussed in this and the previous chapter were anything like the surviving late antique copies of Cicero, Terence, Vergil, Livy, and Pliny, they were written in "inch-high" rustic capital or uncial script. Not to mention catching errors in the unfamiliar Latin of most classics, just entering corrections on such pages required specialized skill. Unlike the corrections on modern printer's proofs, whose only function is to pass a message to the printer, these were corrections that formed a permanent part of the book. Where possible, they were entered in the space left by the erasure of the error, in the same script and ink. Deletions and insertions were made as unobtrusively as possible—in the Puteanus of Livy so unobtrusively that they were sometimes missed by later copyists.[205]

We have seen how important correct syllabification was in reading late antique books. Properly trained correctors were expected to check and if necessary correct mistaken word breaks between lines as well as outright errors. Victor of Capua did this systematically in his New Testament, but we can hardly picture a Praetextatus or

---

199. Arns 1953, 63; much information in Teitler 1985.

200. Rapp 1991, 127–48. From the fifth century on Christian books were increasingly produced by scriptoria attached to churches and monasteries. Cutler 1981, 328–34, calculates that over 60 percent of a total of 1,817 identifiable calligraphers between s. IX to XII were monks and ecclesiastics (Cutler 1981, 328–34).

201. S. Lauffer (ed.), *Diocletians Preisedikt* (Berlin 1971), 120.

202. *antiquarios ad bibliothecae codices componendos vel pro vetustate reparandos quattuor Graecos et tres Latinos scribendi peritos legi iubemus*, Cod. *Theod.* xiv. 9. 2. Jerome was evidently proud of his *alumnos qui antiquariae arti serviant* (*Ep.* 5. 2).

203. *Librarii iidem qui et antiquarii vocantur, sed librarii sunt qui nova et vetera scribunt, antiquarii qui tantummodo vetera, unde et nomen sumpserunt*, Isidore, *Orig.* 6. 14, with Gardthausen 1913, 163; *TLL* s.v. *antiquarius* 2, 174; Bischoff 1990, 58–59; Rizzo 1973, 203.

204. *CLA* 4 (1957), 484.

205. F. W. Shipley, *AJA* 7 (1903), 193–97.

a consul like Asterius checking every word break throughout a long text. The scribe of the Morgan fragment of Pliny's *Letters* (ca. 500) was a little less careful than the scribe of the Verona Livy, and an eagle-eyed corrector straightened out his slips. For example, where *exercitu ideo* was broken between lines as *exercitui-deo*, the corrector quite properly deleted the *i* at the end of the first line and replaced it at the beginning of the next, evidently realizing that readers would naturally read *exercitui* as a dative and then be puzzled by *deo*.[206] Only correctors who were also trained scribes could be expected to look out for details like this. Experienced readers must have preferred to use professional correctors whenever possible. Even if an aristocrat was willing (or, like Sidonius, forced) to invest the time in such tedious work, it is unlikely that he would do half so meticulous a job as a trained professional.

Most members of the elite maintained a secretarial staff, but (as the rescript of 372 suggests) competent *antiquarii* may have been harder to find. Symmachus no doubt had adequate facilities for his regular needs, but it is not surprising that they could not cope with multi-book prose classics like Pliny the Elder and Livy. Even assuming that he kept *librarii* capable of producing the requisite script on staff, it will have taken much longer to correct a long prose work. The poets were familiar, as were the stories they told, and defective meter was always a sign of error. But the subject matter of Livy and (especially) Pliny was often unfamiliar, without even the contemporary accentual *cursus* as a guide. While an educated person could correct a new copy of Vergil adequately with only an occasional glance at his exemplar, with Livy and Pliny there was nothing for it but to collate every single word.

Sidonius's bookseller, a professional, copied manuscripts swiftly and elegantly,[207] but found correctors a problem. On one occasion Sidonius did the job himself; on another (as we have seen) the corrector failed to turn up and, since Sidonius was away at the time, the job was left half done.[208] The team of copyists Jerome's rich friend Lucinius sent from Spain to the Holy Land are described as *notarii*, the usual term for stenographers, which may explain Jerome's anxiety about the quality of their work, especially without a competent corrector to oversee it.[209]

Stenographers served an altogether different function from copyists. According to Eusebius, Origen's rich patron Ambrosius provided him with "more than seven shorthand-writers relieving each other at regular intervals when he dictated, and as many copyists, as well as girls skilled in penmanship."[210] Stenographers were invaluable for taking dictation, but most will not have been "skilled in penmanship."

---

206. Lowe and Rand 1922, 29. The better copyists will sometimes (as here perhaps) have doubled as correctors. But if they did the job properly, this will not have represented a saving in either time or fee.
207. *Ep.* ii. 8. 2.
208. *nec semper illo contra legente qui promiserat operam suam, Ep.* v. 15. 1.
209. Elsewhere Jerome uses the word some twenty times, always of stenographers (Teitler 1985, 194). Jerome used stenographers all the time when writing, but *Ep.* 61. 4; 71. 5; and *Vulg. Sal.* pr. make it clear that *librarii* as well were necessary for producing an actual book.
210. Jerome, *Ep.* 61. 4; Euseb. *HE.* vi. 23.

In the circumstances, gentlemen might sometimes be faced with the alternative of either doing the job themselves or leaving it undone. They certainly deserve all due credit for doing what they did, but it would be a serious mistake to infer from the surviving subscriptions that more than a handful willingly undertook such drudgery unaided—or for long. The real grandees hired professors to do the grunt work. Of the two celebrated consular correctors, neither can have spent more than a day or so on the modest task that has attracted so much attention down the years: Asterius cos. 494 checked Vergil's *Bucolics*, Mavortius cos. 527 Horace's *Epodes*, both familiar texts of fewer than thirty modern pages, both with the help of professionals.[211] While the younger Flavianus spent a few days on a copy of Livy, Symmachus never did anything of the sort himself. To judge from his correspondence, it was only a tiny minority of his peers who devoted any significant part of their leisure to serious study of the classics in their adult years. And it was a minority of even these people who occasionally spent a day or so correcting a text.

Correcting texts was not a central part of the life of the late antique man of letters, nor did it bring him prestige. Not only does it not mark off pagans from Christians, it does not even mark off lay Christians from ecclesiastics. The most thorough job of late antique correcting we can actually identify is Victor of Capua's New Testament.

---

211. To judge from the location of the subscriptions. Both *may* have gone further, but if (as I believe) the Asterius subscription is a copy, we cannot infer anything from the contemporary corrections in the Medicean.

14

THE LIVIAN REVIVAL

1

The most famous of all Latin subscriptions, familiar to everyone interested in the transmission of classical texts, are those that, in various forms and combinations, close each of the first nine books of Livy in a number of manuscripts:[1]

1. Victorianus v.c. emendabam domnis Symmachis (Bks 1–9).
2a. Nicomachus Dexter v.c. emendavi (3–4).
2b. Nicomachus Dexter v.c. emendavi ad exemplum parentis mei Clementiani (5).
3a. Nicomachus Flavianus v.c. III praefectus urbis emendavi (6).
3b. Emendavi Nicomachus Flavianus v.c. ter praef(ectus) urbis apud Hennam (7).
3c. Emendavi Nicomachus Flavianus v.c. ter praef(ectus) urbis apud Term(as) (8).

It has hitherto been taken for granted that these three names imply three separate revisions,[2] and as a consequence it has come to be believed that the "editing" of Livy was a "family tradition" among the Symmachi and Nicomachi; that the job was done afresh in successive generations, with the aid of new manuscripts.[3] Some write of a "text prepared by the Symmachi and Nicomachi," or (even more anachronistically) a "programme promoted and financed by the Symmachi,"[4] as though of a long-term collective project to improve the text of Livy.[5] It is the prime (in effect the only) text for the view that the aristocrats of Rome devoted their leisure to editing the classics, in the case of Livy, aristocrats well known for their paganism. Not to mention many earlier studies, a recent essay on the "pagan historiography" of the fourth century has proclaimed Symmachus a leading figure in the "Livian revival" of the age.[6] For

---

1. The basic study is Zetzel 1980, 38–59; see too Pecere 1986, 59–69. On the historical side, there is still much of value in de Rossi 1849. I am grateful to Stephen Oakley for helpful comments.
2. "At various times...three Roman aristocrats," Zetzel 1980, 38; "tre nuclei distinti di sottoscrizioni," Pecere 1986, 59; "plusieurs étapes," Dain 1975, 119; most elaborately, J. Bayet, *Tite-Live: Livre I* (Paris 1954), xcii–c.
3. McGeachy 1942, 171; Chastagnol 1962, 244; *PLRE* ii. 357; Reynolds and Wilson 1991, 40.
4. Billanovich 1959, 108; Pecere 1986, 63.
5. "Symmachus not only wanted to procure a correct Livy for himself; his plan was to circulate it, to publish, so to speak, this emended text" (Bayet 1954, xciv).
6. Schiatti 1998, 259; so too Zecchini 1993, 46, 55, 156, 187.

Grünewald, the younger Flavian's activity as "editor" of Livy is the clearest proof that he remained a pagan at heart even after his purely nominal conversion in 394.[7]

The role of the Symmachi in this project is clarified by a letter of Q. Aurelius Symmachus, promising a friend called Valerianus a complete text of Livy, which was being held up by the need for careful correction (*munus totius Liviani operis quod spopondi etiam nunc diligentia emendationis moratur*).[8] Evidently, Symmachus himself owned a complete text, which he was having copied. Valerianus is often identified with a man of that name who was prefect of Rome twenty years earlier (381), but on no firmer basis than the shared name.[9] Fortunately, the letter itself can be dated to within a couple of months. The next sentence refers to the preparations for the praetorian games of Symmachus's son Memmius, due to be held in July 401. So Symmachus's "emendation" of Livy was still in progress early in 401.

A complete Livy[10] must have been a rare and precious item by Symmachus's day. People were still reading the first five decades, but nothing later than this survived into the Carolingian age.[11] One hundred forty-two (perhaps rather 140)[12] books were just too much. The subject matter could be acquired with less effort from Livian derivatives like Valerius Maximus, Florus, Eutropius, or the various epitomes. Even the epitomes of the last seven decades are briefer and scrappier.[13] Long historical works had never really appealed to Roman readers. It is no coincidence that not one, from Cato to Ammianus, has survived in its entirety. It was his moralizing and his style that won Sallust his place in the Roman literary pantheon, and even so it was his two monographs that survived, not his much longer and more ambitious *Historiae*.

Livy undoubtedly enjoyed considerable fame and popularity for a century or so, universally accepted as *the* historian of Republican Rome.[14] But it is another question how many of these admirers read, much less owned, all 142 books. It is not likely that many complete texts ever existed, even in the first century. Then came the archaizing movement, and Livy was not only too long but out of style. It is exclusively the pre-Livian historians that Gellius read; he quotes Claudius Quadrigarius forty-four times with admiration, but never so much as mentions Livy.[15] Livy no doubt continued to find the odd reader during the late second and third centuries, but there is not likely to have been much demand for new copies of the complete text. If it was really complete, Symmachus's Livy must have been a very old copy, in all probability in roll

---

7. Grünewald 1992, 481, 485. For Mazzarino 1966, 328, for the Romans of the late empire "il livianismo era...un fatto di cultura religiosa (o quasi)."

8. *Ep.* ix. 13, with Roda 1981, 119–22.

9. There are better grounds for identifying him with the Valerianus of *Ep.* viii. 69 (before 391), an elderly literary friend (so Callu in his note).

10. Sym. *Ep.* iv. 18. 5 proves (as we shall see) that it went at least as far as Bk 108.

11. The bifolium from Bk 91 (below) is no exception, since (like the Veronensis) it was palimpsested in s. VIII.

12. Barnes 1998, 209–12, plausibly argues that the last three *Periochae* should be collapsed into one, giving 140.

13. Begbie 1967, 332–38; P. Schmidt 1968; see too O. Rossbach's edition (1910), xxiv.

14. Schanz-Hosius 2⁴ (1935), 315–17; C. Giarratano, *Tito Livio²* (Rome 1943), Ch. 12.

15. For Gellius's taste in historians, Holford-Strevens 2003, 241–59.

form (like the Oxyrynchus Livy of ca. 300),[16] passing from one aristocratic library to another until it reached the Symmachi. In fact, it may have been the library that changed hands rather than the book that moved.

From the peculiar nature of many corruptions in the fifth-century Vindobonensis of the fifth decade, Zelzer argued that it was copied from an exemplar in an early cursive script.[17] Such misreadings of early cursive have been detected in the transmission of other Latin texts as well, notably Lucretius.[18] But they are so systematic in the Vindobonensis as to suggest that its copyist found the script of his exemplar altogether unfamiliar. That suggests in turn that the exemplar was of some antiquity. Symmachus's complete text may likewise have been a couple of centuries old.[19] Indeed, it is legitimate to wonder whether the entire text of Livy was ever copied in codex form.

There is a paradox here. Symmachus is supposed to have sponsored a major attempt to improve the text of Livy. But he already owned what was acknowledged to be an authoritative complete, probably early text. It was to Symmachus that his friends turned when in search of a text of Livy, not only Valerianus, but Protadius in Gaul (more below). Antiquity does not in itself guarantee accuracy,[20] but the fewer transcriptions the less likelihood of serious degradation of the text. Why the need to check so old a text against other manuscripts? How many other copies of the complete text were available even in the libraries of Roman aristocrats? And where does Valerianus fit into this project?

The letter promises the whole of Livy. The subscriptions record the "emendation" of Bks 1–9 for the "Lords Symmachus" (*domnis Symmachis*). Not indeed a complete Livy, but since it begins with Bk 1, quite possibly a projected complete Livy that was never completed. The subscriptions imply that the project got no further than Bk 10 (the absence of a subscription to 10 itself is presumably accidental; no surviving manuscript has a subscription for every book).[21] The third (the second being completely lost), fourth, and fifth decades all descend from different fifth-century archetypes.[22] So we have no means of knowing whether the "Nicomachean edition," now conventionally known as **N**, got further than just the first decade.[23]

It should be noted that Symmachus apologizes to Valerianus precisely because the projected complete Livy was being held up. If the delay continued a little longer, the job may never have been completed, since within the year Symmachus was dead. But

---

16. P. Oxy. 1379 (1. 5. 6–6. 1); *CLA* ii. 247; perhaps only Bk 1. The Oxyrynchus Livy epitome (P. Oxy. 668) of approximately the same date is also in roll form.
17. B misread as D, R as S, and S as F: Zelzer 1972, 487–501. To a lesser extent, she found some of the same errors in the Veronensis of the first decade.
18. Brunhölzl 1971, 16–31; Timpanaro 1981, 118–19.
19. Though that is no sufficient basis for Zelzer's suggestion (1972, 500) that it was because of the difficulty of deciphering an unfamiliar script that Valerianus's copy was delayed.
20. Reynolds and Wilson 1991, 216–18.
21. The fifth-century Puteanus lacks the end of Bk 30 and so its final subscription. But it is unclear why the corrector left the surviving end of Bk 27 unsubscribed.
22. Different in that none of them preserve Symmachan or Nicomachean subscriptions (more below).
23. Since we know nothing about the transmission of the entirely lost second decade, it is *possible* that it too was "Nicomachean." But that would be pure speculation.

some of it was ready, for he goes on to tell Valerianus to send a porter to pick it up, since his own were all busy running errands for Memmius's praetorian games. It is hard to resist the commonsense inference that the books awaiting collection consisted of (or at least included) the first decade.

Over and above general considerations of probability, there are two specific reasons for identifying these two incomplete Symmachan attempts to produce a corrected Livy. In the first place, the letter explains why the subscriptions distinguish the Lords Symmachus from those who did the actual correcting. Symmachus simply had both copy and correction done for him. Second, the plural "Lords Symmachus" implies a date before Symmachus's death in 402, the other Symmachus being his only son Memmius. That yields a window of 401–2, too narrow for coincidence. Victorianus's work on Livy 1–9 must have begun before Symmachus's letter to Valerianus in early 401; and the surviving subscriptions cannot be later than 402.

To the best of my knowledge no one has ever attempted to distinguish the copy made for Valerianus from the copy attested by the subscriptions. Yet at the same time no one has drawn the full consequences of identifying them. For Symmachus could hardly have written the letter he did to Valerianus if he had been contemplating anything in the nature of a scholarly revision of the whole of Livy,[24] 142 books, the equivalent of twenty-eight Oxford text volumes, some eight thousand modern pages.[25] Systematic collation of no more than a handful of manuscripts throughout would have taken many years. But the letter to Valerianus implies a delay of weeks rather than years. If he really planned to give Valerianus a complete Livy, Symmachus can hardly have had anything more in mind than a routine checking of the new copy against its exemplar, the complete text that he evidently owned himself.

Furthermore, if **N** is the copy Valerianus was impatiently waiting for in 401, how is it that it carries (on the traditional view) the signs of two later revisions, those of Flavian (generally assigned to 408) and Dexter (up to a generation later still)? And if this was Valerianus's copy, how did it "find its way" into the possession of the Nicomachi? To reply that they "kept" a copy of their work[26] is to underestimate the sheer time and labor involved in making not one but two copies of even ten books of Livy. It also presupposes the point at issue: that the copy given to Valerianus was an "edition" that differed significantly from its source, the complete text already owned by Symmachus. Of course it may be that Valerianus's man never came for his parcel, and then Symmachus died and the gift was forgotten, so that the copy remained in Symmachus's library, to be corrected again and again over the years. But on the natural interpretation, N passed into the possession of Valerianus in 401, complete with whatever subscriptions it carried at the time.

---

24. So briefly Pasquali 1952, 366.
25. The average length of the surviving books in Weissenborn-Müller pages is fifty-six (Stadter 1972, 304–5).
26. So McGeachy 1942, 171; cf. Callu, *Symmaque* ii. 237.

In the fifth-century Verona palimpsest (**V**) we have a surviving copy of the first decade perhaps as early as **N**. But common errors, omissions, and dislocations make it clear that, with the sole exception of **V**, all surviving manuscripts of the first decade derive ultimately from a common source, and since eight of the most authoritative of these manuscripts[27] (and many later copies) carry one or more Nicomachean subscriptions, there can be little doubt that this common source derived, at an indeterminate number of removes,[28] from **N**.

A masterly study by Mommsen originally published in 1869 showed that **V** represented a different tradition, disagreeing with **N** and its derivatives in both truth and error.[29] Despite its great antiquity, **V** is actually a less valuable witness than the reconstructed text of **N**. One difference between **V** and **N**, highly relevant in the present context, is that **V** was never corrected.[30] The original scribe made a few corrections, but there was clearly no systematic *emendatio*. In its present state we have the end of only one book (5), and there is no subscription.

In his admirably thorough and balanced recent study of the manuscript tradition of the first decade, Oakley explains that he "found it convenient to employ the word 'edition';" of **N**, but "in a neutral sense," not implying that it "resembled a modern critical edition in any significant way."[31] It would have been better to use the genuinely neutral term "copy."[32] For (disclaimer notwithstanding) "edition" automatically implies (as indeed Oakley assumed) consultation of more than one manuscript and some attempt, however amateurish, to decide between variants.[33] We shall see that the celebrated Symmachan "edition" of Livy was in fact no more than a copy duly corrected against its own exemplar. Since the exemplar belonged to Symmachus himself, the text of the copy is unlikely to have marked any improvement beyond the occasional correction of obvious errors. The reason copy rather than exemplar became the archetype of the medieval tradition was partly pure chance, partly (no doubt) the impression of authority created by the subscriber's famous names, but more straightforwardly because the copy was a sturdy new codex written on parchment in the clear uncial script generally employed for late antique Livy manuscripts.

It has in the past been taken for granted that the relative excellence of the **N**-tradition is a consequence of the *emendatio* of Victorianus and the Nicomachi. There is obviously some truth in this assumption. If Symmachus had decided to send Valerianus an uncorrected Livy as he sent Ausonius an uncorrected Pliny (*Ep.* i. 24), our text of Livy 1–10 would no doubt have been worse than it is. How much worse would depend on the competence of the copyist and the quality of his exemplar. If as poor a copy as the inadequately

---

27. All "uneliminable," to use Oakley's term; Zetzel 1980, passim.

28. On the question of these removes, Reeve 1996, 87–88.

29. Mommsen 1909, 96–148 (119–27 on divergences from **N**); *CLA* 4 (1947), 499; Oakley 1997, 164–65. On the remarkable accuracy of Mommsen's decipherment, Grazia Nistri 1982, 193–96.

30. "Correctorem liber non nactus est," Mommsen 1909, 106.

31. Oakley 1997, 152–327 at 165 n. 30.

32. So Reeve 1996, 75.

33. Oakley 1997, 320.

corrected Puteanus of the third decade or Vindobonensis of the fifth decade (both fifth-century), then considerably worse; if more like the uncorrected Veronensis, only a little worse. When **V** and **N** differ, **N** is more often right than **V**, but **V** is right nearly a third of the time.[34] The primary credit for the quality of **N**'s text must go to the exemplar from which it was copied rather than the corrections of the Nicomachi, for the simple reason that the great majority of those corrections were surely made against that very exemplar.

The surviving manuscript generally thought to offer the most satisfactory text of Livy 1–10 is the tenth-century Medicean (Laur. 53. 19), known as **M**.[35] It is probably therefore the manuscript that reflects the text of **N** most closely. It has three other idiosyncratic features: twenty-one marginal notes in Bk 8;[36] twenty similar notes in Bks 7 and 8 (and one in nine) that have been thoughtlessly copied into the text;[37] and a number of doublets[38] throughout that presumably originated as interlinear variants, subsequently incorporated into the text by a copyist who mistakenly supposed them to be omissions. All these features may well derive from **N**. But not necessarily from the earliest stage of **N**, the condition in which it left Victorianus and the Nicomachi.

Five of the doublets are reduced to gibberish in **M** by a seemingly meaningless *ia*, which Heraeus acutely recognized as an abbreviation found regularly in the fifth-century Vatican Fronto palimpsest and occasionally in late antique scholiasts, standing for *i(n) a(lio codice)* and identifying a variant found by collation in another manuscript.[39] Two examples may be cited. First, *Licinio ia Cilnio* at 10. 5. 13, where all other manuscripts have just *Licinio*. Since *Cilnio* is undoubtedly what Livy wrote, there can be no question that it was a genuine variant introduced into **N** by collation, not conjecture. Second, 4. 13. 6, where the correct text (offered by all Nicomachean manuscripts but **M**) is *Agrippa Menenius*. **M** has *Agrippam ia manilius enenius*, namely a variant *Manilius*, which Ogilvie plausibly explained as "a correction of the hapolography *Menius*."[40] *Mallius* (= *Manlius*) in the contemporary Veronensis (**V**) implies that the variant was well established and the haplography early.

Though this abbreviation is not as rare in medieval manuscripts as Heraeus supposed,[41] there is a presumption that these variants are late antique rather than

34. For figures and examples, Oakley 1997, 164–65; in addition, "V often shows that the Nicomachean mss are corrupt in passages where one might not have suspected it" (165).

35. See now Oakley 1997, 168–84.

36. Published by L. Voit, *Philol.* 91 (1936), 308–21; Oakley 1997, 168.

37. Walters and Conway (OCT) 2 (1919), vii–viii; Oakley 1997, 168–69.

38. By "doublets" I mean cases where a scribe has mechanically copied both of two alternatives instead of making a choice: for example, *fruantur utantur* at 2. 34. 10 or *inciderunt fuerunt* at 5. 3. 4, where the other MSS have just *fruantur* and *fuerunt*; for a list, Ogilvie, *CQ* 7 (1957), 76.

39. Heraeus 1925, 5–14; more examples now in M. P. J. Van den Hout, *Fronto Epistulae*[2] (1988), xxxviii–xliii.

40. Ogilvie 1965, 554.

41. There are many cases where *ia* must surely be interpreted *i(n) a(lio)* rather than (with Schwartz) *ia(cet)* in the notes of the deacon Rusticus (writing in 564) on the Chalcedon Acta in Paris. lat. 11611 (s. IX) and occasionally 1458 (s. X): *ACO* II. iii. 1 [1935], pp. 39. 12; 57. 3; 88. 23; 132. 16; 201. 31; 202. 14; 208. 5; 226. 29; 227. 15; 230. 2; 243. 19; 259. 18; a senseless *iam* introducing a variant at p. 132. 1 must also surely be read the same way (compare the *iam* in Livy 3. At p. 33. 8 and 243. 19 we have *in alio* in full. While the copyist of the Medicean evidently did not recognize the abbreviation, those of the two Parisini apparently did.

medieval. The *ia Manilius* variant was clearly inserted one letter too early in a text written in capital script without word division, in other words a late antique rather than a Carolingian copy.[42] Not surprisingly, scholars have generally succumbed to the temptation of assigning such variants to Victorianus and the Nicomachi. So Oakley, concluding that their editorial performance was "notably diligent and scholarly, and well merited their proud subscriptions." So too Zetzel, with the following conclusion:[43]

> The significant facts are two: that the correctors did consult what must have been a manuscript other than the exemplar from which their copy of the text was taken, and that they did, at least on occasion, give some indication (*in alio*) that they had done so.... Late antique manuscripts do not, as a rule, contain *variants* at all: they have only corrections by addition or expunction. That the emenders of the first decade of Livy did more places them in a different class from most correctors.

This apparently uncontroversial claim rests on two dubious assumptions. First, that the variants go back to Victorianus and the Nicomachi; second, that they formed part of the *emendatio* described in the subscriptions. To take the second first, we saw in the last chapter that the subscription *emendavi* normally indicates the routine correction of a newly copied manuscript. That is why, as Zetzel rightly says, "late antique manuscripts do not, as a rule, contain variants." If correctors had consulted more than one exemplar, they would immeasurably have extended and complicated their labors. Instead of just checking that the copy was an accurate reproduction of its exemplar (difficult and time consuming enough in itself if done conscientiously, especially in a prose text), they would have been faced with a task of an altogether different order: collecting, comparing, and adjudicating between variants.

In the present case there are two further arguments in favor of confining the correctors' *emendavi* to simple correction. In the first place, there is the fact that this copy was made for a friend. As we saw in the last chapter, given the difficulty of obtaining books in the ancient world, at all periods but especially in late antiquity, this was a favor often asked. Apologies for delay and reference to the speed of copyists in replies to such requests make it clear that (as we might expect) people normally wanted their copies as soon as possible.[44] To judge from Symmachus's apology, Valerianus was getting impatient. So long as we identify the copy behind the subscriptions with the gift to Valerianus, we are bound to assume that Symmachus asked no more of Victorianus and the Nicomachi than correction against exemplar. After all, both letter and subscriptions use the same word: *emendatio*.

---

42. The final M of AGRIPPAM belongs with ENENIUS; this is a mistake that could not have been made if the words had been written separately.
43. Oakley 1997, 320; Zetzel 1980, 46.
44. Auson. *Ep.* XXVII. 9, p. 201 Green; Sidon. *Ep.* v. 15. 1; Symm. *Ep.* i. 24 as well as ix. 13.

In the second place, as Zetzel has already underlined, the location of the subscriptions makes it clear that each book had already been completely copied, right down to the explicits and incipits, *before* the correctors set to work. As the nonsense lines that close each book reveal (*emendavi Nicomachus Flavianus Titi Livii ter praefectus*...and the like), each subscription was centrally written in the convenient gaps left by the copyist between the body of the text and the explicits and incipits of successive books. Book 7 (e.g.) evidently closed as follows:

emendavi Nicomachus Flavianus
TITI LIVII
ter praefectus urbis apud Hennam
AB URBE CONDITA
Victorianus v. c. emendabam domnis Symmachis
EXPLICIT LIBER VII

If **N** had really been, as Billanovich called it, a "text prepared by the Symmachi and Nicomachi," we should expect the "preparation" to have been completed *before* the final copy was made. The final copy would have to have been subjected to the usual process of correction in any case. This, not some undocumented "preparation," is what the subscriptions attest. The very fact that each book is separately subscribed supports the natural assumption of routine book-by-book correction.[45] If successive subscriptions had been dated exactly (as in Victor of Capua's New Testament or Theodorus's Priscian), each would have been a few days later than its predecessor.

As for the marginalia, there are a number of obvious transcriptional errors, implying that they have been copied more than once and so probably late antique rather than medieval. Since they are restricted to Bk 8, one of the books subscribed by the younger Flavian, few have been able to resist the temptation of crediting him with any that look late antique. There is in fact only one of any significance, a note on 8. 15. 7, the burial of the Vestal Minucia in 337 B.C. on suspicion of being unchaste. The first half of the note simply paraphrases Livy, but the second offers a learned comment:[46]

I am astonished [*miror*], since [Livy] mentions her burial, that he neglects to say it was laid down in the Sibylline books, as I recollect [*recolo*] having read in actual verses of that date in Phlegon.

---

45. As illustrated by the many "interim" subscriptions listed in the preceding chapter.
46. *Minutia virgo Vestalis, mundioris* [*minutioris* cod.] *primo suspecta cultus mox(que) flagitii servo accusante convicta, ad portam Collinam viva defoditur locusque Sceleratus ex eo ca<m>pus dictus. miror autem, cum defossam indicat, omisisse illum ex libris Sibyllinis hoc esse praeceptum, ut legisse me in ipsis apud Flegontem temporis illius versibus recolo*: Voit 1936, 315–20; Zetzel 1980, 48; Pecere 1986, 68; Oakley 1997, 168.

The author of this note is remarkably well informed. The Sibylline Oracles were indeed consulted when Vestal Virgins were found to be unchaste;[47] and the surviving excerpts of Phlegon, a freedman of Hadrian who wrote antiquarian works in Greek,[48] do indeed quote Sibylline Oracles, no fewer than four of them from at least two different works, two complete with authenticating acrostics and consular dates.[49] Since the note in **M** focuses on the name of the place where Minucia was entombed, we should probably accept Voit's suggestion that the reference is to Phlegon's lost work *On places in Rome and how they got their names*.[50]

But where did the writer get his information? By 400 Phlegon was no more than a name in the Latin-speaking West: three plainly bogus citations in the *Historia Augusta* and two in Jerome taken over from earlier sources.[51] No one will believe that a fifth-century western reader of Livy simply happened to "recall" (*recolo*) so recondite yet so apposite a passage in a Greek book that failed to survive even in the East. This is no casual recollection by a reader. It is an excerpt from a learned work. If we take into account the elegant word order and metrical clausulas,[52] there can be little doubt that the ultimate source is an antiquarian work in Latin.

The polemical attitude to Livy would suit the age of Gellius. But the affectation of a conversational manner (*legisse… recolo, miror*) suggests a work with literary pretensions rather than a scholarly monograph, perhaps a speech in one of the lost parts of Macrobius's *Saturnalia*. In what survives there are no fewer than three examples of *legisse… memini*, not to mention other passages where interlocutors are represented (improbably enough) as "remembering" (*memini, recordor*) the countless texts they cite.[53] As for *miror*, one Macrobian interlocutor is "astonished" (*miror*) at Valerius Probus's ignorance of the source of a story in Vergil and "embarrassed" (*me pudet*) at a similar display of ignorance on the part of Cornutus.[54] And two more are represented as "astonished" (*miror* again) that other interlocutors have not raised certain issues. We shall see elsewhere that Macrobius liked to spice up his dialogue with an occasional note of polemic. But there are no such formulas in Gellius.[55]

---

47. Dion. Hal. iii. 67. 3; Plut. *Quaest. Rom.* 83 = *Mor.* 284B; apparently in 228, 216, and 114 B.C.: Parke 1988, 196, 198, 205.

48. F. Jacoby, *FGrH* 255; see too W. Hansen 1996.

49. Diels 1890; Jacoby, *FGrH* 257, F 36, X; F 37, V. 2, 4; Hansen 1996, 40–43, 55–57, 126–37, 183–89. The oracle on the secular games is also quoted in Zosimus ii. 6 (see the notes in Paschoud 2000, 201–5).

50. Περὶ τῶν ἐν Ῥώμῃ τόπων καὶ ὧν ἐπικέκληνται ὀνομάτων, Suda s.v. Φλέγων; Voit, *Philol.* 91 (1936), 319.

51. Syme 1968, 60; Courcelle 1969, 78 n. 146.

52. Oakley 1997, 168. There are traces of clausulae in the note on 8. 38. 7 (Oakley 1997, 168), but it is just summary of the Livian text, with no rhetoric and no citations.

53. ii. 2. 16 (Symmachus); vii. 6. 15 (Flavian); vii. 13. 11 (Caecina Albinus); ii. 7. 10 (*memini*); i. 4. 24 (*ut recordor*); vii. 5. 12 (*si bene recordor*).

54. *Sat.* v. 22. 10; v. 19. 3; on the ignorance Macrobius (mistakenly) ascribes to these scholars, see J. Rauk, *CP* 90 (1995), 345–54.

55. *Sat.* iii. 3. 1; iii. 14. 1. *memini* is common enough in Gellius, but of reminiscences by the author and his friends rather than as an affectation of "remembering" long lists of obscure quotations. And no sign of Macrobius's polemical *miror*.

If Macrobius's *Saturnalia* (ca. 430) was indeed the source of this note, that would be a generation too late for Flavian's contribution to the text of Livy. Not that he was a scholar in any case, as we have already seen. On the other hand, the *Saturnalia* is just the sort of text we would expect to find on the bookshelf of a late fifth- or sixth-century reader of Livy. The other marginalia are no more than summaries or excerpts, of no scholarly value. A single example will suffice: "this was the first trial held for poisoning at Rome" against 8. 18. 11, simply a summary of the chapter in question. As Zetzel rightly remarks, they are not in any sense a commentary, "nor would they be of interest to anyone but the writer himself."[56] There are a few marginalia of the same sort in the uncorrected Veronensis, some interestingly enough in Greek.[57] These are in fact the sort of jottings an owner makes in the margins of a book of his own to remind himself of points of interest.

No less important, Flavian was not the owner of **N**. If we identify, as we surely must, the two Symmachan copies of Livy, Flavian simply corrected a text destined for Valerianus. The fact that it was Valerianus who had asked Symmachus for a complete Livy in the first place argues considerable interest in Republican antiquities. Valerianus is a better bet than Flavian for the earliest stratum of marginalia and variants in **M**.

To return to the three different subscribers, on any hypothesis the apparent duplication of attention to Bks 1–9 is puzzling. Why (on the standard interpretation) did each of the three begin again with the first decade? If the main function of *emendatio* was to correct copy against exemplar, how many times did this need to be done? If the object of the enterprise was to correct the whole of Livy (*totius Liviani operis*), why not move on to the second and third decades? This is surely what Valerianus would have wanted.

The standard assumption that the later correctors continued to "improve" the text by collating fresh manuscripts is more problematic than generally supposed. In the first place, it is improbable in the extreme that amateur critics, rich men with a busy social life, careers, and estates to run, would collate manuscripts in their entirety rather than simply check problem passages. Second, collating manuscripts should not be equated straightforwardly with "improving the text." Systematic collation of a number of manuscripts (if only for key passages) will provide an experienced editor with useful information about the nature of the transmission.[58] But collation of one or two by an amateur is all too likely to overwhelm him with a mass of trivial variants. Even if he is fortunate enough to hit on a superior manuscript, he still needs the knowledge and experience to distinguish its superior readings from its errors.

---

56. Zetzel 1980, 48–49.
57. Mommsen 1909, 106–7; for a plate showing one of the Greek scholia, Grazia Nistri 1982.
58. For example, Felix's reference to the *mendosissima exemplaria* of Martianus Capella may mean that all manuscripts he consulted shared the same errors and so offered no help where he could see the text was corrupt.

As already remarked, collating manuscripts and weighing variants is not just an extension of correcting, but something altogether different. Many of **M**'s variants are trivial. For example, its text at 2. 15. 3 suggests a variant *ea esse vota* for *eam esse voluntatem* (or vice versa). In the handful of cases where the *ia* formula allows us to be sure which was the variant, *Cilnio* for *Licinio* at 10. 5. 13 is certainly right while *Manilius* for *Menenius* at 4. 13. 6 is certainly wrong. But then as now the average reader seldom had the historical knowledge or feel for style to make authoritative decisions when presented with a choice between variants like this when both made perfectly satisfactory sense. And in this case it is clear that no such decisions were made. The reader who quoted these random variants evidently did not indicate whether he preferred the variant to the original reading.

The only one of our three correctors to mention another exemplar is Dexter, one belonging to his *parens* Clementianus. If we make the traditional assumption that our correctors were engaged in serious collation, it becomes natural to assume that one of them collated Clementianus's exemplar throughout. But it is only mentioned in the subscription to Bk 5. Nor does Dexter claim to have used it *in addition* to another exemplar. Nor do either of his fellow correctors claim to have used this copy. Indeed, the very fact that only Dexter mentions it suggests that the others did not. It is conceivable (as often assumed) that Dexter corrected 3 and 4 against this manuscript as well as 5,[59] but he does not say so. We cannot even be sure that it contained 3 and 4, much less the whole of the first decade. If, like the Oxyrynchus Livy of ca. 300, it was a roll rather a codex,[60] it will have contained only one book. Even if it contained more, the assumption that either Dexter or one of the other two used it throughout is based on the prior assumption that they were exploiting all manuscripts available to them rather than (on my assumption) just checking Valerianus's copy for obvious errors. Without any specific indication to the contrary, the natural inference from the only evidence we have is that 1–4 and 6–9 were simply checked against the exemplar in Symmachus's library. The presumption is that Flavian and Dexter used only this exemplar for 3–4 and 6–8; and that Dexter used only Clementianus's exemplar for 5.

I would like to suggest a different interpretation of the three subscriptions based on a more careful examination of their dates and interrelationship, one that better explains both the subscriptions and the letter to Valerianus. In my view, the three correctors divided the first decade between them and worked simultaneously. If so, the probability is that Dexter used Clementianus's copy while (and because) Flavian was using Symmachus's.

If we combine the evidence of the letter and subscriptions, we can date Victorianus's work between ca. 400 and Symmachus's death in 402. What of his two colleagues? The younger Flavian's long career can be traced from a proconsulship of Asia in 382–83

---

59. Pecere 1986, 66, argued that all the *ia(m)* dittographies derived from Clementianus, even in Bk 10.
60. So too in all probability Symmachus's complete Livy.

to the prefecture of Italy in 431–32.[61] His subscription, which is only found at the end of Bks 6, 7, and 8, refers to a third tenure of the urban prefecture (PVR). According to all modern authorities, he was PVR in 392/4, 399–400, and 408. So on the face of it, his corrections belong in 408 (after laying down office he would have described himself as ex-prefect, *ex praefecto*). Since Dexter was Flavian's son (below), his corrections are generally placed a generation later.[62] His only known office is a city prefecture held in the vicinity of 430.[63]

But these later dates at once raise a problem. Both the Flavian and the Dexter subscriptions invariably appear above and before Victorianus's. As we have seen, the subscriptions were not just scribbled in the margin, but carefully and centrally written, with the dignity appropriate to the subscriber's rank (which is recorded in full) in the gaps between the body of the text and the explicits and incipits of individual books.[64]

It is difficult to see how the subscriptions of Flavian and Dexter could *always* have preceded Victorianus's unless they were written first. It is theoretically possible that Victorianus wrote first but for no obvious reason always chose to inscribe his name in the lowest available gap between books, so that Flavian and Dexter, though writing later, were obliged to enter their names above his. Yet we should hardly expect such consistency in the utilization of these gaps. The only reasonable explanation of this invariable sequence is that Flavian and Dexter wrote before Victorianus. And Victorianus was writing between 400 and 402.

As for the assumption that Dexter's corrections represent a separate, third stage, it should be noted that he subscribes Bks 3–5, while Flavian subscribes 6–8. That is to say, the son's subscriptions *precede* the father's in the sequence of Livian books. Once again, it could be that, though working later, he simply corrected earlier books. But if Flavian worked first, we have to wonder why he left 3–5 uncorrected. The *natural* interpretation is certainly that Dexter corrected 3–5 before (or at the same time as) Flavian corrected 6–8.

According to his subscription, Flavian was prefect of Rome for the third time when he made his corrections. Now his *second* prefecture (on the traditional reckoning) fell in 399–400, to be precise from (at any rate) 6 June 399 till 8 November 400. That is to say, Flavian was in office as prefect at exactly the time Victorianus set to work. It would be a remarkable coincidence if Flavian had been PVR for the *second* time when Victorianus wrote, and then added his own name above Victorianus's on some later occasion when he happened to be PVR again, for the third time. I suggest that the prefecture of 399–400 was not his second, but his third, and that all three wrote their names in sequence as part of the same operation within a period of a few weeks in the year 400.

---

61. For the basic facts, *PLRE* i. 345–47.
62. Though Bloch 1963, 216, allowed that "Dexter helped his father"; so too Pecere 1986, 65.
63. *PLRE* ii. 357–58.
64. Zetzel 1980, 44; Oakley 1997, 167.

The only realistic way to accomplish the task of correcting so massive a text as Livy was to rope in as many correctors as possible. In the case of the first decade, Victorianus and the two Nicomachi. The only other context in which we encounter Victorianus is as a copyist or corrector working for the elder Flavian (Ch. 15). It is an exaggeration to describe him as a "friend of Symmachus";[65] he is nowhere mentioned in the correspondence, so abundant for just this period. He participated less as a fellow aristocrat whiling away his leisure hours than as a professional scholar, engaged by Symmachus to do the real work.[66] Note the way he claims to be making his corrections "for the Lords Symmachus," as if, though himself of senatorial rank (*v. c.*),[67] he was the social inferior of such grandees. He began and finished the first decade on his own, while the two Nicomachi helped him out with Bks 3–8.

Clementianus is usually identified as Dexter's father.[68] Yet we might have expected Symmachus to mention the fact somewhere if the younger Flavian had a brother, and it would be disrespectfully unbalanced for Dexter to give himself two names and a title but his own father only one name and no title. The single name and lack of title in this highly formal context suggest that Clementianus was not even a social equal, much less kin. In late antiquity relationship terms like *parens, frater,* and *filius* were often used in an extended sense: *frater* of a friend (or just someone of the same social class); *filius* of younger friends; and *parens* as a term of respect for those who were older or senior.[69] In view of Dexter's youth (below), the natural inference is that *parens* is simply a respectful form of address. In the context Clementianus is perhaps a teacher,[70] another professional scholar engaged to assist the aristocrats (which would explain why he brought his own copy of Livy).

On the evidence of the subscriptions, Victorianus corrected some books (1, 2, 9) entirely on his own, but received help from the Nicomachi for the others. This hypothesis would explain the curious distribution of the Nicomachean contributions: Dexter 3, 4, and 5; Flavian 6, 7, and 8. No one manuscript preserves all the subscriptions and we cannot exclude the possibility that another Flavian or Dexter subscription may be lost. But it is hard to believe it coincidence that, (a) of the three, only Victorianus's appears at the close of all nine books in one or more of the eight manuscripts; and (b) that no manuscript offers both a Flavian and a Dexter subscription for the same book.

In the books on which two collaborated it is natural to assume that one read the exemplar aloud while the other checked the copy in the usual way. As we have seen, this was the standard way of correcting copy against exemplar. But it was labor intensive and time consuming. A faster if riskier method (as any experienced

---

65. "ami de Symmaque," Chastagnol 1962, 323.
66. So first de Rossi 1849, 328; cf. Pecere 1986, 61.
67. Perhaps, as in the case of Securus Melior Felix, a reward for "services to scholarship."
68. *PLRE* ii. 303; bibliography in Cecconi 2002, 195.
69. For *frater*, very frequent in Symmachus in the sense "fellow senator," Marcone 1983, 65.
70. For teachers characterized as their students' father, see Cribiore 2007, 138–41.

proofreader knows) is for one person to read the copy and simply check the exemplar himself when in doubt. In view of the bulk of text to be covered and the need for speed, this may be what Victorianus and the Nicomachi did, perhaps dividing books and each correcting his own part separately. This might explain why (like the Lupicinus and Constantinus subscriptions to Caesar's *Gallic War*) they signed their names separately. In any case, it seems clear that Victorianus did the lion's share of the work, assisted from time to time by the two aristocrats. It is thus doubly misleading to refer to the result as a "Nicomachean edition." It was in no sense an edition, and the Nicomachi played a subsidiary role.

To many it has always seemed self-evident that it was the paganism of the Symmachi and Nicomachi that drew them to Livy. Billanovich[71] wrote lyrically of

> the loving preoccupation bestowed by the Symmachi and the Nicomachi on the *restoration* of the text of the first Decade, which was treated by those last faithful supporters of *pagan orthodoxy* as if it were a *Bible* which, in the final stand against the barbarians and the converts to the new faith, *upheld a cult* in which the gods seemed as indispensable as memories of the fatherland.

It is a nice thought that Symmachus read and reread Livy's stirring narrative with patriotic pride, savoring the lists of prodigies and portents and encouraging others to do the same. But while full of conventional admiration for the heroes and glories of Rome, his knowledge of both comes from the rhetorical rather than historiographical tradition, and his main sources are demonstrably Cicero and Valerius Maximus.[72] His debt to the latter is proved less by verbal parallels than by the fact that he uses the stories in question in exactly the way they are categorized in Valerius's handbook, as moral exempla.[73] Kroll's careful study of classical texts known to Symmachus found not a single unmistakable indication that he had read Livy. Nor Caesar either, despite owning a copy of the *Gallic Wars* that he presented to his Gallic friend Protadius.[74]

Lack of verbal echoes does not in itself (of course) prove lack of knowledge, and perhaps we should not expect to find many traces of a prose writer of unremarkable style.[75] Yet there are dozens of verbal echoes of Livy in Ammianus,[76] and dozens of Sallust (e.g.) in Symmachus. On the criteria that establish his knowledge

---

71. Billanovich 1951, 199 (my italics).
72. Kroll 1891, 17–22, 82–88.
73. E.g., where Symmachus mentions Scipio Africanus's indulgence in Greek dress in Sicily during the Hannibalic War (*Or.* i. 16), Kroll cited Livy (29. 19. 12) when Valerius Maximus lists the story in a section devoted to "famous men who behaved in dress... more licentiously than national custom permitted" (3. 6. 1).
74. Kroll 1891, 80–82. His remark to Protadius that Caesar "will tell you all about the origin, geography, battles, customs and laws of the Gauls" (*Ep.* iv. 18) need not argue any great familiarity.
75. By which I mean no more than that Livy's style is not distinguished by striking turns of phrase or memorable epigrams, like (e.g.) that of Sallust or Tacitus.
76. Collected by Fletcher 1937, 383–86.

of Terence, Vergil, Cicero, Sallust, and a number of other classics, he cannot be shown to have known Livy at all. There is certainly nothing in the letters that survive in such abundance from the last decade of his life to suggest a rediscovery in Livy of the religious traditions of archaic Rome. Not surprisingly if (as the subscriptions to Bks 7 and 8 suggest) he kept his precious copy on an estate in Sicily he seldom if ever visited.[77]

It is the same story with Claudian. His later poems especially are full of references to early Roman history, and an industrious nineteenth-century dissertation filled fifty-six pages with citations from Livy and the Livian epitomators, taking it for granted that he had a deep firsthand knowledge of Livy. But all the closest parallels are with the epitomators (particularly Florus)[78] and Valerius Maximus.[79] The only case where the verbal similarity is close enough to suggest knowledge of Livy himself comes, significantly enough, from Bk 1.[80] The later poems regularly portray Alaric as a second Hannibal, with Stilicho playing by turns the role of Marcellus, Fabius Maximus, and Scipio. But Dewar has shown that Claudian's principal inspiration here was actually the *Punica* of Silius.[81] Symmachus too seems to have known Silius, who is also quoted a number of times by Ausonius and Paulinus of Nola.[82] It is perhaps not surprising that a poetical account in the Vergilian style of Rome's most triumphant recovery from near disaster should appeal to readers living in the shadow of Alaric. I am not (of course) implying that Symmachus had *never* read *any* Livy. He no doubt read a few of the early books, but there can be no question that it was the poets, epitomators, and rhetoricians from whom he derived most of his knowledge of Roman history.

Servius too has been cited as an early fifth-century pagan reader of Livy.[83] There are indeed almost forty citations. But very little of the older material in the Servian corpus is the fruit of Servius's own reading; the Livian quotations in particular, mostly parallel or alternative versions of the Aeneas saga (no fewer than fourteen from Bk 1), almost certainly go back to the earliest stage of the tradition, to the second-century Asper at latest. Some at least of these citations were certainly not firsthand. For example, on *Aen*. i. 242 Servius claims that "according to Livy" Aeneas and Antenor betrayed Troy to the Greeks. There was indeed such a tradition, which Dionysius attributes to Menecrates of Xanthus. But it is *not* in Livy.[84] It is also striking

---

77. On the evidence of the correspondence he did not visit Sicily in at any rate the last few decades of his life.

78. Claud. *Gild*. 108, *ipsa nocet moles* (of the size of the Roman Empire) ~ *ipsa moles exitio fuit*, Flor. ii. 21. 5; Claud. *Get*. 291 ~ Flor. i. 7. 17; Cameron 1970, 333.

79. Claud. *Get*. 140, *Marcellus vinci docuit* (of Hannibal) ~ *Marcellus...Hannibalem vinci...posse docuit*, Val. Max. iv. 1. 7.

80. Claud. *Eutrop*. i. 132 (*contemptu...liber*, "free because he was despised") ~ Livy 1. 56. 7 (*contemptu...tutus*).

81. Dewar 1994, 349–72.

82. Kroll 1891, 57–58; R. Green 1991, 773; and 1971, 49. For other late fourth-century readers of Silius, E. L. Bassett, *Catal. Transl. et Comm*. 3 (Washington, D.C. 1976), 345.

83. Schmidt 1968, 229.

84. Dion. Hal. i. 48. 3; *FGrH* 769 F 3; Erskine 2001, 138.

that so devoted an antiquarian as Macrobius never cites Livy.[85] The author of the *HA* goes so far as to depreciate Livy as untruthful.[86] In fact, the only fourth-century pagans who can be shown to have read Livy are those with a professional interest, historians of the Republic like Eutropius, Rufius Festus, the authors of the so-called *Origo gentis Romanae* and *De viris illustribus*—and Ammianus. Then there is the scholiast on Lucan, with ten quotations, five of them verbatim.[87] Three give book numbers, following a curious feature also found in the *periochae*, which count Bks 109–16 as Bks 1–8 of the civil war.[88] Not then a casual reader, but a scholar who conscientiously consulted specific books of Livy because they were known to be Lucan's main historical source.[89] When Symmachus's cultivated Christian friend Protadius asked him for Livy, it was with a very specific agenda in mind: studying the early history of his native Gaul.[90]

The explanation for this lack of interest in an otherwise cultivated man like Symmachus is not in doubt. History as such never really formed a central part of the culture of a Roman gentleman.[91] "Knowing" Greek and Roman history comprised little more than the ability to make and recognize allusions to famous stories, above all examples of virtue and vice.[92] Symmachus was not unusual in acquiring his historical culture in the school of the rhetorician. It was not chance that only the most moralizing of the historians, Sallust, won a place in the school curriculum. Nor is it chance that there are no late antique scholia on Livy (we have already seen that the occasional marginalia in **M** are readers' jottings rather than authentic scholia).

Paradoxically enough, in the age of Symmachus and the Nicomachi it was mainly Christians who turned to Livy, but as a historical source rather than a classic, searching for evidence that the pagan past was as full of disasters as the Christian present. In the case of Augustine and Orosius there has been a tendency to dogmatism one way or the other, most insisting that they used only Eutropius or an epitome. But we are not entitled to generalize from a few passages that are closer to Florus, Eutropius, or the *Periochae* than the full Livian text. The best way to search so long a text would be to use both, discovering from the epitome which parts (if available) were worth reading in full (it is important to bear in mind that, outside a handful of major libraries, few potential readers are likely to have had access to more than one or two decades,

---

85. This would not be inconsistent with the criticism of Livy implied in the Phlegon note. Martianus names Livy as an illustration of history as opposed to fable (v. 550, p. 193. 10 Willis), but shows no other knowledge.

86. Syme 1991, 358–71, 451–58; there is no reason to believe Livy was known to the *HA* (Ch. 20).

87. fr. 32a, 32b, 32c, 32d, 33, 33a, 34a, 39a, 40, 41. I am assuming that the surviving s. IX scholia go back to a late antique commentary: Zetzel 1981, 194–99.

88. *in primo libro belli civilis* (fr. 32a) ~ *per.* 109, *qui est civilis belli primus*; it is immaterial whether this division goes back to Livy (Syme 1979, 407) or not (Stadter 1972, 296–98).

89. On the historical sources of the Lucan scholia, Rawson 1987, 163–80; Fantham 1987, 89–96.

90. *Ep.* iv. 18. 5; 36. 2.

91. Holford-Strevens 2003, Ch. 13.

92. Marrou 1965, 405; 1958, 131–35. See too Ch. 1 ("Die Geschichte in der Jugendbildung") in Peter 1897.

perhaps just individual books).[93] Augustine, for example, undoubtedly used both Florus and Eutropius, but in a number of passages he no less clearly gives details found only in Livy himself.[94] The same applies to Orosius, who also knew Tacitus at first-hand. On the Vestal Minucia he refers with Livy to the place where she was executed, not mentioned in the surviving *periocha*;[95] on Pyrrhus he copied some details in Livy 7 verbatim; two citations from Bk 109 correspond to nothing in the *periochae*; and the same is true of a few other passages.[96]

Jerome mentions Livy four times, directly quotes from one of the later books (114), and tells three historical anecdotes that may derive from Livy.[97] When discussing the origins of the Lupercalia in 495, Pope Gelasius not only cited Livy, but precisely the "second decade" (*Livius in secunda decade*), the latest identifiable witness to Bks 11–20.[98] A much earlier (and unpolemical) case of a Christian reader of Livy is provided by the Oxyrhynchus Epitome of Bks 37–55, in a "handsome uncial hand of the first half of the third century." The papyrus was reused for a copy of the Epistle to the Hebrews, in such a way as to suggest that the owner wanted to be able to read both texts.[99]

According to E. Lommatzsch, in a study still cited by historians as authoritative, "But for the activity of [Symmachus and the Nicomachi] we would have almost no original Livy."[100] If by this he meant no Livy at all, that is pure nonsense. **N** is not known to have reached further than Bk 10, and we have the full text of a further twenty-five books. Furthermore, while in the case of many classical texts we have no manuscript earlier than the High Middle Ages, in the case of Livy 21–45, all or part of no fewer than six fifth-century codices have actually survived. Our primary source for the entire third decade is the Puteanus, a "superbly calligraphic uncial of the oldest type"; eight books carry a subscription (unfortunately anonymous and undated) affixed at Avellino (near Naples), no doubt (as already remarked) on some aristocratic estate.[101] As for the fifth, the only surviving witness is yet another fifth-century manuscript, now in Vienna.[102] For the fourth decade we have the Bamberg and Vatican fragments

---

93. We might have expected to find the *Periochae* prefixed to individual books of Livy as a sort of table of contents. In fact, they seem to have reached the Middle Ages in the company of Florus, as shown by Reeve 1988, 477–91, and its sequel 1991, 453–83.

94. See the full list in Hagendahl 1967, 650–66.

95. Oros. vii. 2 and vi. 15 = fr. 31–32 Weissenborn and Schlesinger; Oros. iii. 9. 5 ~ Livy 8. 15. 8.

96. Oros. iii. 8. 1 ~ Liv. vii. 29. 1; Oros. v. 4 and v. 11. 4–5 with the notes in Lippold 1976; cf. too ib. xxxvii.

97. Luebeck 1872, 201–3; Hagendahl 1958, 186, 187, 189, 218, 226; add *Adv Jov.* i. 41 ~ Livy 8. 15. 7–8 on the Vestal Minucia (F. Münzer, *Philol.* 92 [1937/8], 56 n. 31), though perhaps via the intermediary of Seneca's lost *De matrimonio*, from which this work draws much of its erudition (Hagendahl 150–52). The story about L. Flamininus executing a condemned man at a banquet in *Comm. Matt.* ii. 14 is verbally much closer to Seneca, *Contr.* 9. 2. 1–29 (esp. 1) than Livy 29. 43 (for Jerome's knowledge of Seneca rhetor, Hagendahl 1958, 297).

98. *Tract.* 6, p. 601 Thiel = *Coll. Avell.* 100. 12, p. 457 Guenther.

99. P. Oxy. 668; *CLA* ii². 208; Roberts 1979, 10.

100. Lommatzsch 1904, 185, quoted with approval by Wytzes 1977, 85.

101. *CLA* v. 562; Walters and Conway OCT 3 (1929), vi–xi; Bks 22 and 23 are subscribed *recognobi ubi supra* (Mommsen 1909, 150), 21, 24, 25 *recognobi Abellini*, and 26, 28, 29 just *recognobi*.

102. *CLA* x. 1472; Reynolds 1983, 214; Pecere 1986, 62; see now J. Briscoe's Teubner edition of 1986.

(**R** and **V**), again both fifth-century;[103] and a leaf from a fifth-century copy of Bk 11 has recently been found in a Coptic monastery in the Fayyum.[104] There is not the remotest reason to believe that any of these manuscripts were influenced by the "Nicomachean" Livy. Given their date, most must have been copied both by and for Christians. **N** was not even the only early fifth-century copy made of Bks 1–10. If it had perished before generating medieval copies, we would still have the almost exactly contemporary Veronensis,[105] not to mention the Oxyrynchus fragment from Bk 1.

Livy was neither a pagan nor even an unusual taste in fifth-century Italy. To quote another purple passage of Billanovich:[106]

> All the most ancient surviving codices [of Livy] seem to have been written in Italy while the Italian eagles were beating the air with their wings for the last time at Rome or at Ravenna, or when they had only just ceased to fly and had finally come to rest.

It is also significant that none of these manuscripts go beyond Bk 45, closing with the final defeat of Macedon at Pydna in 167. It was early Roman history people wanted to read about, the myth of Rome and the growth of Roman power. It is surely no coincidence that this surge of interest in the romantic origins and greatest triumphs of Rome coincides with the rapid decline in the reality of Roman power in the West. It is not "pagan orthodoxy" but the romanticized literary paganism we encounter in the cult of Vergil and the preoccupation with archaic Roman religion in Macrobius.[107] The parallel is neatly symbolized in the luxury scripts in which late antique Vergil and Livy manuscripts were copied: capitals for Vergil, uncials for Livy.[108]

The reader who added the Phlegon note in **M** could perfectly well have been a Christian. It was not just pagans but Christians too who consoled themselves for the defeats they had lived through with the victories they could still read about. The early fifth-century Veronensis of Augustine's *City of God* may have been produced in the same scriptorium as the Puteanus of Livy.[109] As for the assumption that Livy's late antique readers were mainly Roman aristocrats, the Gallic aristocrat Protadius, a Christian, is as close as we have come. We have even seen that one of the earliest owners of the Veronensis of Livy was a Greek-speaker.

The reason Symmachus had his celebrated copy made was mundane enough. A friend, knowing that Symmachus owned a complete Livy, had asked for a copy.

---

103. *CLA* viii. 1028; i. 57; L. Traube, *Abhandl. Bay. Akad., Hist. Kl.* 24 (1909), 5–29; Reynolds 1983, 212–13.
104. Bravo and Griffin 1988, 447–521 (with tav. 1–4).
105. The Veronensis now has only fragments of 3–6, but no doubt originally contained the whole first decade.
106. Billanovich 1951, 199; E. A. Lowe, *CLA* 4 (1947), xv; H. Bloch, *Speculum* 25 (1950), 278–79.
107. It may be that the Veronensis of Livy and the Veronensis of Vergil, palimpsested together in the eighth century, originally formed part of the same aristocratic library.
108. As pointed out by Lowe, *CLA* 4, xv. The new fragment of Bk 11 is also in a fine uncial.
109. So Lowe in *CLA* 4 (1947), 491.

The initiative came from Valerianus. Symmachus's role seems to have been limited to having the copy made (a common gesture among those with well-stocked libraries) and the Nicomachi did no more than correct a few books of this copy, an essential part in the production of a reliable text and no doubt efficiently executed, but scarcely "restoration" (Billanovich's term).

2: THE YOUNGER FLAVIAN'S THREE CITY PREFECTURES

On my interpretation, the three subscribers worked not consecutively but simultaneously on the text of Livy. As already remarked, for this to have been possible the prefecture Flavian held in 400 must have been his third, not his second.[110] It remains to show that this is possible, by reexamining the chronology of Flavian's three urban prefectures, hitherto dated to 392/4, 399–400, and 408. The matter is complicated by the fact that one of them was held during the period of Eugenius's usurpation (392–94) and so subsequently cancelled.

It is from a letter of Symmachus that we learn about the prefecture held under Eugenius (392–94), and the one in 399–400 can be pinned down by five dated laws.[111] But the evidence for the prefecture hitherto assigned to 408 is far weaker than generally recognized: a single law (*CJ* ii. 15. 1) that is agreed to be in error, the only question being how best to correct the error. The addressee of this law, dated to 29 November 408 (*Basso et Philippo consulibus*), is *Flaviano p(raefecto) p(raetorio)*. But another man, Theodorus, is securely and continuously attested as praetorian prefect of Italy by some twenty laws between September 408 and January 409. So one element at least must be incorrect: either the office or the year. The office, according to Seeck, who "corrected" PP to PVR and turned an impossible praetorian prefecture into the third urban prefecture attested by the Livy subscription. Both Chastagnol and *PLRE* followed him, without indicating that there could be either a doubt or an alternative.

Yet the moment we consider the possibility that the year might be in error, an all but compelling alternative suggests itself. It was Seeck himself who documented the different sorts of confusion that occur among the consular datings of imperial laws, and in this case there is an obvious and easy potential source of confusion, an example of what he called "supplemented consulships" ("ergänzte Konsulate"). Up till 410 the two consuls of each year were always proclaimed together as a pair, even when the empire was divided between a plurality of emperors.[112] From 411[113] the western and eastern courts began to

---

110. There is one other possibility, which I mention for the sake of completeness: III in the subscription *could* be an error for II. Two of the three Latin dedications for Praetextatus (*CIL* VI. 1778–79) call him PPO II, when we know that he held the office only once (Chastagnol 1962, 177–78).
111. Symm. *Ep.* vii. 104; *PLRE* i. 346.
112. Seeck 1919, 88–96; Cameron in *CLRE* 13–16.
113. Not from 395 or 399, as hitherto supposed: *CLRE* 16–17.

proclaim one consul each, neither waiting for the other. Since the dissemination of the new consular names got slower and slower as the century progressed,[114] it was often not till quite late in the year that the name of the new eastern consul was added to the consular dating formula of western documents. Till then, laws, private documents, and inscriptions alike would be dated by the name of the local consul alone, or (more fully) by his name followed by the formula "and whoever shall have been proclaimed" (*et qui nuntiatus fuerit*). The Theodosian compilers did their best to eliminate such "provisional" formulas in laws they included in the Code, retroactively adding the second name on the basis of consular lists.[115] But they worked hastily and often made errors.

CJ ii. 15. 1 must fall under suspicion of suffering this corruption, for two reasons. In the first place, if the law had originally been dated just *Basso consule*, the compilers would not have known whether to supplement *Basso et Philippo* (408) or *Basso et Antiocho* (431). If the date were in fact 431, the heading *p(raefecto) p(raetorio)* could stand and all would be well, since Flavian was indeed praetorian prefect in 431.[116] It is hard to believe this a coincidence. It should be added that *CJ* ii. 15. 1 concerns the privileges of imperial estates, not an area that would normally concern the PVR, whose authority was limited to the city of Rome and its environs to a radius of 100 miles. There is obviously a strong case for correcting the year rather than the office, in which case the evidence for Flavian's urban prefecture in 408 simply vanishes.

We are left with the prefectures of 392/4 and 399–400. The two surviving dedications are unhelpful: one in Rome (*AE* 1934, 147) from a statue to Arcadius, and so later than 383; and another from Naples (*ILS* 8985) recording a second prefecture, unfortunately undatable. But there is no longer any reason why 399–400 should be his second or 392/4 his first. I suggest that Flavian was first appointed prefect in 389/90.

Here is the relevant part of the Fasti of the prefecture of Rome as currently established:

Pinianus	24 Feb. 385–8 Feb. 387[117]
Julianus	387/8 (under Maximus)
Victor	388/9
Albinus	17 June 389–24 Feb. 391[118]
Alypius	12 June 391
Philippus	391
Flavianus	392/4

---

114. The evidence is assembled in *CLRE* 26–35.

115. Seeck, *Regesten* 88f.; cf. *CLRE* 77–79.

116. Securely attested in office between 29 April 431 and 24 March 432: *PLRE* i. 246. The same suggestion was already made briefly in another context by Demandt and Brummer 1977, 495.

117. For Pinianus's dates and the sequence of his four predecessors see Martínez-Fazio 1972, summarized by Vera 1978, 48–54: Bassus (382–83); Aventius (383–84); Symmachus (spring 384–summer/autumn 385); Sallustius (summer/autumn 385–June 386); Pinianus (June 386–September 387).

118. The law that bears this latter date (*Cod. Theod.* 16. 10. 10) actually addresses Albinus as PPO, an office that he is not otherwise attested as holding and that was in addition held by the elder Flavian at this time (*CLRE* 655). It seems inevitable to correct the office to PVR (so already Tillemont).

The prefectures of Pinianus, Julianus, Albinus, Alypius, and Flavian are all securely fixed by legal or literary sources. But the dates suggested for Victor and Philippus are purely conjectural.

Fl. Philippus is known from four inscriptions. Three (p. 49) record his restoration of a *nymphaeum* while urban prefect; the other, very fragmentary, runs around the base of a column that originally stood not far from the altar of the Basilica of S. Paolo fuori le mura.[119] In Chastagnol's generally accepted restoration the relevant part runs as follows: *natale X[III Kal. Dec. post consulat(um) D.N.] Valentin[i] ani IIII et Neoteri v.c., administrante Fl. Filippo, v.[c. praef(ecto) urb(is)]*. Valentinian IIII and Neoterius were the consular pair for 390, so the postconsulate of this year would be 391. But there are serious objections. The formula *administrante X* would fit a city prefect well enough, but is also found of other officials, and it is normally the architect's name that we find at the bottom of a column inside a church.[120]

More important, the year is impossible. Postconsulates were not used randomly whenever a man could not remember the current consuls. They are found early in the year in places where news of the new consuls had not yet arrived. This is why they are particularly common in Africa and Egypt, cut off by the *mare clausum* at the beginning of the year.[121] Furthermore, a study of the two sites where we have a substantial body of evidence—Egypt and the city of Rome—has shown that postconsulates were used uniformly: that is to say, the postconsulate was superseded by the new formula once it arrived.[122] This is certainly true of Egypt, and if there are a few exceptions at Rome, they are normally private epitaphs, erected by people who had not taken the trouble to consult up-to-date official sources. We have no fewer than eighteen inscriptions from Rome dated to 391, and not one is dated by the postconsulate of 390. And since the case under discussion concerns a major new public building in Rome, a postconsulate would be altogether incredible.

Chastagnol thought the fact that the consular names were in the genitive pointed to the formula *post consulatum*. It is true that the ablative followed by *consulibus* was the standard formula; but *consulatu* followed by the genitive (first attested in 338) was also common.[123] There can be little doubt that the dedication of S. Paolo fuori le mura took place not in 391, but in 390. If so, Philippus cannot then have been PVR, since Albinus was still in office. Whatever part he played in the dedication must have been in some other capacity.

---

119. *ILCV* 1857 = *ICUR* n. s. II. 4778, with Chastagnol 1966, 428–32 = 1994, 309–27 (with plate).
120. Pietri 1976, 515–16.
121. Cameron in *CLRE* 77–84; even Seeck went seriously astray on the matter of postconsulates.
122. See *CLRE* 30–33; 65–66.
123. Presumably in imitation of the standard Greek formula ὑπατείᾳ followed by the genitive: *CLRE* 63, and for a collection of examples from *ILCV* see Diehl's index to vol. 3, 220–221.

As for Victor, he dedicated a statue to Theodosius while in office (*ILS* 2945), that is to say between 379–87 or 388–92.[124] No fewer than fourteen prefects are already attested between 379 and 387. So 388/89 and 391/92 look more promising, though 391/92 would be excluded if Ammianus, who mentions Victor's prefecture, published by 390 (p. 632). Since Flavian was undoubtedly PVR under Eugenius sometime during the period 392–94, it is perhaps unlikely that he was also prefect in 391/92.[125] But given the prevalence of very short tenures (at least six and perhaps eight in the three years 380–82), Julianus, Victor, and a first prefecture for Flavian could all be squeezed into 388/9.

This would have two advantages over the current sequence. First, it would make the younger Flavian's prefecture coincide exactly with the elder's promotion to *quaestor sacri palatii* (388–89). It would have been a precocious promotion, but Junior had already held the proconsulship of Asia in 382–83. After a proconsulship the logical next step for an aristocrat with a father in high places would have been the prefecture of Rome. Second, it provides a better explanation of a letter of Symmachus to Rufinus about the recent promotion of Junior to some post unspecified, clearly implying that Rufinus had had a hand in the promotion.[126] The standard assumption is that this refers to his appointment to the proconsulate of Asia in 383. But in 383 Rufinus was a minor civil servant in the East; it is unlikely that Symmachus even knew him then (Ch. 17. 2). It would be more natural to suppose that Symmachus was writing to him as *magister officiorum* at Theodosius's court at Milan in 389/91, in which case the post in question could be identified as Junior's first urban prefecture. The fasti of the urban prefecture between 387 and 400 could then be reconstituted as follows:

Julianus	387/8
Flavianus I	388/9
Victor	388/9
Albinus	June 389–Feb. 391
Alypius	June 391
Flavianus II	392/4
Basilius	395
Andromachus	395
Florentinus	395–97
Lampadius	398
Felix	398
Laetus	398–99
Flavianus III	June 399–Nov. 400
Protadius	400/401

---

124. Chastagnol 1962, 232.

125. Note however the case of Orfitus, PVR from 353 to 355 and then again from 357 to 359.

126. "I would commend my son Flavian to you if he had not already been summoned (*accitus*) on your wishes," Symm. *Ep.* iii. 89.

The one solid piece of evidence, not lightly to be brushed aside, is the subscription that formed our point of departure, with its clear implication (*domnis Symmachis*) that Flavian's third prefecture fell before Symmachus's death in 402.

The joint enterprise of the two Nicomachi and Victorianus belongs in 400, before Symmachus's letter to Valerianus (which implies that the business of correction had begun) and while Flavian was still PVR—what we may now regard as his third tenure—between 6 June 399 and (at least) 8 November 400.[127]

The reference to Henna in the subscription to Bk 7 locates the subscribing in Sicily. Strictly speaking, the prefect of Rome was not supposed to leave Rome while in office. But such a technicality is not likely to have bothered a man of Flavian's well-documented arrogance, and the absence of letters from Symmachus proves nothing in itself. The subscriptions to Bks 7 and 8 are indisputable evidence that at some point during his third tenure (whenever dated) he did visit both Henna and (as we shall see) Sciacca as well. It would not have been worth writing if he went on a short trip. In this connection it may be worth drawing attention to the fact that, during his prefecture, Flavian was yet again embroiled in a scandal, this time embezzlement.[128] He may have welcomed the opportunity of absenting himself from the inquiry into his conduct. It may have been on his return from this very trip that he brought back from Henna the books of Livy that Symmachus had ready to give Valerianus.

This brings us to the puzzle of the inscription to the statue rehabilitating the elder Flavian in 431 (*ILS* 2948). The *damnatio memoriae* that followed his death in 394 was soon lifted, and his career up to his service under Eugenius restored. But he could not be given back the honors conferred by the usurper. Thus no mention of his cancelled consulate for 394. The younger Flavian was in the same position. He had lived in disgrace from 394 to January 399, after which he too could reclaim his pre-Eugenian career. The puzzle is that the younger Flavian (now praetorian prefect), instead of being credited straightforwardly with his two legitimate urban prefectures, is styled *praefectus urbi saepius*. For O'Donnell the *saepius* was "merely a bit of boasting" to suggest to "the unwary reader" that the number of Flavian's urban prefectures "was larger than three."[129] This is certainly mistaken. But not even the standard explanation that this was a "tactful" way of glossing over the "embarrassment" of his prefecture under Eugenius will do. The protocol for offices held under usurpers was well established and invariable: they were simply ignored.

The formula is not in fact unique.[130] Silvio Panciera published a dedication of Manilius Rusticianus, praetorian prefect under Maxentius, that describes the emperor as [*consuli*] *saepius*.[131] For a variety of reasons Panciera identified the consulate as

---

127. The tenure of his successor Protadius cannot be fixed with any precision: Chastagnol 1962, 254; *PLRE* i. 751.

128. Symm. *Ep.* vii. 96. 3 (with Callu's note); Vera 1981, 261.

129. O'Donnell 1978, 131. There would have been little point in such a boast, since (as we shall see) no one ever held more than three urban prefectures.

130. "totalmente anomalo," according to Vera 1983, 37.

131. Panciera 1992, 249–63 at 254–57.

Maxentius's third in 310,[132] citing the parallel of L. Egnatius Victor Lollianus, described in two of six parallel dedications as proconsul of Asia "often" (πολλάκις). The other four all specify that he was proconsul for three years. The three Greek dedications all express this three-year tenure in different terms,[133] and πολλάκις was apparently thought of as a fourth variation.[134] The common idiom *semel et saepius, iterum et saepius* suggests that *saepius* = three times was in line with ordinary usage.[135]

So there was nothing actually anomalous in the formula *saepius* taken by itself. Nonetheless it was portentously rare, and it is hard to doubt that in so carefully worded a document Flavian employed it advisedly. There was (I suggest) a particular reason he resented the loss of his third prefecture. In the last two hundred years of the Western Empire only one man held three legitimate urban prefectures, Anicius Acilius Glabrio Faustus (421/23; 425; 425/37). No one ever held more. Glabrio Faustus's third prefecture fell at a date unknown between 425 and 437. There is a slightly more than even chance that it fell before rather than after the rehabilitation of the elder Flavian, in September 431.[136] In the thirty years between then and 400 only two men had equaled Flavian's record of two prefectures. And of course Flavian had the private satisfaction of knowing that he was the only man in history who had really been PVR three times. This privilege was taken from him at a stroke by the third legitimate prefecture of Glabrio Faustus. Flavian could not claim equality by openly styling himself PVR III, and yet was naturally reluctant to be content with the now outclassed PVR II. So he compromised with the rare formula *saepius*, implying three (or even more) tenures without actually saying so.

It is often held that Dexter was Flavian's nephew, son of the Clementianus he refers to as his *parens*,[137] more probably (as we have seen) a professional scholar in his employ. Although it has no direct bearing on the thesis here advanced,[138] I should like to return to Seeck's view that Dexter was Flavian's son.[139] This is surely the most natural explanation of the fact that the only two sources to mention him do so in such close connection with Flavian. First *ILS* 2948, Dexter's dedication of the monument rehabilitating the elder Flavian, "best of grandfathers" (*avus optimus*), "in honor of his son Nicomachus Flavian." Such a dedication would come more naturally from a son

---

132. Chastagnol 1993, 856–59, argued that the Maxentius dedication dates from when he was *bis consul* but designated for a third term; he explains the Lollianus πολλάκις the same way. Against, Panciera 2006, 1141.

133. κατὰ τὸ ἐξῆς ἐτῶν τριῶν, τὸ γ* and ἐπὶ τρίετες (*ter* in the one Latin dedication: *AE* 1923, 41); *Inschriften von Ephesos* vii. 1. 3164; iii. 664A; iii. 664 (for fuller references, Panciera 1992, 255).

134. *AE* 1902, 244 (from Miletus); *AE* 1996, 1480 (from Aphrodisias).

135. *OLD* s. v. *saepe* 2. In Cicero, *Att.* 407E. 1 and 407F. 1, *saepius* "seems to mean no more than *iterum*," Shackleton Bailey, vol. 6, 1967, 278.

136. If so, then Faustus's three tenures would fall within a decade, an exact parallel to my suggested reconstruction of Flavian's three prefectures.

137. So Chastagnol (1962, 244) and *PLRE* ii. 357; 303; Pecere 1986, 65.

138. Dexter could just as easily have corrected manuscripts with his uncle as his father.

139. Seeck implausibly claimed that the younger Flavian married twice; against, Chastagnol 1962, 239–40.

than a nephew. Then there are the Livy subscriptions, which (on the most natural interpretation) show them working together in a domestic context.

Given a date of ca. 387 for Flavian's marriage, Dexter would have been no more than twelve or thirteen in 400, which would square nicely with the fact that, while Flavian's rank is fully reported, Dexter gives himself no more than the courtesy title *v. c.*[140] But he would have been quite old enough at any rate to act as a reader. Renaissance printing houses employed children as readers; Plantin used his own daughters, but only up to the age of twelve, on grounds of decency. The great Henri Estienne "had begun to correct Greek texts as a teenager, working with his father on the proofs of Robert's edition of Dionysius of Halicarnassus."[141] At least four other subscriptions in our manuscripts are the work of schoolboys (Ch. 12. 6). So much for the view that "the Symmachi and the Nicomachi…led the way in the recension of texts." All we have is a gentleman and a small boy whiling away a few idle days proofreading a copy of a few books of Livy before giving it to a friend.

The subscription to Bk 7 localizes Flavian's work "in Henna" (*apud Hennam*), while the subscription to Bk 8 offers *apud Term.*, that is to say *T(h)erm(as)*. The latter is usually either ignored or dismissed as no more than an error,[142] but there were in fact two spa towns of that name in Sicily: Thermae Himeraeae (modern Termini Imeresi) near Himera; and Thermae Selinuntiae (modern Sciacca) near Selinus.[143] The fact that none other than Symmachus's father-in-law, Memmius Vitrasius Orfitus, built a new post for the cursus publicus at Thermae Selinuntiae when governor of Sicily (340/350)[144] is strongly in favor of accepting *Term.* as an authentic variant and so identifying the place. Orfitus may have owned property there himself, property that in due course passed into the hands of Symmachus. Such a post would have greatly facilitated access to the baths and any villas in the neighborhood.

Henna is probably to be identified as the large villa excavated at Piazza Armerina.[145] It is hard to believe there was another villa large and splendid enough to have suited such grandees any closer to Henna than Piazza Armerina.[146] It has often been assumed that the villa belonged to the Nicomachi.[147] But why was Victorianus doing a job for

---

140. So already Jahn 1851, 337. The title *v. c.* need not imply that he was an adult. Sons of senators automatically became senators themselves on election to the quaestorship, which normally came at an early age in the old families; the title *v. c.* was often informally used by those of senatorial birth even before the quaestorship: Jones, *LRE* iii. 152 n. 19.

141. *Correspondance de Christophe Plantin* 2 (Anvers 1885), 176; Grafton 1998, 68; 2001, 143.

142. Not even mentioned in Bloch 1963, 215; Ogilvie's Oxford text (1974), vii; Pecere 1986, 68; Oakley 1997, 166; treated as an error by Zetzel 1980, 40; among recent writers taken seriously only by Vera, *Quaderni catanesi* 10 (1988), 116 n. 2.

143. R. Wilson 1990, 166, 228; Vera, 1988, 116.

144. *ILS* 5905, with R. Wilson 1990, 393 n. 175.

145. There is no clear evidence that the villa belonged to the same owner as the nearby estate identified by brickstamps as Filosofiana: Wilson 1990, 216–17, 232–33.

146. So (e.g.) Ogilvie, in his edition of Livy 1–5 (1974), vii. On the fanciful suggestions made by Carandini, Ricci, and de Vos 1982, see D. Vera, *Opus* 2 (1983), 583–84; "Polyonomy in the Roman Aristocracy," Cameron 1985, 175–76.

147. Symm. *Ep.* iv. 77; vi. 57; and vi. 66. 2 refer to the younger Flavian's legal problems in Sicily, whence it is usually (but not altogether securely) inferred that he owned property there; see too Wilson 1990, 217–18.

"the Lords Symmachus" in a Nicomachean villa? And what was Symmachus's Livy doing in a Nicomachean villa? If (as suggested above) it was in roll form, a bulky and fragile item. No one would transport 142 papyrus rolls to Sicily for transcription without a good reason. The simplest explanation is that it was in the library of the Sicilian villa we know Symmachus himself owned[148] that he kept his Livy. Cicero and Varro kept substantial parts of their libraries divided among their various country houses, and since it was while relaxing on his estates that Symmachus most enjoyed reading (Ch. 10. 6), he surely did the same.[149] There would be nothing surprising in Flavian moving from one to another of his father-in-law's villas, accompanied by his young son.

On the other hand, if he was doing his correcting in the intervals of a trip around Sicily, it is not likely that he was carrying anything much in the way of scholarly paraphernalia with him. Furthermore, the new date falls during Symmachus's lifetime, at a time when Symmachus was writing to Flavian regularly. But no mention of Livy. Making a copy for a friend was routine, and proofreading was drudgery—not the sort of thing aristocrats bothered to write to each other about.

3: PROTADIUS'S LIVY

The routine nature of Symmachus's gift to Valerianus is illustrated by another letter (*Ep.* iv. 18. 5), overlooked in this context, to his Gallic friend Protadius five years earlier (396):

> You ask for the earliest records of the Gauls to be delivered into your hands. Read the last books of the writer from Patavium, describing the exploits of Caesar; or if Livy does not answer your needs, try Caesar's journal (*ephemeridem*), plucked from my own humble library as a gift for you. It will tell you all about the origin, geography, battles, customs and laws of the Gauls. I will do my best, if luck is with me, to look out (*conquirere*) a copy of Pliny's *German Wars*. Meanwhile, you can happily rely on the material I have given you (*fide operis oblati*).

It has been generally assumed that it was only Caesar Symmachus actually sent Protadius a copy of. By itself, this might well seem a reasonable inference from the singular *operis* and the fact that only Caesar is said to have been "plucked" from Symmachus's own library. What then of Livy?

According to Wightman,[150] Protadius "had his own copy of Livy." She took Symmachus's reference to Livy to be no more than bibliographical advice. But in a

---

148. *Ep.* vi. 66. 2; ix. 52 (with Roda's commentary).
149. Rawson 1985, 40–41. Symmachus may well have acquired the books together with the estate.
150. Wightman 1975, 93–107 at 94, the only detailed discussion of this passage known to me.

letter to Protadius's brother Minervius written about the same time (iv. 36. 2), Symmachus remarks that Protadius had "asked him to *have copies made* of the early histories of Gaul to while away his leisure" (*sibi Galliarum prisca monumenta iuvando otio* exscribenda *mandaverat*). And he prefaces his mention of Livy in the other letter by remarking that Protadius had asked for "the earliest histories of Gaul to be delivered into [his] hands" (*deferri in manus tuas postulas*). That is to say, Protadius had *not* asked for bibliography, but for actual copies of specific texts. This is why Symmachus has nothing to say about Pliny except that he will try to find a copy.[151] Protadius had evidently asked for all three, and Symmachus could only supply Livy and Caesar.

Not that Symmachus's words suit a bibliographical reference anyway. Protadius was one of the most cultivated of all his friends: the eighteen letters to him are stuffed with more literary allusions and flourishes than any other sequence in the entire correspondence. Symmachus would hardly have been so tactless as to imply that Protadius would not by himself have thought to check Livy—especially if he owned a text. It would also have been unhelpful to refer him so vaguely to the "end" (*extrema*) of a work in 142 books when the relevant portion began 39 books before the end (103–8).

With the exception of Orosius and the Lucan scholiast, from the fourth century on the handful of surviving quotations from the lost books come entirely from grammarians and scholiasts, almost certainly at second- or thirdhand. We have seen that it was only the early books that still found readers. The surviving late antique copies contain nothing later than the first five decades.[152] From the last seven decades we have just one isolated palimpsest fragment of Bk 91 in fourth-century rustic capitals. Both hand and layout are similar to the Verona palimpsest, though there are sufficient differences to make it unlikely that both derive from a single copy.[153] We are not obliged to infer that this fragment derived from a complete Livy[154] rather than just a copy of the ninth decade, though the odd complete Livy was no doubt still to be found here and there in the year 400. But there is no sign of a Livian revival in fourth-century Gaul. No trace (e.g.) in the Gallic panegyrists, Ausonius, Paulinus of Nola, or Rutilius Namatianus.[155] And while Sidonius refers to Livy for "the glories of the invincible dictator," the same sentence also cites two highly suspect works, the history of Juventius Martialis and the journal of Balbus, and identifies the author of Caesar's *Commentaries* as Suetonius![156] Sulpicius Severus knew Sallust, Tacitus, and Justin,[157] but his only

---

151. Apparently, without success, since there is no mention of it in subsequent letters to Protadius.

152. From that point of view at least the newly discovered Fayyum fragment of Bk 11 is no surprise.

153. *CLA* i. 75; Mommsen 1909, 148; for a revised text and commentary, Ogilvie 1984, 116–25.

154. As assumed (e.g.) by Ogilvie 1984, 119. Nor is there any reason to believe that the Puteanus or Vindobonensis were ever part of complete texts.

155. C. Green 1991, 357; Nixon and Rodgers 1994, 18 (citing one or two unconvincing parallels). No mention of Livy in the section on history in Haarhoff 1920, 209–19.

156. Sidon. *Ep.* ix. 14. 7; for the ascription to Suetonius, see too Orosius vi. 7.

157. Van Andel 1976, 24, 40–48 (Tacitus), 70–74 (Sallust); 37–39 (Justin); the one parallel cited from Livy (p. 9) is commonplace.

Livian allusion is the opening sentence of the preface to Bk 1, quoted verbatim in the preface to his *Life of St. Martin*.[158] It is not impossible that Protadius owned some of the early books, but hardly a complete text.[159]

Yet Symmachus did have a complete Livy, and could easily have had the relevant books copied. If Protadius had only asked for Caesar and Pliny, why mention Livy at all? We are surely bound to infer that Symmachus sent Protadius Livy 103–8 as well as Caesar's *Gallic Wars*.[160] This would explain the vagueness of his reference: *extrema* was enough in a letter that accompanied the relevant books.

Both Symmachus's other letters about having copies made mention correction. So why no reference to the correction of the copies sent to Protadius? The fact that the Caesar is said to have come from Symmachus's own library suggests that it was not in fact a new copy specially made, but an old copy Symmachus felt he could spare, no doubt a duplicate.[161] He mentions the fact because Protadius might otherwise have wondered whether he had been sent the wrong book in error, original instead of copy. But since only the Caesar is said to come from Symmachus's library, it follows that the Livy *was* a new copy, in the ordinary way requiring correction.

The explanation of Symmachus's silence on the point is as simple as it is revealing. Correction (as we have seen) was an integral part of the production of an ancient book—so integral that, apart from the subscription on the book itself, it was seldom mentioned except in its absence or the delay it occasioned. Members of the elite with large libraries routinely sent friends copies of their treasures on request. Unless otherwise specified, the recipient would take it for granted that his copy had been duly corrected. But we have also seen that it seems to have become less and less easy to find competent correctors. Symmachus apologized to Valerianus for the delay in correcting his Livy.[162] Sidonius too apologized for sending friends uncorrected manuscripts.[163] Since Symmachus does *not* apologize to Protadius, a close friend of discriminating taste, the natural inference is that both the texts he sent him were adequately corrected without undue delay.

This sets the apology to Valerianus in a quite different light. On the traditional view (which tacitly ignores the copy he sent Protadius) Symmachus and Flavian were trying to "improve" the text of Livy, implying (a) recognition that it stood in need of

---

158. *unde facturus mihi operae pretium videor si…perscripsero* (Sev. i. 6) ~ *facturusne operae pretium sim si…perscripserim* (Liv. i pr. 1).

159. On the location of Protadius's Gallic estates, Wightman 1975, 94.

160. Wightman 1975, 94–101, makes unnecessarily heavy weather of Symmachus's *ephemeris* (= journals) of Caesar's commentaries, given that it is found as a title in some MSS for Bk 8, and in a poem by Arator (*Ep. Parth.* 40), not to mention two Greek writers (Plutarch, *Caes.* 22. 2; Appian, *Celt.* 18).

161. The new estates aristocrats were constantly acquiring, whether through marriage, inheritance, or purchase, must often have included libraries. A man like Symmachus with three town houses and at least sixteen villas (McGeachy 1942, 57–58; *PLRE* i. 870) must have had many libraries and a fair number of duplicates.

162. *malui enim tibi probari mei muneris celeritate*, *Ep.* i. 24.

163. Sidon. *Ep.* v. 15. 1.

improvement and (b) collation of new manuscripts in addition to Symmachus's personal copy. Yet apparently no such "improvement" was thought necessary five years earlier.

There are no grounds for distinguishing between an "edition" prepared for Valerianus in 401 and a mere copy sent to Protadius in 396. The only difference between Valerianus's Livy and Protadius's Livy is that Valerianus had asked for more, a lot more, all 142 books as against a mere 6. Naturally, it took correspondingly longer to correct,[164] whence the delays for which Symmachus apologized. But neither was anything more than a copy made from Symmachus's personal exemplar and duly corrected against that exemplar.

---

164. As for Pliny's *Natural History*, Ausonius had evidently asked for all thirty-seven books. Symmachus did not have it all, but sent what he had (*en tibi libellos, quorum mihi praesentanea copia fuit, Ep.* i. 24). It would certainly have been a time-consuming task to correct even part of so long and difficult a work.

15

GREEK TEXTS AND LATIN TRANSLATION

1: INTRODUCTION

From the age of Cicero to the age of Marcus Aurelius, the more cultivated members of the Roman elite were, if not bilingual, at any rate fluent in Greek.[1] As late as Gellius and Apuleius we find well-to-do westerners spending years of study in the university towns of the Greek East.[2] Greek was the language in which the elite studied philosophy, both as students in Athens itself and later in life with Greek scholars who shared their houses in Rome. We hear little of Latin translations, because most Romans who wanted to read Greek books could read them in the original. The few translations we know of from the late Republic and early empire are mainly adaptations with artistic ambitions of their own rather than straightforward attempts to make the work in question available to Greekless readers.[3] No one who was not, in the telling formula, "skilled in both languages" (*utraque lingua peritus*) could lay any claim to be truly cultivated.

Greek philosophy was still thriving in late third-century Rome. From 243 to 270 Plotinus presided over the most famous philosophical school of the age. Among those who flocked to his classes were "men and women of the highest rank."[4] Porphyry mentions a mother and daughter both called Gemina, in whose city house Plotinus lived, and a man called Castricius Firmus, at whose country estate near Minturnae he was a frequent visitor. It had always been common for Roman notables to retain a Greek philosopher as a sort of domestic chaplain. But Plotinus was the spiritual director of a far wider circle than normally fell to the most fashionable philosopher's lot. Even the empress Salonina fell under his spell. We need not believe they all took their philosophy seriously, but some did. One senator called Rogatianus renounced his praetorship when the lictors were waiting at his front door, dismissed his servants, sold his property, made do with eating alternate days, and in no time was cured of the gout—a classic illustration of the value of philosophy.

The keenest philosophers among the senators were Marcellus Arruntius and Sabinillus, the latter at any rate a person of real consequence if he was the Sabinillus

---

1. See now Swain 2004, 3–40.
2. Fronto belittles his own command of Greek, but clearly read and even wrote it fluently: Swain 2004, 17–28.
3. For a general outline, Kaimio 1979, 271–94.
4. Porph. *Vita Plot.* 7 and 9.

who was ordinary consul in 266 with Gallienus as colleague.[5] On Plotinus's death Porphyry seems to have assumed the leadership of the school. His *De abstinentia* was dedicated to Castricius Firmus (presumably the Firmus cited as a commentator on Plato's *Parmenides* by Damascius).[6] More important is the Chrysaorius to whom ca. 270 he dedicated his introduction to Aristotle's *Categories* and two other works. Chrysaorius was "a leading man in the senate of Rome, for he was descended from that Symmachus of whom it was written, 'Symmachus, son of Symmachus, man of many allies, ally of Rome.'"[7] He was a "consul of Rome" (evidently suffect), a man of affairs who "devoted more time to generalship than literature,"[8] who is said to have written to Porphyry asking for guidance when unable to make head or tail of Aristotle's *Categories*. Porphyry sent him the *Isagoge* by way of reply.[9] The picture may be conventional,[10] but there is no reason to doubt that Chrysaorius dabbled in Greek philosophy. The verse Porphyry quoted must have come from a panegyric by some itinerant Greek poet.

To all appearances Greek culture was still thriving in Rome in the late third century, and a great-great-grandfather of Symmachus cos. 391 was one of its doyens. Neoplatonism continued to find serious adherents among the Roman elite for another generation or so. Not the least interesting poem to survive from the early decades of the fourth century is a translation of a Greek hymn to the creator by Tiberianus. The combination of Platonic, Orphic, and magical elements points to some third-century Platonist as author of the Greek original. Tiberianus was clearly still in contact with Greek philosophical thought. He is usually identified as the cultivated Annius Tiberianus, whose career culminated with the prefecture of the Gauls in 336–37, but might equally be one of the two Iunii Tiberiani, prefects of Rome in 291–92 and 303–4.[11] Then there is Caeionius Rufius Albinus cos. 335, proclaimed *philosophus* on a dedication in Rome dating from his city prefecture in 335–37, traditionally identified as the Albinus whom Boethius mentions as having written on logic and geometry (p. 360).

But as the fourth century progressed, there was a sharp decline in knowledge of Greek in the West. Given the enormous consequences of this decline for East-West relations in the centuries that followed (political and ecclesiastical no less than cultural), it has attracted surprisingly little scholarly attention.[12] This is partly because

---

5. *PIR* S. 15; Christol 1986, 106.

6. J. Bouffartigue and M. Patillon, *Porphyre: De l'Abstinence* 1 (Paris 1977), xviii–xxiv.

7. Σύμμαχε Συμμαχίδη, πολυσύμμαχε, σύμμαχε Ρώμης, Elias, *Comm. in Isag. Porph.* 15 (CAG xviii. 1), Busse (ed.) (1900), p. 39. 8–11; Cameron 1999, 504–5.

8. *Schol. Arist.* Brandis (ed.) (Berlin 1836), p. 11 *b*. 14; David, *In Porph. Isag.*, Busse (ed.) (*CAG* xviii. 1904), p. 92. 18.

9. Ammon. *Comm. in Isag Porph.* (CAG iv. 3) Busse (ed.) (1891), 22.

10. For many examples of the motif of the dedicatee represented as soliciting the dedicated work, see A. Gudeman, *Tacitus Dialogus*[2] (Leipzig 1914), 41.

11. Smolak in Herzog 1989, § 552; Cameron 1984, 224; Courtney 1993, 429–46.

12. The basic work is Courcelle 1948, ET 1969, with a supplementary bibliography (including a further thirty-four items by Courcelle himself). But a comprehensive new study taking into account the research Courcelle inspired is urgently needed. Nor do we yet have the volume Courcelle once promised on the fourth century.

notions like "decline" have so often seemed self-explanatory; partly because the external forms remained unchanged, making it difficult to measure the degree or pace of change. Greek was still studied in school, but people knew less. For Marrou the decline of Greek was an inevitable consequence of the growth of a national Roman literature: Vergil, Terence, and Sallust superseded Homer, Menander, and Thucydides both in the schools and in the culture of the elite.[13] It may be true that the Greek culture of (say) the younger Pliny and Quintilian was inferior to Cicero's, but there was certainly no steady decline. Indeed, Greek influence at Rome reached a new high in the second century A.D.[14] Another factor was now at work: many of the leading figures in the second-century Greek resurgence were easterners, people who spoke Greek as a first language. Though a native Latin speaker, the emperor Marcus was not the only westerner with a culture more Greek than Latin.

The decisive factor in the decline of Greek in Rome was the de facto division of the empire by Diocletian and the creation by the tetrarchs of a series of new administrative capitals, especially those in the East. By the fourth century, Trier and Milan, Nicomedia, Antioch, and (most important of all) Constantinople were taking over many of the roles previously monopolized by Rome. From the age of the Scipios to the reign of Gallienus, Rome had been the central and inevitable source of patronage for ambitious Greeks. But from Diocletian on, court followed emperor from one to another of these secondary capitals, paying no more than the occasional brief visit to Rome. At the same time, the central government was tightening its grip at every level. The vast expansion of Roman administrative control in the East transformed both cultural and political life for the old Greek elites, who increasingly withdrew from their traditional role in the cities to seek positions in the imperial service. Rome rapidly became a cultural as well as a political backwater. The aristocracy of Rome might continue to regard itself as *pars melior humani generis*, but by Symmachus's day prominent Greek intellectuals had long been looking elsewhere for patronage. We do not know the name of a single Greek grammaticus in late antique Rome, as against nine Latin grammatici in Constantinople;[15] and no certainly identifiable Greek rhetor either. A rescript of Gratian fixing the salaries of professors for Trier, then an imperial capital, envisaged difficulty in finding a competent Greek grammaticus.[16]

In the late Republic and early empire it was altogether exceptional for Greeks to learn Latin—a situation transformed in the fourth century by the rapid growth of a Latin-speaking civil service in the East (p. 641). The gains made by Latin in the East may have played a part in the decline of Greek in the West. According to Matthews, Ammianus and Claudian "were the tip of an iceberg, for the west was full of such

---

13. Marrou 1958 (1938), 38–46; Marrou 1965, 380–85.
14. Syme 1958, 504–19; Swain 1996.
15. Ranging from s. IV to VI: Chrestus, Cledonius, Corippus, Evanthius, Eutyches, Priscian, Speciosus, Theophilus, Urbanus (nos. 27, 31, 37, 54, 57, 126, 138, 154, and 164 in the prosopography included in Kaster 1988).
16. *Graeco etiam, si qui dignus repperiri potuerit…*, Cod. *Theod.* xiii. 3. 11 (376).

Latin-speaking Greeks."[17] It depends what is implied by the word "such." There may well have been many Greeks who spoke and read enough Latin to cope with the demands of the imperial service, but surely few with a wide knowledge of both literatures. Modern research into bilingual cultures has shown that bilingual speakers are not normally at home in more than one of the literatures of their two languages. Nor does it follow that it is the literature of their first language they know best. In the United States a child of Hispanic parents may be proud of her Hispanic heritage and speak both English and Spanish with native fluency, but acquire through school and college an almost entirely English literary culture.

Even so familiar a case as Ammianus may be less straightforward than often assumed. It is true that he refers to "us Greeks" and often cites Greek writers and philosophers, but we should bear in mind that he joined the army in his early twenties, retired to Rome, and wrote a long and ambitious history in Latin that reveals a wide familiarity with the Latin classics. That Claudian should have a deep and extensive familiarity with all the major Roman poets is not surprising. He was after all a poet. But Ammianus not only has just as deep a knowledge of Vergil, but makes extensive use of poetical language and an originally poetic device that gradually took hold in later prose, the so-called poetic plural.[18] As for Vergilian influence, this is not a case of occasional direct quotations, but a prose that is steeped in Vergilian phraseology. Here is a single inconspicuous illustration. At 18. 7. 4 he describes how the Romans burned crops to prevent the enemy using them: the fire completely consumed "the young vegetation and the grain, which was already swelling on its yellow stalks" (*frumenta omnia cum iam stipula flaventi turgerent herbasque pubentes*). The casual reader will sense a certain elevation in the diction here, but the fact is that Ammianus is combining details from two different passages of Vergil: *frumenta in viridi stipula lactentia turgent* from *Georg*. i. 315; and *pubentes herbae* from *Aen*. 4. 514. He is not, of course, alone in writing this sort of Vergil-laden prose, but such writers are normally westerners who grew up as native Latin speakers, learning Vergil by heart in the school of the grammaticus from an early age. To have acquired so deep and extensive a knowledge of Vergil Ammianus must have studied the text line by line as a child with a grammaticus rather than simply read it as an adult. Claudian's remarkable familiarity with both Vergil and the Silver Age poets likewise implies years of study with a grammaticus rather than the more literary reading of the adult. In addition to knowing Vergil by heart, Ammianus must also have been intimately familiar with this sort of prose. The likelihood is that he either grew up in a bilingual household or lived for a significant part of his school days in a Latin-speaking area.

If (as Matthews conjectures) his mother was Greek and his father a Latin-speaking official stationed at Antioch, he may have grown up entirely bilingual (though with dominant Greek), which would at once put him in a different category from Greeks who

---

17. Matthews 1989, 467.
18. All three features are treated in detail in Hagendahl 1921. For Vergilian influence, see too Kelly 2008.

learned Latin as a second language. At some stage he received a Greek education and read Homer (the only Greek poet with whom he reveals indisputably firsthand familiarity), but once in the army he must have relied increasingly on his Latin. The evidence of his history suggests that most of the reading he did in his adult years was in Latin. By the time he came to write in Rome in his fifties it may well be true, as Lana and Fornara have argued, that he was better read in Latin than Greek. Many of his incidental references to classical Greek writers and philosophers are anecdotal, redolent of secondary sources (whether Greek or Latin) rather than firsthand acquaintance.[19]

Barnes has recently questioned this approach, arguing on the basis of the many Grecisms in Ammianus's prose and his failure to use purely Latin constructions like the historic infinitive, so common in other Latin historians, that (as Norden famously put it) Ammianus "thought in Greek."[20] On this basis he argues that it is "improbable a priori that one who thought in Greek preferred Latin over Greek sources." This is a dubious claim. I have asked many native French- and German-speakers who have lived for long periods in the United Kingdom or United States whether they still think in French or German, and even those with heavily French- or German-influenced English say that as soon as they start thinking in words at all, the words are English. While Ammianus was living in Rome among Latin-speakers and writing in Latin, he too surely "thought" in Latin, though the same heavily Greek-influenced Latin he wrote. This has nothing whatever to do with either the extent or currency of his Greek literary culture.

To return to the decline of Greek in the West, it has been generally assumed that a small group of cultivated pagan aristocrats successfully resisted the trend and even contrived something of a revival of Greek culture. Hadot writes of pagan members of the senate "possessing a considerable bilingual culture." Surprisingly enough, even Marrou was prepared to take Roman aristocrats at their own valuation and identify them as the last bastion of Greek in the West.[21] As we shall see, it has long been axiomatic that they read Plotinus and (especially) Porphyry in Greek, thus acquiring a firm philosophical underpinning for their religious convictions.

To a much larger extent than anyone seems to have recognized, this assumption presupposes the literal historicity of Macrobius's *Saturnalia*. Courcelle began his celebrated book *Les lettres grecques en occident* with Macrobius on the grounds that the *Saturnalia* gives a "very precise idea . . . of the state of pagan culture . . . and the position that Hellenism still retained" in the West at the death of Theodosius.[22] And Haverling's more recent discussion of Symmachus's knowledge of Greek begins by citing the discussions on Greek literature and philosophy by "the group of pagans which Macrobius depicts in his *Saturnalia*."[23]

---

19. Lana 1993, 23–40; Fornara 1992, 420–38.
20. Barnes 1998, 67, 76, 79.
21. Courcelle 1969, 13; Haverling 1990, 190; Hadot 2005, 248, 378; Marrou 1965, 384.
22. Courcelle 1969, 13 (395 was Courcelle's dramatic date).
23. Haverling 1990, 188–205.

Yet Macrobius was not a historian trying to give a picture of Hellenism at the death of Theodosius. He simply used the names of people from that period as mouthpieces for material he had collected himself. The Greek material in the *Saturnalia* is evidence of *Macrobius*'s culture, not his interlocutors'. Nor are its character and extent easy to determine. He quotes from more than sixty different Greek authors in the *Saturnalia* alone. But the overwhelming bulk of these quotations is taken over verbatim from a series of secondary sources. There can be no doubt that Macrobius was fluent in Greek and drew much of his erudition from Greek sources. But the number of Greek texts he knew at firsthand was small, and most were writers of the imperial age. There is no clear evidence that he knew *any* pre-imperial Greek literature at firsthand, not even Homer, from whom he cites some three hundred lines. For example, the long lists of Vergilian borrowings from Homer in *Sat.* v were simply copied from first-century pamphlets on Vergil's plagiarism (Ch. 16. 6); all twenty-six Homeric quotations in *Sat.* vii were lifted, complete with context, from surviving works of Gellius, Plutarch, and Alexander of Aphrodisias.[24] Not a single Homeric quotation can be ascribed with any degree of confidence to spontaneous reminiscence on the part of Macrobius himself.

Not only does Macrobius's Greek culture (such as it is) tell us nothing about the culture of his interlocutors. If we look to the contributions of individual interlocutors within the fiction of his dialogue rather than to Macrobius's actual sources, it is the Greeks Eusebius and Eustathius who are assigned the task of discussing Vergil's debt to the Greek poets and the Greek arts of philosophy, astrology, and rhetoric. When the Roman senator Euangelus makes a casual remark about Plato and wine, it is Eustathius who corrects him, and Eustathius who supplements Praetextatus's discourse on the Roman calendar by invoking Egyptian influence on Caesar's calendar reforms.[25] In Bk 7 Dysarius answers a series of questions from the other interlocutors on medicine and natural science. The only one who contradicts him is Eustathius, and they have a sharp exchange on the relative claims of medicine and philosophy.[26] That is to say, on any issue where the sources are Greek, the Roman interlocutors are represented as deferring to Greeks for authoritative opinions. It is also noteworthy that Eustathius is praised for his fluency in Latin and his ability to "act as his own interpreter," a clear implication that Macrobius himself did not believe his interlocutors capable of following a discussion in Greek.[27] For all the Greek quotations he puts in their mouths, not even Macrobius rep-resents his Roman interlocutors as fluent Greek-speakers, much less Greek scholars.

Servius too has the reputation of being a Greek scholar, a Neoplatonist who read Plotinus and Porphyry in the original.[28] Once again, he undoubtedly knew Greek and read Porphyry, and his commentary contains a fair amount of Greek lore of one sort

---

24. Flamant 1977, 298–301.
25. *Sat.* v. 2–22; i. 24. 14, 18, 21; ii. 8. 4–16; i. 16. 38–44.
26. vii. 14–16: Kaster, *HSCP* 84 (1980), 240–41.
27. *sui locuples interpres est, Sat.* i. 5. 16; Flamant 1977, 67.
28. Courcelle 1969, Ch. 1; Flamant 1977, 662–67; Setaioli 1995.

or another, from technical terms of grammar and rhetoric to quotations from Greek classics. Yet there is little evidence that he had any *firsthand* knowledge of classical or Hellenistic literature, either verse or prose.[29] He knew about Vergil's debt to Homer, Hesiod, Theocritus, Euphorion, and Apollonius, of course, and he even cites a few other great names, Pindar, Aeschylus, and Euripides. But when he says of *Eclogue* vii that "this eclogue is almost pure Theocritus," it is obvious that he had never actually read a poem of Theocritus. He simply knows the lines he found ready quoted in his Donatus or Asper. The same applies to his claim that the whole of *Aeneid* iv was "translated" from Bk iii of Apollonius's *Argonautica*,[30] and that Gallus "translated" Euphorion into Latin.[31] A recent study of citations of Homer in the ancient commentaries on Vergil is based on the assumption that both Servius himself and his students, mostly children of the Roman elite, had a firsthand familiarity with Homer.[32] Most of Servius's Homer citations almost certainly derive from earlier commentaries.

As though it was established fact, I. Hadot writes of the "strange world of the Neoplatonic circle described by Macrobius."[33] In a recent discussion of the influence of Plotinus and Porphyry on Ammianus, Szidat regretted the lack of detailed documentation in what he represented as a growing recognition of the influence of Neoplatonism on cultivated fourth-century pagans. It might seem that Ammianus's relevance to this theme was marginal, given that he grew up in the East as a native Greek speaker. But on the basis of parallels with Macrobius and Servius, Szidat paradoxically argued that he picked up his Neoplatonism in the West.[34] That is to say, he took it for granted that firsthand knowledge of Greek philosophy was widespread among the western elite as late as the 380s.[35] Certainly some westerners still read Plotinus and Porphyry in the original: the rhetorician Marius Victorinus (e.g.) in the 350s; Symmachus's critic Ambrose, a much better Greek scholar than Symmachus, who adapted long tracts from Plotinus and (perhaps more surprisingly) Philo in some of his sermons; and (using Victorinus's Latin translations) the young Augustine, though it is uncertain whether Plotinus or Porphyry were among the "Platonic" writers Victorinus translated.[36] All (it will be noted) men who ended their days as Christians.

The question asked in this chapter is not just whether aristocrats like Praetextatus, Symmachus, and Flavian "knew" Greek, but how much and what sort of Greek they knew. Did they (as so often simply assumed) have an easy firsthand familiarity with the Greek literary classics? Classical scholars inevitably tend to think of Greek as the

---

29. For more detail on Servius's knowledge of Greek, see Cameron 2004, 192–208.
30. For a brilliant and just appraisal of Servius's learning, Goold 1970, 134–39.
31. On *Buc.* vi. 72; x. 1, 50.
32. Scaffai 2006.
33. I. Hadot 2005, 152.
34. Szidat 1982; so too Matthews 1989, 429–32. But there seems no reason to doubt that he knew Plotinus (whom he mentions twice) at firsthand (Barnes 1998, 76–78). More on Ammianus's culture below.
35. According to Ammianus, on the other hand, aristocrats preferred singers to philosophers (14. 6. 18).
36. Courcelle 1968; Hadot 1968; 1971; Madec 1974; Runia 1993, 291–311.

language of culture for educated Romans. But this was never more than half the truth. Even in the first and second centuries many people used what Greek they had to read philosophy (or what passed for philosophy) rather than the classical poets—the less cultivated disciples of teachers like Musonius Rufus and Epictetus, for example. Such people had no doubt read some Homer, tragedy, and Menander when they studied Greek in school, and could understand and perhaps even memorize and quote the moral maxims from the poets cited by Musonius and Epictetus. But they did not read the Greek classics in and for themselves in their adult lives.

By the fourth century more people learned Greek to study Scripture than to read the classics. To cite only examples from the higher aristocracy, Rufinus praises the "skill in both languages" of his patron Apronianus.[37] Another of his patrons, the elder Melania, is said to have read the whole of Origen, Basil, and other Greek writers, "not once only but seven or eight times."[38] As for the younger Melania, according to her biographer "when she read in Latin, it was as if she knew no Greek, and when she read in Greek, it was as if she knew no Latin." Jerome makes exactly the same claim about one of his young female disciples, Paula's daughter Blesilla. Jerome also implies that Blesilla's sister Eustochium and their mother, Paula, had fluent Greek.[39] So too Pammachius, another of Jerome's Roman patrons and the dedicatee of several of his biblical commentaries.[40] Paulinus's cultivated (and apparently still pagan) kinsman Jovius knew and read Greek, though Paulinus himself did not.[41] Since all these claims take the form of compliments addressed to rich patrons (in the case of Blesilla to her mother), we are hardly obliged to take them literally—especially since Blesilla died at the age of twenty after living what Jerome himself reproachfully characterized as an overly secular life till she was widowed at the age of eighteen. Nonetheless it would be unreasonable to doubt that they had a working knowledge of Greek, sufficient to check passages in the Latin New Testament against the Greek original.

As Luebeck showed long ago and Courcelle put beyond serious doubt, Jerome himself, while clearly capable of reading prose writers of the empire like Philo, Clement, Porphyry, and the Greek Fathers, had little or no firsthand knowledge of the Greek classics.[42] His very occasional quotations from Homer, Euripides, and Aristophanes are demonstrably taken at secondhand from surviving passages of Cicero, Plutarch, and Clement. His citation of Herodotus for Sennacherib's siege of Pelusium is taken from Josephus.[43] Naturally he knew a good deal about the classical poets and philosophers from his extensive knowledge of well-read Latin writers like Cicero, but it is unlikely that he had ever opened an original text of (say) Homer or Euripides.

---

37. *tu qui utriusque linguae habes peritiam*, A. Engelbrecht (ed.), *Tyrannii Rufini Opera* i (CSEL 46) 1910, 5.

38. Pallad. *Hist. Laus.* 55, p. 149 Butler.

39. *Vita Melan.* 26, p. 181 Gorce; Jer. *Ep.* 39. 1; *Epp.* 108. 26; 33. 1, 5—claims taken seriously in the entries for all three women in *PCBE*: ii. 1 (1999), 310 (Blesilla); ii. 1. 714 (Eustochium); ii. 2 (2000), 1618 (Paula).

40. The passages are collected in *PCBE* ii. 2. 1576.

41. *Ep.* 16. 6; *Carm.* 22. 20–23; Mratschek 2002, 171, 336–37.

42. Luebeck 1872; Courcelle 1969, 58–127.

43. All relevant texts are set out in parallel columns by Courcelle 1969, 80.

There was also a more mundane, practical use for Greek: as a means of communication with Greek-speakers. Jerome, Rufinus, and John Cassian, for example, must have greatly improved their fluency during their years of residence in the East, and could presumably speak as well as read Greek. Symmachus, as we shall see, corresponded with only three native Greek-speakers (Iamblichus, Andronicus, and Hierophantes, one letter each), and whether or not he could understand their Greek, Symmachus himself wrote to all three in Latin. All the other Roman notables of the age we know to have corresponded with Greeks are Christians. For example, three prominent Roman ladies, Anicia Faltonia Proba, her daughter-in-law Anicia Iuliana, and Italica, perhaps another daughter-in-law, corresponded with John Chrysostom.[44] Ambrose wrote to Basil to inform him of his election to the see of Milan and request the return of the bones of his orthodox predecessor Dionysius, who had died in Cappadocia.[45] And a variety of other western bishops, above all the bishop of Rome, corresponded with a variety of eastern bishops. Much of this correspondence was concerned with momentous theological and ecclesiastical issues, and it was essential that each party understood the other. Most bishops must have depended on translators, but some at least of these westerners, notably Ambrose, were surely able to read replies to their letters in the original and perhaps also write their side of the exchange in Greek. Christian notables had a motive for acquiring at any rate some knowledge of Greek to check theological details.[46]

But theology and ecclesiastical politics were not the only reason Christian members of the elite learned Greek. We have seen that Ausonius praises Petronius Probus for his eloquence in Greek, and his son Anicius Probinus cos. 395 also read secular classics. One of his contributions to the *Epigrammata Bobiensia* is a rambling but accurate translation of an epigram by Lucillius.[47] Seen against this wider context, there is no obvious sense in which we can credit pagans like Symmachus, Flavian, and Praetextatus with sponsoring a Greek revival. But did they at any rate read the classics? Did they read the Neoplatonists in the original? Did they make important pagan works more widely available by translating them into Latin?

2: SYMMACHUS

In 395 Symmachus told Protadius that his son Memmius (then about eleven years old) was beginning Greek and that he himself (then about fifty-five) was joining in his studies "as though his peer" (*velud aequalis*).[48] Not to be taken altogether seriously, of course, but surely more than a rueful admission that his Greek was rusty. For if (as

---

44. Chrys. *Epp.* 168–70 (*PG* 52. 709–10); for the two last named, *PCBE* ii. 1 (1999), 1162, 1169.
45. Known only from Basil's reply, *Ep.* 19 (iii. 90–99 Deferrari); Homes Dudden 1935, 69.
46. Much information, not always accurate, in Bardy 1948.
47. *Ep. Bob.* 65 ~ *AP* xi. 104; Speyer 1959, 113–20.
48. Symm. *Ep.* iv. 20. 2.

widely believed) it was good enough to read not only Homer but Porphyry in the original, it would have been absurd rather than merely self-deprecating to represent himself taking elementary classes. The natural implication of this remark, that Greek was a language he had learned at school but not kept up in adult years, is amply borne out by the nature of his references to Greek writers.

To be sure his letters and speeches are full of allusions to Greek literature, philosophy, and history. But little if any of all this needs to have come from Greek sources. The enormous debt of late antique culture to the art, literature, and philosophy of classical and Hellenistic Greece is amply reflected in central Latin texts like Cicero, Vergil, and Horace. In some important respects Symmachus's Greek culture resembles that of entirely Greekless medieval writers. Dante, for example, like Symmachus, knew more about the philosophers (colorful figures often mentioned in Latin texts) than the poets, with whom, inevitably, he had no direct acquaintance. Homer alone Dante mentions a number of times, having learned from Latin writers that he was the "poeta sovrano."[49] Symmachus too refers more than a dozen times to the *Iliad* and *Odyssey*, but never a direct quotation. It is true that (unlike Dante) Symmachus occasionally uses a Greek word in his correspondence, but never casually (like Cicero), only in letters to literary friends who knew Greek, surely a calculated artifice (p. 385).

Typical of his often elaborate Homeric allusions is the comparison of the attractions of Praetextatus's estate at Baiae to lotus trees, the alluring potions of Circe (*suada Circae pocula*) and the "trio of winged maidens" (*tricinium semivolucrum puellarum*). All passages often alluded to in Latin texts, with *Circae pocula* coming from Horace, not Homer. Homer's Sirens are neither winged nor said to number three. Symmachus's source here is perhaps sarcophagi of the Roman period, where Sirens regularly appear as winged trios.[50] It is instructive to compare the allusions in Greekless Elizabethan writers to Odysseus stopping up his ears with wax to resist the Sirens, an un-Homeric detail that can be traced to Erasmus's *Similia*.[51] With these vague Homeric reminiscences in Symmachus we may contrast the sixteen Homeric references in Ammianus, two direct quotations, and a number of clear allusions to specific passages. Another Symmachan letter suggests that, while hunting, Praetextatus met Apollo in the woods "like Hesiod." But Hesiod did not meet Apollo in the woods. Symmachus misunderstood a reference to Hesiod in Vergil.[52]

There is in fact nothing in the speeches and letters as extant that demonstrably derives from firsthand knowledge of a Greek text. This might seem an excessively rigorous standard to require, but it is a mistake (with Haverling) to take refuge in a

---

49. Paratore 1968, 90–92 (the key passages are *Inf.* 4 and *Purg.* 22). For references to Homer in Dante's various works, Teodolinda Barini, *Dante's Poets* (Princeton 1984), 189, 293; see too G. Cerri, *Dante e Omero* (Lecce 2007).
50. *Ep.* i. 47; Hor. *Ep.* i. 2. 23; Courcelle 1944, at 78–91.
51. Bush 1960, 28 n. 4; M. P. Tilley, *CP* 21 (1926), 162–64.
52. *Ep.* i. 53. 1; Verg. *Buc.* vi. 69–73.

supposed reluctance to quote verbatim. It is true that writers with a sense of style preferred allusion or paraphrase to verbatim quotation, but such allusions were meant to be recognized and admired just the same (Ch. 20. 6). This is particularly true of Symmachus, given the distinction drawn in chapter 10 between his "literary" and "standard" letters. Most of his literary allusions are to be found in a small number of letters addressed to the sort of cultivated friends who would appreciate them. For example, he represents Protadius, perhaps the most cultivated of all his correspondents, complaining that he entrusts his letters *periturae chartae*, "to the perishable medium of parchment." Not exactly a quotation, but the well-read Protadius would have detected the allusion to the beginning of Juvenal's first satire, *periturae parcere chartae*, even though the sense in Juvenal is quite different ("spare parchment that will be wasted anyway").[53] Symmachus always incorporates enough of the original for such allusions to Latin classics to be recognized. But there are no such specific allusions to any Greek text.

While conceding that most of Symmachus's "Greek" allusions can be traced to Latin sources he certainly knew (above all Cicero and Valerius Maximus),[54] Haverling nonetheless found "some evidence" that he "had read some of the most important Greek classics in the original." But if a man as anxious as Symmachus to advertise his cultural attainments really knew even a few Greek classics in the original, he would not have left his correspondents (or us) in any doubt.

According to Courcelle, Symmachus had enough Greek "to listen to and appreciate" Greek orators who declaimed in Rome.[55] A single text lies behind this sweeping claim: a reference to the supposedly Athenian rhetor Palladius, whom Symmachus commended to three different dignitaries of the late 370s.[56] But the only evidence that Palladius declaimed in Greek is the Greek word Seeck introduced by emendation (*movit* λόγος *Athenaei hospitis*) into a corrupt passage that can be solved more simply and plausibly.[57] It is not just a question of whether or not Symmachus "knew" Greek. I have no doubt that he had read a book or two of Homer and Demosthenes in school, and in later years may still have been able to struggle through a Greek quotation in a Latin text or a letter or document in Greek, just as a modern English tourist may be able to dredge up enough of his schoolboy French to navigate a label in a museum, a menu in a restaurant, or a newspaper headline. But it would require an altogether different level of fluency to understand fourth-century spoken Greek, much less follow the highly artificial Greek of

---

53. *Ep.* iv. 34. 3 ~ Juv. i. 18.
54. So already Kroll 1891, passim; Montana 1961, 297–316; Haverling 1990, 188–205.
55. *Ep.* i. 15; Courcelle 1969, 15, developed by Haverling 1990, 203.
56. *Ep.* i. 15 (to Ausonius); i. 94 (to Syagrius); iii. 50 (to Eutropius); *PLRE.* i. 660.
57. *Ep.* i. 15. 2; Thraede's *movit novus Athenaei hospes* (*Rhein. Mus.* 111 [1968], 287–89) would eliminate the anomalous use of *Athenaeus* = "Athenian" for the normal *Atheniensis*, and leave Symmachus simply listening to a recent visiting speaker at the Athenaeum, an odeum in Rome where recitations took place (the MSS offer *nouus, uos,* and *nouos*). For the Athenaeum, Braunert 1964, 9–41, with Cameron 1965, 248.

a contemporary declamation. And the expertise and authority with which Symmachus assessed Palladius's performance (*divisionis arte, inventionum copia, gravitate sensuum, luce verborum*) make it clear that he claimed to follow it as a connoisseur.

It is worth inquiring how Symmachus might have acquired that level of fluency in Greek. In earlier times, once they had acquired the elements through formal instruction, members of the Roman elite would normally spend a year or two studying in Athens or Rhodes,[58] and subsequently retain a Greek man of letters (usually a philosopher) to live with them and accompany them on journeys. Cicero and Diodotus the Stoic, Lucullus and Antiochus of Ascalon, Pompey and Theophanes of Mytilene are merely the best-known examples.[59] In his consular year Symmachus wrote a letter to Libanius, known only from Libanius's reply, which reminisces about a visit to Antioch by Avianius Symmachus in 361.[60] At the time (it seems) Avianius was considering sending his son to study with Libanius. A year in Antioch would have made all the difference to the younger Symmachus's Greek.[61] As things turned out, he grew up in an increasingly monolingual Rome, and never visited the Greek-speaking parts of the empire. Nor is there any indication in his 776 letters extending over more than twenty-five years that he was ever on intimate terms with any Greek men of letters.

We should not be misled by the four learned Greek interlocutors of Macrobius's *Saturnalia*: Horus, Dysarius, Eustathius, and Eusebius. Horus and Dysarius were at any rate real people, mentioned in Symmachus's correspondence. Horus he describes as a "long-time dear friend" and Dysarius as "brother," but in letters of commendation, where such characterizations are not to be taken too seriously. The fact that he never actually wrote to either of them is enough to prove that they were not among his intimates. As for Eustathius and Eusebius, it is far from certain that they existed, at any rate as they appear in the pages of Macrobius. Peter Schmidt has recently identified Eustathius as Eustathius of Cappadocia, the disciple of Iamblichus. Eustathius must have been dead by 382, though he might be counted as one of Macrobius's deliberate anachronisms.[62] But Macrobius describes his Eustathius as Academic, Stoic, and Peripatetic combined (i. 5. 13–16), in words copied verbatim from Gellius (vi. 14. 8–10), whereas the Cappadocian was a Neoplatonist. As for the Greek rhetor Eusebius, there were a number of Greek rhetors of this name,[63] one of whom was recommended for a chair in Rome by his teacher Prohaeresius ca. 350.[64] He too would be rather early for Macrobius's Eusebius, even though he is described as being on the verge of old age in 382 (vii. 10. 1).

---

58. Daly 1950, 40–58; Rawson 1985, 6–12.
59. Balsdon 1979, 54–58; Rawson 1985, 79–83.
60. Lib. *Ep.* 1004. It is curious that a letter to so distinguished a figure was not included in Symmachus's published correspondence.
61. Praetextatus spent a year as proconsul of Achaea, and the younger Flavian a year in Antioch as proconsul of Asia.
62. Penella 1990, 53–58 for his dates; P. Schmidt 2009, 76–78.
63. *PLRE* i. 302–5, nos. 10, 12, 13, 14, 16, 17, 24, and 25.
64. Eunapius, *Vit. Soph.* 493; P. Hadot 1971, 33–34.

It may be that we should just concede the existence of two otherwise unattested Greeks resident in Rome who fit Macrobius's specifications better. But the specifications are probably no more than dramatic fiction, like the philosophical and rhetorical expertise Cicero puts in the mouths of his interlocutors. Macrobius needed Greeks to vouch for Vergil's knowledge of Greek literature and rhetoric. If he had Eustathius of Cappadocia in mind, the resemblance goes no further than name and profession. For his purposes it did not matter whether the real-life counterparts of his Greek interlocutors lived in Rome, read Vergil, or even spoke Latin. Quite apart from the fact that the Academy, Stoa, and Peripatos no longer existed as organized philosophical schools, no one could be a follower of all three (Academics, after all, were sceptics). And Horus is surely portrayed as a Cynic because a Cynic interlocutor was one of the standard requirements of a literary symposium,[65] not because in real life he was "a follower of Antisthenes, Crates and Diogenes himself" (i. 7. 3) who owned but a single cloak (vii. 13. 17). Macrobius's Greeks are nothing but literary stereotypes.

The literary discussions Libanius claims to have had with Avianius Symmachus during his visit to Antioch might have been conducted through interpreters (Libanius certainly had no Latin), but the fact that Avianius undertook at least two embassies to Greek-speaking provinces (something his son never did) suggests the possibility of some sort of speaking knowledge of Greek.[66] It may be no coincidence that Praetextatus, who had good enough Greek to translate philosophical texts, spent a year as proconsul of Achaea, a post to which he was appointed by Julian during a visit to Constantinople "on private business."[67] As already remarked, the ability of Jerome and Rufinus to draw on the Greek Fathers as extensively as they did must have been helped by their many years in the East.

Thanks to the political division between East and West from the death of Julian on, by the last quarter of the fourth century it became less and less common for westerners to serve in the eastern provinces, surely another factor contributing to the decline of Greek. While easterners now had strong motives of self-interest to learn Latin, westerners had less and less reason to maintain and improve their schoolboy Greek. By Symmachus's day many of his Roman peers had never enjoyed the sort of contact with native Greek-speakers that had been routine for their class a century earlier. Fewer still now enjoyed the advantage of a domestic mentor, someone with whom to discuss literature and philosophy in Greek on a daily basis. Certainly Symmachus himself never mentions any such figure. Only one of Macrobius's Greek interlocutors is said to have arrived with one of his aristocrats, Dysarius with Euangelus,[68] though there is no hint elsewhere in the dialogue of a relationship between them.

---

65. Martin 1931, 69, 72–76.
66. I infer an official visit to Constantinople from the gold statue erected there: *PLRE* i. 863–65.
67. Amm. Marc. 22. 7. 6.
68. *Euangelum adesse nuntiat* [a slave] *cum Dysario, Sat.* i. 7. 1.

Under the circumstances, there is little likelihood that Symmachus's Greek was good enough to follow what was evidently a virtuoso declamation in Greek. We are surely bound to conclude that Palladius spoke in Latin. Indeed, on another possible reconstruction of the text in question there is no reason to suppose that he was Greek at all. The fact that he soon embarked on a brilliant career in the imperial service in the West leaves little doubt that, whatever his origin, he was competent in Latin.

The Greek poet Andronicus of Hermupolis sent Symmachus a collection of his poems. Symmachus replied in Latin: "the Muse of Cecrops flourishes on your lips, while my language is Latin." He describes himself as a "grateful reader," but (unlike, e.g., his letter to Ausonius on the latter's *Mosella*) betrays no hint of subject or treatment, nothing (in short) to suggest that he had actually read Andronicus's poems, let alone with any appreciation.[69] We only have Libanius's side of his exchange with Symmachus, and Haverling regrets that we do not know "whether it was written in Greek or Latin." In fact, we do, since Libanius mentions that he had to find a translator before he could read it! Symmachus also wrote in Latin to the younger Iamblichus (below). This proves nothing in itself, since a stylist like Symmachus would naturally prefer to write in the language of which he was an acknowledged master.[70] Nonetheless, Fronto and Marcus corresponded in Greek as well as Latin, as did Cicero.[71]

Symmachus would no doubt dearly have wished for good enough Greek to read Homer, Plato, and the orators in the original. But that level of competence would have been very hard to attain in late fourth-century Rome. As for his knowledge of philosophy, Symmachus twice emphatically professes complete ignorance.[72] And while such self-deprecation is conventional, all that we find in the letters and speeches is trivial anecdotes about philosophers of old (Anaxagoras, Pythagoras, Socrates, etc.). He wrote commendations for several otherwise unknown professors of philosophy (Barachus, Celsus, Horus, Priscianus, Serapammon), all general character references without any mention of doctrines or expertise. Presumably, schoolteachers rather than scholars if they "instructed the nobility," some of them on public salaries.[73] There is no indication that he had a personal relationship with any of these nonentities. But he did write to one real philosopher, Iamblichus, grandson of Sopater, one of the leading disciples of the great Iamblichus. This younger Iamblichus seems to have established Athens as the new home of Neoplatonism.[74] The letter is instructive: most people collect precious objects; Symmachus collects students of philosophy, among whom "the experts" agree that Iamblichus is supreme, in particular his friend Eudoxius, a "careful judge."[75] Here even

---

69. *In tuo ore vernat Musa Cecropia, mihi lingua Latiaris est, Ep.* viii. 22; *PLRE* i. 65–66.
70. Libanius absurdly enough admires the style of the letter he could not read!
71. On the Greek letters of Cicero and Fronto, see now Swain 2004.
72. *tune, inquies, audeas de philosophis iudicare?* (*Ep.* i. 29 to Ausonius); ii. 61 to Flavian (judging Serapammon a philosopher by his long hair).
73. *Ep.* i. 29; i. 41; i. 79; ii. 39; ii. 61; *Rel.* 5; McGeachy 1942, 189–91.
74. Raubitschek 1964, 63–68; Cameron 1967, 143–53; Saffrey and Westerink 1968, xlvi.
75. *Ep.* ix. 2, with S. Roda's commentary; a Platonist philosopher called Eudoxius of unknown date is attested on a late antique mosaic from Heliopolis (M. Chéhab, *Mosaiques du Liban* [Paris 1958], 44–46, pl. xxi. 3).

more than in his other references to philosophers, Symmachus ostentatiously disavows any basis for personal judgment.

Yet many modern scholars nonetheless believe that he was influenced by Neoplatonic teachings, in particular that he "almost certainly owes much to Porphyry."[76] The basis for this claim boils down to just two sentences in his celebrated statement of the case for religious pluralism:[77]

> Everyone has his own customs, his own religious practices; the divine mind has assigned to different cities different religions to be their guardians.... Not by one avenue alone can we arrive at so great a secret (*uno itinere non potest perveniri ad tam grande secretum*).

The idea that peoples, like individuals, had their own guardian spirits, though by no means exclusively Neoplatonic, can be traced to Porphyry. Both Themistius (in 364) and Libanius (in 386) say something similar to the first sentence in pronouncements of their own on religious pluralism.[78] Of the three, Themistius undoubtedly had some philosophical training, though his main interest was Aristotle.[79] Libanius might have read Themistius, but the fact that Praetextatus translated Themistius's Aristotelian paraphrases, written in simple Greek, does not mean that Symmachus could read the highly wrought and exceptionally difficult Greek of his speeches.[80] Of course it is possible that they "exchanged views" during one of Themistius's Roman visits (357 and 376).[81] But that is an awful lot of "mights" and "coulds," the similarities are very general,[82] and even if we grant such exchanges, that still falls far short of crediting Symmachus with firsthand knowledge of Porphyry.

In the ordinary way, a philosophical motif that appears in three orators is most plausibly identified as a rhetorical commonplace. In an age when many pagans were faced with claiming tolerance for their beliefs, it is hardly necessary to suppose that they could only have got this simple and obvious argument from independently reading Porphyry at firsthand. We have already seen that Symmachus was acting as spokesman for his senatorial colleagues when he addressed his celebrated *Relatio* to court in 384. Being an orator, not a philosopher, he doubtless consulted colleagues better qualified than himself in these areas. The names of Praetextatus and Flavian naturally come to mind, though (as we shall see) there must be considerable doubt whether they knew Porphyry at firsthand either. In earlier times we would have postulated the assistance of a Greek domestic mentor. Guardian spirits are hardly an abstruse philosophical notion.

76. Vanderspoel 1995, 25; Courcelle in Momigliano 1963, 175; Wytzes 1977, 271–80; Vera, *Comm.* 1981, 37–41.
77. *Rel.* 10. 8, 10, trans. R. H. Barrow; e.g., Klein 1971, 84–91; Szidat 1982, 132.
78. *Them. Or.* 5. 70a (p. 102–3 Downey), with L. J. Daly, *GRBS* 12 (1971), 74–77; Liban. *Or.* 30. 4–5; Cracco Ruggini 1972, 178–88.
79. G. Dagron, *Thémistios* (1968), 154–55; Vanderspoel 1995, 26.
80. So Cracco Ruggini 1972, 3 n. 8; and in *CP* 82 (1987), 202–3.
81. So Vanderspoel 1995, 25.
82. See the detailed discussion of the three texts by J. Streeter in de Ste Croix 2006, 237–42.

As for the second Symmachan sentence, neither Themistius nor Libanius has anything at all similar, and when Augustine says "According to Porphyry, no doctrine has yet been established...which offers a universal way (*universalem...viam*) for the liberation of the soul" (*CD* x. 32. 1), the emphasis is surely very different. If he could go on to infer that Porphyry "admits without any doubt that such a way exists, but confesses that it had never come to his notice," Porphyry can hardly have asserted that there must be *many* ways. In fact, the closest parallel comes from an early work of Augustine, at *Solil.* i. 13. 23: "wisdom is not reached by only one road" (*sed non ad [sapientiam] una via pervenitur*). Here too scholars have reconstructed Porphyry as a common source behind Symmachus and Augustine. When Augustine later expressed regret for implying that there was any other way but Christ (*Retr.* iv. 3), according to Vanderspoel he is renouncing his earlier dependence on Porphyry.[83]

But there is considerable doubt whether Augustine had even read Porphyry at this stage of his career,[84] and there is a much simpler and more natural explanation of this undeniably striking parallel. Whether consciously or not, Augustine was surely echoing Symmachus.[85] This is in fact put beyond doubt by the fact that it is not just the idea Augustine echoes, but precisely Symmachus's formulation *in Latin*. First, both use the same verb in the passive (*perveniri ~ pervenitur*). Second, in the slightly later *De vera rel.* 28. 51 we find the other half of Symmachus's famous sentence, *tam grande secretum*. Time and place conspire to provide a perfect context: Symmachus wrote in 384, at the very time Augustine was in Rome; Augustine wrote in 386. Both as a rhetor himself and as an applicant for a post in rhetoric decided by Symmachus, it is highly probable that Augustine took the trouble to read Symmachus's famous recent speech.

It would be one thing if we were dealing with an author known to have philosophical interests. But these two sentences are quite insufficient to outweigh the emphatically unphilosophical impression given by the rest of Symmachus's extensive oeuvre.

3: PRAETEXTATUS

We have seen there is little basis for the notion that Praetextatus was in any sense a genuine scholar. Macrobius's interlocutors are full of praise for his religious expertise, but never suggest that he was more learned than the rest in other matters.[86] Allusions to Homer and Hesiod in three of Symmachus's letters to him imply that he knew some Greek, and one or two other remarks that he was something of a philosopher.[87] It has been suggested that he is the "man of monstrous vanity" (*hominem immanissimo typho*

---

83. Vanderspoel 1990, 179–93.
84. Rist 1994, 16–17.
85. Trout 1988, 141; O'Donnell on *Conf.* v. 13. 23 (ii. 321).
86. *Sat.* i. 17. 7; i. 2. 20; i. 11. 1; i. 24. 21.
87. *Ep.* i. 45, 47, 53; Ch. 10. 4.

turgidum) who introduced the young Augustine to Neoplatonic writings,[88] surely in fact Mallius Theodorus, the future consul of 399, to whom Augustine dedicated his *De beata vita* soon after his conversion, with fulsome acknowledgement of his debt to many discussions on philosophical questions. It would have been a delightful paradox if Praetextatus had set Augustine on the road that was to lead to his becoming the greatest doctor of the western church.[89] But that would require him to have been a serious Neoplatonist, for which there is simply no evidence.

The widespread belief that Praetextatus was a student of Porphyry rests entirely on the speech about solar theology put in his mouth by Macrobius.[90] This material does indeed ultimately derive from Porphyry, but (as we have seen) it has nothing to do with the real Praetextatus. Macrobius found it in Cornelius Labeo (p. 267). There is no authentic evidence that Praetextatus had any knowledge of Neoplatonism. His attested philosophical interests were more austere. As we learn from Boethius, he translated Themistius's paraphrases of Aristotle's *Prior* and *Posterior Analytics* (both lost).

These Latin versions were no doubt a boon to Greekless students of logic. But scarcely scholarship. In the first place, all Praetextatus did was translate Themistius. And not (as often loosely stated) *commentaries* by Themistius, but simply *paraphrases*, several of which are extant, including the one on the *Posterior Analytics*. Not abstracts (the one on the *Posterior Analytics* is sixty-five pages long, not much shorter than the original), but summaries that embody a certain amount of interpretation. Nonetheless they are Aristotle made easy, an introduction to the real thing in simple Greek.

In the second place, Praetextatus was not blazing any new trails. It was Porphyry who revived interest in Aristotle's logic at Rome, with his influential *Eisagoge* (dedicated to an ancestor of Symmachus) and various commentaries. A generation before Praetextatus Marius Victorinus, professor of rhetoric at Rome, translated the *Eisagoge* and perhaps both *Categories* and *De interpretatione* as well. He also wrote logical treatises of his own in Latin, a lost *De syllogismis hypotheticis* and a surviving *De definitionibus*.[91] Since Victorinus was born ca. 290/300 and with a statue in the Forum of Trajan in 354, Praetextatus, born in 324, was surely his pupil. Not only did Praetextatus derive his interest in Aristotelian logic from Victorinus, the various works of Victorinus must have provided him with all the Latin terminology he needed for his own versions of Themistius. His actual copies of the Themistian paraphrases he may have picked up during his visit to Constantinople in 361.[92]

Boethius, our only source for these versions, goes on to imply that Praetextatus concealed his debt to Themistius. Praetextatus, he wrote, did not produce his versions by translating Aristotle, but "by translating Themistius, as anyone who reads both will

---

88. *Confess.* 7. 9. 13; Rist 1991, 138–43; for earlier views, O'Donnell 1992, 419–24.
89. In addition to the irony that Symmachus sent him to Milan where he met Ambrose.
90. So Wytzes 1977, 141; Turcan 1984, 209–26 at 225. And many others.
91. Hadot 1971, passim.
92. Amm. 22. 7. 6; Matthews 1989, 23.

see at once."[93] The imputation of dishonesty we may probably ascribe to the same professional rivalry that led Boethius to depreciate even Victorinus's achievements.[94] A Latin paraphrase of the *Categories* mistakenly ascribed to Augustine has often been attributed to Praetextatus, the one man (as it happens) who cannot have been the author, since he is named in the text.[95] Since the anonymous translator praises "Agorius" for his learning and mentions Themistius (as a contemporary), he at any rate does not seem to have regarded Praetextatus as a plagiarist. But we need not take his praise of so important a contemporary too seriously. There may have been other ways in which Praetextatus demonstrated his philosophical erudition and acumen, but the Aristotelian paraphrases required little more than a knowledge of Greek and familiarity with the writings of Victorinus.

Themistius was no Neoplatonist, and the very fact that Praetextatus was attracted to his paraphrases of Aristotle's logical writings militates against the assumption that he sought support for his paganism in Neoplatonism. Like Boethius a century later, Praetextatus occupied himself with the formal and (from the religious point of view) uncontroversial problems of logic. It might be added that, unlike his frequent allusions to Flavian's philosophical expertise (below), Symmachus drops only one very oblique reference to philosophy in his letters to Praetextatus. After making a trite remark about man being born to suffer adversity (Praetextatus's wife was sick), he suggests "leaving that to the disputations of philosophers" (i. 48).

4: THE ELDER FLAVIAN

We have seen (Ch. 10. 4) that Flavian affected some philosophical expertise, and suggested that he should be identified as the otherwise unknown Flavianus to whom John of Salisbury ascribes a work titled *De dogmatibus philosophorum* or *De vestigiis sive de dogmate philosophorum*.[96]

According to Wytzes, Flavian's philosophical master was "undoubtedly Porphyry." Evidently he did not bother to check the citations in John of Salisbury, which spectacularly fail to support any such notion. Two are trivial anecdotes: the first tells how Plato went into a decline and died when unable to answer a question put him by some sailors; the second how Plato used to carry a mirror to see what changes travel and study had wrought in his face. Another cites Flavian's book for sayings of Epicurus.[97] That is to say,

---

93. *Vettius Praetextatus priores postremosque Analyticos non vertendo Aristotelem latino sermoni tradidit, sed transferendo Themistium, quod qui utrosque legit facile intellegit,* (Boethius, *De interpretatione*[2] pp. 3–4 Meiser).
94. Chadwick 1981, 115–18.
95. So L. Minio-Paluello, *CQ* 39 (1945), 67; and Chadwick 1981, 114. Around 374 we find the twenty-year-old Augustine reading the *Categories* and perhaps other logical works of Aristotle at Carthage, presumably in Victorinus's translation (Hadot 1971, 193–98; Aug. *Conf.* iv. 16, with O'Donnell 1992, 264–65).
96. So Schaarschmidt 1862, 103–7; C. C. J. Webb's edition, vol. 1 (Oxford 1909), xlvi.
97. Wytzes 1977, 154; John, *Policraticus* ii. 26 (460B = i. 141 Webb); viii. 11 (761A = ii. 314); viii. 11 (ii. 294).

not a Neoplatonist tract at all, but a collection of silly anecdotes about the philosophers of old—much like the one Symmachus quotes in his letter to Flavian.

Much more dubious is John's claim that his Flavian treated Petronius's story about the Widow of Ephesus as fact rather than fiction (claiming that she was subsequently punished for adultery and murder).[98] Here we need to bear in mind John's admission in his preface that, "like Plato, Cicero and Macrobius," he will sometimes quote unknown or imaginary sources (i. 17. 30). Given the admission, he cannot have been hoping to deceive, as when he stretches out a list of historians who wrote about the miserable ends of tyrants by including both Suetonius and Tranquillus![99] The fact that he transcribed Petronius's story is certainly proof that he had read and enjoyed it, but a good Christian could not let the widow get away with such scandalous behavior. Whence the playful claim that she paid the penalty.

But the fact that this citation may be bogus need not discredit the others. Doubts have indeed been expressed, and a medieval compilation suggested instead.[100] But why invent a source for anecdotes about Plato? To be sure they are almost all unhistorical, but then so is the one about Socrates in Symmachus's letter to Flavian. Indeed, it is tempting to conjecture that it was in Flavian's book that Symmachus found it. In the course of his *Policraticus* John cites fifteen more anecdotes about Plato, all but six attested in surviving ancient sources. Seven (nos. 1, 2, 4, 11, 12, 13, 14 in Riginos's catalogue) agree closely with the version in Apuleius's *De Platone et dogmate eius*; nos. 71 and 76 derive from Jerome; 3 is closest to the versions in Cicero or Valerius Maximus and 7 to Seneca or Censorinus. The six otherwise unattested (including the two ascribed to Flavian) are 19, 28, 36, 76b, 122, and 147. None are likely to be medieval inventions.[101] There is also the point that John borrowed the puzzling *de vestigiis* in Flavian's title to form a part of his own subtitle (*de nugis curialium et vestigiis philosophorum*).[102] He cites the work four times, and in all probability drew on it in many other passages as well.

This and his knowledge of Philostratus's *Life of Apollonius of Tyana* (see § 5) is the totality of the evidence about Flavian's philosophical attainments. It is by no means impossible that, in addition to a taste for biographies of philosophers, Flavian actually read real philosophical texts in Greek. He may even have read some Porphyry. But we are not entitled simply to assume that he did on the grounds that we would expect a pagan champion to read the pagan philosopher par excellence. Nor are we entitled to assume that he did so on the analogy of Servius and Macrobius. Servius was a

---

98. *Pol.* viii. 11 (755A = ii. 304 Webb).

99. viii. 18, ii. 364 Webb; Janet Martin, *Viator* 10 (1979), 67–68.

100. Lehmann 1927, 25–27.

101. Riginos 1976, no. 36 (Plato's dream that he would be captured by pirates); 76b (Plato deliberately chose a site vulnerable to earthquakes for the academy); witty repartees by Socrates to Plato (19) and Plato to the tyrant Dionysius (28). The reference to Thersites in 19 would seem to exclude medieval invention.

102. As noted by Schaarschmidt 1862, 103.

professional scholar, and while Macrobius was more a gentleman than a scholar, he wrote a half-century later than the lifetime of his interlocutors. Servius and Macrobius tell us nothing about the real intellectual interests and attainments of the last generation of pagan aristocrats. For the point at issue is precisely whether they *did* have a philosophical underpinning for their convictions.

5: A LATIN TRANSLATION OF PHILOSTRATUS'S *LIFE OF APOLLONIUS OF TYANA?*

The rapid decline in knowledge of Greek was accompanied (tellingly) by a rise in the use and number of translations—a unique opportunity to make a direct comparison between the sort of works pagans and Christians translated. If we choose to treat the comparison as a contest, there can be no question that the Christians won. Bilingual Christians skillfully exploited the opportunity of making a number of key Christian books available to monolingual westerners.

Book 8 of Augustine's *Confessions* vividly evokes the effect a reading of the *Life of Antony* in Latin translation had on a group of young western intellectuals hovering on the brink of conversion. In fact, two different translations (both extant) had appeared by ca. 375, one now anonymous, literal but ungraceful, a second, more elegant but much less literal, by Evagrius of Antioch.[103] The so-called *Historia Monachorum in Aegypto* was translated by Rufinus before the end of the century. In addition, Rufinus produced version after version of works by Eusebius, Origen, Gregory Nazianzen, and Basil the Great for his aristocratic Roman patron Apronianus. Apronianus's wife, Avita, confessed to Rufinus that she found this sort of thing rather heavy going, and the tactful (and practical) Rufinus responded with some of Origen's easier homilies, on Psalms 36–38, remarking in a preface addressed to Apronianus that their simplicity will appeal even to the unintelligent, "so that the inspired utterance may reach not only men but also devout ladies." Soon afterward he had an even better idea, and produced a version of the *Sentences of Sextus*, which became an instant best seller.[104] Jerome complained about its popularity on the grounds that Sextus had been a pagan. Whether or not he was right about this, Rufinus was shrewd enough to capture the *Sentences* definitively for a wide Christian market. Jerome himself, of course, with his translations and commentaries was likewise aiming to make the results of Greek patristic scholarship available to a wide public. Jerome's greatest and most lasting achievement was a new translation of substantial parts of both Old and New Testaments.

---

103. J. Quasten, *Patrology* (Utrecht 1960), 40; for a comparison of the two versions, Rousseau 1978, 248–50.
104. For all the details, Chadwick 1959.

Did pagans make any comparable use of the opportunity? The prime example (really, as so often, the only example) is the supposed translation of Philostratus's *Life* of the pagan miracle worker Apollonius of Tyana (hereafter *VA*) by Flavian. At the turn of the third and fourth centuries, Porphyry and Sossianus Hierocles published attacks on Christianity that extolled Apollonius's miracles over those performed by Christ. Lactantius devoted a chapter of his *Divine Institutes* to a refutation of Hierocles, and Eusebius (if he is the author) an entire book.[105] With Apollonius acquiring something of the status of a pagan holy man, a Latin translation (so it is held) should be seen as a pagan counterpart to contemporary Christian translations of the lives of the Desert Fathers. Dzielska was only reflecting a long standard modern view when she identified Flavian's goal as nothing less than "to popularize the figure of a pagan thaumaturge and a prophet of the old religion among Roman citizens who did not know the Greek language." Flavian's translation is a central element in the modern view of an aggressive pagan reaction.[106]

The only evidence is a couple of puzzling sentences in a letter of Sidonius Apollinaris to his learned friend Leo ca. 476. I give first the Latin text (not itself in any doubt) and then (with a couple of supplements) W. B. Anderson's careful Loeb translation:[107]

> Apollonii Pythagorici vitam, non ut Nicomachus senior e Philostrati sed ut Tascius Victorianus e Nicomachi schedio exscripsit, quia iusseras, misi; quam, dum parere festino, celeriter eiecit in tumultuarium exemplar turbida et prae-ceps et Opica translatio... Sane, cum primum reduci aliquid otii fuit, inpoli-tum hunc semicrudumque et, ut aiunt, tamquam musteum librum plus desiderii tui quam officii mei memor obtuli.

> I have sent, at your command, the *Life of Apollonius the Pythagorean*, not as the elder Nicomachus [copied it] from [the manuscript] of Philostratus, but as Tascius Victorianus copied it from Nicomachus's manuscript. In my haste to obey your wish, I hurriedly flung the work into a haphazard copy, making a wild, pre-cipitate, barbarous transcription.... Certainly, in offering you this inelegant, half-raw, and, as the saying is, newly-vinted book at my first spare moment after getting home again, I have paid more regard to your desire than to my own duty.

Whatever this means, there is no getting away from the fact that it is allusively and obscurely expressed. Sidonius seems to distinguish between three different versions of

105. Lact. *Div. Inst.* 5. 3; for Eusebius's book see now vol. 3 (2006) of C. P. Jones's new Loeb; Dzielska 1986, 96–99, 154–57; E. Junod, *Rev. de théol. et de philos.* 120 (1988), 475–82. For well-founded doubts about Eusebian authorship, Hägg 1992, 138–50; against, Jones 2006, at 49–52.

106. Lommatzsch 1904, 182; Alföldi and Alföldi 1990, 54, firmly restated (after many others) in Dzielska 1986, 170–77; see too now Horsfall 1995, 169–75.

107. *Ep.* viii. 3. 1; W. B. Anderson, *Sidonius: Poems and Letters* 2 (Cambridge 1965), 404–7.

Philostratus's book: by the elder Nicomachus, by Victorianus, and (in more detail) by himself. How did they differ? Sidonius calls his own a *translatio*, and uses the verb *exscripsit* for the activity of both Nicomachus and Victorianus. The word *translatio* can certainly mean "translation," but also "transcription"; *exscribo* means "transcribe" or "represent."[108]

The difficulty of pinning down so imprecise a writer is well brought out by another letter (ii. 9. 5), in which Sidonius claims that Rufinus's Latin version of Origen was

> sic...ad verbum sententiamque *translatus* ut nec Apuleius Phaedonem sic Platonis neque Tullius Ctesiphontem sic Demosthenis in usum regulamque Romani sermonis *exscripserint*.

> translated into Latin with such faithfulness to the letter and the spirit that Apuleius could not be said to have turned Plato's *Phaedo* or Tully Demosthenes's *Ctesiphon* into such a perfect expression of the theory and the usage of Latin speech.

Here at least *translatus* undoubtedly means "translated," though of course the idea is considerably helped out by the Cicero and Apuleius parallels, not to mention the qualifying phrases *ad verbum sententiamque* and *in usum regulamque Romani sermonis*.[109] As for *exscripserint*, though it describes the activity of Apuleius and Cicero as translators, in context the word actually means something closer to "represent" than "translate."[110] Elsewhere Sidonius uses *transferre* of "transcribe" (ix. 11. 6, put beyond doubt by the mention of correcting errors and adding punctuation) and both the noun *translator* and the same verb *exscripsi* of his own transcription of the letters that make up Bk ix of his *Epistles* (ix. 16. 2, put beyond doubt by the mention of the winter's cold freezing the ink on his pen). It should also be borne in mind that Leo did not need Sidonius's covering letter to tell him whether the manuscript he received was in Latin or Greek!

On the standard interpretation (which goes back to Mommsen) Nicomachus translated from the original Greek, Victorianus revised or edited this translation, and Sidonius either just transcribed or further revised it.[111] But there are other possibilities. According to Pricoco and Loyen, Nicomachus and Victorianus both transcribed the original Greek, which Sidonius then translated into Latin.[112] I hope to show that all three simply transcribed the text in Greek.[113]

---

108. *Translatio* also = "metaphor," and in the rhetoricians there are various more technical meanings: see *OLD* s.v. 3b, or C. Halm, *Rhetores Latini Minores* (1863), 656–57. For *exscribo*, *TLL* v. ii. 2. 1830–31.
109. The verb is found twenty-six times in Cassiodorus's *Institutiones* in the sense "translate," though it is worth adding that in every case there is an *ex Graeco* or *in Latinum* in the context.
110. Compare *Ep.* vii. 13. 5, where *tuam temperantiam, religionem...exscripsit* means "give a picture of your moderation and piety," a natural extension of "copy," but not in the direction of "translate."
111. Briefly stated in his index to C. Luetjohann's edition (1887), p. 420. Mommsen himself said nothing about Sidonius's copy.
112. Pricoco 1965, at 71–98, endorsed by Loyen 1968, 83–86; and *Sidoine Apollinaire* 3 (Paris 1970), 196–97; so too Horsfall 1993, 321–22.
113. So Anderson in a footnote (ii. 404 n. 5)—immediately contradicted by his editor Warmington.

Let us begin with Sidonius's copy, about which we have the most information. The assumption that Sidonius translated rests almost entirely on the word *translatio*. But there is nothing in the context (contrast the passage on Rufinus's translations from Origen) to suggest translation rather than transcription. Nor is it likely that Sidonius's Greek was good enough to take on so ambitious a task as translating so long and difficult a work.[114] The context is in fact remarkably rich in colorful epithets (all negative) that suggest transcription. Sidonius describes how in his haste his "wild, precipitate and crude *translatio* has hurriedly flung the *Life of Apollonius* into a rushed copy." A few sentences later we have a fresh set of apologies for "this inelegant, half-raw, and (as it were) newly-vinted book."

Pricoco and Loyen rather surprisingly argued that these exaggerated excuses imply more than just transcription. Yet if Sidonius had *translated* Philostratus, somewhere among these interminable apologies there should have been some reference to the one central requirement of any translation, fidelity to the original. Did Sidonius translate *ad verbum* or *ad sensum*? What about the specific problems presented by Philostratus's often extravagant style? Why was he so desperately apologetic about stylistic shortcomings but apparently oblivious to the possibility of misunderstanding or mistranslation? No fewer than six of the words in Sidonius's litany of apologies imply speed or haste (*festino, celeriter, tumultuarium, turbida, praeceps, eiecit*) and those that do not (*Opica, impolitum, semicrudum, museum*) are all metaphors of style. While it is true that Sidonius was first and foremost a stylist, his judgment of Rufinus's translations from Origen reveals him well aware of the importance of accuracy and fidelity. It would surely be very odd for even Sidonius to have characterized a translation of his own in *exclusively* stylistic terms.

Pricoco and Loyen point out that the preface to Jerome's *Chronicle* refers to it as a *tumultuarium opus*. It is true that the *Chronicle* was (in the main) a translation, but that does not make *tumultuarium* "better applicable to a translation...than to the essentially mechanical act of copying." A hastily executed copy is just as flawed as a hastily executed translation. In any case, this is the only reference to haste; the rest of Jerome's long preface is entirely devoted to the problems of translating and the character of this particular translation.[115] It is also true that, in a letter to Augustine comparing his own and earlier translations of the Bible, Jerome contrasts the "old wine" some people prefer with his own "unfermented vintage."[116] The metaphor suits a new translation well enough, but would also suit any freshly written work in need of polishing. Both writers almost certainly derive it from the younger Pliny, who had characterized a draft copy of his own poems as an *adhuc museum librum*, inviting improvements.[117]

---

114. On Sidonius's Greek culture, Loyen 1943, 26–30; Courcelle 1969, 251–58.

115. Horsfall 1993, 322; R. Helm, *Die Chronik des Hieronymus* (Berlin 1956), 1–7.

116. *bibat vinum vetus cum suavitate, et nostra musta contemnat, Ep.* 112. 20.

117. Pliny, *Ep.* viii. 21. 6, with more positive connotations ("before it has lost its freshness," Radice); *TLL* viii. 1711. 81–84.

With Jerome's one appeal for indulgence on the grounds that he had had to work fast, contrast Sidonius's *six* references to haste. Here we may compare the one other passage in his correspondence where Sidonius describes himself making a copy for a friend (ix. 16. 2). Once again he emphasizes how fast he had worked: "I copied out hastily and under pressure" (*raptim coactimque...festinus exscripsi*). In conclusion he warns his friend not to expect "two entirely incompatible things, finish and speed" (*res omnino discrepantissimas, maturitatem celeritatemque*). Once again, six separate details implying speed prompted by his anxiety to fulfill a commission for a friend, in this case indisputably a copy.

As for *Opica, impolitum, semicrudum*, and *musteum*, all are metaphors for lack of polish. Exaggerated affectations of modesty are common enough in late antique writers, but even by Sidonius's standards this is excessive, implying that the text he sent Leo was *especially* clumsy and uncouth. If he had translated from the Greek he might have mis-understood a number of details, but even working in haste he would never have written clumsy, uncouth *Latin*.[118] And if (as sometimes supposed) he had simply transcribed an existing Latin translation by Nicomachus, such extravagant apologies would be even more out of place. However fast he worked, he would still have made the same sort of slips we all make when copying. Yet his extravagant language suggests the possibility of gross and elementary blunders, not routine miscopyings.

Of all these epithets, the most eloquent is *Opica. Opicus*, properly an ancient inhab-itant of Italy, implies "barbarous, rustic, uncivilized...with particular reference to *lack of knowledge of Greek*."[119] According to the elder Cato, Greeks insulted Romans by calling them barbarians and *Opici*.[120] The second-century grammarian Terentius Scaurus remarks that anyone who is not *Opicus* knows that Greek words beginning with *upsilon* are aspirated, whether or not they are spelled with initial *h* in Latin. Philodemus describes as *Opike* an Italian girl who cannot sing Sappho.[121] Gellius describes as *Opicus* someone who had missed the negative connotations of a Greek word; in another passage he equates *veteres Romani...rudes Graecae linguae* with *nostri Opici*, where Rolfe's transla-tion "rude forefathers" misses the specific implication of ignorance of Greek. Finally, two passages in the correspondence of Fronto: first, Fronto asking Marcus to check a letter he had written in Greek to Marcus's mother for solecisms (*barbarismus*), so that she would not look down on him as *Opicus*; then a letter from Marcus to Fronto claiming that he himself was "all but a breathing *Opicus*" because of his ignorance of Greek.[122]

---

118. That is to say, Latin beneath his own stylistic standards (it is irrelevant that a modern critic might judge Sidonius's usual style as uncouth).

119. E. Courtney on Juvenal iii. 207 (*Opici rodebant carmina mures*, i.e., mice with no understanding of literature); the scholia vetera comment "ὀπικίζειν *Graeci dicunt de iis qui imperite loquuntur*"; for more passages, A. Otto, *Die Sprichwörter der Römer* (Leipzig 1890), 256–57; Dubuisson 1983, 522–45; Swain 2004, 38–39.

120. Plin. *NH* xxix. 14, with Dubuisson 1983, 522–26.

121. Ter. Scaur. *GLK* vii. 23. 1; *Anth. Pal.* v. 132. 7; D. Sider, *The Epigrams of Philodemos* (Oxford 1997), 108.

122. Gell. xiii. 9. 4; Pliny, *NH* 29. 14; Fronto p. 21. 15 and 31. 6 van den Hout² = i. 124 and 142 Haines.

Sidonius refers to Fronto a number of times (not least in this very letter),[123] and in the context there can be little doubt that he deliberately selected this word in a pleasingly learned evocation of his anxiety about the correctness of his Greek.

The explanation of Sidonius's anxiety is inescapable: he copied Philostratus *in Greek*. Anyone who copies by hand a long work in a language of which he is not master knows that, over and above the routine transcriptional errors to which even the most expert and cultivated are prone, he is bound to make embarrassing elementary blunders (incorrect verbal forms, case-endings, genders, and the like) springing from ignorance—especially when the work being copied is written in different characters. However carefully he revised, a man whose Greek was shaky could not count on catching every slip in phonology or grammar. Whence the exaggerated emphasis on the excuse of haste. A man in a hurry does not have time to check every detail. By making the excuse he does, Sidonius hopes that all his errors will be put down to haste rather than ignorance, a haste that is unavoidable because Leo is so anxious to have the book without delay.

If Sidonius copied Philostratus in Greek, it follows that Nicomachus and Victorianus must have done the same. If his copy was (as he states) like Victorianus's rather than Nicomachus's, Victorianus's cannot have been in Latin. And it would be absurd to suppose that Victorianus translated Nicomachus's Latin version back into Greek. What then was the distinction Sidonius seems to be drawing between the copies of Nicomachus and Victorianus? On the standard view, Nicomachus translated, Victorianus revised, and Sidonius transcribed; according to Pricoco and Loyen, Nicomachus transcribed in Greek, Victorianus *abbreviated* Nicomachus's Greek text, and Sidonius *translated* this abbreviated text into Latin. That is to say, on both views Nicomachus, Victorianus, and Sidonius each did something different to the text of Philostratus. According to Mazzarino, Victorianus purged Nicomachus's translation of its more objectionably pagan features.[124]

Yet however reasonable in itself the hypothesis that Victorianus revised, edited, abridged, or even bowdlerized what Nicomachus wrote, it is difficult to see how any of these meanings can be extracted from Sidonius's actual words.[125] Here is the most problematic clause again: *non ut Nicomachus senior e Philostrati sed ut Tascius Victorianus e Nicomachi schedio exscripsit*. The opposition *non ut ... sed ut* implies an antithesis, but not a straightforward one (e.g., between original and translation): "not as Nicomachus <copied from the manuscript> of Philostratus but as Tascius Victorianus copied from

123. Set out in full in van den Hout's edition (pp. 272–73), together with a reference in Sidonius's friend Claudianus Mamertus.

124. Mazzarino 1974, 457 n. 148. In fact (as we shall see), there are no objectionably pagan features.

125. To be sure Philostratus's book cries out for abbreviation (C. P. Jones's abridged Penguin translation of 1970 gains rather than loses by omitting "unimportant digressions and ... overblown rhetoric"). Fictional works like the Lucianic *Ass* and perhaps the *Ephesiaka* of Xenophon of Ephesus were abridged, and it may be that Flavian had an abbreviated text of the *Life of Apollonius*. But nothing in Sidonius supports the idea.

the manuscript of Nicomachus." The apparent sharpness of the antithesis is at once blurred by the fact that Nicomachus appears in both halves; and Sidonius uses the same word *exscripsit* for the activity and the same word *schedium* for the books of both Nicomachus and Victorianus. The Mommsen interpretation requires that *exscripsit* should mean both translate and transcribe simultaneously, and Loyen/Pricoco that it should mean transcribe the first time and abbreviate the second. Yet the carefully wrought balance of the sentence surely requires that it should mean *exactly the same* both times: *whatever* Nicomachus did to Philostratus, Victorianus did to Nicomachus. Yet while Nicomachus might (in theory at least) have translated Philostratus, obviously Victorianus cannot have translated Nicomachus. On no hypothesis can *both* have translated. So if both did the same, it follows that both transcribed the original Greek.

The same objection applies to Traube's suggestion, revived by Pecere and Zetzel, that "all Victorianus did was to copy out for public circulation the unfinished draft of Nicomachus' translation."[126] Properly something produced extempore,[127] *schedium* is sometimes assimilated to *scheda*, which from ca. 400 is often found in the sense "draft," notably of a writer's rough draft awaiting final revision, as in a famous dispute between Jerome and Rufinus.[128] Once again, if Sidonius had written no more than *ut Tascius Victorianus e Nicomachi schedio exscripsit*, it might be a reasonable inference that Victorianus published an unfinished draft of the elder Flavian. As it is, *schedio exscripsit* has to do double duty for Nicomachus's activity as well, and we should have to identify Philostratus's original as a rough draft! In any case, Sidonius is clearly trying to distinguish two copies that might be confused, and no one would ever confuse the unpublished draft and published version of the same work. Sidonius uses *schedium* twice elsewhere, of a scrap of paper and a published book, respectively,[129] and we must surely take it here in the quite general sense "book."[130]

Where did Sidonius get the information that enabled him to draw this distinction that generations of scholars have found it so hard to pin down? Traube suggested that by his day the papers of the Symmachi had found their way to Gaul, where somehow Sidonius got hold of them. But the Symmachi remained leading lights in the social and intellectual life of Rome well into the sixth century, long after Sidonius's death. How could he have got hold of such documents? Much simpler to suppose that Victorianus was fulfilling another commission "for the Lords Symmachus." We know that Symmachus sent copies of Livy and Caesar to Protadius in Gaul, and the Livy subscriptions show that Victorianus was involved in correcting these copies. Another Gallic friend (perhaps Protadius again) had asked for the *VA*, and Victorianus duly

126. Traube 1909, 16; Zetzel 1980, 48 n. 32; cf. Pecere 1986, 60.
127. As σχεδιάζω, σχεδίασμα in Greek: *LSJ* and *OLD* s. vv.; Zetzel 1980, 48 n. 32.
128. Also of the original version of a document, complete with final corrections and duly signed and witnessed, as opposed to a copy. For *scheda*, Tengström 1962, 35–49; Rizzo 1973, 305–6.
129. *si quod schedium temere iacens* (ix. 16. 2); *declamationum tuarum schedio* (*Ep.* 9. 7. 1).
130. For examples, Arns 1954, 21–22.

sent a copy. This would explain how a text bearing the names of Victorianus and one of the Nicomachi found its way to Gaul.

It was Mommsen who came closest to the truth when he cited the parallel of the Livy subscriptions. The explanation is surely that Sidonius's exemplar was *subscribed* with the names of both Flavian and Victorianus.[131] I suggest that, when he originally told Leo about his precious copy of Philostratus, Sidonius mistakenly claimed, on the basis of a hasty reading of its subscription, that he owned the very copy subscribed by the elder Flavian. On closer inspection he discovered his mistake, and explained that it was not after all Flavian's own copy but the next best thing, a copy made from it by Victorianus (a scholar known to have been patronized by the Symmachi and Nicomachi). Victorianus had no doubt subscribed his text with some such formula as *emendavi ego Tascius Victorianus de codice Nicomachi Flaviani senioris*. When Mommsen suggested that Victorianus "revised" Nicomachus, all he had in mind was the *emendavi* or *recognovi* of a corrector checking his copy against its exemplar.[132] This would explain the care Sidonius took to distinguish between two copies that, seen as texts of Philostratus, were to all intents and purposes identical. The only difference between them[133] was the fact that the first (which Sidonius never saw) was subscribed in the hand of the elder Flavian; the second (the exemplar from which Sidonius made his copy) was Victorianus's copy of the first.

Various objections have been raised to the notion that Nicomachus transcribed the original Greek. Pecere found it "hard to believe that the name of this man, well known for his literary no less than his political activity, would be recorded merely for having made a copy in the original Greek." According to Horsfall, "The likes of Nicomachus, Tascius and Sidonius did not make copies (and certainly did not boast of it if they had to)." Consequently, the idea "that Nicomachus, Tascius and Sidonius solemnly copied, one after the other, 350-odd Teubner pages of Greek is clearly absurd."[134] But there is no need to suppose that either Nicomachus or Victorianus actually copied the *text* in person. That was done by professionals. All they did, no doubt assisted by professionals, was check and then subscribe their copies in the way illustrated in the last three chapters. The case of Sidonius is entirely different. In the ordinary way he too relied on professionals, but he spent the year or more (475–77) in which he copied Philostratus imprisoned by Euric the Goth in the fortress of Liviana.[135] This was a difficult and depressing period for Sidonius, and Anderson plausibly suggested that it was "to give him a task which would take his mind off his troubles" that Leo, a loyal friend at Euric's court, asked him to make this copy.[136]

---

131. So too Pecere 1986, 60.
132. His exact words were *Significatur opinor Nicomachi senioris cura Philostrati Graeca latine versa esse, Victorianum eam versionem recognovisse* (Luetjohann's *Sidonius*, p. 420).
133. Not counting the transcriptional errors that are inevitable in even the most careful copy.
134. Pecere 1986, 232 n. 230; Horsfall 1993, 322.
135. Stevens 1933, 162–63; Harries 1994, 175–76, 238–39.
136. Anderson, *Sidonius* 1 (1936), xlix.

There is no reason to believe that Flavian edited, translated, or even copied a Greek text of the *VA*. But he owned a copy, which Victorianus copied and subscribed, probably for a Gallic friend, which would explain how it eventually came into Sidonius's hands. Sidonius made his own copy of this text. On this evidence, there never was a Latin translation of the *Life of Apollonius*.

6: APOLLONIUS OF TYANA

Previous discussions of the reputation of Apollonius in the West have been dominated by Alföldi's thesis about the contorniates (Ch. 19. 1). Alföldi himself considered the appearance of Apollonius among the "culture heroes" represented on contorniates the clearest single illustration of his thesis. If the contorniates were pagan propaganda, then Apollonius was a pagan symbol. There are six contorniate obverses bearing the head of Apollonius, two backed by the legend *Diva Faustina Aug(usta)*, the other four by charioteers. Despite these innocuous reverses, Alföldi had no doubt that Apollonius owed his place on the obverse to his status as a pagan symbol, and he interpreted all contemporary references to Apollonius in this light.[137]

With the lapse of his thesis, the case must be made on the basis of the literary texts alone. Until Philostratus wrote his biography ca. 220, knowledge of this "minor mystic from a remote city in Cappadocia"[138] was confined to the few Greek cities he had visited: Aegaeae, Antioch, Ephesus, Tarsus, and (of course) his native Tyana.[139] It was Philostratus who turned him into a major holy man, and it was two more Greek writers, Porphyry and Hierocles, building on Philostratus, who turned him into a rival to Christ. As Eusebius put it, "Hierocles, of all the writers who have ever attacked us, stands alone in selecting Apollonius, as he has recently done, for the purposes of comparison and contrast with our Savior."[140]

In some circles in the Greek-speaking East, Apollonius became a pagan symbol, rejected and ridiculed by Christians, and correspondingly admired by pagans like Eunapius. In the Latin-speaking West the situation is more complicated than Alföldi and his followers assumed. There is virtually no evidence that western pagans treated Apollonius as a pagan symbol, nor did Philostratus's book play any part in the debate, such as it was. Inevitably, the fact that there was (as we now know) no Latin translation meant that Greekless westerners were simply unable to read it. But that is not the only or even the principal reason.

---

137. Alföldi and Alföldi 1976, 32; two more added in 1990, 102–3.
138. Bowersock in Jones and Bowersock 1970, 9.
139. Dzielska 1986, Ch. 2; Jones 1980, 190–94.
140. *Contra Hieroclem* 1. Evidently, Celsus, who also accused Jesus of being a common sorcerer but wrote before Philostratus, had *not* cited the parallel of Apollonius. It might also seem that Eusebius had not yet read Porphyry, who undoubtedly made the same comparison (so Barnes, *HSCP* 80 [1976], 241). This would have a bearing on the date, if Eusebius of Caesarea is the author, since at some point he certainly did read Porphyry.

The truth is that the *VA* is not *in itself* an anti-Christian book, and even after Hierocles and Porphyry it was not universally read as such. It is a complex work, which modern critics have found hard to classify, though they are more likely to discuss it in books on ancient fiction than books on ancient religion.[141] The frequent digressions on every conceivable subject are reminiscent of the *Leucippe and Clitophon* of Achilles Tatius. Indeed, it shares a great many features with both the novels of the age (except for their love interest, Apollonius being a celibate) and the *Alexander Romance* (Apollonius visits many of the same places as Alexander, and, like him, debates with the Brahmins or "naked philosophers" of India). It seems to have been Apollonius's travels that readers enjoyed most, even Christians: "travel along with our man from Tyana [said Sidonius], now to the Caucasus or the Indus, now to the gymnosophists of Ethiopia and the Brahmins of India." So too Jerome (quoted below), and the only reference to the *VA* in a late antique scholiast, Lactantius Placidus on Statius's reference to Dionysus visiting the Ganges: "first visitor Dionysus, second Alexander, third Apollonius."[142] Religion plays a relatively minor role—and not the one we might have expected. Wherever he goes Apollonius criticizes local cult practices.[143] He attacks gladiatorial games, chariot-racing, public baths, luxury in every form and, above all, blood sacrifice. As he proclaims in his trial before Domitian: "I would do anything to save my fellow-men, but I have never made a sacrifice for them, nor would I do so. I would never touch offerings in which there was any blood, or pray with my eyes on a knife or on the kind of sacrifice my accuser alleges."[144]

To be sure he is represented as a healer, but Philostratus is careful not to exaggerate his magical powers. The people of Tyana believed he was the son of Zeus, but Apollonius (adds Philostratus) "called himself the son of Apollonius." His first act of healing is given a thoroughly rationalizing explanation; he told a dropsical youth to cut down on his rich diet and drinking. And when he raised a woman from the dead, it is suggested that he "may have seen a spark of life in her which her doctors had not noticed, since apparently the sky was drizzling and steam was coming from her face."[145] First and foremost he is a philosopher who disavows supernatural powers and repeatedly rebuts the accusation that he is a magician. So far from this being the sort of stuff to rally pagans, much of it would have seemed exemplary even to Christian readers.

This is certainly how Sidonius read the book he spent so many weeks laboriously transcribing for his Christian friend Leo:

---

141. Bowie in Morgan and Stoneman 1994, 181–99; Schirren 2005; Dall'Astra 2008; Bowie and Elsner 2009; Demoen and Praet 2009.

142. Sid. *Ep.* viii. 3. 4; Stat. *Theb.* iv. 387; Lact. Plac. p. 281 Sweeney.

143. iv. 19; v. 12; vi. 41; viii. 7. 10.

144. iv. 22; v. 26; i. 16; on sacrifice (e.g.) i. 11; iv. 11; iv. 19; v. 12; vi. 41; viii. 7. 10 (quoted above, trans. Jones). Apoll. *Ep.* 27 also attacks blood sacrifice. Whether or not the letter is authentic, it is obviously significant that Philostratus chose to emphasize this aspect of the tradition.

145. *VA* i. 6; i. 9; iv. 45 (trans. Jones, Loeb 2005).

Read of a man who—be it said with all due deference to the Catholic faith—was in most respects like you, that is, sought after by the rich but not seeking riches for himself; greedy for knowledge but chary of money-making; abstemious in feasts, clad in plain linen among the purple-robed, severe as a censor amid luxurious perfumes.

For Sidonius, the *VA* was an unsurpassed evocation of "the philosopher's life."

According to Dzielska, who took the existence of Flavian's Latin translation for granted, references to Apollonius become common in Latin sources by the last decades of the fourth century.[146] Setting the Sidonius passage on one side for the moment, I can find eight fourth- or early fifth-century Latin writers who show some knowledge of Apollonius: Lactantius, Ammianus, Jerome, Augustine, Augustine's friend Marcellinus, Ps-Ambrose, Lactantius Placidus, and the author of the *HA*. We should note straightaway that at least five of the eight were Christians; and five could have read Philostratus in Greek: Lactantius, Jerome, Ammianus, Lactantius Placidus, and the author of the *HA* (Ch. 20. 10).

That leaves only Augustine, Marcellinus, and Ps-Ambrose probably incapable of reading the *VA* in Greek. But there is no reason to believe that more than four of the eight actually read Philostratus at all. Marcellinus wrote to Augustine for guidance on pagan claims about the miracles of Apuleius and Apollonius. Augustine's two references also link the miracles of Apuleius and Apollonius.[147] Jerome too links the miracles of Apuleius and Apollonius, directly citing Porphyry in the context.[148] But Philostratus himself did not compare Apollonius and Christ, nor (of course) did he mention the Latin writer Apuleius. It was not in Philostratus that any of them found these claims, but, via a Latin intermediary, in Porphyry or Hierocles. One obvious intermediary known to most of them is Lactantius, who expressed surprise that Hierocles did not link Apuleius and Apollonius.[149] There were also anonymous Latin collections of pagan objections to Christianity. An African priest called Deogratias sent Augustine a series of six such objections, deriving ultimately from Porphyry, and it is in Augustine's response that we find one of his references to Apollonius and Apuleius.[150] Ps-Ambrose refers to Apollonius's supposedly miraculous disappearance when on trial before Domitian. But he did not get the story from Philostratus either. Verbal parallels prove that he simply copied it from Jerome, who had got it in turn from Lactantius.[151] Nor did even Lactantius get it from Philostratus. While Eusebius's

146. Dzielska 1986, 172.
147. Aug. *Ep.* 136. 1 (from Marcellinus), 102. 6. 32 (to Deogratias), and 138. 4. 18 (to Marcellinus).
148. Jer. *Tract. de Psalm.* 81 = *PL* 26. 1130.
149. Lact. *Div. Inst.* 5. 3.
150. *Ep.* 102 (to Deogratias); cf. *Retract.* ii. 31; Courcelle 1969, 210–11.
151. Ps-Ambrose, *De Trin.* 29 = *PL* 17. 570B, or 540D in the 1985 reprint (*cum ante Domitianum imperatorem staret in consistorio, repente non comparuisset*) ~ Jerome, *Contra Joh. Hier.* 34 = *PL* 23. 404C (*cum ante Domitianum staret in consistorio, repente non comparuisse*) ~ Lact. *Div. Inst.* 5. 3 (*cum Domitianus eum punire vellet, repente in iudicio non comparuit*). It is plain that Ps-Ambrose drew on Jerome rather than Lactantius.

detailed refutation goes through the *VA* methodically book by book, there was no need for Lactantius to read Philostratus as well as Hierocles for his single chapter.[152]

So of the five western Christians who mention pagan claims about Apollonius, every one (it seems) got his information from a Latin summary of Hierocles or Porphyry rather than Philostratus. In some cases from a summary that already included a refutation, such as Lactantius, or Augustine's letter to Deogratias. Of the eight westerners who show any knowledge of Apollonius, only four give any indication of having read the *VA* itself: Ammianus, Jerome, Lactantius Placidus, and the author of the *HA*. Given the fact that there was no Latin translation, it is obviously significant that all four knew Greek.

Ammianus's two references carry no significant pagan charge. One describes a well sacred to Zeus Asbamaios near Tyana that he seems actually to have visited in person.[153] The second is a list of great men who had a close relationship with their guardian spirits (*genii*). A list that included the elder Scipio, Marius, and Augustus as well as Pythagoras, Socrates, and Apollonius[154] could hardly be said to have a specifically pagan purpose.

A letter of Jerome to Paulinus of Nola is particularly instructive. Though appropriately indignant at pagan comparisons of Apollonius and Christ, Jerome nonetheless found nothing bad to say about the *VA* itself. In the course of a discussion of wandering sages that begins with Pythagoras and ends with Paul, he gives a remarkably favorable summary of the biography as a whole:[155]

> Apollonius the magician (as he is popularly known) or philosopher (as the Pythagoreans call him) was also a traveller. He entered Persia, traversed the Caucasus. . . . Then returning to Alexandria, he made his way to Ethiopia to see the gymnosophists and the famous table of the sun spread in the sands of the desert. Everywhere he found something to learn, and as he was going to new places, he became constantly wiser and better. Philostratus has written his story in eight books.

Like Sidonius, Jerome was willing to call him a philosopher. Augustine too, while naturally rejecting the comparison with Christ, nonetheless conceded that Apollonius was "better than the perpetrator of all those outrages whom they call Jupiter," that is to say, a better moral exemplar.[156] A western pilgrim who traveled from Bordeaux to the Holy Land in 333 went out of his way to take in Tyana, "where Apollonius the *magus* came from."[157] Five lines later he mentions Tarsus, "where the Apostle Paul

---

152. For the limited range of Greek texts known to Lactantius at firsthand, Ogilvie 1978, 19–38.
153. Amm. xxiii. 6. 19; it is mentioned at *VA* i. 6.
154. Amm. xxi. 14. 3–5; R. L. Rike, *Apex Omnium* (1987), 20–23.
155. *Ep.* 53. 1, with the qualifications in Adkin 2000, 70–72); the citation of Philostratus was deleted as a gloss by Hillberg, initiating a long debate on the question (Adkin 75–78).
156. *Ep.* 138. 18 (to Marcellinus).
157. *Itinerarium Burdigalense* 578 (*CC* 175, 1965), with M. Fuhrmann in Herzog and Schmidt 5, § 517.

came from." Even in the Greek East, while Byzantine churchmen denounced the comparison with Christ, the *VA* continued to find enthusiastic readers. Photius devoted twenty-six columns of his *Bibliotheca* to the *VA*. Though dismissing the miracles, he evidently found the rest of the book entertaining and enjoyable, quoting page after page of "beautiful phrases." A depaganized Apollonius plays a major role in the mythology of medieval Constantinople; late texts represent him advising Constantine on the foundation of the city and even prophesying the birth of Christ.[158]

7: THE *HISTORIA AUGUSTA*

That leaves only two references in the *HA*, both regularly proclaimed pagan propaganda. First the claim that Alexander Severus had a private chapel in which he kept statues of "Apollonius and, according to a contemporary writer, Christ, Abraham, Orpheus and others of this sort." Given the very small proportion of fact in this life (a fiftieth, according to one estimate),[159] this is unlikely to be true. Yet I cannot see any real grounds for detecting the bitterness of a writer who regrets that paganism has lost its monopoly,[160] much less for seeing the passage as characteristic of the Theodosian age.[161] Enthusiasm for the sage of Tyana would be perfectly natural in the grand-nephew of Julia Domna, who had inspired Philostratus to write the *VA*.[162] The Christian author of the so-called Tübingen *Theosophia* quotes with approval a presumably third-century Hermetic oracle claiming Hermes, Apollonius, and Moses as the only mortals who have drawn near to God.[163]

More important is a passage in the *Life of Aurelian*, always a favorite with those looking for pagan propaganda. Section 24 describes how, when Aurelian was laying siege to Tyana in 272, Apollonius appeared to him in a vision and urged him to spare the inhabitants. Alföldi went so far as to claim that Aurelian's vision of Apollonius was intended to offer a pagan counterpart to Constantine's vision before the Battle of the Milvian Bridge. In the climate of fantasy and credulity that has enveloped current *HA* studies, it should come as no surprise that this extraordinary suggestion has been recently restated and even embellished.[164] But the incident is simply too trivial to bear the weight of such a comparison. While the writer may have exaggerated the significance of Apollonius, it cannot be said that he dragged him into his narrative. He picked the one moment in the entire period covered by the *HA* when a Roman emperor went

158. Photius, *Bibl.* cod. 44 and 241; W. Speyer, *JbAC* 17 (1974), 62–63; Dzielska 1986, 125–27; and especially Dagron 1984, 102–15; Potter 1994, 32–35; Jones 2006, 49–64.
159. Barnes 1978, 57.
160. Chastagnol 1994, cxlv; "an argument of pagan polemists," Syme 1968, 138; and many others.
161. E. Alföldi-Rosenbaum, *Pro Arte Antiqua: Festschrift H. Kenner* (1982), 11.
162. *VA* i. 3; Dzielska 1986, 188–92.
163. W. Scott, *Hermetica* 4 (1936), 228–29; H. Erbse, *Theosophorum Graecorum Fragmenta* (1995), 29.
164. Alföldi and Alföldi 1990, 54; Chastagnol 1994, cxlii; Brandt 1995, 107–17.

to Tyana. The siege of Tyana was no watershed confrontation for Aurelian. According to the writer's own narrative Aurelian had already taken the city by treachery when Apollonius appeared. Nor does he claim any significant change in Aurelian's religious beliefs or policies afterwards. Where Constantine's vision had affected the whole empire, Aurelian's was confined to Tyana, nothing more than the story of a local hero protecting his birthplace. The vision of Apollonius is also somewhat undermined by the silly claim that he spoke to Aurelian in Latin (24. 3)![165]

After praising Apollonius's holiness and claiming that he brought the dead back to life and did things beyond the power of man, the *HA* writer mentions "Greek books written about his life," and announces his own intention to write about "the deeds of this great man" (24. 3–9), presumably in Latin. A few chapters later in another context he quotes an undoubtedly fictitious Nicomachus as having translated a letter of Queen Zenobia from Syriac into Greek (27. 6). According to most modern scholars, we are meant to combine a projected *Latin* biography of Apollonius by the writer and a *Greek* translation of a letter of Zenobia by this Nicomachus into a cryptic allusion to a Latin translation of Philostratus by Nicomachus Flavianus a century later! But why so convoluted and indirect an allusion? As usual, Alföldi explained the indirectness by postulating fear of Christian reprisals. But even on that dubious postulate, what was to stop the writer saying (e.g.), in keeping with his purported early fourth-century date, "if only someone would translate Philostratus's excellent biography into Latin?" And now we know that Flavian did not translate Philostratus at all, this whole tenuous fantasy loses its raison d'être.

But true believers are reluctant to let it go. While conceding that Sidonius's *exscripsit* does not provide the necessary support for the supposed Latin translation, some insist on the importance of the fact that Flavian "concerned himself" in some way with Philostratus's book.[166] According to Zecchini, we are still entitled to infer that he took a keen interest in spreading Apollonius's "religious message," by preparing a carefully revised Greek text for some other pagan activist to translate.[167] But insofar as Apollonius had a "religious message," he agreed with Christianity in seeking to stop blood sacrifice. The very idea of an aristocrat preparing a critical edition of a Greek text in late fourth-century Rome is incredible, and Flavian was no philologist. All we know for certain is that he owned a copy of Philostratus. Naturally, the fact that he read the *VA* remains significant of his pagan sympathies, and the fact that he read it in Greek is a valuable index of his culture. But he can no longer be seen as doing anything to popularize the figure of a pagan counterpart to Christ for Greekless western readers.

---

165. Against this fantasy, see now J. Long in Drake 2006, 231–33.

166. So, for example, Paschoud 1996, 143; Speyer 1974, 53 ("beschäftigen sich mit dem Text"). After sensibly conceding that he did not translate the *Life of Apollonius* into Latin, Paschoud brought Flavian in through the back door by deriving this part of the *Life of Aurelian* from Flavian's *Annales*! Even if this phantom covered this period, it is unlikely in the extreme that a Roman aristocrat not known to have visited the East gave so full an account of the siege of this remote Cappadocian city.

167. Zecchini 1993, 44–45.

8: ALEXANDER LITERATURE

If the *VA* had been translated into Latin, it might well have won more readers, like
(e.g.) the *Alexander Romance*, translated by Julius Valerius. The now lost codex
Taurinensis adds the names Alexander Polemius, who is often identified with Polemius
cos. 338.[168] Valerius is also often identified with the anonymous author of the *Itinerarium
Alexandri*, a more rhetorical account of Alexander's invasion of Persia addressed to
and designed to inspire and guide Constantius II when he was planning to do the
same ca. 340[169] (its now missing conclusion reinforced the point by adding an
account of Trajan's Parthian War).[170] Whether or not Valerius wrote the *Itinerarium*,
according to a lost codex owned by Salmasius, his translation of the *Alexander Romance*
was also dedicated to Constantius.[171] From the same general period we have the
more mundane *Epitoma rerum gestarum Alexandri* and *Liber de morte Alexandri*
(the latter another translation), anonymous, but almost certainly both by the same
author.[172] In a detailed study of late antique Latin Alexander literature, Cracco Ruggini
has emphasized the paganism of all these texts, an approach taken for granted in the
new book by Richard Stoneman, who writes of Alexander becoming "a kind of symbol
for the 'pagan revival' of the fourth century."[173] Cracco Ruggini identified the *Epitoma*
and *Liber de morte* with cultivated rather than popular taste, and went so far as to
associate them with the "circle of the Symmachi and Nicomachi."

But the arguments are desperately weak: Flavian's supposed historical interests
(Ch. 17–18); the parallel of his supposed Latin translation of the *VA*, a work that shares
a number of features with the *Alexander Romance*; and the popularity of Alexander on
the contorniates. Though expressing reservations about Alföldi's thesis (Ch. 19. 1),
Cracco Ruggini was in no doubt about their basically "pagan" character. Yet the most
that can be said for the notion of Alexander as a pagan symbol is that Alexander amulets are known to have been popular good luck charms.[174] It is hardly surprising that
portraits of the most successful man who ever lived[175] were thought to bring good
luck, especially in the context of the games, where luck is so important. J. C. Christiansen
has recently published a coin bearing the image of Alexander incised with a
Christogram. "The addition of this symbol to the coin," suggests Sande, "is probably

---

168. Lane Fox 1997, 240–47; against, Schmidt in Herzog and Schmidt 5, § 540. 1, on the grounds that the
     consul's name, according to consular papyri, was Fl. Polemius. But Flavius is more a title than a name:
     Cameron 1988.
169. For the date, Barnes, *JRS* 75 (1985), 135.
170. See now R. Tabacco, *Itinerarium Alexandri* (2000).
171. Schmidt § 540, T.1; Reeve, *Riv. Fil.* 123 (1995), 370; Lane Fox 1997, 242; questioned by Tabacco 2000,
     xiii–xv.
172. As argued most recently by Baynham 1995, 60–77.
173. Cracco Ruggini 1961 (esp. 350–56); and 1965 (esp. 8–13); Stoneman 2008, 200, with more detail in
     Hofmann 1999, 174–83. See too Callu 2006, 565–82.
174. As described in *HA XXX Tyr.* 14. 3–6.
175. On the role played by fortune in Alexander's career, Tarn, *Alexander the Great* 2 (1948), 64–65, 95, 99.

not an attempt to 'Christianize' a pagan amulet, but rather a wish to add a powerful symbol to the already powerful image of Alexander."[176] And before too much is made of John Chrysostom's condemnation of those who "tie bronze coins of Alexander of Macedon around their heads and feet," it should be borne in mind that it is Christian members of his congregation he has in mind, not pagans. Christians long continued to wear Alexander-amulets.[177] All the Alexander contorniates do is illustrate in a very general way the popularity of Alexander in late fourth-century Rome.

Two of the Alexander texts are translations of much earlier Greek texts, and the other two follow earlier sources fairly closely (the *Epitoma* Curtius Rufus, the *Itinerarium* Arrian). Their contemporary pagan content is close to zero. The fact that they reproduce one or two cult references in their sources is not enough even to prove the writers pagans, nor would it have deterred Christian readers (we have seen how popular Livy was with Christian readers). One phrase in the preface to the *Itinerarium* suggests a pagan author, but since the preface addresses Constantius II, evidently a pagan hoping for favor at a Christian court in the East rather than the salons of Rome. The fact that Flavian wrote (if he did) on Roman history need not imply that he took any interest in Hellenistic history. And (of course) the famed translation of the *VA* never existed. The only aristocrat of the age whose work we can examine is Symmachus himself. He never mentions Apollonius and shows no sign of familiarity with either the *VA* or any of this Alexander literature. He refers to Alexander four times, always as a rhetorical exemplum, at least twice drawing his information from Cicero.[178]

Weakest of all is the argument that the classicizing diction of these works supports the notion that they were aimed at pagan nobles. The truth is that the Latin Alexander Romance is written in a clumsy mixture of archaisms and neologisms.[179] It is difficult to believe that Symmachus would have shared Valerius's enthusiasm for initial *enim*. And while the *Epitoma* and *Liber de morte* are more consistently archaizing (and closer to history than romance), they are still pretty feeble products. Symmachus would have been scandalized at their sheer lack of style, above all their monotonous sentence structure (six sentences in the first three pages of the *Epitoma* beginning with *deinde*; *id ubi X audivit* or *vidit* four times in sixteen lines).

More intriguing is the *Collatio Alexandri et Dindimi*, an imaginary exchange of letters between Alexander and Dindimus, the king of the Brahmans.[180] Dindimus's letters proclaim that the Brahmans are ascetics, and attack the pagans' gods and the sacrifices made at their temples. Since he specifically mentions shows and baths, it is obviously pagan Rome rather than fourth-century Macedon he has in mind. If we had

---

176. Sande 1999, 230.
177. Chrys. *De illum. cat.* ii. 5 (*PG.* 49. 240); Maguire 1995, 4.
178. Symm. *Ep.* i. 20; ix. 72; *Or.* iii. 6, 7, 10; Kroll 1891, 10, 15.
179. For Valerius's language and style, Romano 1974, 65–87; the many borrowings from the Republican poets and Apuleius reveal him still a child of the archaizing movement.
180. For an English translation, Stoneman 1994, 57–66; on the historiography of Alexander and the Brahmans, Stoneman 1994; 1995.

only Dindimus's contribution, few would doubt that the author was a Christian. But Alexander attacks the Brahmans' asceticism, and since he is given the last word, many have concluded that the author rejected Dindimus's polemic. But his arguments against asceticism are distinctly frivolous (Brahman women were unattractive and so did not arouse their men), nor is there any response to the attacks on the gods and sacrifice. It is not easy to find any serious purpose in either direction.

Some details about the topography of Alexandria added to his Greek source have been thought to suggest that Valerius was an Alexandrian,[181] and if he dedicated his translation to Constantius II, then he too may have written for the eastern court, not Roman senators. If so, then the revival of interest in Alexander would have a much simpler explanation, nothing to do with pagan symbols: Constantius's determination to check the aggression of a resurgent Persia. In much the same way Festus's *Breviarium* (dedicated to Valens), two-thirds of which is devoted to the eastern provinces of the empire, was clearly written with a view to Valens's projected Persian expedition of 370.[182] Polyaenus's collection of strategems purports to have been written to help Marcus and Verus during their Persian expedition of 162–66. Polyaenus makes the most of his own Macedonian heritage and devotes one whole book (iv) to the strategems of Alexander and other Macedonian generals.[183] Like Festus and the *Itinerarium*, the *Epitoma* and *Liber de morte* were also surely written to instruct ignorant eastern courtiers rather than amuse idle Roman aristocrats, whether under Constantius again, or possibly Julian (Julian's enthusiasm for Alexander was notorious).[184]

More relevant in this context, Liénard drew attention to an interesting parallel between the *Collatio* and an early letter of Symmachus.[185] "They say," Symmachus wrote to Ausonius, "that men's minds shine under a clear sky but fall apart when clouds gather." According to the *Collatio*, "Men's minds...shine under a clear sky, but fall apart when clouds gather."[186] The sentiment is proverbial, but the verbal parallel so close as to suggest that one writer is directly quoting the other. So did Symmachus know the *Collatio*? Steinmann has recently drawn attention to another parallel with Symmachus.[187] With Dindimus's claim that he has no eloquence to draw on in replying to Alexander (*nec mihi ullum suppetit uber eloquii*), compare Symmachus: *tantum tibi suppetit uber eloquii.*[188]

---

181. Romano 1974, 11–17; Callu 2006, 563–64; for some doubts, Lane Fox 1997, 243.
182. Lenski 2002, 188.
183. Hammond 1996, 23–53. There may well be a connection between Arrian's history of Alexander and Trajan's Parthian War (which he also wrote about); F. A. Lepper, *Trajan's Parthian War* (Oxford 1948), 132, 195–98.
184. So Schmidt in Herzog and Schmidt 5, § 541. 1; for Julian and Alexander, Lane Fox 1997, 247–52.
185. Liénard 1936, 833.
186. *Non frustra praedicant mentes hominum* **nitere liquido die, coacta nube fatiscere** (Symm. *Ep.* i. 37. 1) ~ *animorum quin etiam species cum caeli mutatione vertuntur, et* **liquido quidem die nitent, coacta vero nube fatiscunt** (*Coll.* 5. 5). *fatiscere* has been restored in Symmachus on the basis of *Coll.* (see Callu ad loc.).
187. Steinmann 2000, 24; for a less striking parallel, cf. *rumorum licentia*(*m*) in *Coll.* 1. 1 and Symm. *Ep.* vi. 65. 1.
188. Symm. *Ep.* iii. 22. 1 ~ *Coll.* 2. 1.

The combination of the striking phrase *uber eloquii* ("udder of eloquence") with the same verb *suppetit* makes it hard to doubt direct influence one way or the other. Yet who will believe that the sophisticated Symmachus copied entire phrases unaltered from so trivial a pamphlet, while the *Collatio* is positively stuffed with crude borrowings from the classics, both prose and (especially) verse.[189] Take its opening words: *saepius ad aures meas fando pervenit*, reproducing almost unaltered Vergil's *fando … tuas pervenit ad aures* (*Aen.* ii. 81). The explanation is surely that the author of the *Collatio* was copying Symmachus, a popular stylistic model down into the sixth century.[190] The only other occurrences of the collocation *uber eloquii* appear to be in Ennodius, who undoubtedly knew and frequently imitated Symmachus.[191] Note too that *suppetit* = "be available" is something of an affectation of Symmachus (another twenty-four examples); and that he uses the same uncommon verb *fatiscit* again in an earlier letter in the same book (i. 10), literally this time, of one of his villas falling apart. If Symmachus was the source rather than the borrower, then the *Collatio* belongs (at earliest) in the fifth rather than fourth century.

There is in fact only one other translation from the Greek that we can link to a Roman aristocrat. A certain L. Septimius dedicated his translation of the journal of Dictys of Crete to Q. Aradius Rufinus. This work purports to be the memoirs of Diomedes's squire at Troy, found in his grave on Crete when it was struck by lightning during the reign of Nero. This need not mean that Rufinus himself was an aficionado of mythological fiction—or even that he read further than the dedication. But it does at least place Septimius in Rome. When, and which Rufinus? The usual identification, on no solid grounds, is Aradius Rufinus (no praenomen recorded) cos. 311. On no better grounds Syme proposed Aradius Rufinus prefect of Rome in 376,[192] a perfect illustration of the way a literary revival under the auspices of the late fourth-century aristocracy is manufactured. The family is securely attested from the early third century on, and a tenth-century library catalogue from Bobbio identifies the author as Septimius Serenus the mid-third-century poet, author of a book titled *Ruralia*.[193] This could be a guess, but it is not good method to disregard the only piece of actual evidence we have, especially when it fits the manuscript evidence. As I read that evidence, the dedicatory letter is headed *L. Septimius Q. Aradio salutem*, with Rufinus appearing only in an apostrophe (*Rufine mi*) in the body of the text. Not only does the carefully wrought balance explain the omission of the Serenus; the fact that both are given a praenomen points to the third rather than the fourth century, by when the praenomen had largely fallen out of use.[194]

---

189. See the *loci similes* quoted beneath the text in Steinmann's edition (not all persuasive). The extent of the writer's debt to the Latin classics makes it unlikely (as often assumed) that he too is translating a Greek text.

190. Polara 1972, 3–16.

191. *Ep.* i. 16. 2 (p. 24. 17 Vogel); *Carm.* i. 7, pr. (p. 27. 17 V); for other Symmachan echoes, Vogel's index, p. 332.

192. Chastagnol 1962, 62; *PLRE* i Rufinus 10; Syme 1968, 128 ("why not to the time of Theodosius?").

193. Cameron 1980, 172–75; Courtney 1993, 407; Champlin 1981.

194. The Symmachi were one of the very few exceptions: Cameron 1999, 485–88.

The heavily Sallustian style also points to the third rather than late fourth century, by when the archaizing movement was largely spent.

9: OTHER TRANSLATIONS

As for the few other pagan translations of the age, Ausonius translated nearly fifty epigrams from the Greek, and the various poets (among them Naucellius) whose work is collected in the *Epigrammata Bobiensia* (*EB*) more than forty (p. 374). Ten epigrams are translated in both collections, but differently. In addition, both Ausonius and the poets of the *EB* draw on exactly the same range of earlier collections, Meleager, Philip, Diogenian, Rufinus, and even the early fourth-century Palladas. It seems unlikely that they all drew on all these collections independently at firsthand, and selected so many of the same epigrams to translate independently. The probability is that both drew on a probably mid-fourth-century omnibus anthology based on all these earlier collections.[195] As so often at this period, an abridgment, though in this case an abridgment that at any rate offered the complete text of the epigrams it included.[196]

Both sets of translations include a handful of erotic epigrams, but demonstrate a clear preference for epideictic and ecphrastic poetry. This no doubt reflected the bias of the new anthology, itself a consequence of the fourth-century Greek revival of classicizing epigram, with its most notable practitioners the pagan Palladas and the Christian Gregory Nazianzen. This unexpected vogue for Hellenistic epigram in the West was predictably short-lived. It is natural to infer that the Italian poets were inspired by Ausonius's example. Both Ausonius and Naucellius were friends of Symmachus, but there is no sign that Symmachus himself was interested. It is true that a letter to Ausonius mentions Myron's cow, perhaps the most popular of all epigrammatic themes, treated four times in the *EB* and eight or nine times by Ausonius.[197] But in Symmachus, Myron's cow is just one in a list of famous Greek statues taken from Cicero's *Verrines*.[198] If he had known Ausonius's sequence on the theme, he would surely have treated it very differently in a letter to Ausonius himself. It might be added that no secular genre was more easily adapted to Christian themes than ecphrastic epigram, as Gregory's illustrate. We now know that Naucellius, like Ausonius, was a Christian (p. 375), as was the only other identifiable contributor to the *EB*, Anicius Probinus cos. 395.

Naucellius also translated a historical work of some sort. The text is unfortunately corrupt at the crucial point, but the most plausible guess is that the original was an

---

195. For the identification of this fourth-century anthology, Cameron 1993, 78–96; Wilkinson 2009 plausibly dates it earlier than I did, on the basis of an earlier date for Palladas.
196. But the absence of ascriptions in both Ausonius and the *EB* suggests that individual authors' names (as often in such anthologies) were not included.
197. R. Green 1991, 404–5; *EB* 10–13.
198. *Verr.* 4. 5; 135. In Symmachus's day Myron's statue was actually in Rome: Gow and Page, *Hellenistic Epigrams* (1965), 63–64.

abridged version of the Aristotelian *Constitutions* of the various Greek states. A wide-ranging study by Callu has attempted to fit Naucellius's project into a revival of interest in the Aristotelian *Constitutions* in the fourth-century Greek world, and also to link it to Ausonius's translation of the *Peplos* dubiously ascribed to Aristotle.[199] But this supposed revival is no more than a hypothesis, nor do either Ausonius or Naucellius seem to have had any idea that the works they translated had any connection with Aristotle. All Ausonius translated was a series of elegiac distichs on Homeric heroes that he says he came across "in a certain scholar," probably referring to the *Homeric Researches* of Porphyry, whom he was no doubt reluctant to name.[200] All Symmachus says about Naucellius's "little book" (*opusculum*) is that it was translated "from the Greek." It is difficult to see how it can have had any relevance to late fourth-century Roman paganism, and there are no grounds for assigning any initiative in the project to Symmachus.[201] In addition, Rufius Festus Avienius published a series of fairly free Latin versions of Greek astronomical and geographical poetry: one each of Dionysius Periegetes and Aratus, and a third of some unidentified Greek source. In addition to his basic sources, he seems also to have drawn on a variety of subsidiary sources, scholia, and the like.[202] Avienius himself was undoubtedly a pagan, but his translations are of purely antiquarian inspiration, quite uninfluenced by contemporary issues. In connection with his knowledge of Greek, it might be added that he was a generation older than Symmachus, and, like Praetextatus, once held office as proconsul of Achaca.

Then there is Firmicus Maternus's astrological handbook, little more than a translation of various Greek astrological treatises.[203] Maternus quotes both Plotinus and Porphyry, though only for their relevance to his astrological themes.[204] The *Mathesis* should not be seen as the product of a pagan party. Book i is devoted to answering critics of astrology, some of them clearly pagans ("you also claim...that we dissuade men from worshipping the gods," i. 6. 1), and is contemptuous of the emasculated servants of Cybele (vii. 25. 10; 14). In addition (of course), Maternus ended his days as a Christian.

10: CONCLUSION

In the East, with an unbroken succession in both Athens and Alexandria, pagan Neoplatonism managed to maintain itself, among tiny groups of the faithful, down into the sixth century.[205] In the West (it seems) it was effectively dead before the end

---

199. Callu 1975, 268–315; for the *Peplos*, Cameron 1993, 388–93.
200. Auson. p. 59 Green (with p. 364); Cameron 1993, 388–89.
201. As implied (e.g.) by Callu 1975, 309.
202. K. Smolak in Herzog and Schmidt 5, § 557, for the scanty modern bibliography.
203. Schanz-Hosius iv. 1 (1914), 131–32; W. Hübner in Herzog and Schmidt 5, § 515. 1.
204. i. 7. 14–22; vii. 1. 1.
205. Cameron 2007, 21–22.

of the fourth. There is simply no basis for the assumption that Praetextatus, Flavian, and Symmachus were well-informed and devoted students of Porphyry, where they found an intellectual underpinning for their pagan convictions. Given their social pre-eminence in Rome and the traditional priesthoods this brought them, inevitably they were in some sense leaders of what passed for a pagan party in late fourth-century Rome. But there is no reason to believe that they were in any sense its intellectual leaders.

The last pagan who can be assigned any such role is Marius Victorinus, a professor of rhetoric whose study of Cicero's rhetorical writings led him to Aristotle's dialectic and Porphyry's introduction, which he translated. There can be little doubt that Victorinus was responsible for a brief vogue for Aristotelian logic in Latin a century before Boethius.[206] Praetextatus was simply one of Victorinus's disciples. Augustine calls Victorinus the "teacher of countless noble senators," and as a consequence he won a statue in the Forum of Trajan.[207] But then, according to Augustine, late in life he shocked Rome by announcing his conversion. The rest of his days were spent writing commentaries on the Pauline epistles and an elaborate attack on Arianism (it is significant, and typical, that, once a Christian, Victorinus saw heresy rather than paganism as the enemy).

The true heirs to Plotinus and Porphyry as spiritual mentors of the Roman nobility at the end of the fourth century were Christian scholars like Jerome, Rufinus, and Pelagius. All three were supported by patrons among the aristocracy, all three counted aristocratic ladies among their most devoted admirers. By now Christianity had not only defeated paganism on the political and intellectual fronts; more important still, it was fashionable. Paradoxically, or perhaps predictably, it is western Christians rather than pagans who both read and (more important) exploited Plotinus and Porphyry. This was the momentous discovery that the young Augustine made at Milan in 386. One cannot help feeling that if Augustine, or any other intelligent but disillusioned young intellectual in search of the truth, had walked into the lecture room of Plutarch the Neoplatonist at Athens rather than Ambrose's church or Mallius Theodorus's villa, his story might have been very different. But there was no Plutarch in Rome or Milan, no subtle and learned pagan Neoplatonist to present him with the full truth according to Plato rather than just the bits that were consistent with Christianity. Significantly enough, like Marius Victorinus before him, in Neoplatonism Augustine found a bridge to Christianity.

---

206. Around 374 we find the twenty-year-old Augustine reading the *Categories* and perhaps other logical works of Aristotle at Carthage, presumably in Victorinus's translation (Hadot 1971, 193–98; Aug. *Conf.* iv. 16, with O'Donnell 1992, 264–65).

207. *Conf.* viii. 2. 3; the statue is also mentioned in Jerome's *Chron.* s.a. 353.

16

PAGAN SCHOLARSHIP
Vergil and His Commentators

1

Arnaldo Momigliano once remarked that it was not so much pagan historians that disturbed Augustine, "who knew where to look for the real enemy," as "the idealization of the Roman past which he found in fourth-century Latin antiquarians, poets and commentators of poets." This, he argued, is why Augustine "went back to the sources of their antiquarianism, and primarily to Varro, in order to undermine the foundations of their work."[1] It is time to follow up, and qualify, this important insight.

Enough has already been said about the popularity of classicizing poetry at the Christian courts of Milan and Ravenna.[2] It is easy to see why people like Augustine were distressed to see Christians applauding poems on Christian emperors decked out with pagan gods and goddesses, elaborately described in all their traditional dress and paraphernalia. Among the antiquarians the prime exhibits are the *Saturnalia* of Macrobius, largely devoted to Vergil, and the massive Vergil commentary of the grammarian Servius, partly because both have been generally assumed committed pagans, but also because of the often stated but never justified modern doctrine of Vergil as a "pagan bible," a book "venerated, copied and expounded as a sacred text" (p. 608). A more modest illustration is the so-called *Origo Gentis Romanae*, the first part in a tripartite corpus of texts covering all Roman history down to Constantius II.[3] The *Origo* goes from Janus and Saturnus to Romulus and Remus, with the first third largely devoted to reconciling Vergil with other traditions. At 1. 6 indeed the anonymous pagan author claims to have "begun to write" a commentary on Vergil. As Christopher Smith has recently remarked, "the *Origo* is very close throughout to the Virgilian commentators," and though they often disagree "they are recognizably inhabiting the same mental world."[4]

That late fourth- and fifth-century western culture was dominated by Vergil needs no demonstration. The writings, prose as well as verse, of all educated people,

---

1. Momigliano 1963, 98–99.
2. And at the eastern court in Constantinople, where the tradition lasted much longer.
3. The basic study remains Momigliano 1958, 56–73 = *Secondo Contributo* (Rome 1960), 145–76.
4. C. J. Smith 2005, 97–136, at 101.

Christians no less than pagans, were steeped in Vergilian echoes and quotations.[5] All or part of no fewer than seven late antique manuscripts of Vergil survive, two of them illustrated. The fact that the miniatures in the Vatican Vergil depict scenes of sacrifice has, inevitably, been held to point to pagan patrons (Ch. 19. 3). And the fact that Macrobius and Servius devote so many pages and so much learning to Vergil's treatment of sacrifice has naturally seemed to fill out this picture of a pagan revival centering on Vergil.[6] According to Mario Geymonat, the cultural revival sponsored by the Nicomachi and Symmachi "led at the time to an exceptional flowering, particularly in Italy, of work on Virgil."[7]

But the cultural dominance of Vergil began centuries before the age of Symmachus. The Vatican Vergil might as easily date from 350 or 450 as 400.[8] And the very idea of a general classical revival is no longer taken seriously by serious students of the transmission of classical texts. The story varies so much from text to text. Nor did any text stand so little in need of revival as the ever-popular Vergil. The idea that Symmachus himself played a key role in this supposed revival is based on his reputation as a pagan champion rather than the evidence of his writings. Certainly, his letters and speeches are full of Vergilian echoes,[9] but there is no trace of anything deeper. If Macrobius were really any guide to their interests, we might have expected to find Symmachus and his friends discussing in their (real) correspondence as they do in the pages of the (fictitious) *Saturnalia* topics like Vergil's expertise in Roman religion. Yet not only does Symmachus himself never even hint at any such dimension in Vergil, for all his undoubtedly genuine devotion to the classics, he never *discusses* them at all, not even with his closest literary friends. He treats them as a quarry for anecdotes, elegant phrases, and choice archaisms. Above all, as one might expect in an orator, he treats them as a source of encomiastic tropes. It is worth glancing at the handful of passages where he directly quotes (as distinct from echoing or paraphrasing) the two supreme classics, Cicero and Vergil.[10] They are good test cases, since several occur in letters addressed to pagans.

In almost every passage the reference is adapted to an encomiastic purpose. Beside his father's poetry, his own, he claims (i. 1. 4), is a goose honking among swans (*Buc.* ix. 36); piety overcoming a difficult journey (*Aen.* vi. 688) is applied to a visit from his father under difficult circumstances (i. 9); it is not only bad news that travels fast, as Vergil claimed (*Aen.* iv. 174), because the news of Siburius's acquittal brings pleasure (iii. 45); in i. 14. 5 he compares Ausonius's *Mosella* to Vergil; finally, he adapted *Buc.* iv as a whole to a panegyric (*Or.* iii) on the Christian emperor Gratian. References to Cicero are likewise

---

5. For brief studies of the most important cases, see the various contributions in Rees 2004.
6. Most recently D. Wright 1993 and 2001, criticized by Cameron 2004, 502–25.
7. M. Geymonat in Horsfall 1995, 303.
8. See Cameron 1998 and 2004.
9. Kroll 1891, 42–51, lists about ninety Vergilian echoes, of which I would disallow nearly half.
10. I am not suggesting that these are more interesting or characteristic than the far more numerous unidentified quotations and allusions. But they are the passages where he comes closest to making a comment on the writer.

adapted to compliments on a correspondent's style: i. 3. 2 (Avianius); i. 31. 1 (Ausonius); iii. 12. 2 (Naucellius); ix. 110. 2 (Anonymus). In iv. 60 he twists Cicero's remark that the Romans of old were parsimonious in private but extravagant in public (*Pro Flacco* 28) into a rhetorical justification for begging a Spanish friend to get him the best racehorses for Memmius's games. Particularly revealing is a letter (i. 32. 3) praising Ausonius for combining the *opulentia* of Cicero with the *proprietas* of Vergil. We have substantial specimens of both the prose and verse of Ausonius, and the one is as unlike Cicero as the other is unlike Vergil. Symmachus was not suggesting a genuine literary comparison at all: the names simply exemplify generalized excellence.

Of course, it would be wrong to suppose that this was all Vergil meant to Symmachus. He no doubt read and reread his illustrated codex in rustic capitals with deep satisfaction. As a boy he must have studied the *Aeneid* with Donatus's commentary and imbibed the standard view (treated in detail below) that Aeneas was a *pontifex* avant la lettre and that there were countless allusions to old Roman rituals throughout the poem. But he never mentions this aspect of the poem in letters to even his closest pagan friends, nor is there any indication that it played any part in his attitude to the cults of his own day.

To be sure he added a few Vergilian touches to his *relatio* on the altar of Victory, claiming that it was not weeds (*avenae*) or mildew (*rubigo*) but sacrilege (Gratian's measures) that led to the famine of 383, causing men to return to eating acorns, recalling several phrases from *Georgics* i. 147–59. This is a doubly instructive case. First, because Symmachus was not here turning to Vergil as a religious authority, but simply to elevate his own diction. Second, because Ambrose outdid him, not just rejecting the argument, but doing so in even more elaborate Vergilian colors of his own, alluding to eight different passages from both *Aeneid* and *Georgics*.[11] Unlike Augustine, here as often elsewhere Ambrose drew on the classics he knew so well with a clear conscience. His *De officiis* is openly modeled on Cicero's *De officiis*, and his exegetical masterpiece, the *Hexaemeron*, offers "an average of around three Vergilian echoes per page."[12] Well aware that Vergilian diction swayed educated Christians no less than pagans, he deliberately and skilfully outbid the pagan orator at his own game.

2

Unlike Symmachus, Servius and Macrobius have a great deal to say about cult and ritual in Vergil, with frequent reference to pontifical law.[13] Was there a serious religious

---

11. *Ep.* 18. 17–20; M. Diederich 1931, 107–14; Gualandri in Consolino 1995, 242–49.

12. I. Davidson in Rees 2004, 104; for a full list of Vergilian imitations in the *Hexaemeron*, Diederich 1931, 6–32.

13. *pontifex* and *pontificalis* appear thirty-six times in *Sat.* i and iii, the books most concerned with cult and sacrifice.

dimension to their undoubted interest in these subjects? Did they actually conduct research in ancient texts to support their religious convictions? A recent study by Clifford Ando rejects the idea (implicit in my own earlier work) that Macrobian antiquarianism is no more than "a retreat from cult and its topographic concerns to the discursive world of texts," and argues that "Symmachus, Servius, Praetextatus, and Macrobius" were "engaged in the preservation of a cultural system then under assault by the government of their empire."[14] Even before we turn to specific arguments, this is a curiously ill-assorted quartet. The classical revival of which modern scholars have made so much is dated to the generation of Symmachus and Praetextatus, that is to say to the 380s and early 390s. But Macrobius and Servius wrote almost a half-century later, in a now largely Christian world. Ando nonetheless assumed without argument that he could treat what he calls their antiquarian "researches" as representing the views of "the last pagan generation."

Macrobius certainly saw himself as preserving Rome's cultural heritage, but it was not "government" policy he saw as the enemy, but narrow-minded, pedantic schoolteachers (*grammatici*), the sort of people we might have expected to be his natural allies. For Ando it was self-evident that Servius shared the goals he ascribes to Macrobius, but (as we shall see) the truth is that, for all their common concerns, Servius was not at all the died-in-the-wool antiquarian Macrobius was. For Ando, Macrobius's *Saturnalia* is "a loving and passionate investigation of Rome's pagan past."[15] Loving, certainly, but hardly passionate, and his antiquarian interests are by no means restricted to pagan aspects of the Roman past. A long section in Bk ii (1. 8–7. 19) is devoted to jokes of the ancients; Bk vii, much the longest surviving book (though even so incomplete) ranges over a wide variety of pseudo-scientific topics (why women get drunk less but feel the cold more; why people blush and go bald; why we wear rings on certain fingers; and so on). If the *Saturnalia* had survived complete, the emphasis on specifically pagan topics would have been much less striking. For modern readers in search of information on a pagan reaction, the passages on the old festivals and rituals seem to stand out. But secular-minded contemporaries who read the book from cover to cover forty years after the end of the cults would have been more likely to see these passages as simply one aspect of its wide-ranging antiquarianism.

Since Macrobius and Servius are by far the best candidates for identifying any sort of specifically pagan scholarship in late antique Rome, it is essential to begin by establishing their credentials as scholars. The fact is that the works they produced were entirely derivative compilations, copied, often verbatim, from a modest number of secondary works rather than based on firsthand study of original texts. Above all, despite the interest both profess in pontifical and augural law, heavily emphasized in modern writings, their knowledge of these subjects was entirely derived at second- or thirdhand from earlier Vergil commentators.

---

14. Ando 2001, 369–410 at 370–74.
15. Ando 2001, 389.

Let us begin with Servius. Thousands of pages of ancient commentaries on classical writers (especially poets) have come down to us in the form of marginal scholia in manuscripts of the relevant writers. The Homeric scholia are especially illuminating on the ways ancient critics read and taught a major classic,[16] and also very important for the understanding of both Vergil and (more particularly) the ancient commentators on Vergil.[17] But with few exceptions, in the form in which they have reached us, marginal scholia are the work of medieval scribes and represent excerpts from different commentators of often very different dates and interests. Servius's commentary, despite (and also because of) its shortcomings, is uniquely revealing as the only commentary on any major classic to survive in its original form. When we read Servius, we are reading the very words a well-known grammaticus wrote for his students in an early fifth-century Roman schoolroom. On the whole it is a dispiriting read. The greater part is thoroughly pedestrian. On Kaster's estimate, notes on language amount to "two out of every three," while only "one note in seven, by contrast, is concerned with the broader mythical, historical, and literary background of the poetry, and of this small minority only another small proportion amounts to more than perfunctory references or glosses."[18]

Kaster perhaps understated the scale of mythological notes, which are both frequent and often extensive. But they are also peculiar. Servius has no interest in explaining *how* Vergil uses myth. Instead of commenting on the mythological detail relevant to the Vergilian passage in question, he always tells the whole story, often with variants and usually with a source reference. In fact, he offers a mythical "story" for almost every person, place, and even plant Vergil mentions, using the fact that Vergil happens to mention these people, plants, and animals as a peg on which to hang his own mythological erudition. This erudition derives from a first- or second-century Latin monograph on mythology in Vergil, modeled on a late Hellenistic monograph on Homeric mythology of which we now have a number of papyrus fragments.[19] Typically, Servius never mentions this Latin text, only the obscure Greek sources it cited.[20] It is unclear how early this mythological material was integrated into the commentary tradition. Systematic mythological notes were not a feature of the earliest Homer commentaries, and it is not known whether they were part of the earliest Vergil commentaries either. In the first and second centuries basic knowledge of mythology may have been taken for granted in readers of the classics. Its routine inclusion in later commentaries is probably to be seen as one more indication of the narrowing of literary culture in late antiquity. Uhl has recently studied the way Servius's linguistic notes (improbably) use Vergil (of all writers) as a tool to instil the principles of good Latin, warning students off

---

16. On the Greek side we now have the marvellously complete collection of information provided by Dickey 2007.
17. As clearly seen by E. Fraenkel, *JRS* 39 (1949), 154; see Cameron 2004, 84–85; and Farrell 2008.
18. Kaster 1988, 170.
19. For full details on this, see Cameron 2004, Ch. 8.
20. For a list of such citations, Cameron 2004, 208.

his "licences."[21] The goal of the mythological notes is no less clearly didactic, to teach mythology, a central element in the culture of the late antique gentleman.[22]

This was the way Servius himself had been taught to read Vergil as a boy. His notes on language were no doubt influenced by his own practice over the years. Here we may be hearing the authentic voice of Servius in his classroom. But the only original contribution of any substance to the commentary tradition he can be credited with is the introduction of parallels from the Silver Age poets—Lucan, Statius, and Juvenal— almost entirely absent from his predecessors. As a counterpart to this he omitted most of the citations of archaic Latin writers that were still a regular feature in Donatus (Ch. 11. 5). As we shall see, in the present context the most relevant of Servius's omissions is the mass of information about Roman cults, priests, and rituals that we know from the DS additions were such a conspicuous feature of Donatus.

But the most remarkable feature of the thousand-odd pages of Servius's commentary is that at no point does he step back and offer any general guidance or analysis of any sort. Vergil's overwhelming excellence is simply taken for granted. His single sentence on the purpose of the *Aeneid* has become notorious: "To imitate Homer and praise Augustus through his ancestors."[23] But his remarks on style are scarcely more satisfactory: "the style is grandiloquent, which consists of high language and great sentiments; for we know that there are three types of style, the plain, middle and grandiloquent."[24] Here we may compare the only part of Donatus's commentary to survive intact, his introduction to the *Bucolics*. Why did Vergil write *Bucolics*, *Georgics*, and *Aeneïd* in that order? Either to represent the three stages of man's life (shepherd, agriculturalist, warrior);[25] or according to the three forms of style, the *Bucolics* in the plain, the *Georgics* in the middle, and the *Aeneïd* in the grand style, "for he excelled in every style."[26] No comment on the radical incommensurability of these suggestions, and no attempt to weigh their respective merits. The implication is that Servius too thought the style of the *Aeneïd* grandiloquent throughout. Clearly, neither had given any serious thought to the claim they threw out with such an air of authority before passing on to the next topic.

It is beyond dispute that Servius preserves a mass of information of the highest value for the understanding of Vergil. Nonetheless, the fact is that his commentary represents less research than a drastic and systematic reduction of the learned material assembled by his predecessors, principally Aemilius Asper and Aelius Donatus. Of course, that is not necessarily a bad thing in a commentary. Every commentary on a

---

21. Uhl 1998; see too Kaster 1988.
22. Discussed in detail by Cameron 2004, Ch. 8.
23. *Homerum imitari et laudare Augustum a parentibus*, p. 4 Harv.
24. *est autem stilus grandiloquus, qui constat alto sermone magnisque sententiis; scimus enim tria esse genera dicendi, humile medium grandiloquum*: p. 4 Harv. = I. 4 Thilo.
25. Repeated by Servius in his preface, acknowledging Donatus (iii. 3. 30 Thilo).
26. *utpote qui in omni genere valuit*, § 58 K. Bayer (ed.) in *Vergil: Landleben*², J. Götte and M. Götte (eds.) (Darmstadt 1970), 320 (not included in Hardie's OCT of the *Vitae Vergilianae*, 1954).

classic is bound to include much tralatician learning,[27] and much of the Donatan material Servius omitted was too advanced and discursive for schoolchildren. Servius's commentary has a definite character of its own. Nonetheless, it can hardly, as so often, be viewed as a "flowering," much less a "revival" of interest in Vergil. Commentaries on Vergil had existed since at least the second century,[28] each being replaced by another as the centuries passed. Servius's survives in essentially its original form because he was the end of the line; no one cannibalized Servius as he had cannibalized Donatus, Donatus Asper, and so on. What his commentary documents is no more than the continuing interest paid to a minute reading of Vergil in the late Roman West. For us moderns it casts a flood of light on the way Vergil was read in late Roman schools. But that is only because we have no comparable earlier work.

3

It is common knowledge that the Servian Vergil commentary has come down to us in two very different forms: a short version, and the longer version first published by P. Daniel in 1600.[29] It was at first thought that the long version, D(anielis) S(ervius), was the original Servius and the shorter version (S) an abridgment. But it is now firmly established that S is the original Servius, and DS a conflation, probably made in the early seventh century, between S and a larger but clearly related commentary (D),[30] the same larger commentary from which S itself was compiled. Servius, the shorter version, is a coherent, well-articulated whole, while the DS additions are obviously stitched onto a text of Servius, not infrequently repeating details already in Servius, thereby proving that the main source of both S and DS was a single commentary like Servius, only fuller. Some of the shorter DS additions actually complete sentences begun in S. Since an influential paper by E. K. Rand, D has generally been identified as the commentary of Aelius Donatus.[31] DS is often styled Servius Auctus (or even Ps-Servius), but I follow the convention of citing it as DS, not least because the D suggests Donatus as well as Daniel. For the interpretation of Vergil it makes little difference whether a particular note comes from S or DS. But for anyone trying to reconstruct the views of Servius himself it makes a great deal of difference. Ando, for example, more than once cites as illustrating Servius's personal convictions about the

---

27. So, frankly, E. Courtney, *A Commentary on the Satires of Juvenal* (London 1980), x, "by far the greater proportion of my commentary is not original."
28. And perhaps earlier. While there was abundant scholarly writing on Vergil from soon after his death (Ziolkowski and Putnam 2008, 623–30), there is no clear evidence for continuous, comprehensive commentaries before Asper.
29. Schmidt in Herzog and Schmidt 5 § 527. 3; Brugnoli, *EV* 4 (1988), 805–13; Timpanaro, *MD* 22 (1989), 123–82.
30. For the complex manuscript tradition (early for both S and DS), Marshall's summary in Reynolds 1983, 385–88.
31. Rand 1916, 158–64.

pagan cults passages that appear only in the DS additions, passages (that is) that Servius himself deliberately omitted. I say "deliberately" because we are bound to assume that Servius had a complete text of Donatus in front of him as he wrote.

For a while it was hoped that the original text of Donatus might be recovered by a simple process of subtracting S from DS, but we now know that the seventh-century scholar who conflated D and S adapted his material more freely and carelessly than Rand had supposed. Daintree has questioned the very idea of reconstructing Donatus, but when he claims that the sources at our disposal do not allow us to "do more than touch the hem of Donatus' garment," he goes too far.[32] The DS additions share so many common features that there can be little doubt that the greater part of them derives from a single work with a certain character and unity of interests. For example, (1) as already noted, they cite scores of early Republican authors never quoted at all by Servius; (2) DS citations of Republican texts are usually more accurate than Servius and regularly include titles and book numbers omitted by Servius; (3) the DS additions include much recondite mythological lore. Above all (4), and most relevant to this chapter, they offer a mass of material on the old Roman cults and priests missing in Servius.

While the DS additions may well include a few details from other sources, there can be little doubt that most derive from a single variorum commentary on Vergil, not only fuller than Servius, but fuller in certain well-defined respects. The source of the DS additions was evidently a learned commentary, aimed at advanced students, while Servius was a shorter and more elementary commentary. Countless Servian notes are summaries or abridgments of longer and more learned DS notes. Probably Donatus, but the early third-century commentary of Asper is cited by Ausonius, Jerome, and Augustine as if a standard work still in use.[33] Donatus famously boasted of not naming his predecessors,[34] but the scholia in the probably mid-fifth-century Veronensis of Vergil cite numerous sources by name, Asper no fewer than eighteen times.[35] Since we know from the dedicatory letter transmitted with his *Life of Vergil* that Donatus claimed to have reproduced the very words of his sources,[36] many DS additions, though taken from Donatus, may in fact have been reproduced more or less verbatim from Asper. Donatus's *Life of Vergil* is usually assumed to be almost pure Suetonius, as is the *Life* prefixed to his commentary on Terence.[37]

The actual text the seventh-century DS compiler used to supplement his Servius may not have been pure Donatus. Its margins may have carried notes from a variety of other sources. But since there are DS additions to all books of all three of Vergil's

---

32. Daintree 1990, 65–79, at 72.
33. Tomsin 1952.
34. *Unde praeceptor meus Donatus ... "pereant" inquit "qui ante nos nostra dixerunt,"* Jerome, *Comm. in Eccles.* i. 9/10; bizarrely misinterpreted by Holtz 1981, 41–43; see Kaster, *Speculum* 58 (1983), 482.
35. Baschera 1999, 50.
36. *maluimus ... eorum etiam verba servare,* Don. *Ep.* in C. Hardie, *Vitae Verg. Ant.* (Oxford 1964).
37. In the latter case acknowledged (*haec Suetonius Tranquillus,* § 8, p. 9 Wessner).

poems, it must have been a complete commentary on all of Vergil.[38] But there is one note that seems to prove that the core of the source of DS was Donatus rather than Asper. On *Aen.* x. 272–73 Servius cites a work on comets by "Avienus, who put the stories of Vergil into iambics."[39] A long DS addition supplies another forty-six lines from this Avienus, more properly the mid-fourth-century poet (Postumius Rufius Festus) Avien*i*us.[40] Avienius must have been a (perhaps slightly younger) contemporary of Donatus. No commentary earlier than that of Donatus can have quoted Avienius; and both Servius and DS clearly drew on a commentary that quoted Avienius.

4

While we will never be able to reconstruct the text of Donatus, some details can be recovered with a fair degree of confidence from the DS additions. By comparing DS and Servius, in some cases we can identify the actual words as well as the substance of Donatus.[41] In the present context, the most instructive examples come in the many references to *pontifices, flamines,* and details of sacrificial practice in DS. These notes are almost always in the present tense, as we should expect in Donatus, who wrote ca. 350, nearly a half-century before the banning of sacrifice. For example, "the double toga, in which the *flamines* sacrifice" and "the knife . . . which the *flamines* . . . and *pontifices* use for sacrifice" (DS on *Aen.* iv. 262). Servius, however, routinely writes of pagan cult in the imperfect tense.[42] The note on *Aen.* xii. 170 is a particularly clear example: Servius has the imperfects *sacrificabant* and *immolabant,* while the additional DS material that he omitted has the present tense (*quam pontifices . . . vocant*). On *Aen.* viii. 641 Servius has an imperfect: "a pig *used to* be employed for this sort of sacrifice" (*ad hoc genus sacrificii porcus adhibebatur*); while the parallel DS note on xii. 170 has a present ("some say that it is customary to sacrifice a pig, not a sow when making treaties").[43] When Aeneas refers to auspices (*Aen.* iv. 340), according to Servius this is "because our ancestors *used to* do everything according to auspices" (*maiores omnia auspicato gerebant*). With Servius's note (in the imperfect) on *Aen.* xi. 339 (*futtile vas . . . quo utebantur in sacris Vestae*) we may also compare a note (in the present) from

---

38. Why did this compiler supplement a short commentary from a long commentary instead of simply copying the long commentary? The obvious guess is that he already owned a Servius, and, given the massive overlap between the two texts, chose to supplement his own copy when he came across the longer version in a library somewhere.

39. Servius gives *Livii fabulas,* but for reasons given by Murgia 1970, DS's *Vergilii fabulas* must be right.

40. Cameron 1995, 252–62; Cameron 2004, 212–16.

41. "we often find in the non-Servian comment of Servius Auctus the very voice of Donatus," Murgia 1987, 289.

42. Murgia 2003, 45–69.

43. *non nulli autem porcum, non porcam in foederibus adserunt solere mactari.* We find the same variation between present and imperfect in DS and Servius on xii. 169.

Donatus's Terence commentary (*vas quod futile dicitur, quod non deponunt ministri sacrificiorum*).[44] Scores more examples might be cited.[45]

Since Servius's career did not begin till within a year or two of the disestablishment of the cults in 382, there can be little doubt that this is the explanation for his systematic change of tense. Horsfall has challenged the argument, on two grounds. First, that there are a number of presents as well as imperfects in Servius.[46] Yet it is not the presents that need explaining, but the imperfects. If Servius had been writing before the end of sacrifice, why did he change *any* of these presents? Why not just reproduce *all* the original presents he must have found in every source he consulted? There are at least two explanations for the occasional presents. Even in explanations of cult details the present tense did not always need to be changed. For example, on *Aen.* x. 228 Servius writes "this *is* sacral language" (*verba sunt sacrorum*), before illustrating the use of the formula in the imperfect (*nam virgines Vestae…dicebant*). Even when no longer used, the words remained a sacral formula; there was no need to change that *sunt* to *erant*. On *Aen.* v. 45, after explaining that the difference between *deus* and *divus* lay in the fact that *divi* were once mortals, Servius adds "whence we call emperors too *divi*." Whatever the merits of the explanation, *divus* did in fact continue to be used of deceased emperors down into the sixth century.[47]

But most of Servius's occasional presents are simply the result of inattention. This can sometimes be demonstrated. For example, on *Aen.* iv. 57: "it *used to be* (*erat*) the custom to pick perfect sheep for sacrifice," where a few lines later in the note there is an uncorrected present, "those that *are* (*sunt*) suitable for sacrifice." This last present is the more striking in that Servius repeats the whole phrase on vi. 39 (with a cross-reference to his note on iv. 57), verbatim—except that the second time he remembered to correct the present (*quae erant aptae sacrificiis*). Clearly, the original note he was reproducing gave presents throughout, and his intention was to substitute imperfects throughout.

We also find occasional imperfects in DS notes, but only in reference to practices already obsolete by Donatus's day. For example, people *used to* sacrifice in their own hearths (*veteres in focis sacrificabant*); in the old days, you *used not* to be able to marry a wife or plough a field without sacrificing; in the old days people *used* to relate the deeds of their ancestors at banquets.[48]

Horsfall's second objection was that "repetition of the same prohibitions [of sacrifice] down to the late 430s" renders 391–5 an insecure terminus. But the argument does not depend on a terminus of 391–5, at any rate as applied to Servius, who was writing in the 420s. And while sacrifice no doubt continued for years in remote country districts, the state festivals had to be performed publicly in the center of Rome itself. The supervising

---

44. See his note on *Andria* 609.

45. See the notes on *Aen.* iii. 12 (*di magni…Romae colebantur*); iv. 301; iv. 694; v. 64 (burial customs).

46. Horsfall 1995, 308 n. 55, citing *Aen.* i. 292, 335; ii. 104, 134, 148, 202; iii. 21, 118, 231; vi. 224.

47. L. Koep, "Divus," *RAC* 3 (1957), 1255–57; in formulas such as *divae memoriae, divae recordationis* the original associations of divinity were further attenuated.

48. *Aen.* i. 704 (DS); iii. 136 (DS); i. 641 (DS).

priests were members of the aristocracy, public figures who (as we have seen) would not have dared to defy imperial authority. It may be regarded as certain that 391–5 does indeed mark a terminus for the traditional Roman rituals the commentators talk about.

Furthermore, Servius was by no means the only commentator to change presents to imperfects in cult references—though given his known dates he may have been the earliest. The Horace scholiast conventionally known as Pseudo-Acro[49] routinely changed the earlier Porphyrio's presents to imperfects. For example, on *Odes* iii. 8. 1, where Porphyrio wrote "to this very day the first of March *is* the festal day for married women," Pseudo-Acro dropped the *hodieque* and changed *est* to *erat*. According to Porphyrio's note on i. 36. 1, "Everyone knows they *use* lyre-players for sacrifices at Rome";[50] according to Pseudo-Acro, "they *used to* (*consueverant*) use lyre-players for sacrifices." Where Porphyrio refers on i. 37. 2 to the priestly banquets the Salii *hold* (*faciunt*), Ps-Acro has "*used to* hold" (*faciebant*). On *Epodes* 17. 58 Porphyrio remarks that pontiffs "*render* judgments on sacral matters" and on iii. 5. 10 that eternal flames *are* maintained on the altar of Vesta; in both cases Ps-Acro has imperfects.[51]

Then there are the Juvenal scholia. Although we do not have an earlier set with which to compare the surviving scholia, which are no earlier than the mid-fifth century, here too we find the same use of the imperfect. For example, "sterile women *used to* offer themselves to the Luperci for purification"; "this *was* the penalty that *used to* be laid down for Vestal Virgins, that if they had been debauched, they *used to* be walled up alive."[52] At the same time, in the Juvenal and Pseudo-Acro Horace scholia, as in Servius, we also find the occasional uncorrected present.[53] Once again, the explanation is inattention. For example, the Juvenal scholiast describes the *simpuvium* as a vessel "suited for sacrifice, from which the pontiffs *used to* offer libations"—and then added that the assistant who held it "*is* called a *simpuviatrix*."[54] There can be no serious doubt that all these scholiasts found present tenses in their sources and did their best to change them all to imperfects.

We also find present tenses in the few but telling references to sacrifice in the very different Vergil commentary of Tiberius Claudius Donatus: "whence we still have the custom that a cow and bull with gilded forehead and horns *are* sacrificed to Capitoline Jupiter"; "those who deal with sacrifices have vessels dedicated to the gods that they

---

49. Known mainly from marginal notes in Par. lat. 7900 of s. IX/X: Tarrant in Reynolds 1983, 183, 186; for the other MSS, Noske 1969, summarized by M. J. McGann, *CR* 86 (1972), 110.
50. *fidicines hodieque Romae ad sacrificia adhiberi* [*adh. consueverant, Acro*] *sicut tibicines nemo est qui nesciat.*
51. For further examples, see both commentaries on *Odes* i. 5. 12; ii. 16. 14; iii. 18. 9; 28. 16.
52. *steriles mulieres februantibus Lupercis se efferebant et ferula verberabantur* (ii. 142); *haec virginibus Vestae poena fuerat decreta, ut, si vitiatae fuissent, vivae in parietibus struebantur* (iv. 37). For the date of the Juvenal scholia, Cameron 2010.
53. For example, *id est pollutis, secundum pontificum et aruspicum dicta, qui dicunt numquam fieri fulmina nisi in lucis pollutione alique alienis* (Pseudo-Acro on *Odes* i. 12. 59); *Silvano mulieres non licet sacrificare* (Schol. Juv. vi. 447); *quotienscumque pontifex dispersos ignes in unum redigit* (vi. 587; cf. vi. 47).
54. *sacrificiis aptum, in quo pontifices libare solebant; inde illa dicitur simpuviatrix quae porrigit poculum ipsud* (vi. 343); on the *simpuvium*, A. Brinkmann, *ALL* 15 (1908), 139–43. It might also be argued that, even after the rite ceased to be performed, the name of the assistant who held the *simpuvium* continued to be *simpuviatrix*.

use for performing divine service."[55] Since Tiberius Donatus did not copy his material from earlier scholars like the other commentators (his only virtue), there can be little doubt that he was a pagan who wrote before the end of sacrifice. Indeed, it is hard to believe he could have written that "festal days (*dies festi*) *are* those counted above the rest and consecrated to the honor of some deity" after the abolition of pagan festal days in 389.[56] Particularly telling here is Servius's discussion of the sort of robes priests "*used to wear* when about to perform sacrifices on festal days" (*vesti qua festis diebus uti consueverant sacra celebraturi*). Once again, the lengthy DS additions to this note all have the present tense.[57]

This use of the present tense is by no means restricted to pre-Servian commentators on the poets. Gellius's chapters on Vestal Virgins and the *flamen Dialis* (*NA* i. 12; x. 15) and countless entries on cult details in the dictionary of S. Pompeius Festus, both of the second century, are written throughout in the present tense. Gellius drew heavily on the Augustan jurists Veranius, Antistius Labeo, and Ateius Capito, scholars who wrote extensively on pontifical law. And Festus's book was an epitome of the *De verborum significatu* of the Augustan Verrius Flaccus. There can be little doubt that the work of Verrius and the jurists is the ultimate source, via intermediaries like Gellius and Festus, of most references to cult practices in Macrobius and the late antique commentators.[58] Writing as they were in the early first century, they naturally used the present tense of current practices they expected to continue indefinitely, and down to at any rate Aelius Donatus in the mid-fourth century, the commentators just as naturally followed suit.

The change of tense cannot be ascribed to later Christian scribes. Christian scribes did not censor the pagan texts they copied—at any rate not in details like this. None of the manuscripts of Gellius, Festus, Porphyrio, or Tiberius Claudius Donatus change any of these present tenses to imperfects. And the seventh-century compiler who added all that Donatan material to his copy of Servius did not change any of Donatus's present tenses. It was only writers who *reused* such material *in works of their own* who did so. After 391 it was not so much dangerous as simply incorrect to use the present tense of pagan rituals that everyone knew no longer took place. A revealing illustration is provided by the abridgement of Festus's dictionary made by the Carolingian scholar Paul the Deacon. For part of the work we have original Festus, preserved on a single incomplete and in part illegible manuscript, so it is often possible to make a direct comparison. Since Paul was adapting Festus's material into a new work published under his own name for Christian readers, he too systematically changed Festus's

---

55. *unde consuetudo permansit ut vacca simul et taurus auratis fronte et cornibus Iovi Capitolino mactentur*, ix. 627; *sacrum idcirco posuit, quia quibus sacrorum cura est habent dicata numinibus vasa quibus obsequia divina perficiunt*, viii. 279; *quod magnopere desideramus inpleri commendamus diis, in quorum potestate sunt quae inter homines aguntur*, *Aen*. vii. 260. I owe this point to Charles Murgia.

56. *festi dies sunt qui praeponuntur ceteris et in honorem cuiuslibet numinis consecrati numerantur*, vi. 70 (not in Georgii's edition; published by Marshall 1993, 9).

57. Serv. on *Aen*. xii. 169; he let Donatus's presents stand on *Geo*. i. 268 and 270, but (as we shall see) it is the imperfects that are significant.

58. Most of the few fragments are preserved by Festus and Macrobius.

presents to imperfects in cult references.[59] But like his late antique predecessors, he too missed a fair number, especially toward the end of the longer entries. To give a single illustration, in the long entry on *februarius* (from *februare*, "to purify"), the first seven verbs are in the imperfect, but the last four in the present. Obviously, Festus had used presents throughout, and Paul began intending to change them all to imperfects but grew careless (or could not be bothered) toward the end of a long entry.[60]

By substituting imperfects for presents in references to sacrifice were commentators simply trying to protect themselves? Pagan teachers would not want to antagonize Christian pupils, but we should not assume that all commentators were pagans (the Juvenal scholiast at any rate was certainly a Christian). If there had been any real risk, it would have been simpler and safer just to omit such details. Pseudo-Acro dropped much of the erudition he found in Porphyrio (notably on Horace's Greek sources), just as Porphyrio abridged what he found in the second-century commentary of the real Helenius Acro.[61] Yet significantly enough Pseudo-Acro did not omit the pagan cult references he found in Porphyrio, despite the fact that, given his date, he must have been writing for Christian readers. The seventh-century compiler who replaced several score such Donatan references that the pagan Servius had omitted was likewise a Christian.[62] The answer is that, while the banning of sacrifice stopped public celebration of the cults themselves, it did not stop Christians continuing to read the classical poets and wanting to understand the many references to these celebrations they found there. This is the sort of antiquarianism that Augustine understandably found so worrying. To give an obvious example, in order to understand the opening of Horace, *Odes* iii. 8 ("What am I, a bachelor, doing on 1 March?"), it is essential to know that 1 March was the beginning of the Matronalia, when married men gave their wives presents. Many passages in Vergil are practically unintelligible without such knowledge.

Macrobius's usage is a special case. Despite writing a half-century after the end of sacrifice, all the innumerable references to pagan cult practices in the *Saturnalia* are in the present tense. This is almost certainly the main reason so many modern readers have taken him for a contemporary and participant of the discussions he records, not to mention a practicing pagan. But as already remarked, the real explanation lies in his choice of genre: dialogue rather than commentary. Obviously, the interlocutors in a dialogue have to be shown speaking in the present tense. If Macrobius had chosen a dramatic date in the 430s, like Servius and his scholiastic successors he too would have had to change Donatus's present tenses. He could not realistically have represented his interlocutors saying that such and such an animal *is* sacrificed to such or

---

59. As first noticed by Antonio Agustín (1559): Grafton 1983, 141–42; see now Glinister et al. 2007.
60. Paul's abridgment is printed in full in Lindsay's Festus, on facing pages where the original Festus survives; quotation from Festus p. 75. 23–76. 5 Lindsay.
61. This last point is difficult to gauge, since it is likely that what has been transmitted under the name of Porphyrio is itself abridged.
62. This compiler was writing so long after the end of sacrifice that no one was likely to suspect him of paganism for adding either the material or Donatus's original present tenses.

such a god, or that the pontiffs *say* this or that. It would have been not so much impious or dangerous as simply and obviously incorrect. But by fixing his dramatic date before the end of sacrifice, he was able to keep the presents. Pagans discussing pagan cult before 382 would naturally have used the present tense.

The present tenses put in the mouths of Macrobius's interlocutors are thus entirely irrelevant to the writer's personal attitude to the pagan practices to which he devotes so many pages. Since he used only pagans for interlocutors, it seems that Macrobius at any rate regarded Servius as a pagan, though nothing in his works suggests a committed pagan. Nor are we obliged to assume that he remained a pagan all his life. In 382 Servius was little more than twenty years old, and the world of Roman paganism was overturned between the dramatic date of the *Saturnalia* in 382 and the 420s. Some of his notes on cult matters imply a very distanced attitude. Where Aeneas says *sacra deosque dabo* at *Aen.* xii. 192, Servius blandly comments that "our ancestors paid a lot of attention to cult matters." On Vergil's suggestion that Octavian might one day become a constellation filling the space between Virgo and Libra (*Geo.* i. 33), he remarks that "our ancestors (*maiores*) placed the home of the gods between these signs."

There is certainly no basis for seeing his occasional present tenses as polemical. Writing *sacrificant* instead of *sacrificabant* was not going to bring sacrifice back. But the combination of imperfects and uncorrected presents may after all tell us something about the nature of Servius's attitude to the old cults. While the imperfects make it clear that he wrote after the end of sacrifice, his only detectable reaction was to correct the present tenses in his sources. There is no hint of indignation or regret. And the fact that he so often forgot only enhances the impression that the end of sacrifice was not a subject that deeply engaged him.

5

The DS additions also have a number of extended points of contact with Macrobius, especially in passages bearing on pagan cult. The standard explanation is a common source, and the usual assumption that both derive from Donatus. Nonetheless, Türk rejected the common source assumption entirely and argued instead that the DS notes derive directly from Macrobius.[63] The implications of this hypothesis would be far-reaching. Türk dated the *Saturnalia* between 384 and 387, and took it for granted that Macrobius was himself a pagan and an active member of the circle of Symmachus, engaged in a cultural battle against Christianity. Macrobius (he insisted) was not the plagiarist he is usually depicted, but a conscientious and diligent researcher who assembled all those citations from Republican antiquarians from the original texts.

---

63. Türk 1963, 327–49.

The now agreed later date for Macrobius (ca. 430) puts Türk's point of departure out of court, but that does not in itself disprove the idea that he conducted research in the literature of pagan cults (as Ando too now assumes), which might have been argued to lend some support to the view that there was a second "pagan revival" in the 430s. What puts this possibility too out of court is the proof that Macrobius and the DS notes do indeed derive from a common source. No one is ever entirely happy about postulating lost common sources. But this is a case where no other solution can explain the facts. It is also a very natural and reasonable assumption. While the seventh-century DS compiler may well have had a somewhat degraded, interpolated copy of Donatus, it would be surprising if Servius and Macrobius, both writing in Rome within a few decades of Donatus's death, did not have access to complete, accurate copies of so basic a resource.

In some of the parallels between DS and Macrobius, DS preserves details missing in Macrobius; in others Macrobius preserves details missing in DS—the classic pointers to a common source.[64] A single illustration must suffice: their comments on Vergil's use of the word *delubrum* (shrine) in *Aen*. ii. 225. For reasons that will soon become clear I also cite Servius's comment on the same word in a later note and a note of Pseudo-Asconius on Cicero. I do not include a translation, because it is the verbal parallels that bring out the nature and extent of the relationship between these texts:

DS on *Aen*. ii. 225:	**Macrobius iii. 4. 2:**	*Serv. Aen*. iv. 56:	Ps-Ascon. *Div*. 3:
Varro autem *Rerum Divinarum* **libro XIX** delubrum esse dicit **aut ubi plura numina sub uno tecto sunt, ut Capitolium, aut** ubi *praeter aedem area sit adsumpta deum causa, ut in circo Flaminio Iovi Statoris* in quo loco dei dicatum sit simulacrum, ut, <*sicut*> *in quo figunt candelabrum appellant, sic in quo deum ponant delubrum dicant*....	**Varro libro octavo** *Rerum Divinarum* delubrum ait alios aestimare in quo *praeter aedem sit area adsumpta deum causa, ut est in Circo Flaminio Iovis Statoris*, alios in quo loco dei simulacrum dedicatum sit; et adiecit, *sicut locum in quo figerent candelam candelabrum appellatum, ita in quo deum ponerent nominatum delubrum*.	Delubrum dictum, ut supra diximus (ii 225), propter lacum in quo manus abluuntur, vel propter tectum coniunctum, aut certe ligneum simulacrum, 'delubrum' dicimus **a 'libro,' hoc est raso ligno factum, quod Graeci ξόανον dicitur.** Sane in secundo libro [ii. 225] de singulis speciebus delubri iuxta Varronem relatum est.	Sunt qui templa esse dicant singulorum dis attributorum locorum, delubra multarum aedium sub uno tecto a diluvio pluviae munitarum. alii delubra dicunt ea templa in quibus sunt labra corporum abluendorum more Dodonaei Iovis aut Apollinis Delphici, in quorum delubris lebetes tripodesque visuntur.

---

64. *Sat*. iii. 4. 1 ~ DS *Aen*. ii. 225; *Sat*. iii. 6. 6–7 ~ DS *Aen*. iii. 84; *Sat*. iii. 6. 15 ~ DS *Aen*. xi. 836; *Sat*. iii. 7. 3 ~ DS *Aen*. x. 419; *Sat*. iii. 8. 1 ~ DS *Aen*. ii. 632. For many more illustrations, Santoro 1946 and Marinone 1946.

Masurius Sabinus *delubrum* effigies, a delibratione corticis; nam antiqui felicium arborum ramos cortice detracto in effigies deorum formabant, unde Graeci ξόανον dicunt.	sunt etiam qui delubra ligna delibrata, id est decorticata, pro simulacris deorum more veterum existiment, sed male.

To begin with DS and Macrobius, the italicized words unmistakably establish a connection between the two passages. But the DS compiler added another clause to the quotation from Varro, clearly authentic since it appears in a slightly fuller form in Servius's note on the passage. As so often, the DS compiler carelessly repeated a detail already included in Servius's abridgment of their common source (one of innumerable proofs that DS and Servius drew on the same source). He also added a quotation from the first-century jurist Masurius Sabinus. Türk would no doubt argue that DS added this from another source, but Servius's note on *Aen.* iv. 56 proves that the Masurius quotation was part of the same original note. Remembering that he had already discussed the etymology of *delubrum* in an earlier note, Servius gave a cross-reference, but did not take the trouble to check what he had written there, and in his second note gives a *different* abridgment of the much longer note in his source. Without mentioning Masurius Sabinus, he summarizes the view DS attributes to him: a *delubrum* was an effigy carved from a tree branch from which the bark had been removed (*delibrare, delibratio*),[65] "whence the Greeks call it a *xoanon*." The final clause is a garbled reference to the derivation of Greek *xoanon*, a statue, from *xeo*, to carve, though of course a *delubrum* was a building or demarcated area, not a statue.

Pseudo-Asconius was a probably fifth-century commentator on Cicero's *Verrines*. The few modern critics to pay any attention to his work have emphasized his debt to Servius,[66] but the passages in question might as easily derive from Donatus as Servius. While he did not copy verbatim like DS or Servius, Pseudo-Asconius evidently drew on a long list of etymologies of *delubrum* closely related to all these other texts (including the removal of bark from logs of wood). It is a further pointer to a common source that each of these four witnesses preserves at least one detail missing in all the others. There can be little doubt that all derive from Donatus (or, more remotely, Asper).

Nonetheless, it is a misunderstanding of Macrobius's purpose and method to present the issue, as Türk did, as a choice between researcher or plagiarist, nor need the fact that he followed the sources we can identify closely imply that he drew on only a few.[67] Listen to his own words:

---

65. For these exceptionally rare words, see *TLL* v. 442.
66. G. Thilo, *Servius* 1 (1881), xxxi; Gessner 1888; Zetzel 1981, 172–76.
67. Türk 1963, 332.

> You should not count it a fault if I often set out the borrowings from my mis-
> cellaneous reading in the authors' own words (*si res quas ex lectione varia mutu-
> abor ipsis saepe verbis quibus ab ipsis auctoribus enarratae sunt explicabo*). The
> present work sets out to be a collection of noteworthy facts, not a display of
> fine style. You must be satisfied if you find knowledge about the ancient world
> (*notitiam vetustatis*) sometimes set out plainly (*non obscure*) in my own words,
> sometimes faithfully recorded in the actual words of ancient writers, as each
> topic has seemed to call for an exposition or a transcription (*prout quaeque se
> vel enarranda vel transferenda suggesserint*).

Not only does he admit that he has "often" reproduced his sources verbatim, it has not always been appreciated that the final clause distinguishes *two* procedures: *enarrare* and *transferre*. *Transferre* must refer to the verbatim transcription of texts, *enarrare* to expounding what he calls *notitia vetustatis* in his own words. He makes no claim of original research for either procedure. The clearest illustration of transcription is the use he makes of Gellius. Since Gellius has survived almost complete, we can see that Macrobius incorporates scores of pages into his own text virtually verbatim. A subtle investigation by G. Lögdberg has shown that the few slight verbal differences between Macrobius and Gellius in such borrowed passages are almost invariably to be explained by deliberate alteration of Gellius's often archaising language to more "classical" forms (c.g., *necesse est* for Gellius's *necessum est*; *enarrat* for Gellius's rare *denarrat*) to harmonize with Macrobius's own more classicizing style.[68] As for material "set out plainly in his own words," one example we can identify is Plutarch's *Table Talk*, also drawn on very extensively, where (of course) he had to translate Plutarch's Greek into Latin.

It is true that he never names either Gellius or Plutarch or (above all) Donatus,[69] to all of whom he owes so much. But it does not follow that he was furtively conceal-ing his debt. Many late antique writers (above all grammarians) copied material more or less verbatim from sources they do not name. It was standard practice for antiquar-ians not to name the late intermediaries where they found the classical texts and anec-dotes they took such pleasure in collecting[70]—much as moderns do not feel it necessary to name the dictionaries of quotations and Web sites from which they draw material they assume to be in the public domain. Macrobius seems to have looked on books like Gellius and Plutarch's *Table Talk* as quarries rather than authorities. Nonius Marcellus, an early fourth-century (perhaps amateur) *grammaticus*,[71] likewise drew extensively on Gellius without acknowledgement in his *De compendiosa doctrina*, a collection of lexicographical and antiquarian material in twenty books.[72] But Nonius

---

68. Lögdberg 1936, Ch. 1.
69. He does name Plutarch once together with Aristotle and Apuleius as writers on skommata (vii. 3. 24), but not in such a way as to suggest that he was a major source.
70. See the studies in section 3 of Braund and Wilkins 2000; Cameron 2004, 158–59.
71. So Kaster 1988, 417–18.
72. Chahoud 2007, 69–96.

was not so much concealing his source as deliberately (even ostentatiously) not naming it, since he cites it a number of times anonymously as "an old writer" *auctoritatis
incertae, obscurae, incognitae,* or (more significantly) *non receptae.*[73] For Macrobius, as
for Nonius, Gellius was simply too recent to merit citation *as an authority.* The latest
source he cites by name is the Severan polymath Serenus Sammonicus, and Marinone
not implausibly argues from the very fact that he is named that Macrobius cites him
though a later intermediary.[74] By the same token the fact that he nowhere names
Athenaeus might (paradoxically) be argued to imply that Macrobius knew him at
firsthand.[75]

Literary trimmings aside, the *Saturnalia* is more a collection of extracts than an
original work of scholarship. Informed contemporary readers would have taken it for
granted that he came by his ancient learning through more recent intermediaries.
After all, he openly admits to "often" copying his sources verbatim, and all his readers
must have been familiar with Donatus from reading Vergil in school. If one of them
had subsequently come across a text of (say) Gellius, his first reaction (I suspect)
would not have been indignation at unmasking a plagiarist, but pleasure at discovering
that Gellius contained so much congenial material that Macrobius had omitted.

Moderns have always treated Macrobius in turn as a quarry, on the whole unimpressed by the literary pretensions of his dialogue. For while we can trace fifty or so
pages back to surviving sources, much the greater part derives from sources now lost.
The *Saturnalia* preserves an enormous number of otherwise unknown texts.
Contemporary readers with antiquarian tastes would have been as delighted as we are
by all these arcane fragments,[76] but they would also have appreciated the effort he put
into turning his borrowed material into a secular version of the literary dialogue so
fashionable at this period.[77]

On occasion, even a passage in other respects plagiarized word for word is by a
minimal change neatly adapted to its new context.[78] What in Gellius was a vivid portrait of the flamboyant Sophist Favorinus rebuking a young man for using ostentatiously archaic language, in Macrobius serves to characterize the young Avienus—
a warning that we should beware what we read into the characterizations of
other interlocutors in the *Saturnalia.* Favorinus's speech is a sensible rebuke of a
pretentious youth by an older man, while Avienus is an ignorant youth about to
be rebuked himself in turn. So Macrobius changed Favorinus's imperative "live

---

73. See the index auctorum to W. M. Lindsay's edition of Nonius, vol. 3 (1903), 943–44; Chahoud 2007,
    81; *non receptae* in particular seems to excludes the possibility that Nonius's copy of Gellius had just
    lost its title page; his decision was deliberate.
74. *Sat.* iii. 9. 6; 16. 8; 16. 9; 17. 4; Marinone 1967, 46.
75. Courcelle 1969, 22–25, argues for indirect consultation of Athenaeus.
76. I use the word *fragment* advisedly, since so many of Macrobius's quotations are garbled, corrupt, or
    incomplete.
77. Schmidt in Fuhrmann 1977, 174–80, lists forty-three "early Christian" dialogues, thirty-four of them
    from the late fourth to early fifth century.
78. Macrobius i. 5. 1 ~ Gellius *NA* i. 10.

according to the morals of the past, but speak in the language of the present," entirely appropriate for Favorinus but striking the wrong note in an impertinent youth, to "*let us* live according to the morals of the past, but speak in the language of the present."

The literary artistry of the *Saturnalia* has perhaps been undervalued. There is a rich field here for investigation (for some illustrations, Ch. 7. 10–11). Nonetheless, although he may fairly be called an antiquarian, given his obvious delight in archaic Roman texts and customs, he can hardly be called a scholar. As far as concerns his material, he was an entirely derivative compiler. Türk's thesis that he originated the material on pagan cult that he shares with DS is mistaken.

6

Yet the fact that so much of Macrobius's material is simply copied from earlier sources does not in itself mean that it had no contemporary relevance in its new context. Both Servius and Macrobius pay considerable attention to Vergil's treatment of cult and ritual. Is it possible that late antique Vergilian commentators did indeed read the pagan/Christian issues of their own day into their beloved Vergil?

Perhaps the most intriguing Macrobian conception is Vergil the *pontifex maximus*. In i. 24 he represents his interlocutors mapping out the course of their future discussions. Symmachus announces that he will cover rhetoric in Vergil. Next comes Praetextatus, in a passage regularly quoted out of context:

> Of all the high qualities for which Vergil is praised, my constant reading of his poems leads me to admire the great learning with which he has observed the rules of pontifical law in many different parts of his work, as if he had made a special study of it. If my discourse does not prove unequal to so lofty a topic, I undertake to show that our Vergil may fairly be regarded as a *pontifex maximus*. (i. 24. 16)

According to Türk, "The idea of seeing Vergil as the supreme pontiff must have originated in the circle of Symmachus," as a sort of discreet response to Gratian's repudiation of the title "from the Roman nobility, conscious of the importance of the role of the supreme pontificate for the old religion." Hedrick mistakenly claims that Macrobius so styles the poet "several times." No, once only.[79]

Taken by itself, it might well seem an attractive notion that pagans assigned to Vergil the religious duties (supposedly) rejected by the imperial pontifex.[80] But the long discourse of Praetextatus that follows (iii. 1–12) makes it clear that the reference is not to religious secrets or respect for the gods, but simply to details in the Vergilian

---

79. Türk 1963, 336; Hedrick 2000, 85 ("Vergil…is imagined as the head of the official state religion").
80. So (e.g.) P. Brown 1967, 301.

text alleged to reflect the minutiae of pontifical law—the province of the *pontifex*. Even in chapters that appear to be straightforward discussions of textual points, the underlying purpose is to argue for the reading that implies the deepest knowledge of correct cult practice. For example, at *Aen.* v. 238, where the best MSS offer *extaque... pro-iciam*, Servius insists that the correct reading is *porriciam*, quoting *exta porriciunto... in altaria*, as cited by Veranius from Fabius Pictor.[81] For Macrobius, the key factor is the learning displayed by the citation. In context, *pontifex maximus* has less the modern associations of "high priest" than "religious expert."

The same applies to the immediately following sentence, in which Flavian announces the topic of his contribution:

> I find in our poet such knowledge of augural law that, even if he were unskilled in all other branches of learning, the exhibition of this knowledge alone would win him high esteem.

Though regularly cited as proof that he was a passionate and dedicated pagan, all Macrobius is saying here is that he has chosen Flavian as the mouthpiece for *his own* collection of material on *Vergil's* knowledge of augural law. In the next sentence the Greek Eustathius announces that he will treat Vergil's knowledge of Greek, philosophy, and astronomy as well as literature. Then the two Albini promise to discuss Vergil's knowledge of Roman poetry.

According to Ando, Macrobius "advocat[ed] the truth and efficacy of pontifical law."[82] But it is not pontifical law itself he is concerned with, but *Vergil's* knowledge of the subject. If this were a theme confined to Macrobius and no earlier than 382, it might still be worth exploring the idea of a link with the disestablishment of the cults. But it is by no means confined to Macrobius. Servius nowhere directly calls either Vergil or Aeneas *pontifex maximus*, but he does assert that Vergil "everywhere" presents Aeneas as "both a *pontifex* and an expert in sacred matters," and DS notes find "hidden allusions" to pontifical law in a number of other passages—most of them (it must be said) wildly implausible.[83] The fact that most of these allusions occur in DS notes proves that this fascination with pontifical knowledge goes back (at least) to Donatus, long before what is generally perceived as the "crisis" of late Roman paganism.

The most quoted note in this category is the one on *Aen.* iii. 80, referring to Anius the priest-king of Delos, where Servius remarks "whence we call emperors

---

81. *Sat.* iii. 2. 1. In this case some editors agree, but while *porricere* is no doubt the correct term for placing entrails on an altar, in Vergil they are being cast into the sea. Praetextatus implausibly argues that the sea is being regarded as equivalent to an altar, but in the light of Livy 29. 27. 5 (*exta caesa victima, uti mos est, in mare proiecit*), *proiciam* might actually be the ritually correct term in context.

82. Ando 2001, 392.

83. *et pontificem et sacrorum inducit peritum, Aen.* x. 228; *ius pontificum latenter attingit*, on *Aen.* i. 179; *hic ius pontificale quibusdam videtur subtiliter tangere*, on *Aen.* viii. 363; see too the notes on i. 305; ii. 57, 119; iv. 262; viii. 552, 610; ix. 4.

pontiffs (*pontifices*) to this very day (*hodieque*)." The obvious inference (so it might seem) is that Servius was writing before Gratian's (supposed) repudiation of the title of *pontifex maximus*. Yet his representation as a young man at Macrobius's dramatic date of 382 forbids so early a chronology for his commentary (in fact, a work of the 420s). What then are we to make of the *hodieque*? Writers of all sorts and dates regularly use this formula when describing activities or objects that have lasted for centuries.[84] It is especially common in commentaries on classical texts, a teacher's device to underline the continuing relevance of the classics.[85] Only a few lines earlier in this very note on Anius, a DS passage, after describing how his three daughters were transformed into doves, adds "whence to this very day it is forbidden to kill doves on Delos."[86] No one will believe that Donatus had up-to-the-minute information on the way doves were treated on Delos ca. 350. In both cases the emphasis falls on the *origin* of a long-standing custom (*unde hodieque*). In all probability both aetiologies stood, complete with the *hodieque*, in Servius's source. Quite properly judging the doves irrelevant to his purpose, he included only the story about why the emperor was called *pontifex*. So this detail would date to the 350s rather than the 420s, if not earlier still.[87] On any hypothesis, Servius's note is not concerned with the importance of the emperor in the state cults. It traces the *origin* of his title back to a mythical king of Delos!

In addition to all these pontifical references (forty-two in all), no fewer than twenty-six DS notes (plus three in Servius) claim to detect allusions to the presentation of Aeneas as *flamen Dialis*. More specifically, ten notes in Bk iv claim that Vergil's account of the "marriage" between Dido and Aeneas portrays them throughout as *flamen* and *flaminica*, respectively,[88] with one asserting that Aeneas and Dido are "everywhere" portrayed as *flamen* and *flaminica*.[89] On iv. 29 we are told without further explanation that "according to ancient rites" the *flamen* was allowed to remarry after his wife's death while the *flaminica* could only marry once—which is held to justify Aeneas in marrying Lavinia but not Dido in wanting to marry Aeneas! (When Jerome cites *flamen* and *flaminica* in a list of societies that practice monogamy, he is surely recalling

---

84. For many examples, Krebs and Schmalz, *Antibarbarus* 1 (1905), 654–55; *TLL* 5. 2853.

85. Twenty-one examples in Porphyrio's commentary on Horace (Holder's index, 476); for a nice *unde hodieque*, see p. 208. 14 Holder.

86. *unde hodieque Deli columbas violare nefas est* ~ *unde hodieque imperatores pontifices dicimus*, both on *Aen.* iii. 80. There is no other source for this claim. For cults related to Anius on Delos, Bruneau 1970, 413–30.

87. We may compare the DS reference on *Aen.* iii. 12 to the innermost shrine (*penus*) of Vesta being opened and closed "to this very day" (*hodie quoque*), true for the 350s, but this time quite properly dropped by Servius.

88. DS on *Geo.* i. 21, 31; on *Aen.* i. 179, 305, 706; ii. 57, 683; iii. 607; iv. 19, 29, 103, 137, 262, 263, 339, 374, 518, 646; viii. 363, 552; x. 270; xi. 76; xii. 120, 492, 588, 602. There are also two brief notes (on i. 448 and ii. 683) and one longer note in Servius (on viii. 664), not counting a reference on i. 290 to Julius Caesar's honors including a personal *flamen*. See too Starr 1997, 63–70.

89. DS on *Aen.* iv. 103.

what he learned in Donatus's classroom).[90] On iv. 518 DS has a long note on the sort of footwear permitted a *flaminica*, utterly irrelevant unless Dido is assumed to be or represent a *flaminica* (Servius adopts a simpler and more sensible explanation of the line).[91] On 339 and 374 the form of marriage between *flamen* and *flaminica* is again described as though its relevance to Dido and Aeneas were obvious. It seems clear that this strange fancy must have been deeply entrenched in the exegetical tradition even before Donatus. Apart from one allusive reference to twice-married women not being eligible to hold priesthoods (on iv. 19), Servius does not mention it.[92] Nor does Macrobius in what we have of his dialogue, though his silence is probably to be explained by the loss of the end of Bk iii (below).

As for Servius, insufficient attention has been paid to the fact that so much of this cult material appears only in the DS additions. Whether this means Donatus or Asper or some specialized earlier monograph on cult references in Vergil, we cannot doubt that Servius was aware of it. It follows that Servius deliberately *omitted* much of the cult material in his sources. The fact that he dropped so many of Donatus's references to *pontifices* and *flamines* implies that he did not altogether share this obsession with Vergil's supposed pontifical expertise. Yet the fact that he includes as many as he does[93] suggests that he was not suppressing them out of discretion or fear. There was nothing *more* pagan about flaminical rituals. The very reverse, in fact; by the fourth century they had long ceased to be part of living pagan practice (p. 162).[94] It would be nice to ascribe Servius's restraint in this case to good sense, but more probably he just found the DS notes too detailed, discursive, and obscure for his purposes. Elsewhere he comments freely enough but usually succinctly on Vergil's ritual references. That is to say, the pagan Servius is actually less interested in pagan ritual than the probably Christian Macrobius. And both are less interested than the undoubtedly Christian seventh-century editor who put all that Donatan ritual material Servius had omitted back in the margins of his copy of Servius.

Another passage that has been widely held to support a specifically pagan purpose for the *Saturnalia* is i. 24. 13, put in the mouth of Symmachus:[95]

> But we, who claim to have a finer taste, will not allow the secret places of this sacred poem to remain concealed (*non patiamur abstrusa esse adyta sacri poematos*), but we shall examine the approaches to its hidden meanings (*arcanorum sensuum investigato aditu*) and throw open its inmost shrine (*reclusa penetralia*) for the worship of the learned (*doctorum cultu celebranda*).

---

90. *flamen unius uxoris ad sacerdotium admittitur, flaminica quoque unius mariti eligitur, Ep.* 123. 56.

91. See Austin's note on iv. 518.

92. Serv. on *Aen.* ii. 683; viii. 664; see Austin on ii. 683.

93. For example, ii. 148 (*verba sunt quibus pontifex maximus utitur*); iii. 64, 80; vi. 176, 366; viii. 275; ix. 298.

94. It should be emphasised that by *flamines* Servius always means the *flamines* of the state cult, not the various provincial priests known by this name down into late antiquity.

95. Klingner 1961, 529; Bloch 1963, 210; Türk 1963, 338; Klein 1971, 68–69; Döpp 1978, 631–32.

This has recently been described as "a passage of unmistakeable religious significance."[96] Taken by itself, it might indeed seem to suggest that Macrobius saw Vergil as a sacred text, from which he planned to extract arcane religious truths.[97] But if the sentence is read in context, any such interpretation is completely excluded.[98] The subject is the versatility, the many-sidedness, the *copia rerum* of Vergil. This *copia*, says Symmachus (i. 24. 12),

> almost all the schoolteachers (*litteratores*) gloss over,[99] as though grammarians were not allowed to know anything beyond the explanation of individual words. So those fine fellows (*belli isti homines*) have set hard and fast limits or boundaries to their science. If anyone dares to go beyond them, he would be deemed guilty of as heinous a crime as if he had peeped into the temple of the goddess barred to men [the Bona Dea].

In the course of the next couple of pages we are given a list of these "secret places" and "hidden meanings" in Vergil. Once again, they are simply the themes of the *Saturnalia*: Vergil's knowledge of rhetoric, pontifical law, augural law, Greek writers, Latin poets. They are only "secrets" because (according to Symmachus) they are unknown to most schoolteachers (*litteratores*). Tiberius Donatus too began his *Interpretationes Vergilianae* with an attack on the superficiality of schoolteachers.[100] Macrobius would have included the real Servius in this lowly company; we have seen that his commentary lays disproportionate emphasis on grammatical and linguistic detail, and omits much of the cult material we know from the DS parallels with Macrobius to have stood in Donatus.

Symmachus promises that he and his fellow guests will open up the "innermost recesses" of this sacred poem "for the worship of the learned" (*doctorum cultu*). Ando translates the final phrase "celebrated *in cult* by the learned," but the fact that it is to the cult of the *learned* they will be opened up is enough, in context, to prove that, like all the other religious terms in this passage, the sacral language is simply metaphor. We might compare Servius's remark, in the preface to a treatise on meter, that *velut ad Musarum sacraria venitur.*[101] Phocas, a *grammaticus urbis Romae* of uncertain date, but at earliest late fourth century since he was clearly writing for Christian students, refers to the *Aeneid* as a *sacrum carmen.*[102] Compare too Cicero, who writes of "disclosing the innermost secrets (*mysteria*) of the rhetors."[103] Elsewhere Macrobius refers more than

---

96. Ando 2001, 373 n. 21.

97. "Das ist eine wahre Bibelerklärung," Alföldi and Alföldi 1990, 52, of this very passage.

98. Sinclair 1982, 261–63.

99. *inlotis pedibus*, without waiting for the proper ritual ablutions necessary for performing sacrifice, and so a metaphor for superficiality or lack of preparation (Jan ad loc.).

100. *Sed cum adverterem nihil magistros discipulis conferre quod sapiat* (i. 1. 5 Georgii).

101. Serv. *Centimeter* in *GLK* iv. 456. 6.

102. Phocas, *Vita Verg.* 24; A. Mazzarino 1973/4, 526–27; Kaster 1988, 339–41.

103. *Tusc.* iv. 55; *De or.* i. 206; cf. *Pro Mur.* 25; Quintilian i. 2. 20, v. 13. 60, v. 14. 27. English "mysteries" would have insufficient religious connotations. An imperial law (*Cod. Theod.* i. 15. 8) claims that the emperor will deal with cases referred to court by *vicarii* "lest we should repel their consultations from our shrines as though they were supplications of the profane" (*veluti profanorum preces a nostris adytis repellamus*).

once to the *adyta* of philosophy, and once to its *penetral*.[104] To interpret the *adyta sacri poematos* otherwise would conflict with the clear surface purpose of the passage in context: a list of Vergilian topics to be discussed in the following pages. There is indeed polemic—but against pedantic grammarians. Other passages reveal the same polemic: for example, the reference to obtaining basic information from "the lowest ranks of the grammarians" (*ex plebeia grammaticorum cohorte*, i. 24. 8). At vi. 9. 1 Avienus quotes contemptuously the inadequate response a question of his had elicited from "someone from the rank and file of the grammarians" (*quendam de grammaticorum cohorte*). At v. 22. 12 Eustathius attacks the ignorance of the grammarians.

7

It is understandable that historians unfamiliar with the history of ancient Vergilian scholarship should have been misled by the fact that Macrobius's interlocutors devote so much attention to the old Roman cults. Horsfall has rightly observed that Macrobius and Servius "represent two readings of Vergil more interested than the poet himself in religious detail."[105] But that does not mean that they had a religious purpose. The key factor here is that this interest in ritual detail does not begin with Macrobius and Servius, nor with their source Donatus, nor even with his source, Asper. Indeed, the first ancient critic to raise the issue was a man who might actually have known Vergil himself, C. Julius Hyginus, a freedman of Augustus and friend of Ovid. His various works (*De familiis Troianis, De proprietatibus deorum, De penatibus,* and *De Vergilio*), known from a handful of quotations in Gellius, Servius, and Macrobius, suggest that he was more an antiquarian than a critic, and Gellius described him as "not ignorant of pontifical law." No fewer than four of the nine quotations from his *De Vergilio* are concerned with ritual language, of which three already reveal the same inappropriate insistence on Vergil's ritual accuracy that we find in Servius and Macrobius.[106]

First, *Aen.* vi. 15, where Daedalus is said to have escaped Crete *praepetibus pennis*, "with swift wings." According to Hyginus, this was "incorrect and ignorant" (*inproprie et inscite dictum*), because *praepes* is a word properly applied by augurs to birds that fly past at opportune moments or settle on appropriate perches. It was therefore "inappropriate" (*non apte*) for Vergil to use this word in a non-augural context. Nonsense, retorted Gellius, it is Hyginus who was inappropriate, evidently unaware of parallels in Ennius and Matius.[107] Second, there is xii. 120, where for *lino velati* read by all sur-

---

104. *Sat.* 1.17.2; *Comm.* 1.12.18; *Sat.* vii. 1. 5; cf. Boeth. *Cons. phil.* 2.1; Aug. *c. Acad.* iii.18.41 (*adyta Platonis*).
105. Horsfall, *CR* 41 (1991), 242.
106. For the fragments of Hyginus, see G. Funaioli, *Grammaticae Romanae Fragmenta* (Leipzig 1907), 525–37.
107. For more information on *praepes*, see Wigodsky 1972, 112–13.

viving manuscripts, Hyginus argued that Vergil wrote (or should have written) *limo*, referring to the long apron worn by the officials who killed sacrificial victims. As we shall see in a couple of pages, this was a misguided attempt to introduce a ritual reference where it does not belong.

Third, Hyginus understood *Aen.* vii. 187–88, *ipse Quirinali lituo parvaque sedebat / succinctus trabea*, to imply that a *lituus* was something worn like a *trabea*, claiming that Vergil did not know it was a curved rod carried by augurs. Our source here is Gellius, who cites, and refutes, Hyginus's objection, in a discussion that extends over almost two pages.[108] Macrobius copies it verbatim (*Sat.* vi. 8. 1–6), complete with every argument and every text cited, the only differences resulting from his skilful assignment of Hyginus's argument to Avienus and Gellius's refutation to Servius (a particularly good illustration of the way Macrobius adapts his source while reproducing its substance more or less verbatim).

Hyginus's fourth comment is more successful. On *lanigeras mactabat rite bidentis* at *Aen.* vii. 93, he rejected the apparently widespread view that *bidentes* was a byform of *biennes*, meaning "two-year-olds," and explained instead that it meant with two teeth (referring to the replacement of the two central milk teeth by larger teeth at the age of one year). This is correct, confirmed by the authority of modern sheep farmers,[109] though Vergil's fondness for *bidentes* is surely due more to its metrical convenience (eight times, always at the line end) than (as the commentators assumed) its appropriateness for a given ritual. Once again, our source is Gellius, and once again Macrobius copies the chapter in question verbatim (except for a couple of omissions), again neatly dividing it between Avienus and Servius. The real Servius also reproduces Hyginus's solution, unacknowledged.[110]

But while Hyginus and the fourth-century commentators shared a preoccupation with Vergil's ritual language, there is nonetheless an important difference between their approaches. Hyginus found Vergil insufficiently attentive to ritual language, whereas the later commentators saw him as an expert in all areas of Roman religion, repeatedly characterising him as *sacrorum peritus*. Three other of Hyginus's nine surviving notes accuse Vergil of error of one sort or another,[111] while for Servius and Macrobius Vergil *never* makes errors. Macrobius explicitly states more than once that Vergil was both expert and infallible in all matters.[112] Servius too claims universal expertise for him, and many passages imply infallibility, though he does not make the point explicitly.

When and how did this remarkable doctrine of Vergilian infallibility arise? There can be little doubt that it gradually developed out of the response to early attacks on

---

108. *NA* v. 8. 1–11; see Horsfall's note on *Aen.* vii. 188.
109. See H. Wright 1931, 1–23 at 7–18; Pease on *Aen.* iv. 57; Horsfall on vii. 93.
110. Gell. xvi. 6. 14–15; Macr. *Sat.* vi. 9. 7; Serv. on *Aen.* iv. 57; vi. 39.
111. F 7–9 Funaioli, all quoted in Gellius x. 16.
112. *Vergilius quem nullius umquam disciplinae error involvit* (Macr. *Somn.* ii. 8. 1); *V. quem constat erroris ignarum* (*Sat.* ii. 8. 8); *nullius disciplinae expers* (*Somn.* i. 6. 44); *omnium disciplinarum peritissimus* (*Somn.* i. 15. 12); *omnium disciplinarum peritus* (*Sat.* i. 16. 12).

Vergil.[113] Some early critics compiled lists of his plagiarisms (*furta*), others accused him of faults (*vitia*) both stylistic and moral, not to mention inconsistencies and ignorance of various sorts. A fascinating recent article by Sergio Casali has shown that Ovid's "Aeneid" (*Metamorphoses* 13) reflects some evidently very early criticisms otherwise known from later commentators.[114] In addition to Hyginus, we know of Carvilius Pictor's *Aenaeomastix* and the anonymous *Vergiliomastix*. Perhaps the most interesting thing about the response to this polemic is that, instead of just accepting some criticisms and ignoring the rest, Vergil's more single-minded admirers set out to refute them systematically, in part because from an early date the reception of Vergil was influenced by the reception of Homer. The fullest response we know of was published by Asconius († A.D. 88) under the title *Contra obtrectatores Vergilii*. All these works have perished, but substantial traces survive in parts of Macrobius. To judge from his commentary on Cicero, Asconius's responses were probably judicious, but it is clear that later admirers felt obliged to defend Vergil against *all* criticisms, at any cost.

The most fully developed, it seems, was that of plagiarism, the subject of at least three different works, the *Thefts* (*Furta*) of Perellius Faustus and the *Similarities* (*Homoiotētes*) of Q. Octavius Avitus (the latter providing lists of parallels between Vergil and his predecessors that filled eight books); and Asconius, who defended Vergil against the accusation of plagiarising Homer.[115] Macrobius's lists undoubtedly derive from earlier compilations based on these polemical works, not on his own reading.[116] Given his unqualified admiration for Vergil we might have expected him to offer either a systematic rebuttal, passage by passage, or at any rate a general rebuttal. But plagiarism is not an accusation that can be simply refuted or countered by a better explanation. In most cases Vergil did indeed "imitate" (for want of a more precise term) the passage cited. His only answer to those who accuse Vergil of plagiarism is to call them ignorant or spiteful (*Sat.* vi. 1. 2). Unable to refute the charge and not knowing how else to deal with it, in the main Macrobius simply ignored it and just lists Vergil's "imitations" without comment as proof of his erudition.

As for Servius, though duly quoting many passages alleged to be Vergilian models, he betrays no interest in defining the extent, much less the purpose of an imitation. They are just facts to be registered for their own sake. Of the nearly thirty passages listed by Macrobius as being "copied in their entirety" (*ex integro translatos*) from an earlier poet, most show no more than two and a half feet copied exactly.[117] We cannot

---

113. Ribbeck 1866, 103–7; H. Funaioli, *Gramm. Rom. Fragmenta* 1 (1907), 542–44; W. Görler, *EV* 3 (1987), 807–13.

114. Casali 2007, 181–210.

115. *octo volumina quos et unde versus transtulerit continent*, Don. *V. Verg.* 185; Funaioli, *Gramm. Rom. Frag.* (1907), 544; Asconius, Don. § 190 (*quod pleraque ab Homero sumpsisset*).

116. The most penetrating and systematic analysis of these lists is that of Jocelyn 1964 and 1965, on which I gratefully draw without further acknowledgement. Hollis 2007, 8, mistakenly assumes that Macrobius, a "person of high culture," consulted original texts of poets like Varius Rufus and Furius Bibaculus.

117. Jocelyn 1965, 140.

fairly fault Servius and Macrobius for not being interested in the mechanics of imitation, but we can fault sweeping and inaccurate generalizations. We may compare (out of many examples) "this whole passage is taken from Naevius's *Punic War*" (DS on *Aen.* i. 198); "this whole passage is Ennian" (on viii. 631); and above all "these are all lines of Gallus, borrowed from his poems" (on *Buc.* x. 46). No attempt to specify which lines or even which poems of Gallus. The important point was Vergil's amazing knowledge of earlier poets. Particularly instructive is the note on *Aen.* v. 517, where Servius dismisses criticism as *inanis vituperatio* (characteristically polemical language) because "the whole passage is taken from Homer, and the thing is just a translation" (*res est translata simpliciter*). That is to say, if Vergil was "just translating," he had no option but to translate literally; the accusation of plagiarism cannot apply in such cases!

The doctrine of infallibility is the final stage of this development. On the evidence we have, the first intimations appear at the beginning of the second century in Florus's dialogue *Was Vergil an orator or poet?* (of which, sadly, only the autobiographical preface survives). Next comes Asper. Asper's commentary does not survive, but his approach can in part be reconstructed from citations in Servius, the Verona Scholia, and a fragment of a monograph preserved on a palimpsest.[118] Once again, a single illustration must suffice. At *Aen.* iii. 623, Achaemenes, a companion of Ulysses, describes seeing the Cyclops eat two of their band (*vidi egomet duo de numero*). "Homer says four" [actually six], says Servius, so [Vergil] disagrees with him." It is characteristic of the defensiveness of the commentators that they felt it necessary to explain away even so trivial a discrepancy as this. Evidently, the *obtrectatores* had made much of this proof of Vergil's "ignorance" of Homer. Servius suggests that Vergil's two merely refers to victims whose grisly end Achaemenes had actually seen himself; DS that Achaemenes meant two eaten simultaneously. According to Asper, Vergil was using *duo* for *bini*,[119] meaning "in pairs" (Homer does in fact describe the Cyclops grabbing men in pairs, δύω μάρψας).[120] While all these explanations are possible, none are natural and none of them would ever have occurred to anyone except for a misguided anxiety to reconcile Vergil with Homer. In the present context it is instructive to be able to date such special pleading as early as Asper. Asper also devoted many notes to Vergil's erudition.[121]

There are in fact hundreds of such defensive notes in Servius, with the DS additions usually adding even more excuses. At *Aen.* i. 407–8 Aeneas asks Venus why she "*so often* mocks [him] with false phantoms" (*quid natum totiens...falsis / ludis imaginibus*). As it happens, this is the only time she does this. Servius offers three explanations (DS

---

118. On the latter work, Thilo-Hagen iii. 2. 533–40; Tomsin 1952, 23–34.
119. '*duo* enim posuit pro '*binis*,' Thilo-Hagen iii. 2. 537; Tomsin 1952, 47–48.
120. This may explain Vergil's slip (if such it was); knowing the *Odyssey* well, he may not have reread the entire passage when writing these lines and so not noticed that Homer repeated the formula three times (ix. 285, 311, 344), thus making a total of six. Servius no doubt made the same slip when he said four instead of six.
121. So Tomsin 70–78; Schmidt in Herzog and Schmidt 5 § 443. 2.

adds a fourth), of which the last is especially far-fetched: "many claim that in this very passage he is often deceived, by her dress, her question, her answer, her augury." The sheer number of these alternative defenses of what in many cases stood in no need of defense in the first place, often introduced by polemical language like *reprehendunt* and *refutantur*, suggests that the doctrine of infallibility was already fully developed well before Donatus. It is clearly axiomatic for Servius and Macrobius. It might seem tempting to connect Vergilian infallibility with Christian reliance on the Bible as an infallible source of religious truth, but Vergilian infallibility goes back long before pagan readers of Vergil are likely to have had any knowledge of Christian attitudes to the Bible.

There is a striking illustration from the Christian side in an early work of Augustine addressed to a Manichaean friend who, influenced by Manichaean prejudice against the Old Testament, was unable to appreciate so difficult a book. According to Augustine, the only way to understand difficult texts, whether Scripture or classics, is to read them with sympathetic commentators: "who ever thought of having the recondite and obscure works of Aristotle explained to him by an enemy of Aristotle?" Similarly, he continues, we will never derive any pleasure from Vergil if we begin by hating him and listen to those who say he was mistaken (*errasse*) or mad. But if we read with the help of the experts (in a later chapter he specifies Asper, Cornutus, and Donatus), "even those who do not understand him will at least believe that he made no errors (*peccavisse*) and wrote nothing that was not admirable."[122] His point is not just that the experts will help us to appreciate the beauty of Vergil's poetry. In consecutive sentences he twice raises the possibility that Vergil might be "in error," in the ordinary way a strange reproach to level at a poet, but immediately comprehensible in the light of the sort of criticisms reported by Servius and Macrobius. As early as the 360s, the young Augustine was clearly brought up on the doctrine of Vergilian infallibility, enshrined in defensive commentators, and that in the schools of a small town in North Africa. As Euangelus, the most cantankerous of Macrobius's interlocutors says, "When we were boys, we had an uncritical admiration for Vergil, because our teachers ... *did not allow us* to investigate his faults."[123]

8

It is understandable that modern readers have been tempted to link debates in the *Saturnalia* about cult details in Vergil with the pagan/Christian conflicts of the fourth and fifth centuries. Horsfall was merely restating a long standard view when he recently referred to the "passionately heated religious climate under which details of pagan cult in Virgil were discussed in late antiquity." Fowler refers to Servius's interest in religion

---

122. *De utilitate credendi* 10–17.
123. Macr. *Sat.* i. 24. 6 (Euangelus, who then proceeds to enumerate his faults).

as "reflecting the contemporary struggle between Christianity and paganism."[124] But we have seen that ignorance of ritual was one of the very earliest criticisms made of Vergil. It was because Hyginus and other early critics accused Vergil of ignorance in ritual matters that his defenders were tempted to exaggerate his pontifical and augural expertise. As a consequence, by the second century sacral law had simply become one of the areas of Vergil's omniscience. There is no sign that Macrobius treated it any differently from the others. As for the "debates" about Vergil's knowledge of sacral law, as Ribbeck saw long ago, they are no more than an inescapable element of any dialogue. The issues were long settled (in Vergil's favor), and the polemic simply lifted from the pro- and anti-Vergilian pamphlets of the first century.[125] ✓

Indeed, this literature was surely one of the factors in Macrobius's decision to cast the material he had collected in the form of a dialogue in the first place. In the interest of verisimilitude, whenever he could he liked to add a bit of cut and thrust to the often interminable learned lists he put in the mouths of his interlocutors. Reference has already been made to a couple of passages of Gellius he divided between speakers, and he did the same with a long chapter adapted from Plutarch (vii. 15), cleverly adding a polemical note missing in Plutarch.[126] The first-century pro- and anti-Vergil literature was tailor-made to fit the cut and thrust of a dialogue. All he had to do was divide up the two sides between different interlocutors. And the obvious candidate for delivering the attacks on Vergil was the stock dialogue character of the uninvited guest, a disagreeable person whose function was to provoke the other interlocutors to discuss topics that would not otherwise have arisen among like-minded guests.[127]

The single most influential element in the "pagan reaction" reading of the *Saturnalia* has always been Macrobius's uninvited guest, the boorish Euangelus who repeatedly attacks Vergil. Few have been able to resist the assumption that he is meant to represent Christian hostility to the "pagan culture" venerated by the rest of the company.[128] According to Ando,

> Macrobius exploited the moment of his arrival to discuss explicitly the political and legal implications of religious affiliation in that era. Looking around at the assembled company, Euangelus recognized something that united them and excluded him, and he asked whether they wished to continue without witnesses present. "If that is the case, as I think it is, I will depart rather than mix myself up in your secrets."... Praetextatus rapidly revealed that he had

---

124. Horsfall 2006, on *Aen.* iii. 20; Don Fowler, *Cambridge Companion to Virgil* (Cambridge 1997), 74.
125. Ribbeck 1866, 96–113, still well worth reading.
126. Well discussed by Kaster 1980, 240–42.
127. See the chapter "Der ungebetene Gast" in Martin 1931, 64–79.
128. Klingner 1961, 528; Klein 1971, 70; Smith 1976, 269–70; Marcone 1983, 72; MacCormack 1998, 74, 86–87; most recently Ando 2001, 389; the earliest statement I know is L. Jan's edition, 1 (1848), xxxi.

understood Euangelus to be suggesting that their secret was a shared devotion to illicit religious practices.

This is a complete misunderstanding of the scene. A half-page before this passage Macrobius offers a perfectly satisfactory explanation of the hostile reaction Euangelus senses by introducing him as a spiteful, sharp-tongued fellow "who cared nothing for the dislike which his provocative language, directed against friend and foe alike, stirred up against him everywhere." Furthermore, the reason Euangelus himself gives for suspecting that his presence might disturb the other guests is pure antiquarianism: one of Varro's *Menippean Satires* lays down that the number of guests at a dinner party should not be less than the number of the Graces nor more than the number of the Muses, and he counts nine present already.[129] Praetextatus at once dismisses the idea that he and his guests were "sharing any secret which could not be disclosed to you or, for that matter, to the whole world." The fact that he goes on to refer to the gods and to talk about the "sacred holidays" is simply part of the mise-en-scène of the dialogue. As we have seen, Macrobius regularly inserts details that present his interlocutors as practicing pagans—more such details, indeed, than we would expect in the unself-conscious conversation of "real" pagans (pp. 259 and 271).

Above all, this interpretation presupposes that Euangelus is immediately identifiable as a Christian. This is simply not so. The name itself might *seem* to suggest a Christian, yet it is not in fact a common Christian name.[130] It is not a fictitious name, but the name of a real person taken from Symmachus's correspondence, a person Symmachus criticizes for his "malicious attacks" (*obtrectatio*)—obviously the reason Macrobius selected him for the role of uninvited guest (Ch. 7. 7). His characterization as a sharp-tongued, provocative person is not meant to identify a Christian, but simply to prepare readers for comments and questions that will provoke the other interlocutors.

More important, as we shall see over the next few pages, a number of passages in the *Saturnalia* unmistakably portray him as a pagan who claims to know more about pontifical law than Praetextatus himself. Note i. 24. 2, where he admires Praetextatus's grasp of the complexities of solar theology, and iii. 11. 9, where Praetextatus expects Euangelus to agree with him that on 21 December a pregnant sow is sacrificed to Hercules and Ceres. Despite his contempt for Vergil, we are undoubtedly meant to think of him as a serious, well-informed pagan, only differing from the other interlocutors in his hostility to Vergil. No one depreciated Vergil like that in the fifth century, not even Augustine. The fact that it is Vergil who is the main object of Euangelus's hostility is not a reflection of contemporary attitudes to Vergil, much less Christian hostility to pagan culture. It is simply a reflection of Macrobius's first- and second-century sources, skilfully adapted to provide a foil for his own glorification of Vergil.[131]

---

129. *Sat.* i. 7. 12; cf. Gellius 13. 11. 2.
130. *PCBE* i (1982), 359; ii (1999), 662; *ILS* 3222 (a pagan).
131. "Ipsum vero Aeneomastiga repraesentat apud Macrobium Euangelus," Ribbeck 1866, 103.

To this day no one has described the role of Euangelus more intelligently than Comparetti, as long ago as 1872. As he shrewdly pointed out, Euangelus "sets out to attack just those points in which Vergil is strongest."[132] The most obvious illustration is his petulant denial (v. 2. 1) that "a Venetian, born of peasants and reared amidst forests and scrub, could have acquired even a smattering of Greek letters." As Comparetti saw, this claim "could not so much have occurred to Vergil's bitterest detractor in the Augustan age," and it is inconceivable in fifth-century Rome. The three most prolific Latin Christian writers of the age, Ambrose, Jerome, and Augustine, all steeped in Vergil, while naturally having reservations about the content of his poetry, would have been as astonished as Praetextatus and his friends at the crude and (above all) ill-informed criticisms of Euangelus. The (obviously absurd) accusation that Vergil knew no Greek could have no Christian significance. Its sole purpose in context is to provide a justification for the seventy-five pages on Vergil's knowledge of Greek literature that follow.

Anyone who takes the trouble to look carefully at what Euangelus is actually given to say will discover that he nowhere depreciates anything "pagan" about Vergil. Rather he claims to judge Vergil by stricter standards than the other interlocutors. He constantly and aggressively casts doubt on what he sees as exaggerated claims made for Vergil's scholarly attainments. Ironically enough, most modern readers of Vergil would agree with his general position, if not his actual arguments. For example, at i. 24. 9: "all that remains for you people to do now is to proclaim Vergil an orator as well"—which is (of course) exactly what they proceed to do, indeed had been doing since the early second century, to judge from Annius Florus. In late antiquity it was heresy to doubt that Vergil was the supreme orator (a striking illustration of the assimilation of Vergilian to Homeric criticism: Homer too was universally regarded as the supreme orator).[133] Tiberius Claudius Donatus goes so far as to claim that it should be rhetors, not grammatici, who taught Vergil.[134]

Whether it is Greek literature, rhetoric, or pontifical law, Euangelus is just a foil in the literary frame Macrobius chose to demonstrate Vergil's omniscience. Let us take a closer look at two of his questions together with the answers put in Praetextatus's mouth. After listening to an interpretation by Praetextatus that postulated considerable knowledge of pontifical law on Vergil's part (iii. 9), Euangelus loses his temper: "I too have attended lectures on pontifical law (*et nos cepimus pontificii iuris auditum*)[135] and from what I know of it I shall establish Vergil's ignorance of the discipline" (iii. 10. 2). After citing *Aen.* iii. 21, where Aeneas sacrifices a bull (*taurus*) to Jupiter, he quotes one passage from Bk i of Ateius Capito's *De iure sacrificiorum* forbidding the sacrifice of a bull (*taurus*), boar, or ram to Jupiter; and another from Bk 68 of Antistius Labeo (presumably his *De iure pontificio*) laying down that a *taurus* may only be sacrificed to Neptune, Apollo, and Mars. That is to say, Euangelus is clearly presented as an authority

---

132. Comparetti 1885, 67–68.
133. Kennedy 1957, 23–35. Almost all the Greek rhetorical writers quote Homer more than any other author.
134. *inde intelleges Vergilium non grammaticos sed oratores praecipuos tradere debuisse* (i. 4. 27 Georgii).
135. On these "lectures," see p. 271.

on pontifical law—and so unmistakably as a pagan. As proof that Vergil was well informed about such matters, Praetextatus in response quotes a passage where *tauri* are indeed sacrificed to Neptune and Apollo (*Aen.* iii. 119), and then points out that a terrible portent followed Aeneas's sacrifice of a *taurus* to Jupiter (iii. 26), concluding that "Vergil was looking forward to what was to come when he represented Aeneas as sacrificing a victim unsuited to the occasion" (*Sat.* iii. 10. 7). That is to say, he acknowledges that Vergil represents Aeneas making the wrong sacrifice, but ingeniously claims that the mistake was deliberate. The mistake was a way of foreshadowing the terrible portent that follows, a detail (he implies) that would be picked up by learned readers. This explanation is briefly summarized (without the learned citation) in Servius's notes on *Aen.* iii. 21 and xii. 120, and (with more detail) in a DS note on ii. 202.

Few modern critics have paid much attention to this notion of deliberate mistakes in Vergilian descriptions of rituals. But since it has become a central element in a recent account of Vergil's treatment of sacrifice,[136] it may be worth taking a closer look at so intriguing a feature of the late antique approach to Vergil. First, although there were a few invariable principles (male victims for male gods, female for female, etc.),[137] the system was in fact quite complicated. It is not likely that contemporary readers would have cried out "No! A bull for Jupiter!" in the tones of a peasant in a Dracula movie being asked the way to the count's castle. No contemporary able to read Augustan poets in the light of their Greek models would ever have expected Vergil to offer an accurate description of a Roman ritual. What he would have expected is "fantasy descriptions which are blends of the true facts and of Greek analogues and other models."[138] In an epic poem such as the *Aeneid*, inevitably many of Vergil's ritual descriptions are an amalgam of Roman and Homeric elements. For example, when Vergil has Aeneas sacrifice *taurum Neptuno* (*Aen.* iii. 119), it was not Ateius Capito he had in mind but Homer (*tauron de Poseidāōni*).[139] Although Vergil regularly includes hints of future Roman practices and places in the *Aeneid*, in Bk iii Aeneas himself was still a Trojan who had not yet even reached Italy.[140]

Macrobius knew one and only one thing about sacrifices to Jupiter: bulls were not allowed. What was allowed? Ateius Capito notwithstanding, the Romans undoubtedly did sacrifice large male bovines to Jupiter, as in many scenes of sacrifice in Roman art, most clearly one of the Boscoreale Cups.[141] We know from their acta that the Arval brethren regularly sacrificed a *bos mas* to Jupiter,[142] and according to the protocol for

---

136. Dyson 2001, 9–130, passim.

137. Wissowa 1912, 412–16; Scheid 1998, 72–73.

138. F. Cairns (writing of Propertius) in Galinsky 1992, 67; see too Feeney 1998, Ch. 4.

139. *Il.* 11. 728; cf. 20. 403–4; *Od.* 3. 6; 11. 130–31; 13. 181–82; 23. 277–78; Horsfall on *Aen.* iii. 119.

140. Apropos the *flamen/flaminica* obsession in the notes on *Aen.* iv, it is especially implausible that Dido, Rome's greatest future enemy, should be expected to follow future Roman practice.

141. Kuttner 1995, 133 with pl. 15. Oddly enough Scott Ryberg 1955, 143, characterises this animal, shown with prominent penis, as "the steer prescribed by Roman ritual as the victim appropriate to Jupiter." On bulls and steers in sacrifical scenes, see too Gradel 2002, 167–73, 177–79.

142. Their various sacrificial offerings are tabulated in full by Scheid 1990, 386–423.

the Augustan secular games, both Augustus and Agrippa sacrificed a *bos mas* to Jupiter Optimus Maximus.[143] The difference between *bos mas* and *taurus* must be that one was castrated (steer, ox, or bullock in English usage) and the other not. Oddly enough, scholars disagree about which was which.[144] It has often been thought that the *mas* in *bos mas* implies uncastrated, and that *taurus* must therefore be the castrated animal.[145] But *mas* simply distinguishes biologically male from female. Festus's entry *solitaurilia* (p. 373 L) describes a combined offering of a bull, ram, and boar (*taurus, aries, verres*)— the same trio mentioned by Ateius Capito—"because they are all of whole and complete body" (*quod omnes eae solidi integrique sint corporis*). Capito's ban on *tauri* did not mean another animal altogether; just that the normal offering to Jupiter was a bullock (*bos mas*) rather than a bull (*taurus*).

As for Vergil's *taurus*, Macrobius does not even mention the commonsense explanation that poets have to take meter into account and cannot be expected to use technical terminology. The only defense he puts in Praetextatus's mouth is the claim of deliberate error. If he had really consulted pontifical writings, or even just glanced at any of the prominent inscribed sacrificial monuments in and around Rome, he would have realized that it was simply a question of terminology: if Vergil had written *bovem* all would have been well.[146] The real Praetextatus presumably knew so elementary a fact. But Macrobius did not, nor was he able to consult Praetextatus or any other practising *pontifex*, all long dead by the time he wrote. The citations from Capito and Labeo gives the appearance of research and erudition, but all Macrobius had access to was excerpts cited out of context by first- or second-century Vergil commentators.

In matters of ritual Macrobius and the Vergil commentators were very literal-minded readers. A DS note expresses puzzlement that in the course of 115 lines in Bk 5 Vergil refers to the same animal three times as *taurus*, twice as *iuvencus*, and once as *bos*,[147] and it apparently did not occur to Servius either that the reason Vergil so often used *iŭvēncus* for sacrificial victims was metrical convenience. His note on *Aen*. iii. 21 is very instructive. After repeating the mantra that it was forbidden to sacrifice a *taurus* to Jupiter, whence the prodigy, he comments "for we read everywhere that a calf (*iuvencus*) was sacrificed to Jupiter," adding that "in victims the age too must be taken into account." What was Servius's evidence for this claim? His "everywhere" turns out to mean everywhere *in Vergil*, where there are a dozen references to the sacrifice of

---

143. Pighi 1965, 114, lines 103–4.

144. For an anthology of views, Capdeville 1976, 115–23; Horsfall on *Aen.* iii. 59–60.

145. So Palmer 1969, 11–13.

146. This much is in fact preserved by the so-called *Scholia Bernensia* on *Geo.* i. 45 (p. 179 Hagen): "by *taurum* he means *bovem*," citing *Aen.* ii. 21, "where, unless *bos* is understood (*nisi bos intelligitur*), Vergil is in error (*erravit*)." Essentially, the same note appears in *Brevis Expos. in V. Geo.* i. 45 (Thilo/Hagen iii. 214).

147. *Aen.* v. 366, 382, 472, 473, 477, 481; *cur, cum de uno loquatur, hic bovem, alibi iuvencum, alibi taurum vocat?* (DS on 481). I am not sure what the rest of the note means: *sed videtur pro tempore et diversitate usus, ideoque iuvencum ait.*

iuvenci (all at line end), though only one case specifies an offering to Jupiter (*Aen.* ix. 624). On that passage (the night exploit of Nisus and Euryalus) Servius irrelevantly repeats that this was done "according to Roman rites, because a *taurus* was not sacrificed to Jupiter." But the correct victim for Jupiter was either a *bos mas* or else, on certain occasions (below), a *taurus*.

Servius's *iuvencus* is not based on antiquarian research, but on Vergilian usage alone. Servius was a prisoner of the assumption that Vergil had an infallible knowledge of such things. So since the offering at iii. 21 was followed by the disturbing prodigy of the bleeding tree, he deliberately made it incorrect; but since the offering at ix. 627 was crowned with immediate success (Ascanius's first kill in battle), it must have been correct. Ergo a *iuvencus* was the correct offering to Jupiter.

A couple of other notes show how little Servius really knew or cared about such things. On *Aen.* iv. 543, entirely forgetting his own note on iii. 21 about the ban on *tauri* for Jupiter, he states without comment that a triumphing general *in Capitolio* (and so to Jupiter Optimus Maximus) "sacrifices bulls." On ix. 627, after stating that a *iuvencus* was the proper sacrifice to Jupiter because bulls were not sacrificed to him (*Iovi de tauro non immolabatur*),[148] he suddenly remembered those sacrifices on the Capitol and added "*except* when there was a *suovetaurium* for a triumph" (*nisi cum triumphi nomine suovetaurium fiebat*), with the explanation "this is allowed because sacrifice is not being made to Jupiter alone but also to the other gods who preside over war." This is utter nonsense, but a fascinating illustration of the way Servius deals with contradiction. His sources (earlier commentators) presented him with two contradictory assertions: (1) bulls could not be sacrificed to Jupiter, and (2) bulls were sacrificed to Jupiter by triumphators. Unable to doubt (1), he was forced to conclude that (2) must be some sort of exception to the "rule." The *suovetaurilia* (involving sacrifice of a pig, sheep, and bull) was simply a guess, and a bad guess, since it was a ritual of purification and protection and had nothing to do with victory or triumphs. If we did not know better, we might have been tempted to accept this confidently presented solution to a pseudo-problem.

Servius undoubtedly preserves accurate details about sacrificial practice. He knows that sheep were supposed to be unshorn, that is to say never shorn (so Vergil at *Aen.* xii. 170, *intonsamque bidentem*), for which there was the ritual term *altilaneus*, as he remarks in his note (*quam pontifices altilaneam vocant*). He also knows that oxen were supposed to be not yet broken for the plough (*iniuges*), represented in Vergil by *intactus* (e.g., *intacta…cervice iuvencas, Geo.* iv. 540).[149] But the truth is that he had no real interest in or knowledge of the details of Roman sacrificial ritual except insofar as they confirmed Vergil's expertise in this area. And if they did not so confirm it, then Vergil deliberately got it wrong!

The deliberate mistake axiom helps to fill out the lacuna at the end of *Sat.* iii. 12. Here is Euangelus again:

---

148. Note the characteristic imperfect tenses.
149. H. Wright 1931, 1–23 at 18–23.

Has it never occurred to you, Praetextatus, that Vergil got Dido's marriage sacrifice completely wrong. For he sacrifices "ewes duly chosen for sacrifice to Ceres the lawgiver, to Phoebus, and to father Lyaeus." And then, as though waking up, he added "before all to Juno, who is responsible for the bonds of matrimony" (*mactat…/ legiferae Cereri Phoeboque patrique Lyaeo, / Iunoni ante omnes, cui vincla iugalia curae, Aen.* iv. 56–59).

Tantalizingly enough, the Macrobian text breaks off here, but since Dido's "marriage" to Aeneas turned out so disastrously, it is likely that Praetextatus in reply resorted to the same explanation:[150] Vergil deliberately made her sacrifice to the wrong gods. This assumption is supported by the rambling DS note: "some say that the gods he mentioned are hostile to marriage…so Dido, who wishes to marry Aeneas, was unwise to call upon them."[151] The argument is particularly weak here, for two quite different reasons. First, because the reasons given for Ceres, Apollo, and Bacchus being hostile to marriage are speculations drawn from Greek mythology rather than Roman ritual (Ceres hated marriage because her daughter was kidnapped; Apollo and Bacchus preferred rape to marriage). Second, because Vergil immediately goes on to invoke Juno, beyond question the correct deity, the goddess of marriage. Once again, Macrobius's concern here is not which deity was correct for Roman marriage rituals, but the pseudo-problem created by the deliberate mistake axiom: since the marriage Dido prays for does not happen, there ought to be something wrong with the deities she sacrifices to.

No less instructive is the well-known crux in *Aen.* xii. 116–20, a passage that undoubtedly displays some concern for ritual details:[152] priests of the Latins and Trojans preparing to make a treaty set up hearths and altars while others carry fire and water "veiled in linen" (*velati lino*), their brows bound with vervain (*verbena*). So the manuscripts, but according to Servius the *fetiales* never wore linen when making treaties, citing Caper and Hyginus for the reading *limo* from *limus*, the long apron worn during sacrifice. Despite the fact that all surviving manuscripts offer *lino*, most modern editors and critics prefer *limo*, a reading rejected even by Servius, our only source for it. The argument considered decisive by Timpanaro[153] was adduced by Jocelyn: a recently published municipal decree from Irni in Spain that permitted aediles ca. A.D. 82–84 to be attended by "public slaves girded with a *limus*" (*servos communes…limo cinctos*).[154] *Limus*, Jocelyn concluded "can no longer be regarded as a word likely to have been

---

150. So Georgii 1891, 197–98.
151. The note continues, "but others say that Ceres was in favour of marriage," so clearly there was no unanimity in the exegetical tradition. For the jumble of ancient views on these lines, see A. S. Pease's commentary (1935).
152. Warde Fowler 1927, 53–54; Bailey 1935, 99–100.
153. Timpanaro 2001, 15–17, the fullest recent discussion; against, see now Murgia in Rees 2004, 194–96.
154. *JRS* 76 (1986), 153, 202 (III A 16–17), with Jocelyn, *Gnomon* 60 (1988), 202; the *lex colon. Genet.* lxii. 16–17 mentions (*servos*) *publicos cum cincto limo* (M. Crawford [ed.], *Roman Statutes* 1 (London 1996), 400, 433.

unfamiliar either to Virgil's first readers ... or to his copyists."[155] Perhaps so, but the real question is does it make sense in the context? There are two fatal objections.

In the first place, this law simply confirms that those who wore the *limus* were people of low status, slaves or freedmen. Roman magistrates did not deign to kill sacrificial victims themselves. The blow was delivered by attendants known as *victimarii*, who wore the *limus* to protect them from the inevitable spray of blood.[156] There was a guild of *victimarii*, with various specializations: the *popa* stunned the victim with a mallet, while the *cultrarius* cut its throat. In the case of Vergil this is intriguingly documented by miniatures in the Vatican Vergil (ca. 400) illustrating both scenes just discussed: Aeneas sacrificing to Jupiter at *Aen.* iii. 19–48 and Dido sacrificing to Juno et al. at iv. 56–64. In both cases the Vergilian text implies that Aeneas and Dido themselves strike the fatal blow. But the miniatures show *victimarii* bare to the waist, girded with the *limus* and standing by the victims, axe in hand (Ch. 19. 3). Dido is even shown covering her face with her cloak in the Roman manner (below). In keeping with the late antique tendency to exaggerate Vergil's concern for ritual accuracy, the painter has represented Aeneas and Dido as Roman magistrates, leaving the execution of the sacrifice to servile attendants. Servius himself knew that the *limus* was "a garment by which the private parts of the *popae* are covered from navel to feet." If Vergil had really been aiming at ritual accuracy, he would not have made such a blunder as to represent the future fetiales as slaves girded with the *limus*.

Second, *velati* implies (as regularly in Vergil) covering of the head rather than an ankle-length apron tied around the waist.[157] The Irni law bears out the literary evidence that the proper participle to describe wearing the *limus* was *cinctus*.[158] At *Aen.* iii. 405 the seer Helenus tells Aeneas to cover his hair (*velare comas*) before sacrificing when he arrives on Italian soil, obviously an aetiology of the future Roman custom of sacrificing with the head covered.[159] That *fetiales* were supposed to cover their heads with a fillet when performing their ritual is explicitly stated by Livy. He goes on to say that the material was wool,[160] and this is surely the source of the supposed ban on linen. All we have is Servius's report of the second-century Caper's report of Hyginus's argument. Anyone wishing to check Vergil's account of what was (in the distant future) to become the ritual of the *fetiales* would go to the classic source, Livy,[161] where he would discover that wool, not linen, was specified.[162] The first stage in Hyginus's

---

155. He was alluding to Zetzel's claim (1981, 32) that contemporary readers would be more likely to have thought of *limus* = mud. M. Geymonat's second edition (Rome 2008) reiterates his support for *limo*, citing the lex Irnitana.

156. Scott Ryberg 1955, 35, 46, and passim (index s.v. *popa* and *victimarius*); Volkmann in *KP* 5 (1975), 1256–57; Latte 1960, 383–84; Hurley 1993, 128.

157. *OLD* s.v. 3; *Aen.* iii. 174, 545; v. 72, 134; vii. 154, 815; x. 205; xi. 101; seven times in Livy.

158. E.g., Propertius iv. 3. 62, *succinctique ... popae*; see too Murgia in Rees 2004, 195.

159. See the full note on this in Horsfall ad loc. (p. 306).

160. *capite velato filo* (*lanae velamen est*), Liv. i. 32. 6.

161. Liv. i. 24, 32, with Ogilvy's commentary (1965), 110–12, 127–36; Beard, North, Price 2 (1998), 7–8.

162. For other cases where wool was worn (normally on the head) in Roman rituals, Porte 1989, 80.

argument was probably that Vergil "should have" said wool, the second that linen was forbidden.[163] There is no reason to believe (as sometimes argued) that he emended the text or claimed to have found *limo* in an old manuscript.

Given that students of both Vergil and Roman religion have taken this note so seriously, it is disturbing to discover a long DS note on *puraque in veste sacerdos* fifty lines later in the book (xii. 169) that lays down linen as the *correct* material for priests to wear when about to take part in sacrifice, adding that they should wipe their hand on linen towels. The note actually concludes by citing *velati lino* from xii. 120! No one familiar with the Vergil scholia will be surprised by such inconsistency.

The truth (of course) is that Vergil himself had no thought of simply describing fetial procedure. While outlining something that could be imagined as *evolving* into the procedure of historical times (including the *verbena* mentioned by Livy),[164] he omits (e.g.) the picturesque detail of the flintstone with which the victim (a pig) was supposed to be struck (DS on *Aen.* viii. 641 mentions the flint),[165] adds a sheep, and turns the occasion into a regular sacrifice followed by a banquet.[166] A DS note (on xii. 170) reveals a commentator uncomfortably aware that the sheep does not belong in this context, and claims that it was added *graeco more*—no explanation at all if Vergil's object was to give an accurate description of Roman fetial procedure. It is instructive to contrast the arguments of modern and late antique critics here. Moderns prefer *limo* as a rare technical term liable to be corrupted by ignorant copyists into the more familiar *lino*. We might have expected the late antique commentator likewise to pounce on an obscure ritual term. But he was also faced with another, more compelling imperative: explaining the fact that the treaty comes to nothing. That is why, invoking the deliberate mistake axiom, Servius concluded that, knowing he should have written *limo*, Vergil cunningly substituted *lino* to warn alert readers that the negotiations would fail!

9

While insisting that Vergil was an unsurpassed expert on sacral law, when they came across apparent mistakes commentators were often satisfied with astonishingly weak explanations. The note on viii. 641 suggests two ways of dealing with the sacrifice of a sow (rather than pig): either Vergil was using feminine for masculine (citing *timidi... dammae* at *Buc.* viii. 28), or this was an illustration of the fact that female victims were always "more powerful" (*quia in omnibus sacris feminei generis plus valent victimae*). The DS goes on to add a further, even feebler justification, that the feminine

---

163. All modern authorities say that *fetiales* were not allowed to wear linen, but Servius is the only source.
164. Or what was later imagined as such. There are in fact serious doubts about the historicity of the role of the *fetiales* in both declarations of war and making treaties: Rawson 1991, 89–93.
165. Festus s.v. *Lapidem silicem* (p. 102 Lindsay).
166. So Warde Fowler and Bailey; for the *verbena*, Liv. i. 24. 6.

was used "for the sake of euphony." Of course, it is all wasted effort. Why should Vergil have felt obliged to impose fetial procedure on the age of Romulus?

Servius adds the general principle that "if they could not make a successful offering (*litare*) with a male, a female was offered in substitution (*succidanea dabatur*); if they could not succeed with a female, no <further> substitute could be used." The language looks official: *succidaneus* is the technical term for a substitute offering, and appears again in the DS note on *Aen.* ii. 140, which also gives other ancient (*veteri more*) ritual terms (*effugia* for an animal that escapes from the altar; *forda* for a pregnant cow; *taura* for a sterile cow). It is tempting to think that Servius is here preserving a basic principle of Roman sacrificial practice.[167] But we know from Varro as well as Livy[168] that a pig was indeed the proper victim, and it would be surprising if it had been acceptable, even preferable (*plus valent*), to offer a sow. Almost certainly the doctrine of female substitution is an invention by some commentator to save Vergil the reproach of having erred when he makes Romulus sacrifice a sow.

A different sort of error about a supposed sacrificial custom is provided by Tiberius Donatus on *Aen.* ix. 627, where Vergil describes a *iuvencus* being sacrificed to Jupiter as *pariterque caput cum matre ferentem*, meaning that the calf was already as tall as its mother. According to Tiberius Donatus, "Whence we get the custom of a cow and bull being sacrificed together…to Jupiter Capitolinus." This apparently authoritative claim about sacrificial practice is based on a gross misreading of the text: Tiberius evidently thought that the calf was sacrificed *together with* its mother (*cum matre*). Tiberius was a rhetorician, not an antiquarian, but he was familiar with the doctrine of Vergilian expertise in cult matters, and simply invented this supposed "custom" on the basis of his own misreading of the passage. Here at any rate Servius (on 628) interpreted the phrase correctly (*aequalem matri*).

Servius's note on *Aen.* x. 228–29 has been much discussed in the modern literature on archaic Roman religion. A sea nymph grasps Aeneas's ship and addresses him thus: "Are you on the alert, Aeneas, scion of gods? Be alert!" (*vigilasne, deum gens, Aenea, vigila*).[169] According to Servius,

> this is a cult formula (*verba sacrorum*): for the Vestal virgins used on a certain day to go to the *rex sacrorum* and say *vigilasne rex? vigila*. Vergil quite properly gives these words to Aeneas, as though to a king, everywhere representing him as *pontifex* also and as an authority on religion (*sacrorum peritum*).

If this is authentic information, as all modern studies assume, then Vergil's allusion would indeed be appropriate in an address by a female character to Aeneas.[170] But

---

167. So Capdeville 1971, 283–323 at 303.
168. Livy 1. 24. 9; Varro *RR* ii. 49.
169. Not "wake up," since Vergil has just said that Aeneas was *not* asleep (x. 217).
170. Serv. on *Aen.* x. 228–29; S. J. Harrison, *Vergil Aeneid* 10 (Oxford 1991), 134.

another Servian note offers what seems to be a different version: "*vigilasne deum gens* are the words used by the *pontifex maximus* at the sacred couches" (*verba sunt quibus pontifex maximus utitur in pulvinaribus*).[171] Koch assumed that this was an entirely different ritual, in which the *pontifex* addressed the assembled gods at a *lectisternium* (a sacrificial feast with couches set up for the images of certain gods).[172] But the *verba* Servius quotes (*vigilasne deum gens*) are *not* a cult formula but Vergil's words at *Aen*. x. 228, which suggests that he was thinking of the same ritual, perhaps drawing on the same note in Donatus. Furthermore, even if we assume that his source gave the imperative *vigila* rather than *vigilasne*, the singular would hardly be appropriate for a plurality of gods *in pulvinaribus*, nor does asking the gods if they are alert or asleep seem plausible.

There is also a third text to take into account. On viii. 3 where Turnus "clashes his weapons" (*impulit arma*), Servius claims that the magistrate charged with conducting a war used to enter the shrine (*sacrarium*) of Mars and, after shaking the sacred shields (*ancilia*), would also shake the spear of the statue itself, saying "*Mars, vigila*."[173] The singular imperative makes better sense here. There may well have been one or even two archaic rituals in which some official or priest cried *vigila*, but it is not easy to believe that these three notes of Servius are solid evidence (the only evidence) for three entirely different rituals.

As for the ascription of the *vigila* formula to the Vestals, in historical times they were responsible to the *pontifex maximus*. Various ingenious theories have been devised to produce an "original" relationship between Vestals and *rex sacrorum*, and while that is perfectly possible, this text would be the only evidence.[174] Naturally, these theories were based on the assumption that Servius was a disinterested antiquarian who preserves priceless cult material. Sometimes he does, but we have seen that both Servius himself and the sources on which he depended not only handled cult material irresponsibly, but did so because they had an agenda that renders suspect any otherwise unsupported claims they make. In this case the suspicious feature is precisely the fact that a female addressing a *rex* fits Vergil's supposed "allusion" to the ritual so neatly. At the very least we ought to ask whether a Vestal was likely to begin her address to the *rex sacrorum* with a reproachful *vigilasne?* and allow the possibility that *rex sacrorum* is just a guess based on the fact that he was the only Roman priest whose title included the word *rex*.

Nor would this be the only note that confuses one Roman priest with another. A twenty-four-line DS note on *Aen*. viii. 552 begins: "many reproach (*reprehendunt*) Vergil because, although he shows Aeneas everywhere (*ubique*) as *pontifex* and *pontifices* were not allowed to ride horses...why does he show Aeneas riding a horse?" Another gross blunder. It was not *pontifices* but the *flamen Dialis* who was not allowed

---

171. Serv. on *Aen*. ii. 148; for *pulvinaria* and *lectisternia*, Weinstock 1971, 284–85.
172. Koch 1960, 100–101.
173. Norden 1939, 154–56; see too the note on *Aen*. vii. 603.
174. Latte 1960, 110; Guizzi 1968, 109; Dumézil 1970, 586; Beard, North, and Price 1 (1998), 58.

to ride a horse.[175] A reference later in the note to the *flamen Martialis* and *flamen Quirinalis* not being bound by so many taboos implies an earlier version that correctly assigned the horse taboo to the *flamen Dialis*. The original version of the note must have reproached Vergil for making Aeneas ride a horse despite being *flamen Dialis*. According to another DS note, Vergil "everywhere" (*ubique*) portrays Aeneas as *flamen Dialis*.[176] Since (as we have just seen) the DS note on x. 228 claims that Vergil "everywhere" (*ubique*) portrays Aeneas as *pontifex*, a confusion between the two priesthoods is understandable. But it should be emphasized that, since the confusion occurs in the DS commentary rather than Servius, it must go back at any rate to Donatus, which means that it must have been an even earlier commentator who originated the fantasy of Aeneas as *flamen Dialis*. It is certainly not a notion invented by the last pagans.

When considering such claims about supposed cultic allusions, we also have to ask ourselves a more general question: how likely it is that Vergil repeatedly evoked archaic rituals and formulas?[177] The ancient commentators were so obsessed with this assumption that in the case of x. 228 they entirely overlooked the primary allusion, which is poetic and Greek, not Roman: *vigilasne?* evokes one of several nighttime dream visions in Homer all reproachfully beginning "are you asleep?" (εὕδεις),[178] while the Roman formula refers to vigilance in protection of the city. Since he does not cite any of these passages, it does not look as if Servius was even aware of the Homeric allusion. On any hypothesis we must surely exclude the interrogative formulation *vigilasne* from the ritual utterance.

10

To return to Vergil's use of *praepes*, Macrobius does not cite Gellius's account of Hyginus's criticism in what we have of the *Saturnalia*, but Gellius's answer to the criticism appears almost word for word in the DS note on the passage in question (*Aen.* vi. 15) and in simplified form in the Servian note.[179] Since Macrobius cites Gellius so extensively elsewhere, he was surely familiar with both criticism and defense. In all probability, since it concerns Vergil's knowledge of augural law, he saved it for the detailed treatment of the subject assigned to Flavian in the major lacuna in *Sat.* ii–iii. Indeed, it is tempting to conjecture that the section began with Euangelus aggressively raising the objection that *praepetibus pennis* was *inproprie et*

---

175. So Wissowa 1912, 506 n. 1.
176. On *Aen*. iv. 103; as often, it is clear from the context that the bare term *flamen* here means *flamen Dialis*.
177. Modern critics (Julia Dyson excepted) are generally more sceptical. Stefan Weinstock, according to Nicholas Horsfall, would "be amused and delighted (*more suo*) at my present state of scepticism about the presence of religious language and learning in the text" (*Aeneid* 7, 2000, preface,).
178. *Il.* ii. 23; xxiii. 69; *Od.* iv. 804; Harrison 1991, 228–29.
179. See Georgii 1891, 270–71.

inscite dictum, and Flavian responding with Gellius's defense: "have you not read, Euangelus, that *praepes* can also be applied to the places where birds settle" and so on. Since Daedalus's flight from Crete was such a notorious disaster, Flavian could have gone on to claim that the "improper" use of ritual language foreshadowed Icarus's fall.

Historians of the pagan revival regret the loss of Flavian's speech, assuming that it would have provided priceless information about his views on augury. If so, it would have been very different from all other speeches in the *Saturnalia*, which simply put in the mouths of his various interlocutors Macrobius's own antiquarian research. How would Macrobius have gone about constructing a speech on augural law?

He would not (could not) have turned to the learned ancient literature on the subject, long lost by the 430s.[180] The latest scholarly treatment was Ateius Capito's *De iure augurali*, written under Augustus, of which only three brief quotations in Festus survive, plus another four or five quotations in Festus conjecturally assigned to the work.[181] One of this handful of quotations (fr. 4 Bremer) appears to have been the source of Servius's note on *Aen.* iii. 117. At iii. 3. 8 Macrobius ascribes to Cicero's jurist friend Servius Sulpicius a definition of *religio* that corresponds verbatim with a passage of Gellius (iv. 9. 8)—except that Gellius cites it from the *De indigenis* of Masurius Sabinus. So precise a citation in Gellius, who certainly knew the jurists at firsthand,[182] must be preferred. No one will believe that Macrobius drew directly on Sulpicius,[183] but the first-century Sabinus may well have quoted Sulpicius. The most likely explanation (as Bremer saw) is that Macrobius misread some intermediary source that quoted both names. It is unlikely that he had ever seen an original copy of any of these works. The few fragments he cites all have a bearing on passages of Vergil, and it was undoubtedly in the Vergil commentators that he found them, ready excerpted. It was surely in the Vergil commentators that he found most (if not all) of the material for the speeches he put in the mouths of both Flavian and Praetextatus. Like Praetextatus's speech, Flavian's must have been designed to illustrate the poet's erudition, specifically his expertise (*peritia*) in augural science. There is no reason to believe that it had anything more to do with the real life of the speaker than any other speech in the dialogue.

Something of its character and contents may confidently be reconstructed from notes on passages in Vergil that the scholiasts thought (often mistakenly) touched on Roman augural practice. "Fortunately for us," as Linderski put it, "the commentators of Vergil, in their effort to explain [signs he described], applied technical augural concepts and formulas (which they quite often did not understand)."[184] Almost all these

---

180. For the various books and records attested for the augurs, Linderski 1986.
181. F. P. Bremer, *Iurisprudentiae antehadrianae quae supersunt* II. 1 (1898), 28–82, with Reitzenstein 1887, 47–52.
182. Holford-Strevens 2003, 298–300.
183. Here at least Gellius cannot be Macrobius's source, since Gellius does not mention Sulpicius.
184. Linderski 1986, 2235.

notes are confined to the DS additions,[185] and none have any counterpart in the surviving portions of the *Saturnalia*, presumably because Macrobius saved them up to
put in Flavian's speech, now lost. The fact that most of this augural material was omitted by Servius nicely illustrates Macrobius's promise to rescue from oblivion arcane
material that "almost all the schoolteachers gloss over."

To give a couple of illustrations, Servius refers three times to *extemplo* as in origin
an augural term (*sermo augurum*), though the reason Vergil uses the word so often
(fifteen times) is surely its "archaic dignity"[186] rather than (as Servius thought) a
learned, "hidden" allusion to Aeneas's status as an augur. Where Picus is described as
sitting (*sedebat*) holding a *lituus*, Servius notes that the *lituus* was the emblem of the
augur and that augurs sat to watch for omens. While this is true enough,[187] we may
doubt whether this is really why Vergil wrote *sedebat* here (kings are regularly shown
seated on thrones), even more so the claim that this is why Turnus is represented
sitting in a later book.[188] The DS note on *Aen.* i. 398 is typically more recondite, citing
augurales commentari and *libri reconditi*, and distinguishing between an *augurium*
(sought, and revealed by certain birds), and an *auspicium* (not sought, and not revealed
by any bird). Then come the ominous words "But Vergil loves hidden allusions" (*amat
secretiora dicere*). A fanciful illustration is provided by the note on iii. 537–43 where
Anchises finds an omen in the behavior of some horses.

It is on the basis of this focus of Macrobius and the commentators on his knowledge
of cult that Vergil has so often been proclaimed the pagan bible. He might perhaps be
called the *Roman* bible, in the sense that Homer was the Greek bible, a text regarded
by all educated speakers of the language as canonical, the source of all knowledge and
a continuing subject of (often polemical, often defensive) exegesis. But hardly a *pagan*
bible.[189] There is a world of difference between the conviction that there are numerous
hidden allusions to Roman priesthoods and cult practices in Vergil, treated as proof of
his erudition, and the modern claim that Vergil was "venerated, copied and expounded
as a sacred text"—naturally by pagans.[190]

The practice of treating verses of Vergil selected at random as oracles (the so-called
Sortes Vergilianae) should certainly not be so interpreted. Not only is it based on the
wisdom attributed to Vergil rather than any belief that he was divinely inspired, more
important, outside the *Historia Augusta* there is no evidence that the practice even

---

185. Here is a list of some of the more important notes together with Linderski's learned comments (all
　　　DS): *Aen.* iv. 161, 339 (Linderski 2170); *Aen.* iii. 117 (2220); *Geo.* iv. 424 (2222); *Aen.* iii. 463 (2223); *Aen*
　　　iii. 246, iv. 453, v. 7 (2234–36); *Aen.* ii. 719 (2253); *Aen.* xii. 176 (2254); *Aen.* i. 446, iv. 200 and ix. 4
　　　(2272); *Aen.* iv. 200 (2275); *Aen.* ii. 178 (2278); *Aen.* iii. 361 (2279). Note too Serv. on *Aen.* xii. 259 and
　　　v. 530 (2254), and i. 92, vi. 191, and vii. 187 (2271); and the notes in both commentaries on *Aen.* i.
　　　393–401 and ii. 679–702.
186. R. G. Austin's note on *Aen.* i. 92; Serv. on *Aen.* i. 92, ii. 699, and vi. 210.
187. Linderski 1986, 2246 and 2258.
188. Serv. on *Aen.* vii. 187–90 and ix. 4; see the commentaries of Horsfall (2000) and Hardie (1994).
189. Except in the sense of "pagan" as referring to pre-Christian times (Ch. 2. 2).
190. Markus 1974, 130; cf. Bloch 1945, 210 ("pagan Bible"); Klingner 1961, 530, 536 ("heilige Schrift");
　　　Levine 1966, 211 ("pagan scripture").

existed before the sixteenth century. Contrary to widespread popular belief (based on Comparetti, who relied entirely on the *HA*), there is no evidence that it was known throughout the Middle Ages.[191] Moreover, as Syme remarked, the *HA*'s use of Vergil is "doubly peculiar." First, while Hadrian is alleged to have consulted a text of Vergil, in later passages various oracles (Apollo at Cumae, Fortuna at Praeneste) improbably give their reponses in the form of Vergilian quotations! Second, most of these quotations come from the same passage of Vergil, Anchises's speech in *Aeneid* vi. There can be little doubt that these passages are idiosyncratic fabrications by the compiler of the *HA*. Many have argued that using Vergil this way is a "discreet pagan response" to the Christian use of *Sortes biblicae*, most famously Augustine's *tolle lege* story.[192] But this would not explain the eccentric use the compiler made of the motif, and pagans had long been reading random verses culled from Homer as oracles,[193] while Christians had been reading the Fourth Eclogue as a prophecy of the birth of Christ from as early as the beginning of the fourth century.[194]

11

The truth is that Donatus, Servius, and Macrobius were simply not interested in what we would call the *religious* issues involved in Vergil's cult references. Above all, there is not the slightest indication that they were responding to Christian criticisms of Vergil. Bruggisser devoted a book to the claim that Romulus's fratricide became an issue between pagans and Christians, with Augustine making the most of the opportunity to attack the founder of Rome and Servius taking a consistently favorable view. But this was an embarrassing episode long before it was exploited by Christians.[195] It was only to be expected that Christian apologists who set out systematically to undermine the pagan roots of the Roman tradition would seize on such a detail. But it is hard to believe that pagans would be troubled enough by such trite polemic to feel the need to reply to it. Other objections aside, it is a fundamental misunderstanding of Servius's method to suppose that his commentary might represent a personal view on a subject like Romulus and Remus. He simply selected from the vast mass of material assembled by his predecessors. Of course, up to a point selection implies approval, but Servius could only select from the material at his disposal. And since in his only two references to Remus Vergil chose to portray him working in harmony with his brother,[196] there was simply no call for any Vergilian commentator to deal with the accusation of fratricide.

---

191. Hamilton 1993, 309–36; Katz 1994, 245–58; Ziolkowski and Putnam 2008, 829–30.
192. Aug. *Conf.* viii. 29; Syme 1968, 127; de Kisch 1970, 321–62; den Hengst, in Rees 2004, 172–88.
193. van der Horst 1998, 143–73 at 160–66; more generally, Courcelle 1963, 143–97.
194. Courcelle 1957, 294–319; Ziolkowski and Putnam 2008, 487–503.
195. Bruggisser 1987; see the sensible review by N. Horsfall, *CR* 51 (1991), 242–43; Wiseman 1995, passim.
196. *Geo.* ii. 532–33; *Aen.* i. 292–33; MacCormack 1998, 7–10.

Ando too claims to find serious contemporary issues in Macrobius and Servius, devoting a detailed discussion to talismans[197] of the eternity of Rome such as the Palladium, and the early Roman practice of *evocatio*. He writes of Romans and Constantinopolitans "contest[ing] the sacred topography of the Roman Empire" through and with "pontifical law and ancient artifacts."[198] It is indeed fascinating to find Christians in sixth-century Constantinople claiming that Constantine "secretly" took the Palladium from Rome and buried it beneath the column that bore his statue in the Forum of his new capital. But it is a mistake to interpret these claims as "rivalry" between the New and Old Rome. The very fact that they are not heard of before the sixth century, long after the fall of Old Rome, is enough to show that they bear witness to something quite different: the transference of power from Old to New Rome, the *translatio imperii* so dear to medieval historians. As Le Goff put it, the "transfer of power, the *translatio imperii*, was above all a transfer of knowledge and culture, a *translatio studii*."[199] There was no "debate" about these talismans in the early fifth-century West. Macrobius does not so much as mention the Palladium, despite its prominent role in *Aeneid* ii. Servian and DS notes mention it a number of times, but nowhere suggest any contemporary relevance. While briefly reporting the tradition that *imperium fore ubi et Palladium*, Servius is more interested in the stories about how it reached Rome, given that it was two Greeks, Diomede and Ulysses, who took it from Troy. Three separate notes claim that it was the early Republican family of the Nautii (not the Iulii) who acquired the Palladium from Diomedes, citing Varro's *De familiis Troianis*.[200] Another note reports the strange tradition that the Trojans simply hid it (which doesn't even explain the fall of Troy), and that it was rediscovered there by Fimbria during the First Mithradatic War.[201] Given this unremittingly antiquarian focus, it is unlikely that either Servius or Macrobius were implicitly attacking the notion (not in itself Christian) that *imperium* had now passed to Constantinople.

Macrobius discusses at length the *evocatio* of local gods from cities the Romans were at war with, linking it to the care they took that the name of the tutelary god of Rome itself should not be known, so that enemies could not do the same to them. According to Ando, "The contemporary relevance of this piece of antiquarian lore was clear even before 410," citing "parallels" in Symmachus, Servius, Claudian, and Rutilius Namatianus, all pagans.[202] But Rome was not sacked because the Goths practised *evocatio* or discovered the secret name of Rome—a name (remember) that no one knew.[203]

---

197. For the importance of talismans in Greek myth and ritual, see Faraone 1992.

198. Ando 2001, 404.

199. Le Goff 1988, 171, with a number of illustrations.

200. Serv. on *Aen.* ii. 166, iii. 407, v. 704; on the "Trojan" families of Rome, Wiseman 1987, 207–18; and 2004, 18–21.

201. Serv. on *Aen.* ii. 166 (p. 369. 30 Harv.); for the historical basis for this late tradition, Erskine 2001, 237–45.

202. *Sat.* iii. 9; Ando 2001, 392–96.

203. Cracco Ruggini 1968, 433–47.

The notion of a contemporary reference in this passage of Macrobius is excluded by a small but telling linguistic detail. The verbs in the sentences linking *evocatio* and secret names (iii. 9. 2–3) are, most unusually for Macrobian dialogue, in the past tense. We have seen that Donatus and even Varro used past tenses of rituals they regarded as obsolete in their day. Ando also cites a note on *Aen.* ii. 351 clearly related to the passage of Macrobius, repeating that the Romans kept secret the name of their tutelary god "lest they be deconsecrated" (*ne exaugurari possent*); and another note (on *Aen.* ii. 244) that describes the rite of *evocatio* and quotes some of the same formula given in full by Macrobius. On this basis, according to Ando, "we can say for certain … that Servius in the late fourth century firmly believed that Juno had been summoned forth from Carthage and her rites transferred to Rome during the third Punic war."[204] But both these notes are DS additions. Servius himself was apparently not interested in the subject of *evocatio*. The inevitable explanation of the parallels between the DS notes and Macrobius is a common source. Ando's "firmly believed" is presumably based on *constat* in a brief summary in a later note by Servius himself which, in keeping with his general lack of interest in archaic texts, dismisses the actual rites with a vague *sacris quibusdam*.[205] But this *constat* is no more than a formula used more than two hundred times in the *Aeneid* commentary alone (and more than seventy times in Macrobius), simply identifying a standard interpretation. It need not even imply the writer's agreement. Macrobius was just repeating information compiled (at latest) ca. 350, and probably much earlier.

In itself this does not prove that the passage had no contemporary resonance. But two further details do. First, both the DS notes are also in the past tense. The common source of DS and Macrobius must likewise have offered past tenses, treating *evocatio* as an obsolete practice. In general, Macrobius is careful to make his pagan interlocutors speak in the present tense of pagan practices he (often mistakenly) believed current at his dramatic date.[206] His unusual use of the past in this case shows that he was content to follow his sources in treating *evocatio* as no longer relevant to pagan practice in the 380s.

Second, we know why Donatus (DS) and Macrobius cited this material. Both were explaining *Aen.* ii. 351–52:

> excessere omnes adytis arisque relictis
> di quibus imperium hoc steterat.

All the gods by whose aid this realm once stood have left, forsaking their shrines and altars.

Few lines in the *Aeneid* can have had more poignant contemporary resonance for pagans living in Rome in the 420s and 430s, a city still disfigured by stark reminders of

---

204. Ando 2001, 392–96.
205. *constat bello Punico secundo exoratam Iunonem, tertio vero bello a Scipione sacris quibusdam etiam Romam esse translatam*, Serv. on *Aen.* xii. 841.
206. E.g., iii. 2. 5, "when sacrifice *is* to be made to the gods above, purification *is* effected by ablution of the body."

the Gothic sack. Augustine quotes these very lines no fewer than ten times in the first three books of the *City of God*, citing example after example of earlier disasters that those gods had done nothing to avert.[207] But for Macrobius, they are a learned allusion to the archaic Roman practice of *evocatio*. The very fact that he treats secret names and *evocatio* as illustrating Vergil's *erudition* is enough to prove that they were not a central element in current pagan belief. Indeed, this chapter might be held a particularly striking illustration of Macrobius's retreat "to the discursive world of texts."

Ando was impressed by a muddled reference in John the Lydian to Constantinople having a "hieratic" name Anthusa to match the name Flora borne by Rome. The same passage also refers to a secret name, known only to "high priests" for use in rituals. Once again, this does not reflect an East/West, Christian/pagan debate on the issue. Though dimly reflecting the Roman tradition of an unnamed tutelary deity, there is no evidence outside this passage that the unnamed deity was Flora (Macrobius suggests four names, concluding that "even the most learned of men do not know the name").[208] Flora is pure Constantinopolitan invention, the closest Latin name some Byzantine antiquarian could come up with to match Anthusa, a standing epithet for Constantinople from the mid-fourth century. But the match is imperfect: Anthusa was no deity, but a feminine participle agreeing with city (*polis*) understood, a formula reflected in contemporary Latin texts as *urbs florentissima*, the flourishing city.[209] John also claims that none other than "Praetextatus the hierophant" took part in the ceremonies for the foundation of Constantinople with "Sopater the initiate" and Constantine.[210] This is said to show that Constantine scrupulously followed Roman tradition in consulting the pontifical college about his new foundation.[211] But nothing in this passage deserves to be taken seriously. In the first place, whether the reference is to Constantine's initial decision to found a new city in 324 or its "consecration" in 330, Praetextatus, born in 324, cannot possibly have played a part.[212] Nor does John style him *pontifex*, a Latin term he knew well and loved to quote in Greek transliteration, but "hierophant," a more exotic term that fits his description of Sopater as "initiate." John had something much grander and more mystical than pontifical participation in mind for the foundation of the greatest city in the world, something from which nothing so mundane as mere facts can be salvaged.

To suggest that the rise of Constantinople "detracted from the ... *religious* preeminence of Rome"[213] is to take altogether too seriously the (exaggerated) boast of a

---

207. They are cited in full in Hagendahl 1967, 331–32, with brief commentary by MacCormack 1997, 164–65.

208. *Sat.* iii. 9. 4 (Jupiter, Angeronia, Lua, Ops Consivia).

209. *Cod. Theod.* xv. 2. 4 (381 or 382: Seeck, *Regesten* 91; *PLRE* i. 664) and vii. 8. 14 (427). Possibly also reflected in art by the cornucopiae in the hand of early representations of Constantinople as a Tyche-figure: Toynbee 1947, 136–37; Bühl 1995, 56–58.

210. *De mens.* iv. 2 (p. 65. 20 Wuensch).

211. Ando 2001, 401–3. I shall be discussing this view in detail in a forthcoming book.

212. For bibliography on this problem, Fraschetti 1999, 65–70.

213. Ando 2001, 375.

handful of ecclesiastical writers that Constantinople was a wholly Christian foundation from the start. It was the Roman church, not Roman pagans, that was disturbed by the proclamation of Constantinople as New Rome.[214]

Convinced that "pagan" talismans were a hot topic in late antique Rome, Ando cites the following note on *Aen.* vii. 188:[215]

> There were seven *pignora* that maintained the Roman empire: the stone of the Mother of the Gods, the terracotta chariot of the Veientines, the ashes of Orestes, the sceptre of Priam, the veil of Iliona, the *Palladium*, and the *ancilia*.

This is a curiously mixed bag. Four of these *pignora* were at least material objects of some sort, but the ashes of Orestes,[216] the sceptre of Priam,[217] and the veil of Iliona "only ever existed on paper."[218] They are mentioned nowhere else in ancient literature, let alone as talismans of the eternity of Rome. No context or authority is cited, though it is tempting (with Latte) to conjecture that the list was an invention of Varro's (who is known to have written about the omen of the chariot of the Veientines).[219] Varro was famously fascinated by the number seven. His *Hebdomades* contained seven hundred portraits of famous men, arranged in groups of seven, with an introduction on the number seven itself.[220] The work has not survived, but according to Gellius (*NA* iii. 10), this introduction listed the seven wonders, the seven sages, the seven laps of the circus, and the seven against Thebes. So why not seven *pignora imperii*? It is also a problem that the word *pignora* is a modern emendation (for *paria*), and if the writer of the note considered these items continuing talismans of empire, it is puzzling that he used the past tense (*fuerunt*).[221] Even so, if Servius had included the list with some approving comment, it might have merited a brief discussion. But Servius did not include it at all.[222] Once again, this is a DS note that Servius *omitted*. Why would any fourth- or fifth-century pagan take seriously a list eked out with items from Greek mythology?

---

214. I shall be discussing all these issues in a forthcoming study, *Constantinople New Rome*.

215. For a thorough treatment of the various items, Gross 1935; Ando 2001, 394–95.

216. Perhaps = the bones of Orestes Augustus is said to have transferred from Aricia to Rome (Green 2007, 41–48), though not if Varro is the author.

217. Buchheit 1963, 161, takes the sceptre of Priam more seriously on the basis of *Aen.* vii. 246–48 (Horsfall's commentary is more sceptical). Yet there is not even a tradition that Priam's sceptre was brought to Rome, let alone a material object housed somewhere in Rome.

218. Latte 1960, 292.

219. Pliny, *NH* xxviii. 16, with Münzer 1897, 178–80.

220. For a brief recent account, J. Geiger in *CQ* 48 (1998), 305–09.

221. Timpanaro 1978, 431 n. 3, suggests *sunt*, which does not explain *fuerunt*.

222. The note is also included in the two manuscripts G. Ramires classifies as the *a* tradition of Servius (*Commento al libro IX dell'Eneide di Virgilio* [Bologna 1996], xxxi–xxxii; *Commento al libro VII...* [Bologna 2003], xxxvii–xlix), but all other critics more plausibly argue that they derive from the DS tradition: see H. D. Jocelyn, *Latomus* 57 (1998), 435–36, and in more detail an online discussion by Charles Murgia ("Where Is the APA/Harvard Servius?").

12

Why does Augustine's polemic against paganism in the *City of God* focus so exclusively on Varro? It might have been expected that he would make more use than he
does of Cicero's *De natura deorum*, a rich source of ammunition against paganism
exploited by Christian apologists since Minucius Felix.[223] One reason is surely Varro's
reputation as *the* authority on the traditional cults. Another, the fact that many passages
reveal Varro himself as a sceptic, who (perhaps even more than Cicero) thought that
the cults should be maintained for their utility to the state.[224] Third, the (to a monotheist) mind-boggling detail he supplied about the sheer number of gods in Roman
polytheism, detail that needed only to be stated to provoke ridicule and disbelief.

No less important, according to O'Daly, "he was read and invoked by educated
pagan contemporaries."[225] According to Robert Markus, Varro's *Antiquitates* "carried
weighty authority in fifth-century pagan circles such as the fictitiously assembled
group represented in Macrobius's *Saturnalia*."[226] But did they? And which pagans?
Certainly not Symmachus, who mentions Varro just once, when his father had the
short-lived idea of writing epigrams on famous contemporaries in the manner of
Varro's *Hebdomades*.[227]

Barnes argued that the author of *Saturnalia* and *Commentary* "corresponds to the
pagan audience envisaged in the *City of God* in details large and small."[228] Where
Macrobius reveres Cicero and Vergil, Augustine attacks them—while drawing his
ammunition from the same sources. Augustine's refutation is by far the most important single surviving source of our knowledge of Varro's *Antiquitates* (and so in effect
of our knowledge of Roman paganism); and it is an instructive coincidence that between them Macrobius and Augustine are our two most important sources (outside
the Vatican palimpsest) for Cicero's lost *De republica*.[229] On the old date for Macrobius
it might have been wondered whether Augustine had *Commentary* and *Saturnalia* in
mind, but the polemical early books of the *City of God* were published by 417, the
complete work by 427 at latest, and the *Saturnalia* not before ca. 430. If there is a relationship between them, it must go the other way. Is it possible that Macrobius had
read Augustine? Is it possible that he was in some sense responding to Augustine's
polemic?

However attractive the notion, it does not survive a serious comparison of *City of
God* and *Saturnalia*. To start with, Augustine's attack on Roman paganism was based

---

223. Zielinski 1908, 145–59; briefly, Walsh 1997, xxxix–xli.
224. Aug. *CD* iv. 27, 31; Arnob. *Adv nat.* vii. 1; Jocelyn 1982, 148–205; Momigliano 1987, 58–73.
225. O'Daly 1999, 236.
226. Markus, in Sommerstein 1996, 77; see too Maslakov 1983, 100–106.
227. Symm. *Ep.* i. 2, 4; Ausonius too ostentatiously refers to the *Hebdomades* at *Mosella* 305–7, with Green's
     commentary (pp. 496–97).
228. Barnes 1982, 79.
229. Hagendahl 1967, 265–316, 589–630 (Varro); 112–31, 540–53 (*De republica*).

on a thorough firsthand study of Varro. In addition to citing Varro by name at least eighty times,[230] he provides a very precise and detailed account of the contents and structure of the *Antiquitates* (presumably drawn from Varro's own introduction), which is reflected in his own citations.[231] Augustine must have had a complete text of the *Antiquitates* (not to mention other works of Varro he cites from time to time), and, whether or not he studied every word, he must at least have skimmed the entire work and read at firsthand and excerpted whatever struck him as relevant to his purpose (mainly Bks 1 and 14–16). Perhaps the clearest proof that he relied on his own direct knowledge of the book is the fact that the great majority of his quotations are not found or paralleled in earlier writers, whether pagan or Christian.

What now of Macrobius's knowledge of Varro? There are in the *Saturnalia* just eight citations from *Antiquitates rerum divinarum*, five of them in passages discussing Vergil, the other three concerning the calendaric material collected in Bk i. We have already seen that one of the first group (iii. 4. 2), about the derivation of the word *delubrum*, was copied verbatim by Macrobius from Asper or Donatus, proved by close verbal similarities with Servius, DS, and Pseudo-Asconius. The same applies to *Sat.* iii. 2. 7–8, proved by the parallel version in DS on *Aen.* iv. 219:[232]

Macrobius: multifariam enim legimus quod litare sola non possit oratio, nisi ut is qui deos precatur etiam aras manibus adprehendat. Inde Varro *Divinarum* libro quinto dicit 'aras' primum 'asas' dictas, quod esset necessarium a sacrificantibus eas teneri; *ansis* autem teneri solere vasa quis dubitet? Commutatione ergo litterarum aras dici coeptas, ut Valesios et Fusios dictos prius, nunc Valerios et Furios dici.	DS: veteres aras 'asas' dicebant, postea immutata littera 's' in 'r' aras dixerunt, sicut Valesios Valerios, Fusios Furios; quod Varro *Rerum divinarum* in libro quinto plenius narrat. necesse enim erat *ansis* eas a sacrificantibus teneri, quod nisi fieret, diis sacrificatio grata non esset.

The mysterious "handles" (*ansis*) are supported by the Servian note on *Aen.* vi. 124, "people used to pray (*rogabant*) to the gods holding the handles of the altars" (*ararum ansas tenentes*). Whether or not early Roman altars were provided with anything that could have been called a handle, Timpanaro and Jocelyn are surely right to suppose

---

230. *CD* vi. 3; Hagendahl 1967, 265–316.

231. "Of the first three books...the first division deals with the pontiffs, the second with the augurs, and the third the quindecimvirs. Of the second three, which deal with places, he speaks in one of them of shrines (*de sacellis*), in another of sacred temples (*de sacris aedibus*), and in the third of religious places. The three following books deal with times, that is with festivals; and one of these deals with holy days, another with the games of the circus, and the third with theatrical performances. The fourth set of three books deals with sacred rites; and here he devotes one book to consecrations, one to private rites, and the final one to public rites. In the remaining three...come the gods themselves, for whom all this care has been expended. First come the "certain gods," then the "uncertain gods," and, third and last of all, the "principal and select gods" (*CD* vi. 3).

232. I give the fourth line of the DS note as in F, supported by Timpanaro (*Nuovi contributi* [Bologna 1994], 382), rather than the Thilo/Harvard text.

"that Varro tracked the noun *ara* back to an older form *asa*, which he then identified with the noun educated people of his own time spelled as *ansa*."[233] Some commentator faced with explaining Vergil's *aras tenere* (*Aen*. iv. 219 and vi. 124) was puzzled by *holding* an altar, and could not resist Varro's etymological speculations. Something is seriously wrong with Macrobius's irrelevant rhetorical question about holding vases (*vasa*) by their handles (*ansis*). Did he (or a source) perhaps misread "ansis *eas a*" preserved in the DS note as "ansis *vasa*"? Whatever the explanation, it is clear that Macrobius cannot have had a text of Varro in front of him. He knew no more than a garbled quotation he had found in some antiquary or Vergil commentary. The archaic adverb *multifariam* ("in many places"), affected by second-century antiquarians, is a pointer: twice in Fronto and Apuleius, and five times in Gellius.

As usual, Macrobius's discussion is supposed to illustrate Vergil's "profound erudition." Many of these illustrations are far-fetched, but this one is positively misguided. If he had been able to consult Pease on *Aen*. iv. 219 instead of Donatus, he would have discovered that there is nothing remotely learned about *tenere aras*, and certainly no allusion to Varro's handles. At all periods it was standard Roman practice to touch an altar when praying or taking an oath, the usual formula being *tangere, contingere*, or *tenere aram*.[234] This is one of many hints that Macrobius's knowledge of pagan ritual owes more to antiquarians and Vergil commentators than living practice.

In the light of this example, we may assume that the other three citations that concern Vergil were likewise found in Vergil commentaries, not an original text of Varro. In all three cases Macrobius's purpose was the same as the commentators', to explain Vergil. As for the three citations from Bk i, a long chapter on the Roman calendar (*Sat*. i. 3) cites Varro by name four times. Every word is copied from a long chapter in Gellius (iii. 2), right down to formulas like *idem Varro in eodem libro scripsit*. In the course of this chapter Macrobius claims that "I have also (*quoque*) read that Q. Mucius...used to say," where the "also" might seem to imply an additional source. In fact, this too comes from Gellius, even down to the "also." The *ultimate* source of much of the calendrical material in Bk i is no doubt Varro, the importance of whose work in this area has been brilliantly put in context by Denis Feeney.[235] But the many often close parallels between Censorinus, Solinus, and Macrobius make it clear that Macrobius's direct source must have been some later compilation, according to Wissowa Suetonius's lost *On the Roman Year*, according to Mastandrea Cornelius Labeo's *Fasti*.[236]

Cornelius Labeo makes another appearance in a complex of antiquarian notes on the origin of the Penates, where there are close parallels not only with DS and Servius, but with Arnobius, who wrote in the first decade of the fourth century:[237]

---

233. Jocelyn 1981, 108–9, with philological parallels.
234. A large number of examples are cited by Pease on *Aen*. iv. 219; see too Scheid 1990, 522–25.
235. Feeney 2007, 358–59 (index s.v. Varro).
236. Flamant 1977, 294–97; Mastandrea 1979, 14–734. The title of Suetonius's book is known from his Suda entry.
237. Simmons 1995, 47–93; Herzog and Schmidt 5 § 569. 1.

Macrobius, Sat. iii. 4:

1) Nigidius...De dis libro nono decimo requirit num di Penates sint Troianorum Apollo et Neptunus, qui muros eis fecisse dicuntur...Cornelius quoque Labeo de dis Penatibus eadem existimat (6).

DS on *Aen.* i. 378:

Alii, ut Nigidius *et Labeo*, deos Penates Aeneae Neptunum et Apollinem tradunt.

Arnobius iii. 40:

Nigidius Penates deos Neptunum esse atque Apollinem prodidit, qui quondam muris immortalibus Ilium condicione adiuncta cinxerunt.

2) Varro Humanarum secundo Dardanum refert deos Penates ex Samothrace in Phrygiam, et Aeneam ex Phrygia in Italiam detulisse (7).

DS on *Aen.* iii. 148: Varro sane Rerum humanarum secundo...hos deos Dardanum ex Samothraca in Phrygiam, Aeneam vero in Italiam ex Phrygia transtulisse idem Varro testatur.

3) Sed qui diligentius eruunt veritatem, Penates esse dixerunt per quos penitus spiramus, per quos habemus corpus, per quod rationem animi possidemus; esse autem medium aethera Iovem, Iunonem vero imum aera cum terra, et Minervam summum aetheris cacumen.(8)

DS on *Aen.* ii. 296: Nonnulli tamen Penates esse dixerunt per quos penitus spiramus et corpus habemus et animi rationes possidemus; eos autem esse Iovem aetherem medium, Iunonem imum aera cum terra, summum aetheris cacumen Minervam.

Nec defuerunt qui scriberent Iovem, Iunonem ac Minervam deos Penates existere, sine quibus vivere ac sapere nequeamus et qui penitus nos regant ratione, calore et spiritu.

4) Cassius vero Hemina dixit Samothracas deos eosdemque Romanorum Penates proprie dici θεοὺς μεγάλους, θεοὺς χρηστούς, θεοὺς δυνατούς (8)

DS on *Aen.* i. 378: Alii autem, ut Cassius Hemina, dicunt deos Penates ex Samothraca appellatos θεοὺς μεγάλους, θεοὺς δυνατούς, θεοὺς χρηστούς.

5) Eodem nomine appellavit et Vestam, quam de numero Penatium aut certe comitem eorum esse manifestum est, adeo ut et consules et praetores seu dictatores, cum adeunt magistratum, Lavinii rem divinam faciant Penatibus pariter et Vestae (11).

DS on *Aen.* ii. 296: Hic ergo quaeritur utrum Vesta et iam de numero Penatium sit, an comes eorum accipiatur, quod cum consules et praetores sive dictatores abeunt magistratu, Lavini sacra Penatibus simul et Vestae faciunt.

6)

| Serv. on *Aen.* iii. 168: ad ritum referri, de quo dicit Labeo in libris qui appellantur De diis animalibus: in quibus ait esse quaedam sacra quibus animae humanae vertantur in deos, qui appellantur animales, quod de animis fiant. hi autem sunt dii Penates et viales. | Arnob. ii. 62: quod Etruria libris in Acheronticis pollicetur, certorum animalium sanguine numinibus certis dato divinas animas fieri et ab legibus mortalitatis educi. |

The parallels in language, substance, and source citations between Macrobius and the DS notes unmistakably point to a common source. This common source already included the shared citations of Varro, Nigidius Figulus, and Cassius Hemina (that Macrobius and DS came by them independently is excluded by the identical formulation of the opinions ascribed to them).

The second-century B.C. Cassius Hemina was presumably cited by Varro or (more probably) Nigidius, but Varro and Nigidius were contemporaries, unlikely to have cited each other's views at length. The telltale "Varro et Labeo" suggests that the Varronian material at any rate was found ready quoted in Labeo.[238] Arnobius does not cite his source, but the Servian note on *Aen.* iii. 168, which parallels Arnobius ii. 62, explicitly cites Labeo's *De diis animalibus*.[239] Not the least striking detail is the fact that all three texts cited under number 3 ascribe the identification with Jupiter, Juno, and Minerva to an ostentatiously unnamed writer.[240] As Mastandrea saw, this is a more telling pointer to a common source than if they had merely named the same authority. It is improbable that all three should have decided independently to cite this one piece of information anonymously. Evidently, their common source failed to name his authority for this point.

It is important to be clear that in cases like this we are not talking about literary allusion or embellishment. Macrobius is not simply giving his prose a pleasing archaic flavor. He purports to be quoting Varro to support an argument. And yet he had no firsthand knowledge of either side in the debate. Nor was it Augustine he was arguing with, but Nigidius Figulus and Cassius Hemina. He did not even restate the argument in his own words. As the exact verbal correspondences with the Vergil scholia so eloquently demonstrate, he was content to copy verbatim the exact formulation of some anonymous intermediary. If questioned on any point, he could never have offered any further argument. The proof he offered in his text was already an excerpt when he found it. He could not (as Augustine could) have reconsidered any given passage of Varro in context and reformulated his argument to take account of objections. More

---

238. Not that we are entitled to assume that Labeo himself read both at firsthand.
239. Arnob. *Adv. nat.* ii. 62, with Mastandrea 1979, 95, 126–27, 130–33.
240. *nec defuerunt qui scriberent* (Arnobius), *qui diligentius eruunt veritatem...dixerunt* (Macrobius), *nonnulli dixerunt* (Servius).

important, he could not have offered any sort of informed rebuttal of any of Augustine's anti-Varronian arguments because he had no firsthand knowledge of the passages on which Augustine had based those arguments.

Macrobius may have consulted Labeo at firsthand, but when (as here) discussing specific passages of Vergil, his direct source is more likely to have been excerpts quoted by Donatus. This is a passage where his knowledge of Varro was *at best* thirdhand. At some level Macrobius must have known that the majority of Donatus's notes were no more than abridged summaries of earlier sources whose very names had been suppressed. He must have known but was simply not bothered that Varro's views were unlikely to be fully and fairly reflected in the final potted summary he copied so trustingly word for word. As for Servius, he omitted almost all these references to the Penates. All citations but one in the middle column above are DS additions to Servius.[241]

Two final observations. First, none of these texts reveal the slightest interest in the role of the Penates in living fourth-century cult. All are antiquarian speculations about their origin and identity. Second, the speculations are provoked (as so often) by the commentator's need to explain the role of the Penates in Vergil, especially their dream speech to Aeneas in *Aen.* iii. 147–74, nicely illustrated in one of the miniatures of the (more or less contemporary) Vatican Vergil, where they are shown veiled just as Vergil describes them (line 174).[242]

No less telling is a passage later in the book (i. 15. 21): "Varro relates that Verrius Flaccus, an expert on pontifical law, used to say." Verrius Flaccus, of course, wrote *later* than (and drew heavily on) Varro.[243] Some have tried to save Macrobius's credit by supposing that the name cited was not Verrius but Veranius, a well-known authority on pontifical law,[244] who is then further identified with an archaizing writer called Veranius Flaccus mentioned by Suetonius.[245] But the pontifical writer is always cited as just Veranius, nor is it even certain that he wrote early enough to be cited by Varro (though he is frequently cited by Verrius Flaccus).[246] Macrobius no doubt misread a passage in his source that cited both texts, like (e.g.) *alii, sicut Varro et Verrius*, in the DS note on *Aen.* xi. 143. Having never (in all probability) seen a complete, original text of either Varro or Verrius Flaccus, he had no way of knowing which wrote first and guessed wrong. Servius cites Verrius once only, and DS only twice more (one of them the note on xi. 143 just quoted).

Servius too is regularly cited as a pagan of the age who looked to Varro as a religious authority.[247] It is true that there are 87 Varro citations in Servius and 101 in DS.[248] But of these 87 citations, only 4 are to the *Antiquitates rerum divinarum* (with a further

---

241. To the DS citations the notes on *Aen.* ii. 325 and iii. 12 should be added.
242. See now Horsfall's detailed commentary on the passage.
243. Münzer 1897, 299–307; M.-K. Lhommé in F. Glinister et al. 2007, 33–47.
244. Rawson 1985, 93, 303; Linderski 1986, 2186.
245. *PIR* V. 264, 267; Funaioli, *Gramm. Rom. Frag.* (1907), 429–35; Syme, *Roman Papers* 1 (1979), 333.
246. To judge from the numerous citations of Veranius in Festus, largely based on Verrius Flaccus.
247. Burns 2001, 37–64 at 43, 49–50.
248. Figures from Lloyd 1961, 309.

7 in DS). This hardly suggests that he looked to Varro specifically as a religious authority, rather than just as the inevitable source for a wide variety of antiquarian information, in keeping with his reputation as the great Roman polymath. Indeed, in one note, in a statement more frank than anything in Augustine himself, Servius refers to Varro as "everywhere *attacking* religion" (*ubique expugnator religionis*). Three other notes cite Varro for rationalistic explanations of mythical stories.[249]

Not that he got more than a fraction of his eighty-seven quotations from a first-hand consultation of a text of Varro. In several cases he can be shown to have drawn on the same intermediary as Macrobius, sometimes demonstrably Donatus. On *Aen.* vii. 563 Servius cites Varro for a list of volcanic pools like Lake Amsanctus, adding "whence Donatus." Others are that always suspicious phenomenon, double citations (*sed Varro et Ateius, secundum Varronem et Cassium*).[250]

Not the least of the reasons Augustine turned to Varro was (I suggest) precisely that *nobody* was actually reading him anymore. He was no longer a text that people read but an authority they cited, almost always (as Augustine, an experienced reader of texts, could easily see) at second- or thirdhand. Of his more than seventy works in more than six hundred volumes, only one has survived complete.[251] Nonius Marcellus, who preserves almost all of the six hundred surviving fragments of Varro's *Menippean Satires*, might seem an exception. At least one copy of this extraordinary work must have survived into the fourth century,[252] but even so it can hardly be said that Nonius *read* them. He quotes them, a line or so at a time, for details of morphology or vocabulary. What mattered was Varro's authority, usually as reported in some later work, on whether this or that noun was masculine or feminine, or made its genitive in this way or that.[253] In a word, what mattered was *auctoritas Varronis*, a formula we encounter constantly in the grammarians.[254] It was enough that Varro was known to have said this rather than that. Macrobius and Servius constantly appeal to Varro, on a variety of topics, but obviously it was his authority in religious affairs that worried Augustine. He knew the Vergil commentators intimately (citing Asper, Cornutus, and Donatus by name), and must have been disturbed at how often Varro was invoked to explain some cult detail in Vergil. For educated Romans, the combined authority of Vergil and Varro was irresistible. Augustine's brainwave was to sit down and actually *read* this great authority from cover to cover, and show those who appealed to him so trustingly, whether pagans or Christians, what laughable nonsense it was.

---

249. Serv. on *Aen.* xi. 787; Serv. on *Aen.* i. 53; iii. 578; v. 824; Jocelyn 1982, 151.
250. Serv. on *Aen.* v. 45 and DS on xii. 603; for double citations, Cameron 2004, 94, 112, 132, 144, 330–33.
251. The *Res rusticae* in three books (in a corpus of works on agriculture); and six books of the twenty-five-book *De lingua Latina*.
252. Three volumes, according to Lindsay 1901.
253. I. Hadot 2005 has shown that late antique writers did not draw on Varro's lost *Disciplinarum libri* for the cycle of the so-called seven liberal arts.
254. Barabino 2006, 293–305.

If it had really been the purpose of either Servius or Macrobius to "reaffirm" pagan culture against Augustine's "wholesale denigration,"[255] then it would be extraordinary if they had been content to do no more than repeat second- or thirdhand citations of Varro found in Gellius or earlier Vergil commentators. No one who had read even the first five books of the *City of God* could have failed to see the centrality of Varro in Augustine's attack on paganism. Christian readers were likely to applaud the skill with which he exposed the folly and falsity of paganism on the basis of information supplied by its leading authority. Pagan readers must have been indignant at the way he treated Varro's "learned reconstruction of early Roman religion"[256] as if it was the bible of contemporary paganism.

There are two topics Augustine comes back to again and again. First, the religious significance of theatrical games (Conclusion); and second, the hundreds of so-called minor gods, deities with single functions.[257] Here is a typical passage, on the seemingly innumerable deities responsible for crops:

> They set Proserpina over the germinating seeds; the god Nodotus over the joints and nodes of the stems; and the goddess Volutina over the sheaths (*involumenta*) of the ears. When the sheaths open (*patescunt*), the goddess Patelana takes charge of them, so that the ears might emerge. When the wheat stood level in the field, with new ears, this was attributed to the goddess Hostilina, so called because the ancients used the verb *hostire* to mean "make level." When the crops were in flower, the goddess Flora presided; when they were milky (*lactescentibus*), the god Lacturnus; when they ripened (*maturescentibus*), the goddess Matuta; and when the weeds were cleared—that is removed (*runcantur*) from the field—the goddess Runcina. (iv. 8)

Augustine took especial pleasure in making fun of the three deities who presided over doorways: Forculus for the door itself (*fores*), Cardea for the hinges (*cardines*), and Limentinus for the threshhold (*limen*), sarcastically adding that we only need one human doorkeeper. Augustine returned to these topics so often not just because they were so easy to ridicule, but because they were irrefutably documented in Varro.

Any pagan serious enough about the old cults to think of defending them against Augustine's ridicule would have needed to begin by looking at what Varro actually said. He could then have pointed out that neither *ludi* nor "minor" gods played the central part Augustine by implication assigned them in contemporary paganism. Macrobius does nothing of the sort. There is nothing defensive in his dozen or so references to *ludi*. For example, his discussion of the *ludi Apollinares* simply reveals his usual antiquarian preoccupation (were they founded to commemorate a victory, or,

---

255. Barnes 1982, 80.
256. Hagendahl 1967, 608.
257. See now Perfigli 2004.

as some annalists say, to appease the god of heat?).[258] As for the "minor" gods, not a word about Volutina, Patelana, Hostilina, Forculus, Cardea, and company. But he does name three "minor" deities Augustine happens not to mention, Antevorta and Postvorta, "worshipped at Rome as deities most fittingly associated with divination" (i. 7. 20), and Angeronia, the goddess of secrecy, represented with a finger on her sealed mouth. Macrobius's interest is predictably antiquarian: how did she come by her name and what did it mean? Did she banish anxiety (*angores*, so Verrius Flaccus)? Or did she, if duly propitiated, deliver people from quinsy (*angina*, so Julius Modestus)? Or was she, "as some say," the guardian of Rome's secret name?[259]

On this subject we have an interesting note by Servius on Vergil's invocation of all the deities responsible for agriculture (*dique deaeque omnes, studium quibus arva tueri*, *Geo.* i. 21), among those named according to their functions including Sterculinius *a stercoratione* (dung). Commenting on the view that Saturnus was the father of Picus, Augustine reports that Picus's father was in fact Sterces or Stercutius, the man who discovered the value of manure (*stercus*).[260] Much earlier, writing to a pagan grammaticus in 390, Augustine had already made fun of Stercutius and Cloacina (the sewer goddess). He may have been recalling one of three passages in his fellow countryman Tertullian mocking Sterculus as one of the gods who made Rome great.[261] Prudentius too ridicules senators who worship Sterculus (*Per.* ii. 449–51). A defensive pagan would have been well advised quietly to drop the god of manure.

In short, there is not the slightest indication that either Servius or Macrobius had any thought of defending the old gods and their rites against Augustine's mockery. A more specific illustration is the fact that very few of Augustine's quotations find any parallel in Servius or Macrobius. That is to say, there is no indication that either of them was interested in discussing any of his (often unfair and misleading) arguments based on Varro. Complete texts of long works like Varro's *Antiquitates* cannot have been easy to come by in the fifth century. But if Augustine managed to get hold of one in remote Hippo Regius, Macrobius too could surely have done so if he had really looked, whether in Rome itself or in one of the libraries kept in the suburban villas of the old aristocracy, perhaps still in roll form (it is unlikely that much of Varro was ever transferred to codexes).

What does it mean that Macrobius did not take the trouble to track down and actually read a work that had always been an important resource for any serious

---

258. *Sat.* i. 17. 26–27 (the subject of the chapter as a whole is the identification of Apollo as the sun).

259. Macr. *Sat.* i. 10. 7–9; iii. 9. 4; Aug. *CD* iv. 8, 11; for what is known about Angeronia, Latte 1960, 241.

260. The DS addition offers a supplement from the second-century pontifical writer Fabius Pictor (on whom see Herzog and Schmidt 1, 368): *Fabius Pictor hos deos enumerat, quos invocat flamen sacrum Cereale faciens Telluri et Cereri: Vervactorem, Reparatorem, Inporcitorem, Insitorem, Obaratorem, Occatorem, Sarritorem, Subruncinatorem, Messorem, Convectorem, Conditorem, Ptomitorem.*

261. *Quid Stercu<lus> meruit ad divinitatem* (*Ad nat.* ii. 9. 20); *nimirum Sterculus…pro<vexit> hoc imperium* (*Ad nat.* ii. 17. 3; cf. *Apol.* 25. 3).

Roman antiquarian, and had now been transformed by Augustine into a central text in the battle against paganism? Apparently, Varro meant no more to him than the scores of other Republican writers he so lovingly excerpted. Since Varro wrote so much, he quotes him more often than most (forty-three times from various works, including the *Menippean Satires*), but not as often as Ennius (fifty-five times), and not much more often than Lucretius (forty-one times). "Since our generation has deserted Ennius and all the old books, we are ignorant of much that would be clear to us if we were more used to reading the old authors."[262] That was Macrobius's faith, rather than either paganism or Christianity. For all the passion he professes for archaic writers, it was not strong enough to make him search out original texts and actually *read* them. If he really read Ennius and Lucilius, and actively preferred them to the poets of the imperial age, that would be one thing. Who is to say he was not entitled to such a preference? But he did not read them. He was content to savor his old Roman writers in the form of ready-excerpted quotations in antiquarians like Gellius, Sammonicus, and the Vergil commentators. Remarkably enough, he apparently saw no reason to treat Varro any differently from all the other texts he was content to cite at third- or fourthhand.

No less instructive in a different way again is the long chapter on Janus and Saturnus (*Sat.* i. 7). According to Macrobius, Janus was originally a king of Italy, and the story that he had two faces and so could see both behind and before him is "undoubtedly a reference to the foresight and shrewdness of the king" (i. 7. 20). At some point Saturnus arrived, by ship, and, after learning from him the art of husbandry, Janus rewarded Saturnus by sharing the kingdom with him. When Saturnus died Janus devised religious honors for him (21–24). This is pure euhemerism. In earlier centuries a number of pagans had been attracted by the idea that (at least some) gods were originally just outstanding men deified by a grateful posterity. Since pagans often celebrated the birth of their gods (and especially the places where they were born), euhemerism was not as subversive of traditional cults as might at first appear. The Roman ruler cult embraced the idea. But from the second century on Christians siezed on euhemerism as a neat way of attacking pagans through one of their own. We know as much as we do about the lost book of Euhemerus himself because Lactantius chose to quote Ennius's Latin translation at some length.[263] Lactantius even included the same detail as Macrobius of Saturnus arriving in Italy by boat.[264]

This euhemeristic approach is also a conspicuous feature of another late Roman antiquarian work already mentioned in passing, the *Origo gentis Romanae*. The *Origo*

---

262. *Sat.* vi. 9. 9; cf. too *Sat.* iii. 14. 2: *Vetustas quidem nobis semper, si sapimus, adoranda est.*
263. That Lactantius offers direct quotations as well as paraphrase was shown by Laughton and Fraenkel 1951, 35–56; Courtney 1999, 27–39; Ogilvie 1978, 55–57.
264. Lact. i. 13. 7, though citing Ovid (*Fasti* i. 239–40) for the boat.

gives a brief but heavily annotated account of the history of pre-Romulan Italy, with special reference to places and customs that were later to play a part in the story of Rome. The euhemerism is taken even further here, with not only Janus and Saturnus but Picus and Faunus too represented as mortal kings of Italy. Despite its brevity (twenty Teubner pages), the unknown writer cites more than thirty named sources, some of them many times. There are references to oracles, sacrifice, Penates, and the origin of festivals such as the Lupercalia, and among the texts cited are the *Annales pontificum* and *Pontificalium libri*. Beyond question it is a pagan work. But its paganism should not be overstated. While offering, like the two other parts of the tripartite corpus it opens (*De viris illustribus* and Victor's *Caesares*), an account of Roman history from Janus to Constantius II that ignores Christianity, there is nothing either polemical or even defensive about the *Origo*. Nothing suggests that it was intended to provide a pagan counterpart to Christian accounts. Momigliano nicely described it as "a pamphlet in which the origins of Rome were presented in an enlightened euhemeristic fashion with a wealth of references to the fashionable archaic writers: the very thing to be enjoyed by a Macrobius."[265] The latest of the thirty different sources cited is Verrius Flaccus. Such a profusion of such ancient citations in so brief and elementary a work has naturally aroused disquiet. Earlier suspicions of forgery are now generally discredited, but current insistence on the authenticity of the citations is no less simplistic. Like so many of the similar antiquarian citations in Macrobius, they were just copied, unverified, from the latest in a series of earlier and more scholarly works. Like Macrobius, the writer had never seen an actual copy of any of the venerable texts he nonetheless cherished.[266]

It would have been a bad mistake for any pagan apologist to present a euhemeristic account of Janus, Saturnus, Picus, and Faunus as if it were no more than historical fact. So why do Macrobius and the Anonymus do just this? The explanation must be that they were simply reproducing, without any agenda of their own, what we know to have been Varro's approach, as we can reconstruct it from Augustine.[267] Both DS and Servius also claim that Faunus was originally a mortal, with a DS note explicitly citing Varro.[268] A pagan whose goal was to respond, however indirectly, to Augustine's criticisms would hardly have so casually conceded so central a point in contemporary Christian polemic. Anonymus, perhaps writing as early as the 360s, may simply have been unfamiliar with Christian polemic, but it is hard to believe that Macrobius, writing in the 430s, was unaware that he was reproducing the same line of attack Augustine had employed against those very same Italian gods, explicitly citing Varro. In so doing he was, perhaps unintentionally, making his account more acceptable to Christian readers.

---

265. Momigliano 1960, 158.
266. On the source citations, Cameron 2004, 328–34; for more detail, Smith 2005, 97–136.
267. Aug. *CD* 7. 4; 8. 5; 18. 15; P. Fraccaro, *Studi Varroniani* (Padua 1907), 181; Rawson 1985, 245.
268. DS on *Aen.* viii. 275 (citing Varro); DS on *Aen.* x. 551; Serv. on *Aen.* x. 558.

13

So we conclude with a paradox. While it would be interesting to know for certain whether Macrobius was a Christian, that is a secondary issue. On the one hand, it is no longer plausible to maintain that Macrobius and Servius were either promoting or defending paganism. On the other hand, both undoubtedly represent a reading of Vergil more interested than the poet himself in the rituals of paganism. This is not because they were pagans (though Servius, actually less obsessed with this reading than Macrobius, probably was), but because this was the way everyone, pagans and Christians alike, had been reading Vergil for centuries.

While there may still have been a few elderly pagans around when Macrobius wrote, they cannot have been his target audience. We have no information about early readers of the *Saturnalia*, but we do about early readers of the *Commentary*: Symmachus cos. 485 and his son-in-law Boethius, both Christians.[269] Since Macrobius carefully selected interlocutors for his *Saturnalia* with sons or grandsons who held high office in the 420s–440s, it is natural to suppose that here too his target audience was members of the Roman elite of his own day, all almost at any rate nominal Christians. Both works were immensely popular in the Christian Middle Ages.[270]

Members of the late Roman elite continued to devote what must seem an altogether disproportionate amount of their time to Vergil, at many different levels. The sort of thing that so disturbed the older Augustine is perfectly illustrated by the practice of the young Augustine. After his conversion in September 386, he retired to Cassiacum to study philosophy with his friend Alypius, his brother Navigius, and a few disciples. At one point they broke off their philosophical discussions to devote an entire week to "reviewing" and "discussing" three books of the *Aeneid*, and "listened" to a half-book of Vergil before dinner every day.[271]

> These readings, often timed to conclude distinct phases of argument that the group were engaged in, gave shape and rhythm to the days at Cassiacum. Vergil's words penetrated into many aspects of the discussion and were quoted sometimes lightheartedly and playfully and sometimes in a serious sense.

All these young men had already studied Vergil exhaustively in the school of the grammaticus, and then again from a different point of view with the rhetorician. All of them

---

269. For Boethius and Macrobius, Courcelle 1967, 116–24.
270. Kelly 1999.
271. *Contra Acad.* i. 15; ii. 10; *De ordine* i. 8. 26; for the three different verbs, p. 464. Quotation from MacCormack 1998, 46, with illustrations.

considered themselves Christians of some sort, and yet here they are constantly returning to Vergil in their philosophical discussions.[272]

Vergil long continued to be admired for his learning. It might have seemed inevitable that the emphasis on his expertise in pagan ritual would atrophy and disappear with the decline of paganism, but the fact is that it did not. Here as in so many other areas of late antique literary culture, the power of tradition was simply too strong. But it is easy to see why devout Christians would have been disturbed to come across a book written by a prominent imperial official as late as the 430s that positively reveled in such stuff. Idealization of the glorious Roman past (the earlier centuries inevitably pagan) was one thing. We have seen how popular the early books of Livy were at this period. But it was quite another to encourage Christians in the name of tradition to spend their time solemnly learning that pagan priests were forbidden to wear linen, and that steers, not bulls, were sacrificed to Jupiter. Many may have dismissed the *Saturnalia* as harmless antiquarianism. But more serious Christians must have been horrified, nor would they have been reassured to discover that the author was a Christian. Indeed, they might have refused to believe that a man with such interests really was a Christian. Not the least of the reasons Augustine eventually came to disapprove so strongly of the poet he had once loved so deeply was that, as a former student and teacher himself,[273] he knew only too well that, for Christians no less than pagans, the *Aeneid* remained much more than a mythological poem about the founder of Rome. The heady aura of paganism continued to linger around Vergil's poems and (especially) his commentators long after the last pagans were gone.

---

272. Cultivated Christians could (of course) reconcile their faith with continuing study of Vergil through an allegorical reading (for a brief account, MacCormack 1998, 21–31), an approach Augustine himself seems to have rejected (Mestra 2007).

273. Augustine "resta toute sa vie un grammairien," Marrou 1938, 15.

17

THE *ANNALES* OF NICOMACHUS
FLAVIANUS I

1: INTRODUCTION

What was the most important and influential pagan history of the late fourth-century West? In the view of many scholars, not the surviving *Res gestae* of Ammianus Marcellinus, but the lost *Annales* of Nicomachus Flavianus, which offered (so they claim) a full-scale narrative of late third- and fourth-century history from the pagan point of view. According to some, an imperial history from Augustus to the death of Gratian (383); according to others the whole of Roman history, from the foundation of Rome right down to the fall of the usurper Maximus in 388.[1]

Up till the appearance of Bleckmann 1992,[2] Flavian's *Annales* was little more than a shadowy name flitting across more speculative modern accounts of the pagan reaction, and a source postulated for supposedly anti-Christian allusions in more fanciful writings on the *Historia Augusta*. The solid and lasting contribution of Bleckmann's book was to demonstrate just how much good evidence for the late third and early fourth centuries survives in the twelfth-century history of the Byzantine monk Zonaras. At least one lost late antique source needs to be postulated to account for all this material. Unfortunately, Bleckmann was persuaded by Paschoud to identify this lost source as Flavian. This changed the terms of the debate. Flavian's *Annales* could now be seen not only as an ideological cornerstone of the pagan revival but also as a necessary postulate to explain the detailed narrative preserved in the Byzantine historical tradition. Until recently sceptics have been in the majority, and little attention was paid to such fantasies. But thanks in large measure to the energetic advocacy and brilliant rhetoric of François Paschoud, the balance between sceptics and believers has shifted. "Despite his *damnatio memoriae*," writes Bleckmann, "Flavian remained in senatorial circles the historian par excellence, *historicus disertissimus*."[3] Here is the recent verdict of a French critic:[4]

> Today there is no longer any doubt about the existence and importance of this source for late antiquity. It is, in fact, now certain that it exercised enormous

---

1. For the various suggested termini, Zecchini 1993, 51–64; Festy 1997, 465–478; and 2002, xvii–xx.
2. Critical summary in Paschoud 1994, 71–82.
3. Bleckmann 1995, 83–99 at 94; according to Paschoud 1994, 72, "Cette oeuvre est bien attestée."
4. Festy 1997, 465–66. For more recent statements, Baldini 2005, 15–46.

influence, not only on Roman historiography (the *Historia Augusta*, Ammianus Marcellinus, the *Epitome de Caesaribus*), but also on Greek and Byzantine historical writing (Eunapius-Zosimus, Peter the Patrician, Zonaras).

There is indeed such a consensus, at any rate among European scholars, but it is the quality of the argument that counts, not the number of believers.

The problem, of course, is that, being entirely lost, Flavian's history has to be reconstructed on the basis of the surviving works it is supposed to have influenced. In a lively survey of "current problems in the historiography of late antiquity," Paschoud proclaimed the recovery of the *Annales* one of the modern triumphs of source criticism (Quellenforschung). Paschoud himself somewhat disingenuously attributes disagreement to the unpopularity of source criticism, accusing his critics of being unwilling to read "austere texts in German, Italian and French" (which would seem to identify by its absence the language in which he expected to encounter opposition).[5] But while trendier scholars are indeed nowadays impatient with source criticism, Paschoud's three most stubborn critics are all seasoned practitioners.[6] What they are impatient with is *bad* source criticism. Paschoud has recently compared himself to an astronomer, using mathematical calculations to discover unknown planets.[7] This grandiose image might be applied to the identification of the so-called *Kaisergeschichte* (*KG*) or *Imperial History*, whose existence was inferred from the remarkable degree of coincidence in content, structure, and verbal formulation (notably shared errors) in the surviving works of Aurelius Victor, Eutropius, the *Historia Augusta*, and *Epitome de Caesaribus*.[8] But for the method used to "recover" Flavian's *Annales*, astrology would be a more appropriate analogy.

Paschoud proclaimed the recovery of the *KG* and Flavian twin triumphs of source criticism, but the two cases are very different. In the identification of the *KG*, hypothesis arose directly from careful analysis of evidence. Although we do not even know the name of the author, the scale, date, and influence of the work can be inferred with some precision from the evidence; the limited selection of topics in its derivatives implies that the *KG* cannot have been much larger, nor much earlier than the earliest of those derivatives. In the case of Flavian's *Annales* hypothesis came first and evidence was cobbled together afterwards. No verbal or structural parallels and no shared errors.[9]

---

5. Paschoud 1998, 82; and 2002, xviii.
6. Barnes has written extensively on the sources of the *HA*; Cameron's *Greek Anthology* (1993) is in large part an exercise in source criticism, and his *Greek Mythography* (2004) has conjured up a previously unsuspected major source for ancient Vergil commentaries; and what could be more "austere" than Burgess 1999?
7. "in the way astronomers determine with mathematical precision the existence of invisible celestial bodies," *Ant. Tard.* 10 (2002), 487, reviewing Baldini 2000.
8. For brief discussion and bibliography, Herzog and Schmidt 5 § 536, and further below.
9. I hope this answers Paschoud's claim (2006a, 339) that the objection about the lack of direct evidence for Flavian's *Annales* "s'applique aussi à la lettre à l'*EKG*."

The most recent survey of late Latin historiography again gives pride of place to the "recovery" of Flavian's *Annales*, again denouncing sceptics for "refusing to debate."[10] But it is not easy to "debate" mere speculation. It should have been enough to point out, as sceptics repeatedly have,[11] that there is not a shred of evidence that Flavian wrote anything remotely resembling the work fathered on him by the Paschoud équipe. I had originally intended to devote no more than a couple of paragraphs to the subject, but I now realize that such restraint would merely encourage Flavian fanciers, who would see it as a failure to find valid objections to an established consensus. So in view of the difference it would make to my account of the "pagan reaction" if the Bleckmann/Paschoud hypothesis turned out to be true, in the end I decided to demonstrate in detail why, even on its own terms, it simply does not work.

2: FLAVIAN AND THEODOSIUS

What do we actually know about Flavian's *Annales*? Let us be frank. Not a single word survives. Not a single reference in any literary text of any sort or date. This supposedly so important and influential work is known from just two epigraphic dedications. One by his grandson, Nicomachus Dexter, revealing no more than a work called *Annales* dedicated to Theodosius; the other from the base to the statue erected in the family house on the Caelian Hill by his grandson-in-law Memmius Symmachus ca. 402. Both the superlative and the literary reference in the much quoted phrase *historicus disertissimus* were designed to balance the description of Memmius's father as *orator disertissimus*. Sensible people don't take seriously extravagant claims by family members on funerary monuments in private houses. There is also an indirect allusion by yet another kinsman: Aurelius Memmius Symmachus cos. 485 is said to have written his own history "in imitation of his ancestors" (*parentes*). These ancestors included Flavian, but, once again, that tells us no more than that a history of some sort existed.[12]

Thus the entirety of our knowledge of the very existence of Flavian's *Annales* is confined to members of his own family! We have no idea whether it was a large-scale history or the briefest of epitomes, nor even whether it dealt with the empire at all rather than the Republic—or some other period or subject altogether. Those who raise this last objection (notably Barnes, Burgess, and Cameron), are berated for not having read a 1985 paper by Schlumberger that is supposed to have proved that it covered the empire.[13] We have (of course) all read this paper, but found its

---

10. "Le tort des adversaires...est d'avoir refusé le débat," Ratti 2003, 214.

11. See the brief refutations by Cameron 1999, 115; Barnes (*CR* 54 [2004], 121–24); and Burgess (*CR* 100 [2005], 167–69); for a brief but effective earlier refutation, Blockley 1981, 23–24.

12. According to Schlumberger 1985, 329, it is inconceivable ("kaum denkbar") that the younger Symmachus could have said this if Flavian had treated only Republican history. I fail to see any force in this argument.

13. Schlumberger 1985, 305–29.

conclusion unconvincing (its first half actually produces much better evidence for a work on the Republic).

To start with, we should be paying more attention to the one and only fact we know about the *Annales*, the very precise claim in the imperial letter authorizing Flavian's rehabilitation that Theodosius "wished" (*voluit*) the book to be dedicated to himself (p. 201–2). The wishes of a Roman emperor were commands, and *volo* is indeed regularly so used in imperial laws. The natural assumption is that Flavian's book represented the fulfilment of an imperial commission. This at once undermines the presumption on which all modern study of the *Annales* has been based, that it was an openly pagan work.

Valens commissioned histories from two members of his court, Eutropius and Festus, who held the office of *magister memoriae* in succession. Both fulfilled their tasks in a very short time, producing the two briefest epitomes of Roman history that have come down to us, both underlining the importance of conquest and emphasizing the eastern frontier, in obvious anticipation of Valens's projected Persian campaign of 370.[14] A generation earlier we have the so-called *Itinerarium Alexandri*, written with a view to Constantius II's Persian campaign of 340, comparing him to Alexander and Trajan.[15] All three have often been interpreted as illustrating the interest "pagan circles" took in the history of Rome. The truth is that Eutropius and Festus at any rate were enlisted by a Christian emperor to provide literary support in furtherance of his military goals. In this context, the lack of Christian content was immaterial; all the emperor wanted was a convenient summary of facts about past campaigns for a governing class that (especially in the East) was ignorant of the basic facts of Roman history. Festus focused on Rome's eastern frontier, while Eutropius provided a longer perspective on Rome's territorial expansion, giving much information about the terms of treaties made with conquered powers, obviously with implicit reference to Jovian's recent unfavorable treaty with Persia, hopefully to be superseded by Valens. If Theodosius commissioned Flavian to write a history, he too presumably had some such propagandist goal in mind—and wanted something relatively brief, something that (at least in theory) he might read himself.

According to the *Epitome de Caesaribus*, Theodosius took a keen and intelligent interest in ancient history (*sagax plane multumque diligens ad noscenda maiorum gesta*).[16] When Theodosius is represented by Claudian as giving his son Honorius guidance on kingship, there is not a word about poetry, oratory, or philosophy in the section advising him to "cultivate the Muses"; twenty-two out of its twenty-three lines are devoted to the importance of studying history (naturally again in the form of a list of *exempla*, all Republican).[17] Theodosius might well have wanted a member of his

14. See especially Lenski 2002, 185–96.
15. Lane Fox 1997, 239–52; see now Tabacco 2000.
16. *Epit. de Caes.* 48. 11, with Festy's notes in his Budé edition (pp. 233–34).
17. IV Cons. Hon. 395–418; Cameron 1970, 336–40.

court to write a history that would set his own reign in an appropriate historical context (he apparently liked to think of himself as descended from his great Spanish predecessor Trajan). But he is not likely to have wanted a detailed narrative.

The title *Annales* would not suit a history of the empire better than the Republic. It could be applied to any sort of history;[18] Tacitus uses it of Greek history, Ammianus of Egyptian history, and Paulinus of Nola styles the Christian world chronicle of Sulpicius Severus *Annales*.[19] In Flavian's case *Annales* may not have been intended as a *title* at all rather than (as often) a description, simply "a history."[20]

One thing can be fixed with a reasonable degree of certainty: the date of publication. The Flavian dedication of 431 (p. 201) very specifically states that Theodosius wished the *Annales* "to be dedicated to him by his quaestor and prefect" (*consecrari sibi a quaestore et praefecto sibi voluit*). The dedication of the *Annales* must have mentioned Flavian's successive tenure of both offices. Flavian was indeed promoted directly from quaestor to praetorian prefect, as we know from a letter Symmachus wrote to Rufinus (*Ep.* iii. 90):

> You are often the first or only bearer of happy tidings for me: your letter announced the promotion of my brother, previously (*antehac*) quaestor, to the praetorian prefecture. All your letters bring me some great pleasure. Your very words are full of exuberance, and by the brilliance of their style bear witness to the alertness of your mind. Since I cannot respond in kind, I address heaven with my good wishes, that the good fortune of good men may always be agreeable to Your Felicity (*felicitas vestra*).

In context, *antehac* must mean "up till now"; Flavian has been promoted to prefect while still quaestor. The dates at which he held these offices are one of the most controversial problems of fourth-century prosopography.[21]

The two possibilities are 382/3 and 388/90. The evidence is dates in imperial laws (notoriously unreliable) and the letters of Symmachus. To my mind Matthews has produced an all but unanswerable case for the later date. Cecconi has recently tried to revive the earlier date, but without seriously undermining Matthews's arguments or producing new ones of his own. The key item is the quaestorship, and the letter of Symmachus just quoted allows its date to be fixed to 388/9.[22] Some scholars have been prepared to accept this date for the quaestorship, but accept a prefecture in 382/3.

---

18. For a long list of references to *annales* in and by a variety of writers, Verbrugghe 1989, 192–230 at 225–30. The term is rare in late antique texts: see the wide-ranging discussion in Croke 2001, 291–331, esp. 298–99.

19. Tac. *Ann.* ii. 88. 3; Amm. xxii. 16. 14; Paul. Nol. *Ep.* 28. 5 (Sulp. Sev. *Chron.* pr. 2 calls it a *historia*).

20. For examples, Verbrugghe 1989, 196–97. I am ignoring Schlumberger's suggestion that *Annales* evokes the priestly associations of the *Annales Maximi* compiled in early Republican times by the *pontifex maximus*.

21. For a tabulation of the various possibilities with full bibliography, Cecconi 2002, 168–69.

22. See, with a full analysis of earlier discussions, Matthews 1989, 18–25; Honoré 1998, 59–70; and for the prefecture, Matthews 1997, 196–213, rebutting Errington 1992, 439–61; see too Sogno 2006, 73.

That is simply impossible. No one ever took a step down in the imperial hierarchy. Those who dismiss this argument have never produced a counterexample.

Nothing is known of Rufinus's career before he is first attested as *magister officiorum* at the eastern court in 388. Those who want Flavian to be prefect in 382 argue that Symmachus might have got to know Rufinus this early,[23] but it is difficult to see when, where, or how. Before 388 he was a minor eastern bureacrat, and Symmachus never visited the eastern court. Yet this letter obviously treats Rufinus as an equal (to the extent of affecting to be unable to match his literary style). This was Symmachus's manner when writing to those who exercised real power. Rufinus was a nobody before he won the mastership of offices in 388, whereupon he rapidly became Theodosius's chief minister. There can be little doubt that he did not enter Symmachus's world until he arrived in Rome in the retinue of Theodosius in 389.

Then there is the formula *felicitas vestra*. At this period such honorific formulas were becoming increasingly associated with specific offices, a development traced in a recent study by Mathisen.[24] This one is otherwise confined to emperors, kings, and the very highest officials.[25] Symmachus was a connoisseur of such formalities; he uses it twice elsewhere, both times addressing emperors.[26] Writing to Flavian after his promotion to the quaestorship, he playfully refers to the good fortune of "your amplitude" (*de amplitudinis tuae prosperis*). *Amplitudo tua/vestra* is another formula restricted to officials of the very highest rank: in Symmachus, once more of Flavian, and otherwise of an ordinary consul and another quaestor.[27] Like Ambrose, another connoisseur, he was careful to reserve *clementia tua/vestra* for emperors.[28] It is hard to believe that he would have employed so inappropriate a formula as *felicitas vestra* when writing to the minor civil servant Rufinus must still have been in 382. On the contrary, it is the subtlest detail in his flattery of Theodosius's chief minister.

Flavian's quaestorship must be dated to 388/89 and his first prefecture to 389-90. Since the dedication apparently mentioned his recent promotion, we are bound to conclude that it was not before, and probably not long after 390 that Flavian published his *Annales*. That is to say, the entire project was both begun and completed in his spare time as a busy bureaucrat over a period of less than three years.[29]

Since the Paschoud équipe see Ammianus as our earliest witness to Flavian's influence, it is naturally essential for them that Flavian published first. This is immediately problematic, since the best authorities assign Ammianus's last books to the same general date, in or soon after 390.[30] A recent study by Guy Sabbah argues for 394/5 or

---

23. For example, Callu 1999, 94 = 2006, 380.
24. Mathisen 2001, 179–207.
25. O'Brien 1930, 13; *TLL.* vi. 1. 431 § 3. For the imperial associations of formulas like *felicitas saeculi* and *felicitas temporum*, Rösch 1978, 42–43. The formula is in fact very rare.
26. Symm. *Rel.* 18. 1; 35. 1.
27. *Ep.* ii. 8. 1; 21. 1; v. 5. 1; 54. 6; see Cecconi's notes on 170 and 206.
28. O'Brien 1930, 11–12.
29. Paschoud suggests that it was his fame as a (budding) historian that led to his appointment as quaestor.
30. Matthews 1989, 22; Barnes 1998, 184.

even later.[31] But he produced no new arguments or evidence, and it is impossible to believe that Ammianus would have included his extravagant eulogy of the elder Theodosius if he had been writing under Eugenius. Nor is it easy to see why he would have included it if he had been writing after the emperor Theodosius's death. Why not rather a eulogy of the emperor, or Arcadius and Honorius? In a separate article I have argued that numerous indications point to publication before the death of Valentinian II (15 May 392).

Schlumberger took an idiosyncratic line on the relationship between Ammianus and Flavian, providing less support for the Bleckmann/Paschoud hypothesis than their blanket endorsement of his "proof" that Flavian covered empire rather than Republic might seem to imply. Completely undermining the assumption that parallels between Ammianus and Zosimus or Zonaras derive from common use of Flavian, he sensibly argued that Ammianus must have published first. On reading Ammianus (he argued), Flavian judged that this Greek had proved an unworthy continuator of Tacitus and decided to produce a more appropriate continuation of his own, a "traditionalist, Roman, senatorial reaction to Ammianus's work." This (he argued) would explain why he called it *Annales* (to underline its traditionalist, senatorial, even priestly perspective)—and why two works covering the same period appeared in such quick succession in the same city. But however different their perspective, it is hard to believe that two major narratives covering the same period would be published within a couple of years. *If* Flavian wrote an imperial history he must indeed have written after Ammianus. But if so, given the limited time at his disposal while in office, the *Annales* cannot have been much more than an epitome of Ammianus, not based on independent research. Obviously, this would help to explain why it disappeared without trace.

3: THE EVIDENCE OF MACROBIUS AND SYMMACHUS

For believers, it is axiomatic that Flavian's *Annales* were on a large scale and in the grand style, at once recognized as the standard history of the third and fourth centuries. It is thus especially surprising that the letters of his lifelong friend Symmachus and the *Saturnalia* of Macrobius, our only detailed accounts of Flavian's cultural interests, neither mention the *Annales* nor suggest that he took any interest in history.

In one way or another Macrobius indicates the expertise or reputation of each of his interlocutors. The professionals are simply labeled (philosopher, rhetorician, grammarian), while the aristocrats are characterized by what they are given to talk about: Symmachus Vergil's rhetoric, for example. Flavian is assigned Vergil's knowledge of augural law (i. 24. 17), but his more general characterization simply praises him (i. 5. 13) for surpassing his father Venustus in "distinction of character and dignity of life no less

---

31. Sabbah 1997, 89–116; and in his Budé edition, *Ammien Marcellin* 6 (Paris 1999), xlvi–xlix.

than abundance and depth of learning." It is a paradox that, while the subject assigned
to Symmachus perfectly illustrates one-half of the paired dedications in the house on
the Caelian Hill (*orator disertissimus*), nothing in the dialogue as preserved even hints
at Flavian being *historicus disertissimus*.

How is this to be explained? Schlumberger suggests two possibilities. First, that
Flavian's book was not published till after Macrobius's dramatic date, namely 382.[32]
But Servius's Vergil commentary was likewise published after 382, more than thirty
years after. Without ever mentioning the published commentary, Macrobius nonetheless repeatedly represents Servius as the great Vergilian commentator of his age,
undoubtedly the reason he chose him as an interlocutor. Schlumberger's second suggestion is that, since the *Saturnalia* is exclusively concerned with the literature and
institutions of the Republic, the subject matter of an imperial history simply did not
fit. But the *Saturnalia* consists of two quite separate elements: the antiquarian text,
and the dramatic frame. The frame, as we have seen in earlier chapters, is full of details
about the lives and interests of the interlocutors. Macrobius's exclusive concern with
the Republic for his subject matter would certainly be a good reason for not citing an
imperial history *in his text*. But it would be no reason at all for not mentioning the fact
that Flavian was a famous historian in the frame. Symmachus's oratory was (naturally)
devoted to recent affairs, yet it is often mentioned in the frame by the other interlocutors. If Flavian wrote a major history of the empire that was not published till (say)
390, it would have been well within the conventions of the genre for even the most
dyed-in-the-wool antiquarian to have one of his interlocutors say to him *in a frame
passage* something like "How is the great work coming on?" Indeed, if Macrobius had
thought of Flavian as a historian, we might have expected him to be entrusted with a
contribution on Vergil's knowledge of Roman history, obviously a major element in
the *Aeneid*.

As for Symmachus, while it would be vain to look among his brief and functional
missives for the sort of informative letters Pliny wrote to his historian friend Cornelius
Tacitus, most of those addressed to writers do in fact allude to the sort of writing for
which they were known. Ausonius is praised for his poetry (i. 14); letters to Naucellius
refer both to his poetry and to his historical work (Greek, not Roman history);[33]
Praetextatus was a *pontifex* and philhellene (i. 47). There is even an allusion to the
poems of the obscure Messala (vii. 91). Yet not a hint in ninety-one letters to Flavian
that he was even interested in history, much less a historian. In an area where speculation has raged out of control I am reluctant to add one of my own, but, purely as a
speculation, I suggest that Symmachus did not mention Flavian's history because it
was a hastily executed and derivative imperial commission of which Flavian himself
was not especially proud.

---

32. Schlumberger 1985, 318–19 (in fact assuming 384, which is immaterial in the context of his argument).
33. *Ep.* iii. 11, variously identified: Munari 1955, 26; Speyer 1959, 3; above, p. 564.

The anonymous addressee of *Ep.* ix. 110 is reproached for devoting to his history the time he should have been spending on his oratory.[34] Callu has suggested that this might be Flavian, which would supply the missing evidence for his supposed interest in history.[35] But the forced and rather formal compliments of the letter are too distant in tone for Symmachus's oldest friend, and it is clear that Anonymus's fame rests on his oratory, while there is no evidence that Flavian was known as an orator.[36] All Symmachus's letters to Flavian are collected in Bk ii, and it would be incredible if the one letter that alluded to his greatest claim to fame had been omitted and published anonymously years later with the odds and ends in Bk ix.[37]

The combined silence of Macrobius and Symmachus must be held significant, especially since both Bk 2 of Symmachus's correspondence and the *Saturnalia* were published after Flavian's death, by when any *Annales* dedicated to Theodosius must have been published. Nor can we argue that Macrobius and Symmachus were reluctant to mention what is held to have been an aggressively pagan work. For both refer openly and often to Flavian's paganism. Given his obvious concern to pick interlocutors known for their cultural distinction, the silence of Macrobius in particular is a real problem. The simplest solution, one devastating to all the Bleckmann/Paschoud assumptions, is that, outside the family, the *Annales* had already been forgotten by the time Macrobius came to write around 430.

4: THE WESTERN TRADITION

There is also an objection of another sort to the assumption that the *Annales* covered the empire. While making extensive use of the Byzantine historical tradition to reconstruct Flavian's *Annales*, Paschoud and his followers have almost completely ignored the western, Latin tradition.[38] First, the *Romana* and *Getica* of the mid-sixth-century Jordanes. The *Romana* is a history of the world from Adam to Justinian, wholly compiled from surviving sources, both Greek and Latin. For the fourth century it derives the entirety of its information from Eutropius, Jerome's *Chronicle*, the *Epitome de Caesaribus*, Socrates, and Orosius. There is not a single sentence left unaccounted for that might be derived from a lost source.[39] As for the *Getica*, since it traces the history of the Goths rather than the empire, its coverage is erratic, in the fourth

---

34. *omnem te operam condendae historiae deputasse, Ep.* ix. 110. 2; Cameron 1964, 15–28. Conceivably the author of the so-called *Epitome de Caesaribus.*
35. Callu 1999, 95.
36. Symmachus's reference to his eloquence (*tua lingua*) in *Ep.* ii. 22. 2 alludes to his role as quaestor (the official who drafted imperial laws), as recognised by Callu in his edition, quite different from fame as an orator.
37. On the publication of Bk ix, see Ch. 10.
38. On the question whether the *Epitome de Caesaribus* drew on Flavian, see below § 10.
39. Unless, of course, we assume that Flavian transcribed the same sources verbatim, which would undermine any claim for originality and importance for the *Annales.*

century jumping from Constantine to Valens. Its sources for the fourth century are Ammianus, the *Epitome*, and Orosius. From the point where Ammianus breaks off down to the 430s, it draws on an unknown secular source that Mommsen styled *Continuator Ammiani*. In theory the first two or three years of this *could* be Flavian, if (improbably enough) his history extended beyond 378, though the natural assumption is one or both of the known lost Latin sources that undoubtedly covered this period, Sulpicius Alexander and Renatus Profuturus Frigeridus.[40]

Second, the lost *Historia Romana* in seven books by Symmachus cos. 485, only known from the so-called *Anecdoton Holderi* and one extended quotation about the emperor Maximin (A.D. 235–38) in Jordanes's *Getica*, cited from Bk 5. For the fifth century Symmachus no doubt drew on personal research and inquiries, but for earlier centuries he is bound to have relied on existing works, among them naturally Flavian, especially since Symmachus's history was supposedly written "in imitation of his ancestors." But the one quotation we have consists of verbatim excerpts from a known source, the *Historia Augusta*, combined with excerpts from Orosius, apparently his account of Maximin in its entirety. Either Flavian did not cover Maximin at all, or what he said was considered inferior to the entirely fictitious *HA Life of Maximin*.

Bizarrely enough, one scholar has recently argued that the *HA* is, in fact, Flavian's *Annales*,[41] not a view that is likely to commend itself, given the fact that the *HA* was published pseudonymously under six different names and in the form, not of annals, but of biographies of emperors. Another strange view gaining currency in recent years is that the pseudonymous author of the *HA* was the younger Flavian.[42] Other objections (such as the total lack of evidence) aside, if true, this would have the absurdly improbable consequence that father and son both produced detailed accounts of the same period at almost the same time!

Finally, there is the *Historia Romana* of Paul the Deacon, an amplified version of Eutropius's *Breviarium* continued down to the reign of Justinian, compiled between A.D. 761 and 784. Once again, Paul's additions to Eutropius all come from the same surviving sources, mainly Jerome, the *Epitome*, and Orosius.[43] Of course, the fact that Jordanes and Paul knew nothing of any history that could be ascribed to Flavian doesn't in itself prove that he did not write such a work. But the fact that three surviving Latin histories covering the third and fourth centuries can be satisfactorily explained without the need to postulate a substantial lost source certainly lends no support to current speculations about the supposed influence of Flavian's *Annales*. Long before Bleckmann it had always been obvious that a major lost narrative source lay behind Zonaras, but there is simply no basis for any such postulate in the western historical tradition.

---

40. Alexander perhaps covered 375/8 to 395, and Frigeridus perhaps 395–425. For a brief account of what little is known about them, Zecchini in Marasco 2003, 333–35.

41. Ratti 2007; 2007a. Not even Paschoud could swallow this (*An. tard.* 15 [2007], 360–62).

42. Most recently, M. Festy in Bonamente and Brandt 2007, 183–95.

43. See Droysen's edition of Eutropius (1879), xxxviii–lxi, esp. xxxix; A. Crivellucci, *Pauli Diaconi Historia Romana* (Rome 1914); Goffart 2005, 347–69.

5: LATIN IN THE GREEK EAST

We have seen that the lost source Bleckmann postulates behind Zonaras and several other Byzantine historical texts is supposed to have been a large-scale narrative covering the late third and fourth century that was pagan, senatorial in bias, earlier than Ammianus, and written in Latin. According to Bleckmann, the *Annales* is "the only available candidate."[44] What he means (of course) is that, granted this tendentious characterization of a purely hypothetical lost source, granted the traditional picture of Flavian as a pagan fanatic, granted the assumption that the *Annales* was a large-scale narrative, granted considerable licence in handling major chronological objections, and (above all) granted the astonishing claim that this source was written in Latin, Flavian looks the most promising lost source we can actually *name*.

It is tempting to think we should at least be able to put a name to lost works we believe important—though the *KG* should serve as a warning.[45] We shall see that, if a source corresponding to this description existed at all, it must have been Greek rather than Latin. But even among Latin historians, we have already identified another possible candidate: the anonymous addressee of Symmachus *Ep.* ix. 110, a late fourth-century senatorial historian who cannot be Flavian. No less important, the features Bleckmann identified cannot all be predicated of the same parts of this postulated lost source of Zonaras. It is only the narrative of the third-century emperors preceding Diocletian that reveals senatorial bias. The narrative of the house of Constantine in Zonaras does not manifest the same senatorial bias, nor is there any compelling reason to suppose that the third- and fourth-century narratives are both from the same history, much less the work of the same man. Even if the narrative of the entire period 270–365 did all derive from the same fourth-century history, its author cannot have written at firsthand of the third century. This material at least he must have derived from an earlier written source. There is thus little reason to believe that it was this hypothetical late fourth-century author who originated a senatorial bias in the first half of his work, inevitably based on written sources, not apparent in the second, for which he presumably had firsthand sources and a freer hand. Not that the concept "senatorial bias" has any clear-cut meaning in an age when most men of letters were likely to be of senatorial rank. Nor is it clear what is meant by the claim that this source was pagan (rather than just secular). No fourth-century narrative history was likely to be Christian.

The main objection, of course, is the improbability of a Byzantine writer drawing on a Latin text. Before turning to this question it should be emphasized that Paschoud has enormously compounded this improbability by insisting that Eunapius too drew on Flavian's *Annales*. That is to say, we are asked to believe that *two* Greek writers drew on Flavian *independently*. Bleckmann suggests the more

---

44. Bleckmann 1995, 400.
45. For one suggestion about the author, Burgess 1993.

economical possibility that someone produced a "Greek adaptation," not further defined, already in the fourth century, which was used by both Eunapius and (later) Peter the Patrician.[46] But quite apart from the lack of either evidence or parallel for any such "adaptation," the suggestion presupposes (mistakenly, as we shall see) that Flavian wrote before Eunapius.

It is true enough that, once Constantinople became an imperial capital, would-be civil servants found knowledge of Latin an advantage. But Bleckmann exaggerates when he claims that "from the fourth to the sixth century Latin historical works were increasingly translated into Greek or adapted by Greek writers."[47] It is true that a certain amount of Latin literature was read in sixth-century Constantinople, but mainly either legal texts or luxury copies of the classics produced for expatriate western aristocrats.[48] By then the history of the empire was amply covered in a succession of large-scale histories written in Greek: Dio, Herodian, Dexippus, Eunapius, Olympiodorus, Priscus, Malchus, Procopius, and Agathias, with Olympiodorus, Priscus, and Procopius offering extensive coverage of western events. Why would any Greek-speaker have been interested in the Latin histories of Flavian or Symmachus cos. 485?

The fact is that there is only one example of a Latin history translated into Greek— and only two undoubted cases of Greek historians drawing on a published Latin source. First, the one and only translation: Eutropius. The *Breviarium* of Eutropius compressed a thousand years of Roman history into seventy pages, short on analysis but cramming in as many facts as possible. A Greek version by a certain Paeanius, a friend of Libanius, soon appeared, a version even briefer than the original, omitting many minor details (such as Roman *praenomina* and hard-to-translate titles) but adding occasional explanatory notes for Greek-speakers.[49] Over and above the attractions of its brevity and simplicity, there is a very specific reason why the *Breviarium* rather than any other Latin historical work of the age was selected for translation: its comprehensiveness. No other work—certainly no Greek work—covered so much ground in so brief a space. It should be added that Paeanius was an advocate, and so one of the small number of Greek-speakers with a professional motive to learn Latin. The very fact that so brief a work written in such clear and simple Latin was nonetheless translated into Greek is itself an illustration of the fact that it was not otherwise expected to attract Greek-speaking readers. The sheer utility of the book is further illustrated by the fact that another translation was produced in the early sixth century, by Capito, who also wrote historical works in Greek.[50]

---

46. "eine griechische Bearbeitung," Bleckmann 1992, 415.

47. "ins Griechische übertragen oder durch griechische Autoren überarbeitet," Bleckmann 1992, 23.

48. On this phenomenon see Cameron 2004, at 518–25.

49. H. Droysen, *Eutropii Breviarium cum versionibus et continuatoribus* (Berlin 1879), xxi–xxv. For a brief analysis of Paeanius's style, Fisher 1982, 189–93.

50. Droysen 1879, xxv, lxix–lxxii; see now Roberto 2003, 241–71.

Socrates not only cites Rufinus's Latin continuation of Eusebius's *Ecclesiastical History* in his own, but also drew on Eutropius.[51] Both are to some extent special cases. Rufinus was a major figure in the eastern monastic world, praised for his learning in the *Lausiac History* of Palladius. For all its faults, his work represents the first attempt to continue Eusebius, based on original research,[52] and, thanks to his Greek connections, is likely to have circulated in eastern ecclesiastical circles. As for Eutropius, a careful study by P. Périchon has shown, remarkable though it might seem, that Socrates must have had both the original Latin text and Paeanius's translation on his desk as he worked. On two occasions he includes precise details Paeanius omitted.[53] Nonetheless, there can be little doubt that it was the Greek translation that brought Eutropius to his attention. Socrates also drew a number of dates from a consular list maintained in Constantinople that survives in a Latin version. But there may well have been a Greek version as well (not that it required much Latin to use a consular list).[54] It should be added that Socrates sometimes misunderstood Rufinus's Latin.[55]

Sozomen, another lawyer, also drew on (but does not directly cite) Rufinus.[56] But Sabbah points out that, while occasionally citing Greek translations of imperial letters written in Latin, Sozomen never offers translations of his own.[57] Sozomen also mentions three other Latin ecclesiastical writers—Eusebius of Vercelli, Hilary of Poitiers, and Lucifer of Cagliari—known to him by reputation.[58] It is obviously significant that all three spent long periods in exile in the East, where they are bound to have become known in eastern ecclesiastical circles. So while Socrates and Sozomen had good enough Latin to consult Latin sources, the only ones they show any knowledge of are books known to have circulated in the East.

The possibility that Zonaras either knew Latin or had access to a multi-book history in Latin may be excluded without further discussion. Following Patzig, Bleckmann posited an early Byzantine intermediary that was also used by a number of middle Byzantine historians. This text Patzig gave the name "Leo-source" (Leoquelle), after the chronicle published under the name Leo Grammaticus. But Leo Grammaticus is just the name of the scribe responsible for a late and heavily interpolated copy of what has long been known to be the *Chronikon* of Symeon the Logothete.[59] It is thus unfortunate that Bleckmann chose to perpetuate this

---

51. The latest studies doubt the old assumption that Socrates was a lawyer: Leppin 1996, 11; Urbainczyk 1997, 13–14. Unlike Sozomen, he does not draw on imperial legislation (Errington 1997, at 403–6).

52. I follow van Nuffelen 2002 in regarding the so-called *HE* of Gelasius of Caesarea as a pseudonymous forgery of the late fifth century; so too Maraval 2004, 25–28. If Gelasius wrote before and was drawn on by Rufinus, why does Socrates cite only Rufinus, not Gelasius?

53. Périchon 1968, 378–84.

54. Hansen 1995, li–lii; Burgess 1993, 197.

55. See Maraval 2004, 25.

56. Bidez and Hansen 1960, xlviii; Errington 1997, at 410–35.

57. E.g., *HE* iii. 2; Sabbah in Grillet, Sabbah, and Festugière, *Sozomène, Hist. Ecclés.* 1–2 (Paris 1983), 20 n. 1.

58. Soz. *HE* iii. 15. 6, with Sabbah's notes (1996, 142–44).

59. For the evidence, Wahlgren 2001, 251–62; see now his edition in *CFHB* 43. 1 (2006).

antiquated and wholly inappropriate name, regrettably now common coin. It was the author of this "Leo-source" who (according to Bleckmann) cannibalized Flavian's *Annales*. Patzig himself identified the "Leo-source" with the early seventh-century history of John of Antioch;[60] Bleckmann less plausibly (as we shall see) with the mid sixth-century Peter the Patrician.

As a longtime bureaucrat who lived in Italy for five years, Peter presumably knew Latin.[61] But was his Latin good enough to read hundreds of pages of historical narrative written in literary Latin when a detailed Greek history covering the same period (namely Eunapius) was available? In any case, it is not enough for Paschoud that material from Flavian's *Annales* reached Zonaras via Peter the Patrician. We are also asked to believe that Eunapius too read Flavian.

Paschoud himself dismissed the objection that a Greek Sophist was unlikely to know Latin as no more than "long-standing prejudice,"[62] and Baldini relegated the language question to a single offhand footnote toward the end of a lengthy discussion.[63] But while it is an obvious truism that the Roman Empire was bilingual,[64] few individuals were genuinely bilingual. A (fast decreasing) number of Latin-speaking westerners knew some Greek,[65] but very few Greek-speaking easterners knew Latin. As Millar has recently pointed out, the best evidence comes in the abundant *Acta* of the three fifth-century Ecumenical Councils of the Church (431, 449, and 451):[66]

> If we take the several hundred bishops from (almost) all over the Theodosian Empire who attended the three Councils as a reasonably representative sample of (to very varying degrees) educated men, they did not understand spoken Latin, and had to have all written material in Latin translated for them.

It is true that it became less rare for Greeks to learn Latin in late antiquity, but it never became common. Zecchini argued that in the course of the fourth century Latin spread among Greek "intellectuals" as never before, citing Ammianus as typical.[67] Inasmuch as "intellectual" implies what Greeks of the high empire called *pepaideumenoi* (those trained in the traditional Greek *paideia*), this is simply untrue.[68] Greeks

---

60. Patzig 1904, the last of a series of papers beginning with Patzig 1894; so too a series of papers by M. DiMaio in *Byzantion* (50 [1980], 158–85; 51 [1981], 502–10; 58 [1988], 230–55).
61. Bleckmann 1992, 415; Paschoud 1994, 80; *PLRE* iii. 994–95.
62. "un vieux préjugé ténace…une orthodoxie apodictique, un axiome inébranlable," Paschoud 2001, 7 (a nice illustration of Paschoud's lively rhetoric).
63. Baldini 2000, 151 n. 198.
64. P. Veyne, *L'empire gréco-romain* (Paris 2005).
65. See Ch. 15. In this context I am not counting Latin-speaking *easterners* who knew Greek, such as Marcellinus *comes*, Jordanes, and indeed the emperor Justinian, all born in the still partially bilingual Illyricum.
66. Millar 2006, 17.
67. Zecchini 1993, 59, citing the chronicler Marcellinus, but he is the *opposite* phenomenon (n. 65).
68. The concept "intellectual" is not entirely appropriate to the Graeco-Roman world (Zanker 1995, 1–9).

who learned Latin in the fourth century did so more or less exclusively with a view to a career in law or the imperial administration. In the East as in the West, all official communications between the emperor and his administrators were in Latin.[69] It was thus essential that anyone who hoped to hold public office at any level should acquire a functional knowledge of Latin. But such evidence as we have on the teaching of Latin in the fourth- and fifth-century Greek East at this period suggests that only a fairly elementary reading knowledge was required.[70]

Latin-speaking Easterners fall into two main groups:[71] governors and civil servants, men who are not likely to have learned more than the Latin they needed for their jobs; and a handful of Christian clerics (e.g., Athanasius and Evagrius of Antioch), most of whom learned Latin during the extended periods they are known to have spent living in the West. In earlier centuries, a very few Greeks (Dio Cassius, e.g.) picked up some knowledge of Latin poets as well as historians.[72] But then Dio lived for many years in Rome. Plutarch too made many visits to Rome, yet admits that he started Latin late in life and never perfected it. He clearly consulted Latin sources, but may not have been able to read multibook works (such as Livy) unaided. How then did he cope? Presumably he relied on Greek-speaking western friends and (like Cicero and the elder Pliny) bilingual freedmen.[73] So far as we know Eunapius never once visited the West, and if he had Latin-speaking friends in Sardis, they are unlikely to have been able to offer anything more than the basic Latin of the bureaucrat. Jerome's Roman friends regularly sent him copies of books they thought would interest him. But the idea that Eunapius was part of a network in Rome that kept Sardis up to date on the latest Latin publications is, if anything, even less plausible than the idea of Eunapius himself learning Latin.

The only two Greeks of the age we know of with a wide Latin literary culture are Ammianus and Claudian. Both are obviously special cases, and not simply in the quality of their Latin publications. Their familiarity with the Latin classics, prose and verse, is so extensive that it is reasonable to assume that both were products of bilingual homes. No less important, both lived for many years in the West. Ammianus in addition spent many years in the army, where Latin was the normal if not official language.[74] Obviously, a few Greeks with a gift for languages *may* have progressed beyond basic Latin to the poets and historians.[75] It was once fashionable to argue, on the analogy of Claudian, that Nonnus and one or two other Greek poets of the age knew Ovid and Vergil. But a systematic study by Knox of the most favorable example

---

69. Millar 2006, 84–93, and passim.
70. On the papyrological evidence, see especially now Cribiore 2003/4.
71. Evidence collected in Bruno Rochette, *Le latin dans le monde grec* (Brussels 1997).
72. Swain 1996, 403–4.
73. Jones 1971, 81–87. For the freedmen of Cicero and his peers, Treggiari 1969, 110–29.
74. Rochette 1997, 147–50; for more evidence, but objecting to the term "official," Adams 2003, 599–623.
75. Geiger 1999, 606–17, has argued that Latin was "more prevalent in the East than is usually acknowledged," but cites no new evidence of fourth- or fifth-century Greeks with a Latin literary culture.

alleged, the story of Phaethon in Bk 38 of the *Dionysiaca*, has put that assumption out of court.[76] In the case of Quintus of Smyrna it should be noted that if (as generally assumed) he wrote no later than the third century, that would be before the development of Latin teaching that transformed the late Roman East.

Another Sophist with some philosophical expertise was Themistius, author of some thirty-five orations and a few paraphrases of Aristotle. In a response to a speech of Valens written in Latin, Themistius said that he did not know the language, a claim often taken literally.[77] In fact, he was disclaiming the ability to deliver a formal oration in Latin, which is rather different, leaving open the possibility that he had a reading knowledge.[78] We should bear in mind that Themistius spent forty-five years in the service of five successive emperors; he could hardly have avoided picking up *some* Latin in daily dealings with court (Valens at any rate and probably Theodosius too knew little or no Greek).[79] Yet even so he affected not to know the language.

Julian knew Latin well enough to conduct a conversation (*Latine disserendi sufficiens sermo*, as Ammianus patronisingly put it). But there is no indication that he read literary texts in Latin.[80] We might have expected that the many judgments on earlier emperors expressed in his *Caesares* would prove to derive from the fourth-century Latin epitomators, but they are often so different as to suggest that he "had small acquaintance with their work or the historiographical tradition to which they belonged."[81]

It might seem that any Greek planning to write Roman history would need to know Latin, and this is certainly true of the many cases we know of in the early empire: Appian, Dio, Dionysius, Diodorus, Plutarch, Strabo. But two major differences inevitably conditioned the approach of, not just Eunapius, but any would-be Greek historian of Rome in late antiquity. All these early imperial historians wrote on the Republic, for which the sources were very largely Latin; and all lived for long periods in Rome.[82] Eunapius spent his entire adult life in his native Sardis; nor (before Ammianus) were there substantial Latin sources for the period he chose (270–404). He set out to continue Dexippus, a Greek who probably never left his native Athens. Coming as he did from an old family that boasted a succession of Sophists and local dignitaries, Dexippus could easily have become a member of the Roman senate if he

---

76. Knox 1988; so too B. Simon in the Budé Nonnos vol. 14 (Paris 1999), 29–40. On Quintus, see Gärtner 2005, who makes insufficient allowance for the vast amount of Greek mythological poetry that is lost, nor for the influence of mythographic writings (Cameron 2004, passim).

77. *Or.* 6. 81a; Dagron 1968, 60; Vanderspoel 1995, 157.

78. Errington 2000, 879–80.

79. Moroni 2005. Valentinian I could carry on a conversation in Greek: Colombo 2007.

80. Amm. Marc. xvi. 5. 7; Thompson 1944, 49–51; Bouffartigue 1992, 408–12, 500–501.

81. Bowersock 1982, 159–72 at 167.

82. Herodian wrote on the empire, but as a minor official in Rome for several years he obviously acquired Latin for professional purposes, and in fact cites a number of documents that must have been written in Latin: C. R. Whittaker, *Herodian* 1 (Loeb 1969), xxxiv. Appian too spent many years in Roman service.

had wished. Apparently, he did not.[83] Nothing we know about Dexippus's work suggests that he drew on Latin sources, and when Eunapius first formed the idea of continuing Dexippus, there was no reason for him to think that the research that lay ahead of him would call for knowledge of Latin.

As we know from the frequent complaints of Libanius at Antioch, Latin was perceived as a rival to the traditional rhetorical studies in Greek. Many of his students left to study Latin, shorthand, and the law, and students from well-to-do families often completed their course with a period in Italy.[84] Eunapius tells us enough about his own career to exclude the possibility that he followed this path. After studying rhetoric in Sardis, at the age of fifteen he left for another four years of rhetoric in Athens. He then returned to Sardis, where he began to teach rhetoric himself while undertaking a fresh course of study in philosophy. At some point he also made an extensive study of medicine (he is the dedicatee of a substantial medical handbook by his friend Oribasius).[85] That is to say, he devoted himself for many years to three different subjects, all of which required protracted study in the original Greek. His continuing passion for all three is sufficiently illustrated by his *Lives of the Philosophers and Sophists*, men "trained in every kind of learning," as he himself put it.[86] Its theme is excellence in the traditional Greek *paideia* in all its forms. In his history too Eunapius draws attention to the *paideia* of numerous learned Greeks, whether Sophists or philosophers: no fewer than ten such men are named in the surviving fragments, and at least another three in passages of Zosimus deriving from Eunapius.[87] On our present knowledge, a Greek Sophist with expertise in philosophy and medicine who also had a fluent reading knowledge of literary Latin would be unique.

Eunapius's continuator Olympiodorus certainly knew Latin. The part of Zosimus's narrative based on Olympiodorus actually includes four brief quotations in Latin. But Olympiodorus lived for a period in the West, where he must have done much of the research for his history, and even before that he had extensive dealings with court and may already have had some knowledge of Latin. He was, after all, what we would now call a professional diplomat.[88] Eunapius would have been horrified by his heavily Latinate Greek prose style. Priscus of Panium, who continued Olympiodorus, also seems to have used Roman (not necessarily written) sources. Like Olympiodorus, Priscus too was a much-traveled diplomat (best known for his visit to the camp of Attila) who spent some time in Rome.[89]

Libanius lived and worked in a city that, for much of his lifetime, was an imperial capital, where he must have had frequent dealings with Latin-speaking officials. Even

---

83. As remarked by Millar 1969, 12–29 at 21.
84. Liebeschuetz 1972, 242–55; Cribiore 2007, 206–12.
85. See the brief account in Penella 1990, 1–9.
86. πεπαιδευμένων ἀνδρῶν εἰς πᾶσαν παιδείαν, *Vit. Soph.* 463 (vi. 2. 12); cf. 477 (vii. 3. 12).
87. Acacius, Eunapius (of Phrygia), Heraclius, Hilarius, Libanius, Longinus, Maximus, Musonius, Oribasius, Patricius, Priscus, Prohaeresius, Simonides, Sopater, Tuscianus: see Penella 1990, 13–16 and index s.vv.
88. For this aspect of Olympiodorus's activity, see Matthews 1970, 79–97.
89. Roberto 2000/2002, 117–59.

so he never learned Latin, and represents himself as unable even to read letters from Latin-speakers until a translator could be found.[90] It is worth taking a close look at the only two occasions when he praises men for knowing Latin as well as Greek. First Montius Magnus, whom a couple of lines earlier he had described as "best of proconsuls"; and then Julianus, in a letter recommending him for public office. Julianus he also praises for his knowledge of law.[91] That is to say, both had evidently learned Latin with a view to a career in administration. Here we may compare the epigram on the base of the statue of Oecumenius, *praeses* of Caria ca. 400, praising him for his expertise in Latin as well as Greek and for his knowledge of law.[92] Clearly, these were less Libanius's personal beliefs than the sort of compliments expected in eulogies of governors.

Unlike Priscus and Olympiodorus, there is no sign that Eunapius ever had anything to do with the imperial administration; he refers contemptuously to the "the gang at court" and "a miserable mob of clowns."[93] In another passage (*VS* 483) he describes a proconsul as "not one of the uneducated for a Roman" (*hōs Rhomaios*). The context suggests a native Latin-speaker able to appreciate Greek culture at first-hand. It is hard to imagine any figure of his age more exclusively devoted to Greek culture and less likely to know *any* Latin, let alone enough to conduct serious historical research in Latin.

6: ZOSIMUS

For Paschoud, Zosimus's account of the fourth century includes a series of incidents involving anti-Christian polemic, all localized in the West, all concerning Roman religion. He enumerates just four: (1) the significance of the Secular Games for the safety of the empire (ii. 1–7); (2) Constantine's refusal to sacrifice on the Capitol (ii. 29); (3) Gratian's refusal of the pontifical robe (iv. 36); and (4) Theodosius's withdrawal of financial support for the pagan cults of Rome (iv. 59). Paschoud sees these four passages as central and integral elements in the anti-Christian thrust of the narrative.[94] Such a perspective, he infers, must derive from "pagan senatorial circles in Rome," meaning Flavian.

But the four passages in question are singularly ill chosen. Mendelssohn long ago gave excellent reasons (amplified below) for supposing that the first and third do not derive from Eunapius at all, but are Zosiman additions to his basic source. And while the fourth might derive from Eunapius, it cannot possibly reflect the views of Flavian,

---

90. *Ep.* 1004. 4 (Symmachus); 1036. 2 (Postumianus).
91. Montius: Lib. *pr. Arg. Demosth.* (viii. 600. 2–9 Foerster); Julianus 15: Lib. *Ep.* 668; *PLRE* i. 472, 535.
92. Smith 2002, 134–56; Ševčenko 1968, 29–41.
93. ὁ βασιλικὸς τῆς αὐλῆς ὅμιλος ... ὁ κακοδαίμων ... τῶν θυμελῶν χόρος, *VS* 490, p. 498 Wright.
94. Study of Zosimus has been put on an entirely different footing by Paschoud's magnificent Budé edition in five volumes, but (as we shall see) not all his interpretations command assent.

since it refers to the aftermath of the Frigidus, by when Flavian was dead. The second is indeed one of the most discussed passages in Zosimus,[95] but if we look at the context, Constantine's refusal to sacrifice is just one brief section in a long chapter attacking Constantine on a variety of counts. With the four allegedly key passages reduced to one, this western religious emphasis simply vanishes.

In any case, the rest of Zosimus's narrative for the period after Julian's death (Bk iv) simply does not bear out the hypothesis of a western source, least of all in the area of religion. What was the most famous crisis of Roman paganism during this period? Undoubtedly, Gratian's withdrawal of state subsidies from the traditional pagan cults, provoking all those senatorial embassies and Symmachus's plea about the altar of Victory. What does Zosimus have to say about all this? Nothing. Not a single word. *If* Flavian's history reached this point, it must have covered this episode, representing it as a heroic defense of the old cults. Careless though he was, if Flavian had been his guide, how could even Zosimus, given his own passionately pagan agenda, have omitted the affair entirely?

We saw in an earlier chapter that Zosimus mistakenly ascribes the withdrawal of subsidies from the cults to Theodosius (Ch. 2. 6). Paschoud has an ingenious solution that would neatly explain both this error and the omission of Gratian's measures in 382. Since he was using Flavian, Eunapius knew about Gratian's measures, but *deliberately* transferred them to Theodosius, so as to provide the latter with a crime against paganism that led to his death. It was enough for Gratian to be left with the crime of refusing the pontifical robe, which led to his being killed by Maximus soon after. But nothing in the context suggests this crime-followed-by-punishment syndrome in either case.[96] Theodosius is simply said to have died of disease. As for Gratian and the pontifical robe, any western source would have known that Maximus was a Christian who continued Gratian's anti-pagan policies, and the chapter in question (as we shall see) is a Zosiman addition.

As for Eunapius's biggest bête noire, Constantine, it is true that in his *Lives of the Sophists* Eunapius claims to have described in his *History* how Constantine was "punished" for the favors he showed the prefect Ablabius, who was responsible for the death of Eunapius's idol Sopater. But this need not and almost certainly does not refer to Constantine's death. Zosimus, presumably reflecting Eunapius, simply records that Constantine died of a disease. What Eunapius had in mind is surely Libanius's remark that Constantine was *posthumously* punished (for confiscating temple property, he claims) "when the members of his family attacked each other and not a single one was left."[97] There is nothing here or elsewhere to support the idea that Eunapius's history highlighted "deaths of persecutors," which makes it even less likely that he would have deliberately falsified the facts to achieve such an end. The hypothesis is not only implausible, but

---

95. Fraschetti 1999, 1–134; Paschoud, Zosime 1² (2000), 234–40.
96. For this thesis see the paper now reprinted in Paschoud 2006, 367–78 at 372–73.
97. Vit. Soph. vi. 3. 13 (464); Zos. ii. 39. 1; see Penella 1990, 126–27; Lib. *Or.* xxx. 37.

unnecessary. Since Theodosius was well known in East and West alike for banning the pagan cults, there was simply no need to assign him one of Gratian's crimes against paganism to explain his death—if this had been Eunapius's purpose in the first place.

Nor would this hypothesis explain the omission of Gratian's withdrawal of state subsidies, the Altar of Victory, and the senatorial embassies. These are the central episodes in every modern account of the last days of Roman paganism. Even granted Paschoud's hypothesis, why would Zosimus omit these of all details? The chapter on Gratian says no more than that he refused the pontifical robe because he considered it "impious" for a Christian to wear such garb—fairly moderate language compared with the hyperbolic rhetoric of contemporary anti-pagan legislation. No suggestion that he was the emperor responsible for the first major attack on the traditional cults.

The obvious explanation is that whatever (undoubtedly Greek) sources were available to Eunapius simply omitted Gratian's anti-pagan measures of 382 in their entirety. Being limited to the cults of Rome, they may not have made much of an impression in the East. They are unknown to all the fifth-century ecclesiastical historians, and not mentioned in any eastern chronicles. Such an explanation is strengthened by a study of the second half of Bk iv as a whole, in which Gratian is barely mentioned. This silence is in large part a consequence of the fact that, after the death of Valentinian I, Zosimus's narrative is almost entirely devoted to Theodosius and eastern affairs.[98]

According to Bleckmann, the fourth-century pagan history that lies behind Zonaras was characterized by senatorial bias. Yet there is not a trace of senatorial outlook in Zosimus's narrative of the fourth century, nor in the relevant surviving fragments of Eunapius. Perhaps the clearest single proof that Zosimus/Eunapius drew on an eastern source for at any rate the year 375 is a blunder long recognized, the full consequences of which seem nonetheless not to have been drawn. On the proclamation of Valentinian II, according to Zosimus, the western provinces were divided between Gratian and Valentinian: Gratian ruled Gaul, Spain, and Britain; Valentinian Italy, Illyricum, and Africa (iv. 19). Though still occasionally repeated by modern historians, this is undoubtedly false. There was no such division. Gratian alone ruled all the western provinces; Valentinian remained a purely nominal member of the imperial college, an "Auguste sans terre," till Gratian's death in 383.

This cannot be explained as one of Zosimus's many confusions. Since there was no division of territory following the death of Valentinian I, there was nothing to confuse. That the error goes back to Eunapius is put beyond doubt by the claim in one of the longest surviving fragments that Valens was annoyed that his nephews "had divided their realm without referring the division to their uncle."[99] This must have been a guess, perhaps based on the division of the western provinces between Constantine II and Constans in 337. While acknowledging Zosimus's error,[100] Paschoud seems not to

---

98. As can be seen at a glance from Paschoud's useful table of contents to Bk iv (ii. 2. 259–60).
99. διῃρῆσθαι... διανομήν, F 42 MB = *Exc. de Leg.* p. 595. 23–26 de Boor.
100. See his note on Zos. iv. 19 in volume 2. 2 (1979), 370–71.

have realized that it could not possibly have come from any well-informed western source. It is clear from the contemporary evidence of Symmachus that it was Gratian, not Valentinian, who ruled Italy from 375 to 383, and any Roman senator of the 380s must have known this.

According to another fragment of Eunapius, "Despite diligent enquiry I was unable to learn either about individual acts of the Emperor Gratian or what sort of person he was."[101] This text alone is enough to prove that he did not draw on Flavian's *Annales*, which (if they covered this period at all) must have provided a well-informed account of Gratian's reign. Blockley plausibly suggests that this passage introduced Eunapius's account of Gratian's fall. On any hypothesis it implies that he had not previously had much to say about the youthful emperor, confirmed by Zosimus's failure to report anything of significance before his fall. Furthermore, when we bear in mind Eunapius's aggressively pagan agenda, his claim to have no idea what sort of person Gratian was makes it hard to believe that he saw him as one of the major villains of his story.

For Paschoud and his followers the key text is Zosimus iv. 36, not only (they argue) obviously deriving from a western source, but a source written in *Latin*. In view of the importance of this chapter in the story of the fall of Roman paganism, it is necessary to quote it in full and analyse it in detail:[102]

It is worth including here some historical facts not irrelevant to the present narrative. In the priestly hierarchy at Rome, the *pontifices* had first place. They would be called bridge-men (*gephyraioi*) if the name were translated into Greek. The explanation of the name is as follows. When mankind had not yet learned how to worship the gods through cult-statues, the first images of gods were made in Thessaly. Because there were no temples (even their use was as yet unknown), these images of the gods were set up on the bridge over the river Peneios, and those chosen to be priests were called bridge-men from the place where the images were first set up. The Romans took this over from the Greeks and called those who held their highest rank of priesthood *pontifices*, and laid down that kings (*basileas*) should be numbered among them because of their important rank. All the kings (*reges*) after Numa Pompilius (who was the first to do so) and all who succeeded to the monarchy from Octavian on have held this office. As soon as each assumed supreme power, the priestly robe was brought to him by the *pontifices* and he was styled *pontifex maximus*. All the earlier emperors were apparently happy to accept the honor and to use this title, even Constantine (who, when he came to the throne, turned aside from the true path in religion and embraced the Christian faith) and all his

---

101. F 50 Bl = 57 M (Blockley's translation, much adapted).
102. Zos. iv. 36 (Ridley, adapted). The next couple of pages are summarised from Cameron 2007, 343–49.

successors, including Valentinian and Valens. But when the *pontifices* brought the robes to Gratian in the usual way, he rejected their request, considering it impious for a Christian to wear such garb. When the robe was given back to the priests, their leader is reputed to have said: "If the emperor does not want to be called *pontifex*, soon enough there will be a *pontifex* Maximus."[103]

As early as Sylburg (1590) it was realized that the final sentence is a punning *post eventum* prophecy alluding to Gratian's deposition by the usurper Maximus. But Paschoud argues for a *second* pun as well, again detected (or imagined) by Sylburg. According to the preceding chapter in Zosimus (iv. 35. 6), Gratian was killed on a bridge at Singidunum.[104] Preferring the evidence of Ambrose that Gratian was in fact treacherously killed at a banquet,[105] Paschoud inferred that Zosimus's bridge is a fabrication to lead up to the *pontifex* pun at iv. 36. The etymology of *pontifex* (*pontem facere*) is supposed to suggest *pontem inficere* (i.e., *sangine*), "stain the bridge," that is to say with Gratian's blood. But Socrates and Sozomen both mention the bridge, and according to Sozomen Gratian was *captured* on the bridge and killed soon after.[106] The natural explanation is that Zosimus simply telescoped capture and killing and placed both on the bridge.

The second pun is much too complicated to carry conviction. Both the simple verb *facio* and its many other compounds (*afficio, conficio, deficio, efficio, officio, perficio, praeficio, proficio, sufficio*) can mean so many different things that it is not easy to see why *pontifex* should suggest *inficio* rather than any of the other compounds, much less suggest combining it with the mention of a bridge a page earlier to a mind already struggling to grasp the first pun. In any case, *inficere sanguine* is an elevated usage, at home in the poets and in historians rather than conversation.[107] There is no need to postulate a written Latin source for the Maximus pun; though obviously first made in Latin, it is reflected perfectly in Zosimus's Greek.

More important, is it really credible that this nonsense derives from a Roman *pontifex*? Despite Zosimus's evident pride in his antiquarian erudition, the chapter is a tissue of ignorance and misinformation from start to finish.[108] There was no genuine tradition that Numa was *pontifex maximus*, and no tradition that the other kings of Rome were pontiffs. More important, the unhistorical continuity between kings and emperors (ignoring five centuries of civilian holders of the office) suggests Byzantine

---

103. εἰ μὴ βούλεται ποντίφεξ ὁ βασιλεὺς ὀνομάζεθαι, τάχιστα γενήσεται ποντίφεξ Μάξιμος.

104. Probably a scribal error for Lugdunum, Lyon; Paschoud 1975, 88–91; and in *Zosime* 2. 2 (1979), 415.

105. Ambrose, *In Ps.* 61 *enarr.* 23–25; Homes Dudden 1935, 221.

106. Soc. *HE* v. 11. 7–8 (placing it at Lugdunum); Soz. *HE* vii. 13. 8–9.

107. E. Skard, *Ennius und Sallustius* (Oslo 1933), 40. Paschoud appeals to the many puns in the *Historia Augusta*, but almost all are simple (not to say childish) jokes about proper names (Dessau 1889, 384–86).

108. Paschoud (ii. 2. 418) indulgently claims that, apart from its alleged Greek origin, nothing Zosimus says about the college of pontiffs "n'est positivement faux." Rüpke 2008, 63–64, follows Paschoud too closely.

ignorance rather than Roman erudition. We find the same leap from kings to emperors in the slightly later chronicle of Malalas, who (except for a bizarre story linking the aetiology of February to Manlius and the geese) proceeds directly from Tarquinius to Julius Caesar.[109] Zosimus's account implicitly presupposes that private citizens were not eligible for so important an office. How could Flavian, a *pontifex* himself, have made such a colossal blunder?

Equally unhistorical is the supposed Greek origin of the college of pontiffs and (above all) the Greek derivation of the word *pontifex* itself, supposedly from the first statues of the gods worshipped on a bridge over a river in Thessaly. We find the same bizarre derivation in the sixth-century antiquarian John the Lydian, with *pontifices* again glossed as "bridge-men" (*gephyraioi*), after a bridge over another river in Thessaly.[110] Why *gephyraioi* rather than the more accurate *gephyropoios*, bridge--maker (= *ponti-fex*, from *facio*), that we find in Plutarch?[111] John goes on to explain that "Roman priests are called *pontifices*, just as at Athens all priests and interpreters of sacred traditions were once known as *gephyraioi*...because they made offerings to a statue of Athena [Palladium] on a bridge over the Spercheios." The mention of Athena gives a glimpse of what lies behind this pseudoscholarship: an old Athenian priestly clan *named* Gephyraioi. This is put beyond doubt by John's additional remark that the pontiffs were also known as "praxiergiai," because of their power to get things done. The lexica offer no comment on this mysterious word, found nowhere else in literature, papyri, or inscriptions. The explanation is that John failed to recognize the name of *another* Athenian priestly clan, the Praxiergidai.[112] The ultimate source of this material must be some antiquarian comparison of Greek and Roman institutions. This source derived the Gephyraioi from a bridge in Athens on the analogy of the derivation of *pontifex* from a bridge in Rome, so that both Roman and Athenian priests might be named after bridges! But John obviously failed fully to understand the Athenian connection, or he would not have linked his Gephyraioi to a bridge in Thessaly. Thessaly presumably comes from a later section of this source, listing the various different locations of Palladia, most claiming to be the original stolen from Troy by Odysseus and Diomede.[113] Since Zosimus shares John's blunder of deriving Gephyraioi from a bridge in Thessaly, clearly his source came late in this disreputable tradition.

---

109. Malalas 140–42 Thurn; at 161. Thurn, he simply refers to 460 years of (unnamed) consuls.

110. *De mens.* iv. 15, p. 78 Wuensch (Leipzig 1898); briefly again at *De mens.* iv. 102 and *De magg.* ii. 4.

111. Most scholars accept Varro's view that *pontifex* derives from *pontem facere*; Varro, *De lingua latina* 5. 15. 83; Plutarch, *Numa* 9; Livy i. 33. 6 (with Ogilvie's note); see the appendix "Pons and Pontifex" in L. A. Holland, *Janus and the Bridge* (Rome 1961), 332–42; J. P. Hallet, *TAPA* 101 (1970), 219–27; van Haeperen 2002, 11–45.

112. For both Γεφυραῖοι and Πραξιεργίδαι, see R. Parker, *Athenian Religion* (Oxford 1996), 288–89, 307–8; F. Jacoby, *FGrH* 333 F 4, with III b (Suppl.) 499–500. On this basis we should probably (with Wilamowitz, *Hermes* 34 (1899), 607–8) read πραξιεργί<δ>αι in Lydus, or at any rate assume that this is what stood in his source.

113. They are listed in Erskine 2001, 117, 141–42, 144.

For Paschoud, the claim of a Greek origin for the college was a pagan attempt to enhance its antiquity and thereby accentuate the enormity of the sacrilege committed by Gratian. This is unconvincing. No pagan senator of Rome was likely to feel that the importance of so uniquely Roman an institution as the college of pontiffs was enhanced by tracing its origin to prehistoric Thessaly! For Zosimus/Eunapius, the emperors responsible for the fall of paganism were Constantine and Theodosius. Flavian's history *might* have included a digression on the *pontifex maximus*. But it is preposterous (with Baldini) to recognize "the expert hand of Nicomachus Flavianus" in this mixture of garbled Greek nonsense and gross historical error.[114] Above all (of course), it is impossible that Flavian should have said that Gratian refused the office when he did not. The demonstrably Greek origin of this of all chapters is perhaps the clearest single proof that Eunapius/Zosimus did *not* draw on a western source for the late fourth century.

What we find in this chapter is rather the enthusiasm of Christian Byzantines for investigating the Roman roots of their institutions that we find a generation after Zosimus in John the Lydian, and Hesychius of Miletus.[115] Mendelssohn was right to derive it from a secondary source, an antiquarian account of the college of pontiffs in *Greek*.[116] It has clear links to the very similar account in John himself. There are a handful of other such antiquarian digressions here and there in Zosimus (i. 57–59; ii. 1–6; ii. 32, 36–37). Paschoud argues that they all reflect the pagan propaganda he detected in iv. 36 and that all derive from Eunapius.[117] But since Zosimus himself was a pagan there is no need to derive all his pagan material from Eunapius.[118]

It will clarify the situation to take a closer look at two of them. First, the remarkable digression on the Secular games, which quotes a Sibylline Oracle and concludes as follows:[119]

> Thus, as the oracle says and the facts confirm, so long as these rites were duly performed, the Roman empire was safe and Rome remained in control of virtually the whole inhabited world. But once the festival was neglected after Diocletian's abdication [305], the empire gradually collapsed and became imperceptibly barbarized.... The period of 110 years elapsed in the third consulship of Constantine and Licinius [313], and they ought to have held the festival according to tradition. Since they did not, matters were bound to come to their present unhappy state.

---

114. "qui, però, è presente la mano esperta di Nicomaco Flaviano," Baldini 1999, 22.
115. Maas 1992; 1986; Dagron 1984, 55–58; R. Scott in Jeffreys, Croke, and Scott 1990, 67–76.
116. Mendelssohn 1887, xxxviii; P. Athanassiadi 1999, 354–55, argues, in part on linguistic grounds, for a Greek source, more precisely "a piece of late Neoplatonic propaganda."
117. Mendlessohn 1887, xxxvii–xxxviii; for a recent summary of Paschoud's views, *Zosime* 1² (2000), xlvi–xlviii, lxv.
118. Liebeschuetz 2003, at 207–14.
119. Zos. ii. 7. 2, with Paschoud's notes (192–205); for the oracle, *FGrH* 257 F 37; Hansen 1996, 56, 186–89.

This is a confused and puzzling comment. Paschoud focuses on the two final sentences, which he interprets straightforwardly as anti-Christian propaganda, blaming Constantine for the decline of Rome. For Paschoud, Zosimus's source here is Flavian via Eunapius. But three consular dates in as many sentences, complete with iteration numbers, would be utterly foreign to the style of Eunapius, whose preface pours scorn on Dexippus's obsession (as he saw it) with Olympiads and consuls, and promises that his own history will do without dates.[120] It should also be noted that, by linking Constantine's name with that of his pagan colleague Licinius in the third of these dates, Zosimus blunts the specifically Christian element in the polemic. The fact is that he does *not* directly blame Constantine for the neglect of the festival.

The ultimate source must be the (lost) *On Roman Festivals* of Phlegon of Tralles, a freedman of Hadrian.[121] A series of extracts from Phlegon quotes the same thirty-seven-line Sibylline Oracle as Zosimus. Since the entire oracle is devoted to various details of the Secular Games, it made sense in the context of his book for Phlegon to include it all, but only the last three lines are relevant to Zosimus's claim that the survival of the empire depended on their continued performance. Though fond of oracles, the longest Eunapius quotes is no more than seven lines, adding that it was "preceded" (meaning in his source) by "other prayers and sacrifices" that "are not appropriate for inclusion in a serious formal history; for to include every detail is not the action of one who respects the truth, but of one who is carried away by idle curiosity and slips into empty prattle."[122] For all his faults Eunapius had a better sense of the proportion appropriate to a historical narrative than Zosimus.

Of course, the passage in question (ii. 7. 2) postdates Phlegon's lifetime, so an intermediary must be postulated. Yet it is not just the consular dates that argue against identifying this intermediary as Eunapius, but the disproportionate antiquarian detail of the entire section (ii. 1–7, eleven Budé pages), nine-tenths of it completely irrelevant to the anti-Christian purpose on which Paschoud lays such emphasis. That this intermediary was no earlier than ca. 450 is clearly implied by the claim (ii. 7. 1) that neglect of the Games has led to the present collapse and barbarization of the empire. This was simply not true at the date Eunapius (still less Flavian) wrote. Zosimus found this material in some (probably fifth-century) antiquarian work,[123] but lacked the judgment to select the details most telling for his purpose.

---

120. Nor would it help to assign these dates to Flavian, simply repeated by Eunapius. Eunapius must have omitted consular dates given in his various sources, to judge from their absence from the rest of Zosimus's narrative.

121. Mendelssohn 1887, xxxvii and notes on 54–55. For Paschoud (of course), Flavian drew on Phlegon, Eunapius on Flavian, and finally Zosimus on Eunapius.

122. F 28. 6 Blockley = *FHG* iv. 25, no. 27 = *Exc. de Sent.* 29 (Blockley's translation).

123. Jo. Lyd., *De mensibus*, R. Wuensch (ed.) (1898), p. 11. 14 cites Phlegon.

A similar illustration is provided by ii. 36–37:

> I have often wondered why, since the city of Byzantium has grown so great that no other surpasses it in prosperity or size, no divine prophecy was given to our predecessors concerning its progress and destiny. After thinking about this for a long time and consulting many historical works and collections of oracles and spending time puzzling over them, I finally came across an oracle said to be of the Sibyl or Erythrae or Phaennis in Epirus (who is said to have been inspired and given out some oracles). Nicomedes, son of Prusias…[twenty-seven lines of oracle].…This oracle tells, albeit ambiguously and in riddles…how "power will swiftly pass to the men who dwell in Byzas's seat" [lines 10–11 of the oracle].

According to Paschoud, Zosimus's purpose, as always, was anti-Christian polemic, a pagan prophecy of the future greatness of Constantinople to match Christian prophecies.[124] On that basis he assumes that here too the source must be Eunapius. But the oracle is only pagan in the sense that it is pre-Christian. There is no more than a single passing mention of Zeus and a reference to "god-built walls." Nor (it seems) did Zosimus himself set much store by his own interpretation. He admits that the "swiftly" does not fit the five hundred-year interval between Nicomedes—in fact Nicomedes I (279–50? B.C.) not II (149–25? B.C.)—and Constantine, and concludes with the words "if anyone has a different interpretation, he is welcome to it."

As Dagron put it, "The history of Byzantium before Constantine…seems to be a discovery of the sixth century."[125] Its first representatives are Hesychius of Miletus, Stephanus of Byzantium, and John the Lydian—all Christians.[126] All would have echoed Zosimus's first sentence, and most do in fact cite "pagan" oracles from the remote past foretelling the destiny of the future New Rome.[127] Zonaras too describes Constantine as deciding to found his new capital "according to a divine oracle." These Christian antiquarians even invented a pseudo-pagan mythological past for the city, involving Io, metamorphosed into a cow by Hera, who fled to the place named (after her) Bos-porus, where she gave birth to a daughter called Keroessa (named after Keras, the Golden Horn), who subsequently gave birth to Byzas, the founder of Byzantium![128] The antiquarian origin of the chapter is sufficiently illustrated by the

---

124. Paschoud 1². 255; so too Kaegi 1968, 137–38.
125. Dagron 1974, 14.
126. Kaldellis 2003 and 2005 argues that John, Hesychius and indeed most other classicizing Greek writers of the sixth century (including Procopius and Agathias) were pagans. This is not the place to debate this claim. It is enough to say that it would make it impossible to understand the continuing attraction of Classicism and antiquarianism for educated Byzantines.
127. Hesychius Mil. § 3 in T. Preger (ed.), *Scriptores Originum Constantinopolitanarum* (1901); H. Erbse (ed.), *Theosophorum Graecorum Fragmenta* (1995), 14–15; Zon. xiii. 3. 1. John the Lydian reports an oracle given to Romulus that fortune would abandon the Romans if they forgot their ancestral tongue (*De mag.* iii. 42).
128. Hesychius Mil. §§ 4–20; Jo. Ant. F 256 R; cf. Dagron 1984, 24–26, and passim.

citation of the whole oracle when no more than two lines are by any stretch of the imagination relevant, and by the pedantic hesitation about the identity of the Sibyl concerned.[129] As for the date of this source, the description of Constantinople as "surpassing all other cities in prosperity and size" fits 500 better than 400 (when Rome, Alexandria, and Antioch may still have been larger, or at any rate as large).[130]

For Paschoud, Zosimus was incapable of combining more than one source. But Photius's sweeping claim that he did not so much write a history as transcribe Eunapius's should not be taken so literally.[131] Quite apart from the fact that Photius himself adds not one but two qualifications ("one might say" and "virtually"), he had obviously not noticed that the last fifty pages are abridged Olympiodorus. Neither Eunapius nor Zosimus are among the texts Photius excerpted or summarized at length, nor did he read them one after the other.[132] Once he had noticed the obvious debt of Zosimus to Eunapius (an impression naturally enhanced by their shared paganism) it is unlikely that he bothered to read Zosimus as carefully as he read Eunapius. In any case, combining two detailed sources into a coherent narrative is very different from just adding the occasional detail based on his own knowledge or reading. To take a trivial example, even Paschoud concedes that Zosimus must have added the reference to the new walls of Constantinople built by Theodosius II, which Eunapius cannot have lived to see.[133]

The five digressions singled out above share three common features. All are antiquarian, with three out of the five dealing with specifically Roman antiquities. In four (the beginning of one is missing), the opening words imply supplementary research on the part of Zosimus himself: i. 57. 1 and 59. 1 ("It is worth recording in detail the events that preceded the fall of Palmyra.... But it is time to return to the point from which I digressed."); ii. 36. 1 ("I have often wondered... consulting many historical works and collections of oracles"); iii. 32. 1 ("Having arrived at this point of my history I have often wondered."); iv. 36. 1 ("it is worth including here some historical facts not irrelevant to the present narrative"). And the very similar laments about the loss of territory and increasing barbarization of the empire in the chapters on the fall of Palmyra (i. 57. 1 and 58. 4), the Secular Games (ii. 7. 1), the oracle about Constantinople (ii. 7. 1), Jovian's treaty (iii. 32. 6), and the epilogue to Bk iv on the abolition of pagan rites at Rome all imply a much longer perspective than the closing date of Eunapius's *History* (404). Eunapius wrote well before the loss of Africa, Gaul, and Italy to barbarians.

In at least two of these cases Paschoud dismissed as fraudulent Zosimus's claims to have engaged in personal research.[134] But the fact that these claims always precede antiquarian digressions and always imply a long perspective surely combine to exclude

---

129. For further details about the oracle, see H. W. Parke, in CQ 32 (1982), 441–44.
130. For various estimates for the size of all these cities, Dagron 1974, 524–25.
131. See the sensible remarks of Blockley 1980, 393–402.
132. Eunapius is Cod. 77 in the *Bibliotheca*, Zosimus Cod. 98.
133. Zos. ii. 35. 2; Paschoud 2000, 254–55.
134. Paschoud 2000, xlviii.

such gratuitous scepticism. The fact that Zosimus's history as we have it breaks off in 410 has tended to obscure the fact that he was undoubtedly planning to take the story down close to his own day, probably to the death of Zeno (491).[135] His often-repeated promise that his future narrative will illustrate in detail the loss of territory and barbarization of the empire clearly refers to his own day, a century after Eunapius.[136]

In addition, Zosimus's search for an oracle predicting the future greatness of Constantinople implies an admiration for his native city that contrasts sharply with the contempt for the new capital shown by Eunapius in his *Lives of the Sophists*. In classical times, Eunapius bitterly remarked, Byzantium used to supply Athens with grain. Now it takes much of the rest of the world to supply "the intoxicated multitude which Constantine transported to Byzantium by emptying other cities, and established near him because he loved to be applauded in the theatres by men so drunk that they could not hold their liquor."[137] We find the same hostility in contemporaries like Libanius, who describes Constantinople as "growing fat on the sweat of other cities."[138] Inevitably, citizens from former capitals of ancient kingdoms like Antioch and Sardis resented watching them eclipsed by a parasitic upstart that had always enjoyed a reputation for luxury and drunkenness. Athenaeus cites four texts for the habitual drunkenness of the Byzantines from as early as the fourth century B.C.[139]

By Zosimus's day a century later Constantinople's dual role as the greatest of Greek cities and capital of the Roman world was established and uncontroversial. Living and writing as he was in the very different world of the sixth century, Zosimus shared the developing enthusiasm of his age for the Roman and antiquarian traditions of Constantinople. For this reason it is likely that the section on Constantine's supposed first attempt to build his new capital near ancient Troy is also a Zosiman addition to Eunapius, partly because the story is not likely to be earlier than the fifth century, but more because the legend of Constantine being guided by heaven in his search for the perfect site, so dear to the Byzantines, is unlikely to have appealed to Eunapius.[140] Despite sharing Eunapius's paganism, Zosimus was a "Byzantine" in a way that Eunapius, a traditionalist Hellene, was most emphatically not.

7: ZOSIMUS ON CONSTANTINE AND THEODOSIUS

If the chapters on the Secular Games and *pontifex maximus* are Zosiman additions, that reduces Paschoud's "western pagan perspective" to vanishing point. Beyond

---

135. So Paschoud 2000, xxv–xxvi.

136. As in effect acknowledged by Paschoud, *Zosime* 1^2 (2000), xvi. Zosimus was writing before the Justinianic reconquest.

137. *Vit. Soph.* 462/3; so too Zos. ii. 30–31; ii. 32. 1, probably reflecting Eunapius here rather than his own view.

138. Lib. *Or.* i. 279.

139. Athen. x. 442C–D (esp. Phylarchus, *FGrH* 81, F 7) and xii. 526D–F (Theopompus, *FGrH* 115, F 62).

140. Zos. ii. 30. 1–2; I shall be discussing this point in detail elsewhere.

question, for Eunapius/Zosimus the great enemies of paganism were Constantine and Theodosius. Not surprisingly, perhaps, Zosimus is more explicit and bitter about Constantine. Setting aside Theodosius's address to the Roman senate after the Frigidus (problematic on many counts), there is only one clear reference to anti-pagan legislation.[141] Yet there is an interesting pattern in Zosimus's portrayal of Constantine and Theodosius as persecutors, more consistent and pervasive than any "western perspective." As Buck has emphasized, he systematically accuses the two emperors of the same faults, often in the same words.[142] Before long both abandoned making war and devoted themselves to luxury (*tryphē*). Theodosius's reorganization of the *magistri militum* is described in almost exactly the same terms as Constantine's reorganization of his praetorian prefects.[143] Theodosius's reforms (iv. 29. 1), like Constantine's (ii. 38. 4), lead to the ruins of the cities. Both are condemned for their excessive taxation (ii. 38; iv. 32; and 41). I would add two further correspondences. Both dealt treacherously with rivals; and the policies of both were the beginning of the fall of the empire.[144]

To be sure, some of these criticisms are commonplace, but in combination they do suggest that Eunapius saw Theodosius as the Constantine of his age. In one respect the parallelism goes the other way. The accusation that Constantine's weakening of frontier defenses was "the beginning of the destruction of the empire" (ii. 34. 2) was surely influenced by criticism of Theodosius enrolling barbarians in his armies.[145]

It is usually assumed that Eunapius's criticisms of Constantine and Theodosius were inspired by his passionate paganism, and while this is no doubt true, I would prefer a slightly different emphasis. It was not just that abandoning and proscribing the old gods lost mankind their favor. Rulers who pursued such policies were corrupted in a variety of ways, and in turn corrupted the empire they ruled. This is particularly clear in the case of the least commonplace of the shared criticisms: surrender to *tryphē*, luxury or extravagance.[146] The idea that *tryphē* corrupts both ruler and ruled by weakening their energy and morals is a popular concept in Hellenistic historians and moral philosophers. Book 12 of Athenaeus's *Deipnosophists* collects an astonishing dossier of illustrations.[147] It was Julian who originated the reproach of *tryphē* against Constantine. Julian himself followed an ascetic lifestyle, and was famously shocked by the luxury of the imperial court in Constantinople.[148] But as Dagron has shown, the context in Zosimus favors a more concrete sense than mere personal luxury for Constantine: "having permanently abandoned warfare and given himself up to luxury,

141. Zos. iv. 33. 4, implying legislation in 382 not otherwise known (Paschoud, ii. 2. 405). iv. 37. 3 refers to violent action by Cynegius, but does not directly lay the responsibility on Theodosius.

142. Buck 1988, 36–53, summarized and in part quoted below.

143. Theodosius τὰς μὲν προεστώσας ἀρχὰς συνετάραξε (iv. 27. 1); Constantine συνετάραξε δὲ καὶ τὰς πάλαι καθεσταμένας ἀρχάς (ii. 32. 1).

144. Con.: ii. 18. 1 and 28. 2; Theod.: iv. 37. 3 and 57. 1; Eun. F 60; Con.: ii. 34. 2; Theod: iv. 28. 2 and 59. 3.

145. Buck 1988, 42–44; Heather and Matthews 1991.

146. The excerpt from Theopompus cited above uses the word τρυφή.

147. Zecchini 1989; Braund and Wilkins 2000; Gorman and Gorman 2007.

148. Caesares 30 and 38 (329a and 336a); Amm. Marc. xxii. 4 and xxv. 4. 4–5.

he distributed an allowance of grain to the people of Byzantium at state expense."[149] This is the classic doctrine of *tryphē*: a ruler's *tryphē* infects the people he rules. Once Constantine was free from the need to make war, he not only degenerated himself but freed the people of his new capital from the need to work. That it was Eunapius, not Flavian, who originated this particular application of *tryphē* to Constantine is put beyond serious question by the contemptuous account of Constantine's institution of the grain dole in his *Lives of the Sophists*, where it is linked to his need for flattery.[150]

That this was not an idea limited to Eunapius is illustrated by a number of passages in other Greek writers of the age. According to Themistius the usurper Procopius withdrew "their customary extravagance" (*tryphēn*) from the "pampered population" (*demos ho tryphōn*) of Constantinople. As Dagron saw, here too the reference must be to the grain allowance.[151] In another speech Themistius defends himself against the charge of using allocations of grain and oil and other items from the "long catalogue of extravagance" (*tryphē* again) at his disposal as proconsul of Constantinople in order to attract students.[152] Like the practiced panegyrist he was, Themistius has it both ways when praising Constantius II: "while far from being given to extravagance (*tryphē*) himself, he gave it to his city in abundance."[153] In one of his earliest speeches he proclaimed that he did not like a city with a "sumptuous marketplace (*tryphōsas agoras*), in which there are hordes of men drunk on wine…in which the theatre's gates never close and horses are continuously racing."[154] Given the combination of drunkenness and chariot racing, his listeners were bound to think of Constantinople. Libanius three times refers to Constantinople as "Fat City" (*tryphōsa polis*), once as "the extravagance (*tryphē*) on the Bosporus," and describes its inhabitants as "wallowing in base extravagance" (*kakōs tryphōntōn*).[155]

Only two passages of Zosimus refer to Constantine's *tryphē*,[156] but no fewer than five to Theodosius's, not counting at least two more that criticize his luxurious lifestyle without actually using the word.[157] One links what might have seemed to be a weakness of the emperor's private life with military misjudgment: "having begun his reign with luxury (*tryphē*) and neglect, he threw the senior offices into confusion." Here we have an excerpt of Eunapius that, without using the word, corresponds to this passage: "No sooner had he become emperor than he behaved like a youth who is heir to new wealth accumulated over a long time by the foresight and

---

149. Zos. ii. 32. 1; by splitting this sentence into two, Ridley blurs the causal link between its two propositions.
150. Eun. Vit. Soph. 462/3 = vi. 2–vii–8 Giangrande.
151. Them. *Or.* vii. 92bc; Dagron 1974, 304; cf. 522, 542.
152. *Or.* 23. 292b = p. 86. 25 Downey-Norman; Penella 2000, 19, 118.
153. ἥκιστα αὐτὸς τρυφῶν χορηγεῖ τῇ πόλει τρυφῆς ἀφθονίαν, Them. *Or.* 4. 58c (p. 83. 15 Downey).
154. *Or.* 24. 307b; see Penella 2000, 22–24, 128–37.
155. *Or.* i. 215; 279; *Ep.* 772. 2; *Ep.* 633. 2; *Or.* xxx. 37.
156. ii. 32. 1; ii. 34. 2.
157. Zos. iv. 27. 1; iv. 33. 1; iv. 41. 1; iv. 43. 2; iv. 50. 1–2; Eun. F 46. 1B = 48M; cf. iv. 28. 1–2; iv. 44. 1.

thrift of his father...using every manner of wickedness and excess towards the ruin of the state."[158] According to another Zosiman passage (iv. 43. 2), once he had decided to attack the usurper Maximus, "he to some extent forgot his excessive *tryphē*," though after the defeat of Maximus he once more gave himself up to *tryphē* (iv. 50. 1–2), recalling the claim that Constantine gave up warfare for *tryphē* (ii. 34. 2). Here we also have an excerpt from Eunapius on the period before Maximus's defeat, describing how the Goths ambushed Theodosius's army: "it was clear to all that if the Roman state rejected luxury (*tryphē*) and embraced war, it would conquer and enslave the whole world," but God has brought it about that emperors turn to pleasure rather than glory.[159]

Particularly telling is iv. 33. 1, describing Theodosius's arrival in Constantinople, where he "extended boundless extravagance (*tryphēs ametrian*) in proportion to the greatness of the city." That this directly reflects Eunapius's original words is proved by Philostorgius's application of the very same phrase (*tryphēs ametria*) to Theodosius.[160] Most critics have interpreted *tryphē* here as the emperor's personal extravagance, and explained "greatness" in terms of the importance of Constantinople. But this would make it hard to understand the correlation between extravagance and city. If Dagron was right to read *tryphē* as a sort of moralizing code word for the grain dole, then this is surely a reference to Theodosius's extension of public grain distributions in 392.[161] A law of 416 refers to Constantine establishing and Theodosius extending the ration and so the number of recipients. No further extension is recorded. If this is what Eunapius meant (Zosimus's abridgment has no doubt eliminated some clarifying detail), then, once again, he was implicitly representing Theodosius as another Constantine. His motive in repeatedly so doing is not in doubt. Instead of directly attacking the specifically religious aspect of Theodosius's anti-pagan policies, Eunapius preferred to focus on what he saw as their consequences.

What factual truth is there in the charge of *tryphē*? Pagans were bound to disapprove of the extravagant sums Constantine spent on churches and his confiscation of the treasures of pagan temples to beautify his new capital.[162] He was also believed to be too generous to his courtiers and too indulgent of their rapacity.[163] At a personal level, he dressed extravagantly, "his bright mantle...decorated with the dazzling brilliance of gold and precious stones," in the admiring description of one contemporary observer.[164] More generally, a philosopher was bound to disapprove of

---

158. Zos. iv. 27. 1; Eun. F 46. 1B = 48M.
159. Eun. F 58M = 55B; the relevant chapters of Zosimus are iv. 48–50.
160. Phil. *HE* xi. 2, p. 134. 7 Bidez.
161. *Cod. Just.* xi. 25. 2 (392); *Cod. Theod.* xiv. 17. 14 (402); xiv. 16. 2 (416); Jones, *LRE* ii. 696–97; Dagron 1974, 521–22.
162. Liban. *Or.* xxx. 6; *Anon. de rebus bell.* ii. 1–2; Jul. *Or.* vii. 22bB.
163. Amm. xvi. 8. 12; even Euseb. *V. Con.* iv. 31; 54.
164. Euseb. *Vita Const.* iii. 10. 3 (trans. Cameron and Hall).

the "orientalizing" spectacle of the imperial court in the early Byzantine world,[165] though it is unclear how far Constantine and Theodosius went beyond standard practice.

It is also important to appreciate that the charge of *tryphē*, which forms so large a part of Eunapius's indictment of both Constantine and Theodosius, is not directly linked to their Christianity. In an article that has had less impact than it deserved, Sacks argued that it is misleading to see Eunapius's history as driven exclusively by his hatred of Christianity.[166] There is also a strong moralizing streak, stressing the importance of character and the corrupting effect of power. Eunapius's view was not simply that neglect of pagan cult led to the decline and fall of Roman power, but that Christian values were more likely than the usual factors of greed and ambition to lead to the corruption of rulers and their ministers. It was the responsibility of emperors to defend the empire, but Christian emperors allowed themselves to be sidetracked by other concerns (as Gibbon memorably put it, "the attention of emperors was diverted from camps to synods"). Like so many non-Christians down the ages, it was not so much Christianity he despised as what Christians did in the name of Christianity. And what is so striking in these texts about Constantine and Theodosius is that Eunapius expressed his disapproval through the traditional Hellenistic concept of *tryphē*, evoked no fewer than sixteen times in Zosimus, with another six occurrences in what survives of Eunapius himself. In additions to passages already cited, four generals are attacked for the vice, and the new tax that provoked the riot of the statues at Antioch in 387 is said to have been yet another product of Theodosius's *tryphē*.[167] Nor is it confined to Christian emperors. Carinus is condemned for his *tryphē* in the strongest terms.[168] The wholly Greek nature of all this material makes it absurd, if not perverse, to trace it back to the Latin text of Nicomachus Flavianus.

There is also another inference to be drawn here. Eunapius's picture of Theodosius is so systematically hostile that it can hardly have been published before his death in 395. And this hostility is clear from the very start. Here is the first excerpt from Eunapius to mention Theodosius: "When Theodosius became emperor…a wise observer could see as if from a watchtower that the emperor was using every manner of wickedness and excess towards the ruin of the state."[169] It follows that this part of Eunapius's narrative *cannot* have been based on Flavian, who died before Theodosius.

---

165. Victor disapproved of Diocletian's introduction of *adoratio* and jewel-encrusted robes (*Caes.* 39. 2–4).
166. Sacks 1986, 52–67.
167. Zos. v. 7. 2; v. 16. 5; v. 25. 3, 4; Eun. F 67. 8B; Zos. iv. 41. 1.
168. Zos. v. 7. 2; v. 16. 5; v. 25. 3, 4; Eun. F 67. 8B; Zos. iv. 41. 1; Zos. i. 72. 1 with Eun. F 5. 1–2.
169. F 46 = *Exc. de Sent.* 48.

18

THE *ANNALES* OF NICOMACHUS FLAVIANUS II

8: GREEK HISTORIANS AND LATIN SOURCES

For a variety of reasons Flavianus's lost *Annales* simply cannot play the role for which it has increasingly often been cast in recent years. But both Bleckmann and Paschoud insist that their argument for an ultimate Latin source for the Byzantine tradition is entirely independent of its identification as Flavian's *Annales*. Paschoud himself has of late begun to berate his critics for their failure to realize that this identification is no more than a distraction and a detail. The real issue is the necessity of postulating a lost *Latin* history—the identification of which as Flavian's *Annales* remains (of course) "seductive and plausible."[1] Is it possible that we do in fact need to postulate a lost Latin history of the fourth century?

Bleckmann, Paschoud, and Festy have done their best to come up with linguistic proof, words in Byzantine texts alleged either to reflect a Latin source or to mistranslate a Latin term.[2] Given enough convincing examples, this is a thesis capable of proof. Yet they have barely been able to get into double figures, and not one comes close to passing muster. Seven are (just) worth scrutiny.

1) The pièce de résistance has already been discussed at length: Zosimus's chapter on the *pontifex maximus*, with its supposed double Latin pun. So far from deriving from a Latin source, the information in this chapter is wholly Greek.

2) The Anonymus Continuator of Dio, on inadequate grounds often identified as Peter the Patrician,[3] describes a certain Cledonius, an official at Valerian's court in 260, as "the man who brings judges (*dikastas*) into the imperial presence."[4] According to Bleckmann, Cledonius is being anachronistically described as *magister admissionum*, the official who regulated audiences with the emperor, and the translator did not realize that *iudices* in his Latin source was being used in the late antique sense of civil servant or official. He cites a passage of Lactantius describing how "a few civilian

---

1. See his significantly titled paper "Preuves de la présence d'une source occidentale latine dans la tradition grecque pour l'histoire du 4ᵉ siècle," now in Paschoud 2006, 413–22; and his most recent statement, 2006a, 338–44.
2. "countless words derived from Latin," Bleckmann 1995, 84.
3. In favor, de Boor 1892, 13–33; Bleckmann 1992, 51–53, 411–15; against, Mazzarino 1980, 69–103; Potter 1990, 395–97; M. R. Cataudella, in Marasco 2003, 437–40. Treadgold 2007, 48–49, suggests Heliconius of Byzantium, whose lost *Chronological Epitome* stopped in 379.
4. ἄνδρα τοὺς δικαστὰς εἰσάγοντα τῷ βασιλεῖ, Anon. Cont. F 3 (*FHG* iv. 193); Bleckmann 1995, 86.

officials and a few military officers were admitted" (*admissi ergo iudices pauci et pauci militares*) into Diocletian's consistory. But the *magister admissionum* oversaw *all* audiences with the emperor, private citizens, foreign ambassadors, magistrates, and generals alike.[5] Lactantius just happens to mention an occasion when *iudices* (among others) were admitted. No one wishing to identify the office of *magister admissionum* would have singled out admission of *iudices*.

There can be little doubt that Cledonius held the post of *a cognitionibus*, the official responsible in the high empire for organizing and scheduling legal cases (*cognitiones*) heard by the emperor.[6] Philostratus describes how the Sophist Heliodorus was "called in" (*eskaloumenos*) to plead a case sooner than he expected and tried to persuade "the official who introduced the cases" (*ho tas dikas eskalōn*) to postpone his hearing. And Dio describes how Septimius Severus ordered the "man who arranged the cases" to "bring in a particular case" (*diken tina eisagein*).[7] The very same verb *eisagein* used by Peter (*eisagein diken* was the standard term for bringing a case to court).[8] These parallels suggest that the true reading in Anonymus might be *dikas* rather than *dikastas*,[9] but in other respects his words are a perfect description of the function of *a cognitionibus*. If so, no translation error.

In any case, since *iudex* was the standard Latin term for an official in the early Byzantine world, what we should expect in this hypothesized Byzantine translator is exactly the reverse mistake: judges wrongly identified as officials. Furthermore, since Peter the Patrician wrote the protocol for the promotion of what in his day was called the *comes admissionum*,[10] he would be the very last person to make such a mistake. The care Peter took with titles centuries before his own day is nicely illustrated by an excerpt in which a *magister memoriae* in 298/9 is correctly described as *antigrapheus tēs mnemēs*, the standard Greek equivalent for the period.[11]

Peter's history is perhaps the least promising place imaginable to look for traces of a Latin source. We have substantial extracts from another of his works, on imperial ceremonial.[12] Not surprisingly for a life-long bureaucrat, Peter wrote in a heavily Latinate Greek. When reporting the text of Peter's arguments as envoy negotiating a treaty with the Persians, Menander remarks that he "made no substitutions of vocabulary, except for altering excessively lowly expressions into better Attic."[13] The most prominent element in what made Peter's style too low for Menander's pages is bound to have been its Latinisms. Just so when Photius condemns the "vulgarity" of

---

5. Lact. *De mort. pers.* 11. 6; Delmaire 1995, 43–44.

6. *PIR* C² 1133; Millar 1977, 232, 235.

7. Phil. *Vit. Soph.* ii. 33; on the incident, Millar, *JRS* 59 (1969), 12–13; Dio lxxvi. 15. 5.

8. For a brief selection of passages, *LSJ* s.v. εἰσάγω II. 3; the magistrate who brought cases to court was called εἰσαγωγεύς in inscriptions and papyri from all over the Greek world (*LSJ* s.v. II).

9. Perhaps an abridgment from something like τὸν τὰς δίκας τὰς <ἐπὶ τοῦ βασίλεως λεγομένας> εἰσαγόντα.

10. *De caerimoniis* i. 84; Delmaire 1995, 43.

11. Peter, F 14 (*FHG* iv. 189); J. B. Bury, *HSCP* 21 (1910), 24–25; Delmaire 1995, 67–68.

12. Preserved in *De caerimoniis* i. 84–95; briefly, J. B. Bury, *EHR* 86 (1907), 212–13; Averil Cameron in Cannadine and Price 1987, 126. For a new fragment of Peter, see A. Laniado, *BZ* 90 (1997), 405–12.

13. τὸ χθαμαλώτερον, F 6. 2 in Blockley 1985, 88–89.

Olympiodorus, it must be mainly his Latinisms he has in mind.[14] Whatever traces of Latin we find in Peter surely derive from Peter himself rather than any hypothetical fourth-century Latin source.

3) Peter's account of an embassy of the usurper Magnentius lists a general (*stratelates*) called Marcellinus.[15] Now Marcellinus was the name of Magnentius's *magister officiorum*.[16] On the already questionable assumption that Magnentius could not have had two officers called Marcellinus, Bleckmann argued that his hypothetical Latin source, instead of giving the correct term *magister officiorum* in full, described Marcellinus simply as *magister*, which Peter mistakenly identified as *magister militum* (normally rendered *stratelates* in Greek).[17] This is doubly implausible. In the first place, in Byzantine usage *magister* by itself (transliterated as *magistros*) invariably denoted the *magister officiorum*.[18] This is therefore one confusion Peter of all people, author of a book on the *magister officiorum* (p. 664), an office he himself held for an unprecedented twenty-five years, would *never* have made.

In the second place, published too late for *PLRE* and so overlooked by Bleckmann and Paschoud, a dozen or so graffiti name a Marcellianus together with a Romulus as owners of the Kaiseraugst treasure.[19] This treasure was found in a fort evidently manned by a unit of Magnentius's army. Moreover, we happen to know that another of his *magistri militum* was indeed called Romulus.[20] This Marcellianus (a name not infrequently confused with the much commoner Marcellinus)[21] is surely the general named by Peter the Patrician.

4) After referring to a man as "head of the troops at court," Zosimus then adds (as often elsewhere) the formal Latin title in a parenthesis (*magistron touton ufficiōn kalousi Romaioi*). According to Festy and Paschoud, because the so-called *Epitome* styles the man *officiorum magistrum*, this proves that both derive from a common source in Latin.[22] But all secular Greek historians (Ch. 6. 3) employed classicizing periphrases for Latin titles, curiously enough often together with the original title. To quote a single example out of scores in Procopius, after styling another *magister officiorum* as "head of the troops at court," he adds the proper title in a parenthesis (*magistron Romaioi ten archen kalein nenomikasi*).[23]

---

14. χυδαιολογία, T 1 in Blockley; Baldini 2004, 146–49.

15. F 16 = *FHG* iv. 190.

16. Zos. ii. 42. 2–5; *PLRE* i. 546, Marcellinus 8, distinguished from the general, Marcellinus 9.

17. For a different explanation, A. Demandt, *RE* s.v. Magister militum, Suppbd 12 (1970), 563.

18. As Bleckmann 1995, 85 n. 10 himself oddly conceded, citing many examples; see too Bury 1911, 29.

19. Cahn and Kaufmann-Heinimann 1984; Textband 182, 388–90, 408–9.

20. Zosimus ii. 52. 2; *PLRE* i. 771; Cahn 1982, 408–9.

21. Marcellinus 6, in *PLRE* ii. 708–10, is regularly called Μαρκελλιανός by Procopius; a bishop at the Council of Ephesus is regularly Marcellianus in Latin and Μαρκελλῖνος in Greek versions of the Acta: *ACO* IV. iii. 2. 2 (1982), 303; note too Marcellinus 46 in *RE* 14. 2 (1930), 1450.

22. Zos. ii. 25. 2; Festy 2002, xvii n. 29; Paschoud, *Zosime* i² (2000), 231. For similar cases, ii. 25. 2; ii. 43. 4; iii. 29. 3; for a useful index of Zosimus's words for civil and military institutions, *Zosime* 3. 2 (1989), 201–12.

23. Proc. *BP* i. 8. 2; for other such expressions in Procopius, above Ch. 6. 3.

5) According to Victor (42. 9) and Eutropius (10. 12. 2), the usurper Magnentius appointed his brother (*frater*) Decentius as his Caesar. But according to the *Epitome*, Decentius was his *consanguineus* (42. 2). This text also describes both Hannibalianus and Delmatius and Valentinian I and Valens as *consanguinei* (41. 20; 45. 4). Technically, *consanguineus* is the term for half-brother,[24] but Valentinian and Valens were full brothers. This use of *consanguineus* as a synonym for *frater* was apparently an idiosyncrasy of the *Epitome*. But Bleckmann and Paschoud will not allow that it is an idiosyncrasy of the author of the *Epitome* himself. It must be a usage he copied from his source, here Flavian.[25] Since Zosimus ii. 45. 2 styles Decentius, not *adelphos*, but *genei sunaptomenos*, this is held to be proof that "behind Zosimus (or rather Eunapius) is a Latin source that used *consanguineus* for *frater*." So both the *Epitome* and Zosimus derive from Flavian.

But if Flavian regularly used *consanguineus* for *frater*, and Zosimus reflects Flavian, why does Zosimus describe Valentinian and Valens as *adelphoi* and Constantine's half-brother Julius Constantius as his *adelphos*? And why does Zonaras, who is also held to derive ultimately from Flavian, describe Decentius twice as Magnentius's *adelphos*?[26] In fact, another passage of Zonaras suggests a quite different interpretation of all these texts. He calls another brother of Magnentius, Desiderius, first his *adelphos* and then seven lines later his *homaimōn*.[27] By derivation *homaimōn* is a vague term for a kinsman of any degree, but it (and its by-forms *homaimos* and *synaimos*) is common in the classical tragedians specifically for brother or sister.[28] The obvious explanation here is that Zonaras's ultimate source was a classicizing Greek writer who used *homaimōn* for brother.[29] This usage was unfamiliar to Zosimus and the author of the *Epitome*; the former resorted to paraphrase, the latter used the closest Latin equivalent he could think of (*consanguineus*).

6) Paschoud compared passages from three obituary notices on the emperor Jovian:

Amm. 25. 10. 14:	Epitome 44. 3:	Zonaras 13. 14. 19:
vultu laetissimo…vasta	hic fuit insignis	εὐσεβὴς ἦν περὶ τὸ δόγμα καὶ
proceritate et ardua, adeo	corpore, laetus	ἀγαθοθελής. οἴνου δ' ἥττητο καὶ
ut nullum indumentum	ingenio, litterarum	ἀφροδισίων, καὶ τὴν τοῦ
regium ad mensuram eius	studiosus.	σώματος ἀναδρομὴν εὐμήκης
aptum inveniretur		ἐτύγχανε καὶ γραμμάτων οὐκ
		ἄπειρος.

---

24. Ammianus calls Valentinian II the *consanguineus* of Gratian (30. 10. 6): same father but different mothers.
25. Bleckmann, *Göttinger Forum für Altertumswissenschaft* 2 (1999), 85–87; Paschoud 2006, 415–6.
26. Zonaras xiii. 8. 2; 9. 6 (neither text cited by Bleckmann or Paschoud).
27. ὁμαίμων, Zonaras xiii. 9. 4, 7 (Desiderius is not known from any other source: *PLRE* i. 249–50).
28. See *LSJ* s.v. ὅμαιμος 2 for a selection of examples.
29. Zonaras himself uses ὁμαίμων for brother or sister no fewer than forty-one times (*TLG*).

[15]....Christianae legis
idem studiosus et
nonnumquam
honorificus, mediocriter
eruditus, magisque
benivolus...edax tamen et
vino Venerique indulgens.

According to Paschoud it is "obvious" (a) that Ammianus, the *Epitome*, and Zonaras all derive from the same source; and (b) that this source was written in Latin and contained the word *benivolus*, rendered in Zonaras by the unclassical *agathothelēs*.[30] I would concede that a classicizing Greek writer is unlikely to have used so unliterary a word, but why would anyone when there were so many acceptable classical equivalents?[31] Any one of these would have been a more satisfactory choice, and other representatives of the Byzantine tradition do indeed use one of them. So the chronicle preserved under the name of Georgius Cedrenus: "a very kindly man and an orthodox Christian...so tall that none of the imperial robes would fit him."[32] This notice just as obviously goes back to the same ultimate source, even preserving Ammianus's circumstantial detail (like him using a consecutive clause) about the imperial robes being too short for Jovian. But in George, Ammianus's *benivolus* is rendered by *prāotatos*. Somewhat less of this ultimate source survives in Symeon, but it is sugges-tive that he too uses classical terms, one of them the same as Cedrenus.[33] It may be that Zonaras's *agathothelēs* does not represent *benivolus* at all, but in the context means "right-thinking," that is to say orthodox (rather than Arian). Here we may note that Cedrenus carefully specifies that Jovian was orthodox.

We might also bear in mind that Flavian had never seen Jovian, whereas Ammianus had the opportunity to observe him at close quarters during most of his short reign. Why then would he copy his description of Jovian from Flavian? Since he uses *benivolus* five times elsewhere in his history, the natural conclusion is that it was simply part of his normal vocabulary.

7) Fragments 13 and 14 of Peter, the longest surviving episode from his history, describe the treaty negotiated between Persians and Romans in 298/9 by Sicorius Probus the *magister memoriae*.[34] When the Persians asked Galerius to treat their king's harem (which the Romans had captured) kindly, Galerius angrily reminded them of their shameful treatment of Valerian, adding that he would follow in the footsteps

---

30. Paschoud 2006, 419 ("saute aux yeux"), listing the very few occurrences of the word.
31. ἐπιεικής, εὔνους, εὐγνώμων, εὐμενής, εὔφρων, πρᾶος, προσφιλής, πρόφρων, φιλόφρων etc.
32. ἀνὴρ πραότατος καὶ ὀρθόδοξος Χριστιανός...εὐμήκης ὥστε μηδὲ ἓν τῶν βασιλικῶν ἱματίων ἁρμόζειν αὐτῷ, Cedrenus p. 539. 16 B.
33. πραΰς καὶ ἐπιεικής, Symeon § 91. 1 Wahlgren; πραΰς is the Byzantine form for πρᾶος.
34. F 13–14 = FHG iv. 188–89; *The Roman Eastern Frontier and the Persian Wars AD 226–363*, M. H. Dodgeon and S. N. C. Lieu (eds.) (London 1991), 131–33; date, Barnes, *Phoenix* 30 (1976), 185–86; negotiations, Blockley 1984.

of his ancestors, whose custom it was "to spare those who surrendered but conquer those who resisted." These words are a close translation of Vergil's *parcere subiectis et debellare superbos*.[35] Bleckmann saw this as a reflection of western historiography during the late fourth-century pagan reaction—meaning Flavian. But quite apart from the baseless assumption of a fourth-century Vergil revival (Ch. 16), how would Flavian working in Rome have come by such a detailed account of these negotiations? Bleckmann suggests that Sicorius Probus was "related to the Anicii and Petronii," and that Flavian was thus able to draw on a "Roman senatorial source." But no *magister memoriae* in 298/9 would even have been a senator, much less an aristocrat. Palatine secretariats, formerly held by freedmen, were at this period manned by *equites*.[36]

Eunapius is one obvious possible source.[37] But we should bear in mind that Peter was not only a diplomat himself, but wrote a detailed study both of his own diplomatic missions and of the mastership of the offices he himself held for so many years, the office responsible for dealing with all foreign embassies at court.[38] Under the circumstances it is natural to suppose that it was Peter who searched out a contemporary account of these negotiations in the archives of his own office, in which case it may be that Galerius himself (or at any rate Sicorius Probus) quoted Vergil. If the soldier emperor Valentinian I could compose a Vergilian cento,[39] there is no call to deny Galerius the one line even soldier emperors surely knew.[40] If these excerpts are indeed based on Peter's own documentary research, this would undermine the assumption that he simply copied out some earlier history, whether Flavian or Eunapius.

One final case. Immediately after the proclamation of Valentinian I, the officers who had chosen him insisted that he take a colleague. The *magister militum* Dagalaifus boldly advised him as follows, according to Ammianus: "If you love your kin, best of emperors, you have a brother; if you love the state, look for someone [else] to invest" (*si tuos amas, inquit, imperator optime, habes fratrem; si rempublicam, quaere quem vestias*). Dagalaifus's advice is reported in exactly the same terms by both Symeon Logothete and Cedrenus.[41] The articulation of the two versions is identical down to the last detail, and no one could be in any doubt that one is a translation of the other. So which is the original? While *respublica* is common and idiomatic in Latin for "the public good," *politeia* is not normally so used in Greek. And the final phrase is no less telling: the translator evidently could not think of a one-word Greek equivalent to

35. φείδεσθαι μὲν τῶν ὑπηκόων, καταγωνίζεσθαι δὲ τῶν ἀντιταττομένων, Bleckmann 1992, 154; Paschoud 1994, 75.
36. Bleckmann 1992, 413; S. Corcoran in N. Lenski, *Cambridge Companion to the Age of Constantine* (2006), 45.
37. At *Vit. Soph.* 465/6 Eunapius gives interesting details about the role of the philosopher Eustathius of Cappadocia on an embassy to Persia in 358: Blockley 1992, 21.
38. Boak and Dunlap 1924, 93–98; Treadgold 2007, 264–69. For a modern history, Peachin 1989, 168–208.
39. Ausonius, intro to *Cento Nupt.*, p. 133 Green, with Green's notes (p. 518).
40. For some of the many quotations of this line, Courcelle 1984, 497–99.
41. Amm. Marc. xxvi. 4. 1; εἰ τοὺς σοὺς φιλεῖς, κράτιστε αὐτοκράτορ, ἔχεις ἀδελφόν· εἰ δὲ τὴν πολιτείαν, σκόπησον ὅτῳ ἂν τὴν ἁλουργίδα περιβάλῃς, Symeon § 92. 2 Wahlgren; Cedrenus p. 541. 13 Bekker (with περιβαλεῖς).

vestire with the connotation "dress in the purple robe of empire."[42] But even if the Latin version is original, that does not prove that Symeon and Cedrenus derive from a Latin narrative source. For the advice itself may have been given in Latin, so that Greek writers were bound to give it in translation. The text offered by Symeon and Cedrenus could perfectly well be as early as Eunapius, who (to judge from Philostorgius and Sozomen) gave an account similar to Ammianus's.[43]

9: A GREEK *KG*?

More than one scholar has posited a common source for the Latin epitomators and the later Greek historians for the third century.[44] Festy has recently emphasized similarities between Zosimus and Victor, concluding that they prove derivation from the *KG*.[45] But it is important to bear in mind that mere agreement in facts proves nothing in itself (especially in a history, where events are bound to follow a certain sequence) unless the selection of facts is idiosyncratic or marked by verbal similarities. Festy's list offers none of the verbal parallels and shared errors that establish the *KG* as the common source of Victor, Eutropius, and other Latin texts. And how did material from the *KG* reach Zosimus? According to Festy, it was first included in Flavian's *Annales*, whence it passed into Eunapius and finally Zosimus—a tortuous and improbable odyssey. Why introduce the complication of Flavian? Much simpler to suppose that Eunapius read a source we know existed, the *KG*, rather than a source we have no reason to believe even covered this period. But there is no need to posit a Latin source for Eunapius at all. Why not a Greek translation of the *KG*, made for the same reason as the translation of Eutropius: the sheer utility of so comprehensive a manual. There are in fact good reasons for postulating such a translation.

In the first place, Alden Mosshammer has pointed out that, in addition to many details in the early ninth-century Byzantine chronicle of George Syncellus that seem to derive from Eutropius, there are a number of other details that, though absent from Eutropius, appear in much the same form in Victor or Festus.[46] While it is easy enough to believe that Syncellus consulted one of the Greek translations of Eutropius, how did he come to know Victor or Festus? Here we have more than mere agreement in fact: in the case of Festus there is a striking shared error. In A.D. 3 Augustus sent his grandson Gaius Caesar to Armenia, where he received a wound from which he died. According to Syncellus it was his grandson *Claudius* Caesar that Augustus sent to

---

42. For which, see Symm. *Or. in Grat.* 2 (p. 330. 22 Seeck).

43. Neri 1985, 169.

44. Earlier bibliography in Bleckmann 1992, 24.

45. Festy 1998, at 160–63, with Burgess's critique in the same volume (85–86).

46. A. A. Mosshammer, *Georgius Syncellus* (Leipzig 1984), xxix; see too W. Adler and P. Tuffin, *The Chronography of George Syncellus* (Oxford 2002), lxi.

Armenia. The only other surviving text to make this error is Festus.[47] The likely source
of the error is a mistaken expansion of "C. Caesar" in a Latin text. The obvious explanation is that it goes back to the *KG*, whence it was repeated by Festus alone of the
Latin epitomators, and, via a Greek translation, by Syncellus.

Second, it has long been known that the first few pages of the chronicle of
Theophanes (which begins with Diocletian) draw on the later books of Eutropius.[48] It
is also common knowledge that the surviving excerpts from the *Chronike Historia* of
John of Antioch draw extensively on what appears to be a Greek translation of Eutropius,
from Bks 1 to 10, from the early Republic down to the death of Jovian.[49] Since the translation John cites is completely different throughout from Paeanius's, it has always been
assumed that he used Capito's somewhat later translation (ca. 500), known from an
entry in the Suda. But in 1885 Carl de Boor pointed out that Theophanes (p. 10. 20–26
de Boor) offers a close translation of Eutropius x. 1 that is completely different both
from that of Paeanius and from the relevant excerpt in John of Antioch.[50]

Some popular literary texts were translated more than once (the five Latin versions of Aratus are a famous case), but two of so utilitarian a work as Eutropius's
Breviarium are surprising enough, and three would be remarkable. Furthermore, all
who have studied the "Eutropian" excerpts in John of Antioch have noticed that John
often offers a somewhat fuller version than the Latin original.[51] In many cases the
explanation is that John includes details from genuine sources that can actually be
identified. But in other cases there is no additional information, just a more expansive
narrative than the bare bones offered by Eutropius. Köcher long ago suggested two
possible explanations: either John drew on a fuller version of Eutropius, or on
Eutropius's source.[52] Writing as he was in 1871, before the identification of the *KG*,
Köcher opted for his first alternative. But a fuller version of Eutropius is pretty much
a definition of his source, the *KG*. I suggest that it is Theophanes who reflects Capito's
translation, while John of Antioch drew on the *KG*, presumably in a Greek translation.
In this connection it is worth pointing out that, while Eutropius/*KG* provides John
with his framework for a thousand years of Roman history, he never names Eutropius,
despite the fact that he does in fact occasionally cite sources by name.[53]

The most suggestive single illustration is the long passage published from an Athos
manuscript by Lambros in 1904, where, after (as it seems) translating Eutropius on

---

47. Sync. p. 376. 1 Mosshammer; Fest. *Brev.* 19; it is also found in Jordanes (*Rom.* 240), who used Festus
    extensively elsewhere. Festus's source for the events seems to be Florus ii. 32.
48. Theophanes's chronicle is a continuation of Syncellus's, in large part based on material collected by
    Syncellus (who drew on the earlier books of Eutropius): see C. Mango and R. Scott, *The Chronicle of
    Theophanes Confessor* (Oxford 1997), lxxvi; A. A. Mosshammer, *Georgius Syncellus* (1984), xxix.
49. See the notes on sources in F 37–181 in Müller, *FHG* 4.
50. *Hermes* 20 (1885), 325–26; for another example (Theoph. p. 9. 1–16), E. Condurachi, *RFIC* 65 (1937),
    47–50.
51. Sotiroudis 1989, 110–17; see too now, superceding all earlier work, Roberto 2005, cxxxii–cxxxiii.
52. Köcher 1871, 20. Sotiroudis weakly suggests that John was simply more verbose than the text he was
    copying.
53. Roberto 2005, cxxv–clvii.

Sulla, John adds a quotation from Sallust: "the Roman historian Sallust rightly remarked that Sulla made an excellent beginning but reached a shocking end."[54] This is an accurate translation of *Catiline* 11. 4 (*L. Sulla... bonis initiis malos eventus habuit*). John may have had a little Latin, but it is incredible that a seventh-century Byzantine knew Sallust so well that he was able to recall so apposite a quotation and then put it into accurate Greek.[55] Obviously, it is far more likely that he was translating a Latin text that already included the quotation, or (more probably) using an existing Greek translation of such a text. Most of the sources John cites by name are Greek texts he might have consulted himself (Diodorus, Dionysius, Plutarch), but he also twice cites Livy, in both cases lost books, once again suggesting the possibility of a fuller Latin source that might have drawn on books of Livy lost by John's day.[56] Later in his narrative, after paraphrasing the Eutropian account of the parsimonious Constantius Chlorus borrowing other people's silver plate when holding a large dinner party, John concludes with a detail missing in Eutropius: "whence he was known as Pauper."[57] This could be pure invention by John, but the Latin word suggests a Latin source, a source not fully understood by the Greek translator, who took Pauper for a proper name rather than a nickname.

Particularly striking is F 180M = 272R, an obituary of Julian that, while seeming to follow Eutropius fairly closely at the beginning and end, gives more detail (and a different emphasis) in the middle. For example, where Eutropius offers *Liberalibus disciplinis apprime eruditus; Graece doctior, atque ideo ut Latina eruditione nequaquam cum Graeca scientia conveniret*, John has "he had an intimate grasp of the entire learning of the Romans, especially the Greek language, quick to spot what needed to be done but even prompter to articulate and interpret it, with a firm recall of every detail, wise in matters divine, prudent in human affairs."[58] Once again, John himself might have inserted the additional material from another source favorable to Julian (Eunapius, e.g.) or even invented it himself, but why would a Christian writer go to such lengths to expand an already favorable account of the Apostate?

Over the years there has been much debate about the terminal point of the *KG*. Burgess has recently argued for successive redactions, running from 337 to 378.[59] One possibility is that John used a later redaction of the original Latin *KG*. Another is that the Greek version he used itself included a continuation of the Latin original to the translator's own day, just as Eutropius continued the *KG* to his day. Here is a concrete illustration, kindly drawn to my attention by Burgess: Jerome's account of Diocletian's Roman triumph in 303: Jerome (227m Helm):

---

54. F 145. 2. 269, p. 240 Roberto; on the Lambros fragment, Roberto 2005, cxi–cxvii.
55. Suda s.v. Zenobios claims that the Hadrianic Sophist of this name translated Sallust's Histories into Greek, but does not mention his *Catiline*.
56. F 145. 2. 63; F 147. 16 Roberto.
57. ὅθεν καὶ Παῦπερ ὠνομάξετο, F 168 Mueller = 252 Roberto; Eutr. x. 1. 2.
58. F 180, *FHG* iv. 606.
59. Burgess 1995; 2005; see too Paschoud 2006a, 337–44.

| Diocletianus et Maximianus Augusti insigni pompa Romae triumpharunt, antecedentibus currum eorum Narsei coniuge sororibus liberis et omni praeda, qua Parthos spoliaverunt. | Eutropius (ix. 27. 2): ...triumphum inclitum, quem Romae ex numerosis gentibus egerent [Diocletianus et Maximianus], pompa ferculorum inlustri, qua Narsei coniuges sororesque et liberi ante currum ducti sunt. | Zonaras (12. 32, p. 618. 14): ἐν Ῥώμῃ κατήγαγον θρίαμβον, ἐν ᾧ τάς τε τοῦ Ναρσοῦ γαμετὰς καὶ τὰ τέκνα καὶ τὰς ὁμαίμονας ἐθριάμβευσαν καὶ ἀρχηγοὺς ἑτέρων ἐθνῶν καὶ τὸν πλοῦτον ὅσον ἐκ Περσῶν ἐληΐσαντο. |

This is one of many proofs that Jerome drew on the *KG*. It must have been here that he found the detail about Persian booty that Eutropius omitted, a detail that also appears in Zonaras. The fact that all three texts include Narses's sisters (*homaimonas*) in the triumphal procession is a further link between them. The preceding section in both Eutropius and Zonaras deals with Diocletian's introduction of *adoratio* and jewel-encrusted clothing. Here the key detail is that both (like Victor) single out jewel-encrusted *shoes*.[60] Zonaras could have got this from Capito's translation of Eutropius (Paeanius translates it quite differently), but since he shares with Jerome the Persian booty Eutropius omitted (in both cases in a relative clause), the *KG* is a more likely ultimate source, perhaps (as we shall see in § 12) mediated by John of Antioch.

It will be obvious that a Greek translation of the *KG* would transform the debate about the supposed influence of Flavian's *Annales*.[61] Anything in Byzantine texts up to the death of Jovian suspected of deriving from Flavian might equally derive from the Greek version of the *KG*. The postulate of Flavian would turn out to be not only baseless but also superfluous.

10: EUNAPIUS

The most important part of Zonaras's narrative for the Flavian hypothesis is his remarkably full account of the years 350–64, from the rebellion of Magnentius and proclamation of Gallus to the death of Jovian. This account has many close similarities with the narrative of Ammianus, but also significant differences, the classic pointers to a common source, for Bleckmann and Paschoud (of course), Flavian's *Annales*.[62]

---

60. Zonaras 12. 32; Eutr. ix. 26; Victor, *Caes.* 39. 2. Zonaras's ἀρχηγοὺς ἑτέρων ἐθνῶν also parallels Eutropius's *ex numerosis gentibus*, a detail omitted by Jerome.

61. Which is why Paschoud 2006a, 334–35 ridicules, mainly by use of exclamation marks, my brief statement in *BMCR* 2006, characterizing my arguments as "ressorts pipés de l'acrobatie sophistique." But a Greek translation of the *KG* would be no more surprising than the Greek translation of Eutropius we know to have existed—and incomparably less surprising than a Greek translation of Nicomachus Flavianus!

62. Zonaras xiii. 9–14 (pp. 44–71 Büttner-Wobst); see the comparison in Bleckmann 1992, 336–95.

It should now be clear why it is so essential for the Flavian hypothesis that he should have published before Ammianus. For we are not here concerned with Ammianus's last books, but the earliest surviving books (the fall of Gallus is described in Bk xiv). Whether or not Bks xiv–xxv were published earlier than xxvi–xxxi, we are bound to assume that Ammianus did the research for these books before before writing the later books. If the later books were published not long after 390, and Flavian published not before 390, Ammianus cannot possibly have used Flavian when composing his earlier books.

The *Epitome de Caesaribus* has played a significant part in recent discussions. The most recent editor assumes that it is mainly based on Flavian, and Baldini goes so far as to claim that its purpose was "to perpetuate the memory of the *historicus disertissimus* Nicomachus Flavianus."[63] Since it closes with the death of Theodosius I (17 January 395) and is written in Latin, Epitomator (so to style him, for the convenience of a name) certainly could have used Flavian (if he wrote on the history of the empire). But what is the evidence that he did? In one of the more outrageous of his recent contributions to the debate, Paschoud has asserted that "there is no indication that the *Epitome* ever drew on a Greek source."[64] Outrageous, because there are more than a dozen passages in the last third of the book where the closest parallel to the *Epitome* comes in a Greek text.[65] But since in most of these cases the parallel text is Zosimus or Zonaras, and since for the Flavian équipe it is axiomatic that *Epitome* + Zosimus/Zonaras = Flavian, by a remarkable paradox parallels from the Greek tradition are regarded as proof that the *Epitome* derives here from a Latin source!

More than half the work can be explained perfectly satisfactorily in terms of known sources like the *KG* and the biographies of Marius Maximus, a work we know from a disapproving remark of Ammianus to have been all the rage in late fourth-century Rome. It remains possible that Epitomator drew on Flavian (if he covered the empire), but we would now have to devise new criteria for identifying any such debts; passages paralleled in Greek texts would have to be excluded from consideration. With the lapse of the hypothesis that Flavian can be reconstructed from Zosimus and the Byzantine tradition, we may return to the commonsense alternative that Epitomator drew on Greek sources.

There is one puzzle here that seems to have escaped attention in recent discussions. If Epitomator, writing in the mid- to late 390s, could have used Flavian, he could also have used Ammianus. And yet, since we have Bks xiv–xxxi of Ammianus complete, we can say with confidence that he did not. It is easy to see why the compiler of a trivial epitome might not take the trouble to read Ammianus from cover to cover, but it would be rather surprising if he had paid him no attention at all. Even more surprisingly, he apparently did read a Greek history of the period. How is this paradox to be

---

63. Festy 2002, xv–xx, xxvii–xxxviii, liv–lv; Baldini 1999, 16.
64. "il n'y a aucun indice que l'*Epitome* ait jamais exploité une source grecque," Paschoud 2006, 415.
65. Conveniently tabulated by Barnes 1976, 264–67. Add the use of *consanguineus* for brother (? = ὁμαίμων).

explained? It has always been taken for granted that Epitomator was an associate of pagan senators and wrote in Rome (whence the assumption that he "channelled" Flavian). But there is no support for any of these assumptions in the work itself, least of all in its vulgar Latin and clumsy and repetitious style.[66]

There is another possibility. What if he wrote in the East? The two latest occasions on which he records where an emperor was buried are in Constantinople (Constantine and Theodosius).[67] Why would this have interested a Roman audience? It should be borne in mind that both Eutropius and Festus produced their Breviaria at and for eastern courts. It was the East where potted imperial histories seem to have been in most demand, and the only sixth-century texts that can be shown to have used the Epitome are eastern.[68] More important, the final chapter draws on a consular list maintained in Constantinople from 356 to 388.[69] The obvious implication is that Epitomator was living in Constantinople when he wrote. If so, that would explain why for his last few emperors he turned to a recent Greek history rather than a recent Latin history. He may never have seen either Ammianus or Flavian.

Which Greek sources did he use? Since he shares so many details with Zosimus, and Zosimus is said to have "copied out" Eunapius,[70] the simplest solution would be Eunapius.[71] It used to be thought that Eunapius wrote too late for Ammianus or even Epitomator. But in 1976 Barnes argued that the first edition of Eunapius went down to Adrianople (378) and was published soon after. That would make it possible for both Epitomator (especially if he wrote in the East) and Ammianus to read it.[72] Paschoud claimed to have "refuted" the argument and "proved" that the first installment was not published till 395. But this is to go beyond the possibilities of the evidence.

The circumstances attending the publication of Eunapius's History are a notorious puzzle. More than a dozen passages in his *Lives of the Sophists* (ca. 399) refer to books already published and promise another installment to come; and Photius knew two "editions" (*ekdoseis*), both of which he claims to have read.[73] Photius makes three points: (1) both editions covered the same period; (2) the second cut out the anti-Christian polemic; (3) these cuts left the second edition incoherent. He particularly emphasizes the last point: "many passages of the new edition are obscure because of

66. For some useful remarks on Epitomator's Latinity, see E. Wölfflin, *ALL* 12 (1902), 445–53.
67. Cameron 2001, 324–27 argued that the final sentence about the burial of Theodosius's body in Constantinople was interpolated from Marcellinus, *Chron.* s.a. 395. But in the light of § 41. 17 (*corpus sepultum in Byzantio, Constantinopoli dicta*) I am no longer so sure. Festy 2002, xlviii, cites several passages that imply (he suggests) personal knowledge of Rome, but they might easily have been taken over from an earlier source; *vidimus* (20. 6) in such a context need imply no more than "still survives."
68. Jordanes (Mommsen's edition [1882], xxvii); and perhaps Marcellinus (Croke 2001, 206).
69. Burgess 1993, 194–96, 203–4; see Festy's notes on *Epit.* 48.
70. εἴποι δ ' ἄν τις οὐ γράψαι αὐτὸν ἱστορίαν ἀλλὰ μεταγράψαι τὴν Εὐναπίου, according to Photius, who had read both (F 1–2 Blockley).
71. Remember that Epitomator followed Eunapius rather than Ammianus in numbering Equitius among those responsible for proclaiming Valentinian II in 375.
72. The following pages will provide abundant evidence that Ammianus did indeed draw on Eunapius.
73. For all these questions, see Paschoud 2006, 153–99, with a complete list of the cross-references. But for the most plausible and convincing solution, see Baker 1988, 389–402.

excisions (*perikopas*) in the text.... Because in the second edition he did not properly adjust his language to accord with the excisions, he destroys the sense of what is read." For reasons that are not clear to me, most recent critics insist that Eunapius himself was responsible for both editions,[74] and link or identify successive editions with successive installments. That is to say, they accept what can only have been Photius's guess about who was responsible for the "new" edition, but ignore his observation that the excisions left the text incoherent, and reject his claim that both editions covered the same period. Yet Photius was an expert on style,[75] and his remark about the clumsiness of the excisions was presumably based on a firsthand comparison of one or two sample passages in the two editions. It is particularly unlikely that he was wrong about so simple a point as the terminal date of the history. All he had to do, after all, was check the final page of both editions, a moment's work in a codex.

For a variety of reasons, true second editions were rare in the ancient world.[76] In particular, while many histories were published in installments (Livy and Polybius are uncontroversial examples), the only known case of a history that appeared in more than one edition is Eusebius's Ecclesiastical History.[77] Nor did even Eusebius revise his history as a whole.[78] He added three new books and then revised a few details in those additional books to accommodate his narrative to the dramatic changes in the fortunes of the church since the first edition.[79] Baldini's theory that Eunapius's second edition represents a radical revision of the entire work in the light of another history published since the first edition (namely Flavian's) would be without parallel in ancient historical writing. Eunapius might have decided that it was prudent to tone down his anti-Christian polemic, but so self-conscious a stylist would never have done so by making clumsy excisions that left the surrounding context unintelligible. The "new" edition must (as Niebuhr saw) be a copy bowdlerized by a later editor anxious to render so useful a work less offensive to pious readers—incidentally an intriguing illustration of its continuing popularity and influence.

Since the Constantinian excerpts are said to have been taken from the new edition, it follows, as Aaron Baker pointed out, that excerpts and Suda quotations alike must derive from this bowdlerized edition. There is also another proof. The first and longest of the *Excerpta de Sententiis* is Eunapius's preface, largely consisting of polemic against Dexippus and giving as justification for his own undertaking the lack of a worthy history covering the period from the death of Claudius II (270) to the present day. Nothing in these rambling reflections in the preface to what is described as a "new

74. Blockley 1981, 3; cf. Treadgold 2007, 82.

75. See the index s.v. Photius in G. L. Kustas, *Studies in Byzantine Rhetoric* (Thessalonica 1973), 209.

76. H. Emonds, *Zweite Auflage im Altertum* (Leipzig 1941); Cameron 1995, 114–18.

77. H. *Emonds, Zweite Auflage im Altertum* (Leipzig 1941), 25–44; Barnes 1981, 191–201; Burgess 1997, 471–504.

78. Grafton and Williams 2006, 213–14.

79. Socrates revised the first draft of his first two books after discovering that he had been misled by Rufinus's chronology, but there is no suggestion that they were actually published in their original form (Hansen 1995, xliii).

edition" in the immediately preceding title suggests that what followed was a second or revised edition inspired by a recent competitor.[80]

What do we know about the publication of the first installment? One passage in *Lives of the Sophists* describes the destruction of the Serapeum of Alexandria in 391 and the temples of Canopus, and then goes on to report that "they imported monks (as they call them) into the sacred places" and continues with a diatribe against monks, concluding "all this I have described in my universal history." As Barnes pointed out, it does not follow that Eunapius described the destruction of the Serapeum in his History. It is enough that he dealt with the excesses of the monks, already a popular theme in anti-Christian polemic as early as Julian.[81] Another passage reports the prophecy of an Eleusinian hierophant that his successor would be unworthy and in consequence that the sacred temples would be destroyed and the worship of the goddesses would end. A Mithraic pater became hierophant, and disasters duly came in a flood, some of which Eunapius says he has already described in his History. Then he mentions Alaric's invasion of Greece through the pass of Thermopylae, betrayed to him by Christian monks. "All this (he concludes) happened in later days."[82] Paschoud concedes that Alaric's invasion belongs in the "later days," but argues that the destruction of the temples must have been a consequence of Theodosius's legislation of 391–92, and that the first edition must therefore have described this legislation and so (presumably) terminated with Theodosius's death in 395.[83] This is certainly a possible, perhaps even a reasonable interpretation of Eunapius's words, but it is not a necessary interpretation. It is sometimes important to bear in mind that, when the evidence is inadequate, what might seem a natural, reasonable, or plausible conclusion based on that evidence may nonetheless be mistaken. At the time he wrote the *Lives of the Sophists*, round 399, inevitably Eunapius saw Theodosius's laws as the definitive fulfillment of the hierophant's prophecy. But if the first installment dated from the 380s, he may then have seen earlier disasters as fulfilling the prophecy just as well. Modern Christian sects that emphasize the fulfillment of biblical prophecy are constantly obliged to update the supposedly contemporary reference of such prophecies.

There is also another consideration. As already remarked, it is not easy to believe that Eunapius published his extraordinarily hostile account of Theodosius in the emperor's lifetime. It might be argued that the first installment appeared soon after Theodosius's death (17 January 395), though it would be unparalleled for any historian to continue a full-scale narrative right up to the moment of publication.[84] Even so, it

80. F 1: Paschoud 2006, 223–40. It is true that the last few lines of the excerpt are illegible, but any reference to major revisions must have come earlier than this. Baker 1988, 399–402, has also shown that τὰ μὲν οὖν πρῶτα τῆς συγγραφῆς at the beginning of F 41 M = 41. 1 B need not refer to either installments or editions.
81. Vit. Soph. vii. 3, 4 (476D); Barnes 1978, 114–23.
82. *Vit. Soph.* vi. 11. 17 (472D).
83. Paschoud 1980, now in Paschoud 2006, 93–106 (plus polemical addenda).
84. Thus Victor's *Caesares* is no real parallel.

would have to be very soon indeed after Theodosius's death, before Alaric's invasion of Greece in late 395, which was apparently not included. Note too that Eunapius hopes to include in a later installment the deaths of several friends during Alaric's invasion.[85] If the first installment really stopped as late as January 395, it would also be strange that none of the fourteen other cross-references in the Lives of the Sophists refers to anything later than the reign of Valens. There is no proof that the first installment closed with the death of Valens, but there is certainly no proof that it continued to the death of Theodosius either. Eunapius was born in 347/8, and might perfectly well have published a first installment in plenty of time for Ammianus (390/91) and Epitomator (395). Oribasius composed a detailed memoir on Julian specially for Eunapius, and it seems unlikely that either waited thirty years.

Paschoud thought he had provided a specific demonstration that Peter the Patrician at any rate did not depend on Eunapius. A long fragment of Eunapius describes in detail the emperor Julian's negotiations with a defeated barbarian tribe, the Chamavi. By good fortune we have a summary of the same anecdote in an excerpt of Peter.[86] Julian demanded hostages, including the king's son, whom he was in fact already holding as a prisoner. The king burst into tears, explaining that his son had been killed in the fighting, whereupon Julian produced him alive and dictated conditions for a peace treaty. Paschoud points out that the Peter excerpt closes with a detail not in Eunapius: "this was an indication that he [Julian] did not want peace." According to Paschoud, this non-Eunapian detail proves that Eunapius was not Peter's source.[87] But the syntax of this final sentence is abrupt, and the content makes no sense in the context of the anecdote. Of course Julian wanted peace, and with the king's son as hostage was in a strong position to dictate whatever terms he wanted. Opening and closing sentences in sequences of excerpts are often summaries by the excerptor rather than verbatim quotation. In an article that should be required (re)reading for anyone who works with historical fragments, excerpts, and epitomes, Brunt cites many examples of excerpts from texts that also survive complete where the excerptor's final sentence gives an entirely false impression of what follows.[88] This is surely the explanation of the final sentence in this excerpt, the last in the sequence.[89] The excerptor was visibly getting impatient;[90] he did not even bother to finish the story. His remark is based on a hasty reading of Julian's concluding threat to attack the barbarians if they break the peace. In all other respects the excerpt is little more than a paraphrase of Eunapius. There are three clear verbal parallels. (1) In Eunapius, the barbarians beg Julian "not to

---

85. *Vit. Soph.* viii. 1–2 (481–82).

86. Eun. F 12M = F 18. 6B; Petr. Patr. F 18 (*FHG* iv. 191); there is another summary in Zos. iii. 7. 6–7. See Paschoud 2000, now in Paschoud 2006, 395–402, restated in 2006a, 343.

87. τοῦτο δὲ τεκμήριον εἶναι τοῦ σπονδὰς αὐτὸν μὴ ἐθέλειν ποιήσασθαι, Paschoud 2002, xviii; and 2000, 60.

88. "The beginnings and endings of excerpts are at times arbitrary and misleading," Brunt 1980, 477–94, at 484.

89. Inasmuch as it refers to Julian as "the Apostate," the first sentence too must be largely the work of the excerptor.

90. "As he draws to a close the excerptor may lose patience," Brunt 1980, 484.

make impossible demands: it would be impossible to raise the fallen and deliver the dead as hostages"; in Peter, they beg him "not to seek the impossible, asking for the dead as hostages."[91] (2) In Eunapius the king's son is described as "alone a guarantee of peace"; in Peter "alone sufficing in place of many."[92] (3) In Eunapius, Julian claims that (indirect speech) "now he was seeking the best men among them lest they use deceit in the matter of peace"; in Peter, Julian claims that (same construction) "now he was seeking sureties for peace if there were any men among them reliable in this matter."[93] Either both texts derive from the same Greek source or (much more probably) Peter is summarizing Eunapius.[94] Note that all three passages occur in reported speech or speeches. That is to say, this is not a case where similarities can be explained by common subject matter. In the form in which we have it, which consists of little but speeches delivered by a barbarian king (and so not likely to have been recorded by court stenographers), Eunapius may have virtually invented the episode. Not even Ammianus's ample narrative of Julian's campaigns finds room for the story.[95] Since Peter is the only remotely plausible candidate for a Byzantine historian with a reading knowledge of Latin and a potential source of Zonaras, this is virtually enough by itself to scotch the Bleckmann-Paschoud solution.

Bleckmann and Paschoud dismissed the possibility that the lost source of Zonaras was Eunapius without serious discussion, more on the basis of their conviction that they had firmly established the superior credentials of Flavian's *Annales* than from any positive objections to Eunapius. The fact that some parts of Zonaras's account of the years 350–64 actually offer more detail than Ammianus clearly implies an extremely full narrative. This at once narrows the field of possible candidates. The only large-scale near-contemporary narrative we know of apart from Ammianus is Eunapius. Other objections aside, the claim that Flavian's *Annales* provided a large-scale narrative is circular, an assumption based on what it is supposed to be proving: that Flavian was Zonaras's source. The larger and more influential we assume the *Annales* to have been, the more of a problem it becomes that not a single reference to or quotation from it survives.

Let us take for comparison an undoubtedly influential lost work that is nowhere directly attested: the *KG*. The *KG* cannot have been significantly more detailed than its various derivatives and continuations, which in turn explains why it disappeared without trace. This cannot have been true of Flavian's *Annales* as imagined by its modern admirers. Why then did it disappear so completely? If its disappearance is attributed to

---

91. Eunapius: δεόμενοι μηδὲν ἀδύνατον ἐπιτάττεσθαι· ἀδύνατον δὲ αὐτοῖς εἶναι καὶ τοὺς πεσόντας ἀναστῆσαι καὶ ὁμήρους δοῦναι τοὺς τετελευτηκότας. Peter: ἐδέοντο τοῦ Καίσαρος ἀδύνατα μὴ ζητεῖν, ἀπαιτοῦντα τοὺς ἤδη τεθνεῶτας ὁμήρους.

92. Eunapius: μόνον ἀντάξιον εἰρήνης. Peter: ἀντὶ πολλῶν μόνον ἀρκοῦντα.

93. Eunapius: νυνὶ δὲ ζητεῖν παρ' αὐτῶν τοὺς ἀρίστους, εἰ μὴ τεχνάζουσι περὶ τὴν εἰρήνην; Peter: νῦν δὲ ζητεῖν εἰρήνης ἐνέχυρα, εἴ τινες εἶεν πρὸς τοῦτο παρ᾽ αὐτοῖς ἐπιτήδειοι.

94. So (e.g.) Blockley 1981, 98; and Ochoa 1990, 259–62.

95. *pacem hoc tribuit pacto ut ad sua redirent incolumes* is all he says of the treaty with the Chamavi (xvii. 8. 5).

its aggressive paganism, that conflicts with its supposed enormous influence on the Christian Byzantine tradition, an uncomfortable and improbable paradox. Eunapius was also aggressively anti-Christian, yet although his history did not survive in its entirety, we have hundreds of quotations and what amounts to an abridgement in Zosimus. The obvious, inevitable explanation for the fact that whatever Flavian wrote disappeared so completely is that it was not an influential work and disappeared early.

One other obvious objection to the identification of this common source as Flavian is that much of the relevant part of Zonaras's narrative concerns eastern affairs. Since Flavian seems never to have visited the East,[96] his history cannot have contained any firsthand coverage of fourth-century eastern affairs. He cannot have visited the sites or interrogated participants over many years as Ammianus did. It is difficult to believe that Ammianus would have paid any serious attention to anything Flavian wrote about eastern affairs. Why would easterners want a Greek version of a Latin history that (if it existed at all) must have been largely based on Greek sources? However unsatisfactory Eunapius's History, for eastern affairs he is bound to have had much better sources than an armchair historian writing in Rome.

Bleckmann's objections to Eunapius as (ultimate) source are in essence (1) that there are no significant parallels between this section of Zonaras and Zosimus; and (2) that (citing Paschoud as his authority), Eunapius's history was a "trivial historical pamphlet."[97] Even on its own terms the first objection makes no sense. There are certainly some parallels, and Bleckmann and Paschoud appear to have forgotten that, on their own hypothesis, Zosimus/Eunapius also derives from Flavian! On their own theory, the fact that Zonaras is closer here to Ammianus than Zosimus would not prove that Zonaras did not use Eunapius; only that Eunapius followed Flavian less closely in this section than Zonaras's direct source, for them Peter the Patrician. Flavian is supposed to be the ultimate source of all these writers.[98]

As for the objection that Eunapius is "trivial," that is a subjective judgement by a modern scholar, and it is absurd to use the depreciatory term "pamphlet" of a work in the grand style (set speeches, battle descriptions, digressions, historical exempla, moralising reflections)[99] in fourteen books. Whatever its shortcomings, in the Byzantine world Eunapius's was undoubtedly considered the standard history of the period it covered (270–404).

There are only two respects in which Eunapius's history does not fit Bleckmann's characterization of the lost source as well as Flavian's *Annales*. First, senatorial bias. But such bias as we find in Zonaras's narrative for the late third century is likely to reflect the bias of the written sources available to any later historian, pagan or Christian, Greek or

---

96. On the early chronology, Flavian was quaestor at court in Constantinople, but that chronology cannot be sustained. Not that a busy bureaucrat would have had much spare time for historical research while in office.

97. "ein triviales Geschichtspamphlet," Bleckmann 1992, 398–99; cf. Paschoud 1994, 79.

98. As can be seen from the stemma in Paschoud 1994, 80.

99. On all these features of Eunapius's History, see Blockley 1981, 10–15.

Roman. There is little trace of senatorial perspective for the fourth century, when Flavian would have been writing from personal knowledge. It is true that Zonaras's surprisingly favorable obituary for Constantius II praises him for, among other excellent qualities, "never admitting anyone into the senate who was not a man of culture, a good speaker and a skilled composer in both prose and verse." For Bleckmann, this "clearly betrays the outlook of senatorial circles,"[100] which would fit Flavian. But it would be odd for Flavian to praise so warmly the emperor who first removed the altar of Victory from the senate house, and when did Constantius concern himself with the composition of the Roman senate? On the other hand, in 359 Constantius famously gave Themistius the job of recruiting 1,700 new members for the senate of Constantinople.[101] Predictably enough, Themistius praised his literary culture.[102] Zonaras's remark surely reflects the perspective of a Greek writing about the radical expansion of the senate of Constantinople. As for the condition that the lost source should be Latin, that we may surely now forget about. It is impossible to believe that any Byzantine writer would weigh a detailed narrative in Greek by a well-known writer against a similarly detailed Latin source and reject the Greek text. In one crucial respect Eunapius actually fits the blueprint better: unlike Flavian, he wrote before Ammianus.

Yet another problem with the postulate of Flavian's *Annales* as the lost source is (paradoxically) what true believers see as its greatest advantage: the very fact that we know nothing about it. It is not surprising that what is in effect an imaginary work can be argued to fit the bill so perfectly. It is impossible to raise concrete objections to a work about which we know absolutely nothing. Believers are free to assume that Zonaras reproduces Flavian's narrative in extenso more or less exactly and literally, right down to mistranslations of the original Latin. We should also bear in mind that our impression of Eunapius is largely based on Zosimus's undoubtedly incompetent abridgment, which may be more misleading than we are in a position to appreciate. Epitomes of long historical works are usually less systematic abridgements than anthologies, reproducing some episodes almost in full while completing omitting many others. This is particularly clear in the case of Xiphilinus's epitome of Dio, which is less a précis of the whole than an eccentric selection of excerpts.[103]

Bleckmann was not even deterred by the fact that, to judge from Zonaras, this supposed Latin source evidently quoted Greek oracles at length and entire lines of Homer, unthinkable in the traditionalist Roman history the *Annales* is supposed to be. Here we might add that the Anonymus Continuator represents Licinius (a man of peasant stock) quoting two lines of Homer.[104] This is not the sort of detail the down-to-earth

---

100. Zonaras xiii. 11. 13; surprising, because Constantius was an Arian (as Zonaras notes); Bleckmann 1992, 369–70.

101. On Constantius's senate, see Heather 1994, 11–33. Libanius mocked the new senators as parvenus, but he was an old-fashioned civic patriot who hated the drain of local elites to the capital.

102. Them. *Or.* 4. 6, 54 AB.

103. F. Millar, *A Study of Cassius Dio* (Oxford 1964), 2; Brunt 1980, at 487–92.

104. F 14 = *FHG* iv. 199 = *Exc.* 188 in Boissevain's Dio, vol. 3. 748.

Peter would have added to his source, which must therefore have been Greek, not Latin. Bleckmann misleadingly cites Ammianus as a parallel, but then Ammianus not only quite openly wrote as a Greek,[105] but undoubtedly consulted Greek sources. Even more misleadingly Bleckmann cites Macrobius's *Saturnalia* as proof that the "cultivated senatorial circles" frequented by Symmachus and Flavian liked to cite Greek verses.[106] But not only is this to confuse genres; it is to make the more serious error of supposing that Macrobius's dialogue reflects genuine contemporary symposia when in fact he derived all his Homer quotations from secondary sources (p. 532). The one name Bleckmann does not cite is Eunapius. Yet even the scanty surviving fragments of his *History* cite two oracles, an epitaph in four hexameters, and a number of complete lines of Homer (*Lives of the Sophists* is also full of oracles and Homer quotations).[107] If we are looking for a large-scale fourth-century pagan history with a taste for oracles and quotations from Homer, Eunapius is clearly the front-runner.

According to Ammianus, when Constantius II clad Julian in the imperial purple and proclaimed him Caesar, Julian punningly whispered to himself the Homeric line "I am in the grip of purple death and irresistible fate." One of the Salmasian excerpts of John of Antioch repeats the anecdote.[108] While no one will believe that Licinius quoted Homer, Julian cites Homer by name no fewer than forty-five times in various writings. It is entirely plausible that he thought of this line as he donned the purple. Eunapius undoubtedly knew the story, because he refers in *Lives of the Sophists* to a failed usurper "being brought purple death instead of a purple robe."[109]

Ammianus, Zosimus, and Zonaras all preserve an astrological prophecy of the date of Constantius II's death in four hexameters that supposedly came to Julian in a dream.[110] Bleckmann's claim that Zonaras's text agrees with Ammianus against Zosimus overstates the case (the only significant variant in Zosimus might as easily be late as early). More important, how did two such personal stories get into the main historical tradition? The obvious guess is that Julian told them to Oribasius, who included them in the memoir he wrote for the exclusive use of Eunapius.[111]

Finally, there are the three separate Homeric quotations in John of Antioch's account of the hostile reception of Jovian in Antioch after his unfavorable peace treaty with Persia. First, three complete lines with a neat parodic alteration: where Odysseus threatens to send Thersites "back to the ships" (*epi nēas*), some wit substituted "back

---

105. For example, "visa nocturna, quas φαντασίας *nos* appell*amus*" (xiv. 11. 18) and similar passages (Matthews 1989, 462) where he speaks as a Greek in his text.

106. Bleckmann 1995, 86.

107. F 28. 6B = 26M (oracle); F 28. 4B = 24M (oracle); F 43. 3B = 45M (epitaph); F 56, 59, 72. 1B = 65, 60, 87M (1, 2 and 2 lines of Homer); F 27. 7 = 27M (from the Suda) = *Anth. Pal.* xiv. 148, though described as an oracle, is really from a panegyric on Julian, and may not derive from Eunapius.

108. ἔλλαβε πορφύρεος θάνατος καὶ μοῖρα κραταιή, *Iliad* v. 83; Amm. xv. 8. 17; John F 176 M = 263 R.

109. Bouffartigue 1992, 60–61; *Vit. Soph.* vi. 3. 13 (464).

110. Amm. xxi. 2. 2; Zos. iii. 9. 6; Zon. xiii. 11. 10; the astrology seems to be correct (Paschoud on ii. 1 [1979], 89).

111. Eun. F 15 B = 8 M. There is simply no basis for Paschoud's assertion (*Zosime* 1² [2000], 1) that Ammianus too consulted Oribasius's memoir: Bowersock 1978, 8.

to the Persians" (*epi Persas*). Second, Hector's reproach to Paris, opening "Paris, you handsome fellow," ironically alluding to Jovian's good looks. Third, Helen to Paris: "You have come from the battlefield; I wish you had died there."[112] Ammianus was in Antioch at the time and must have known about Jovian's reception, but in his own account of the emperor's brief stay he chose to focus on omens of his death, no doubt reckoning that appreciation of this sophisticated abuse required a deeper Greek culture than he could count on in his Latin-speaking readers. Then in the very next paragraph Ammianus describes Jovian adorning the tomb of Julian by the river Cydnus just outside Tarsus. In parallel accounts (all three locate the monument in a "suburb" of Tarsus)[113] Zosimus and Zonaras both include the inscription on the tomb, four hexameter lines.[114] Again, Ammianus was there and must have seen and read the inscription in person, but he did not include it. Zonaras omitted Jovian's reception in Antioch but included the inscription, adding that Julian's body was subsequently moved from Tarsus to Constantinople. It looks as if Zonaras's source included at least eight and a half lines of Greek hexameters[115] that Ammianus omitted. This source cannot possibly have been a traditional history written in Latin.

11: JOHN OF ANTIOCH

While building on the work of Patzig and even using his antiquated terminology, Bleckmann rejected Patzig's identification of the "Leo-source," the text that allegedly mediated Flavian's *Annales* to the Byzantine world, as John of Antioch and substituted Peter the Patrician, an identification accepted without question or discussion by his followers.[116] But there is nothing beyond Peter's likely knowledge of Latin in favor of this identification. As elsewhere, the Achilles' heel of the Bleckmann-Paschoud doctrine is evidence.

In the first place, our excerpts of Peter stop in 358, with Julian as Caesar in Gaul; and the excerpts of the Anonymus Continuator stop with Constantine. It is true that the Vatican palimpsest that alone carries the latter excerpts is missing a folio at this point, leaving open the possibility that the excerpts continued for a few more years. But given the uncertainty of the identification with Peter, this falls well short of proving that Peter himself continued beyond 358. On the evidence we have, Peter's history did not reach as far as the period where Zonaras's narrative runs in parallel with Ammianus's.

---

112. Jo. Ant. F 181 M = 273 R = Eun. F 29 Blockley; Homer, *Il.* ii. 261–63; iii. 39 (Δύσπαρι, εἶδος ἄριστε, καὶ τὰ ἑξῆς, Hector to Paris); iii. 428 (ἤλυθες ἐκ πολέμου· ὡς ὤφελες αὐτόθ' ὀλέσθαι, Helen to Paris).

113. ἐν προαστείῳ, Zon. and Zos.; *in pomerio situm itineris* (more pretentiously) Ammianus.

114. On the various versions of the inscription, P. Grierson, *DOP* 16 (1962), 40–41.

115. At least, because καὶ τὰ ἑξῆς after three words of iii. 39 implies that the original text included a few more lines.

116. Ratti 1997, 503, even seems to have thought that the identification with Peter was Patzig's idea!

The reason the identification of Peter with Continuator is so important to Bleckmann is that the evidence for a link with Zonaras is much stronger for Continuator[117] than it is for Peter. While there is no doubt that Zonaras drew on Continuator or a closely related source for the third century, there are no comparable links between Zonaras and the relevant surviving excerpts of Peter.[118] For the period 350–64 only three excerpts of Peter come into question, and of these three only one is reflected in Zonaras, the account of an embassy to Constantius II from the usurpers Magnentius and Vetranio.[119] Even if we include Continuator, there are no excerpts that reach 350.

Nor is there any evidence that Peter's history exercised the influence on middle Byzantine chroniclers and historians that led Patzig to postulate his "Leo-source" in the first place. With the exception of a couple of quotations in an eleventh-century grammatical text,[120] Peter's history is known to us exclusively from the Constantinian excerpts. John of Antioch, on the other hand, fits the role of intermediary in every respect. His narrative continues down to the beginning of the seventh century, was clearly well known to the middle Byzantine historians, and (unlike Peter's) is represented in several different sets of excerpts.[121] More specifically, four excerpts of John offer close parallels with Ammianus, and six episodes treated in surviving excerpts of John (including two of the four just mentioned) reappear, usually with verbal parallels, in Zonaras.

Study of John has been bedeviled by a long-standing debate about the date and nature of his history. For the period of the empire we have two different sets of excerpts: the Constantinian and Salmasian. The Salmasian are less classicizing in language, more anecdotal, and appear to derive from different sources. The standard way of resolving the debate has been to dismiss one or the other sets as inauthentic, and Bleckmann falls into the camp that dismisses the Salmasian, the source of six out of the eight under discussion. The new edition of Mariev not only omits the Salmasian excerpts, but any Constantinian excerpts that do not come up to his stylistic standard.[122] There are less simplistic solutions. Since his narrative runs from the Creation (via the Trojan War) to his own day, inevitably John drew on a wide variety of sources, some in popular (Malalas), some in elevated Greek (Eunapius). Since he copied his sources almost verbatim, the linguistic and stylistic level of his work must have varied wildly according to the source he was following at the time. Furthermore, the long

---

117. See de Boor 1892, 21; Potter 1990, 360–61; Bleckmann 1992, 44; see Mueller's notes in *FHG* iv. 193–99.

118. Zonaras xii. 31 mentions Galerius's defeat of Persia and the peace treaty of 299, but there is no hint of the detailed account of the negotiations in Peter F 13–14, discussed above.

119. Peter F 16 ~ Zonaras xiii. 7. 18–22.

120. F 1 in *FHG* iv. 184: Lex. Seg. in Bekker, *Anecd. Gr.* i. 117 and 130: Krumbacher, *Gesch. Byz. Lit.*[2] (1897), 572.

121. Tabulated in the editions of Roberto (2005), clvii–clxvi; and Mariev (2008), 17~–30~.

122. On Roberto's edition (2005), Cameron 2006; on Mariev's, M. Whittow, *BMCR* 2009.12.06; Roberto, *JÖB* 2010; Treadgold, *Speculum* 2010.

Athos fragment on the late Republic (our closest witness to the original form of the work) has revealed that John systematically combined two or more sources, adding details from Dio and Plutarch to a basic "Eutropian" framework. Thus the apparent difference in sources between the two series proves no more than the difference in style, especially in short excerpts. Mariev dates John to the 520s on the grounds that excerpts that go down to the seventh century do not come up to his stylistic standards. But the last few decades are likely to have been his own work, in what was no doubt his own rather popular Greek.[123]

The stylistic difference may also be explained by another factor. Roberto plausibly argues that the Salmasian excerpts represent an epitome of the full text. This epitome rather than the full history would be Patzig's Leo-source. But whether the Salmasian excerpts derive from real John or Pseudo-John, their links with Ammianus and Zonaras are real, and cannot be excluded from the discussion. Here is the most explicit of these links, the trial of a certain Numerius, a former governor of Gallia Narbonensis accused of embezzlement:

Amm. xviii. 1. 4:	John F 178 M = 269 R:	Zonaras 13. 12.8–9:
Numerius defended himself by denying the charge, and his defense could not be shaken. The lack of proof so infuriated Delphidius, who was attacking him violently in a fiery speech for the prosecution, that he exclaimed: "Can anyone, mighty Caesar, ever be found guilty if it be enough to deny the charge?" On the spur of the moment Julian shrewdly replied: "Will anyone ever be acquitted if accusation is enough to secure a conviction?"	Numerius was being accused by someone for embezzling public funds (ὡς κεκλοφὼς δημόσια χρήματα). He denied the charge. The prosecutor, having no proofs, said: "Will any defendant (τίς, ἔφη), best of emperors, be found guilty if denial is enough to secure acquittal?" Julian replied: "Who (καὶ τίς) will be found innocent if the prosecutor is believed without proofs" (εἰ ὁ κατήγορος ἐλέγχων χωρὶς πιστεύοιτο)?	[Julian] was once trying a man who was accused of embezzling public funds (κεκλοφέναι...δημόσια χρήματα) but denied the charge. "Who, emperor," said the prosecutor (τίς, ἔφη), "will be found guilty when accused if it benefits the accused simply to deny the charge?" Julian replied: "Who (καὶ τίς) will be found innocent if prosecutors are believed without proofs" (εἰ ἐλέγχων ἄνευ πιστεύοιντο οἱ κατήγοροι)?

The articulation of the two speeches is identical in all three accounts. Patzig improbably assumed that John drew directly on Ammianus, but it is impossible to believe that his Latin was good enough to read so long and difficult a Latin text. A common

---

123. Whitby 1990; Whittow 2009; see too Treadgold 2007, 311–29.

Greek source is the inevitable solution. In theory, Flavian might have told the story (if he covered the period at all), but this was not a major event that might have been recorded in any history of the period. The original source must have been someone present in court during this minor (and apparently unsuccessful) prosecution in Gaul. Neither Flavian nor Ammianus was with Julian in Gaul. The obvious guess is Julian's friend Oribasius, who was there. An excerpt from Eunapius reports another saying of Julian, this time actually addressed to Oribasius, and so certainly deriving from this memoir.[124] The clinching detail here is that John undoubtedly drew on Eunapius elsewhere, in one case copying him verbatim.[125] We may confidently conclude that Ammianus and John both got the Numerius story from Eunapius, and that Zonaras got it (as the verbal parallels prove beyond question) from John. In the juxtaposition of these three texts we have a perfect illustration of (Salmasian) John of Antioch serving as intermediary between a fourth-century history (whoever the author) and Zonaras.

There are also three other cases. (1) John F 176 M = 265 R offers a parallel with Ammianus not repeated in Zonaras: among a series of omens, Constantius II had a vision a few days before his death in which his father held out to him a beautiful child who knocked the globe he was holding—a symbol of imperial rule—out of his right hand and threw it some distance away.[126] (2) Both Ammianus and John tell the story just quoted of Julian whispering a line of Homer as he donned the purple for the first time. Finally (3), John and Zonaras give parallel accounts of the cruelty of the Persian prince Adarnarses followed by the story of the escape to the Romans of his imprisoned brother Hormisdas. There is a similar account of Hormisdas's escape in Zosimus, and since Ammianus states that he too gave an account in one of his lost books,[127] this may fairly be counted as another parallel between Ammianus and Zonaras. Paschoud assumed that Ammianus and Zosimus derived here from Flavian,[128] but both Zosimus and John are known to have drawn on Eunapius. Yet whatever the ultimate common source in any of these cases, John's role as intermediary is firmly established.

There are also a number of episodes that, though missing from Ammianus, appear not only in John and Zonaras but also in the Chronikon of Symeon Logothete and in Cedrenus. For example, while still a tribune, Jovian once trod on Julian's purple robe. The emperor turned round and said "at least it's a man," apparently interpreting the accident as an omen of Jovian's future elevation.[129] Then there is the story that Valentinian had the chamberlain Rhodanus burned alive for defrauding a widow.[130]

---

124. πρὸς τὸν Ὀριβάσιον εἰπόντα... εἶπεν, F 24 M = 28. 2 B.
125. Sotiroudis 1989, 129–35; Roberto 2005, cxli–cxliii.
126. Alföldi 1970, 235–38. Opinions differ as to whether the child is Constantius's genius or Julian: see the commentary by den Boeft, den Hengst, and Teitler (1991).
127. Jo. F 178 M = 266 B; Zonaras xiii. 5. 21–24; Zos. ii. 27; Amm. xvi. 10. 16.
128. "on songe évidemment aux *Annales* de Nicomache Flavien," *Zosime* 1² (2000), 232.
129. Jo. F 178. 4 M = 270 R; Symeon § 91. 1 Wahlgren; Cedrenus 539. 10–15; Zonaras xiii. 14. 21–23.
130. Jo. F 183 M = 275 R; Symeon § 92. 4; Cedrenus 544. 5–12; Zonaras xiii. 15. 14.

Though not including this case, Ammianus mentions another official Valentinian burned alive. The incident is placed in Constantinople, so must have fallen in March or April 364, before Valentinian left to spend the rest of his reign in the West.[131] Here we might add the stories about Dagalaifus's advice to Valentinian (also located in Constantinople) and Jovian being too tall for the imperial robes, both of which appear in Ammianus, Symeon, and Cedrenus.

For Bleckmann, such details illustrate the central role played by his "Leo-source." But why single out Leo—or rather Symeon? Thanks to Wahlgren, we now have what is in effect the editio princeps of the Chronikon of Symeon Logothete. Among other things, we have learned that countless details (including the transfer of Julian's body to Constantinople, and the lack of a purple robe long enough to fit Jovian), do not appear in the earliest manuscripts.[132] The chronicle was evidently expanded piecemeal over the years. The version to which Bleckmann, Paschoud, and company appeal, the so-called Leo Grammaticus edited by Bekker (1842), is in fact the most interpolated of all. The information on these topics offered by later manuscripts is not likely to have come from the same source Symeon himself consulted centuries earlier.[133] That is to say, there was not even a single "Leo-source."

Let us recapitulate the episodes just discussed, identifying the texts that include them by letters of the alphabet: A (= Ammianus), J (= John), S (= Symeon), and Z (= Zonaras); (1) the Numerius story (AJZ); (2) the Adanarses/Hormisdas stories (AJZ); (3) the child and globe story (AJ); the "purple death" story (AJ); (5) Jovian treading on Julian's robe (JSZ); (6) the burning of Rhodanus (JSZ); (7) imperial robes too short for Jovian (AS); Dagalaifus's advice (AS). John appears in six of the eight, and the fact that episodes (7) and (8) are missing from the fairly random selection of excerpts that have come down to us does not prove that they were not in the full text of his history. All but one of the eight date from after the last datable event recorded by Peter the Patrician.

All four episodes that appear in Symeon also appear in Cedrenus, who has already been mentioned a number of times in the preceding pages. Georgius Cedrenus himself is a late eleventh- or twelfth-century historian whose direct source for this period is known to have been an unpublished tenth-century text known faute de mieux as Pseudo-Symeon.[134] Fortunately, the question of Pseudo-Symeon's main source for the period is also established; he is known to have drawn extensively on John of Antioch.[135] Sometimes (e.g., in the case of Dagalaifus's advice to Valentinian) Cedrenus gives verbatim the same version as Symeon. But there are also cases where he offers significant additional information or information entirely missing in Symeon. First, two linked

131. Amm. xxvii. 7. 5; Lenski 2002, 105, 273.
132. Wahlgren 2003, 269–77.
133. Which is not to say that it did not derive, directly or indirectly, from a different redaction of the same chronicle.
134. Chron. Par. gr. 1712ff. 18ᵛ–272; for bibliography, Markopoulos 1985, 208.
135. Markopoulos 1978, 66–73; Roberto 2005, clxiii–clxvi.

stories: the usurper Procopius was executed by being tied to two trees bent over and then released, and Valens took his revenge on Chalcedon for supporting Procopius by demolishing its walls and discovering an oracle written on one of the stones.[136] Here Cedrenus offers essentially the same version as Zonaras, and an excerpt of John a somewhat abbreviated version. But there is nothing at all in Symeon. This is a particularly intriguing case, because there can be little doubt that John's direct source was Socrates, who tells both stories in quick succession. Where did Socrates find them? To judge from Zosimus, Eunapius did not have the tree story, which first appears in Socrates.[137] But in view of his well-documented interest in oracles, it is tempting to infer that Eunapius was the common source of Ammianus and Socrates for the oracle. Both, like Cedrenus and Zonaras (but not Symeon), cite the entire text, nine hexameters, in full, making another link between Ammianus and Zonaras. But whatever the chain of transmission, Zonaras's direct source was not the "Leo-source" (Symeon), but once again the full text of John of Antioch.

According to Ammianus, those who accuse Julian of starting war with Persia "should be aware that it was Constantine, not Julian, who kindled the Parthian conflagration, because his greed led him to believe the lies of Metrodorus, of which I gave a full account earlier." According to Cedrenus, a philosopher called Metrodorus went to India, whence he brought back jewels he was planning (he said) to present to Constantine, but the Persians intercepted and refused to surrender them, and war resulted.[138] Not surprisingly, no one has ever taken this very seriously, but Ammianus's reference to both lies and Constantine's greed suggests that he was alluding to something very like Cedrenus's story, and Metrodorus the philosopher and his voyage to India are known from other sources.[139] Whatever the value of the story as an explanation of war with Persia, clearly Cedrenus did not make it up. The ultimate source must have been a contemporary defense of Julian's unsuccessful Persian campaign, probably pagan and surely Greek (Libanius, e.g., accuses Constantine of "sowing the seeds of war with Persia").[140] The obvious guess is Eunapius, but we are on firmer ground in concluding that, here as elsewhere, Cedrenus's direct source was John of Antioch.

Bleckmann and his followers took it for granted that Zonaras's account of the century or so preceding the period of overlap with Ammianus also derived from the "Leo-source." Nearly two hundred pages of Baldini's *Storie Perdute* (2000) are devoted to reconstructing what is alleged to be Flavian's narrative of the third century on this basis. Yet there are remarkably few significant parallels between Symeon and Zonaras for the period from Aurelian to Diocletian—not nearly so many (e.g.) as between the

---

136. Jo. F 184. 1 M = 276 R; Cedrenus 542. 19–543. 12; Zonaras xiii. 16. 29–32.

137. According to Ammianus (xxvi. 9. 9), he was simply beheaded; for the various versions, Lenski 2002, 81.

138. Amm. xxv. 4. 23 (Hamilton, adapted); Cedrenus 516. 15–517. 4 (simplified).

139. *PLRE* i. 601; Warmington 1981, 464–68; Matthews 1989, 135–36; Bleckmann 1991, 358–62.

140. Lib. *Or.* 49. 2; cf. 18. 206.

Anonymus Continuator and Zonaras. Nor are there any significant parallels between Continuator and Symeon, although both are supposed to be versions of the "Leo-source," namely Flavian's *Annales*.

The few there are between Symeon and Zonaras derive from John of Antioch, not Peter or Continuator. For example, one of the three sentences Symeon allots to the emperor Probus (276–82) describes the miracle of the thunderstorm that rained grain, which people gathered up in heaps. This story first appears in Zosimus, then in Symeon, Cedrenus, and finally Zonaras. The Symeon/Cedrenus version is copied verbatim from a Salmasian excerpt of John of Antioch, while the Zonaras version gives a little more detail, a classic case of Symeon following the epitome of John (the real "Leo-source") while Zonaras derives from a fuller version.[141]

When mentioning Diocletian's Roman triumph of 303, Symeon, Cedrenus, and Zonaras all digress on the word *triumph* (*thriambos*), offering a series of overlapping etymologies. It was not inevitable that three different Byzantine writers should pick on this rather than countless earlier Roman triumphs as a peg on which to hang an etymology of the word (the earlier books of Zonaras list more than twenty triumphs), and a common source is obviously indicated. By good fortune it survives: an excerpt (naturally) of John of Antioch.[142] All four texts mention *thria*, fig-leaves sacred to Dionysus; Cedrenus follows John with poems on Dionysus (known as *thriamboi*);[143] Symeon and Cedrenus follow John in suggesting "poetic rapture" (*thriasis*); and Zonaras has an explanation missing in all the others: the three elements that made up the procession—senate, people, and soldiers—with the *tau* in *treis* changed to a *theta* for euphony.[144] All in all the classic pointers to a common source. There can be little doubt that Symeon, Cedrenus, and Zonaras all derive from a fuller text of John.

It might seem tempting to trace a digression on so basic a Roman institution as the triumph back to Nicomachus Flavianus. But the phonetic change alone proves that the Greek term came to Rome via Etruria, and Roman triumphs had nothing to do with Dionysus.[145] The etymologies collected by John are purely Greek, some of them obviously fanciful. Zonaras's explanation in terms of the three elements in society might look Roman, but his *theta* reveals that it is the Greek term he is explaining (in Latin, both *tres* and *triumphus* begin with a *t*). John's etymologies are the same sort of Byzantine pseudo-Roman antiquarianism we identified in Zosimus's chapter on the pontifex maximus, and, predictably enough, there is a selection of etymologies for *triumphus* (or rather *thriambos*) in John the Lydian, all different from those offered by John of Antioch, but, like his, all Greek, not Roman.

---

141. Zos. i. 67. 1; Jo. Ant. F 159 M = 242R; Symeon § 84. 1; Cedrenus 463. 12; Zonaras xii. 29 (iii. 155. 19–22 D).
142. Jo. Ant. F 167. 1 M = 250 R (Suda Θ 494, with a briefer Salmasian excerpt); Symeon § 86. 2; Cedren. 470. 22–472. 4; Zonar. xii. 32 (iii. 163. 20–164. 6 Dindorf).
143. A. W. Pickard-Cambridge, *Dithyramb, Tragedy and Comedy*[2] (Oxford 1962), 8.
144. An etymology found in Suetonius (Isidore, *Orig*. 18. 2. 3); M. Beard, *The Roman Triumph* (2007), 313.
145. Weinstock 1971, 65–66; H. J. Versnel, *Triumphus* (Leiden 1970); Bonfante Warren 1970, 108–20.

A more complex case is the various explanations for the sudden death of Jovian after a reign of only six months on 17 February 364. Eutropius offers three possibilities: (1) vapours from newly plastered walls; (2) fumes from the brazier in his bedroom; (3) overeating.[146] Jerome and the Epitome each repeat two of these, Ammianus all three, though Ammianus, like Jerome, includes the place, Dadastana, missing from Eutropius. The simplest hypothesis is that all four derive from a common source, the *KG*, most fully reproduced by Ammianus. Zonaras has plaster, fumes, too much wine (instead of food), and Dadastana, but also adds a fourth possibility, poisoned mushrooms. The poisoned mushrooms first appear in John of Antioch and then, in the identical participial phrase, in Symeon and Cedrenus.[147] But the John excerpt has only the mushrooms. According to Ratti, this proves that Zonaras cannot have got his information from John.[148] Not so fast. The excerpt in question devotes one of its two sentences to the mushroom story, and the second translates Eutropius/*KG*, who (as we have seen) had the other three explanations. Since he undoubtedly had the relevant section of Eutropius/*KG* in front of him as he wrote, John must have known the other three explanations as well, and it is likely that the full text of his narrative included them. Symeon just has John's three words, but Cedrenus, who (as we have seen) drew on John at one remove, begins with the first two of Eutropius's three and then adds "but as some say" before repeating John's three words.[149] That the full text of John listed Eutropius's three explanations and then the mushrooms separately is strongly suggested by Zonaras, who also offers two groups, introduced by similar formulas ("as some say" the mushroom story; "as others" the other three versions). Here we have the sequence Eutropius/*KG* > John of Antioch > Symeon/Cedrenus > Zonaras. But since Zonaras preserves more of the John version than either Symeon or Cedrenus, the natural conclusion is that Zonaras derived from the original text of John, or at any rate from a much fuller epitome than the Salmasian excerpts. The author of the surviving excerpt, understandably feeling that one explanation was quite enough for so short-lived an emperor, dropped the second group and made do with the more colorful poisoned mushrooms. One final direct link between John and Zonaras is that both use the same phrase "since it was winter," in Zonaras's detailed version explaining the need for a brazier.[150]

Ratti's explanation (of course) was that all these texts derive from Flavian's *Annales*. It is just a bizarre coincidence that Zonaras, writing in Greek in the twelfth century,

---

146. The three suggestions are not so much alternatives as contributory factors (the combined effect of damp plaster and fumes on a man unable to shake off an unusually heavy sleep).

147. μύκητα πεφαρμαγμένον φαγών, Jo. Ant. F 181 note = 273. 2. 22; Symeon § 91. 2 Wahlgren; Cedrenus 540. 17–21; Zonaras xiii. 14. 11–12.

148. Ratti 1997, 503.

149. For Cedrenus's use of John, see Roberto in *JÖB* 2010.

150. χειμῶνος ὄντος; a further link between Symeon, Cedrenus, and Zonaras is that they are the only surviving sources to record the name of Jovian's wife, Charito. It is hard to doubt that this too stood in the full text of John.

preserves more of this Latin Urtext than Eutropius and Ammianus, who (unlike Flavian) were both present in Dadastana at the time! But other objections aside, in this case there are two additional problems. First, the poisoned mushrooms are surely a later embellishment,[151] nor can their source be in doubt: the most famous poisoned mushrooms in history, those that are supposed to have killed an earlier emperor, Claudius. By a lucky chance we have John's account of Claudius's death, excerpted from Dio:[152] Claudius was so drunk that he did not suspect anything. This is why John, followed by Zonaras, substituted an excess of wine for food in his account of Jovian's death. Second, in order to serve as a source for Eutropius, Flavian's *Annales* would have to have been published before 370. Discarding the only two facts we have (dedication to Theodosius and publication in or soon after 390), Ratti posits a "first edition" published more than thirty years earlier![153]

12: CONCLUSION

But the real problem with the Bleckmann-Paschoud doctrine is not just the many different objections in detail raised throughout this and the last chapter. It is the mere idea that any single late antique source lies, in anything approaching its original state, behind any Byzantine historical epitome. In his earlier books Zonaras never confines himself to a single source unless it was all he had. For example, he devotes five books (7–11) to Roman history from Aeneas to Nerva, mainly based on Dio but with extensive insertions from the relevant biographies of Plutarch.[154] Since so much Plutarch survives, it is a simple matter to isolate Dio by subtracting Plutarch. But if either had completely perished, we would have been reduced to guesswork.

To judge from the material collected in the last two sections, much of the Zonaras/ Ammianus overlap probably derives from Eunapius via John. But it should not be thought that I am playing the same game as Bleckmann/Paschoud, simply changing the names (John of Antioch and Eunapius instead of Peter the Patrician and Flavian). For the late third-century Zonaras drew extensively on the Anonymus Continuator as well as John (his Dio manuscript may have been equipped with the same sort of continuation as the surviving Vaticanus graecus 73). There are no straightforward solutions in the identification of the ancient sources of Byzantine historical epitomes. For the fourth century John himself drew on a variety of sources. As before, he

---

151. Chrysostom claims that an unnamed emperor who must be Jovian was "plotted against by his own guards" (*PG* 48. 605; B. Grillet and G. R. Ettlinger, *Jean Chrys. À une jeune veuve* (Paris 1968), 138; and another passage of Chrysostom alleges poison (*PG* 62. 295), but no hint of mushrooms.

152. F 89 M = 171 R; cf. Boissevain's *Dio* iii. 16 and 754–55.

153. Ratti 1997, 507–8; 2003, 213–14, following Paschoud, *RÉL* 53 (1975), 94. Baldini 1999 postulates a Nicomachus continuatus that takes the story down to 410, where Flavian himself would have stopped if he had been allowed to live another twenty years.

154. For the sources of Zonaras 1–12, the detailed 1839 analysis by W. A. Schmidt reprinted in volume 6 (1875) of Dindorf's edition (pp. iii–lx) is still indispensable.

continued to use Eutropius (or the *KG*) for a general framework, and for detail he used not only Eunapius but also Zosimus and (more surprisingly) Socrates.

It might have seemed obvious that it would be for church history that he turned to Socrates, but the fact is that John virtually ignores church affairs and used Socrates exclusively for his rather modest contributions to the secular history of the period. That he used Socrates at firsthand is put beyond doubt by occasional extended verbal parallels. In one excerpt he describes Julian staying up all night to write speeches for the senate, and holding men of culture in great respect, especially philosophers, two entire sentences copied virtually verbatim from Socrates. Whatever the ultimate source of the stories of Procopius's execution and the Chalcedon oracle, we have seen that Zonaras's source was Socrates mediated by John. So when, discussing Julian's ban on Christians teaching the classics, Zonaras cites the story of Apolinarius writing a classicizing paraphrase of the psalms, a story best known from Socrates, it is a reasonable guess that here too his source was Socrates mediated by John.[155] As for Eutropius, we have just seen that Zonaras's source for the various explanations of Jovian's death was Eutropius or the *KG*, again as adapted and amplified by John.

Introductory excerpts from Eutropius often frame longer narrative excerpts (the best illustration is the abuse of Jovian at Antioch). But one excerpt reveals a more intricate interweaving of sources: Magnus Maximus rebelled against Gratian, and Theodosius defeated him; Theodosius then went to Rome with Honorius (whom he had summoned from the East), where he pardoned Symmachus the former consul for delivering a panegyric on Maximus.[156] What is intriguing about the four paragraphs of this excerpt is that, while the second derives from Eunapius (four complete lines recur verbatim in Zosimus, plus a couple of additional phrases Zosimus presumably omitted when abridging Eunapius), the first, third, and fourth all derive from Socrates, much of it verbatim. Rather surprisingly, John must have collated Eunapius and Socrates and combined details from both into a composite narrative.[157] We have seen that Eunapius was weak on western material, and what John took from Socrates here are western details missing in Zosimus (and presumably Eunapius too). It is instructive to reflect that, if Socrates had not survived, it would have been assumed on the basis of the Zosiman parallel that the entire excerpt derived from Eunapius. Obviously, we must beware of making such assumptions.

What then of Peter the Patrician? Zonaras's account of Magnentius's embassy to Constantius certainly reflects both the language and content of an excerpt of Peter.[158] This might seem to prove that, here at any rate, Zonaras drew directly on Peter (in

---

155. Socr. *HE* iii. i. 54–55 ~ John F 179 M = 271 R. Zon. xiii. 12. 22; Socr. *HE* iii. 16.

156. Jo. Ant. F 186 M = 279 R (my summary omits some details); all the relevant texts are cited in Roberto's notes.

157. It might seem curious that, having so carefully collated different sources, John transcribed the result more or less verbatim, but clearly this was now standard practice. There was little point in rephrasing borrowed material.

158. Peter F 16 ~ Zonaras xiii. 7. 18–22.

addition to, not instead of, John). But there are two other possibilities. First, we have seen that in the Chamavi episode Peter closely followed Eunapius, in both language and content. On occasion John too copied Eunapius verbatim, and it may be that Zonaras here reproduces John's version rather than Peter's version of the same passage of Eunapius. Second, just as the occasional traces of Socrates in Zonaras were mediated by John, Peter too may have been mediated by John. There is no trace of Peter's history in the surviving excerpts of John, but he certainly knew Peter's work on ceremonial. As Patzig pointed out, John's account of the proclamation of Anastasius in 491 draws details from Peter's detailed account preserved in the *Book of Ceremonies*. Cedrenus shares one of these details (an exhortation to ban *delatores*) and has another not in the excerpt of John.[159] It is hard to believe that Cedrenus did firsthand documentary research on such a matter, and the obvious explanation is that, here as so often elsewhere, he got his account (via Pseudo-Symeon) from the full text of John. If John drew on one work of Peter's, obviously he might have drawn on another. Given the abundant evidence that Zonaras drew on John, it would be unwise to make too much of this one parallel between Zonaras and Peter.

The clear traces of Eutropius, Eunapius, and Socrates in this part of Zonaras's narrative, all known sources of John, are unmistakable proof that John was the intermediary, almost certainly his direct source. But there is also a further complication. To posit a single intermediary for the secular history of the hundred and more years preceding the period of overlap with Ammianus is to overlook the fact that Zonaras's account of the sole reign of Constantius II (350–61), thirty pages in Büttner-Wobst's edition, is completely out of proportion to his treatment of preceding and following reigns. No fewer than eighteen of these pages are devoted to the usurpation of Magnentius (350–53), by far the fullest account that has come down to us. Furthermore, no more than two of these thirty pages are concerned with church affairs, an astonishing proportion for any Byzantine historical epitome. More remarkable still, most of these thirty pages are pure narrative, covering the events of a very brief period in considerable detail, again highly unusual in such a work.

The one peculiarity of Zonaras's account of these years that no one has really addressed is why this disproportionately detailed narrative begins and ends where it does (neither Ammianus nor Eunapius began or ended at either date, nor is there any reason to believe that Flavian or any other source we know of did either). It is tempting to conjecture that Zonaras used a different source for these years. Instead of continuing to follow his regular source for secular events, he turned to a fragment of a more detailed secular history he found somewhere among his collections of excerpts, a fragment that just happened to open and close at these dates (just as, e.g., our surviving text of Ammianus happens to begin with Bk xiv in 353).

159. Patzig 1897, 351–53; Roberto 2005, cl; Jo. Ant. F 214b M = 308 R; Petr. Patr., in *De Caer.* i. 92 (421. 2; 424. 18); Cedr. 626. 18–22.

We have seen that the concept of a "Leo-source" is of little help in our quest, but if it existed at all, it was surely the *Epitome* of John of Antioch now identified by Roberto. What Zonaras used for the overlap with Ammianus may have been an extract from the full text of John's *Chronica Historia*. We have just such an extract in the Athos manuscript published by Lambros, more than a dozen pages covering the period of Marius and Sulla, based on Eutropius/KG but amplified by material from Plutarch's *Lives* of Marius and Sulla. John continued to write the same sort of history right down to the reign of Heraclius, turning to Priscus when Eunapius gave out, combining him too with Socrates.[160] But Zonaras seems not to have known the later books of John's history. It is important to keep in mind how often ancient and medieval writers depended on incomplete texts and excerpts rather than complete copies of the books they read, especially multivolume books.[161] Take Dio. Zonaras seems to have had a complete text for Bks 1–32 and 44–67. For the subject matter of 67–80 he drew on Xiphilinus's *Epitome* of Dio, but he complains of having no sources at all between 146 and 44 B.C. and simply jumped from the sack of Carthage to Caesar and Pompey.[162] Zonaras seems to have had only limited extracts of even so relatively recent a work as John. His copy apparently gave out early in the reign of Valentinian and Valens.

It is time to abandon the quest for a single lost fourth-century source for Zonaras, and settle for a seventh-century chronicler who combined different sources from different periods into a composite narrative. This in turn means that it is idle to look for any single, consistent voice or perspective (such as "senatorial bias") in this narrative. To give just one illustration, it is tempting to feel that we should be able to identify the obviously contemporary voice that praised Constantius II for not appointing anyone to the senate who could not compose in prose and verse. John may on occasion have inserted an excerpt from a wholly unknown fourth-century writer.[163]

According to Bleckmann and Paschoud, the idea of a historical attack on Christianity, such as we first find fully developed in Zosimus, was invented by Nicomachus Flavianus. It is true that Augustine wrote his *City of God* as a reply "to those who hold the Christian religion responsible for the wars with which the whole world is now tormented, and in particular for the recent sack of Rome by the barbarians."[164] But the frequency with which he returns to aspects of the sack that (he claims) were less terrible than they might have been because of the Christianity of Alaric and his Goths makes it clear that it was *not* a general attack on Christianity he was responding to, but, very precisely, the claim that it was the ban on pagan sacrifice that was responsible for the sack of Rome. This was a very simple claim, that would not gain in plausibility by

160. For John's use of Priscus, Roberto 2005, cxliv–cxlvi.
161. Even in the high empire: Cameron 2004, 119–23.
162. ἀπορίᾳ βίβλων, Zon. ix. 31 (ii. 339 D).
163. In this case possibly an edict, such as *Cod. Theod.* xiv. 1.1 (360), insisting on the importance of training and practice in the liberal arts for positions in the bureaucracy.
164. Aug. *Civ. Dei* ii. 2.

being set in an ambitious narrative blaming all the ills of the past century on Christianity. Furthermore, this was a generation later than Flavian. There is no evidence and little probability that any westerner was inspired to write such a history twenty years before the sack of Rome.

Given the total lack of evidence of any sort or date, we are on safe ground in concluding that, despite its pretentious title (if title it was), Flavian's *Annales* was a trivial epitome, whatever period it covered offering little or nothing not available in earlier epitomes such as the *KG*, Eutropius, and Victor. If it really dealt with the empire and continued Eutropius, then it was superseded within less than a decade by the *Epitome de Caesaribus*. Not surprisingly, it vanished without trace, forgotten by everyone except family members.

Quite apart from the improbability of Eunapius having read Flavian, his notorious explanation of Constantine's conversion as an attempt to win the forgiveness for his crimes that pagan cults could not provide undoubtedly derives from Julian.[165] His eastern perspective is made particularly clear by his apparent ignorance of the best western illustration of pagan resistance, Symmachus's speech on behalf of the altar of Victory. Eunapius's approach can be traced to the pagan Neoplatonic circles of the East and to his own admiration for Julian. Eunapius's pervasive emphasis on the effects of extravagance (*tryphē*) is exclusively Greek, and in its application to Constantine again derives from Julian. Its extension to Theodosius must be the work of Eunapius. Nor is there any evidence in what we have of Eunapius himself that, like Zosimus, he saw Christianity as responsible for the loss of imperial territories, nor is this simply an argument from silence. It is not a thesis that is likely to have occurred to anyone before the end of the fifth century, when most of the former western provinces had passed into the control of barbarians.

---

165. As underlined by Paschoud himself (1975, 32).

19

CLASSICAL REVIVALS AND "PAGAN" ART

1: CONTORNIATES

Scholars have long sought evidence for a pagan reaction in the art as well as the literature of the late fourth century. Alföldi saw the classicizing silver plate and ivory carving of the age as part of a concerted campaign of pagan propaganda sponsored by the aristocracy of Rome. Despite the fact that he did no more than sketch out this thesis in the course of expounding his theory about the contorniates, it has been enormously influential. The reprinting of his brilliant 1943 chapter unchanged in the 1990 revision of his famous book has given the theory a perhaps undeserved fresh lease of life.[1] While conceding that Alföldi's formulation went too far, many scholars nonetheless cling to a modified version, assuming that the artifacts he discussed do at any rate reflect lingering pagan sympathies. Even this goes too far.

First, the contorniates. Contorniates, so called from their turned up edges, are bronze medallions produced in the city of Rome from the mid fourth to the late fifth century (figure 1).[2] A high proportion carry representations of the games and their stars, and most are also decorated with symbols of victory (palms, crowns, etc.). Alföldi thought they were distributed to the plebs by aristocratic families at the new year festival games each year. He distinguished three main series, two struck and a third cast.[3] The two struck series seem to have been produced at the Roman mint. There is a die-link between one of the earliest contorniate types and a coin produced at the mint between 354 and 360,[4] and many of the second series bear the bust of the reigning emperor. On Alföldi's view, the first series closed in 394, and the second began in 410. The cast series he placed in the gap between these two groups (394–410).

Unfortunately, there is no independent evidence for any of these dates. They are not only conjectural, they are entirely based on the theory they are supposed to be proving. The year 394 derives from Alföldi's assumption that pagan propaganda "must

---

1. Alföldi and Alföldi 1976–90. The Alföldi thesis is stated without reservation on the basis of the 1990 edition (25–63) by Lançon 1995, 98–100, ignoring the reservations in my own accompanying supplement (ib. 63–74).
2. For an excellent brief characterization, Toynbee 1986, 234–36; also Mazzarino's entry "Contorniati" in *Enc. Arte Antica* 11 (1959), 784–91; Mittag 1999.
3. Contorniates of the second series are now included along with regular coins and medallions in *RIC* x.
4. D. G. Wigg, *JRA* 8 (1995), 527.

FIGURE 1a & 1b: Contorniates of Apollonius of Tyana and Nero

have" stopped (if only temporarily) on the defeat of the pagan cause at the Frigidus; 410 derives from his conviction that a new sort of pagan propaganda "must have" begun after the sack of Rome by the Goths in 410; and the cast series is placed between these dates on the assumption that the pagan party "must have" been weakened by their defeat in 394, and so unable to use the mint until reenergized in 410.

There is no evidence whatever for the supposedly abrupt end of the first series in 394. For Alföldi, the first series comprised a fresh set of issues each new year from ca. 354 to 394. But a meticulous study by Curtis Clay has shown that the first series falls into two main die-linked groups, that is to say, groups struck from the same dies. On the most natural interpretation of this evidence, the contorniates in question were struck, not annually over the course of forty years, but within a short space of time on only two occasions.[5] As for the cast contorniates, some do copy struck types of the first series, but there is no evidence that they are later as a group than the first series as a whole, and E. Alföldi now concedes that they might be contemporary with the first series.[6] There is no evidence whatever for dating any of them to the fifteen-year gap Alföldi himself created between his arbitrary termini for the two struck series.

---

5. See Clay's appendix in Alföldi 1976, 217–32; and with Wigg, *JRA* 8 (1995), 528.
6. Wigg 1995, 527; E. Alföldi 1990, 11.

In fact, it is far from clear that any such gap exists—or even that Alföldi divided the two series at the right point. Apart from the fact that most of the second series are a little bigger and cruder, the only significant difference is that many in the second series bear portraits of reigning emperors, from Honorius (394–423) to Anthemius (467–72). On this evidence, the second series could begin as early as 394 or as late as 423 rather than precisely in 410. Or even earlier. For no stated reason, Alföldi assigned nine contorniates bearing the portrait of Theodosius I (379–95) to the first series.[7] This seems strange, given that the most obvious difference between the two series seems to be precisely the presence or absence of the portrait of a reigning emperor. If we assign the Theodosius contorniates to the second series, we would have one series with and the other entirely without current imperial portraits, and the dividing line between them might fall as early as 379. On this reconstruction, the first series, which contains most of Alföldi's "propaganda," would end *before* the period generally characterized as a "pagan reaction," the 380s.

Alföldi also argued that it was the prefect of Rome, in his capacity as representative of the Roman senate, who was responsible for striking the contorniates. This suited his propaganda hypothesis nicely, since many fourth-century prefects of Rome were pagans. More specifically, during much of the time he dated the first contorniates (354/60), the office was held by none other than Symmachus's father-in-law, Memmius Vitrasius Orfitus. Alföldi could not resist selecting Orfitus as the mastermind, arguing that it was Constantius's removal of the altar of Victory from the senate house in 357 that inspired him. Everything seemed to fit. Unfortunately, if the contorniates were struck at the mint, they cannot have been issued by the prefect of Rome. The official in charge of the mint was a procurator answerable to the *comes sacrarum largitionum* at court.[8] No prefect of Rome could have used the mint to produce medallions for private citizens to distribute.

There are two further problems with Orfitus. Though undoubtedly a pagan, being "less instructed in the liberal arts than befitted a member of the nobility," he is a far from plausible author for the notion of using Graeco-Roman cultural heroes as pagan propaganda. Like all Constantius's urban prefects, Orfitus had previously demonstrated conspicuous loyalty to the dynasty. He had served at court with Constantius during the war against Magnentius, and after eight prefects in four and a half years, his first tenure of nearly two years was unusual enough in itself; but his reappointment after less than a year for a further two years was altogether exceptional.[9] Constantius's other prefects during this period included his kinsman Naeratius Cerealis and the trusted easterner Fl. Leontius. The only other Roman aristocrat he appointed was the Christian Junius Bassus. Clearly, Orfitus was the only pagan aristocrat that this most suspicious and insecure of Christian emperors trusted. Indeed, he may actually have

---

7. Alföldi 1976, 148–49 (1943 ed. 17).

8. Delmaire 1989, 495–525.

9. For the duration of Orfitus's two prefectures, Barnes 1992, 257–59.

married a niece of Constantius.[10] Hardly the sort of person to wage ideological warfare against his benefactor.

One further problem. Alföldi did not distinguish between propaganda in favor of the traditional cults (credible, and potentially effective) and outright attacks on Christianity (not credible, and surely counterproductive). The most that pagans could hope for by the second half of the fourth century was toleration; this is all Symmachus asked for in his speech on the altar of Victory. The tolerant, cultivated Christians who were swayed by Symmachus's eloquence would have been outraged by the petty anti-Christian jibes Alföldi claimed to detect.

Many of the same objections apply to Alföldi's no less celebrated thesis that another series of Roman medallions bearing the obverse legend VOTA PVBLICA with reverses of Isis, Anubis, the Nile, and the Sphinx are likewise pagan propaganda, distributed (again) as new year's gifts by (again) the pagan aristocracy of Rome.[11] One series of these medallions bears the heads of every emperor from Diocletian to Gratian and Valentinian II, but not Theodosius, from which Alföldi (reasonably) concluded that they were discontinued by 379 (with legends like *deo Sarapidi* and *dea Isis* they are more openly pagan than the contorniates).

There is also another series with busts of Isis and Serapis on the obverse instead of imperial busts. This series Alföldi more speculatively claimed to have been issued by the pagan aristocracy as *covert* propaganda, stopping in 394, because "the pagan party was annihilated in Rome in 394," and would not have been able to use the mint at all after this date.[12] The Isis medallions were undoubtedly produced at the mint, but, as with the contorniates, there can be no question of a "pagan party" choosing types.[13] Furthermore, Alföldi himself drew attention to die-links between his second series and medallions in the earlier series bearing the head of Valentinian I. He saw this as proof that the second series was produced not long after the Valentinianic medallions (namely, between 379 and 394).[14] It would be more natural to infer that they were produced *simultaneously* with the Valentinianic medallions. If so, it would follow that both series stopped in or around 379, in which case, whatever the occasions for which these curious pieces were struck, they could no longer be considered evidence of a covert pagan *reaction*.

Furthermore, the commonest single motif on these coins is Isis in a ship, laying her hands on the sail as it catches the wind (the so-called *Isis Pelagia*), and many bear the legend *Isis Pharia*, "Isis of Alexandria," underlining her role as the goddess who presides over travel by sea.[15] As Alföldi himself showed in a later study, with his usual

---

10. Cameron 1996, 295–301, on a gold-glass commemorating the marriage of Orfitus and Constantia.

11. Alföldi 1937; for some objections, T. A. Brady, *JRS* 28 (1938), 88–90; and Meslin 1970, 59–60, 63–64. For a recent catalogue, L. Vagi, *Coinage and History of the Roman Empire* 2 (Chicago 2002), 566–76. The pagan propaganda thesis is still swallowed whole by Turcan 1996, 123–24.

12. Alföldi 1937, 25.

13. J. W. E. Pearce, following Alföldi, weakly argued from the existence of the medallions that pagan aristocrats must have been able to influence the mint (*RIC* 7 [1953], 108).

14. Alföldi 1937, 25–26, arguing that they were issued in very small numbers once a year for the new year.

15. For *Isis Pharia*, Bruneau 1961, 435–46; Alföldi 1965/66, 64–65; for *Pharius* = Alexandrian, Rouché 1989, 108.

wealth of illustrations in every medium from every corner of the Graeco-Roman world, in Rome and Ostia Isis is often little more than a symbol for the Roman corn supply, the bulk of which came by sea from Egypt and Africa.[16] Other common reverse motifs on these medallions are the Nile recumbent and the Sphinx, both more naturally identified as symbols of Egypt in general than specifically the cult of Isis. It is true that, after the foundation of Constantinople, Egyptian corn ceased to feed Rome, but by then *Isis Pharia* had become the patron of the African cornfleet as well. The last known pagan temple to be renovated at public expense was an Iseum at the Claudian harbor of Portus, with a dedication naming Valens, Gratian, and Valentinian II, datable to between 375 and 378. The official responsible, predictably enough, was the prefect of the *annona*.[17] The linking of Isiac imagery with the public vows of 3 January is sufficiently explained as an allusive wish that there will be no problems with the year's corn supply.[18] It is easy to see why, with Gratian's change of policy toward paganism, the tradition was discontinued.

To return to the contorniates, in the last analysis, Alföldi's thesis stands or falls on the evidence of the contorniates themselves. If they had illustrated the main figures of the Roman Pantheon, the great temples of Rome, and scenes of sacrifice, that might have amounted to evidence worth taking seriously. But we find none of these things. The only pagan deities who appear on obverse types are Serapis and Dea Roma, the latter a personification easily and soon Christianized (most notably in Prudentius's reply to Symmachus). Even on the reverses, we find only a handful of Roman deities: a solitary Mars, three Herculeses, three Apollos, and two Minervas with Hercules. A few more "oriental" deities (Sol, Bacchus, Cybele, Attis, and a solitary Isis), but a most unimpressive proportion of the whole. The overwhelming majority of the obverses are emperors and figures from Graeco-Roman history and literature.

Among the emperors represented, far and away the most popular are Nero (figure 1a) and Trajan, with well over a thousand examples between them. For Alföldi, they were singled out as arch-persecutors of the Christians.[19] But was this really their *popular* reputation? Only Christians ever saw either as persecutors. If we turn to the *Historia Augusta*, the classic source, according to Alföldi himself, for the beliefs and aspirations of the pagan elite of Rome ca. 395, we find Nero portrayed throughout as the worst of the bad emperors. Ten passages give short lists of bad emperors: Caligula appears on five, Domitian on six, but Nero on all ten.[20] According to Jocelyn Toynbee, "Nero and Trajan were far more famous as beautifiers of the city and as patrons of the games."[21] A strong argument in favor of a connection with the games is provided by a

---

16. Alföldi 1965/66, at 55–65, with pl. 1–16; Isis is a common name for ships: Casson 1971, 359.
17. Chastagnol 1969, 135–44, rightly emphasizing the connection with the corn supply.
18. So Alföldi 1965/66, 78, as if unaware how far such a conclusion undermined his pagan propaganda thesis.
19. Alföldi and Alföldi 1990, 37.
20. *HA Marc.* 28. 10; *Ver.* 4. 6; *Clod. Alb.* 13. 5; *Av. Cass.* 8. 4; *Elag.* 1. 1; 33. 1; *Sev. Alex.* 9. 4; *Tac.* 6. 4; *Aur.* 42. 6; *Car.* 1. 4.
21. *JRS* 35 (1945), 118 (reviewing Alföldi 1943); cf. Murray 1965, 44; Syme 1971, 109; Griffin 1984, 109 ("the greatest showman of them all").

late antique (probably fifth-century) gem showing Nero (explicitly identified by label) in frontal quadriga wearing a radiate crown and brandishing an eagle-sceptre and *mappa*.[22] Why the *mappa*? The explanation is provided by an anecdote found in Cassiodorus:[23]

> When Nero was prolonging his dinner and the people, greedy for the spectacle, were making their customary demands for haste, he ordered that the napkin he was using to wipe his hands should be thrown from the window, to give permission for the requested contest.

Of course, this is no more than a silly story explaining why a table napkin (*mappa*) was used to start circus races—and in effect became a symbol of the games.[24] But it is nonetheless significant that the emperor chosen for this aetiology was Nero. And the fact that the story is told in so late a source as Cassiodorus and reflected in a gem of the fifth century vividly illustrates Nero's continuing reputation as a patron of the games.

If Nero and Trajan were chosen for persecuting Christians, why not a single example of Diocletian or Julian? Augustus, Galba, and Vespasian were not persecutors, and why so many empresses (both Faustinas, Agrippina, and Lucilla)? One contorniate unknown to Alföldi in 1943 represents Philip the Arab, believed by some to have been a Christian. One cast contorniate features Constantine's mother, the pious empress Helena. And no one trying to show pagan cults in a favorable light would have included Hadrian's boyfriend Antinous represented as Pan! It is hard to believe that any fourth-century pagan would have cared to defend Antinous's qualifications for deification, universally ridiculed by Christians as a scandal and abomination.[25]

The featured writers are said to be propaganda for "pagan" culture. But we have already seen that the "conflict" over classical culture was entirely one-sided. While some Christians condemned it, there is no evidence that pagans "promoted" it—whatever that might mean. "Propaganda" for what we would now call high culture aimed at those who by definition did not participate in it, namely the masses, makes no sense.

To be sure, none of the writers represented were Christians, but the only significantly pagan figure among them is Apollonius of Tyana (figure 1b). Alföldi saw Apollonius as the best and clearest proof of his thesis. But in the West at any rate Apollonius was not at all the pagan symbol he may have been in the East (Ch. 15. 6–7). As for the other writers, what specifically pagan significance, especially in the eyes of the Latin-speaking populace of late fourth-century Rome, could there have

---

22. Megow 1987, 216 (A 104), with Taf. 35. 6; Alföldi and Alföldi 1990, Taf. 250. 3; Champlin 2003, 31–32.
23. *Variae* iii. 51. 9.
24. Providers of games are regularly so identified by being shown holding up a *mappa*, as on consular diptychs.
25. For Christian attacks on the deification of Antinous, Lambert 1984, 193–94, and passim. Prudentius draws a savage picture of Hadrian's *deliciae* listening to prayers in temples "with his husband" (*Contra Symm.* i. 271–77).

been in Demosthenes, Euripides, or Theophrastus? There was simply no need to "publicize" standard school authors like Terence and Sallust.

It is a common rhetorical ploy among modern students of the "pagan reaction" to disarm criticism by conceding that Alföldi (of course) pushed his theory too far, but to stand firm on the "undeniably pagan character" of the contorniates. But this is to remain within the orbit of Alföldi's unrealistic polarization of the issue. For Alföldi, all art and literature was either pagan or Christian. He allowed no middle ground. The truth is that, devotional works aside, most art and literature falls into the middle ground we now call secular. The countless representations of charioteers, racehorses, pantomimes, and other scenes from circus, theatre, and amphitheatre amply establish the usual assumption that they were mementos of the games.[26] Most Roman games were in origin religious festivals, and two recent studies have argued that as late as the close of the fourth century pagan associations were still strong, one of them specifically invoking the contorniates.[27] That is not likely (Conclusion). While the more obviously pagan themes disappear in the course of the fifth century, the fact that no Christian themes take their place even as late as the 470s is enough to show that it is more satisfactory to regard contorniates as a secular rather than pagan genre.

Certainly, they provide a gallery of Graeco-Roman culture heroes. But not specifically *fourth-century* culture heroes, much less pagan symbols. They are simply a fairly random selection of figures from Greek and Roman history and literature, chosen from whatever was available in the files of the mint, without much conscious thought for their contemporary relevance. Elizabeth Alföldi once remarked to me that, to judge from the range of models drawn on by the contorniates, both geographical and chronological, the Roman mint must have had an extensive numismatic museum. Contorniates are copied from the coins of many different periods and many different parts of the empire. The Antinous-Pan type (e.g.) is copied from a Hadrianic issue of Smyrna or Ephesus,[28] surely a chance selection simply because it happened to be available. The Greek writers included (with legends in Greek characters) and early poets like Accius, surely not read since the archaizing revival, point to (at latest) second-century models. Nowadays we place such culture heroes on our postage stamps.

For Alföldi, the link between contorniates and aristocrats was axiomatic. Yet other objections aside, there is the low artistic quality of the representations and the poorly spelled legends (APOLLONIUS TEANEUS and ROMA HETERNA, to give a couple of examples). If the subjects were selected by sophisticated aristocrats anxious to publicize their cultural heritage, why did they consistently leave the execution of this grand design to semiliterate craftsmen? There is nothing peculiarly pagan and nothing whatever aristocratic about contorniates. Contorniates are more than just one plank in Alföldi's thesis. Alföldi himself and most of his many followers have

---

26. Listed in Alföldi and Alföldi 1976, 156–66, 184–86, 206–15; and 1990, passim.
27. Curran 2000, 218–59; and Lim 1999, 274.
28. E. Alföldi 1991, 14–18.

treated them as its cornerstone. So if they fail, "pagan" representations in the other minor arts have to bear a heavy weight, heavier (perhaps) than they can bear.

2: CLASSICAL REVIVALS

Contorniates scarcely rise to the level of art. But much high-quality silver plate, ivory work, and manuscript illumination has also been assigned to the patronage of the last generation of pagan aristocrats. It is not just the "pagan" themes of this work, but its "classical" style that has led to its being associated with pagan aristocrats. This view is heavily dependent on the notion of a pagan revival of classical texts and forms in the closing decades of the fourth century. In much modern writing the terms "pagan revival," "classical revival," and even "classical renaissance"[29] are often used more or less interchangeably. Art historians in particular refer confidently to "the classical revival that flourished around AD 400" as a natural context for the silver plate, ivory diptychs, and illustrated classical manuscripts that, on the basis of this supposed revival, they date to this period.[30]

But there was no general classical revival in late fourth-century Rome—certainly nothing that can be associated with pagan rather than Christian members of the elite. We know of a number of Christian aristocrats (Apronianus, the elder Melania, Pammachius) who fostered the efforts of scholarly protégés like Jerome, Rufinus, Jovinian, and Pelagius. Yet while there must have been *some* pagan literary patrons, contemporary texts do not allow us to identify any.

Furthermore, critics often write as if "classical" and "classicizing" were unproblematic terms.[31] There is in fact no simple sense in which the literary revival of the fourth century could be characterized as classical. Unsurprisingly enough, most secular writing involves classical forms such as oratory and poetry, to be sure in classicizing diction and meters, but it does not represent a rediscovery of those forms. Such poetry as we have from the third century is written in the same idiom and the same meters.

Insofar as there was a revival of neglected texts, the most striking new development in the fourth-century West is its rediscovery of what we now think of as *post*-classical literature (Ch. 11). Pre- and postclassical are modern labels, but they nonetheless reflect a real and important change of taste in the course of the fourth century. If asked to identify the high-water mark of fourth-century neoclassicism in literature, most scholars would probably point to Claudian. Claudian is the one poet of the fourth century who could pass for a contemporary of Statius or Juvenal. Yet he could never pass for a contemporary of Vergil or Horace. His vocabulary, style, and metrical technique are modeled on the poets of the Silver Age. There is a sense in which Servius

---

29. Often identified as a "Theodosian renaissance": for bibliography, Kiilerich 1993, esp. Ch. 1.
30. E.g., Wright 1996, 44.
31. Porter 2006; Hölscher 2004.

and Macrobius provide a literary context for the luxury Vergil manuscripts of late antiquity. All are aspects of the fast-growing cult of Vergil. But not the same context, nor a context that has anything to do with the "pagan reaction" assigned to the generation before they wrote. Nor is there any straightforward sense in which either Servius or Macrobius fit so simplistic a concept as a "classical" revival. Macrobius was an uncompromising archaizer, while Servius pioneered the introduction of postclassical texts into the curriculum.

As for the further notion that this supposedly Symmachi-sponsored classical revival extended to the arts, the one and only piece of real evidence is the NICOMACHORVM/SYMMACHORVM diptych. This is the umbrella under which modern scholars have thrown every artifact with a "pagan" theme for which a Roman provenance might be claimed and which can be characterized in one way or another as classicizing.

Quite an imposing dossier has been compiled. But there are problems with the method. In the first place, none of the objects in question is independently dated and only one can be placed in Rome. Second, two significant categories of artifact have to be tacitly set on one side: classicizing objects that are clearly Christian; and non-classicizing pagan objects. For example, the two best-documented classicizing artifacts after the SYMMACHORVM diptych are the Junius Bassus sarcophagus (in addition to its celebrated reliefs, its lid is decorated with a poem in classicizing elegiac couplets)[32] and the Esquiline treasure. Both can be fairly closely dated, and both associated with aristocratic Roman families. But at least some members of both families were Christian. The sarcophagus can be dated to 359; the Esquiline treasure to 360/80. On this evidence we might as plausibly proclaim a classicizing revival sponsored by Christian aristocrats a generation before Praetextatus and Symmachus.

Alföldi and his followers made much of the abundant Dionysiac imagery on late antique silverware, interpreting it in the light of the many Dionysiac sarcophagi of the early empire as a pagan promise of afterlife (e.g., the probably fourth-century Mildenhall plate (see figure 2).[33]

For Alföldi himself, it was active propaganda for a pagan alternative; for others, simply a personal statement of belief. It should be said straightaway that both are very dated readings of the sarcophagi. Most would probably now follow Zanker in seeing such scenes as aimed at those who attended family festivals at the tomb, occasions characterized by the drinking, dancing, and conviviality depicted on the sarcophagi. This reading is obviously supported by the frequency of Dionysiac imagery on the wall paintings, mosaic floors, and silver plate of private houses.[34] The very ubiquity of Dionysiac imagery in the art and poetry of late antiquity makes it an important test

---

32. Cameron 2002, 288–92.
33. E.g., Painter 1977, 18.
34. Zanker and Ewald 2004, 135–67; Dunbabin 1978, Ch. 10.

FIGURE 2: the Mildenhall Plate

case. If its religious connotations are to be taken seriously, paganism remained a powerful force well down into the Byzantine world.

The most comprehensive and elaborate late antique treatment of myths associated with Dionysus is the flamboyant forty-eight-book *Dionysiaca* of Nonnus, an early fifth-century poet from Panopolis in Upper Egypt. Despite its profound influence on later Christian poets,[35] the pervasive sensuality and astrological preoccupation of this extraordinary work have often in the past been held to prove its author a convinced pagan.[36] The fact that he is also credited with a paraphrase of St. John's Gospel in the same style was generally explained as an act of repentance for the *Dionysiaca* after conversion. But some important recent studies by Vian have turned this picture upside down. We now know that the *Paraphrase* came first.[37] Interpretation of the *Dionysiaca* must in future proceed on the assumption that its author was a Christian.

Furthermore, if Nonnus's purpose had been to represent Dionysus as a savior god, there should be some hint of this purpose in the poem. Yet there is none. One line has always seemed to leap out of its context:

> Bakchos anax dakrūse, brotōn hina dakrua lūsē,
> Lord Bacchus has wept tears that he may wipe away man's tears.

---

35. Illustrated in detail by Miguélez Cavero 2008.
36. R. Keydell, "Nonnos," in *RE* 33 (1936), 915–16; Chuvin 1986, 387–96.
37. Vian 1997, 143–60; the next two paragraphs are adapted from Cameron 2000, 175–88.

The more so after Golega spotted that both thought and formulation were borrowed from Cyril of Alexandria's commentary on St. John's Gospel (425–28), a work Nonnus studied carefully when writing the *Paraphrase*.[38] On the assumption that he wrote as a pagan, it was naturally tempting to read this as a polemical proclamation of Dionysus as a suffering redeemer. But the context cannot possibly support so extravagant a notion. It is the Fate Atropos who is speaking; impressed by Dionysus's grief for the death of his young friend Ampelos, she turns him into a living vine-shoot. For all its trappings, this is simply an old-fashioned aetiology. It is not even Dionysus himself who performs the metamorphosis. For all its Christian resonance, the line in question is just a formula that came naturally to the pen of a Christian, without any wider implications beyond its immediate context.

Dionysus is *not* portrayed as a savior or redeemer. His mission is simply to bring men and (especially) women joy in the form of wine. He betrays no interest whatever in the afterlife, and though one or two of his favorites (like Ampelos) win a kind of apotheosis, the general run of mankind has no such expectations. One striking passage proclaims that the only relief for mortals burdened with unbearable suffering is... getting drunk![39] There are countless references in the *Dionysiaca* to pagan cults, rites, temples, altars, sacrifices, and statues, but all are literary and antiquarian rather than specific and devotional—as put beyond doubt by the fact that most of the terms he uses he had already used metaphorically of Christian rites in the *Paraphrase*.[40]

Nonnus is not trying to portray Dionysus as a rival of Christ, nor is he trying to assimilate Dionysus and Christ. Dionysiac imagery was pervasive in the ancient world, even in Christian art.[41] There is conspicuous Dionysiac imagery in the account of the wedding at Cana in Nonnus's own *Paraphrase*.[42] A fascinating recent find is a textile with a number of Dionysiac figures framed under a series of arches, attached to several fragments from a series of New Testament scenes.[43] A Christian was evidently buried with Dionysiac tapestries. None of this proves that Dionysiac iconography *never* has specifically Dionysiac, pagan connotations in late antique art. But if a forty-eight-book work entirely dedicated to Dionysus in a highly classicizing style turns out to have no real pagan content or purpose, Dionysiac scenes in traditional domestic contexts like silver plate and textiles are best read as decorative rather than devotional.

The fact that the Mildenhall treasure was found in Britain hardly supports the conjectural attribution to a Roman workshop. While Alföldi saw the procession of Attis

---

38. *Dion.* xii. 171; δακρύει δὲ ὁ κύριος...ἵνα ἡμῶν περιστείλῃ δάκρυον, Golega 1930, 79; on the debt of the *Paraphrase* to this commentary, Golega 126–32, and Livrea's commentaries on *Par.* 2 (2000) and 18 (1989).

39. *Dion.* xii. 265–69; in general, Vian 1994, 197–233, esp. 222–33.

40. As shown in detail by Vian 1988.

41. Mathews 1994, 45. For numerous examples from Coptic textiles, see Rutschowscaya 1990, 83–92 (unnecessarily linking them to "la forte réaction païenne du IVᵉ siècle en face de la montée du christianisme," p. 82).

42. Morton Smith 1974, 815–29.

43. Bowersock 1990, 52–53 (with color plates 10–11); Willers 1992, 141–51.

FIGURE 3: the Parabiago Plate

and Cybele on the Parabiago plate (figure 3) as another pagan promise of eternal life,[44] Musso came up with a different but even more fanciful interpretation. Because it was found near Milan, she suggested that it was a present from Symmachus to Flavian at Eugenius's court there in 394, commemorating the Hilaria, a festival of Attis. Other objections aside (most obviously, some authorities still prefer a second- or third-century date),[45] this interpretation presupposes that both were devotees of "oriental" cults, and (more specifically) is based on a passage of the *Carmen contra paganos* (*CCP*). Moderns are drawn to "pagan" imagery, but the Sevso and Cesena hunting plates both show hunters finishing their day with a picnic eaten off just such plates.

While Attis and Cybele, Dionysus and dancing maenads do reflect, however remotely, actual religious rituals, some of the most popular mythological themes in late antique art—Achilles, Hippolytus, Phaedra—have no specific cult connotations.[46] A plate in the mid-fourth-century Kaiseraugst treasure is decorated with a cycle of ten scenes from Achilles's childhood around its rim and, singled out for special treatment in a large central medallion, his exposure by Odysseus in

44. Alföldi 1949, 68–73; Wright 1993, 104–5. Wright's thesis (1998, 358–59) that an ivory diptych in Sens (61V) illustrates "a pagan promise of afterlife" is improbable in itself, and, once again, the suggested Roman context is no more than a guess.

45. Musso 1983, 143–48; Kiilerich 1993, 176–77; against, Leader-Newby 2004, 146. There is no basis for extending the exchange of *largitio* silver plate in this way: Cameron 1992; 2006; and Leader-Newby 2004, 152.

46. On the interpretation of all these figures on the sarcophagi, see Zanker and Ewald 2004, passim.

female dress. Individual scenes from this cycle are already commonplace on Pompeian wall paintings, and appear regularly on sarcophagus reliefs and mosaics.[47] Long after the Christianization of the Roman state, the ability to identify the main figures and stories of classical mythology remained a central component of a liberal education, indispensable for understanding not only the classics, but contemporary poetry and oratory as well as art.[48] This is why late antique commentators, most of them undoubtedly Christian, devoted so much care to explaining mythological allusions in the classics—and why so many mythological handbooks survive.

Up till a couple of decades ago, no one would have pursued the search for "pagan" themes into sculpture in the round. It had long been taken for granted that mythological statuary ceased to be produced by (at latest) the third century. A group of such statues (Hercules, Zeus, Poseidon, Helius, and Satyr with infant Dionysus) was discovered on the Esquiline Hill in the 1880s. The inscribed plinths identified the sculptors as Fl. Zenon, Fl. Andronicus, and Fl. Chryseros of Aphrodisias; all were assigned to the second century.[49] Then in 1982 Charlotte Rouché and Kenan Erim published dedications of Zeno and Andronicus from Aphrodisias itself, and on a variety of grounds redated all three to the first half of the fourth century.[50] Thanks to the rich finds made there over the past forty years, we now know that Aphrodisias was a major sculptural center in both the early imperial and late antique period. On the basis of this material similar mythological sculptures at a number of different sites have been identified as either imports from Aphrodisias or the work of itinerant Aphrodisian craftsmen: Constantinople, Carthage, and two sites in Gaul, Saint Georges de Montagne (near Bordeaux), and Chiragan (50 km west of Toulouse). The latest expert opinion dates all these works, most previously assigned to the second century, to the fourth.[51] All were found in substantial villas, the Roman group in a grand house not far from where the Esquiline treasure was found. All therefore reflect the private taste of members of the elite. The complex at Saint Georges de Montagne (statuettes of Diana, Venus and erotes, Mars, Apollo, Meleager) is particularly interesting because of the proximity of the site to Bordeaux, home of Ausonius. It is tempting to identify it as one of Ausonius's villas, perhaps his Lucaniacus, where he describes a statue of Bacchus with the attributes of the other gods. Bergmann's recent survey could not resist linking this "pagan" statuary with the patronage of the pagan aristocracy of Rome and Gaul.[52] Stirling's study of Saint Georges de Montagne resisted this facile assumption, well aware that by the mid-fourth century many members of the Gallic

47. For representations of Achilles, Cameron 2009, 1–22.
48. Liebeschuetz 1995, 193–208; Cameron 2004, passim.
49. All now in Copenhagen: see Moltesen 1990, 133–46.
50. Rouché 1989, 25–29, nos. 11–13.
51. Kiilerich and Torp 1994; Hannestad 1994, 105 60; Bergmann 1999; Stirling 1996; 2005.
52. *mixobarbaron Liberi Patris signo marmoreo in villa nostra omnium deorum argumenta habenti, Ep.* 32–33, with Green's commentary (1991, 392–93). For Ausonius's villas, see the Sivan 1993, 68–73. Bergmann 1999, 70.

elite were Christians—but Christians with traditional cultural tastes, like Ausonius. We should bear in mind that Constantine brought statues from all over the empire to decorate his new capital, much of it representations of pagan deities from cult centers. Eusebius implausibly claimed that he was exposing them to ridicule, but obviously the real reason was to equip Constantinople with the traditional artistic trappings befitting a capital city.[53] It was similarly traditional to equip villas with colonnades and gardens peopled with classicizing statues (Ch. 10. 6).

When Alföldi was developing his thesis in the 1930s, much less late antique mythological art was available. The Mildenhall, Kaiseraugst, and Sevso treasures were not published till the 1940s, 1960s, and 1990s respectively, and the Aphrodisian sculpture not redated till the 1980s. Thus the artefacts Alföldi studied stood out more than they would today. The sheer amount of mythological statuary and silverware we can now identify from the fourth century reduces the likelihood of any specifically pagan element in the minds of the patrons who commissioned them.

This is not to say that classical myths *never* carried a deeper meaning, but their very familiarity and ubiquity makes it hard to imagine them as vehicles of propaganda. A further complication is that they sometimes have a serious purpose without it being specifically religious (whether pagan or Christian). One remarkable example is a series of paintings or mosaics in some public building in early sixth-century Gaza described by the Christian rhetor and biblical scholar Procopius of Gaza: the stories of Phaedra and Hippolytus, Theseus and Ariadne, and some episodes from the Trojan cycle, mainly involving Menelaus, Paris, and Helen.[54] It is clear from his introduction that Procopius sees these paintings as a warning of the dangers of sexual passion: "Eros and the arrows of Eros fly everywhere and transfix everyone. Not even Zeus is free when the Erotes will it; but he who is high and mighty 'whose strength is not to be resisted' longs for Semele and chases after Hera and appears as a bull to Europa and navigates the sea steered by Eros."[55] This is a moral purpose of which all Christians would approve, but it is expressed in wholly pagan or (better) secular terms.[56]

Nor was it only in the East that Christian audiences continued to find mythological themes and imagery acceptable in the work of poets and rhetoricians.[57] For the West, Claudian is a particularly important witness, not so much because his imagery is more "pagan" than that of Nonnus, but because of the precise information we have about the date and context (both social and geographical) in which he wrote. His very first Latin poem, a panegyric of the consuls of 395, opens with an apostrophe to the sun and an appeal for inspiration from Apollo, and then describes Roma in the guise of Minerva flying to beg Theodosius (who is compared to Mars, and twice addresses

---

53. Dagron 1974, 36–37; Caseau 2007, 117–41; Wilkinson 2009.
54. See Friedlaender 1969.
55. § 1 p. 5 Friedlaender (quoting Homer, Il. 8. 32).
56. So Liebeschuetz 1995, 195–96.
57. Raby 1957, Ch. 2–3.

her as "goddess") to appoint Olybrius and Probinus consuls. Their pious mother Proba is compared to Thetis and Juno "summoned by sacred incense" (195). Once upon a time it was fashionable to treat Claudian as a pagan propagandist.[58] Yet he recited this poem on 1 January 395, less than four months after the Frigidus, under the auspices of the most powerful Christian family in Rome.

Late antique poets describe just the sort of Dionysiac processions and mythological tableaux that are so common on the silver plate of the age. Cybele with her cymbals and turreted crown and lions appear in Claudian much as they do on the Parabiago plate, and a combination of marine and Dionysiac imagery (as on the Mildenhall plate) closes the third book of Claudian's panegyric on Stilicho.[59] No responsible critic of Claudian has ventured to discern any religious dimension in such passages. As Fargues rightly remarked, he describes goddesses more often than gods because female figures lent themselves better to picturesque description.[60] We should be cautious about reading a religious purpose into the similar tableaux on silver plates.

There is also an important difference between poetry and art. In that it consists of words, poetry cannot help identifying its ultimate pagan inspiration. Even in classical poetry, Apollo, Minerva, Jupiter, Mars, and Venus may function metonymically as little more than personifications, but the names themselves were bound to retain, however vestigially, something of their original connotations. But the pagan sources of late antique art carry no labels. To take a familiar example, a classically educated person looking at the standard representation of Jonah resting under his vine on Christian sarcophagi might be a little surprised to identify, minimally adapted, the sleeping Endymion awaiting the arrival of his lover Selene. An uneducated Christian viewer would simply recognize Jonah. If he gave any thought to the languid pose and naked body, he might see them as a way of representing innocence or the repose of the blessed.[61] An uneducated person looking at (say) a consular diptych would recognize the familiar image of Roma with helmet and shield—perhaps a little puzzled by the one bare breast. A more educated viewer would identify (with Claudian) the guise of Minerva.[62]

In considering the possibility of specifically pagan connotations in this sort of iconography it is also important to bear in mind that classicizing mythological scenes on silverware continue down into the seventh century.[63] It is inconceivable that the sixth- and seventh-century patrons who commissioned such work were polemical pagans. What these continuing "pagan" themes really illustrate—and illustrate abundantly—is the routine acceptance of such themes by the now-Christian elite of the

---

58. E.g., (among many others) Mazzarino 1938, 243; against, Cameron 1970, 237f.

59. *Rapt.* i. 202–13; *Eutr.* i. 277–80; ii. 279–303; *Gild.* 117–20.

60. Fargues 1933, 288f.

61. Mathews 1994, 30–33.

62. *innuptae ritus imitata Minervae, Pan. Prob.* 84.

63. It will be enough to refer to Weitzman 1979, 126–98. Some of the very latest are dated precisely by stamps.

Roman world. Not only are they not pagan propaganda, more interestingly and ultimately more important, they represent common ground between pagans and Christians, common ground that allowed my center-pagan group, more interested in culture than cult, to slip into a respectable center-Christianity without having to give up their classicizing tastes in art and literature.

This brings us to an important caveat. This enthusiasm among (center)-Christians for classicizing motifs and "pagan" iconography is limited to cultivated members of the elite. While a classically educated Christian dignitary of ca. 400 would have smiled with satisfaction as he identified successive scenes in an Achilles or Hercules cycle on his host's silverware, mosaic floors, or wall paintings, a peasant or an uneducated monk would have seen only nude bodies and pagan monsters. Denunciations tend to be overrepresented in the Christian texts that have come down to us. Alföldi cited Jerome's boast that he had never "had his dinner plates engraved with idols, or, at a Christian banquet, set satyrs embracing maenads before the eyes of virgins."[64] But the "silent majority" who continued to commission and admire such silverware has left no record. Satyrs in a state of arousal are pursuing maenads all over two large picture plates and a number of caskets and ewers in the fourth-century Sevso treasure. But the Hunt plate that gives us the owner's name reveals that he was a Christian.[65] Educated contemporary observers would not have batted an eye, but the uneducated, unfamiliar with traditional representations of satyrs, would no doubt have been outraged. For all his professed indignation at such scenes, even Jerome would have been embarrassed if he had failed to identify a labor of Hercules or a stage in the education of Achilles.

3: ILLUMINATED MANUSCRIPTS

One of the two media in which we find the depiction of more specifically Roman cult scenes is in manuscripts of Vergil. We have two illustrated late antique copies, the Vatican and Roman Vergils. The Vatican Vergil is generally dated to ca. 400. The two most recent studies, though disagreeing on most other issues, are at one in proclaiming it a central document of the "pagan revival." For Stevenson, its lavish decoration proclaims it "the vehicle of a holy text," and he explicitly compares the *Saturnalia* of Macrobius, whom he describes as "the movement's leading propagandist."[66] For Wright, it is a "key example" of the "last flowering of the pagan intellegentsia among senatorial families," which it is "natural" to date to the era of Servius and Macrobius,

---

64. Jer. *Ep.* 27. 2; Alföldi and Alföldi 1990, 47.
65. For abundant photos and full description, Mundell Mango and Bennett 1994. Also certainly Christian was the patron who commissioned the Veroli casket (s. X), on one plaque of which, representing the rape of Europa, a putto is shown performing fellatio on a horse (Weitzmann 1984, fig. 247).
66. Vat. lat. 3225 and 3867; see Wright 1992; 1993; and 2001; for a more detailed criticism of Wright's approach, Cameron 2004 501–25, summarized in the next couple of pages; Stevenson 1983, 114.

assumed to be ca. 400. Wright, Geymonat, and Pratesi all explicitly associate it with the "circle" of Symmachus,[67] with Wright insisting that "no Christian is likely to have commissioned a fine illustrated edition, especially one containing many scenes of pagan sacrifice."[68]

Such an interpretation of the Vatican miniatures rests on a number of false assumptions. First, the grounds adduced for the date are much more fragile than generally appreciated. Wright conceded that palaeographical considerations do no more than support a "relatively early date" compared to two other surviving books in Rustic capitals that have often been thought to be precisely dated. Unfortunately, both these dates (ca. 527 for Par. lat. 8084 and 494 for Vat. lat. 3225) have turned out to be based on misconceptions. Neither manuscript can be dated to within a half-century of ca. 500. The Vatican Vergil may be up to a century earlier than this, but if it is even as late as ca. 420/30[69] (the true date of Servius and Macrobius), a specifically pagan commission becomes unlikely.

Wright was impressed by the frequency of scenes of sacrifice. He was right to find them worthy of comment. No illustrator of the *Aeneid* could very well avoid representing its many mythological characters, whether human or divine. But specifically Roman scenes of sacrifice might well seem another matter. Salzman has drawn attention to the rarity of scenes of animal sacrifice on "mid-fourth century Roman artifacts with markedly pagan iconography," such as contorniates and pagan scenes from the Via Latina catacomb. Unlike earlier calendars illustrating pagan festivals, the Calendar of 354 shows only scenes of incense burning.[70] This she plausibly explains in terms of deliberate accommodation, a minimizing of features likely to offend Christians. The SYMMACHORVM/NICOMACHORVM diptych is often proclaimed an artifact of pagan "propaganda" (below), but it should be noted that both panels show scenes of incense burning, not animal sacrifice. If the Vaticanus is as late as 400, then its scenes of sacrifice certainly do not fit this trend. It is also worth noting that none of the twenty-odd medieval illustrated *Aeneid* manuscripts (tenth to fifteenth centuries) include such scenes.[71]

Four of the Vatican miniatures illustrate Roman sacrificial practice. One shows Laocoon as a Roman *victimarius*, bare to the waist and girded with an ankle-length apron (the *limus*); another Aeneas sacrificing a lamb and the Sibyl anointing a heifer; two more, Aeneas and Dido, respectively, preparing for sacrifice attended by *victimarii* and also *camilli* carrying the "bowl of fruits and cakes familiar in scenes of Roman sacrifice."[72] The last two are especially relevant in that Vergil himself simply described

67. Pratesi 1985, 5–33, referring to the "spirito pagano" and "intento propagandistico" of the illustrations; Geymonat in Horsfall 1995, 304.
68. Wright 1993, 3, 102–3; even Peter Brown (1971, 121 pl. 85) wrote of "the pagan illuminator of Vergil."
69. Wright 1993, 91, sets outside limits of 380–420; Pratesi 1985, 28, limits of 375–425; Cameron 1998, 33–39.
70. Salzman 1990, 226.
71. Courcelle and Courcelle 1984, 264–65.
72. Wright 1993, 22, 28, 33, 36; Ryberg 1955, 40–41.

FIGURE 4: the Vatican Vergil

Aeneas and Dido (shown *capite velato*) sacrificing (figure 4). Although victims were normally killed with a knife, *victimarii* are always shown with axes, again as regularly on Roman monuments. It was the painter who added these well-informed ritual details. Clearly the artist's ultimate models date from the early empire, when such scenes were commonly represented on monuments all over the Roman world. As early as the Ara Pacis Aeneas is represented performing a sacrifice that "reflects the formal ritual of the Roman state religion."[73]

But that does not prove either painter or patron a pagan. Just as late antique commentators repeated the ritual details they found in the early imperial commentaries on which they drew (Ch. 16), so painters unthinkingly repeated "pagan" details in their models, regardless of their own religious views. Commentaries and miniatures alike helped readers to understand what was after all a central and inescapable element in the Vergilian text. To suppose that only a pagan would commission such scenes is greatly to underestimate the power of secular traditions in Christian art and literature, above all among precisely the sort of people likely to commission luxury editions of the classics.

Our other illustrated Vergil codex, the Romanus of (probably) the mid-sixth century,[74] is effectively guaranteed by its date to have been commissioned by a Christian. Yet one of its nine surviving *Aeneid* illustrations represents Aeneas's sacrifice

73. Ryberg 1955, 40, with pl. X. 21, and passim.
74. For the date, Cameron 2004, 503; Wright 2001, 11, argues for ca. 480, mainly on the basis of a seriously mistaken date for the Basilius diptych (480 instead of 541).

of a sheep before the tomb of Anchises.[75] But instead of Aeneas himself sacrificing, we see three Trojans seated on thrones over a lower register of crowns and palms while an assistant sacrifices the sheep to one side (figure 5). As Wright saw, the artist was clearly influenced here by contemporary diptychs and other artefacts issued by magistrates who provided games. As we shall see later in this chapter, they regularly portray enthroned figures in the loge of circus or amphitheatre above garlands and palms in a lower register. The garlands and palms Wright identified as "generic prizes typical of official sponsorship of the games in the fifth century," and because the three Trojans are shown with the "imperial attributes of throne, nimbus and purple mantle," he identified them as representing "imperial authority authorizing pagan sacrifice."[76]

The argument fails to convince. In the first place, the miniature is surely to be seen as a combination of two entirely separate scenes, as we find in a number of the Vatican miniatures.[77] Most of the corresponding details in the Vergilian text are at least consecutive and sometimes (as in the Laocoön miniature) closely related. But f. 49ʳ fuses two unrelated episodes in what Wright himself characterizes as "meaningless amalgamation."[78] Such combinations are common in narrative illustrations (e.g., in the miniatures of the more or less contemporary Ambrosian *Iliad*),[79] and although there is no other case in the Romanus, it is the most natural interpretation here. Wright fancifully suggests that the central Trojan "looks at the scene of sacrifice, apparently authorizing it." But since the games *follow* the sacrifice in Vergil, it would be paradoxical if the later scene were supposed to "authorize" the earlier (not that there is any evidence for sacrifice *at* the games in any case). It would have been a most improbable stroke of creative antiquarianism for even the most devout late antique pagan to think that representing Aeneas "authorizing" sacrifice at the games would be recognized by fellow pagans as a "visual statement of pagan sacrifice." The explanation is much simpler. The Vergilian context—Aeneas presiding at Anchises's funeral games—prompted the artist to use the contemporary iconography of magistrates presiding at the games.

And since the entire scene—temple, snake, and sacrifice—is confined to a narrow strip to the left of the three Trojans presiding at the games, it is natural to conclude that it is meant to be thought of as an entirely separate event. Since the man actually performing the sacrifice has no nimbus and is dressed like the servants at Dido's banquet (f. 100ᵛ), he cannot be identified as Aeneas. In all probability he is to be seen, like the sacrificers in the Vaticanus miniatures, as a *victimarius*. In the fuller version of this scene that the Romanus painter has compressed, Aeneas was no doubt shown standing to one side of the *victimarius*, like Dido in figure 4.

---

75. fol. 76 ᵛ; color photo in Wright 2001, 32.

76. Wright 1998, 367; 1992, 366–68; 2001, 33, 53.

77. Wright 1993, 22–23, 50–51, 52–53, 56–57, 68–69.

78. And f. 53ᵛ combines three scenes in what Wright characterizes as "the squeezing together of what must have been two or three separate scenes in the iconographic model" (1993, 52, 57).

79. In three of the four Ambrosian miniatures included in Weitzmann 1977, nos. 7–10.

FIGURE 5: the Roman Vergil

In the second place, magistrate diptychs have nothing to do with official sanction of the games. Contrary to widespread belief, they were *private* mementos of public office, distributed by officeholders to commemorate their promotion. Their iconography was likewise conventional rather than official.[80] The Trojans are simply shown anachronistically in the contemporary guise of Roman magistrates presiding at the games. The crowns and palms do indeed represent the prizes offered for victory in the games, but have nothing whatever to do with "official sponsorship" of the games. They appear on the diptychs because the magistrate shown presiding at the games had paid for them out of his own pocket and was naturally anxious to claim the credit.

Still less do throne, nimbus, or purple mantle identify the three Trojans as representing imperial authority. To be sure, we might so identify a real person so portrayed. But not a mythological character in one of the classics. More specifically,

---

80. As I shall be explaining in a forthcoming catalogue of such diptychs to be published jointly with Anthony Cutler.

readers of the Romanus would have noticed that *all* the main characters in the *Aeneid* are shown with a nimbus (Priam, Dido, Ascanius, the Sibyl, the gods) and that Aeneas is regularly shown with a purple robe. Nor would any contemporary have associated thrones specifically with the emperor rather than any magistrate with judicial authority. Not only are prefects and governors regularly shown dispensing justice seated on a high throne, epigrams inscribed on the base of statues honoring such officials regularly single out the throne as the most characteristic symbol of their authority.[81] It is true that some imperial medallions show emperors enthroned with palms and sacks of coins in the exergue beneath them, but it is misleading to identify the combination of throne and palm leaves in this context as imperial symbols. These are *consular* medallions, and this is consular imagery;[82] the consulate was the one office emperors shared with private citizens. For a better (as well as chronologically closer) parallel, we might compare the consular diptych of Boethius (figure 6), where the consul sits on a throne holding aloft the *mappa* to start the games he has paid for. The palms in the lower register are prizes, but the sacks of gold are for the distributions (*sparsio*) he was expected to make during his consular procession.

There are many representations of pagan gods in both manuscripts. In the Romanus, for example, Iris appearing to Turnus (f. 74r), and, most elaborately, two full-page representations of the principal presiding deities of the *Aeneid* in council: Jupiter with Minerva, Mercury, Vulcan, and Juno; and Neptune with Diana, Apollo, Venus, and Mars.[83] Wright saw "pagan sympathies" here too, arguing that they are "devotional images." There is in fact a fair amount of evidence for pagan devotional images.[84] Though little studied, at least sixty have survived (almost all from Egypt),[85] and there are a few literary references as well.[86] Images of Isis and Suchos were discovered in a private house in Tebtynis, "one complete with its frame and the hemp cord by which it hung from the wall." Another showing Isis enthroned nursing Harpocrates—a particularly striking anticipation of Christian Virgin and child icons—was "painted directly on a house wall in Karanis."[87] All feature *individual* local deities (occasionally with an attendant) conspicuously displayed. A group of ten *dramatis personae* from the *Aeneid* who can only be located by finding the right page in a book can hardly be seen as a devotional image. They are simply illustrations. Readers were naturally curious to see what Vergil's gods looked like.

---

81. For many examples, Robert 1948, 35–47.
82. As Wright 1992, 101, acknowledges; for a different emphasis, Wright 2001, 33, 53.
83. Romanus fol. 74r, 234ᵛ and 235ʳ; Wright 1996, 152.
84. Mathews 1994, 177–90; 2001, 168–77.
85. Mathews 2001 lists thirty, but in November 2009 he told me that he and Norman Muller now know of sixty-two.
86. Pliny, *NH* 35. 5 (referring to people keeping images of Epicurus in their bedrooms). Clem. Alex. *Protr.* 61. 10 (p. 94 Marcovich) refers to *erotic* pictures people display in their homes "*as though* images of their gods."
87. Mathews 1994, 180, 182.

FIGURE 6: the Boethius Diptych

The original owner of the Vatican Vergil *could* have been a pagan. But not the man who commissioned the Romanus more than a century later. Six out of the seven calligraphic Vergil manuscripts in square or rustic capitals are now generally dated later than ca. 450 and so almost certainly Christian commissions. The (no doubt Christian) painters simply copied the content and placing of sacrificial scenes along with their illustrations from earlier illustrated Vergils.[88] It is no more likely that Christian patrons gave specific instructions for their exclusion than that pagans did for their inclusion.

4: PAGAN IVORIES

In every discussion of pagan art patronage, pride of place has always been taken by the celebrated ivory diptych of the Symmachi and Nicomachi now divided between

---

88. Pratesi 1985, 5–33. For earlier representations of *victimarii* on sacrificial monuments, Ryberg 1955, passim.

FIGURE 7. Symmachorum/Nicomachorum diptych

London and Paris (figure 7).[89] Kitzinger explicitly linked these panels with the "pagan revival" of the 390s, describing them as "exercises in nostalgia undertaken in the service of a very specific cause," "professions of unswerving devotion to the ancient gods."[90]

This "classical revival" sponsored by the pagan aristocracy had (he argued) a profound impact on the whole development of western art. This influence he traced in two areas. First in the "official" ivories of the age, the series of presentation diptychs inaugurated by the [L]AMPADIORVM, Probianus and Probus ivories (1, 54, 62V). And second, in two fine Christian ivories of this approximate period, the Munich Ascension panel and the Milan Marys at the Tomb panel (59, 60V). "There is rich

89. Volbach 1976, no. 55; for its history, Williamson 2010, 34–39. Doubts about the authenticity of SYMMACHORVM are misconceived (Kinney and Cutler 1994, 457–80); a recent radiocarbon test has revealed that the elephant died no later than ca. 350 (Williamson 2003). Ivories are cited by their number in Volbach (e.g., 55V).

90. Kitzinger 1977, 34–40. The rest of this chapter incorporates a revised and abridged version of "Pagan Ivories" (Cameron 1986), answering objections and adding new arguments.

irony," he concluded, "in the thought that it was the Nicomachi, Symmachi and other like-minded patrons who thus helped to bring about a massive transfer of pure classical forms into Christian art."

Kitzinger's discussions of the individual ivories are sensitive and illuminating. Yet the framework in which he arranged them is a perfect example of the dangers of attempting to write history without independently ascertained dates. There is an obvious sense in which a style derived from the study of classical models was at this period adapted both to official art and to Christian art. But what Kitzinger has done is, in effect, to treat a logical sequence as a chronological sequence. The pages that follow will argue that it is in fact the reverse of the true historical sequence; that NICOMACHORVM/SYMMACHORVM is not the earliest but the latest of this group of secular ivories. Naturally, this will involve a rethinking of the link Kitzinger postulated between paganism and Classicism.

Much ink has been spilt on the identification and meaning of the scenes depicted on the two panels of this diptych. Each panel show a woman wearing an ivy garland standing in front of an altar framed by a tree. On SYMMACHORVM the woman is dropping some grains of incense on the altar, and the tree is an oak; on NICOMACHORVM the woman holds two long, downward-pointing torches, and the tree is a pine, with cymbals hanging from its branches. On the long-standard view of Delbrueck, both women are priestesses: on SYMMACHORVM a priestess of Bacchus sacrificing to Jupiter (the oak); on NICOMACHORVM of Ceres sacrificing to Cybele (pine and cymbals).[91]

For Bloch, this is the sort of "syncretism" we should expect to find in late paganism: "a very appropriate subject if we think of Fabia Paulina's titles *sacrata ... Libero et Cereri et Corae*."[92] But this is not what is generally understood by syncretism. It is one thing to identify (say) Roman Ceres with Greek Demeter or Egyptian Isis, or to represent Ceres with attributes of Demeter or Isis (that is to say, assume that, apparent differences notwithstanding, they are in essence the same divine figure), but quite another to construct a composite scene deliberately combining specific elements from different Roman cults. It makes no sense in cult terms for the priestess of one cult to be represented sacrificing to the god of another. Delbrueck created a category of "priest-diptychs" on the analogy of consular diptychs, supposedly distributed by priests to inform colleagues of their election to the various colleges.[93] His other example was the Asclepius and Hygieia diptych, generally dated to ca. 400 and assumed to be the product of a Roman workshop.[94] But this makes no sense in Roman terms either. The temple of Aesculapius on the Tiber Island functioned as a Greek Asclepieum, with incubation and dream cures. Its priests must have been Greeks.

---

91. Delbrueck 1929, 212.
92. Bloch 1945, 229; so too (after many others) Kiilerich 1991, 122.
93. Delbrueck 1929, 8–9, 213–14, 217.
94. D 55 = V 57; Gibson 1994, nos. 5–6, pp. 10–15.

Graeven argued that both panels of NICOMACHORVM/SYMMACHORVM represented some mystery initiation or other.[95] Yet neither scene corresponds to the sphere of any one Roman priesthood or any one mystery cult. The most meticulous recent investigation, by Kinney,[96] is devoted to the iconography of the two female figures. The figure on SYMMACHORVM she traces to a representation of Pietas that first appears on coins of Hadrian and Antoninus Pius: a female figure facing right, left leg slightly bent, holding a vessel in her left hand, and dropping kernels of incense with her right into the fire on the low altar in front of her. In both SYMMACHORVM and the coin type this figure's hands are aligned in exactly the same way. It reappears in a slightly different form as a fourth-century contorniate type, based on the reverse of an issue of Pius and labeled Diva Faustina Augusta. The figure on NICOMACHORVM, with its two long, downturned torches, Kinney traces from Athenian coins to a relief from Naples and the so-called Torre Nova casket (second century), decorated with scenes from the Eleusinian mysteries: among them a figure who is either "Kore acting as a priestess, or perhaps a priestess impersonating Kore," with two downturned torches.[97]

Both identifications are iconographically plausible in themselves. But what do we make of the much more complex scenes on our two panels? For it is precisely the additions to these basic types—the ivy garland and oak tree and the cymbal-decked pine—that have inspired most modern readings of the *function* of the diptych. Most scholars have read them as references to Bacchus, Jupiter, and Cybele, respectively. In particular, what are we to make of Kore's bare breast?

Kinney sees oak and pine as purely topographical features, and tries to preserve what she can of the original associations of the figures she has identified. Symmachus's plea for the restoration of the altar of Victory, she claims, "appeals repeatedly to classical notions of *pietas*." Yet he never actually uses the word, and *pietas* on the coinage always refers to the emperor's *pietas*, not "classical notions."[98] Nor is it easy to believe that this otherwise unremarkable sacrificing female could be recognized as Pietas by her pose alone, without the label that identified her on a long defunct coin-type. As for NICOMACHORVM, Kinney argues that both designer and recipient "had knowledge of the statue prototype," and knew (e.g.) that in its Eleusinian context Kore's torches were tools in a ceremony of purification by smoke. That seems a stretch.

Are then the pine, oak, ivy, and cymbals mere space-filling details, or do they reidentify the two figures, or at any rate redefine their roles in the new context? And what is the relationship between the figures? The balancing poses and parallel frames of tree and altar make it hard to doubt that they are being presented as a pair. But what does Greek Kore have to do with Roman Pietas? I quote from Kinney's concluding speculation:

---

95. Graeven 1913, 246–71.
96. Kinney 1994, 64–96, with plates 4–12.
97. Kinney 1994, 82.
98. As Kinney's own well-documented discussion (69–71) makes clear.

Viewed as the modern scholar usually imagines it, splayed open with front and back sides forming a continuum, the diptych offers an obvious, homogeneous subject and a more subtle binary one. The obvious subject is Bacchic, a sacrifice in a rustic landscape with a superhuman female, a bacchante, standing potently by. The cryptic subject involves Pietas and Kore, the one representing Rome, the other Athens. From their opposition, or complementarity, arise any number of meditations on the history, meaning, and value of the Dionysiac mysteries for fourth-century pagans.

Like most of her predecessors, she appeals to the parallel of Praetextatus and his initiations. But it is not *his* name that appears on either of the plaques, but those of Symmachus and Flavian, neither of whom seems to have taken any interest in mystery initiations or ever visited Athens.

Like the diptychs distributed by quaestors, praetors, and consuls, these were presentation objects, sent to a few friends or colleagues. The eye of the art historian focuses on picture first and inscription second. But it was surely the names, prominently engraved at the top of each panel, that first caught the recipient's eye as he unwrapped his parcel, and it must surely be these names that dictate interpretation. Familiar as he was with the conventions of this well-established custom, the recipient would also have noticed two specific features about the names: first that the linking of the two panels links the two names, and second, that both are in the genitive plural. Not Symmachus and Nicomachus, but "the Symmachi" coupled with "the Nicomachi."

It is the linking of the names that has led to widespread acceptance of the hypothesis that the function of the diptych as a whole was to commemorate a wedding. For two weddings between the Symmachi and Nicomachi are directly attested: Symmachus's daughter with the younger Flavian ca. 387, and his son Memmius with a granddaughter of the elder Flavian in 401. But there are problems with this hypothesis. As Graeven remarked long ago, but for the independently attested weddings, no one would ever have made such an inference from the iconography of the diptych.

Simon has recently made an ingenious attempt to identify nuptial themes. She sees the two female figures not as priestesses but as goddesses. The NICOMACH-ORVM goddess with the two torches is Kore, but the artist altered the standard type by baring her right breast, thus conferring on Kore "a connotation of Aphrodite."[99] If Kore takes on the aspect of Venus, continues Simon, "then the torches of the mysteries in her hands take on the aspect of a wedding." The SYMMACHORVM goddess she identifies as Kore-Iuventas, on the grounds that the figure itself is similar to a personified Iuventas sacrificing in front of an altar on a coin of Pius, and Iuventas has links (of a sort) in Roman cult with both Liber (ivy) and Jupiter (oak). The two figures (she

99. Simon 1992, 56–65.

claims) are two aspects of the same goddess: Kore-Venus is "like a bride before marriage" while Kore-Iuventas is "like a young married woman."

This is pretty heady stuff, one equation piled on another, Greek mixed with Roman, till the head spins. Simon concedes that her interpretation is "complicated," but feels that problems are "overcome by Neo-Platonic theology" because, after all (she patronizingly adds) "we are in late antiquity," where (she implies) anything goes. But not all late Roman aristocrats saw the world through Neoplatonic spectacles. More specifically, there is no evidence that Symmachus, Flavian, or even Praetextatus had any knowledge of Neoplatonism (Ch. 15).

The key detail in this interpretation is the bare breast. But it is one thing to detect (e.g.) an allusion to Venus from a slipping garment on a bust of Livia. Informed observers of that age were alert to such allusions to a variety of deities in representations of imperial females (the same cameo of Livia alludes to Cybele and Ceres as well, with a turreted crown and a sheaf of grain in her hand).[100] But NICOMACHORVM is a quite different sort of representation.[101] Cohen has identified a number of contexts in which female figures are shown with one bare breast in classical art.[102] One category is indeed erotic: Danaë or Leda being approached by an amorous Zeus. But there is no such erotic context in NICOMACHORVM. Another well-documented category is victims of physical violence, notably Niobids and Amazons, or Prokris, accidentally killed by the spear of Kephalos, or Dirke, dragged to her death by a bull. As far as NICOMACHORVM is concerned, the most relevant of Cohen's categories may be "garments accidentally loosened or set in disarray through an action or pose of the wearer," such as dancing maenads or flying Nikai. The contemporary Claudian describes a scene of ritual purification in which a priest "swings the smoking torches around his body."[103] In view of the size of the torches the NICOMACHORVM Kore is swinging, it may be that the slipped garment was intended to reflect her physical exertion.

Nor is it easy to believe that, without an identifying label, anyone would identify the SYMMACHORVM-female as Iuventas rather than Kinney's Pietas (in posture a much closer match). Even granted both Simon's identifications, they hardly amount to *wedding* imagery. Since it was the Lord of the Underworld Kore married, she makes a more natural symbol for death than marriage—as indeed her frequent representation on sarcophagus-reliefs so clearly implies.

The conventions and motifs of wedding imagery were well established, in both art and literature. Claudian's *Epithalamium* for Honorius's wedding in 398 and the silver casket of Proiecta (both nearly contemporary with our diptych) give some

---

100. Zanker 1988, 234.
101. The representations of Aphrodite with one bare breast to which Simon 1992, 64 n. 15, refers are misleading, inasmuch as most are copies of one type, in which the goddess is obviously undressing (*LIMC* 2 [1984], 34).
102. Cohen 1997, 66–92.
103. *circum membra rotat, VI Cons. Hon.* 326.

idea of the range of nuptial themes.[104] In the first place, we need Cupids and a Venus, and signs of festivity. What we have here, on the contrary, is an unmistakable and pervasive air of solemnity, not to say melancholy. Above all, a bare breast surely cannot transform downturned torches into marriage torches.[105] Torches were a conspicuous feature of the wedding procession that conducted a Roman bride to her new home. In poetry, indeed, *taedae* became a symbol and synonym for marriage.[106] But *lowered* torches are one of the commonest symbols in Graeco-Roman art and literature for *death*. Torches were lowered for funerals. A putto with a lowered torch is a stock motif on Roman sarcophagi.[107] In mythological scenes on mosaics a putto with downturned torch often indicates a tragic outcome to the story: Hippolytus rejecting Phaedra on a mosaic from Paphos, or Echo and Narcissus on an Antiochene mosaic.[108] Thanatos himself is regularly shown with a lowered torch.[109]

Cracco Ruggini has objected that downturned torches do not invariably imply death.[110] Not *always*, perhaps, but almost always. She suggests only one counter-example. Relying on Simon's ingenious but improbable theory that the Portland Vase celebrates the legendary union between Augustus's mother, Atia, and Apollo, she cites the downturned torch slipping from the nerveless left hand of the reclining female figure. But critics from Josiah Wedgwood to Paul Zanker have read this very detail as a symbol of death and mourning.[111] Of the now "well over fifty" readings of this enigmatic artifact,[112] one of the most recent is the posthumous wedding of Achilles and Helen on the White Island. Its proposer gave the torch nuptial significance—but added that "as it is downturned, it is connected with the underworld or afterlife," thus supporting his suggestion of a "marriage after death."[113]

Since on NICOMACHORVM it is Kore who holds the torches, it is illuminating to turn again to Claudian, who describes how on Kore's disappearance her mother, Demeter, kindled torches in Mount Aetna and *lowered* them for her search (*inclinatque faces*),[114] with the words:

104. M. Roberts 1989, 321–48; Shelton 1981, 72–75.

105. Simon's claim that Kore is lighting one torch from the other, "a poetic periphrasis for the union of the couple," seems to me entirely fanciful.

106. Treggiari 1991, 166–69; Pease on *Aen.* iv. 18, 339. Pairs of torches are also common on monuments of the cult of Cybele, but these torches are almost invariably held upwards, or shown crossed inside a medallion.

107. Cumont 1942, 341, 391, 409–11, 444; McCann 1978, 51–52; Stuveras 1979; see too the section "torche baisée" in the entry "Eros/Amor, Cupido" in *LIMC* 3. 1 (1986), 976–77.

108. Levi 1947, 137; ii pl. 23c; Kondoleon (to whom I owe both references) 1995, 42, fig. 17.

109. W. H. Roscher, *Myth. Lex.* v. 523–26; C. Saletti, *Encicl. Dell'arte antica* vii. 798–99.

110. Cracco Ruggini in Paschoud 1986, 65 (commenting on Cameron 1986.

111. Ashmole 1967, 14; Zanker 1988, 254.

112. Susan Walker, *The Portland Vase* (London 2004), 7.

113. Hind 1995, 153–55.

114. *De Raptu Pros.* iii. 370–442; cf. Ovid, *Met.* 441–42: *illa duabus / flammiferas pinus manibus succendit ab Aetna.*

non tales gestare tibi, Proserpina, taedas
sperabam, sed vota mihi communia matrum,
et thalami festaeque faces caeloque canendus
ante oculos hymenaeus erat.

Not torches such as these did I hope to
bear for you, Proserpine, but—the
wish of all mothers—a wedding, festal
torches, a marriage to be sung of to
heaven, this was my plan.

Claudian had in mind an image of Demeter carrying lowered torches, which he interpreted as the antithesis of marriage torches. The motif of marriage torches lighting the funeral pyre of those who die just before or after marriage is a commonplace of Greek and Roman epitaphs.[115] "Hide your torches, Hymen…far different are the torches that light the somber grave" (Ovid); for Silius, funerary torches are reversed marriage torches (*taedaeque ad funera versae*).[116] Particularly relevant is an epitaph by the first-century Antipater of Thessalonica for a young girl whose mother had "hoped for a different torch, but this one came first, and the torch was lit not as we prayed, but by Persephone."[117] That is to say, a torch lit by Kore-Persephone symbolizes death.

This death symbolism of downturned torches was a commonplace of literature as well as art, from high poetry down to the most mundane inscribed epitaphs.[118] It was also a familiar motif in a much wider and less esoteric range of art than Eleusinian reliefs. It would certainly have been familiar to even such philistines as the average Roman aristocrat. When the Kore figure was extracted from her original Eleusinian context (I suggest), the more universal death symbolism of downturned torches was likely to take over. Could any sensitive craftsman have used so ill-omened a motif for a wedding celebrated by classically educated patrons? Is it not more likely that the diptych was in fact intended to commemorate a family *death*? That would much better explain both the general air of melancholy and a number of specific funerary motifs.

5: THE CONSECRATIO IVORY

Before inquiring which death, let us turn to the surviving half of another diptych, the so-called Consecratio panel in the British Museum (56V), a late antique copy of the apotheosis of a Roman emperor (figure 8). At the bottom of the panel the emperor's statue stands in a wheeled shrine pulled by an elephant quadriga. Behind the elephants is a funeral pyre, from which another quadriga ascends to heaven. Above we see the subject yet again, carried by two wind gods,[119] being welcomed to the left by ancestors already in heaven, while in the top right-hand corner the sun god watches from behind an arc containing six signs of the zodiac.

---

115. A. S. F. Gow and D. L. Page, *Garland of Philip* 2 (1968), 33; add Heliodorus, *Aeth.* 2. 29.
116. Ovid, *Fasti* ii. 561–62; Silius ii. 184, xiii. 547.
117. *Anth.* Pal. vii. 185. 5–6.
118. *Inter utramque facem* in Prop. iv. 11. 46 means "between marriage and death."
119. On this identification of these figures, Cumont 1942, 174–76.

FIGURE 8: the Consecratio Ivory

Most of the literature on this enigmatic panel has been based on the assumption that, as on its (perhaps second-century) model, its subject is an emperor, variously identified. For little better reason than the beard, the sun god, and the elephants ("symbols of eastern campaigns"), the favorite candidate has always been Julian.[120] Adherents of this view fail to explain why the "emperor" is shown in simple toga without diadem, or why he is shown as triumphator when Julian's eastern campaign was a disastrous failure. And before we make too much of the sun god, we should bear in mind that considerations of symmetry suggest that the moon goddess appeared in the corresponding position on the now-lost companion panel, above the other six signs of the zodiac. Here we may compare the sun god and moon goddess in the spandrels of the sixth-century diptych of Christ and the Virgin (figure 9)— incidentally a warning not to press the pagan implications of at any rate this detail in the iconography.[121]

---

120. For example, Straub 1962, 310–26; St. Clair 1964, 205–11.
121. V 137; Weitzmann 1979, no. 474 (with color reproduction on the dust jacket).

FIGURE 9: Christ and the Virgin Diptych

The main reason the panel concerns us here is Weigand's decipherment of the monogram set in the medallion at the top as SYMMACHORVM.[122] The S and the Y at the top left and right-hand sides, respectively, combine naturally with the central M to guide the eye on its way. David Wright has objected that "the cutting of the monogram clearly makes the element at the upper left a C separate from the R or P below it; if it were intended to be an initial S the letter should be larger and the continuity of strokes unmistakable."[123] Ideally, no doubt. But S must be a particularly difficult letter to render exactly in so hard a medium as ivory, especially when the upper curve has to serve as C and the lower as the curved element in P and R. Wright refers to the monogram on the chair of Maximian (140 Volbach), but there only the top curve has to do double duty, and in any case the execution of the monogram as a whole is far more regular and careful. In the monogram on the diptych of Orestes cos. 530 (31 Volbach), a somewhat better executed S does the same double duty as C and the top of R, but it

122. Weigand 1937, 125–26.
123. Wright 1995, 50.

should be noted that the execution differs on the two panels. Neither Wright nor anyone else has ever been able to suggest a plausible alternative decipherment.[124] Symmachus did in fact use a signet ring bearing his monogram (a "ring whereby my name is deciphered rather than read").[125]

For some, the Symmachan link provided support for the Julian identification: the diptych was "propaganda" for the pagan emperor. Yet there is little evidence that Julian's mystical brand of Neoplatonic Hellenism appealed to Roman aristocrats.[126] The emperor in the artist's model may (as is often assumed) have been Antoninus Pius,[127] but it makes no sense to suppose that he is also the actual subject of the panel. Why would anyone wish to commemorate the apotheosis of Pius two and a half centuries after his death—least of all Symmachus, who only mentions him twice, once to comment on his laziness.[128] Nor does it make sense to stress the paganism of the panel.[129] The deification of emperors was no part of the traditional state cults, nor did it interest antiquarians like Macrobius or Servius.[130]

Cracco Ruggini has suggested that the panel depicts the deification of a private citizen, Theodosius *comes*, father of the emperor Theodosius I.[131] This deification, which she infers from a passage of Symmachus, she dates to 384, when Symmachus was city prefect, arguing that this explains the Symmachan monogram. There is only one point I would accept in this influential but improbable thesis: the subject of the panel is not shown as an emperor. Though emperors were regularly shown holding sceptres, so too were both consuls and proconsuls.[132] For the rest, there are at least four objections, collectively fatal.

1. First (and decisive in itself), it would be without parallel for a private citizen to be officially deified by the senate. And why should a pagan senator have been so misguided as to think that a Christian emperor would be pleased if his father was declared a pagan god?

2. The only evidence is the following passage of Symmachus, addressed to Theodosius:[133]

> This noble order of senators has ... solemnly honored with equestrian statues
> and thus consecrated among ancient names (*inter prisca nomina consecravit*),

---

124. The rules of the game are that letters can be read from any angle and any number of times.
125. *non minore sane cura cupio cognoscere, an omnes obsignatas meas sumperis eo anulo, quo nomen meum magis intellegi quam legi promptum est* (*Ep.* 2. 12. 1).
126. Weiss 1978, 135; Cracco Ruggini 1977, 469.
127. This question dominates the recent discussion by Wright 1998, 359–64, to the extent that he identifies the figure on the lost companion panel as Pius's wife, Faustina.
128. *Or.* i. 16; *Ep.* i. 13. 3.
129. So Wright 1998, 359, 364.
130. Servius only mentions it indirectly in passing when explaining the difference between *deus* and *divus*: *divi* were once mortals, "whence we call the emperors *divi* " (*Aen.* v. 45).
131. Cracco Ruggini 1977, 425–89; accepted and supported by Vera 1981, 89–132.
132. For consuls' sceptres, below p. 734; for proconsuls' sceptres, Foss 1983, 196–219.
133. *Rel.* 9. 4 (English Translation Barrow, adapted); for the address, Vera's commentary.

the author of your family and line who was formerly general in Africa and Britain; he had the favor of fortune when he begat a Divinity to bring well-being to the empire. This is the honor given to men whose children by their birth benefit the state.

The commonest formula for deification is *inter divos referri*, where *inter divos* makes it as clear as the eagles on coins, cameos, and reliefs that it is the location of the emperor's soul in another world that is envisaged. By contrast, to place (as here) a statue *inter prisca nomina* was to put a physical object somewhere in this world, among the statues of great men of the past. That this is what Symmachus had in mind is put beyond doubt by his next point: it is fitting so to honor the elder Theodosius because "he sired a Divinity to bring well-being to the empire" (*numen in imperium salutare progenuit*). It is only his son, the emperor, who can lay any claim to divinity.

3. *Consecravit* here bears a meaning abundantly documented from Cicero to Cassiodorus, "immortalize" in the weakened sense "save from oblivion."[134] *Consecrare* even occurs occasionally in dedicatory inscriptions as an alternative to the more common terms for erecting honorific statues (*erigere, statuere*, etc.).[135]

4. How can the decipherment of the monogram as SYMMACHORVM be connected with statues of Theodosius? Even if Symmachus had tried to take personal credit for statues erected by the senate, he would have done so in his capacity as urban prefect. But the genitive plural implies a domestic matter affecting his family rather than a public issue involving the senate. What we need is something that concerns the Symmachi *as a family*. But only the Symmachi? The analogy of the NICOMACH-ORVM/SYMMACHORVM and LAMPADIORVM/RUFIORVM diptychs (below) makes it likely that the missing pair to the Consecratio panel was also inscribed with a family name in the genitive plural.

More later on the remarkable stylistic differences between the Consecratio panel and NICOMACHORVM/SYMMACHORVM. But they do share one striking common feature, over and above the inscription. It has been remarked already how unsuitable both the general tone and the specific iconography of NICOMACH-ORVM/SYMMACHORVM would be for the commemoration of a wedding. This is even more obviously true of the Consecratio panel, entirely concerned as it is with the theme of death and rebirth. If the inscription alludes to an event concerning the family of the Symmachi, it can only be to a death—a family death.

Now these two diptychs might have commemorated different deaths, one shared by the Symmachi and Nicomachi, the other confined to the Symmachi or shared with some other family. But the family with the closest ties to the Symmachi at the turn of the fourth century was undoubtedly the Nicomachi. The simplest explanation is that the name on the missing pair to the Consecratio panel was, again,

---

134. *TLL* iv. 383. 43–74, *latiore sensu, immortalem reddere, beare*.
135. E.g., *ILS* 795 (*consecravit dedicavitque*, a statue of a prefect of Rome); *ILS* 8944.

NICOMACHORVM—and that both diptychs commemorated the same death or deaths.

Which deaths? Given Symmachus's obsessive concern with the health of his kin, we may be sure that none of the principals or products of either of the marriages between the two families died before Symmachus's correspondence was cut short by his own death in 402. I propose an alternative that explains to perfection the linking of the two names.

The elder Flavian died by his own hand in September 394. The younger Flavian converted and lay low. The *infamia* proclaimed in April 395 was lifted a month later (Ch. 5. 4), and, thanks to the efforts of his father-in-law, he was restored to favor in 398 and to a third tenure of the urban prefecture in 399 (Ch. 14. 2). The Symmachi and Nicomachi doubtless mourned the elder Flavian in private in 394, but they were not so indiscreet as to erect a conspicuous monument. It was not till his father's death in 402 that Memmius erected a monument to both men together, in private. In the family house on the Caelian Hill he put up a pair of statues, of which the matching bases survive (p. 155). It has sometimes been inferred that Flavian's statue was erected immediately after his death in 394. But Memmius did not become Flavian's "grandson-in-law" (*prosocero*) until his marriage in 401. The inscriptions were evidently composed to balance each other, and the most plausible explanation is that both statues were put up together as a pair *after* Symmachus's death.

Was it not on this same occasion that Memmius distributed a set of ivory diptychs in memory of these two paladins of the old order, patriarchs of his own and his wife's families? The diptychs were headed, naturally enough: NICOMACHORVM and SYMMACHORVM. Proper names in the genitive plural had long been associated with funerary monuments. Innumerable tombs bear inscriptions headed VRANIORVM, PELAGIORVM, EVTYCHIORVM, and the like. Few seem to have been genuine family tombs; most were apparently private funeral clubs, whose members took, in this context, the name of the founder and builder of the tomb.[136]

Two recent contributions to the interpretation of SYMMACHORVM/NICO-MACHORVM, developing my suggestion of a funerary function in a different direction, have instead identified the deceased honorand as Praetextatus.[137] According to Kiilerich, "The dead person commemorated does not necessarily have to be a Symmachus or a Nicomachus." But if the honorand is someone else, why are the only people named Symmachi and Nicomachi? And while it is conceivable that Symmachus and Flavian might have chosen to commemorate the death of their admired colleague Praetextatus, the genitive plurals show that it is the families, not the individuals, who are being evoked. It seems to me that the honorand *does* have to be a Symmachus or Nicomachus.

---

136. De Rossi 1877, 705f.; Kajanto 1963, 35–39; 1966, 43–50.
137. Kiilerich 1991; and Turcan 1996, 745–67; so too, more cautiously, Kahlos 2002, 207–8.

There is also another problem. This interpretation privileges the paganism of the panels. Both Kiilerich and Turcan took it for granted that nothing could have been dearer to the hearts of Flavian and Symmachus than commemorating the death of a fellow pagan. In fact, this very issue was a source of friction between Symmachus and Flavian on the one hand, and the family of Praetextatus on the other. Symmachus asked the emperors to erect statues in Praetextatus's memory, and while his request was ultimately granted, there was considerable delay in its execution. Despite having submitted all the necessary paperwork, he was required, rather insultingly, to supply further justification.[138] The Vestal Virgins also announced their intention of raising a statue to Praetextatus. Symmachus, conservative to the core, saw this as a dangerous precedent (!), and voted against it. A few other pontiffs agreed with him, but most approved. Our knowledge of the dispute derives from the letter in which Symmachus explained it to Flavian, who had (characteristically) missed the relevant meeting. Symmachus evidently assumed that Flavian would share his point of view. Praetextatus's widow, Paulina, was understandably annoyed, both at the delay in the official statue and at Symmachus's opposition to the Vestals' statue. In fact, she raised a statue of her own to Coelia Concordia, the chief Vestal, pointedly praising her for being the *first* to erect a statue to her husband.[139]

The scenes on these panels were copied from a variety of earlier models. How do we combine the conflicting iconographic details into one harmonious interpretation? The answer (I suggest) is that we should not even try. The details are not in themselves significant. Memmius simply chose a series of classical scenes of generally pagan inspiration that in one way or another suggested death, mourning, rebirth, or apotheosis. Even Kore's bare breast on NICOMACHORVM can be assigned an appropriate significance. One further context in which women are shown with bared breast is scenes of distress. One familiar example is the Barberini suppliant;[140] less familiar is a late antique mosaic illustrating the story of Pyramus and Thisbe from Paphos on Cyprus. Thisbe, one breast bare, is shown fleeing as a leopard finds the cloak she has dropped. In the context this cannot be an allusion to her love for Pyramus, nor is she suffering violence. The most natural interpretation of her slipping chiton is simply that it underlines her fear or distress.[141] One of the commonest literary motifs for mourning in ancient texts is women baring and beating their breasts, and it is surely permissible to read Kore's bare breast as a sign of mourning.

The Consecratio panel shows, not an emperor, but a private citizen, though a *princeps civitatis* (whence the toga rather than contemporary imperial regalia), whose soul is joining his ancestors beyond the stars, just as Cicero had described in his *Somnium Scipionis*, so elaborately expounded a generation later by Macrobius. Symmachus himself in his most famous speech pictures the deceased Valentinian I gazing down

138. Symm. *Rel.* 12; 24, with Vera 1981, 102–7, 180–83.
139. *ILS* 1261 (*quod haec prior eius viro . . . statuam conlocarat*); Polara 1967, 48.
140. Cohen 1997, 66–67, 82.
141. So Kondoleon 1995, 158–59.

from "his citadel among the stars" (*ex arce siderea*, *Rel.* 3. 20). If I am right, then in all probability the face of this *princeps* is a portrait of none other than Symmachus. There can be little doubt that it is a portrait in any case, since both representations of the *princeps* have identical as well as idiosyncratic features. As for the sceptre he holds, Symmachus had been both consul and proconsul.

Such wholesale appropriation of imperial iconography by a private citizen (it has been objected) would have been considered treasonable.[142] Hardly. Zanker has recently remarked on the incorporation of elements of imperial iconography in the funerary art of private citizens already in the early empire.[143] Many imperial motifs appear regularly on a wide range of funerary monuments for private citizens.[144] Even eagles, the symbol par excellence of imperial apotheosis, are found on private monuments.[145] One sarcophagus for a child shows him carried up to heaven on a chariot as well as an eagle.[146] Dionysiac sarcophagi show the apotheosis of the deceased as Dionysus in a chariot drawn by elephants.[147] The closest single analogue to the Consecratio panel is the third-century Mausoleum at Igel near Trier, where the deceased is represented on the rear face as Hercules rising up to heaven in a chariot surrounded by the zodiac, with four wind gods (differently represented) blowing him on his way while Athena extends him a helping hand from above (figure 10).[148]

Above all, it is not as if I am proposing a real-life formal ceremony of consecration; merely the use of certain funerary motifs in a private context. Why should the Christian court of 402 have cared if a private citizen copied motifs from an old pagan imperial apotheosis? Christians believed in a very different sort of afterlife, not restricted to *principes civitatis*, however defined.

What was shown on the missing pair to the Consecratio panel? On the traditional imperial identification, the apotheosis of the emperor's wife, or perhaps his birth, or an adventus. I suggest the apotheosis of another *princeps civitatis* : more precisely, of Flavian. The eagles represent the soul of the deceased flying up to heaven. But why two eagles? There is only one other scene of this type that features two eagles: the apotheosis relief on the base of the column of Antoninus Pius, which in addition to two eagles depicts two souls on their way to heaven, Pius and his wife, Faustina. It has generally and surely rightly been inferred that the two eagles

142. "avrebbe potuto incorrere nel *crimen* di *laesa maiestas*," Cracco Ruggini in Paschoud 1986, 67.
143. "Die Übernahme von Elementen der kaiserliche Bildsprache in die bürgerliche Grabkunst," Zanker and Ewald 2004, 227.
144. Wrede 1981, collects hundreds of examples of what he calls the apotheosis of private persons, often of very humble status. But his criteria are very generous, taking in any monument in which the deceased is implicitly represented as or shown with the attributes of a god (see the criticisms of J. A. North, *JRS* 73 [1983], 172). To forestall Nock's criticism of Cumont, I hasten to make clear that I am only hereconcerned with motifs, not beliefs.
145. Vogel 1973, 40–55. The link between eagles and apotheosis (Cumont 1949, 294–97) was accepted as "a certainty" even by the sceptical Nock 1972, 606.
146. Cumont 1942, 336–37.
147. Turcan 1966, 468–83, 498–502.
148. Strong 1915, 222; Cumont 1942, 174–76 (pl. XIV illustrates both monuments together).

FIGURE 10: Relief from the Igel Mausoleum

represent the two souls.[149] Perhaps here too: two souls and two deceased, Symmachus and Flavian.

There is also another significant parallel between ivory and column base. The deaths of Symmachus and Flavian were separated by eight years.[150] But the relief of Pius shows Pius and Faustina rising together to heaven despite the fact that Faustina died *twenty* years before Pius (141/161), and was separately consecrated at the time. If Marcus Aurelius included his adoptive mother, Faustina, retrospectively when commemorating the consecration of Pius, why should not Memmius Symmachus have included Flavian when commemorating his father, reuniting two old friends as well as two great forbears of his own?

As for NICOMACHORVM/SYMMACHORVM, on this hypothesis the ivy garlands both females wear would at last take on a relevant and appropriate significance as evergreens, universal symbols of rebirth and immortality.[151] The pinecones above

149. Vogel 1973, 40 with pl. 3; Kleiner 1992, 287.
150. Cracco Ruggini in Paschoud 1986, 67.
151. Cumont 1942, 220, 505–6, 522 (index s.v. lierre); more detail in Cumont 1942a.

FIGURE 11: the column of Antoninus Pius

Kore's head on NICOMACHORVM are another common symbol of immortality in funerary art.[152] The point is most explicitly made in the following lines from another contemporary poet, this time the Christian Paulinus of Nola, about a man called *Pinianus*:

> cui Deus a pinu nomen habere dedit,
> natus ut aeternae uitae puer arbore ab illa
> susciperet nomen, quae sine fine uiret. (21. 296–98)

To whom God gave his name from the pine tree, so that a boy born for eternal life might take his name from the tree that is forever green.

6: THE FAUVEL IVORY

There is also a third panel to take into account. In 1719 Bernard de Montfaucon published an engraving of an ivory panel (now lost) in the possession of his friend the Abbé Fauvel, chaplain to Louis XIV.[153] This panel closely resembles the

---

152. Strong 1915, 195–97 ("The pine-cone appears almost as constantly on these tombstones as the cross on Christian graves"); Cumont 1942, 218, 505–6.

153. B. de Montfaucon, *L'Antiquité expliquée et représentée en figures* 2. 1 (Paris 1719), 190, pl. 83. 1; Lasko 1981, 89–93; Cameron 1984, 397–402.

FIGURE 12: the Fauvel Panel

SYMMACHORVM panel. So closely, indeed, that it is not enough to describe it as "influenced by" SYMMACHORVM. It is nothing less than another version of the same design, a copy with a few deliberate variations (figure 12). That it is not a modern copy is put beyond doubt by the replacement of the original inscription with a Carolingian name, Ennobertus. No forger with an eye for the antiquities market would have been so misguided as to substitute an obviously medieval name[154] for the fine Roman name SYMMACHORVM.

A comparison of the Fauvel and SYMMACHORVM panels confirms that both scenes are composite. The basic master design was a Pietas-type figure sacrificing at an altar, but with a different frame and details. The hair of the Fauvel female is bound with a handkerchief instead of Dionysiac ivy garland, and her right forearm is shown bare. The altar is decorated differently, and the assistant holds a differently shaped vessel in his right hand. The tree too is different, to judge from its leaves a laurel. Above all, she is sacrificing in front of a temple, presumably of Mercury, since the heads on the two

---

154. For this name, Cameron 1984, 397–98.

central pillars have little wings. The fillet tied around the column of the left hand herm reveals the same preoccupation with details of ritual that is so striking a feature of the two extant panels (an eastern law of 392 forbids the "binding of trees with fillets").[155]

While SYMMACHORVM is clearly the closest analogue to the Fauvel panel, it also shares one feature with the Consecratio panel: the medallion set in the pediment above the tabula ansata. The diptych of Boethius cos. 487 has a similarly placed medallion inscribed with his monogram (see figure 6), and the diptych of Orestes cos. 530 has a monogram on a medallion beneath the tabula, in both cases on both panels (31 Volbach). When its Carolingian owner reused the Fauvel panel, he apparently had the original inscriptions stripped from both medallion and tabula,[156] reinscribing the tabula with his own name but leaving the medallion blank. Given its close similarity to SYMMACHORVM, it is natural to conjecture that the original inscription to this panel was (again) SYMMACHORVM. I suggest that the original was one of the postulated series of linked scenes commissioned by Memmius Symmachus to commemorate his father's death in 402.

On the traditional assumption that each panel of NICOMACHORVM/ SYMMACHORVM evokes two different deities (Jupiter and Dionysus; Demeter and Cybele), then the two evoked by the Fauvel panel would be Mercury and Apollo (wings and laurel). As before, however, this makes no sense in cult terms. But in a funerary context the laurel becomes once more a standard evergreen symbol of immortality; in Cumont's words, "throughout the whole of antiquity the laurel and the ivy were linked with death and the tomb."[157] And Mercury becomes Hermes Psychopompus, the guider of the dead to the Underworld, best known from literature but also from sarcophagi and funerary monuments.[158]

If we put ourselves in the place of the recipient of one of these diptychs, the first thing he would notice had to be the conspicuously inscribed names. From the genitive plurals he would at once have inferred a family occasion. Seeing none of the standard nuptial motifs, instead of turning to Neoplatonism he would, I suspect, have looked for funerary motifs instead. Having identified an evergreen or a downturned torch, he would then have recognized the rest and identified the occasion.

7: OTHER DIPTYCHS

If we can fix this group of ivories to 402, what of the "official" diptychs that (on Kitzinger's view) these pagan diptychs are supposed to have inspired? We may begin

---

155. *Cod. Theod.* 16. 10. 12. 2, *redimita vittis arbore* ; the practice is mocked by Prudentius, *CS* ii. 1010; for earlier examples, MacMullen 1997, 197 n. 112.

156. The original names may have been painted, as perhaps on the Asclepius and Hygieia diptych, whose tabulae are now bare.

157. Cumont 1942a, 15. As for the SYMMACHORVM oak, many sorts of oak were also evergreen, and oak garlands often in fact appear on Roman sepulchral monuments: Altmann 1905, nos. 46, 71, 243–54.

158. Combet-Farnoux 1980, 353–82; Cumont 1942, 29 n. 2, 520 (index s.v. Hermès psychopompe).

FIGURE 13: the Lampadiorum Panel

with a well-known panel in Brescia (54V). In the top register, beneath the legend [L]AMPADIORVM, "of the Lampadii," three figures stand in a circus loge, the one in the middle dressed in the *trabea* with *mappa* in his left hand and sceptre in his right (figure 13). The circus race they are watching is shown in the lower register. On the face of it, this is a regular consular diptych. But there are two anomalies. First, though the central figure is obviously a consul, the first and only Lampadius to appear on the consular fasti is in 530. Yet [L]AMPADIORVM is utterly different from the numerous surviving sixth-century diptychs. There can be little question that it belongs with the group of more classicizing western ivories dated ca. 400. Second, unlike all other consular diptychs, this one alone does not name the consul himself, but his family, in the genitive plural.

The central figure shown with *trabea* and sceptre must be a Lampadius. But since the consul of 530 is too late, the honorand must have been a *suffect* consul. Now by the late fourth century the suffect consulship had sunk enormously in prestige. It was seldom included in a man's cursus, and if held at all was held at the beginning of his career.[159] The suffect's only known function was to preside at the games for the

---

159. Chastagnol 1958, 231–37.

anniversary of the foundation of Rome, the *Natalis Vrbis*. Nonetheless, it had lost none of its original trappings. Ausonius refers to the *trabea* and *sella curulis* of his young friend Paulinus of Nola (born ca. 354), whose suffect consulship (he adds) precedes his own in the fasti.[160] Since Ausonius was (ordinary) consul in 379, Paulinus must have been suffect consul before then, still in his early twenties. In 401 Symmachus records that the suffect of the year broke his leg in a street accident and had to be carried off in full consular regalia.[161]

So the honorand of the diptych is likely to have been a young man, still in his twenties. What was the occasion? In a twelfth-century inventory at Novara Cathedral Chiara Formis discovered a reference to two ivory panels inscribed LAMPADIORVM and RVFIORVM. No such diptych is now to be found at Novara, while one panel that answers to half the description turned up a few centuries later at nearby Brescia. We can hardly doubt that the Brescia panel is one-half of a LAMPADIORVM/RVFIORVM diptych. The dossier can be further expanded. Yet another example of double genitive plurals has been lurking for more than a century unrecognized in the Capitoline Museum: a plain (probably) fifth-century ivory diptych inscribed BASSIORVM/EVPLVTIORVM, rediscovered in 1984.[162]

By the end of the fourth century the practice of distributing ivory diptychs was apparently getting out of hand. An eastern law of 384 forbids the use of ivory for any but consular diptychs, and all eastern diptychs we know of are in fact consular. But no attempt was made to curb the extravagance of the more ostentatiously wealthy western governing class.[163] Diptychs were issued by the most junior officials to celebrate even sinecures held by boys, such as the quaestorship. The custom also spread (I suggest) to the commemoration of private occasions.[164] The fact that we now have (at least) three different diptychs commemorating shared family events suggests that they were routine rather than exceptional.

The commonest routine event shared by two families must always have been weddings, and given the youth of the honorand of LAMPADIORVM and the obviously celebratory emphasis of circus games, on this occasion a wedding seems the natural working hypothesis. The missing leaf might have represented a nuptial scene (perhaps the bride shown as Venus at her toilet), while the other shows the groom in the one moment of glory allotted to the suffect consul, the presidency of the games held on the *Natalis Vrbis*, on 21 April.[165] It was on his way to preside at these games that the suffect of 401 met with his unfortunate accident.

---

160. Ausonius, *Ep.* 24. 1–6; Mratschek 2002, 52–53.
161. Symm. *Ep.* vi. 40, with Marcone 1983, 117. Even proconsuls continued to be represented in consular dress and insignia, just as if (as in earlier days) they had previously held the consulship (Foss 1983, 206).
162. This unfortunately very damaged diptych was mentioned in passing by De Rossi 1877, 706, but apparently then mislaid until rediscovered in 1984 by Marina Mattei in response to my enquiries.
163. *Cod. Theod.* xv. 9. 1. Art historians have usually assumed that this law applied to the West as well, but see Cameron 1982, 126–29.
164. Delbrueck 1929, 65A, must also be a leaf from a private presentation diptych; Cameron 1986, 55 n. 46a.
165. Chastagnol 1958, 236.

On this hypothesis, we want a wedding that united the Rufii and Lampadii. What do we know of these families? No important Lampadii are known until the very end of the fourth century. The first bearers of the name recorded in high office are Lampadius, city prefect 398 and Postumius Lampadius, city prefect 403/8 and praetorian prefect in 409. The city prefect of 398 was the brother of Mallius Theodorus cos. 399, whom we know from his panegyrist Claudian to have come from undistinguished Milanese stock. He is therefore to be distinguished from Postumius Lampadius, a Campanian aristocrat.[166] This is surely the Roman family that married into the Rufii.

The Rufii must be the Ceionii Rufii, one of the great houses of the age. C. Ceionius Rufius Volusianus city prefect in 365 and his wife, Caecinia Lolliana, had at least five children and numerous grandchildren, many bearing the names Rufius and Caecina.[167] There will have been no shortage of Rufian heiresses for the Lampadius of the Brescia ivory to marry. That he did marry one can hardly be in doubt: for in the next generation we encounter a city prefect with the names *Rufius* Caecina Felix *Lampadius*. This man was one of three successive prefects of Rome who carried out repairs to the Flavian amphitheatre during the joint reign of Theodosius II and Valentinian III, that is, between 425 and 450. Rufius Lampadius was probably the last of the three. Lampadius's repairs, which were evidently extensive, perhaps belong after the earthquake of 443.[168]

The panel itself offers a clue as to its date. The consul's sceptre is surmounted by two imperial busts, symbols of the authority delegated to him as a Roman magistrate. Though the top of the bust on the left is broken off, enough remains to establish that it was larger than the one on the right. The shoulders rise to a greater height quite clearly, and overlap the smaller bust (it was no doubt because its head was taller and carved in higher relief that it broke off). Imperial busts of differing sizes are a common phenomenon whose meaning is unmistakable: at the time of the scene depicted, there was a plurality of emperors, one of whom was a "minor."

The actual age of an emperor was of no constitutional significance: there was no recognized period of legal minority. Valentinian II was proclaimed Augustus at the age of four, Theodosius II before his first birthday. Valentinian did not exercise authority until the death of Gratian in 383 (when he was twelve), but the seven-year-old Theodosius II became sole eastern Augustus on the death of Arcadius in 408. Nonetheless, if one of a plurality of Augusti was less than about fifteen years old, he was shown smaller than his colleagues when they were shown together (whether standing, seated, or in bust) on the coinage, medallions, weight-standards, or diptychs commemorating the conferment of public offices.[169] There was no agreed age

---

166. *PLRE* ii. 654–56. An unfortunately undatable letter of Symmachus (*Ep.* ix. 34) refers to the death of a senator called Lampadius who left sons behind him.

167. The Rufii Festi of Volsinii were a solid but not especially prominent family until the mid-fifth century (Matthews 1967, 484–509); PLRE i, stemma 13, p. 1138.

168. Chastagnol 1966, 6–19; PLRE ii. 655; Orlandi 2004, 492–93.

169. Between the death of Constantine (337) and the elevation of Gratian in 367 there were no boy emperors, and tableaux of co-emperors always show them equal in height. Between 367 and 474 I have found twenty-two examples on coins, diptychs, and weight-standards; for a shorter list, Cameron 1986, 58–59.

of "majority." Western artists showed Theodosius II smaller at thirteen and Honorius smaller at twelve, but Valentinian III equal at nine; eastern artists showed Valentinian smaller at fifteen. No emperor over the age of fifteen is shown smaller in either East or West.

The LAMPADIORVM busts are both shown draped with the *trabea*, the consular robe (schematically represented like a broad modern scarf crossing itself beneath the chin).[170] So the diptych dates from a year with two imperial consuls (396, 402, 407, 409, 411, 415), one of them younger than about fifteen. In January 396 Honorius was ten, in 402, eighteen; in January 407, 409, 411, and 415 Theodosius was six, eight, eleven, and fourteen, respectively. We find the same motif on two other diptychs. First the Stilicho diptych (63V), with unequal imperial *trabea* -draped busts on Stilicho's shield.[171] Stilicho's son Eucherius is shown so small that the artist must have had the seven-year-old of 396 in mind rather than the thirteen-year-old of 402. The other diptych (62V) commemorates Rufius Probianus as *vicarius Vrbis Romae* (figure 14). In the top left-hand corner of each leaf, ensconced on a special stand, are pairs of imperial busts, one larger than the other, both clean-shaven, both shown with the *trabea*. Since Honorius is shown with a beard on the consular diptych of Probus in 406, that would exclude not only 407, but all occasions when Honorius was shown larger than the infant Theodosius II. That leaves only 396.[172]

Since the head of the larger bust on LAMPADIORVM is broken off, we are prevented from seeing whether it represented the bearded Honorius (408 or later) or his beardless brother Arcadius (396). A man with the right connections might expect to reach the city prefecture in his forties. Praetextatus (367–68) was forty-three, Symmachus (384) forty-five. So a Rufius Lampadius who was city prefect ca. 445 is likely to have been born in the neighborhood of 400, which would place his parents' wedding a year or two before 400. If so, Rufius Lampadius city prefect ca. 445 might easily be the *grandson* of Postumius Lampadius prefect 403/8. A man at the height of his career might well have had a son in his twenties just entering public life and looking around for a suitable wife. So while we cannot exclude 407, 409, 411, or 415 (Honorius larger), 396 (Honorius smaller) would fit these data very nicely. The games at which the suffect consul presided were those of the *Natalis Vrbis*. In all probability, then, the scene depicted on the Lampadiorum diptych can be dated as exactly as any regular consular diptych, to 21 April 396.

Though the two flanking figures on [L]AMPADIORVM both hold the *mappa* in exactly the same pose as the central figure, and the figure on the right is shown as an older man, the fact that they are shown barely half his size makes clear that he is the

---

170. Delbrueck 1929, 52–58; Grierson and Mays 1992, 75.
171. Kiilerich and Torp 1989 object that the emperors' dress cannot certainly be identified as the *trabea*, and that emperors also wore it on other occasions, surely mistaken on both counts: J. P. C. Kent, *RIC* 10 (1994), 48–49.
172. There is a gap in the fasti of the vicariate of Rome between January 395 and late 397. He could be the Probianus to whom Symmachus wrote in 401 (*Ep.* viii. 14).

FIGURE 14: the Probianus Diptych

principal honorand. Who are these flanking figures? If the interpretation of the diptych offered here is correct, the older man might be Lampadius's father, and the other
the father of his bride (no doubt somewhat younger, since the bride might be much
younger than the groom). The motif of three presiding magistrates in the circus or
amphitheatre loge was common. So, for example, an ivory panel in Liverpool (59V)
where three similar figures holding a mappa are shown presiding at a wild beast show.
This time all three are shown the same size, but the central figure is clearly much
younger than the older figure to his left. Though it seems natural to assume that the
central figure is the presiding magistrate, it is the figure on his right who holds the
mappa; the older man on the left gestures toward the central figure, who holds a silver
bowl in his right hand (figure 15). We also have three different fragmentary copies of a
clay plate with three figures in an amphitheatre loge, and a clay copy of a diptych panel
with, again, three figures in a loge; in both cases the central figure is shown larger than
his two companions.[173] That the flanking figures are to be understood as kinsmen is
supported by the history of the motif (medallions with frontal representations of

---

173. Illustrated and discussed by Salomonson 1973, 11–17.

FIGURE 15: the Liverpool Venatio Panel

Constantine I enthroned flanked by his two older sons or Constantine II flanked by his brother emperors Constantius II and Constans).[174] It is because of the influence of this schema that the miniature of Aeneas presiding at the funeral games of Anchises in the Vergilius Romanus (figure 5) shows him with a companion on either side (nothing in the text of Vergil suggests any such trio).

At the turn of the fourth and fifth century the most elaborate games were provided by praetors, or rather, since praetors often held office in their teens, by their fathers in their name. A famous fragment of Olympiodorus lists the three most extravagant cases he knew, in every case naming the praetor's father (in one case not naming the son at all).[175] The bulk of Symmachus's correspondence for three full years is devoted to the preparations for Memmius's games.[176] Under the circumstances it would not be surprising if Symmachus felt that his own likeness belonged together with Memmius's on the diptychs we know he issued to commemorate the event. In Memmius's case we

174. Brilliant 1963, 204–7, for the gestures that identify the central figure as the most important.
175. Olympiodorus F 44 M = 41. 2 B, with Cameron 1984, 193–96.
176. For a list of all the relevant letters, Seeck 1883, lxxi–lxxii.

can go further. As we have already seen, in 401, the year of his praetorian games, he married the granddaughter of the elder Flavian. It is tempting to conjecture that his praetorian diptychs showed him, like Lampadius, standing in the circus loge with his father on one side and Flavian on the other. All diptychs that show three magistrates (one at least older than the central figure) presiding at the games probably commemorate games given by praetors or suffect consuls.

If I am right, then the Probianus, Stilicho, and probably LAMPADIORVM diptychs all date to 396; and the two SYMMACHORVM diptychs commemorate Symmachus's death in 402. That is to say, the so-called "pagan" ivories are later, not earlier than the "official" diptychs. The interval is not great, but is enough to remove what slight basis there ever was for Kitzinger's thesis that militant paganism was the inspiration for this revival of classicizing ivory carving.

There is no call to question the deeply pagan character of the SYMMACHORVM diptychs. Yet (if I am right) they were made several years after the collapse of the so-called "last pagan stand" of 394—after the deaths of both Symmachus and Flavian. Symmachus himself had withdrawn from active promotion of pagan issues for some years before his death, and the younger Flavian cannot have been willing to jeopardize his hard-won rehabilitation after a period of public disgrace. SYMMACHORVM/NICOMACHORVM is often proclaimed an artifact of pagan "propaganda," but both panels show scenes of incense burning, not sacrifice. The diptychs may well reflect the religious sympathies of Symmachus and Flavian, but the patron who actually commissioned them was young Memmius Symmachus, who was born after the withdrawal of public subsidies for the cults and grew to manhood in a world where public sacrifice was a thing of the past. They must surely be seen as nostalgic mementoes rather than religious propaganda.

NICOMACHORVM/SYMMACHORVM has been generally judged the purest example of the classicizing style of the age. According to Kiilerich, the "classicistic formal language [of the diptych] was a deliberate choice of style…in part to be explained by the conservative and pro-pagan outlooks of the Symmachi and Nicomachi."[177] But we have seen again and again that there is no straightforward sense in which classicism implies paganism. It seems to me most unlikely that Symmachus (the only true aristocrat of the age who has left us anything to judge the literary tastes of his class by) had any clear concept of what we would call "classical" even in his own field of literature, much less in art. He admired what we would call the classics, but (like the grammarians of the age) he always uses vague terms like *veteres, antiqui*, and *maiores*, making no distinction between Ennius and Vergil. The *veteres* were all pagan, but they had acquired their classic status long before the triumph of Christianity. It was not for their occasional mention of pagan gods that Symmachus and his peers read and reread what his friend Naucellius tellingly called "*docta* scripta virum

---

177. Elsner 1998, 191–92; Kiilerich 1991, 117; and 1993, 144–49.

veterum" (*Ep. Bob.* 5. 4). It was *doctrina*, diction, and above all antiquity that drew them to these texts.

In his own writings Symmachus affected a scattering of archaic words, and when he praises the letters of his friends, it is never what we would call style that he singles out for comment, but archaic diction, *verborum vetustas* (Ch. 10. 4). Yet his own oratorical style is quintessentially late antique, full of abstract nouns and circumlocutions, utterly unlike the style of Cicero to which he so often appeals as the ultimate yardstick. He contrasts Naucellius's letters "written in the hand of Nestor" with his own, written "in the language (*lingua*) of today"; Naucellius's represents "a model of ancient times" (*vetustas*), Symmachus "modernity" (*novitas*).[178] There is no indication that he had any clear-cut concept either of what we would call "classical" or indeed of "style" as distinct from diction.

There is also another complicating factor in Kitzinger's picture of pagan aristocrats reviving and preserving the forms of classical art. For if NICOMACHORVM/ SYMMACHORVM is the high-water mark of a revived Classicism, the Consecratio panel is perhaps the most unclassical ivory of the age. It is conspicuous for its total rejection of any attempt at spatial illusion. Three successive scenes are shown simultaneously in the same space. The canopy, the chariot wheels, and the elephants' legs are all at cross-purposes; the simplified, stocky figures stare and gesticulate at each other in rigid poses. Kiilerich's book deals with what she called "fourth-century classicism," and so understandably omits the Consecratio panel. But if its monogram is correctly identified, it was commissioned by the same family as SYMMACHORVM/ NICOMACHORVM, and has an obvious bearing on their taste in art, calling into question the concept of a deliberate, polemical, pagan revival of classicizing forms. In art as in literature, style varied according to genre and purpose. We do not need to believe that SYMMACHORVM/NICOMACHORVM and the Consecratio panel were made by the same craftsman. But there is no serious reason to doubt that both were made in the same workshops, workshops that catered to Christian as well as pagan patrons, and employed whichever style was either requested or best suited to the representation requested.

Weigand remarked that there was an "unbridgable stylistic gap, indeed a world" between the Consecratio and SYMMACHORVM ivories.[179] Yet the fact remains that we find the same family simultaneously patronizing the "classical" and the "modern." What then are the grounds for supposing that there was any straightforward sense in which they preferred one to the other, or that they thought one more "pagan" than the other? Kiilerich's claim that classicizing style is "best suited for pagan subject matter" is only half true. Many surviving representations of cult acts of the state religion do happen to be in a more or less classicizing style. But this is because scenes of sacrifice tend to consist of groups or processions of figures (priests, officials, the

---

178. *Ep.* iii. 11. 1–2; cf. *Ep.* i. 53. 2; *Ep.* iii. 22.
179. Weigand 1937, 135.

FIGURE 16: the Leningrad Lion Hunt Diptych

emperor) where the authoritative models (the Ara Pacis, the Column of Trajan) are basically classicizing.[180] But there were few classicizing representations of imperial apotheosis.[181]

The Leningrad Lion hunt diptych (60V) is very similar in style and composition to the Consecratio panel. Lions and hunters are disposed paratactically around the rectangular space of each panel, each on their own ground lines, without any attempt to create an illusion of depth (figure 16). This is a form of composition best known to us from the hunt mosaics of late Roman North Africa,[182] where many Roman aristocrats had vast estates. It was undoubtedly a style popular among rich fourth-century pagans. The Leningrad diptych no doubt commemorated some young aristocrat's praetorian games. Given its similarity of style and technique to the Consecratio panel, conceivably those of young Memmius Symmachus in 401.

As it happens, the only type of art on which Symmachus expresses an opinion is mosaics. He advises his son-in-law that a swimming pool should be decorated with

---

180. Most are collected in Ryberg 1955; see Hölscher 2004 for the thesis that content dictates style.
181. Vogel 1973, 44–55; Elsner 1998, 28–35.
182. Lavin 1963, 179–286; Dunbabin 1978, Ch. 4.

mosaics rather than paintings, and he admired the mosaics of some unnamed friend for their originality, which he hoped to be able to copy in rooms of his own.[183] We may in fact have a specimen. The recent excavations in the area on the Caelian Hill known to have been the site of a grand mansion belonging to the Symmachi have turned up a striking piece of *opus sectile* floor in colored marble.[184] There is no way of dating this work to the lifetime of Symmachus himself, but mosaics that were "new and untried by earlier artists" do not suggest classicizing work on traditional themes.[185]

In conclusion, let us take a brief look at the Christian ivories that, according to Kitzinger, were later Christian responses to this pagan initiative. The lotus and palmette border that surrounds the door of Christ's tomb on the Milan Marys panel (figure 17) is identical to the border of SYMMACHORVM/NICOMACHORVM and Probianus. It is details like this that are workshop trademarks,[186] and the final touch is added by the Fauvel panel, whose border is identical to the outer border of the Milan Marys. This is to say, the inner border of this Christian ivory matches the border of SYMMACHORVM / NICOMACHORVM and Probianus; its outer border the border of the Fauvel panel. It looks as if all four ivories were made in the same workshop, where these slightly differing borders were used in alternation.

There is no reason to believe that the pagan ivories are earlier. We know from the Esquiline treasure that Christian patrons were having high-class silverware made as early as the 360s–380s. There is also the Junius Bassus sarcophagus, securely dated to within a matter of months by the known date of Bassus's death (25 August 359). The most celebrated calligrapher of the age, Furius Dionysius Filocalus, is only known to have worked for Christian patrons: Valentinus, owner of the so-called Calendar of 354; the elder Melania; and Pope Damasus.[187] His activity can be traced from the 350s to the 370s. We know that luxury calligraphic copies of the Scriptures and works of the fathers existed by the end of the fourth century.

Kitzinger finely analyses the similarities in style and atmosphere between NICOMACHORVM/SYMMACHORVM and the Munich ascension panel (figure 18). I would draw attention to a perhaps more significant parallel, the conspicuous tree that frames the scene, in this case not Jupiter's oak or Apollo's laurel, but an olive with perching doves, symbolizing the peace of the Holy Spirit. More striking still, however, is the iconographic parallel with the Consecratio panel. Both ivories show ascents to heaven: just as Christ is welcomed by the hand of God, so "Symmachus" is greeted by the hands of his ancestors. If NICOMACHORVM/SYMMACHORVM

---

183. *novum quippe musivi genus et intemptatum superioribus repperisti, Ep.* viii. 42. 2; *Ep.* vi. 49. 1.

184. See Carignani's description in the entry "La *domus* dei Symmachi," in Ensoli and La Rocca 2000, 150–51.

185. For the decline of mythological themes in favor of hunting, circus, amphitheatre, and genre themes, Dunbabin 1978, Ch. 3–6.

186. Borders and ornamental patterns have long been recognized as workshop pointers, Dunbabin 1978, 22.

187. Cameron 1992, 143.

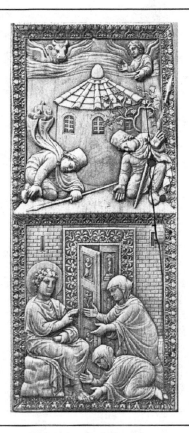

FIGURE 17: the Milan Marys

and the Consecratio panel commemorate a death, it is tempting to wonder whether the Christian panels likewise originally formed part of diptychs issued to commemorate the deaths of prominent Christians.

If there is any polemical purpose in the confrontation of these two conceptions of apotheosis, it is fascinating to observe that the Christian versions are more successfully and consistently classicizing in style. There is in any case no way of telling which is earlier. That is to say, this is another case where we cannot take it for granted that Christian was inspired by and modeled on pagan. After all, the afterlife was far more central to Christians than pagans.

It was evidently important to some members of the Christian elite that Christianity should be made to look as classical as possible. It would be hard to parallel such wholly Hellenized work as these two Christian ivories: classical poses and draperies, wingless angels; no supernatural ascension, but a handsome, beardless young Christ striding gracefully up a mountain behind an "artfully wrought tempietto in some sacred grove."[188] And why not? Purists might disparage the reading and imitation of classical

---

188. Kitzinger 1977, 39.

FIGURE 18: the Munich Ascension Panel

poets, but then the poets had been pagans and often mention pagan gods. There was no such overt link between classicizing art and "pagan" themes.

It was not the Nicomachi or the Symmachi who were the first Roman patrons of the classicizing poet Claudian, but the Christian Anicii. If we are to have any hope of understanding the classicizing taste of the aristocracy of late antique Rome, we must first give up the idea that it has any connection with their religious beliefs. There is no such easy key to the problems of patronage.

20

THE *HISTORIA AUGUSTA*

1

The so-called *Historia Augusta* (hereafter *HA*) is a corpus of imperial biographies from Hadrian to Carinus (117–285) that purports to be the work of six different writers, all otherwise wholly unknown, all purportedly writing between ca. 305 and 325. It had always been obvious that these *Lives* were products of low quality. Not only are they full of errors, absurdities, and manifestly forged documents, they cite as authorities no fewer than thirty-five otherwise unknown and for the most part surely bogus historians and biographers.[1] But it was not until 1889 that Dessau branded the entire work a forgery, written by a single author at the end of the fourth century.[2]

His arguments fell into four main categories. (1) The numerous dedications and autobiographical remarks that appear to date the various Lives so securely are shot through with improbabilities, inconsistencies, and outright contradictions; (2) the many similarities of style and diction among the six supposedly different writers suggest that there was in fact only one, (3) a passage in the *Life of Severus* derives from the *Caesares* of Aurelius Victor, published in 361;[3] and (4) a number of the personal names in fictitious passages are first found in the second half of the fourth century.

While willing to concede that the author(s) forged documents and even sources on a massive scale, for a long time conservative critics rejected the hypothesis that the *HA* itself was a forgery, postulating instead a late fourth-century editor who revised or edited an early fourth-century corpus. Some details can be explained well enough this way (the Victor passage and even the late names), but the contradictions between the dedications and autobiographical remarks (clearly and persuasively restated by Barnes)[4] resist such simple measures. For all their contradictions, these passages are internally homogeneous, and why would a late fourth-century editor interpolate what is after all the only evidence for an early fourth-century date? If he did, then is there any real difference between this interpolator and Dessau's forger?

---

1. Syme 1983, 98–108.
2. Dessau 1889, 337–92. This remarkable article remains the best introduction to the problems of the *HA*; little or nothing written since has added anything of importance to the sum of knowledge. The most useful single resource is now Chastagnol 1994, with text, French translation, brief notes, long general introduction, and separate introductions to each Life.
3. Dessau 1889, 361–74; Chastagnol 1994, 199–215; for Victor's date, C. E. V. Nixon, *CP* 86 (1991), 113–25.
4. Barnes 1978, 13–16.

It is the evidence for single authorship (a topic little discussed in recent years) that is decisive. The most comprehensive treatment of the shared themes, attitudes, and tricks of composition remains an article by Peter White.[5] A certain number can be explained by a common biographical tradition or one writer imitating another. But two at least cannot: all six cite forged documents, and (especially revealing) all include lives of pretenders and co-emperors. "Spartianus" announces a policy of writing separate lives of co-emperors (*Hel.* 1. 1; 7. 5), then "Gallicanus" extends the principle to usurpers (*Avid.* 3. 3); all the rest treat both without further comment. "Lampridius" considers but rejects the possibility of combining the *Life of Diadumenus* with that of his father Macrinus (*Diad.* 6. 1), a policy that is then put into practice by "Capitolinus" (*Max.* 1. 1–3) and followed without comment by "Pollio" and "Vopiscus," who successively reduce the space allotted to subsidiary rulers. That is to say, the series of secondary lives is introduced as an innovation, extended, modified, and gradually abandoned: the "stages through which it passes are fully intelligible as parts of a single development, but they bear no relation to the appearance and disappearance of the several Scriptores."[6]

When they first appeared, Marriot's computer-based studies of sentence length and word types at the beginning and end of sentences were acclaimed as conclusive proof of single authorship. But more recent work has called into question both his definition of a sentence and his conclusions.[7] A study by B. Meissner, based on variations in the frequency of very common words (*et, in, cum,* and so forth), found Pollio and Vopiscus homogeneous enough to be one author, but the rest less so.[8] Given the undoubted fact that the earlier lives are largely based on Marius Maximus and/or (if he existed) Syme's Ignotus,[9] few individual pages of any given life ascribed to Capitolinus, Lampridius, or Spartianus are likely to contain more than a handful of sentences that are entirely the work of the author (better compiler). In the circumstances, it is unlikely that the quantitative method will ever yield definitive results, and more traditional linguistic approaches may be more revealing.

Adams has traced a series of unobtrusive mannerisms running through the work of all five main *HA* authors.[10] Two illustrations must suffice. First, their preference in forming the pluperfect passive. In late Latin we find *amatus fuerat* and *fuisset* alongside *amatus erat* and *esset*. Each of the five prefers *fuerat* for the indicative with an occasional *erat*, but for the subjunctive always *esset*, never *fuisset*. Second, certain idiosyncrasies in their use of the synonyms *interficio* and *occido*. For example, they prefer *interficio* in

5. White 1967, 115–33.
6. White 1967, 123.
7. I. Marriot, *JRS* 69 (1979), 65–77, criticised by D. Sansone, *JRS* 80 (1990), 174–77.
8. Meissner 1997, 175–215. Other technical studies cast more doubt on the single authorship theory: E. K. Tse, F. J. Tweedie, B. D. Frischer, in *Literary and Linguistic Computing* 13 (1998), 148–49; and J. Rudman, ib. 151–57.
9. For a general account of Latin sources, Barnes 1978, Ch. 6 and 7, with Barnes 1995, 1–28.
10. Adams 1971; 1972; 1977; five rather than six since "Vulcacius Gallicanus v.c." is credited with only one life of a dozen pages—itself a puzzle.

the passive and *occido* in relative clauses; they write *quo interfecto* and *eo occiso*, but never *quo occiso* or *eo interfecto*; and when *posse* is needed with a verb of killing, they almost always prefer *occido*. These are idiosyncratic preferences, not paralleled in any of Adams's comparison texts, and yet too unobtrusive (and trivial) to allow the explanation that one author was imitating another. They are also preferences that a compiler might unconsciously substitute when in other respects closely following an earlier source.

If we are dealing with a single author who concealed his true identity behind six invented pseudonyms,[11] then nothing "they" say about themselves can be taken at face value—not least the dates at which they so insistently claim to have written.[12] On the contrary, we are almost compelled to infer that the real, single author wrote at a different, later date.

The scholarship of the past half-century has attempted to go beyond Dessau and determine the true date of the collection and (above all) its purpose. Most of this scholarship, following in succession the leadership of Alföldi, Hartke, Straub, Chastagnol, and Paschoud, has solved both problems with a single hypothesis: the *HA* is alleged to be a covert attack on Christianity, a product of the "pagan reaction" at Rome in or soon after 395. This hypothesis (it is claimed) also explains both the senatorial bias and the pseudonyms. The author was a pagan senator, or perhaps rather a scholar in the service of Symmachus and the Nicomachi; and he hid behind the pseudonyms because (what else?) he was afraid of Christian reprisals.

This is the reason the *HA* finds a place in this book. It has come to be treated as the high point of the "pagan reaction," less because of the virulence of its (inevitably covert) polemic than for the assumption that it needed to be concealed.[13] Alföldi saw the *HA* as a bitter attack on Christianity, Straub as a plea for toleration, a pagan response to Orosius's *Historia adversus paganos*. The sheer improbability of both these views (which are, of course, mutually contradictory and exclusive) has often been noted, as has the lack of evidence for the assumption that pagans were afraid to state their views openly. It is striking that Ronald Syme, a much more sensitive and intelligent reader of texts, while arguing strongly for a date ca. 395, nonetheless entirely rejected the notion of pagan propaganda.

But whatever the arguments for and against, the entire house of cards rests on the date. If a date in or after the 390s could be firmly established, then it might well seem legitimate, especially in a pseudonymous work, to look for allusions to the threat that hung over Roman paganism. But not if it can be dated (as I hope to show) some twenty years earlier (375/80), before Gratian's withdrawal of the cult subsidies in 382. We have already seen what a difference it makes if the *Carmen contra paganos* dates from 384 rather than 395.

---

11. For the pseudo-biographical data, Barnes 1971, 14–15; Momigliano 1960, 136–37.
12. The very number of dating references is suspicious. In Suetonius (e.g.) there are none.
13. Alföldi wrote of its "versteckte christenfeindliche Polemik" in *BHAC* 1963 (1964), 1.

2

Given the importance of the 395 (or later) date for the pagan propaganda school and the confidence with which they maintain it, it is astonishing how little solid evidence they have managed to produce in well over a century. Dessau himself found nothing that pointed later than the 370s. Over the past three or four decades countless allegedly anachronistic allusions to persons, events, and books of the 390s have been announced. Johne's survey of 1974 listed more than a dozen as decisive. Not one of them passes the more rigorous standards of proof required in other fields of scholarship.[14] Certainly no "smoking gun."

A couple of illustrations. In his *Life of Aurelian* "Vopiscus" refers to the "official carriage" (*iudiciale carpentum*) of Tiberianus, prefect of Rome in 303/4. According to Chastagnol, it was not until 382 that the prefect acquired an official carriage.[15] Even on its own terms the argument fails, since Chastagnol misinterpreted the text on which he relied. Symmachus's claim that "people look for the dignified restraint of a private vehicle" does not mean that, until 382, city prefects had used their own carriages.[16] The innovation was not an official carriage, but a more ornate and ostentatious official carriage.[17] Symmachus's repeated emphasis on the appearance of the new carriage makes this clear: a "foreign and pretentious type of conveyance," an "opulent equipage," decorated with chased silver panels, compared to the hybristic mythical chariot of Salmoneus of Elis.[18] Whether or not official carriages existed as early as 303, if the governor of Pannonia had one in 371,[19] it can hardly be doubted that prefects of Rome enjoyed the same privilege long before 382.[20]

Or to take an old favorite, in 251 Decius is said to have planned to revive the censorship and confer it on the future emperor Valerian. Despite the enthusiastic approval of the senate, Valerian refused, on the grounds that only the emperor deserved such powers. This is alleged to postdate 397, the year Symmachus published a speech opposing a proposal made by Honorius a year or two earlier to restore the censorship,

---

14. Johne 1974, 178–79. Honoré 1987, 156–76, simply presupposes ca. 395, without a word of argument.

15. Chastagnol 1960, 203–5; and 1994, cxvii.

16. *oculi quaerunt civitatis privati vehiculi nobilem modum* (*Rel.* 4. 2); see *OLD* s.v. *modus* 4–6 (a due measure that ought not to be exceeded, limited, or restrained). Similarly, the context of *carpenti novitate submota* in *Rel.* 20. 3 suggests the new silver panels (so Barrow) rather than the innovation of a public carriage.

17. So Momigliano 1964, 225–30; and Vera 1981, 55–56. Chastagnol 1994, cxvii, does not even mention Momigliano's analysis, accepted by Vera. His claim that the description of Tiberianus as *vir inlustris* is another anachronism also fails, since there is no necessity to take it as an official designation of rank.

18. *peregrini ac superbi vehiculi usus...dives pompa...submovete vehiculum, cuius cultus insignior est; illus maluimus, cuius usus antiquior* (*Rel.* 4); for the silver, *Rel.* 20.

19. Amm. Marc. 29. 6. 7 (*iudiciale carpentum* again); Chastagnol 1960, 204 n. 6, outrageously suggests that this too might be an anachronism.

20. The rescript of 386 that allows a wide range of officials to use their official carriages (*vehiculis dignitatis suae*) in Constantinople (*Cod. Theod.* 14. 12. 1) does not imply (pace Chastagnol) that the carriage rather than the practice was new.

an issue supposedly dear to the hearts of pagan senators.[21] But the argument is fatally undermined by the fact that the senate of 251 is represented as enthusiastically supporting a proposal that, according to Symmachus, the senate of the 390s decisively rejected. In the *HA* the censorship is represented as obviously desirable in itself and a great honor to the senator selected. In real life things were not so simple. The censor would have real and substantial powers over the lives and fortunes of his fellow senators, whence Symmachus's fear that its revival would inspire divisive competition among his peers.[22] Whether or not Honorius appointed a Christian, Symmachus had many personal enemies (p. 11). It is hard to see any contemporary relevance in the *HA* passage, and it seems to me far likelier that it was written *before* the censorship unexpectedly became a live political issue in the 390s.[23]

No less important than specific objections, is it credible that a person who took such pains to pretend that he was writing no later than 325 would be so careless as to allude to an innovation of 382 or an event of 397? Anyone pretending to write fifty or seventy-five years before his own day was likely to slip up occasionally: two fairly clear examples in the *HA* are regional praetorian prefects (no earlier than the 340s) and the election of suffect consuls by the senate (335/7).[24] To give a modern analogy, if in the year 2000 I forged a journal purporting to have been written in 1950, I might have inadvertently antedated the arrival of television or Elvis Presley by a few years, but I would not have been so careless as to mention the Beatles or the Internet.[25]

Yet many scholars seem to believe that the author of the *HA* repeatedly mentions the equivalent of the Internet. For example, the reference at *Aur.* 15. 4 to the "recent" consular games of Furius Placidus. Chastagnol (after many others) insists that this must be Furius Placidus cos. 343—as if the forger of that 1950 journal would absentmindedly refer to 1975![26] One of the most popular current approaches is the "detection" of allusions to works not published until the 390s. Chastagnol claims to have detected twenty-five allusions to Claudian, the latest poems "quoted" dating from only a few months before his date for the completion of the *HA* (399)! Even more

---

21. *Val.* 5. 4–6. 9; Hartke 1940, 85–103; more sensibly, McGeachy 1942, 32–33; most recently, Chastagnol 1995, 139–50 (dropping some of the more absurd of Hartke's arguments, but no more persuasive overall).

22. *ne sub specioso nomine fores inpotentiae ambire solitis panderentur* (*Ep.* iv. 29. 2; cf. v. 9. 2); Marcone 1987, 70–71.

23. As for Johne's other arguments, even if accepted, the alleged "disguised polemic" against Constantinople need not take us as late as the 390s (Cameron 2001, 45–52).

24. *XXX Tyr.* 18. 5; *Tac.* ix. 6; on the establishment of regional prefectures, see Barnes 1987; 1992.

25. Much has been made of the (obviously forged) dedication to Gordian III's praetorian prefect and father-in-law, Timisitheus: *Misitheo eminenti viro, parenti principum, praet<orio praefec>to* (*Gord.* 27. 10), claiming that it must postdate Stilicho, who was styled *parens principum* from 395 on (most recently Kolb 1997). But what would be the point of such an allusion? Even after 395, why use the plural *principum* of a time when there was only one emperor with no children? A glance at Hohl's app. crit. will show that the text of these lines is very corrupt.

26. Presumably, the writer is just playing games. Of course, even if he were referring to the year of Furius Placidus cos. 343 as recent, that would lend no support to a late fourth-century date. Even more absurdly, B. Pottier, *An. Tard.* 14 (2006), 225–34, detects references to Aurelian cos. 400 in the *Vita Aureliani*!

incredibly, he finds fifty-nine references to the military treatise of Vegetius, and a number to letters of Jerome,[27] in both cases works written only a year or two before 399. Many scholars also now believe that the *HA* knew and poked fun at the history of Ammianus, not completed until ca. 390. Others (notably Paschoud) insist that one of its major sources was the *Annales* of Nicomachus Flavian, not published until 390.

We must not be misled by the one indisputable case of an anachronistic quotation, Aurelius Victor. Victor's account of the second and third centuries (in any case thirty-five years old in 395) was brief and derivative, closely based on the now lost *KG*. I am sure it never occurred to the *HA* author that Victor's account of Septimius Severus might be idiosyncratic enough to give him away. It is most unlikely that contemporary readers spotted the traces of Victor or the anachronistic regional prefects. But they could hardly fail to spot echoes of such idiosyncratic writers as Ammianus, Claudian, and Jerome, published only a year or two before!

Can our forger really be such a bungler? There is a disturbing ambiguity, not to say incoherence in much of this anachronism hunting. While some are allowed to be just telltale slips (Victor, the regional prefectures), others (allusions to Jerome, the censorship) are identified as deliberate, polemical clues, intended to be spotted by alert pagan readers. But who could believe the unstated corollary: that Christian readers were too stupid or ignorant to notice these clues? Many Christians of the 390s (Ambrose, Jerome, Augustine, Sulpicius Severus, Paulinus of Nola, Prudentius) were at least as well read as pagans like Symmachus. It is utterly implausible to suppose that only the intended readership would see through the imposture and pick up these supposedly subversive contemporary allusions.[28] What in any case would be the point of pagan propaganda that only pagans recognized? On the appeal-for-toleration hypothesis it should have been aimed at non-pagans.

Over and above such improbabilities, the similarities alleged with all these writers are very slight and general, with only one exception never involving the sort of close verbal parallels that alone can establish dependence one way or the other between two texts. Furthermore, even in cases where there are unmistakable verbal parallels between texts, literary scholars often disagree about which wrote first. In the case of the *HA* it is obviously significant that virtually all these alleged parallels have been adduced by historians committed to a date in the 390s or later, not one of whom appears to have even considered the possibility that the relationship might go the other way. In virtually none of these cases has any qualified philologist attempted to produce a serious philological argument.

I am by no means alone in my scepticism. One critic fully persuaded of a date in the last decade of the century found only one of Chastagnol's twenty-five "reminiscences" of Claudian convincing.[29] The one that did persuade him is a description of

---

27. Chastagnol 1970, 444–63; 1974, 59–80; 1970, 12–16, 72–77, 82–86; 1994, xciii–xcvii.

28. Not to mention the fact that Christians would be far more likely to pick up allusions to Jerome than pagans.

29. den Hengst 1991, 168–69; Chastagnol 1970, 444–63.

theatrical games in the *Life of Carus*, allegedly based on the games described by Claudian in his panegyric on the consulate of Mallius Theodorus in 399. But one set of games is much like another, and what he considered the decisive detail is nothing of the sort: Claudian describes make-believe fireballs rolling across the stage, while Carus's games end in an accidental fire that destroys the stage. In my judgement not one of the parallels so far alleged comes even close to establishing the dependence of the *HA* on any writer later than Aurelius Victor.

No one wrote more entertainingly and instructively on the *HA* between the late 1960s and the early 1980s than Ronald Syme. But while repeatedly asserting his belief in a date ca. 395, he was curiously unconcerned to prove it. A chapter in his first *HA* book lists one standard argument after another, only (quite rightly) to set them all aside as inconclusive,[30] in the last analysis resting his case on the claim that a handful of passages show knowledge of Ammianus. Even then Syme himself conceded that not one of the ten parallels he adduced was individually decisive, but felt that the cumulative effect was.[31] I would allow perhaps two or three *if* there were secure independent evidence that the *HA* postdated Ammianus. But two or three possibles are not enough to prove dependence. Disregarding his own warning to beware of "the merely plausible," Syme was in fact seduced by just this.

In the case of Ammianus there is a further objection over and above the weakness of the parallels adduced. His history began in A.D. 96, and the surviving books take up the story in 353 with Bk xiv. We do not know how the events of these 250 years were distributed between the missing books, but it is clear from the many back-references in the surviving books that he was well informed about the second and third centuries. Indeed, some of the cross-references imply a more detailed account than could be plausibly contained in just thirteen books. For example, he refers to extensive digressions (*late digessimus*) on Egypt under both Hadrian and Severus, and to "several" (*aliquoties*) digressions on the Saracens under Marcus and "later." Under Commodus he refers to a digression on the arrival of the image of the Magna Mater in Rome during the Second Punic War, presumably under the influence of Herodian, who has a similar digression in his account of Commodus (an entire book of fifty modern pages).[32] To create space for the detailed narrative these back-references imply, I myself am still attracted by H. Michael's thesis that (like Tacitus) Ammianus wrote two separate histories, one from Nerva to Constantine, the other from Constantine to the death of Valens. The surviving books would then be the second half of the second work. Recognizing the problem but unwilling to postulate an entire second history, Barnes has suggested another solution, emending the number of the first surviving book from xiiii to xviiii, thus giving seventeen lost books.[33] An even

---

30. Note too his sceptical review of Johne 1976 in Syme 1983, 109–30.
31. Those who attended the Oxford seminars of Eduard Fraenkel will recall his mantra: "ten bad arguments do not make one good argument."
32. xxii. 15. 1; xiv. 4. 2; xxii. 9. 5–6 ~ Herodian i. 11.
33. Barnes 1998, 26–31.

simpler correction would be xxiv for xiv, giving twenty-three lost books. Whichever solution we pick, there can be little doubt that Ammianus must have provided a more accurate and sober account of the second and third centuries than the *HA*. A valuable study by Gilliam listed more than twenty passages of Ammianus alluding to material missing from the *HA*, concluding that it is "highly doubtful that the biographer knew or made use of Ammianus's account of the period from Hadrian to Carinus."[34] More generally, the obvious explanation for the increasingly fictionalized content of the later lives of the *HA* is that the writer was running out of sources. It is unlikely that he would have indulged in so much sheer invention if he had written with Ammianus's detailed factual narrative available to him or (more important) his readers. In the event the question simply does not arise, whether for Ammianus, Claudian, Vegetius, Jerome, or Nicomachus Flavianus. For we shall see that the *HA* can be shown to have been published *before* any of them put pen to paper.[35]

Some of the favorite arguments for 395 or later in fact fit the late 370s just as well. Three of the more conspicuous recurring motifs in the *HA* are hostility to eunuchs, child emperors, and the *princeps clausus* (the emperor who never leaves his palace).[36] Johne linked the *HA*'s tirades against eunuchs to Claudian's attack on the eunuch Eutropius in 399. But hostility to the influence of eunuchs at court goes back to at least the 350s. Baynes claimed it as an argument for dating the *HA* to the reign of Julian, Stern to the reign of Constantius II.[37]

The key passage on child emperors is a speech by a (fictitious) senator called Maecius Faltonius Nicomachus on the proclamation of the elderly emperor Tacitus. According to a characteristic judgement of Tim Barnes,

> it has long been clear to all competent judges that an author who knows of and laments the political perils of boy emperors (*Tac.* 6. 5, *dii avertant principes pueros...*) and observes that an *imperator qui domi clausus est vera non novit* (*Aur.* 43. 4) can hardly have been writing before the death of the emperor Theodosius (17 January 395), which left his young and ineffectual sons Arcadius and Honorius as nominal rulers of East and West respectively.[38]

But a date two decades earlier fits the facts just as well—in fact, better. A plurality of child emperors undoubtedly posed dangers (power in the hands of unworthy favorites, rivalry between courts, risk of usurpations, etc.). Yet it is none of these real dangers that "Nicomachus" foresees. He goes on to assert that child emperors turn out monsters, instancing Nero, Elagabalus, and Commodus, and closes with the hope that, instead of

---

34. Gilliam 1972, 125–47 at 146.
35. Vegetius's date is uncertain, but in any case later than the death of Gratian (i. 20).
36. First identified by Stroheker 1970, 273–83; Chastagnol, *BHAC* 1982/83 (1985), 149–61.
37. Hopkins 1978, 172–96; Baynes 1926, 123–24, 138–39; Stern 1953, 78–80; Cameron 1965, 155–58, reviewing Straub. Court eunuchs are frequently mentioned in Lactantius's *De mortibus persecutorum*.
38. Barnes 1999, 39.

making young children his own heirs, Tacitus will select the best man, like Nerva, Trajan, and Hadrian. More than a dozen other passages likewise link condemnation of child emperors to praise of adoption, especially in the case of emperors with unworthy sons, instancing Marcus, Severus, and Carus.[39] Yet the problem with Honorius was scarcely that he might turn out a monster. No one writing after the failure of the tetrarchy was likely to believe in or even wish for adoption rather than hereditary descent. Indeed, the improbable insistence on the virtues of adoption might more plausibly be interpreted as part of the pretence to be writing under the tetrarchy.[40]

In complete contradiction to the emphasis on adoption, we also find frequent glorification of the dynasty of Constantine, mainly through its claim to descent from Claudius II, a fictitious claim to be sure, but one that does in fact go back to the age of Constantine.[41] Which are the author's "real" views? The 395 school are in no doubt: condemnation of child emperors. Why then devote so much space and emphasis to descent from Claudius and adoption? Are they just red herrings, intended to divert attention from his true date and purpose? But if he is trying to put across a genuine, deeply felt political message, why make it so difficult for his readers?

There are two further objections. First, while anxiety about child emperors certainly points later than the age of Diocletian and Constantine, Arcadius and Honorius are *not* in fact the inevitable objects of such anxiety. It is only in retrospect that their joint accession in 395[42] stands out as a turning point in Roman history, and less because of their minority (Arcadius was eighteen in 395) than the fatal combination of personal ineffectiveness and feuding ministers during a period of crisis. Westerners surely found the proclamation of Gratian and Valentinian II no less alarming. Unlike the co-emperors of Constantine and Constantius II, both had been elevated directly to the rank of Augustus as children: Gratian in 367 at the age of eight, Valentinian II in 375 at the age of four.

Kolb insisted that the child emperor motif was "unthinkable" before 395, explicitly rejecting the elevation of Valentinian II, on the grounds that he had adult co-emperors, first Valens and Gratian, then Gratian and Theodosius.[43] Not so. On his father's death in 375 Gratian became sole western Augustus at the age of sixteen, and on Valens's death in 378, sole ruling Augustus at the age of nineteen, only one year older than Arcadius at the death of Theodosius. Even after the proclamation of Theodosius in 379, the West remained in the hands of an inexperienced nineteen-year-old with a seven-year-old colleague. According to Zosimus, both were dependent on (unnamed) counsellors, "since the emperors themselves had no authority because of their age." Later on he claims that "because of their youth the emperors of the West were dependent on the slanders of

39. *Avid.* 2. 8; *Marc.* 18. 4; 27. 11–12; 28. 10; *Nig.* 4. 7; *Clod.* 3. 4; *Carac.* 11. 3 (cf. *Marc.* 5. 1; 16. 6; *Pert.* 6. 9); *Car.* 17. 6; 3. 8; *Prob.* 24. 4; cf. *Prob.* 10. 8; 11. 3; 14. 1; *Claud.* 12. 3; Baynes, *JRS* 43 (1953), 137–38.
40. For the tetrarchy as "Adoptivkaisertum," Kolb 1987, 143, 157.
41. On which, Syme 1983, 66–79.
42. Using the term "accession" loosely to indicate their joint assumption of independent power on Theodosius's death; Arcadius had been Augustus since 383, Honorius since 393.
43. Kolb 1997, 157.

eunuch chamberlains," making no distinction between Gratian and Valentinian.[44] In a panegyric on Gratian delivered shortly after his elevation at court in 367/8, Symmachus repeatedly emphasises his extreme youth,[45] at one point stating that Gratian was "the one whom we thought had been chosen almost inopportunely" (*quem paene intempestive putabamus electum*). He goes on to cite examples of great kings who received their thrones young (Alexander, Antiochus III, Ptolemy Epiphanes), but (as Sogno notes) that *intempestive* is a damaging admission, implying that Gratian's youth was a source of criticism in Roman circles, even if (as Symmachus predictably argues) he soon won everyone over.[46] As late as 376, in a speech delivered in Rome, Themistius repeatedly addressed Gratian as "child" or "boy" (παῖ), once (surprisingly) "beautiful boy" (ὦ παῖ καλέ).[47] John Chrysostom, writing in 380, still characterises Gratian as "very young and inexperienced," evidently a continuing popular perception.[48] Valentinian was a purely titular Augustus till Gratian's death in 383, when at the age of twelve he acquired a court of his own at Milan, where he was to remain the puppet of his mother, ministers, and eunuchs, the classic child emperor.[49]

Second, why should pagans feel more apprehensive about child emperors than Christians?[50] It is remarkable how little attention has been paid in this context to a striking passage in Ambrose's *Hexaemeron* of 386/8 that links child emperors and eunuchs. It is an elaborate comparison between the society of bees and humans, a free translation of a similar comparison in the slightly earlier *Hexaemeron* of St. Basil.[51] Like Basil, Ambrose argues that the "king" bee is not chosen by lot or popular vote or inheritance, expanding on Basil in his treatment of the idea of inheritance by evoking the luxury and flattery that corrupts the sons of kings, going on to specify the influence of eunuchs. There can be no question about the source of these additions: Ambrose's own experience of the power of eunuchs at the courts of first Gratian and then Valentinian II. Paulinus embellishes a story about Ambrose's dealings with two arrogant eunuch chamberlains of Gratian that can be dated to 381.[52] And in 386 Valentinian's chamberlain Calligonus threatened to have Ambrose beheaded.[53]

---

44. Zos. iv. 19. 2 (αὐτοὶ γὰρ οἱ βασιλεῖσ οὐκ ἦσαν κύριοι διὰ τὴν ἡλικίαν); iv. 22. 4 (ἐκδόντων ἑαυτοὺς εὐνούχων ἐπὶ τῷ κοιτῶνι τεταγμένων διαβολαῖς).

45. *in gremio rei publicae nutricis adolesce...adolescentem...puer...liberis nostris aequavus...pueri...regni impuberem candidatum...ante robur aetatis...teneritudo primaeva*, all in the first six paragraphs of *Or.* iii.

46. *Or.* iii. 23; Sogno 2006, 18; see now Callu 2009, 60–63.

47. Them. *Or.* xiii. 165d (three times) and 171a (Gratian himself was not present at the time).

48. διὰ τὸ σφόδρα ἔτι νέον εἶναι καὶ ἄπειρον, B. Grillet and G. H. Ettlinger, *Jean Chrysostome, À une jeune veuve*...(Paris 1968), § 4, p. 138 (unnamed, but Gratian is clearly meant: see the notes ad loc.; for the date, ib. 11).

49. McLynn 1994, 171; PCBE ii. 1. 1209 (Justina 1).

50. Despite its title, Molè Ventura's *Principi Fanciulli* (1992) is limited to Rufinus and the *Chronica Gallica* of 452, and contributes nothing to HA studies.

51. Basil, *Hex.* viii. 4; Ambrose, *Hex.* v. 68; see Ruggini 1963, 67–79; for the date of the work, Madec 1974, 72.

52. Paulin. *V. Ambros.* 18, with Palanque 1933, 507; McLynn 1994, 149.

53. PLRE i. 173; PCBE ii. 380. Paulinus (*V. Ambros.* 18) mentions a run-in with two of Gratian's eunuchs.

If the tirades against child emperors are indeed to be taken seriously, they make perfect sense at the court of Valentinian II in the 380s. The *princeps clausus* motif also happens to be first applied to Valentinian II, in the history of Sulpicius Alexander, who wrote in Gaul perhaps around 400.[54] Interestingly enough, the otherwise baffling glorification of the dynasty of Constantine,[55] seemingly pointless after the death of Julian,[56] can also be made to fit the early 380s—but no later. In 374 Gratian married Constantia, the posthumous daughter of Constantius II and so granddaughter of Constantine.[57] Obviously, he must have been hoping to have a son who would carry the blood of Constantine in his veins. In the event she died in 382/3, but it is a measure of her importance that her body was carried to Constantinople and interred in the newly completed Church of the Holy Apostles, only the second imperial person (after Valentinian I) to be buried there.[58]

3

In 1920 Hohl sought evidence of a Theodosian date for the *HA* in its literary interests. The *HA* (he argued) had a "not contemptible" knowledge of classical authors, and there was a revival of classical authors at the end of the fourth century.[59] More recently, Syme too has eloquently evoked the milieu and reading public presupposed by the *HA*: "Where is it to be discovered save in the renascence of letters towards the end of the fourth century?"[60] But as we have seen in earlier chapters, the so-called "renascence of letters" was no sudden phenomenon of the 390s, nor did it begin in Rome. Ammianus and Claudian may represent its high point, but the rediscovery of early imperial literature had been going on steadily for a half-century by then. Most of the authors Hohl listed were as widely read in the age of the tetrarchs and Constantine as the Theodosian age.

Syme's work has undoubtedly contributed to a better understanding of the literary techniques of the *HA*, but his famous characterization of the author as a "rogue grammaticus," while neatly catching an important aspect of his personality, has encouraged the false notion (which Syme himself did not share) that he was a learned man of wide culture, more specifically a worthy member of that notorious non-entity, the "circle of the Symmachi and Nicomachi."[61] The truth is that the *HA* is

---

54. *clauso apud Viennam palatii aedibus principe Valentiniano*, quoted by Greg. Tur. *Hist. Franc.* ii. 9; *PLRE* ii. 59–60; M. Oldoni, *Gregorio di Tours: La storia dei Franchi* 1 (1981), liv.

55. *Elag.* 35. 2; *Gall.* 7. 1; 14. 3; *Claud.* 1. 3; 9. 9; 10. 7; *Aur.* 44. 5.

56. Whence Baynes's insistence that it only made sense if the *HA* was propaganda for Julian (Baynes 1926, 53–57), and Stern's that it fitted Constantius II (Stern 1953, 32–51).

57. *PLRE* i. 221; O. Hirschfeld, *Kleine Schriften* (Berlin 1913), 889–90; Birley 1991, 53.

58. *Chron. Pasch.* s. a. 383 (p. 563); *Cons. Const.* s. a. 383 (*Chron Min.* i. 244), in both places correcting Constantine to Constantius; Grierson 1962, 25.

59. Hohl 1920, 296–310.

60. *The Historia Augusta: A call for Clarity* (Bonn 1971), 112.

61. For the most extravagant list of writers allegedly known to the *HA*, Chastagnol 1994, lxxiv–xcix.

a work of very limited and conventional culture,[62] distinguished by a triviality of interest and vulgarity of tone that Praetextatus and Symmachus would have found just as offensive as their Christian peers.[63]

The question is, does the *HA* show knowledge of authors we have reason to believe were *not* part of the conventional literary culture of the age of the tetrarchs and Constantine? In 1964 I attempted such a demonstration, drawing attention to a modest number of reminiscences of Juvenal.[64] We have seen in detail in an earlier chapter that Juvenal was perhaps the most conspicuous of the Silver Age poets who came back into favor in the course of the fourth century after a long period of neglect. In the circumstances, we cannot fall back on the explanation that Juvenal allusions in the *HA* were already present in its sources, since without exception they appear in obviously fraudulent passages. They must derive from the impostor himself. Writing as he was in the second rather than first half of the fourth century, his work naturally reflects the literary enthusiasms of his own age.

Several scholars have attempted to develop this approach further, so far with little success. In 1966 J. Schwartz listed another thirty-six passages allegedly inspired by Juvenal.[65] I have to confess that I find no more than one persuasive, and would add no more than one more of my own.[66] Schwartz even thought he could prove dependence on the Juvenal scholia and thus win a secure terminus post quem, assuming Mommsen's late fourth-century date for the scholia. But not only are none of his parallels remotely convincing,[67] more important, the Juvenal scholia are much later than Mommsen believed, in the form in which we have them no earlier than ca. 450. One seemingly tempting example actually proves the exact opposite. A confused scholion on Juv. 4. 81 amalgamates two quite different people, C. *Vibius* Crispus (cos. II 45) and C. *Passienus* Crispus (cos. III ?83). One of the least reliable lives mentions an almost certainly fictitious proconsul of Africa called Vibius Passienus. Some have been tempted to derive this imaginary proconsul from the notice in the scholion.[68] Yet the scholiast, like the passage of Juvenal he is annotating, gives only the one name Crispus. So the scholiast *cannot* be the source of the biographer, nor would it help to posit an

---

62. den Hengst 1991 is sensible as far as it goes (which is not very far). A. Lippold's recent survey briefly notes the exaggeration of the author's culture in recent studies (*RAC* 15 [1990], 722).

63. So rightly Syme 1968, 196.

64. Cameron 1964, 363–77.

65. Schwartz 1966; 1982; and 1992.

66. *Quad. Tyr.* 8. 6 (of the Egyptians) *unus illis deus nummus est*, supposedly taking one stage further Juvenal's *nullas nummorum ereximus aras* (1. 116). *Quad. Tyr.* 10. 2, *ipsi custodes timentur* recalls Juv. 6. 347–48, *quis custodiet ipsos/custodes*, though fearing your own guards is very different from guarding your own guards. With Elagabalus promoting men according to the size of their genitals (*pudibilium enormitate membrorum*, *Hel.* 12. 2), compare the men who earned legacies *partes quisque suas ad mensuram inguinis* (Juv. 1. 41).

67. To give one particularly egregious example, the (admittedly rare) word *quemadmodumcumque* in *Alex.* 49. 6 is held to have been taken from its occurrence in Schol. Juv. vi. 329! For the date of the scholia, Cameron 2010.

68. Chastagnol 1994, lxxxvii; Syme, *BHAC* 1964/65 (1966), 263; Syme 1968, 86–87; Momigliano, *EHR* 84 (1969), 566–69.

earlier and fuller version of the scholion. If the scholiast confused Passienus with Vibius, it follows that he can never have given both names of either!

It may be that one or two more Juvenalian echoes await discovery, and it would be a welcome confirmation to find echoes of other Silver Age writers out of fashion at the turn of the third and fourth centuries: Lucan, Statius, Pliny, or Tacitus. An entire poem of Martial is cited in *Alex.* 38. 1–2, and a line of Persius six pages later in the same life (44. 9). We also find a neat adaptation of another line of Persius in a supposed letter of Septimius Severus.[69] But there is no real evidence that Persius and Martial shared in the general eclipse of Silver Age literature. There was something of a revival of Greek epigrammatic poetry in the age of Hadrian and the Antonines,[70] and it would be surprising if the only outstanding Latin epigrammatist had not shared in the vogue. Aelius Caesar, Hadrian's first choice as heir, is said to have loved Martial so much that he called him his Vergil. Both Martial and Persius are cited with approval by the early fourth-century grammarian Charisius, and if little is certainly known about Charisius,[71] the one thing we do know is that he copied his sources verbatim. These citations of Persius and Martial are not the fruit of his own reading, but taken over from a succession of second- and third-century grammarians. More telling still, he shows no knowledge of Lucan, Statius, or Juvenal. On any hypothesis, Charisius is witness to a period when people were reading Persius and Martial but not Lucan, Statius, and Juvenal. Persius is also quoted by Lactantius.[72]

Quotations of Persius and Martial do not stand out in the way allusions to Juvenal do. As for the other Silver Age writers, Chastagnol cited a passage in the *Life of the Gordians* for knowledge of Statius,[73] but all it says is that, just as Vergil wrote an *Aeneid*, Statius an *Achilleid*, and others *Alexandreids*, the elder Gordian once wrote an *Antoniniad*. Knowing titles is hardly the same as reading poems, and few believe that Gordian's *Antoniniad* ever existed. Much has also been made of three references to Tacitus, two of them as one member of a rather surprising quartet: Sallust, Livy, Tacitus, and Pompeius Trogus. Sallust had long been a standard school text, and Trogus surely long since lost and forgotten except via the epitome of Junianius Justinus. Livy and Tacitus do at least fall into the category of writers neglected in the third century, but there is no reason to believe that the author of the *HA* had read them.

First and most notorious, the claim that the emperor Tacitus ordered ten copies of the works of his namesake and (alleged) ancestor to be copied every year and placed in public libraries (*Tac.* 10. 3). According to G. Zecchini, this "concern for the preservation of the text of Tacitus" proves that the writer considered Tacitus "an important author, but rare and difficult to find." So he follows Hohl in seeing this concern as a pointer to the end of the fourth century. What they have in mind (of course) is the

---

69. *Pesc.* 3. 11 ~ Pers. i. 103–4.
70. Cameron 1993, 65–69, 84–90.
71. *HA Ael.* 5. 9; Schmidt in Herzog and Schmidt 5 § 523. 2, with Kaster 1988, 253, 394.
72. ii. 61 ~ *Div. Inst.* ii. 2. 18: Ogilvie 1978, 15.
73. *Gord.* 3. 3; Chastagnol 1994, lxxxiii.

supposed "editing" of classical texts by pagan aristocrats (in fact nothing to do with the preservation of rare books: Ch. 12–14), more specifically the edict of 372 recommending the appointment of copyists to copy and repair manuscripts (in any case Greek texts in Constantinople, not Latin texts in Rome).[74]

But it is simply not true that imperial support for the conservation of classical texts was an innovation of the closing decades of the century. Already in 356 Constantius II had established a team of copyists in Constantinople trained to make new copies of texts that were "crumbling through long neglect...in danger of being utterly destroyed."[75] As for knowledge of Tacitus in particular, there can be no doubt that the African Aurelius Victor, writing in 361 and reflecting a culture formed two or three decades earlier still, knew the *Annals*. His account of both Augustus and Tiberius is heavily influenced by Tacitus's hostile treatment of both emperors.[76] No less important, this view presses beyond all reasonable limits a joke inspired by the coincidence of an emperor bearing the name of a famous writer. If the emperor's name had happened to be Terentius, it would have been Terence he supposedly had copied, regardless of the fact that Terence was never in danger of perishing and had not been recently rediscovered. It is absurd to read a serious concern for the preservation of texts into so inconsequential a context. The preceding and following sentences praise the emperor Tacitus for closing public baths before dark and legislating against silk garments, respectively!

Paschoud went even further, arguing that the passage was intended to evoke the efforts of the Symmachi and Nicomachi to preserve and disseminate the text of Livy, an author (he claims) dear to the heart of the *HA*.[77] We have already seen that there is not the slightest reason to associate the Symmachi and Nicomachi with a Livian revival. Least of all is there any real evidence that the *HA* knew Livy. We have already seen how difficult it is to prove direct knowledge of Livy in a late antique writer. For obvious reasons, anyone in search of information about early Roman history would turn first to Florus or one of the Livian epitomes rather than the eight thousand unindexed pages of the original text. Chastagnol and Paschoud list a number of passages allegedly inspired by Livy.[78] They have one thing in common: factual details and rare words, just the sort of items that could have been found in epitomes, antiquarian works, or scholia.[79] And as

---

74. Zecchini 1993, 181–91; Hohl 1920, 300–302; *Cod. Theod.* xiv. 9. 2.
75. Themistius, *Or.* iv. 59d–60c (i. 85 Downey), of 1 January 357 (reading μακρᾶς in l. 5); Cavallo 1986, 90.
76. Bird 1984, 95.
77. Hohl 1920, 300, 302; Paschoud 1996, 287.
78. Chastagnol 1994, lxxxii; and Paschoud 1994, 97–99.
79. *scriba pontificis, quos hodie pontifices minores vocant* in *Macr.* 7. 2 comes verbatim from Liv. 22. 57. 3; as perhaps *camellis quos dromadas vocitant* (*Aur.* 28. 3) from *cameli quos appellant dromadas* (Liv. 37. 40. 12). But surely via some scholiast or dictionary like Festus (Paschoud cites Festus for the *toga palmata*). Chastagnol derives some military terms in *Alex.* 50. 5; 56. 3–5 from Liv. 37. 40. The claim that the equites were *seminarium senatus* (*Alex.* 19. 4) no doubt derives ultimately from Livy 42. 61. 5, but it is a memorable phrase that was surely quoted as often in ancient as modern times (e.g., Brunt, *Fall of the Roman Republic* [1988], 147).

Syme has observed, "Various indications conspire to put the author in the ambience of the scholiasts."[80]

A chapter in the *Life of Aurelian* (13. 3) ascribed to Vopiscus gives an immense list of decorations and honors supposedly awarded to the future emperor. According to Paschoud, Vopiscus culled them from a half-dozen different passages of Livy, not to mention Gellius and Ammianus, "working like an Alexandrian poet, varying and contaminating his models." Not only is a single antiquarian source that already combined all this material infinitely more likely, the analogy is grotesquely inappropriate. Alexandrian poets integrated their borrowings into something new and individual that nonetheless contrived to recall their separate models. Vopiscus is simply compiling a shopping list.

Even less probably, another scholar argued that many of the portents and omens that are such a feature of the *HA* derive from Livy.[81] But no one searching for portents would turn to Livy rather than the fifty-odd pages of a late antique portent collection like Julius Obsequens, where he could survey the entire range of Livian portents uncluttered by the thousands of pages of narrative.[82] Not one of the parallels alleged has any verbal similarity with the original text of Livy. In the only case that falls within the dates covered by Obsequens, Obsequens is undoubtedly the source.[83] It is instructive to contrast the evidence for Ammianus's knowledge of Livy: tightly packed pages of verbal and stylistic parallels, the sort of similarities that *cannot* be found in epitomes.[84] It was not for facts that Ammianus read Livy, but as a stylistic and moral exemplar. The author of the *HA* read Sallust this way, but not Livy—and certainly not Tacitus.

Even Chastagnol conceded that no one has ever found the slightest hint of Tacitean influence in the *HA*.[85] Paschoud inferred from the three mentions of Tacitus that Vopiscus was writing during a Tacitean renaissance, but the texts themselves are strongly against such an interpretation. The emperor's reason for making copies of his namesake was supposedly "lest his works perish completely through the indifference of readers" (*ne lectorum incuria deperiret*). As for the other two passages, one depreciates historians in the grand style "like Sallust, Livy, Tacitus and Trogus" in favor of biographers;[86] the other accuses Livy, Sallust, Tacitus, "and finally Trogus" of being liars.

It may prove instructive to look a little more closely at the last name on both these lists. Was there a Trogus renaissance as well? So some believe, identifying Vopiscus's

---

80. Syme 1968, 86.

81. de Kisch 1970, 191–95; Chastagnol 1994, lxxxii n. 4.

82. Only thirty modern pages as extant, but the period before 190 B.C. is missing in the only MS (now lost). For the date of Obsequens, Ch. 6. 4.

83. So T. Pekáry, *BHAC* 1968/69 (1970), 162; the loss of the early chapters explains why de Kisch was unable to find counterparts in Obsequens for the earlier Livian parallels.

84. M. Hertz, *Hermes* 8 (1874), 265 n. 1; H. Wirz, *Philologus* 36 (1877), 633–34; Fletcher 1937, 383–86.

85. Chastagnol 1994, lxxxii; so too Syme 1968, 189; and now J. Velava, *HAC Bonnense* (Bari 1997), 241–53.

86. *Prob.* 2. 7 (running from Marius Maximus and Suetonius to his own pseudo-colleagues Julius Capitolinus and Aelius Lampridius); *Aurel.* 2. 2.

Trogus, not with the forty-four book original, but with the (according to Syme) recently published epitome of Justin.[87] There are no solid grounds for accepting either proposition. Syme's case rests essentially on the argument from silence. But the claim that he is not "cited (or surmised) in the long and vivid Gallic excursus" in Ammianus Bk xv backfires. Not there, perhaps, but Ammianus certainly drew on Justin in Bks xxiii and xxvi.[88]

Sulpicius Severus's account of the period from Cyrus to the Maccabees in his *Chronicle* (ca. 403) has both verbal and factual parallels with Justin, but in addition a few details missing from Justin. It is possible that he used Trogus.[89] But Severus, engaged in research for his *Chronicle*, would have had a serious motive to search out the full text. It must have been mainly for rhetoricians that Justin made his epitome, omitting (as he says in his preface) whatever was not pleasing or exemplary.

Even on Syme's date, there was no Trogus renaissance in the sense that there was a Livy or Tacitus renaissance. By the end of the fourth century, people were undoubtedly reading Livy and Tacitus again. But no one was reading Trogus. The appearance of Justin had consigned the original to oblivion. What did happen is that Justin's epitome unexpectedly found a new group of readers around the first decade of the fifth century. But not because a neglected classic had come back into fashion. It was Christians (Sulpicius Severus,[90] Jerome, Augustine, Orosius)[91] who discovered that Justin supplied the only available account in Latin of the succession of world monarchies, so necessary to anyone constructing a Christian world history. There was nothing in Justin's subject matter (mainly Near Eastern and Hellenistic history) to appeal to a fourth-century Roman pagan. It was presumably the praise of Trogus as *vir priscae eloquentiae* in Justin's preface that led him to include Trogus in the quartet of "eloquent" historians.[92] But there is no implication that either he or his readers were actually reading Trogus (or Livy or Tacitus, for that matter). On the contrary, he is implying that, compared with simple, down-to-earth biographies like his own, history in the grand style is overrated. Given his own obvious mendacity and fraudulence, such an attitude is hardly to be taken at face value. But neither does it provide evidence of firsthand familiarity with Trogus, Livy, or Tacitus.[93]

---

87. Syme 1991, 358–71, 451–58; really nothing that comes close to proof; Zecchini 1993, 157–58.
88. 26. 9. 3 ~ Just. vii. 2. 5–12, with M.-A. Marié's notes to the Budé edition of Bk xxvi (1984), 227 n. 123; the chapter on the Arsacids (xxiii. 6. 2–6) is a précis of Just. 41. 4: see J. Fontaine's notes in the Budé (1977), 57–59. For verbal parallels, Fletcher 1937, 394–95.
89. van Andel 1976, 37–39; Stancliffe 1983, 59 n. 17.
90. Even if Severus drew on Trogus, he may well have used Justin as well, just as readers of Livy would also have used an epitome.
91. Writing in 407, Jerome cites "Pompeius Trogus *and* Justinus," characteristically implying that he had consulted two authorities (prol. Daniel = *PL* 25. 494); Orosius in 417 more straightforwardly cites "Pompeius the historian and his abbreviator Justinus" (i. 8. 1), and subsequently "Pompeius and/or Justinus" (i. 8. 1; i. 10. 2; iv. 6. 1, 6); so too Augustine *CD* iv. 6. All three knew only Justin, but knew that his work was an epitome of Trogus.
92. *disertissimos…viros*, Prob. 2. 7; *quos historicae eloquentiae miramur auctores*, Aur. 2. 1.
93. Sallust (of course) the writer knew intimately: see, p. ###.

Only Juvenal stands out as a genuine new taste of late fourth-century Rome (Ch. 12. 7). It is precisely because the *HA* is a work of such limited culture that its knowledge of Juvenal impresses. Its compiler is surely one of those trivial folk derided by Ammianus for reading nothing but Juvenal and Marius Maximus. After all, the *HA* is our only source for all but one of the twenty-seven fragments of Marius Maximus. And the source for that one other fragment is the scholia to Juvenal. When he deplored this vogue for Marius Maximus, Ammianus may in fact have been including what he no doubt saw as its continuation, the *HA*.

4

The Juvenalian allusions suggest a date no earlier than the 360s, which fits nicely with the only secure terminus post quem for the *HA* so far established, the use of Aurelius Victor (361). A text hitherto neglected in this context provides a terminus ante quem. In or soon after 395 an unknown person compiled a brief *Epitome* of Roman history from Augustus to the death of Theodosius (p. 669). For the first eleven lives the work has close affinities with the *Caesares* of Aurelius Victor, but diverges widely thereafter.

Before turning to the relevant chapter, on Hadrian's philhellenism (*Epit.* 14), let us consider the corresponding chapter in the *HA Life of Hadrian*, where the emperor is said to have befriended "*grammaticos rhetores musicos geometras pictores* astrologos" (*Hadr*. 16. 10). Beyond question, this echoes one of the best known diatribes in Juvenal:

> Grammaticus rhetor geometres pictor aliptes
> Augur schoenobates medicus magus, omnia novit
> Graeculus esuriens. (3. 76–8)

In both cases these professions are associated with Greeks, and the four italicized words appear in the same order in both texts. Furthermore, the final word in line 76, *aliptes* (properly one who rubs the body with oil and more generally an athletic trainer),[94] turns up in a supposed letter of Hadrian about the Egyptians quoted in a later Life.[95] The chapter on Hadrian in the *Epitome* has close affinities with the *HA*. For example:

---

94. See the passages cited by J. E. B. Mayor, *Thirteen Satires of Juvenal* 1⁴ (1886), 357–58; the word is rare in Latin (*TLL* i. 1598).

95. There is no archisynagogus of the Jews, no Samaritan, no presbyter of the Christians who is "non mathematicus, non haruspex, non *aliptes*" (*Saturn.* 8. 3); a "curious reproach" (J. Geffcken, *Hermes* 55 [1920], 286 n. 4), but easily explained if Juvenal was running around in the author's head.

imbutusque impensius Graecis studiis, ingenio eius sic ad ea declinante ut a nonnullis Graeculus diceretur. (*HA Hadr.* 1. 5)	hic Graecis litteris impensius eruditus a plerisque Graeculus appellatus est. (*Epit.* 14. 2)

Schlumberger's detailed investigation of such similarities reached the conclusion that they are to be explained by use of a common source (probably Marius Maximus),[96] and this could well be the explanation here. But compare too the following passages:

fuit enim poematum et litterarum studiosissimus, arithmeticae, geometriae, picturae peritissimus. iam psallendi et cantandi scientiam prae se ferebat (*Hadr.* 14. 8)…in summa familiaritate …grammaticos rhetores musicos geometras pictores astrologos habuit. (ib. 16. 10)	Atheniensium studia moresque hausit potitus non sermone tantum, sed et ceteris disciplinis, canendi psallendi medendique scientia, musicus geometra pictor fictorque ex aere vel marmore proxime Polycletus et Euphranoras. (*Epit.* 14. 2)

There are two separate parallels here. First *psallendi et cantandi scientiam ~ canendi psallendi…scientia*. Second, and more telling, *musicus geometra pictor ~ musicos geometras pictores*. It might have been argued that both recalled *geometra pictor* independently from Juvenal—if they had not also shared *musicus/-os*, absent from Juvenal. The explanation must be that one copied the other, and the copier must be Epitomator, who not only combined two passages from the *HA*, but evidently spotted the Juvenalian echo, since he threw in another of his own. Having added *fictor* (sculptor) to the *pictor* in both *HA* and Juvenal, he illustrated the claim with the hyperbole that Hadrian was as good a sculptor as Polyclitus or Euphranor. Where did he get these famous names? From later in the same satire of Juvenal:[97]

> hic aliquid praeclarum Euphranoris et Polycliti
> this man brings some famous statue of Euphranor and Polyclitus

The proof is Epitomator's incorrect nominative *Euphranoras*, based on a failure to recognize that Juvenal's genitive *Euphranoris* derives from a nominative *Euphranor*. In Juvenal the context and point of the reference to famous sculptors is quite different. He is no longer attacking Greeks, but lamenting the lot of the poor in Rome. The poor man loses everything if his house burns down, but if the same thing happens to a rich man, his friends rally around at once to replace his valuable statues. But once

---

96. Schlumberger 1974, 92; so too T. Barnes 1976, 263.

97. 3. 217; noted by E. Courtney, *BICS* 29 (1982), 52; missed by Schlumberger 1974, 92. If *HA Pert.* 12. 2–4 and *Epit.* 24. 5 echo Juvenal 14. 130–32 (as Courtney suggests) both are too free to have influenced each other.

Epitomator had written *fictor*, with Juvenal 3 on his mind after *geometra pictor*, Polyclitus and Euphranor naturally popped into his head as illustrations.

The role played in this process by Juvenal is enough to exclude the hypothesis of a common source here, whether Marius Maximus or Syme's Ignotus. Given their third-century dates, neither is likely to have known or quoted Juvenal. The possibility that the *Epitome* drew on the *HA* has usually been rejected out of hand, nominally on the grounds that elsewhere it has anecdotal material absent from the *HA*, but mainly (I suspect) because it provides too early a terminus ante quem for most scholars. It may be that most parallels between *Epitome* and *HA* are to be explained by joint use of Marius Maximus. But why should Epitomator not have had access to both Maximus and the *HA*? It is often assumed that the author of the *HA* used Victor, Eutropius, and the *KG*, three overlapping and closely related works. Maximus only went up to Elagabalus, and there is no reason why Epitomator should not occasionally have consulted the *HA* (if available) before Maximus ran out. That he did not use it more often need only prove that it was much too detailed for his very modest purposes.

On this basis I conclude that the *Epitome* drew on the *HA*, which was therefore available *before* the close of the fourth century. The following section will take the terminus back another fifteen years, to ca. 380.

5

In 1927 Schmeidler drew attention to a striking parallel between the preface to the *Life of Probus* and the preface to Jerome's *Life of Hilarion*, conventionally dated to 390. No one paid much attention until Johannes Straub resurrected the idea in 1963, turning it into a key part of his claim that the *HA* was a work of pagan propaganda.[98] Both Jerome and Vopiscus[99] open by alluding to Sallust's dictum that a man's fame depends on the talent of his historian, and then both tell, after Cicero, the story of Alexander the Great's visit to the tomb of Achilles.

In 1964 Janson argued for a common source, citing the introduction to Fronto's *Principia historiae*.[100] But the anecdote is missing here, as is the key point about fame depending on the historian. There is also a third parallel between the two texts. Vopiscus continues with the announcement that he is going to tell of *tanti viri et talis historia*, Jerome of *tanti ac talis viri conversatio vitaque*. There is actually a fourth parallel as well. Both go on to complain about the inadequacy of written accounts of their respective subjects. The third and fourth items are not impressive in themselves, but coming on top of the other two, all four in the same sequence in the prefaces to

98. Schmeidler 1927, 955–60; Straub 1963, Ch. 3.

99. For the convenience of a personal name, in what follows I am dropping the scare quotes.

100. The text of this passage (p. 203 van den Hout) is uncertain; Janson 1964, 150; den Hengst 1981, 123.

biographies, they are (I submit) enough to exclude the hypothesis of a common source. One of the two directly imitated the other.

But which? Schmeidler hesitantly decided for Vopiscus, and Straub simply took this for granted, making no attempt to *prove* the priority of Jerome. Straub also took it for granted that the imitation was calculated and significant: that the *Life of Probus* was intended as a "polemical juxtaposition" of the pagan emperor Probus with the Christian saint Hilarion. He admitted that it was difficult to say *why* the *Life of Probus* was selected for this purpose, but was in no doubt that Vopiscus's purpose was polemical.[101] Difficult indeed. Probus's achievements were military, Hilarion's reluctantly performed miracles of healing.

Many scholars since Straub have accepted the terminus post quem of 390, but all have tacitly dropped his hypothesis of a polemical purpose. The only parallels between the two Lives are the purely literary ones in the prefaces. In 1965 I subjected the two prefaces to a detailed comparison, concluding that Vopiscus wrote first.[102] Most of the many scholars committed on other grounds to a later date simply ignored my demonstration. Four advanced specific objections, though without attempting fresh literary analyses of their own.[103]

The only scholar to do so (the only Jerome expert among them) agreed with me, as did the only scholar since Straub to produce a detailed literary analysis of Jerome's saints' lives.[104] The question of the relationship between the two prefaces may be divided into two parts. First, the Sallustian aphorism, where Jerome is closer to the original than Vopiscus; second, their treatment of the Ciceronian anecdote, where it is Vopiscus who is closer to the original. But before we get down to details, three preliminary remarks.

First, the third parallel. Barnes points out that Jerome's *conversatio vitaque* "renders the common Greek phrase *bios kai politeia*, which is frequently employed by hagiographers to describe their accounts of holy men and ascetics." But that does not make it a "clear indication of his priority."[105] We have to bear in mind that whichever of the two wrote second was bound to adapt his borrowing to his own context and purpose. Vopiscus would not have wanted the (to him unfamiliar) Christian usage *conversatio*, and Jerome would be likely to substitute a phrase more appropriate for the life of a saint than an emperor. Second, Schmeidler rightly observed that the Jerome version is "clearer, sharper and more straightforward," and Adkin illustrated its stylistic superiority in detail.[106] But that proves no more than that Jerome was the more elegant writer, which has never been in dispute. Third (and most important),

---

101. Straub 1963, 104–5.
102. Cameron 1965, 244–45, restated in 1971, 258–59 (reviewing Syme 1968).
103. Syme 1968, 80–82; Chastagnol 1970, 12–16; 1994, xciii–xciv; Barnes 1991, 19–28; den Hengst 1981, 122–27; see too Barnes 1999, 34–35.
104. Adkin 1997, 459–67; Fuhrmann 1977, 90.
105. Barnes 1991, 27; Adkin 1997, 461 n. 15.
106. Schmeidler 1927, 958 (though "straightforward" perhaps undertranslates "ehrlicher"); Adkin 1997.

on no hypothesis could Jerome be the *sole* source of Vopiscus, who in addition to Sallust cites *Marcus Cato et Gellius historici*, not mentioned by Jerome. On the other hand, Vopiscus *could* be the sole source of Jerome.[107]

Now for the Sallust citations. To quote Syme's formulation, Jerome's preface puts together two separate passages from Sallust "in exact quotation," while Vopiscus "has only a vague and verbose reflection of the second quotation from that historian." "It was unfortunate for his thesis," Syme added in a footnote, "that Cameron missed this vital fact."[108] Perhaps not so vital. Let us have a closer look at the two passages (Sallustian words in italics):

Jerome: Scripturus vitam beati Hilarionis, habitatorem eius invoco Spiritum sanctum: ut qui illi virtutes largitus est, mihi ad narrandas eas sermonem tribuat, *ut facta dictis exaequentur* (*Cat.* 3. 2). *eorum* enim *qui fecere virtus* (ut ait Crispus) *tanta habetur quantum* eam *verbis potuere extollere praeclara ingenia.* (*Cat.* 8. 4)

Vopiscus: certum est quod Sallustius Crispus quodque Marcus Cato et Gellius historici sententiae modo in litteras rettulerunt, omnes omnium virtutes *tantas* esse *quantas* videri eas voluerint eorum *ingenia* qui unius cuiusque *facta* descripserint.

According to Syme, "On the criterion of literary priority, namely power and originality, which has been used to establish Minucius Felix as the imitator, not Tertullian, it would seem that similarly the *HA* follows Jerome." This is a misleading criterion at best, since it would be easy to cite counterexamples, where the borrower has improved on a borrowed phrase or idea. And whereas it is at least an appropriate criterion where it can be presumed that one of two authors is adapting the other, how is it even relevant where both are simply quoting from a third party? Jerome is more "powerful," not because he wrote first, but because he quotes Sallust's words accurately. Vopiscus paraphrases—and paraphrases inaccurately: fame is said to be dependent on the intention (*voluerint*) rather than the ability of the historian. The misquotation serves no purpose and merely blurs the force of the epigram.

Den Hengst made two points. First, Sallustian echoes in the *HA* are mainly short phrases, whereas Jerome preferred complete *sententiae*, as here.[109] Second, there are seven prefaces of Jerome "in which Sallust is quoted at least once," concluding that "this seems decisive."[110] But the author of the *HA* also knew Sallust well, quotes him

---

107. Sole secular source, not counting his additions from biblical sources (Romans and Daniel): see Bastiaensen's notes in Mohrmann 1998. Obviously, if Vopiscus wrote second, he would have omitted these Christian additions.

108. Syme 1968, 80–83.

109. den Hengst 1981, 125, firmly endorsed by T. Barnes 1991, 26.

110. Hagendahl 1958, 294, to whom he refers, actually lists only six, but Adkin has now added a seventh (*Hermes* 125 [1997], 241).

often, and *could* have quoted him here without prompting from Jerome.[111] Both are in any case irrelevant. For Vopiscus does not purport to be *quoting* Sallust at all. Rather he is *paraphrasing* the consensus of three different writers:

> It is a fact, as Sallustius Crispus and the historians Marcus Cato and Gellius have put into their writings as a sort of maxim, that all the virtues of all men are as great as the talents of those who have described the deeds of each have wished them to appear.

By Cato and Gellius what he had in mind was a fragment of Cato quoted by Aulus Gellius, describing a suicide mission led by the tribune Q. Caedicius, no less heroic than Leonidas the Spartan (Cato claimed) but winning less renown. There is no verbal trace of Cato in Vopiscus, and the only traces of Sallust are the *tant-/quant-* construction and the words *facta* and *ingenia*. Not only does this sentence misrepresent Sallust, it also misrepresents Cato, who only mentions historians in passing, making the rather different point that all Greece combined to honor Leonidas, while Caedicius was an obscure military tribune.[112]

Vopiscus begins with "a sort of maxim," based on his vague recollection of two sources he apparently did not bother to verify, and then proceeds to give a specific illustration of his point from a speech of Cicero, which (as we shall see) he did verify. Even so, it is hard to believe that he would have paraphrased Sallust so inaccurately if he had been confronted with Jerome's two accurate quotations. On the other hand, if Jerome had been confronted with Vopiscus's garbled para-phrase, the explicit mention of Sallust would have ensured that he recognized the allusion, and, knowing Sallust so well, it is entirely credible that he should have straightened it out. But not knowing Gellius,[113] he was baffled by *Cato et Gellius historici*. So he dropped the last two names on Vopiscus's list and concentrated on Sallust.

6

The Alexander anecdote derives from Cicero's *pro Archia* (§ 24). Hagendahl, evidently unaware of the *HA* parallel, simply assumed that Jerome drew directly on Cicero.[114] But let us compare all three versions:

---

111. This is the argument Barnes used against my analysis of the Cicero borrowing. E. Klebs, *Rh. Mus.* 47 (1892), 537–40, lists twenty-nine Sallustian echoes in the *HA*; den Hengst 1991, 164.

112. *omnis Graecia...decoravere...signis, statuis, elogiis, historiis aliisque rebus*, Cato fr. 83 Peter=Gell. *NA* iii. 7. 1–21.

113. If Jerome had been acquainted with so convenient a transmitter of classical lore some trace would have been found by now in the studies of Hagendahl, Courcelle, and Adkin.

114. Hagendahl 1958, 118–19.

Cicero: atque is tamen [Magnus ille Alexander] cum in Sigeo ad Achillis tumulum adstitisset; "o fortunate, inquit, adulescens, qui tuae virtutis Homerum praeconem inveneris." et vere: nam nisi Ilias illa exstitisset, idem tumulus, qui corpus eius contexerat, nomen eius obruisset.

Vopiscus: Alexander Magnus Macedo, cum ad Achillis sepulchrum venisset, graviter ingemiscens "felicem te," inquit, "iuvenis, qui talem praeconem tuarum virtutum repperisti," Homerum intellegi volens, qui Achillem tantum in virtutum studio fecit, quantum ipse valebat ingenio…occidit (pro pudor!) tanti viri et talis historia, qualem non habent bella Punica, non terror Gallicus.

Jerome: Alexander Magnus Macedo, quem vel aes vel pardum vel hircum caprarum Daniel vocat, cum ad Achillis tumulum pervenisset: "felicem te," ait, "o iuvenis, qui magno frueris praecone meritorum," Homerum videlicet significans. porro mihi tanti ac talis viri conversatio vitaque dicenda est, ut Homerus quoque, si adesset, vel invideret materiae vel succumberet.

For all their similarity there are slight verbal differences between the three versions, the sort of trivial alterations an imitator usually makes, some deliberate, some inadvertent. Careful analysis of these differences suggests that only one of the two later writers directly copied Cicero and was in turn copied by the other. Both (1) omit Cicero's *in Sigeo*; (2) replace his *Magnus ille Alexander* with *Alexander Magnus Macedo*; (3) replace his *o fortunate* with the exclamatory accusative *felicem te*; (4) replace his *adulescens* with *iuvenis*; (5) replace his *adstitisset* with *(per)venisset*; and (6) transfer Homer's name from the *qui* clause to an explanatory participial gloss.

If both had been either copying or recalling Cicero direct, it is inconceivable that both should have made all these identical minor alterations independently of one another. Closer scrutiny reveals that in no fewer than four of his divergences from Jerome, Vopiscus agrees with Cicero. If Vopiscus had been confronted with Jerome's free *frueris praecone meritorum*, why did he write *praeconem tuarum virtutum repperisti*, thus returning almost exactly to Cicero's *tuae virtutis…praeconem inveneris*? It was Jerome who deliberately changed Vopiscus's *virtutum* to *meritorum*. Especially in the plural, *virtus* was standard Christian Latin for "miracle."[115] It is the term Jerome himself regularly used in his translation of the Gospels, completed only a year or so before, and he uses it twice of Hilarion's miracles in the course of this very preface (i. 1 and 5). He was bound to substitute a different word for the deeds of a mythical hero.

The fact that both transfer Homer's name from the direct speech into an explanatory gloss governed by a present participle is not only the most telling single indication that one copied the other, it is also a clear pointer to the priority of Vopiscus. In

115. E. Löfstedt, *Phil. Komm. zu Per. Aeth.* (1911), 112; Stancliffe 1983, 9, 99, and passim (index s.v. p. 396).

Jerome, the participial gloss serves no purpose, whereas in Vopiscus (as Adkin has seen) it provides a convenient antecedent for his long relative clause about Homer (*qui Achillem...*). If, following Cicero, Vopiscus had left *Homerum* in direct speech, he could not then have added his second *qui* clause ("felicem te... *qui* Homerum... *qui* Achillem"), because the natural rhetoric of the sentence would then have referred the second *qui*, like the first, to Achilles, not Homer. Moving *Homerum* to a participial clause solved this problem. In Jerome the participial clause has no such rationale, and it is difficult to see what could have prompted him to modify Cicero's formulation in this way if it was Cicero alone he had in front of him.

Three further details put the priority of Vopiscus beyond serious doubt, two of them hitherto unnoticed. First, which of the two changed Cicero's *Magnus ille Alexander* into the less common formula *Alexander Magnus Macedo*, not found in earlier literary texts? This exact formula appears in two other passages of the *HA*, but nowhere else in Jerome.[116] Second, there is the way each of the three writers rounds off the Alexander story with a general reflection about the power of Homer's poetry:

| **Cicero**: If the *Iliad* had not existed, the same tomb that covered [Achilles's] body would have obliterated his name as well. | **Vopiscus**: [Homer} made Achilles as outstanding in pursuit of virtue as he himself was outstanding in talent. | **Jerome**:[117] I have to describe the life of a man so outstanding that if Homer were alive, he would envy me my subject or prove unequal to it. |

There is no trace of Cicero's reflection in Jerome, but (as Adkin saw) Vopiscus adapts it to a Roman context a page later (2. 4): "as for P. Scipio Africanus, or indeed all the Scipios... would they not lie hidden in darkness, had not historians, both famous and obscure, arisen to praise their deeds?" The same formulation, "if X had not existed, Y would be forgotten," with the first clause framed by the same words *nisi... exstitisse(n)t*, a clear verbal and structural parallel with Cicero that has no counterpart in Jerome.

Third, having moved Cicero's reflection to a later point in his preface, Vopiscus replaced it with one of his own that, like Cicero's, links Homer to the fame of Achilles. But Jerome moved on from Achilles to Hilarion, transforming Homer into an encomiastic trope, with the conceit that not even Homer's genius could have done justice to Hilarion. Where Cicero and Vopiscus simply labor a point already made well enough in Alexander's exclamation, Jerome turned Homer into an elegant bridge between mythical hero and Christian saint.[118]

---

116. *Carac.* 2. 1; *XXX Tyr.* 14. 4.

117. Carolinne White, *Early Christian Lives* (New York 1998), 89.

118. This trope is one of the few details in Jerome's book that Sulpicius Severus directly imitated in his Life of Martin: on Martin's ceaseless fasts and vigils, *vere fatebor, non si ipse, ut aiunt, ab inferis Homerus emergeret, posset exponere* (*VM* 26. 3; Stancliffe 1983, 68).

If Vopiscus had been copying Jerome, why did he not simply adapt this conceit to Probus? What could he have objected to in so neat a transition, so well suited to the extravagant eulogies he himself was proposing to heap on Probus? What prompted him to separate the two elements in Jerome's sentence, adapting *tanti viri et talis* to Probus but turning the Homer conceit into a colorless restatement of the Homer/ Achilles motif? The natural explanation is that Vopiscus wrote with Cicero and only Cicero in front of him. Jerome's conceit, on the other hand, was surely inspired by Vopiscus's *matching* of Homer's talent with Achilles's achievements (*tantum… quantum*) rather than Cicero's unfulfilled conditional. That Vopiscus drew directly on a text of the *Pro Archia* can be confirmed on other grounds. In Cicero, the formulation *Magnus ille Alexander* prepares us for the evocation, two sentences later, of *noster hic Magnus,*[119] namely Pompey the Great. A page later Vopiscus too adds a Roman example: who would have heard of the three triumphs of *Pompey* but for Cicero and Livy?

This conclusion was naturally not welcome to those convinced on other grounds that the *HA* dates from the 390s. Accepting the force of my 1965 analysis of the texts, Chastagnol evaded my conclusion by the hypothesis that Jerome and Vopiscus *both* had a *pro Archia* open on their tables as they wrote.[120] This would allow Vopiscus to have got the Alexander anecdote from Jerome in the first place, but to have "improved" it against the original. Barnes was prepared to dispense with a text, arguing that, since both Jerome and Vopiscus "knew the speeches of Cicero well… either… was capable of using the other but changing the wording to accord better with his recollection of the Ciceronian original."[121]

Yet why should either have bothered, especially Vopiscus, who did not bother to check his own inaccurate paraphrase of Sallust. Why should a writer who preferred inventing fictitious sources to consulting real ones have given himself the trouble of comparing two almost identical versions of the same anecdote? But suppose for the sake of argument that Vopiscus wrote second and did check. Even so he did *not* "correct" Jerome against Cicero. Even where the Vopiscus version is closer to Cicero, it is still different. According to den Hengst, Vopiscus was scholar enough to check Jerome against Cicero (thus meeting my objection) but reluctant to reinstate Cicero's actual words because he "dislikes literal quotations."[122]

Apparently, this "dislike" of literal quotations only applies to Cicero, since on den Hengst's own hypothesis Vopiscus copied a half-dozen lines of Jerome all but verbatim! Such desperate attempts to evade the obvious are not only implausible in themselves, but fail to distinguish between at least three different ways in which writers draw on their predecessors: allusion, direct quotation, and simple use as a factual source. Many scholars now prefer to talk of intertextuality rather than allusion,

119. As recognized by den Hengst 1981, 125, though without appreciating that it undermined his own position.
120. Chastagnol 1970, 12–13; 1994, 1061.
121. Barnes 1991, 25, following den Hengst 1981, 124–25.
122. den Hengst 1981, 125: "it would have been out of character had he copied his source verbatim."

and elide the distinction I am trying to draw between allusion and quotation. Intertextuality is no doubt a helpful concept for analyzing poetry, typically a mosaic of allusions (conscious and unconscious) to earlier writers. But we are here concerned with biography, where learned allusion is rare, but use and quotation of factual sources common. By quotation here I mean quoting a specific earlier text either verbatim or by author's name, as opposed to simply drawing factual information from it without attempting to acknowledge or reproduce it accurately. Thus Vopiscus's *quod Sallustius Crispus* is a quotation,[123] while (as we shall see) the Alexander anecdote is not.

Despite his loose terminology, it was apparently what I am calling literary allusion that den Hengst had in mind when he claimed that Vopiscus "dislikes literal quotations." The claim is true but trivial: allusions are by definition allusive, not verbatim quotations. No ancient writer with a sense of style (and this applies to Jerome no less than the *HA*) actually reproduces more than a word or two of a stylistic model unchanged when adapting it to his own context and syntax.[124]

A typical example is the elegant Juvenalian adaptation in *Aurel.* 5. 6: "Aurelian was the only private citizen to own an elephant" (*solusque omnium privatus Aurelianus elephanti dominus fuit*), which shares just one word with its Juvenalian model (*nulli servire paratum/privato*), but nonetheless recalls while reversing Juvenal's claim that only emperors could own elephants (12. 106–7). Given the vogue for Juvenal in late fourth-century Rome, this is undoubtedly a deliberate allusion that he hoped would be identified and admired. How are we to classify Vopiscus's Alexander anecdote? Not a quotation: no *ut dicit Cicero* or the like, and no attempt to preserve Cicero's phraseology. Chastagnol and his followers assume that cultivated readers were nonetheless expected to recognize Cicero as his source and admire his erudition. That is to say, they treat it as (in my terminology) a learned allusion. Yet they apply the criteria appropriate to a quotation. Whence their talk of Vopiscus "improving" or "correcting" the Jerome version "to accord better with...the Ciceronian original." Yet while a quotation can be corrected by collating it against its source, an allusion cannot. A quotation can be misquoted; an allusion can be neat or clumsy, obscure or obvious, but it cannot be either correct or incorrect. The most elegant and successful preserve no more than a single word of the original (sometimes not even that), and normally make a different, even opposite point. A particularly brilliant Juvenalian allusion in Claudian turns the *verbosa et grandis epistula* from Tiberius that brought down Sejanus into the *exigua charta* from Arcadius that brought down Eutropius. Not one word in common, but anyone who knew his Juvenal would at once appreciate the literary link between the missives that wrought the doom of the two imperial favorites.[125]

---

123. Despite its inaccuracy; many quotations are inaccurate. In the *HA* (of course) many are also fraudulent.
124. Hagendahl 1947, 114–28; and (on Jerome) 1958, 298–309.
125. Cameron 1974, 149; unaware of my paper, M. Dewar made the same point again in *CQ* 40 (1990), 582–84, welcome confirmation that the allusion is real.

Writing *felicem te…iuvenis* instead of *o fortunate…adulescens* did not transform Vopiscus's version of the Alexander anecdote into an elegant Ciceronian allusion. The version in the *Pro Archia* is not to be treated as an original Ciceronian thought or turn of phrase (*faex Romuli, quousque tandem…Catilina* or the like) such as might add a touch of learned color to any writer's prose. Anecdotes were common property, and no one ever copied them verbatim.[126] They were freely adapted to suit the writer's purpose and context. This is why so many appear in such widely differing versions. The "punch line" tends to remain the same, but the setting, date, and even protagonists vary.[127] The Alexander anecdote is found in almost a dozen surviving sources, Greek and Latin.[128] Cicero himself did no more than translate a version preserved in an anonymous collection of apophthegms.[129]

Not only would it never have occurred to Vopiscus, if he had written second, to "correct" Jerome against Cicero. The truth is that his divergences were designed to *conceal* rather than advertise his debt to Cicero. This is plain from his opening words, which seek to create the impression that he found the Alexander story at firsthand while reading the classical historians he names, "M. Cato and Gellius the historians" and Sallust. So too in the following paragraph he implies that he has read about Pompey in Cicero *and Livy*. No one will believe that he read as far as Bk 103 of Livy.[130] Cicero sufficed for the little he says but he knew that Livy must talk about Pompey somewhere. Note the telltale *et* in *Cato et Gellius*, so characteristic of the late antique writer anxious to give the impression that he has consulted two different books when in fact he only knows the earlier through the later.[131]

Anyone with any pretensions to literary culture was expected to show familiarity with Cicero. Much of the Greek culture of the Greekless Middle Ages derives ultimately from Cicero, often indirectly through innumerable late antique authors. Many of Symmachus's allusions to Greek literature, philosophy, and art derive from Cicero. This debt he does not advertise in the same way as he does his verbal borrowings from the speeches. We find the same duality in Jerome. On the one hand he constantly quotes Cicero by name and echoes phrases from the speeches; on the other, he drew much information from the philosophical works unacknowledged, often implying that he had consulted Cicero's sources himself.[132] He introduces another Alexander

---

126. For a useful discussion, Saller 1980, 69–83.

127. In a "sample of fifty-two Suetonian anecdotes with parallel versions the chronological element changes…more frequently than it remains constant" and the setting "is only slightly more stable" (Saller 1980, 75).

128. For the various versions, Straub 1963, 96–97, omitting however L. Sternbach, *Gnomologium Vaticanum* (Berlin 1963), no. 78, pp. 35–37 (originally published in *Wien. Stud.* 1887–89 from Vat. gr. 743 of s. XIV).

129. Sternbach (preceding note) 1963, no. 78.

130. Except perhaps Paschoud, *HAC Mac.* (1995), 270, building on the myth of the "Symmachan" edition.

131. For this use of *et* in Jerome, Hagendahl 1958, 255; many examples in Cameron 2004, 47, and Appendix 5.

132. Hagendahl 1958, 284–92, and passim.

anecdote with the formula "Greek history tells us," when his direct source was Quintilian.[133] Alexander anecdotes are a case where there was more credit to be gained by implying familiarity with earlier and more recondite sources.[134]

Over and above the many details in which Vopiscus's version of the anecdote is closer to Cicero's than Jerome's, two other facts establish his direct consultation of a text of the *Pro Archia*: knowledge of the sentence following the anecdote itself, and mention of Pompey. There is no trace of either in Jerome. This is more than can be plausibly ascribed to a good memory. Evidently, Vopiscus checked the *Pro Archia*, where he also found the reference to Pompey, which he added to his own list of Roman worthies who owed their fame to their historians. With the lapse of the Chastagnol-Barnes escape route—"correction" of Jerome against Cicero—we are left with only one alternative: Vopiscus copied Cicero, and Jerome copied Vopiscus.

7

The *Life of Malchus* and *Life of Hilarion* are generally dated ca. 390, on the basis of the order in which Jerome lists his own works in the *de viris illustribus* of 392. By then Jerome had been living in Bethlehem for four or five years. But an earlier date is possible. Syme connected the wish in *Life of Malchus* 1 that Jerome's detractors should cease hounding him in his "flight" (*fugientem*) with his flight from Rome in 385, described in a letter to Asella, one of his most devoted aristocratic disciples.[135]

In support of this earlier date we may compare a prayer for the same Asella preserved in one family of manuscripts of the *Life of Hilarion*. The first (*in sanctis orationibus tuis memento mei decus ac dignitas virginum nonna Asella*) unmistakably echoes the conclusion of that letter (*memento mei, exemplum pudicitiae et virginitatis insigne*).[136] It would be surprising if prayer and letter had been separated by any great interval of time.[137] If so, then we would not need to postulate a copy of the *HA* in Bethlehem. Jerome could have read it in Rome, where he lived from 382 to 385 and where (e.g.) he picked up his knowledge of Juvenal. As we know from Ammianus, it was not only Juvenal but also the imperial biographies of Marius Maximus to which the Roman nobility devoted their leisure. The *HA* cites Maximus twenty-six times by name and was obviously courting the same readership.

---

133. *Ep.* 107. 4 ~ Quintil. i. 1. 9, with Courcelle 1969, 78, with 71 n. 95. Quintilian himself cites Diogenes of Babylon as his source, but even Jerome drew the line at claiming to have read so recondite an author.

134. For the derivation of fraudulent details from Cicero, Syme 1968, 168–69, 184.

135. *Ep.* 45; Syme 1968, 82; for Asella, see now *PCBE* ii. 1 (1999), 199–200.

136. For these prayers, see P. Leclerc, E. M. Morales, and A. de Vogüé, *Jerome: Trois Vies de Moines* (Paris 2007), 92–93. Unfortunately, they do not discuss the relationship between Jerome and the *Vita Probi*.

137. Note too C. Mohrmann's "poco tempo dopo il suo arrivo a Betlemme," in *Vite dei santi* 4 (Milan 1998⁴), xl.

Chastagnol dismissed the possibility that Jerome was the imitator as "improbable" without further comment.[138] But why is it so improbable that a man who prided himself on his classical learning should borrow a couple of appropriate classical illustrations from an imperial biography for a biography of his own? Barnes has recently drawn attention to the similarity between protestations of veracity in the *HA* and Sulpicius Severus's *Life of St. Martin*.[139] As formulated, the thesis is unconvincing. There are similar protestations in the prefaces to the *Life of Antony* and Paulinus's *Life of Ambrose*. Nonetheless, Severus was a cultivated member of the elite with an appreciation of the classical genres. The preface and dedicatory letter to his *Life of Martin* make clear that he was aiming at a cultivated public.[140] He quotes the opening sentence of Livy's preface to Bk 1 verbatim in his own preface.[141]

It is entirely credible that Jerome should have looked at a recently published series of imperial biographies before writing a biography of his own. The *Life of Hilarion* was not his first essay in hagiography, but it was a much longer and more ambitious work than his earlier *Life of Paul*, with higher literary pretensions.[142] We know he had read Philostratus's *Life of Apollonius* (the model for Hilarion's travels), and it would be natural enough, given his intention to return to hagiography, if he had glanced at the new imperial biographies everyone was reading during the period he lived in Rome.

What may have most attracted him in the *HA* is its many idiosyncratic and entertaining prefaces.[143] Since he often added new prefaces to successive books of multivolume works, Jerome ended up producing no fewer than 120. They reveal considerable familiarity with all the traditional conventions (the author's inability to do justice to his subject, stylistic shortcomings, etc.),[144] and would repay a detailed modern study.[145] Many are crammed with classical allusions. For example, the preface to the invective on Jovinianus quotes Horace, Persius, Plautus, Vergil, and even Heraclitus.[146] Sallust is quoted in seven different prefaces; Terence in at least four.[147] The preface to the invective against Vigilantius is full of classical mythology rather than literary quotations: "the world has given birth to many monsters.... Cerberus and the birds of Stymphalus, the Erymanthian boar and the Nemean lion, the Chimaera and the many-headed Hydra ... Spain has produced Geryon with his three bodies." The list concludes with the claim that "Gaul alone has had no monsters"—until Vigilantius! As if unable to stop, he

---

138. Chastagnol 1994, xciv, "pas vraisemblable."

139. Barnes 1999, 39, referring to Barnes 1996, 25–32.

140. J. Fontaine (ed.) 1967, 72–133; Stancliffe 1983, 40.

141. *unde facturus mihi operae pretium videor si...perscripsero* (Sev. i. 6) ~ *facturusne operae pretium sim si...perscripserim* (Liv. i pr. 1).

142. Fuhrmann 1977, 41–58.

143. On which we have den Hengst 1981.

144. For an exemplary treatment of one such preface, Scourfield 1993, 76–80.

145. There is useful material in Stade 1925; Favez 1958; and Janson 1964. Favez counted 111, but Janson added another 9 from the longer letters (136 n. 21). W. H. Fremantle, *St. Jerome: Letters and Select Works* (1892), 483–502, translates a selection of prefaces. In general, see Curtius 1953, 85–89.

146. *PL* 23. 221; Hagendahl 1958, 142–43.

147. See the list in Stade 1925, 93–98.

then adds that Vigilantius is Jovinianus reborn, "as Euphorbus is said to have been born again in the person of Pythagoras." The preface to the *Life of Probus* offered exactly the sort of thing he was looking for: something ideal for the life of a holy man little known and underrated. Like A. E. Housman, Jerome probably kept a notebook for choice items, and skimmed the *HA* before he left Rome, putting his knowledge to use later.

One of the main reasons scholars have been so reluctant to entertain the possibility that he imitated Vopiscus is their conviction that the *HA* is full of allusions to Jerome.[148] According to one critic, "The ever-increasing detection of familiarity with Jerome" is one of the most promising current approaches to understanding the religious attitude of the *HA*.[149] The more than twenty such "parallels" now on record might seem an impressive dossier, but (as already remarked) it must be borne in mind that all were "detected" by historians who took the priority of Jerome for granted. Not one of them treated their "discoveries" as cases where priority needed to be argued rather than simply assumed.

Den Hengst and Barnes had enough common sense and literary sensitivity to be sceptical of most of these parallels, but felt that the Hilarion case lent support to some of the others.[150] The truth is the exact reverse. If Jerome was able to read the *HA* as early as 385, then it must have been written *before* any of the relevant works of Jerome.

8

So the preface to the *Life of Probus* was written between 361 (the date of Aurelius Victor) and 385/6 (the date of the *Life of Hilarion*). If we conclude (as I think we must) that this preface is not an editorial interpolation but an integral part of the *Life* and indeed of the *HA* as a whole, then the *HA* was written between 361 and 386. That is not only before most of Jerome's writings; it is also before Ammianus, Nicomachus Flavianus, Claudian, and Vegetius.

One advantage of these termini is that it allows us to accept what even such notable sceptics as Mommsen and Momigliano conceded to be perhaps the clearest single prima facie pointer (after the borrowing from Victor) to a post-Constantinian date. At the end of the same *Vita Probi*, the writer reports that the descendants of the emperor Probus left Rome and went to live in Verona. When a portrait of Probus at Verona was struck by lightning, the *haruspices* proclaimed "that future generations of the family would rise to such distinction in the senate that they would all hold the highest posts."[151]

---

148. Chastagnol 1970, 12–16, 72–77, 82–86, 93, 96–98; Chastagnol 1994, xciii–xcvii; 2000; 2002; for a sceptical assessment of most of these suggestions, Lippold 1991, 127–31.

149. Birley 1991, 48 n. 40.

150. den Hengst 1981, 126–27; Barnes 1991, 27–28.

151. *haruspices responderunt huius familiae posteros tantae in senatu claritudinis fore ut omnes summis honoribus fungerentur*, 24. 3–4.

Any prophecy in a pseudonymous work purporting to date from an earlier age is open to the suspicion of being a post eventum retrojection from the writer's own day. And when (as here) the prophecy involves a specific name connected to a specific place, we are bound to look for prominent senatorial Probi from Verona. As Dessau saw in 1889, it can hardly be a coincidence that Sex. Petronius Probus, the most famous and powerful Roman aristocrat of his age, holder of four praetorian prefectures and consul in 371, is associated with Verona.[152] A statue base found in Verona describes Probus as its *civis*, and another from Rome was erected by the Veneti and Histri, who call themselves his "own people" (*peculiares*). It has generally and surely correctly been inferred that Probus himself was born in Verona.[153]

If Probus is the subject of the oracle, it cannot be earlier than ca. 370 or later than his death in or around 390. Baynes, while accepting the Probus oracle as "Dessau's strongest argument for the Theodosian dating,"[154] did his best to reconcile what he conceded to be a reference to Petronius Probus with his own theory that the *HA* was written in 362. The writer (he argued) was predicting a distinguished career for Probus on the basis of the consulates of his father (Petronius Probinus, cos. 341) and grandfather (Petronius Probianus, cos. 322). But it would make no sense to invent such an oracle for an as yet undistinguished (and unmarried) thirty-four-year-old. Crees too thought that the Probus oracle "could as easily refer to other distinguished men called Probus, for example, Petronius Probianus."[155] But the point of inventing such an oracle must be to link one famous *Probus* with another, and ancestors called Probianus and Probinus simply will not do.[156] Dessau was right to insist that the oracle must refer to Probus himself, not to his father or grandfather. And Probus must already have been a man of consequence at the time. Surely no earlier than his consulate in 371.

But how much later can we go? Surprisingly enough, most scholars have assumed a reference less to Probus himself than to the shared consulate of his sons Anicius Olybrius and Anicius Probinus in 395.[157] Even Momigliano conceded that "an allusion to the great consul Probus and his sons would be the best interpretation of the prophecy as a prophecy *post eventum*." Seeck added the consulate of his third son Anicius Probus in 406. There are serious objections to such an interpretation of the oracle.

(1) If the author were writing as late as 395, it would obviously be Olybrius and Probinus whose favor he was hoping to win, not Probus, dead for five years. Why then fashion an oracle that fits the father better than either of his sons, neither of whom was even called Probus? (2) The emphasis on Verona points to Probus himself as the primary reference. There is nothing to connect either of his sons with Verona, and for

---

152. Dessau 1889, 355–59, still the best discussion of the issues; for his prefectures, Cameron 1985, 178–82.

153. *ILS* 1266 (Verona) and 1265 (Veneti); Dessau 1889, 537; Cecconi 1994, 52, 99.

154. Baynes 1926, 24–30 at p. 24.

155. Crees 1911, 41.

156. There is no reason to believe that Pompeius Probus cos. 310 was an ancestor.

157. Syme 1968, 164; Johne 1976, 139, 178; Zecchini 1993, 41, to cite three examples at random; most emphatically Barnes 1971, 18 ("the clearest is a humorous reference to the consuls of 395").

what it is worth Claudian places their birth in Rome (*Prob.* 142–45). Why draw such attention to the birthplace of Probus when he was dead and his sons had succeeded to his wealth and position?

(3) According to *HA Prob.* 3. 3, "Many say that Probus was related to Claudius, that most excellent and revered emperor, but since it is only recorded by one Greek historian, I shall not venture an opinion." No one has ever been in any doubt that the relationship to Claudius is as fictitious as the unnamed Greek historian. But *why* invent such a detail? At one level no doubt to link the emperor Probus to the much admired Claudius II, but at the same time it was bound to imply that the senatorial Probi of the future were related to Claudius as well as Probus. This made no sense until 1972,[158] when a dedication was found at Capua styling the consul of 371 *Claudius Petronius Probus*.[159] The Claudius was apparently not a name or connection that Petronius Probus valued, since it appears in only one of eighteen dedications and no literary source. Nor is it a name he chose to pass on to any of his four surviving children. Nonetheless, it is clear proof of a Claudian connection somewhere.

(4) It is the names he did pass on to his children that are the main objection. All are called Anicius, and unquestionably saw the Anician side of the family tree as outweighing the Petronian in importance. Although Petronius Probus is often styled the head of the Anician house, the truth is that he had not a drop of Anician blood in his veins. He acquired his ascendancy among the Anicii by marrying an Anician heiress, Anicia Faltonia Proba.[160] All four of his children bore the Anician family name, but only the youngest son the Petronian name as well (Anicius Petronius Probus, cos. 406). It is clear from Claudian's panegyric on the consuls of 395 that they were perceived as Anicii first and foremost, not Petronii. If tracing Petronius Probus's line back to the emperor Probus (276–82) was intended as a compliment, then the Petronii must at the time of writing have been a fairly new family, who would be flattered to look to a great soldier-emperor of the 270s as ancestor. According to his biographer, the emperor Probus was born in Sirmium: "his mother was of nobler birth than his father, his private fortune was modest, and his kindred unimportant."[161] Petronius Probus's only identifiable ancestors are Probianus and Probinus, the consuls of 322 and 341. No sign of anyone important before the beginning of the fourth century. The Anicii, on the other hand, can be traced a full century further back in wealth and power, to the age of the Severi.[162] No one wanting to flatter Anicius Olybrius and Anicius Probinus in 395 would have invented a fable about descent from the emperor Probus.

---

158. And was in fact tacitly ignored in most discussions of the oracle.

159. On this basis the Petronius Claudius who was proconsul of Africa (*PLRE* i. 208), a post normally held by Roman aristocrats, in 368–70, is probably to be identified as a younger brother who did not live to rise any higher.

160. Barnes, *CP* 111 (1990), 417–18.

161. *Prob.* 3. 1; he had evidently forgotten about the alleged connection with the emperor Claudius when writing the last phrase.

162. To at any rate Q. Anicius Faustus, a legate of Septimius Severus whose career is documented by more than 50 inscriptions: Christol 1986, 141–46; Wilkins 1988, 377–82.

The oracle fits Petronius Probus himself and only him. As early as the mid-370s Probus himself had all the honors, power, and wealth a private citizen of that age could expect to win, and anyone could have foretold a brilliant future for his sons. Indeed, some did. In a poem addressed to Probus a year or two after his consulate (371), Ausonius predicts a consulate for his (at the time apparently) only son.[163] Even then, when obviously cultivating father rather than baby son, Ausonius gives equal emphasis to the Anician and Petronian sides of the future consul's descent. No one hoping to win the favor of his sons after Probus's death would have invented an ancestry that ignored the Anician side. The most obvious proof of this is the fact that the Anician name is conspicuous by its absence in the *HA*, despite the fact that Anicii were already prominent in the late second century.

9

The Probus oracle has received little attention or emphasis in recent studies. Even as a dating handle it has been considered superseded by supposed pointers to the 390s and later. Nor is the reason for this lack of interest in doubt. Petronius Probus ended his days a Christian, and nowadays it is axiomatic that the *HA* is a product of the pagan reaction. Forty years ago J. Schwartz suggested in passing that the man responsible for the *HA* was some grammaticus in the service of Petronius Probus. Without either denying the reference to Probus or offering an alternative explanation, Chastagnol dismissed the suggestion out of hand simply and solely on the grounds that Probus was "one of the heads of the Christian party in the senate."[164]

It is the Symmachi and the Nicomachi the pagan propaganda school see behind the *HA* these days.[165] If so, then it is their names rather than that of Probus we should expect to find among the many "spurious characters ostensibly belonging to the third century" who actually reflect the nomenclature of the late fourth.[166] But the name "Symmachus" never appears, and now that we know there was no Latin translation of the *Life of Apollonius*, we can forget the idea that the Nicomachus who translated a letter of Zenobia from Syriac is a "discreet" allusion to the elder Flavian. What little basis there ever was for seeing him behind "Maecius Faltonius Nicomachus," famous for his speech denouncing child emperors,[167] is removed by the new terminus ante quem. The elder Flavian was not a person of any consequence until the late 380s, and before then the name "Nicomachus" was prominently featured in a far more

---

163. Auson. *Epp.* 27. 9b. 32.
164. J. Schwartz 1961, 174–75; Chastagnol 1964, 208.
165. To give the merest handful of recent references, Callu, *Histoire Auguste* 1. 1 (1992), lxxiii; Zecchini 1993, 39–49; Chastagnol 1994, clii.
166. Syme 1971, 1.
167. Which Honoré, in a flight of fancy remarkable even for *HA* scholarship, identifies as a "historic and moving speech" of the elder Flavian "at Rome in the spring of 394, energetically promoting a pagan revival" (Honoré 1987, 173–75)!

distinguished family, the Anicii.[168] "Nicomachus" is only one element in this porten-
tous name—and in the wrong position if it was the Nicomachi Flaviani the writer
had in mind.[169]

The rarest of the three elements is "Faltonius," which leads us rather to the kin of
Petronius Probus. According to the Probus oracle, "Future generations of the family
would rise to such distinction in the senate that they would all hold the highest posts."
Many kinsmen of Probus did indeed hold high office—and leave traces in the pages of
the *HA*.[170] A fictitious Faltonius Probus was proconsul of Asia in 275.[171] Petronius
Probus's wife was called Anicia *Faltonia* Proba, her uncle *Faltonius Probus* Alypius
(prefect of Rome late in life in 391), and her grandmother Betitia *Faltonia* Proba, the
well-known Christian poetess. The name Faltonius is not found in the aristocracy at
all before the mid-fourth century, and the *HA*'s combination Faltonius Probus can
hardly be a coincidence.[172] And there is more. The husband of Betitia Faltonia Proba
and father of Faltonius Probus Alypius was Clodius Celsinus, prefect of Rome in
351–54. A fictitious Clodius Celsinus is said to have been praised by the senate under
Severus, and another Celsinus is said to have been an adviser of Diocletian, presumably intended to be the same Celsinus represented as a friend of Vopiscus.[173] Is it just
coincidence that, when conjuring up fictitious characters to fill out his narrative, the
writer selected names of in-laws of Petronius Probus. The *Life of Probus* is actually
dedicated to a Celsinus.

Michel Festy has recently produced an ingenious (if unconvincing) new argument
for Nicomachan authorship.[174] The imperial letter commemorating the elder Flavian's
rehabilitation in 431 claims that his disgrace was the result of imperial favor exciting
the "jealousy of scoundrels" (*livorem inproborum*). This phrase Festy connects to the
epilogue of the *HA Life of Elagabalus*, where the writer, who claims to have dedicated
his book to Constantine, says he is apprehensive of the "jealousy of scoundrels"
(*livorem inproborum*). Unable to find any other occurrence of the phrase and arguing
that both texts refer to histories dedicated to emperors, Festy insists that coincidence
can be ruled out: "the two authors are one and the same; Nicomachus Flavianus is the
compiler of the HA." But the two texts are not in fact nearly so similar as Festy suggests. In the *HA* passage, the writer is afraid he will provoke jealousy by flattering
Claudius in a forthcoming biography. In the Flavian dedication, Theodosius's favor
provokes the jealousy that led to Flavian's death and *damnatio memoriae* (his history is

168. For example, Amnius Manius Caesonius Nicomachus Anicius Paulinus cos. 334 and (presumably)
     his son M. Iunius Caesonius Nicomachus Anicius Faustus Paulinus, praetor in 321 (*PLRE* i. 679, 681,
     with Chastagnol 1962, 32; and Christol, 1986, 124).
169. Note the sequence Virius Nicomachus Flavianus, Appius Nicomachus Dexter. There are many other
     cases where the family name seldom or never comes in last place, notably the Anicii and Macrobii.
170. So again Dessau 1889, 352–54.
171. *Aur.* 40. 4; *PIR*² F. 108.
172. *PLRE* i. 49, 732–33; Syme 1968, 156.
173. *Sev.* 11. 3; *Aur.* 44. 3; *Prob.* 1. 3.
174. Festy 2007, 183–95.

simply cited as an illustration of this favor). Nor is the conjunction of *livor* and *improborum* especially striking. The late Roman aristocracy lived in a world of feuds. If he does not use this exact phrase, Symmachus uses many similar (Ch. 5. 4). The words *livor, invidia,* and *improbi* pepper his pages. On any hypothesis, the 430s would be improbably late for the *HA*, and even if there were a direct relationship between the two texts, that would fall far short of proving the identity of the two authors. It is at least as likely that the dedication echoes the biographer.

Why so indirect a hint anyway? Why no reference to the brilliant careers we know some Symmachi to have enjoyed as early as the 270s?[175] While it is not in itself an argument against sponsorship by the Symmachi or Nicomachi that their names do not appear, it must be held significant that another aristocratic faction of an earlier generation has left such unmistakable traces. It is hard to resist the conclusion that "Vopiscus," whoever he was, was hoping to please powerful patrons by slipping the names of Petronius Probus and his kin into his work. Jerome's use of the *Life of Probus* gives us a terminus ante quem of 385, and Petronius Probus's consulate a terminus post quem of 371. The third and longest of his four praetorian prefectures lasted from 368 to 375. When Magnus Maximus invaded Gaul and eliminated Gratian in summer 383, Probus came out of retirement to assume his fourth and final prefecture, heading the resistance to Maximus at the court of Valentinian II.[176] It has indeed been conjectured that the purpose of Maximus's rebellion was precisely to rid the West of "a dilettante youth and a child."[177] Honoré has argued that the author of the *HA* was a bureaucrat,[178] and if he was a member of Probus's staff, he would have witnessed the problems of child emperors at close quarters, something that clearly made a deep impression, whether or not we take his treatment of the motif seriously.

Chastagnol's objection to identifying Probus and his kin as the writer's patrons was their Christianity. There are two issues here. In the first place, Chastagnol took it for granted that the *HA* was a work of markedly pagan character. That the writer was a pagan no one would dispute, but only the most imaginative special pleading can detect pagan propaganda, much less anything positively anti-Christian.[179] On a more balanced reading, there is little or nothing to offend a classically educated person who happened also to be a Christian.

In the second place, while Petronius Probus's wife, Anicia Faltonia Proba, may have been a pillar of the church, there is no evidence that Probus himself (not baptized till his deathbed) was an active Christian in his lifetime, much less head of any "Christian party." As we saw in chapter 10, he was a typical Roman aristocrat of the old school, eager for power and wealth and proud of his literary culture. The fact that the

---

175. See Ch. 15, p. 528.
176. Socrates *HE* v. 11, with Cameron 1985, 181; Matthews 1975, 174.
177. Matthews 1975, 175.
178. Honoré, 1998, 190–211.
179. The writer shows no interest in oriental cults and actually makes fun of *haruspices* (Syme 1968, 140). Birley 1991, 29–52, exaggerates the distinctively pagan character of the work.

poem on his tomb[180] makes so much of his deathbed baptism suggests of itself that he had not been a prominent Christian in his lifetime. We have also seen that Faltonius Probus Alypius may actually have been a pagan (p. 380). There is simply no evidence for the widespread view that the Anicii and their dependents were a homogeneous and politically active Christian faction in Probus's lifetime.

Given a terminus ante quem of ca. 385, it is tempting to refine it further in light of the possibility that the extraordinary emphasis on the dynastic descent of Constantine reflects Gratian's marriage to Constantine's granddaughter Constantia. This would yield a window of 374–382/3 (p. 753). If so, then the *HA* might already have been written before Gratian's anti-pagan measures of 382/3. If so, that would fatally undermine the claim that it was intended as a "plea for toleration." There was no need for toleration before the cults were threatened. Nor would it have been necessary for the writer to conceal his identity.

10

What then was the purpose of the *HA*? The answer is disappointingly simple and banal. The author may have set out intending to do no more than continue and supersede the newly fashionable Marius Maximus. But faced with the scarcity of sources after Maximus (the early books of Ammianus had not yet appeared), he gave ever-freer rein to his powers of invention. He[181] discovered a genuine talent for fiction, and by the time he started calling himself Vopiscus, things had got out of hand. On the usual view, the pseudonyms and pretence of an earlier date were devices to enable the writer to put across his "message" without fear of discovery. But the most conspicuous and idiosyncratic features of the *HA*—the bogus source citations, fake documents, invented characters, forged poems, silly jokes, childish puns, hobbyhorses (adoption, eunuchs, child emperors), the fascination with food, drink, and clothes—contribute nothing whatever to the religious and political agendas detected by modern scholars.

Let us take a brief look at just two of these features: bogus source citations and fake documents. But first it is necessary to underline the pride the writer evidently took in his knowledge of Greek and use of Greek sources. Perhaps not for the early lives, where he had ample Latin sources (there is some doubt as to whether he used even Dio), but once Marius Maximus ran out he turned to Herodian and Dexippus. Herodian he cites by name ten times, several times emphasizing that he was a *Graecus scriptor*, Dexippus fourteen times. On three further occasions where he appears to be drawing on Herodian he cites his source as Arrianus. This might be a scribal corruption

---

180. *CLE* ii. 1347b=*ICLV* i. 63b=*ICVR* n. s. ii. 4219b; see now the new edition by Schmidt 1999, 99–116.
181. She, according to Paschoud's entertaining novel *Le dernier païen* (2008), a daughter of the elder Nicomachus Flavianus, married to an illegitimate son of Julian!

for Herodianus, but might equally be a deceptive attempt to imply consultation of an additional source. He also twice cites Asinius Quadratus. We do not need to believe that these citations are fully authentic (in the sense that they reflect direct consultation of the text in question for the point in question), but there can be no serious doubt that the writer knew and at least occasionally consulted the basic Greek sources for his period. Several of the bogus sources he cites by name either look Greek or are explicitly said to be Greek. For example, in the preface to the *Life of Aurelian* (i. 4) he complains that, while there were several Greek biographies, there was none in Latin. He goes on to cite no fewer than three Greek biographers: Asclepiodotus (44. 2), Callicrates of Tyre (4. 2), and Theoclius (6. 3). There are in fact indications that the *Life of Aurelian* does draw on Greek sources (if not the ones he names).[182] Elsewhere the writer draws on Greek Sibyllines (p. 214). Critics have on the whole been more interested in unmasking bogus sources and identifying actual sources than paying attention to this ostentatious (and not wholly false) parade of Greek culture.

It has not been noticed in this connection that bogus source citations had for centuries been one of the hallmarks of the more disreputable forms of Greek historiography, mythography, and paradoxography in the late Hellenistic and Roman worlds.[183] The prime cases are the *New History* of Ptolemy the Quail, Pseudo-Plutarch's *Roman Parallels*, and *On Rivers*, and the *Phoenician History* of Herennius Philo. The more dubious the subject matter, the more important (it seems) it was considered to cite an authority. Many are completely bogus, but often mixed in with genuine texts that *might* have provided the information cited—but probably did not.[184] As for fake documents, a sizable number are imperial letters. Here one obvious influence is Suetonius, who famously cites letters of Augustus (though none from any later emperors).[185] But we should not overlook the *Alexander Romance* (translated into Latin in the early fourth century), full of blatantly forged letters of Alexander. There are also a great many collections of pseudonymous letters by famous Greeks dating from the early empire.[186] I suggest that bogus sources and fake letters in the *HA* are best understood as an aspect of the author's affectation of Greek culture.

The pseudo-controversy about the birthplace of the emperor Carus provides a perfect illustration:[187]

There is such divergence among the various writers that I am unable to say where it really was. For Onesimus, who wrote a very thorough *Life of Probus*, maintains that he was born at Rome but of Illyrian parents. Yet Fabius Ceryllianus, who covered the *Times of Carus, Carinus and Numerian* with great

---

182. Barnes 1978, 112.
183. On which, see in general Gabba 1981, 50–62; Mazza 1999.
184. Cameron 2004, 89–163, discusses the subject in detail with many illustrations.
185. A. Wallace-Hadrill, *Suetonius* (London 1983), 91–95.
186. Rosenmeyer 2001; on the Alexander letters, Fraser 1986, 205–25.
187. *SHA Car.* 4. 4; Chastagnol 1994, 1137–38; Cameron 2004 (same case from the opposite perspective).

skill, declares that he was not born in Rome but in Illyricum, but that his parents were Carthaginian, not Pannonian. I myself recall having read in a certain journal (*ephemeris*) that he was born in Milan but enrolled in the senate of Aquileia.

As it happens, it is securely, uncontroversially, and abundantly documented that Carus was born at Narbonne in Gaul. If the writer had really investigated the topic he must have known this. Yet he chose instead to pretend that there was serious debate among a number of quite different alternatives. Many of the *HA*'s fabrications concern events where little reliable information was available, but here we find him taking a solid fact for which genuine sources could easily have been cited and creating a nonexistent controversy on the basis of nonexistent authorities.[188] Compare now Ptolemy Quail, on the wife of King Candaules of Lydia; though not named by Herodotus,[189] she was in fact (he claims) called Nysia, coincidentally the name of the girlfriend of Herodotus's boyfriend:[190]

> Others say her name was Tudun (Τουδοῦν), others Clytia, while Abas says that she was called Abro. They say that Herodotus suppressed the woman's name because his lover Plesirrhoos was in love with a woman called Nysia, a Halicarnassian, and hanged himself when this hetaira rejected him. This is why Herodotus could not bring himself to mention the name Nysia, which was hateful to him.

For Nysia we have a fuller version in Tzetzes, who provides the source Photius omitted: the *Samian Tales* (*Logoi*) of Aeneas,[191] where the form of the title is surely modelled on Herodotus's own use of *Assyrioi Logoi* and *Libykoi Logoi* (i. 184; ii. 161. 3). A writer called Abas is cited once by Servius for a *Troïca*, no more likely a source for the name of an oriental queen than a book called *Samian Tales*.[192] Evidently, Ptolemy presented Nysia as front-runner, and Tudun as simply one of many other possibilities. Yet Tudun (or Tudo) is in fact the only name attested by an authentic source, Xanthus of Lydia (quoted by Nicholas of Damascus).[193] As in the case of Carus's birthplace, if Ptolemy had really investigated the question at all, he must have known this. It is not likely that any amount of research could have come up with another name. Yet rather

---

188. Another illustration in the spirit of Ptolemy concerns the diet of the monstrous emperor Maximin: "it is agreed that he often drank a Capitoline amphora of wine in a single day and ate 40 pounds of meat, or (according to Cordus) no less than 60 pounds. It is also agreed that he abstained wholly from vegetables" (*V. Max.* 4. 1).
189. Herod. i. 10; Plato, *Rep.* 360B, did not give the name either.
190. Quoted by Photius, *Bibl.* 150b. 18–28.
191. Quoted by Chatzis p. 33 from Cramer, *Anecd. Oxon.* iii. 351.
192. *FGrH* 46 described as a "Schwindelautor" by Jacoby.
193. τρυδωνου Μυσῶν βασιλέως, the only MS; Τουδὼ τοῦ Mueller, *FHG* iii. 384, on the basis of Ptolemy; now Nic. Dam. F 47. 6 in *FGrH* 90.

than triumphantly produce a name unknown to Herodotus from a source earlier than Herodotus, Ptolemy chose instead to create the impression of a scholarly controversy, with many possible answers—on the basis of invented citations.

This is certainly Syme's "rogue grammaticus." Syme himself put his rogue "in the ambience of the scholiasts," meaning the likes of Servius. But Servius was no faker. It was from writers like Ptolemy Quail or Pseudo-Plutarch that the writer derived his fondness for the spoof scholarly controversy based on multiple forged citations. One of the features that long prevented scholars acknowledging the full extent of Ptolemy's fakery was his habit of citing genuine sources for fake facts, another device found in the *HA*. For example, there was a real historian called Onesimus, son of Apsines, a Cypriot, who wrote on Constantine.[194] But that does not make the citation about Carus's birthplace genuine. Nobody was likely to find a copy of the real Onesimus in late fourth-century Rome, much less check it for this detail. It should also be added that there are countless examples of invented characters, silly jokes, childish puns, and even forged poems in Ptolemy.[195] There can be little doubt that the author of the *HA* was familiar with the shady Greek mythhistorical literature of the early empire (it may be significant that the only occurrences of the words *mythistoria* and *mythistoricus* in Greek or Latin literature are in the *HA*).[196] There was no need or place for any of this if all the writer was trying to do was cover his tracks. Indeed, it would have had the double disadvantage of distracting attention from his "real" purpose while advertising the imposture. In short, I entirely agree with Syme that the imposture is not a means to an end, but the end itself.

If the *HA* was written, not ca. 330, but in the very different world of the 380s, how is it (Momigliano asked) that "none of the prominent features of the period between AD 330 and 380—such as the struggles inside the Christian church, Julian's apostasy, the Germanic menace, the abandon of Rome—seem to have left a clear mark. . . . Is it likely that the author(s) were unsubtle forgers of documents but clever composer(s) of the context?"[197] If the author was writing (as most fanciers of the late date believe) with a contemporary agenda, this is a serious question that deserves (and has not so far received) a serious answer. My own answer would be that the *HA* really is as trivial a product as everyone used to think. Its author was just not interested in heresy, Julian, Germans, or Constantinople. His political views, if they deserve to be so described, were utopian fantasies such as good emperors respecting the senate and choosing the best men to succeed them. The author of the *HA* was a frivolous, ignorant person with no agenda worthy of the name at all.[198]

---

194. Suda s.v. Ὀνάσιμος; Jacoby, *FGrH* 216, with Komm. pp. 631–32.
195. Many cases of all these things are discussed in detail in Cameron 2004, 134–55.
196. *Macrin.* 1; *Firm.* 1.
197. Momigliano 1960, 128–29.
198. "It is at least arguable that lazy and irresponsible people find it more difficult to inform themselves about almost contemporary events than on events of which authoritative accounts are already existing," Momigliano, l. c. According to Dessau, *Hermes* 27 (1892), 585, the author was "eine Persönlichkeit die der Politik fern stand."

It is not surprising that he was reluctant to put his own name to a work that ended up more fiction than fact. But if all he wanted was to conceal his identity, he would have been better advised either to publish anonymously, or to adopt a single, plausible pseudonym (the very idea of a team of collaborators is unprecedented and arouses suspicion). Nor was there any need to drop all those chronological pointers in the prefaces. Yet once he had developed into a full-fledged forger, the fellow was tempted to indulge his taste for mystification to the hilt, and conjured up six imaginary biographers of an earlier age. He even made a perfunctory attempt to give them biographies of their own, but did not take the trouble to make all the details consistent, perhaps half deliberately. At some level most forgers want to receive the credit due their handiwork and, given the triviality of the final product, it is not as if he stood in any danger if a few friends or patrons pierced his true identity.

CONCLUSION

So when did paganism really, finally, end? This is a question that depends on a series of further questions, of definition, interpretation, and context. Above all, it depends on constantly changing perceptions of paganism. Many people still claim to be pagans (a student once gave me a "born-again pagan" button), but nowadays that implies a rejection of established religion that was alien to ancient paganism. If we define paganism as the civic cults of the pre-Christian Graeco-Roman world, official Roman paganism really did effectively end with the disappearance of the priestly colleges in the early fifth century. To use the term in the wider but well-established sense of any and all religious beliefs and practices that preceded conversion in what became Christian societies, Gothic paganism ended in the mid-fourth century, Viking paganism not till the mid-twelfth. We should not confuse the end of paganism with the victory of Christianity, nor should we assume that it was active pagan opposition that kept certain pagan practices alive.

A mass of evidence for pagan "resistance" from all over the Roman (and post-Roman) world was thrown together in a curiously haphazard but (as always) lively and entertaining book by MacMullen.[1] But since the evidence is virtually all Christian, that makes it peculiarly difficult to use. The non-Christian evidence consists almost entirely of Neoplatonist biographies, thanks to which we are remarkably well informed about the philosophers of fifth-century Athens and Alexandria, colorful characters disproportionately prominent in modern accounts of the last pagans. But there can never have been more than a few dozen of them at any one time, and they kept to themselves.[2] According to Lizzi Testa, "The most intractable problem lies in reconstructing pagan attitudes through hostile Christian sources, which are often apt to exaggerate."[3] Actually, the problem is far more complex than just exaggeration. Many Christian texts imply situations that a modern (or contemporary pagan) observer would have described entirely differently.

Traditional religious practices no doubt lingered in remote country areas for many years, in some cases for centuries. John of Ephesus famously claimed to have converted seventy thousand pagans and built ninety-six churches in mid-sixth-century

---

1. MacMullen 1997; see too the less lively volumes of Trombley 1993–94.
2. Chuvin 1990; Cameron 2007, 21–46.
3. Lizzi Testa 1990, 161.

Asia Minor.[4] But even here it depends what is meant by "pagans." There are bound to
have been many places so remote that they had never heard of Christianity. Such people were certainly "pagans," but their practices are not likely to have had much in
common with the civic cults of the Graeco-Roman world in their heyday. To cite them
as proof of the "tenacity" of paganism misleadingly implies a continuing entity that
defiantly resisted the influence of Christianity—a Christian perspective.

To turn to the West, late fourth- and early fifth-century sermons constantly rail
against landowners for not destroying the pagan shrines and temples on their estates,
implying that the landowners themselves were pagans or at least sympathetic to
paganism. Modern scholars tend to take such evidence at face value, but there are
problems with so apparently reasonable an assumption. These texts certainly reveal
Christians anxious about what they saw as the continuing threat of paganism. But how
realistic was this perception? In the first place, we should not be picturing just two or
three rural shrines on a large estate, but scores, if not hundreds, most of them centuries old, many long abandoned.[5]

David Riggs cites canons 58 and 60 of the church council held at Carthage in 401:[6]

> 58: There remain still other requirements to be sought from the most pious
> emperors: that they should command the remaining idols throughout all
> Africa to be utterly destroyed, for in a number of coastal areas and in various
> rural estates (*possessionibus*) the wickedness of such error flourishes.... They
> should direct both the idols themselves to be utterly destroyed (*penitus ampu-
> tari*) and their temples which have been set up in rural parts (*in agris*) or
> remote sites without identification (*in locis abditis nullo ornamento*).

> 60: This too is to be requested that, inasmuch as banquets (*convivia*) occur in
> many places contrary to the decrees, brought together by pagan error, so that
> now Christians are forced (*cogantur*) by pagans to join in such celebra-
> tions... the emperors should order that they be prohibited and banned from
> both cities and rural estates.

According to Riggs, these canons are "good testimony to the vitality of rural pagan
worship at the beginning of the fifth century." But are they? He compares a sermon of Augustine dated to 399, reproaching Christians for participating in a
"pagan" banquet held in front of the statue and altar of the Genius of Carthage,
but mistakenly claims "that these temples, which *continued to function in defiance
of the recent anti-pagan laws*, were those located on rural estates in the Carthaginian

---

4. Whitby 1991, 111–31. It has been claimed that "paganism" survived in Harran (ancient Carrhae) till the
    tenth century: J. Hämeen-Antilla, *The Last Pagans of Iraq* (Leiden 2006).
5. Caseau, 2004, 105–44.
6. Riggs 2001; 2006.

countryside."[7] Actually, both Augustine and canon 60 refer to cities as well as the countryside.

To take the banquets first, this request had already been submitted to court once—and firmly rejected. A law sent to the proconsul of Africa on 20 August 399 expressly forbade attempts to abolish "the festal assemblies of citizens and the common pleasure of all."[8] So long as there was no sacrificing, festal banquets "according to ancient custom...shall be furnished to the people." Not only were they not forbidden; they were to be provided at public expense. The claim that Christians were "forced" to take part is absurd. Most Christians were happy to join in traditional local festivities they now considered safely depaganized. But that was not good enough for a rigorist minority. They got their way in 408, with a law that forbade "banquets in honor of sacrilegious rites in polluted places (*funestioribus locis*)," and also ordered landowners to destroy rural temples.[9] But if these banquets had really followed forbidden public sacrifices, Augustine could not have failed to denounce so flagrant a violation of now established law.[10] As it is, he represents participating Christians thinking that they have committed an entirely venial sin.[11] We may wonder whether the law of 408 finally stopped the practice. A century and a half later we find Caesarius of Arles († 542) still telling his parishioners (obviously Christians) "to avoid devilish banquets held in the vicinity of a shrine or spring or particular trees."[12]

As for rural temples, while some at least were no doubt still functioning, the phrase *nullo ornamento* in canon 58 implies abandoned buildings already stripped of their statues and ornaments. The law of 399 had laid down that statues were only to be removed (*not* destroyed) if an investigation showed that they were still receiving cult. In the eyes of the rigorists,[13] anything that had ever been tainted by paganism had to go. The goal of the civil authorities was to stamp out public pagan practice. The goal of the church triumphant was to eradicate every trace of paganism, including abandoned shrines in remote areas that could no longer be identified. The rigorists wanted even these destroyed. Demons lived in such places, and who knew when pagans might sneak in and perform forbidden rites? One paranoid correspondent of Augustine anxiously asks the bishop whether it is safe to drink from a spring in a disused temple.[14]

---

7. *Sermo* 62. 9: "ecce, in quem verum Deum peccas, dum discumbis apud deos falsos," which Edmund Hill (*Works of S. Augustine* 3. 3 [1990], 161) mistranslates "lounging around in the company of false gods." *Discumbo* is the *vox propia* for reclining at a formal dinner. For the date, Perler 1969, 225–26, 443; and the introduction to the new CCL edition (*Sermones in Matthaeum* 1 [2008], 292–94). Riggs 2001, 294.

8. *Cod. Theod.* xvi. 10. 17, 18.

9. *Cod. Theod.* xvi. 19. 2–3; the implication of *funestioribus* is that these sites should *never* be used by Christians.

10. As noted by Lepelley 2001, 50.

11. *ne...leve duceres peccatum ac parvipenderes, Sermo* 62. 9 (l. 213).

12. Caes. *Sermo* 54. 6.

13. *districtiores Christiani*, Anon. *Consultationes Zacchei* i. 28. 8 (ed. J. L. Feiertag, Paris 1994, i, p. 175).

14. Augustine, *Epp.* 46; 47; see Lepelley 2002, 83–96.

Taken by itself the 408 law *seems* to be solid evidence that rural temples in North Africa were still functioning and banquet tables still laden with sacrificial meat. That is because the central government got its information from the rigorists in Carthage. This is a rare occasion when we are able to identify the information on which they acted. But there must be countless other laws based on distorted information supplied by clerics with an agenda that has misled modern scholars.

According to Dill, "The edict which closes the long series of anti-pagan laws [438] shows, by the fierceness of its tone, and the severity of the penalties with which it threatens the offender, that the spirit of paganism was not yet crushed."[15] But the ferocity of the legislator's rhetoric is simply routine, bearing no relation to the persistence of the practices condemned. Another critic, convinced that paganism persisted well into the sixth century, solemnly remarked of a reference in an eastern law of 423 to "surviving pagans, though we do not believe there are any" that the law was "formulated on the basis of inadequate data."[16] This is to misunderstand both the rhetoric and the purpose of imperial legislation. What we have here is a wish or exhortation expressed as though an established fact.

Obviously, it must have taken many years and much devoted missionary work to Christianize the countryside, and many traditional rituals were assimilated into church practice. But much of what *appears* to be evidence is variously problematic. Here is one out of many similar passages in the sermons of Maximus of Turin, writing in the early decades of the fifth century:[17]

> Apart from a few religious people, hardly anyone's field is unpolluted by idols, hardly any property is kept free from the cult of demons. Everywhere the Christian eye is offended, everywhere the devout mind is assailed; wherever you turn you see either the altars of the devil or the profane auguries of the pagans or the heads of animals fixed to boundary posts.

He does not say that there are *pagans* everywhere, just idols. The term "idol" might identify a multitude of objects: not only statues, but trees, springs, or odd-shaped stones (Caesarius distinguished three sorts of tree idols: profane, sacrilegious, and "fanatical").[18] That is why they are to be seen everywhere. It is not clear that they are all functioning, or that it was only pagans who paid them respect. Lizzi Testa cites as a "manifestation of paganism in Turin" Maximus's complaint about people shouting to help the moon through an eclipse.[19] But this was a popular superstition rather than a surviving element

---

15. Dill 1899, 4.

16. *Nov. Theod.* 3; Dill 1899, 4; *paganos qui supersunt, quamquam iam nullos esse credamus, Cod. Theod.* xvi. 10. 22; Trombley 1 (1993), 1.

17. Max. Taur. *Sermo* 91. 2; see too 30, 63, 106, 107, 108.

18. Filotas 2005, 86–95, and index p. 423; and the section "Trees, Springs and Stones" (145–48); Dowden 2000, Ch. 4.

19. Max. *sermo* 30. 2–3; Lizzi Testa 1990, 167.

of Roman paganism,[20] and Maximus himself concedes that it was "seemingly devout Christians" who did the shouting. A century and a half later Caesarius attacks the very same practice (adding bells and trumpets to the shouting). Did Caesarius really live in a world where paganism was still thriving? As Klingshirn has aptly put it,[21]

> The most serious barrier to our interpretation of Caesarius's sermons against paganism is their indiscriminate polemic. It was (and is) difficult enough for an outsider to deduce religious intentions from observed or reported behavior. But Caesarius further obliterated distinctions in religious intention, and hence religious loyalty, by the wide range of behavior and belief he condemned as pagan: from the sacrifices and dedications of traditional Gallo-Roman religion to such activities as bathing in rivers on the feast of John the Baptist (*serm.* 33. 4) and exchanging presents on New Year's Day (*serm.* 192. 3; 193. 3), activities which had either been adapted to Christian purposes, or drained of their religious content.

In short, any ritual activity that was not unmistakably Christian, above all any such activity that evaded his control, was pagan.

New Year's celebrations make a particularly good illustration, since there is so much evidence over so long a period and so wide a geographical area. A number of Christian attacks on "pagan" New Year's celebrations have come down to us, notably by Augustine, Maximus, Peter Chrysologus, and Caesarius.[22] The earliest is a recently discovered sermon of Augustine, preached on 1 January 404.[23] It might seem tempting to infer that he was referring to the traditional public ceremonies held in the first week of January. But what the sermon actually attacks is, first the well-known mutual gift giving (*strenae*) of New Year's Day, an informal, private custom, before devoting a long section to pagan worship of images of their gods (specifying Neptune, Tellus, Juno, Vulcan, and Mercury, §§ 17–24). What do pagan images have to do with New Year's celebrations? Scheid rightly compared a New Year's sermon delivered at Ravenna ca. 430 by Peter Chrysologus, offering a detailed description of a "procession of demons" (*daemonum pompa*) parading through the streets, naming Saturn, Iupiter, Hercules, Diana, Vulcan, and others.[24] Once again, it is tempting to identify this as a full-fledged pagan festival, perhaps the *pompa circensis* that Christians caricatured as *pompa diaboli*.[25] But the *pompa circensis* was associated with the Ludi Romani of September. Closer study of Peter's sermon shows that he is describing people wearing masks

20. So too livestock heads on stakes; Maximus is the earliest known text for this practice; Filotas 2005, 143.
21. Klingshirn 1994, 210.
22. Meslin 1970, 51–118; Graf 1998, 199–216; Filotas 2005, 155–72. I am leaving out of count here eastern texts by John Chrysostom (*In Kalendas,* PG 48. 951 62, in 387) and Asterius of Amaseia (*Hom.* 4, C. Datema [ed.], 1970, pp. 39–43, in 400).
23. Dolbeau 1996, 345–417 (Mainz 62 = Dolbeau 26); Hill 1997, 180–237.
24. Scheid 1998, 353–65.
25. Waszink 1947, 13–41.

representing these gods, together with others pretending to be animals, particularly stags (*cervi, cervuli*).[26] These masks are surely what prompted Augustine to focus on *images* of pagan gods.

What Augustine, Peter, Caesarius, and the other writers are all attacking is not the continuing performance of official, public ceremonies or processions, but *private* New Year's customs, masked revellers going into private houses, the houses of Christians. "Christians are seeing this [the procession], Christians are waiting for it, letting it into their houses; Christians are welcoming it in their own houses," indignantly protests Peter.[27] All these writers repeatedly stigmatize these practices as "pagan," but it would be rash to suppose that either performers or spectators were actually pagans at all. These customs are simply popular traditions extending back before Christian times.

Augustine reproaches his congregation for giving *strenae* to each other instead of alms to the poor, a reproach echoed in Caesarius's New Year's sermons and other later writers.[28] The *strenae* too go back many centuries, though the masks described most fully by Peter and Caesarius (who adds cross-dressing) are only known from late antique Christian sources. They have nothing whatever to do with official Roman paganism.[29] Indeed, they are best attested in northern Italy, Gaul, and Spain.[30] Likewise, when Caesarius attacks people looking for "auguries" (*auguria*), it is not the official auspice taking of the Roman state he has in mind, but (again) private individuals speculating in a variety of ways (as they still do today) about what the New Year will bring them.[31] What most disturbed not just Caesarius but all the other bishops about New Year's customs was less their character, content, or purpose than the fact that rituals that gave such obvious and universal enjoyment were not only not Christian but beyond the control of the church.

Such customs are often called pagan survivals, but (as Robert Markus pointed out in a classic study) this is a tricky concept, a concept that "fails to take into account ... the sheer vitality of non-religious, secular institutions and traditions and their power to resist change."[32] We have seen that, while many of the traditional festivals recorded in the Calendar of 354 continued to be celebrated down to at least the end of the fourth century, the more objectionably pagan elements—most obviously animal sacrifice—were gradually removed (Ch. 2. 4). Up to a certain point in time, so long as there was

---

26. The phrase is *cervulum facere*, meaning to play the part of a stag (perhaps by wearing antlers): Arbesmann 1979, 89–119.

27. Petr. Chrys. *Sermo* clv bis. 2 = *CCL* 24B. 967; cf. Caesarius, *Sermo* 193 = *CCL* 104. 786.

28. Caesarius, *Serm*. 192; 193; Filotas 2005, 157, 166.

29. With Peter's list: Saturn, Iupiter, Hercules, Diana, and Vulcan; compare Caesarius's: Mars, Mercury, Jupiter, Venus, and Saturn (*Serm*. 193. 4 = *CC* 104. 785). The difference is that Caesarius is attacking not so much pagan deities as the pagan eponyms of the days of the week. We can have no confidence that Peter's list accurately reflects masks he had actually seen, and it may be that the custom he is alluding to involved personifications of the days of the week (for later Christian polemic on the pagan eponyms of days of the week, Filotas 2005, 135–37).

30. Arbesmann 1979; Filotas 2005, 161.

31. Filotas 2005, 168–71.

32. Markus 1990, 9.

still a sizable pagan minority left, that is to say up till around 400, the church was prepared to settle for this compromise. But once the temples were closed, public manifestations of pagan cult banned, and few practicing pagans left, the church grew confident enough to attempt to stamp out all traces of paganism. That included depaganized festivals that had passed muster a few decades earlier, together with traditional customs that were less specifically pagan than simply pre-Christian. Bearing in mind that "paganism" never existed as an entity in itself, we should stop talking about its persistence and focus instead on the limits of Christianization.[33]

It is essential to appreciate the enormous difference between simply banning the public performance of pagan rituals and subsequent attempts to eradicate all traces of paganism from the life of every community. This is why early fifth-century Christians triumphantly credit Theodosius with destroying paganism, while late fifth- and sixth-century preachers write as if it was as big a threat as ever. It is not so much a question of its "tenacity," as a changing, far more comprehensive definition of paganism, a definition that eventually came to include any custom or practice not demonstrably Christian.

Above all, this definition included attendance at the games. This was an area where the church had always been in advance of the civil authorities. Any reader of Augustine's *City of God* must have been struck by how often he returns to the perils of the theater, constantly harping on its pagan roots. Nor was it just roots in the remote past. In a sermon he proclaims that "the demons delight...in the manifold indecencies of the theater, in the mad frenzy of chariot races, in the cruelty of the amphitheater."[34] John Chrysostom repeatedly insists on "the damage that the theater...did to the soul of the spectator."[35] According to one Augustinian scholar, the games were the one element of Roman paganism that remained vital into the fifth century, "the last pagan ritual capable of drawing crowds."[36] Others have recently reasserted Alföldi's view that "pagan senators used the public games to assert 'traditional' values in the face of a rising Christian challenge."[37] It is true that Roman games were in origin religious festivals, but if Alföldi was right, how do we explain the fact that their popularity continued unabated down into the sixth century, when both providers and spectators had long been Christians? No less telling is the fact that the apostate Julian shared the view of the church. In what amounts to an encyclical to pagan priests, he forbade them to attend the theatre or wild beast shows, or even to admit pantomimes, mimes, or charioteers into their houses, adding that he would abolish such licentiousness if he could.[38]

There is no evidence that it was these "pagan roots" (more real to Christians than contemporary pagans) that motivated even known pagans like Symmachus to spend fortunes on games to commemorate their sons' praetorships. In the aristocratic

---

33. See particularly here P. Brown 1995.
34. *Sermo* 198/26 Dolbeau § 3.
35. Webb 2008, 175.
36. Mandouze 1968, 308–10.
37. Lim 1999, 274; Curran 2000, 218–59.
38. Julian, *Ep.* 89 (303bd), pp. 172–73 Bidez, with pp. 102–5; Webb 2008, 35–36.

context, the purpose of these games, quite simply, was to make a splash and outdo the efforts of their peers, pagan and Christian alike. Ambrose, himself by birth a member of the governing class and so more in touch with reality than many western clerics, distinguishes in his *De Officiis* between generosity and extravagance, illustrating the latter with people who exhaust their wealth with theatrical and gladiatorial shows, circus racing, and wild beast shows for the sake of popular favour, *so that they may outdo the fame of their predecessors.*[39] Not a word about pagan roots or the threat to their immortal souls. Thanks to the survival of a remarkably large number of letters about his son Memmius's praetorian games, we know that Symmachus began his preparations three years in advance. He anxiously wrote to one friend he was asking to get him the best racehorses: "I must outdo the fame of my earlier displays, which after the consular magnificence of our house and the quaestorian exhibition of my son portend nothing mediocre from us." And in other letters: "we must satisfy the expectation which has increased because of our own examples," and "make your preparations, so that the second magistracy of my son may surpass the magnificence of his quaestorship."[40] If Augustine had attended any of Symmachus's games, he would doubtless have been shocked at what he saw as their deeply pagan character, but there is no hint of this in any of Symmachus's letters.

According to Olympiodorus, Memmius's praetorian games (401) cost two thousand pounds of gold. The games of Petronius Maximus ca. 415, the future consul of 433 and 443 and short-lived Augustus in 455, cost four thousand pounds. Claudian describes the elaborate consular games of Mallius Theodorus cos. 399, a Christian friend of the young Augustine. The future emperor Justinian spent four thousand pounds on his consular games.[41]

There is a mass of material on spectacles in the circus, theatre, and amphitheatre in sixth-century Rome and Ravenna.[42] There can be no doubt that both the Ostrogothic kings of Italy and the consuls of the year (almost exclusively now members of the oldest and richest noble families, all now Christian) continued to spend fortunes on the games until the Gothic Wars of 536–52 put an end to such extravagance. Theodoric twice encourages consuls to be generous in their games. His surviving consular diptych shows that Basilius cos. 541 provided chariot races for his consular games, the last ever given in the West.[43] Perhaps the most illuminating single document is the very personal poem Apronianus Asterius cos. 494 wrote in his manuscript of Vergil, apparently soon after his consular games:[44]

---

39. *popularis favoris gratia...ut vincant superiorum celebritates,* Ambr. *De Off.* ii. 109.
40. Symm. *Epp.* iv. 60. 2; 58. 2; 59. 2.
41. For all the figures, Cameron and Schauer 1982.
42. Fauvinet-Ranson 2006, esp. 380–440; Ward-Perkins 1984, Ch. 6, and index s.v. entertainments.
43. Cameron and Schauer 1982.
44. For a recent text, Cameron 1998, 33; the poem, in the s. v/vi Medicean Vergil, is often said to be in Asterius's own hand, but I hope to have shown that it is a copy of his autograph. For example, *parcas...opes* in the last line must be a copying error; Asterius undoubtedly wrote *partas...opes,* "the wealth I have won."

I provided banners in the circus and erected a temporary stage on the spina, so that Rome might rejoice and hold games, races and different sorts of wild beast shows. Three times did I earn cheers, three times the people sang out my praises in the theater. My fortune vanished into my fame, for such losses bear the fruit of glory. Thus do the games preserve the expenditure of my riches, and the single day that saw three spectacles will last, and hand on Asterius to a lively future, Asterius who spent the wealth he had won on his consulship.

Asterius beggared himself to provide shows in all three arenas: circus, theater, and amphitheater.

So why did Christian preachers wax so indignant about the popularity of the games? Over and above their endless protests about the immorality of pantomime and gladiator shows, their corrupting effect on the minds of spectators, and the shocking misuse of funds that would have been better spent feeding the poor,[45] there were two factors seldom put into words. First, Christians could not help seeing pagan festivals as an evil counterpart to the festivals of the church.[46] Second, simply because they drew the crowds. No festival of the church could hope to generate the excitement of a major festival day in theatre, amphitheatre, or circus, excitement that the church could not control. Augustine delivered a series of sermons on the psalms at Carthage in December 409, apparently at the invitation of the bishop of Carthage, in the hope that Augustine's fame would deter the faithful from going to the games held at this period. If this was the plan, it was a failure.[47] Christian emperors rejected all appeals by bishops to ban such universally popular entertainments, except for Sundays and major Christian holidays. Indeed, circus and theater became increasingly important as places where the people could express their views about current issues and demonstrate their approval or disapproval.[48]

To return to Augustine's sermon of 1 January 404. It carries the title *Against the pagans* (*Contra paganos*) and, as already remarked, contains some rather erudite polemic, directed (as Augustine himself put it) at "the more learned among the pagans" (*paganis quasi doctioribus*). Sections 17–24 refute the traditional philosophical argument that pagans don't adore the image itself, but what is signified by the image, the elements of nature: thus Neptune is the sea, Juno the air,[49] Vulcan fire, and so on. He mocks their philosophical pretentions and initiation rituals (they say to themselves "Am I to be like my doorkeeper rather than Plato or Pythagoras?").[50] These sophisticated arguments (it has been claimed) provide valuable evidence for the survival of paganism among cultivated members of the African elite in the early fifth century.[51]

---

45. See especially Lepelley 1 (1979), 376–85; 2 (1981), 44–47.
46. Emphasized by Harl 1981.
47. La Bonnardière, 1976, 52–90; Lepelley 1 (1979), 378.
48. Cameron 1976, Ch. 7, "The Emperor and His People at the Games."
49. The Greek argument that Ἥρα = ἀήρ.
50. *Sermo* 26/198 Dolbeau §§ 59, 28, 36.
51. See particularly Lepelley 1998, 327–42.

There is no doubt some truth in this. Yet we should bear in mind that, though titled *Contra paganos* and clearly targeting pagan beliefs, pagans cannot have been Augustine's primary audience. That must have been the Christian congregation in church at the time. In addition, this is the longest known sermon of Augustine, a sermon that (it has been calculated) must have lasted for a good three hours. From the concluding remarks of another sermon, we know that Augustine sometimes spoke for longer than usual on the day of a big pagan festival so as to distract his congregation from attending the festivities.[52] *Contra paganos* was delivered on the Kalends of January. From time to time the odd pagan no doubt came to hear Augustine preach, if only to see whether he deserved his reputation as a man of eloquence and learning. Another of the new sermons provides an explicit illustration. Number 25 Dolbeau, delivered in an otherwise unknown town called Boseth, bears the subtitle "When the pagans were allowed in," and the notation "and after the pagans had left" before the final paragraph.[53] The last third of the sermon deals with the "sacrilegious practices of the gentiles," astrology, idols, amulets. It seems that Augustine had invited local pagan dignitaries to attend, though they were apparently asked to leave before the Eucharist.

But even granted a handful of pagan listeners, how many are likely to have sat through a three-hour sermon? No, the audience Augustine was preaching to in this as in most of his other sermons was primarily *former* pagans, cultivated members of the elite about whose Christian convictions he was not confident, the sort of people whose faith was to be given a rude shock by the sack of Rome six years later. That event provoked Augustine to rehearse countless arguments against paganism in his *City of God*. The 404 sermon reveals that, six years earlier, he was already apprehensive that recent converts, members of the elite brought up on the classics, might fall back into the old ways if faced with adversity. Augustine's arguments were aimed less at converting practicing pagans than providing vulnerable Christians with the ammunition to resist the seductive arguments of their remaining pagan peers. He as good as says as much in § 13: "Pay attention to this story, brothers and sisters, *so that you may be strong and have a good defense against the pagans*, even the grander ones among them (*lautiores*). But why do I call them grander, when they are the ones in greater peril? The more learned they think they are, the more unteachable they become. They seem ashamed to learn, because that would mean admitting their ignorance." Augustine is not addressing such folk, but warning his flock against them.

This brings us to the anti-pagan polemic of Augustine's *City of God*, which has always puzzled thoughtful readers. The early books, attacking paganism, might seem to imply a still living and threatening target. Yet the polemic is almost entirely directed against the religion of the Roman Republic, as reconstructed from Varro and illustrated by Vergil (Ch. 16). It has often been noticed that Augustine says nothing about

---

52. *Etsi aliquanto vos diutius tenuimus, consilii fuit ut importunae horae transirent; arbitramur iam illos* [i.e., the pagans] *peregisse vanitatem suam, Tract. in Ev. Jo.* 7. 24; Chadwick 1996, 71.

53. *cum pagani ingrederentur...et postquam pagani egressi sunt, Sermo* 25 (Dolbeau 1996, 243–44, 248, 267).

the "oriental" religions that modern scholars used to see as the driving force in late Roman paganism. We have seen that by the late fourth century these cults were probably less important than generally believed, but they were not totally insignificant. Some have argued that Augustine was out of touch with living, contemporary paganism. We have seen that this may be true of some Christian writers (Prudentius, e.g.). Yet it is hard to believe it of so intelligent a man as Augustine, who had devoted so much thought, effort, and serious research to the problem of paganism—and who was actually living in Rome during the altar of Victory affair.

Others have explained the silence by assuming that such rites were extinct by the early fifth century. Some no doubt, but they are prominent in all the verse invectives discussed in chapters 8–9. Indeed, I would argue that they play a larger role in fourth-century anti-pagan invective than in the lives of fourth-century pagans precisely because they were so easy to ridicule (Roman nobles with shaven heads waving tambourines). So why did Augustine pass up so easy a target?

The explanation (I suspect) is twofold. On the one hand, in the cities at any rate, with the temples closed and sacrifice forbidden, he may not have seen contemporary public paganism as posing much of a threat. If a few diehards were still performing the old rituals in the privacy of their homes, that was nothing to worry about. On the other hand, like the sermons just discussed, the *City of God* was surely not primarily addressed to practicing pagans. Augustine cannot realistically have expected hard-core pagans even to read, much less be persuaded by, so massive and polemical a work. His primary audience must have been Christians, many of them recent converts, most as yet unbaptized, whose motives and sincerity alike were suspect. In another of the new sermons he says, addressing his congregation: "You were pagans a few years ago, now you are Christians; your parents used to serve demons." Elsewhere he remarks that "everyone here had a pagan grandfather or great-grandfather."[54] Members of the elite, for this purpose defining the term as anyone who had received a secondary education, continued to be brought up on the classics. As we saw in chapter 16, late Roman schoolteachers laid heavy emphasis on Vergil's knowledge of cult and sacrifice. Augustine was worried at the mass of what he saw as deeply pagan material Christians were still reading. Whether or not this actually seduced people away from the true faith, it was at the very least unhealthy that they should spend so much time on stuff like this instead of studying Scripture. Whence the protracted attempt to show them how false it was.

From the reigns of Gratian and Theodosius on we find a series of laws against apostates, in 381, 383, 391, 396, and 426.[55] From as early as 381 "Christians who have become pagans shall be deprived of the power and right to make testaments." Over the years the language of such laws became harsher and harsher: "if any persons shall betray the holy faith..." or "if any persons have defiled themselves with the impious superstition of idolatry when they were Christians...." By 391, any apostates of rank

---

54. *Sermo* 21. 16 Dolbeau (Dolbeau 1996, 285; Hill 1997, 161); Aug. *Enarr.* in *Psalmos* 96. 7.
55. Cococcia 2008, 457–66.

"who have given themselves over to sacrifices" shall lose their rank and "shall not be numbered even among the lowest dregs of the ignoble crowd."[56] Is it really the case that, as Dill put it, "apostasy to heathenism became so frequent that Gratian and Theodosius felt bound to restrain it by severe legislation."[57] If apostasy was a serious problem, that might be thought to imply that paganism still had the power to attract converts back from Christianity.

But what exactly is meant by the term? "Apostate," like "pagan," is an entirely Christian concept.[58] No pagan would have found fault with anyone who, after (say) being initiated into the cult of Isis in his youth, gradually lost interest and turned to another cult. It is worth underlining the anachronistic, wholly Christian viewpoint of the author of the *Carmen ad quendam senatorem* (*CAS*), describing an apostate begging Isis for forgiveness (35–36):

> rumor et ad nostros pervenit publicus aures
> te dixisse "Dea, erravi; ignosce, redivi."

According to the general report you said "Goddess, I have sinned, forgive me, I have returned."

In the fourth century the classic example of an apostate was the emperor Julian, a man brought up a Christian who not only repudiated his faith but did his best to resurrect and reform paganism on the model of Christianity. It may be that a fair number (at least briefly) followed his example in the 360s, but the reigns of Gratian and Theodosius are generally supposed to be the period when mass conversions took place. It is hard to believe this was also a period when large numbers of converts were repudiating their new faith.

I suspect that these laws were primarily aimed less at those who formally renounced their faith than at Christians (especially baptized Christians) seen (or suspected of) performing rites the authorities judged, rightly or wrongly, to be pagan or (no less worrying) Jewish. Not that Christians were actually converting to Judaism. As we saw in chapter 9. 1, in some eastern cities (especially Antioch) some Christians continued to observe aspects of Jewish law and attend certain Jewish festivals. It is unlikely that baptized Christians knowingly performed pagan rituals, but many may have continued to consult astrologers or *haruspices*, follow some details of pagan funerary practices, or watch the picturesque (now depaganized) festivals they had loved as children. For example, the peasant converts in the Val di Non who shocked their priests by wanting to participate in a *lustratio*. It was bad enough that pagans did such things. But they at least had the excuse of being pagans. The offenders themselves, though judged

---

56. *Cod. Theod.* xvi. 7. 1, 4, 6, 5.
57. Dill 1899, 13.
58. Later (of course) also a Muslim concept.

apostates by the church, may have continued to think of themselves as good Christians. Furthermore, since the central element in all legislation on apostasy concerned testamentary rights, there must always have been family members who stood to gain financially by making the accusation.

In addition to the laws there are also four literary texts that have been thought to support the idea of wholesale apostasy.[59] In one of his letters to Valentinian II, Ambrose claims that pagans are asking for [the restoration of] privileges, "those privileges by which even Christians have often been deceived." What does this mean? Ambrose's own explanation is, if anything, even more obscure: "[the pagans] wanted to ensnare many by means of these privileges, exploiting the inadvertency (*imprudentia*) of some and the anxiety of others to avoid disagreeable public duties. And because not all men prove strong, a substantial number lapsed, even under Christian emperors." What are these privileges, and how is it that they "deceived" people into turning away from Christianity? According to Liebeschuetz, "Ambrose is now referring to privileges claimed for pagan priests other than Vestal Virgins."[60] So the context suggests, but Ambrose can hardly be claiming that Christians were becoming pontiffs and augurs.

Yet a similar, and no less puzzling, accusation seems to lie behind the claim of the exactly contemporary *CCP*: namely that Praetextatus provoked apostasies by giving Christians "honors" (*honores*), undermining their faith with offices and bribes (*muneribus cupiens quorundam frangere mentes/aut alios facere prava mercede profanos*).[61] Praetextatus was praetorian prefect of Italy, and so an official with many appointments in his gift. But what sort of *honores* could have seduced Christians away from the faith? While some noble who briefly professed Christianity might have later recanted and become a pontiff or augur, both these texts not only imply that it was the *honor*/immunity itself that led to apostasy, but claim that it happened in large numbers. The numbers are no doubt an exaggeration, and the imputation of pecuniary motives we may ignore as part and parcel of Ambrose's attempt to depict pagans as caring about nothing but money (p. 42). But we are surely bound to accept that, however distorted, there is some basis in fact behind so precise, if allusively expressed, an accusation, attested by two contemporary texts.

I suggest that Ambrose's reference is indeed to the immunities of priests, but to provincial, not Roman priests. A law of 371 exempts provincial priests from curial duties, confirmed by another law as late as 428.[62] The 428 law explicitly refers to Africa, where we know of a number of provincial *sacerdotes* or *sacerdotales* and no fewer than thirteen municipal *flamines* later than 383, some as late as the Vandal period.[63]

---

59. "In the late fourth century Christian writers seem to have been particularly worried about apostasies," Kahlos 2002, 169.
60. *Ep.* 72 [17]. 4, Liebeschuetz and Hill, adapted, with p. 64 n. 4; for the various privileges and immunities of priests, see Vera's note on Symm. *rel.* iii. 11b (p. 45).
61. *CCP* 79–82; no explanation anywhere in the now-abundant literature on this poem.
62. *Qui ad sacerdotium provinciae...pervenerint...habeantur immunes, Cod. Theod.* xii. 1. 75 (371); vii. 13. 22 (428).
63. Chastagnol and Duval 1974, 87–118; Lepelley 1979, 362–79.

While a few of these were doubtless still pagans, many were certainly Christian, one as early as 364/66.[64] The explanation is presumably that, by as early as the 360s, all specifically pagan elements had been removed from the ceremonies at which these officials presided (p. 59). *Flamines* and *sacerdotes provinciae* were chosen from the leading families and provided games at festivals in honour of the emperor.

Thus the distinction of the office answers to the *honores* and *munera* of CCP; and the accompanying immunity from curial responsibilities to Ambrose's "disagreeable public duties." In addition, it would nicely explain Ambrose's puzzling *imprudentia*. Although these priesthoods no longer involved sacrifice, rigorists evidently saw them as tainted by their pagan origin: some Christians took them on because of the immunities they carried, some (Ambrose claimed) because they were "unaware" of their pagan origin. The real attraction, of course, was the distinction of the office. It is a curious fact that, while unrelenting in his opposition to the games, Augustine never mentions these Christian *flamines* and *sacerdotales*,[65] perhaps because they were a long-established and accepted feature of African civic life. In Italy, the altar of Victory affair must have made it impossible for pagan priesthoods to lose their pagan associations in this way. If this interpretation of these two passages is correct, then neither refers to apostasy in the strict sense at all, but to Christians holding offices that a minority of rigorists thought defiled by pagan associations.

Third, a misinterpreted passage in the treatise *Against the Pagans* by the so-called Ambrosiaster, written in Rome in the mid-380s.[66] Satan, the writer claims, skillfully endowed pagan ceremonies with a "certain artifice" (*quaedam praestigia*), through which he enticed people into error, and they got used to these deceits. For what is shameful can seem less so when you are used to it. When people are dishonored, to start with they are embarrassed; but when habit lends it a certain charm, embarrassment recedes, especially if they see many others in the same situation. The greatest triumph of this shame is the so-called nobility. When the nobility is dishonored, it easily finds imitators (*facile enim imitatores invenit dehonestata nobilitas*). But there is no suggestion in this last sentence (as often alleged) that it was *Christians* who imitated the paganism of the nobility.[67] Ambrosiaster is simply making the general point that people follow their example: the glamour of the nobility has made paganism seem less shameful than it should be.

That leaves the *Carmen ad quendam senatorem*, discussed in an earlier chapter. At best, this is an attack on a single apostate, but if Bloch had been right to assign it to the reign of Eugenius, it might indeed have been argued to provide "testimony for the spirit of defection which spread among the Christian members of the Roman aristocracy at this time." But if the solution suggested in chapter 9. 1 is accepted, it dates from the very different world of the early 370s. Men who had converted and held office

---

64. Lepelley 1(1979), 368; Chastagnol 1978, 44–48.
65. Lepelley 1 (1979), 365.
66. Ps. Aug. *Quaest. Vet. et Novi Testamenti* 114. 13 = p. 132–34 Bussières (pp. 40–42 for the date and place).
67. As claimed (e.g.) by Cracco Ruggini 1979, 35; and Consolino 1995, 315.

under Constantius II had a very strong motive to revert to paganism when Julian came to the throne. This was not a situation that would ever recur. Repudiating Christianity in the 380s or later became an entirely different sort of decision, based on conscience and belief, not considerations of personal advantage. The *CAS* can no longer be treated as evidence for this second sort of apostasy.

No one will dispute that a certain number of converts relapsed into what contemporary Christians *called* paganism, especially after the sack of Rome in 410. It is unlikely that many formally renounced rather than quietly (perhaps temporarily) abandoned (or neglected) their faith. But it is less clear what they would have lapsed into.

Take Rufius Volusianus, born ca. 375,[68] often considered a pagan right up till his deathbed baptism in 437, but more probably a catechumen for many years by then (p. 196). What sort of "paganism" was available to such a man at Rome during his adult years? The power and attraction of paganism as a living system lay in the public performance of its rituals, and its temples and sacred routes. MacMullen has vividly evoked the sheer excitement, noise, and color of a big festival day.[69] Some of those rituals were still performed, but without the specifically pagan elements—above all without sacrifice. The temples still stood, but no one went into them or hung votive offerings there. Volusianus had surely never seen public sacrifice, at any rate not as an adult. In all probability the various priestly colleges were also gone by his adult years. No Vestal Virgin tended the sacred flame. Some no doubt quietly maintained their household cults, but it cannot have been easy for anyone born later than the 370s to form any idea what it was like to attend one of the great Roman festivals in its heyday.

Momigliano perceptively put his finger on what he called "a strange absence of information about religious education" in Rome. How did a young Roman learn about the cults? Parents (he assumed) "would teach a minimum of prayers to be recited in given circumstances and to given gods," but beyond that (he conjectures) "the way to find out about religious practices was to be taken around or, if grown up, to go around the city" and just observe.[70] By the fifth century this was no longer an option. Christians simply assumed that lapsed Christians fell back into full-fledged paganism, wallowing in the blood of sacrifice. Paradoxically, long after the closing of the temples and banning of sacrifice, paganism continued to exist for Christians, who had always thought of it as a device of the devil to lure people into error, and who saw the gods pagans worshipped as demons.

There is one other category of evidence that has been much discussed in the past: violent confrontations between pagans and Christians. Such confrontations can be read in one of two ways. Either as forcible conversion of pagans by Christians, an interpretation argued with characteristic verve by MacMullen,[71] or as vigorous pagan resistance to Christianisation. Both interpretations presuppose a still-flourishing

---

68. So Chastagnol 1962, 277.
69. MacMullen 1981, Ch. 1. 2.
70. Momigliano 1987, 85–86.
71. MacMullen 1984, 86–101; 1997, Ch. 1.

paganism. There are certainly cases of both, but fewer of either than generally assumed.

Lives of saints love to portray their heroes cutting down holy trees, smashing idols, and demolishing temples, stories that tend to grow in the telling. But it is not easy from the temple ruins that litter the Mediterranean world to distinguish the destruction of a functioning shrine from the dismantling of one long disused. Schenute of Atripe led bands of monks to smash statues, though there is serious doubt whether they were functioning cult statues, or even whether their owners were pagans.[72] But down to at any rate the first decade of the fifth century, there is little evidence that the state ever used force. Eusebius claims that Constantine abolished the cult of Aphrodite at Baalbek and built a church there. According to Sozomen he *destroyed* the temple and built a church on its ruins, while Malalas claims that it was Theodosius who destroyed the temple and built a church on its ruins. Yet sixth-century sources claim that temple and cult survived till the age of Justinian, when both were destroyed by fire from heaven. The temple is certainly now in ruins, but no church was ever built on its foundations; a basilica was built on its forecourt, but probably later than even Theodosius.[73] If we had only Malalas (and the site had been built over by a modern city), inevitably this text would have featured prominently in the myth of Theodosius, hammer of paganism.

According to Augustine, on 19 March 399 the counts Gaudentius and Iovius "overturned the temples of the false gods and smashed their statues" in Carthage.[74] But the law they were supposed to be executing specified no more than closing temples and removing *functioning* cult statues. Did they exceed their brief? Not according to Quodvultdeus, bishop of Carthage between 431/9 and 454, who limits their activity to closing and stripping the temples—though mistakenly (if significantly) dates it to the reign of Theodosius.[75] It has always been assumed that Theodosius's praetorian prefect Maternus Cynegius was an energetic destroyer of temples, but a recent paper by McLynn has cast doubt on the evidence.[76] This would be the only case of a top Theodosian official directly involved in anti-pagan violence.

Then there is the destruction of the temple of Marnas in Gaza by Porphyry, bishop of Gaza in the early fifth century. According to the *Life of Porphyry*, supposedly written by his deacon Mark, the bishop went to court, secured troops and authorization from the emperor (by a trick), and then returned to Gaza, where the temple of Marnas was destroyed and a church built on the site, with many conversions. This is regularly cited as the classic illustration of forcible conversion. According to Trombley, who devoted almost a hundred pages to the case of Gaza, it "offers the most complete example of

72. Cameron in Bagnall 2007, 39–41.
73. For all the evidence (and much more) see Hahn, Emmel, and Gotter 2008, at 1–2.
74. *falsorum deorum templa everterunt et simulacra fregerunt, CD* ix. 54.
75. *De promissionibus et praedictionibus, Dei* iii. 41 (ii. 569, R. Braun [ed.], SC 101–2, Paris 1964); *PCBE* i. 947–49; see too Riggs in Drake 2006 (n. 5), 298–99.
76. McLynn 2005, 111–19.

how the Christian episcopal infrastructure manipulated the social hierarchy of the cities in the interests of accelerating Christianization."[77] The problem here is that Mark's *Life* is a much later forgery; outside its pages there is no evidence that either bishop Porphyry or his church even existed. Trombley did his best to rehabilitate the *Life*, but Barnes has now put the matter beyond serious doubt.[78] According to Procopius, in the 530s Justinian "destroyed" the temples of Philae, widely identified as the last bastion of paganism in Egypt. But no priests are attested after the 450s, Christianity was thriving there from the early fourth century, and the temples themselves are among the best preserved in the ancient world.[79]

On the Christian side, most violence was unofficial (bands of monks in the East, Martin of Tours in Gaul), and its importance as a factor in actually converting (rather than just intimidating) pagans was overrated by Christian contemporaries, as it has been by many moderns.[80] Just so today, many of those who "come forward" at revivalist meetings slip away again when the excitement has died down. On the pagan side, most violence took the form of pagans defending themselves against provocation or outright aggression by Christians.

Take the destruction of the Serapeum in Alexandria. Christians had provoked pagans by holding sacred objects up to public ridicule and a riot ensued, in which first the Serapeum and subsequently other pagan shrines were overturned. Rufinus pronounced the end of idolatry (in fact, we have abundant evidence that unofficial Alexandrian paganism lasted for at least another century).[81] The ecclesiastical historians insist that bishop Theophilus was simply executing an order from Theodosius in the form of a rescript. But we saw in an earlier chapter that this rescript went no further than banning sacrifice and entry into temples (Ch. 2. 4). No emperor ever ordered the destruction of a major functioning temple in a major city. It was undoubtedly the Christians who provoked and initiated the violence; the pagans simply defended themselves.

Three Christian priests were killed in the Val di Non in the Tyrol in 397, a region (Maximus remarks) "where the Christian name had not been known before" (which suggests that regions nearer Turin where he complains of pagan practices were at least partly Christianized). As we have seen, the violence was provoked by the priests trying to stop some converts from participating in a *lustratio* pagans were leading around their fields (it is easy to see why recent converts felt that they could not risk abandoning a ritual they had been brought up to believe guaranteed their crops). Two incidents in early fifth-century North Africa have been much discussed.[82] In 399 some

---

77. Trombley 1 (1995), 243 (incidentally a good illustration of Trombley's style!).
78. Barnes 2010, 260–83.
79. Proc BP. i. 19.37; J. H. F. Dijkstra, *Philae and the End of Ancient Egyptian Religion* (Leiden 2008).
80. On this see especially Salzman 2006, 265–85.
81. Cameron in Bagnall 2007; McLynn 2009, 579; see now E. J. Watts, *Riot in Alexandria: Tradition and Group Dynamics in Late Antique Pagan and Christian Communities* (Berkeley 2010).
82. Lepelley 1981, 305–7, 97–101; for a legal study of the Calama riots, Hermanowicz 2004, 481–521.

Christians at Sufes in Byzacena destroyed a cult image of Hercules, the patron deity of the town,[83] emboldened by a law of that year ordering that idols be removed from temples. This led to a riot in which, according to Augustine, sixty "innocent" Christians (he does not say how many pagans) were killed. Second, in 408 at Calama a pagan procession was celebrated in violation of a law issued (once more) that very year. The pagans danced and jeered in front of a church. The bishop tried to stop them, exploiting a provision of the new law that gave clergy the authority to prohibit such practices.[84] In the ensuing riot the church was burned and one "innocent" Christian killed (these Christians may not have seemed so "innocent" to the pagans).

Both incidents are known exclusively from letters of Augustine, who complains that the authorities did nothing to stop such atrocities. According to Lepelley, after many others, this proves that "the pagan reaction originated in the curia," an indication of "the persistence of paganism among the notables in many cities." But such inferences go beyond the evidence. In the first place, even assuming (improbably, in view of his exaggerated claim that Theodosius ordered "that the statues of the pagans should be everywhere overthrown")[85] that Augustine is giving an accurate and impartial account, in the absence of a trained police force it would not have been easy for anyone to stop these riots once they had started. Second, while there may still have been many pagans in Sufes and Calama, it is unlikely that they were maintaining public sacrifice. That would have been a far more serious violation of the law than the isolated incidents that so outraged Augustine, and he could hardly have failed to mention the fact.

In both cases Christians provoked and initiated the violence. To be sure, they had the law on their side, but in both cases the law was new and unpopular. These laws are in fact further illustrations of the redefinition of paganism. It was no longer enough that sacrifice was forbidden. The new laws authorized the removal of cult statues and gave the church the authority to prohibit (what they deemed to be) any manifestation of paganism. The council of Calama, no doubt reluctant in the first place to ban a beloved, centuries-old procession, probably long stripped of all offensive pagan trimmings, cannot have been happy at the church usurping its jurisdiction. Nor need it have been only pagans who were upset by the insult offered to the patron deity of Sufes. When Augustine reproached Christians for taking part in a banquet in honor of the Genius of Carthage, he represents one of them objecting, "It isn't a god, it's the Genius of Carthage."[86] The fact that the councils of Sufes and Calama were unwilling to be bullied by the church into enforcing unwelcome new laws need not prove them

---

83. *deus Hercules, genius patriae* (*ILS* 6835), obviously a Graeco-Roman name for a local deity: Rives 1995, 137–38.

84. *Const. Sirm.* 12, p. 917. 2 Mommsen (extracts in *Cod. Theod.* xvi. 2. 38; 5. 41), with Lepelley 2 (1981), 97 n. 25.

85. *simulacra gentilium ubique evertenda praecepit*, Aug. *CD* v. 26. 48.

86. "Non est," inquit, "deus, quia genium est Carthaginis," *Sermo* 62. 10 (for the surprising but well-attested form *genium* here, see Lepelley 2001, 49 n. 51). For a photo of a recently discovered bust of the Genius of Carthage, see Lepelley's frontispiece.

militant pagans. The councils of both towns may well still have contained quite a few pagans, but isolated clashes such as these need not involve outright hostility to the church, much less an entrenched "pagan reaction."

It might seem that much of the argument of this book has been negative. There was no pagan revival in the West, no pagan party, no pagan literary circles, no pagan patronage of the classics, no pagan propaganda in art or literature, no pagans editing classical texts, above all, no last pagan stand. But all these apparent negatives actually add up to a resounding positive. So many of the activities, artifacts, and enthusiasms that have been identified as hallmarks of an elaborate, concerted campaign to combat Christianity turn out to have been central elements in the life of cultivated Christians. This is the one area in which paganism (defined as the Roman tradition, Rome's glorious past) continued to exercise real power and influence on men's minds. Despite the best attempts of Augustine and other rigorists, the Roman literary tradition played a vital and continuing role in shaping the thought-world of Christians, both at the time and in the centuries to come.

APPENDIX

The Poem against the Pagans

Dicite, qui colitis lucos antrumque Sibyllae
Idaeumque nemus, Capitolia celsa Tonantis,
Palladium, Priamique Lares Vestaeque sacellum
incestosque deos, nuptam cum fratre sororem,
inmitem puerum, Veneris monumenta nefandae,   5
purpureă quos sola facit praetexta **sacratos**,
quis numquam verum Phoebi cortina locuta est,
Etruscus ludit semper quos vanus haruspex.
Iuppiter hic vester, Ledae superatus amore,
fingeret ut cycnum, voluit canescere pluma.   10
perditus ad Danaen flueret subito aureus imber,
per freta Parthenopes taurus mugiret adulter.
haec si monstra placent nullă **sacrata** pudica,
pellitur arma Iovis fugiens regnator Olympi:
et quisquam supplex veneratur templa tyranni,   15
cum patrem videat nato cogente fugatum?
postremum, regitur fato si Iuppiter ipse,
quid prodest miseris perituras fundere voces?
plangitur in templis iuvenis formonsus Adonis:
nuda Venus deflet, gaudet Mavortius heros.   20
Iuppiter in medium nescit finire querellas,
iurgantesque deos stimulat Bellona flagello.
Convenit his ducibus, proceres, sperare salutem?
sacratis vestris liceat conponere lites?
dicite: praefectus vester quid profuit urbi,   25
quem Iovis ad solium raptum iactatis abisse,
cum poena<s> scelerum tracta vix morte rependat?
mensibus iste tribus totam qui concitus urbem
lustravit, metas tandem pervenit ad aevi!
quae fuit haec rabies animi? quae insania mentis?   30
†sedovt† vestram posset turbare quietem?
quis tibi iustitium incussit, pulcherrima Roma?
ad saga confugeret populus, quae non habet olim?

　　　sed fuit in terris nullus **sacratior** illo,
quem Numa Pompiliŭs, e multis primus haruspex,　　　35
edocuit vano ritu pecudumque cruore
polluere insanum busti\<s\> putentibus aras.
non ipse est †vinum patriae qui prodidit† olim
antiqua\<s\>que domos, turres a\<c\> tecta priorum
subvertens, urbi vellet cum inferre ruinam?　　　40
ornaret lauro postes, convivia dăret,
pollutos panes infectans ture vaporo
poneret, in risum quaerens quos dedere morti
gallăribus subito membră circumdare suetus,
fraude nova semper miseros profănare paratus?　　　45
　　　sacratus vestĕr urbi quid praestitit, oro,
qui hierium docuit sub terra quaerere solem,
cum sibi forte pirum fossor de rure dolasset,
diceret[que] esse deum comitem Bacchique magistrum,
Sarapidis cultŏr, Etruscis semper amicus?　　　50
fundere qui incautis studuit concepta venena,
mille nocendī vias, totidem cum quaereret artes;
perdere quos voluit, percussit, luridus anguis,
contrā deum verum frustra bellare paratus,
qui tacitus semper lugeret tempora pacis　　　55
ne\<c\> proprium interius posset vulgare dolorem.
　　　Quis tibi, taurobolus, vestem mutare suăsit,
inflatus dives subito mendicus ut esses
obsitus et pannis, modica stipe factus epaeta,
sub terram missus, pollutus sanguine tauri,　　　60
sordidus infectus? vestes servare cruentas,
vivere cum speras viginti mundus in annos?
†ambieras censor meliorum laedere vitam†,
hinc tua confisus possent quod facta latere,
cum canibus Megales semper circumdatus esses,　　　65
quem lasciva cohors (monstrum) comitaret ovantem.
　　　sexagintā senex annis duravit ephebus,
Saturni cultor, Bellonae semper amicus,
qui cunctis Faunosque deos persuaserat esse,
Egeriae nymphae comites, Satyrosque Pānasque,　　　70
nympharum Bacchique comes Triviaeque sacerdos;
quem lustrare choros ac molles sumere thyrsos
cymbalaque imbuerat quaterĕ Berecyntia mater;
quis Galatea potens iussit Ioue prosata summo,
iudicio Paridis pulchrum sortita decorem.　　　75

sacrato nulli liceat servare pudorem,
frangere cum vocem soleant Megalensibus actis.

   Christicolas multos voluit sic perdere demens,
qui vellent sine lege mori, donaret honores
oblitosque sui caperet quos daemonis arte,   80
muneribus cupiens quorundam frangere mentes
aut alios facerĕ prava mercede profanos
mittereque inferias miseros sub Tartara secum.
solvere qui […] voluit pia foedera, leges,
Leucadium fecit fundos curaret Afrorum,   85
perdere Marcianum †sibi† proconsul ut esset.

   Quid tibi diva Paphi custos, quid pronuba Iuno
Saturnusque senex potuit praestare *sacrato*?
quid tibi Neptuni promisit fuscina, demens?
reddere quas potuit sortes Tritonia virgo?   90
dic mihi, Sarapidis templum cur nocte petebas?
quid tibi Mercurius fallax promisit eunti?
quid prodest coluisse Lares Ianumque bifrontem?
quid tibi Terra potens, mater formonsa deorum,
quid tibi *sacrato* placuit latrator Anubis,   95
quid miseranda Ceres, subrepta Proserpina matri,
   quid tibi Vulcanus claudus, pede debilis uno?
quis te plangentem non risit, calvus ad aras
sistriferam Phariam supplex cum forte rogares,
cumque Osĩrim miserum lugens latrator Anubis   100
quaereret, inventum rursum quem perdere posset,
post lacrimas ramum fractum portarēs olivae?
vidimus argento facto iuga ferre leones,
lignea cum traherent iuncti stridentia plaustra,
dextra istum laevaque argentea frena tenere,   105
egregios proceres currum servare Cybelae,
quem trahere<t> conducta manus Megalensibus actis,
arboris excisae truncum portare per urbem,
Attin castratum subito praedicere solem.

   artibus heu magicis procerum dum quaeris honores,   110
sic, miserande, iaces parvo donate sepulcro.
sola tamen gaudet meretrix te consule Flora,
ludorum turpis genetrix Venerisque magistra,
composuit templum nuper cui Symmachus heres.
omnia quae in templis posită, quot monstra colebas.   115
   ipsa mola manibus coniunx altaria supplex
dum cumulat donis votăque in limine templi

solvere dis deabusque parat superisque minatur,
carminibus magicis cupiens Acheronta movere,
praecipitem inferias miserum sub Tartara misit.   120
desine post hydropem talem deflere maritum,
de Iove qui Latio voluit sperare salutem.

Translation

Tell me, you who worship the Sibyl's groves and cave and the forest of Ida; the lofty Capitol of Jupiter the thunderer, the Palladium and the Lares of Priam; the shrine of Vesta, and incestuous gods, a sister married to her brother, a cruel boy [Cupid], the statues of wicked Venus (5), you whom only the purple toga consecrates, you to whom the oracle of Phoebus has never spoken true, you whom the quack Etruscan diviner forever mocks (8). Was this Jupiter of yours so overwhelmed with love for Leda that he covered himself with white feathers to play the swan (10)? Or did he descend on Danaë as a golden shower in his infamy? Or did the adulterer bellow through the straits of Parthenope [Naples] in the form of a bull (12)? If these horrors please you, nothing consecrated is chaste. Is the ruler of Olympus [Saturn] driven in flight by the weapons of Jupiter (14)? What suppliant would venerate the temples of the tyrant, when he sees a father banished by his own son? Finally, if Jupiter himself is ruled by Fate, what is the point of us wretches pouring forth prayers that are doomed to fail (18)? The handsome young Adonis is mourned in the temples. Naked Venus weeps and Mars rejoices, with Jupiter in the middle unable to end their strife, and Bellona urging on the quarrelling gods with her whip (22).

Are these appropriate leaders to look to for salvation, senators? Can your consecrated ones settle these quarrels (24)? Tell me, what has your prefect done to help the city, the man you boast was snatched away to the throne of Jupiter, whose agonizing death scarcely atones for his crimes? The man who feverishly traversed the whole city for three months finally reached the terminus of his life (29). What madness of soul was this, what insanity of mind? What […] might disturb your peace? Who proclaimed this period of mourning for you, beautiful Rome? Are the people to resort to the military cloaks they have not worn for so long (33)?

No one in the world was more consecrated than our hero, whom Numa Pompilius, the first haruspex of many, taught to pollute altars with empty rites and cattle blood on stinking tombs (37). Is this not the man who once †betrayed his country's wine†, destroying ancient houses, towers, and residences of the nobility in his plan to wreck the city? He would deck his doorposts with laurel, give banquets, and offer bread tainted with the smoke of incense, asking whom he should put to death for amusement, accustomed as he was to bind their limbs with chains, forever ready to desecrate the wretches with some new trick (45).

What did your consecrated one do for the city, I ask? He taught Hierius to look for the Sun beneath the ground, when a country digger happened to cut down a pear tree and said it was a god and master of Bacchus (49). He was a worshipper of Serapis and a ready friend to the Etruscans, eager to spray the poisons he had devised on the unwary, seeking a thousand ways of doing harm and as many contrivances (52). Those he wanted to ruin he struck down like a ghastly snake, ready as he was to fight the true

God in vain. He would always lament in silence times of peace, unable to proclaim his own deep grief (57).

Who persuaded you to change your dress, tauroboliate, puffed-up rich man, so that you might suddenly become a beggar, covered in rags, turned into a pauper for a tiny tip, sent underground, stained with bull's blood, dirty, disgusting? Who persuaded you to keep your bloodied garments, since you hope to live pure for twenty years(62). †As a censor you tried to destroy the life of your betters†, confident that your sins would remain hidden because you were always surrounded by the dogs of the Great Mother, you whom a band of perverts (horror!) accompanied in your procession (66).

He lived for sixty years as an ephebe, a worshipper of Saturn and constant friend of Bellona, a companion of nymphs and Bacchus and priest of Trivia [Hecate]. It was you who persuaded all men that the Fauns were gods, companions of the nymph Egeria, and the Satyrs and Pans (70). You whom the Berecynthian Mother [Cybele] inspired to lead her dances and hold the girlish thyrsus and clash the cymbals that great Galatea [Venus] commanded, daughter of lofty Jove who won the prize of beauty by the vote of Paris. Not one of these consecrated men should be allowed to preserve his modesty when they follow their custom of chanting falsetto during the Megalensian games (77).

In his madness he wanted to destroy many Christians. He gave rewards to those who were willing to die outside the <Christian> law, men whom, forgetful of themselves, he would ensnare through demonic artifice, seeking to weaken the minds of some by gifts and turn others away from God for a paltry reward (82), sending the wretches down with him to hell as an offering to the dead. Being eager to break the sacred laws amd pious commandments, he persuaded Leucadius, in charge of the estates of Africa, to corrupt Marcianus so that he might be his proconsul (86).

What could the divine guardian of Paphos [Venus], or Juno goddess of marriage or old Saturn do for a consecrated man? What did Neptune's trident hold out for you, madman? What responses could the Tritonian maiden [Minerva] give you (90)? Tell me, why did you seek the temple of Serapis by night? What did trickster Mercury promise you as you sped on your way? What do you gain from worshipping the Lares and two-faced Janus? What good did mighty Earth, fair mother of the gods, do you? What did barking Anubis do for a consecrated man (95)? What about mother Ceres, you wretch, what Proserpina stolen away from her mother? What lame Vulcan, with his one bad foot (97)?

Who did not laugh at you as you mourned, when you came to the altars with shaven head as a suppliant to pray to rattle-bearing Faria [Isis] and when, after lamentation, you carried the broken olive branch when mourning wretched Osiris, as barking Anubis sought the one he would lose again once found (102)? We have seen lions bearing yokes wrought in silver, pulling creaking wooden wagons in pairs; <we have seen> him holding silver reins in both his hands (105). <We have seen> prominent senators following the chariot of Cybele, dragged by a hired band at the Megalensian festival, carrying through the city a lopped-off tree trunk and suddenly proclaiming castrated Attis to be the Sun (109).

Alas, while seeking the honors of the nobility by your magic arts, you are brought thus low, wretch, rewarded with a tiny tomb. The only one to rejoice in your consulship is Flora the whore, shameful mother of games and teacher of Venus, for whom your heir Symmachus recently built a temple (114). Every monstrosity placed in the temples you used to worship.

Your suppliant wife with her hands heaps up the altars with grain and gifts and prepares to fulfil her vows to the gods and goddesses on the threshold of the temple, threatening the deities (118). Yet while hoping to to sway Acheron with her magic incantations, instead she sent the wretch headlong down to Tartarus. After the dropsy stop weeping for such a husband, who looked to Latian Jupiter for salvation.

The text is my own and the translation acknowledges a debt to Croke and Harries 1982, 80–83. Given the shortcomings of both MS and author, a number of passages remain insoluble. For information about MS readings and useful commentary, see Bartalucci 1998.

SELECTED BIBLIOGRAPHY

All works cited in the notes by author surname and year of publication are listed with full details in the bibliography. In order to keep it within bounds I have not included encyclopedia entries, most editions of texts used, and a few passing references or reviews cited only once or for a marginal detail. References to commentaries (mainly on Vergil) are given in the traditional manner (Pease on *Aen.* iv. 18, Horsfall on *Aen.* iii...). Again, to save space, in the case of articles published more than once, I usually cite only the first version, unless the later version is more accessible. When the writer cited has published more than one item in a given year, I normally assume that readers will be guided by the title, subject matter, and pagination, but where there is ambiguity I have distinguished items by adding *a* or *b*. Note that I cite *Prosopography of the Later Roman Empire* as PLRE, *Consuls of the Later Roman Empire* (ed. R. S. Bagnall, A. Cameron, S. Schwartz and K. A. Worp) as CLRE, and *Prosopographie chrétienne du Bas-Empire* as PCBE. Most other abbreviations follow the usual conventions. I cite R. Herzog and P. L. Schmidt (eds.), *Handbuch der lateinischen Literatur der Antike* (1989-) by volume and section numbers, which are the same in the French translation (*Nouvelle histoire de la littérature latine*, 1993-).

Adamik, B. "Das sog. Carmen contra paganos," *Acta Antiqua Acad. Scient. Hungar.* 36 (1995), 185–233.

Adams, J. N. "A type of hyperbaton in Latin Prose," *Proc. Camb. Phil. Soc.* 17 (1971), 1–16.

——— . "The authorship of the Historia Augusta," CQ 22 (1972), 186–94.

——— . "The linguistic unity of the Historia Augusta," *Antichthon* 11 (1977), 93–102.

——— . *The Latin Sexual Vocabulary* (Baltimore 1982).

——— . *Bilingualism and the Latin Language* (Cambridge 2003).

Adkin, N. "Juvenal and Jerome," CP 89 (1994), 69–72.

——— . "Terence's Eunuchus and Jerome," *Rhein. Mus.* 137 (1994), 187–95.

——— . "The Historia Augusta and Jerome again," *Klio* 79 (1997), 459–67.

——— . "Jerome's vow never to reread the classics: Some observations," *REA* 101 (1999), 165.

——— . "Apollonius of Tyana in Jerome," *Sacris Erudiri* 39 (2000), 67–79.

——— . "Jerome, Seneca, Juvenal," *Rev. belge de phil. et d'hist.* 78 (2000), 119–28.

Adler, M. *Drawing Down the Moon: Witches, Druids, Goddess-Worshippers, and Other Pagans in America Today* (Boston 1986).

Aland, K., and B. Aland. *The Text of the New Testament* (Grand Rapids 1989).

Alexander, P. J. *The Oracle of Baalbek: The Tiburtine Sibyl in Greek Dress* (Washington, D.C. 1967).

Alföldi, A. *A Festival of Isis in Rome under the Christian Emperors of the IVth Century* (Budapest 1937).

——— . *Die Kontorniaten. Ein verkanntes Propagandamittel der stadtrömische Aristokratie in ihrem Kampfe gegen das christliche Kaisertum* (Budapest 1942–43).

——— . *The Conversion of Constantine and Pagan Rome* (Oxford 1948).

——— . "Die Spätantike," *Atlantis* 21 (1949), 68–73.

——— . *A Conflict of Ideas in the Late Roman Empire* (Oxford 1952).

——— . "Cornuti," *DOP* 13 (1959), 169–83.

——— . "Die Alexandrinische Götter und die Vota Publica am Jahresbeginn," *JbAC* 8/9 (1965/66), 54–87.

——— . *Die monarchische Repräsentation im römischen Kaiserreiche* (Darmstadt 1970).

Alföldi, A., and E. Alföldi. *Die Kontorniat-Medaillons* 1 (Berlin 1976), 2 (Berlin 1990).

Alföldi, E. "Hadrian and Antinous on the contorniates and in the Vita Hadriani," in Bonamente (ed.) 1991, 11–18.

Alföldy, G. "Gallicanus noster," *Chiron* 9 (1979), 507–44.

Allen, T. W. *Homer: The Origins and Transmission* (Oxford 1924).

Altmann, W. *Die römische Grabaltäre der Kaiserzeit* (Berlin 1905).

Amidon, P. R. *The Church History of Rufinus of Aquileia: Books 10 and 11* (Oxford 1997).

Anderson, J. K. *Hunting in the Ancient World* (Berkeley 1985).

Ando, C. "The Palladium and the Pentateuch," *Phoenix* 55 (2001), 369–410 at 370–74 (reprinted with a few minor changes in Ando, *The Matter of the Gods: Religion and the Roman Empire* [Berkeley 2008], Ch. 7).

André, J. M. *L'otium dans la vie morale et intellectuelle romaine* (Paris 1966).

Arbesmann, R. "The cervuli and anniculae in Caesarius of Arles," *Traditio* 35 (1979), 89–119.

Armisen-Marchetti, M. *Macrobe: Commentaire au Songe de Scipion Livre I*² (Paris 2003).

Arns, E. *La technique du livre d'après saint Jérôme* (Paris 1953).

Ashmole, B. "A new interpretation of the Portland Vase," *JHS* 87 (1967), 1–17.

Astin, A. E. *Scipio Aemilianus* (Oxford 1967).

Athanassiadi, P. *Damascius: The Philosophical History* (Athens 1999).

Athanassiadi, P., and M. Frede (eds.), *Pagan Monotheism in Late Antiquity* (Oxford 1999).

Aubineau, M. "Publication des undecim novae homiliae de saint Jean Chrysostome," *Studia Patristica* 22 (1989), 83–88.

Babcock, R. G. "A revival of Claudian in the tenth century," *Class. et Med.* 37 (1986), 203–21.

Badel, Christophe. *La noblesse de l'empire romain* (Mayenne 2005).

Badian, E. "Cicero and the Commission of 146 BC," *Hommages M. Renard* 1 (Brussels 1969), 54–65.

Bagnall, R. S. *Egypt in Late Antiquity* (Princeton 1993).

——— (ed.). *Egypt in the Byzantine World 300–700* (Cambridge 2007).

——— . *Early Christian Books in Egypt* (Princeton 2009).

Bailey, C. *Religion in Virgil* (Oxford 1935).

Baker, Aaron. "Eunapius's NEA EKDOSIS and Photius," *GRBS* 29 (1988), 389–402.

Baldini, A. "Problemi della tradizione sulla 'distruzione' del Serapeo di Alessandria," *Riv. stor. dell'antichità* 15 (1985), 97–152.

——— . "Un'ipotesi su una tradizione occidentale post-Flavianea," *Hist. Aug. Coll. Genevense* (Bari 1999), 14–31.

——— . *Storie Perdute (III secolo d. C.)* (Bologna 2000).

——— . "Considerazioni ulteriori su Sozomenos HE i.5.1. e sulle edizioni della Storia di Eunapio," *Ant. tard.* 12 (2004), 387–91.

——— . "Considerazioni in tema di *Annales* ed *Historia Augusta*," in Bonamente and Brandt 2005, 15–46.

Baldwin, B. "Athenaeus and his work," *Acta Classica* 19 (1976), 21–42.

——— . "Tacitus, the Panegyrici Latini and the *Historia Augusta*," *Eranos* 78 (1980), 175–80.

Balsdon, J. P. V. D. *Romans and Aliens* (London 1979).

Banchich, T. M., and E. N. Lane. *The History of Zonaras from Alexander Severus to the Death of Theodosius the Great* (London 2009).

Barabino, G. "L'*auctoritas* di Varrone in Nonio Marcello," *Scripta Noniana* (Genoa 2006), 293–305.

Bardy, G. *La question des langues dans l'église ancienne* (Rennes 1948).

Barkowski, O. *De carmine adversus Flavianum anonymo* (Königsberg 1912).

Barns, J. "A new gnomologium," *CQ* 44 (1950), at 132–34.

Barnes, T. D. *Tertullian* (Oxford 1971).

——. "Who were the nobility of the Roman Empire?" *Phoenix* 28 (1974), 444–49.

——. "Publilius Optatianus Porphyrius," *AJP* 96 (1975), 173–86.

——. "Two senators under Constantine," *JRS* 65 (1975), 40–49.

——. "The Epitome de Caesaribus and its sources," *CP* 71 (1976), 258–68.

——. "The fragments of Tacitus's *Histories*," *CP* 72 (1977), 341–45.

——. *The Sources of the Historia Augusta* (Brussels 1978).

——. *Constantine and Eusebius* (Cambridge, Mass. 1981).

——. "The editions of Eusebius' *Ecclesiastical History*," *GRBS* 21 (1981), 191–201.

——. "Aspects of the background of the *City of God*," *University of Ottawa Quarterly* 52 (1982), 69–85.

——. *The New Empire of Diocletian and Constantine* (Cambridge, Mass. 1982).

——. "Regional prefectures," *Bonner Historia-Augusta-Colloquium 1984/85* (1987), 13–23.

——. "Jerome and the *Historia Augusta*," *HAC Paris. 1990* (Macerata 1991), 19–28.

——. "The capitulation of Liberius and Hilary of Poitiers," *Phoenix* 46 (1992), 256–65.

——. "Praetorian prefects 337–61," *ZPE* 94 (1992), 249–60.

——. *Athanasius and Constantius* (Cambridge Mass. 1993).

——. *From Eusebius to Augustine* (Brookfield 1994), no. 21, 160.

——. "The religious affiliation of consuls and prefects, 317–361," Ch. 7 of *From Eusebius to Augustine* (Variorum 1994). [1994a]

——. "The sources of the HA (1967–92)," in *HA Coll. Maceratense* (Bari 1995), 1–28.

——. "Statistics and the conversion of the Roman aristocracy," *JRS* 85 (1995), 135–47. [1995a]

——. "The military career of Martin of Tours," *Anal. Boll.* 114 (1996), 25–32.

——. "Oppressor, persecutor, usurper: The meaning of *tyrannus* in the fourth century," in Bonamente and Mayer 1996, 55–65.

——. *Ammianus Marcellinus and the Representation of Historical Reality* (Ithaca 1998).

——. "Ambrose and Gratian," *Ant. Tard.* 7 (1999), 165–74.

——. "The Historia Augusta and Christian hagiography," *HA Coll. Genevense* (Bari 1999), 33–41.

——. "Monotheists all?" *Phoenix* 55 (2001), 142–62.

——. "A neglected letter of Ambrose," *Studia Patristica* 38 (2001), 357–61.

——. "An urban prefect and his wife," *CQ* 56 (2006), 249–56.

——. *Early Christian Hagiography and Roman History* (Tübingen 2010).

——. *Roman Emperors, 284–602: Dates, Titles, Itineraries, Jurisdiction* (forthcoming).

Barnes, T. D., and R. W. Westall. "The conversion of the Roman aristocracy in Prudentius' *Contra Symmachum*," *Phoenix* 45 (1991), 50–61.

Bartalucci, A. "*Contro i pagani*": *Carmen cod. Par. lat. 8084* (Pisa 1998).

Bartsch, Shadi. *Actors in the Audience* (Cambridge Mass. 1994).

Baschera, C. *Gli scolii veronesi a Virgilio* (Verona 1999).

Bastien, P. *Le monnayage de Magnence (350–353)²* (Wetteren 1983).

Baynes, N. H. *The Historia Augusta: Its Date and Purpose* (Oxford 1926).

——. *Byzantine Studies* (London 1955).

Baynham, E. "An introduction to the Metz Epitome," *Antichthon* 29 (1995), 60–77.

Beard, M., and J. A. North. *Pagan Priests* (London 1990).

Beard, M., J. A. North, and S. Price. *Religions of Rome* 1–2 (Cambridge 1998).

Begbie, C. M. "The Epitome of Livy," *CQ* 17 (1967), 332–38.

Berger, P. *The Insignia of the Notitia Dignitatum* (New York 1981).

Bergmann, M. *Chiragan, Aphrodisias, Konstantinopel: Zur mythologischen Skulptur der Spätantike* (Wiesbaden 1999).

Bertoletti, M., M. Cima, and E. Talamo. *Centrale Montemartini: Musei Capitolini*² (Milan 2006).

Bickel, E. *Diatribe in Senecae philosophi fragmenta, volumen 1: Fragmenta de matrimonio* (Leipzig 1915).

——— . "Pagani: Kaiseranbeter in den Laren-Kapellen der pagi urbani im Rom Neros und der Apostels Petrus," *Rhein. Museum* 97 (1954), 1–47.

Bidez, J., and F. Cumont. *Les mages hellénisés* 1–2 (Paris 1938).

Bidez, J., and G. C. Hansen. *Sozomenus Kirchengeschichte* (Berlin 1960).

Billanovich, G. "Petrarch and the textual tradition of Livy," *Journal of the Warburg and Courtauld Institutes* 14 (1951), 137–208.

——— . "Dall'antica Ravenna alle biblioteche umanistiche," *Annuario dell'Università cattolica del sacro Cuore* (1955/57), 73–107.

——— . "Dal Livio di Raterio al Livio di Petrarca," *IMU* 2 (1959), 103–78.

——— . "Il testo di Livio," *IMU* 36 (1993), 107–74.

Bird, H. W. *Sextus Aurelius Victor: A historiographical study* (Liverpool 1984).

Birley, A. R. "Magnus Maximus and the persecution of heresy," *Bulletin of the John Rylands Library* 66 (1983), 13–43.

——— . "Religion in the *HA*," *HAC Parisinum* (1991), 29–52.

Bischoff, B. *Latin Palaeography*, trans. Dáibhí ó Cróinín and David Ganz (Cambridge 1990).

Bleckmann, B. "Die Chronik des Ioannes Zonaras und eine pagane Quelle zur Geschichte Konstantins," *Historia* 40 (1991), 343–65.

——— . *Die Reichskrise des III. Jahrhunderts in der spätantiken und byzantinischen Geschichtsschreibung: Untersuchungen zu den nachdionischen Quellen der Chronik des Johannes Zonaras* (Munich 1992).

——— . "Bemerkungen zu den *Annales* des Nicomachus Flavianus," *Historia* 44 (1995), 83–99.

——— . "Die Schlacht von Mursa und die zeitgenössische Deutung eines spätantiken Bürgerkrieges," in Brandt 1999, 58–68.

Bloch, H. "A new document of the last pagan revival in the West," *Harvard Theological Review* 38 (1945), 199–244.

——— . "The pagan revival in the West at the end of the fourth century," in Momigliano 1963, 193–218.

Blockley, R. C. *Ammianus Marcellinus: A Study of his Historiography and Political Thought* (Brussels 1975).

——— . "Was the first book of Zosimus' New History based on more than one source?" *Byzantion* 50 (1980), 393–402.

——— . *The Fragmentary Classicizing Historians of the Later Roman Empire* 1 (Liverpool 1981) and 2 (Liverpool 1983).

——— . "The Romano-Persian Peace Treaties of AD 299 and 363," *Florilegium* 6 (1984), 27–49.

——— . *The History of Menander the Guardsman* (Liverpool 1985).

——— . *East Roman Foreign Policy* (Leeds 1992).

Boak, A. E. R., and J. E. Dunlap. *Two Studies in Later Roman and Byzantine Administration* (London 1924).

Bodei Giglioni, G. "Pecunia fanatica: L'incidenza economica dei templi laziali," *Riv. Stor. Ital.* 89 (1977), 33–76.

Boin, D. R. "A hall for Hercules at Ostia and a farewell to the Late Antique 'pagan revival,'" *AJA* 114 (2010), 253–66.

Boissier, G. *La fin du paganisme* 1–2 (Paris 1891).

Bonamente, G. "Potere politico e autorità religiosa nel *De obitu Theodosii*," in *Chiesa e società dal secolo IV ai nostri giorni. Studi storici in onore del P. Ilarino da Milano* 1 (Rome 1979), 83–106.

Bonamente, G., and H. Brandt (eds.). *Historiae Augustae Colloquium Colloquium Barcinonense* (Bari 2005).

——— . *Historiae Augustae Colloquium Bambergense* (Bari 2007).

Bonamente, G., and M. Mayer (eds.). *Historiae Augustae Colloquium Barcinonense* (Bari 1996).

Bonamente, G., and K. Rosen (eds.). *Historiae Augustae Colloquium Bonnense* (Bari 1997).

Bonaria, M. "Echi lucanei in Paneg. Lat. x(4). 29. 5," *Latomus* 17 (1958), 497–99.

Bonfante Warren, L. "Roman triumphs and Etruscan kings: The Latin word *triumphus*," in R. C. Lugton and M. G. Borgehammar, S. *How the Holy Cross Was Found* (Stockholm 1991).

Borg, Barbara. *A Matter of Life and Death: A Social History of Tombs and Burial Customs in Second- and Third-Century AD Rome* (forthcoming).

Borgomeo, P. *L'église de ce temps* (Paris 1972).

Borret, M. *Origène Contre Celse* 1, SC 132 (Paris 1967), 23–24.

Boswell, J. *Christianity, Social Tolerance, and Homosexuality* (Chicago 1980).

Bouffartigue, J. "Julien, ou l'hellénisme décomposé," in S. Saïd, ΕΛΛΗΝΙΣΜΟΣ: *Quelques jalons pour une histoire de l'identité grecque* (Leiden 1991), 251–66.

——— . *L'Empereur Julien et la culture de son temps* (Paris 1992).

Bowersock, G. W. *Julian the Apostate* (Cambridge Mass. 1978).

——— . "The emperor Julian on his predecessors," *Yale Classical Studies* 27 (1982), 159–72.

——— . "From emperor to bishop: The self-conscious transformation of political power in the fourth century AD," *CP* 81 (1986), 298–307.

——— . *Hellenism in Late Antiquity* (Ann Arbor 1990).

Bowie, E., and J. Elsner. *Philostratus* (Cambridge 2009), (eds.).

Bradbury, S. "Julian's pagan revival and the decline of blood sacrifice," *Phoenix* 49 (1995), 331–56.

Bramble, J. C. *Persius and the Programmatic Satire* (Cambridge 1974).

Brandenburg, Hugo. "Das Ende der antiken Sarkophagkunst in Rom: Pagane und christliche Sarkophage im 4. Jahrhundert," in K. Kirchhainer (ed.), *Akten des Symposiums "Frühchristliche Sarkophage" Marburg 1999* (Mainz 2002), 19–39.

Brandt, H. "Die 'heidnische Vision' Aurelians (*HA A.* 24, 2–8) und die 'christliche Vision' Konstantins des großen," *Historiae Augustae Colloquium Maceratense* (Bari 1995), 107–17.

Brandt, H. (ed.). *Gedeutete Realität: Krisen, Wirklichkeiten, Interpretationen (3.–6. Jh. n. Chr.)* (Stuttgart 1999).

Brasseur, A. "Le songe de Théodose le Grand," *Latomus* 2 (1938), 190–95.

Bratož, R. (ed.). *Westillyricum und Nordostitalien in der spätrömischen Zeit* (Ljubljana 1996).

Braund, D. *Georgia in Antiquity* (Oxford 1994), 246–52.

Braund, D., and J. Wilkins (eds.). *Athenaeus and His World* (Exeter 2000).

Braunert, H. "Das Athenaeum zu Rom...," *Bonner Historia-Augusta-Colloquium 1963* (1964), 9–41.

Bravo, B., and M. Griffin. "Un frammento del libro XI di Tito Livio?" *Athenaeum* 66 (1988), 447–521.

Brennan, P. "The Notitia Dignitatum," *Les Littératures techniques dans l'antiquité romaine* (Geneva 1996), 147–78.

Brilliant, R. *Gesture and Rank in Roman Art* (Copenhagen 1963).

Brink, C. O. *Horace on Poetry* 2 (Cambridge 1971).

Briquel, D. *Chrétiens et haruspices: La réligion Étrusque, dernier rempart du paganisme romain* (Paris 1997).

Brock, S. "Origen's aims as a textual critic of the Old Testament," *Studia Patristica* 10. 1 (Berlin 1970), 215–18.

Brottier, L. "Jean Chrysostome: Un pasteur face à des demi-chrétiens," *Topoi*, Suppl. 5 (2004), 439–57.

Brown, P. "Aspects of the Christianisation of the Roman aristocracy," *JRS* 51 (1961), 1–2.

———. *Augustine of Hippo* (London 1967).

———. "The rise and function of the holy man," *JRS* 61 (1971), 80–101 = *Society and the Holy* (1982), 103–52.

———. *The World of Late Antiquity* (1971).

———. *Religion and Society in the Age of Saint Augustine* (1972).

———. *Power and Persuasion in Late Antiquity* (Madison 1992).

———. *Authority and the Sacred: Aspects of the Christianisation of the Roman World* (Cambridge 1995).

———. *The Rise of Western Christendom*[2] (Oxford 2003).

Brown, V. "Latin manuscripts of Caesar's *Gallic War*," *Palaeographica Diplomatica et Archivistica: Studi in onore G. Battelli* (Rome 1979), 105–57.

Bruggisser, P. "Précaution de Macrobe et datation de Servius," *Mus. Helv.* 41 (1984), 162–73.

———. *Romulus Servianus: La légende de Romulus dans les Commentaires à Virgile de Servius: mythographie et idéologie à l'époque de la dynastie théodosienne* (Bonn 1987).

———. *Symmaque ou le rituel épistolaire de l'amitié littéraire* (Fribourg 1993).

Bruhl, A. *Liber Pater* (Paris 1953).

Bruit Zaidman, L., and P. Schmitt Pantel, *Religion in the Ancient Greek City* (Cambridge 1992).

Bruneau, P. "Isis Pélagia à Délos," *BCH* 85 (1961), 435–46.

———. *Recherches sur les cultes de Délos* (Paris 1970).

Brunhölzl, F. "Zu den sogenannten codices archetypi der römischen Literatur," *Festschrift B. Bischoff* (Stuttgart 1971), 16–31.

Brunt, P. "On historical fragments and epitomes," *CQ* 74 (1980), 477–94.

Buchheit, V. *Vergil über die Sendung Roms* (Heidelberg 1963).

Buck, D. F. "Eunapius of Sardis and Theodosius the Great," *Byzantion* 58 (1988), 36–53.

———. "Did Sozomen use Eunapius' Histories?" *MH* 56 (1999), 15–25.

Burdeau, F. *Aspects de l'empire romain* (Paris 1964).

Burgess, R. W. *The Chronicle of Hydatius and the Consularia Constantinopolitana* (Oxford 1993).

———. "Principes cum tyrannis," *CQ* 43 (1993), 491–500.

———. "On the date of the Kaisergeschichte," *CP* 90 (1995), 111–28.

———. "Dates and editions of Eusebius' … HE," *JTS* 48 (1997), 471–504.

———. *Studies in Eusebian and Post-Eusebian Chronography* (Stuttgart 1999).

———. "A common source for Jerome, Eutropius, Festus, Ammianus, and the *Epitome de Caesaribus* between 358 and 378, along with further thoughts on the date and nature of the *Kaisergeschichte*," *CP* 100 (2005), 166–92.

Burkert, W. *Ancient Mystery Cults* (Cambridge Mass. 1987).

Burns, P. C. "Augustine's use of Varro's *Antiquitates Rerum Divinarum* in his *De Civitate Dei*," *Augustinian Studies* 32 (2001), 37–64.

Bury, J. B. *Imperial Administrative System in the Ninth Century* (London 1911).

Bush, D. *Mythology and the Renaissance Tradition in English Poetry*² (New York 1960).

Bussières, M.-P. *Ambrosiaster: Contre les Païens*, SC 512 (Paris 2007).

Bühl, G. *Constantinopolis und Roma* (Zürich 1995).

Cahn, H. A., and A. Kaufmann-Heiniman. *Der spätrömische Silberschatz von Kaiseraugst* (Derendingen 1984).

Callu, J.-P. *Symmaque: Lettres* 1–4 (Paris 1972–2002); and *Symmaque: Discours—Rapports* (Paris 2009).

"Les *Constitutions* d'Aristote et leur fortune au Bas-Empire," *RéL* 33 (1975), 268–315 (also in Callu 2006).

———. "Date et genèse du premier livre de Prudence Contre Symmaque," *RÉL* 59 (1981), 235–59.

———. "En amont de l'Histoire Auguste, 357–387," *Historiae Augustae Colloquium Genevense* (Bari 1999), 87–107 (also in Callu 2006, 371–93).

———. "Alexandre dans la littérature latine de l'antiquité tardive," in Callu (2006), 565–82.

——— *Culture profane et critique des sources* (Rome 2006).

Cameron, Alan. "Literary Allusions in the *Historia Augusta*," *Hermes* 92 (1964), 363–77.

———. "The Roman Friends of Ammianus," *JRS* 54 (1964), 15–28.

———. "The Fate of Pliny's *Letters* in the Late Empire," *CQ* 15 (1965), 289–98.

———. "Wandering poets: A literary movement in Byzantine Egypt," *Historia* 14 (1965), 470–509.

———. Review/Discussion of J. Straub, *Heidnische Geschichtsapologetik in der christlichen Spätantike* (Bonn 1963), in *JRS* 55 (1965), 240–48.

———. "The date and identity of Macrobius," *JRS* 56 (1966), 25–38.

———. "Iamblichus at Athens," *Athenaeum* 45 (1967), 143–53.

——— "Macrobius, Avienus and Avianus," *CQ* 27 (1967), 385–95. [1967a]

——— "Rutilius Namatianus, St. Augustine and the date of the *De Reditu*," *JRS* 57 (1967), 31–39.

———. "Tacitus and the date of Curiatius Maternus' death," *CR* 17 (1967), 258–61.

———. "The treatise *De Verbo* ascribed to Macrobius," *BICS* 14 (1967), 91–92.

———. "Celestial consulates: A note on the Pelagian letter *Humanae referunt*," *JTS* 29 (1968), 213–15.

———. "Gratian's repudiation of the pontifical robe," *JRS* 58 (1968), 96–102.

———. "Notes on Claudian's Invectives," *CQ* 18 (1968), 387–411.

———. "Theodosius the Great and the Regency of Stilico," *HSCP* 73 (1968), 247–80.

———. *Claudian: Poetry and Propaganda at the Court of Honorius* (Oxford 1970).

———. Review/Discussion of R. Syme, *Ammianus and the Historia Augusta* (1968), in *JRS* 61 (1971), 255–67.

———. "Claudian," in J. W. Binns (ed.), *Latin Literature of the Fourth Century* (London 1974), 134–59.

———. *Circus Factions: Blues and Greens at Rome and Byzantium* (Oxford 1976).

———. "Paganism and literature in fourth century Rome," in *Christianisme et formes littéraires de l'antiquité tardive en occident*, Entretiens sur l'antiquité classique 23 (Geneva 1977), 1–30.

———. "Poetae Novelli," *HSCP* 84 (1980), 127–75.

———. "The empress and the poet: Paganism and poetry at the court of Theodosius II," *YCS* 27 (1982), 217–89.

———. "The Latin Revival of the fourth century," in Warren Treadgold (ed.), *Renaissances before the Renaissance* (Stanford 1984), 42–58, 182–84.

———. "A new Late Antique ivory," *AJA* 88 (1984), 397–402.

————. "The Pervigilium Veneris," *La poesia tardoantica: tra retorica, teologia e politica:* Atti del V corso della scuola superiore di archeologia e civiltà medievali presso il centro di cultura scientifica "E.Majorana," Erice (Trapani) 6–12 Dicembre 1981 (Messina 1984), 209–34. [also in Cameron 1985]

————. "Probus' Praetorian games," *GRBS* 25 (1984), 193–96.

————. "The date and owners of the Esquiline treasure," *AJA* 89 (1985), 135–45. [1985a]

————. *Literature and Society in the Early Byzantine World* (London 1985).

————. "Nonius Atticus Maximus," *Epigraphica* 47 (1985), 109–10.

————. "Polyonomy in the Roman aristocracy: The case of Petronius Probus," *JRS* 75 (1985), 164–82.

————. "Martianus Capella and his first editor," *CP* 81 (1986), 320–28.

————. "Pagan ivories" in F. Paschoud (ed.), *Symmaque à l'occasion du mille six centième anniversaire du conflit de l'autel de la Victoire* (Paris 1986), 41–64.

———— "Flavius: A Nicety of Protocol": *Latomus* 47 (1988), 26–33.

————. "Biondo's Ammianus: Constantius and Hormisdas at Rome," *HSCP* 92 (1989), 423–36.

————. "Forschungen zum Thema der 'Heidnischen Reaktion' in der Literatur seit 1943," in A. Alföldi and E. Alföldi, *Die Kontorniat-Medaillons* 2: *Text* (Berlin 1990), 63–74. [1990a]

————. "Isidore of Miletus and Hypatia: On the editing of mathematical texts," *GRBS* 31 (1990), 103–27.

————. "Filocalus and Melania," *CP* 86 (1992), 140–44.

————. "Observations on the distribution and ownership of late Roman silver plate," *JRA* 5 (1992), 178–87.

————. *The Greek Anthology: From Meleager to Planudes* (Oxford 1993).

————. "Julian and Hellenism," *Ancient World* 24 (1993), 25–29.

————. "Avienus or Avienius," *ZPE* 108 (1995), 252–62.

————. *Callimachus and His Critics* (Princeton 1995). [1995a]

————. "Orfitus and Constantius: A note on Roman gold-glasses," *JRA* 9 (1996), 295–301.

————. "Basilius, Mavortius, Asterius," in I. Sevenko and I. Hutter (eds.), *ΑΕΤΟΣ: Studies in Honour of Cyril Mango* (Stuttgart and Leipzig 1998), 28–39.

————. "Consular diptychs in their social context: New eastern evidence," *JRA* 11 (1998), 384–403.

————. "The antiquity of the Symmachi," *Historia* 48 (1999), 477–505.

————. "The last pagans of Rome," in W. V. Harris (ed.), *The Transformations of Urbs Roma in Late Antiquity* (Portsmouth 1999), 109–21.

————. "Claudian Revisited," in Franca Ela Consolino (ed.), *Letteratura e propaganda nell'occidente latino da Augusto ai regni romanobarbarici* (Rome 2000), 127–44 [2000a].

————. "The poet, the bishop, and the harlot," *GRBS* 41 (2000), 175–88.

————. "The *Epitome de Caesaribus* and the *Chronicle* of Marcellinus," *CQ* 51 (2001), 324–27.

————. "Oracles and earthquakes: A note on the Theodosian Sibyl," in C. Sode and S. Takáks (eds.), *Novum Millenium: Studies on Byzantine history and culture dedicated to Paul Speck* (Aldershot 2001), 45–52.

————. "The funeral of Junius Bassus," *ZPE* 139 (2002), 288–92.

————. "Petronius Probus, Aemilius Probus and the transmission of Nepos: A note on late Roman calligraphers," in J.-M. Carrié and R. Lizzi Testa (eds.), *"Humana Sapit": Études d'antiquité tardive offertes à Lellia Cracco Ruggini* (Brepols 2002), 121–30.

————. *Greek Mythography in the Roman World* (Oxford 2004).

——— . "Poetry and literary culture in Late Antiquity," in S. Swain and M. Edwards (eds.), *Approaching Late Antiquity: The Transformation from Early to Late Empire* (Oxford 2004), 327–54.

——— . "Vergil illustrated, between pagans and Christians," *JRA* 17 (2004), 501–25.

——— . "More pieces from the Kaiseraugst treasure and the issue of imperial and senatorial *largitio* plate," *JRA* 19 (2006), 695–702.

——— . Review of Umberto Roberto, *Ioannis Antiocheni Fragmenta* (Berlin 2005) in *Bryn Mawr Classical Review* 2006.07.37.

——— . "The Imperial Pontifex," *HSCP* 103 (2007), 341–84.

——— . "Poets and pagans in Byzantine Egypt," in R. S. Bagnall (ed.), *Egypt in the Byzantine World* (Cambridge 2007), 21–46.

——— . "The Probus Diptych and Christian Apologetic," in H. Amirav and Bas ter Haar Romeny (eds.), *From Rome to Constantinople: Studies in Honour of Averil Cameron* (Leiden 2007), 191–202.

——— "Young Achilles in the Roman World," *JRS* 99 (2009), 1–22.

——— . "The date of the Scholia Vetustiora on Juvenal," *CQ* 60 (2010), 569–76.

——— "The Transmission of Cassian," *Revue d'histoire des textes* n.s. 6 (2011).

——— "Psyche and her Sisters," *Latomus* 69 (2010), 1070–77.

——— "The date of the last books of Ammianus Marcellinus," Forthcoming.

Cameron, Alan, and J. Long. *Barbarians and Politics at the Court of Arcadius* (Berkeley 1993).

Cameron, Alan, and D. Schauer. "The last consul: Basilius and his diptych," *JRS* 72 (1982), 126–45.

Cameron, Averil. *Agathias* (Oxford 1970).

——— . *Procopius* (Berkeley 1985).

Cameron, Averil, and Alan Cameron. "Christianity and tradition in the historiography of the Late Empire," *CQ* 14 (1964), 316–28.

Campbell, B. *The Writings of the Roman Land Surveyors* (London 2000).

Canivet, P. *Théodoret de Cyr: Thérapeutique des Maladies Helléniques* 1² (Paris 2000).

Cannadine, D.. and S. Price (eds.). *Rituals of Royalty* (Cambridge 1987).

Capdeville, G. "Substitution de victimes dans les sacrifices des animaux à Rome," *MEFRA* 83 (1971), 283–323.

——— . "*Taurus* et *bos mas*," *Mélanges…Jacques Heurgon* 1 (Rome 1976), 115–23.

Cappelletto, R. *Recuperi ammianei da Biondo Flavio* (Rome 1983).

Carandini, A., A. Ricci, and M. de Vos. *Filosofiana: La villa di Piazza Armerina* (1982).

Carriker, A. J. *The Library of Eusebius of Caesarea* (Leiden 2003).

Carson, R. A. G. *Principal Coins of the Romans*. Volume 3: *The Dominate* (London 1981).

Casali, S. "Correcting Aeneas's voyage: Ovid's commentary on *Aeneid* 3," *TAPA* 137 (2007), 181–210.

Caseau, B. "The fate of rural temples in Late Antiquity," in W. Bowden, L. Lavan, and C. Machado (eds.), *Recent Research on the Late Antique Countryside* (Leiden 2004), 105–44.

——— . "Firmicus Maternus, un astrologue converti au christianisme, ou la rhétorique du reject sans appel," in D. Toller (ed.), *La religion que j'ai quittée* (Paris 2007), 39–63, with earlier bibliography.

——— . "Rire des dieux," in E. Crouzet-Pavan and J. Verger (eds.), *La dérision au Moyen Âge* (Paris 2007), 117–41.

Casson, L. *Ships and Seamanship in the Ancient World* (Princeton 1971).

——— . *Libraries in the Ancient World* (New Haven 2001).

Castelli, E. "Gender, theory and *The Rise of Christianity*: A response to Rodney Stark," *JECS* 6 (1998), 227–57.

Castorina, E. *Claudio Rutilio Namaziano: De reditu* (Florence 1967).

Cavallera, F. *Saint Jérôme: Sa vie et son oeuvre* 2 (Louvain 1922).

Cavallo, G. (ed.). *Libri, editori e pubblico nel mondo antico* (Rome 1977).

———— (ed.). *Libri scritture scribi a Ercolano* (Naples 1983).

———— (ed.). *Le biblioteche nel mondo antico e medievale* (Roma 1988).

————. "Conservazione e perdita dei testi greci: Fattori materiali, sociali, culturali," in A. Giardina (ed.), *Società romana e impero tardoantico: Tradizione dei classici, Trasformazione della cultura* (Bari 1986), 83–172.

————. "La storia dei testi antichi a Bizanzio: Qualche riflessione," in J. Hamesse, *Les problèmes posés par l'édition critique des textes anciens et médiévaux* (Louvain-la-Neuve 1992), 98–104.

————. "Qualche annotazione sulla trasmissione dei classici nella tarda antichità," *Riv. di Fil.* 125 (1997), 205–19.

Cavarzere, A. *Orazio: Il libro degli Epodi* (Venice 1992).

Cecconi, G. A. *Governo imperiale e élites dirigenti nell' Italia tardoantica* (Como 1994).

————. *Commento storico al libro II dell epistolario di Q. A. Simmaco* (Pisa 2002).

Chadwick, H. *The Sentences of Sextus* (Cambridge 1959).

————. *Priscillian of Avila: The Occult and the Charismatic in the Early Church* (Oxford 1976).

————. *Boethius: The Consolations of Music, Logic, Theology and Philosophy* (Oxford 1981).

————. "Oracles of the end in the conflict of paganism and Christianity in the fourth century," in E. Lucchesi and H. D. Saffrey (eds.), *Mémorial André-Jean Festugière* (Geneva 1984), 125–26.

————. "Augustine on pagans and Christians," in D. Beales and G. Best (eds.), *History, Society and the Churches: Essays in Honour of Owen Chadwick* (Cambridge 1985), 9–27.

————. "New sermons of Augustine," *JTS* 47 (1996), 69–91.

Chahoud, A. "Antiquity and authority in Nonius Marcellus," in J. H. D. Scourfield (ed.), *Texts and Culture in Late Antiquity* (Swansea 2007), 69–96.

Champlin, E. "Serenus Sammonicus," *HSCP* 85 (1981), 189–212.

————. "The epitaph of Naucellius," *ZPE* 49 (1982), 184.

————. *Final judgments: Duty and emotion in Roman wills 200 B.C. – A.D. 250* (Berkeley 1991).

————. *Nero* (Cambridge, Mass. 2003).

Chantraine, H. "Die Kreuzesvision von 351. Fakten und Probleme," *Byz. Zeitschr.* 86/87 (1993/94), 430–41.

Chastagnol, A. "Le sénateur Volusien et la conversion d'une famille de l'aristocratie romaine au bas-empire," *RÉA* 58 (1956), 241–53.

————. "Observations sur le consulat suffect et la préture du bas-empire," *Rev. hist.* 219 (1958), 221–53.

———— "La carrière du proconsul d'Afrique M. Aurelius Consus Quartus," Libyca 7 (1959), 191–203.

———— *La prefecture urbaine à Rome sous le Bas-Empire* (Paris 1960).

————. *Les Fastes de la préfecture de Rome au Bas-Empire* (Paris 1962).

————. "L' Administration du Diocèse Italien au Bas-Empire," *Historia* 12 (1963), 348–79.

————. "L' Histoire Auguste," *Assoc. G. Budé: Actes du VIIᵉ congrès Aix-en-Provence 1963* (Paris 1964), 187–212.

————. "Les espagnoles dans l'aristocratie gouvernementale à l'époque de Théodose," in *Les empereurs romains d'Espagne* (Paris 1965), 269–72.

————. *Le sénat romain sous le règne d'Odoacre*, Antiquitas 3. 3 (Bonn 1966).

———. "Sur quelques documents relatifs à la basilique de Saint-Paul-hors-les-murs," *Mélanges…A. Piganiol* 1 (Paris 1966), 428–32.

———. "La restauration du temple d'Isis au *Portus Romae* sous le règne de Gratien," *Hommages…Renard* 2 (Brussels 1969), 135–44.

———. "Le poète Claudien et l'Histoire Auguste," *Historia* 19 (1970), 444–63.

———. *Recherches sur l'Histoire Auguste* (Bonn 1970).

———. "Vegèce et l'Histoire Auguste," *Bonner Historia-Augusta-Colloquium 1971* (1974), 59–80.

———. "Constantin et le Sénat," *Atti dell'Accademia Romanistica costantiniana* (Perugia 1976), 51–69.

———. *L'album municipal de Timgad* (Bonn 1978).

———. "La carrière sénatoriale du bas-empire," *Tituli* 4 (1982), 167–94.

———. *L'Italie et l'Afrique au Bas-Empire: Scripta Varia* (Lille 1987).

———. *Le sénat romain à l'époque impériale* (Paris 1992), 336.

———. "Consul saepius," *Latomus* 52 (1993), 856–59.

———. *Aspects de l'antiquité tardive* (Rome 1994).

———. *Histoire Auguste: Les empereurs romains des IIᵉ et IIIᵉ siècles* (Paris 1994).

———. "La censure de Valérien," *HAC Maceratense* (Bari 1995), 139–50.

———. *Le Bas-Empire³* (Paris 1997).

Chastagnol, A., and N. Duval. "Les survivances du culte impérial dans l'Afrique du nord à l'époque vandale," *Mélanges…W. Seston* (Paris 1974), 87–118.

Chatillon, F. "Arator déclamateur antijuif," *Revue du moyen âge latin* 19 (1963), 71–78.

Christol, M. *Essai sur l'évolution des carrières sénatoriales* (Paris 1986).

———. "A propos des Anicii: Le IIIᵉ siècle," *MEFRA* 98 (1986), 141–46.

Christol, M., et al. (eds.). *Institutions, Societé et vie politique dans l'empire Romain au IVᵉ siècle… A. Chastagnol* (Rome 1992.)

Chuvin, P. "Nonnos de Panopolis entre paganisme et christianisme," *Bulletin de l'Association Guillaume Budé* 45 (1986), 387–96.

———. *A Chronicle of the Last Pagans* (Cambridge, Mass. 1990).

———. "Sur les origines de l'équation *paganus* = païen," in L. Mary and M. Sot (eds.), *Impies et païens entre Antiquité et Moyen Age* (Paris 2002), 7–15.

Clark, E. A. *The Life of Melania the Younger* (New York 1984).

Clark, E A., and D. F. Hatch. *The Golden Bough, the Oaken Cross* (Chico 1981).

Clarke, G. W. *The Octavius of M. Minucius Felix* (New York 1974).

Clausen, W. V. "Sabinus's MS of Persius," *Hermes* 91 (1963), 252–56.

Clauss, M. *Cultores Mithrae: Die Anhängerschaft des Mithras-Kultes* (Stuttgart 1992).

———. *The Roman Cult of Mithras* (Edinburgh 2000).

Coarelli, F. *Rome and Environs: An Archaeological Guide* (Berkeley 2007).

Coates-Stephens, R. "The re-use of statuary in walls on the Esquiline and Caelian," *JRA* 14 (2001), at 228–31.

Cococcia, A. "La législation sur l'apostasie dans le Code Théodosien," in J.-N. Guinot and F. Richard (eds.), *Empire chrétien et Église aux IVᵉ et Vᵉ siècles: Intégration ou concordat* (Paris 2008), 457–66.

Cohen, B. "Divesting the female breast of clothes in classical sculpture," in A. O. Koloski-Ostrow and C. L. Lyons (eds.), *Naked Truths: Women, Sexuality, and Gender in Classical Art and Archaeology* (London 1997).

Collins-Clinton, J. *A Late Antique Shrine of Liber Pater at Cosa* (Leiden 1977).

Colombo, M. "Il bilinguismo di Valentiniano I," *Rhein. Mus.* 150 (2007), 396–406.

Combet-Farnoux, B. *Mercure romain* (Rome 1980).

Comparetti, D. *Vergil in the Middle Ages*, English translation 1885, reprinted with intro. by Jan Ziolkowski (Princeton 1997).

Consolino, F. E. (ed.). "Il significativo dell' *inventio crucis* nel *De obitu Theodosii*," *Annali della facoltà di lettere e filosofia, Università di Siena* 5 (1984), 161–80.

——— . "Girolamo poeta…" *Disiecti Membra Poetae* 3 (Foggia 1988), 226–42.

——— . "Teodosio e il ruolo del principe cristiano dal *De obitu* di Ambrogio alle storie ecclesiastiche," *Cristianesimo nella storia* 15 (1994), 257–77.

——— (ed.). *Pagani e cristiani da Giuliano l'Apostata al sacco di Roma* (Messina 1995).

——— (ed.). *Letteratura e propaganda nell'occidente latino da Augusto ai regni Romanobarbarici* (Rome 2000).

——— . "Poetry and Politics in Claudian's *carmina minora* 22 and 50," in W. Ehlers, F. Felgentreu, S. M. Wheeler, *Aetas Claudianea* (Leipzig 2004), 142–74.

Conte, G. B. *The Rhetoric of Imitation* (Ithaca 1986).

——— . *Latin Literature: A History*, trans. J. B. Solodow (Baltimore 1994).

Cooper, K., and J. Hillner (eds.), *Religion, Dynasty and Patronage in Early Christian Rome, 300–900* (Cambridge 2007).

Corcoran, S. *The Empire of the Tetrarchs* (Oxford 1996).

Corsano, M. "Un incontro problematico," *Orpheus* 21 (2000), 26–43.

Corsaro, F. *Studi rutiliani* (Bologna 1981).

Corssen, P. "Die Subskriptionen des Bischofs Victor in dem Codex Fuldensis," *Zeitschr. f. neutest. Wiss.* 10 (1909), 175–77.

Coşkun, A. "Virius Nicomachus Flavianus, der praefectus und consul des *Carmen Contra Paganos*," *Vigiliae Christianae* 57 (2004), 152–78.

Courcelle, P. "Quelques symboles funéraires du néoplatonisme latin," *REA* 346 (1944), 65–93.

——— . "Mille nocendi artes," *Mélanges…P. Boyancé* (Rome 1947), 219–27.

——— . *Les lettres grecques en occident*² (Paris 1948).

——— *Recherches sur les Confessions de Saint Augustin* (Paris 1950).

——— . "Les exégèses chrétiennes de la quatrième Églogue," *RÉA* 61 (1957), 294–319.

——— . *Les confessions de Saint Augustin dans la tradition littéraire* (Paris 1963).

——— . *Histoire littéraire des grandes invasions germaniques*³ (Paris 1964).

——— . *La Consolation de Philosophie dans la tradition littéraire* (Paris 1967).

——— . "Nouveaux aspects de la culture lérinienne," *RÉL* 46 (1968), 379–409.

——— . *Recherches sur les Confessions de S. Augustin*² (Paris 1968).

——— . "Jugements de Rufin et de Saint Augustin sur les empereurs du IVᵉ siècle et la défaite suprème du paganisme," *RÉA* 71 (1969), 100–130.

——— . *Late Latin Writers and Their Greek Sources* (Cambridge, Mass. 1969).

——— . "Ambroise de Milan face au comique latins," *RÉL* 50 (1972), 223–31.

Courcelle, P., and J. Courcelle. *Lecteurs païens et lecteurs chrétiens de L'Énéide* 1–2 (Paris 1984).

Courtney, E. "The transmission of Juvenal's text," *BICS* 14 (1967), 38–50.

——— . *Fragmentary Latin Poets* (Oxford 1993).

——— . *Archaic Latin Prose* (Atlanta 1999).

——— . "The Formation of the Text of Vergil," *BICS* 28 (1981), 13–29 (with second thoughts, ib. 46 [2002–3], 189–94).

Cova, P. V. *La critica letteraria di Plinio il Giovane* (Brescia 1966).

Cracco Ruggini, L. "L'Epitoma Rerum Gestarum Alexandri Magni e il Liber de Morte Testamentoque eius," *Athenaeum* 39 (1961), 285–357.

——— . "Sulla cristianizazione della cultura pagana: Il mito greco e latino di Alessandro dall' età antonina al medioevo," *Athenaeum* 43 (1965), 3–80.

———. "De morte persecutorum e polemica antibarbarica nella storiografica pagana e cristiana: A proposito della disgrazia di Stilicone," *Riv. di storia e letteratura religiosa* 4 (1968), 433–47.

———. "La leggenda dei Dioscuri tra paganesimo e cristianesimo," in *Studi storici O. Bertolini* (Pisa 1972), 265–72.

———. "Simboli di battaglia ideologica nel tardo ellenismo," *Studi Storici O. Bertolini* (Pisa 1972), 178–300.

———. "Apoteosi e politica senatoria nel IV secolo D. C. Il dittico dei Simmachi al British Museum," *Riv. stor. ital.* 89 (1977), 425–89.

———. *Il paganesimo romano tra religione e politica (384–394 d.C.): Per una reinterpretazione del Carmen contra paganos*, Memorie Accad. Lincei 8. 23. 1 (Rome 1979).

———. "Un cinquantennio di polemica antipagana a Roma," in *Paradoxos Politeia: Studi patristici in onore di G. Lazzati* (Milan 1979), 119–44 [1979a].

———. "En marge d'une 'mésalliance': Prétextat, Damase et le *Carmen contra paganos*," *CRAI* (1998), 493–516.

Crees, J. H. E. *The Reign of the Emperor Probus* (London 1911).

Cribiore, R. "Latin literacy in Egypt," *Kodai: Journal of Ancient History* 13/14 (2003/4), 111–18.

——— *The School of Libanius in Late Antique Antioch* (Princeton 2007).

Croke, B. "The editing of Symmachus' letters to Eugenius and Arbogast," *Latomus* 35 (1976), 533–49.

———. "AD 476: The manufacture of a turning point," *Chiron* 13 (1983), 81–119.

———. "Chronicles, annals and 'consular' annals in Late Antiquity," *Chiron* 31 (2001), 291–331.

———. *Count Marcellinus and His Chronicle* (Oxford 2001).

Croke, B., and J. Harries. *Religious Conflict in Fourth-Century Rome* (Sydney 1982).

Cumont, F. *Textes et monuments figurés relatifs aux mystères de Mithra* 1–2 (Brussels 1899).

———. *Les religions orientales dans le paganisme romain*⁴ (Paris 1929).

———. *Recherches sur le symbolisme funéraire des romains* (Paris 1942).

———. *La stèle du danseur d'Antibes et son décor végétal: étude sur le symbolisme funéraire des plantes* (Paris 1942) [1942a].

———. *Lux Perpetua* (Paris 1949).

Cunningham, M. P. "Some Facts about the Puteanus of Prudentius," *TAPA* 89 (1958), 32–37.

Curran, J. *Pagan City and Christian Capital: Rome in the Fourth Century* (Oxford 2000).

Curtius, E. R. *European Literature and the Latin Middle Ages* (Princeton 1953).

Cutler, A. "The social status of Byzantine scribes," *Byz. Zeit.* 74 (1981), 328–34.

D'Arms, J. H. *Romans on the Bay of Naples* (Cambridge, Mass. 1970).

Dagron, G. *L'empire romain d'orient au IVe siècle et les tradition politiques de l'hellénisme: Le témoignage de Thémistios*, Travaux et Mémoires 3 (Paris 1968).

———. *Naissance d'une capitale* (Paris 1974).

———. *Constantinople imaginaire: Études sur le recueil des Patria* (Paris 1984).

———. "L'organisation et le déroulement des course d'après le Livre des Cérémonies," *Travaux et Mémoires* 13 (2000), 3–200.

———. *Emperor and Priest* (Cambridge 2003).

Dain, A. *Les manuscrits*³ (Paris 1975).

Daintree, D. "The Virgil commentary of Aelius Donatus: Black hole or eminence grise," *Greece and Rome* 37 (1990), 65–79.

Dall'Astra, M. *Philosoph, Magier, Scharlatan und Antichrist: Zur Rezeption von Philostrat's Vita Apollonii in der Renaissance* (Heidelberg 2008).

Daly, L. W. "Roman Study Abroad," *AJP* 71 (1950), 40–58.

Davidson, I. *Ambrose De officiis 1–2* (Oxford 2001).

de Boor, C. "Römische Kaisergeschichte in byzantinischer Fassung," *BZ* 1 (1892), 13–33.

———. "Suidas und die Konstantinische Exzerptsammlung," *BZ* 21 (1912), 381–424; and 23 (1914/19), 1–127.

de Bruyn, T. *Pelagius's Commentary on St Paul's Epistle to the Romans* (Oxford 1993).

de Ghellinck, J. *Patristique et Moyen Age* (Brussels-Paris 1946).

De Labriolle, P. *La reaction paienne* (Paris 1934).

Deichman, F. W., G. Bovini, and H. Brandenburg. *Repertorium der christlich-antiken Sarkophage I: Rom und Ostia* (Wiesbaden 1967).

de Kisch, Y. "Les sortes vergilianae dans l'Histoire Auguste," *MEFR* 82 (1970), 321–62.

Dekkers, E. "Les autographes des pères latins," *Colligere Fragmenta: Festschrift A. Dold* (1952), 127–39.

DeLaine, J. "The 'cella solearis' of the Baths of Caracalla," *PBSR* 55 (1987), 147–56.

Delbrueck, R. *Die Consulardiptychen und verwandte Denkmäler* (Berlin 1929).

Delehaye, H. *Les origines du culte des martyrs* (Brussels 1933).

Delmaire, R. *Largesses sacrées et res privata: L'aerarium impérial et son administration du IVe au VIe siècle* (Rome 1989).

———. *Les responsables des finances impériales au Bas-Empire romain* (Brussels 1989).

———. *Les institutions du bas-empire romain de Constantin à Justinien 1* (Paris 1995).

Delvigo, M. L. "L' *emendatio* del filologo, del critico, dell'autore: Tre modi di corregere il testo?" *Materiali e discussione* 24 (1990), 71–110.

Demandt, A. *Verformungstendenzen in der Überlieferung antiker Sonnen- und Mondfinsternisse* (Mainz 1970).

———. "Römische Entscheidungsschlachten," in Bratož 1996, 31–44.

———. *Die Spätantike: Römische Geschichte von Diocletian bis Justinian 284–565 n. Chr.²* (Munich 2007).

Demandt, A., and G. Brummer. "Der Prozess gegen Serena im Jahre 408," *Historia* 26 (1977), 479–502.

Demoen, K., and D. Praet. *Theios Sophistes: Essays on Flavius Philostratus' Vita Apollonii* (Leiden 2009).

Demougeot, E. *De l'unité à la division de l'empire romain* (Paris 1951).

———. "Saint Jérôme, les oracles sibyllins et Stilicon," *RÉA* 54 (1952), 83–92.

———. "Remarques sur l'emploi de paganus," *Studi… Calderini-Paribeni 1* (Milan 1956), 337–50.

———. "*Paganus*, Mithra et Tertullien," *Studia Patristica 3* (1961), 354–65.

den Boeft, J., J. W. Drijvers, D. den Hengst, and H. C. Teitler. *Ammianus after Julian* (Leiden 2007).

den Hengst, D. *The Prefaces in the Historia Augusta* (Amsterdam 1981).

———. "The author's literary culture," *Historiae Augustae Colloquium Parisinum* (Macerata 1991), 161–69.

———. "The Plato of Poets: Vergil in the *Historia Augusta*," in R. Rees (ed.), *Romane Memento: Vergil in the Fourth Century* (London 2004), 172–88.

Dennis, G. T. "Byzantine Battle Flags," *Byzantinische Forschungen 8* (1982), 51–59.

de Paolis, P. "Macrobio 1934–1984," *Lustrum* 28–29 (1986–87), 107–254.

———. *De verborum graeci et latini differentiis et societatibus* (Urbino 1990).

de Rossi, G. B. "Iscrizione onoraria di Nicomaco Flaviano," *Annali dell'Instituto di corrispondenza archeologica* (1849), 283–363.

———. "Il culto idolatrico in Roma nel 394. Notizie raccolte da un inedito carme scoperto in Parigi," *Bull. di arch. cristiana 6* (1868), 49–58, 61–75.

———. "I collegii funeraticii famigliari e privati e le loro denominazioni," *Commentationes philol. in honorem Th. Mommsen* (Berlin 1877), 705–11.

Dessau, H. "Über Zeit und Persönlichkeit der Scriptores Historiae Augustae," *Hermes* 24 (1889), 337–92.

de Ste Croix, G. E. M. *Christian Persecution, Martyrdom, and Orthodoxy* (Oxford 2006), 237–42.

Devréesse, R. *Introduction à l'Étude des manuscrits grecs* (1954).

Dewar, M. "Hannibal and Alaric in the later poems of Claudian," *Mnemosyne* 47 (1994), 349–72.

———. *Claudian: Panegyricus de sexto consulatu Honorii Augusti* (Oxford 1996).

Dickey, E. *Ancient Greek Scholarship* (Oxford 2007).

Diederich, M. D. *Vergil in the Works of St. Ambrose* (Washington, D.C. 1931).

Diederich, S. *Der Horazkommentar des Porphyrio im Rahmen der kaiserzeitlichen Schul- und Bildungstradition* (Berlin 1999).

Diels, H. *Sibyllinische Blätter* (Berlin 1890).

Dill, S. *Roman Society in the Last Century of the Roman Empire*[2] (London 1899).

Diller, A. *The Tradition of the Minor Greek Geographers* (Lancaster 1952).

Doblhofer, E. *Rutilius Claudius Namatianus De Reditu suo* 2 (Heidelberg 1977).

Dobschütz, E. von. "Wann las Victor von Capua sein Neues Testament?" *Zeitschr. f. neutest. Wiss.* 10 (1909), 90–96.

Doignon, J. "Oracles, prophéties, 'on-dit' sur la chute de Rome (395–410)," *Rev. Ét. Aug.* 36 (1990), 120–46.

Dolbeau, F. "Un nouveau catalogue de manuscrits de Lobbes aux XI–XII siècles," *Rech. Augustiniennes* 13 (1978), 3–36.

———. "Damase, le *Carmen contra paganos* et Hériger de Lobbes," *RÉAug.* 27 (1981), 38–43.

———. *Augustin d'Hippone. Vingt six Sermon au peuple d'Afrique* (Paris 1996).

Dowden, Ken. *European Paganism: The Realities of Cult from Antiquity to the Middle Ages* (London 2000).

Downey, G. *A History of Antioch in Syria* (Princeton 1961).

Döpp, S. "Theodosius I. Ein zweites Mal in Rom?" in A. Patzer (ed.), *Apophoreta für Uvo Hölscher* (Bonn 1975), 73–83.

———. "Zur Datierung von Macrobius' *Saturnalia*," *Hermes* 106 (1978), 619–32.

Drake, H. A. *Constantine and the Bishops* (Baltimore 2000).

——— (ed.). *Violence in Later Antiquity* (Burlington 2006).

Dresken-Weiland, Jutta. *Sarkophagbestattungen des 4.–6. Jahrhunderts im Westen des römischen Reiches* (Freiburg 2003).

Drijvers, J. W. *Helena Augusta: The Mother of Constantine and the Legend of Her Finding of the True Cross* (Leiden 1992).

Drinkwater, J. F. *The Gallic Empire* (Stuttgart 1987).

Dubuisson, M. "Les opici, Osques, Occidentaux ou barbares," *Latomus* 42 (1983), 522–45.

Dufourcq, A. "Rutilius Namatianus contre saint Augustin," *Revue d'histoire et de litt. relig.* 10 (1905), 488–92.

Dumézil, G. *Archaic Roman Religion* 2 (Chicago 1970).

Dunbabin, K. M. D. *The Mosaics of Roman North Africa* (Oxford 1978).

Duthoy, R. *The Taurobolium: its evolution and terminology* (Leiden 1969).

Duval, Y.-M. (ed.). "L'éloge De Théodose dans la *Cité de Dieu* (v. 26. 1)," *Recherches Augustiniennes* 4 (1966), 156–57.

——— (ed.). *Ambroise de Milan: XVI*[e] *Centenaire de son élection épiscopale* (Paris 1974).

———. "Formes profanes et formes bibliques dans les oraisons funèbres de Saint Ambroise," *Entretiens Fondation Hardt* 23 (1977), 274–86.

———. "Les *aurea fulmina* des Alpes Juliennes: le rôle des statues divines dans les lieux stratégiques," in Bratož 1996, 95–107.

———. *L'affaire Jovinien: D'une crise de la société romaine à une crise de la pensée chrétienne à la fin du IVe et au debut du Ve siècle* (Rome 2003).

Dyson, J. T. *King of the Wood: The Sacrificial Victor in Virgil's Aeneid* (Norman 2001).

Dzielska, M. *Apollonius of Tyana in Legend and History* (Rome 1986).

Ebbeler, J. V., and C. Sogno. "Religious identity and the politics of patronage: Symmachus and Augustine," *Historia* 56 (2007), 230–42.

Eck, W. et al. (eds.). *Senatores Populi Romani* (Stuttgart 2005).

Economou, G. D. *The Goddess Natura in Medieval Literature* (Cambridge, Mass. 1972).

Egger, R. *Römisches Antike u. frühes Christentum* 1 (1962).

Ellis, R. "On a recently discovered Latin poem…" *Journal of Philology* 1 (1868), 66–80.

Elsner, Jás. *Imperial Rome and Christian Triumph* (Oxford 1998).

Engemann, Josef. *Untersuchungen zur Sepulchralsymbolik der späteren römischen Kaiserzeit, JbAC Erg.* 2 (Münster 1973).

Eno, R. B. *St Augustine, Letters VI (1*–29*)* (Washington, D.C. 1989).

Ensoli, S., and E. La Rocca (eds.). *Aurea Roma: Dalla città pagana alla città cristiana* (Rome 2000).

Ensslin, W. "War Kaiser Theodosius I zweimal in Rome?" *Hermes* 81 (1953), 500–507.

Errington, R. M. "The Praetorian Prefectures of Virius Nicomachus Flavianus," *Historia* 41 (1992), 439–61.

——— "The Accession of Theodosius I," *Klio* 78 (1996), 438–53.

———. "Christian accounts of the religious legislation of Theodosius I," *Klio* 79 (1997), 398–443.

———. "Church and state in the first years of Theodosius I," *Chiron* 27 (1997), 21–72 [1997a].

———. "Themistius and his emperors," *Chiron* 30 (2000), 861–904.

———. *Roman Imperial Policy from Julian to Theodosius* (Chapel Hill 2006).

Erskine, A. *Troy between Greece and Rome* (Oxford 2001).

Étienne, R. *Bordeaux antique* (Bordeaux 1962).

Fagan, G. G. *Bathing in Public in the Roman World* (Ann Arbor 1999).

Faguet, E. *De Aurelii Prudentii Clementis carminibus lyricis* (Bordeaux 1883).

Fantham, E. "Lucan, his Scholia, and the victims of Marius," *Ancient History Bulletin* 1 (1987), 89–96.

Faraone, C. A. *Talismans and Trojan Horses* (Oxford 1992).

Fargues, P. *Claudien: Études sur sa poésie et son temps* (Paris 1933).

Farrell, J. "Servius and the Homeric Scholia," in S. Casali and F. Stok (eds.), *Servio: Stratificazioni esegetiche e modelli culturali* (Brussels 2008), 112–31.

Fauvinet-Ranson, V. *Decor Civitatis, Decor Italiae: Monuments, travaux publics et spectacles au VIe siècle d'après les Variae de Cassiodore* (Bari 2006).

Favez, C. *Saint Jérôme peint par lui-même* (Brussels 1958).

Feeney, D. *Literature and Religion at Rome* (Cambridge 1998).

———. *Caesar's Calendar: Ancient Time and the Beginnings of History* (Berkeley 2007).

Ferrari, M. "Spigolature bobbiesi," *IMU* 16 (1973), 1–41.

Ferrua, A. *Epigrammata Damasiana* (Vatican 1942).

Festugière, A. J. *Trois dévots païens* (Paris 1944).

Festy, M. "Le début et la fin des *Annales* de Nicomaque Flavien," *Historia* 46 (1997), 465–78.

———. "En éditant l'*Epitome de Caesaribus*," *Hist. Aug. Coll. Argentoratense* (Bari 1998), 153–66.

——— . *Pseudo-Aurélius Victor: Abrégé des Césars*² (Paris 2002).

——— . "L'Histoire Auguste et les Nicomaques," in Bonamente and Brandt (eds.) 2007, 183–95.

Filotas, B. *Pagan Survivals, Superstitions and Popular Cultures in Early Medieval Pastoral Literature* (Toronto 2005).

Fischer, B. "Bibelausgaben des frühen Mittelalters," in *La bibbia nel alto medioevo* (*Settimane di studio del centro italiano di studi sull'alto medioevo* 10) (Spoleto 1963), at 545–57.

Fisher, E. "Greek translations of Latin literature in the fourth century AD," in *Yale Classical Studies* 27 (1982), 173–215.

Fishwick, D. *The Imperial Cult in the Latin West* 1. 1 (Leiden 1993).

Flamant, J. *Macrobe et le Néo-Platonisme latin à la fin du IVᵉ siècle* (Leiden 1977).

Fletcher, G. B. A. "Stylistic borrowings and parallels in Ammianus Marcellinus," *Rev. de Phil.* 63 (1937), 377–95.

Fletcher, R. *The Conversion of Europe* (London 1997).

Flower, Harriet I. *The Art of Forgetting: Disgrace and Oblivion in Roman Political Culture* (Chapel Hill 2006).

Fo, A. *Rutilio Namaziano: Il ritorno* (Turin 1992).

Fontaine, J. *Sulpice Sévère: Vie de Saint Martin* 1–3 (Paris 1968).

——— . "Valeurs antiques et valeurs chrétiennes dans la spiritualité des grands propriétaires terriens à la fin du IVᵉ siècle occidental," *Epektasis: Mélanges…Daniélou* (Beauchesne 1972), 571–602.

——— . "L'affaire Priscillien ou l'ère des nouveaux Catilina," *Classica et Iberica: Festschrift… J. M.-F. Marique* (Worcester 1975), 355–92.

——— . "L'aristocratie occidentale devant le monachisme au IVème et Vème siècles," *Rivista si storia e letteratura religiosa* 15 (1979), 28–53.

. *Naissance de la poésie dans l'occident chrétien* (Paris 1981).

. "Damase poète Théodosien: L'imaginaire poétique des *Epigrammata*," *Saecularia damasiana: Atti del convegno internazionale per il XVI centenario della morte di Papa Damaso I* (Rome 1986), 115–45.

Forbes, C. A. *Firmicus Maternus: The Error of the Pagan Religions* (New York 1970).

Formis, C. "Il dittico eburneo della Cattedrale di Novara," *Contributi dell'Istituto di Archeologia* (Pubblicazioni dell'Università cattolica del Sacro Cuore 3. 9) (Milan 1967), 171–91.

Fornara, C. W. "Studies in Ammianus Marcellinus II," *Historia* 41 (1992), 420–38.

Foss, C. "Stephanus, proconsul of Asia, and related statues," *Okeanos: Essays…I. Sevcenko*, Harvard Ukrainian Studies 7, (1983), 196–219.

Fowden, G. "Bishops and Temples in the Eastern Roman Empire 320–435," *JTS* 29 (1978), 53–78.

——— . "Between Pagans and Christians," *JRS* 78 (1988), 173–82.

——— . "Constantine's porphyry column: The earliest literary allusion," *JRS* 81 (1991), 119–31.

——— . *Empire to Commonwealth: Consequences of Monotheism in Late Antiquity* (Princeton 1993).

Fowler, R. "Genealogical thinking, Hesiod's catalogue, and the creation of the Hellenes," *Proc. Camb. Phil. Soc.* 44 (1999), 1–19.

Fowler, W. W. *The Death of Turnus* (Oxford 1927).

Frank, R. I. *Scholae Palatinae: The Palace Guards of the Later Roman Empire* (Rome 1969).

Franklin, C. V., and P. J. Meyvaert. "Has Bede's version of the Passio S. Anastasii come down to us?" *Anal. Boll.* 100 (1982), 373–400.

Fraschetti, A. *Roma e il principe* (Rome 1990).

——— . *La Conversione: Da Roma pagana a Roma cristiana* (Rome 1999).

Fraser, P. M. *Cities of Alexander the Great* (Oxford 1986).

Frend, W. H. C. *The Rise of the Monophysite Movement* (Cambridge 1972).

Friedheim, E. *Rabbinisme et Paganisme en Palestine romaine* (Leiden 2006).

Friedlaender, P. *Spätantiker Gemäldezyklus des Procopius von Gaza* (Rome 1939), reprinted together with his 1912 *Johannes von Gaza und Paulus Silentiarius* (Hildesheim 1969).

Frier, B. W. *Libri Annales Pontificum Maximorum: The Origins of the Annalistic Tradition*[2] (Ann Arbor 1999).

Fuhrmann, M. (ed.). *Christianisme et Formes littéraires de l'antiquité tardive* (Vandoeuvres 1977).

——— . "Die Mönchgeschichten des Hieronymus: Formexperimente in erzählender Literatur," in Fuhrman (ed.) 1977, 41–89.

——— . *Rom in der Spätantike* (Zürich 1994).

Fuller, C. J. *The Camphor Flame: Popular Hinduism and Society in India* (Princeton 1992).

Gabba, E. "True history and false history in Classical Antiquity," *JRS* 71 (1981), 50–62.

Gager, J. *The Origins of Anti-Semitism* (Oxford 1985).

Galinsky, K. (ed.). *The Interpretation of Roman Poetry* (Frankfurt 1992).

Gardthausen, V. *Griechische Paläographie* 1–2[2] (Leipzig 1913).

Garnsey, P. *Social Status and Legal Privilege in the Roman Empire* (Oxford 1970).

Gaudemet, J. "La condamnation des pratiques paiennes en 391," *Epektasis: Mélanges J. Daniélou* (Beauchesne 1972), 597–602.

Gärtner, U. *Quintus Smyrnaeus und die Aeneis: Zur Nachwirkung Vergils in der griech. Literatur der Kaiserzeit* (Munich 2005).

Geffcken, J. *Der Ausgang des griechisch-römischen Heidentums* (Heidelberg 1920).

Geiger, J. "Some Latin authors from the Greek East," *CQ* 49 (1999), 606–17.

Gelzer, M. *The Roman Nobility* (Oxford 1969).

Georgii, H. *Die antike Äneiskritik aus den Scholien und anderen Quellen* (Stuttgart 1891).

——— . "Zur Bestimmung der Zeit des Servius," *Philologus* 71 (1912), 518–26.

Georgoudi, S., R. Koch Piettre, and F. Schmidt. *La cuisine et l'autel* (Turnhout 2005).

Gerbenne, B. "Modèles bibliques pour un empereur: Le *De obitu Theodosii* d'Ambroise de Milan," in *Rois et reines de la Bible au miroir des Pères* (Strasburg 1999), 161–76.

Gernentz, W. *Laudes Romae* (Rostoch 1918).

Gerritsen, J. "Printing at Froben's: An eye-witness account," *Studies in Bibliography* 44 (1991), 144–63.

Gessner, J. A. *Servius und Pseudo-Asconius* (Zürich 1888).

Geymonat, M. "Servius as commentator on Horace," in P. Knox and C. Foss (eds.), *Style and Tradition: Studies in Honor of W. Clausen* (Stuttgart 1998), 30–39.

Ghilardi, M., C. J. Goddard, and P. Porena (eds.). *Les cités de l'Italie tardo-antique (IVe–VIe siècle)* (Rome 2006).

Gibson, Margaret (ed.). *Boethius: His Life, Thought and Influence* (Oxford 1981).

——— . *The Liverpool Ivories* (London 1994).

Gillett, Andrew. "The date and circumstances of Olympiodorus of Thebes," *Traditio* 48 (1993), 1–29.

Gilliam, J. F. "Paganus in B.G.U. 696," *AJP* 73 (1952), 75–78.

——— . "Ammianus and the Historia Augusta: The lost books and the period 117–285," *Bonner Historia-Augusta-Colloquium 1970* (1972), 125–47.

Girardet, K. "Die Erhebung Kaiser Valentinian II. Politische Umstände und Folgen (375/76)," *Chiron* 34 (2004), 109–44.

Glinister, F., C. Woods, J. A. North, and M. H. Crawford, *Verrius, Festus and Paul* (London 2007).

Goar, R. J. *Cicero and the State Religion* (Amsterdam 1972).

Goddard, C. J. "The evolution of pagan sanctuaries in late antique Italy," in Ghilardi et al. (eds.) 2006, 281–308.

——— . "La divination à l'époque tardive," *Mètis* 5 (2007).

Goette, H. R. *Studien zu römischen Togadarstellungen* (Mainz 1989).

Goffart, W. *The Narrators of Barbarian History (AD 550–800)*[2] (Notre Dame 2005).

Golega, J. *Studien über die Evangeliendichtung des Nonnos von Panopolis* (Breslau 1930).

Goold, G. P. "The Helen Episode," *HSCP* 74 (1970), 101–68.

Gordini, G. D. "L'opposizione al monachesimo a Roma nel IV secolo," in *Dalla Chiesa antica alla Chiesa moderna* (Rome 1983), 19–35.

Gorman, M. M. "Chapter headings for Augustine's De genesi ad litteram," *Rev. Ét. Aug.* 26 (1980), 88–104.

——— . "Eugippius and the origins of the manuscript tradition of Augustine's De genesi ad litteram," *Rev. Bén.* 93 (1983), 7–30.

Gorman, R. J., and V. B. Gorman. "The Tryphê of the Sybarites: A historiographical problem in Athenaeus," *JHS* 127 (2007), 38–60.

Grabar, André. *Early Christian Art: From the Rise of Christianity to the Death of Theodosius* (New York 1968).

Gradel, I. *Emperor Worship and Roman Religion* (Oxford 2002).

Graeven, H. "Heidnische Diptychen," *Röm. Mitt.* 28 (1913), 246–71.

Graf, F. (ed.). *Einleitung in die lateinische Philologie* (Stuttgart and Leipzig 1997).

——— . "Kalendae Ianuariae," in *Ansichten griechischer Rituale: Geburtstags...W. Burkert* (Stuttgart 1998).

Grafton, A. *Joseph Scaliger* 1 (Oxford 1983).

——— . *Commerce with the Classics* (Ann Arbor 1997).

——— . "Correctores corruptores? Notes on the Social History of Editing," in G. W. Most (ed.), *Editing Texts/Texte edieren* (Göttingen 1998), 54–76.

——— . *Bring Out Your Dead: The Past as Revelation* (Cambridge, Mass. 2001).

Grafton, A., and M. Williams. *Christianity and the Transformation of the Book* (Cambridge, Mass. 2006).

Grant, J. N. *Studies in the Textual Tradition of Terence* (Toronto 1986).

Grazia Nistri, M. "Nuovi lezioni del palinsesto veronese di Tito Livio," *Annali della Facoltà di lettere dell'università di Siena* 3 (1982), 193–96.

Green, C. M. C. *Roman Religion and the Cult of Diana at Aricia* (Cambridge 2007).

Green, R. P. H. *The Poetry of Paulinus of Nola* (Brussels 1971).

——— . "Ausonius' use of the classical Latin poets," *CQ* 27 (1977), 441–52.

——— . "Marius Maximus and Ausonius' *Caesares*," *CQ* 31 (1981), 226–36.

——— . *The Works of Ausonius* (Oxford 1991).

——— . "Proba's Cento: Its date, purpose and reception," *CQ* 45 (1995), 551–63.

——— . "Proba's introduction to her Cento," *CQ* 47 (1997), 548–59.

——— . *Latin Epics of the New Testament* (Oxford 2006).

Grégoire, H., and P. Orgels. "*Paganus*: Étude de sémantique et d'histoire," *Mélanges Georges Smets* (Brussels 1952), 363–400.

Grierson, P. "The tombs and obits of the Byzantine Emperors," *DOP* 16 (1962), 3–60.

Grierson, P., and M. Mays. *Catalogue of Late Roman Coins in the Dumbarton Oaks Collection* (Washington, D.C. 1992).

Griffin, M. T. *Nero: The End of a Dynasty* (London 1984).

Griffiths, Alison. "Mithraism in the private and public lives of the 4th-c. senators in Rome," *Electronic Journal of Mithraic Studies* 1 (2000).

Griffiths, J. G. "The survival of the longer of the so-called Oxford fragments of Juvenal," *Hermes* 91 (1963), 104–14.

Grimal, P. *Les jardins romains*² (Paris 1969).

Groag, E. "Der Dichter Porphyrios in einer stadrömischen Inschrift," *Wien. Stud.* 45 (1926/7), 102–9.

Gross, P. K. *Die Unterpfänder der römischen Herrschaft* (Berlin 1935).

Grünewald, T. "Der letzte Kampf des Heidentums in Rom?" *Historia* 41 (1992), 462–87.

Gryson, R. *Scolies ariennes sur le concile d'Aquilée* (Paris 1980).

Gualandri, I. "La risposta di Ambrogio a Simmaco: Destinatari pagani e destinatari cristiani," in Consolino 1995, 241–56.

Guignebert, R. "Les demi-chrétiens et leur place dans l'église antique," *Rev. de l'histoire des religions* 88 (1923), 65–102.

Guillemin, A. M. *Pline et la vie littéraire se son temps* (Paris 1929).

Guizzi, F. *Aspetti giuridici del sacerdozio Romano* (1968).

Guttila, G. "Il panegyricus de S. Paolino di Nola," *Koinonia* 14 (1990), 139–54.

Gwyn Griffiths, J. *Apuleius of Madauros: The Isis-Book* (Leiden 1975).

Haarhoff, T. J. *Schools of Gaul* (Oxford 1920).

Hackethal, I. M. "Studien zum Mithraskult in Rom," *ZPE* 3 (1968), 221–54.

Hadot, I. *Arts libéraux et philosophie dans la pensée antique* (2nd exp. ed. 2005).

Hadot, P. (ed.). *Marius Victorinus: Traités théologiques sur la Trinité* 1 (Paris 1960).

———. *Porphyre et Victorinus* 1–2 (Paris 1968).

———. *Marius Victorinus: Recherches sur sa vie et ses oeuvres* (Paris 1971).

Hadot, P., and M. Cordier. *Ambroise de Milan: Apologie de David* (Paris 1977).

Hagendahl, H. *Studia Ammianea* (Uppsala 1921).

———. "Methods of citation in post-classical prose," *Eranos* 45 (1947), 114–28.

——— *Latin Fathers and the Classics* (Göteborg 1958).

———. *Augustine and the Latin Classics* 1–2 (Göteborg 1967).

———. "Jerome and the Latin Classics," *Vig. Christ.* 28 (1974), 216–27.

Hahn, J. "The conversion of the cult statues: The destruction of the Serapeum 392 AD and the transformation of Alexandria into the 'Christ-loving' city," in J. Hahn, S. Emmel, and U. Gotter (eds.), *From Temple to Church: Destruction and Renewal of Local Cultic Topography in Late Antiquity* (Leiden 2008), 335–65.

Hamilton, R. "Fatal Texts: The *Sortes Vergilianae*," *Classical and Modern Literature* 13 (1993), 309–36.

Hammond, N. G. L. "Some passages of Polyaenus..." *GRBS* 37 (1996), 23–53.

Hannestad, N. *Tradition in Late Antique Sculpture* (Aarhus 1994).

Hansen, G. C. *Sokrates Kirchengeschichte* (Berlin 1995).

Hansen, W. *Phlegon of Tralles' Book of Marvels* (Exeter 1996).

Hanson, A. "Galen: Author and critic" in G. W. Most (ed.), *Editing Texts* (Göttingen 1998), 22–53.

Harl, K. W. "Sacrifice and pagan belief in fifth- and sixth-century Byzantium," *Past and Present* 128 (1990), 7–27.

Harl, M. "La dénonciation des festivités profanes dans le discours épiscopal et monastique, en orient chrétien, à la fin du IVe siècle," in *La fête, pratique et discours* (Annales littéraires de l'université de Besançon 262) (Paris 1981), 123–47.

Harmand, L. *Le patronat sur les collectivités publiques* (Paris 1957).

Harries, J. "Prudentius and Theodosius," *Latomus* 43 (1984), 69–84.

———. "The Roman Imperial Quaestor from Constantine to Theodosius II," *JRS* 78 (1988), 148–72.

———. *Sidonius Apollinaris and the Fall of Rome* (Oxford 1994).

———. *Law and Empire in Late Antiquity* (Cambridge 1999).

Harries, J., and Ian Wood (eds.). *The Theodosian Code* (Ithaca 1993).

Harris, W. V. "Why did the Codex supplant the Book-Roll?" in *Renaissance Society and Culture: Essays in Honor of Eugene F. Rice, Jr.* (New York 1991), 71–85.

——— (ed.). *The Transformations of Urbs Roma in Late Antiquity* (Portsmouth 1999).

———. "Constantine's dream," *Klio* 87 (2005), 488–94.

———. *Dreams and Experience in Classical Antiquity* (Cambridge, Mass. 2009).

Harrison, S. J. *Vergil: Aeneid 10* (Oxford 1991).

Hartke, W. *Geschichte und Politik im spätantiken Rom* (= *Klio*, Beiheft 32) (Leipzig 1940).

Haverling, G. *Studies on Symmachus' Language and Style* (Göteborg 1988).

———. "Symmachus and Greek literature," in S.-V. Teodorsson (ed.), *Greek and Latin Studies in Memory of Cajus Fabricius* (Göteborg 1990), 188–205.

Hägg, T. "Hierocles the lover of truth and Eusebius the Sophist," *Symbol. Osl.* 67 (1992), 138–50.

Heath, T. L. *Euclid: The Thirteen Books of the Elements* 1^2 (London 1926), 46–63.

Heather, P. "New men for new Constantines? Creating an imperial elite in the eastern Mediterranean," in P. Magdalino (ed.), *New Constantines: The Rhythm of Imperial Renewal in Byzantium* (Aldershot 1994), 11–33.

Heather, P., and J. Matthews. *The Goths in the Fourth Century* (Liverpool 1991).

Hedrick, C. *History and Silence: Purge and Rehabilitation of Memory in Late Antiquity* (Austin 2000).

Heim, F. "Le thème de la 'victoire sans combat' chez Ambroise," in Duval 1974, 267–81.

——— "Les auspices publics de Constantin à Théodose," *Ktéma* 13 (1988), 41–53.

——— *La théologie de la victoire de Constantin à Théodose* (Paris 1992).

Heinzberger, F. *Heidnische und Christliche Reaktion auf die Krisen des weströmischen Reiches in den Jahren 395–410 n. Chr.* (Bonn 1976).

Henig, M., and A. King (eds.). *Pagan Gods and Shrines of the Roman Empire* (Oxford 1986).

Heraeus, W. *Die Sprache des Petronius und die Glossen* (Leipzig 1899).

———. "Über einige Variantenzeichen," *Paleographia Latina* 4 (1925), 5–14.

Hermanowicz, E. T. "Catholic bishops and appeals to the imperial court," *JECS* 12 (2004), 481–521.

Highet, G. *Juvenal the Satirist* (Oxford 1954).

Hill, E. *Works of Saint Augustine: Sermons* III. 11 (New York 1997).

Hind, J. "The Portland vase: New clues towards old solutions," *JHS* 115 (1995), 153–55.

Hinds, S. *Allusion and Intertext: Dynamics of Appropriation in Roman Poetry* (Cambridge 1998).

Hoffer, E. *The Anxieties of Pliny the Younger* (Atlanta 1999).

Lewis, M.W.H. *The Official Priests of Rome under the Julio-Claudians* (Rome 1955).

Hofmann H. (ed.). *Latin Fiction* (London 1999).

Hohl, E. "Über den Ursprung der Historia Augusta," *Hermes* 55 (1920), 296–310.

Holford-Strevens, L. *Aulus Gellius*² (Oxford 2003).

———, and A. Vardi (eds.). *The Worlds of Aulus Gellius* (Oxford 2004).

Hollis, A. *Fragments of Roman Poetry* (Oxford 2007).

Holtz, L. *Donat et la tradition de l'enseignement grammatical* (Paris 1981).

Homes Dudden, F. *The Life and Times of St Ambrose* 1–2 (Oxford 1935).

Honoré, T. "Scriptor Historiae Augustae," *JRS* 77 (1987), 156–76.

———. *Law in the Crisis of Empire 379–455 AD* (Oxford 1998), 59–70.

Honoré, T., and J. Matthews. *Virius Nicomachus Flavianus, Xenia* 23 (Konstanz 1989).

Hopkins, K. "The Age of Roman Girls at Marriage," *Population Studies* 18 (1965), 309–27.

———. *Conquerors and Slaves* (Cambridge 1978).

Horsfall, N. "Two problems of late imperial literary history," *Tria Lustra: Essays and Notes Presented to John Pinsent* (Liverpool 1993), 321–22.

———. "Apollonius of Tyana, Bibliomancy," *Historiae Augustae Colloquium Maceratense* 3 (Bari 1995), 169–77.

——— (ed.). *A Companion to the Study of Virgil* (Leiden 1995).

Hölscher, T. *The Language of Images in Roman Art*, English translation by A. Snodgrass and A. Künzl-Snodgrass (Cambridge 2004).

Hubaux, J. "La crise de la trois cent soixante cinquième année," *L'Antiquité classique* 17 (1948), 343–54.

Hubert, K. "Zur indirekten Überlieferung der Tischgespräche Plutarchs," *Hermes* 73 (1938), 307–17.

Hunger, H., O. Stegmüller, H. Erbse (eds.). *Geschichte der Textüberlieferung der antiken und mittelalterlichen Literatur* 1 (Munich 1961).

Hunter, D. G. *Marriage, Celibacy and Heresy in Ancient Christianity: The Jovinianist Controversy* (Oxford 2007).

Hurley, D. *Historical Commentary on Suetonius' Caligula* (Atlanta 1993).

Ihm, M. "Die Epigramme des Damasus," *Rhein. Mus.* 59 (1895), 191–204.

———. "Zu lateinischen Dichtern," *Rhein. Mus.* 52 (1899), 191–204.

Instinsky, H. U. "Formalien im Briefwechsel des Plinius mit Kaiser Trajan," *Abhandl. d. Akad. d. Wiss. in Mainz* (1969), 12.

Jahn, O. "Über die Subscriptionen in den Handschriften römischer Classiker," *Berichte der sächs. Gesell. der Wiss. zu Leipzig* (1851), 327–72.

Janson, T. *Latin Prose Prefaces: Studies in Literary Conventions* (Stockholm 1964).

Jeffreys, E., B. Croke, and R. Scott (eds.). *Studies in John Malalas* (Sydney 1990).

Jenkins, R. G. "Colophons of the Syrohexapla and the Textgeschichte of the recensions of Origen," *VII Congress of the International Organization for Septuagint and Cognate Studies* (Atlanta 1991), 261–77.

Jenkyns, R. *The Victorians and Ancient Greece* (Cambridge, Mass. 1980).

Jocelyn, H. D. "Ancient scholarship and Virgil's use of Republican Latin poetry," *CQ* 14 (1964), 280–95; and 15 (1965), 126–44.

———. "The quotations of Republican drama in Priscian's De metris," *Antichthon* 1 (1967), 60–69.

———. "Servius Daniel. ad Aen iv. 219…," *GIF* 12 (1981), 107–16.

———. "Varro's *Antiquitates rerum divinarum* and religious affairs in the late Roman Republic," *Bull. John Rylands Library* 65 (1982), 148–205.

———. "The Annotations of M. Valerius Probus," *CQ* 34 (1984), 464–72; 35 (1985), 149–61, 473–79.

Johne, K.-P. *Kaiserbiographie und Senatsaristokratie: Untersuchungen zur Datierung und sozialen Herkunft der Historia Augusta* (Berlin 1974).

Jones, C. P. *Plutarch and Rome* (Oxford 1971).

———. "An epigram on Apollonius of Tyana," *JHS* 100 (1980), 190–94.

———. "Apollonius of Tyana in Late Antiquity," in S. F. Johnson (ed.), *Greek Literature in Late Antiquity* (Ashgate 2006), 49–52.

———. Obituary of Herbert Bloch, *Proc. Amer. Phil. Soc.* 152 (2008), 533–40.

Jones, C. P., and G. W. Bowersock. *Philostratus, Life of Apollonius* (Penguin 1970).

Jones, P., and N. Pennick. *A History of Pagan Europe* (London 1995).

Jones, R. E. "Cicero's accuracy of characterization in his dialogues," *AJP* 60 (1939), 307–25.

Jüthner, J. *Hellenen und Barbaren* (Leipzig 1923).

Kaegi, W. E. *Byzantium and the Decline of Rome* (Princeton 1968).

Kahlos, M. "The Restoration Policy of V. A. Praetextatus," *Arctos* 29 (1995), 39–47.

——— . *Vettius Agorius Praetextatus* (Rome 2002).

——— . *Debate and Dialogue: Christian and Pagan Culture c. 360–430* (Ashgate 2007).

Kaimio, J. *The Romans and the Greek Language.* Comm. Hum. Litt. 64 (Helsinki 1979).

Kajanto, I. *Onomastic Studies in the Early Christian Inscriptions of Rome and Carthage* (Helsinki 1963).

——— . *Supernomina: A Study in Latin Epigraphy* (Helsinki 1966).

Kaldellis, A. "The religion of Ioannes Lydos," *Phoenix* 57 (2003), 300–316.

——— . *Procopius of Caesarea*(Philadelphia 2004).

——— . "The works and days of Hesychius the Illoustrios from Miletos," *GRBS* 45 (2005), 381–403.

Kaster, R. A. "Macrobius and Servius: Verecundia and the grammarian's function," *HSCP* 84 (1980), 219–62.

——— *Guardians of Language* (Berkeley 1988).

Katz, P. B. "The *Sortes Vergilianae*: Fact and fiction," Classical and Modern Literature 14 (1994), 245–58.

Keenan, M. E. *The Life and Times of Augustine as Revealed in His Letters* (Washington 1935).

Kelly, D. *The Conspiracy of Allusion: Description, Rewriting, and Authorship from Macrobius to Medieval Romance* (Leiden 1999).

Kelly, G. *Ammianus Marcellinus: The Allusive Historian* (Cambridge 2008).

Kelly, J. N. D. *Jerome: His Life, Writings, and Controversies* (London 1975).

Kennedy, G. A. "The ancient dispute over rhetoric in Homer," *AJP* 78 (1957), 23–35.

Kienast, D. *Römische Kaisertabelle. Grundzüge einer römischen Kaiserchronologie*, 2 ed. Darmstadt 1990).

Kiilerich, B. "A different interpretation of the Nicomachorum-Symmachorum diptych," *JbAC* 34 (1991), 115–28.

——— . *Late Fourth Century Classicism in the Plastic Arts* (Odense 1993).

Kiilerich, B., and H. Torp. "Hic est, hic Stilicho. The date and interpretation of a notable diptych," *JDAI* 104 (1989), 319–71.

——— . "Mythological sculpture in the fourth century AD: The Esquiline group and the Silahtarağa statues," *Istanbuler Mittheilungen* 44 (1994), 307–16.

King, C. "Ammianus Marcellinus' description of the Huns," *AJAH* 12 (1987), 77–95.

King, N. Q. *Theodosius* (1960 Philadelphia).

Kinney, D. "The iconography of the Ivory Diptych Nicomachorum-Symmachorum," *Jahrbuch für Antike und Christentum* 37 (1994), 64–96, with plates 4–12.

Kinzig, W. " 'Trample upon me'..., the Sophist Asterius and Hecebolius: Turncoats in the fourth century AD," *Christian Faith and Greek Philosophy: Essays...G. C. Stead* (Leiden 1993), 92–111.

Kitzinger, E. *Early Medieval Art* (London 1940).

——— . *Byzantine Art in the Making* (Cambridge, Mass. 1977).

Klein, R. *Symmachus* (Darmstadt 1971).

Kleiner, D. E. E. *Roman Sculpture* (New Haven 1992).

Klingner, F. "Vom Geisteswesen im Rom des ausgehendes Altertums," in *Römisches Geisteswelt*[4] (Munich 1961).

Klingshirn, W. *Caesarius of Arles: The Making of a Christian Community in Late Antique Gaul* (Cambridge 1994).

Klotz, A. "Studien zu den Panegyrici Latini," *Rh. Mus.* 66 (1911), 513–72.

———. "Studien zu Valerius Maxcimus und den Exempla," *Sitzungber. Bay. Akad.* 5 (1942), 5–104.

Knoche, U. *Handschriftliche Grundlagen der Juvenaltextes*, Philol. Suppl. 33 (1940).

Knox, P. E. "Phaethon in Ovid and Nonnus," *CQ* 38 (1988), 536–51.

Koch, C. *Religio* (Nürnberg 1960).

Koetschau, P. *Die Textüberlieferung der Bücher des Origenes gegen Celsus*, Texte und Unters 6 1 (Leipzig 1889).

Kofsky, A. *Eusebius of Caesarea against Paganism* (Brill 2000).

Kohns, H.-P. *Versorgungskrisen und Hungerrevolten im spätantiken Rom* (Bonn 1961).

Kolb, F. *Diocletian und die erste Tetrarchie* (Berlin 1987).

———. "Politische Terminologie und historisches Milieu: Kinderkaiser und Parens Principis in der Historia Augusta," in Bonamente and Rosen (eds.) 1997, 153–60.

Kondoleon, C. *Domestic and Divine: Roman Mosaics in the House of Dionysos* (Ithaca 1995).

Kovač, M. "Bora or summer storm: Meteorological aspects of the battle at Frigidus," in Bratož (ed.) 1996, 109–18.

Köcher, A. *De Ioannis Antiocheni aetate fontibus auctoritate* (Bonn 1871), 20.

Kragelund, P. "Epicurus, Ps-Quintilian and the rhetor at Trajan's forum," *Classica et Mediaevalia* 42 (1991), 259–75.

Krautheimer, R. *Three Christian Capitals* (Berkeley 1983).

Kroll, W. *De Q. Aurelii Symmachi studiis graecis et latinis* (Breslau 1891).

Kudlien, F. "Krankheitsmetaphorik im Laurentius hymnus des Prudentius," *Hermes* 90 (1962), 104–15.

Kunkel, W. *Herkunft und soziale Stellung der römischen Juristen* (Weimar 1952).

Kuttner, A. *Dynasty and Empire in the Age of Augustus: The Case of the Boscoreale Cups* (Berkeley 1995).

Küppers, J. *Die Fabeln Avians* (Bonn 1977).

La Bonnardière, A.-M. "Les *enarrationes in psalmos* prêchées par saint Augustin à Carthage en décembre 409," *Rech. Augustin.* 11 (1976), 52–90.

Labrousse, M. *Optat de Milève: Traité contre les donatistes* 1 (Paris 1995).

Lamirande, É. *Paulin de Milan et la Vita Ambrosii* (Montreal 1983).

Lana, I. *Rutilio Namaziano* (Turin 1961).

———. "Ammiano Marcellino e la sua conoscenza degli autori greci," in F. Conca, I. Gualandri, and G. Lozza (eds.), *Politica, cultura e religione nell'impero romano (s. IV–VI) tra oriente e occidente* (Naples 1993), 23–40.

———. "Q. Giulio Ilariano e il problema della storiografia latina cristiana nel IV secolo," *Riv. di Fil.* 123 (1995), 73–89.

Lançon, B. *Rome dans l'Antiquité tardive* (Paris 1995).

Lane Fox, R. *Pagans and Christians* (New York 1987).

———. "The itinerary of Alexander," *CQ* 47 (1997), at 240–47.

Langlois, P. "Sur la correspondance de Symmaque," *Rev. de Phil.* 48 (1974), 92–95.

Lasko, P. "An unnoticed leaf of a late antique ivory diptych and the temple of Mercury in Rome," in A. Borg and A. Martindale (eds.), *The Vanishing Past: Studies of Medieval Art, Literature and Metrology Presented to Christopher Hohler*, BAR International Series 111 (Oxford 1981), 89–93.

Latte, K. *Römische Religionsgeschichte* (Munich 1960).

Laughton, E. "The Prose of Ennius," *Eranos* 49 (1951), 35–49 (with E. Fraenkel ib. 50–56).

Lausberg, H. *Handbook of Literary Rhetoric*, English translation (Leiden 1998).

Lavin, I. "Hunting mosaics of Antioch and their sources," *DOP* 17 (1963), 179–286.

Lawlor, H. J., and J. E. L. Oulton. *Eusebius: The Ecclesiastical History* 2 (London 1928).

Leader-Newby, Ruth E. *Silver and Society in Late Antiquity: Functions and Meanings of Silver Plate in the Fourth to Seventh Centuries* (Ashgate 2004).

Lebek, W. *Verba Prisca* (Göttingen 1970).

Lee, A. D. *Pagans and Christians in Late Antiquity* (London 2000).

———. *War in Late Antiquity: A Social History* (Oxford 2007).

Le Gall, J. "Jupiter et les grands cols des Alpes Occidentales," in R. Chevallier (ed.), *Actes du Colloque international sur les Cols des Alpes* (Bourg-en-Bresse 1969), 171–78.

Le Goff, J. *Time, Work and Culture in the Middle Ages*, English translation (Chicago 1980).

———. *Medieval History*, trans. J. Barrow (Oxford 1988).

Lehmann, P. *Pseudo-antike Literatur des Mittelalters* (Leipzig 1927).

Leitschuh, F. *Katalog der Handschriften der Königlichen Bibliothek zu Bamberg* 1. 2 (Bamberg 1895).

Lemerle, P. *Le premier humanisme byzantin* (Paris 1971).

———. *Byzantine Humanism*, English translation by H. Lindsay and A. Moffat (Canberra 1986).

Lenaz, L. *Martiani Capellae…liber secundus* (Padua 1975).

———. "Annotazioni sul *Carmen contra paganos*," *Studia patavina* 25 (1978), 541–72.

———. "Regitur fato si Iuppiter ipse…," *Perennitas: Studi in onore di Angelo Brelich* (Rome 1980), 293–309.

Lendon, J. E. *Empire of Honour* (Oxford 1997).

Lenski, N. *Failure of Empire: Valens and the Roman State in the Fourth Century AD* (Berkeley 2002).

Lepelley, C. *Les cités de l'Afrique romaine au Bas-Empire* 1–2 (Paris 1979, 1981).

———. "L'aristocratie lettrée païenne: Une menace aux yeux d'Augustin," in G. Madec (ed.), *Augustin prédicateur (395–411)* (Paris 1998), 327–42.

———. *Aspects de l'Afrique romaine* (Bari 2001).

———. "La diabolisation du paganisme et ses conséquences psychologiques," in L. Mary and M. Sot, *Impies et païens entre Antiquité et Moyen Age* (Paris 2002), 83–96.

Leppin, H. *Von Constantin dem Grossen zu Theodosius II: Das christliche Kaisertum bei den Kirchenhistorikern Socrates, Sozomenus und Theodoret* (Göttingen 1996).

———. "Heretical historiography: Philostorgius," *Studia Patristica* 34 (2001), 111–24.

———. *Theodosius der Grosse: Auf dem Weg zum christlichen Imperium* (Darmstadt 2003).

Lersch, L. "Römische Diorthosen," *Museum der Rheinische Westphälischen Schulmänner-Vereins* 3 (1845), 229–74.

Levi, D. *Antioch Mosaic Pavements* 1 (Princeton 1947).

Levine, P. "The continuity and preservation of the Roman tradition," in L. White Jr. (ed.), *The Transformation of the Roman World* (Berkeley 1966).

Lewis, N. *Papyrus in Classical Antiquity* (Oxford 1974).

Liebenam, W. *Städteverwaltung im römischen Kaiserreiche* (Leipzig 1900).

Liebeschuetz, J. H. W. G. *Antioch: City and Imperial Administration in the Later Roman Empire* (Oxford 1972).

———. *Continuity and Change in Roman Religion* (Oxford 1979).

———. "The significance of the speech of Praetextatus," in P. Athanassiadi and M. Frede (eds.), *Pagan Monotheism in Late Antiquity* (Oxford 1999), 186.

———. *The Decline and Fall of the Roman City* (Oxford 2001).

———. "Pagan historiography and the decline of the Empire," in Marasco 2003, 177–218.

Liebeschuetz, J. H. W. G., and Carole Hill. *Ambrose of Milan: Political Letters and Speeches* (Liverpool 2005).

Liénard, É. "La Collatio Alexandri et Dindymi," *Rev. belge de phil.* 15 (1936), 819–38.

Lim, R. "People as power: Games, munificence, and contested topography," in Harris (ed.) 1999, 265–81.

Linderski, J. "*Exta* and *aves*: An emendation in Rufinus, *Origenis in Numeros Homilia* 17. 2," *HSCP* 85 (1981), 213–15 = *Roman Questions* (Stuttgart 1995), 524–26.

———. "The Augural Law," in *ANRW* 2. 16. 3 (1986), 2146–312.

Lindsay, W. M. *Nonius Marcellus' Dictionary of Republican Latin* (Oxford 1901).

———. *Ancient Editions of Martial* (Oxford 1903).

Lippold, A. (ed.). *Orosio: Le storie contro i pagani* 1–2 (Verona 1976).

———. *Theodosius der Grosse*² (1980).

———. *Kommentar zur Vita Maximini Duo der Historia Augusta* (Bonn 1991).

Litchfield, H. W. "National *Exempla Virtutis* in Roman literature," *HSCP* 25 (1914), 1–71.

Lizzi Testa, R. *Vescovi e strutture ecclesiastiche nella città tardoantica* (1989).

———. "Ambrose's contemporaries and the Christianization of northern Italy," *JRS* 80 (1990), 156–73.

———. "Vergini di Dio-vergini di Vesta: Il sesso negato e la sacralità," in S. Pricoco (ed.), *L'Eros Difficile: Amore e sessualità nell'antico cristianesimo* (1998), 89–132.

———. "Paganesimo politico e politica edilizia: La 'cura urbis' nella tarda antichità," in *Atti dell'Accademia Romanistica Costantiniana* 13 (2001), 671–707.

———. *Senatori, popolo, papi: Il governo di Roma al tempo dei Valentiniani* (Bari 2004).

———. "Christian emperor, Vestal virgins and priestly colleges: Reconsidering the end of Roman paganism," *An. Tard.* 15 (2007), 251–62.

Llewellyn, P. *Rome in the Dark Ages* (London 1970).

Lloyd, R. B. "Republican authors in Servius and the Scholia Danielis," *HSCP* 65 (1961), 291–341.

Lommatzsch, E. "Literarische Bewegungen in Rom im vierten und fünften Jahrhundert n. Christ," *Zeitschr. für vergleichende Literaturgeschichte* 15 (1904), 177–92.

Lo Monaco, F. "Note sull'esegesi oraziana antica," *Studia Classica I. Tarditi oblata* (Milan 1995), 1203–24.

Long, J. *Claudian's In Eutropium: Or, How, When, and Why to Slander a Eunuch* (Chapel Hill 1996).

———. "Juvenal Renewed in Claudian's *In Eutropium*," *International Journal of the Classical Tradition* 2 (1996), 321–35 [1996a].

Lorenz, R. "Die Anfänge des abendländischen Mönchtums im 4. Jahrhundert," *Zeitschrift für Kirchengeschichte* 77 (1966), 1–61.

Lowe, E. A. *Palaeographical Papers* 1–2 (Oxford 1972).

Lowe, E. A., and E. K. Rand. *A Sixth-Century Fragment of the Letters of Pliny the Younger* (Washington, D.C. 1922).

Loyen, A. *Sidoine et l'esprit précieux en Gaule aux derniers jours de l'empire* (Paris 1943).

———. "Études sur Sidoine Apollinaire," *RÉL* 46 (1968), 83–90.

———. *Sidoine Apollinaire* 3 (Paris 1970).

Löfstedt, E. *Philologischer Kommentar zur Peregrinatio Aetheriae* (Uppsala 1911).

Lögdberg, G. *In Macrobii Saturnalia Adnotationes* (Uppsala 1936).

Luebeck, A. *Hieronymus quos noverit scriptores* (Leipzig 1872).

Lugton, R. C., and M. G. Saltzer (eds.). *Studies in Honor of J. Alexander Kerns* (The Hague 1970), 108–20.

Maas, M. "Roman history and Christian ideology in Justinianic reform legislation," in *Dumbarton Oaks Papers* 40 (1986), 17–31.

———. *John Lydus and the Roman Past* (London 1992).

MacBain, B. *Prodigy and Expiation* (Brussels 1982).

MacCormack, S. *Art and Ceremony in Late Antiquity* (Berkeley 1981), 150.

———. *The Shadows of Poetry: Vergil in the Mind of Augustine* (Berkeley 1998).

MacMullen, R. *Paganism in the Roman Empire* (New Haven 1981).

———. *Christianizing the Roman Empire* (New Haven 1984).

———. "Judicial savagery in the Roman Empire," *Chiron* 16 (1986), 147–66.

———. *Christianity and Paganism in the Fourth to Eighth Centuries* (New Haven 1997).

Madec, G. *Saint Ambroise et la philosophie* (Paris 1974).

———. "L'historicité des *Dialogues* de Cassiacum," *Revue des Études Augustiniennes* 32 (1986), 207–31.

Maenchen-Helfen, O. J. "The date of Ammianus Marcellinus' last books," *AJP* 76 (1955), 384–99.

Maguire, H. *Byzantine Magic* (Washington, D.C. 1995).

Maier, Harry O. "The topography of heresy and dissent in late-fourth-century Rome," *Historia* 44 (1995), 232–49.

Mandouze, A. *Saint Augustin: L'aventure de la raison et de la grâce* (Paris 1968).

Manganaro, G. "La reazione pagana a Roma nel 408–9 d.C. e il poemetto anonimo Contra Paganos," *GIF* 13 (1960), 210–24.

———. "Il poemetto anonimo *Contra Paganos*," *Nuovo Didaskaleion* 11 (1961), 23–45.

Mango, C. *Le développement urbain de Constantinople (IVᵉ–VIᵉ siècles)* (Paris 1985).

Mannix, M. D. S. *Ambrosii oratio de obitu Theodosii* (Washington, D.C. 1925).

Marache, R. *La Critique littéraire de langue latine et le développement du goût archaïsant au IIᵉ siècle de notre ère* (Rennes 1952).

———. *Mots nouveaux et mots archaïques chez Fronton et Aulu-Gelle* (1957).

Marasco, G. (ed.). *Greek and Roman Historiography in Late Antiquity* (Leiden 2003).

Maraval, P. *Socrate de Constantinople, Histoire Ecclésiastique* 1 (Paris 2004).

Marcone, A. *Commento storico al libro vi dell'epistolario di Q. Aur. Simmaco* (Pisa 1983).

———. *Commento storico al libro iv dell'epistolario di Q. Aur. Simmaco* (Pisa 1987).

———. *Di tarda antichità: Scritti scelti* (Milan 2008).

Marié, M.-A. *Ammien Marcellin: Livres 26–28* (Paris 1984).

Mariev, Sergei. *Ioannis Antiocheni Fragmenta quae supersunt omnia* (Berlin 2008).

Marinone, N. *Elio Donato, Macrobio e Servio* (Vercelli 1946).

———. *I Saturnali di Macrobio Teodosio* (Turin 1967).

———. "Per la cronologia di Servio," *Atti della Accademia delle Scienze di Torino* 104 (1970), 181–211.

Markopoulos, A. Ἡ χρονογραφία τοῦ Ψευδοσυμεών καὶ οἱ πηγές της (Ioannina 1978).

———. "Kedrenos, Pseudo-Symeon, and the Last Oracle at Delphi," *GRBS* 26 (1985), 207–10.

Markschies, C. "Leben wir nicht alle unter demselben Sternenzelt?" in R. Feldmeier and U. Heckel (eds.), *Die Heiden: Juden, Christen und das Problem des Fremden* (Tübingen 1994), 325–77.

Markus, D., and G. Schwendner. "Seneca's *Medea* in Egypt," *ZPE* 117 (1997), 73–80.

Markus, R. A. *Christianity in the Roman World* (London 1974), 130.

———. *The End of Ancient Christianity* (Cambridge 1990).

———. Response in A. H. Sommerstein (ed.), *Religion and Superstition in Latin Literature* (Bari 1996), 77–80.

Marquardt, J. *Römische Staatsverwaltung* 2², H. Dessau and A. von Domaszewski (eds.) (Leipzig 1884).

Marriot, Ian. "The authorship of the *Historia Augusta*: Two computer studies," *JRS* 69 (1979), 65–77.

Marrou, H.-I. "La vie intellectuelle au Forum de Trajan et au Forum d'Auguste," *MEFR* 49 (1932), 93–110 = *Patristique et humanisme* (Paris 1976), 65–80 (with additions).

———. *Saint Augustin et la fin de la culture antique* (Paris 1938, 1958²).

———. "La technique de l'édition à l'époque patristique," *Vig. Christ.* 3 (1949), 208–24.

———. "La division en chapitres des livres de *La Cité du Dieu*," *Mélanges J. de Ghellinck* 1 (Gembloux 1951), 247–49.

———. *Histoire de l'éducation dans l'antiquité*⁶ (Paris 1965).

Marshall, P. K. *The Manuscript Tradition of Cornelius Nepos*, BICS Suppl. 37 (London 1977).

Martin, D. E. "The Statilius-subscription and the editions of late antiquity," in D. F. Bright and E. S. Ramage (eds.), *Classical Texts and Their Traditions* (Chicago 1984), 147–54.

Martin, J. *Symposion: Die Geschichte einer literarischen Form* (Paderborn 1931).

Martindale, C. (ed.). *Cambridge Companion to Virgil* (Cambridge 1997).

Martínez-Fazio, L. M. *La segunda basilica de San Pablo extramuros* (Rome 1972).

Marzano, A. *Roman Villas in Central Italy: A Social and Economic History* (Leiden 2007).

Maslakov, G. "The Roman antiquarian tradition in Late Antiquity," in B. Croke and A. Emmett, *History and Historians in Late Antiquity* (Sydney 1983), 100–106.

Mason, H. J. *Greek Terms for Roman Institutions* (Toronto 1974).

Mastandrea, P. "Il dossier Longiniano nell'epistolario di sant'Agostino," *Studia patavina* 25 (1978), 523–40.

——— *Un neoplatonico latino: Cornelio Labeone* (Leiden 1969).

Mathews, T. *The Clash of Gods: A Reinterpretation of Early Christian Art*² (Princeton 1994).

———. "The emperor and the icon," *Acta ad archaeologiam et artium historiam pertinentia* 15 (2001), 168–77.

Mathisen, R. W. *Ecclesiastical Factionalism and Religious Controversy in Fifth-Century Gaul* (Washington, D.C. 1989).

———. "Imperial honorifics and senatorial status," in R. W. Mathisen (ed.), *Law, Society and Authority in Late Antiquity* (Oxford 2001), 179–207.

Matthews, J. "Continuity in a Roman family: The Rufii Festi of Volsinii," *Historia* 16 (1967), 484–509.

———. "The historical setting of the Carmen Contra Paganos," *Historia* 19 (1970), 464–79.

———. "Olympiodorus of Thebes and the history of the West (407–425)," *JRS* 60 (1970), 79–97.

——— "Symmachus and the *magister militum* Theodosius," *Historia* 20 (1971), 122–28.

———. "Symmachus and the Oriental cults," *JRS* 63 (1973), 175–95.

———. "The letters of Symmachus," in J. W. Binns (ed.), *Latin Literature of the Fourth Century* (London 1974), 75–77.

———. *Western Aristocracies and Imperial Court* (Oxford 1975, 1990²).

———. *Political Life and Culture in Late Roman Society* (London 1985).

———. "Symmachus and his enemies," in Paschoud (ed.) 1986, 163–75.

———. "Nicomachus Flavianus' Quaestorship: The historical evidence," in W. Schuller (ed.), *Xenia: Konstanzer althistorische Vorträge und Forschungen* 23 (1989), 18–25.

———. *The Roman Empire of Ammianus* (London 1989).

———. "The poetess Proba and fourth-century Rome," in Christol et al. (eds.) 1992, 277–304.

———. "The origin of Ammianus," *CQ* 44 (1994), 252–69.

———. "Codex Theodosianus 9.4.13 and Nicomachus Flavianus," *Historia* 46 (1997), 196–213.

———. *Laying Down the Law* (New Haven 2000).

Mazza, M. *Il vero e l'immaginato: Profezia, narrativa e storiografia nel mondo romano* (Rome 1999).

Mazzarino, A. "Intorno all età e all'opera di Foca," *Helikon* 13/14 (1973/4), 505–27.

——— . "Paignia," *Helikon* 15–16 (1975–76), 556–58.

Mazzarino, S. "La politica religiosa di Stilicone," *Rendiconti Istituto Lombardo* 71 (1938), 236–63.

——— . *Stilicone: La crisi imperiale dopo Teodosio* (1942).

——— . "La propaganda senatoria nel tardo impero," *Doxa* 4 (1951), 121–48.

——— . *Il Pensiero storico classico* ii (Bari 1966).

——— . *Antico, tardoantico ed èra costantiniana* 1–2 (Rome 1974–80).

McCann, A. M. *Roman Sarcophagi in The Metropolitan Museum of Art* (New York 1978).

McCormick, M. *Eternal Victory* (Cambridge 1986).

McDonnell, M. "Writing, copying and autograph manuscripts in ancient Rome," *CQ* 46 (1996), 474–77.

McDonough, C. M. "Women at the Ara Maxima in the fourth century AD?" *CQ* 54 (2004), 655–58.

McGeachy, J. A. Jr. *Q. Aurelius Symmachus and the Senatorial Aristocracy of the West* (Chicago 1942).

——— . "The editing of the *Letters* of Symmachus," *CP* 44 (1949), 222–29.

McLynn, N. B. *Ambrose of Milan: Church and Court in a Christian Capital* (Berkeley 1994).

——— . "The fourth-century *taurobolium*," *Phoenix* 50 (1996), 312–30.

——— . "*Genere Hispanus*: Theodosius, Spain and Nicene orthodoxy," in K. Bowes and M. Kulikowski (eds.), *Hispania in N. Late Antiquity* (Leiden 2005), 121–49.

——— . "Crying wolf: The Pope and the Lupercalia," *JRS* 98 (2008), 161–75.

——— . "Pagans in a Christian empire," in P. Rousseau (ed.), *A Companion to Late Antiquity* (Oxford 2009), 572–87.

McNamee, K. *Abbreviations in Greek Literary Papyri* (1981).

——— . "Aristarchus and 'Everyman's' Homer," *GRBS* 22 (1981), 247–55.

——— . "Greek literary papyri revised by two or more hands," *Proceedings of the XVI International Congress of Papyrology* (Chico 1981), 79–91.

——— . *Papiri letterari greci e latini*, ed. M. Capasso (Lecce 1992), 15–51.

——— . "Another chapter in the history of scholia," *CQ* 48 (1998), 269–88.

——— . *Annotations in Greek and Latin Texts from Egypt*, American Studies in Papyrology 45 (2007).

McNeil, M. D. "The Latin manuscript tradition of the *Vita Sancti Hilarionis*," in W. A. Oldfather (ed.), *Studies in the Text Tradition of St. Jerome's Vitae Patrum* (Urbana 1943), 251–305.

Megow, W.-R. *Kameen von Augustus bis Alexander Severus* (Berlin 1987).

Meiggs, R. *Roman Ostia*² (Oxford 1973).

Meissner, B. "Computergestützte Untersuchungen zur stilistichen Einheitlichkeit der Historia Augusta," in Bonamente and Rosen (eds.) (1997), 175–215.

Mendelssohn, L. *Zosimi Historia Nova* (Leipzig 1887).

Mercati, G. *Nuove Note di letteratura biblica e cristiana antica* (Vatican 1941).

Mesk, J. "Zur Technik der lateinischen Panegyriker," *WS* 34 (1912), 246–52.

Meslin, A. *La fête des kalendes de Janvier dans l'empire Romain* (Brussels 1970).

Mestra, H. J. "Augustine and Poetic Exegesis," in W. Otten and K. Pollmann (eds.), *Poetry and Exegesis in Premodern Latin Christianity* (Leiden 2007), 11–28.

Méthy, N. *Les lettres de Pline the Jeune* (Paris 2007).

Miguélez Cavero, L. *Poems in Context: Greek Poetry in the Egyptian Thebaid* (Berlin 2008).

Millar, F. "P. Herennius Dexippus: The Greek world and the third century invasions," *JRS* 59 (1969), 12–29.

———. *The Emperor in the Roman World* (London 1977).

———. *A Greek Roman Empire: Power and Belief under Theodosius II (408–450)* (Berkeley 2006).

Mitchell, S. *A History of the Later Roman Empire AD 284–641* (Oxford 2007), 88–89.

Mittag, P. F. *Alte Köpfe in neuen Händen: Urheber und Funktion der Kontorniaten* (Bonn 1999).

Mohrmann, C. "Encore une fois: *paganus*," *Vig. Christ.* 6 (1952), 109–21 = *Étude sur le latin des chrétiens* 3 (Rome 1965), 277–89.

Mohrmann, C., and A. A. R. Bastiaensen (eds.). *Vite dei Santi* 3 (*Vite di Cipriano, Ambrogio, Agostino*) (Milan 1975).

Moine, N. "Melaniana," *Rech. Augustiniennes* 15 (1980), 3–79.

Molè Ventura, C. *Principi fanciulli: Legittimismo costituzionale e storiografia cristiana nella tarda antichità* (Catania 1992).

Moltesen, M. "The Aphrodisian sculptures in the Ny Carlsberg Glyptotek," in C. Roueché and K. T. Erim (eds.), *Aphrodisias Papers* (Ann Arbor 1990), 133–46.

Momigliano, A. *Secondo Contributo alla Storia degli Studi Classici* (Rome 1960).

———. "Some observations on the *Origo Gentis Romanae*," *JRS* 48 (1958), 56–73 = (1960), 145–76.

——— (ed.). *The Conflict between Paganism and Christianity in the Fourth Century* (1963).

———. "Per la interpretatione di Simmaco Relatio 4," *Rendiconti Acc. Lincei* 19 (1964), 225–30.

———. *Essays in Ancient and Modern Historiography* (Oxford 1977).

———. *On Pagans, Jews and Christians* (Middletown 1987).

Mommsen, T. "Carmen codicis Parisini 8084," *Hermes* 4 (1870), 350–64 = *Gesammelte Schriften* 7 (1909), 485–98.

———. "T. Livii ab Urbe condita…in codice rescripto Veronensi," *Ges. Schriften* 7 (Berlin 1909), 96–148.

Montana, M. F. "Note all'epistolario di Q. Aurelio Simmaco: Simmaco e la cultura greca," *Rendiconti Istituto Lombardo* 95 (1961), 297–316.

Montanari, F. "Zenodotus, Aristarchus and the *Ekdosis* of Homer," in Most (ed.) 1998, 1–20.

Moorhead, J. *Ambrose: Church and Society in the Late Roman World* (London 1999).

Moreau, M. "Le dossier Marcellinus…" *Rech. Aug.* 9 (1974), 6–181.

Morel, C. "Le poème latin du ms. 8084 de la bibliothèque impériale," *Revue critique d'histoire et littérature* 20 (1869), 300–304.

Morelli, C. "L'autore del cosidetto *Poeta ultimum* attribuito a Paolino di Nola," *Didaskaleion* 1 (1912), 481–98.

Morgan, J. R., and R. Stoneman (eds.). *Greek Fiction* (London 1994).

Moroni, B. "Dopo Giuliano: Lingua e cultura greca nella famiglia imperiale fino a Teodosio," in I. Gualandri, F. Conca, R. Passarella (eds.), *Nuovo e antico nella cultura greco-latina di IV–VI secolo* (Milan 2005), 47–99.

Most, G. W. (ed.). *Editing Texts/Texte Edieren*, Aporemata 2 (Göttingen 1998).

Mountford, J. F. *The Scholia Bembina* (Liverpool 1934).

Mratschek, S. *Die Briefwechsel des Paulinus von Nola* (Göttingen 2002).

Munari, F. *Epigrammata Bobiensia* (Rome 1955), 21–22.

Mundell Mango, M., and A. Bennett. *The Sevso Treasure*, part 1 (Ann Arbor 1994).

Munk Olsen, B. *L'Etude des auteurs classiques latins aux XIe et XIIe siècles I: Catalogue des manuscrits classiques latins copiés du IXe–XIIe siècle: Apicius-Juvénal* (Paris 1982).

Murgia, C. E. "Avienus's supposed iambic version of Livy," *CSCA* 3 (1970), 185–97.

———. "Aldhelm and Donatus's Commentary on Vergil," *Philologus* 131 (1987), 289–99.

———. "The Dating of Servius Revisited," *CP* 98 (2003), 45.69.

Murphy, F. X. *Rufinus of Aquileia (345–411); His Life and Works* (Washington, D.C. 1945).

Murray, O. "The quinquennium Neronis and the Stoics," *Historia* 14 (1965), 41–61.

Musso, L. "Il *praefectus* del *carmen contra pagana*: Tra vecchie e nuove interpretazioni," *Archeologia classica* 31 (1979), 185–240 at 215–19.

——— . *Manifattura suntuaria e committenza pagana nella Roma del IV secolo: Indagine sulla lanx di Parabiago* (Rome 1983).

Musurillo, H. *Acts of the Christian Martyrs* (Oxford 1972).

Münzer, F. *Beiträge zur Quellenkritik der Naturgeschichte des Plinius* (Berlin 1897).

Naudé, C. P. T. "The date of the later books of Ammianus Marcellinus," *AJAH* 9 (1984 [in fact, 1990]), 70–94.

Nautin, P. "Les premières relations d'Ambroise avec l'empereur Gratien," in Y.-M. Duval (ed.), *Ambroise de Milan* (Paris 1974), 229–44.

Neri, V. "L'elogio della cultura e l'elogio delle virtù politiche nell'epigrafia latina del IV secolo d. C." *Epigraphica* 43 (1981), 175–201.

——— . "Ammiano Marcellino e l'elezione di Valentiniano," *Rivista storica dell'antichità* 15 (1985), 169.

——— . "Usurpatore come tiranno nel lessico politico della tarda antichità," in F. Paschoud and J. Szidat (eds.), *Usurpationen in der Spätantike* (Stuttgart 1997), 71–86.

Neugebauer, O., and H. B. van Hoesen. *Greek Horoscopes* (Philadelphia 1959).

Nilsson, M. P. *Opuscula Selecta* (Lund 1952).

——— . *The Dionysiac Mysteries of the Hellenistic and Roman Age* (Lund 1957).

Niquet, H. *Monumenta virtutum titulique: Senatorische Selbstdarstellung im spätantiken Rom im Spiegel der epigraphischen Denkmäler* (Stuttgart 2000).

Nisbet, R. G. M. *Collected Papers on Latin Literature* (Oxford 1995).

Nixon, C. E. V. "Aurelius Victor and Julian," *CP* 86 (1991), 113–25.

Nixon, C. E. V., and B. S. Rodgers. *In Praise of Later Roman Emperors: The Panegyrici Latini* (Berkeley 1994).

Nock, A. D. *Essays on Religion and the Ancient World* 1–2 (Oxford 1972).

Noethlichs, K.-L. *Die gesetzgeberischen Massnamen der christlicher Kaiser des vierten Jahrhunderts gegen Häretiker, Heiden und Juden* (Cologne 1971).

Norden, E. *Ennius und Vergilius* (Leipzig 1915).

——— . *Aus altrömischen Priesterbüchen* (Lund 1939).

Norman, A. F. "The book trade in fourth-century Antioch," *JHS* 80 (1960), 122–26.

——— . *Libanius: Autobiography and Selected Letters* 1–2 (Loeb 1992).

North, John. "The development of religious pluralism," in J. Lieu, J. North, and T. Rajak, (eds.), *The Jews among Pagans and Christians in the Roman Empire* (London 1992), 174–93.

——— . "Pagans, polytheists and the pendulum," in W. V. Harris (ed.), *The Spread of Christianity in the FirstFfour Centuries* (Leiden 2005), 125–43.

Noske, G. *Quaestiones Pseudoacroneae* (Munich 1969).

Novak, D. M. "Constantine and the Senate: An early phase of the Christianization of the Roman aristocracy," *Ancient Society* 10 (1979), 271–310.

Oakley, S. P. *A Commentary on Livy Books VI–X* vol. 1 (Oxford 1997).

O'Brien, M. B. *Titles of Address in Christian Latin Epistolography to 543 AD* (Washington, D.C., 1930).

Ochoa, José A. *La transmisión de la Historia de Eunapio* (Madrid 1990).

O'Daly, G. *The Poetry of Boethius* (London 1991).

——— . *Augustine's City of God: A Reader's Guide* (Oxford 1999).

O'Donnell, J. J. "The Demise of Paganism," *Traditio* 35 (1970), 66–67.

——— . "Paganus," *Classical Folia* 31 (1977), 163–69.

———. "The career of Virius Nicomachus Flavianus," *Phoenix* 32 (1978), 129–43.

———. "Augustine's classical readings," *Rech. Aug.* 15 (1980), 144–75.

———. *Augustine: Confessions 1–3* (Oxford 1992).

O'Flynn, John M. "A Greek on the Roman throne: The fate of Anthemius," *Historia* 40 (1991), 122–28.

Ogilvie, R. M. "The manuscript tradition of Livy's first decade," *CQ* 7 (1957), 68–81.

———. *A Commentary on Livy Books 1–5* (Oxford 1965).

———. *The Library of Lactantius* (Oxford 1978).

———. "Titi Livi Lib. XCI," *Proc. Camb. Phil. Soc.* 30 (1984), 116–25.

Oikonomidès, N. *Les listes de préséance byzantines des IXᵉ et Xᵉ siècles* (Paris 1972).

O'Meara, J. J. *Porphyry's Philosophy from Oracles in Augustine* (Paris 1959).

Oost, S. I. *Galla Placidia Augusta* (Chicago 1968).

Orlandi, S. *Epigrafia anfiteatrale dell'Occidente Romano 6: Roma. Anfiteatri e strutture annesse con una nuova edizione e commento delle iscrizioni del Colosseo* (Rome 2004).

Overbeck, M. *Untersuchungen zum afrikanischen Senatsadel in der Spätantike* (Kallmünz 1973).

Pabst, A. *Q. Aurelius Symmachus: Reden* (Darmstadt 1989).

Painter, Kenneth. *The Mildenhall Treasure* (London 1977).

Palanque, J.-R. *Saint Ambroise et l'empire romain* (Paris 1933).

———. "Collégialité et partages dans l'empire romain," *RÉA* 46 (1944), 47–64, 280–98.

Palla, R., and M. Corsano. *Ps.-Paolino, Poema ultimum* (Pisa 2002).

Palma, B. "Un gruppo ostiense dei musei vaticani: le fatiche di Eracle," *Rendic. Pont. Acc. rom. di arch.* 51–52 (1978–80), 137–56.

Palmer, A.-M. *Prudentius on the Martyrs* (Oxford 1989).

Palmer, R. E. A. *The King and the Comitium* (Wiesbaden 1969).

Panciera, S. "Un prefetto del pretorio di Massenzio: Manilius Rusticianus," *Institutions… A. Chastagnol* (Rome 1992), 249–63.

———. "Il precettore di Valentiniano III," *Studi… A. Garzetti* (Brescia 1996), 277–97.

———. *Epigrafi, Epigrafia, Epigrafisti: Scritti varii editi e inediti (1956–2005) 1–3* (Rome 2006).

Paratore, E. *Tradizione e struttura in Dante* (Florence 1968).

Paredi, A. "Ambrose of Milan," *Sacris Erudiri* 14 (1963), 206–30.

Parke, H. W. *Sibyls and Sibylline Prophecy in Classical Antiquity* (London 1988).

Parkes, M. B. *Pause and Effect: An Introduction to the History of Punctuation in the West* (Berkeley 1993).

Paschoud, F. *Roma Aeterna* (Rome 1967).

———. *Cinq Études sur Zosime* (Paris 1975).

———. *Zosime, Histoire nouvelle,* 5 vols. (Paris 1979–2000).

——— (ed.). *Colloque génévois sur Symmaque à l'occasion du mille six centième anniversaire du conflit de l'autel de la Victoire* (Paris 1986).

———. "Nicomaque Flavien et la connexion byzantine," *Ant. Tard.* 2 (1994), 71–82.

———. "Les sources du récit des campagnes orientales d'Aurélien," in G. Bonamente and G. Paci (eds.), *Hist. Aug. Coll. Maceratense* (Bari 1995), 281–95.

———. *Histoire Auguste: Vies d'Aurélien et Tacite* (Paris 1996).

———. "Pour un mille six centième anniversaire: Le Frigidus en ebullition," *Antiquité tardive* 5 (1997), 275–80.

———. "Quelques problèmes actuels relatifs à l'historiographie de l'antiquité tardive," *Symbolae Osloenses* 73 (1998), 74–87.

———. "Symmaque, Jérôme et l'Histoire Auguste," *Mus. Helv.* 57 (2000), 176–81.

———. *Histoire Auguste 2* (Paris 2002).

————. "L'auteur de l'Histoire Auguste, est-il un apostat?" in F. Chausson and E. Wolff (eds.), *Consuetudinis Amor: Fragments d'histoire romaine offerts à J. P. Callu* (Rome 2002), 362–68.

————. "Chronographie d'historiographie tardive," *An. tard.* 14 (2006), 325–44 [2006a].

————. *Eunape, Olympiodore, Zosime: Scripta Minora* (Bari 2006).

Paschoud, F., and J. Szidat (eds.). *Usurpationen in der Spätantike* (Stuttgart 1997).

Pasquali, G. *Storia della tradizione e critica del testo*² (Florence 1952).

Patzig, E. "Leo grammaticus und seine Sippe," *BZ* 3 (1894), 470–97.

————. "Über einige Quellen des Zonaras," *BZ* 5 (1896), 24–53; and 6 (1897), at 322–56.

————. "Die römischen Quellen des salmasischen Johannes Antiochenus," *BZ* 13 (1904), 13–50.

Peachin, M. "The Office of the Memory," in E. Chrysos (ed.), *Studien zur Geschichte der röm. Spätantike: Festgabe J. Straub* (Athens 1989), 168–208.

Pease, A. S. "The Attitude of Jerome toward Pagan Literature," *TAPA* 50 (1919), 150–67.

Pecere, O. "La subscriptio di Statilio Massimo," *IMU* 25 (1982), 73–123.

————. "La tradizione dei testi latini tra IV e V secolo attraverso i libri sottoscritti," in A. Giardina (ed.), *Tradizione dei classici: Trasformazioni della cultura* (Bari 1986), 19–81; and "I meccanismi della tradizione testuale," in *Lo spazio letterario di Roma antica* 3 (Rome 1990), 297–386 (both illustrated).

Pellegrino, M. *Paolino: Vita di Ambrogio* (Rome 1961).

Pellizzari, A. *Commento storico al libro iii del epistolario di Q. Aurelio Simmaco* (Pisa 1998).

Penella, R. J. *Greek Philosophers and Sophists in the Fourth Century AD: Studies in Eunapius of Sardis* (Leeds 1990).

————. "Julian the Persecutor in fifth-century church historians," *The Ancient World* 24 (1993), 31–43.

————. *The Private Orations of Themistius* (Berkeley 2000).

Perelli, A. "Nefanda Venus," *GIF* 40 (1988), 241–54.

————. "Suggestioni Claudianee nel *Carmen contra paganos*," in *Disiecti Membra Poetae* 3, V. Tandoi (ed.) (Foggia 1988), 209–25.

Perfigli, M. *Indigitamenta: Divinità funzionali e Funzionalità divina nella Religione Romana* (Pisa 2004).

Perler, O. *Les Voyages de Saint Augustin* (Paris 1969).

Perrelli, R. "La vittoria 'cristiana' del Frigido," in Consolino 1995, 261–62.

Peter, H. *Geschichtliche Literatur über die römische Kaiserzeit bis Theodosius I* 1–2 (Leipzig 1897).

————. *Die Brief in der röm. Literatur* (1901).

Petitmengin, P. "Que signifie la souscription 'contuli'?" *Les lettres de saint Augustin découvertes par Johannes Divjak: Communications présentées au colloque des 20 et 21 Septembre 1982* (Paris 1983), 365–74.

Petitmengin, P., and B. Flusin. "Le livre antique et la dictée," *Mémorial André-Jean Festugière* (Geneva 1984), 249–51.

Petropoulou, M.-Z. *Animal Sacrifice in Ancient Greek Religion, Judaism, and Christianity* (Oxford 2008).

Périchon, P. "Eutrope ou Paeanius? L'historien Socrate se référait-il à une source latine ou grecque?" *REG* 81 (1968), 378–84.

Phillips, C. R. III. "The Compitalia and the Carmen Contra Paganos," *Historia* 37 (1988), 383–84.

Pietri, C. *Roma Christiana: Recherches sur l'Église de Rome* 1–2 (Rome 1976).

————. "Aristocratie et societé cléricale dans l'Italie chrétienne au temps d'Odoacre et de Théodoric," *MEFRA* 93 (1981), 417–67.

Pietri, L. "Évergétisme chrétien et fondations privées dans l'Italie de l'antiquité tardive," in J.-M. Carrié and R. Lizzi Testa (eds.), *Humana Sapit: Études…Lellia Cracco Ruggini* (Turnhout 2002), 253–63.

Piganiol, A. *L'empereur Constantin* (Paris 1932).

——. *L'Empire chrétien*[2] (Paris 1975).

Pighi, I. B. *De ludis saecularibus populi Romani Quiritium,* 2nd ed. (Chicago 1965).

Platner, S. B., and T. Ashby. *Topographical Dictionary of Ancient Rome* (Oxford 1929).

Pohlsander, H. A. "Victory: The story of a statue," *Historia* 18 (1969), 588–97.

Poinsotte, J.-M. "La présence des poèmes antipaïens anonymes dans l'oeuvre de Prudence," *Rev. Ét. Aug.* 28 (1982), 33–58.

Polara, G. "Le iscrizioni sul cippo tombale di Vezzio Agorio Pretestato," *Vichiana* 4 (1967), 40–65.

——. "La fortuna di Simmaco dalla tarda antichità al secolo xvii," *Vichiana* 1 (1972), 250–63.

Porte, D. *Le prêtre à Rome* (Paris 1989).

Porter, James I. *Classical Pasts. The Classical Traditions of Greece and Rome* (Princeton 2006).

Potter, D. S. *Prophecy and History in the Crisis of the Roman Empire: A Historical Commentary on the Thirteenth Sibylline Oracle* (Oxford 1990).

——. *Prophets and Emperors* (Cambridge, Mass. 1994).

——. *The Roman Empire at Bay AD 180–395* (London 2004).

Pratesi, A. "Nuove divagazioni per uno studio della scrittura capitale: I codices Vergiliani antiquiores," *Scrittura e civiltà* 9 (1985), 5–33.

Prete, S. *Il Codice di Terenzio Vat. Lat. 3226,* Studi e Testi 262 (Vatican City 1970).

Préaux, J. "Securus Melior Felix, l'ultime orator urbis Romae," *Corona Gratiarum…E. Dekkers* (Wetteren 1975), 101–21.

Pricoco, S. "Studi su Sidonio Apollinare," *Nuovo Didaskaleion* 15 (1965), 69–150.

Pritchett, W. K. *The Greek State at War* 3 (Berkeley 1979).

Puglisi, G. *Politica e religione nel IV secolo: Le prefetture del 384 e il "Carmen contra paganos"* (Catania 1981).

Raby, F. J. E. *A History of Christian Latin Poetry*[2] (Oxford 1953).

——. *Secular Latin Poetry in the Middle Ages*[2] 1 (Oxford 1957).

Rand, E. K. "Is Donatus's commentary on Virgil lost?" *CQ* 10 (1916), 158–64.

Rapp, C. "Christians and their manuscripts," in G. Cavallo (ed.), *Scritture, libri e testi nelle aree provinciali di Bisanzio* (Spoleto 1991), 127–48.

Ratti, S. "Jérome et Nicomaque Flavien," *Historia* 56 (1997), 479–508.

——. "L'historiographie latine tardive, IIIe–IVe siècle: État des recherches 1987–2002," *Pallas* 63 (2003), 214.

——. "Nicomaque Flavien senior et l'Histoire Auguste: La découverte de nouveaux liens," *RÉA* 85 (2007), 204–19.

——. "Nicomaque senior auteur de l'Histoire Auguste," in Bonamente and Brandt (eds.) 2007, 305–17 [2007a].

Raubitschek, A. E. "Iamblichus at Athens," *Hesperia* 33 (1964), 63–68.

Rawson, E. *Intellectual Life in the Late Roman Republic* (Baltimore 1985).

——. "Sallust on the eighties?" *CQ* 37 (1987), 163–80.

——. *Roman Culture and Society* (Oxford 1991).

Rebenich, S. *Hieronymus und sein Kreis* (Stuttgart 1992).

Rees, R. *Layers of Loyalty in Latin Panegyric AD 289–307* (Oxford 2002).

—— (ed.). *Romane Memento: Vergil in the Fourth Century* (London 2004).

Reeve, M. D. "Some manuscripts of Ausonius," *Prometheus* 3 (1977), 112–20.

——— . "The transmission of Florus's *Epitoma de Tito Livio* and the *Periochae*," in *CQ* 38 (1988), 477–91; and 41 (1991), 453–83.

——— . "The Place of P in the Stemma of Livy 1–10," in C. A. Chavannes-Mazel and M. M. Smith (eds.), *Medieval Manuscripts of the Latin Classics: Production and Use* (London 1996), 87–88.

Reifferscheid, A. *De latinorum codicum subscriptionibus* (Index Schol. Vratisl. 1873).

Reitzenstein, R. *Verrianische Forschungen* (= *Breslauer Philol. Abhandlungen* 1887).

Reynolds, L. D. (ed.). *Texts and Transmission* (Oxford 1983).

Reynolds, L. D., and N. G. Wilson. *Scribes and Scholars*[3] (Oxford 1991).

Ribbeck, O. "De obtrectatoribus Vergilii," in *Prolegomena critica ad P. Vergili Maronis opera maiora* (Leipzig 1866).

Richard, M. "ἀπὸ φωνῆς," *Byzantion* 20 (1950), 191–222.

Riché, P. *Éducation et culture dans l'occident barbare*[4] (Paris 1995).

Riggs, D. "Paganism between the cities and countryside of Late Roman Africa," in T. S. Burns and J. W. Eadie (eds.), *Urban Centers and Rural Contexts in Late Antiquity* (East Lansing 2001), 285–300.

——— . "Christianizing the Rural Communities of Late Roman Africa," in H. A. Drake (ed.), *Violence in Late Antiquity* (Ashgate 2006), 297–308.

Riginos, A. S. *Platonica: The Anecdotes Concerning the Life and Writings of Plato* (Leiden 1976).

Rist, J. M. "A man of monstrous vanity," *JTS* 42 (1991), 138–43.

——— . *Augustine: Ancient Thought Baptized* (Cambridge 1994).

Rives, J. B. *Religion and Authority in Roman Carthage from Augustus to Constantine* (Oxford 1995).

Rivolta Tiberga, P. *Comm. stor. al libro v dell'epistolario di Simmaco* (Pisa 1992).

Rizzo, S. *Il lessico filologico degli umanisti* (Rome 1973).

Robert, L. "Épigrammes du Bas-Empire," *Hellenica* 4 (Paris 1948).

——— . *Le martyre de Pionios, prêtre de Smyrne* (Washington, D.C. 1994).

Roberto, U. "Prisco e una fonte Romana del IV secolo," *Romanobarbarica* 17 (2000/2002), 117–59.

——— . "Il *Breviarium* di Eutropio nella cultura greca tardoantica e bizantina," *Medioevo Greco* 3 (2003), 241–71.

——— . *Ioannis Antiocheni Fragmenta ex Historia Chronica*, Texte und Unters. 154 (Berlin 2005).

Roberts, C. H. "The Antinoë fragment of Juvenal," *JEA* 31 (1935), 199–209.

——— . *Manuscript, Society and Christian Belief in Early Christian Egypt* (Oxford 1979).

Roberts, C. H., and T. C. Skeat. *The Birth of the Codex* (Oxford 1987).

Roberts, M. *Biblical Epic and Rhetorical Paraphrase in Late Antiquity* (Liverpool 1985).

——— . "The use of myth in Latin Epithalamia from Statius to Venantius Fortunatus," *TAPA* 119 (1989), 321–48.

Robinson, D. W. "An analysis of the pagan revival of the late fourth century, with special reference to Symmachus," *TAPA* 46 (1915), 87–101.

Rochette, B. *Le latin dans le monde grec* (Brussels 1997).

Rochow, I. "Der Vorwurf des Heidentums als Mittel der innenpolitischen Polemik in Byzanz," in Salamon (ed.) 1991, 133–56.

Roda, S. "Simmaco nel gioco politico del suo tempo," *SDHI* 39 (1973), 53–114.

——— . "Alcune ipotesi sulla prima edizione dell'epistolario di Q. Aurelio Simmaco," *Parola del Passato* 34 (1979), 31–54.

——— . *Commento storico al libro ix dell'epistolario di Q. Aurelio Simmaco* (Pisa 1981) [1981a].

————. "Uno nuova lettera di Simmaco ad Ausonio?" *REA* 83 (1981), 273–80 [1981b].

————. "Fuga nel privato e nostalgia del potere nel IV sec. d. c.," in *Le trasformazioni della cultura nella tarda antichità* (Rome 1985), 95–108.

Rösch, G. *ONOMA BASILEIAS: Studien zur offiziellen Gebrauch der Kaisertitel in spätantiker und frühbyzantinischer Zeit* (Vienna 1978).

Romano, D. *Giulio Romano* (Palermo 1974).

————. *L'ultimo pagano: Flaviano nello specchio del Carmen contra paganos* (Palermo 1998).

Rosen, K. "Ein Wanderer zwischen zwei Welten," *Klassisches Altertum, Spätantike und frühes Christentum: Adolf Lippold…gewidmet* (Würzburg 1993), 393–408.

Rosenmeyer, P. *Ancient Epistolary Fictions* (Cambridge 2001).

Rossbach, O. "Der Prodigiorum liber des Iulius Obsequens," *Rhein. Mus.* 52 (1897), 3f.

Rouché, Charlotte. *Aphrodisias in Late Antiquity* (London 1989).

Rougé, J. "La pseudo-bigamie de Valentinien Ier," *Cahiers d'histoire* 3 (1958), 5–15.

Rougé, J., R. Delmaire, and F. Richard. *Les lois religieuses des empereurs romains de Constantine à Théodose II*, vol. 1 (312–438), SC 497 (Paris 2005).

Rousseau, P. *Ascetics, Authority and the Church in the age of Jerome and Cassian* (Oxford 1978).

Rowell, H. T. "Aelius Donatus and the D scholia on…Naevius," *YCS* 15 (1957), 113–19.

Rubin, Z. "Pagan propaganda under Magnentius," *Scripta Classica Israelica* 17 (1998), 124–41.

Ruggini, L. "Il vescovo Ambrogio e la Historia Augusta: Attualità di un topos politico-letterario," *Atti del colloquio patavino sulla Historia Augusta* (Rome 1963), 67–79.

————. *Economia e Società nell Italia annonaria²* (Bari 1995).

Runia, D. T. *Philo in Early Christian Literature* (Assen 1993).

————. "Caesarea Maritima and the survival of Hellenistic-Jewish literature," in A. Raban and K. G. Holum (eds.), *Caesarea Maritima: A Retrospective after Two Millenia* (Leiden 1996), 476–95.

Russell, D. A. *Antonine Literature* (Oxford 1990), (ed.).

Rutschowscaya, M.-H. *Tissus coptes* (Paris 1990).

Rutter, J. "The Three Phases of the Taurobolium," *Phoenix* 22 (1968), 226–49.

Rüpke, J. *Fasti Sacerdotum* 1–2 (Stuttgart 2005); one-volume English translation (Oxford 2008).

————. *Religion of the Romans* (Cambridge 2007).

Sabbah, G. *La Méthode d' Ammien Marcellin* (Paris 1978).

————. "Présences Féminines dans l'Histoire d'Ammien Marcellin," in J. den Boeft, D. den Hengst, H. C. Teitler, (eds.), *Cognitio Gestorum: The Historiographic Art of Ammianus Marcellinus* (Amsterdam 1992), 91–105 at 99–101.

————. "Ammien Marcellin, Libanius, Antioche et la date des derniers livres des *Res Gestae*," *Cassiodorus* 3 (1997), 89–116.

Sacks, K. "The Meaning of Eunapius's History," *History and Theory* 25 (1986), 52–67.

Saenger, Paul. *Space between Words: The Origins of Silent Reading* (Stanford 1997).

Saffrey, H. D., and L. G. Westerink. *Proclus: Théologie platonicienne* 1 (Paris 1968).

Saggioro, A. "Il sacrificio pagano nella reazione al cristianesimo: Giuliano e Macrobio," *Annali di storia dell'esegesi* 19 (2002), 237–54.

Salamon, M. (ed.). *Paganism in the Later Roman Empire* (Kraków 1991).

Salomonson, J. W. "Kunstgeschichtliche und ikonographische Untersuchungen zu einem Tonfragment der Sammlung Benaki in Athen," *Bulletin Antieke Beschaving* 48 (1973), 4–82.

Salzman, M. *On Roman Time: The Codex-Calendar of 354 and the Rhythms of Urban Life in Late Antiquity* (Berkeley 1990).

————. *The Making of a Christian Aristocracy: Social and Religious Change in the Western Roman Empire* (Berkeley 2002).

———. "Rethinking Pagan-Christian violence," in Drake (ed.) 2006, 265–85.

———. "Symmachus and the 'barbarian' generals," *Historia* 55 (2006), 352–67.

Sande, S. "Famous persons as bringers of good luck," in D. R. Jordan, H. Montgomery and E. Thomassen (eds.), *The World of Ancient Magic* (Bergen 1999), 227–38.

Sandwell, I. *Religious Identity in Late Antiquity: Greeks, Jews and Christians in Antioch* (2007).

Santoro, A. *Esegeti virgiliani antichi: Donato, Macrobio, Servio* (Bari 1946).

Savon, H. "Saint Ambroise a-t-il imité le recueil de lettres de Pline le jeune?" *REAug* 41 (1995), 3–17.

Scaffai, M. *La presenza di Omero nei commenti antichi a Virgilio* (Bologna 2006).

Schaarschmidt, C. *Johannes Saresberiensis nach Leben und Studien* (Leipzig 1862).

Scheid, J. "La thiase du Metropolitan Museum," in *L'Association dionysiaque dans les societés anciennes* (Rome 1986), 275–90.

———. *Le collège des frères arvales. Étude prosopographique du recrutement (69–304)* (Rome 1990) [1990b].

———. *Romulus et ses frères* (Rome 1990) [1990b].

———. "Le dernier Arvale," in *Institutions...A. Chastagnol* (Rome 1992), 219–23.

———. *Commentarii fratrum arvalium qui supersunt: les copies épigraphiques des protocoles annuels de la confrérie arvale (21 av.–304 ap. J.-C.)* (Rome 1998).

———. *La religion des romains* (Paris 1998).

———. "Les réjouissances des calendes de janvier d'après le sermon Dolbeau 26. Nouvelles lumières sur une fête mal connue," in G. Madec (ed.), *Augustin Prédicateur (395–411)* (Paris 1998), 353–65.

———. *Quand faire, c'est croire. Les rites sacrificiels des Romains* (Mayenne 2005).

Scheid, J., and H. Broise. *Le balneum des frères arvales* (Rome 1987).

———. "Deux nouveaux fragments des Actes des frères arvales...," *MEFRA* 92 (1980), 215–48.

Schenkl, C. "Zur lateinischen Anthologie," *Wien. Stud.* 1 (1879), 59–74.

Schenkl, H. "Ein spätrömischer Dichter und sein Glaubensbekenntnis," *Rhein. Mus.* 66 (1911), 392–410.

Schiatti, S. "La storiografia pagana nel IV secolo: Eutropio e la tradizione liviana," *Cultura latina pagana fra terzo e quinto secolo dopo Cristo: Atti del Convegno Mantova, 9–11 ottobre 1995* (Florence 1998), 259.

Schindel, U. *Die lateinischen Figurenlehren des 5. bis 7. Jahrhunderts und Donats Vergilkommentar* (Göttingen 1975), 34–36.

Schirren, T. *Philosophos Bios: Die antike Philosophen-biographie als symbolische Form. Studien zur Vita Apollonii des Philostrat* (Heidlelberg 2005).

Schlumberger, J. *Die Epitome De Caesaribus: Untersuchungen zur heidnischen Geschichtsschreibung des 4. Jhdts n. Chr.* (Munich 1974).

———. "Die verlorenen Annalen des Nicomachus Flavianus: ein Werk über Geschichte der römischen Republik oder Kaiserzeit?" *Bonner Historia-Augusta-Colloquium 1982/1983* (1985), 305–29.

Schmeidler, B. "Die SHA und der heilige Hieronymus," *Philol. Woch.* 47 (1927), 955–60.

Schmidt, M. G. "Ambrosii carmen de obitu Probi," *Hermes* 127 (1999), 99–116.

Schmidt, P. L. *Iulius Obsequens und das Problem der Livius-Epitome* (Mainz 1968).

———. "Rezeption und Überlieferung der Tragödien Senecas," in E. Lefèvre, *Der Einfluss Senecas auf das europäische Drama* (Darmstadt 1972), 12–73.

———. "Macrobius Theodosius und das Personal der Saturnalia," *RFIC* 137 (2009), 47–83.

Schneider, C. "Littérature et propagande au ive siècle de notre ère dans le recueil des *grandes dèclamations* pseudo-quintiliennes," in Consolino (ed.) (2000), 45–66 [2000a].

——— . "Quelques réflexions sur la date de publication des *Grandes déclamations* pseudo-quintiliennes," *Latomus* 59 (2000), 614–32 [2000b].

Schulz, F. *A History of Roman Legal Science* (Oxford 1946).

Schulze, W. *Zur Gesch. latein. Eigennamen* (Göttingen 1904).

Schumacher, W. N. "Zum Sarkophag eines christlichen Konsuls," *Röm. Mitt.* 65 (1958), 100–120.

Schürer, Emil, Geza Vermes, Fergus Millar, and Matthew Black (eds.). *History of the Jewish People in the Age of Jesus Christ* 1–2 (Edinburgh 1973/79).

Schwartz, E. "Aus den Akten des Concils von Chalkedon," *Abhandl. Bay. Akad.* (1925).

Schwartz, J. "Sur la date de l'Histoire Auguste," *Bulletin de la faculté des lettres de Strasbourg* 40 (1961), 174–75.

——— . "Arguments philologiques pour dater l'Histoire Auguste," *Historia* 16 (1966), 454–65.

——— . "L'Histoire Auguste, Suétone et Juvénal," *Romanitas-Christianitas: Untersuchungen…* J. Straub (Berlin 1982), 634–44.

——— . "La lettre de l'empereur Hadrien…selon l'Histoire Auguste," *Institutions, société et vie politique dans l'empire romain au IVe siècle ap. J.C.* (Rome 1992), 29–34.

Schwartz, S. *Imperialism and Jewish Society, 200 BCE to 640 CE* (Princeton 2001).

Scott Ryberg, I. *Rites of the Roman State Religion in Roman Art* (New Haven 1955).

Scourfield, J. H. D. *Consoling Heliodorus: A Commentary on Jerome, Letter 60* (Oxford 1993), 76–80.

Sebesta, J. L., and L. Bonfante (eds.). *The World of Roman Costume* (Madison 1994).

Seeck, O. *Die Briefe des Libanius* (Leipzig 1906).

——— . *Gesch. d. Untergangs der antiken Welt* 5 (Berlin 1913).

——— . *Regesten der Kaiser und Päpste* (Stuttgart 1919).

Seeck, O., and G. Veith. "Die Schlacht am Frigidus," *Klio* 13 (1913), 451–67.

Setaioli, A. "La discesa dell'anima in Servio," *Atti dell'Accademia Romanistica Costantiniana* (Naples 1995), 629–49.

Sfameni, C. *Ville residenziali nell' Italia tardoantica* (Bari 2006).

Shackleton Bailey, D. R. *Profile of Horace* (London 1982).

Shanzer, D. "The anonymous *Carmen Contra Paganos* and the date and identity of the Centonist Proba," *RÉAug* 32 (1986), 232–48.

——— . *A Philosophical and Literary Commentary on Martianus Capella…Book 1* (Berkeley 1986).

——— . "The date and composition of Prudentius' *Contra Orationem Symmachi*," *RIFC* 117 (1989), 442–62.

——— . "The date and identity of the Centonist Proba," *Rech. Augustiniennes* 27 (1994), 75–96.

Shaw, B. D. "The age of Roman girls at marriage: Some reconsiderations," *JRS* 77 (1987), 30–46.

Shelton, K. J. *The Esquiline Treasure* (London 1981).

Sheridan, J. A. *The Vestis Militaris Codex*, Columbia Papyri 9 (Atlanta 1998).

Sheridan, J. J. "The Altar of Victory: Paganism's last battle," *L'Antiquité classique* 35 (1966), at 186–206.

Sherwin-White, A. N. *The Letters of Pliny* (Oxford 1966).

Simmons, M. B. *Arnobius of Sicca* (Oxford 1995).

Simon, E. "The Diptych of the Symmachi and Nicomachi: An interpretation," *Greece and Rome* 39 (1992), 56–65.

Sinclair, B. W. "Vergil's sacrum poema in Macrobius's Satuirnalia," *Maia* 34 (1982), 261–63.

Sivan, H. "Redating Ausonius's Moselle," *AJP* 111 (1990), 383–94.

——— . "The historian Eusebius (of Nantes)," *JHS* 112 (1992), 158–63.

————. "Anician Women, the Cento of Proba, and aristocratic conversion in the fourth century," *Vigiliae Christianae* 47 (1993), 140–57.

————. *Ausonius of Bordeaux* (London 1993).

————. "The last Gallic prose panegyrist," in C. Deroux (ed.), *Studies in Latin Literature and Roman History* 7 (Brussels 1994), 577–94.

Skutsch, O. *The Annals of Quintus Ennius* (Oxford 1985).

Smith, C. J. "The *Origo Gentis Romanae*: Facts and fictions," *BICS* 48 (2005), 97–136.

Smith, Macklin. *Prudentius' Psychomachia* (Princeton 1976).

Smith, Morton. "On the Wine God in Palestine (Gen. 18, Jn 2 and Achilles Tatius)," *Salo Wittmayer Baron Jubilee* 2 (Jerusalem 1974), 815–29.

Smith, R. R. R. "The statue monument of Oecumenius," *JRS* 92 (2002), 134–56.

Sogno, C. *Q. Aurelius Symmacus: A political biography* (Ann Arbor 2006).

Solari, A. "Tolleranza verso il Paganesimo nella prima metà del sec. Vᵒ," *Philologus* 91 (1936), 357–60.

Solmsen, F. "The Conclusion of Theodosius' Oration in Prudentius' *Contra Symmachum*," *Philologus* 109 (1965), 310–13.

Sordi, M. "È di Cipriano il *Carmen ad quendam senatorem*," *Aevum* 82 (2008), 149–54.

Sotiroudis, P. *Untersuchungen zum Geschichtswerk des Johannes von Antiocheia* (Salonica 1989).

Speidel, M. P. *Roman Army Studies* 2 (Stuttgart 1992).

————. *Riding for Caesar: The Roman Emperor's Horse Guards* (Cambridge, Mass. 1994).

Speyer, W. *Naucellius und sein Kreis: Studien zu den Epigrammata Bobiensia* (Munich 1959).

————. "Zum Bild des Apollonius von Tyana bei Heiden und Christen," *JbAC* 17 (1974), 47–63.

Spier, J. "A lost consular diptych of Anicius Auchenius Bassus," *JRA* 16 (2003), 350–54.

Springer, C. P. E. "Jerome and the *Cento* of Proba," *Studia Patristica* 28 (1993), 96–105.

Springer, M. "Die Schlacht am Frigidus als quellenkundliches und literaturgeschichtliches Problem," in Bratoz̆ (ed.) 1996, 15–93.

Stade, W. *Hieronymus in prooemiis quid tractaverit et quos auctores quasque leges rhetoricas secutus sit* (Rostock 1925).

Stadter, P. A. "The structure of Livy's History," *Historia* 21 (1972), 287–307.

Stahl, W. H., R. Johnson, and E. L. Burge, *Martianus Capella* (New York 1971).

Stancliffe, C. *St Martin and His Hagiographer* (Oxford 1983).

Stangl, T. *Boethiana, vel Boethii commentariorum in Ciceronis Topica emendationes* (Munich 1882).

Stark, R. *Cities of God* (New York 2006).

Starr, R. J. "The circulation of literary texts in the Roman world," *CQ* 37 (1987), 213–23.

————. "Vergil as the Flamen Dialis?" *Vergilius* 43 (1997), 63–70.

St. Clair, A. "The apotheosis diptych," *Art Bulletin* 64 (1964), 205–11.

Steidle, W. "Die Leichenrede des Ambrosius für Kaiser Theodosius und die Helena-Legende," *Vigiliae Christianae* 32 (1978), 94.112.

Stein, E. *Histoire du Bas-Empire* I (Brussels 1959).

Steinmann, M. *Collatio Alexandri et Dindimi* (Göttingen 2000).

Stern, H. *Date et destinataire de l'Histoire Auguste* (Paris 1953).

————. *Le calendrier de 354* (Paris 1953).

————. "Les calendriers romains illustrés," in *ANRW* 2. 12. 2 (1981), 431–75.

Stevens, C. E. *Sidonius Apollinaris* (Oxford 1933).

Stevenson, T. B. *Miniature Decoration in the Vatican Virgil* (Tübingen 1983).

Stirling, L. "Divinities and heroes in the age of Ausonius: A late-antique villa and sculptural collection at Saint-George-de-Montagne (Gironde)," *Revue archéologique* (1996), 1, 103–43.

——— . *The Learned Collector: Mythological Statuettes and Classical Taste in Late Antique Gaul* (Ann Arbor 2005).

Stoneman, R. *Legends of Alexander the Great* (London 1994).

——— . "Who are the Brahmans?" *CQ* 44 (1994), 500–510.

——— . "Naked philosophers," *JHS* 115 (1995), 99–114.

——— . *Alexander the Great: A Life in Legend* (New Haven 2008).

Straub, J. *Vom Herrscherideal in der Spätantike* (Stuttgart 1939).

——— . *Studien zur Historia Augusta* (Bern 1952).

——— . "Die Himmelfahrt des Iulianus Apostata," *Gymnasium* 69 (1962), 310–26.

——— . *Heidnische Geschichtsapologetik in der christlichen Spatantike* (Bonn 1963).

Strelitz, A. *De antiquo Ciceronis de re publica librorum emendatore* (Gnesnae 1874).

Stroheker, K. F. "Princeps clausus," *BHAC 1968/69* (1970), 273–83.

Strong, E. S. *Apotheosis and Afterlife* (New York 1915).

Stuveras, R. *Le putto dans l'art romain*, Coll. Latomus 99 (Brussels 1979).

Sumner, G. V. *The Orators in Cicero's Brutus* (Toronto 1973).

Sundwall, J. *Weströmische Studien* (Berlin 1915).

Sussman, L. A. *The Declamations of Calpurnius Flaccus* (Leiden 1994).

——— . *The Major Declamations Ascribed to Quintilian* (Frankfurt 1987).

Svennung, J. *Untersuchungen zur Palladius* (Uppsala 1935).

Swain, S. *Hellenism and Empire* (Oxford 1996).

——— . "Bilingualism and biculturalism in Antonine Rome," in Holford-Strevens and Vardi (eds.) 2004, 3–40.

Syme, R. *Tacitus* 1–2 (Oxford 1958).

——— . *Ammianus and the Histora Augusta* (Oxford 1968).

——— . *Emperors and Biography* (Oxford 1971).

——— . *Roman papers* 1–7 (Oxford 1979–91).

——— . *Some Arval Brethren* (Oxford 1980).

——— . *Historia Augusta Papers* (1983).

——— . *The Augustan Aristocracy* (Oxford 1986).

Szidat, J. "Die Usurpation des Eugenius," *Historia* 28 (1979), 487–508.

——— . "Der Neuplatonismus und die Gebildeten im Westen des Reiches," *Mus. Helv.* 39 (1982), 132–45.

——— . "Imperator legitime declaratus," in *Historia testis: Mélanges… T. Zawadski* (Friburg 1989), 174–88.

Ševčenko, I. "A Late Antique epigram…," *Synthronon: Art et archéologie… Receuil d'études* (Paris 1968), 29–41.

Tabacco, R. *Itinerarium Alexandri* (Turin 2000).

Talbert, R. J. A. *The Senate of Imperial Rome* (Princeton 1984).

Tantillo, I. "L'ideologia imperiale tra centro e periferie," *RFIC* 127 (1999), 73–95.

Tarrant, R. J. "Classical Latin literature," D. C. Greetham (ed.), *Scholarly Editing: A Guide to Research* (New York 1995), 95–148.

Taylor, P. R. "Pre-history in the ninth-century manuscripts of the *Ad Herennium*," *Class. et Med.* 44 (1993), 181–254, at 243–50.

Teitler, H. C. *Notarii and Exceptores* (Amsterdam 1985).

Tengström, E. *Die Protokollierung der Collatio Carthaginiensis* (Göteborg 1962).

Thélamon, F. *Païens et chrétiens au IVᵉ siècle: L'apport de l'Histoire ecclésiastique de Rufin d'Aquilée* (Paris 1981).

Thomas, R. *Reading Virgil and His Texts* (Ann Arbor 1999).

Thompson, E. A. "The Emperor Julian's knowledge of Latin," *CR* 58 (1944), 49–51.

——— . *The Historical Work of Ammianus Marcellinus* (Cambridge 1947).

——— . *The Visigoths in the Time of Ulfila* (Oxford 1966).

Thrams, P. *Christianisierung der Römerreiches und heidnischer Widerstand* (Heidelberg 1992).

Thylander, H. *Étude sur l'épigraphie latine* (1952).

Timpanaro, S. *Contributi di filologia* (Rome 1978).

——— . *La genesi del metodo di Lachmann*^{2} (Padua 1981).

——— . *Per la storia della filologia virgiliana antica* (Rome 1986).

——— . *Virgilianisti antichi e tradizione indiretta* (Florence 2001).

Tjäder, J.-O. *Die nichtlit. latein. Papyri Italiens* 2 (Stockholm 1982).

Tomlin, R. S. O. "Christianity and the Roman army," in S. N. C. Lieu and D. Montserrat
   (eds.), *Constantine: History, Hagiography and Legend* (1998), 21–51.

Tomsin, A. *Étude sur le Commentaire Virgilien d'Aemilius Asper* (Paris 1952).

Townend, G. B. "Some problems of punctuation in the Latin hexameter," *CQ* 19 (1969), 330–44.

Toynbee, J. M. C. "Roma and Constantinopolis in Late-Antique Art," *JRS* 37 (1947), 136–37.

——— . *Roman Medallions*^{2} (New York 1986).

Traube, L. *Bamberger Fragmente der vierten Dekade des Livius.* Abhandl. Bay. Akad., Hist. Kl.
   24 (1909).

Treadgold, W. "The diplomatic career and historical work of Olympiodorus of Thebes,"
   International History Review 16 (2004), 709–33.

——— . *The Early Byzantine Historians* (New York 2007).

Treggiari, S. *Roman Freedman during the Late Republic* (Oxford 1969).

——— . *Roman Marriage* (Oxford 1991).

Trombley, F. *Hellenic Religion and Christianisation c. 370–529* (Leiden 1993, 1994).

Trout, D. R. "Augustine at Cassiacum: Otium honestum and the social dimensions of
   conversion," *Vig. Chr.* 42 (1988), 132–46.

——— . "Re-Textualizing Lucretia: Cultural Subversion in the *City of God*," *JECS* 2 (1994),
   53–70.

——— . "*Lex* and *Iussio* in the Theodosian Age," in Mathisen 1997, 162–78.

——— . *Paulinus of Nola: Life, Letters and Poems* (Berkeley 1999).

——— . "The Verse Epitaph(s) of Petronius Probus," *New England Classical Journal* 28
   (2000), 157–76.

——— . "Damasus and the Invention of Early Christian Rome," *Journal of Medieval and Early
   Modern Studies* 33 (2003), 517–36.

Turcan, R. *Mithras Platonicus: Recherches sur l'hellénisation philosophique de Mithra* (Leiden
   1975).

——— . "Intolérance chrétienne et la fin du mithriacisme au IVe siècle ap JC," *Actes du VIIe
   Congrès FIEC* 2 (Budapest 1984), 209–26.

——— . "Les monuments figurés dans l'*Histoire Auguste*," *HAC Parisinum 1990* (Macerata
   1991), 287–309.

——— . *Les cultes orientaux dans le monde romain*^{2} (Paris 1992).

——— . *The Cults of the Roman Empire* (Oxford 1996).

——— . "Corè-Libéra?" *CRAI* (1996), 745–67.

——— . *The Gods of Ancient Rome* (Edinburgh 2000).

Turcan-Verkerk, A.-M. *Un poète latin chrétien redécouvert: Latinius Pacatus Drepanius,
   panégyriste de Théodose*, Collection Latomus 276 (Brussels 2003).

Turner, E. G. *Greek Papyri* (Oxford 1968).

——— . *Greek Manuscripts of the Ancient World*^{2} (London 1987).

Türk, E. *Macrobius und die Quellen seiner Saturnalien: Eine Untersuchung über die
   Bildungsbestrebungen im Symmachuskreis*, diss. (Freiburgs 1961).

—— . "Les *Saturnales* de Macrobe source de Servius Danielis," *RÉL* 41 (1963), 327–49.

Twyman, B. L. "Aetius and the aristocracy," *Historia* 19 (1970), 480–503.

Uhl, A. *Servius als Sprachlehrer: Zur Sprachrichtigheit in der exegetischen Praxis des spätantiken Grammatikerunterrichts* (Göttingen 1998).

Ullmann, W. "The constitutional significance of Constantine the Great's settlement," *Journal of Ecclesiastical History* 27 (1976), 1–16.

—— . "Über die rechtliche Bedeutung der spätrömischen Kaisertitulatur für das Pappstum," in *Scholarship and Politics in the Middle Ages: Collected Studies* (1978), Ch. 2.

Urbainczyk, T. *Socrates of Constantinople* (Ann Arbor 1997).

—— . *Theodoret of Cyrrhus: The Bishop and the Holy Man* (Ann Arbor 2002).

Urso, A. M. "Sopravvivenze e metonomasie nel processo di denominazione greco di alcune patologie," in A. Debru and G. Sabbah (eds.), *Nommer la maladie: Recherches sur le lexique gréco-romain de la pathologie* (Saint-Étienne 2000), 39–60.

Vaganay, L., and C.-B. Amphoux. *An Introduction to New Testament Textual Criticism*[2] (Cambridge 1991).

van Andel, G. K. *The Christian Concept of History in the Chronicle of Sulpicius Severus* (Amsterdam 1976).

van Buren, A. W. *The Palimpsest of Cicero's De Re Publica* (1907).

van Dam, R. *Kingdom of Snow: Roman Rule and Greek Culture in Cappadocia* (Philadelphia 2002).

—— . *The Roman Revolution of Constantine* (Cambridge 2007).

van der Horst, P. W. "*Sortes*: Sacred books as instant oracles," in L. V. Rutgers (ed.), *The Use of Sacred Books in the Ancient World* (Leuven 1998), 143–73.

van der Meer, F. *Augustine the Bishop* (London 1961).

Vanderspoel, J. "Claudian, Christ and the cult of the saints," *CQ* 36 (1986), 244–55.

—— . "The background to Augustine's denial of religious plurality," in H. A. Meynell (ed.), *Grace, Politics and Desire: Essays on Augustine* (Calgary 1990), 179–93.

—— . *Themistius and the Imperial Court* (Ann Arbor 1995).

—— . "Symmachus, *Ep.* iii. 47: Books are children," *Hermes* 129 (2001), 284–85.

van der Valk, M. *Researches on the Text and Scholia of the Iliad* 1 (Leiden 1963).

Vangaard, J. H. *The Flamen: A Study in the History and Sociology of Roman Religion* (Copenhagen 1988).

van Groningen, B. "ΕΚΔΟΣΙΣ," Mnemosyne 16 (1963), 1–17.

van Haeperen, F. *Le collège pontifical* (Brussels 2002).

van Nuffelen, P. "Gélase de Césarée, un compilateur du cinquième siècle," *Byz. Zeitschr.* 95 (2002), 621–39.

van Oort, J. *Studia Patristica* 27 (1993), 417–23.

Varady, L. "Jordanes-Studien," *Chiron* 6 (1976), 441–87.

Varner, E. R., (ed.). *From Caligula to Constantine: Tyranny and Transformation in Roman Culture* (Atlanta 2000).

—— . *Mutilation and Transformation: Damnatio Memoriae and Roman Imperial Portraiture* (Leiden 2004).

Vassili, L. "La cultura di Antemio," *Athenaeum* 16 (1938), 38–43.

Vera, D. "I rapporti tra Magno Massimo, Teodosio e Valentiniano II nel 383–384," *Athenaeum* 53 (1975), 277–82.

—— . "Sulle edizioni antiche delle Relationes di Simmaco," *Latomus* 36 (1977), 1003–36.

—— . "Lo scandalo edilizio di Cyriades e Auxentius...," *Studia et Documenta Historiae Iuris* 44 (1978), 45–94.

———. "Le statue del senato di Roma in onore di Flavio Teodosio…" *Athenaeum* 91 (1979), 381–403.

———. "La polemica contro l'abuso imperiale del trionfo: rapporti fra ideologia, economia e propaganda nel basso impero," *Rivista storica dell'antichità* 10 (1980), 89–132.

———. *Commento storico alle Relationes di…Simmaco* (Pisa 1981).

———. "Lotta politica e antagonismi religiosi nella Roma tardoantica," *Koinonia* 7 (1983), 133–55.

Verbrugghe, G. P. "On the Meaning of *Annales* and Annalist," *Philologus* 133 (1989), 192–230.

Vermander, J.-M. "La polémique des Apologistes latins contre les Dieux du paganisme," *Rech. Augustiniennes* 17 (1982), 3–128.

Vermaseren, M. J. *Cybele and Attis: The Myth and the Cult* (London 1977).

Vian, F. "Les cultes païens dans les *Dionysiaques* de Nonnos: Étude de vocabulaire," *RÉA* 90 (1988), 399–410.

———. "Théogamies et sotériologie dans les *Dionysiaques* de Nonnos," *Journal des savants* (1994), 197–233.

———. "Martus chez Nonnos de Panopolis: etude de sémantique et de chronologie," *REG* 110 (1997), 143–60.

Vidén, G. *The Roman Chancery Tradition: Studies in the Language of Codex Theodosianus and Cassiodorus' Variae* (Göteborg 1984), 82.

Vidman, L. "Inferiae und Iustitium," *Klio* 53 (1971), 209–12.

Ville, G. "Les jeux de gladiateurs dans l'empire chrétien," *MÉFR* 72 (1960), 273–335.

———. *La gladiature en occident* (Rome 1981).

Vinchesi, M. A. "Servio e la riscoperta di Lucano," *Atene e Roma* 24 (1979), 2–40.

Voelkl, L. *Die Kirchenstiftungen des Kaisers Konstantin im Licht des römischen Sakralrechts* (Opladen 1964).

Vogel, L. *The Column of Antoninus Pius* (Cambridge, Mass. 1973).

Vogel, M., and V. Gardthausen. *Die griechischen Schreiber des Mittelalters und der Renaissance* (Leipzig 1909).

Volbach, W. F. *Elfenbeinarbeiten der Spätantike und des frühen Mittelalters*³ (Mainz 1976).

Vollmer, F. "De funere publico Romanorum," *Fleckeisens Jahrbuch für classische Philologie*, Suppl. 19. 3 (1893), 321–64.

Von Haehling, R. *Die Religionzugehörigkeit der hohen Amtsträger des römischen Reiches* (Bonn 1978).

Wahlgren, S. "Symeon the Logothete: Some philological remarks," *Byzantion* 71 (2001), 251–62.

———. "Original und Archetypus: zu Zustandekommen und Transformation einer byzantinischen Weltchronik," *BZ* 96 (2003), 269–77.

Walsh, P. G. *The Poems of Paulinus of Nola* (New York 1975).

———. *Cicero: The Nature of the Gods* (Oxford 1997).

Ward-Perkins, B. *From Classical Antiquity to the Middle Ages: Urban Public Building in Northern and Central Italy AD 300–850* (Oxford 1984).

Ware, C. "Claudian, Virgil and the two battles of Frigidus," in Rees (ed.) 2004, 168–69.

Warmington, B. H. "Ammianus Marcellinus and the lies of Metrodorus," *CQ* 31 (1981), 464–68.

Waszink, J. H. "Pompa Diaboli," *Vig. Christ.* 1 (1947), 13–41.

Watson, A. *Aurelian and the Third Century* (London 1999).

Wattenbach, W. *Das Schriftwesen im Mittelalter*³ (Leipzig 1896).

Webb, Ruth. *Demons and Dancers: Performance in Late Antiquity* (Cambridge, Mass. 2008).

Weigand, E. "Ein bisher verkanntes Diptychon Symmachorum," *JDAI* 52 (1937), 121–26.

Weinstock, S. *Divus Julius* (Oxford 1971).

Weiss, J.-P. "Julien, Rome et les Romains," in R. Braun and J. Richer (eds.), *L'empereur Julien: De l'histoire à la légende (331–1715)* (Paris 1978), 125–40.

Weisweiler, J. "Inscribing imperial power: Letters from emperors in Late-Antique Rome," in R. Behrwald and C. Witschel (eds.), *Historische Erinnerung im städtischen Raum: Rom in der Spätantike* (Stuttgart 2010).

Weitzmann, K. *Late Antique and Early Christian Book Illumination* (New York 1977).

——— . (ed.). *Age of Spirituality: Late Antique and Early Christian Art, Third to Seventh Century* (New York 1979).

——— . *Greek Mythology in Byzantine Art*[2] (Princeton 1984).

Wenger, A. "La tradition des oeuvres de saint Jean Chrysostome," *RÉB* 14 (1956), 5–47.

Werner, S. *The Transmission and Scholia to Lucan's Bellum Civile* (Hamburg 1998).

Wesch-Klein, G. *Funus publicum* (Stuttgart 1993).

Wessner, P. *Scholia in Iuvenalem vetustiora* (Leipzig 1931).

West, M. L. *Studies in Aeschylus* (Stuttgart 1990).

Whitby, Mary. "Paul the Silentiary and Claudian," *CQ* 35 (1985), 507–16.

Whitby, Michael. "John of Antioch," *CR* 40 (1990), 255–56.

——— . "John of Ephesus and the pagans: Pagan survivals in the sixth century," in Salamon (ed.) 1991, 111–31.

White, P. "The authorship of the *HA*," *JRS* 57 (1967), 115–33.

——— . "The friends of Martial, Statius and Pliny and the dispersal of patronage," *HSCP* 79 (1975), 265–300.

Wickham, C. *Framing the Early Middle Ages: Europe and the Mediterranean, 400–800* (Oxford 2005).

Wiedemann, T. *Emperors and Gladiators* (London 1992).

Wiesen, D. S. *St. Jerome as a Satirist* (Ithaca 1964).

Wightman, E. "*Priscae Gallorum Memoriae*: Some comments on sources for a history of Gaul," in *The Ancient Historian and His Materials: Essays in Honour of C. E. Stevens* (Farnborough 1975), 93–107.

Wigodsky, M. *Vergil and Early Latin Poetry* (Wiesbaden 1972).

Wildfang, R. L. "The Vestals and annual public rites," *Class. et Med.* 52 (2001), 223–56.

——— . *Rome's Vestal Virgins* (London 2006).

Wilken, R. L. *John Chrysostom and the Jews* (Berkeley 1983).

Wilkins, P. I. "The African Anicii: A neglected text and a new genealogy," *Chiron* 18 (1988), 377–82.

Wilkinson, Kevin W. "Palladas and the Age of Constantine," *JRS* 99 (2009), 36–60.

Willers, D. "Dionysos und Christus: Ein archäologisches Zeugnis zur 'Konfessionsangehörigkeit' des Nonnos," *Mus. Helv.* 49 (1992), 141–51.

Williams, S., and G. Friell. *Theodosius: The Empire at Bay* (New Haven 1994).

Williamson, Paul. "On the date of the Symmachi panel and the so-called Grado Chair ivories," in C. Entwistle (ed.), *Through a Glass Brightly: Studies in Byzantine and Medieval Art and Archaeology Presented to David Buckton* (Exeter 2003), 47–50.

——— . *Medieval Ivory Carvings: Early Christian to Romanesque* (2010).

Wilmart, A. "L'odyssée du manuscrit de San Pietro qui renferme les oeuvres de s. Hilaire," *Classical and Mediaeval Studies in Honor of E. K. Rand* (New York 1938), 293–305.

Wilson, L. M. *The Clothing of the Ancient Romans* (Baltimore 1938).

Wilson, N. G. *Scholars of Byzantium* (London 1983).

Wilson, R. J. A. *Sicily under the Roman Empire* (Warminster 1990).

Wingo, E. O. *Latin Punctuation* (Mouton 1972).

Winstedt, E. O. "Mavortius' copy of Prudentius," *CR* 18 (1904), 112–15.

Winterbottom, M. *The Minor Declamations Ascribed to Quintilian* (Berlin 1984).

Wiseman, T. P. *Roman Studies* (1987).

———. *Remus: A Roman Myth* (Cambridge 1995).

———. *The Myths of Rome* (Exeter 2004).

Wissowa, G. *De Macrobii Saturnaliorum fontibus* (Breslau 1880).

———. *Religion und Kultus der Römer*² (1912).

Wistrand, E. "Textkritisches und Interpretatorisches zu Symmachus," *Symbolae Gotoburgenses* 56 (1950), 87–89 = *Opera Selecta* (Stockholm 1972), 229–31.

Wolff, É., S. Lancel, and J. Soler. *Rutilius Namazianus: Sur son retour* (Paris 2007).

Woodman, A. J., and R. H. Martin. *Annals of Tacitus: Book 3* (Cambridge 1996).

Woods, D. "Ammianus Marcellinus and the Deaths of Bonosus and Maximilianus," *Hagiographica* 2 (1995), 25–55.

———. "Julian, Arbogastes and the *signa* of the *Ioviani* and *Herculiani*," *Journal of Roman Military Equipment Studies* 6 (1995), 61–68.

———. "Eusebius, *VC* 4. 21, and the *Notitia Dignitatum*," *Studia Patristica* 29 (1997), 195–202.

———. "Valentinian I, Severa, Marina and Justina," *Class. et Med.* 57 (2006), 173–87.

Woolf, G. *Becoming Roman: The Origins of Provincial Civilization in Gaul* (Cambridge 1998).

Worp, K. A., and A. Rijksbaron. *The Kellis Isocrates Codex* (Oxford 1997).

Wrede, H. *Consecratio in formam deorum: Vergöttliche Privatpersonen in der röm. Kaiserzeit* (Mainz 1981).

Wright, D. H. *Codicological Notes on the Vergilius Romanus* (Vatican 1992).

———. *The Vatican Vergil: A Masterpiece of Late Antique Art* (Berkeley 1993).

———. *Twenty-first Annual Byzantine Studies Conference: Abstracts of Papers* (New York 1995).

———. "The Organization of the Lost Late Antique Illustrated Terence," in Claudine A. Chavannes-Mazel and Margaret M. Smith (eds.), *Medieval Manuscripts of the Latin Classics: Production and Use* (London 1996), 41–56.

———. "The persistence of pagan art patronage in fifth-century Rome," *ΑΕΤΟΣ: Studies in Honour of Cyril Mango* (Stuttgart 1998), 354–69.

———. *The Roman Vergil and the Origins of Medieval Book Design* (Toronto 2001).

Wright, H. W. "The age of Roman sacrificial victims," *Studies in the Humanities* (Lehigh University) 12 (1931), 1–23.

Wytzes, J. *Der letzte Kampf des Heidentums in Rom* (Leiden 1977).

Zanker, P. *The Power of Images in the Age of Augustus* (Ann Arbor 1988).

———. *The Mask of Socrates: The Image of the Intellectual in Antiquity* (Berkeley 1995).

Zanker, Paul, and Björn Ewald. *Mit Mythen leben: Die Bilderwelt der römischen Sarkophage* (Munich 2004).

Zecchini, G. "S. Ambrogio e le origini della vittoria incruenta," *Rivista di storia della chiesa in Italia* 38 (1984), 391–404.

———. "Barbari e Romani in Rufino di Concordia," in *Rufino di Concordia e il suo tempo* 2 (Udine 1987), 47–48.

———. *La cultura storica di Ateneo* (Milan 1989).

———. *Ricerche di storiografia latina tardoantica* (Rome 1993).

Zeiller, J. *Paganus: Étude de terminologie historique* (Fribourg 1917).

Zelzer, M. "Paleographische Bemerkungen zur Vorlage der Wiener Livius handschrift," *Antidosis: Festschrift W. Kraus, Wien. Stud.* Beiheft 5 (1972), 487–501.

———. "Zu Aufbau und Absicht des zehnten Briefbuches des Ambrosius," *Latinität und alte Kirche: Festschrift ... R. Hanslik* (Vienna 1977), 351–62.

——— . *Sancti Ambrosii Opera 10. 3: Epistularum liber decimus, epistulae extra collectionem,* CSEL 82 (1983).

Zetzel, J. E. G. "Cicero and the Scipionic Circle," *HSCP* 76 (1972), 173–79.

——— . "Emendavi ad Tironem: Some notes on classical scholarship in the second century AD," *HSCP* 77 (1973), 225–43.

——— . "Statilius Maximus and Ciceronian studies in the Antonine age," *BICS* 21 (1974), 107–23.

——— . "The subscriptions in the manuscripts of Livy and Fronto and the meaning of *emendatio*," *CP* 75 (1980), 38–59.

——— . *Latin Textual Criticism in Antiquity* (New York 1981).

——— . *Cicero: De re publica, Selections* (Cambridge 1995).

——— . *Marginal Scholarship and Textual Deviance: The Commentum Cornuti and the Early Scholia on Persius* (London 2005).

Ziegler, J. *Zur religiösen Haltung der Gegenkaiser im 4 h. n. Chr.* (Kallmünz 1970).

Zielinski, T. *Cicero im Wandel der Jahrhunderte* (Leipzig 1908).

Ziolkowski, J. M., and M. C. J. Putnam. *The Virgilian Tradition* (New Haven 2008).

Zuntz, G. *The Ancestry of the Harklean New Testament* (London 1945).

——— . "Die Subscriptionen der Syra Harclensis," *ZDMG* 101 (1951), 174–96.

——— . *The Text of the Epistles: A Disquisition upon the Corpus Paulinum* (London 1953).

——— . *An Inquiry into the Transmission of the Plays of Euripides* (Cambridge 1965).

Zwierlein, O. *Prolegomena zu einer kritischen Ausgabe der Tragödien Senecas* (Mainz 1983).

——— . *Senecas Hercules im Lichte kaiserzeitlicher und Spätantiker Deutung* (Mainz 1984).

INDEX